WRITERS' & ARTISTS'
YEARBOOK 1995

Peter,
from Mirian
Christmas '94

Use it well and
I expect to see
your name there one day.

Writers' & Artists' Yearbook 1995

EIGHTY-EIGHTH YEAR OF ISSUE

*A directory for writers, artists, playwrights,
writers for film, radio and television,
photographers and composers*

A&C BLACK · LONDON

A CIP catalogue record for this book
is available from the British Library.

ISBN 0-7136-3931-8

Typeset by Page Bros., Norwich, England
Printed and bound in Great Britain by
BPC Paperbacks Ltd.

Contents

PART ONE: Markets

Illustration and design

Photography

Picture research

Music

Agents

PART TWO: General Information

Preparation of materials, resources

Publishing practice

Copyright and libel

Finance

Societies and prizes

Index

Phoneday – code changes

Preface

In its 88th year of publication, *Writers' & Artists' Yearbook* is the essential guide to markets in all areas of the media – for writers, artists, composers, photographers and others. All sections are revised and updated annually, each directory entry and all other information being checked at source.

This 1995 edition includes a new article on *Publishing Agreements* by Michael Legat. Of interest to many writers – particularly perhaps to novices – is a new feature *Writing Courses in Higher Education*. A *Self-publishing Success Story* gives help and inspiration to writers contemplating 'doing it themselves'. The *broadcasting* section has been enlarged by the addition of a list of independent radio producers. The list of *picture agencies and libraries* has been classified by subject area to aid both photographers looking for outlets and picture researchers. The *classified list of periodicals* has been extended to cover markets for puzzles, quizzes and cartoons. Entries for the larger *UK publishers* have been rearranged and consolidated for ease of reference. Other new and updated material includes *Writing for Broadcasting*, *Writing for the EU* and a *Journalists' Calendar* for 1995.

Writers' & Artists' Yearbook is arranged in two main parts with fourteen clearly defined sections.

Part One provides *Markets* for articles, books, scripts, poetry, illustrations, photographs, music and includes articles on picture research and self-publishing.

Part Two offers *General Information*, with articles on many practical and legal matters of importance to writers and artists, together with lists of resources and useful addresses. This part also provides details of societies, associations and clubs, as well as a list of prizes, awards and competitions.

Vanity publishing Every edition of the *Yearbook* contains a strong warning that authors who pay for the publication of their work are almost invariably making an expensive mistake. It has been suggested that several distinguished poets have found it necessary to underwrite their first books in order to establish themselves, and in this respect the cautionary note on 'vanity publishing' on page 276 has been mildly modified; but unhappily there is still ample evidence that an emphatic general warning is necessary. Writers who cannot resist the temptation of seeing their work in print should read the advice given in the article on self-publishing which begins on page 268.

It should be repeated, too, that the publishers of the *Yearbook* cannot provide an advisory service, and that to rely on an out-of-date edition is to invite inevitable difficulties and disappointments.

PART ONE
Markets

Articles, reports
and short stories

Newspapers and Magazines

SUBMITTING MATERIAL

More than nine hundred titles are included in the newspapers and magazines section of the *Yearbook*, almost all of them offering opportunities to the writer. Some overseas titles have little space for freelance contributions, but many of them will always consider outstanding work. Many do not appear in our lists because the market they offer for the freelance writer is either too small or too specialised, or both. Those who wish to offer contributions to technical, specialist or local journals are likely to know their names and can find their addresses; before submitting a manuscript to any such periodical it is advisable to write a preliminary letter to its editor.

Magazine editors frequently complain to us about the unsuitability of many manuscripts submitted to them. Not only are these unsuitable, but no postage is sent for their return. In their own interests, writers and others are advised to *enclose postage for the return of unsuitable material*. It is also advisable to send the material to the correct person. Each section of the main newspapers and magazines nowadays has its own commissioning editor. A telephone call to the main switchboard will establish the name of the editor in question.

Before submitting manuscripts, writers should study carefully the editorial requirements of a magazine; not only for the subjects dealt with, but for the approach, treatment, style and length. Obvious though these comments may be to the practised writer, the beginner would be spared much disappointment by studying the market more carefully (but should not expect editors to send free specimen copies of their magazines). An article or short story suitable for *Woman's Weekly* is unlikely to appeal to the readers of *The Literary Review*. The importance of studying the market cannot be over-emphasised. It is an editor's job to know what readers want, and to see that they get it. Thus freelance contributions must be tailored to fit a specific market; subject, theme, treatment, length, etc., must meet the editor's requirements.

Editors also prefer, and expect, material to be well presented. Neatly typed, double-spaced, with good margins, on A4 paper is the standard to aim at – see the *Typescripts* section on page 465 and Randall McMullan's article, *Word Processing*, on page 481.

When submitting illustrations, be they colour or b&w prints or transparencies, line drawings or cartoons, it is advisable not to send these 'on spec', but to check with the editor first. See also page 118.

It has always been our aim to obtain and publish the rates of payment offered for contributions by newspapers and magazines. Many journals, however, are reluctant to state a standard rate of payment, since the value of a contribution may be dependent not upon length but upon the standing of the writer or of the information given. Many other periodicals, in spite of efforts to extract more precise information from them, prefer to state 'by negotiation' or 'by arrangement'.

A number of magazines and newspapers will accept and pay for letters to the editor, brief fillers and gossip paragraphs, as well as puzzles and quizzes. For a list of these see the **Classified index** on page 125. This index provides only a rough guide to markets and must be used with discrimination. For lists of recent mergers, changes of title, and terminations, see page 124. For a list of magazines and newspapers willing to pay for cartoons, see page 347.

Readers are reminded that potential contributors living outside the UK should always enclose return postage in the form of International Reply Coupons when submitting queries or MSS. They might also consider approaching an agent to syndicate their material. Most agents operate on an international basis and are more aware of current market requirements. Again, return postage should always be included. See **Syndicates, news and press agencies** on page 139.

WRITING FOR DIFFERENT MARKETS

Writing for newspapers See Jill Dick's article on page 110.

Writing magazine articles See John Hines' article on page 113.

Writing for EU markets See Barbara Wood-Kaczmar's article on page 119.

Writing for other markets outside the UK The lists of overseas newspapers and magazines contain only a selection of those journals which offer some market for the freelance (*Willings Press Guide Volume 2 Overseas* provides fuller listings). The overseas market for stories and articles is small and editors often prefer their fiction to have a local setting.

The larger newspapers and magazines buy many of their stories, as the smaller papers buy general articles, through one or other of the well-known syndicates, and a writer may be well advised to send printed copies of stories he/she has had published at home to an agent for syndication overseas.

Most of the big newspapers depend for news on their own staffs and the press agencies. The most important papers have permanent representatives in Britain who keep them supplied, not only with news of especial interest to the country concerned, but also with regular summaries of British news and with articles on events of particular importance. While many overseas newspapers and magazines have a London office, it is usual for MSS from freelance contributors to be submitted to the headquarters' editorial office overseas.

When sending MSS abroad it is important to remember to enclose International Reply Coupons; these can be exchanged in any foreign country for stamps representing the minimum postage payable on a letter sent from that country to this country.

See also Journalists' Calendar
in **Preparation of materials,
resources**

UNITED KINGDOM

(For Northern Ireland publications, see under Irish listings, page 100.)

Aberdeen Evening Express, R.J. Williamson, Aberdeen Journals Ltd, PO Box 43, Lang Stracht, Mastrick, Aberdeen AB9 8AF   *tel* (0224) 690222   *telex* 739244 JNLSAB G   *fax* (0224) 699575.
24p. D. Lively evening paper reading. *Illustrations:* colour and b&w, cartoons. *Payment:* by arrangement.

Accountancy (1889), Brian Singleton-Green, 40 Bernard Street, London WC1N 1LD   *tel* 071-833 3291   *fax* 071-833 2085.
£3.35. M. Articles on accounting, taxation, financial, legal and other subjects likely to be of professional interest to accountants in practice or industry, and to top management generally; cartoons. *Payment:* £100 per page.

Accountancy Age (1969), Robert Outram, VNU Business Publications, VNU House, 32-34 Broadwick Street, London W1A 2HG   *tel* 071-439 4242   *telex* 23918 VNU G   *fax* 071-437 7001.
£1.50. W. Articles of accounting, financial and business interest. *Illustrations:* colour photos; freelance assignments commissioned. *Payment:* by arrangement; NUJ rates.

Accounting World (1920), Garry Carter, Chartergate Publishing, 1 Northumberland Avenue, Trafalgar Square, London WC2N 5BW   *tel* 071-872 5522   *fax* 071-872 5611. Journal of The Institute of Financial Accountants and The International Association of Book-keepers, Burford House, 44 London Road, Sevenoaks, Kent TN13 1AS   *tel* (0732) 458080.
£12.00 p.a. Bi-M. Articles on accounting, management, company law, data processing, information technology, pensions, factoring, investment, insurance, fraud prevention and general business administration. *Length:* 1000-2000 words. *Illustrations:* offset litho (mono or colour). *Payment:* by arrangement.

Achievement, World Trade Magazines Ltd, World Trade House, 49 Dartford Road, Sevenoaks, Kent TN13 3TE   *tel* (0732) 458144   *fax* (0732) 456295.
£2.00. Q. Lively articles relating to British business achievements in international project management. *Illustrations:* first-class photos. *Payment:* by arrangement.

Active Life (1989), Helene Hodge, Aspen Specialist Media, Christ Church, Cosway Street, London NW1 5NJ   *tel* 071-262 2622.
£1.75. Bi-M. Lifestyle advice for the over 55s, including holidays and health, fashion and food, finance and fiction, hobbies and home, plus personality profiles. *Submit ideas in writing. Length:* 600-1200 words. *Illustrations:* colour. *Payment:* £100 per 1000 words; photos by negotiation.

Acumen (1985), Patricia Oxley, 6 The Mount, Higher Furzeham, Brixham, South Devon TQ5 8QY   *tel* (0803) 851098.
£5.50 p.a. Bi-annual (Apr/Oct). Poetry, literary articles, interviews with poets on poetry; 100pp. or more. Send sae with submissions. *Illustrations:* line drawings. *Payment:* by negotiation.

Administrator (1971), 16 Park Crescent, London W1N 4AH   *tel* 071-580 4741   *fax* 071-323 1132.
£3.75. M. (£34.00 p.a. post free UK) Official Journal of The Institute of Chartered Secretaries and Administrators. Practical and topical articles (750-1600 words) on law, finance and management affecting company secretaries and other senior administrators in business, nationalised industries, local and

central government and other institutions in Britain and overseas. Most articles commissioned from leading administrators. *Payment:* by arrangement.

Aeromodeller (1935), John Stroud, Argus Specialist Publications, Argus House, Boundary Way, Hemel Hempstead, Herts. HP2 7ST   *tel* (0442) 66551   *fax* (0442) 66998.
£1.95. M. Articles and news concerning model aircraft. Suitable articles and first-class photos by outside contributors are always considered. *Length:* 750-2000 words, or by arrangement. *Illustrations:* photos and line drawings to scale. *Payment:* by negotiation.

Aeroplane Monthly (1973), Richard T. Riding, IPC Magazines Ltd, King's Reach Tower, Stamford Street, London SE1 9LS   *tel* 071-261 5551   *fax* 071-261 7851.
£2.20. M. Articles and photos relating to historical aviation. *Length:* up to 3000 words. *Illustrations:* line, half-tone, colour, cartoons. *Payment:* £45 per 1000 words, payable on publication; photos £10; colour £80 per page.

Africa Confidential (1960), Patrick Smith, Miramoor Publications Ltd, 73 Farringdon Road, London EC1M 3JB   *tel* 071-831 3511   *fax* 071-831 6778.
£145.00 p.a. F. News and analysis of political and economic developments in Africa. Unsolicited contributions welcomed, but must be exclusive and not published elsewhere. *Length:* 1200-word features, 200-word pointers. *Payment:* £180 per 1000 words. *No* illustrations or advertising.

African Business (1978), Linda Van Buren, IC Publications Ltd, 7 Coldbath Square, London EC1R 4LQ   *tel* 071-713 7711   *telex* 8811757 ARABY G   *fax* 071-713 7970.
£1.50. M. Articles on business, economic and financial topics of interest to businessmen, ministers, officials concerned with African affairs. *Length:* 400-750 words; shorter coverage 100-400 words. *Illustrations:* line, half-tone. *Payment:* £70 per 1000 words; £1 per column cm.

Agenda, William Cookson and Peter Dale, 5 Cranbourne Court, Albert Bridge Road, London SW11 4PE   *tel* 071-228 0700.
£18.00 p.a. Q. (libraries, institutions and overseas: rates on application) Poetry and criticism. Contributors should study the journal before submitting MSS with an sae. *Illustrations:* half-tone. *Payment:* £12 per poem or per page of poetry, £8 per page for reviews and criticism; illustrations £35.

Air International (1971), Malcolm English, Key Publishing Ltd, PO Box 100, Stamford, Lincs. PE9 1XQ   *tel* (0780) 55131   *telex* 9312134113 (KPG)   *fax* (0780) 57261.
£1.95. M. Technical articles on aircraft; features on topical aviation subjects – civil and military; historical aviation subjects. *Length:* up to 5000 words. *Illustrations:* colour transparencies/prints, b&w prints/line drawings, cartoons. *Payment:* £50 per 1000 words or by negotiation; £25 colour, £10 b&w.

Air Pictorial International, Barry C. Wheeler, HPC Publishing, Drury Lane, St Leonards-on-Sea, East Sussex TN38 9BJ   *tel* (0424) 720477   *fax* (0424) 443693/434086.
£1.95. M. Covers all aspects of aviation. Many articles commissioned, and the editor is glad to consider competent articles exploring fresh ground or presenting an individual point of view on technical matters. All articles are *illustrated*, mainly with photos. *Payment:* by arrangement.

Amateur Gardening (1884), G. Clarke, IPC Magazines Ltd, Westover House, West Quay Road, Poole, Dorset BH15 1JG   *tel* (0202) 680586   *fax* (0202) 674335.

77p. W. Articles up to 700 words about any aspect of gardening. *Payment:* by arrangement. *Illustrations:* colour.

Amateur Photographer (1884), Keith Wilson, IPC Magazines Ltd, King's Reach Tower, Stamford Street, London SE1 9LS   *tel* 071-261 5100.
£1.30. W. Original articles of pictorial or technical interest, preferably illustrated with either photos or diagrams. Good instructional features especially sought. *Length preferred:* (unillustrated) 400-800 words: articles up to 1500 words; (illustrated) 2 to 4 pages. *Payment:* weekly, at rates according to usage. *Illustrations* unaccompanied by text will be considered for covers or feature illustrations, please indicate if we can hold on file; cartoons.

Amateur Stage (1946), Charles Vance, Platform Publications Ltd, 83 George Street, London W1H 5PL   *tel* 071-486 1732/7930   *fax* 071-224 2215.
£1.50. M. Articles on all aspects of the amateur theatre, preferably practical and factual. *Length:* 600-2000 words. *Illustrations:* photos and line drawings. *Payment:* none.

Ambit (1959), Dr Martin Bax, 17 Priory Gardens, Highgate, London N6 5QY   *tel* 081-340 3566.
£5.00. Q. Poems, short stories, criticism. *Payment:* by arrangement. *Illustrations:* line, half-tone.

Angler's Mail, Roy Westwood, IPC Magazines Ltd, King's Reach Tower, Stamford Street, London SE1 9LS   *tel* 071-261 5778   *fax* 071-261 6016.
70p. W. Features and news items about sea, coarse and game fishing. *Length:* 650-800 words. *Payment:* by arrangement. *Illustrations:* colour.

Angling Times (1953), Keith Higginbottom, EMAP Pursuit Publishing Ltd, PO Box 231, Bretton Court, Bretton, Peterborough PE3 8EN   *tel* (0733) 266222/264666   *fax* (0733) 265515.
62p. W. Articles, pictures, news stories, on all forms of angling. *Illustrations:* line, half-tone, colour. *Payment:* by arrangement.

Annabel, D.C. Thomson & Co. Ltd, 80 Kingsway East, Dundee DD4 8SL   *tel* (0382) 23131   *telex* 76380 DCTHOM G   *fax* (0382) 452491; and 185 Fleet Street, London EC4A 2HS   *tel* 071-242 5086   *fax* 071-404 5694.
£1.00. M. Colour gravure monthly for the modern woman with wide interests. Biographical stories of well-known personalities, family and parenthood topics, fashion, cookery, knitting, fiction. Art *illustrations* and photos in full colour and b&w, cartoons. *Payment:* on acceptance.   Ceased publication.

The Antique Collector (1930), Susan Morris, Orpheus Publications Ltd, 7 St John's Road, Harrow-on-the-Hill, Middlesex HA1 2EE.
£3.00. 10 p.a. Authoritative, topical and fully illustrated information for those interested in extending their knowledge and enjoyment of all aspects of antiques and the fine and decorative arts. *Illustrations:* fine b&w photos or colour transparencies. *Payment:* £250 per feature; at cost.

The Antique Dealer & Collectors Guide, Philip Bartlam, PO Box 805, Greenwich, London SE10 8TD   *tel* 081-318 5868.
£2.75. M. Articles on antique collecting and art. *Length:* 1500-2000 words. *Payment:* £76 per 1000 words. *Illustrations:* half-tone, colour.

Apollo (1925), Robin Simon, 29 Chesham Place, London SW1X 8HB   *tel* 071-235 1676   *fax* 071-235 1673.
£7.80. M. Knowledgeable articles of about 2500 words on art, architecture, ceramics, furniture, armour, glass, sculpture, and any subject connected with art and collecting. *Payment:* by arrangement. *Illustrations:* half-tone, colour.

The Aquarist and Pondkeeper (1924), John Dawes, Dog World Ltd, 9 Tufton Street, Ashford, Kent TN23 1QN   *tel* (0233) 621877   *fax* (0233) 645669.
£1.60. M. Illustrated authoritative articles by professional and amateur biologists, naturalists and aquarium hobbyists on all matters concerning life in and near water, conservation and herpetology. *Length:* about 1500 words. *Illustrations:* line, half-tone, colour, cartoons. *Payment:* by arrangement.

The Architects' Journal (1895), Paul Finch, EMAP Architecture, 33-35 Bowling Green Lane, London EC1R 0DA   *tel* 071-837 1212   *fax* 071-833 3073.
£1.35. W. Articles (mainly technical) on architecture, planning and building accepted only with prior agreement of synopsis. *Illustrations:* photos and drawings. *Payment:* by arrangement.

Architectural Design (1930), Maggie Toy, Academy Group Ltd, 42 Leinster Gardens, London W2 3AN   *tel* 071-402 2141   *fax* 071-723 9540.
£65.00 p.a. 6 double issues (£45.00 p.a. students) International magazine comprising an extensively illustrated thematic profile presenting architecture and critical interpretations of architectural history, theory and practice. Uncommissioned articles not accepted. *Illustrations:* drawings and photos, colour, half-tone, line (colour preferred). *Payment:* by arrangement.

Architectural Review (1896), Peter Davey, EMAP Architecture, 33-35 Bowling Green Lane, London EC1R 0DA   *tel* 071-837 1212   *fax* 071-278 4003.
£5.25. M. Articles on architecture and the allied arts. Writers must be thoroughly qualified. *Length:* up to 3000 words. *Payment:* by arrangement. *Illustrations:* photos, drawings, etc.

Arena (1986), 3rd Floor Block A, Exmouth House, Pine Street, London EC1R 0JL   *tel* 071-837 7270   *fax* 071-837 3906.
£2.00. Bi-M. Profiles, articles on a wide range of subjects intelligently treated; art, architecture, politics, sport, business, music, film, design, media, fashion. *Length:* up to 3000 words. *Illustrations:* b&w and colour photos. *Payment:* £150 per 1000 words; varies.

Army Quarterly & Defence Journal (1829), T.D. Bridge, 1 West Street, Tavistock, Devon PL19 8DS   *tel* (0822) 613577/612785   *fax* (0822) 612785.
£49.80 p.a. Q. (£132.00 3-yr saver contract) Articles on a wide range of British, UN, Commonwealth and international defence issues, historical and current; also Quarterly Diary, Defence Contracts, International Defence Reports, book and video reviews. *Preliminary letter preferred. Length:* 1000-6000 words. *Illustrations:* b&w photos, line drawings, maps. *Payment:* by arrangement.

Aromatherapy Quarterly (1983), Séza Eccles, 5 Ranelagh Avenue, Barnes, London SW13 0BY   *tel/fax* 081-392 1691.
£4.00. Q. (£16.00 p.a.) Articles and case studies on aromatherapy, herbalism, massage and health-related issues. *Length:* 1500-3000 words. *Illustrations:* b&w photos and line. *Payment:* by arrangement.

Art & Craft (1936), Eileen Lowcock, Scholastic Publications (Magazines) Ltd, Villiers House, Clarendon Avenue, Leamington Spa, Warks. CV32 5PR   *tel* (0926) 887799   *fax* (0926) 883331.
£1.75. M. Articles offering fresh, creative ideas of a practical nature, based on teaching art, design and technology in the National Curriculum, for the infant/junior school teacher. Articles by teachers for teachers. *Illustrations:* colour and b&w line drawings. *Payment:* by arrangement.

Art & Design (1985), Nicola Hodges, Academy Group Ltd, 42 Leinster Gardens, London W2 3AN   *tel* 071-402 2141   *fax* 071-723 9540.

£65.00 p.a. 6 double issues (£45.00 p.a. students) International magazine covering the whole spectrum of the arts, with particular emphasis on New Art. Each issue comprises extensively illustrated thematic features together with critical articles from well-known writers. Feature articles, exhibition reviews/previews, book reviews. Uncommissioned articles not accepted. *Illustrations:* line, half-tone, colour (colour preferred). *Payment:* by arrangement.

Art Business Today (1991), Imogen McEvedy, The Fine Art Trade Guild, 16-18 Empress Place, London SW6 1TT   *tel* 071-381 6616   *fax* 071-381 2596.
£13.50 p.a. Q. Distributed to the fine art and framing industry. Covers essential information on new products and technology, market trends and business analysis. *Length:* 800-1600 words. *Illustrations:* colour photos, cartoons. *Payment:* by arrangement.

Art Monthly (1976), Patricia Bickers, Britannia Art Publications Ltd, Suite 17, 26 Charing Cross Road, London WC2H 0DG   *tel* 071-240 0389   *fax* 071-240 0389.
£2.25. 10 p.a. Features on modern and contemporary artists and art history, art theory and art-related issues; exhibition and book reviews. *All material commissioned. Length:* 1000-2000 words. *Illustrations:* b&w photos. *Payment:* features £100 per 1000 words; none for photos.

The Art Newspaper (1990), Anna Somers Cocks, Mitre House, 44-46 Fleet Street, London EC4Y 1BN   *tel* 071-936 2886   *fax* 071-583 6897.
£3.50. 10 p.a. (£30.00 p.a.) International, up-to-date coverage of the art market, news, commentary. *Length:* 200-1000 words. *Illustrations:* b&w photos. *Payment:* £120 per 1000 words; negotiable (£40 per photo).

Art Review (1949), David Lee, Art Review Ltd, 20 Prescott Place, London SW4 6BT   *tel* 071-978 1000   *fax* 071-978 1102.
£3.50. M. Art criticism and reviews. Commissioned work only. *Payment:* modest. *Illustrations:* line, half-tone, colour.

The Artist (1931), Sally Bulgin, The Artists' Publishing Co. Ltd, Caxton House, 63-65 High Street, Tenterden, Kent TN30 6BD   *tel* (058076) 3673.
£1.85. M. Practical, instructional articles on painting for all amateur and professional artists. *Payment:* by arrangement. *Illustrations:* line, half-tone, colour.

Artists and Illustrators (1986), Rada Petrovic, 4th Floor, The Fitzpatrick Building, 188-194 York Way, London N7 9QR   *tel* 071-609 2177   *fax* 071-700 4985.
£2.25. M. Mainly technical and practical articles on all the artistic media. *Length:* 1500 words. *Illustrations:* colour transparencies. *Payment:* variable.

Artrage, Black Arts Quarterly (1982), Julian Brutus, Minority Arts Advisory Service, 4th Floor, 28 Shacklewell Lane, London E8 2EZ   *tel* 071-254 7275   *fax* 071-923 1596.
£2.00. Q. Black literature, performing arts and media arts, including arts reviews, interviews, poetry. *Length/payment:* 500-1000 words, £30; 1000-1800 words, £50-£80. *Illustrations:* line, half-tone.

Asian Times (1983), Arif Ali, Hansib Publishing Ltd, Tower House, 141/149 Fonthill Road, London N4 3HF   *tel* 071-281 1191   *fax* 071-263 9656.
45p. W. News stories, articles and features of interest to Britain's Asian community. *Illustrations:* line, half-tone. *Payment:* by negotiation; £10 minimum.

Astronomy Now (1987), Steven Young, Intra Press, Intra House, 193 Uxbridge Road, London W12 9RA   *tel* 081-743 8888   *fax* 081-743 3062.

£1.95. M. Aimed at amateur astronomers. Interested in news items and longer features on astronomy and some space-related activities. Writers' guidelines available (send sae). *Length:* 1500-3000 words. *Illustrations:* line, half-tone, colour. *Payment:* 5p per word; from £10 per photo.

Athletics Weekly (1946), David Clarke, EMAP Pursuit Publishing Ltd, Bretton Court, Bretton, Peterborough PE3 8DZ   *tel* (0733) 261144   *fax* (0733) 265515.
85p. W. News and features on track and field athletics. Material *mostly commissioned. Length:* 1000-3000 words. *Illustrations:* b&w action and head/ shoulder photos, line, cartoons. *Payment:* varies.

audIT, the audit automation magazine (1990), Brian O'Kane, Cork Publishing Ltd, 19 Rutland Street, Cork, Republic of Ireland   *tel* (021) 313855   *fax* (021) 313496.
£115.00 p.a. UK/Eire. Bi-M. (£135.00 p.a. rest of world). Articles on audit automation, product reviews, etc. Material *mostly commissioned. Length:* 2000-4000 words. *Illustrations:* b&w photos, computer screen images. *Payment:* £250 per article; by negotiation.

The Author (1890), Derek Parker, 84 Drayton Gardens, London SW10 9SB   *tel* 071-373 6642.
£6.00. Q. Organ of The Society of Authors. Commissioned articles from 1000-2000 words on any subject connected with the legal, commercial or technical side of authorship. Little scope for the freelance writer: *preliminary letter* advisable. *Payment:* by arrangement.

Auto Express (1988), David Johns, Express Newspapers, Ludgate House, 245 Blackfriars Road, London SE1 9UX   *tel* 071-928 8000   *fax* 071-928 2847.
£1.00. W. News stories, and general interest features about drivers as well as cars. *Illustrations:* colour photos. *Payment:* features £200 per 1000 words; photos, varies.

Autocar & Motor (1895), Michael Harvey, Haymarket Publishing Ltd, 38-42 Hampton Road, Teddington, Middlesex TW11 0JE   *tel* 081-943 5013   *telex* 8952440   *fax* 081-943 5653.
£1.35. W. Articles on all aspects of cars, motoring and motor industries: general, practical, competition and technical. *Illustrations:* tone, line (litho) and colour. Press day news: Friday. *Payment:* varies; mid-month following publication.

Back Street Heroes (1983), Caz Carroll, PO Box 28, Altrincham, Cheshire WA15 8SH   *tel* 061-928 3480   *fax* 061-941 6897.
£2.20. M. Custom motorcycle features plus informed life style pieces; biker fiction. *Illustrations:* colour, cartoons. *Payment:* by arrangement.

Bad Attitude (1992), 121 Railton Road, London SE24 0LR   *tel* 071-978 9057.
£1.00. Bi-M. Feminist newspaper. News, features, reviews, short stories – feminist/relating to women. *Length:* up to 3000 words. *Illustrations:* b&w photos, line, cartoons. *Payment:* £3 per article/photo.

Balance (1935), Lesley Hallett, British Diabetic Association, 10 Queen Anne Street, London W1M 0BD   *tel* 071-323 1531   *fax* 071-637 3644.
£1.50. Bi-M. Articles on diabetes or related topics. *Length:* 1000-2000 words. *Payment:* £75 per 1000 words. *Illustrations:* colour.

Ballroom Dancing Times (1956), Executive Editor: Mary Clarke, The Dancing Times Ltd, Clerkenwell House, 45-47 Clerkenwell Green, London EC1R 0EB   *tel* 071-250 3006   *fax* 071-253 6679.
80p. M. Ballroom dancing from every aspect, but chiefly from the serious competitive, teaching and medal test angles. Well-informed freelance articles

are occasionally used, but only after preliminary arrangements. *Payment:* by arrangement. *Illustrations:* action photos preferred.

The Banker (1926), Stephen Timewell, Greystoke Place, Fetter Lane, London EC4A 1ND   *tel* 071-405 6969   *telex* 23700 FINBI G   *fax* 071-831 9136. £4.00. M. Articles on capital markets, trade finance, bank analysis and top 1000 listings. *Illustrations:* half-tones of people, charts, tables. *Payment:* by negotiation.

Banking World (1983), Garth Hewitt, 10 Salters' Hall Court, London EC4N 5AP   *tel* 071-283 3355   *fax* 071-626 2113. £3.25. M. Commissioned articles on developments in retail banking worldwide. *Length:* 200-2000 words. *Illustrations:* line, half-tone. *Payment:* by arrangement.

Baptist Times (1855), John Capon, PO Box 54, Didcot, Oxon OX11 8XB   *tel* (0235) 512012   *fax* (0235) 512013. 40p. W. Religious or social affairs material, up to 1000 words. *Payment:* by arrangement. *Illustrations:* half-tone, cartoons.

BBC Gardeners' World Magazine (1991), Adam Pasco, BBC Magazines, 101 Bayham Street, London NW1 0AG   *tel* 071-331 8000   *fax* 071-331 8162. £1.60. M. Features and ideas on plants, garden design and garden visits. *All material commissioned.* Study of magazine essential before submitting ideas. *Length:* varies, mainly 800-1000 words. *Illustrations:* colour transparencies; all artwork commissioned. *Payment:* by negotiation.

BBC GoodFood (1989), Sarah Jane Evans, BBC Magazines, 101 Bayham Street, London NW1 0AG   *tel* 071-331 8000   *fax* 071-331 8001. £1.45. M. Recipes from TV and radio, cookery features, food and wine news. *No* unsolicited material. *Length:* 700-1400 words. *Illustrations:* colour photos and line. *Payment:* by arrangement.

BBC Holidays (1992), Alison Rice, BBC Magazines, 101 Bayham Street, London NW1 0AG   *tel* 071-331 8000   *fax* 071-331 8030. £1.40. M. Articles and features of general and practical interest on all aspects of travel. *All material commissioned*; preliminary letter with outline and cuttings essential. *Length:* varies. *Illustrations:* commissioned illustrations, cartoons. *Payment:* £350 per 1000 words; depending on size.

BBC Homes & Antiques (1993), Judith Hall, BBC Magazines, 101 Bayham Street, London NW1 0AG   *tel* 071-331 8000   *fax* 071-331 8001. £1.60. M. Features on homes or antiques-related subjects. *Send synopsis* first, or brief outline. *Length:* 500-1000 words. *Illustrations:* colour. *Payment:* by arrangement.

BBC Music Magazine (1992), Fiona Maddocks, BBC Enterprises Ltd, Room A1130, Woodlands, 80 Wood Lane, London W12 0TT   *tel* 081-576 3283   *fax* 081-576 3292. £3.75. M. Articles, features, news and reviews on classical music. *All material commissioned. Length:* up to 2000 words. *Illustrations:* line, half-tone, colour. *Payment:* £150 per 1000 words; varies.

BBC Vegetarian GoodFood (1992), Mary Gwynn, BBC Magazines, 101 Bayham Street, London NW1 0AG   *tel* 071-331 8281   *fax* 071-331 8161. £1.65. M. Cooking, nutrition, environmental issues. Accepts only single-page feature outlines; *no* unsolicited material. *Illustrated. Payment:* by arrangement.

BBC Wildlife Magazine, Rosamund Kidman Cox, Broadcasting House, White-ladies Road, Bristol BS8 2LR   *tel* (0272) 732211   *fax* (0272) 467075.

£2.10. M. Popular but scientifically accurate articles about wildlife and conservation (national and international), some linked by subject to TV and radio programmes. Two news sections for short, topical biological and environmental stories. *Length of articles:* 3000 words. *Illustrations:* top-quality colour photos. *Payment:* £200-£350 per article; photos according to reproduction size, £40-£140.

The Beano, D.C. Thomson & Co. Ltd, Courier Place, Dundee DD1 9QJ *tel* (0382) 23131 *fax* (0382) 22214; and 185 Fleet Street, London EC4A 2HS *tel* 071-242 5086 *fax* 071-404 5694.
35p. W. Comic strips for children. Series, 11-22 pictures. *Payment:* on acceptance.

Beano Library, D.C. Thomson & Co. Ltd, Courier Place, Dundee DD1 9QJ *tel* (0382) 23131 *fax* (0382) 22214; and 185 Fleet Street, London EC4A 2HS *tel* 071-242 5086 *fax* 071-404 5694.
50p. 2 p.m. Extra-long comic adventure stories featuring well-known characters from the weekly Beano publication.

Beano Puzzle Library, D.C. Thomson & Co. Ltd, Courier Place, Dundee DD1 9QJ *tel* (0382) 23131 *fax* (0382) 22214; and 185 Fleet Street, London EC4A 2HS *tel* 071-242 5086 *fax* 071-404 5694.
50p. M. 64 pages of puzzles, word-games and teasers featuring the well-known characters from the weekly Beano and Dandy publications.

Bedfordshire Magazine (1947), Betty Chambers, White Crescent Press, 50 Shefford Road, Meppershall, Shefford SG17 5LL *tel* Hitchin (0462) 813363.
£2.25. Q. Articles of Bedfordshire interest, especially history and biography. *Length:* up to 1500 words. *Illustrations:* line, half-tone. *Payment:* £1.05 per 1000 words; by agreement.

Bella (1987), Jackie Highe, Shirley House, 25 Camden Road, London NW1 9LL *tel* 071-284 0909 *fax* 071-485 3774.
50p. W. General interest magazine for women: practical articles on fashion and beauty, health, cooking, home, travel; real life stories, plus romantic fiction up to 2000 words. *Payment:* by arrangement. *Illustrations:* line including cartoons, half-tone, colour.

Best (1987), Dennis Neeld, 10th Floor, Portland House, Stag Place, London SW1E 5AU *tel* 071-245 8700 *fax* 071-245 8825.
50p. W. Short stories. No other uncommissioned work accepted, but always willing to look at ideas/outlines. *Length:* variable. *Illustrations:* line, half-tone, colour, cartoons. *Payment:* by agreement.

The Big Issue (1991), A. John Bird, 57-61 Clerkenwell Road, London EC1M 5NP *tel* 071-490 4130.
60p. W. Features, news, reviews, interviews – of general interest and on social issues, especially homelessness. *Length:* 1200-word features. *Illustrations:* colour and b&w photos and line. *Payment:* £100 per feature; front cover only, £100.

Bird Watching (1986), David Cromack, EMAP Pursuit Publishing Ltd, Bretton Court, Bretton, Peterborough PE3 8DZ *tel* (0733) 264666 *fax* (0773) 265515.
£2.10. M. Practical advice articles on birdwatching techniques or places to visit. Send synopsis first. *Length:* 850 words. *Illustrations:* colour and b&w photos, cartoons. *Payment:* by negotiation.

Birdwatch (1991), Dominic Mitchell, Solo Publishing Ltd, 215 Bow House Business Centre, 153-159 Bow Road, London E3 2SE *tel* 081-983 1855 *fax* 081-983 0246.

£2.10. M. Topical articles on all aspects of birds and birding, including conservation, identification, sites and habitats, equipment, overseas expeditions. *Length:* 700-1500 words. *Illustrations:* colour slides, b&w photos, colour and b&w line. *Payment:* from £40 per 1000 words; colour: photos £15-£40, cover £70, line by negotiation; b&w: photos £10, line £10-£40.

Birmingham Evening Mail (1870), I. Dowell, 28 Colmore Circus, Queensway, Birmingham B4 6AX   *tel* 021-236 3366   *telex* 337552; *London office:* 11 Buckingham Street, WC2N 6DF   *tel* 071-409 7409   *fax* 071-495 2742.
26p. D. Ind. Features of topical Midland interest considered. *Length:* 400-800 words. *Payment:* by arrangement.

The Birmingham Post, N. Hastilow, PO Box 18, 28 Colmore Circus, Birmingham B4 6AX   *tel* 021-236 3366   *fax* 021-625 1105; *London office:* 11 Buckingham Street, WC2N 6DF   *tel* 071-409 7409   *fax* 071-495 2742.
35p. D. Authoritative and well-written articles of industrial, political or general interest are considered, especially if they have relevance to the Midlands. *Length:* up to 1000 words. *Payment:* by arrangement.

Black Beauty & Hair (1982), Irene Shelley, Hawker Publications, 13 Park House, 140 Battersea Park Road, London SW11 4NB   *tel* 071-720 2108   *fax* 071-498 3023.
£2.00. Q. Beauty and style articles relating specifically to the black woman; celebrity features. *No* short stories. *Length:* approx. 1000 words. *Illustrations:* colour and b&w photos. *Payment:* £85 per 1000 words; £50-£100.

Boards (1982), Bill Dawes, Yachting Press Ltd, 196 Eastern Esplanade, Southend-on-Sea, Essex SS1 3AB   *tel* (0702) 582245   *fax* (0702) 588434.
£2.25. 10 p.a. (M. during summer, Bi-M. during winter) Articles, photos and reports on all aspects of windsurfing and boardsailing. *Payment:* by arrangement. *Illustrations:* line, half-tone, colour, cartoons.

Bolton Evening News (1867), Newspaper House, Churchgate, Bolton, Lancs. BL1 1DE   *tel* (0204) 22345   *telegraphic address* Newspapers, Bolton.
26p. D. Articles, particularly those with South Lancashire appeal. *Length:* up to 500 words. *Illustrations:* photos; considered at usual rates. *Payment:* by arrangement.

The Book Collector (1952) (incorporating **Bibliographical Notes and Queries**), Editorial Board: Nicolas Barker (Editor), A. Bell, J. Commander, J. Fergusson, T. Hofmann, D. McKitterick, The Collector Ltd, 43 Gordon Square, London WC1H 0PD   *tel* 071-388 0846   *fax* 071-388 0854.
£26.00 p.a. ($47.00), postage extra. Q. Articles, biographical and bibliographical, on the collection and study of printed books and MSS. *Payment:* for reviews only.

Books in Wales—see **Llais Llyfrau.**

Books Magazine (1987), Richard Mabb, 43 Museum Street, London WC1A 1LY   *tel* 071-404 0304   *fax* 071-242 0762.
£1.50. Bi-M. Reviews, features, interviews with authors. *Payment:* negotiable.

The Bookseller (1858), Louis Baum, J. Whitaker and Sons Ltd, 12 Dyott Street, London WC1A 1DF   *tel* 071-836 8911   *fax* 071-836 6381.
£105.00 p.a. W. Journal of the publishing and bookselling trades. While outside contributions are welcomed, most of the journal's contents are commissioned. *Length:* about 1000-1500 words. *Payment:* by arrangement.

Bowls International (1981), Chris Mills, Key Publishing Ltd, PO Box 100, Stamford, Lincs. PE9 1XQ   *tel* (0780) 55131   *telex* 265871 MONREF G attn YQQ332   *fax* (0780) 57261.

£1.70. M. Sport and news items and features; occasional, bowls-oriented short stories. *Illustrations:* colour transparencies, b&w photos, occasional line, cartoons. *Payment:* sport/news approx. 25p per line, features approx. £50 per page; colour £25, b&w £10.

Brewing & Distilling International (1865), Bruce Stevens, 52 Glenhouse Road, Eltham, London SE9 1JQ *tel* 081-859 4300 *fax* 081-859 5813.
Controlled circulation. M. Journal for brewers, maltsters, hop merchants, distillers, soft drinks manufacturers, bottlers and allied traders, circulating in over 80 countries. Technical and marketing articles (average 1000 words) accepted, by prior arrangement, from authors with specialist knowledge. *Illustrations:* line drawings, photos. *Payment:* by prior agreement with editor.

Bridge (formerly **Bridge International**) (1926), Chess & Bridge Ltd, 369 Euston Road, London NW1 3AR *tel* 071-388 2404 *fax* 071-388 2407.
£23.95 p.a. M. Articles on bidding and play; instruction, competitions, tournament reports and humour. *Payment:* by arrangement. *Illustrations:* line, half-tone.

Bristol Evening Post (1932), A. King, Temple Way, Bristol BS99 7HD *tel* (0272) 260080.
25p. D.

La Brita Esperantisto (1905), W. Auld, 140 Holland Park Avenue, London W11 4UF *tel* 071-727 7821.
£2.50. M. (£14.00 p.a.) Journal of the Esperanto Asocio de Britio. Articles in Esperanto and English, by arrangement, on the applications of the International Language, Esperanto, to education, commerce, travel, international affairs, scouting, radio, television, literature, linguistics, etc. *Illustrations:* photos by arrangement. *Payment:* by arrangement.

British Birds (1907), Dr J.T.R. Sharrock, Fountains, Park Lane, Blunham, Bedford MK44 3NJ *tel/fax* (0767) 640025.
£47.25 p.a. M. Original observations relating to birds of Britain, Europe and North Africa. *Illustrations:* line, half-tone, colour. *Payment:* none for articles, nominal for illustrations.

British Chess Magazine (1881), M. Chandler, BCM Chess Shop, 69 Masbro Road, London W14 0LS.
£2.20. M. (£24.00 p.a. post free) Commisioned articles, 800-2500 words, on historical and cultural aspects of chess. *Payment:* by arrangement.

The British Deaf News (1955), Mrs Irene Hall, The British Deaf Association, 38 Victoria Place, Carlisle CA1 1HU *tel* (0228) 48844 (Voice), (0228) 48844 (DCT) *fax* (0228) 41420.
70p. M. (£8.00 p.a.) Articles, news items, letters dealing with deafness. *Payment:* by arrangement. *Illustrations:* line, half-tone.

British Journal of General Practice (formerly **Journal of the Royal College of General Practitioners**), Dr A.F. Wright MBE, FRCGP, 12 Queen Street, Edinburgh EH2 1JE *tel* 031-225 7629 *fax* 031-220 6750.
£110.00 p.a. M. (£125 overseas, £141.50 by airmail) Articles relevant to general medical practice. *Illustrations:* half-tone, colour. *Payment:* none.

The British Journal of Photography (1854), Reuel Golden, Henry Greenwood & Co. Ltd, 186-187 Temple Chambers, Temple Avenue, London EC4Y 0DT *tel* 071-583 3030 *fax* 071-583 4068.
£1.00. W. Articles on professional, commercial and press photography, and on the more advanced aspects of amateur, technical, industrial, medical, scientific and colour photography. *Illustrations:* line, half-tone, colour. *Payment:* by arrangement.

British Journal of Special Education, Margaret Peter, 12 Hollycroft Avenue, London NW3 7QL   *tel* 071-794 7109.
£26.00 p.a. Q. (£51.50 p.a. UK institutions) Official Journal of the National Association for Special Educational Needs. Articles by specialists on the education of children and young people with all kinds of special educational needs, including the medical, therapeutic and sociological aspects of special education. *Length:* about 2000-3000 words. *Payment:* by arrangement. *Illustrations:* line, half-tone.

British Journalism Review (1989), Geoffrey Goodman, BJR Publishing Ltd, c/o Cassell plc, Villiers House, 41-47 Strand, London WC2N 5JE   *tel* 071-839 4900   *fax* 071-839 1804.
£7.50. Q. (£25.00 p.a., £50.00 p.a. institutions) Comment/criticism/review of matters published by, or of interest to, the media. *Length:* 1000-3000 words. *Illustrations:* b&w photos. *Payment:* by arrangement.

British Medical Journal (1840), Richard Smith BSc, MB, ChBEd, MSc, MFPHM, FRCPE, British Medical Association House, Tavistock Square, London WC1H 9JR   *tel* 071-387 4499   *fax* 071-383 6418.
£5.95. W. Medical and related articles.

British Printer (1888), Andy Thomas, Maclean Hunter House, Chalk Lane, Cockfosters Road, Barnet, Herts. EN4 0BU   *tel* 081-975 9759.
£50.00 p.a. M. Articles on technical and aesthetic aspects of printing processes and graphic reproduction. *Payment:* by arrangement. *Illustrations:* offset litho from photos, line drawings and diagrams, cartoons.

Broadcast, EMAP Media, 33-39 Bowling Green Lane, London EC1R 0DA   *tel* 071-837 1212.
£1.80. W. News and authoritative articles designed for all concerned with the UK and international television and radio industry, and with programmes and advertising on television, radio, video, cable, satellite, business. *Payment:* by arrangement.

Brownie, Marion Thompson, The Guide Association, 17-19 Buckingham Palace Road, London SW1W 0PT   *tel* 071-834 6242.
£1.15. M. Official Magazine of The Guide Association. Short articles for Brownies (girls 7-10 years); fiction with Brownie background (500-800 words); puzzles; 'things to make', etc. *Illustrations:* line, colour. *Payment:* £40 per 1000 words; varies.

Budgerigar World (1982), The County Press, Bala, Gwynedd LL23 7PG   *tel* (0678) 520262; *editor:* Terry A. Tuxford, 145 Western Way, Basingstoke, Hants RG22 6EX   *tel* (0256) 28898.
£2.00. M. (£24.00 p.a.) Articles about exhibition budgerigars. *Payment:* by arrangement. *Illustrations:* half-tone, colour.

Building (1842), Peter Bill, The Builder Group, Builder House, 1 Millharbour, London E14 9RA   *tel* 071-537 2222   *fax* 071-537 2007.
£2.00. W. Covers the entire professional, industrial and manufacturing aspects of the building industry. Articles on architecture and techniques at home and abroad considered, also news and photos. *Payment:* by arrangement.

Built Environment, Professor Peter Hall, Alexandrine Press, PO Box 15, 51 Cornmarket Street, Oxford OX1 3EB   *tel* (0865) 724627   *fax* (0865) 792309.
£55.00 p.a. Q. Articles about architecture, planning and the environment. *Preliminary letter* advisable. *Length:* 1000-5000 words. *Payment:* by arrangement. *Illustrations:* photos and line.

Bulletin of Hispanic Studies (1923), D.S. Severin and A.L. Mackenzie, 2 Abercromby Square, The University, PO Box 147, Liverpool L69 3BX   *tel* 051-794 2774   *fax* 051-708 6502. Published by the Liverpool University Press, PO Box 147, Liverpool L69 3BX.
£25.00 p.a. Q. (£64.00 p.a. institutions, £12.00 p.a. students) Specialist articles on the languages and literatures of Spain, Portugal and Latin America, written in English, Spanish, Portuguese, Catalan or French. *Payment:* none.

Bunty, D.C. Thomson & Co. Ltd, Courier Place, Dundee DD1 9QJ   *tel* (0382) 23131   *fax* (0382) 22214; and 185 Fleet Street, London EC4A 2HS   *tel* 071-242 5086   *fax* 071-404 5694.
45p. W. Vividly told picture-story serials for young girls of school age: 16-18 frames in each 2-page instalment; 23-24 frames in each 3-page instalment. Comic strips and features. Special encouragement to promising scriptwriters and artists. *Payment:* on acceptance.

Bunty Library, D.C. Thomson & Co. Ltd, Courier Place, Dundee DD1 9QJ   *tel* (0382) 23131   *fax* (0382) 22214; and 185 Fleet Street, London EC4A 2HS   *tel* 071-242 5086   *fax* 071-404 5694.
50p. M. Picture-stories for schoolgirls, 64 pages (about 140 line drawings): ballet, school, adventure, theatre, sport. Scripts considered; promising artists and scriptwriters encouraged. *Payment:* on acceptance.

Burlington Magazine (1903), Caroline Elam, 14-16 Duke's Road, London WC1H 9AD   *tel* 071-388 1228   *fax* 071-388 1229.
£9.30. M. Deals with the history and criticism of art. Average *length* of article, 500-3000 words. The editor can use only articles by those who have special knowledge of the subjects treated and cannot accept MSS compiled from works of reference. Book and exhibition reviews and an illustrated monthly Calendar section. No verse. *Payment:* up to £100. *Illustrations:* almost invariably made from photos.

Burton Mail (1898), Brian J. Vertigen, Burton Daily Mail Ltd, 65-68 High Street, Burton on Trent DE14 1LE   *tel* (0283) 512345   *fax* (0283) 515351.
24p. D. Features, news and articles of interest to Burton and south Derbyshire. *Length:* 400-500 words. *Illustrations:* colour and b&w. *Payment:* by negotiation.

Buses (1949), Coombelands House, Coombelands Lane, Addlestone, Surrey KT15 1HY   *tel* (0932) 855909   *fax* (0932) 854750.
£1.90. M. Articles of interest to both road passenger transport operators and bus enthusiasts. *Preliminary enquiry* essential. *Illustrations:* colour transparencies, half-tone, line maps, cartoons. *Payment:* on application.

Business Life (1985), Sandra Harris, Premier Magazines, Berger House, 36-38 Berkeley Square, London W1X 5DA   *tel* 071-495 8788   *fax* 071-499 5379.
Free. 10 p.a. Inflight magazine for British Airways. Articles and features of interest to the European business traveller. *All material commissioned*; approach in writing with ideas. *Length:* 850-1500 words. *Illustrations:* colour photos and line. *Payment:* £300 per 1000 words; £100-£400.

Business Scotland (1947), Graham Lironi, Peebles Publishing Group, Bergius House, Clifton Street, Glasgow G3 7LA   *tel* 041-331 1022   *fax* 041-331 1395.
Controlled circulation. M. Features, profiles and news items of interest to business and finance in Scotland. *Payment:* by arrangement.

Buster (1960), Fleetway Editions Ltd, Egmont House, 25/31 Tavistock Place, London WC1H 9SU   *tel* 071-344 6400   *fax* 071-388 4020.
60p. W. Juvenile comic. Comedy characters in picture strips, for children aged 6 to 12. Full colour. *Payment:* by arrangement.

Cage and Aviary Birds (1902), Brian Byles, IPC Magazines Ltd, King's Reach Tower, Stamford Street, London SE1 9LS   *tel* 071-261 6116   *fax* 071-261 6095.
83p. W. Practical articles on aviculture. First-hand knowledge only. *Illustrations:* line, half-tone, colour, cartoons. *Payment:* by arrangement.

Camcorder User (incorporating **Video Editing** and **Camcorder Buyer**) (1988), Robert Uhlig, WV Publications, 57-59 Rochester Place, London NW1 9JU   *tel* 071-485 0011   *fax* 071-482 6269/284 2145.
£2.00. M. Features on film/video-making techniques, specifically tailored to the amateur enthusiast. *Material mostly commissioned. Length:* 1000-2500 words. *Illustrations:* colour and b&w; contact editor for details. *Payment:* by arrangement.

Campaign, Dominic Mills, Haymarket Campaign Magazines Ltd, 22 Lancaster Gate, London W2 3LY   *tel* 071-413 4036   *fax* 071-413 4507.
£1.50. W. News and articles covering the whole of the mass communications field, particularly advertising in all its forms, marketing and the media. Features should not exceed 2000 words. News items also welcome. Press day, Wednesday. *Payment:* by arrangement.

Camping Magazine (1961), John Lloyd, Link House, Dingwall Avenue, Croydon CR9 2TA   *tel* 081-686 2599   *fax* 081-781 6044.
£2.00. M. Covers the spectrum of camping and related activities in all shapes and forms – camping is more than a tent on a site! Lively, anecdotal articles and photos are welcome, but call to discuss your ideas with the editor first. *Length:* 500-1500 words on average. *Illustrations:* line, half-tone, colour. *Payment:* by arrangement.

Car (1962), Gavin Green, EMAP National Publications Ltd, Abbots Court, 34 Farringdon Lane, London EC1R 3AV   *tel* 071-216 6200   *fax* 071-216 6259.
£2.50. M. Top-grade journalistic features on car driving, car people and cars. *Length:* 1000-2500 words. *Payment:* minimum £260 per 1000 words. *Illustrations:* b&w and colour photos to professional standards.

Car Mechanics, Gordon Wright, Kelsey House, 77 High Street, Beckenham, Kent BR3 1AN   *tel* 081-658 3131.
£1.80. M. Practical articles on maintaining, repairing and uprating modern cars for the DIY and enthusiast market. *Preliminary letter* outlining feature necessary. *Length:* average 1500-2000 words. *Payment:* by arrangement. *Illustrations:* line drawings, colour and b&w.

Caravan Magazine (1933), Barry Williams, Link House, Dingwall Avenue, Croydon CR9 2TA   *tel* 081-686 2599   *fax* 081-781 6044/760 0973.
£1.95. M. Lively articles based on real experience of touring caravanning, especially if well illustrated by photos. General countryside or motoring material not wanted. *Payment:* by arrangement.

Carers World (1993), Chris Cattrall, 1 Coverdale Road, Lancaster LA1 5PY   *tel/fax* (0524) 39241.
£1.50. M. Factual and informative articles aimed at the disabled, carers and the elderly. *Length:* up to 1200 words. *Illustrations:* line, half-tone, cartoons. *Payment:* by arrangement; £25 colour, £5 b&w.

Caribbean Times (1981; incorporating African Times), Arif Ali, Hansib Publishing Ltd, Tower House, 141/149 Fonthill Road, London N4 3HF   *tel* 071-281 1191   *fax* 071-263 9656.
45p. W. News stories, articles and features of interest to Britain's Afro-Caribbean community. *Illustrations:* half-tone, line. *Payment:* by negotiation; £10 minimum.

Cat World (1981), Joan Moore, 10 Western Road, Shoreham-by-Sea, West Sussex BN43 5WD   *tel* (0273) 462000   *fax* (0273) 455994.
£1.50. M. Bright, lively articles on any aspect of cat ownership. Articles on breeds of cats and veterinary articles by acknowledged experts only. No unsolicited fiction. *Illustrations:* b&w and colour photos, cartoons. *Payment:* by arrangement; £7.50 each.

Catch, D.C. Thomson & Co. Ltd, Courier Place, Dundee DD1 9QJ   *tel* (0382) 23131   *fax* (0382) 22214; and 185 Fleet Street, London EC4A 2HS   *tel* 071-242 5086   *fax* 071-404 5694.
£1.20. M. 92-page gravure monthly for 17-21-year-old women. Fiction (up to 1800 words), fashion, beauty, features. *Illustrations:* art illustrations in full colour, colour photos, cartoons. *Payment:* on acceptance.

Caterer & Hotelkeeper (1893), Gary Crossley, Reed Business Publishing, Quadrant House, The Quadrant, Sutton, Surrey SM2 5AS   *tel* 081-652 8680   *telex* 892084 REEDBP G   *fax* 081-652 8973/8947.
£1.35. W. Articles on all aspects of the hotel and catering industries. *Length:* up to 1500 words. *Illustrations:* line, half-tone, colour. *Payment:* by arrangement.

Catholic Gazette (1910), Fr. Paul Billington, 114 West Heath Road, London NW3 7TX   *tel* 081-458 3316   *fax* 081-905 5780.
80p. M. Articles on evangelisation and the Christian life. *Length:* up to 1500 words. *Illustrations:* b&w photos, line, cartoons. *Payment:* by arrangement.

The Catholic Herald, Cristina Odone, Herald House, Lambs Passage, Bunhill Row, London EC1Y 8TQ   *tel* 071-588 3101   *fax* 071-256 9728.
45p. W. Independent newspaper covering national and international affairs from a Catholic/Christian viewpoint as well as church news. *Length:* articles 600-1100 words. *Illustrations:* photos of Catholic and Christian interest, cartoons. *Payment:* by arrangement.

Catholic Pictorial (1961), David Mahon, Media House, Mann Island, Pier Head, Liverpool L3 1DQ   *tel* 051-236 2191   *fax* 051-236 2216.
40p. W. News and photo features (maximum 800 words plus illustration) of Merseyside, regional and national Catholic interest only. Has a strongly social editorial and is a trenchant tabloid. *Payment:* by arrangement.

Catholic Times (relaunched 1993), Norman Cresswell, 1st Floor, St James's Buildings, Oxford Street, Manchester M1 6FP   *tel* 061-236 8856   *fax* 061-237 5590.
40p. W. News (400 words) and news features (800 words) of Catholic interest. *Illustrations:* b&w photos. *Payment:* £30-£80; £50.

Cencrastus: Scottish & International Literature, Arts and Affairs (1979), Raymond Ross and Thom Nairn, Unit One, Abbeymount Techbase, 8 Easter Road, Abbeymount, Edinburgh EH8 8EJ   *tel* 031-661 5687.
£1.80 (back copies £2.00). Q. Articles, short stories, poetry, reviews. *Payment:* by arrangement. *Illustrations:* line, half-tone.

Certified Accountant, Brian O'Kane, Cork Publishing Ltd, 19 Rutland Street, Cork, Republic of Ireland   *tel* (21) 313855   *fax* (21) 313496.
£2.00. M. Journal of the Chartered Association of Certified Accountants. Articles of accounting and financial interest. *Payment:* £120 per 1000 words.

Chapman (1969), Joy Hendry, 4 Broughton Place, Edinburgh EH1 3RX   *tel* 031-557 2207   *fax* 031-556 9565.
£2.95. Q. (£12.00 p.a.) 'Scotland's Quality Literary Magazine.' Poetry, short stories, reviews, criticism, articles on Scottish culture. *Illustrations:* line, half-tone, cartoons. *Payment:* £8.50 per page; by negotiation.

Chat (1986), Terry Tavner, IPC Magazines Ltd, King's Reach Tower, Stamford Street, London SE1 9LS   *tel* 071-261 6565   *fax* 071-261 6534.
49p. W. Tabloid weekly for women; fiction. *Length:* up to 1000 words. *Illustrations:* half-tone, colour, cartoons. *Payment:* by arrangement.

Cheshire Life (1934), Patrick O'Neill, Town & County Magazines, Oyston Mill, Strand Road, Preston PR1 8UR   *tel* (0772) 722022   *fax* (0772) 736496.
£1.90. M. Articles of county interest. *Length:* 800-1000 words. *Illustrations:* line and half-tone, 4-colour positives. Photos of definite Cheshire interest. *Payment:* by arrangement.

Child Education (1924), Gill Moore, Scholastic Publications Ltd, Villiers House, Clarendon Avenue, Leamington Spa, Warks. CV32 5PR   *tel* (0926) 887799   *fax* (0926) 883331.
£2.10. M. For teachers, pre-school staff, nursery nurses and parents concerned with children aged 3-8. Articles by specialists on practical teaching ideas and methods, child development, education news. *Length:* 800-1600 words. *Payment:* by arrangement. Profusely illustrated with photos and line drawings; also large pictures in full colour. Also **Infant Projects** (formerly Child Education Special) (1978). Margot O'Keeffe. £2.00. Bi-M.

The China Quarterly, Dr David Shambaugh, School of Oriental and African Studies, Thornhaugh Street, Russell Square, London WC1H 0XG   *tel* 071-323 6129   *fax* 071-580 6836.
£29/$56 p.a. Q. (£36/$70 institutions, £15/$28 students) Articles on contemporary China. *Length:* 8000 words approx. *Payment:* on specially commissioned articles only.

Choice (1974), Apex House, Oundle Road, Peterborough PE2 9NP   *tel* (0733) 555123   *fax* (0733) 898487.
£1.75. M. Life style magazine for the 50+ market. Editor insists that writers should read and digest magazine before making contact with her. Travel is not commissioned, but news/feature ideas with colour photos can be. *Payment:* by agreement.

Christian Herald (1866), Herald House Ltd, 96 Dominion Road, Worthing, West Sussex BN14 8JP   *tel* (0903) 821082   *fax* (0903) 821081.
40p. W. Evangelical Christian paper intended for families. News, well-illustrated 'it really happened' and general filler items up to 800 words. *No* short stories. *Payment:* £20-£50, depending on length/pictures used.

Chronicle & Echo, Northampton (1931), Robin Fletcher, EMAP Newspapers Ltd, Upper Mounts, Northampton NN1 3HR   *tel* (0604) 231122   *fax* (0604) 233000.
25p. D. Articles, features and news – mostly commissioned – of interest to the Northampton area. *Length/Illustrations:* varies. *Payment:* by negotiation.

Church of England Newspaper (1828), Christian Weekly Newspapers, 12-13 Clerkenwell Green, London EC1R 0DP   *tel* 071-490 0898   *fax* 071-490 0861.
40p. W. Anglican news and articles relating the Christian faith to everyday life. Evangelical basis; almost exclusively commissioned articles. Study of paper desirable. *Length:* up to 1000 words. *Illustrations:* photos, line drawings, cartoons. *Payment:* c. £25 per 1000 words; photos £18, line by arrangement.

Church Times (1863), John Whale, 33 Upper Street, London N1 0PN   *tel* 071-359 4570   *fax* 071-226 3073.
35p. W. Articles on religious topics are considered. No verse or fiction. *Length:* up to 800 words. *Illustrations:* news photos. *Payment:* £100 per 1000 words; Periodical Publishers' Association negotiated rates.

Classic & Sportscar (1982), Ian Bond, Haymarket Magazines Ltd, 60 Waldegrave Road, Teddington, Middlesex TW11 8LG *tel* 081-943 5000 *telex* 8952440 HAYMRT G *fax* 081-943 5844.
£2.40. M. Features on classic cars and sportscars; show news and reviews. *Length:* varies. *Illustrations:* half-tone, colour. *Payment:* £150 per 1000 words; varies.

Classic Boat (1987), Robin Gates, Boating Publications Ltd, Link House, Dingwall Avenue, Croydon CR9 2TA *tel* 081-686 2599 *fax* 081-781 6535.
£2.95. M. Articles and features – technical, nautical science, how-to, maritime history; news. *Study of magazine essential:* read 3-4 back issues and send for contributors' guidelines. *Length:* 500-2000 words. *Illustrations:* colour and b&w photos; line drawings of hulls. *Payment:* £75-£100 per published page.

Classic Cars, Malcolm McKay, IPC Magazines Ltd, King's Reach Tower, Stamford Street, London SE1 9LS *tel* 071-261 5858 *fax* 071-261 6731.
£2.30. M. Specialist articles on older cars. *Length:* from 500-4000 words (subject to prior contract). *Illustrations:* half-tone, colour, cartoons. *Payment:* by negotiation.

Classic CD (1990), Rob Ainsley, Future Publishing, 30 Monmouth Street, Beauford Court, Bath BA1 2BW *tel* (0225) 442244 *fax* (0225) 312228.
£3.50. M. Aims to inform, educate and entertain, with features – historical, and on composers and performers, reviews, news and session reports. *Commissioned* material only. *Length:* up to 2000 words. *Illustrations:* colour and b&w photos, b&w line, including collage and cartoons. *Payment:* £125 per 1000 words; colour up to £300, b&w £35 ⅛ page.

Classical Music (1976), Keith Clarke, 241 Shaftesbury Avenue, London WC2H 8EH *tel* 071-333 1742 *fax* 071-333 1769.
£2.45. F. News, opinion, features on classical music. All material commissioned. *Illustrations:* b&w photos and line; colour covers. *Payment:* minimum £75 per 1000 words; from £35.

Climber and Hill Walker (1962), Tom Prentice, The Plaza Tower, The Plaza, East Kilbride, Glasgow G74 1LW *tel* (03552) 46444.
£1.95. M. Articles on all aspects of mountaineering and hill walking in Great Britain and abroad, and on related subjects. *Study of magazine* essential. *Length:* 1500-2000 words, illustrated. *Illustrations:* colour transparencies/ prints. *Payment:* according to merit.

Clocks (1978), John Hunter, Argus Specialist Publications. Editorial address: 28 Gillespie Crescent, Edinburgh EH10 4HU *tel* 031-229 5550.
£2.40. M. Well-researched articles on antique clocks and their makers, clock repair and restoration, and in general anything of interest to knowledgeable horologists. Sundials, barometers and associated scientific instruments are minority interests of Clocks readers. *Length:* 1500-3000 words. *Illustrations:* line, half-tone, colour; no cartoons. *Payment:* £30 per 1000 words, £5 per b&w photo, £8 per colour print/transparency.

Clothes Show Magazine (1990), Pam Mayers, BBC Magazines, Woodlands, 80 Wood Lane, London W12 0AG *tel* 081-576 2445 *fax* 081-576 2424.
£1.50. M. Articles relating to fashion and beauty in a practical, accessible way. Submit ideas first, in writing, to the editor. *Length:* 2000-word, 4-page main feature; 800-word, 1-page. *Illustrations:* commissioned as necessary. *Payment:* up to £500 for main feature, £150 for 1-page; £150.

Club Mirror (1969), Lewis Eckett, Quantum Publishing Ltd, 29-31 Lower Coombe Street, Croydon, Surrey CR9 1LX *tel* 081-681 2099 *fax* 081-680 8828.

£30.00 p.a. M. Features, news, drink news, catering news, legal and financial advice as a guide to the successful management of clubs. *Payment:* by arrangement. *Illustrations:* line, half-tone.

Coin News (1964), John W. Mussell, Token Publishing Ltd, 105 High Street, Honiton, Devon EX14 8PE *tel* (0404) 45414 *fax* (0404) 45313.
£1.85. M. Articles of high standard on coins, tokens, paper money. *Length:* up to 2000 words. *Payment:* by arrangement.

Commando, D.C. Thomson & Co. Ltd, Albert Square, Dundee DD1 9QJ *tel* (0382) 23131 *fax* (0382) 22214; and 185 Fleet Street, London EC4A 2HS *tel* 071-242 5086 *fax* 071-404 5694.
50p. 8 p.m. Fictional war stories of World War II told in pictures. Scripts should be of about 135 pictures. Synopsis required as an opener. New writers encouraged; send for details. *Payment:* on acceptance.

Commercial Motor (1905), Brian Weatherley, Reed Business Publishing, Quadrant House, The Quadrant, Sutton, Surrey SM2 5AS *tel* 081-652 3302/3303 *fax* 081-652 8969.
£1.15. W. Technical and road transport articles only. *Length:* up to 1500 words. *Payment:* varies. *Illustrations:* drawings and photos.

Communicate (1980), Annie Turner, The Economist Group, 15 Regent Street, London SW1Y 4LR *tel* 071-830 7000 *fax* 071-839 1475.
Controlled circulation. M. Covers all aspects of communication management: analysis pieces (200-700 words), features (700-1600 words), case studies (1200 words). *All material commissioned. Illustrations:* colour and b&w photos, line, diagrams. *Payment:* £165 per 1000 words; by negotiation.

Community Care (1974), Terry Philpot, Quadrant House, The Quadrant, Sutton, Surrey SM2 5AS *tel* 081-652 4861 *fax* 081-652 4739.
£1.20. W. Articles of professional interest to local authority and voluntary body social workers, managers, teachers and students. *Preliminary letter* advisable. *Length:* 800-1400 words. *Payment:* at current rates. *Illustrations:* line, half-tone.

Company (1978), Mandi Norwood, National Magazine House, 72 Broadwick Street, London W1V 2BP *tel* 071-439 5000.
£1.60. M. Articles on a wide variety of subjects, relevant to young, independent women. Most articles commissioned. *Payment:* usual magazine rate. *Illustrated.*

Computer Weekly (1966), Editor: John Lamb, News Editor: David Bicknell, Features Editor: Lindsay Nicolle, Reed Business Publishing Group, Quadrant House, The Quadrant, Sutton, Surrey SM2 5AS *tel* 081-652 3122 *telex* 892084 REEDBP G *fax* 081-652 3038.
£1.70. W. Feature articles on computer-related topics for business/industry users. *Length:* 1200 words. *Illustrations:* b&w photos, line, cartoons. *Payment:* £150 per feature; negotiable.

Computing (1973), Jerry Sanders, 32-34 Broadwick Street, London W1A 2HG *tel* 071-439 4242 *fax* 071-437 3516.
£70.00 p.a. W. Features and news items on the computer industry and on applications and implications of computers and electronics. *Length:* up to 1800 words. *Payment:* £130 per 1000 words. *Illustrations:* colour photos, line drawings, cartoons.

Construction Europe, Paul Marsden, Southfields, Southview Road, Wadhurst, East Sussex TN5 6TP *tel* (0892) 784088.
Controlled circulation. M. Aimed at contractors, consultants and government/international authorities. *Payment:* by negotiation.

Contemporary Art (1992), Keith Spencer and Lynne Green, 2 Sydney Place, Bath BA2 6NF *tel/fax* (0225) 332527.
£3.95. Q. Articles and reviews on all aspects of contemporary art; book reviews. *Length:* 1000-2000 words. *Illustrations:* colour and b&w photos. *Payment:* from £70 per 1000 words; none for photos.

Contemporary Review (incorporating the **Fortnightly**) (1866), Dr Richard Mullen, Contemporary Review Co. Ltd, Cheam Business Centre, 14 Upper Mulgrave Road, Cheam, Surrey SM2 7AZ *tel* 081-643 4846.
£2.75. M. Independent review dealing with questions of the day, chiefly politics, international affairs, theology, literature, the arts. Mostly commissioned, but with limited scope for freelance authors with authoritative knowledge. Articles must be typewritten and double-spaced; 2000-3000 words. TS returned *only if sae enclosed*. Intending contributors should *study journal* before submitting (sample copy: £3.00 from the above address). *Payment:* £5 per page (500 words), 2 complimentary copies.

Control & Instrumentation (1958), Brian J. Tinham BSc, CEng, MInstMC, Morgan-Grampian (Process Press) Ltd, 30 Calderwood Street, Woolwich, London SE18 6QH *tel* 081-855 7777.
£60.00 p.a. M. Authoritative main feature articles on measurement, automation, control systems, instrumentation and data processing; also export, business and engineering news. *Length of articles:* 750 words for highly technical pieces, 1000-2500 words main features. *Payment:* according to value. *Illustrations:* photos and drawings of equipment using automatic techniques, control engineering personalities, cartoons.

Cosmetic World News (1949), M.A. Murray-Pearce, Caroline Marcuse, Norman Clare, 130 Wigmore Street, London W1H 0AT *tel* 071-486 6757/8 *fax* 071-487 5436.
£90.00 p.a. Bi-M. International news magazine of perfumery, cosmetics and toiletries industry. World-wide reports, photo-news stories, articles (500-1000 words) on essential oils and new cosmetic raw materials, and exclusive information on industry's companies and personalities welcomed. *Payment:* by arrangement, minimum 10p per word. *Illustrations:* b&w and colour photos or colour separations.

Cosmopolitan (1972), Marcelle D'Argy Smith, National Magazine House, 72 Broadwick Street, London W1V 2BP *tel* 071-439 5000 *fax* 071-439 5016.
£1.70. M. Short stories, articles. Commissioned material only. *Payment:* by arrangement. *Illustrated*.

Country (1901), Anthony Bush, The Country Gentlemen's Association, Hill Crest Mews, London Road, Baldock, Herts. SG7 6ND *tel* (0462) 490206.
£1.70. M. The Magazine of the Country Gentlemen's Association. Authoritative articles on wildlife, countryside and general interest. Gardening, cookery, fashion, travel. *Length:* 500-1000 words. *Payment:* by arrangement.

Country Homes & Interiors (1986), Julia Watson, IPC Magazines Ltd, King's Reach Tower, Stamford Street, London SE1 9LS *tel* 071-261 6451 *fax* 071-261 6895.
£1.95. M. Articles on property, country homes, interior designs. *Illustrations:* colour. *Payment:* from £150 per 1000 words.

Country Life (1897), Clive Aslet, IPC Magazines Ltd, King's Reach Tower, Stamford Street, London SE1 9LS *tel* 071-261 7058 *fax* 071-261 5139.
£1.80. W. Illustrated journal chiefly concerned with British country life, social history, architecture and the fine arts, natural history, agriculture, gardening and sport. *Length of articles:* about 700, 1000 or 1300 words. *Illustrations:*

mainly colour photos, cartoons. *Payment:* according to merit; £40 b&w, £60 colour.

Country Living (1985), Francine Lawrence, National Magazine House, 72 Broadwick Street, London W1V 2BP   *tel* 071-439 5000   *fax* 071-439 5093.
£1.95. M. Up-market magazine for country dwellers and townies who have the country at heart. *No* unsolicited material and *do not* send valuable transparencies; magazine cannot accept responsibility for loss of unsolicited material. *Illustrations:* line, half-tone, colour. *Payment:* by arrangement.

Country Quest, Joe Kelly, North Wales Newspapers, Business Park, Mold, Clwyd CH7 1XY   *tel* (0352) 700022.
90p. M. Illustrated articles on matters relating to countryside, history and personalities of Wales and border counties. No fiction. Illustrated work preferred. *Length:* 500-1500 words. *Illustrations:* line, half-tone. *Payment:* by arrangement.

The Countryman (1927), Christopher Hall, Sheep Street, Burford, Oxon OX18 4LH   *tel* (0993) 822258.
£2.00. Bi-M. Every department of rural life and progress except field sports. Party politics and sentimentalising about the country barred. Copy must be trustworthy, well-written, brisk, cogent and light in hand. Articles up to 1500 words. Good paragraphs and notes, first-class poetry and skilful sketches of life and character from personal knowledge and experience. Dependable natural history based on writer's own observation. Really good matter from old unpublished letters and MSS. *Illustrations:* b&w photos and drawings, but all must be exclusive and out of the ordinary, and bear close scrutiny. Humour welcomed if genuine. *Payment:* £40 per 1000 words minimum; £10 minimum. Payment is usually much in excess of these figures, according to merit.

Country-Side (1905), Dr David Applin, PO Box 87, Cambridge CB1 3UP   *tel/fax* (0933) 314672.
£12.00 p.a. Q. Official organ of the British Naturalists' Association (BNA), the national body for naturalists. Original observations on wildlife and its protection, and on natural history generally, but not on killing for sport. *Preliminary letter* or study of magazine advisable. *Payment:* 1200 words plus pictures £50, shorter articles pro-rata. *Illustrations:* photos, drawings, cartoons.

County (1992), Howard M. Reynolds, Enterprise Magazines Ltd, Post & Mail House, 28 Colmore Circus, Birmingham B4 6AX   *tel* 021-212 4141   *fax* 021-212 2468.
£1.25. M. Articles of topical relevance or historical interest relating to Heart of England region of Birmingham, Warwickshire and Worcestershire. Prefer illustrated material. *Length:* 1200 words. *Illustrations:* line, half-tone, colour. *Payment:* £50 per 1200 words; according to quality.

The Courier and Advertiser (1816 and 1801), D.C. Thomson & Co. Ltd, 80 Kingsway East, Dundee DD4 8SL   *tel* (0382) 23131   *telex* DCTHOM G 76380   *fax* (0382) 454590; and 185 Fleet Street, London EC4A 2HS   *tel* 071-242 5086.
28p. D. Ind.

Coventry Evening Telegraph, Dan Mason, Corporation Street, Coventry CV1 1FP   *tel* (0203) 633633   *fax* (0203) 550869.
26p. D. Topical, illustrated articles, those with a Warwickshire interest particularly acceptable. *Length:* up to 600 words.

Creative Camera (1968), David Brittain, CC Publishing, Sadler's Wells, Rosebery Avenue, London EC1R 4TN   *tel* 071-713 0671.

£3.95. Bi-M. Illustrated articles and pictures dealing with creative photography, sociology of, history of and criticism of photos; book and exhibition reviews. Arts Council supported. *Payment:* by arrangement. *Illustrations:* b&w, colour.

The Cricketer International (1921), Peter Perchard, Third Street, Langton Green, Tunbridge Wells, Kent TN3 0EN   *tel* (0892) 862551   *fax* (0892) 863755.
£2.20. M. Articles on cricket at any level. *Illustrations:* line, half-tone, colour, cartoons. *Payment:* £50 per 1000 words; minimum £15.

The Criminologist (1966), R.W. Stone, East Row, Little London, Chichester, West Sussex PO19 1PG   *tel* (0243) 775552   *fax* (0243) 779278.
£34.50 p.a. post free. Q. Specialised material designed for an expert and professional readership on national and international criminology, the police, forensic science, the law, penology, sociology and law enforcement. Articles welcomed, up to 4000 words, from those familiar with the journal's style and requirements. *A preliminary letter* with a brief résumé is requested. *Payment:* according to merit. *Illustrations:* line and photos.

Critical Quarterly (1959), Editorial Board: C.B. Cox, Kate Pahl, Colin MacCabe. The Secretary, Programme in Literary Linguistics, University of Strathclyde, Glasgow G1 1XH.
£19.50 p.a. Q. (£32.50 p.a. institutions) Fiction, poems, literary criticism. *Length:* 2000-5000 words. Interested contributors should *study magazine* before submitting MSS. *Payment:* by arrangement.

Critical Wave: The European Science Fiction & Fantasy Review (1987), Steve Green, Martin Tudor, 33 Scott Road, Olton, Solihull B92 7LQ   *tel* 021-706 0108.
£1.95. Bi-M. (£8.50 p.a.) Interviews with leading figures in the sf/fantasy/horror field; features on the genres; book reviews; market reports; art portfolios (by arrangement). *No* fiction or poetry. *Length:* by arrangement. *Illustrations:* b&w photos and line – send photocopy samples of portfolios (single illustrations rarely used). *Payment:* none, but receive one complimentary copy of magazine.

CTN (Confectioner, Tobacconist, Newsagent), Anne Bingham, Maclaren House, 19 Scarbrook Road, Croydon CR9 1QH   *tel* 081-688 7788   *fax* 081-688 9657.
90p. W. (£45.00 p.a.) Trade news and brief articles illustrated when possible with photos or line drawings. Must be of current interest to retail confectioner-tobacconists and newsagents. *Length:* articles 600-800 words. *Payment:* by negotiation.

Cumbria (1951), Terry Fletcher, Dalesman Publishing Company Ltd, Stable Courtyard, Broughton Hall, Skipton, North Yorkshire BD23 3AE   *tel* (0756) 701381   *fax* (0756) 701326.
75p. M. Articles of genuine rural interest concerning Lakeland and Cumbria. Short *length* preferred. *Illustrations:* line drawings and first-class photos. *Payment:* according to merit.

Custom Car (1970), Tim Baggaley, Kelsey Publishing Ltd, Kelsey House, 77 High Street, Beckenham, Kent BR3 1AN   *tel* 081-658 3531   *fax* 081-650 8035.
£2.20. M. Customising, drag racing and hot rods. *Length:* by arrangement. *Payment:* by arrangement.

Cycling Weekly (1891), Andrew Sutcliffe, IPC Magazines Ltd, King's Reach Tower, Stamford Street, London SE1 9LS   *tel* 071-261 5588   *fax* 071-261 5758.
£1.20. W. Racing and technical articles not exceeding 1500 words. Topical photos with a cycling interest also considered. *Payment:* by arrangement.

The Daily Awaz International (1992), Shirley Rizvi, Middlesex Business Centre, Unit K, Bridge Road, Southall, Middlesex UB2 4AB   *tel* 081-813 9933   *fax* 081-813 8822.
40p. Mon.-Sun. Asian-related features and news stories. *Length:* 1200-word features. *Illustrations:* colour and b&w photos. *Payment:* by agreement; none for photos.

Daily Express, Sir Nicholas Lloyd, Ludgate House, 245 Blackfriars Road, London SE1 9UX   *tel* 071-928 8000   *cables* Lon Express   *telex* 21841/21842   *fax* 071-633 0244; Great Ancoats Street, Manchester M60 4HB   *tel* 061-236 2112.
32p. D. Exclusive news: striking photos. Leader page articles, 600 words; facts preferred to opinions. *Payment:* according to value.

Daily Mail (1896), Paul Dacre, Northcliffe House, 2 Derry Street, London W8 5TT   *tel* 071-938 6000   *fax* 071-937 3251.
32p. D. Highest *payment* for good, exclusive news. Ideas welcomed for leader page articles, 500-800 words average. Exclusive news photos always wanted.

Daily Mirror (1903), Colin Myler, 1 Canada Square, Canary Wharf, London E14 5AP   *tel* 071-293 3000   *fax* 071-293 3758.
27p. D. Top *payment* for exclusive news and news pictures. Articles from freelances used, and ideas bought: send synopsis only. 'Unusual' pictures and those giving a new angle on the news are welcomed.

Daily Post (1855), Keith Ely, PO Box 48, Old Hall Street, Liverpool L69 3EB   *tel* 051-227 2000   *fax* 051-236 4682.
30p. D. Ind. Articles of general interest and topical features of special interest to North West England and North Wales. No verse or fiction. *Payment:* according to value. News and feature illustrations.

Daily Record, Editor-in-Chief: E.J. Laird, Anderston Quay, Glasgow G3 8DA   *tel* 041-248 7000   *telex* 778277; *London office:* 33 Holborn, EC1P 1DQ   *tel* 071-353 0246.
27p. D. Topical articles, from 300-700 words; exclusive stories of Scottish interest and exclusive colour photos.

Daily Sport (1988), Jeff McGowan, 19 Great Ancoats Street, Manchester M60 4BT   *tel* 061-236 4466   *fax* 061-236 4535   *Mercury Link* 19045750.
30p. Mon.-Fri. Factual stories and series. *Length:* up to 1000 words. *Illustrations:* b&w and colour photos, cartoons. *Payment:* £30-£5000.

Daily Star (1978), Brian Hitchen CBE, Ludgate House, 245 Blackfriars Road, London SE1 9UX   *tel* 071-928 8000   *cables* Lon Express   *telex* 21841/ 21842   *fax* 071-620 1641.
25p. D. Hard news exclusives, commanding substantial payment. Major interviews with big-star personalities; short features; series based on people rather than things; picture features. *Payment:* short features £75-£100; full page £250-£300; double page £400-£600, otherwise by negotiation. *Illustrations:* line, half-tone, cartoons.

The Daily Telegraph (1855), Editor-in-Chief: Max Hastings, 1 Canada Square, Canary Wharf, London E14 5DT   *tel* 071-538 5000   *telex* 22874/5/6   *fax* 071-538 6242.
48p. D. 60p. Sat. Ind. Articles on a wide range of subjects of topical interest considered. *Preliminary letter* and synopsis required. *Length:* 700-1000 words. *Payment:* by arrangement.

Dairy Farmer and Dairy Beef Producer, David Shead, Morgan Grampian Farming Press Ltd, Wharfedale Road, Ipswich IP1 4LG   *tel* (0473) 241122   *fax* (0473) 240501.

Controlled circulation. M. Authoritative articles dealing in practical, lively style with dairy farming. Topical controversial articles invited. Well-written, illustrated accounts of new ideas being tried on dairy farms are especially wanted. *Length:* normally up to 1500 words. *Payment:* by arrangement. *Illustrations:* line, half-tone, colour.

Dairy Industries International (1936), Sarah McRitchie, Wilmington House, Church Hill, Wilmington, Dartford, Kent DA2 7EF *tel* (0322) 277788 *fax* (0322) 276474.
£54.00 post free (UK). M. Covers the entire field of milk processing, the manufacture of products from liquid milk, and ice cream. Articles relating to dairy plant, butter and cheese making, ice cream making, new product developments and marketing, etc. *Payment:* by arrangement. *Illustrations:* colour transparencies/prints and Indian ink diagrams.

The Dalesman (1939), Terry Fletcher, Dalesman Publishing Company Ltd, Stable Courtyard, Broughton Hall, Skipton, North Yorkshire BD23 3AE *tel* (0756) 701381 *fax* (0756) 701326.
85p. M. Articles and stories of genuine rural interest concerning Yorkshire. Short *length* preferred. *Payment:* according to merit. *Illustrations:* line drawings and first-class photos preferably featuring people.

DAM (Disability Arts Magazine) (1991), Roland Humphrey, DAM Publishing Ltd, 10 Woad Lane, Great Coates, Grimsby DN37 9NH *tel/minicom* (0472) 280031 *fax* (0472) 886631.
£12.00 p.a. Q. (£6.00 unwaged; £2.00 sample copy) Focuses on all aspects of creative work by disabled people and on disability culture. News and features, venues, exhibitions, artists and cabarets. *Length:* 500-2000 words. *Illustrations:* line, half-tone, colour, cartoons. *Payment:* (disabled people only) £80 per 1000 words; varies.

Dance & Dancers (1950), John Percival, 214 Panther House, 38 Mount Pleasant, London WC1X 0AP *tel/fax* 071-837 2711.
£1.75. M. Specialist features, reviews on modern/classical dance, dancers. *Length:* by prior arrangement. *Payment:* by arrangement. *Illustrations:* line, half-tone; colour covers.

Dancing Times (1910), Editor: Mary Clarke, Editorial Adviser: Ivor Guest, The Dancing Times Ltd, Clerkenwell House, 45-47 Clerkenwell Green, London EC1R 0EB *tel* 071-250 3006 *fax* 071-253 6679.
£1.50. M. Ballet and stage dancing, both from general, historical, critical and technical angles. Well-informed freelance articles are occasionally used, but only after preliminary arrangements. *Payment:* by arrangement. *Illustrations:* occasional line, action photos always preferred; colour invited.

The Dandy, D.C. Thomson & Co. Ltd, Courier Place, Dundee DD1 9QJ *tel* (0382) 23131 *fax* (0382) 22214; and 185 Fleet Street, London EC4A 2HS *tel* 071-242 5086 *fax* 071-404 5694.
35p. W. Comic strips for children. 10-12 pictures per single page story, 18-20 pictures per 2-page story. Promising artists encouraged. *Payment:* on acceptance.

Dandy Cartoon Library, D.C. Thomson & Co. Ltd, Courier Place, Dundee DD1 9QJ *tel* (0382) 23131 *fax* (0382) 22214; and 185 Fleet Street, London EC4A 2HS *tel* 071-242 5086 *fax* 071-404 5694.
50p. M. 64 pages of jokes and gags in cartoon form featuring the well-known characters from the weekly Beano and Dandy publications.

Dandy Library, D.C. Thomson & Co. Ltd, Courier Place, Dundee DD1 9QJ *tel* (0382) 23131 *fax* (0382) 22214; and 185 Fleet Street, London EC4A 2HS *tel* 071-242 5086 *fax* 071-404 5694.
50p. 2 p.m. Extra-long comic adventure stories featuring the well-known characters from the weekly Dandy publication.

Darts World (1972), Tony Wood, World Magazines Limited, 9 Kelsey Park Road, Beckenham, Kent BR3 2LH *tel* 081-650 6580 *fax* 081-650 2534.
£1.40. M. Articles and stories with darts theme. *Illustrations:* half-tone, cartoons. *Payment:* £40-£50 per 1000 words; by arrangement.

Day by Day (1963), Patrick Richards, Woolacombe House, 141 Woolacombe Road, Blackheath, London SE3 8QP *tel* 081-856 6249.
70p. M. Articles and news on non-violence and social justice. Reviews of art, books, films, plays, musicals and opera. Cricket reports. Occasional poems and very occasional short stories in keeping with editorial viewpoint. *Payment:* £2 per 1000 words. No *illustrations* required.

Debbie Library, D.C. Thomson & Co. Ltd, Courier Place, Dundee DD1 9QJ *tel* (0382) 23131 *fax* (0382) 22214; and 185 Fleet Street, London EC4A 2HS *tel* 071-242 5086 *fax* 071-404 5694.
50p. M. 64-page picture-stories for schoolgirls (about 140 line drawings). Adventure, animal, mystery, school, sport. Scripts considered; promising scriptwriters and artists encouraged. *Payment:* on acceptance.

Dental Update (1973), Susan Joyce, George Warman Publications (UK) Ltd, 20 Leas Road, Guildford, Surrey GU1 4QT *tel* (0483) 304944 *fax* (0483) 303191.
£45.00 p.a. 10 p.a. (£20.00 p.a. students) Clinical articles, clinical quizzes. *Illustrations:* line, colour. *Payment:* £50-£100 per 1000 words; £50 cover photos only.

Derby Evening Telegraph, Mike Lowe, Northcliffe House, Meadow Road, Derby DE1 2DW *tel* (0332) 291111 *fax* (0322) 290280.
25p. Mon.-Sat. Articles and news of local interest. *Payment:* by negotiation.

Derbyshire Life and Countryside (1931), Lodge Lane, Derby DE1 3HE *tel* (0332) 347087/8/9 *fax* (0332) 290688.
£1.00. M. Articles, preferably illustrated, about Derbyshire life, people and history. *Length:* up to 800 words. Some short stories set in Derbyshire accepted, but verse not used. *Payment:* according to nature and quality of contribution. *Illustrations:* photos of Derbyshire subjects.

The Dickensian, Dickens House, 48 Doughty Street, London WC1N 2LF.
£9.00 p.a. 3 p.a. (£11.00 p.a. institutions; overseas rates on application) Published by The Dickens Fellowship. Welcomes articles on all aspects of Dickens' life, works and character. *Payment:* none. Contributions (enclose sae if return required) and editorial correspondence to the editor: Dr Malcolm Andrews, Eliot College, University of Kent, Canterbury, Kent CT2 7NS *fax* (0227) 475471.

Digests with one or two exceptions are not included since they seldom use original material, but reprint articles previously published elsewhere and extracts from books. But see **The Reader's Digest.**

Director (1947), Stuart Rock, Mountbarrow House, 12-20 Elizabeth Street, London SW1W 9RB *tel* 071-730 8320 *fax* 071-235 5627.
£3.00. M. Authoritative business-related articles. Send synopsis of proposed article and examples of printed work. *Length:* 500-3000 words. *Payment:* by arrangement. *Illustrated* mainly in colour.

Dirt Bike Rider (1981), Mike Greenough, Key Publishing Ltd, PO Box 100, Stamford, Lincs. PE9 1XQ *tel* (0780) 55131 *fax* (0780) 57261.
£1.85. M. Features, track tests, coverage on all aspects of off-road motorcycling. *Length:* up to 1000 words. *Payment:* £80 per 1000 words. *Illustrations:* half-tone, colour, cartoons.

Disability Now (1957), Mary Wilkinson, The Spastics Society, 12 Park Crescent, London W1N 4EQ *tel* 071-636 5020 *fax* 071-436 4582.
£10.00 p.a. M. (£15.00 organisations, £20.00 overseas) Topical, authoritative articles of interest to people with a wide range of disabilities, carers and professionals; also arts and book reviews. Contributions from people with disabilities particularly welcome. *Preliminary letter desirable. Length:* up to 1000 words. *Illustrations:* b&w news photos, cartoons. *Payment:* £75 per 1000 words; by arrangement.

Diver (1953), Bernard Eaton, 55 High Street, Teddington, Middlesex TW11 8HA *tel* 081-943 4288 *fax* 081-943 4312.
£2.30. M. Articles on sub aqua diving and underwater developments. *Length:* 1500-2000 words. *Illustrations:* line, half-tone, colour. *Payment:* by arrangement.

Doctor (1971), Helena Sturridge, Reed Elsevier Medical, Quadrant House, The Quadrant, Sutton, Surrey SM2 5AS *tel* 081-652 8740 *telex* 892084 REEDBP G *fax* 081-652 8701.
£2.00. W. Commissioned articles and features of interest to GPs. *Length:* various. *Illustrations:* colour photos – news, features, clinical; some line. *Payment:* NUJ rates.

Dorset Evening Echo (1923), Mike Woods, Southern Newspapers plc, 57 St Thomas Street, Weymouth, Dorset DT4 8EU *tel* (0305) 784804 *fax* (0305) 760387.
22p. D. News and occasional features (1000-2000 words). *Illustrations:* b&w photos. *Payment:* NUJ rates.

Dorset Life – The Dorset Magazine (1967), John Newth, Trinity Lane, Wareham, Dorset BH20 4LN *tel* (0929) 551264.
£1.20. M. Articles (500-1500 words), photos (colour or b&w) and line drawings with a *specifically* Dorset theme. *Payment:* by arrangement.

The Downside Review, Dom Daniel Rees, Downside Abbey, Stratton-on-the-Fosse, Nr Bath, Somerset BA3 4RH *tel* Stratton-on-the-Fosse (0761) 232 295.
£5.00. Q. (£20.00 p.a.) Articles and book reviews on theology, metaphysics, mysticism and modernism, and monastic and church history. *Payment:* not usual.

Drapers Record (formerly **DR The Fashion Business**) (1887), Juliet Warkentin, EMAP Maclaren, 67 Clerkenwell Road, London EC1R 5BH *tel* 071-404 0429 *fax* 071-404 0396.
£1.50. W. Editorial aimed at fashion retailers, large and small. No unsolicited material. *Payment:* by negotiation. *Illustrations:* colour and b&w: photos, drawings and cartoons.

Dundee Evening Telegraph and Post, D.C. Thomson & Co. Ltd, 80 Kingsway East, Dundee DD4 8SL *tel* (0382) 23131 *telex* DCTHOM 76380 *fax* (0382) 454590; and 185 Fleet Street, London EC4A 2HS *tel* 071-242 5086 *fax* 071-404 5694.
24p. D.

Early Music (1973), Tess Knighton, Oxford University Press, 3 Park Road, London NW1 6XN *tel* 071-724 1707 *fax* 071-723 5033.

£9.50. Q. (£35.00 p.a., institutions £45.00 p.a.) Lively, informative and scholarly articles on aspects of medieval, renaissance, baroque and classical music. *Payment:* £20 per 1000 words. *Illustrations:* line, half-tone, colour.

Early Times (1988), Dolly Clew, 2/4 Leigham Court Road, London SW16 2PD   *tel* 081-769 4444   *fax* 081-769 6052.
50p. W. Serious weekly newspaper for children. News and features of interest to 10-16-year-olds; two pages dedicated to young reporters' articles. *Payment:* by arrangement. *Illustrations:* line, half-tone.

East Anglian Daily Times (1874), Malcolm Pheby, 30 Lower Brook Street, Ipswich, Suffolk IP4 1AN   *tel* (0473) 230023   *fax* (0473) 225296.
33p. D. Features of East Anglian interest, preferably with pics. *Length:* 500 words. *Illustrations:* colour, b&w. *Payment:* £50 per feature; NUJ rates.

East Lothian Life (1989), Pauline Jaffray, 2 Beveridge Row, Belhaven, Dunbar, East Lothian EH42 1TP   *tel* (0368) 863593.
£2.00. Q. Articles and features with an East Lothian slant. *Length:* up to 1000 words. *Illustrations:* b&w photos, line, cartoons. *Payment:* negotiable.

Eastern Art Report (1989), Sajid Rizvi, Eastern Art Publishing/NEAR, Acre House, 69-76 Long Acre, London WC2E 9AS   *tel* 071-379 3939/081-392 1122   *fax* 081-392 1422.
£5.00. Bi-M. (£25.00 p.a.) Original, well-researched articles on all aspects of the visual arts – Islamic, Indian, Chinese and Japanese; reviews. *Length* of articles: min. 1500 words. *Illustrations:* colour transparencies, b&w photos; no responsibility accepted for unsolicited material. *Payment:* by arrangement.

Eastern Daily Press (1870), L. Sear, Prospect House, Rouen Road, Norwich NR1 1RE   *tel* (0603) 628311   *telex* 975276 ECNNCH G   *fax* (0603) 612930; *London office:* AMRA Ltd, Park Place, 12 Lawn Lane, SW8 1UD   *tel* 071-820 1000   *fax* 071-820 0304/5.
35p. D. Ind. Limited market for articles of East Anglian interest not exceeding 900 words.

Eastern Evening News (1882), Peter Ware, Prospect House, Rouen Road, Norwich NR1 1RE   *tel* (0603) 628311   *telex* 975276 ECNNCH G   *fax* (0603) 612930; *London office:* AMRA Ltd, Park Place, 12 Lawn Lane, SW8 1UD *tel* 071-820 1000   *fax* 071-820 0304/5.
26p. D. Ind. Interested in news-based features, material for advert features and cartoons. *Length:* up to 500 words. *Payment:* NUJ or agreed rates.

Eastern Eye (1989), Sarwar Ahmed, Eastern Eye Publications Ltd, 138-148 Cambridge Heath Road, London E1 5QJ   *tel* 071-702 8012   *fax* 071-702 7937.
45p. W. Articles, features and news of interest to Asians aged 16-36. *Length:* features, 1800 words. *Illustrations:* colour and b&w photos. *Payment:* £75 per 1000 words; £10.

The Ecologist, Edward Goldsmith, Nicholas Hildyard, Agriculture House, Bath Road, Sturminster Newton, Dorset DT10 1DU   *tel* (0258) 473476.
£3.50. 6 p.a. Fully-referenced articles on economic, social and environmental affairs from an ecological standpoint. *Study* magazine for level and approach. *Length:* 1000-5000 words. *Illustrations:* line, half-tone. *Payment:* by arrangement.

Economic Journal (1891), John D. Hey, Department of Economics, University of York, York YO1 5DD   *tel/fax* (0904) 433575.

Free to members. Bi-M. (£95.00 p.a.) Organ of the Royal Economic Society. Economic theory, applied economics and the development of economic thinking in relation to current problems. Statistical and economic diagrams. Reviews of new books, software and other publications. *Payment:* none.

Economica (1921. New Series, 1934), Editors: Dr F.A. Cowell, Dr D.C. Webb, STICERD, London School of Economics, Houghton Street, London WC2A 2AE   *tel* 071-955 7855   *fax* 071-242 2357.
£12.00. Q. (subscription rates on application) Learned journal covering the fields of economics, economic history and statistics. *Payment:* none.

The Economist (1843), Bill Emmott, 25 St James's Street, London SW1A 1HG   *tel* 071-839 7000.
£1.80. W. Articles staff-written.

Edinburgh Evening News, Harry Roulston, 20 North Bridge, Edinburgh EH1 1YT   *tel* 031-225 2468   *fax* 031-225 7302.
22p. D. Ind. Features on current affairs, preferably in relation to our circulation area. Women's talking points, local historical articles; subjects of general interest.

Edinburgh Review (1969), Murdo Macdonald, 22 George Square, Edinburgh EH8 9LF   *tel* 031-650 4689   *fax* 031-662 0053.
£6.95. Bi-A. (£12.00 p.a.) Fiction, clearly written articles on Scottish and international cultural and philosophical ideas. *Payment:* by arrangement.

Education (1903), George Low, 21-27 Lamb's Conduit Street, London WC1N 3NJ   *tel* 071-242 2548   *fax* 071-831 2855.
£1.46. W. Specialist articles on educational administration, all branches of education; technical education; universities; school building; playing fields; environmental studies; physical education; school equipment; school meals and health; teaching aids. *Length:* 1000 words. *Illustrations:* photos, cartoons. *Payment:* by arrangement.

Electrical Review (1872), T. Tunbridge, Reed Business Publishing, Quadrant House, The Quadrant, Sutton, Surrey SM2 5AS   *tel* 081-652 3113   *telex* 892084 REEDBP G   *fax* 081-652 8951.
£2.50. F. Technical and business articles on electrical and control engineering; outside contributions considered. Electrical news welcomed. *Illustrations:* photos and drawings, cartoons. *Payment:* according to merit.

The Electrical Times (1891), Bill Evett, Reed Business Publishing, Quadrant House, The Quadrant, Sutton, Surrey SM2 5AS   *tel* 081-652 3115   *telex* 892084 REEDBP G   *fax* 081-652 8972.
£2.25. M. Business and technical articles of interest to managers in the electrical industries, with illustrations as necessary. *Length:* 750 words. *Payment:* £100 per article. *Illustrations:* line, half-tone, colour, cartoons.

Elle (UK) (1985), Nicola Jeal, EMAP Women's Group, 20 Orange Street, London WC2H 7ED   *tel* 071-957 8383.
£1.80. M. Commissioned material only. *Payment:* by arrangement. *Illustrations:* colour.

Embroidery, The Embroiderers' Guild, PO Box 42B, East Molesey, Surrey KT8 9BB   *tel* 081-943 1229.
£2.50. Q. (£12.40 p.a.) Articles on historical and contemporary embroidery by curators, artists and craftsmen; exhibition and book reviews; saleroom report; diary of events. *Illustrations:* line, half-tone, colour. *Payment:* by arrangement.

Empire (1989), Philip Thomas, Mappin House, 4 Winsley Street, London W1N 7AR   *tel* 071-436 1515/1601   *fax* 071-323 0276.
£1.85. M. Monthly guide to film and video: articles, features, news. *Length:* various. *Illustrations:* colour and b&w photos. *Payment:* approx. £125 per 1000 words; varies.

The Engineer (1856), Richard Northcote, 30 Calderwood Street, London SE18 6QH   *tel* 081-855 7777.
£3.50. W. (£84.00 p.a.) Covers the business and technology of the engineering industry. Outside contributions paid for if accepted.

English Historical Review (1886), Dr R.J.W. Evans, Dr J.R. Maddicott, Longman Higher Education, Burnt Mill, Harlow, Essex CM20 2JE   *tel* (0279) 426721.
£76.00 p.a. Q. High-class scholarly articles, documents, and reviews or short notices of books. Contributions are not accepted unless they supply original information and should be sent direct to Dr R.J.W. Evans, Editor, E.H.R., Brasenose College, Oxford OX1 4AJ. Books for review should be sent to Dr J.R. Maddicott, Editor, E.H.R., Exeter College, Oxford OX1 3DP. *Payment:* none.

Entomologist's Monthly Magazine (1864), K.G.V. Smith, Gem Publishing Co., Brightwood, Bell Lane, Brightwell cum Sotwell, Wallingford, Oxon OX10 0QD   *tel* (0491) 833882   *fax* (0491) 825161.
£25.00 p.a. 3 p.a. Articles on all orders of insects and terrestrial arthropods, foreign and British. *Payment:* none.

Envoi (1957), Roger Elkin, 44 Rudyard Road, Biddulph Moor, Stoke-on-Trent, Staffs. ST8 7JN   *tel* (0782) 517892.
£9.00 p.a. 3 p.a. New poetry, including sequences, collaborative works and translations, reviews, articles on modern poets and poetic style; poetry competitions; editorial criticism of subscribers' poems (with sae) at no charge. Sample copy: £2.00. *Payment:* 2 complimentary copies.

ES Magazine (1987), Emma Soames, Northcliffe House, 2 Derry Street, London W8 5EE   *tel* 071-938 6000   *fax* 071-937 9302.
Free with the Evening Standard. W. Feature ideas, *exclusively* about London. *Payment:* by negotiation. *Illustrations:* all types.

Esquire (1991), Rosie Boycott, National Magazine House, 72 Broadwick Street, London W1V 2BP   *tel* 071-439 5000   *telegraphic address* Shanmag, London W1   *telex* 263879 NATMAG G   *fax* 071-439 5067.
£2.20. M. Quality men's interest magazine – articles, features. *No* unsolicited material or short stories. *Length:* various. *Illustrations:* colour and b&w photos, line. *Payment:* by arrangement.

Essentials (1988), IPC Magazines Ltd, King's Reach Tower, Stamford Street, London SE1 9LS   *tel* 071-261 5540.
£1.40. M. Features, plus fashion, health and beauty, cookery; also short stories, up to 2000 words. *Illustrations:* colour, cartoons. *Payment:* by negotiation.

Essex Countryside (1952), Suzanne Kuyser, Market Link House, Tye Green, Elsenham, Bishop's Stortford CM22 6DY   *tel* (0279) 647555   *fax* (0279) 815300.
£1.10. M. Articles of county interest. *Length:* approximately 1000 words. *Illustrations:* line, half-tone, colour.

Euromoney (1969), Garry Evans, Nestor House, Playhouse Yard, London EC4V 5EX   *tel* 071-779 8888   *telex* 928726/7 (editorial/research), 914553/4/5 (adv./survey/prod.)   *fax* 071-779 8641.

£145.00 p.a. M. Articles of general interest on finance, banking and capital markets. *Length:* up to 6000 words. *Illustrations:* colour photos, cartoons. *Payment:* £250 per 1000 words; £50.

The European, Herbert Pearson, Orbit House, 5 New Fetter Lane, London EC4A 1AP *tel* 071-418 7777 *fax* 071-353 4386.
75p. Thu. News reports, analytical articles and features on subjects of interest and importance to Europe as a whole, including business affairs, sport, arts, literature, leisure, fashion. *Illustrations:* line, half-tone, colour transparencies, cartoons. *Payment:* by arrangement.

European Bookseller (1990), Marc Beishon, 3 Queen Square, London WC1N 3AR *tel* 071-837 1357 *fax* 071-837 7004.
£66.00 p.a. Bi-M. Articles, features, news, statistics for the European book trade. Database of Europe-wide, recently published titles (approx. 1000), subject classified. *All material commissioned. Length:* 200-2000 words. *Illustrations:* b&w photos. *Payment:* £75 per article; photos by agreement.

European Chemical News, John Baker, Reed Business Publishing, Quadrant House, The Quadrant, Sutton, Surrey SM2 5AS *tel* 081-652 3187.
£4.25. W. Articles and features concerning business, markets and investments in the chemical industry. *Length:* 1000-2000 words; news items up to 400 words. *Payment:* £120-£150 per 1000 words.

European Drinks Buyer (1991), Heather Buckle, Crier Publications, Arctic House, Rye Lane, Dunton Green, Sevenoaks, Kent TN14 5HB *tel* (0732) 451515 *fax* (0732) 451383.
Controlled free circulation. Bi-M. Articles of European interest on business, marketing, branding, catering, retail, duty free, EU legislation, packaging, labelling, product surveys, consumption trends. *No* unsolicited material but enquiries for editorial guidelines welcome (enclose sae/samples of published work). Overseas correspondents wanted. *Length:* features, profiles, interviews, opinion pieces 1000-2000 words, news 150-500 words. *Illustrations:* half-tone, colour. *Payment:* from £80 per 1000 words; none.

European Frozen Food Buyer (1989), Alwyn Brice, Crier Publications, Arctic House, Rye Lane, Dunton Green, Sevenoaks, Kent TN14 5HB *tel* (0732) 451515 *fax* (0732) 451383.
Controlled free circulation. Bi-M. Articles of European interest on business, marketing, branding, catering, retail, EU legislation, packaging, labelling, product surveys, food hygiene, consumption trends. *No* unsolicited material but enquiries for editorial guidelines welcome (enclose sae/samples of published work). Overseas correspondents wanted. *Length:* features, profiles, interviews 1000-2000 words, news 150-500 words. *Illustrations:* half-tone, colour. *Payment:* £80 per 1000 words; none.

European Plastics News (1929), Andrew Beevers, EMAP Maclaren, PO Box 109, Maclaren House, Scarbrook Road, Croydon, Surrey CR9 1QH *tel* 081-688 7788 *fax* 081-688 8375.
£10.00. M. (£75.00 p.a.) Technical articles dealing with plastics and allied subjects. *Length:* depending on subject. *Illustrations:* b&w or colour photos/diagrams. *Payment:* by arrangement; none.

Evangelical Quarterly (1929), Professor I.H. Marshall, Department of Divinity with Religious Studies, King's College, Aberdeen AB9 2UB. Published by Paternoster Periodicals, PO Box 300, Carlisle, Cumbria CA3 0QS *tel* (0228) 512512.
£4.25. Q. International review of Bible and theology in defence of the historic Christian faith. Articles on the defence or exposition of biblical theology as exhibited in the great Reformed Confessions. *Payment:* none.

Evening Chronicle, Neil Benson, Newcastle Chronicle and Journal Ltd, Thomson House, Groat Market, Newcastle upon Tyne NE1 1ED *tel* 091-232 7500 *fax* 091-232 2256.
25p. D. News, photos and features covering almost every subject of interest to readers in Tyne and Wear, Northumberland and Durham. *Payment:* according to value.

Evening Echo (1900), Gareth Weekes, Richmond Hill, Bournemouth, Dorset BH2 6HH *tel* (0202) 554601 *fax* (0202) 292115.
26p. Mon.-Sat. News and features. *Length:* up to 500 words. *Illustrations:* line, half-tone, colour, cartoons. *Payment:* by arrangement.

Evening Gazette (Teesside) (1869), Ranald Allan, North Eastern Evening Gazette Ltd, Borough Road, Middlesbrough TS1 3AZ *tel* (0642) 245401 *fax* (0642) 232014.
23p. Mon.-Sat. News, and topical and life style features. *Length:* 600-800 words. *Illustrations:* line, half-tone, colour, graphics, cartoons. *Payment:* £50 per 1000 words; scale rate or by agreement.

Evening Post (1965), Kim Chapman, 8 Tessa Road, Reading, Berks. RG1 8NS *tel* (0734) 575833 *fax* (0734) 599363.
22p. D. Topical articles based on current news. *Length:* 800-1200 words. *Payment:* based on lineage rates. *Illustrations:* half-tone.

Evening Standard (1827), Stewart Steven, Northcliffe House, 2 Derry Street, London W8 5EE *tel* 071-938 6000.
30p. D. Ind. Articles of general interest considered, 1500 words or shorter; also news, pictures and ideas.

Eventing (1984), Kate Green, IPC Magazines Ltd, Room 2105, King's Reach Tower, Stamford Street, London SE1 9LS *tel* 071-261 5388 *fax* 071-261 5429.
£2.25. M. News, articles, features, event reports and opinion pieces – all with bias towards the sport of horse trials. *Material mostly commissioned,* but all ideas welcome. Length: up to 1500 words. *Illustrations:* colour and b&w, mostly commissioned. *Payment:* by arrangement; £30-£45.

Everyday with Practical Electronics (1971), Mike Kenward, Wimborne Publishing Ltd, 6 Church Street, Wimborne, Dorset BH21 1JH *tel* (0202) 881749 *fax* (0202) 841692.
£1.95. M. Constructional and theoretical articles aimed at the student and hobbyist. *Length:* 1000-5500 words. *Payment:* £55-£90 per 1000 words depending on type of article. *Illustrations:* line, half-tone, cartoons.

Everywoman (1985), Barbara Rogers, 34 Islington Green, London N1 8DU *tel* 071-359 5496.
£1.75. M. Features, especially news features. *Study* of this feminist magazine essential; covering note should state which section a piece is for. *No* short stories. *Illustrations:* line, half-tone, cartoons. *Payment:* for commissions, £40 per 1000 words.

Exchange and Mart (1868), Link House, West Street, Poole, Dorset BH15 1LL *tel* (0202) 445180 *fax* (0202) 445189.
£1.00. W. No editorial matter used.

Executive PA (1991), Claire Gillman, Astley House, 33 Notting Hill Gate, Notting Hill, London W11 3JQ *tel* 071-243 5000 *fax* 071-727 4222.
Complimentary. Q. Business to business for working senior secretaries. *Length:* 1500 or 2250 words. *Illustrations:* colour. *Payment:* £110 per 1000 words; by negotiation.

Express and Star (1874), Keith Parker, Queen Street, Wolverhampton WV1 3BU   *tel* (0902) 313131; *London office:* Hamilton House, 1 Temple Avenue, Victoria Embankment, EC4Y 0HA.
25p. D. Will consider topical contributions up to 750 words with or without illustrations. *Payment:* by arrangement.

Expression (1984), Sue Thomas, Redwood Publishing Ltd, 101 Bayham Street, London NW1 0AG   *tel* 071-331 8000   *fax* 071-331 8346.
Free to American Express Cardmembers. Bi-M. Travel, leisure, business and personalities. *All material commissioned. Length:* 500-2000 words. *Payment:* varies. *Illustrated.*

The Face (1980), Sheryl Garratt, Exmouth House, Pine Street, London EC1R 0JL   *tel* 071-837 7270   *fax* 071-837 3906.
£1.90. M. Articles on music, fashion, films, popular youth culture. Contributors *must* be familiar with the magazine, its audience and culture. *Illustrations:* half-tone, colour. *Payment:* £120 per 1000 words; approx. £120 per page.

Family Circle, IPC Magazines Ltd, King's Reach Tower, Stamford Street, London SE1 9LS   *tel* 071-261 5000   *fax* 071-261 5929.
£1.10. 13 p.a. Practical, medical human interest material; short stories. *Length:* 650-2000 words. *Illustrated. Payment:* NUJ rates.

Family Law (1971), Elizabeth Walsh, Miles McColl, 21 St Thomas Street, Bristol BS1 6JS   *tel* (0272) 230600   *telex* 449119   *fax* (0272) 250486   *DX* 78161 Bristol.
£75.00 p.a. M. Articles dealing with all aspects of the law as it affects the family, written from a legal or socio-legal point of view. *Length:* from 1000 words. *Payment:* £15 per 1000 words, or by arrangement. No *illustrations*.

Family Tree Magazine (1984), Avril Cross, 61 Great Whyte, Ramsey, Huntingdon, Cambs. PE17 1HL   *tel* (0487) 814050.
£1.70. M. (£19.40 p.a.) Articles on any genealogically related topics. *Illustrations:* half-tone, line, cartoons. *Payment:* £20 per 1000 words; by arrangement.

Farmers Weekly (incorporating **Power Farming**) (1934), Stephen Howe, Reed Business Publishing, Quadrant House, The Quadrant, Sutton, Surrey SM2 5AS   *tel* 081-652 4911   *fax* 081-652 8901.
90p. W. Articles on agriculture from freelance contributors will be accepted subject to negotiation.

Farming News (1983), Donald Taylor, Morgan-Grampian Farming Press, 30 Calderwood Street, London SE18 6QH   *tel* 081-855 3579   *telex* 896238   *fax* 081-854 6795.
70p. W. (£60.00 p.a.) News, business, technical, leisure articles; crosswords, features. *Payment:* NUJ freelance rates. *Illustrations:* half-tone, colour, cartoons.

Fashion Forecast International (1946), Managing Editor: Stephen Higginson, 23 Bloomsbury Square, London WC1A 2JP   *tel* 071-637 2211   *telex* 8954884   *fax* 071-637 2248.
£24.00 p.a. UK/Europe, £35.00 p.a. outside Europe. 2 p.a. (Feb, Aug) **Hosiery Forecast** and **Lingerie Forecast** are included in each issue. Factual articles on fashions and accessories with forecast trends. *Length:* 800-1000 words. *Illustrations:* line, half-tone. *Payment:* by arrangement.

Fashion Weekly (1959), Martin Raymond, EMAP Maclaren, 67 Clerkenwell Road, London EC1R 5BH   *tel* 071-404 0431   *fax* 071-404 0428.
£1.20. W. Fashion business newspaper primarily for retailers and wholesalers. *Payment:* by arrangement. *Illustrations:* line, half-tone, colour.

The Field (1853) (incorporating **Land and Water**, **The Country Gentleman** and **Country Times and Landscape**), Astley House, 33 Notting Hill Gate, London W11 3JQ   *tel* 071-243 5000   *fax* 071-727 4222/4333.
£2.50. M. Specific, topical and informed features on the British countryside and country pursuits, including natural history, field sports, gardening and farming. Overseas subjects considered but opportunities for such articles are limited. No fiction or children's material. Articles, *length* 800-2000 words, by outside contributors considered; also topical 'shorts' of 200-300 words on all countryside matters. *Illustrations:* colour photos of a high standard. *Payment:* on merit.

Filtration & Separation (1964), Steve Barrett, Elsevier Advanced Technology, PO Box 150, Kidlington, Oxford OX5 1AS   *tel* (0865) 512242   *fax* (0865) 310981.
£75.00 p.a. 8 p.a. Articles on the design, contruction and application of filtration and separation equipment and dust control and air cleaning equipment for all industrial purposes; articles on filtration and separation and dust control and air cleaning operations and techniques in all industries. *Illustrations:* line, half-tone. *Payment:* by arrangement; none.

Financial Adviser (1987), Ceri Jones, FT Business Information Ltd, Boundary House, 91-3 Charterhouse Street, London EC1M 6HR   *tel* 071-608 3471   *fax* 071-250 0004.
Free to SRO members. W. (£75.00 p.a.) Topical personal finance news and features. *Length:* variable. *Payment:* by arrangement.

Financial Director (1984), Jane Simms, VNU Business Publications, VNU House, 32-34 Broadwick Street, London W1A 2HG   *tel* 071-439 4242   *telex* 23918 VNU G   *fax* 071-437 7001.
£2.00 (free to finance directors). M. Features on financial and strategic management issues. *Length:* 1500-2000 words. *Illustrations:* colour and b&w photos, line drawings. *Payment:* £150 per 1000 words; photos, variable; line, £250-£300.

Financial Times (1888), Richard Lambert, Number One, Southwark Bridge, London SE1 9HL   *tel* 071-873 3000.
65p. D. Articles of financial, commercial, industrial and economic interest. *Length:* 800-1000 words. *Payment:* by arrangement.

Fire (1908), Simon Hoffman, Queensway House, 2 Queensway, Redhill, Surrey RH1 1QS   *tel* (0737) 768611   *telex* 948669 TOPJNL G   *fax* (0737) 761685.
£3.50. M. (£44.80 p.a.) Articles on firefighting and fire prevention from acknowledged experts only. *Length:* 1000 words. *Illustrations:* dramatic firefighting or fire brigade rescue colour photos sometimes bought. *Payment:* by arrangement.

Flight International (1909), A. Winn, Reed Business Publishing, Quadrant House, The Quadrant, Sutton, Surrey SM2 5AS   *tel* 081-652 3882   *telex* 892084 REEDBP G   *fax* 081-652 3840.
£1.95. W. Deals with all branches of aerospace: operational and technical articles, illustrated by photos, engineering cutaway drawings; also news, paragraphs, reports of lectures, etc. News press days: Thu, Fri. *Illustrations:* tone, line, 2- and 4-colour. *Payment:* varies; by agreement.

Flightpath Magazine, Diana Breadmore, Kingsclere Contract Publishing, Furlongs House, Peasemore, Newbury, Berks. RG16 0JE   *tel* (0635) 248031.

Free. Q. Inflight magazine for Longanair. General features suitable for an inflight magazine. *Length:* 800 words. *Illustrations:* colour, b&w. *Payment:* £100 per 1000 words; usually included in editorial fee.

Fly-Fishing & Fly-Tying (1990), Mark Bowler, 8 The Square, Aberfeldy, Perthshire PH15 2DD	*tel* (0887) 820082	*fax* (0887) 829626.
£2.00. Bi-M. Fishing and fly-tying articles, fishery features, short stories. *Length:* 800-1500 words. *Illustrations:* colour and b&w photos, cartoons. *Payment:* by arrangement.

Football Picture Story Library, D.C. Thomson & Co. Ltd, Courier Place, Dundee DD1 9QJ	*tel* (0382) 23131	*fax* (0382) 22214; and 185 Fleet Street, London EC4A 2HS	*tel* 071-242 5086	*fax* 071-404 5694.
50p. 2 p.m. Football stories for boys told in pictures.

For Him (FHM) (1987), EMAP Metro, Mappin House, 4 Winsley Street, London W1N 7AR	*tel* 071-436 1515	*fax* 071-323 0680.
£2.50. 10 p.a. Features, fashion, grooming, travel (adventure) and men's interests. *Length:* 2000-3000 words. *Illustrations:* colour and b&w photos. *Payment:* £150 per 1000 words; by negotiation.

Forensic Photography, incorporating **Medico-Legal Photography** (1972), Ewart Kemp, 87 London Street, Chertsey, Surrey KT16 8AN	*tel* (0932) 562933.
£18.00 p.a. Q. Available on subscription only. The editor is always interested in articles (illustrated or not) concerned with photographic techniques slanted to the professional and concerned with any aspect of the journal's title. *Payment:* by arrangement. *Illustrations:* line, half-tone.

Fortean Times (1973), Bob Rickard and Paul Sieveking, Box 2409, London NW5 4NP	*tel/fax* 071-485 5002.
£2.00. Bi-M. The journal of strange phenomena, experiences, related subjects and philosophies. Articles, features, news, reviews. *Length:* 500-2500 words; longer by arrangement. *Illustrations:* colour cover; b&w photos, line and tone art, cartoons. *Payment:* by negotiation.

Fourth World Review (1984), John Papworth, Fourth World Educational Research Association Trust, 24 Abercorn Place, London NW8 9XP	*tel* 071-286 4366	*fax* 071-286 2186.
£ – at reader's discretion. Bi-M. For small nations, small communities and the human spirit. Original material on all aspects of society from the perspective of the human scale. Politics, but *not* party political. *Length:* 3000-5000 words. *Illustrations:* b&w cartoons. *Payment:* £10 per page; £25.

France Magazine (1989), Philip Faiers, France Magazine Ltd, Dormer House, The Square, Stow-on-the-Wold, Glos. GL54 1BN	*tel* (0451) 831398	*fax* (0451) 830869.
£3.00. Q. An armchair journey to the real France – features and articles ranging from cuisine to customs to architecture to exploring the hidden France. Material *mostly commissioned. Length:* 800-2500 words. *Illustrations:* colour transparencies, cartoons. *Payment:* £100 per 1000 words; £50 per page/pro rata.

Freelance Market News—see **Freelance Press Services** on page 502.

Freelance Writing & Photography (1965), John T. Wilson, Weavers Press Publishing, Tregeraint House, Zennor, St Ives, Cornwall TR26 3DB	*tel/fax* (0736) 797061.
£2.50. Bi-M. (£16.50 p.a.) Articles, features, reviews, interviews, market news, competitions, tips and hints for the freelance writer and photographer. *No work will be considered* unless accompanied by an sae. Letter of enquiry or outline preferred in first instance. *Length:* 250-1000 words. *Illustrations:* line,

half-tone, cartoons. *Payment:* £20 per 1000 words on acceptance; £5 per photo/ illustration, £10 for cover picture.

Fresh Produce Journal (1895), David Hope-Mason, Lockwood Press Ltd, 430-438 Market Towers, New Covent Garden, 1 Nine Elms Lane, London SW8 5NN *tel* 071-622 6677 *fax* 071-720 2047.
£1.40. W. Articles dealing with above trades on the marketing aspects of production but particularly importing, distribution and post-harvest handling; articles should average 500-700 words. *Payment:* by arrangement. *Illustrations:* half-tone.

The Friend (1843), Deborah Padfield, Drayton House, 30 Gordon Street, London WC1H 0BQ *tel* 071-387 7549.
70p. W. Quaker weekly paper. Material of interest to the Religious Society of Friends and like-minded people; political, social, economic or devotional, considered from outside contributors. No fiction. *Length:* up to 1000 words. *Illustrations:* b&w or colour prints. *Payment:* none.

The Garden (1866), Ian Hodgson, 80 Vincent Square, London SW1P 2PE *tel* 071-834 4333 *fax* 071-821 0140.
£2.50. M. Journal of The Royal Horticultural Society. Features of horticultural or botanical interest on a wide range of subjects. *Commissioned material only. Length:* 1200-2500 words. *Illustrations:* 35mm or medium format colour transparencies, occasional b&w prints, botanical line drawings. *Payment:* £100 per 1000 words; varies.

Garden Answers (1982), Adrienne Wild, EMAP Apex Publications Ltd, Apex House, Oundle Road, Peterborough PE2 9NP *tel* (0733) 898100 *fax* (0733) 898433.
£1.55. M. Commissioned features and articles on all aspects of gardening. *Study of magazine* essential. Approach by letter with examples of published work. *Length:* 750 words. *Illustrations:* colour transparencies and artwork. *Payment:* by negotiation.

Garden News (1958), Andrew Blackford, EMAP National Publications Ltd, Apex House, Oundle Road, Peterborough PE2 9NP *tel* (0733) 898100 *fax* (0733) 898433.
60p. W. Gardening news and features on gardeners and their methods of success. *Illustrations:* line, half-tone, colour, cartoons. *Payment:* from £25 per 1000 words; higher rate for good short pieces and suited to our style; from £12.

Gas World International (1884), Alan Bakalor, Petroleum Economist Ltd, 25/31 Ironmonger Row, London EC1V 3PN *tel* 071-251 3501 *fax* 071-253 1224.
£8.00. M. (£75.00 p.a., £95/$180 p.a. USA/Europe) Full news coverage and technical articles on all aspects of engineering and management in the gas industry. *Length:* up to 1800 words. Pictures and news items of topical interest accepted. *Payment:* by arrangement.

Gay Times (1982), David Smith, Ground Floor, Worldwide House, 116-134 Bayham Street, London NW1 0BA *tel* 071-482 2576 *fax* 071-284 0329.
£2.00. M. Feature articles, full news and review coverage of all aspects of gay and lesbian life. *Length:* up to 2000 words. *Illustrations:* colour, line and half-tone, cartoons. *Payment:* by arrangement.

Gemmological Newsletter (1969), Michael O'Donoghue, 7 Hillingdon Avenue, Sevenoaks, Kent TN13 3RB *tel* (0732) 453503.
£8.00 p.a. 30 p.a. (Oct-Jul) Articles about minerals, gemstones, man-made crystals and lapidary. *Length:* up to 800-1000 words. *Payment:* by arrangement. *Illustrated.*

Geographical Journal (1893), Dr R.W. Bradnock, Royal Geographical Society, Kensington Gore, London SW7 2AR   *tel* 071-589 5466   *fax* 071-584 4447. £16.00 (post free). 3 p.a. (£47.50 p.a.) Papers on all aspects of geography, including some read before the Royal Geographical Society. *Length:* up to 4500 words. *Payment:* for reviews. *Illustrations:* photos, maps and diagrams.

Geographical Magazine (1935), Alexander Goldsmith, Centurion Publications Ltd, under licence from the Royal Geographical Society, 48 George Street, London W1H 5RF   *tel* 071-487 4284. £1.80. M. Topical geography in a broad sense. *Length:* 2000 words. *Illustrations:* colour slides, b&w prints or vintage material; maps and graphs always needed; cartoons. *Payment:* £150 per 1000 words; by negotiation.

Geological Magazine (1864), Dr C.P. Hughes, Professor I.N. McCave, Dr N.H. Woodcock, Dr M.J. Bickle, Cambridge University Press, The Edinburgh Building, Shaftesbury Road, Cambridge CB2 2RU   *tel* (0223) 312393. £133.00 p.a. Bi-M. (US$249 USA/Canada/Mexico) Original articles on all earth science topics containing the results of independent research by experts. Also reviews and notices of current geological literature, correspondence on geological subjects – illustrated. *Length:* variable. *Payment:* none.

Gibbons Stamp Monthly, Hugh Jefferies, Stanley Gibbons Ltd, 5 Parkside, Ringwood, Hants BH24 3SH   *tel* (0425) 472363   *fax* (0425) 470247. £1.65. M. (£19.20 p.a.) Articles on philatelic topics. Previous reference to the editor advisable. *Length:* 500-2500 words. *Payment:* by arrangement, £25 or more per 1000 words. *Illustrations:* photos.

Gifts International, Alison Jarman, Bouverie Publishing Co. Ltd, 147-151 Temple Chambers, Temple Avenue, London EC4Y 0BA   *tel* 071-583 3030   *fax* 071-583 4068. £38.00 p.a. M. (£48.00 p.a. overseas) News of gift industry – products, trends, shops; articles on retailing, exporting, importing, manufacturing, crafts (UK and abroad). *Payment:* by agreement. *Illustrations:* products, news, personal photos, cartoons.

Girl About Town Magazine (1973), Editor-in-Chief: Bill Williamson, CPP, 9 Rathbone Street, London W1P 1AF   *tel* 071-872 0022   *fax* 071-255 2352. Free. W. Articles of general interest to London women. *Length:* about 800 words. *Illustrations:* line, half-tone, colour. *Payment:* £120 per 1000 words (average).

Glasgow Evening Times (1876), George McKechnie, 195 Albion Street, Glasgow G1 1QP   *tel* 041-552 6255; *London office:* 127 Clerkenwell Road, EC1R 5DB   *tel* 071-405 2121   *fax* 041-405 1888. 27p. D.

Glaucus (1990), Andy Horton, 14 Corbyn Crescent, Shoreham-by-Sea, West Sussex BN43 6PQ   *tel* (0273) 465433. £18.00 p.a. Q. Official journal of the British Marine Life Study Society, aimed at the popular market. Observations and scientific research on the natural history, and related subjects, of the marine environment surrounding the British Isles. Send sae for Guide to Submissions. *Length:* up to 2000 words. *Illustrations:* b&w line drawings, occasional b&w photos. *Payment:* expenses only.

Gloucestershire Echo (1873), Anita Syvret, Cheltenham Newspaper Co. Ltd, 1 Clarence Parade, Cheltenham, Glos. GL50 3NZ   *tel* (0242) 526261   *fax* (0242) 578395. 27p. D. Specialist articles with Gloucestershire connections; no fiction. *Material mostly commissioned. Length:* 350 words. *Payment:* £30 per article.

Golf Monthly (1911), Colin Callander, IPC Magazines Ltd, King's Reach Tower, Stamford Street, London SE1 9LS *tel* 071-261 7237 *fax* 071-261 7240.
£2.40. M. Original articles on golf considered (not reports), golf clinics, handy hints. *Illustrations:* half-tone, colour, cartoons. *Payment:* by arrangement.

Golf Weekly, Paul Trow, Advance House, 37 Millharbour, Isle of Dogs, London E14 9TX *tel* 071-538 1031 *fax* 071-537 2503.
£1.20. W. News, tournament reports and articles on golf and of interest to golfers. *Payment:* by arrangement. *Illustrations:* photos of golfers and golf courses.

Golf World (1962), Robert Green, Advance House, 37 Millharbour, Isle of Dogs, London E14 9TX *tel* 071-538 1031 *fax* 071-538 4106.
£2.70. M. Expert golf instructional articles, 500-3000 words; general interest articles, personality features 500-3000 words. Little fiction. *Payment:* by negotiation. *Illustrations:* line, half-tone, colour, cartoons.

Good Housekeeping (1922), Sally O'Sullivan, National Magazine House, 72 Broadwick Street, London W1V 2BP *tel* 071-439 5000.
£1.80. M. Articles of 1000-2500 words from qualified writers are invited on topics of interest to intelligent women. Domestic subjects covered by staff writers. Personal experiences and humorous articles occasionally used. *Payment:* magazine standards. *Illustrations:* mainly commissioned.

GQ (1988), Michael VerMeulen, Vogue House, Hanover Square, London W1R 0AD *tel* 071-499 9080 *telex* 27338 VOLON G *fax* 071-495 1679.
£2.20. M. Articles relating to the life style of the successful, stylish man. *Illustrations:* b&w and colour photos, line drawings, cartoons. *Payment:* by arrangement.

Gramophone, James Jolly, 177-179 Kenton Road, Harrow, Middlesex HA3 0HA *tel* 081-907 4476 *fax* 081-909 1599.
£2.60. M. Outside contributions are rarely used. Features on recording artists, technical articles, and articles about gramophone needs. *Length:* 500-1000 words preferred. *Payment:* by arrangement. *Illustrations:* line, half-tone.

Granta (1889; new series 1979), Editor: Bill Buford, Managing Director: Catherine Eccles, 2/3 Hanover Yard, Noel Road, Islington, London N1 8BE *tel* 071-704 9776 *fax* 071-704 0474. Published in association with Penguin Books UK Ltd.
£6.99. Q. Original fiction and journalism. *Length:* determined by content. *Illustrations:* photos. *Payment:* by arrangement.

The Great Outdoors (1978), Cameron McNeish, Caledonian Magazines Ltd, 7th Floor, The Plaza Tower, East Kilbride, Glasgow G74 1LW *tel* (03552) 46444 *fax* (03552) 63013.
£2.25. M. (£25.00 p.a.) Articles on walking or lightweight camping in specific areas, preferably illustrated. *Length:* 1200-1800 words. *Payment:* by arrangement. *Illustrations:* colour, cartoons.

Green Magazine (1989), Alistair Townley, Mouse Lane, Steyning, West Sussex BN44 3DG *tel* (0903) 879323.
£1.95. M. Feature articles and topical news items covering all aspects of the environment. No fiction. *Length:* features 1000-2500 words. *Illustrations:* colour and b&w photos and line. *Payment:* £120 per 1000 words; by arrangement.

Greenscene (1988), Glynne Steele, The Vegetarian Society, Parkdale, Dunham Road, Altrincham, Cheshire WA14 4QG *tel* 061-928 0793 *fax* 061-926 9182.

85p. Q. 'The only magazine for young vegetarians!' Features on vegetarian issues, i.e. animals/environment/health/developing world; short stories relating to animal welfare or the environment. *Length:* 700 or 1500 words. *Illustrations:* b&w photos and line, cartoons. *Payment:* £50 per 1000 words; £30.

Greetings Magazine (1992), Publisher: Malcolm Naish, Editor: Terri Mousley, Lema Publishing Co., Unit No. 1, Queen Mary's Avenue, Watford, Herts. WD4 8PP   *tel* (0923) 250909   *fax* (0923) 250995.
£20.00 p.a. 8 p.a. Official journal of the Greeting Card and Calendar Association. Articles, features and news related to the greetings card and giftwrap industry. Mainly written in-house; some material taken from outside. *Length:* varies. *Illustrations:* line, colour and b&w photos. *Payment:* by arrangement.

Grimsby Evening Telegraph (1897), Peter Moore, 80 Cleethorpe Road, Grimsby, South Humberside DN31 3EH   *tel* (0472) 359232   *fax* (0472) 352272.
26p. D. Considers general interest articles. *Illustrations:* line, half-tone, colour, cartoons. *Payment:* by arrangement.

The Grocer (1861), A. de Angeli, William Reed, Broadfield Park, Crawley, West Sussex RH11 9RT   *tel* (0293) 613400   *fax* (0293) 515174.
40p. W. Trade journal: articles or news or illustrations of general interest to the grocery and provision trades. *Payment:* by arrangement.

The Grower (1923), Peter Rogers, Nexus Business Communications Ltd, Warwick House, Swanley, Kent BR8 8HY   *tel* (0322) 660070   *fax* (0322) 667633.
£1.05. W. News and practical articles on commercial horticulture, preferably illustrated. *Illustrations:* photos, line drawings. *Payment:* by arrangement.

The Guardian (1821), Peter Preston, 119 Farringdon Road, London EC1R 3ER   *tel* 071-278 2332   *telex* 8811746/7/8 GUARDN G; 164 Deansgate, Manchester M60 2RR   *tel* 061-832 7200.
Mon.-Fri. 45p. Sat. 50p. D. Ind. The paper takes few articles from outside contributors except on its specialist pages. Articles should not normally exceed 1200 words in *length. Illustrations:* news and features photos. *Payment:* from £142.60 per 1000 words; from £26.50.

Guiding, Nora Warner, 17-19 Buckingham Palace Road, London SW1W 0PT   *tel* 071-834 6242   *fax* 071-828 8317.
£1.10. M. Official Organ of The Guide Association. Articles of interest to women of all ages, with special emphasis on youth work and the Guide Movement. *Length:* 500-1500 words. *Illustrations:* line, half-tone, colour, cartoons. *Payment:* £70 per 1000 words; £100 full colour page, £60 b&w – negotiable.

The Haiku Quarterly (1990), Kevin Bailey, 39 Exmouth Street, Kingshill, Swindon, Wilts. SN1 3PU   *tel* (0793) 523927.
£2.40. Q. (£8.00 p.a.) Haiku, Tanka, Englyn and epigrams, etc.; also longer traditional and experimental poetry. Book and magazine reviews. *Payment:* small. Commissioned *illustrations.*

Hairflair (1985), Hellena Barnes, Hairflair Publishing Ltd, 4th Floor, 27 Maddox Street, London W1R 9LE   *tel* 071-493 1081   *fax* 071-499 6686.
£1.20. M. Hair, beauty, fashion – and related features – for the 16-35 age group. *Preliminary letter* essential. *Length:* 800-1000 words. *Illustrations:* colour and b&w photos, occasional line drawings. *Payment:* £100-£120 per 1000 words.

Hampshire—The County Magazine, Dennis Stevens, 74 Bedford Place, Southampton SO1 2DF   *tel* (0703) 223591/333457.
£1.20. M. Factual articles concerning all aspects of Hampshire and Hampshire life, past and present. *Length:* 500-1500 words. *Payment:* £10 per 1000 words. *Illustrations:* photos and line drawings.

Harpers & Queen (1929), National Magazine House, 72 Broadwick Street, London W1V 2BP   *tel* 071-439 5000   *fax* 071-439 5506.
£2.70. M. Features, fashion, beauty, art, theatre, films, travel, interior decoration, mainly commissioned. *Illustrations:* line, wash, full colour and two- and three-colour, and photos.

Hartlepool Mail (1877), Christopher Cox, Northeast Press Ltd, Clarence Road, Hartlepool, Cleveland TS24 8BU   *tel* (0429) 274441   *fax* (0429) 869024.
25p. D. Features of local interest. *Length:* 500 words. *Illustrations:* colour, b&w photos, line, cartoons. *Payment:* by negotiation.

Health & Efficiency International (1900), Kate Sturdy, 28 Charles Square, Pitfield Street, London N1 6HT   *tel* 071-253 4037   *fax* 071-253 0539.
£2.00. M. (also publishes separate Q. and Bi-A. editions) Articles on naturist and human relationship matters. Naturist travel features; some health and humour. Wide scope for new writers; guidelines on request. *Length:* 750-1500 words. *Illustrations:* line, half-tone, colour transparencies, colour prints, cartoons. *Payment:* by negotiation.

Health & Fitness (1984), Sharon Walker, HHL Publishing, Greater London House, Hampstead Road, London NW1 7QQ   *tel* 071-388 3171   *fax* 071-377 4890.
£1.95. M. Articles on all aspects of health and fitness. *Illustrations:* line, half-tone, colour. *Payment:* by arrangement; varies.

Hello! (1988), Maggie Koumi, Wellington House, 69/71 Upper Ground, London SE1 9PQ   *tel* 071-334 7404   *fax* 071-334 7412.
£1.25. W. Personality-based features – showbusiness, celebrity, royalty; exclusive interviews; gossip. *Payment:* by arrangement. *Illustrated.*

The Herald (1783), Arnold Kemp, Caledonian Newspapers Ltd, 195 Albion Street, Glasgow G1 1QP   *tel* 041-552 6255   *fax* 041-552 2288; *London office:* Gray's Inn House, 127 Clerkenwell Road, EC1R 5DB   *tel* 071-405 2121.
42p. D. Ind. Articles up to 1000 words.

Heredity: An International Journal of Genetics (1947), M.J. Kearsey, School of Biological Sciences, The University of Birmingham, Edgbaston, Birmingham B15 2TT.
£164.00 (Europe), US$295.00 (USA/Canada), £180.00 (rest of world) (two volumes each of six parts yearly). Research and review articles in genetics of 1000-15,000 words with summary and bibliography. Book reviews and abstracts of conferences. *Illustrations:* line, half-tone. *Payment:* none.

Here's Health, Ramuné Burns, EMAP Élan, Victory House, Leicester Place, London WC2H 7BP   *tel* 071-437 9011   *telex* 266400   *fax* 071-434 0656.
£1.80. M. Articles on nutrition, alternative medicine, environment and health, natural treatment success stories. *Preliminary letter and clippings essential. Length:* 750-1800 words. *Payment:* on publication. *Illustrated.*

Heritage (1984), Siân Ellis, Bulldog Magazines Ltd, 4 The Courtyard, Denmark Street, Wokingham, Berks. RG11 2AZ   *tel* (0734) 771677   *fax* (0734) 772903.
£2.25. Bi-M. Features on British topics only: towns and villages to visit, tours/off the beaten track, customs, craftsmen, people, all historic/heritage subjects with a contemporary angle. *Length:* 1200-1500 words. *Illustrations:* colour transparencies. *Payment:* £100 per feature; by negotiation.

Hertfordshire Countryside (1946), Ken Washbrook, Beaumonde Publications Ltd, 4 Mill Bridge, Hertford, Herts. SG14 1PY   *tel* (0992) 553571   *fax* (0992) 587713.

£1.00. M. Articles of county interest, 1000 words. *Payment:* £25 per 1000 words. *Illustrations:* line, half-tone, cartoons.

The Heythrop Journal (1960), Dr T.J. Deidun, Heythrop College, University of London, Kensington Square, London W8 5HQ   *tel* 071-795 6600   *fax* 071-795 4200.
£22.00 p.a. (UK/Europe; institutions/overseas rates on application). Q. Accept articles on philosophy, theology – speculative and positive, scripture, canon law, church relations, moral and pastoral psychology, of general interest but of technical merit. *Length:* 5000-8000 words. *Payment:* 5 free copies of issue in which article appears.

Hi-Fi News & Record Review (1956), Steve Harris, Link House, Dingwall Avenue, Croydon CR9 2TA   *tel* 081-686 2599   *fax* 081-760 0973.
£2.50. M. Articles on all aspects of high quality sound recording and reproduction; also extensive record review section and supporting musical feature articles. Audio matter is essentially technical, but should be presented in a manner suitable for music lovers interested in the nature of sound. *Length:* 2000-3000 words. *Illustrations:* line and/or half-tone. *Payment:* by arrangement.

Higher Education Quarterly (1946), Michael Shattock, University of Warwick, Coventry CV4 7AL   *tel* (0203) 523523.
£26.00 p.a. Q. (£62.00 p.a. institutions) (subscriptions from Basil Blackwell Ltd, 108 Cowley Road, Oxford OX4 1JF) Articles on national and international higher education policy. *Length:* 2000-6000 words. *Payment:* 6 copies of issue.

HIM magazine (1987), Mark Smith, Worldwide House, 116-134 Bayham Street, London NW1 0BA   *tel* 071-482 2576   *fax* 071-284 0329.
£2.50. M. Lifestyle magazine. Features, news, reviews. *Length:* 2000 words. *Illustrations:* colour and b&w photos for photo-spreads, b&w line illustrations for features, cartoons. *Payment:* £60-£100 per 1000 words; photos from £30; line £60-£100.

History (1916), H.T. Dickinson BA, DipEd, MA, PhD, DLitt. Editorial: History Department, University of Edinburgh, Edinburgh EH8 9JY   *tel* 031-650 3785. Published by the Historical Association, 59A Kennington Park Road, London SE11 4JH   *tel* 071-735 3901.
£13.00 for Historical Association members; £33.00 p.a. non-members. 3 p.a. Historical articles and reviews by experts. *Length:* usually up to 8000 words. *Illustrations:* only exceptionally. *Payment:* none.

History Today (1951), Gordon Marsden, 20 Old Compton Street, London W1V 5PE   *tel* 071-439 8315.
£2.65. M. History in the widest sense – political, economic, social, biography, relating past to present; world history as well as British. *Length:* articles 3500 words; shorter news/views pieces 600-1200 words. *Illustrations:* from prints and original photos. Please do not send original material until publication is agreed. *Payment:* by arrangement.

Home and Country (1919), Penny Kitchen, 104 New King's Road, London SW6 4LY   *tel* 071-731 5777   *fax* 071-736 4061.
58p. M. Official Journal of the National Federation of Women's Institutes for England and Wales. Publishes material related to the Federation's and members' activities; also considers articles of general interest to women, particularly country women, of 800-1200 words. *Illustrations:* colour and b&w photos and drawings, cartoons. *Payment:* by arrangement.

Home and Family (1954), Margaret Duggan, The Mothers' Union, The Mary Sumner House, 24 Tufton Street, London SW1P 3RB   *tel* 071-222 5533.

80p. Q. Short articles related to Christian family life. *Payment:* approx. £30-£40 per 1000 words. *Illustrations:* line, half-tone, colour, usually commissioned.

Home Words (1870), PO Box 44, Guildford, Surrey GU1 1XL *tel* (0483) 33944. M. Illustrated C of E magazine insert. Articles of popular Christian interest with an Anglican slant (400-800 words) with relevant photos. *Payment:* by arrangement.

Homes and Gardens (1919), Amanda Evans, IPC Magazines Ltd, King's Reach Tower, Stamford Street, London SE1 9LS *tel* 071-261 5000 *fax* 071-261 6247.
£1.90. M. Articles on home interest or design. *Length:* articles, 900-1000 words. *Illustrations:* all types. *Payment:* generous, but exceptional work required; varies.

Homes & Ideas (1993), Penny Harris, IPC Magazines Ltd, King's Reach Tower, Stamford Street, London SE1 9LS *tel* 071-261 7325 *fax* 071-261 7495.
£1.20. M. Features on any aspect of style for the home. *Send* cuttings to the editor. *Length:* by arrangement. *Illustrations:* colour photos and drawings. *Payment:* NUJ rates plus; illustrations by arrangement.

Horse and Hound, M.A. Clayton, IPC Magazines Ltd, King's Reach Tower, Stamford Street, London SE1 9LS *tel* 071-261 6315.
£1.20. W. Special articles, news items, photos, on all matters appertaining to horses, hunting. *Payment:* by negotiation.

Horse & Pony (1980), Sarah Haw, EMAP Pursuit Publishing Ltd, Bretton Court, Bretton, Peterborough PE3 8DZ *tel* (0733) 264666 *fax* (0733) 265515.
99p. F. All material relevant to young people with equestrian interests. *Payment:* on value to publication rather than length. *Illustrations:* colour, with a strong story line, cartoons.

Horse and Rider (1959), Managing Editor: Kate Austin, Editor: Alison Bridge, 296 Ewell Road, Surbiton, Surrey KT6 7AQ *tel* 081-390 8547 *fax* 081-390 8696.
£1.70. M. Sophisticated magazine covering all forms of equestrian activity at home and abroad. Good writing and technical accuracy essential. *Length:* 1500-2000 words. *Illustrations:* photos and drawings, the latter usually commissioned. *Payment:* by arrangement.

Horticulture Week, Stovin Hayter, Haymarket Magazines Ltd, 38-42 Hampton Road, Teddington, Middlesex TW11 0JE *tel* 081-943 5719.
90p. W. (£55.00 p.a.) Practical horticultural and business journal for the nursery and garden centre trade, landscape industry and public parks and sports ground staff. Outside contributions considered and, if accepted, paid for. No fiction. *Length:* 500-1500 words. *Illustrations:* line, half-tone, colour. *Payment:* by arrangement.

Hortus (1987), David Wheeler, Bryan's Ground, Stapleton, Nr Presteigne, Herefordshire LD8 2LP *tel* (0544) 260001 *fax* (0544) 260015.
£25.00 p.a. Q. Articles on decorative horticulture: plants, gardens, history, design, literature, people; book reviews. *Length:* 1500-5000 words, longer by arrangement. *Illustrations:* line, half-tone and wood-engravings. *Payment:* by arrangement.

Hospitality (1980), Consultant Editor: Alan Sutton, 58 Collingdon Street, Luton, Beds. LU1 1RX *tel* (0582) 480065 *fax* (0582) 33531.
£4.00. Bi-M. Official magazine of the Hotel Catering & Institutional Management Association. Articles for a management readership on food, accommodation services and related topics in hotels, restaurants, tourism,

educational establishments, the health service, industrial situations, educational and other institutions. *Illustrations:* photos, line, cartoons. *Payment:* by arrangement.

Hot Air (1984), Alex Finer, The Boathouse, Crabtree Lane, London SW6 6LU   *tel* 071-381 6007   *fax* 071-381 3930.
Free. Q. Inflight magazine for Virgin Atlantic Airways. Sport, trends/lifestyle, celebrities. *Length:* 1500-3000 words. *Illustrations:* high quality colour transparencies. *Payment:* by negotiation.

House & Garden, Susan Crewe, Vogue House, Hanover Square, London W1R 0AD   *tel* 071-499 9080   *telex* 27338 VOLON G   *fax* 071-629 2907.
£2.20. M. Articles (always commissioned), on subjects relating to domestic architecture, interior decorating, furnishing, gardening, household equipment, food and wine.

House Beautiful (1989), Pat Roberts, National Magazine House, 72 Broadwick Street, London W1V 2BP   *tel* 071-439 5500   *fax* 071-439 5595.
£1.30. M. Specialist 'home' features for the homes of today. *Preliminary study* of magazine advisable. *Payment:* according to merit. *Illustrated.*

House Builder, Phillip Cooke, 82 New Cavendish Street, London W1M 8AD   *tel* 071-580 5588   *fax* 071-323 0890.
£6.00. M. Official Journal of the House-Builders Federation and National House-Building Council. Technical articles on design, construction and equipment of dwellings, estate planning and development, and technical aspects of house-building, aimed at those engaged in house and flat construction and the development of housing estates. *Preliminary letter* advisable. *Length:* articles from 500 words, preferably with illustrations. *Payment:* by arrangement. *Illustrations:* photos, plans, construction details, cartoons.

i-D Magazine (1980), Terry Jones, Level Print Ltd, Seven Dials Warehouse, 44 Earlham Street, London WC2H 9LA   *tel* 071-240 3282   *fax* 071-240 3250.
£1.95. M. Youth and general interest magazine: i-Deas, fashion, clubs, music, people. Will consider unsolicited material. *Illustrations:* colour and b&w photos. *Payment:* £80 per 1000 words; £45 per page.

Ideal Home (1920), Terence Whelan, IPC Magazines Ltd, King's Reach Tower, Stamford Street, London SE1 9LS   *tel* 071-261 6474.
£1.60. M. Specialised home subjects magazine, and articles usually commissioned. Contributors advised to *study editorial content* before submitting material. *Payment:* according to material. *Illustrations:* usually commissioned.

The Illustrated London News (1842), James Bishop, 20 Upper Ground, London SE1 9PF   *tel* 071-928 2111   *fax* 071-620 1594.
£2.50. 2-3 p.a. Magazine dealing chiefly with London and the UK, travel, adventure, environment and the quality of life. Interesting articles accepted; but most material commissioned. *Payment:* usual rates; special rates for exclusive material.

In Britain (1930), Sue Rose, HHL Publishing, Greater London House, Hampstead Road, London NW1 7QQ   *tel* 071-377 4633   *fax* 071-387 9518.
£1.50. M. (£17.50 p.a.) Upmarket features magazine about places and people in Britain. Some freelance material accepted. *Illustrated. Payment:* by arrangement.

Incentive Today (1982), Charles Ford, Blenheim Group plc, 630 Chiswick High Road, London W4 5BG   *tel* 081-742 2828   *fax* 081-742 0329.
£2.50. M. Articles on sales promotion, marketing, motivation and travel. *Illustrations:* line, half-tone, colour. *Payment:* by negotiation.

The Independent (1986), Andreas Whittam Smith, 40 City Road, London EC1Y 2DB *tel* 071-253 1222.
50p. D. 50p. Sat. Occasional freelance contributions; *preliminary letter* advisable. *Payment:* by arrangement.
The Independent Magazine (1988), John Walsh. Free with newspaper. W. Profiles and illustrated articles of topical interest; *all material commissioned. Preliminary study* of the magazine essential. *Length:* 500-3000 words. *Illustrations:* cartoons; commissioned colour and b&w photos. *Payment:* by arrangement.

The Independent on Sunday (1990), Ian Jack, 40 City Road, London EC1Y 2DB *tel* 071-253 1222 *telex* 9419611 *fax* 071-956 1469.
£1.00. W. News, features and articles. *Illustrated. Payment:* by negotiation.

The Independent/The Independent on Sunday moving, October 1994, to 1 Canada Square, Canary Wharf, London E14 5AP.

Index on Censorship (1972), Ursula Owen, Lancaster House, 33 Islington High Street, London N1 *tel* 071-278 2313 *fax* 071-278 1878.
£5.99. Bi-M. (£30.00 p.a.) Articles up to 5000 words dealing with all aspects of free speech and political censorship, book reviews 800-1200 words. *Payment:* £60 per 1000 words.

The Indexer (1958), Hazel Bell, 139 The Ryde, Hatfield, Herts. AL9 5DP *tel* (0707) 265201 *fax* (0707) 273601.
Free to members. 2 p.a. (subscription £25.00 p.a. from Journal Subscriptions Officer, Huntersquay, 33 Marlow Bottom, Marlow, Bucks. SL7 3LZ). Journal of the Society of Indexers, American Society of Indexers, Australian Society of Indexers, and Indexing & Abstracting Society of Canada. Articles of interest to professional indexers, authors, publishers, documentalists and users of indexes. *Payment:* none.

Information and Software Technology (1959), Butterworth-Heinemann Ltd, Linacre House, Jordan Hill, Oxford OX2 8DP *tel* (0865) 310366 *fax* (0865) 310898.
£200.00 p.a. M. (£210.00 p.a. outside UK/Europe) Papers on software design and development and the application of information processing in large organisations, especially multinationals. *Length:* 5000 words. *Illustrations:* line, half-tone.

The Inquirer (1842), Keith Gilley, 1-6 Essex Street, London WC2R 2HY *tel* 071-240 2384.
35p. F. Journal of news and comment for Unitarians and religious liberals. Articles, liberal and progressive in tone, of general religious, social, cultural and international interest. *Length:* up to 750 words. *Payment:* none.

Insurance Brokers' Monthly (1950), Brian Susman, 7 Stourbridge Road, Lye, Stourbridge, West Midlands DY9 7DG *tel* Lye (0384) 895228.
£2.50. M. Articles of technical and non-technical interest to insurance brokers and others engaged in the insurance industry. Occasional articles of general interest to the City, on finance, etc. *Length:* 1000-1500 words. *Payment:* from £25 per 1000 words on last day of month following publication. Authoritative material written under true name and qualification receives highest payment. *Illustrations:* line and half-tone, 100-120 screen.

InterMedia (1970), Assistant Editor: Rex Winsbury, International Institute of Communications, Tavistock House South, Tavistock Square, London WC1H 9LF *tel* 071-388 0671 *telex* 24578 IICLDN G *fax* 071-380 0623.
£50.00 p.a. Bi-M. (£70.00 p.a. institutions) International journal concerned with policies, events, trends and research in the field of communications,

broadcasting, telecommunications and associated issues, particularly cultural and social. *Preliminary letter* essential. *Illustrations:* b&w line. *Payment:* by arrangement.

International Affairs (1922), Royal Institute of International Affairs, Chatham House, 10 St James's Square, London SW1Y 4LE   *tel* 071-957 5700   *fax* 071-957 5710.
£13.00. Q. (£35.00 p.a., institutions £48.00 p.a.) Serious long-term articles on international affairs and reviews of books. *Preliminary letter* advisable. *Length:* average 7000 words. *Illustrations:* none. *Payment:* by arrangement.

International Broadcast Engineer, David Kirk, Argus Business Publications Ltd, Queensway House, 2 Queensway, Redhill, Surrey RH1 1QS   *tel* (0737) 768611   *telex* 948669 TOPJNL G   *fax* (0737) 760564.
£66.00 p.a. Bi-M. Independent journal devoted to the structure and operation of professional television and radio broadcast equipment. Circulates to over 144 countries and technical aspect is emphasised. *Preliminary letter* essential. *Illustrations:* line, half-tone. *Payment:* by arrangement.

International Construction, A.J. Peterson, Maclean Hunter Ltd, Maclean Hunter House, Chalk Lane, Cockfosters Road, Barnet, Herts. EN4 0BU   *tel* 081-242 3193   *telex* 299072 MACHUN G   *fax* 081-242 3186.
Controlled circulation. M. Articles dealing with new techniques of construction, applications of construction equipment and use of construction materials in any part of the world. *Length:* maximum 1500 words plus illustrations. *Illustrations:* line, half-tone, colour; some two-colour line illustrations used, cartoons. *Payment:* from £100 per 1000 words, plus illustrations.

Interzone (1982), David Pringle, 217 Preston Drove, Brighton, East Sussex BN1 6FL   *tel* (0273) 504710.
£2.50. M. (£28.00 p.a.) Science fiction and fantasy short stories, articles, interviews and reviews. *Please read magazine* before submitting. *Length:* 2000-6000 words. *Illustrations:* line, half-tone, colour. *Payment:* by arrangement.

Inverness Courier (1817), John Macdonald, PO Box 13, 9-11 Bank Lane, Inverness IV1 1QW   *tel* (0463) 233059   *fax* (0463) 243439.
35p. Tue./Fri. Articles of Highland interest only. Unsolicited material accepted. *Payment:* by arrangement.

Investors Chronicle, Gillian O'Connor, Greystoke Place, Fetter Lane, London EC4A 1ND   *tel* 071-405 6969   *fax* 071-405 5276.
£1.70. W. Journal covering investment and personal finance. Occasional outside contributions for surveys are accepted. *Payment:* by negotiation.

Involvement & Participation (1884), Anthony Barry, 42 Colebrooke Row, London N1 8AF   *tel* 071-354 8040.
£29.00 p.a. UK, £41.00 p.a. overseas, post free. Q. Journal of the Involvement & Participation Association. Articles, mostly commissioned, on participation and involvement in industry, employee shareholding, joint consultation, the sharing of information, labour-management relations, workers participation, and kindred industrial subjects from the operational angle, with emphasis on the practice of particular enterprises, usually written by a member of the team involved, whether manager or workers, and with a strong factual background. *Length:* up to 2500 words. *Payment:* by negotiation.

Iron (1973), Peter Mortimer, 5 Marden Terrace, Cullercoats, North Shields, Northumberland NE30 4PD   *tel* Tyneside (091) 2531901.
£3.00 inc. postage. 3 p.a. Poems; short stories up to 6000 words in total. *Illustrations:* line, half-tone. *Payment:* £10 per page; £5.

i-to-i (1989), Yannis Andricopoulos, 92 Prince of Wales Road, London NW5 3NE *tel* 071-267 7094 *fax* 071-284 3063.
£2.45. Q. 'A forum for change.' News, stories and features on 'New Age', green issues, spirituality, human rights, science and politics. *Commissioned material only. Length:* news 200 words, features 1000 words. *Illustrations:* colour photos, cartoons. *Payment:* by negotiation.

Jane's Defence Weekly (1984), Peter Howard, Sentinel House, 163 Brighton Road, Coulsdon, Surrey CR5 2NH *tel* 081-763 1030 *telex* 916907 JANES G *fax* 081-763 1007.
£121.00 p.a. W. Defence news, military, political, industrial; analysis or briefing articles. *Length:* up to 1250 words. *Payment:* minimum £100 per 1000 words used. *Illustrations:* line, half-tone, colour.

Jazz Journal International (1948), Publisher and Editor-in-Chief: Eddie Cook, Jazz Journal Ltd, 1/5 Clerkenwell Road, London EC1M 5PA *tel* 071-608 1348/1362 *fax* 071-608 1292.
£2.50. M. Articles on jazz, record reviews. Prospective contributors are advised to call or write before submitting material. *Payment:* by arrangement. *Illustrations:* photos.

Jewish Chronicle (1841), Edward J. Temko, 25 Furnival Street, London EC4A 1JT *tel* 071-405 9252.
40p. W. Authentic and exclusive news stories and articles of Jewish interest from 500-1500 words are considered. There is a lively arts and leisure section, as well as regular travel pages. **JC Impressions** (free, Bi-M). Commissioned features and interviews, colour and b&w photos. *Payment:* by arrangement. *Illustrations:* of Jewish interest, either topical or feature.

Jewish Quarterly (1953), Colin Shindler, PO Box 1148, London NW5 2AZ *tel* 071-485 4062.
£3.50. Q. (£12.50 p.a., £17.50 p.a. overseas) Articles of Jewish interest, literature, history, music, politics, poetry, book reviews, fiction. *Length:* 2000-3000 words. *Illustrations:* half-tone.

Jewish Telegraph (1950), Paul Harris, Telegraph House, 11 Park Hill, Bury Old Road, Prestwich, Manchester M25 0HH *tel* 061-740 9321 *fax* 061-740 9325; 4A Roman View, Leeds LS8 2LW *tel* (0532) 695044; Harold House, Dunbabin Road, Liverpool L15 6XL *tel* 051-475 6666/2222; 43 Queen Square, Glasgow G41 2BD *tel/fax* 041-423 9200.
26p (Man.), 15p (Leeds), 21p (Liv.), 35p (Glas.). W. Non-fiction articles of Jewish interest, especially humour. Exclusive Jewish news stories and pictures, international, national and local. *Length:* 1000-1500 words. *Payment:* by arrangement. *Illustrations:* line, half-tone, cartoons.

The Journal (1912), Susan Sheen, The Chartered Insurance Institute, 20 Aldermanbury, London EC2V 7HY *tel* 071-606 3835 *fax* 071-726 0131.
Free to members. Bi-M. (£3.00) Journal of The Chartered Insurance Institute. Technical articles on all aspects of insurance. *Material mostly commissioned. Length:* 1200 words. *Payment:* £140 per 1000 words.

The Journal, Bill Bradshaw, Thomson House, Groat Market, Newcastle upon Tyne NE1 1ED *tel* 091-232 7500 *fax* 091-261 8869.
28p. D. Ind.

Journal of Alternative and Complementary Medicine (1983), Leon Chaitow, Homewood House, Guildford Road, Chertsey, Surrey KT16 0QA *tel* (0932) 874333 *fax* (0932) 872777.
£2.25. M. (£27.50 p.a.) Feature articles (*length:* up to 2000 words) and news stories (*length:* up to 250 words). Unsolicited material welcome but not eligible

for payment unless commissioned. *Illustrations:* line, half-tone, colour. *Payment:* by negotiation.

Journalist, NUJ, Acorn House, 314 Gray's Inn Road, London WC1X 8DP *tel* 071-278 7916 *telex* 892384 *fax* 071-837 8143.
45p. Bi-M. (£9.50 p.a., £13.00 p.a. overseas) Magazine of the National Union of Journalists (mailed to all members). Accepts material relating to journalism, trade unionism and general conditions in the newspaper industry. Mainly contributed by members, and outside written contributions not paid.

Judy Library, D.C. Thomson & Co. Ltd, Courier Place, Dundee DD1 9QJ *tel* (0382) 23131 *fax* (0382) 22214; and 185 Fleet Street, London EC4A 2HS *tel* 071-242 5086 *fax* 071-404 5694.
50p. M. 64-page (about 140 line drawings) picture-stories for schoolgirls: ballet, school, adventure, theatre, sport. Scripts considered; promising artists and scriptwriters encouraged. *Payment:* on acceptance.

Junior Bookshelf, Marsh Hall, Thurstonland, Huddersfield HD4 6XB *tel* (0484) 661811.
£2.00. 6 p.a. (£9.80 p.a., overseas £12.00 p.a.) Articles on children's books and authors. *Length:* about 1200-1500 words. *Payment:* nominal.

Junior Education (1977), Mrs Terry Saunders, Scholastic Publications Ltd, Villiers House, Clarendon Avenue, Leamington Spa, Warks. CV32 5PR *tel* (0926) 887799 *fax* (0926) 883331.
£2.10. M. For teachers, educationalists and students concerned with children aged 7-12. Articles by specialists on practical teaching ideas and methods, plus in-depth coverage and debate on news issues in education. *Length:* 800-1200 words. *Payment:* by arrangement. *Illustrated* with b&w photos and line drawings; includes colour poster.

Junior Focus (1982), Margot O'Keeffe, Scholastic Publications Ltd, Villiers House, Clarendon Avenue, Leamington Spa, Warks. CV32 5PR *tel* (0926) 887799 *fax* (0926) 883331.
£2.00. M. Aimed at teachers of 7-12 year olds, each issue is based on a theme, closely linked with the National Curriculum. Includes A1 and A3 full-colour posters, 4 pages of photocopiable material and 12 pages of project notes. *All material commissioned. Length:* 1-4 pages. *Illustrations:* commissioned b&w line; welcomes samples of work from new illustrators. *Payment:* £90 per double-page spread; varies.

Just Seventeen (1983), Toni Rodgers, EMAP Women's Group, 20 Orange Street, London WC2H 7ED *tel* 071-957 8383 *fax* 071-957 8400.
70p. W. Articles of interest to girls aged between 12 and 18: fashion, beauty, pop, and various features; short stories up to 1500 words; quizzes. *Payment:* £110 per 1000 words. *Illustrations:* line, half-tone, colour, cartoons.

Justice of the Peace and Local Government Law (1837), F.W. Davies and Mark Watson-Gandy, Little London, Chichester, West Sussex PO19 1PG *tel* (0243) 775552.
£125.00 p.a. inc. postage. W. Professional journal. Articles on magisterial and local government law and associated subjects including family law, criminology, medico-legal matters, penology, police, probation (length preferred, under 1400 words). *Preliminary letter* welcomed although not essential. *Payment:* articles minimum £10 per column except when otherwise commissioned.

Kent, Fred Nixon, Little Theobald, Sandy Cross, Heathfield, East Sussex TN21 8BT *tel* (0435) 866653.

Free to members. Q. Journal of the Men of Kent and Kentish Men. Articles referring to County of Kent or former Kent people of interest. *Length:* maximum 500-600 words. *Payment:* very modest, by arrangement. *Illustrations:* photos and line.

Kent Messenger, 6 and 7 Middle Row, Maidstone, Kent ME14 1TG *tel* (0622) 695666; *London office:* Suite 12, Chancery House, 53/64 Chancery Lane, WC2A 1QX.
40p. Fri. Articles of special interest to Kent particularly Maidstone and Mid-Kent areas. *Payment:* state price. *Illustrations:* any format.

Kent Today, 395 High Street, Chatham, Kent ME4 4PG *tel* Medway (0634) 830999 *fax* (0634) 829479.
23p. Mon.-Fri. Paper with emphasis on news and sport, plus regular feature pages and a weekly business supplement. National news; with editions covering the Medway Towns, Gravesend, Dartford, Swale, Maidstone, Ashford and Canterbury. *Illustrations:* line, half-tone.

Kerrang! (1981), Phil Alexander, EMAP Metro Ltd, 5th Floor, Mappin House, 4 Winsley Street, London W1N 7AR *tel* 071-436 1515 *fax* 071-323 0276.
£1.30. W. News, views and reviews on the heaviest of heavy metal. *All material commissioned. Length:* 1000 words. *Illustrations:* half-tone. *Payment:* £88.75 per 1000 words; varies.

The Lady (1885), Arline Usden, 39-40 Bedford Street, Strand, London WC2E 9ER *tel* 071-379 4717 *fax* 071-497 2137.
60p. W. British and foreign travel, countryside, human-interest, celebrity interviews, animals, cookery, art and antiques, historic-interest and commemorative articles (*preliminary letter* advisable for articles dealing with anniversaries). *Length:* 700-1000 words; Viewpoint: 600 words. *Illustrations:* colour transparencies, b&w photos and drawings. *Payment:* from £60 per 1000 words; varies.

Lancashire Evening Post, Oliver's Place, Fulwood, Preston PR2 4ZA *tel* (0772) 254841 *fax* (0772) 880173.
23p. D. Topical articles on all subjects. Area of interest Wigan to Lake District and coast. *Length:* 600-900 words. *Payment:* by arrangement.

Lancashire Evening Telegraph (1886), Peter Butterfield, Newspaper House, High Street, Blackburn, Lancs. BB1 1HT *tel* (0254) 678678.
25p. D. Will consider general interest articles, such as holidays, property, motoring, finance, etc.

Lancashire Life, Brian Hargreaves, Town & County Magazines, Oyston Mill, Strand Road, Preston PR1 8UR *tel* (0772) 722022 *fax* (0772) 736496.
£1.90. M. Quality features and photographic material of regional interest. *Payment:* by negotiation.

Lancashire Magazine (1977), Winston Halstead, Barclays Bank Chambers, Sowerby Bridge, West Yorkshire HX6 2DX *tel/fax* (0422) 885678.
£1.00. Bi-M. Articles about people, life and character of all parts of Lancashire. *Length:* 1500 words. *Payment:* £30-£35 approx. per published page. *Illustrations:* line, half-tone, colour.

Lancet (1823), Robin Fox FRCPE, 42 Bedford Square, London WC1B 3SL *tel* 071-436 4981 *fax* 071-436 7550.
£2.75. W. Research papers, review articles, editorials, correspondence and commentaries on the international medicosocial scene. Regular contributors are paid by arrangement; others should consult the editor before submitting.

Land & Liberty (1894), Fred Harrison, 177 Vauxhall Bridge Road, London SW1V 1EU *tel* 071-834 4266.
£2.00. Bi-M. (£12.00 p.a.) Articles on land economics, land taxation, land prices, land speculation as they relate to housing, the economy, production, politics. *Study of journal* essential. *Length:* up to 3000 words. *Payment:* by arrangement. *Illustrations:* half-tone.

Learned Publishing (1988) (successor to **ALPSP Bulletin**), Hazel K. Bell, 139 The Ryde, Hatfield, Herts. AL9 5DP *tel* (0707) 265201 *fax* (0707) 273601.
Free to members. Q. (£60.00 p.a.) Journal of the Association of Learned and Professional Society Publishers. Articles, reports and book reviews on publishing and learned societies: editorial, production, marketing and distribution, copyright. *Length:* 1000-1500 words. *Illustrations:* line, half-tone. *Payment:* none.

The Leisure Manager (1985), Matthew Moggridge, International Trade Publications, Queensway House, 2 Queensway, Redhill, Surrey RH1 1QS *tel* (0737) 768611 *fax* (0737) 760564.
£5.00. M. Official Journal of The Institute of Leisure and Amenity Management. Articles on amenity, leisure, parks, entertainment, recreation and sports management. *Payment:* by arrangement. *Illustrations:* line, half-tone.

Leisure Painter (1966), Irene Briers, 63-65 High Street, Tenterden, Kent TN30 6BD *tel* (0580) 763315.
£1.85. M. Instructional articles on painting and fine arts. *Payment:* £60 per 1000 words. *Illustrations:* line, half-tone, colour, original artwork.

Leisureweek (1989), Michael Nutley, Centaur Publishing Ltd, St Giles House, 50 Poland Street, London W1V 4AX *tel* 071-494 0300 *fax* 071-734 2741.
£1.00. W. News and features relating to the leisure industry. *All material commissioned. Length:* features from 800 words, news from 200 words. *Illustrations:* line, half-tone. *Payment:* by agreement.

Liberal Democrats News, David Boyle, 4 Cowley Street, London SW1P 3NB *tel* 071-222 7999 *fax* 071-222 7904.
60p. W. (£26.00 p.a.) Official newspaper of the Liberal Democrats. News, political and social features. *Payment:* none.

The Library (1889), M.C. Davies, Incunabula, Humanities & Social Sciences, The British Library, Great Russell Street, London WC1B 3DG *tel* 071-323 7579 *fax* 071-323 7736. Oxford University Press for the Bibliographical Society.
£10.00. Q. (£32.00 p.a.) Articles up to 15,000 words as well as shorter Notes, embodying original research on subjects connected with bibliography. *Illustrations:* line, half-tone. *Payment:* none.

Life and Work: Record of the Church of Scotland, 121 George Street, Edinburgh EH2 4YN *tel* 031-225 5722 *fax* 031-220 3113.
50p. M. Articles not exceeding 1200 words and news; poems and occasional stories. *Study* the magazine. *Payment:* up to £45 per 1000 words, or by arrangement. *Illustrations:* photos and line, cartoons.

Lincolnshire Life (1961), Jenny Walton, PO Box 81, Lincoln LN1 1HD *tel* (0522) 527127 *fax* (0522) 560035.
£1.20. M. Articles and news of county interest. *Length:* up to 1200 words. *Illustrations:* b&w photos and line drawings. *Payment:* varies.

Lines Review (1952), Tessa Ransford, Edgefield Road, Loanhead, Edinburgh, Midlothian EH20 9SY *tel* 031-440 0246 *fax* 031-440 0315.
£1.80. Q. (£8.50 p.a.) Poetry, essays, criticism, reviews. *Illustrations:* line/half-tone for frontispiece only. *Payment:* £20 per 1000 words; £10.

The Linguist, Dr J.L. Kettle-Williams, The Institute of Linguists, 24A Highbury Grove, London N5 2EA *tel* 071-359 7445 *fax* 071-354 0202.
£5.00. Bi-M. (£25.00 p.a.) Articles of interest to professional linguists in translating, interpreting and teaching fields. Articles usually contributed, but *payment* by arrangement. All contributors have special knowledge of the subjects with which they deal. *Length:* 2000-3000 words. *Illustrations:* line, half-tone.

The Literary Review (1979), Auberon Waugh, 51 Beak Street, London W1R 3LF *tel* 071-437 9392 *fax* 071-734 1844.
£2.00. M. (£22.00 p.a.) Reviews, articles of cultural interest, interviews, profiles, monthly poetry competitions. Material mostly commissioned. *Length:* articles and reviews 800-1500 words. *Illustrations:* line and b&w photos. *Payment:* £25 per article; none.

Liverpool Echo, John Griffith, PO Box 48, Old Hall Street, Liverpool L69 3EB *tel* 051-227 2000.
26p. D. Ind. Articles of up to 600-800 words of local or topical interest. *Payment:* according to merit; special rates for exceptional material. This newspaper is connected with, but independent of, the Liverpool **Daily Post.** Articles not interchangeable.

Living (1967), Sharon Brown, IPC Magazines Ltd, King's Reach Tower, Stamford Street, London SE1 9LS *tel* 071-261 5000.
£1.30. M. General interest and human interest features; money, health, leisure, home, food, fashion and beauty. *Payment:* by arrangement. *Illustrated.*

Llais Llyfrau/Books in Wales (1964), R. Gerallt Jones, Ian Bell, Geraint Lewis, Welsh Books Council, Castell Brychan, Aberystwyth, Dyfed SY23 2JB *tel* (0970) 624151 *fax* (0970) 625385.
£5.00 p.a. Q. Articles in Welsh and English on authors and their books, Welsh publishing; reviews and book lists. Mainly commissioned. *Payment:* by arrangement.

Local Council Review, Paul Smith, Plus Public Relations, Press House, 130a Godinton Road, Ashford, Kent TN23 1LJ *tel* (0233) 643574 *fax* (0233) 641816.
£7.50 p.a. post free. Bi-M. Official Journal of the National Association of Local Councils. Local government in relation to parish, town and community councils in England and Wales.

Local Government Chronicle (1855), David Pead, EMAP Business Publishing, 33-39 Bowling Green Lane, London EC1R 0DA *tel* 071-837 1212 *fax* 071-837 2725.
£2.05. W. Articles relating to financial, political, legal and administrative work of the local government manager. *Payment:* by arrangement. *Illustrations:* half-tone, cartoons.

The Local Historian (formerly **The Amateur Historian**) (1952), Dr Margaret Bonney, 7 Carisbrooke Park, Knighton, Leicester LE2 3PQ *tel* (0533) 705028. British Association for Local History, Shopwyke Manor Barn, Chichester, West Sussex PO20 6BG *tel* (0243) 787639.
£5.00. Q. Articles, popular in style but based on knowledge of research, covering methods of research, sources and background material helpful to regional, local and family historians – histories of particular places, people or incidents *not* wanted. *Length:* maximum 7000 words. *Illustrations:* line and photos. *Payment:* none.

LOGOS (1990), Gordon Graham, 5 Beechwood Drive, Marlow, Bucks. SL7 2DH *tel/fax* (0628) 477577.

£38.00 p.a. Q. (£59.00 p.a. institutions) In-depth articles on publishing, librarianship and bookselling with international or inter-disciplinary appeal. *Length:* 3500-7000 words. *Payment:* 25 offprints/copy of issue.

London Magazine: A Review of the Arts (1954), Editor: Alan Ross, Deputy Editor: Jeremy Lewis, 30 Thurloe Place, London SW7 2HQ   *tel* 071-589 0618. £5.99. Bi-M. (£28.50 p.a.) Poems, stories, literary memoirs, critical articles, features on art, photography, sport, theatre, cinema, music, architecture, events, reports from abroad, drawings. Sae necessary. *Payment:* by arrangement.

London Review of Books (1979), Mary-Kay Wilmers, 28-30 Little Russell Street, London WC1A 2HN   *tel* 071-404 3336   *fax* 071-404 3337. £2.10. Bi-M. Features, essays, poems. *Payment:* by arrangement. *Illustrations:* line, half-tone.

LOOKS Magazine, Annabel Goldstaub, EMAP Women's Group, 20 Orange Street, London WC2H 7ED   *tel* 071-957 8383   *fax* 071-930 4191. £1.30. M. Fashion, beauty and hair for 15-22 age range; features, especially with a celebrity bias. *Length:* up to 2000 words. *Illustrations:* colour, b&w. *Payment:* £150 per 1000 words; £100-£200.

Love Story (1987), Ann Jaloba, Roderick Hudson, Argus Specialist Publications, Argus House, Boundary Way, Hemel Hempstead, Herts. HP2 7ST   *tel* (0442) 66551. £1.00. M. Contemporary and historical romantic stories, 4500-7000 words. *No freelance fiction can be considered*; unsolicited MSS will not be returned.

Loving (1970), Jo Pink, Room 2725, IPC Magazines Ltd, King's Reach Tower, Stamford Street, London SE1 9LS   *tel* 081-390 5833   *fax* 081-261 6032. 99p. M. General romantic fiction stories; can be first or third person, male or female viewpoint, for 18-30 market. Do not accept uncommissioned features material, but unsolicited stories welcome. *Length:* 1000-4000 words. All *illustrations* commissioned. *Payment:* by arrangement.

Mail on Sunday (1982), Jonathan Holborow, Northcliffe House, 2 Derry Street, London W8 5TT   *tel* 071-938 6000. 60p. W. Articles. *Payment:* by arrangement. *Illustrations:* line, half-tone. Includes **You** colour supplement, and **Night & Day** general interest supplement.

Making Music (1986), Jon Lewin, Making Music Ltd, 20 Bowling Green Lane, London EC1R 0BD   *tel* 071-251 1900   *fax* 071-251 2619. £12.00 p.a. M. Technical, musicianly and instrumental features on rock, pop, blues, dance, world, jazz, soul; little classical. *Length:* 500-1500 words. *Payment:* £80 per 1000 words. *Illustrations:* colour; b&w cartoons.

Management Today (1966), Dennis Hackett, 22 Lancaster Gate, London W2 3LY   *tel* 071-413 4566   *fax* 071-413 4138. £2.10. M. Company profiles and analysis – columns from 1000 words, features up to 3000 words. *Payment:* £250 per 1000 words. *Illustrations:* colour transparencies, usually commissioned.

Manchester Evening News, Michael Unger, 164 Deansgate, Manchester M60 2RD   *tel* 061-832 7200. 30p. D. Feature articles of up to 1000 words, topical or general interest and illustrated where appropriate, should be addressed to the Features Editor. *Payment:* on acceptance.

Mandy/Judy, D.C. Thomson & Co. Ltd, Courier Place, Dundee DD1 9QJ   *tel* (0382) 23131   *fax* (0382) 22214; and 185 Fleet Street, London EC4A 2HS   *tel* 071-242 5086   *fax* 071-404 5694.

45p. W. Picture-story paper for schoolgirls. Serials and series in line drawings: 2 and 3 page instalments, 8-9 frames per page. Editorial co-operation offered to promising scriptwriters. *Payment:* on acceptance.

Mandy Library, D.C. Thomson & Co. Ltd, Courier Place, Dundee DD1 9QJ *tel* (0382) 23131 *fax* (0382) 22214; and 185 Fleet Street, London EC4A 2HS *tel* 071-242 5086 *fax* 071-404 5694.
50p. M. 64-page (about 140 line drawings) picture-stories for schoolgirls: adventure, animal, mystery, school, sport. Scripts considered; promising script-writers and artists encouraged. *Payment:* on acceptance.

Manx Life (1971), Ian Faulds, Trafalgar Press Ltd, 12 Douglas Street, Peel, Isle of Man *tel* (0624) 843881.
£1.00. M. Factual articles on historical or topical aspects of the social, commercial, agricultural or cultural activities and interests of the Isle of Man. *Payment:* £20 per 1000 words on publication or by arrangement. *Illustrations:* line, half-tone.

Marie Claire (1988), Glenda Bailey, European Magazines Ltd, 2 Hatfields, London SE1 9PG *tel* 071-261 5240 *fax* 071-261 5277.
£1.90. M. Feature articles of interest to today's woman; plus fashion, beauty, health, food, drink and travel. *Commissioned material* only. *Payment:* by negotiation. *Illustrated* in colour.

Market Newsletter (1965), John Tracy, Focus House, 497 Green Lanes, London N13 4BP *tel* 081-882 3315/6.
Private circulation. M. Published by the Bureau of Freelance Photographers. Current information on markets and editorial requirements of interest to writers and photographers.

Marketing Week (1978), Stuart Smith, St Giles House, 50 Poland Street, London W1V 4AX *tel* 071-439 4222 *fax* 071-439 9669.
£1.40. W. Aimed at marketing management. Accepts occasional features and analysis. *Length:* 1000-2000 words. *Payment:* £150 per 1000 words.

Masonic Square (1975), Coombelands House, Coombelands Lane, Addlestone, Surrey TW17 8AS *tel* (0932) 820560 *fax* (0932) 821258.
£2.00. Q. (£9.00 p.a.) Biographies, history, symbolism, news items – all relevant to Freemasonry or affiliated subjects. *Length:* 1000-1500 words. *Illustrations:* line, half-tone, colour.

Mayfair (1966), Stephen Bleach, 2 Archer Street, London W1V 7HE *tel* 071-734 9191.
£1.95. M. Short humorous articles, sport, music, motoring. *Payment:* by arrangement. *Illustrations:* colour transparencies to illustrate highly visual feature ideas.

Me (1989), Simon Geller, G E Magazines Ltd, Elme House, 133 Long Acre, London WC2E 9AD *tel* 071-836 0519 *fax* 071-497 2364.
55p. W. Features include: celebrities, reviews, women and home. *Commissioned material* only. *Payment:* by negotiation. *Illustrated* in colour.

Medal News (1989), Diana Birch, Token Publishing Ltd, 105 High Street, Honiton, Devon EX14 8PE *tel* (0404) 45414 *fax* (0404) 45313.
£2.20. 10 p.a. Well-researched articles on military history with a bias towards medals. *Length:* up to 2000 words. *Illustrations:* b&w preferred. *Payment:* £20 per 1000 words; none.

Media Week (1985), Phoebe Corke, EMAP Media, 33-35 Bowling Green Lane, London EC1R 0DA *tel* 071-837 1212 *fax* 071-837 3285.

£1.50. W. News and analysis of UK and international advertising media. *Illustrations:* half-tone, cartoons.

Melody Maker, Allan Jones, IPC Magazines Ltd, King's Reach Tower, Stamford Street, London SE1 9LS *tel* 071-261 6229 *fax* 071-261 6706.
60p. W. Technical, entertaining and informative articles on rock and pop music. *Payment:* by arrangement. *Illustrations:* line, half-tone, colour.

Men Only (published by Paul Raymond: 1971), Nevile Player, 2 Archer Street, London W1V 7HF *tel* 071-734 9191 *fax* 071-734 5030.
£1.95. M. Erotic fiction; humour; glamour photography. *Payment:* by arrangement.

Methodist Recorder (1861), Michael Taylor, 122 Golden Lane, London EC1Y 0TL *tel* 071-251 8414.
40p. W. Methodist and Free Church newspaper; ecumenically involved. Limited opportunities for freelance contributors. *Preliminary letter* advised.

Middle East International (1971), Michael Wall, 21 Collingham Road, London SW5 0NU *tel* 071-373 5228 *fax* 071-370 5956.
£60.00 p.a. F. (other rates on application) Articles (1200-1600 words) and news stories on Middle East and Arab world related topics. *Payment:* £80 per 1000 words.

Military Modelling, Kenneth M. Jones, Argus Specialist Publications, Argus House, Boundary Way, Hemel Hempstead, Herts. HP2 7ST *tel* (0442) 66551 *fax* (0442) 66998.
£1.75. M. Articles on military modelling. *Length:* up to 2000 words. *Payment:* by arrangement. *Illustrations:* line, half-tone, colour.

Millennium—Journal of International Studies (1971), Bice Maiguashca, Mairi Johnson, London School of Economics, Houghton Street, London WC2A 2AE *tel* 071-955 7438 *fax* 071-955 7446.
£5.00. 3 p.a. (£16.00 p.a., institutions £35.00 p.a.) Serious articles on International Studies; original research work published, as well as topical articles on all aspects of international affairs. *Length:* 4500-8000 words (in triplicate with abstract). *Payment:* none. No *illustrations.*

Mind (1876), Professor Mark Sainsbury, Oxford University Press, Walton Street, Oxford OX2 6DP *tel* (0865) 56767 *fax* (0865) 267773.
£31.00 p.a. Q. Review of philosophy intended for those who have studied and thought on this subject. Articles from about 5000 words; shorter discussion notes; critical notices and reviews. *Payment:* none.

Mizz (1985), Jeanette Baker, IPC Magazines Ltd, King's Reach Tower, Stamford Street, London SE1 9LS *tel* 071-261 6319 *fax* 071-261 6032.
70p. F. Articles on any subject of interest to 15-19-year-old girls. *Approach* in writing. *Payment:* by arrangement. *Illustrated.*

Mobile & Holiday Homes (1960), Anne Webb, Link House, Dingwall Avenue, Croydon CR9 2TA *tel* 081-686 2599 *fax* 081-781 6044.
£1.90. M. Informative articles on residential mobile homes (park homes) and holiday static caravans – personal experience articles, site features, news items. No preliminary letter. *Payment:* by arrangement. *Illustrations:* line, half-tone, colour transparencies, cartoons.

Model Boats (1964), John L. Cundell, Argus Specialist Publications, Argus House, Boundary Way, Hemel Hempstead, Herts. HP2 7ST *tel* (0442) 66551 *fax* (0442) 66998.
£1.75. M. Articles, drawings, plans, sketches of model boats. *Payment:* £25 per page; plans £100. *Illustrations:* line, half-tone.

Model Engineer (1898), Ted Jolliffe, Argus Specialist Publications, Argus House, Boundary Way, Hemel Hempstead, Herts. HP2 7ST *tel* (0442) 66551 *fax* (0442) 66998.
£1.50. 2 p.m. Detailed description of the construction of models, small workshop equipment, machine tools and small electrical and mechanical devices; articles on small power engineering, mechanics, electricity, workshop methods, clocks and experiments. *Payment:* up to £35 per page. *Illustrations:* line, halftone, colour.

Model Railways (1971), Roy Johnstone, Argus Specialist Publications, Argus House, Boundary Way, Hemel Hempstead, Herts. HP2 7ST *tel* (0442) 66551 *fax* (0442) 66998.   Publication suspended.
£19.20 p.a. M. Descriptive articles on model railways and prototype railways suitable for modelling. Articles covering all aspects of construction, planning, electrical wiring, experimental model railway engineering, and operation of model layouts. *Payment:* by arrangement. *Illustrations:* photos, line.

Modern Churchman (1911), The Modern Churchpeople's Union, The School House, Leysters, Leominster, Hereford HR6 0HS *tel* (056 887) 271.
£1.30. Q. Covers contemporary and pastoral theology, ethics, politics, current affairs. *Length:* 1500-3500 words. Contributions voluntary.

Modern Language Review (1905), Modern Humanities Research Association, King's College, Strand, London WC2R 2LS.
£62.00 p.a. Q. (£74.00 overseas, $148.00 USA) Articles and reviews of a scholarly or specialist character on English, Romance, Germanic and Slavonic languages and literatures. *Payment:* none, but offprints are given.

The Modern Review (1991), Toby Young, 6 Hopgood Street, London W12 7JU *tel/fax* 081-749 0593.
£1.95. Bi-M. Intelligently written profiles, features, reviews of any aspect of popular culture. *Study of magazine* essential. Approach editor by phone. *Length:* 800-1500 words. *Illustrations:* photos, collages, caricatures, doodles, strips. *Payment:* £50 per 1000 words; £75.

Modus, Geoffrey Thompson, Hamilton House, Mabledon Place, London WC1H 9BJ *tel* 071-387 1441 *fax* 071-383 7230.
£3.00. 8 p.a. (£24.00 p.a.) Official Journal of the National Association of Teachers of Home Economics and Technology: aimed at teachers and educationists. Articles on the teaching of home economics and technology, including textiles, nutrition, and social and technical background information for teachers. *Length:* up to 1500 words. *Payment:* by arrangement. *Illustrations:* line, half-tone, cartoons.

MoneyMarketing (1985), Tim Potter, Centaur Communications Ltd, St Giles House, 50 Poland Street, London W1V 4AX *tel* 071-287 5678 *fax* 071-734 9379.
£1.00. W. News, features, surveys, viewpoints; cartoons. *Length:* features – from 900 words. *Illustrations:* b&w photos, colour and b&w line. *Payment:* £100 per 1000 words; colour line £150, b&w line £100, b&w photos £80.

Moneywise (1990), Christine Michael, Berkeley Magazines Ltd, 10 Old Bailey, London EC4M 7NB *tel* 071-409 5273 *fax* 071-409 5261.
£2.25. M. The magazine for a richer way of life. Financial and consumer interest features, articles and news stories. *Length:* 1500-2000 words. *Illustrations:* willing to see designers, illustrators and photographers for fresh new ideas. *Payment:* by arrangement.

The Month (1864), John McDade sj, 114 Mount Street, London W1Y 6AH *tel* 071-491 7596 *fax* 071-495 1673.

£1.20. M. Review of Christian thought, and world affairs, with arts and literary sections, edited by the Jesuit Fathers. *Preliminary letter* desirable. *Length:* up to 3000 words. *Payment:* by arrangement. *Illustrations:* b&w photos.

More! (1988), Marie O'Riordan, EMAP Women's Group, 20 Orange Street, London WC2H 7ED *tel* 071-957 8383 *fax* 071-930 4637.
£1.10. F. News, features, 'how to' articles aimed at young, working women. *No* fiction. *Study of magazine* essential. *Length:* 1800 words. *Payment:* £150 per 1000 words. *Illustrated.*

Morning Star (formerly **Daily Worker,** 1930), Tony Chater, The Morning Star Co-operative Society Ltd, 1-3 Ardleigh Road, London N1 4HS *tel* 071-254 0033 *telex* 916463 *fax* 071-254 5950.
40p. Daily newspaper for the Labour movement. Articles of general interest. *Illustrations:* photos, cartoons and drawings.

Mortgage Finance Gazette (1869), Neil Madden, Franey & Co. Ltd, South Quay Plaza, 183 Marsh Wall, London E14 9FS *tel* 071-538 5386 *fax* 071-538 8624.
£41.60 p.a. M. Articles on all aspects of building society management, mortgage finance, retail financial services. *Length:* up to 2000 words. *Payment:* by arrangement. *Illustrations:* line, half-tone.

Mother & Baby (1956), Stephanie Neuman, EMAP Élan, Victory House, Leicester Place, Leicester Square, London WC2H 7BP *tel* 071-437 9011 *telex* 266400 *fax* 071-434 0656.
£1.20. M. Features and practical articles. *Length:* 1200-2800 words. *Payment:* by negotiation. *Illustrated.*

Motor Boat and Yachting (1904), Alan Harper, IPC Magazines Ltd, King's Reach Tower, Stamford Street, London SE1 9LS *tel* 071-261 5333.
£2.35. M. General interest as well as specialist motor boating material welcomed. Features up to 2000 words considered on all aspects, sea-going and on inland waterways. *Payment:* varies. *Illustrations:* photos (mostly colour and transparencies preferred) and line, cartoons.

Motor Caravan Magazine (1985), Paul Carter, Link House Magazines Ltd, Link House, Dingwall Avenue, Croydon CR9 2TA *tel* 081-686 2599 *fax* 081-781 6044.
£1.95. M. Practical features, touring features (home and abroad). *Length:* up to 1500 words. *Payment:* £35-£40 per page. *Illustrations:* line, half-tone, colour, cartoons.

Motor Cycle News (1955), EMAP National Publications Ltd, 20-22 Station Road, Kettering NN15 7HH *tel* (0536) 411111 *fax* (0536) 411750.
77p. W. Features (up to 1000 words), photos and news stories of interest to motor cyclists.

Motorcaravan and Motorhome Monthly (MMM) (1966 as Motor Caravan and Camping), Penny Smith, 8 Swan Meadow, Pewsey, Wilts. SN9 5HW *tel* (0980) 630349 *fax* (0980) 630770.
£1.90. M. Articles including motorcaravan travel, owner reports and DIY. *Length:* up to 3000 words. *Payment:* from £15 per printed page. *Illustrations:* line, half-tone, colourprint.

Motorcycle International (1985), Justin Evans, 3 Acton Hill Mews, 310/328 Uxbridge Road, London W3 9QU *tel* 081-993 4136 *fax* 081-993 8702.
£2.45. M. Motorcycle-related features, news and travel articles. *Length:* from 1000 words. *Illustrations:* colour transparencies. *Payment:* £120 per 1000 words; by negotiation.

Ms London (1968), Editor-in-Chief: Bill Williamson, The Commuter Publishing Partnership, 7-9 Rathbone Street, London W1P 1AF *tel* 071-636 3666.
Free. W. Features and life style pieces of interest to young professional working women. *All material commissioned*; contributors *must* live in the capital. *Length:* 1000-2000 words. *Illustrations:* no unsolicited illustrations; enquire first. *Payment:* £125 per 1000 words or by negotiation.

Museums Journal (1901), The Museums Association, 42 Clerkenwell Close, London EC1R 0PA *tel* 071-250 1834 *fax* 071-250 1929.
£5.00. M. (free to members; £40.00 p.a. individuals; £60.00 p.a. institutions) Articles and news items on museum and art gallery policy, administration, architecture and display, notes on technical developments, book reviews. *Length:* 100-2500 words. *Illustrations:* line, half-tone, colour, cartoons. *Payment:* by agreement.

Music and Letters (1920). Editorial: Dr Nigel Fortune, Dr Tim Carter, Music Department, Royal Holloway, University of London, Egham, Surrey TW20 0EX *tel* (0784) 443532. Other matters: Oxford University Press (Journals Production), 60 Walton Street, Oxford OX2 6DP.
£9.00. Q. Scholarly articles, up to 10,000 words, on musical subjects, neither merely topical nor purely descriptive. Technical, historical and research matter preferred. *Illustrations:* music quotations and plates. *Payment:* none.

The Music Review (1940), A.F. Leighton Thomas, Glyneithin, Burry Port, Dyfed SA16 0TA. Other matters: Black Bear Press, King's Hedges Road, Cambridge CB4 2PQ.
£15.00. Q. (£50.00 p.a.) Articles from 1500-8000 words dealing with any aspect of standard or classical music (no jazz). *Payment:* small, by arrangement.

Music Teacher (1908), Tim Homfray, Rhinegold Publishing Ltd, 241 Shaftesbury Avenue, London WC2H 8EH *tel* 071-333 1747 *fax* 071-333 1769.
£2.45. M. Provides information and articles for both school and private music teachers. Articles and illustrations must have a teacher, as well as a musical, interest. *Length:* articles 1000-3000 words. *Payment:* by arrangement.

Music Week (1959), Steve Redmond, Eighth Floor, Ludgate House, 245 Blackfriars Road, London SE1 9UL *tel* 071-620 3636 *fax* 071-401 8035.
£2.80. W. (£103.00 p.a.) News and features on all aspects of producing, manufacturing, marketing and retailing music. *Payment:* by negotiation.

Musical Opinion (1877), Denby Richards, 2 Princes Road, St Leonards-on-Sea, East Sussex TN37 6EL *tel* (0424) 715167 *fax* (0424) 712214.
£1.50. M. Suggestions for contributions of musical interest, scholastic, educational, anniversaries, ethnic, and relating to the organ world. Record, opera, festival, book, music reviews. All editorial matter must be commissioned. *Payment:* on publication. *Illustrations:* b&w photos, cartoons.

Musical Times (1844), Antony Bye and Gavin Thomas, Orpheus Publications, 4th Floor, Centro House, Mandela Street, London NW1 0DU *tel* 071-387 3848 *fax* 071-388 8532.
£1.95. M. Musical articles, reviews, 150-2500 words. Intending contributors are advised to *study recent numbers of the journal; material mostly commissioned*. *Payment:* by arrangement. *Illustrations:* photos and music.

My Weekly (1910), D.C. Thomson & Co. Ltd, 80 Kingsway East, Dundee DD4 8SL *tel* (0382) 23131 *fax* (0382) 452491; and 185 Fleet Street, London EC4A 2HS *tel* 071-242 5086 *fax* 071-404 5694.
40p. W. Serials, from 30,000-80,000 words, suitable for family reading. Short complete stories of 1500-5000 words with humorous, romantic or strong emotional theme. Articles on prominent people and on all subjects of feminine

interest. All contributions should make their appeal to the modern woman. *No preliminary letter* required. *Payment:* on acceptance. *Illustrations:* colour and b&w.

My Weekly Puzzle Time (1993), D.C. Thomson & Co. Ltd, Albert Square, Dundee DD1 9QJ *tel* (0382) 23131 *fax* (0382) 22214.
£1.10. M. Broad range of puzzles appealing mainly to women. Entertainment value more important than intellectual. *Payment:* by arrangement. No *illustrations*.

My Weekly Story Library, D.C. Thomson & Co. Ltd, Courier Place, Dundee DD1 9QJ *tel* (0382) 23131 *fax* (0382) 22214; and 185 Fleet Street, London EC4A 2HS *tel* 071-242 5086 *fax* 071-404 5694.
50p. 4 p.m. 35,000-37,500-word romantic stories aimed at the post-teenage market. *Payment:* by arrangement; competitive for the market. No *illustrations*.

Natural World (1981), Linda Bennett, 20 Upper Ground, London SE1 9PF *tel* 071-928 2111 *fax* 071-620 1594.
Free to members. 3 p.a. Magazine of RSNC · The Wildlife Trusts Partnership. Short articles on UK nature conservation, particularly the work of the Partnership; contributors normally have special knowledge of subjects on which they write. *Length:* up to 1500 words. *Payment:* by arrangement. *Illustrations:* line, half-tone, colour.

Naturalist (1875), Professor M.R.D. Seaward MSc, PhD, DSc, The University, Bradford BD7 1DP *tel* (0274) 384212 *telex* 51309 UNIBFD G *fax* (0274) 384231.
£15.00 p.a. Q. Original papers on all kinds of British natural history subjects, including various aspects of geology, archaeology and environmental science. *Length:* immaterial. *Illustrations:* photos and line drawings. *Payment:* none.

Nature (1869), John Maddox, Macmillan Magazines Ltd, 4 Little Essex Street, London WC2R 3LF *tel* 071-836 6633 *fax* 071-836 9934.
£4.00. W. Devoted to scientific matters and to their bearing upon public affairs. All contributors of articles have specialised knowledge of the subjects with which they deal. *Illustrations:* line, half-tone.

Nautical Magazine (1832), L. Ingram-Brown FInstSMM, MBIM, MRIN, Brown, Son & Ferguson, Ltd, 4-10 Darnley Street, Glasgow G41 2SD *tel* 041-429 1234 *telegraphic address* Skipper, Glasgow *fax* 041-420 1694.
£25.32 p.a. inc. postage (£29.40 p.a. overseas); 3 years £75.50 (£88.00 overseas). M. Articles relating to nautical and shipping profession, from 1500-2000 words; also translations. *Payment:* by arrangement. No *illustrations*.

Navy International, Anthony J. Watts, Hunters Moon, Hogspudding Lane, Newdigate, Nr Dorking, Surrey RH5 5DS *tel* (0306) 631442 *fax* (0306) 631226.
£33.00 p.a. M. Geo-political, strategic and technical articles on current world naval affairs. *Length:* 1500-2000 words. *Payment:* £70 per 1000 words. *Illustrations* used.

New Beacon (1930; as **Beacon** 1917), Ann Lee, RNIB, 224 Great Portland Street, London W1N 6AA *tel* 071-388 1266.
£1.20. M. Articles on all aspects of visual impairment. *Length:* from 500 words. *Payment:* £30 per 1000 words: *Illustrations:* half-tone. Also Braille edition.

New Blackfriars (1920), Rev. Allan White OP, The English Dominicans, Blackfriars, Oxford OX1 3LY *tel/fax* (0865) 278414.
£1.70. M. (£15.50 p.a.) Critical review, surveying the field of theology, philosophy, sociology and the arts, from the standpoint of Christian principles and

their application to the problems of the modern world. Incorporates *Life of the Spirit. Length:* 2500-6000 words. *Payment:* by arrangement.

New DIY (1957), John McGowan, Link House, Dingwall Avenue, Croydon CR9 2TA   *tel* 081-686 2599   *fax* 081-760 0973/781 6046.
£1.80. M. Authoritative articles on every aspect of DIY in the house, garden, workshop and garage. Press 3 months ahead. Leaflet describing style requirements available on request. *Length:* up to 1000 words unless negotiated. *Illustrations:* line drawings and photos. *Payment:* by arrangement.

New Humanist (1885), Jim Herrick, Rationalist Press Association, 15 Lamb's Conduit Passage, London WC1R 4RH   *tel* 071-430 1371   *fax* 071-430 1271.
£1.50. Q. Articles on current affairs, philosophy and humanism. *Length:* 1000-3000 words. *Illustrations:* b&w photos. *Payment:* nominal; none for photos.

New Internationalist (1973), Vanessa Baird, Chris Brazier, David Ransom, Nikki van der Gaag, 55 Rectory Road, Oxford OX4 1BW   *tel* (0865) 728181   *telegraphic address* Newint, Oxford   *telex* 83147 NEWINT VIAOR G   *fax* (0865) 793152.
£1.50. M. (£18.40 p.a.) World issues, ranging from food to feminism to peace – examines one subject each month. *Length:* up to 2000 words. *Illustrations:* line, half-tone, colour, cartoons. *Payment:* £100 per 1000 words; b&w photos, £100 full page, £45 ¼ page.

New Law Journal (1975), James Morton, Butterworth & Co. (Publishers) Ltd, 9/12 Bell Yard, London WC2A 2JR   *tel* 071-405 6900   *fax* 071-405 7083.
£3.00. 48 p.a. Articles and news on all aspects of the legal profession. *Length:* up to 1800 words. *Payment:* by arrangement.

New Library World (1898), MCB University Press, 60/62 Toller Lane, Bradford, West Yorkshire BD8 9BY   *tel* (0274) 499821.
£359.95 p.a. 7 p.a. Professional and bibliographical articles. *Payment:* none.

New Musical Express, Steve Sutherland, IPC Magazines Ltd, 25th Floor, King's Reach Tower, Stamford Street, London SE1 9LS   *tel* 071-261 5000   *fax* 071-261 5185.
75p. W. Authoritative articles and news stories on the world's rock and movie personalities. *Length:* by arrangement. *Preliminary letter or phone call* desirable. *Payment:* by arrangement. *Illustrations:* action photos with strong news-angle of recording personalities, cartoons.

New Scientist, Alun Anderson, IPC Magazines Ltd, King's Reach Tower, Stamford Street, London SE1 9LS   *tel* 071-261 5000   *fax* 071-261 6464   *electronic mailbox* Telecom Gold/Dialcom: 83:NSM007.
£1.60. W. Authoritative articles of topical importance on all aspects of science and technology (*length:* 1000-3000 words); preliminary letter or telephone call desirable. Short items from specialists also considered for *Science, This Week, Forum* and *Technology.* Intending contributors should study recent copies of the magazine. *Payment:* varies but average £160 per 1000 words. *Illustrations:* line, half-tone, colour, cartoons.

New Statesman & Society (1988), Steve Platt, Foundation House, Perseverance Works, 38 Kingsland Road, London E2 8DQ   *tel* 071-739 3211   *fax* 071-739 9307.
£1.50. W. Interested in news, reportage and analysis of current political and social issues at home and overseas, plus book reviews, general articles and coverage of the arts, environment and science seen from the perspective of the British Left but written in a stylish, witty and unpredictable way. *Length:* strictly according to the value of the piece. *Payment:* by agreement.

New Theatre Quarterly (1985; as **Theatre Quarterly** 1971), Clive Barker, Simon Trussler, Great Robhurst, Woodchurch, Ashford, Kent TN26 3TB.
£11.00. Q. (£24.00 p.a.) Articles, interviews, documentation, reference material covering all aspects of live theatre. An informed, factual and serious approach essential. Preliminary discussion and synopsis desirable. *Payment:* by arrangement. *Illustrations:* line, half-tone.

The New Welsh Review (1988), Robin Reeves, 49 Park Place, Cardiff CF1 3AT *tel* (0222) 665529/515014.
£3.60. Q. (£15.00 p.a.) Articles, short stories, poetry; plus reviews, interviews and profiles. Especially, but not exclusively, concerned with Welsh literature in English. *Length:* (articles) up to 4000 words; short poems preferred. *Illustrations:* line, half-tone, cartoons; colour cover. *Payment:* £7-£15 per page prose; £8-£20 per poem; £10-£20 per review; £10-£20 per illustration.

New Woman (1988), Gill Hudson, EMAP Women's Group, 20 Orange Street, London WC2H 7ED *tel* 071-957 8383 *fax* 071-957 8400.
£1.70. M. Features up to 2000 words. Occasionally accepts unsolicited articles; enclose sae for return. *Payment:* at or above NUJ rates. *Illustrated.*

New World, United Nations Association, 3 Whitehall Court, London SW1A 2EL *tel* 071-930 2931 *fax* 071-930 5893.
50p. 4 p.a. Review of UN activities, of UNA campaigns and of different viewpoints on major international issues confronting the United Nations.

The News, Portsmouth (1877), Geoffrey Elliott, The News Centre, Hilsea, Portsmouth PO2 9SX *tel* (0705) 664488 *fax* (0705) 673363.
25p. D. Articles of relevance to south-east Hampshire and West Sussex. *Length:* 600 words. *Illustrations:* photos, preferably in colour, cartoons. *Payment:* £50.

News of the World (1843), Piers Morgan (acting), 1 Virginia Street, London E1 9XR *tel* 071-782 4000 *fax* 071-583 9504.
50p. W.

19 (1968), April Joyce, IPC Magazines Ltd, King's Reach Tower, Stamford Street, London SE1 9LS *tel* 071-261 6360.
£1.20. M. Glossy fashion and general interest magazine for young women aged 17 to 22 including beauty, music and social features of strong contemporary interest. All *illustrations* commissioned. *Payment:* by arrangement.

90 Minutes (1990), Paul Hawksbee, IPC Magazines Ltd, King's Reach Tower, Stamford Street, London SE1 9LS *tel* 071-261 7450 *fax* 071-261 7474.
70p. W. Football features, news stories, interviews. *Length:* 50-1500 words. *Illustrations:* colour photos. *Payment:* £10-£80.

The Northern Echo (1870), David Flintham, Priestgate, Darlington, Co. Durham DL1 1NF *tel* (0325) 381313 *fax* (0325) 380539.
30p. D. Articles of interest to North-East and North Yorkshire; *all material commissioned. Preliminary study* of newspaper advisable. *Length:* 800-1000 words. *Illustrations:* line, half-tone, colour – mostly commissioned. *Payment:* by negotiation.

Nottingham Evening Post (1878), Forman Street, Nottingham NG1 4AB *tel* (0602) 482000 *fax* (0602) 484116.
25p. D. Will consider material on local issues.

Numismatic Chronicle (1839), Mark Blackburn, Department of Coins and Medals, Fitzwilliam Museum, Cambridge CB2 1RB *tel* (0223) 332917.

£24.00 per annual volume. Journal of the Royal Numismatic Society. Articles on coins and medals. Memoirs relating to coins and medals are unpaid, and contributions should reach a high standard of quality.

Nursery World, Lindsey Blythe, The School House Workshop, 51 Calthorpe Street, London WC1X 0HH *tel* 071-837 7224   *fax* 071-278 3896.
80p. W. For all grades of primary school, nursery and child care staff, nannies, foster parents and all concerned with the care of expectant mothers, babies and young children. Authoritative and informative articles, 800 or 1600 words, and photos, on all aspects of child welfare and early education, from 0-8 years, in the UK. Practical ideas and leisure crafts. *No* short stories. *Payment:* by arrangement. *Illustrations:* line, half-tone, colour.

Nursing Times and Nursing Mirror (1905), Macmillan Magazines Ltd, 4 Little Essex Street, London WC2R 3LF *tel* 071-379 0970   *fax* 071-497 2664.
95p. W. Articles of clinical interest, nursing education and nursing policy. *Illustrated* articles not longer than 1500 words. Contributions from other than health professionals sometimes accepted. Press day, Monday. *Payment:* NUJ rates.

The Observer (1791), Jonathan Fenby, 119 Farringdon Road, London EC1R 3ER *tel* 071-278 2332.
90p. Sun. Ind. Some articles and illustrations commissioned.

Office Secretary (1986), Jane Slade, Trade Media Ltd, Brookmead House, Two Rivers, Station Lane, Witney, Oxon OX8 6BH *tel* (0993) 775545   *fax* (0993) 778884; *London editorial office:* Studio A132, The Riverside Business Centre, Bendon Valley, SW18 4LZ *tel/fax* 081-875 0343/0344.
£9.50 p.a. Q. Serious features on anything of interest to senior secretaries/ working women. *No* unsolicited MSS; ideas only. *Illustrations:* colour transparencies, cartoons. *Payment:* £100 per 1000 words, or by negotiation.

Oldham Evening Chronicle (1854), Philip Hirst, PO Box 47, Union Street, Oldham, Lancs. OL1 1EQ *tel* 061-633 2121   *fax* 061-627 0905.
26p. Mon.-Fri. News and features on current topics and local history. *Length:* 1000 words. *Illustrations:* colour and b&w photos and line. *Payment:* £20-£25 per 1000 words; £13.60-£18.26.

The Oldie (1992), Richard Ingrams, 26 Charlotte Street, London W1P 1HJ *tel* 071-636 3686   *fax* 071-636 3685.
£1.60. F. General interest magazine reflecting attitudes of older people but aimed at a wider audience. Welcomes features (500-700 words) and ideas on all subjects. No interviews but profiles (900 words) for *Still With Us* section. *Payment:* approx. £100 per 1000 words. Welcomes b&w cartoons. *Payment:* minimum £40. Would prefer not to have to return MSS.

Opera, Rodney Milnes, 1A Mountgrove Road, London N5 2LU *tel* 071-359 1037   *fax* 071-354 2700. Seymour Press Ltd, Windsor House, 1270 London Road, London SW16 4DH.
£2.25. 13 p.a. Articles on general subjects appertaining to opera; reviews; criticisms. *Length:* up to 2000 words. *Payment:* by arrangement. *Illustrations:* photos.

Opera Now (1989), Graeme Kay, 241 Shaftesbury Avenue, London WC2H 8EH *tel* 071-333 1740   *fax* 071-333 1769.
£3.45. M. Articles, news, reviews on opera. All material commissioned only. *Length:* 150-1500 words. *Illustrations:* colour and b&w photos, line, cartoons. *Payment:* £120 per 1000 words.

Options (1982), Maureen Rice, IPC Magazines Ltd, King's Reach Tower, Stamford Street, London SE1 9LS *tel* 071-261 5000.

£1.60. M. Aimed at women aged 25-35. Careers, emotional and sexual matters, health and well-being, women's issues, first-class celebrity interviews and profiles. *Mostly commissioned. Length:* 1000-3000 words. *Payment:* by arrangement.

Orbis (1968), Mike Shields, 199 The Long Shoot, Nuneaton, Warks. CV11 6JQ   *tel* (0203) 327440/385551   *fax* (0203) 642402.
£15.00 p.a. Q. Poetry, prose pieces (up to 1000 words), reviews, letters. Annual competition for rhymed poetry. *Payment:* by arrangement. *Illustrations:* line.

The Organ (1921), Dr Brian Hick, 5 Aldborough Road, St Leonards-on-Sea, East Sussex TN37 6SE   *tel* (0424) 422225.
£15.00 p.a. Q. (£19.00 p.a. overseas) Articles, 1000-5000 words, relating to the organ: historical, technical and artistic; reviews of music, records. *Payment:* small. *Illustrations:* line, half-tone, colour.

Organic Gardening (1988), Basil Caplan, Wardnest Ltd, PO Box 4, Wiveliscombe, Taunton, Somerset TA4 2QY   *tel* (0984) 623998   *fax* (0984) 623998.
£1.75. M. Articles and features on all aspects of organic gardening. *All material commissioned. Length:* 800-2000 words. *Illustrations:* colour and b&w photos, line drawings, cartoons. *Payment:* by arrangement.

Our Dogs (1895), William Moores, Oxford Road Station Approach, Manchester M60 1SX   *tel* 061-236 2660   *fax* 061-236 5534/0892.
£1.10. W. Articles and news on the breeding and showing of pedigree dogs. *Illustrations:* b&w photos. *Payment:* NUJ rates; £7.50 per photo.

Outdoor (1993; formerly **Outdoor Action**), Moira Crawford, Mark Allen Publishing Ltd, Croxted Mews, 288 Croxted Road, London SE24 9BY   *tel* 081-671 7521   *fax* 081-671 1722.
£2.00. M. Feature articles about walking and walking areas, particularly in the UK but also more exotic places. *Length:* up to 1200 words. *Illustrations:* colour transparencies. *Payment:* £100 per 1000 words; by negotiation.

Outposts Poetry Quarterly (1943), Roland John, 22 Whitewell Road, Frome, Somerset BA11 4EL   *tel* (0373) 466653. *Founder:* Howard Sergeant MBE.
£4.00. Q. (£12.00 p.a.) Poems, essays and critical articles on poets and their work; poetry competitions. *Payment:* by arrangement.

Overkill (1992), Jacqui Papp, Marvel UK Ltd, Arundel House, 13/15 Arundel Street, London WC2R 3DX   *tel* 071-497 2121   *fax* 071-497 2234.
99p. F. Comic strip stories featuring range of previously created characters and situations. Submit ideas to editor for discussion. *Length:* 11-22 pages. *Illustrations:* colour and b&w line art. *Payment:* £35 per page; £110 per page; £200+ per cover.

Oxford Poetry (1983), Sinéad Garrigan, Ian Sansom, Magdalen College, Oxford OX1 4AU.
£2.00. 3 p.a. Previously unpublished poems, both unsolicited and commissioned. *Payment:* none.

Parents (1976), Sarah Kilby, EMAP Élan, Victory House, Leicester Place, London WC2H 7BP   *tel* 071-437 9011   *fax* 071-434 0656.
£1.40. M. Articles on pregnancy, childbirth, general family health, food, fashion, child upbringing and development up to aged three and marital relations. MSS with sae only. *Illustrations:* b&w or colour. *Payment:* in accordance with national magazine standards; by arrangement.

Parks & Sports Grounds (1935), Alan Guthrie, 61 London Road, Staines, Middlesex TW18 4BN *tel* (0784) 461326 *fax* (0784) 462073.
£25.00 p.a. M. Articles on the design, construction, maintenance and management of parks, sports grounds, golf courses, open spaces and amenity areas. *Length:* 750-2000 words. *Payment:* £70 per 1000 words. *Illustrations:* line, half-tone.

PC Direct (1991), Karen Packham, Ziff-Davis UK Ltd, Cottons Centre, Hay's Lane, London SE1 2QT *tel* 071-378 6800 *fax* 071-378 1192.
£1.70. M. News, features and technical information for the direct business computer buyer. *All material commissioned. Length:* 800-6000 words. *Illustrations:* colour photos and illustrations, including computer generated. *Payment:* £180 per 1000 words; varies for illustrations according to subject/media.

PC Review, Christina Erskine, EMAP Images, Priory Court, 30-32 Farringdon Lane, London EC1R 3AU *tel* 071-972 6700 *fax* 071-972 6710.
£3.95. M. Features, previews, reviews of PC entertainment – commissioned only, by arrangement with the editor. *Illustrations:* colour transparencies; ideas for line art, diagrams, charts, etc. *Payment:* by negotiation.

Peace News for nonviolent revolution (1936), 5 Caledonian Road, London N1 9DX *tel* 071-278 3344 *fax* 071-278 0444.
80p. M. Political articles based on nonviolence in every aspect of human life. *Illustrations:* line, half-tone. *Payment:* none.

Pensions World (1972), Stephanie Hawthorne, Tolley Publishing Co. Ltd, Tolley House, 2 Addiscombe Road, Croydon, Surrey CR9 5AF *tel* 081-686 9141 *fax* 081-760 0588.
£46.00 p.a. M. Specialist articles on pensions and investment law. *No* unsolicited articles; all material is *commissioned. Length:* 1500 words. *Payment:* by negotiation.

Penthouse Magazine, The International Magazine for Men (1965), Deric Botham, Northern & Shell Tower, PO Box 381, City Harbour, London E14 9GL *tel* 071-987 5090 *fax* 071-987 2160.
£2.95. M. Serious and light-hearted factual articles on sex, relationships, motoring, adventure, general interest. *No* fiction. *Length:* 2000-3000 words. *Payment:* by arrangement. *Illustrations:* cartoon strips, colour photo sets on 35 mm slide, and photos.

The People, Bridget Rowe, 1 Canada Square, Canary Wharf, London E14 5AP *tel* 071-293 3000 *fax* 071-293 3758.
50p. Sun. Investigative features, single articles and series considered; pictures should be supplied with contributions if possible. Features should be of deep human interest, whether the subject is serious or light-hearted. Very strong sports following. Exclusive news and news-feature stories also considered. *Payment:* rates high, even for tips that lead to published news stories.

People's Friend (1869), D.C. Thomson & Co. Ltd, 80 Kingsway East, Dundee DD4 8SL *tel* (0382) 23131 *telex* 76380 DCTHOM G *fax* (0382) 452491; and 185 Fleet Street, London EC4A 2HS *tel* 071-242 5086 *fax* 071-404 5694.
40p. W. Illustrated weekly appealing to women of all ages and devoted to their personal and home interests, especially knitting, fashion and cookery. Serials (60,000-70,000 words) and complete stories (1500-3000 words) of strong romantic and emotional appeal. Stories for children considered. *No preliminary letter* required. *Illustrations:* colour and b&w. *Payment:* on acceptance.

People's Friend Library, D.C. Thomson & Co. Ltd, 80 Kingsway East, Dundee DD4 8SL *tel* (0382) 23131 *telex* 76380 DCTHOM G *fax* (0382) 452491; and 185 Fleet Street, London EC4A 2HS *tel* 071-242 5086 *fax* 071-404 5694.
80p. 2 p.m. 50,000-55,000-word family and romantic stories aimed at 30+ age group. *Payment:* by arrangement. No *illustrations*.

Perfect Home (1992), Julia Smith, DMG Home Interest Magazines Ltd, Times House, Station Approach, Ruislip, Middlesex HA4 8NB *tel* (0895) 677677 *fax* (0895) 676027.
£1.10. M. Home-related features: craft, travel, cookery, finance, DIY, houses, product testing/reviews, gardening. *Length:* 800-1000 words. *Payment:* £300 per 1000 words. *Illustrated.*

Performance Car (1983), Paul Clark, EMAP National Publications Ltd, Bushfield House, Orton Centre, Peterborough PE2 5UW *tel* (0733) 237111.
£2.20. M. Articles, 2000-3000 words, on all aspects of cars. *Payment:* by arrangement. *Illustrations:* half-tone, colour, cartoons.

Period Living & Traditional Homes (1990), Isobel McKenzie-Price, EMAP Élan, Victory House, 14 Leicester Place, London WC2H 7BP *tel* 071-437 9011 *fax* 071-434 0656.
£2.20. M. Articles and features on decoration, furnishings, renovation of period homes; traditional cookery; gardens, crafts, decorating in a period style. *Illustrated. Payment:* varies, according to work required.

Personal Computer World (1977), Ben Tisdall, VNU House, 32-34 Broadwick Street, London W1A 2HG *tel* 071-439 4242 *fax* 071-895 8098 *e-mail* ben@compulink.co.uk.
£1.95. M. Articles about computers; reviews. *Length:* 800-5000 words. *Payment:* from £130 per 1000 words. *Illustrations:* line, half-tone, colour.

Personnel Management, Rob MacLachlan, Personnel Publications Ltd, 17 Britton Street, London EC1M 5NQ *tel* 071-336 7888 *fax* 071-336 7635.
£5.00. M. (£52.00 p.a.) Journal of the Institute of Personnel Management. Features and news items on recruitment and selection, training and development; wage and salary administration; industrial psychology; employee relations; labour law; welfare schemes, working practices and new practical ideas in personnel management in industry and commerce. *Length:* up to 2500 words. *Payment:* by arrangement. *Illustrations:* photographers and illustrators should contact art editor.

The Pharmaceutical Journal (1841), D. Simpson MRPharmS, 1 Lambeth High Street, London SE1 7JN *tel* 071-735 9141 *telegraphic address/cables* Pharmakon, London SE1 *fax* 071-735 7629.
£1.50. W. Official Journal of the Royal Pharmaceutical Society of Great Britain. Articles on any aspect of pharmacy may be submitted. *Payment:* by arrangement. *Illustrations:* half-tone, colour.

Photo Answers, Steve Moore, EMAP Apex Publications, Apex House, Oundle Road, Peterborough PE2 9NP *tel* (0733) 898100 *fax* (0733) 894472.
£1.95. M. Magazine appealing to everyone interested in photography. Little opportunity for freelance writers, but always interested in seeing quality photos. *Payment:* upwards of £25 per published page, colour or mono. *Illustrations:* print, slide, line, half-tone.

Physiotherapy, Jill Whitehouse, 14 Bedford Row, London WC1R 4ED *tel* 071-242 1941.
£4.50. M. Journal of the Chartered Society of Physiotherapy. Articles on physiotherapy and related subjects, technical items and news regarding activities of members of the Society. Contributions welcomed from physiotherapists

and doctors. *Length:* 2000 words (average). *Illustrations:* photos, line. *Payment:* none.

PIC (People in Camera) (1989), Shawn Russell, PIC (1994) Ltd, 34 Church Road, Hove, East Sussex BN3 2GJ *tel* (0273) 779797 *fax* (0273) 733371. £2.45. M. Photographic or image-making articles, concentrating on people – models as well as photographers – generally illustrated with photos. *Length:* up to 2000 words. *Illustrations:* colour transparencies/prints. *Payment:* by negotiation.

Pig Farming, Bryan Kelly, Morgan-Grampian Farming Press, Wharfedale Road, Ipswich IP1 4LG *tel* (0473) 241122 *fax* (0473) 240501. £23.00 p.a. M. Practical, well-illustrated articles on all aspects of pigmeat production required, particularly those dealing with new ideas in pig management, feeding, housing and processing. *Length:* 800-1200 words. *Payment:* by arrangement. *Illustrations:* line, half-tone, colour, cartoons.

Pilot (1968), James Gilbert, The Clock House, 28 Old Town, Clapham, London SW4 0LB *tel* 071-498 2506 *fax* 071-498 6920. £2.10. M. Feature articles on general aviation, private and business flying. *Illustrations:* line, half-tone, colour, cartoons. *Payment:* £100-£800 per article on acceptance; £25 for each photo used.

The Pink Paper (1988), Alison Gregory, 13 Hercules Street, London N7 6AT *tel* 071-272 2155 *fax* 071-263 2572. Free. W. The national newspaper for lesbians and gay men. Features (500-1000 words) and news (100-400 words) on any subject of interest. *Illustrations:* b&w photos and line. *Payment:* £100 per 1000 words; £30-£50.

Planet (1970-9; relaunched 1985), John Barnie, PO Box 44, Aberystwyth, Dyfed SY23 5BS *tel* (0970) 611255 *fax* (0970) 623311. £2.50. 6 p.a. (£12.00 p.a.) Short stories, poems, topical articles on Welsh current affairs, politics and society; articles on minority cultures throughout the world. New literature in English. *Length* of articles: 1000-3500 words. *Payment:* £40 per 1000 words for prose; £25 minimum per poem. *Illustrations:* line, half-tone, cartoons.

Plays & Players, Sandra Rennie, 18 Friern Park, London N12 9DA *tel* 081-343 8515 *fax* 081-446 4959. £2.50. M. Articles, reviews and photos on world theatre. *Payment:* by arrangement. *Illustrations:* line, photos.

PN Review, formerly **Poetry Nation** (1973), Michael Schmidt, 208 Corn Exchange Buildings, Manchester M4 3BQ *tel* 061-834 8730 *fax* 061-832 0084. £4.00. Q. (£24.50 p.a.) Poems, essays, reviews, translations. *Payment:* by arrangement.

Poetry Durham (1982), David Hartnett, Michael O'Neill, Gareth Reeves, School of English, University of Durham, Elvet Riverside, New Elvet, Durham DH1 3JT *tel* (091) 374 2730. £6.00 p.a. 3 p.a. Poems and review essays on contemporary poetry. *Payment:* on publication.

Poetry London Newsletter (1988), Leon Cych, Pascale Petit, Katherine Gallagher, 26 Clacton Road, London E17 8AR *tel* 081-520 6693 *tel/fax* 071-637 4575. £12.00 p.a. 3 p.a. Poems of the highest standard, articles/reviews on any aspect of modern poetry; listings. Contributors must be very knowledgeable about contemporary poetry. *Illustrations:* line or digitised photos, cartoons. *Payment:* £10 per review or three copies of the magazine; poets £10 per issue and two copies of magazine.

Poetry Nottingham (1941), Martin Holroyd, 39 Cavendish Road, Long Eaton, Nottingham NG10 4HY.
£2.00. Q. Poems. *Length:* not more than 30 lines. *Illustrations:* line. *Payment:* none, but complimentary copy.

Poetry Review, Peter Forbes, 22 Betterton Street, London WC2H 9BU   *tel* 071-240 4810   *fax* 071-240 4818.
£20.00 p.a. Q. (£26.00 p.a. institutions, schools and libraries) Poems, features and reviews. Send no more than six poems with sae. *Preliminary study* of magazine essential. *Payment:* £25-£30 per poem.

Poetry Wales (1965), Richard Poole, Glan-y-Werydd, Llandanwg, Harlech LL46 2SD Cymru/Wales. Subscriptions and books for review to: Amy Wack, And-mar House, Trewsfield Road, Bridgend CF31 4LJ.
£2.50. Q. (£10.00 p.a. inc. postage) Poems mainly in English and mainly by Welsh people or resident: other contributors (and Welsh language poetry) also published. Articles on Welsh literature in English and in Welsh, as well as on poetry from other countries. Special features; reviews on poetry and wider matters. *Payment:* by arrangement.

Police Journal (1928), R.W. Stone QPM, Little London, Chichester, West Sussex PO19 1PG   *tel* (0243) 787841   *fax* (0243) 779278.
£50.00 p.a. Q. Articles of technical or professional interest to the Police Service throughout the world. *Payment:* by negotiation. *Illustrations:* half-tone.

The Political Quarterly (1930), Basil Blackwell Ltd, 108 Cowley Road, Oxford OX4 1JF   *tel* (0865) 791100. Editors: Colin Crouch (Trinity College, Oxford OX1 3BH   *tel* (0865) 279879/279900   *fax* (0865) 279911) and David Marquand (University of Sheffield, Sheffield S10 2TN   *tel* (0742) 768555). Books for review to be sent to the Literary Editor, Bernard Crick, 8A Bellevue Terrace, Edinburgh EH7 4DT.
£53.50 p.a. 5 p.a. Journal devoted to topical aspects of national and international politics and public administration; takes a progressive, but not a party, point of view. *Length:* average 5000 words. *Payment:* c. £60 per article.

Pony (1949), Managing Editor: Kate Austin, 296 Ewell Road, Surbiton, Surrey KT6 7AQ   *tel* 081-390 8547   *fax* 081-390 8696.
£1.05. M. Lively articles and short stories with a horsy theme aimed at young readers, 8 to 16 years old. Technical accuracy and young, fresh writing essential. *Length:* up to 800 words. *Payment:* by arrangement. *Illustrations:* drawings (commissioned) and interesting photos, cartoons.

Popular Crafts, Brenda Ross, Argus Specialist Publications, Argus House, Boundary Way, Hemel Hempstead, Herts. HP2 7ST   *tel* (0442) 66551.
£1.75. M. Covers all kinds of crafts. Projects with full instructions, profiles and successes of craftspeople, news on craft group activities, collecting crafts, personal anecdotes, general craft-related articles. Welcomes written outlines of ideas. *Payment:* by arrangement. *Illustrated.*

Port of London, Port of London Authority, Devon House, 58-60 St Katherine's Way, London E1 9LB   *tel* 071-265 2656   *fax* 071-256 2699.
£2.50. Q. The magazine of the Port of London Authority. Articles up to 2500 words considered; semi-technical, historical or having bearing on trade and commerce of London essential. *Preliminary letter* essential. *Payment:* £80 per 1000 words. *Illustrations:* line, half-tone, colour.

Poultry World, John Farrant, Quadrant House, The Quadrant, Sutton, Surrey SM2 5AS   *tel* 081-652 4021   *fax* 081-652 4748.

£1.60. M. Articles on poultry breeding, production, marketing and packaging. News of international poultry interest. *Payment:* by arrangement. *Illustrations:* photos, line.

PR Week (1984), Stephen Farish, Haymarket Marketing Publications, 22 Lancaster Gate, London W2 3LP   *tel* 071-413 4520.
Controlled circulation. W. (£50.00 p.a.) News and features on public relations. *Length:* approx. 800 words. *Payment:* £150 per 1000 words. *Illustrations:* halftone, cartoons.

Practical Boat Owner (1967), George Taylor, Westover House, West Quay Road, Poole, Dorset BH15 1JG   *tel* (0202) 680593.
£2.35. M. Articles of up to 2000 words in *length*, about practical matters concerning the boating enthusiast. *Payment:* by negotiation. *Illustrations:* photos or drawings.

Practical Fishkeeping (1966), Steve Windsor, EMAP Pursuit Publishing Ltd, Bretton Court, Bretton, Peterborough PE3 8DZ   *tel* (0733) 264666.
£1.90. M. Instructional articles on fishkeeping with heavy emphasis on easily-absorbed information. *Payment:* by arrangement. *Illustrations:* line, half-tone, high quality colour transparencies of tropical fish, cartoons.

Practical Gardening (1960), Susie Johns, EMAP Garden Publications, Apex House, Oundle Road, Peterborough PE2 9NP   *tel* (0733) 898100   *fax* (0733) 898433.
£1.90. M. 500-1000 words on inspirational gardening subjects, particularly if oriented towards ideas for garden design, and well illustrated. *Payment:* from £120 per 1000 words. *Illustrations:* line, half-tone, colour.

Practical Householder (1955), Martyn Hocking, Greater London House, Hampstead Road, London NW1 7QQ   *tel* 071-388 3171   *fax* 071-387 9518.
£1.50. M. Articles about 1500 words in *length*, about practical matters concerning home improvement. *Payment:* according to subject. *Illustrations:* line, half-tone, cartoons.

Practical Motorist (1934), David Orrick, Arrowsmith Court, Station Approach, Broadstone, Dorset BH18 8PW   *tel* (0202) 659910   *fax* (0202) 659950.
£1.70. M. Practical articles on upkeep, servicing and repair and customising and performance improvements of all makes of cars; also practical hints and tips. *Payment:* according to merit. *Illustrations:* b&w, colour prints or transparencies, line drawings, cartoons.

Practical Parenting (1987), Helen Gill, IPC Magazines Ltd, King's Reach Tower, Stamford Street, London SE1 9LS   *tel* 071-261 5058   *fax* 071-261 5366.
£1.35. M. Articles on parenting, baby and childcare, health, psychology, education, children's activities, personal birth/parenting experiences. *Send synopsis*, with sae. *Illustrations: commissioned only*; colour: photos, line, cartoons. *Payment:* £100-£150 per 1000 words; by agreement.

Practical Photography (1959), William Cheung, EMAP Apex Publications Ltd, 5th Floor, Apex House, Oundle Road, Peterborough PE2 9NP   *tel* (0733) 898100   *fax* (0733) 894472.
£2.00. M. Features on any aspect of photography with practical bias. Mostly written by staff journalists, but freelance ideas welcome. Send brief synopsis *only* in first instance. *Illustrations:* line, half-tone, colour, cartoons. *Payment:* from £50 per 1000 words; from £10 b&w or colour.

Practical Wireless (1932), Rob Mannion, G3XFD, PW Publishing Ltd, Arrowsmith Court, Station Approach, Broadstone, Dorset BH18 8PW   *tel* (0202) 659910   *fax* (0202) 659950.

72p. M. Articles on the practical and theoretical aspects of amateur radio and communications. Constructional projects. *Illustrations:* b&w and colour photos, line drawings and wash half-tone for offset litho. *Payment:* by arrangement.

Practical Woodworking, Alan Mitchell, IPC Magazines Ltd, King's Reach Tower, Stamford Street, London SE1 9LS   *tel* 071-261 6602.
£1.90. M. Articles of a practical nature covering any aspect of woodworking, including woodworking projects, tools, joints or timber technology. *Payment:* £60 per published page. *Illustrated.*

The Practitioner (1868), Howard Griffiths, Morgan-Grampian (Professional Press) Ltd, 30 Calderwood Street, London SE18 6QH   *tel* 081-855 7777.
£6.50. M. (£52.00 p.a., $120.00 p.a. overseas) Articles of interest to GPs and vocational trainees, and others in the medical profession. *Payment:* approx. £100 per 1000 words.

Prediction (1936), Jo Logan, Link House, Dingwall Avenue, Croydon CR9 2TA   *tel* 081-686 2599   *fax* 081-760 0973.
£1.60. M. Articles on all occult subjects. *Length:* up to 2000 words. *Payment:* by arrangement. *Illustrations:* for cover use only: large colour transparencies (i.e. not 35 mm).

Prep School, Anne Kiggell, Straight Ash, Ashampstead Common, Pangbourne, Berks. RG8 8QT   *tel* (0635) 201385.
£7.00 p.a. (on subscription) 3 p.a. Journal of the Preparatory School world: the magazine of IAPS and SATIPS. Articles of educational interest covering ages 4-13. *Length:* about 1000 words. *Illustrations:* line, half-tone. *Payment:* by arrangement.

The Press and Journal (1748), Derek Tucker, Lang Stracht, Aberdeen AB9 8AF   *tel* (0224) 690222; *London office:* Marylebone House, 52 St John Street, EC1M 4DT   *tel* 071-490 5581.
23p. D. Contributions of Scottish interest. *Payment:* by arrangement. *Illustrations:* half-tone.

Priests & People, Rev. D.C. Sanders OP, 1 King Street Cloisters, Clifton Walk, London W6 0QZ   *tel* 081-748 8484   *fax* 081-748 1550.
£2.00. M. Journal of pastoral theology especially for parish ministry and for Christians of English-speaking countries. *Length* and *payment* by arrangement.

Prima (1986), Editor in Chief: Sue James, Portland House, Stag Place, London SW1E 5AU   *tel* 071-245 8700.
£1.40. M. Articles on fashion, crafts, health and beauty, cookery; features. *Illustrations:* half-tone, colour.

Printing World (1878), Gareth Ward, Benn Publications Ltd, Benn House, Sovereign Way, Tonbridge, Kent TN9 1RW   *tel* (0732) 364422   *fax* (0732) 361534.
£2.20. W. (£70.00 p.a., overseas £105.00 p.a.) Commercial, technical, financial and labour news covering all aspects of the printing industry in the UK and abroad. Outside contributions. *Payment:* by arrangement. *Illustrations:* line, half-tone, colour, cartoons.

Private Eye (1962), Ian Hislop, 6 Carlisle Street, London W1V 5RG   *tel* 071-437 4017   *fax* 071-437 0705.
80p. F. Satire. *Payment:* by arrangement. *Illustrations:* b&w, line, cartoons.

Professional Nurse (1985), Ann Shuttleworth, Austen Cornish Publishers, Lynton House, 7-12 Tavistock Place, London WC1B 9LB   *tel* 071-388 7676   *fax* 071-411 3118.

£32.00 p.a. M. Articles of interest to the professional nurse. *Length:* articles: 2000-2500 words; factsheets: 1400 words; letters: 250-500 words. *Payment:* by arrangement. *Illustrations:* line, half-tone, colour.

Public Service & Local Government, Kathy Stansfield, EMAP Maclaren Ltd, Maclaren House, 19 Scarbrook Road, Croydon CR9 1QU *tel* 081-688 7788 *fax* 081-680 5892.
Controlled circulation. M. News and views, technical features on planning and architecture, building and housing, information technology, environment, transport and roads. Send sae for Editorial Programme of special features. *Length:* 800 words, occasionally 1200 words. *Illustrations:* half-tone, colour. *Payment:* £120 per 1000 words; by negotiation.

Publishing News (1979), Fred Newman, 43 Museum Street, London WC1A 1LY *tel* 071-404 0304.
£1.40. W. Articles and news items on books and publishers. *Payment:* £60-£80 per 1000 words. *Illustrations:* half-tone, cartoons.

Pulse, Howard Griffiths, Morgan-Grampian (Professional Press) Ltd, Morgan-Grampian House, 30 Calderwood Street, Woolwich, London SE18 6QH *tel* 081-855 7777 *fax* 081-855 2406.
£150.00 p.a. W. Articles and photos of direct interest to GPs. Purely clinical material can only be accepted from medically qualified authors. *Length:* up to 750 words. *Payment:* £150 average. *Illustrations:* b&w and colour photos.

Q Magazine (1987), Danny Kelly, EMAP Metro, Mappin House, 4 Winsley Street, London W1N 7AR *tel* 071-436 1515 *fax* 071-323 0680.
£2.10. M. Glossy modern guide to more than just rock music. *All material commissioned. Length:* 1200-2500 words. *Illustrations:* colour and b&w photos. *Payment:* £180 per 1000 words; by arrangement.

Quaker Monthly (1921), Elizabeth Cave, Quaker Home Service, Friends House, Euston Road, London NW1 2BJ *tel* 071-387 3601 *fax* 071-388 1977.
65p. M. (£10.50 p.a.) Articles, poems, reviews, expanding the Quaker approach to the spiritual life. Writers should be members or attenders of a Quaker meeting. *Illustrations:* line, half-tone. *Payment:* none.

Quarterly Journal of Medicine (1907). *Publisher:* Oxford University Press, Walton Street, Oxford OX2 6DP; *executive editor:* Dr J.M. Hopkin, Churchill Hospital, Oxford OX3 7LJ.
£105.00 p.a. M. Devoted to the publication of original papers and critical reviews dealing with clinical medicine and medical science. *Payment:* none.

RA Magazine (1983), Nick Tite, Royal Academy of Arts, Burlington House, Piccadilly, London W1V 0DS *tel* 071-494 5657 *fax* 071-287 9023.
£3.50. Q. Topical articles relating to the Royal Academy, its history and its exhibitions. *Length:* 500-1500 words. *Illustrations:* consult editor. *Payment:* £100 per 1000 words; by negotiation.

Radio Control Models and Electronics (1960), Kevin Crozier, Argus Specialist Publications, Argus House, Boundary Way, Hemel Hempstead, Herts. HP2 7ST *tel* (0442) 66551 *fax* (0442) 66998.
£1.70. M. Well-illustrated articles on topics related to radio control. *Payment:* £30 per published page. *Illustrations:* line, half-tone.

Radio Times, BBC Enterprises Ltd, Woodlands, 80 Wood Lane, London W12 0TT *tel* 081-576 2000.
65p. W. Articles support and enlarge BBC Television and Radio programmes, and ITV, Channel 4 and satellite programmes, and are, therefore, on every subject broadcast. *Length:* 600-2500 words. *Payment:* by arrangement. *Illustrations:* in colour and b&w; photos, graphic designs or drawings.

Railway Gazette International, Murray Hughes, Reed Business Publishing Group, Quadrant House, The Quadrant, Sutton, Surrey SM2 5AS *tel* 081-652 3739 *telex* 892084 REEDBP G *fax* 081-652 3738.
£35.00 p.a. M. Deals with management, engineering, operation and finance of railways world-wide. Articles of practical interest on these subjects are considered and paid for if accepted. Illustrated articles, of 1000-3000 words, are preferred. A *preliminary letter* is desirable.

Railway Magazine (1897), Peter Kelly, IPC Magazines Ltd, King's Reach Tower, Stamford Street, London SE1 9LS *tel* 071-261 5821 *fax* 071-261 5269.
£1.95. M. Illustrated magazine dealing with all railway subjects; no fiction or verse. Articles from 1500-2000 words accompanied by photos. *Preliminary letter* desirable. *Payment:* by arrangement. *Illustrations:* colour transparencies, half-tone and line.

Rambling Today (1935), Annabelle Birchall, 1-5 Wandsworth Road, London SW8 2XX *tel* 071-582 6878 *fax* 071-587 3799.
Free to members. Q. Official magazine of The Ramblers' Association. Articles on walking, access to countryside and related issues. *Material mostly commissioned. Length:* about 1000 words. *Illustrations:* colour and b&w photos. *Payment:* by agreement.

Rattler's Tale (1989), Anthony North, BCM Keyhole, London WC1N 3XX.
£8.00 p.a. Q. Horror/SF/crime/life fiction/satirical stories; articles on mysteries/religions/politics/psychology/criminology/New Age philosophy. *Length:* up to 2000 words. *Payment:* £2 per piece.

Reader's Digest, Russell Twisk, The Reader's Digest Association Ltd, Berkeley Square House, Berkeley Square, London W1X 6AB *tel* 071-629 8144.
£1.80. M. Original anecdotes – £150 for up to 300 words – are required for humorous features.

Red Tape (1911), Amanda Fingleson, Civil and Public Services Association, 160 Falcon Road, Clapham Junction, London SW11 2LN *tel* 071-924 2727 *fax* 071-924 1847.
Free to members. 11 p.a. (50p per issue non-members) Well-written articles on Civil Service, trade union and general subjects considered. *Length:* 750-1400 words. Also photos and humorous drawings of interest to Civil Servants. *Illustrations:* line, half-tone. *Payment:* NUJ rates.

Reform (1972), Norman Hart, 86 Tavistock Place, London WC1H 9RT *tel* 071-916 2020 *fax* 071-916 2021 (mark: for 'Reform').
75p. M. Published by United Reformed Church. Articles of religious or social comment. *Length:* 600-1000 words. *Illustrations:* line, half-tone, colour, cartoons. *Payment:* by arrangement.

Report, 7 Northumberland Street, London WC2N 5DA *tel* 071-930 6441 *fax* 071-930 1359.
£8.00 p.a. 8 p.a. (£12.00 p.a. overseas) Journal of the Association of Teachers and Lecturers (formerly Assistant Masters and Mistresses Association). Features, articles, comment, news about primary, secondary and further education; no poems. *Payment:* minimum £60 per 1000 words.

Retail Week (1988), Ian McGarrigle, EMAP Business Publishing, Maclaren House, 19 Scarbrook Road, Croydon, Surrey CR9 1QH *tel* 081-688 7788 *fax* 081-688 8375.
Controlled circulation. W. (£60.00 p.a.) Features and news stories on all aspects of retail management. *Length:* up to 1000 words. *Illustrations:* colour and b&w photos. *Payment:* £120 per 1000 words; market rates.

The Rialto (1984), Michael Mackmín, John Wakeman, 32 Grosvenor Road, Norwich, Norfolk NR2 2PZ *tel* (0603) 666455.
£2.90. 3 p.a. (£8.00 p.a., £6.50 p.a. low income) Poetry and criticism. Sae essential. *Illustrations:* line. *Payment:* by arrangement.

Right Start (1989), Anita Bevan, Needmarsh Publishing Ltd, 71 Newcomen Street, London SE1 1YT *tel* 071-403 0840 *fax* 071-378 6883.
£1.75. Bi-M. Features on all aspects of pre-school and infant education, baby and child health and behaviour. *No* unsolicited MSS. *Length:* 1200-1500 words. *Illustrations:* colour photos, line. *Payment:* varies.

Risqué (1991), Ian Jackson, Rockzone Publications Ltd, 61 Old Street, London EC1V 9HX *tel* 071-608 2112 *fax* 071-608 2668.
£1.95. M. Interviews, articles, features, men's interest, fiction. Unsolicited MSS considered. *Length:* 1500-3000 words. *Illustrations:* colour illustrations, line, cartoons; erotic photography. *Payment:* by negotiation.

Runner's World (1979), Nick Troop, 67-71 Goswell Road, London EC1V 7EN *tel* 071-972 9119.
£2.00. M. Articles on jogging, running and fitness. *Payment:* by arrangement. *Illustrations:* line, half-tone, colour, cartoons.

RUSI Journal, Editorial Manager: Alexandra Citron, Whitehall, London SW1A 2ET *tel* 071-930 5854 *fax* 071-321 0943.
£6.00. Bi-M. Journal of the Royal United Services Institute for Defence Studies. Articles on international security, the military sciences, defence technology and procurement, and military history; also book reviews and correspondence. *Length:* 3000-4000 words. *Illustrations:* b&w photos, maps and diagrams. *Payment:* £12.50 per printed page upon publication.

Safety Education (1966; founded 1937 as **Child Safety**; 1940 became **Safety Training**), Carole Wale, Royal Society for the Prevention of Accidents, Cannon House, The Priory Queensway, Birmingham B4 6BS *tel* 021-200 2461 *telex* 336546 *fax* 021-200 1254.
£6.00 p.a. for members of Safety Education Department. 3 p.a. (£12.00 p.a. non-members) Articles on every aspect of safety for children and in particular articles on the teaching of road, home, water and leisure safety by means of established subjects on the school curriculum. All ages. *Illustrations:* line, half-tone, colour. *Payment:* by negotiation.

Saga Magazine (1984), Paul Bach, The Saga Building, Middelburg Square, Folkestone, Kent CT20 1AZ *tel* (0303) 857523 *telex* 966331 *fax* (0303) 220391.
£1.25. 10 p.a. Articles relevant to interests of 55+ age group, and profiles of celebrities in same age group. *Length:* up to 1800 words. *Illustrations:* colour transparencies, commissioned colour artwork. *Payment:* negotiable, approx. £200 per 1200 words; £120 per page and pro rata.

Satellite Times (1988), Eric Woods, 23 Mitcham Lane, Streatham, London SW16 6LQ *tel* 081-677 7822 *fax* 081-677 8223.
£1.95. M. Television and film personality articles and interviews, sports articles, music, competitions. *Payment:* by negotiation.

Scale Models International, Kelvin Barber, Argus House, Boundary Way, Hemel Hempstead, Herts. HP2 7ST *tel* (0442) 66551 *fax* (0442) 66998.
£1.70. M. Articles on scale models. *Length:* up to 2500 words. *Payment:* £30 per page. *Illustrations:* line, half-tone, colour.

School Librarian (1937), Editor: Sheila Ray; Review Editor: Keith Barker, The School Library Association, Liden Library, Barrington Close, Liden, Swindon, Wilts. SN3 6HF *tel* (0793) 617838.

Free to members. Q. (£45.00 p.a. post free) Official Journal of the School Library Association. Reviews of books from pre-school to young adult age range with articles on authors and illustrators; also articles on school library organisation, use and skills. *Length:* up to 3000 words. *Payment:* by arrangement.

Science Progress, Professor David Phillips, Professor Robin Rowbury, Science Reviews, 18 Oaklands Gate, Northwood, Middlesex. HA6 3DY   *tel* (0923) 823586   *fax* (0923) 825066   *e-mail* scitech.demon.co.uk.
£86.50 p.a. Q. (£95.00 p.a. overseas) Articles of 6000 words on new scientific developments, written so as to be intelligible to workers in other disciplines. Imperative to submit synopsis before full-length article. *Payment:* by arrangement. *Illustrations:* line, half-tone.

Scootering (1985), Stuart Lanning, PO Box 46, Weston-super-Mare, Avon BS23 1AF   *tel* (0934) 414785.
£2.20. M. Custom, racing and vintage scooter features, plus technical information. Music features and related life style pieces. *Payment:* by arrangement. *Illustrations:* half-tone, colour, cartoons.

Scotland on Sunday (1988), Andrew Jaspan, North Bridge, Edinburgh EH1 1YT   *tel* 031-225 2468   *telex* 72255   *fax* 031-220 2443; Glasgow office   *tel* 041-221 6007.
60p. W. Features on all subjects, not necessarily Scottish. *Payment:* £88 per 1000 words.

The Scots Magazine (1739), D.C. Thomson & Co. Ltd, 2 Albert Square, Dundee DD1 9QJ   *tel* (0382) 23131   *fax* (0382) 25511.
95p. M. Articles on all subjects of Scottish interest. Short stories, poetry, but must be Scottish. *Payment:* by arrangement. *Illustrations:* colour and b&w photos, drawings, cartoons.

The Scotsman (1817), Magnus Linklater, 20 North Bridge, Edinburgh EH1 1YT   *tel* 031-225 2468   *fax* 031-226 7420.
42p. D. Ind. Considers articles, 800-1000 words, on political, economic and general themes, which add substantially to current information. Prepared to commission topical and controversial series from proved authorities. *Illustrations:* outstanding news pictures, cartoons. *Payment:* by arrangement.

Scottish Book Collector (1987), Jennie Renton, 11A Forth Street, Edinburgh EH1 3LE   *tel* 031-228 4837.
£1.50. Bi-M. Articles on collecting Scottish books; literary/bibliographical articles on books published in Scotland or by Scottish writers. *Length:* 1500-2500 words. *Payment:* £25 per article.

Scottish Educational Journal, Simon Macaulay, Educational Institute of Scotland, 46 Moray Place, Edinburgh EH3 6BH   *tel* 031-225 6244   *fax* 031-220 3151.
£8.10 p.a. 6 p.a., plus Specials.

The Scottish Farmer (1893), Angus MacDonald, The Plaza Tower, East Kilbride, Glasgow G74 1LW   *tel* (03552) 46444.
95p. W. Articles on agricultural subjects. *Length:* 1000-1500 words. *Payment:* £80 per 1000 words. *Illustrations:* line, half-tone, cartoons.

Scottish Field (1903), Peter Evans, Caledonian Magazines Ltd, The Plaza Tower, East Kilbride, Glasgow G74 1LW   *tel* (03552) 46444   *fax* (03552) 63013.
£1.90. M. Will consider all material with a Scottish link and good photos. *Payment:* by negotiation.

Scottish Historical Review, Dr A. Grant and Professor S.J. Brown, Company of Scottish History Ltd. Distributed by Edinburgh University Press, 22 George Square, Edinburgh EH8 9LF *tel* 031-650 4218 *fax* 031-667 7938.
£15.00 p.a. 2 p.a. (£18.00 p.a. through booksellers; £28.00 p.a. institutions) Contributions to the advancement of knowledge in any aspect of Scottish history. *Length:* up to 8000 words. *Illustrations:* line, half-tone. *Payment:* none; contributors are given offprints.

Scottish Home and Country (1924), Stella Roberts, 42A Heriot Row, Edinburgh EH3 6ES *tel* 031-225 1934.
52p. M. Articles on crafts, cookery, travel, personal experience, village histories, country customs, DIY, antiques, farming; humorous rural stories; fashion, health, books. *Length:* up to 1000 words, preferably illustrated. *Illustrations:* colour prints/transparencies, b&w, cartoons. *Payment:* by arrangement.

Scouting, David Easton, The Scout Association, Baden-Powell House, Queens Gate, London SW7 5JS *tel* 071-584 7030 *fax* 071-581 9953.
£1.10. M. National Magazine of The Scout Association. Ideas, news, views, features and programme resources for Leaders and Supporters. Training material, accounts of Scouting events and articles of general interest with Scouting connections. *Illustrations:* photos – action shots preferred rather than static posed shots for use with articles or as fillers or cover potential, cartoons. *Payment:* on publication by arrangement.

Screen International, Oscar Moore, EMAP Business Publishing, 33-39 Bowling Green Lane, London EC1R 0DA *tel* 071-837 1212 *fax* 071-837 8326.
£1.60. W. International news and features on every aspect of films, television and associated media. *Length:* variable. *Payment:* by arrangement.

Sea Angler (1973), Melvyn Russ, EMAP Pursuit Publishing Ltd, Bretton Court, Bretton, Peterborough PE3 8DZ *tel* (0733) 264666 *fax* (0733) 265515.
£1.70. M. Topical articles on all aspects of sea-fishing around the British Isles. *Payment:* by arrangement. *Illustrations:* line, half-tone, colour.

Sea Breezes (1919), C.H. Milsom, 202 Cotton Exchange Building, Old Hall Street, Liverpool L3 9LA *tel* 051-236 3935.
£1.80. M. Factual articles on ships and the sea past and present, preferably illustrated. *Length:* up to 4000 words. *Illustrations:* line, half-tone, colour. *Payment:* by arrangement.

Secrets Story Library, D.C. Thomson & Co. Ltd, Courier Place, Dundee DD1 9QJ *tel* (0382) 23131 *fax* (0382) 22214; and 185 Fleet Street, London EC4A 2HS *tel* 071-242 5086 *fax* 071-404 5694.
50p. M. Exciting and romantic stories in text, 35,000-37,000 words.

Select Magazine (1990), Andrew Harrison, EMAP Metro, Mappin House, 4 Winsley Street, London W1N 5AR *tel* 071-436 1515 *fax* 071-637 0456.
£1.75. M. Off-the-wall youth/music feature ideas for hip 18-25-year-olds. *Length:* decided on commissioning. *Illustrations:* colour and b&w rock/pop photography with an arty/provocative bent. *Payment:* £100 per 1000 words; £110 per page.

She (1955), Linda Kelsey, National Magazine House, 72 Broadwick Street, London W1V 2BP *tel* 071-439 5000 *fax* 071-439 5350.
£1.60. M. No unsolicited manuscripts. Ideas with synopses welcome on subjects ranging from health and relationships to child-care and careers. *Payment:* NUJ freelance rates. *Illustrations:* photos, cartoons.

Ship & Boat International (incorporating **Small Craft**), Richard White, Royal Institution of Naval Architects, 10 Upper Belgrave Street, London SW1X 8BQ *tel* 071-235 4622 *telex* 265844 SINAI G *fax* 071-245 6959.

£50.00 p.a. M. Technical articles on the design, construction and operation of all types of specialised small ships and workboats. *Length:* 500-1500 words. *Payment:* by arrangement. *Illustrations:* line and half-tone, photos and diagrams.

Ships Monthly (1966), Robert Shopland, Waterway Productions Ltd, Kottingham House, Dale Street, Burton-on-Trent DE14 3TD *tel* (0283) 64290 *fax* (0283) 61077.
£1.80. M. Illustrated articles of shipping interest – both mercantile and naval, preferably of 20th century ships. Well-researched, factual material only. No short stories or poetry. 'Notes for Contributors' available. Mainly commissioned material; preliminary letter essential. *Payment:* by arrangement. *Illustrations:* half-tone and line, colour transparencies and prints.

Shooting Times and Country Magazine (1882), John Gregson, Astley House, 33 Notting Hill Gate, London W11 3JQ *tel* 071-243 5000.
£1.30. W. Articles on fieldsports especially shooting, and on related natural history and countryside topics. *Length:* up to 1000 words. *Payment:* by arrangement. *Illustrations:* photos, drawings, colour transparencies.

Shout (1993), D.C. Thomson & Co. Ltd, Albert Square, Dundee DD1 9QJ *tel* (0382) 23131 *fax* (0382) 22214; and 185 Fleet Street, London EC4A 2HS *tel* 071-242 5086 *fax* 071-404 5694.
75p. F. 56-page colour gravure magazine for 13-16-year-old girls. Pop and film features and pin-ups; general features of teen interest; emotional/astrological, fashion and beauty advice. *Illustrations:* colour transparencies. *Payment:* on acceptance.

The Short Wave Magazine (1937), Dick Ganderton, G8VFH, Arrowsmith Court, Station Approach, Broadstone, Dorset BH18 8PW *tel* (0202) 659910 *fax* (0202) 659950.
£1.90. M. (£22.00 p.a.) Technical and semi-technical articles, 500-5000 words, dealing with design, construction and operation of radio receiving equipment. Radio related photo features welcome. *Payment:* £55 per page. *Illustrations:* line, half-tone, cartoons.

The Shropshire Magazine (1950), Pam Green, The Leopard Press Ltd, 77 Wyle Cop, Shrewsbury, Shropshire SY1 1UT *tel* (0743) 362175.
95p. M. Articles on topics related to Shropshire, including countryside, history, characters, legends, education, food; also home and garden features. *Length:* up to 1500 words. *Illustrations:* b&w photos, line drawings. *Payment:* £15-£20; by arrangement.

Shropshire Star (1964), Warren Wilson, Ketley, Telford TF1 4HU *tel* (0952) 242424 *fax* (0952) 254605.
25p. D. Evening paper – news and features. *No* unsolicited material; write to editor with outline of feature ideas. *Payment:* by arrangement.

Sight and Sound (1932), Philip Dodd, 21 Stephen Street, London W1P 1PL *tel* 071-255 1444 *telex* 27624 BFILDN G *fax* 071-436 2327. Published by the British Film Institute.
£2.20. M. Topical and critical articles on the cinema of any country; book reviews; reviews of every film theatrically released in London; reviews of every video released; regular columns from the USA and Europe. *Length:* 1000-5000 words. *Payment:* by arrangement. *Illustrations:* relevant photos, cartoons.

The Sign (1905), Chansitor Publications Ltd, St Mary's Works, St Mary's Plain, Norwich, Norfolk NR3 3BH *tel* (0603) 615995.
5p. M. Leading national insert for C of E parish magazines. Articles of interest to parishes. Items should bear the author's name and address; return postage

essential. *Length:* up to 400 words. *Illustrations:* unusual b&w photos, drawings considered. *Payment:* by arrangement.

Signal, Approaches to Children's Books (1970), Nancy Chambers, Lockwood, Station Road, South Woodchester, Stroud, Glos. GL5 5EQ *tel* (0453 87) 3716/2208.
£3.75. 3 p.a. (£11.25 p.a.) Articles on any aspect of children's books or the children's book world. *Length:* no limit but average 2500-3000 words. *Payment:* £3 per printed page. *Illustrations:* line occasionally.

The Skier and The Snowboarder (1984), Frank Baldwin, 48 London Road, Sevenoaks, Kent TN13 1AS *tel* (0732) 743644 *fax* (0732) 742769.
£2.25. 6 p.a. (Sept-May) Ski features, based around a good story. *Length:* 800-1000 words. *Illustrations:* colour action ski photos. *Payment:* £100 per 1000 words.

Sky Magazine, Angela Holden, Hachette Emap, Mappin House, 4 Winsley Street, London W1N 7AR *tel* 071-436 1515 *fax* 071-323 0276.
£1.60. M. People, movies, music and style. *Length:* varies. *Illustrations:* colour and b&w photos. *Payment:* by arrangement.

Slimmer Magazine (1972), Claire Crowther, Turret Group plc, 177 Hagden Lane, Watford, Herts WD1 8LN *tel* (0923) 228577 *fax* (0923) 221346.
£1.55. Bi-M. Features on health, nutrition, slimming. Personal weight loss stories. Sae essential. *Length:* 500 or 1500 words. *Payment:* £10 per 100 words.

Slimming Magazine (1969), Michele Simmons, Victory House, 14 Leicester Place, London WC2H 7BP *tel* 071-437 9011 *telex* 266400 *fax* 071-434 0656.
£1.60. 10 p.a. Scientifically based articles on slimming-related subjects. *Approach* editor in writing with ideas. *Length:* 1000-1500 words. *Payment:* by negotiation.

Smallholder (1985), Liz Wright, Hook House, Hook Road, Wimblington, March, Cambs. PE15 0QL *tel* (0354) 740719/(0366) 501035 *fax* (0354) 741182.
£1.75. M. Articles of relevance to small farmers about livestock and crops; items relating to the countryside considered. *Payment:* £20 per 1000 words or by arrangement. *Illustrations:* line, half-tone, cartoons.

Smash Hits, Mark Frith, 2nd Floor, Mappin House, 4 Winsley Street, London W1N 7AR *tel* 071-436 1516 *fax* 071-636 5792.
75p. F. News interviews and posters of pop, TV and film stars. *Illustrations:* colour photos. *Payment:* £100 per page; £100.

Snooker Scene (1971), Clive Everton, Cavalier House, 202 Hagley Road, Edgbaston, Birmingham B16 9PQ *tel* 021-454 2931 *fax* 021-452 1822.
£1.30. M. News and articles about snooker. *Payment:* by arrangement. *Illustrations:* photos.

Solicitors Journal (1856), 21-27 Lamb's Conduit Street, London WC1N 3NJ *tel* 071-242 2548 *fax* 071-430 1729.
£1.65. W. Articles, by practising lawyers or specialist journalists, on subjects of practical interest to solicitors. Articles sent on spec should be on computer disk. *Length:* up to 1800 words. *Payment:* by negotiation.

Somerset Magazine (1977 as Somerset & West), Roy Smart, Smart Print Publications Ltd, 23 Market Street, Crewkerne, Somerset TA18 7JU *tel* (0460) 78000 *fax* (0460) 76718.
£1.20. M. Articles, features with particular reference to county locations, facilities and other interests. *Length:* 1000-2000 words. *Illustrations:* line, half-tone, colour (transparencies or prints). *Payment:* by arrangement.

Songwriting and Composing (1986), General Secretary: Carole Jones, Sovereign House, 12 Trewartha Road, Praa Sands, Penzance, Cornwall TR20 9ST   *tel* (0736) 762826   *fax* (0736) 763328.
Free to members. Q. Magazine of the Guild of International Songwriters and Composers. Short stories, articles, letters relating to songwriting, publishing, recording and the music industry. *Payment:* negotiable upon content £25-£60. *Illustrations:* line, half-tone.

South Wales Echo (1884), Keith Perch, Thomson House, Havelock Street, Cardiff CF1 1WR   *tel* (0222) 223333   *fax* (0222) 583624.
25p. D. Evening paper – features, showbiz, news features, personality interviews. *Length:* up to 700 words. *Payment:* by negotiation.

The Southern Daily Echo (1888), Patrick Fleming, 45 Above Bar, Southampton SO9 7BA   *tel* (0703) 634134   *fax* (0703) 630289.
26p. D. News, articles, features, sport. *Length:* varies. *Illustrations:* line, half-tone, colour. *Payment:* NUJ rates.

Spaceflight (1956), Professor G.V. Groves, 27-29 South Lambeth Road, London SW8 1SZ   *tel* 071-735 3160   *fax* 071-820 1504. Published by The British Interplanetary Society.
Free to members. M. (£1.95) Articles up to 2500 words dealing with topics of astronomy, space and astronautics. *Illustrations:* line, half-tone, colour. *Payment:* none.

The Spectator (1828), Dominic Lawson, 56 Doughty Street, London WC1N 2LL   *tel* 071-405 1706   *fax* 071-242-0603.
£1.80. W. Articles on current affairs, politics and the arts. *Payment:* rate depends upon the nature and length of the article.

Speech and Drama (1951), Dr Paul Ranger, 4 Fane Road, Old Marston, Oxford OX3 0SA   *tel* (0865) 728304.
£6.50 p.a. 2 p.a. Covers theatre, drama and all levels of education relating to speech and drama; specialist articles only; preliminary abstract of 300 words; photos welcome. *Length:* 1500-2000 words. *Payment:* none, complimentary copy.

Spoken English (1968), Malcolm Dale, English Speaking Board (International), 26A Princes Street, Southport, Merseyside PR8 1EQ   *tel* (0704) 501730.
£14.00 p.a. (ESB membership inc. 2 issues of journal) Serious articles (1000+ words) on spoken English, communication ventures and training, poetry, drama, and English-teaching from primary to university levels, in Britain and overseas.

Sport and Leisure (1949), Louise Fyfe, The Sports Council, 16 Upper Woburn Place, London WC1H 0QP   *tel* 071-388 1277   *fax* 071-383 5740.
£2.50. 6 p.a. Articles on various sport development, physical education, sports politics, the leisure boom, sponsorship, facilities, equipment and outdoor activities. *Length:* 500-1000 words. *Illustrations:* sports photographers encouraged; b&w photos. *Payment:* £100 per 1000 words; £50 per ½ page.

The Sporting Life, Tom Clarke, Mirror Group Newspapers Ltd, 1 Canada Square, Canary Wharf, London E14 5AP   *tel* 071-293 3000   *fax* 071-293 3758.
70p. D. National racing daily, with wide news and feature coverage, including bloodstock and betting; plus daily Sportslife feature on general sports and betting. Also **Greyhound Life,** a daily pull-out, covering every angle of greyhound racing and betting. Interested in relevant news stories; features, photos and graphics are commissioned. *Payment:* by negotiation.

Squash Player (1971), Nick Troop, 67-71 Goswell Road, London EC1V 7EN *tel* 071-410 9410 *fax* 071-410 9440.
£1.75. 10 p.a. Covers all aspects of playing squash. All features are commissioned – discuss ideas with editor. *Length:* 1000-1500 words. *Illustrations:* unusual photos (e.g. celebrities), cartoons. *Payment:* £75 per 1000 words; £25-£40.

The Stage and Television Today (1880), Jeremy Jehu, Stage House, 47 Bermondsey Street, London SE1 3XT *tel* 071-403 1818 *fax* 071-403 1418.
60p. W. Original and interesting articles on professional stage and television topics may be sent for the editor's consideration. *Length:* 500-800 words. *Payment:* £100 per 1000 words.

Stamp Lover (1908), Michael Furnell, National Philatelic Society, British Philatelic Centre, 107 Charterhouse Street, London EC1M 6PT *tel* 071-251 5040.
£1.50. 6 p.a. Original articles on stamps and postal history. *Illustrations:* line, half-tone. *Payment:* by arrangement.

Stamp Magazine (1934), Richard West, Link House Publications, Link House, Dingwall Avenue, Croydon CR9 2TA *tel* 081-686 2599 *fax* 081-781 6044.
£1.80. M. Informative articles and exclusive news items on stamp collecting and postal history. *No preliminary letter. Payment:* by arrangement. *Illustrations:* line, half-tone, colour.

Stand Magazine (1952), Jon Silkin, Lorna Tracy, Rodney Pybus, 179 Wingrove Road, Newcastle upon Tyne NE4 9DA *tel* 091-273 3280/281 2614.
£3.15 (inc. p&p). Q. (£10.95 p.a.) Poetry, short stories, translations, literary criticism. Send sae for return. Biennial Short Story Competition for unpublished original short story in English (see page 682). *Payment:* £30 per 1000 words of prose; £30 per poem.

Staple (1982), Bob Windsor, Donald Measham, Gilderoy East, Upperwood Road, Matlock Bath, Derbyshire DE4 3PD *tel* (0629) 583867/582764.
£10.00 p.a. 4 p.a. (£15.00 outside Europe) Mainstream poems and short stories. *Payment:* £5-£10.

The Star (1887), Peter Charlton, York Street, Sheffield S1 1PU *tel* (0742) 767676 *fax* (0742) 725978.
26p. D. Well-written articles of local character. *Length:* about 500 words. *Payment:* by negotiation. *Illustrations:* topical photos, line drawings, graphics, cartoons.

Steam Classic (1990), Peter Herring, Argus Specialist Publications, Argus House, Boundary Way, Hemel Hempstead, Herts. HP2 7ST *tel* (0442) 66551/(0932) 225330 *fax* (0442) 66998/(0932) 254639.
£1.95. M. Features on the history, design and performance of British-built steam locomotives; news stories and features on present-day steam locomotive preservation. *Length:* 2000-3000 words. *Illustrations:* archive and contemporary colour transparencies and b&w photos; apply for list of specific required material (topical material always welcome). *Payment:* approx. £50 per 1000 words; £20 colour, £10 b&w.

Street Machine (1979), Russ Smith, EMAP National Publications Ltd, Bushfield House, Orton Centre, Peterborough PE2 5UW *tel* (0733) 237111 *fax* (0733) 231137.
£2.00. M. Articles on all modified cars and bodywork. *Length:* 800-1500 words. *Payment:* by arrangement. *Illustrations:* line, half-tone, colour.

Studio Sound (1959), Tim Goodyer, Spotlight Publications, Ludgate House, 245 Blackfriars Road, London SE1 9UR *tel* 071-620 3636 *fax* 071-401 8036.

£2.00. M. Articles on all aspects of professional sound recording. Technical and operational features on the functional aspects of studio equipment; general features on studio affairs. *Length:* widely variable. *Payment:* by arrangement. *Illustrations:* line, half-tone, colour.

The Sun (1969), Stuart Higgins, News Group Newspapers Ltd, Virginia Street, London E1 9XP   *tel* 071-782 7000   *telex* 262135 SUNEWS G   *fax* 071-488 3253. 20p. D.

Sunday Express (1918), Eve Pollard, Ludgate House, 245 Blackfriars Road, London SE1 9UX   *tel* 071-928 8000   *cables* Lon Express   *telex* 21841/ 21842   *fax* 071-620 1656.
65p. W. Exclusive news stories, photos, personality profiles and features of controversial or lively interest. *Length:* 800-1000 words. *Payment:* top rates.

Sunday Express Magazine, Jean Carr, Ludgate House, 245 Blackfriars Road, London SE1 9UX   *tel* 071-928 8000   *cables* Lon Express   *telex* 21841/ 21842   *fax* 071-928 7262.
Free with newspaper. W. General interest features. *Length:* 1500 words. *Payment:* from £150 per 1000 words. *Illustrations:* colour, half-tone, artwork.

Sunday Magazine (1981), Tony Harris, Phase 2, 5th Floor, 1 Virginia Street, Wapping, London E1 9BD   *tel* 071-782 7900   *fax* 071-782 7474.
Free with News of the World. W. Freelance writers' ideas and material always welcome. *Payment:* by arrangement.

Sunday Mail, Jim Cassidy, Anderston Quay, Glasgow G3 8DA   *tel* 041-242 3403   *fax* 041-242 3145; *London office:* 33 Holborn Circus, EC1P 1DQ.
50p. W. Exclusive stories and pictures (in colour if possible) of national and Scottish interest. *Payment:* above average.

Sunday Mercury, Peter Whitehouse, Colmore Circus, Birmingham B4 6AZ   *tel* 021-236 3366   *fax* 021-233 0271.
47p. W. News specials or features of Midland interest. *Illustrations:* colour, b&w, cartoons. Special rates for special matter.

Sunday Mirror (1915), Tessa Hilton, 1 Canada Square, Canary Wharf, London E14 5AP   *tel* 071-293 3000   *fax* 071-293 3758.
50p. W. Concentrates on human interest news features, social documentaries, dramatic news and feature photos. Ideas, as well as articles, bought. *Payment:* high, especially for exclusives.

Sunday Mirror Magazine (1988), Katharine Hadley, Third Floor, Orbit House, 1 New Fetter Lane, Holborn Circus, London EC1P 1DQ   *tel* 071-822 2094   *fax* 071-583 4151.
Free with Sunday Mirror. W. Human interest and celebrity articles. *Length:* 1000 words. *Illustrations:* colour photos, cartoons. *Payment:* articles £250+; photos £50+.

Sunday Post, D.C. Thomson & Co. Ltd, 144 Port Dundas Road, Glasgow G4 0HZ   *tel* 041-332 9933   *fax* 041-331 1595; Courier Place, Dundee DD1 9QJ   *tel* (0382) 23131   *fax* (0382) 201064; 185 Fleet Street, London EC4A 2HS   *tel* 071-404 0199   *fax* 071-404 5694.
50p. W. Human interest, topical, domestic and humorous articles, and exclusive news; and short stories up to 2000 words. *Illustrations:* humorous drawings. *Payment:* on acceptance.

The Sunday Post Magazine (1988), Maggie Dun, D.C. Thomson & Co. Ltd, Albert Square, Dundee DD1 9QJ   *tel* (0382) 23131 ext 4147   *fax* (0382) 201064.

Free. M. General interest articles. *Length:* 1000-2000 words. *Illustrations:* colour transparencies. *Payment:* varies.

Sunday Sport (1986), Tony Livesey, 19 Great Ancoats Street, Manchester M60 4BT   *tel* 061-236 4466   *fax* 061-236 2427.
50p. W.

The Sunday Sun (1919), Chris Rushton, Thomson House, Groat Market, Newcastle upon Tyne NE1 1ED   *tel* 091-232 7500   *fax* 091-230 0238.
45p. W. Immediate topicality and human sidelights on current problems are the keynote of the Sunday Sun's requirements. Particularly welcomed are special features of family appeal and news stories of special interest to the North-East of England. Photos used to illustrate articles. *Length:* 200-800 words. *Payment:* normal lineage rates, or by arrangement. *Illustrations:* photos and line, cartoons.

Sunday Telegraph, Charles Moore, 1 Canada Square, Canary Wharf, London E14 5DT   *tel* 071-538 5000.
70p. W. Occasional freelance material accepted.

The Sunday Times (1822), Acting Editor: John Witherow, 1 Pennington Street, London E1 9XW   *tel* 071-782 5000.
£1.00. W. Special articles by authoritative writers on politics, literature, art, drama, music, finance and science, and topical matters. *Payment:* top rate for exclusive features. *Illustrations:* first-class photos of topical interest and pictorial merit very welcome; also topical drawings and cartoons.

Sunday Times Magazine, 1 Pennington Street, London E1 9XW   *tel* 071-782 7000.
Free with paper. W. Articles and pictures. *Illustrations:* colour and b&w photos. *Payment:* by negotiation.

SuperBike, John Cutts, Link House Magazines Ltd, Link House, Dingwall Avenue, Croydon CR9 2TA   *tel* 081-686 2599   *fax* 081-760 0973.
£1.90. M. Anything to do with high-powered motorcycles and the associated life style, including touring stories and fiction. *Payment:* by arrangement. *Illustrations:* half-tone, colour.

The Tablet (1840), John Wilkins, 1 King Street Cloisters, Clifton Walk, London W6 0QZ   *tel* 081-748 8484   *fax* 081-748 1550.
£1.25. W. The senior Catholic weekly. Religion, philosophy, politics, society, the arts. International coverage. Freelance work welcomed. *Length:* 1500 words. *Payment:* by arrangement.

Take a Break (1990), John Dale, 25-27 Camden Road, London NW1 9LL   *tel* 071-284 0909   *fax* 071-284 3778.
46p. W. Lively, tabloid women's weekly. True life features, celebrities, health and beauty, family, travel; short stories (up to 1500 words); lots of puzzles. *Payment:* by arrangement. *Illustrated.*

The Tatler (1709), Jane Procter, Vogue House, Hanover Square, London W1R 0AD   *tel* 071-499 9080   *fax* 071-409 0451.
£2.20. M. Smart society magazine favouring sharp articles, profiles, fashion and the arts. *Illustrations:* colour, b&w, but all commissioned.

Telegraph & Argus (1868), Perry Austin-Clarke, Hall Ings, Bradford, West Yorkshire BD1 1JR   *tel* (0274) 729511   *fax* (0274) 723634.
27p. D. Evening paper – news, articles and features relevant to or about the people of West Yorkshire. *Length:* up to 1000 words. *Illustrations:* line, half-tone, colour. *Payment:* features from £15; line from £5, b&w photos from £14.40, colour photos from £19.50.

Telegraph Magazine (1964), Nigel Horne, 1 Canada Square, Canary Wharf, London E14 5DT *tel* 071-538 5000 *telegraphic address* Teleweek, London. Free with Sat. paper. W. Short profiles (about 1600 words), articles of topical interest. *Preliminary study* of the magazine essential. *Illustrations:* all types. *Payment:* by arrangement.

Television (1950), Reed Business Publishing Ltd, Quadrant House, The Quadrant, Sutton, Surrey SM2 5AS *tel* 081-652 8120 *fax* 081-652 8956. £2.20. M. Articles on the technical aspects of domestic TV and video equipment, especially servicing, long-distance television, constructional projects, satellite TV, video recording, teletext and viewdata, test equipment. *Payment:* by arrangement. *Illustrations:* photos and line drawings for litho.

Tempo, Calum MacDonald, Boosey & Hawkes, Music Publishers, Ltd, 295 Regent Street, London W1R 8JH *tel* 071-580 2060 *fax* 071-436 5675. £2.50. Q. (£13.00 p.a.) Authoritative articles about 2000-4000 words on contemporary music. *Payment:* by arrangement. *Illustrations:* music type, occasional photographic or musical supplements.

Tennis World, Alastair McIver, Presswatch Ltd, The Spendlove Centre, Enstone Road, Charlbury, Oxford OX7 3PQ *tel* (0608) 811446. £2.00. M. Tournament reports, topical features, personality profiles, instructional articles. *Length:* 600-1500 words. *Payment:* by arrangement. *Illustrations:* line, half-tone, colour.

Theology (1920), Ann Loades, Theology Department, Abbey House, Palace Green, Durham DH1 3RS *tel* 091-374 2052. £2.50. Bi-M. Articles and reviews on theology, ethics, Church and Society. *Length:* up to 3500 words. *Payment:* none.

Therapy Weekly (1974 as **Therapy**), Carol Harris, Macmillan Magazines Ltd, 4 Little Essex Street, London WC2R 3LF *tel* 071-379 6144 *fax* 071-836 0798. Free to NHS and local authority therapists. W. (£41.50 p.a.) Articles of interest to physiotherapists, occupational therapists and speech and language therapists. Guidelines to contributors available. *Send proposals only* initially. *Length:* up to 1000 words. *Illustrations:* colour and b&w photos, line, cartoons. *Payment:* by arrangement.

Third Way (1977), St Peters, Sumner Road, Harrow, Middlesex HA2 4BX *tel* 081-423 8494 *fax* 081-423 5367. £2.90. 10 p.a. Aims to present biblical perspectives on a wide range of current issues, e.g. sociology, politics, education, economics, industry and the arts. *Payment:* for articles: on publication.

This Caring Business (1985), Michael J. Monk, 1 St Thomas' Road, Hastings, East Sussex TN34 3LG *tel* (0424) 718406 *fax* (0424) 718460. £50.00 p.a. M. Specialist contributions relating to the commercial aspects of nursing and residential care, including hospitals. *Payment:* £75 per 1000 words. *Illustrations:* line, half-tone.

This England (1968), Roy Faiers, PO Box 52, Cheltenham, Glos. GL50 1HT *tel* (0242) 577775. £2.90. Q. Articles on towns, villages, traditions, customs, legends, crafts of England; stories of people. *Length:* 250-2000 words. *Payment:* £20 per page and pro rata. *Illustrations:* line, half-tone, colour.

The Times (1785), Peter Stothard, 1 Pennington Street, London E1 9XN *tel* 071-782 5000 *telex* 262141 *fax* 071-782 5142. 30p. D. 40p. Sat. Ind. Outside contributions considered from (1) experts in subjects of current interest; (2) writers who can make first-hand experience or reflection come readably alive. *No preliminary letter* is required, but telephone call to appropriate section editor is recommended. *Length:* up to 1200 words.

The Times Educational Supplement, Admiral House, 66-68 East Smithfield, London E1 9XY *tel* 071-782 3000 *fax* 071-782 3200.
80p. W. Articles on education written with special knowledge or experience; news items; books, arts and equipment reviews. Advisable to check with features, news or picture editor before submitting. *Illustrations:* suitable photos and drawings of educational interest, cartoons. *Payment:* standard rates, or by arrangement.

Times Educational Supplement Scotland (1965), Willis Pickard, 37 George Street, Edinburgh EH2 2HN *tel* 031-220 1100 *fax* 031-220 1616.
80p. W. Articles on education, preferably 1100 words, written with special knowledge or experience. News items about Scottish educational affairs. *Illustrations:* line, half-tone. *Payment:* by arrangement.

Times Higher Education Supplement (1971), Auriol Stevens, Admiral House, 66-68 East Smithfield, London E1 9XY *tel* 071-782 3000 *fax* 071-782 3300.
90p. W. Articles on higher education written with special knowledge or experience, or articles dealing with academic topics. News items. *Illustrations:* suitable photos and drawings of educational interest. *Payment:* by arrangement.

The Times Literary Supplement, Ferdinand Mount, Admiral House, 66-68 East Smithfield, London E1 9XY *tel* 071-782 3000 *dx* 98956 WAPPING *fax* 071-782 3100.
£1.75. W. Will consider poems for publication, literary discoveries and articles, particularly of an opinionated kind, on literary and cultural affairs. *Payment:* by arrangement.

Titbits (1881), Leonard Holdsworth, Caversham Communications, 2 Caversham Street, London SW3 4AH *tel* 071-351 4995.
£1.20. M. Human interest articles; also show business, pop stars and medical, especially men's interest. No fiction. *Illustrations:* colour transparencies and photos, cartoons. *No* b&w. *Payment:* details on application.

Today (1986), Martin Dunn, 1 Virginia Street, London E1 9BS *tel* 071-782 4600.
25p. D. Feature and news-type articles. *Length:* 300-3000 words. *Payment:* by arrangement. *Illustrations:* line, half-tone, colour, cartoons.

Today's Golfer (1988), Martin Vousden, EMAP Pursuit Publishing Ltd, Bretton Court, Bretton, Peterborough PE3 8DZ *tel* (0733) 264666 *fax* (0733) 267198.
£2.35. M. Features and articles on golf. *Payment:* £150 per 1000 words. *Illustrations:* line, half-tone, colour.

Today's Runner (1985), Allan Haines, EMAP Pursuit Publishing, Bretton Court, Bretton, Peterborough PE3 8DZ *tel* (0733) 264666 *fax* (0733) 227198.
£1.80. M. Practical articles on all aspects of running, especially road running training and events, and advice on health, fitness and injury. *Illustrations:* mainly colour and b&w photos, cartoons. *Payment:* by negotiation.

Together (1956), Dorothy Jamal, The National Society, Church House, Great Smith Street, London SW1P 3NZ *tel* 071-222 1672 *fax* 071-233 2592.
80p. M. (£10.00 p.a.) Short, practical or topical articles dealing with all forms of children's Christian education and all-age learning and worship. *Length:* up to 1200 words. *Illustrations:* line, half-tone. *Payment:* by arrangement.

Town and Country Planning, Nick Mathews, 17 Carlton House Terrace, London SW1Y 5AS *tel* 071-930 8903/4/5.

£49.50 p.a. M. Journal of the Town and Country Planning Association. Informative articles on town and country planning, regional planning, land use, new towns, green belts, countryside preservation, industrial, business and social life in great and small towns, environment in general and community development. *Length:* 1000 words. *Illustrations:* photos and drawings. *Payment:* none.

Toy Trader (1908), David Coombs, Turret Group plc, Turret House, 171 High Street, Rickmansworth, Herts WD3 1SN *tel* (0923) 777000 *fax* (0923) 771297.
£48.00 p.a. M. Trade journal specialising in anything to do with games and toys, circulated to manufacturers and retailers. *Length:* by negotiation. *Payment:* by negotiation.

Traveller (1970), Wexas Ltd, 45 Brompton Road, London SW3 1DE *tel* 071-581 4130 *telegraphic address* Wexas, London SW3 *telex* 297155 WEXAS G *fax* 071-581 1357.
£39.58 p.a. Q. Features usually based on long-haul and offbeat destinations, with a particular emphasis on cultural or anthropological angles. Recent features include: The Annual Cattle Crossing in Mali; The Textiles of Rajasthan; The Gypsies of Bulgaria. *Length:* 1000-2000 words. *Illustrations:* first-class transparencies. *Payment:* £125 per 1000 words; £25 (£50 cover).

The Trefoil, Myra Street, C.H.Q., The Guide Association, 17-19 Buckingham Palace Road, London SW1W 0PT *tel* 071-834 6242 *fax* 071-828 8317.
Q. Official Journal of the Trefoil Guild (non-members £4.50 p.a., overseas £7.00 p.a.) Articles on the activities of the Guild and of Guiding in the UK and overseas and on the work of voluntary organisations. *Length:* not more than 500 words. No fiction. *Illustrations:* photos. *Payment:* by arrangement.

Tribune, Editor: Mark Seddon; Reviews Editor: Jeff Lovitt; Features Editor: Caroline Rees, 308 Gray's Inn Road, London WC1X 8DY *tel* 071-278 0911.
£1.00. W. Political, literary, with Socialist outlook. Informative articles (about 800 words), news stories (250-300 words), some poetry. No unsolicited reviews or fiction. *Payment:* by arrangement. *Illustrations:* cartoons and photos.

Trout and Salmon (1955), Sandy Leventon, EMAP Pursuit Publishing Ltd, Bretton Court, Bretton Centre, Peterborough PE3 8DZ *tel* (0733) 264666 *fax* (0733) 265515.
£1.90. M. Articles of good quality with strong trout or salmon angling interest. *Length:* 400-2000 words, accompanied if possible by colour transparencies or good-quality colour prints. *Payment:* by arrangement. *Illustrations:* line, colour transparencies and prints, cartoons.

True Romances, Ann Jaloba, Roderick Hudson, Argus Specialist Publications, Argus House, Boundary Way, Hemel Hempstead, Herts. HP2 7ST *tel* (0442) 66551 *fax* (0442) 66998.
£1.00. M. First-person stories with strong love interest, aimed at the 16-19 reader, 2500-4000 words. *No freelance fiction can be considered*; unsolicited MSS will not be returned.

True Story, Ann Jaloba, Roderick Hudson, Argus Specialist Publications, Argus House, Boundary Way, Hemel Hempstead, Herts. HP2 7ST *tel* (0442) 66551 *fax* (0442) 66998.
£1.00. M. First person short stories with a strong woman-interest plot, 2500-4000 words. *No freelance fiction can be considered*; unsolicited MSS will not be returned.

TV Times, Liz Murphy, IPC Magazines Ltd, 10th Floor, King's Reach Tower, Stamford Street, London SE1 9LS *tel* 071-261 7000 *fax* 071-261 7777.
55p. W. Features with an affinity to ITV, BBC1, BBC2, Channel 4, satellite and radio personalities and television generally. *Length:* by arrangement. *Photographs:* only those of outstanding quality. *Payment:* by arrangement.

Twinkle, D.C. Thomson & Co. Ltd, Albert Square, Dundee DD1 9QJ *tel* (0382) 23131 *fax* (0382) 22214; and 185 Fleet Street, London EC4A 2HS *tel* 071-242 5086 *fax* 071-404 5694.
40p. W. Picture stories, features and comic strips, specially for little girls. Drawings in line or colour for gravure. Special encouragement to promising writers and artists. *Payment:* on acceptance.

UCW Journal (1920), Julia Simpson, UCW House, 16 Crescent Lane, Clapham, London SW4 9RN *tel* 071-622 9977 *telex* 913585 *fax* 071-720 6853.
Free to members. M. Journal of the Union of Communication Workers. Articles on postal workers and operators in the UK and abroad and on other questions of interest to a trade union readership. *Length:* 1000 words or less. *Payment:* by arrangement. *Illustrations:* line and half-tone occasionally.

The Unesco Courier (1948), Bahgat Elnadi, Adel Rifaat, Unesco, 31 rue François Bonvin, Paris 75015, France *tel* (1) 45 68 47 15 *telegraphic address* Unesco, Paris *fax* (1) 45 66 92 70.
£17.00 p.a. Monthly in 36 language editions plus Braille editions in French, English, Spanish and Korean. Illustrated feature articles in the fields of science, culture, education and communication; promotion of international understanding; human rights. *Length:* 2000 words. *Illustrations:* colour and b&w photos, drawings, graphs, maps.

The Universe (1860), Mrs Ann Knowles, 1st Floor, St James's Buildings, Oxford Street, Manchester M1 6FP *tel* 061-236 8856 *fax* 061-236 8530.
40p. W. Newspaper and review for Catholics. News stories, features and photos on all aspects of Catholic life required. MSS should not be submitted without sae. *Payment:* by arrangement.

The Use of English, Roger Knight, School of Education, 21 University Road, Leicester LE1 7RF. *Publishers:* The English Association, University of Leicester, 128 Regent Road, Leicester LE1 7PA *tel* (0533) 551725.
£13.50 p.a. 3 p.a. (£15.50 p.a. institutions) For teachers in all fields of English in Great Britain and overseas. *Length:* usually up to 3500 words. *Payment:* none.

Vanity Fair, The Condé Nast Publications Ltd, Vogue House, Hanover Square, London W1R 0AD *tel* 071-499 9080 *fax* 071-499 4415. London Editor: Henry Porter *tel* 071-221 6228 *fax* 071-221 6269.
£2.00. M. Style, media and politics for grown-up readers. *No* unsolicited MSS or illustrations. *Payment:* by arrangement. *Illustrated.*

The Vegan (1944), Richard Farhall, The Vegan Society, 7 Battle Road, St Leonards-on-Sea, East Sussex TN37 7AA *tel* (0424) 427393.
£1.25. Q. Articles on animal rights, nutrition, cookery, agriculture, Third World, health. *Length:* approx. 1500 words. *Payment:* by arrangement. *Illustrations:* photos, cartoons, line drawings – foods, animals, livestock systems, crops, people, events; colour for cover.

Vegetarian Living, Nicola Graimes, HHL Publishing Ltd, Greater London House, Hampstead Road, London NW1 7QQ *tel* 071-388 3171 *fax* 071-377 4890.

£1.20. M. Articles on animal welfare, nutrition, recipes, health, vegetarian life styles; interviews with vegetarian celebrities; the environment. *Payment:* by arrangement. *Illustrations:* photos and drawings of foods, animals, relevant events, nature studies; colour, cartoons.

Verse (1984), Robert Crawford, David Kinloch, Henry Hart, Richard Price, School of English, University of St Andrews, St Andrews, Fife KY16 9AL   *tel* (0334) 76161 ext 2666   *fax* (0334) 62655.
£3.00. 3 p.a. Poems in English, Scots, or translation; critical pieces on contemporary poetry. *Payment:* none.

Video Camera (1989), Chris George, IPC Magazines Ltd, King's Reach Tower, Stamford Street, London SE1 9LS   *tel* 071-261 5000   *fax* 071-261 6050.
£2.00. M. Technique articles on how to use camcorders, especially for specific tricks or events. Material *mostly commissioned. Length:* 800-1000 words. *Illustrations:* colour photos, cartoons, diagrams. *Payment:* £80 per 1000 words; £90 per page.

Viz (1979), Chris Donald, John Brown Publishing Ltd, The Boat House, Crabtree Lane, London SW6 8NJ.
£1.25. 6 p.a. Cartoons, cartoon scripts, articles. *Illustrations:* half-tone, line, cartoons. *Payment:* £200 per page (cartoons).

Vogue, Alexandra Shulman, Vogue House, Hanover Square, London W1R 0AD   *tel* 071-499 9080   *telex* 27338 VOLON G.
£2.50. M. Fashion, beauty, health, decorating, art, theatre, films, literature, music, travel, food and wine. *Length:* articles from 1000 words. *Illustrated.*

The Voice (1982), Winsome Cornish, 370 Coldharbour Lane, London SW9 8PL   *tel* 071-737 7377   *fax* 071-274 8994.
65p. W. News stories, general and arts features of interest to black readers. *Illustrations:* colour and b&w photos, cartoons. *Payment:* £100 per 1000 words; £20-£35.

Voice Intelligence Report (1972), Ann Morris, 15A Lowndes Street, London SW1X 9EY   *tel* 071-235 5966   *fax* 071-259 6694.
£18.00. Q. (£48.00 p.a.) Background intelligence reports on the Press, media, Parliament, European Parliament, banking, diplomats, Saudi Arabia and the Arab Gulf countries, with specific reference to Middle East. All material commissioned. *Write* for specimen copy. *Illustrations:* none.

Vox (1990), Paul Colbert, IPC Magazines Ltd, 25th Floor, King's Reach Tower, Stamford Street, London SE1 9LS   *tel* 071-261 6312   *fax* 071-261 5627.
£1.90. M. Music and movies, aimed at 18-35 market – interviews, non-interview features, reviews. *Illustrations:* colour and b&w photos; commissioned illustrations and cartoons. *Payment:* by negotiation/NUJ rates; by negotiation.

Wales on Sunday (1989), Thomson House, Havelock Street, Cardiff CF1 1XR   *tel* (0222) 583583   *fax* (0222) 583725.
50p. W. Ind. General interest articles preferably with a Welsh connection, suitable for use in the national Sunday newspaper of Wales which offers comprehensive news, features and entertainments coverage at the weekend, with a particular focus on events in Wales.

War Cry (1879), Captain Charles King, 101 Queen Victoria Street, London EC4P 4EP   *tel* 071-236 5222   *fax* 071-236 3491. Published by The Salvation Army.
15p. W. (£22.50 p.a. UK) Voluntary contributions; puzzles. *Illustrations:* line and photos, cartoons.

Wasafiri (1984), Susheila Nasta, Queen Mary & Westfield College, Mile End Road, London E1 4NS.
£12.00 p.a. Bi-A. (£16.00 p.a. institutions) Published at University of Kent. Short stories, poetry, reviews, essays on literature and film. Submit MSS in duplicate, with an sae. *Illustrations:* b&w photos. *Payment:* none.

Waterways World (1972), Hugh Potter, Waterway Productions Ltd, Kottingham House, Dale Street, Burton-on-Trent, Staffs. DE14 3TD *tel* (0283) 64290.
£1.80. M. Feature articles on all aspects of inland waterways in Britain and abroad, including historical material; factual and technical articles preferred. No short stories or poetry. Send sae for 'Notes for WW Contributors'. *Payment:* £35 per 1000 words. *Illustrations:* b&w photos, colour transparencies, line.

Wedding and Home (1985), Debbie Djordjević, IPC Magazines Ltd, King's Reach Tower, Stamford Street, London SE1 9LS *tel* 071-261 7471 *fax* 071-261 7459.
£2.75. Bi-M. Financial, travel, home and style, emotional, humour. Approach in writing. *Length:* 500-1500 words. *Illustrations:* colour and b&w photos. *Payment:* by negotiation.

Weekend Guardian, Deborah Orr, 119 Farringdon Road, London EC1R 3ER *tel* 071-278 2332 *telex* 8811746/7/8 GUARDN G *fax* 071-837 2114; 164 Deansgate, Manchester M60 2RR *tel* 061-832 7200.
Free with Sat. *Guardian*. W. Features on world affairs, food and drink, home life, the arts, travel, leisure, etc. Also good reportage on social and political subjects. *Illustrations:* half-tone, line, cartoons. *Payment:* apply for rates.

The Weekly Journal (1992), Isabel Appio, Vee Tee Ay (Media Resources) Co. Ltd, 370 Coldharbour Lane, London SW9 8PL *tel* 071-738 5500 *fax* 071-924 0134.
55p. W. Features, news, interviews, arts, society, business – from a black perspective. *Length:* 300-3000 words. *Illustrations:* half-tone, cartoons. *Payment:* £100 per 1000 words; varies.

The Weekly News, D.C. Thomson & Co. Ltd, Courier Place, Dundee DD1 9QJ *tel* (0382) 23131; 137 Chapel Street, Manchester M3 6AA *tel* 061-834 5122; 144 Port Dundas Road, Glasgow G4 0HZ *tel* 041-332 9933; and 185 Fleet Street, London EC4A 2HS *tel* 071-242 5086.
37p. W. Real-life dramas of around 2000 words told in the first person. Non-fiction series with lively themes or about interesting people. Keynote throughout is strong human interest. Joke sketches. *Payment:* on acceptance.

Weight Watchers Magazine, Barbara Thompson, Harmsworth Magazines Ltd, Astley House, 33 Notting Hill Gate, London W11 3JQ *tel* 071-243 5000 *fax* 071-727 4222.
£1.35. 8 p.a. Features page – health, beauty, news, astrology; food-orientated articles; success stories. *All material commissioned. Length:* ½-3 pages. *Illustrations:* colour photos and cartoons. *Payment:* by arrangement.

West Africa, Editor-in-Chief: Kaye Whiteman, 43-45 Coldharbour Lane, London SE5 9NR *tel* 071-737 2946 *telex* 892420 WEST AF G *fax* 071-978 8334.
£1.50. W. Weekly summary of West African news, with articles on political, economic and commercial matters, and on all matters of general interest affecting West Africa; also book reviews. Covers Ghana, Nigeria, Sierra Leone, The Gambia, French-speaking African States, former Portuguese West Africa, Liberia, South Africa, Namibia and Zaire. *Length:* articles about 1200 words. *Payment:* as arranged. *Illustrations:* half-tone.

Western Daily Press (1858), Ian Beales, Bristol United Press Ltd, Temple Way, Bristol BS99 7HD *tel* (0272) 260080 *fax* (0272) 279568.

30p. D. National, international or West Country topics for features or news items, from established journalists, with or without *illustrations. Payment:* by negotiation.

Western Mail (1869), David Hughes, Thomson House, Cardiff CF1 1WR *tel* (0222) 223333 *fax* (0222) 583652.
32p. D. Ind. Articles of political, industrial, literary or general and Welsh interest are considered. *Illustrations:* topical general news and feature pictures, cartoons. *Payment:* according to value; special fees for exclusive news.

The Western Morning News (1860), Colin Davison, 17 Brest Road, Derriford Business Park, Plymouth PL6 5AA *tel* (0752) 765500 *fax* (0752) 765535.
30p. D. Articles of 600-800 words, plus illustrations, considered on West Country subjects.

What Car? (1973), Ralph Morton, Haymarket Motoring Magazines Ltd, 38-42 Hampton Road, Teddington, Middlesex TW11 0JE *tel* 081-943 5637 *fax* 081-943 5659.
£2.50. M. Road tests, buying guide and used car features. *No* unsolicited material. *Length:* varies. *Illustrations:* colour and b&w photos. *Payment:* £175 per 1000 words.

What's on TV (1991), Mike Hollingsworth, IPC Magazines Ltd, 10th Floor, King's Reach Tower, Stamford Street, London SE1 9LS *tel* 071-261 7769 *fax* 071-261 7739.
38p. W. Features on TV programmes and personalities. *All material commissioned. Length:* up to 500 words. *Illustrations:* colour and b&w photos, cartoons. *Payment:* by agreement.

Which Computer? (1977), David Dobson, 33-39 Bowling Green Lane, London EC1R 0DA *tel* 071-837 1212 *fax* 071-278 4003.
£2.45. M. Will consider proposals for equipment reviews and general features about business computing. *Preliminary letter* essential. *Payment:* by negotiation. *Illustrations:* line, half-tone, colour.

Wisden Cricket Monthly (1979), David Frith, 6 Beech Lane, Guildford, Surrey GU2 5ES *tel* (0483) 32573 *fax* (0483) 33153.
£2.20. M. Cricket articles of general interest. *Length:* up to 1000 words. *Payment:* by arrangement. *Illustrations:* half-tone, colour.

Woman (1937), David Durman, IPC Magazines Ltd, King's Reach Tower, Stamford Street, London SE1 9LS *tel* 071-261 5000 *fax* 071-261 5997.
50p. W. Practical articles of varying length on all subjects of interest to women. No unsolicited fiction. *Payment:* by arrangement. *Illustrations:* colour transparencies, photos, sketches, cartoons.

Woman Alive (formerly **Christian Woman**) (1991), Elizabeth Round, Herald House Ltd, 96 Dominion Road, Worthing, West Sussex BN14 8JP *tel* (0903) 821082 *fax* (0903) 821081.
£1.20. M. Aimed at women aged 25-45. Celebrity interviews, topical features, Christian issues, 'Day in the life of' profiles of women in interesting occupations, Christian testimonies, fashion, beauty, health, crafts and puzzles. All unsolicited material should include colour slides or b&w photos. *Length:* fillers 200-300 words, 'Day in the life of'/testimonies 750 words, interviews/features 1200 words. *Illustrations:* humorous photos, cartoons. *Payment:* by negotiation.

Woman and Home (1926), Orlando Murrin, IPC Magazines Ltd, King's Reach Tower, Stamford Street, London SE1 9LS *tel* 071-261 5423 *fax* 071-261 7346.

£1.30. M. Centres on the personal and home interests of the lively-minded woman with or without career and family. Articles dealing with leisure pursuits, crafts, gardening, fashion, beauty and knitting; things to make and buy for the home; features on people and places. Fiction: serial stories 3-5 instalments, and complete stories from 1000-5000 words in *length*, often with some romantic interest. *Illustrations:* commissioned colour photos and sketches.

The Woman Journalist (1894), Jocelyn Glegg, 300 Hills Road, Cambridge CB2 2QG.
Free to members. Q. Periodical of the Society of Women Writers and Journalists. Short articles of interest to professional writers. *Payment:* none.

Woman's Journal (1927), Deirdre Vine, IPC Magazines Ltd, King's Reach Tower, Stamford Street, London SE1 9LS *tel* 071-261 6622 *fax* 071-261 7061.
£1.60. M. Magazine devoted to the looks and lives of intelligent women: interviews and articles (1000-2500 words) dealing with topical subjects and personalities; fashion, beauty and health, food and houses. *Illustrations:* full colour, line and wash, first-rate photos. *Payment:* by arrangement.

Woman's Own, Keith McNeill, IPC Magazines Ltd, King's Reach Tower, Stamford Street, London SE1 9LS *tel* 071-261 5474.
50p. W. Modern women's magazine aimed at the 20-35 age group. No unsolicited features; no unsolicited fiction accepted except for annual short story competition. *Illustrations:* in full colour and mono. Original knitting, interior decorating and furnishing ideas, fashion. Please address work to relevant department editor. *Payment:* by arrangement.

Woman's Realm (1958), IPC Magazines Ltd, King's Reach Tower, Stamford Street, London SE1 9LS *tel* 071-261 5000.
48p. W. Lively general interest weekly magazine aimed at women with growing families. Articles on personalities, topical subjects, cookery, fashion, beauty, home. Human interest real-life features; dramatic emotional stories, strong adventure and chilling ghost/supernatural stories. (Regretfully, no unsolicited fiction accepted.) *Length:* features 1500 words. *Payment:* by arrangement. *Illustrations:* 4- and 2-colour drawings, photos in colour and b&w.

Woman's Weekly (1911), Olwen Rice, IPC Magazines Ltd, King's Reach Tower, Stamford Street, London SE1 9LS *tel* 071-261 5000 *fax* 071-261 6322.
44p. W. Lively, family-interest magazine. One serial, averaging 4600 words each instalment of strong romantic interest, and several short stories of 1000-4500 words of general emotional interest. Personality and strong human interest features; inspirational and entertaining personal stories, and general interest stories. *Payment:* by arrangement. *Illustrations:* full colour fiction illustrations, small sketches and photos.

Woodworker, Zachary Taylor, Argus Specialist Publications, Argus House, Boundary Way, Hemel Hempstead, Herts. HP2 7ST *tel* (0442) 66551 *telex* 827797 *fax* (0442) 66998.
£2.00. M. For the craft and professional woodworker. Practical illustrated articles on cabinet work, carpentry, wood polishing, wood turning, wood carving, rural crafts, craft history, antique and period furniture; also wooden toys and models, musical instruments; timber procurement, conditioning, seasoning; tool, machinery and equipment reviews. *Payment:* by arrangement. *Illustrations:* line drawings and photos, cartoons.

Work Study, John Heap, Leeds Metropolitan University Learning Support Services, Calverley Street, Leeds LS1 3HE *tel* (0532) 832600 *fax* (0532) 833145.

£199.95. 8 p.a. Authoritative articles on all aspects of work study including work measurement, method study, O&M, industrial engineering, payment systems. *Length:* 2000-4000 words. *Payment:* by arrangement. *Illustrations:* line, half-tone.

Workbox (1984), Audrey Babington, Upcott Hall, Bishop's Hull, Taunton, Somerset TA4 1AQ.
£1.50. Q. Features, of any length, on all aspects of needlecrafts. *No* 'how-to' articles. Send sae with enquiries and submissions. *Illustrations:* good b&w photos and colour transparencies; also line drawings. *Payment:* by agreement.

World Fishing (1952), Martin Gill, Oban Times Ltd, Royston House, Caroline Park, Edinburgh EH5 1QT   *tel* 031-551 2942   *fax* 031-551 2938.
£35.00 p.a. M. International journal of commercial fishing. Technical and management emphasis on catching, processing, farming and marketing of fish and related products; fishery operations and vessels covered world-wide. *Length:* 1000-2000 words. *Payment:* by arrangement. *Illustrations:* photos and diagrams for litho reproduction.

World of Bowls (1993; formerly **World Bowls**), Frank Baldwin, 48 London Road, Sevenoaks, Kent TN13 1AS   *tel* (0732) 743644   *fax* (0732) 742769.
Free to members of the English Bowling Association. £1.50. M. Bowls related stories and features relating to indoor and outdoor bowls. *Illustrations:* colour transparencies and photos. *Payment:* by negotiation.

The World of Interiors (1981), Min Hogg, The Condé Nast Publications Ltd, Vogue House, Hanover Square, London W1R 0AD   *tel* 071-499 9080   *telex* 27338 VOLON G   *fax* 071-499 0052.
£2.80. M. All material commissioned: send synopsis/visual reference for article ideas. *Length:* 1000-1500 words. *Illustrations:* colour photos. *Payment:* £400 per 1000 words; £150.

World Soccer (1960), Keir Radnedge, IPC Magazines Ltd, 25th Floor, King's Reach Tower, Stamford Street, London SE1 9LS   *tel* 071-261 5737   *fax* 071-261 5007.
£1.70. M. Articles, features, news concerning football, its personalities and world-wide development. *Length:* 600-2000 words. *Illustrations:* colour and b&w photos, cartoons. *Payment:* by arrangement; b&w £25, colour £50.

The World Today (1945), Christopher Cviic, The Royal Institute of International Affairs, Chatham House, 10 St James's Square, London SW1Y 4LE   *tel* 071-957 5700   *fax* 071-957 5710.
£2.50. M. Objective and factual articles on current questions of international affairs. *Length:* about 3500 words. *Payment:* £40 each article.

The World's Children (1920), Lotte Hughes and Julia Lewis, 17 Grove Lane, London SE5 8RD   *tel* 071-703 5400   *fax* 071-703 2278.
£5.00 p.a. Q. The magazine of Save the Children. Articles on child welfare related to Save the Children's work overseas and in the UK. *Length:* 700 words. *Payment:* by arrangement. *Illustrations:* photos for cover and article illustration.

Writers News (1989), Richard Bell, PO Box 4, Nairn IV12 4HU   *tel* (0667) 454441   *fax* (0667) 454401.
£39.90 p.a. (£34.90 p.a. CC/DD). M. News, competitions and articles on all aspects of writing. *Length:* 800-1500 words. *Illustrations:* line, half-tone. *Payment:* by arrangement.

Writing Magazine (1992), Richard Bell, PO Box 4, Nairn IV12 4HU   *tel* (0667) 454441   *fax* (0667) 454401.

£2.25. 5 p.a. (free to subscribers of *Writers News*) Articles on all aspects of writing. *Length:* 800-1500 words. *Illustrations:* line, half-tone. *Payment:* by arrangement.

Writing Women (1981), Linda Anderson, Cynthia Fuller, Andrea Badenoch, Margaret Wilkinson, Unit 14, Hawthorn House, Forth Banks, Newcastle upon Tyne NE2 3SG.
£2.00. 3 p.a. Poems, short stories. *Payment:* £15 per poem or per 1000 words.

Xenos (1990), S.V. Copestake, 29 Prebend Street, Bedford MK40 1QN   *tel* (0234) 349067.
£3.45. Bi-M. (£19.50 p.a.) Stories: science fiction, fantasy, horror, occult, humour, detective; ripping yarns. *No* gore, romance, domestic. Annual short story competition. Closing date: 31 May. *Length:* 2000-10,000 words. *Payment:* by negotiation.

Yachting Monthly (1906), Geoff Pack, IPC Magazines Ltd, King's Reach Tower, Stamford Street, London SE1 9LS   *tel* 071-261 6040   *fax* 071-261 7555.
£2.35. M. Technical articles, up to 2250 words, on all aspects of seamanship, navigation, the handling of sailing craft, and their design, construction and equipment. Well-written narrative accounts, up to 2500 words, of cruises in yachts. *Payment:* quoted on acceptance. *Illustrations:* b&w, colour transparencies, line or wash drawings, cartoons.

Yachting World (1894), Andrew Bray, IPC Magazines Ltd, King's Reach Tower, Stamford Street, London SE1 9LS   *tel* 071-261 6800   *fax* 071-261 6818.
£2.40. M. Practical articles of an original nature, dealing with sailing and boats. *Length:* 1500-2000 words. *Payment:* varies. *Illustrations:* colour transparencies, drawings, cartoons.

Yachts and Yachting (1947), Frazer Clark, 196 Eastern Esplanade, Southend-on-Sea, Essex SS1 3AB   *tel* (0702) 582245.
£1.95. F. Short articles which should be technically correct. *Payment:* by arrangement. *Illustrations:* line, half-tone, colour.

Yorkshire Evening Post (1890), C.H. Bye, PO Box 168, Wellington Street, Leeds LS1 1RF   *tel* (0532) 432701   *telex* 55425 YPOST G   *fax* (0532) 443430.
27p. Mon.-Sat. News stories and feature articles. *Illustrations:* colour and b&w, cartoons. *Payment:* by negotiation.

Yorkshire Evening Press (1882), David Nicholson, York and County Press, PO Box 29, 76-86 Walmgate, York YO1 1YN   *tel* (0904) 653051   *fax* (0904) 612853.
27p. D. Articles of Yorkshire or general interest, humour, personal experience of current affairs. *Length:* 500-1000 words. *Payment:* by arrangement. *Illustrations:* line, half-tone, cartoons.

Yorkshire Gazette & Herald Series, Dorothy Blundell, PO Box 29, 76-86 Walmgate, York YO1 1YN   *tel* (0904) 653051   *fax* (0904) 611488.
30p. W. Stories, features and pictures of local interest. *Payment:* varies. *Illustrations:* line, half-tone, colour.

Yorkshire Life (1947), Brian Hargreaves, Town & County Magazines, Oyston Mill, Strand Road, Preston PR1 8UR   *tel* (0772) 722022   *fax* (0772) 736496.
£1.50. M. Topics of Yorkshire interest, with or without photos. *Length:* 200-500 words and 800-1500 words. *Payment:* varies. *Illustrations:* line, half-tone, colour.

Yorkshire Post (1754), Tony Watson, Wellington Street, Leeds LS1 1RF   *tel* (0532) 432701   *telex* 55245   *fax* (0532) 443430; *London office:* Ludgate House, 245 Blackfriars Road, SE1 9UY   *tel* 071-921 5000.

32p. D. Authoritative and well-written articles on new topics or on topical subjects of general, literary or industrial interests. *Length:* 1200-1500 words. Contributions to *People*, a column about personalities in the news, are welcomed. *Illustrations:* photos and frequent pocket cartoons (single column width), topical wherever possible. *Payment:* by arrangement.

Yorkshire Ridings Magazine (1964), Winston Halstead, Barclays Bank Chambers, Sowerby Bridge, West Yorkshire HX6 2DX   *tel* (0422) 885678. £1.00. Bi-M. Articles exclusively about people, life and character of the three Ridings of Yorkshire. *Length:* up to 1500 words. *Payment:* approx. £30-£35 per published page. *Illustrations:* line, half-tone, colour.

You (1982), Dee Nolan, Northcliffe House, 2 Derry Street, Kensington, London W8 5TS   *tel* 071-938 6000   *telex* 28301 LDM G   *fax* 071-938 1488. Free with *Mail on Sunday*. W. Features on all subjects. *Length:* 1000-2500 words. *Payment:* by arrangement. *Illustrations:* line, half-tone, colour photos, cartoons, generally commissioned.

Young People Now (1989), Mary Durkin, National Youth Agency, 17-23 Albion Street, Leicester LE1 6GD   *tel* (0533) 471200   *fax* (0533) 471043. £2.00. M. (£22.80 p.a.) Informative, general interest articles, highlighting issues of concern to all those who work with young people – including youth, probation and social services, teachers and volunteers. Guidelines for contributors available on request. *Length:* 1000-1500 words. *Illustrations:* line, half-tone. *Payment:* £45 per 1000 words; by negotiation.

The Young Soldier (1881), Philippa Smale, 101 Queen Victoria Street, London EC4P 4EP   *tel* 071-236 5222 ext 2274   *fax* 071-236 3491. 15p W. (£22.50 p.a.) The Salvation Army's children's weekly. Stories, pictures, cartoon strips, puzzles etc., often on Christian themes. *Payment:* by arrangement. *Illustrations:* half-tone, line and three-colour line, cartoons.

Young Telegraph (1990), Caroline Clayton, Young Telegraph Ltd, 346 Old Street, London EC1V 9NQ   *tel* 071-613 3376   *fax* 071-613 3372. Free with Sat. *Daily Telegraph*. Short articles of interest to children aged 8-12 years. *Length:* 100-250 words. *Illustrations:* colour and b&w photos, cartoons. *Payment:* varies.

Your Garden (1993), Graham Clarke, IPC Magazines Ltd, Westover House, West Quay Road, Poole, Dorset BH15 1JG *tel* (0202) 680603   *fax* (0202) 674335. £1.55. M. Anything on gardening for the enthusiastic beginner. *Commissioned material only*; send brief synopsis of ideas. *Length:* 800-2000 words. *Illustrations:* colour photos and line. *Payment:* £100 per published 1000 words.

Yours (1973), Neil Patrick, Apex House, Oundle Road, Peterborough PE2 9NP   *tel* (0733) 555123   *fax* (0733) 898487. 60p. M. Features and news about/of interest to over-60s including nostalgia; short stories. *Study of magazine* essential; approach in writing. *Length:* articles up to 1000 words, short stories up to 1800 words. *Illustrations:* preferably colour transparencies/prints; will consider good b&w prints/line drawings, cartoons. *Payment:* at editor's discretion or by agreement.

YX (Youth Express) (1992), Tess Kingham, PO Box 405, Swindon, Wilts. SN1 1UZ   *tel* (0793) 514596   *fax* (0793) 514654. Free to secondary schools. 3 p.a. (termly) 'Hard'/environmental issues, music and sport, aimed at and mostly written by young people. *Length:* 300-400 words. *Illustrations:* cartoons. *Payment:* varies.

AUSTRALIA

Newspapers are listed under the towns in which they are published.

(Adelaide) Advertiser (1858), Peter Blunden, 121 King William Street, Adelaide, SA 5000 *tel* (08) 218 9218 *fax* (08) 231 1147; London: PO Box 481, 1 Virginia Street, E1 9BD *tel* 071-702 1355 *fax* 071-702 1384.
60c. Mon.-Fri., $1.00 Sat. The only morning daily in South Australia. Descriptive and news background material, 400-800 words, preferably with pictures.

(Adelaide) Sunday Mail (1912), K. Sullivan, 121 King William Street, Adelaide, SA 5000 *postal address* GPO Box 339, Adelaide, SA 5001 *tel* (08) 218 9218 *fax* (08) 212 6264.

Australasian Sporting Shooter, Ray Galea, Yaffa Publishing Group, 17-21 Bellevue Street, Surry Hills, NSW 2010 *tel* (02) 281 2333 *fax* (02) 281 2750.
$3.70. M. All aspects of game shooting, collecting, antiques, archery (associated with hunting), pistol shooting, clay target shooting, reloading, ballistics and articles of a technical nature. *Payment:* by arrangement.

Australian Angler's Fishing World, Gil Schott, Yaffa Publishing Group, 17-21 Bellevue Street, Surry Hills, NSW 2010 *tel* (02) 281 2333 *telex* AA 121887 *fax* (02) 281 2750.
$4.25. M. All aspects of rock, surf, stream, deep sea and game fishing, with comprehensive sections on gear, equipment and boats. *Payment:* by arrangement.

Australian Bookseller & Publisher (1921), John Nieuwenhuizen, D.W. Thorpe, 18 Salmon Street, Port Melbourne, Victoria 3207 *tel* (03) 245 7390 *fax* (03) 245 7395.

The Australian Financial Review, Gregory Hywood, 235-243 Jones Street, Broadway, Sydney, NSW 2007 *tel* (02) 282 2822 *fax* (02) 282 3137; London: 12 Norwich Street, EC4A 1BH *tel* 071-353 9321; New York: Suite 1002, 1500 Broadway, NY 10036 *tel* 212-398-9494.
$1.00. Mon.-Fri. Investment business and economic news and reviews; government and politics, production, banking, commercial, and Stock Exchange statistics; company analysis. General features in Friday *Weekend Review* supplement.

Australian Flying, Paul Phelan, Yaffa Publishing Group, 17-21 Bellevue Street, Surry Hills, NSW 2010 *tel* (02) 281 2333 *fax* (02) 281 2750; London: Robert Logan, 64 The Mall, Ealing, W5 5LS *tel* 081-579 4836.
$4.40. 6 p.a. Appeals to owners of light and medium aircraft, as well as those directly and indirectly associated with the aircraft industry. *Payment:* by arrangement.

Australian Geographic (1986), Howard Whelan, PO Box 321, Terrey Hills, NSW 2084 *tel* (02) 450 2344 *telex* AA 176203 *fax* (02) 450 2990.
$37.40 p.a. Q. (2-yr $74.80) Short articles and features about Australia, particularly life, technology and natural history in remote parts of the country. Material *mostly commissioned. Length:* articles, 300-800 words, features, 2000-3000 words. *Illustrations:* all commissioned. *Payment:* $500 per 1000 words; by negotiation.

Australian Historical Studies, John Rickard, Monash University, Clayton, Victoria 3168.
$36.00 p.a. 2 p.a. *Length:* 8000 words maximum. *Illustrations:* tables and maps. *Payment:* none.

Australian Home Beautiful (1913), A. Fawcett, 32 Walsh Street, West Melbourne, Victoria 3003   *tel* (03) 320 7000   *fax* (03) 320 7020.
$4.00. M. Deals with home building, interior decoration, furnishing, gardening, cookery, etc. Short articles with accompanying photos with Australian slant accepted. *Preliminary letter* advisable. *Payment:* higher than Australian average.

Australian House and Garden (1948), Stephanie King, 54 Park Street, Sydney, NSW 2000   *tel* (02) 282 8413.
$4.20. M. Factual articles dealing with interior decorating, home design, gardening, wine, food. *Preliminary letter* essential. *Payment:* by arrangement. *Illustrations:* line, half-tone, colour.

Australian Journal of International Affairs, Dr Stephanie Lawson, Peace Research Centre, Australian National University, Canberra, ACT 0200   *tel* (06) 249 3861   *fax* (06) 249 0174.
$28.00 p.a. Australia/NZ. 2 p.a. ($39.00 p.a. elsewhere) Scholarly articles on international affairs. *Length:* 4000-7000 words. *Payment:* none.

The Australian Journal of Politics and History, J.A. Moses, Department of History, University of Queensland Press, St Lucia, Queensland 4067   *tel* (07) 365 6477.
$60.00. 3 p.a. (US $58.00, UK £33.00, inc. postage) Australian, Commonwealth, Asian, SW Pacific and international articles. Special feature: regular surveys of Australian Foreign Policy and State and Commonwealth politics. *Length:* 8000 words max. *Illustrations:* line, only when necessary. *Payment:* none.

The Australian Magazine (1988), James Hall, 2 Holt Street, Surry Hills, Sydney, NSW 2010   *tel* (02) 288 2442   *fax* (02) 288 2486.
Free with the Weekend Australian. Articles, features, narrative investigations, profiles, etc. *Length:* 2000-4000 words. *Illustrations:* mostly colour transparencies; will use b&w or artwork. *Payment:* by negotiation.

Australian Mining, Lou Caruana, Thomson Publications Australia, 47 Chippen Street, Chippendale, NSW 2008   *postal address* PO Box 815, Chippendale, NSW 2008   *tel* (02) 699 2411.
$56.00 p.a. in Australia.

Australian Photography (1950), Steve Packer, Yaffa Publishing Group, 17-21 Bellevue Street, Surry Hills, NSW 2010   *tel* (02) 281 2333   *fax* (02) 281 2750.
$3.95. M. Illustrated articles – picture-taking techniques, technical. *Length/ illustrations:* 2000 words/colour and b&w prints or slides. *Payment:* $80 per page.

The Australian Quarterly (1929), Professor Ross Garnaut, Professor Nancy Viviani, Australian Institute of Political Science, Level 4, WEA House, 72 Bathurst Street, Sydney, NSW 2000   *tel* (02) 249 5111   *fax* (02) 267 7900.
$43.00 p.a. Q. ($57.00 p.a. overseas) Articles of high standard on politics, law, economics, social issues, etc. *Length:* 3500 words preferred. *Payment:* none.

Australian Skiing, Matt Johnson, PO Box 746, Darlinghurst, NSW 2010   *tel* (02) 331 5006   *fax* (02) 360 5367.
$4.75. 5 p.a. (May-Sept.) Articles and features on skiing world-wide. *Length:* 1500 words. *Illustrations:* colour transparencies, cartoons. *Payment:* $200 per 1000 words; $300 cover, $190 2-page, $120 1-page.

The Australian Way (1986), Brian Courtis, David Syme & Co. Ltd, 250 Spencer Street, Melbourne, Victoria 3000   *postal address* GPO Box 257c, Melbourne, Victoria 3001   *tel* (03) 601 2917   *fax* (03) 642 0852.

Free. M. Inflight magazine for Australian Airlines. Articles on Australian travel and prominent Australian people. *Length:* 800-1500 words. *Illustrations:* colour transparencies on acceptance of article for publication. *Payment:* by negotiation.

The Australian Women's Weekly, Jennifer Rowe, Australian Consolidated Press Ltd, 54 Park Street, Sydney, NSW 2000 *tel* (02) 282 8000 *fax* (02) 267 4459. $3.30. M. Fiction and features. *Length:* fiction 1000-10,000 words; features 750-2500 words plus colour or b&w photos. *Payment:* according to length and merit. *Fiction illustrations:* sketches by own artists and freelances.

The Australian Worker & Labor News, Steve Harrison, Mike Forshaw, 51-65 Bathurst Street, Sydney, NSW 2000 *tel* (02) 264 2877 *fax* (02) 261 1701. Bi-M. Official Journal of the AWU-FIME Amalgamated Union.

(Brisbane) The Courier-Mail, D. Houghton, Queensland Newspapers Pty Ltd, Campbell Street, Bowen Hills, Brisbane, Queensland 4006 *tel* (07) 252 6011 *fax* (07) 252 6696. 30c. D. Occasional topical special articles required. *Length:* 1000 words.

(Brisbane) Sunday Mail, Bob Gordon, Queensland Newspapers Pty Ltd, PO Box 130, Campbell Street, Bowen Hills, Brisbane, Queensland 4006 *tel* (07) 252 6011. 90c. W. Anything of general interest. *Length:* up to 1500 words. *Illustrations:* line, photos, b&w and colour, cartoons. *Payment:* by arrangement. Rejected MSS returned if postage enclosed.

The Bulletin with Newsweek, Lyndall Crisp, 54 Park Street, Sydney, NSW 2000 *tel* (02) 282 8200 *fax* (02) 267 4359. $3.30. W. General interest articles, features; humour. *Length:* up to 3200 words. *Illustrations:* colour photos and cartoons. *Payment:* $450 per 1000 words published; $100 colour cartoons, colour photos, according to size used.

Cleo (1972), Lisa Wilkinson, 54 Park Street, Sydney, NSW 2000 *tel* (02) 282 8617 *fax* (02) 267 2150. $2.95. M. Articles (relationship, emotional, self-help) up to 3000 words, short quizzes. *Payment:* by negotiation.

The Countryman, John Dare, 219 St Georges Terrace, Perth, Western Australia 6000 *tel* (09) 482 3322 *telegraphic address* Westralian Perth *fax* (09) 482 3324. 70c. W. Agriculture, farming or country interest features and service columns. *Payment:* standard rates. *Illustrations:* line, half-tone, colour, cartoons.

Current Affairs Bulletin (1942), Dr Bob Howard, CAB, 72 Bathurst Street, Sydney, NSW 2000 *tel* (02) 264 5726 *fax* (02) 267 7900. $3.50. 11 p.a. ($40.00 p.a., $57.00 p.a. overseas) Authoritative well-documented articles on all national and international affairs: politics, economics, science, the arts, business and social questions. *Length:* 3000-5000 words. *Illustrations:* line, half-tone. *Payment:* none.

Cycling World (1978), Chuck Smeeton, PO Box 746, Darlinghurst, NSW 2010 *tel* (02) 331 5006 *fax* (02) 360 5367. $4.50. Bi-M. All general cycling features, including technique, training, travel, competition and commuting. *Length:* 1500-2000 words. *Illustrations:* colour transparencies preferred; b&w prints accepted. *Payment:* $150 per 1000 words; $100 per page.

Dance Australia (1980), Karen Van Ulzen, Yaffa Publishing Group, Box 606, GPO Sydney, NSW 2001 *tel* (02) 281 2333 *fax* (02) 281 2750.

$4.75. Bi-M. Articles and features on all aspects of dance in Australia. Material *mostly commissioned*, but will consider unsolicited contributions. *Length:* as appropriate. *Illustrations:* b&w photos, line drawings, cartoons. *Payment:* $100 per 1000 words; by negotiation.

Dolly (1970), Marina Go, 54 Park Street, Sydney, NSW 2000   *tel* (02) 282 8000   *fax* (02) 267 4911.
$2.40. M. Features on fashion, health and beauty, personalities, music, social issues and how to cope with growing up, etc. *Length:* not less than 1000 words. *Payment:* by arrangement.

Electronics Australia with ETI, Jamieson Rowe, PO Box 199, Alexandria, NSW 2015   *tel* (02) 353 0620   *fax* (02) 353 0613/0935.
$4.95. M. Articles on technical television and radio, hi-fi, popular electronics, microcomputers and avionics. *Length:* up to 2000 words. *Payment:* by arrangement. *Illustrations:* line, half-tone, cartoons.

Geo Australasia (1978), Michael Hohensee, Geo Productions Pty Ltd, PO Box 1390, Chatswood, NSW 2057   *tel* (02) 411 1766   *fax* (02) 413 2689.
$7.95. Bi-M. ($55.00 p.a. surface mail) Non-fiction articles on wildlife, adventure, culture and lifestyles, natural history and the environment in Australia, New Zealand, the Pacific and SE Asia. *Length:* 1500-3000 words. *Payment:* $600-$1500 by arrangement. *Illustrations:* photos, colour transparencies.

Guns Australia, Ray Galea, Yaffa Publishing Group Pty Ltd, 17-21 Bellevue Street, Surry Hills, NSW 2010   *tel* (02) 281 2333   *fax* (02) 281 2750.
$3.90. Bi-M. Articles, features, technical pieces, news. *All material commissioned. Length:* 2000 words. *Illustrations:* colour slides, b&w photos. *Payment:* $50 per page.

Herald of the South (1925), Editorial Board: Lilian Ala'i, Barry Anderson, Stephen Beale, Janet Hetaraka, Jennifer Lemon, Gaylene Whenmouth, GPO Box 283, Canberra, ACT 2601   *tel/fax* (02) 970 6710.
$22.00 p.a. Q. Baha'i magazine with particular emphasis on religious approach to unity. Features, fiction and non-fiction. *Length:* up to 3500 words. *Illustrations:* colour and b&w photos. *Payment:* by negotiation.

HQ Magazine (1989), Shona Martyn, 54 Park Street, Sydney, NSW 2000   *tel* (02) 282 8260   *telex* 120514 AA   *fax* (02) 267 3616.
$5.95. Q. General interest features and profiles for a literate readership. *Length:* 1500-5000 words. *Illustrations:* colour and b&w photos. *Payment:* by negotiation.

(Launceston) Examiner, Rod Scott, Box 99A, PO Launceston, Tasmania 7250   *tel* (003) 315 111   *telegraphic address* Examiner, Launceston   *fax* (003) 320 300.
65c. D. Accepts freelance material. *Payment:* by arrangement.

(Melbourne) Age, A. Kohler, David Syme & Co. Ltd, 250 Spencer Street, Melbourne, Victoria 3000   *tel* (03) 600 4211   *telex* 30331/30376/30449   *fax* (03) 670 7514; London: The London International Press Centre, 12 Norwich Street, EC4A 1BH   *tel* 071-353 9321.
80c. Mon.-Fri. $1.20 Sat. Independent liberal morning daily; room occasionally for outside matter. An illustrated weekend magazine and literary review is published on Saturday; accepts occasional freelance material.

(Melbourne) Australasian Post, News Editor: Denis Williams, Southdown Press, 32 Walsh Street, PO Box 1292K GPO, West Melbourne, Victoria 3003   *tel* (03) 320 7000.

$2.20. W. Opening for casual contributions of topical factual illustrated articles of Australian interest. General appeal. *Payment:* by arrangement.

(Melbourne) Herald-Sun, Alan Oakley, 44-74 Flinders Street, Melbourne, Victoria 3000 *tel* (03) 652 1950 *fax* (03) 652 2542.
60c. Mon.-Sat. Accepts freelance articles, preferably with illustrations. *Length:* up to 750 words. *Illustrations:* half-tone, line, cartoons. *Payment:* on merit.

(Melbourne) The Sunday Age (1989), Bruce Guthrie, 250 Spencer Street, Melbourne, Victoria 3000 *tel* (03) 600 4211 *fax* (03) 602 1856; London: The London International Press Centre, 76 Shoe Lane, EC4A 3JB *tel* 071-353 5193.
70c. W. Features. *Length:* 500-2000 words. *Payment:* by arrangement.

(Melbourne) Sunday Herald-Sun, Ian Moore, 44-74 Flinders Street, Melbourne, Victoria 3000 *tel* (03) 652 1111 *telex* 30104/30124 *fax* (03) 652 2080.
90c. W. Accepts freelance articles, preferably with illustrations. *Length:* up to 2000 words. *Illustrations:* colour. *Payment:* on merit.

Mode Australia (1973), Deborah Thomas, ACP Publishing Pty Ltd, 54 Park Street, Sydney, NSW 2001 *tel* (02) 282 8703 *fax* (02) 267 4456.
$5.50. Bi-M. Fashion, health and beauty, celebrity news. *Length:* 3000 words. *Illustrations:* colour and b&w photos. *Payment:* $500 per 1000 words; $150.

Modern Boating (1965), Mark Rothfield, 180 Bourke Road, Alexandria, NSW 2015 *tel* (02) 693 6666 *fax* (02) 317 4615.
$4.50. M. Articles on all types of boats and boating. *Payment:* $130-$200 per 1000 words. *Illustrations:* half-tone, colour.

New Idea (1902), L. Willox, 32 Walsh Street, PO Box 1292K GPO, Melbourne, Victoria 3001 *tel* (03) 320 7000.
$2.20. W. General interest women's magazine; news stories, features, fashion, services, short stories of general interest to women of all ages. *Length:* stories, 500-4000 words: articles, 500-2000 words. *Payment:* on acceptance; minimum $150 per 1000 words.

Overland, John McLaren, PO Box 14146, Melbourne, Victoria 3000 *tel* (03) 380 1152 *fax* (03) 380 2586.
$6.50. Q. Literary and general. Australian material preferred. *Payment:* by arrangement. *Illustrations:* line, half-tone, cartoons.

People Magazine (national weekly news-pictorial), D. Naylor, 54 Park Street, Sydney, NSW 2000 *tel* (02) 282 8743 *fax* (02) 267 4365.
$2.30. W. Mainly people stories, but good documentary subjects needed. Photos depicting exciting happenings, candid camera pictures of events affecting Australians, glamour and show business, modern-living features, and complete series of any subject such as unusual occupations, rites, customs. *Payment:* highest Australian scale.

(Perth) Sunday Times (1897), Don Smith, 34 Stirling Street, Perth, Western Australia 6000 *tel* (09) 326 8326 *fax* (09) 221 1121.
$1.00. W. Topical articles to 800 words. *Payment:* on acceptance.

(Perth) The West Australian (1833), Paul Murray, 219 St Georges Terrace, Perth, Western Australia 6000 *tel* (09) 482 3111 *telegraphic address* Westralian, Perth *fax* (09) 324 1416.
60c. Mon.-Fri. 90c. Sat. Articles and sketches about people and events in Australia and abroad. *Length:* 300-700 words. *Payment:* Award rates or better. *Illustrations:* line, half-tone.

Poetry Australia (1964), John Millett, South Head Press, The Market Place, Berrima, NSW 2577 *tel* (048) 771 421.

$40 p.a. Q. Previously unpublished new poetry, and criticism. *Payment:* copy of magazine.

Portfolio (1984), Alexandra Joel, 15-19 Boundary Street, Rushcutters Bay, NSW 2011 *postal address* PO Box 746, Darlinghurst, NSW 2010 *tel* (02) 331 5006 *fax* (02) 360 5367.
$4.50. 6 p.a. Features for the modern woman: includes – career, relationships, health issues. *No* poetry or fiction. *Length:* 1000-2000 words. *Illustrations:* colour transparencies, b&w photos. *Payment:* by negotiation.

Quadrant, Robert Manne, 46 George Street, Fitzroy, Victoria 3065 *postal address* PO Box 1495, Collingwood, Victoria 3066 *tel* (03) 417 6855 *fax* (03) 416 2980.
$5.00. M. Articles, short stories, verse, etc. *Prose length:* 2000-5000 words. *Payment:* minimum $80 articles/stories, $60 reviews, $30 poems.

Reader's Digest (Australian and New Zealand editions), Hugh Vaughan-Williams, 26-32 Waterloo Street, Surry Hills, NSW 2010 *tel* (02) 690 6111 *fax* (02) 699 8165.
$3.25. M. Articles on Australian/NZ subjects by commission only. No unsolicited MSS accepted. *Length:* 2500-5000 words. *Payment:* up to $4000 per article; brief filler paragraphs, $50-$200. *Illustrations:* half-tone, colour.

Redoubt (1988), Managing Editor: Ruth Sless, Faculty of Communication, University of Canberra, PO Box 1, Belconnen, ACT 2616 *tel* (06) 201 5090 *fax* (06) 201 5300.
$8.50. Bi-A. Literary magazine: mainly poetry, short stories, reviews, articles. *Length:* short poetry; stories/reviews, up to 3000 words. *Illustrations:* b&w line and photos. *Payment:* by arrangement.

The Sun-Herald, Andrew Clark, GPO Box 506, Sydney, NSW 2001 *tel* (02) 282 2822 *fax* (02) 282 1640; London: John Fairfax (UK) Ltd, 12 Norwich Street, EC4A 1BH *tel* 071-353 9321.
$1.00. W. Topical articles to 1000 words; sections on politics, social issues, show business, finance and fashion. *Payment:* by arrangement.

(Sydney) The Daily Telegraph Mirror, Editor-in-Chief: John Hartigan, News Limited, 2 Holt Street, Surry Hills, NSW 2010 *tel* (02) 288 3000 *fax* (02) 288 2300.
60c. D. Modern feature articles and series of Australian or world interest. *Length:* 1000-2000 words. *Payment:* according to merit/length.

The Sydney Morning Herald (1831), Editor-in-Chief: D.J. Hickie, PO Box 506, Sydney, NSW 2001 *tel* (02) 282 2858 *fax* (02) 282 2632; London: 12 Norwich Street, EC4A 1BH *tel* 071-353 9321 *fax* 071-583 0348.
90c. D. Saturday edition has pages of literary criticism and also magazine articles, plus glossy colour magazine. Topical articles 600-4000 words. *Payment:* varies, but minimum $100 per 1000 words. *Illustrations:* all types.

Woman's Day, Nene King, 54-58 Park Street, Sydney, NSW 2000 *tel* (02) 282 8000 *fax* (02) 267 2150.
$2.30. W. National women's magazine; news, show business, fiction, fashion, general articles, cookery, home economy.

CANADA

Newspapers are listed under the towns in which they are published.

ArtsAtlantic (1977), Joseph Sherman, Confederation Centre of the Arts, 145 Richmond Street, Charlottetown, Prince Edward Island C1A 1J1 *tel* 902-628-6138 *fax* 902-566-4648.

$29.95 for 4 issues. 3 p.a. ($45.95 for 8 issues) Features and reviews on the art history of Atlantic Canada, the work of contemporary artists and the ideas and issues affecting Canadian culture. *No* fiction or poetry. *All material commissioned*; send enquiries (+ CV and samples of published work). *Length:* reviews, 300-900 words, features, 1000-3000 words. *Illustrations:* colour and b&w. *Payment:* $65 per review, features 15c per word to $250 maximum; by negotiation.

Aviation & Aerospace (1928), Garth Wallace, Baxter Publishing, 310 Dupont Street, Toronto, Ontario M5R 1U9   *tel* 416-968-7252   *fax* 416-968-2377.
$42.00 p.a. (UK). Bi-M. Stories with a Canadian angle, on civil or military aviation. *Payment:* $250-$400. *Illustrations:* photos; from $25.

The Beaver: Exploring Canada's History, Christopher Dafoe, Hudson's Bay Co., 450 Portage Avenue, Winnipeg, Manitoba R3C 0E7   *tel* 204-786-7048   *fax* 204-774-8624.
$22.50 p.a. Bi-M. ($29.00 p.a. elsewhere) Articles, historical and modern, on Canadian history. *Length:* 1500-5000 words, with illustrations. *Payment:* on acceptance, about 10c a word. *Illustrations:* b&w and colour photos or drawings.

Books in Canada (1971), Paul Stuewe, 130 Spadina Avenue, Suite 603, Toronto, Ontario M5V 2L4   *tel* 416-601 9880.
$3.25. 9 p.a. Commissioned reviews, informed criticism and articles on Canadian literary scene. *Query first* – do not send unsolicited material. *Payment:* 12c per word.

C Magazine (1972), Joyce Mason, PO Box 5, Station B, Toronto, Ontario M5T 2T2   *tel* 416-539-9495   *fax* 416-531-7610.
$7.50. Q. Arts and artists, projects, features, reviews. Accept submissions *only*. *Length:* features, varies; reviews, 750 words. *Illustrations:* b&w photos. *Payment:* $250-$500 features, $125 reviews.

Canadian Author and Bookman, 275 Slater Street, Suite 500, Ottawa, Ontario K1P 5H9.
$15.00 p.a. Q. ($20.00 p.a. overseas) Published by Canadian Authors Association. Interested in an international view on writing techniques, profiles, interviews, freelance opportunities for Canadian writers. *Query only. Payment:* $30 per printed page.

The Canadian Forum, Duncan Cameron, 251 Laurier Avenue W, Suite 804, Ottawa, Ontario K1P 5J6   *tel* 613-230-3078   *fax* 613-233-1458.
$2.00. 10 p.a. ($18.00 p.a.) Articles on public affairs and the arts. *Length:* up to 2500 words. *Payment:* $100 per article. *Illustrations:* line and photos.

Canadian Interiors, Lorraine Tierney, The Maclean Hunter Building, 777 Bay Street, Toronto, Ontario M5W 1A7   *tel* 416-596-5976   *telegraphic address* Macpub   *fax* 416-593-3189.
$40.00 p.a. 8 p.a. ($89.00 p.a. elsewhere) Articles on all aspects of interior design; also technical and business articles. *Payment:* $100-$400 per article. *Illustrations:* half-tone, colour.

Canadian Literature (1959), W.H. New, 2029 West Mall, University of British Columbia, Vancouver, BC V6T 1Z2   *tel* 604-882-2780   *fax* 604-822-9452.
$15.00. Q. Articles on Canadian writers and writing in English and French. *Length:* up to 5000 words. *Payment:* $5 per printed page.

Canadian Yachting (1974), Iain MacMillan, Kerrwil Publications Ltd, 395 Matheson Boulevard East, Mississauga, Ontario L4Z 2H2   *tel* 905-890-1846   *fax* 905-890-5769.

$2.95. 7 p.a. Features, news and views. *Query letters preferred. Length:* regulars, 1000-2000 words; features, 1800-3000 words. *Illustrations:* line, half-tone, colour, cartoons. *Payment:* up to $350 regulars, up to $500 features; $50-$250 line, $30-$100 photos, $200 cover shots.

Chatelaine, Mildred Istona, 777 Bay Street, Toronto, Ontario M5W 1A7   *tel* 416-596-5425.
$2.00. M. Women's interest articles used; Canadian angle preferred. *Payment:* on acceptance; from $1000.

The Dalhousie Review, Dr Alan Andrews, Dalhousie University Press Ltd, Sir James Dunn Building, Suite 314, Halifax, NS B3H 3J5   *tel* 902-494-2541.
$6.50 (plus postage). Q. ($19.00 p.a., $28.00 p.a. outside Canada; or $48.00 for 3 years; $75.00 for 3 years outside Canada) Articles on literary, political, historical, philosophical and social topics; fiction; verse; book reviews. *Length:* prose, normally not more than 5000 words; verse, preferably less than 40 words. *Payment:* $1 per printed page for fiction; $3 for 1st poem, $2 for each subsequent poem (per issue). Contributors receive two copies of issue and 15 offprints of their work. Usually not more than two stories and about 10 or 12 poems in any one issue.

Equinox (1982), Jim Cormier, 7 Queen Victoria Road, Camden East, Ontario K0K 3N0   *tel* 613-378-6661.
$3.95. Bi-M. ($19.98 p.a. Canada; $25.00 p.a. USA; $29.00 elsewhere) Magazine of discovery in science, travel and geography, especially ecology and earth sciences. Accepts articles on hard science topics (*length:* 100-500 words); welcomes queries (2-3-page outline) for specific environmental assignments. *Illustrations:* colour transparencies. *Payment:* by arrangement.

The Fiddlehead (1945), Don Mckay, Campus House, University of New Brunswick, PO Box 4400, Fredericton, NB E3B 5A3   *tel* 506-453-3501.
$6.00. Q. Reviews, poetry, short stories. *Payment:* approx. $10-$12 per printed page.

The Hamilton Spectator (1846), Publisher, Gordon Bullock, 44 Frid Street, Hamilton, Ontario L8N 3G3   *tel* 416-526-3333.
35c. Mon.-Fri. $1.00 Sat. Articles of general interest, political analysis and background; interviews, stories of Canadians abroad. *Length:* 800 words maximum. *Payment:* rate varies.

Inuit Art Quarterly (1986), Marybelle Mitchell, 2081 Merivale Road, Nepean, Ontario K2G 1G9   *tel* 613-224-8189   *fax* 613-224-2907.
$6.25. Q. Features, news and reviews on the Inuit art world. *Length:* varies. *Illustrations:* colour and b&w photos and line. *Payment:* by arrangement; $50.

Journal of Canadian Studies, Michael Peterman, Michèle Lacombe, Joy Manson, Trent University, Peterborough, Ontario K9J 7B8   *tel* 705-748-1279   *fax* 705-748-1655.
$28.00 p.a. Q. ($45.00 p.a. institutions) Major academic review of Canadian studies. Articles of general as well as scholarly interest on history, politics, literature, society, arts. *Length:* 7000-10,000 words.

The Malahat Review (1967), Derk Wynand, University of Victoria, PO Box 1700, Victoria, BC V8W 2Y2   *tel* 604-721-8524.
$18.00 p.a. Q. ($25.00 p.a. overseas) Short stories, poetry, short plays, reviews, some graphics. *Payment:* prose: $40 per 1000 words; poetry: $20 per page. *Illustrations:* half-tone.

Performing Arts & Entertainment in Canada (PA&E) (1961), Karen Bell, 1100 Caledonian Road, Suite 200, Toronto, Ontario M6A 2W5   *tel* 416-785-4300.

$8.00 p.a. Q. ($14.00 p.a. elsewhere) Feature articles on Canadian theatre, music, dance and film artists and organisations; technical articles on scenery, lighting, make-up, costumes, etc. *Length:* 800-1500 words. *Payment:* $150-$250, one month after publication. *Illustrations:* b&w photos, colour slides.

Photo Life (1976), Jerry Kobalenko, 130 Spy Court, Markham, Ontario L3R 5H6 *tel* 905-475-8440 *fax* 905-475-9560.
$2.95. 8 p.a. Covers all aspects of photography of interest to amateur and professional Canadian photographers. *Length:* 1500-2500 words. *Illustrations:* colour and b&w photos. *Payment:* by arrangement.

Quebec Chronicle Telegraph (1764), Karen Macdonald, Quebec Chronicle-Telegraph Inc., 3484 chemin Ste-Foy, Quebec City, Quebec G1X 1S8 *tel* 418-650-1764.
40c. W. Covers local events within English community in Quebec City. Some feature articles.

Quill & Quire (1935), Ted Mumford, 70 The Esplanade, 4th Floor, Toronto, Ontario M5E 1R2 *tel* 416-360-0044 *fax* 416-360-8745.
$55.00 p.a. (in UK; 2-year sub $85.00). 12 p.a. Articles of interest about the Canadian book trade. *Payment:* from $100. *Illustrations:* line, half-tone. Subscription includes *Canadian Publishers Directory*, 2 p.a.

Reader's Digest, Alexander Farrell, 215 Redfern Avenue, Montreal, Quebec H3Z 2V9 *tel* 514-934-0751.
$2.49. M. Original articles on all subjects of broad general appeal, thoroughly researched and professionally written. Outline or query *only*. *Length:* 3000 words approx. *Payment:* from $2700. Also previously published material. *Illustrations:* line, half-tone, colour.

(Toronto) The Globe and Mail (1844), Publisher: C. David Clark, Editor-in-Chief: William Thorsell, 444 Front Street West, Toronto, Ontario M5V 2S9; London: First Floor, The Quadrangle, PO Box 4YG, 180 Wardour Street, W1A 4YG *tel* 071-287 2725.
50c. D. Unsolicited material considered. *Payment:* by arrangement.

Toronto Life (1967), John Macfarlane, 59 Front Street East, Toronto, Ontario M5E 1B3 *tel* 416-364-3333 *fax* 416-861-1169.
$2.50. M. Articles, profiles on Toronto and Torontonians. *Illustrations:* line, half-tone, colour.

Toronto Star (1892), One Yonge Street, Toronto, Ontario M5E 1E6 *tel* 416-367-2000; London: Level 4A, PO Box 495, Virginia Street, E1 9XY *tel* 071-833 0791.
30c. Mon.-Fri. $1.00 Sat. 75c. Sun. Features, life, world/national politics. *Payment:* by arrangement.

(Vancouver) Province (1898), Editor-in-Chief: Brian Butters, 2250 Granville Street, Vancouver, BC V6H 3G2 *tel* 604-732-2007 *fax* 604-732-2223.
50c. Mon.-Fri. $1.00. Sunday.

Vancouver Sun, Editor-in-Chief: Ian R. Haysom, 2250 Granville Street, Vancouver, BC V6H 3G2 *tel* 604-732-2111 *fax* 604-732-2323; London: Southam News, 4th Floor, 8 Bouverie Street, EC4Y 8AX *tel* 071-583 7322.
50c. Mon.-Thu. $1.00 Fri. 75c. Sat. Saturday Review, weekly arts magazine, accepts contributions. Travel, Op-Ed pieces considered. *Payment:* by arrangement.

Wascana Review of Contemporary Poetry & Short Fiction (1966), Kathleen Wall, c/o English Department, University of Regina, Regina, Sask. S4S 0A2 *tel* 306-585-4316.

$7.00 p.a. Bi-A. ($8.00 p.a. outside Canada) Criticism, short stories, poetry, reviews. Manuscripts from freelance writers welcome. *Length:* prose, not more than 6000 words; verse, up to 100 lines. *Payment:* $3 per page for prose; $10 per printed page for verse; $3 per page for reviews. Contributors also receive two free copies of the issue.

Winnipeg Free Press (1872), John Dafoe, PO Box 9500, Winnipeg, Manitoba R2X 3A2 *tel* 204-694-2022.
25c. Mon.-Fri. $1.25 Sat. 35c. Sun. Some freelance articles. *Payment:* $100.

THE REPUBLIC OF IRELAND AND NORTHERN IRELAND

Africa: St Patrick's Missions, Rev. Gary Howley, St Patrick's, Kiltegan, Co. Wicklow *tel* (0508) 73233 *fax* (0508) 73281.
£5.00 p.a. 9 p.a. Articles of missionary and topical religious interest. *Length:* up to 1000 words. *Illustrations:* line, half-tone, colour

Belfast Telegraph (1870), 124-144 Royal Avenue, Belfast BT1 1EB *tel* (0232) 321242 *telex* 74269 *fax* (0232) 242287 (editorial only).
26p. D. Any material relating to Northern Ireland. *Payment:* by negotiation.

Books Ireland (1976), Jeremy Addis, 11 Newgrove Avenue, Dublin 4 *tel/fax* (01) 2692185.
£1.25. M. (exc Jan, Jul, Aug; £15.00 p.a.) Reviews of Irish-interest and Irish-author books, articles of interest to librarians, booksellers and readers. *Length:* 800-1400 words. *Payment:* £35 per 1000 words.

Church of Ireland Gazette (1885, New Series 1963), Rev. Canon C.W.M. Cooper, 36 Bachelor's Walk, Lisburn, Co. Antrim BT28 1XN *tel* (0846) 675743 *fax* (0846) 675743.
25p. W. Church news, articles of religious and general interest. *Length:* 600-1000 words. *Payment:* according to length and interest.

Cork Examiner (1841), Fergus O'Callaghan, 1-6 Academy Street, Cork *tel* (021) 272722 *telex* 76014 *fax* (021) 275477.
70p. D. Features. Material *mostly commissioned. Length:* 1000 words. *Payment:* by arrangement.

Cyphers (1975), Leland Bardwell, Pearse Hutchinson, Eiléan Ní Chuilleanáin, Macdara Woods, 3 Selskar Terrace, Dublin 6 *tel* (01) 978866.
£2.00. 2 or 3 p.a. Poems, fiction, articles on literary subjects, translations. *Payment:* £7 per page (verse), £5 per page (prose).

Evening Herald, 90 Middle Abbey Street, Dublin 1 *tel* (01) 8731333.
55p. D. Articles. *Payment:* by arrangement. *Illustrations:* line, half-tone, cartoons.

Evening Press (1954), Sean Ward, Parnell House, Parnell Square, Dublin 1 *tel* (01) 713333 *fax* (01) 713097.
50p. D. News items, articles. *Payment:* NUJ rates.

Fortnight. An Independent Review of Politics and the Arts (1970), Robin Wilson, 7 Lower Crescent, Belfast BT7 1NR *tel* (0232) 232353/311337 *fax* (0232) 232650.
£1.70. M. Current affairs analysis, reportage, opinion pieces, cultural criticism, book reviews, poems. *Illustrations:* line, half-tone, cartoons. *Payment:* by arrangement.

The Furrow (1950), Rev. Ronan Drury, St Patrick's College, Maynooth, Co. Kildare *tel* (01) 6286215.

£1.35. M. Religious, pastoral, theological, social articles. *Length:* 3000 words. *Payment:* average £15 per page (450 words). *Illustrations:* line, half-tone.

The Honest Ulsterman (1968), Tom Clyde, 14 Shaw Street, Belfast BT4 1PT. £2.00. 3 p.a. Poetry, short stories, reviews, critical articles, poetry pamphlets. *Payment:* by arrangement.

Hotel and Catering Review, Frank Corr, Jemma Publications Ltd, Marino House, 52 Glasthule Road, Sandycove, Co. Dublin *tel* (01) 2800000 *fax* (01) 2801818.
£22.00 p.a. M. Short news and trade news pieces. *Length:* approx. 200 words. Features. *Payment:* £80 per 1000 words. *Illustrations:* half-tone, cartoons.

IMAGE (1974), Jane McDonnell, 22 Crofton Road, Dún Laoghaire, Co. Dublin *tel* (01) 2808415 *fax* (01) 2808309.
£1.50. M. Short stories of a high literary standard and of interest to women. *Length:* up to 3000 words. Interviews with actors, writers, etc.; human interest stories. *Payment:* by arrangement.

In Dublin (1976), Damian Corless, 6-7 Camden Place, Dublin 2 *tel* (01) 4784322 *fax* (01) 4781055.
£1.50. F. Dublin-related news features, oddball items, humour and interviews. *Length:* 500-2000 words. *Payment:* £80 per 1000 words. *Illustrated.*

Ireland of the Welcomes, Irish Tourist Board, Baggot Street Bridge, Dublin 2 *tel* (01) 6765871 *fax* (01) 6764765.
£2.00. Bi-M. Irish items with cultural, sporting or topographical background designed to arouse interest in Irish holidays. Mostly commissioned – *preliminary letter* preferred. *Length:* 1200-1800 words. *Payment:* by arrangement. *Illustrations:* scenic and topical, cartoons.

Ireland's Eye (1979), Lynn Industrial Estate, Mullingar, Co. Westmeath *tel* (044) 48868.
60p. M. Articles, features, short stories with an Irish flavour; cartoons. *Length:* 1200-2000 words. *Payment:* £10-£15; £4 for cartoons.

Ireland's Own (1902), Austen Channing, North Main Street, Wexford *tel* (053) 22155 *fax* (053) 23801.
40p. W. Short stories, written in a non-experimental, traditional manner with an Irish orientation (2000-2500 words); articles of interest to Irish readers at home and abroad (750-1000 words); general and literary articles (750-1000 words). Monthly special bumper editions, each devoted to a particular seasonal topic, i.e. New Year, St Valentine's, Spring, etc. Jokes and funny stories always welcome; suggestions for new features considered. *Payment:* varies according to quality and length. *Illustrations:* photos, cartoons.

Irish Farmers Journal (1948), Matthew Dempsey, Irish Farm Centre, Bluebell, Dublin 12 *tel* (01) 501166 *fax* (01) 520876.
95p. W. Readable, technical articles on any aspect of farming. *Length:* 700-1000 words. *Payment:* £100-£150 per article. *Illustrated.*

Irish Independent, Vincent Doyle, Independent House, 90 Middle Abbey Street, Dublin 1 *tel* (01) 8731666 *fax* (01) 8720304/8731787.
80p. D. Special articles on topical or general subjects. *Length:* 700-1000 words. *Payment:* editor's estimate of value.

Irish Journal of Medical Science (1st series 1832, 6th series January 1926, Volume 162, 1993), Royal Academy of Medicine, 6 Kildare Street, Dublin 2 *tel* (01) 767650 *fax* (01) 611684.
£10.00. M. (EU £60.00 post free; other rates on application) Official Organ of the Royal Academy of Medicine in Ireland. Original contributions in medicine,

surgery, midwifery, public health, etc.; reviews of professional books, reports of medical societies, etc. *Illustrations:* line, half-tone, colour.

Irish Medical Times, Maureen Browne, 15 Harcourt Street, Dublin 2   *tel* (01) 757461   *fax* (01) 757467.
£1.90. W. (£96.90 p.a.) Medical articles, also humorous articles with medical slant. *Length:* 850-1000 words. *Payment:* £60 per 1000 words. *Illustrations:* line, half-tone, colour, cartoons.

The Irish News and Belfast Morning News (1855), Tom Collins, 113-117 Donegall Street, Belfast BT1 2GE   *tel* (0232) 322226   *fax* (0232) 337505.
28p. D. Articles of historical and topical interest. *Payment:* by arrangement.

Irish Press, Hugh Lambert, Burgh Quay, Dublin 2   *tel* (01) 713333.
70p. D. Topical articles about 1000 words. *Payment:* by arrangement. *Illustrations:* topical photos, cartoons.

Irish Printer (1974), Frank Corr, Jemma Publications Ltd, 52 Glasthule Road, Sandycove, Co. Dublin   *tel* (01) 2800000   *fax* (01) 2801818.
£22.00 p.a. M. Technical articles and news of interest to the printing industry. *Length:* 800-1000 words. *Illustrations:* colour and b&w photos. *Payment:* £80 per 1000 words; £30.

Irish Times, Conor Brady, 11-15 D'Olier Street, Dublin 2   *tel* (01) 6792022   *telex* 93639   *fax* (01) 6793910.
75p. D. Mainly staff-written. Specialist contributions (800-2000 words) by commission on basis of ideas submitted. *Payment:* at editor's valuation. *Illustrations:* photos and line drawings.

IT (Irish Tatler), Morag Prunty, 126 Lower Baggot Street, Dublin 2   *tel* (01) 6608264   *fax* (01) 6619757.
£1.40. M. General interest women's magazine: beauty, interiors, fashion, cookery, current affairs, fiction, reportage and celebrity interviews. *Length:* 1000-3000 words. *Payment:* by arrangement.

Krino (1986), Gerald Dawe, Aodan MacPoilin, Eve Patten, Jonathan Williams, PO Box 65, Dún Laoghaire, Co. Dublin.
£5.00. 2 p.a. Poetry; fiction; work-in-progress; critical prose mostly on commissioned basis. *Illustrations:* line, half-tone. *Payment:* none, but complimentary copies of the magazine.

The Nationalist and Munster Advertiser (1890), Tom Corr, Queen Street, Clonmel, Co. Tipperary   *tel* (052) 22211.
55p. W. Requirements by arrangement. *Payment:* £22 per 1000 words. *Illustrations:* artwork.

Poetry Ireland/Éigse Éireann (1981), Pat Boran, Bermingham Tower, Upper Yard, Dublin Castle, Dublin 2   *tel* (01) 6714632   *fax* (01) 6714634.
£4.00. Q. Poetry, short lyric and sections from long poems, articles and reviews. *Payment:* by arrangement.

Portadown Times & Craigavon News (1859), David Armstrong, 14 Church Street, Portadown BT62 1HY   *tel* (0762) 336111.
48p. W. Articles. *Payment:* NUJ rates.

Reality (1936), Rev. Gerry Moloney cssr, Redemptorist Publications, Orwell Road, Rathgar, Dublin 6   *tel* (01) 961488/961688   *fax* (01) 961654.
75p. M. Illustrated magazine for Christian living. Articles on all aspects of modern life, including family, youth, religion, leisure. Illustrated articles, b&w photos only. Short stories. *Length:* 1000-1500 words. *Payment:* by arrangement; average £25 per 1000 words.

The Songwriter (1967), James D. Liddane, International Songwriters Association, PO Box 46, Limerick City   *tel* (061) 228837.
Available to members only as part of membership fee. M. Articles on songwriting and interviews with music publishers and recording company executives. *Length:* 400-5000 words. *Payment:* from £75 per page and by arrangement. *Illustrations:* photos.

Studies, An Irish quarterly review (1912), Rev. Noel Barber sj, 35 Lower Leeson Street, Dublin 2   *tel* (01) 6766785   *fax* (01) 6762984.
£3.00. Q. General review of social comment, literature, history, the arts. Articles written by specialists for the general reader. Critical book reviews. *Preliminary letter. Length:* 3500 words.

The Sunday Business Post (1989), Damien Kiberd, Merchants House, 27-30 Merchants Quay, Dublin 8   *tel* (01) 6799777   *fax* (01) 6796496/6796498.
85p. W. Features on financial, economic and political topics; also life style, media and science articles. *Illustrations:* colour and b&w photos, graphics, cartoons. *Payment:* by negotiation.

Sunday Independent, Aengus Fanning, Independent House, 90 Middle Abbey Street, Dublin 1   *tel* (01) 731333   *fax* (01) 721914.
90p. W. Special articles. *Length:* according to subject. *Illustrations:* topical or general interest, cartoons. *Payment:* at editor's valuation; good.

Sunday Life (1988), Martin Lindsay, 124 Royal Avenue, Belfast BT9 1EB   *tel* (0232) 331133   *telex* Belfast 74269   *fax* (0232) 248968.
45p. W. Items of interest to Northern Ireland Sunday tabloid readers. *Payment:* by arrangement. *Illustrations:* colour and b&w, cartoons.

The Sunday Press, Michael Keane, Burgh Quay, Dublin 2   *tel* (01) 6713333   *telegraphic address* Sceala, Dublin   *fax* (01) 6797452.
90p. W. Articles of general interest. *Length:* 1000 words. *Illustrations:* line, half-tone, cartoons.

Technology Ireland (1969), Mary Mulvihill and Tom Kennedy, Forbairt (Irish Science and Technology Agency), Glasnevin, Dublin 9   *tel* (01) 370101   *fax* (01) 367122.
£23.00 p.a. M. Articles, features, reviews and news on current science and technology. *Length:* 1500-2000 words. *Illustrations:* line, half-tone, colour. *Payment:* varies.

Theatre Ireland Magazine (1982), Justin Binding, 29 Main Street, Castlerock, Co. Derry BT51 4RA   *tel* (0265) 848130 (24 hours)/44141 ext 4167.
£2.50. Q. Irish and international: contemporary theatre practices, documentary and critical forum, book reviews. *Length:* 1000-3000 words. *Payment:* by arrangement. *Illustrations:* colour and b&w.

U magazine (1978), Maura O'Kiely, Smurfit Publications Ltd, 126 Lower Baggot Street, Dublin 2   *tel* (01) 6608264   *fax* (01) 6619757.
£1.50. M. Ireland's review for women today. Special reports, interviews, analysis, fashion, humour, travel, health, arts. Material *mostly commissioned. Length:* 1000 words. *Illustrations:* line, half-tone, colour. *Payment:* varies.

Ulster Grocer (1972), Brian McCalden, Greer Publications, 151 University Street, Belfast BT7 1HR   *tel* (0232) 231634   *fax* (0232) 325736.
£1.50. M. Topical features (500-1000 words) on agribusiness – retail and manufacturing – and exhibitions; news (200 words) with a Northern Ireland bias. *Illustrations:* colour and b&w photos. *Payment:* features £75, news £30; £40.

Ulster News Letter (1737), Geoff Martin, 46-56 Boucher Crescent, Boucher Road, Belfast BT12 6QY *tel* (0232) 680000 *fax* (0232) 664412.
28p. D. Unionist.

Waterford News & Star, Peter Doyle, 25 Michael Street, Waterford *tel* (051) 74951 *fax* (051) 55281.
65p. W. News articles. *Payment:* by arrangement. *Illustrations:* line, half-tone.

Woman's Way (1963), Celine Naughton, Smurfit Publications Ltd, 126 Lower Baggot Street, Dublin 2 *tel* (01) 6608264 *fax* (01) 6619757.
65p. W. Short stories, personality interviews, general features. *Length:* 1500-2000 words. *Payment:* £25-£80 approx. *Illustrations:* line, half-tone, colour.

The Word (1936), Fr Tom Cahill SVD (The Word Press, Hadzor, Droitwich), Divine Word Missionaries, Maynooth, Co. Kildare *tel* (01) 6289564/6286391 *fax* (01) 6289184.
50p. M. Catholic illustrated magazine for the family. Illustrated articles of general interest up to 1000 words and good picture features. *Payment:* by arrangement. *Illustrations:* photos and large colour transparencies, cartoons.

NEW ZEALAND

Newspapers are listed under the towns in which they are published.

(Auckland) New Zealand Herald (1863), P.J. Scherer, PO Box 32, Auckland *tel* (09) 379-5050 *fax* (09) 366-1568.
60c. D. Topical and informative articles 800-1100 words. *Payment:* minimum $50-$150. *Illustrations:* half-tone blocks (72 screen).

(Auckland) Sunday Star-Times, Michael Prain, News Media Auckland Ltd, PO Box 1409, Auckland *tel* (09) 379-7626.
$1.20. Sun.

Boating World (1945), Geoff Green, Private Bag 93209, Parnell, Auckland *tel* (09) 309-8292 *fax* (09) 309-6361.
$5.00. M. Features and photos, of New Zealand interest, on power or sail pleasure boating; also technical and how-to articles. *Payment:* $180 per 1000 words. *Illustrations:* line, half-tone, colour, cartoons.

(Christchurch) The Press, D.W.C. Wilson, Private Bag 4722, Christchurch *tel* (03) 379-0940 *fax* (03) 364-8492.
40c. D. Articles of general interest not more than 1000 words. *Illustrations:* photos and line drawings, cartoons. *Payment:* by arrangement.

Christchurch Star (1868), Mike Fletcher, Tuam Street, Christchurch *tel* (03) 379-7100 *fax* (03) 366-0180.
Free. Bi-W. Will consider freelance material, excluding travel.

(Dunedin) Otago Daily Times (1861), G.T. Adams, PO Box 181, Dunedin *tel* (03) 477-4760 *fax* (03) 477-1313.
50c. D. Any articles of general interest up to 1000 words, but preference is given to NZ writers. Topical illustrations and personalities. *Payment:* current NZ rates.

The Gisborne Herald (1874), Iain Gillies, PO Box 1143, 64 Gladstone Road, Gisborne *tel* (06) 867-2099 *telegraphic address* Herald, Gisborne.
12c. D. Topical features of local interest. *Length:* 1000-1500 words. *Payment:* by arrangement. *Illustrations:* bromides.

Hawke's Bay Herald Tribune, J.E. Morgan, PO Box 180, Karamu Road North, Hastings *tel* (06) 878-5155 *fax* (06) 876-0655.

55c. D. Limited requirements. *Payment:* $30+ for articles, $10+ for photos. *Illustrations:* web offset.

(Invercargill) The Southland Times (1862), C.A. Lind, PO Box 805, Invercargill *tel* (03) 218-1909 *telegraphic address* Times, Invercargill *fax* (03) 214-9905.
60c. D. Articles of up to 800 words on topics of Southland interest. *Payment:* by arrangement. *Illustrations:* line, half-tone, colour, cartoons.

The Listener (1939), Terry Snow, PO Box 7, Auckland *tel* (09) 623-1002 *fax* (09) 623-1011.
$2.20. W. Topical features of NZ and international interest: also features related to television and radio programmes. *Length:* up to 2000 words. *Illustrations:* colour and b&w, cartoons. *Payment:* by arrangement.

Management, Tracey Strange, Profile Publishing, Box 5544, Auckland *tel* (09) 358-5455 *fax* (09) 358-5462.
$5.95. M. Articles on the practice of management skills and techniques, individual and company profiles, coverage of business trends and topics. A NZ/Australian angle or application preferred. *Length:* 2000 words. *Payment:* by arrangement; minimum 23c. per word. *Illustrations:* photos, line drawings.

(Napier) The Daily Telegraph (1871), K.R. Hawker, PO Box 343, Napier *tel* (06) 835-4488 *fax* (06) 835-1129.
50c. D. Limited market for features. *Illustrations:* line, half-tone, colour. *Payment:* $50 upwards per 1000 words; $20 a picture.

The Nelson Evening Mail, David Mitchell, PO Box 244, 15 Bridge Street, Nelson *tel* (03) 548-7079 *fax* (03) 546-2802.
40c. D. Features, articles on NZ subjects. *Length:* 500-1000 words. *Payment:* up to $60 per 1000 words. *Illustrations:* half-tone, colour.

(New Plymouth) The Daily News (1857), Murray Goston, PO Box 444, Currie Street, New Plymouth *tel* (06) 758-0559 *fax* (06) 758-6849.
50c. D. Articles preferably with a Taranaki connection. *Payment:* by negotiation. *Illustrations:* half-tone, cartoons.

New Truth and TV Extra, News Media Auckland Ltd, Hedley Mortlock, 155 New North Road, Auckland, PO Box 1074 *tel* (09) 794-166 *fax* (09) 309-2279.
$1.00. W. Bold investigative reporting, exposés. *Length:* 500-1000 words, preferably accompanied by photos. *Payment:* about $150 per 500 words, extra for photos.

New Zealand Farmer, Hugh Stringleman, NZ Rural Press Ltd, PO Box 4233, 540 Great South Road, Greenlane, Auckland 5 *tel* (09) 579-1124 *fax* (09) 579-9589.
F. Authoritative, simply written articles on new developments in livestock husbandry, grassland farming, cropping, farm machinery, marketing. *Length:* 500 words. *Payment:* $150 per 1000 words.

New Zealand Woman's Weekly (1932), Jenny Lynch, NZ Magazines Ltd (Wilson & Horton), Private Bag, Dominion Road, Auckland 3 *tel* (09) 638-8105 *fax* (09) 630-9128.
$2.50. W. Pictorial features. Illustrated articles of general, family, celebrity interest, particularly with a NZ slant. *Length:* articles 750-1500 words. *Payment:* by arrangement. *Illustrations:* b&w, colour.

NZ Engineering (1946), R.H. Braddell, Engineering Publications Co. Ltd, PO Box 12241, Wellington *tel* (04) 473-9444 *fax* (04) 473-2324.

$4.50. M. Articles of interest to NZ engineers, not necessarily technical. *Preliminary letter* essential. *Payment:* by arrangement.

The Timaru Herald, B.R. Appleby, PO Box 46, Bank Street, Timaru   *tel* (03) 684-4129   *fax* (03) 688-1042.
50c. D. Topical articles. *Payment:* by arrangement. *Illustrations:* colour or b&w prints, cartoons.

TV Times (1993), Frank Nerney, PO Box 10043, Dominion Road, Auckland 3   *tel* (09) 623-6656   *fax* (09) 630-9128.
$1.00. W. Features related to television and films. *Length:* up to 600 words. *Illustrations:* colour, cartoons. *Payment:* by arrangement.

(Wellington) The Evening Post (1865), P.R. Cavanagh, PO Box 3740, 40 Boulcott Street, Wellington   *tel* (04) 474-0444   *fax* (04) 474-0237.
10c. D. General topical articles, 600 words. *Payment:* NZ current rates or by arrangement. News *illustrations*, cartoons.

SOUTH AFRICA

Newspapers are listed under the towns in which they are published.

Argus South African Newspapers
Cape Town: **Argus,** D, R1.20, **Weekend Argus,** Sat., R2.00; Durban: **Daily News,** 90c, **Sunday Tribune,** R2.80; Kimberley: **Diamond Fields Advertiser,** D, 80c; Johannesburg: **The Star,** D, R1.00, **Saturday Star,** R1.50, **Sunday Star,** R3.00; Pretoria: **Pretoria News,** D, R1.00. Accepts articles of general and South African interest. *Payment:* in accordance with an editor's assessment. Contributions should be addressed to the Bureau Chief, Argus South African Newspapers Ltd, 32-33 Hatton Garden, London EC1N 8DL   *tel* 071-831 0882   *fax* 071-831 2339, and not direct.

Bona, Republican Press, PO Box 32083, Mobeni 4060, Natal   *tel* (031) 422-041   *telegraphic address* Keur Durban; UK: Suite 15-17, The Outer Temple, 222-225 Strand, London WC2R 1BA   *tel* 071-353 2580.
R2.85. M. Articles on fashion, cookery, sport, music of interest to black people. *Length:* up to 3000 words. *Payment:* by arrangement. *Illustrations:* line, half-tone, colour, cartoons.

(Cape Town) Cape Times (1876), J.C. Viviers, Newspaper House, 122 St George's Street, Cape Town 8001   *tel* (021) 488-4911   *postal address* PO Box 11, Cape Town 8000; London: 1st Floor, 32-33 Hatton Garden, EC1N 8DL   *tel* 071-405 3742.
70c. D. Contributions must be suitable for a daily newspaper and must not exceed 800 words. *Illustrations:* photos of outstanding South African interest.

Car (1957), David Trebett, PO Box 180, Howard Place 7450   *tel* (021) 531-1391   *telegraphic address* Confrere   *telex* 526 933   *fax* (021) 531-3333.
R4.65. M. New car announcements with pictures and full colour features of motoring interest. *Payment:* by arrangement. *Illustrations:* colour, cartoons.

(Durban) Natal Mercury (1852), J.M. Patten, Natal Newspapers (Pty) Ltd, 18 Osborne Street, Greyville 4001   *tel* (031) 308-2300   *fax* (031) 308-2333.
70c. Mon.-Sat. Serious background news and inside details of world events. *Length:* 700-900 words. *Illustrations:* photos of general interest.

Fair Lady, Liz Butler, National Magazines, PO Box 1802, Cape Town 8000   *tel* (021) 406-2204   *telegraphic address* Ladyfair; London: *tel* 071-323 5843.
R4.00. F. Fashion, beauty, articles and stories for women including showbiz, travel, humour. *Length:* articles up to 2000 words, short stories approx. 3000

words; short novels and serialisation of book material. *Payment:* on quality rather than length – by arrangement.

Farmer's Weekly (1911), M. Fisher, PO Box 32083, Mobeni 4060, Natal *tel* (031) 422-041; UK: Suite 15-17, The Outer Temple, 222-225 Strand, London WC2R 1BA *tel* 071-353 2580 *fax* 071-353 2578.
R4.40. W. Articles, generally illustrated, up to 1000 words in length dealing with all aspects of practical farming and research with particular reference to conditions in Southern Africa. Includes women's section which accepts articles suitably illustrated, on subjects of interest to women. *Illustrations:* line, half-tone, colour, cartoons. *Payment:* according to merit.

Femina Magazine, Jane Raphaely, Associated Magazines, Box 3647, Cape Town 8000 *tel* (021) 462-3070.
R5.35. M. For young married women and those who would like to be. Humour, good fiction, personalities, real-life drama, medical breakthroughs, popular science. *Payment:* by arrangement. *Illustrations:* line, half-tone, colour.

Garden and Home, Margaret Wasserfall, Republican Press, PO Box 32083, Mobeni 4060, Natal *tel* (031) 422-041 *telegraphic address* Keur, Durban; UK: Suite 15-17, The Outer Temple, 222-225 Strand, London WC2R 1BA *tel* 071-353 2580 *fax* 071-353 2578.
R6.56. M. Well-illustrated articles on gardening, suitable for southern hemisphere. Articles for home section on furnishings, flower arrangement, food. *Payment:* by arrangement. *Illustrations:* half-tone, colour, cartoons.

(Johannesburg) Sunday Times, K.F. Owen, PO Box 1090, Johannesburg 2000 *tel* (011) 497-2300; London: South African Morning Newspapers Ltd, 32-33 Hatton Garden, EC1N 8DL *tel* 071-405 3742.
R3.00. Sun. Illustrated articles of political or human interest, from a South African angle if possible. Maximum 1000 words long and two or three photos. Shorter essays, stories and articles of a light nature from 500-750 words. *Payment:* average rate £100 a column. *Illustrations:* photos (colour or b&w) and line.

Living and Loving (1970), Angela Still, Republican Press, PO Box 32083, Mobeni 4060, Natal *tel* (031) 422-041 *telegraphic address* Keur Durban; UK: Suite 15-17, The Outer Temple, 222-225 Strand, London WC2R 1BA *tel* 071-353 2580 *fax* 071-353 2578.
R4.33. M. Romantic fiction, 1500-4000 words. Articles dealing with first-person experiences; baby, family and marriage, medical articles up to 3000 words. *Payment:* by merit.

Natal Witness (1846), D.J. Willers, 244 Longmarket Street, Pietermaritzburg, Natal 3201 *tel* (0331) 942-011 *fax* (0331) 940-468.
80c. D. Accepts topical articles. All material should be submitted direct to the editor in Pietermaritzburg. *Length:* 500-1000 words. *Payment:* average of R70 per 1000 words.

Personality, W. Christopher, Republican Press, PO Box 32083, Mobeni 4060, Natal *tel* (031) 422-041 *telegraphic address* Keur, Durban; UK: Suite 15-17, The Outer Temple, 222-225 Strand, London WC2R 1BA *tel* 071-353 2580.
R3.42. W. Illustrated. Primarily an entertainment-oriented magazine but also a market for articles about people and places, preferably with South African angle. Strong news features and/or photojournalism, 1000-4000 words, with b&w and colour photos. Short stories 1500-5000 words. *Payment:* by arrangement. *Illustrations:* usually commissioned.

Scope, D. Mullany, Republican Press, PO Box 32083, Mobeni 4060, Natal *tel* (031) 422-041 *telegraphic address* Keur, Durban; UK: Suite 15-17, The Outer Temple, 222-225 Strand, London WC2R 1BA *tel* 071-353 2580.
R5.30. F. Strong news features, well illustrated, about people and places in all parts of the world. *Length:* up to 4000 words. Short stories 1500-5000 words, serials from 20,000 words. *Illustrations:* half-tone, colour, cartoons.

South African Yachting (1957), Neil Rusch, PO Box 3473, Cape Town 8000 *tel* (021) 461-7472 *fax* (021) 461-3758.
R5.80. M. Articles on yachting, boating or allied subjects. *Payment:* R10 per 100 words. *Illustrations:* line, half-tone, cartoons; colour covers.

Southern Cross, PO Box 2372, Cape Town 8000 *tel* (021) 455-007 *telegraphic address* Catholic *fax* (021) 453-850 *e-mail* SANGONET SNO194.
R1.00. W. National English-language Catholic weekly. Catholic news reports, world and South African. 1000-word articles, cartoons of Catholic interest acceptable from freelance contributors. *Payment:* 87.5c. per column cm for all copy used. *Illustrations:* photos, R6 per column width, cartoons.

World Airnews, Tom Chalmers, PO Box 35082, Northway, Durban 4065 *tel* (031) 841-319.
£12.50. M. Aviation news and features with an African angle. *Payment:* £55 per 1000 words. *Illustrations:* photos, £35 each (conditional).

Your Family, Angela Waller-Paton, Republican Press, PO Box 32083, Mobeni 4060, Natal *tel* (031) 422-041 *telegraphic address* Keur, Durban; UK: Suite 15-17, The Outer Temple, 222-225 Strand, London WC2R 1BA *tel* 071-353 2580 *fax* 071-353 2578.
R4.33. M. Cookery, knitting, crochet and homecrafts. Short fiction, family drama, happy ending. *Payment:* by arrangement. *Illustrations:* continuous tone, colour and line, cartoons.

ZIMBABWE

The Chronicle (1894), S.A. Mpofu, PO Box 585, Bulawayo *tel* 65471.
90c. Mon.-Sat. Topical articles.

The Farmer, Modern Farming Publications (1928), Felicity Wood, Agriculture House, Leopold Takawira Street, PO Box 1622, Harare *tel* 753278/9 *telex* 22084 CFU ZW *fax* 750754.
Outside Africa: $400 p.a. airmail, $150 p.a. surface mail. W. Official journal of the Commercial Farmers' Union. Articles on all aspects of agriculture. *Payment:* by arrangement. *Illustrated.*

The Herald (1891), T.A.G. Sithole, PO Box 396, Harare *tel* 795771 *telegraphic address* Manherald, Harare *telex* 26196 *fax* 791311.
20c. D. Topical articles of news value. *Payment:* varies, depends on length, content and news value. *Illustrations:* bromides, colour, cartoons.

Mahogany, Gill Beach, PO Box UA589, Harare *tel* 705412 *telex* 4748 zw *fax* 705411.
$1.45. F. Articles concerning events and personalities; standard women's magazine formula. Average *length:* 1500 words. *Payment:* by arrangement. *Illustrations:* line, half-tone, colour.

The Manica Post, J. Gambanga, PO Box 960, Mutare *tel* 62780.
25c. W. Non-fiction articles only. *Length:* up to 500 words. *Payment:* by arrangement. *Illustrations:* half-tone.

Southern Africa Political & Economic Monthly (1987), Dr Ibbo Mandaza, PO Box MP 111, Mount Pleasant, Harare *tel* 727875 *telex* 26464 AAPS ZW *fax* 732735.
£2.00. M. (US$4.50/ZW$3.00) Features, articles, news on political, economic and social aspects of Southern Africa; also columns on culture, gender issues, sport, etc. Portuguese articles also published. *Length:* varies. *Illustrations:* colour and b&w photos. *Payment:* US$200 per 1000 words; Press agency rates.

The Sunday Mail (1935), C. Chikerema, PO Box 396, Harare *tel* 795771 *telegraphic address* Manherald, Harare *telex* 26196 *fax* 791311.
50c. W. Topical articles of news value. *Payment:* varies, depends on length, content and news value. *Illustrations:* bromides, colour, cartoons.

The Sunday News (1930), Lawrence Chikuwira, PO Box 585, Bulawayo *tel* 65471 *telex* 33481 ZMNEWS ZW *fax* 75522.
$1.00. W. Topical articles. *Payment:* by arrangement.

UNITED STATES OF AMERICA

Because of the difficulties in providing an up-to-date list of US magazines and journals, the *Yearbook* does not contain a detailed list. For general reference purposes, readers are referred to the list of US publications in the Overseas volume of *Willings Press Guide* (Reed Information Services), available in most reference libraries.

Readers who are particularly interested in the US market are referred to the following (please note that any payments should be made in US funds). *Writer's Market*, an annual guidebook giving editorial requirements and other details of over 4000 US markets for freelance writing, published by **Writer's Digest Books**, 1507 Dana Avenue, Cincinnati, OH 45207 ($26.95, plus $4.00 postage and handling); *The Writer's Handbook*, a substantial volume published by **The Writer Inc.**, 120 Boylston Street, Boston, MA 02116 ($29.95 plus $17.34 for airmail, $3.97 for surface mail). It contains 110 chapters, each written by an authority, giving practical instruction on a wide variety of aspects of freelance writing and including details of 3000 markets, payment rates and addresses. Also publishes books on writing fiction, non-fiction, poetry, articles, plays, etc.

The Writer Inc. also publish a monthly magazine *The Writer* ($35.00 p.a., must be in US funds) which contains articles of instruction on all writing fields, lists of markets for MSS and special features of interest to freelance writers everywhere.

Writer's Digest Books also publish the monthly magazine *Writer's Digest* ($25.95 per year) and the annual directories, *Novel and Short Story Writer's Market*, *Children's Writer's and Illustrator's Market*, *Poet's Market*, *Artist's Market* and many other books on creating and selling writing and illustrations.

For availability in the UK details may be obtained from: **Freelance Press Services,** Cumberland House, Lissadel Street, Salford M6 6GG *tel* 061-745 8850 *fax* 061-745 8865.

SUBMISSION OF MSS

When submitting material to US journals send your covering letter with the MS, together with International Reply Coupons. Make clear what rights are being offered for sale for some editors like to purchase MSS outright, thus securing world copyright, i.e. the traditional British market as well as the US market. MSS should be sent direct to the US office of the journal and not to any London office.

In many cases it is far better to send a preliminary letter giving a rough outline of your article or story. Enclose International Reply Coupons for reply. Most magazines will send a leaflet giving guidance to authors.

Writing for Newspapers

JILL DICK

Newspapers offer writers an enormous market. As new editions of the UK's estimated 1700 titles appear daily, weekly, fortnightly, monthly or at other regular intervals, there are over 100,000 papers to be filled in any one year.

The majority of these publications welcome – and sometimes rely on – freelance contributions from writers who take pains to provide what is wanted. Entry into the world of newspapers is not restricted to those who have been through an officially recognised course of indenture or instruction and emerge as full-time staff journalists. The abolition of the 'closed shop' extended the freedom of non-union writers but so wide a market may be a jungle for new entrants; it is easy to get lost and a close study of which papers to aim at, what to write, how to write it and how to get it to the paper is – among other prerequisites – essential for sustained success.

MARKETS

With so many to choose from, how do you find the one to target? You can consult the classified list of magazines starting on page 125, or *Willings Press Guide* will give you a more comprehensive indication of where to start your search. *British Rate and Data* (BRAD: Maclean Hunter House, Chalk Lane, Cockfosters, Herts. EN4 0BU) is the most reliable guide to circulation figures and readership profiles; 'studying the market' really means 'studying the readers'. But the best way to find markets is to keep looking for them. Pore over your newsagent's display and delve into the titles owned by Thomson Regional Newspapers, Northern Newspapers, United Newspapers and Reed Regional Newspapers who are some of the giants in the business of regional paid-for papers and freesheets (all those papers pushed through your letterbox without invitation or charge). Above all, read the papers and get to know how they think and what they like. The long-established high-circulation *Manchester Evening News* has an advertising slogan 'A FRIEND DROPPING IN'; be it a daily, weekly, national or local, that's how close you should feel to your chosen market.

WHAT TO WRITE – AND HOW

Sometimes it helps to target a market by defining your potential place in it. What readers want is what sells; and ordinary people are just like you and me. So what do we all want? Health, happiness, a good job, a home and enough money – within reason. We want people to respect us, we want to look after our loved ones and secure the future for our children. Not wishing to harm anyone else, we care most of all about *ourselves*. Write to satisfy that entirely natural wish among readers and you'll always give them what they want to read. Study newspaper advertisements. The popular papers have less need to rely on the revenue they receive from advertisers than do the more serious ones, but adverts reveal a good deal about the readership. They will also tell you about the general health of the newspaper, particularly the 'freesheets' which are the most dependent on selling advertising space. When you write for newspapers you may not be writing for posterity: whatever you write will have a brief life and will soon be lighting someone's fire or wrapping up the fish and chips. But when readers want it, editors buy it.

Regarding *how* to write for a newspaper one golden rule covers all others: your chosen market will reveal all you need to know and there is no better teacher. You're not sure about house style, length of articles, the best 'slant', what is and is not welcome? All the answers are there, in those pages.

FEATURES

Feature-writing is usually the first choice for freelances (although it is not necessarily the easiest way in) and the germ of any feature is an idea. If you can think about the viewpoint your copy is going to take as the idea grows in your mind, the feature will gradually take shape. Originality is always welcome (unlike unwarranted personal opinion) and it pays to look ahead. What will readers want explained? What information will be useful at some likely or known future occurrence? Whatever the topic or your intended treatment of it, you'll almost certainly need to do some serious research and – at least while you're writing it – make yourself an 'expert'. The word *feature* carries that very connotation in the newspaper world: that it is written with authority and accuracy by a writer who knows what (s)he is talking about. It matters not whether it is a 'one-off' item or one of a series of regularly published pieces; it must be *well-written*. If you prefer to call your copy an 'article' the same criteria apply: make yourself an expert before you consider sending your copy to an editor. One of the main reasons for editorial rejection is that the writer is merely dabbling with the story. Make sure, therefore, that your features *demand* attention. Often they will be tagged to news events or subjects of intense public interest or controversy. Whatever the topic, its importance at the time of submission or its value for any other reason, a good feature is only viable if it is relevant to people – and strong enough to hit the editor right between the eyes.

SPECIALITY FEATURES

Study any newspaper and you'll find regularly printed features on a variety of themes from gardening, horoscopes and pop music to pets, cookery and crosswords. These items are usually provided by freelances (a query to the paper will confirm whether this is so) who began their particular 'columns' by putting forward a *new* idea and supporting it with plenty of sample copy. A serious contributor prepares the ground by submitting earlier copy to the editor who will need to be assured of the new columnist's efficiency, dedication and – above all – *ability to meet deadlines*. This last point of timing may have little to do with what you write or how well you write it, but it takes precedence. Perhaps it's sad, but it's true; in practical terms copy that is 'all right' but on time is more acceptable than copy that is 'brilliant' but *too late*.

To start a new column (page, half-page, corner, etc.) you will need a constantly replenished stock of fresh ideas; putting yourself to a private test may reveal weaknesses before submitting the plan to crushing editorial judgement. Do you have the stamina – as well as the ideas – to pound out your copy every week or every *day*, as demanded? A regular column is not an undertaking to be accepted lightly but if it is successful it can open more doors and involve you in other fascinating writing jobs. Not least among the advantages of being a regular columnist is the arrival every month of a pre-negotiated fee.

INTERVIEWS

Interviews with celebrities are popular with readers, 'celebrities' being people readers want to know about; remember local interest may or may not be the same as national interest. As in all writing, the needs and wishes of the readers are the determining factors.

The eventual publication of an interview is preceded by a good deal of work. A subject 'interviewee' must be selected, approached, consent acquired and the date, time and place for the interview agreed. An editor will be pleased if prior publicity can be arranged to the paper's advantage. You will need to do your homework before the actual interview and delving into your interviewee's past will ensure you don't waste time (and cause annoyance) by asking questions you could have found answers to before you met. Ready with your questions and equipped with necessary pen, notebook and tape-recorder if required, arrive promptly. Keeping the preliminary greetings as brief as politeness allows should give your interview a good start but don't worry if a few moments pass before you feel able to relax, particularly if you are new to the task. Initial tenseness (which your interviewee may also experience) will soon fade.

When you come to write up the interview for the paper recall your own personal feelings as you listened to what your interviewee had to say. You will have discussed with the editor or gleaned from published interviews how much of 'you' there should be in your copy (do you appear as a friend, for example, or an unidentified voice and are your questions put directly or do you drop into reported speech?) but at all times it pays to remember how you felt and what you saw. These are the feelings and impressions you have to convey to your readers as you tell them what the interviewee said and did.

NO BEGINNERS, PLEASE

Notable among subjects generally unsuitable for non-staff freelances are sport, travel, reviewing, motoring and business. Normally these topics are covered by staff writers. 'Outside' contributions to these sections, occasional or regular, have to be exceptional, if not unique.

OTHER OPPORTUNITIES

If you enjoy writing small items of copy to keep the mind ticking over, fillers and anecdotes may buy you a few sheets of stamps. To a freelance writer nothing overheard or observed is ever wasted; your chosen market will reveal the type and length required. Because of their brevity it is best to file (i.e. deliver to the paper) them as a batch rather than as single items. Leaven your copy with humour, remembering that newspapers = *people*, and you'll have editors eating out of your hand.

NEWS

While the arrival or non-arrival of feature material can to varying extents be left to chance, the gathering of news must be guaranteed by the employment of regular staff. Nevertheless there is often a place for the news-conscious freelance who has ascertained terms of reference before submitting news items to a paper. When you discuss your prospects ask the editor to give you the telephone number of the newsdesk or the paper's FREEFONE number. Most papers have one but it is not always easy to find out what it is! Developing a nose for news isn't difficult if you have (or cultivate) a genuine interest in people, what they do and what happens to them. Read your chosen paper carefully and regularly to understand what is and what is not news; a successful reporter not only discovers news other people might miss but knows how to write it up and how to get it to the paper as quickly as possible.

HELP

When it comes to researching for commissioned or on-spec work your own cuttings file, compiled with forethought over months and years, will repay you many times. It should be constantly be checked and kept up to date. For published help with research of every type there is nothing to beat Ann Hoffmann's *Research for Writers* (A. & C. Black), while public and newspaper libraries offer a wide variety of assistance. Personal help may be obtained from several bodies and organisations for journalists and from other writers (see *Directory of Writers' Circles* on page 648).

BUSINESS

Visual presentation of your manuscript should follow the accepted pattern; crisp and clean double spacing in unjustified type on white A4 paper with decent margins all round. Each page is numbered (except the first) and carries a catchline at the top to identify it with its brethren should it become detached. Indicate when more pages follow and which is the last. Paragraphs are indented (except the first) and have no extra line spacing between them. Quote a rounded-up number of words at the foot of the last page and repeat your name, address and telephone number. Copy must be titled at the top of the first page but separate title pages are redundant if an accompanying letter *briefly* reminds the editor of the relevant details: what the copy is about, its length, treatment, conditions of sale (e.g. if it is commissioned work) and any fee that has been negotiated. Copyright in the work normally remains yours and although it is not essential to mention you are selling only First British Serial Rights you might feel safer to do so. A detailed account of what you should be paid appears in *Freelance Writing for Newspapers* (A. & C. Black). Don't forget that newspapers, unlike most magazines, expect to be invoiced for published work, whether commissioned or not; *if you fail to send an invoice you are unlikely to be paid.*

Keeping your records straight will save time and trouble; a lined exercise book will itemise each piece of work with an identifying number or on a separate page, giving details of title and length, destination, dates of despatch and acceptance (with the occasional rejection?), fee agreed and paid – and any other information you wish to record. Another equally important book will list your income and expenses; careful attention to the latter is important when submitting a profit/loss account to the Inland Revenue (see article on **Income Tax for Writers and Artists**).

Writing Magazine Articles

JOHN HINES

For the would-be writer there can be little doubt that magazine articles offer the easiest way to get into print. The magazine market is vast and is growing steadily. *Willings Press Guide 1994* recorded no less than 10,152 UK periodicals, excluding newspapers, and the majority of these rely on freelance contributions to fill their pages.

New magazines appear almost daily and, although some founder, most of them survive. The subject material covered by these magazines is so varied that few writers would find their special interests not included.

The magazines range from the modest budget publications to the expensive glossies. Beginners can cut their teeth on the lower end of the market, knowing that, although the fees are modest, the competition is small. These publications provide an excellent start for building skills, self-confidence and credibility. The opportunity for steadily moving up-market is there for the taking, until the writer reaches the level which fulfils his or her ambitions.

The pathway to successful article writing is surprisingly simple:

- have a good idea for a subject
- find a suitable market
- produce an interesting and well-written article for that market
- submit a professional-looking typescript
- have a sound sales strategy throughout

THE IDEA

Established article-writers usually have files bulging with ideas. They will include newspaper and magazine clippings, jottings from TV and radio programmes and personal observations. Almost anything which intrigues the writer or fires the imagination is worth a place in the ideas file.

There is an adage in the writing world that it pays to write about what you know. Certainly this is a good idea, for you write more comfortably and competently on a familiar subject, but the wise diversify as well.

In selecting subjects, it pays to pick those which interest you or, better still, fascinate you. They provide absorbing research and can result in articles rich in original thought with your enthusiasm showing through. As a freelance, you have the luxury of being able to pick and choose, so why not select those articles which are a pleasure to write?

MARKET STUDY

Successful writers know that effective market study is vital. Any editor will tell you that the vast majority of unsolicited material which lands on their desk is quite unsuitable. The material may be wrong in length, style or choice of subject. Yet studying a copy of the magazine could have helped to avoid these mistakes.

Try to read at least two recent copies of the magazine for which you are aiming to write. Analyse it carefully. Check the number of articles which are staff-written. You can usually find the names of the staff in the front of the magazine. By studying several issues you may also discover that there are contributors with regular slots. From this information you can deduce the opportunities which exist for the freelance.

If the magazine looks promising, study the type of subject which the editor favours. Check the approximate length of the average article. Ask yourself if the magazine's style is one with which you would be comfortable or to which you could adapt.

Few writers seem to study the advertisements and this is a big mistake. Advertising agencies spend a great deal of money on painstaking expert research, aimed at identifying the typical reader. By studying the advertisements you can benefit from this valuable information which can be most helpful when slanting your article to the readers' interests.

Studying the *Writers' & Artists' Yearbook* can give you a good insight into the requirements of many magazines, even including the fees they pay.

Freelance Market News is the best market newsletter for the freelance (see the further reading list on page 123). However, the finest market information is that which freelances compile for themselves from personal experience. A card filing system is useful here but, like all market information, its value depends on its being kept up to date.

RESEARCH AND ACCURACY

Although some articles can be written from personal experience or knowledge, most articles require some sound current research. The public libraries can be very helpful, particularly if you enlist the help of the qualified librarian rather than the library assistant.

The copyright libraries, of which the British Library is the best known, are superb. Would-be researchers must establish their bona-fides before being issued with a ticket.

All facts should be checked for accuracy, going back to the source wherever possible. The books of others are not infallible, even reference books. Errors can be embarrassing and inevitably attract unwelcome letters from readers.

Researched material must be filed away for future use and an effective filing system is necessary.

The best book on the subject is undoubtedly *Research for Writers* by Ann Hoffmann (see the further reading list on page 123).

Research may entail interviewing people and this is a skill which the freelance should consider developing. For effective interviews, sound preparation is important. Research in advance as much as possible about the interviewee and their field of interest. Make a list of important questions in logical sequence. But be prepared to divert from your questions and follow any unexpected revelations. If you use a tape-recorder, test it beforehand and always carry spare batteries and tapes. It is essential to have a notebook as a back-up and to carry spare pens.

Sensitivity and courtesy should be the criteria for all interviewing for normal articles. Start with easy general questions. Guide the interview gently, but firmly. Wind up the interview as you began, on an easy note. The interviewee should be left with the feeling that it has been an enjoyable experience.

Some interviewees ask if they can vet the finished article. You should always politely refuse, but do offer to allow them to withdraw anything they may regret saying.

(For more information on interviewing, see both *Freelance Writing for Newspapers* and *The Way to Write Magazine Articles* in the further reading list on page 123.)

NON-LINEAR THINKING

A stumbling block for many inexperienced writers is beginning their article, particularly when faced with a daunting mass of notes, clippings and research references.

Related research material must be associated and the various aspects considered in order of importance. However, when marshalling material, we often tend to arrange it in a linear fashion, rather like a shopping list. This tends to restrict our thinking on each point.

It has been found that non-linear thinking stimulates ideas and their logical development. It is this method which I use as a framework for my articles, particularly those which are complex.

Non-linear flow-of-thought patterns are easy to compile and to use. The subject is written in the centre of a large sheet of paper with the major aspects to be covered radiating out from it. From these, further spurs are drawn, filling in

Organic Gardening (mind map)

ORGANIC GARDENING

WHAT IS IT?
- Growing crops naturally
- Working with rather than against nature

WHY?
- Tastier crops
- Improves soil
- Better plants
  - More resistant to
    - Pests
    - Disease
  - Compete better with weeds
- Healthier
  - No insecticides
  - No poisons
    - Safer for
      - Humans
      - Pets
      - Wildlife
    - No weedkillers
  - No artificial fertilisers
    - Which...
      - Cause nitrogen pollution
      - Are expensive
      - Unbalance soil
      - And destroy soil's structure

HOW?
- Pest control
  - Biological
    - Natural predators
      - Birds
      - Frogs
      - Hedgehogs
      - Ladybirds
      - Hover flies
        - How to encourage?
    - Purchased
  - Organic sprays
  - Special strategies
    - Cabbage root-fly collars
    - Carrot-fly barriers
    - Companion planting
      - Tomatoes/tagetes
      - Onions/carrots
    - Slug traps
- Weed control
  - Hoeing
  - Mulching
    - Organic
      - Newspapers etc.
    - Plastic sheeting
- Organic manures
  - Green manure
  - Farmyard
  - Compost
    - Home-made
    - Commercial
      - Methods
        - Trenches
        - Heaps
        - Commercial containers
          - Boxes

© JOHN HINES 1990

other important material. Less significant points are added on minor spurs until all aspects are covered.

The illustration shows a typical pattern developed for an article on organic gardening. One strong aspect has been highlighted for a possible further article on organic pest control.

Never discard these patterns. They should be filed away for future use as a valuable concise reference to your research material.

THE ARTICLE STRUCTURE

We all develop our own style, but it is important to learn to modify it to suit the requirements of our market. The majority of articles are relatively short and must put over their story crisply without wasting words. Often this can best be done with fairly short sentences and relatively short paragraphs. Never write long convoluted sentences which require reading more than once to understand.

The opening. The first paragraph of an article has special importance. It must grip the editor's attention immediately, its purpose being to force the editor to read on. You can often make your opening irresistible by selecting a point from your article which is intriguing, startling or even audacious.

The body. You will not sell an article on the strength of its opening. The body of the article must fulfil the promise of that good first paragraph. It is here that the main text or message of your article will be unfolded. Your thought patterns will help you to move logically from one aspect to the next in a smooth progression and ensure that nothing important is left out.

The end. The poor article appears to finish when the writer runs out of ideas. A good ending must aim to tie up any loose ends positively. The way it does this depends a great deal on the subject. It can be speculative – a look into the future, perhaps. It might go back to answer a question posed in the beginning.

Avoid a mere recap of the main text for this gives a weak ending. Try to set aside some 'meat' to include in the ending, if possible. This could leave the reader with a strong point to ponder over.

Dialogue. Dialogue can breathe life into an article and give it sparkle. It must be used judiciously, for over-use may unbalance the article. It is often effective when used appropriately as the first sentence of an article.

THE TYPESCRIPT

The conventional layout of the typescript is covered elsewhere in this handbook (see under **Preparation of Materials, Resources**). However, an article for the British magazine market does have the addition of a cover sheet.

The cover sheet. The conventional cover sheet has the writer's name and address in the top right-hand corner. Centred half-way down the page is the article's title, followed by the writer's name. If you are using a pseudonym it goes here, not at the top.

About two-thirds down the page on the left you should type the number of words in the article. Two or three lines' space below, type in the rights which you are offering the editor. For normal practical purposes this would be First British Serial Rights, usually abbreviated to 'FBSR offered' – see below. The cover sheet is not used for USA markets.

ILLUSTRATIONS

Good illustrations enhance an article, making it more saleable. The writer/illustrator also receives an extra fee. It is self-evident that all article-writers should try to produce their editors' delight – the words and pictures package.

If you are a reasonable photographer, you are half-way there. If you are not, there is little excuse for not trying with the modern fully automatic cameras.

Study magazines to see, not only whether they use black and white or colour, but also the way they use illustrations. Do they tend to be small and plentiful to assist in the understanding of the text? Does the editor favour large dramatic pictures, sometimes covering as much as a whole page or even two? Finally, can your pictures match those in the magazine?

Your pictures must be pin-sharp and properly exposed. They must avoid all the basic mistakes of composition which are outlined in any photographic primer.

For black and white you should submit glossy, borderless prints, 254 × 203 mm (10 × 8 in). Transparencies are demanded by most quality magazines for their colour illustrations, although a small but growing number of periodicals will consider colour prints. You must always confirm that a magazine uses colour prints before submitting them.

Most magazines use 35 mm transparencies, but many prefer a larger format for their covers.

Writers who turn to supplementing their writing with photography rarely look back. They report better sales and increased earnings.

(Illustrations are covered in depth in *The Way to Write Magazine Articles*; see further reading list on page 123.)

RIGHTS

In offering First British Serial Rights you are inviting the magazine to publish your article once and for the first time in Britain. You are retaining the right to sell it elsewhere in the world.

Some editors will try to wring all rights from you. Do not give way as it leaves the magazine free to sell your article world-wide and pocket the proceeds.

Second British Serial Rights are rarely sold, but a magazine may ask to buy them if they see your article in print and wish to reproduce it themselves. You would normally accept, but as Second Rights earn lower fees than First Rights, you should not make any particular effort to sell them. It pays to rewrite the original article, reslanting it to suit the new market and possibly introducing some new material. This effectively makes it a new article for which the First Rights may be legitimately offered.

THE SALES STRATEGY

Probably the most common reason for good articles failing to get published is lack of a sound sales strategy. A surprisingly large number of writers complete a good article and then peddle it hopefully around the markets. This is quite the wrong way. Your article must always be written specifically for the market you have in mind.

Your sales strategy should begin the moment you look at your material and can say: 'Yes, there is enough here for a good article.' You then use your market study to find a number of likely magazines which might publish such an article.

Query letters. The sound query letter is essential for sustained success in the article-writing field. Examine your list of possible magazines and arrange them in order of your preference. Select the top one and write your query letter to its editor.

The letter should be brief and should state your idea for the article, mentioning any special slant you have in mind. If you are qualified in any way to write such an article or if you have a 'track-record' of writing in that field, you should say so. Also mention if you have suitable illustrations.

Ask the editor how many words he would like to see. It is particularly important to ask for the magazine's rates for contributors. Always enclose an sae. The query letter is your initial shop-window and its quality should be the best of which you are capable.

If the editor turns down the idea, write immediately to the next magazine on your list and so on.

If the editor likes your idea, you may get a commission, but if you are unknown it is more likely that you will be asked to submit the article on spec. Some editors try to side-step divulging their rates in advance, but you must be professional and insist on knowing them.

An acceptance is the usual outcome from an editor's expression of interest. As you become better at matching subject to magazine, writing shrewd query letters and producing sound articles, your rejections should drop to virtually nil.

On acceptance, the professional freelance looks around for another outlet. Writing is easy, it is the research which takes the time. Make sure you get the maximum from your research (see above).

Payment. Some magazines pay on acceptance, but the majority pay on publication. Avoid those magazines which hold your material on spec with no guarantee of ultimate publication. They are not worthy of consideration.

You should never be afraid to question offers of low rates, for many editors will negotiate. If low rates are not improved upon, be professional and withdraw the offer of your article.

FRESH FIELDS

When you have written articles extensively on a subject, it may be worth considering whether the subject is suitable for a non-fiction book. If so, your articles could be valuable as evidence of your writing skills, your knowledge of the subject and the wide interest the subject can generate. Many writers have used their published articles as a means of gaining an advance contract for a non-fiction book. (This is covered in *The Way to Write Non-fiction*; see further reading on page 123.)

Writing for the European Union

BARBARA WOOD-KACZMAR

Another year, another name. After the Maastricht Treaty of 1993 the 12 countries of the European Community became the European Union, or EU. The new name isn't important as EU is not added to the bottom of addresses like USA, but discerning writers will realise their home market has grown yet again. One of the EU's first acts was to allow six more countries access to the European single market, swelling its size to 372 million. The writer's home market, once restricted to the UK, is now Europe, the world's largest trader.

The addition of the Nordic countries means for the first time British books are sold freely from the Arctic to the Mediterranean. And journalists benefit too. Sports writers gain the ski slopes of Austria, Norway and Sweden, energy specialists acquire Iceland's geothermal electricity and music writers now have Finland's Sibelius. Financial journalists will net the bankers of Liechtenstein whenever that state unravels its customs arrangements with Switzerland – the Swiss voted to remain aloof from this European re-birth.

And yet more change is in the pipeline. On 1 January 1995, Norway, Sweden, Austria and Finland are scheduled to become full EU states, raising the total EU membership to 16.

The birth pangs of creating a European single market have already brought turbulence to British magazine publishing – familiar titles have folded and new ones are launched to fight off the European invaders. But writers now benefit from a larger UK market – German newcomers *Take a Break* and *Bella* head the women's bestseller list while Dutch publisher VNU has expanded the business and computer sectors.

And there is the greater challenge of writing for magazines in the EU. EMAP's aggressive policy of launching and acquiring European consumer titles provides new writing opportunities on the continent but mergers may not be such good news. When Reed International combined with the Dutch publisher Elsevier to create one of the world's largest media empires, British journalists lost their union rights while Dutch writers kept theirs.

Right now, British writers are in a unique position to exploit the European market as the main EU business language is English. Advertisements in the *Guardian*'s media supplement reflect an upsurge in EU demand for English-speaking writers, especially for new radio and TV stations being set up on the continent. And in 1993 the NUJ ran the first UK course to help TV comedy script writers get a foothold in Europe. Journalists fluent in a second European language are also sought by computer, pollution and media titles. However, German will become increasingly dominant when Austria becomes a full EU member – and other EU writers are multilingual.

All speciality writers will find a magazine somewhere in the EU which publishes their topic. The language situation must be checked out first and various pitfalls avoided (see below). Otherwise the usual rules of good writing apply: an article must be tailored to the magazine style and written with respect for the sensitivities of its readers.

EU countries are signatories to the Universal Copyright Convention and in many the author's moral right not to have his/her work distorted has been part of the law for years. However, a single European copyright is still years away.

HOW TO SUBMIT MSS TO EU MAGAZINES

Syndication (see page 139)

This is the easiest method for original MSS and also for articles previously published in the UK, if the UK rights only have been sold. A few syndicates report an increase in British writers selling to Europe but many have noticed little change.

Commission fees are usually around 50%, reflecting higher European payments but both translation facilities and fees may vary. BIPS has no translation fee while Europress Features charges per page. Some syndicates may translate only one language, e.g. Features International translates only German. Illustrated material is preferred and the most popular subjects remain Royalty, international celebrities and science and medicine with a strong human interest. Recently romantic fiction, real life crime and detection and women's interests have become more sellable and travel features are more in demand. Interesting events in Britain have a shelf life of six weeks on the continent but news items and political features are not required.

Pan-European magazines

Pan-European magazines are publications sold throughout the EU and aimed at an all-European readership, e.g. *Euromoney*, *Construction Europe* and *European Chemical News*. These English-language magazines and newspapers, e.g. *The European*, pay well for freelance material tailored to their style. EMAP Images' *PC Review* is aimed at people who use computers for entertainment or non-business applications.

Other pan-Europeans change their language according to the country (e.g. *Prima*) and also their title (*Essentials* is called *Avantage* in France and *Pratica* in Italy). These women's publications are less easy to penetrate: each national title is geared to that market alone and there may be no connection between their different editions.

However some magazine publishers will forward MSS from their London offices to their mainland counterparts. Others hire writers with linguistic skills as editorial consultants for continental editions (e.g. BBC's *Wildlife Magazine*'s German edition) or swap editorial with their continental partners (e.g. Reed Business Publishing's *Motor Transport* and *Commercial Motor*). See *Willings Press Guide* for pan-European publishers' London offices.

Subjects in demand include science, medicine, consumer marketing, pollution and law.

Do it yourself

The go-it-alone approach is not difficult. Choose a country you have some knowledge of and an affinity for: then read the appropriate Department of Trade and Industry country profile for an idea of its business scene and publishing sector. These excellent profiles are in reference libraries or available from the DTI at £11 each – none has been updated yet so buy only new issues.

Select your magazine from *Willings Press Guide*, the one essential tool. EU periodicals are in volume 2, listed according to country. Each entry includes subject, readership, editor's name, publisher and UK representative. An expanded classified list is helpful to speciality writers. English-language magazines are described as such but the few examples may be academic journals, not commercial concerns.

Send a preliminary letter to the editor along with a synopsis, photocopies of previous work and an International Reply Coupon. Never send MSS or photos unless commissioned and stipulate the material is for use only in the country of publication. Otherwise the publisher can claim copyright and peddle the rights world-wide. Similarly, make it clear your work should not be fed into a database or retrieval system without prior consent. Rates of pay should be agreed in advance.

The magazine's UK representative may provide back copies for commissioned writers: s/he may also know if the editor speaks English. Translation costs are sometimes deducted from your fee but double taxation exemption forms are no longer necessary.

Subjects in demand are environmental matters and interviews with famous people – it may be cheaper for an EU magazine editor to commission interviews from British writers on the spot. Hobbies, e.g. sailing, photography, camping and computers are also popular. And high quality photos need no translation – articles with photos are usually easy to sell.

SOLVING THE LANGUAGE PROBLEM

In descending order of English usage the EU countries are: Ireland, Holland, Germany, Belgium, Denmark and Luxembourg; Portugal, Spain, France, Italy and Greece. Generally speaking, editors in countries in the second half expect correspondence as well as articles to be in their own language. But as areas popular with British tourists and expatriates, they may have small English-language publishing sectors worth investigating. And English is commercially acceptable in Nordic countries.

Don't be tempted to translate your MSS yourself. The Institute of Translation and Interpreting (318a Finchley Road, London NW3 5HT   *tel* 071-794 9931; see page 645) maintains a national register of professional translators. Members of the Society of Authors may contact the Translators' Association, a specialised unit within their organisation. Fees for French, German, Italian and Spanish start from £35 per 1000 words but Greek and Scandinavian languages cost more. Highly technical texts can cost from £60 per 1000 words. Local colleges may offer private translation facilities but few provide a 24-hour service.

CHANGES IN BOOK PUBLISHING

With the retail value of the total Union book market estimated at £15 billion, competition is fierce. EU book publishers have already moved into the UK for access to the enormous English-language markets world-wide – see *Willings* for their addresses or consult Cassell's *Directory of Publishing, Continental Europe* 1995. For the best deal on translation rights, a British agent is advisable.

Book sales should continue to hold up while VAT on British books is permitted to remain at zero. And authors should benefit from increased royalties: UK publishers may offer single, exclusive licences for the entire Union based on the UK price.

SOURCES OF INFORMATION

1. *Willings Press Guide*, volume 2 *Overseas*, 121st edn, 1995 (Reed Information Services, Windsor Court, East Grinstead House, East Grinstead, West Sussex RH19 1XA   *tel* (0342) 326972).
2. Cassell's *Directory of Publishing, Continental Europe* 1995 (Cassell plc, Stanley House, 3 Fleet's Lane, Poole, Dorset BH15 3AJ   *tel* (0202) 670581   *fax* (0202) 666219).
3. DTI: Department of Trade and Industry (see page 522). For a country profile or publications catalogue contact DTI Export Publications, PO Box 55, Stratford-upon-Avon, Warks. CV37 9GE   *tel* (0789) 296212   *fax* (0789) 299096. The new address for general queries is Exports to Europe Branch, Kingsgate House, 66-74 Victoria Street, London SW1E 6SW   *tel* 071-215 5336. DTI library facilities are available at London and Regional offices.
4. Embassies (see **Government Offices and Public Services**). Most will supply lists of magazines and newspapers in their countries, publishers' and representatives' addresses (useful as changes are frequent) as well as circulation figures and names of editors. Some lists are more comprehensive than others! Embassies usually know the UK addresses of their countries' major publishers.
5. Chambers of Commerce are comprehensive information centres. Visitors may study reference books on publishing or photocopies may be supplied on request. Some Cultural Institutes are located outside London.
6. The European Commission discusses its proposals with professionals before legislation. Phone the London office (071-973 1992) for information or to air your views.
7. The European Parliament is the only directly elected body in the EU. Your MEP or the London office (*tel* 071-222 0411) should know of changes in the legislative pipeline affecting writers or their specialities.

HELPFUL ASSOCIATIONS

1. The National Union of Journalists can raise grievances, such as non-payment or breach of copyright, with European publishers either on its own or through its affiliated European unions. The NUJ maintains lists of EU unions of journalists (see page 633).
2. The Society of Authors (see page 650) normally advises on problems arising in the UK but it will refer a member having problems with a European publisher to the foreign authors' society, as all these belong to the Congress of European Writers' Organisations. However if disputes arise over payments the cost of going to law may be prohibitive. Writers who regularly or solely write for an EU country should join the relevant authors' society.
3. The Writers' Guild (see page 653) works out common European policies on Public Lending Rights and minimum terms publishing agreements through the biennial European Writers' Congress.

FURTHER READING FOR MAGAZINE WRITERS

Buzan, Tony, *Use Your Head*, BBC, 3rd edn, 1989. Non-linear thinking.

Dick, Jill, *Freelance Writing for Newspapers*, A. & C. Black, 1991. Writing articles for newspapers.

Dick, Jill, *Writing for Magazines*, A. & C. Black, 1994. Writing articles for magazines.

Freelance Market News, Freelance Press Services, Lissadel Street, Salford M6 6GG (on subscription). Monthly.

Hines, John, *The Way to Write Magazine Articles*, Hamish Hamilton, 1987. Writing articles for magazines.

Hines, John, *The Way to Write Non-fiction*, Hamish Hamilton, 1990. Turning articles into books.

Hoffmann, Ann, *Research for Writers*, A. & C. Black, revised edn, 1992. Manual on factual research.

Howard, Godfrey, *The Good English Guide*, Pan Macmillan, 1993.

Legat, Michael, *The Nuts and Bolts of Writing*, Robert Hale, 1989. For those needing to brush up on writing basics.

The Oxford Writers' Dictionary, Oxford Reference, 1990.

Willings Press Guide, Reed Information Services. Annual media directory.

Recent UK Magazine Changes

The following changes have taken place since the last edition of the *Yearbook*.

Changes of Name and Mergers

The Artist's & Illustrator's Magazine *now* Artists and Illustrators
Arts Review *now* Art Review
Cycling *now* Cycling Weekly
Justice of the Peace *now* Justice of the Peace and Local Government Law
Outdoor Action *now* Outdoor
The Post *now* UCW Journal
The Skier *now* The Skier and The Snowboarder
Southern Evening Echo *now* The Southern Daily Echo
Stamp Monthly *now* Gibbons Stamp Monthly
Times Scottish Education Supplement *now* Times Educational Supplement
    Scotland
World Bowls *now* World of Bowls

Newspapers and Magazines Ceased Publication

And What Of Tomorrow?
Annabel
Beezer-Topper
Bestseller
Birds Illustrated
British Book News
Construction Weekly
Cornish Life
Devon Life
Engineering
Film Monthly
Gloucestershire Life
Guide Patrol
Million
Money Week
Scotland on Sunday Magazine
Somerset & Avon Life
Y Faner

Classified Index of Newspapers and Magazines

Commonwealth, Irish and South African Journals

This index can be only a broad classification. It should be regarded as a pointer to possible markets, and should be used with discrimination.
Addresses for newspapers and magazines start on page 5.

Short Stories (*See also* Literary)

Active Life
Ambit
Annabel
*Australian Women's Weekly
Bad Attitude
Bella
Best
Catch
Chat
Christian Herald
Company
Cosmopolitan
Essentials
*Fair Lady (SA)
Family Circle
*Femina (SA)
*Fiddlehead (Can.)
Fly-Fishing & Fly-Tying
Granta
Greenscene
*Honest Ulsterman

*IMAGE (Ire.)
Interzone
*Ireland's Eye
*Ireland's Own
Iron
*IT (Ire.)
*(Johannesburg) Sunday Times
    (SA)
Just Seventeen
*Living and Loving (SA)
London Magazine
Loving
*Malahat Review (Can.)
My Weekly
*New Idea (Aus.)
People's Friend
*Personality (SA)
*Quadrant (Aus.)
Rattler's Tale
*Redoubt (Aus.)

*Reality (Ire.)
Risqué
*Scope (SA)
Scots Magazine
Songwriting and Composing
Stand
Staple
Storm
Sunday Post
SuperBike
Take a Break
*Wascana Review (Can.)
Woman and Home
*Woman's Day (Aus.)
Woman's Own
*Woman's Way (Ire.)
Woman's Weekly
Xenos
*Your Family (SA)
Yours

Long Complete Stories
From 8000 words upwards

My Weekly Story Library

People's Friend Library

Secrets Story Library

Serials

*Fair Lady (SA)
My Weekly

People's Friend
Woman and Home

Woman's Weekly

Letters to the Editor

Annabel
Art & Craft
*Australian Woman's Weekly
BBC Gardeners' World
    Magazine
Best
The Big Issue
Buster
Catch
Chat

Child Education
Choice
Control and Instrumentation
Daily Express
Daily Star
*Dolly (Aus.)
The Electrical Times
Essentials
*Fair Lady (SA)
Family Circle

*Femina (SA)
Freelance Writing &
    Photography
*The Furrow (Ire.)
Garden News
Good Housekeeping
Ideal Home
Junior Education
Living
Mandy/Judy

Me
Mobile & Holiday Homes
Moneywise
Mother & Baby
Motor Caravan Magazine
My Weekly
New DIY
New Woman
News of the World
Penthouse
Police Journal

Practical Householder
Practical Parenting
Practical Photography
Practical Woodworking
Right Start
Saga Magazine
She
Shout
Slimming Magazine
Street Machine
Sunday Mail

Take a Break
Television
True Story
The Weekly News
What's on TV
Woman
*Woman's Day (Aus.)
Woman's Own
Woman's Realm
*Woman's Way (Ire.)
Yours

Gossip Paragraphs

Aberdeen Evening Express
(Aberdeen) Press and Journal
Aeroplane Monthly
African Business
Amateur Gardening
Annabel
The Architects' Journal
Art Business Today
Art Monthly
Auto Express
BBC Music Magazine
The Big Issue
Boards
Bowls International
Bristol Evening Post
Broadcast
Cage and Aviary Birds
Campaign
*Canadian Yachting
*(Cape Town) Cape Times
  (SA)
Car
Caravan Magazine
Carers World
Cat World
Catholic Pictorial
Cheshire Life
*(Christchurch) The Press (NZ)
Classic Boat
Classic Cars
Classical Music
Climber and Hill Walker
Country Life
Cycling Weekly
Daily Mail
Daily Mirror
Daily Star
Daily Telegraph
Derby Evening Telegraph
Dirt Bike Rider
Drapers Record
Edinburgh Evening News
The Electrical Times
Euromoney
*Evening Herald (Ire.)
Evening Post
Eventing

Farming News
Fashion Weekly
Financial Weekly
Fresh Produce Journal
Garden News
Geographical Magazine
Gibbons Stamp Monthly
Gifts International
Glasgow Evening Times
Golf World
The Herald
*The Herald (Zim.)
Horse and Hound
*Hotel and Catering Review
  (Ire.)
The Independent
The Independent on Sunday
*Inuit Art Quarterly (Can.)
Inverness Courier
*Irish Farmers Journal
*Irish Medical Times
*Irish Printer
Jewish Chronicle
*(Johannesburg) Sunday Times
  (SA)
The Journal
Journalist
Justice of the Peace and Local
  Government Law
*The Listener (NZ)
Liverpool Echo
Living
Mail on Sunday
Marketing Week
*(Melbourne) Australasian Post
Men Only
The Mirror
*Mode Australia
Music Week
*(New Plymouth) The Daily
  News (NZ)
New Statesman & Society
The New Welsh Review
News of the World
The News, Portsmouth
Nursing Times and Nursing
  Mirror

The Oldie
Opera Now
Organic Gardening
PC Review
*Photo Life (Can.)
Pilot
The Pink Paper
Practical Fishkeeping
Private Eye
Radio Times
Runner's World
The Scotsman
The Scottish Farmer
Sea Breezes
Shout
*South African Yachting
South Wales Echo
Squash Player
Stage and Television Today
The Sun
*The Sun-Herald (Aus.)
*The Sunday Age (Aus.)
Sunday Express
*Sunday Independent (Ire.)
Sunday Mail
*The Sunday Mail (Zim.)
*The Sunday Press (Ire.)
Sunday Telegraph
The Tablet
Therapy Weekly
The Times
Titbits
Today
Today's Runner
*TV Times (NZ)
Wales on Sunday
Western Daily Press
Western Mail
Woman
Woman's Realm
*Woman's Way (Ire.)
World Soccer
Yachts and Yachting
Yorkshire Evening Post
Yorkshire Evening Press
Yorkshire Life
Yorkshire Post

Brief Filler Paragraphs

(Aberdeen) Press and Journal
Accountancy Age
Active Life
Aeroplane Monthly
Africa Confidential
African Business
Air Pictorial International
Amateur Gardening
Angler's Mail
Annabel
The Architects' Journal
Art Monthly
Athletics Weekly
*Australian Skiing
Auto Express
BBC Music Magazine
The Big Issue
Black Beauty & Hair
Boards
Bowls International
Broadcast
Buses
Cage and Aviary Birds
*Canadian Yachting
*(Cape Town) Cape Times
   (SA)
Car
Caravan Magazine
Carers World
Cat World
Catholic Herald
Catholic Pictorial
Cheshire Life
*(Christchurch) The Press (NZ)
Christian Herald
Classic Boat
Classic Cars
Climber and Hill Walker
Communicate
Country Life
Countryman
Cycling Weekly
Daily Mail
Daily Mirror
Daily Star
Derby Evening Telegraph
Dorset Life – The Dorset
   Magazine
Drapers Record
East Lothian Life
Edinburgh Evening News
The Electrical Times
Euromoney
*Evening Herald (Ire.)
Eventing
Express and Star
Farming News
Fashion Weekly
The Field
Fire

Flight International
Fly-Fishing & Fly-Tying
France Magazine
Freelance Writing &
   Photography
Fresh Produce Journal
Garden News
Geographical Magazine
Gibbons Stamp Monthly
Gifts International
Glasgow Evening Times
Golf Illustrated Weekly
Golf World
The Great Outdoors
Greetings Magazine
Hartlepool Mail
Health & Fitness
The Herald
*The Herald (Zim.)
Heritage
Hi-Fi News & Record Review
HIM Magazine
Horse and Hound
Horticulture Week
Hortus
*Hotel and Catering Review
   (Ire.)
The Illustrated London News
*IMAGE (Ire.)
The Independent
The Independent on Sunday
*Inuit Art Quarterly (Can.)
Inverness Courier
*Ireland's Own
*Irish Farmers Journal
*Irish Medical Times
*Irish Printer
Jane's Defence Weekly
Jewish Chronicle
*(Johannesburg) Sunday Times
   (SA)
The Journal
Journalist
Justice of the Peace and Local
   Government Law
Lancashire Evening Post
*The Listener (NZ)
Liverpool Echo
Living
Mail on Sunday
Manx Life
Marketing Week
Men Only
Mobile & Holiday Homes
*Mode Australia
Model Engineer
Motor Boat and Yachting
Nautical Magazine
Navy International
New Scientist

The New Welsh Review
New Woman
News of the World
Nursing Times and Nursing
   Mirror
The Oldie
Opera Now
Organic Gardening
Overkill
Pig Farming
Pilot
The Pink Paper
Port of London
Practical Fishkeeping
Practical Woodworking
Priests and People
Printing World
Private Eye
Radio Times
Railway Gazette
Railway Magazine
Reader's Digest
*Reader's Digest (Aus.)
Runner's World
Saga Magazine
The Scotsman
The Scottish Farmer
Sea Breezes
Somerset Magazine
*Songwriter (Ire.)
*South African Yachting
South Wales Echo
*Southern Cross (SA)
The Southern Daily Echo
Squash Player
Stage and Television Today
Staple
The Star
Steam Classic
Studio Sound
The Sun
*The Sun-Herald (Aus.)
*The Sunday Business Post
   (Ire.)
Sunday Express
*Sunday Life (Ire.)
Sunday Mail
*The Sunday Mail (Zim.)
*The Sunday Press (Ire.)
The Sunday Sun
The Tablet
*Technology Ireland
*Theatre Ireland Magazine
Therapy Weekly
This England
The Times
Titbits
Today
Today's Runner
Town and Country Planning

*TV Times (NZ)
Vegetarian Living
Wales on Sunday
Waterways World
Weight Watchers Magazine
Western Daily Press

The Western Morning News
Woman
Woman's Realm
Woodworker
*World Airnews (SA)
World Fishing

World Soccer
Yachts and Yachting
Yorkshire Evening Post
Yorkshire Evening Press
Yours

Puzzles and Quizzes

The newspapers and magazines listed below all take puzzles and/or quizzes, on an occasional or, in some cases, regular basis. Ideas must be tailored to suit each magazine or newspaper; approach in writing in the first instance.

Aberdeen Evening Express
*Adelaide Advertiser (Aus.)
*(Adelaide) Sunday Mail
  (Aus.)
Annabel
*Argus South African
  Newspapers
Art Business Today
Athletics Weekly
*(Auckland) Sunday Star-Times
  (NZ)
Baptist Times
BBC Holidays
Bird Watching
Birmingham Evening Mail
Bolton Evening News
*Bona (SA)
Bowls International
*(Brisbane) Sunday Mail (Aus.)
Brownie
Cage and Aviary Birds
*Canadian Yachting
Carers World
Cat World
Catholic Gazette
Catholic Herald
Catholic Pictorial
Choice
*(Christchurch) The Press (NZ)
*Christchurch Star (NZ)
Christian Herald
*The Chronicle (Zim.)
Church of England Newspaper
*Cleo (Aus.)
Country Life
Country-Side
The Cricketer International
Daily Mail
Daily Mirror
Daily Star
*Daily Times (NZ)
The Dandy
Dandy Cartoon Library
Darts World
Dirt Bike Rider
Disability Now
*Dolly (Aus.)
*(Dunedin) Otago Daily Times
  (NZ)

East Lothian Life
Eastern Evening News
The Electrical Times
Essentials
The European
Evening Echo
Evening Gazette (Teesside)
*Evening Herald (Ire.)
Everyday with Practical
  Electronics
*Fair Lady (SA)
*Farmers Weekly (SA)
Financial Adviser
Football Picture Story Library
*Garden and Home (SA)
Garden News
Gifts International
Glasgow Evening Times
Golf Monthly
Golf World
The Great Outdoors
Grimsby Evening Telegraph
Guiding
Health & Efficiency
  International
The Herald
*The Herald (Zim.)
Here's Health
Hertfordshire Countryside
Horse and Hound
Horse & Pony
*Hotel and Catering Review
  (Ire.)
House Builder
The Illustrated London News
The Independent Magazine
The Independent on Sunday
*(Invercargill) The Southland
  Times (NZ)
Inverness Courier
*Ireland's Eye
*Ireland's Own
*Irish Medical Times
The Journal
Journalist
Just Seventeen
The Lady
Lancashire Evening Post
*(Launston) Examiner (Aus.)

*The Listener (NZ)
Liverpool Echo
*Living and Loving (SA)
Mail on Sunday
Mandy/Judy
*(Melbourne) Australasian Post
Men Only
Methodist Recorder
Mobile & Holiday Homes
My Weekly Puzzle Time
*New Idea (Aus.)
*(New Plymouth) The Daily
  News (NZ)
New Scientist
The New Welsh Review
New World
*New Zealand Woman's
  Weekly
The News, Portsmouth
19
Nottingham Evening Post
Nursing Times and Nursing
  Mirror
Opera
Opera Now
*Personality (SA)
*(Perth) The West Australian
Pilot
Pony
Practical Motorist
Practical Photography
The Practitioner
Publishing News
*Reality (Ire.)
Red Tape
Runner's World
*Scope (SA)
The Scotsman
The Scottish Farmer
Scottish Homes and Country
She
The Short Wave Magazine
Shout
Shropshire Star
*South African Yachting
South Wales Echo
*Southern Cross (SA)
The Spectator
Stage and Television Today

Stamp Lover
The Star
The Sun
*The Sun-Herald (Aus.)
*Sunday Life (Ire.)
Sunday Mail
*The Sunday Mail (Zim.)
Sunday Mirror Magazine
*The Sunday News (Zim.)
*The Sunday Press (Ire.)
The Sunday Sun
The Sunday Times
*(Sydney) The Daily Telegraph
    Mirror (Aus.)
The Tablet
Take a Break
Telegraph Magazine
Therapy Weekly

The Times
The Times Educational
    Supplement
Titbits
Today
Today's Runner
Trout and Salmon
*TV Times (NZ)
Twinkle
The Universe
*(Vancouver) Province (Can.)
Vox
Wales on Sunday
War Cry
Waterways World
Weekend Guardian
The Weekly Journal

Weight Watchers Magazine
*(Wellington) The Evening
    Post (NZ)
Western Daily Press
Western Mail
The Western Morning News
Woman
Woman Alive
Woodworker
*The Word (Ire.)
World Soccer
The Young Soldier
Young Telegraph
Yorkshire Evening Post
Yorkshire Evening Press
*Your Family (SA)
Yours

Newspapers

UK National Daily/Sunday Newspapers (*excluding* Northern Ireland)

Daily Express
Daily Mail
Daily Mirror
Daily Sport
Daily Star
The Daily Telegraph
Financial Times
The Guardian

The Independent
The Independent on Sunday
Mail on Sunday
News of the World
The Observer
The People
Scotland on Sunday
The Sun

Sunday Express
Sunday Mirror
Sunday Sport
Sunday Telegraph
The Sunday Times
The Times
Today
Wales on Sunday

UK National Weekly Newspapers (*excluding* Northern Ireland)

Asian Times
Caribbean Times

Eastern Eye
The European

The Voice
The Weekly Journal

UK Regional Newspapers (*excluding* Northern Ireland)

Aberdeen Evening Express
Birmingham Evening Mail
The Birmingham Post
Bolton Evening News
Bristol Evening Post
Burton Mail
Chronicle and Echo
    (Northampton)
The Courier and Advertiser
    (Dundee)
Coventry Evening Telegraph
Daily Awaz International
Daily Post (Liverpool)
Daily Record (Glasgow)
Derby Evening Telegraph
Dorset Evening Echo
Dundee Evening Telegraph &
    Post

East Anglian Daily Times
Eastern Daily Press (Norwich)
Eastern Evening News
    (Norwich)
Edinburgh Evening News
Evening Chronicle
    (Newcastle)
Evening Echo (Bournemouth)
Evening Gazette (Teesside)
Evening Post (Reading)
Evening Standard (London)
Express and Star
    (Wolverhampton)
Glasgow Evening Times
Gloucestershire Echo
Grimsby Evening Telegraph
Hartlepool Mail
The Herald (Glasgow)

Inverness Courier
The Journal (Newcastle)
Kent Messenger
Kent Today
Lancashire Evening Post
Lancashire Evening Telegraph
Liverpool Echo
Manchester Evening News
The News, Portsmouth
The Northern Echo (Durham)
Nottingham Evening Post
Oldham Evening Chronicle
The Press and Journal
    (Aberdeen)
Shropshire Star
South Wales Echo
The Southern Daily Echo
    (Southampton)

The Star (Sheffield)
Sunday Mail (Glasgow)
Sunday Mercury (Birmingham)
Sunday Post (Dundee/ Glasgow)
The Sunday Sun (Newcastle)

Telegraph & Argus (Bradford)
The Weekly News (Scotland)
Western Daily Press (Bristol)
Western Mail (Cardiff)
The Western Morning News (Plymouth)

Yorkshire Evening Post
Yorkshire Evening Press
Yorkshire Gazette & Herald Series
Yorkshire Post

UK Colour Supplements (*excluding* Northern Ireland)

ES Magazine (Evening Standard)
The Independent Magazine
JC Impressions (Jewish Chronicle)

Sunday Express Magazine
Sunday Magazine (News of the World)
Sunday Mirror Magazine
The Sunday Post Magazine

Sunday Times Magazine
Telegraph Magazine (Daily Telegraph)
Weekend Guardian
You (Mail on Sunday)

Women's Magazines
(*See also* Health and Home)

Annabel
*Australian Women's Weekly
Bad Attitude
Bella
Best
Black Beauty & Hair
*Bona (SA)
Catch
Chat
*Chatelaine (Can.)
Clothes Show Magazine
Company
Cosmopolitan
Country Living
Elle (UK)
Essentials
Everywoman
Executive PA
*Fair Lady (SA)
Family Circle
*Femina (SA)
Girl About Town
Good Housekeeping
Hairflair
Harpers & Queen
Hello!

Home and Country
Home Words
*HQ (Aus.)
*IMAGE (Ire.)
*IT (Ire.)
Just Seventeen
Lady
Living
*Living and Loving (SA)
LOOKS
Loving
*Mahogany (Zimbabwe)
Marie Claire
Me
*Mode Australia
More!
Mother & Baby
Ms London
My Weekly
My Weekly Puzzle Time
*New Idea (Aus.)
New Woman
*New Zealand Woman's Weekly
19
Nursery World

Office Secretary
Options
People's Friend
The Pink Paper
*Portfolio (Aus.)
Prima
Right Start
She
Sunday Post
Take a Break
The Tatler
*U magazine (Ire.)
Vanity Fair
Vogue
Wedding and Home
Woman
Woman Alive
Woman and Home
*Woman's Day (Aus.)
Woman's Journal
Woman's Own
Woman's Realm
*Woman's Way (Ire.)
Woman's Weekly
World's Children
*Your Family (SA)

Men's Magazines

Arena
Country
Esquire
For Him
Gay Times

GQ
HIM
Masonic Square
Mayfair

Men Only
Penthouse
The Pink Paper
Risqué

Children's and Young Adult Magazines

The Beano
Beano Library
Beano Puzzle Library
Brownie
Bunty
Bunty Library
Buster
Commando
The Dandy
Dandy Cartoon Library
Dandy Library
Debbie Library

*Dolly (Aus.)
Early Times
Football Picture Story Library
Greenscene
Horse & Pony
i-D Magazine
Judy Library
Junior Bookshelf
Just Seventeen
LOOKS
Mandy/Judy
Mandy Library

Mizz
Overkill
Pony
Scouting
Shout
Sky Magazine
Smash Hits
Twinkle
Vox
Young Telegraph
YX

Subject Articles

Advertising, Design, Printing and Publishing (*See also* Literary)

Arena
*Australian Bookseller &
  Publisher
Bookseller
British Journalism Review
British Printer
Campaign
*Canadian Interiors

Exchange & Mart
The Face
Greetings Magazine
Indexer
Interior Design
InterMedia
*Irish Printer
Journalist

Learned Publishing
Market Newsletter
Media Week
PR Week
Printing World
Publishing News
World of Interiors

Agriculture, Farming and Horticulture

Country Life
Countryman
*Countryman (Aus.)
Country-Side
Dairy Farmer
*The Farmer (Zimbabwe)
Farmer's Weekly

*Farmer's Weekly (SA)
Farming News
The Field
Fresh Produce Journal
Grower
Horticulture Week
*Irish Farmers Journal

*New Zealand Farmer
Pig Farming
Poultry World
Scottish Farmer
Smallholder
Town and Country Planning

Architecture and Building

Architects' Journal
Architectural Design
Architectural Review
Building
Built Environment
Burlington Magazine
Construction Europe
Contemporary Review

Country Homes & Interiors
Country Life
Design
Designers' Journal
Education
Homes and Gardens
House & Garden

House Builder
Ideal Home
International Construction
Local Historian
Mortgage Finance Gazette
Museums Journal
Town and Country Planning

Art and Collecting

Antique Collector
Antique Dealer &
  Collectors Guide
Apollo
Art & Design
Art Business Today
Art Monthly

The Art Newspaper
Art Review
Artist
Artists and Illustrators
*ArtsAtlantic (Can.)
BBC Homes & Antiques
Burlington Magazine

*C Magazine (Can.)
Clocks
Coin News
Contemporary Art
Contemporary Review
Country Life
Creative Camera

Design
Eastern Art Report
Embroidery
Gemmological Newsletter
Gibbons Stamp Monthly

Illustrated London News
*Inuit Art Quarterly (Can.)
Leisure Painter
Medal News
Museums Journal

Numismatic Chronicle
RA Magazine
Stamp Lover
Stamp Magazine
The World of Interiors

Aviation

Aeromodeller
Aeroplane Monthly
Air International
Air Pictorial International

*Australian Flying
*Aviation & Aerospace (Can.)
Flight International
Pilot

Spaceflight
Transport
*World Airnews (SA)

Blind and Deaf-Blind

Published by the Royal National Institute for the Blind (see under **United Kingdom Book Publishers**)

Aphra
Braille Chess Magazine
Braille Journal of
   Physiotherapy
Braille Music Magazine
Braille Radio Times
Braille Rainbow
Braille TV Times
Channels of Blessing
Contention
Daily Bread

Diane
Fleur de Lys
Gleanings
High Browse (in Braille and
   print)
'Law Notes' Extracts
Light of the Moon
Moon Magazine
Moon Rainbow
New Beacon (in Braille and
   print)

Physiotherapists' Quarterly
Piano Tuners' Quarterly
Progress
Rhetoric
Roundabout
Scientific Enquiry
Soundings
Spotlight
Theological Times
The Weekender

Business, Industry and Management

Achievement
Administrator
Brewing & Distilling
   International
Business Life
Business Scotland
Communicate
Contemporary Review
Cosmetic World News
Dairy Industries International
Director
Euromoney
European Chemical News

European Drinks Buyer
European Frozen Food Buyer
European Plastic News
Executive PA
Fashion Forecast International
Fashion Weekly
Financial Director
Fire
Information and Software
   Technology
Involvement & Participation
Land & Liberty

Leisureweek
*Management (NZ)
Management Today
Millennium
Office Secretary
Personnel Management
Political Quarterly
*The Sunday Business Post
   (Ire.)
UCW Journal
Woodworker
Work Study

Cinema and Films

Campaign
Empire
International Broadcast
   Engineer

New Statesman & Society
Screen International
Sight and Sound
Speech and Drama

Stand
Studio Sound
*TV and Radio Times (NZ)

Computers

Computer Weekly
Computing

PC Direct
PC Review

Personal Computer World
Which Computer?

Economics, Accountancy and Finance

Accountancy
Accountancy Age

Accounting World
Active Life

Africa Confidential
African Business

audIT
*Australian Financial Review
Banker
Banking World
Business Scotland
Certified Accountant
Choice
Contemporary Review
Dairy Industries International
Economic Journal
Economica

Economist
Euromoney
Financial Adviser
Financial Director
Financial Times
Financial Weekly
Grower
Insurance Brokers' Monthly
Investors Chronicle
The Journal
Land & Liberty

Local Government Chronicle
MoneyMarketing
Moneywise
Mortgage Finance Gazette
New Statesman & Society
Pensions World
*Southern Africa Political &
  Economic Monthly (Zim.)
*Studies (Ire.)
Tribune
West Africa

Education

Amateur Stage
Art & Craft
La Brita Esperantisto
British Journal of Special
  Education
Child Education
Education
Guiding
Higher Education Quarterly
Junior Bookshelf
Junior Education
Junior Focus
Linguist
Local Historian
Modern Languages
Modus

Month
Museums Journal
Music Teacher
New Blackfriars
New Statesman & Society
Nursery World
Parents
Practical Parenting
Prep School
*Reality (Ire.)
Report
Right Start
Safety Education
School Librarian
Scottish Educational Journal

Speech and Drama
Spoken English
Theology
Times Educational
  Supplement
Times Educational
  Supplement Scotland
Times Higher Education
  Supplement
Together
Tribune
Unesco Courier
Use of English
World's Children
Young People Now

Engineering and Mechanics (*See also* Architecture, Aviation, Business, Motoring, Nautical, Radio, Sciences)

*Australian Mining
*The Australian Worker &
  Labor News
Buses
Car Mechanics
Construction Weekly
Control and Instrumentation
Design
Electrical Review

Electrical Times
*Electronics Australia
Engineer
European Chemical News
Everyday with Practical
  Electronics
Filtration & Separation
Fire
Gas World International

International Construction
Model Engineer
*NZ Engineering
Practical Woodworking
Railway Gazette
Railway Magazine
Spaceflight
Transport

Gardening

Amateur Gardening
BBC Gardeners' World
  Magazine
Country
Country Life

The Field
The Garden
*Garden and Home (SA)
Garden Answers
Garden News

Hortus
House and Garden
Organic Gardening
Practical Gardening
Your Garden

Health and Home (*See also* Women's Magazines)

Active Life
Aromatherapy
*Australian Home Beautiful
*Australian House and Garden
BBC GoodFood
BBC Homes & Antiques
BBC Vegetarian GoodFood

*Canadian Interiors
Choice
Country Homes & Interiors
Embroidery
*Garden and Home (SA)
Greenscene
Health & Efficiency

Health & Fitness
Here's Health
Home and Family
Homes and Gardens
Homes and Ideas
Hospitality
House & Garden

House Beautiful
Ideal Home
Jewish Telegraph
Modus
New DIY
Parents
Perfect Home
Period Living & Traditional
   Homes

Practical Householder
Practical Parenting
Running Magazine
Safety Education
Saga
Scottish Home and Country
Slimmer Magazine
Slimming Magazine

Today's Runner
Vegan
Vegetarian Living
Weight Watchers Magazine
The World of Interiors
*Your Family (SA)
Yours

History and Archaeology

Albion
Bedfordshire Magazine
Coin News
Contemporary Review
Country Quest
English Historical Review

Geographical Magazine
Heythrop Journal
History
History Today
Illustrated London News
In Britain

Lancashire Life
Local Historian
Museums Journal
New Blackfriars
Scottish Historical Review
*Studies (Ire.)

Hotel, Catering and Leisure

Caterer & Hotelkeeper
Club Mirror
European Drinks Buyer
European Frozen Food Buyer

Hospitality
*Hotel and Catering Review
   (Ire.)
Leisure Manager

Leisureweek
Parks & Sports Grounds
Sport and Leisure

Humour

Private Eye

Viz

Inflight Magazines

*The Australian Way
Business Life

Flightpath Magazine

Hot Air

Legal and Police

The Criminologist
Family Law
Forensic Photography

Justice of the Peace and Local
   Government Law
New Law Journal

Police Journal
Solicitors Journal

Literary (*See also* **Poetry**)

Artrage
*Australian Bookseller &
   Publisher
Author
Book Collector
*Books in Canada
*Books Ireland
Books Magazine
Bookseller
British Journalism Review
*Canadian Author
*Canadian Forum
*Canadian Literature
Cencrastus
Chapman
Contemporary Review
Critical Quarterly
Critical Wave

*Dalhousie Review (Can.)
Dickensian
Edinburgh Review
European Bookseller
*Fiddlehead (Can.)
Freelance Writing &
   Photography
Granta
Illustrated London News
Index on Censorship
Indexer
*Journal of Canadian Studies
Journalist
Junior Bookshelf
Learned Publishing
Library
Lines Review
Literary Review

Llais Llyfrau
LOGOS
London Magazine
London Review of Books
*Malahat Review (Can.)
Modern Languages
Modern Review
New Library World
New Statesman & Society
The New Welsh Review
The Oldie
Orbis
Outposts Poetry Quarterly
*Overland (Aus.)
Planet
Publishing News
*Quadrant (Aus.)
*Quill & Quire (Can.)

*Reality (Ire.)
*Redoubt (Aus.)
Scottish Book Collector
Signal
Spectator
Stand

*Studies (Ire.)
Times Literary Supplement
Tribune
Use of English
Wasafiri
*Wascana Review (Can.)

Woman Journalist
Writers News
Writing Magazine
Writing Women
Xenos

Local Government and Civil Service

Justice of the Peace and Local
  Government Law
Local Council Review

Local Government Chronicle
Public Service & Local
  Government

Red Tape

Marketing and Retailing

CTN
Drapers Record
Fashion Weekly
Gifts International

Greetings Magazine
Grocer
Incentive Today
Marketing Week

Retail Week
Toy Trader
*Ulster Grocer

Medicine and Nursing

Balance
British Deaf News
British Journal of General
  Practice
British Medical Journal
Carers World
Community Care
Dental Update
Disability Now

Doctor
*Irish Journal of Medical
  Science
*Irish Medical Times
Journal of Alternative and
  Complementary Medicine
Lancet
Nursery World
Nursing Times

Pharmaceutical Journal
Physiotherapy
The Practitioner
Professional Nurse
Pulse
Quarterly Journal of Medicine
Therapy Weekly
This Caring Business
Young People Now

Motoring and Cycling

Auto Express
Autocar & Motor
Back Street Heroes
Buses
Car
*Car (SA)
Car Mechanics
Caravan Magazine
Classic & Sportscar

Classic Cars
Commercial Motor
Custom Car
Cycling Weekly
*Cycling World (Aus.)
Dirt Bike Rider
Mobile & Holiday Homes
Motor Caravan Magazine
Motor Cycle News

Motorcaravan and Motorhome
  Monthly
Motorcycle International
Performance Car
Practical Motorist
Scootering
Street Machine
Superbike
What Car?

Music and Recording

Arena
BBC Music Magazine
Classic CD
Classical Music
Early Music
The Face
Gramophone
Hi-Fi News
i-D Magazine
Jazz Journal International
Kerrang!

Making Music
Melody Maker
Music and Letters
Music Review
Music Teacher
Music Week
Musical Opinion
Musical Times
New Musical Express
Opera
Opera Now

Organ
Q Magazine
Select Magazine
Sky Magazine
Smash Hits
*Songwriter (Ire.)
Songwriting and Composing
Studio Sound
Tempo
Vox

Natural History (*See also* Agriculture, Rural Life)

Aquarist and
  Pondkeeper
BBC Wildlife Magazine
Bird Watching
Birdwatch
British Birds
Budgerigar World
Cage and Aviary Birds
Cat World
Dalesman

Ecologist
Entomologist's Monthly
  Magazine
*Equinox (Can.)
*Geo (Aus.)
Geographical Magazine
Glaucus
Green Magazine
Guiding

Heredity
Horse & Pony
Museums Journal
Natural World
Naturalist
Nature
Our Dogs
Pony
Practical Fishkeeping

Nautical and Marine

*Boating World (NZ)
*Canadian Yachting
Classic Boat
Diver
*Modern Boating (Aus.)
Motor Boat and Yachting

Nautical Magazine
Navy International
Port of London
Practical Boat Owner
Sea Breezes
Ship & Boat International

Ships Monthly
Transport
Yachting Monthly
Yachting World
Yachts and Yachting

Photography

Amateur Photographer
*Australian Photography
British Journal of Photography
Camcorder User
Creative Camera

Forensic Photography
Freelance Writing &
  Photography
Photo Answers

*Photo Life (Can.)
PIC (People in Camera)
Practical Photography
Video Camera

Poetry

Those magazines marked with a † only take the occasional poem. Check with the editor before submitting.

Acumen
Agenda
Ambit
†Artrage
Cencrastus
Chapman
†The Countryman
Critical Quarterly
*Cyphers (Ire.)
*The Dalhousie Review (Can.)
†Day by Day
Envoi
*The Fiddlehead (Can.)
*Fortnight (Ire.)
The Haiku Quarterly
*The Honest Ulsterman
Iron
†Jewish Quarterly

*Krino (Ire.)
†Life and Work
Lines Review
The Literary Review
London Magazine
London Review of Books
*The Malahat Review (Can.)
New Statesman & Society
The New Welsh Review
Orbis
Outposts Poetry Quarterly
Oxford Poetry
Planet
PN Review
*Poetry Australia
Poetry Durham
*Poetry Ireland/Éigse Éireann
Poetry London Newsletter

Poetry Nottingham
Poetry Review
Poetry Wales
*Quadrant (Aus.)
†Quaker Monthly
*Redoubt (Aus.)
The Rialto
†The Scots Magazine
Stand Magazine
Staple
†The Times Literary
  Supplement
†Tribune
Verse
Wasafiri
*Wascana Review (Can.)
Writing Women

Politics

Africa Confidential
*Australian Journal of
  International Affairs
*Australian Journal of Politics
  and History

*Australian Quarterly
China Quarterly
Contemporary Review
*Current Affairs Bulletin
  (Aus.)

*Fortnight (Ire.)
Fourth World Review
Illustrated London News
International Affairs
Justice of the Peace

Liberal Democrats News
Local Government Chronicle
Middle East International
New Blackfriars
New Internationalist
New Statesman & Society

Peace News
Political Quarterly
*Southern Africa Political &
  Economic Monthly (Zim.)
*Studies (Ire.)
Town and Country Planning

Tribune
Unesco Courier
Voice Intelligence Report
West Africa
World Today

Radio, Television and Video

Broadcast
Campaign
*Electronics Australia
Empire
Gramophone
Hi-Fi News
InterMedia
International Broadcast
  Engineer

New Statesman & Society
*The Listener (NZ)
Opera Now
Practical Wireless
Radio Times
Satellite Times
Short-Wave Magazine

Stage and Television Today
Studio Sound
Television
Tribune
TV Times
*TV Times (NZ)
What's on TV

Religion, Philosophy and New Age

Baptist Times
Catholic Gazette
Catholic Herald
Catholic Pictorial
Catholic Times
Christian Herald
Church of England Newspaper
*Church of Ireland Gazette
Church Times
Contemporary Review
Day by Day
Downside Review
Evangelical Quarterly
Fortean Times
Friend
*The Furrow (Ire.)
*Herald of the South (Aus.)

Heythrop Journal
Home and Family
Home Words
Inquirer
i-to-i
Jewish Chronicle
Jewish Quarterly
Jewish Telegraph
Life and Work
Methodist Recorder
Mind
Modern Churchman
Month
New Blackfriars
New Humanist
Priests & People

Quaker Monthly
*Reality (Ire.)
Reform
Sign
*Southern Cross (SA)
*Studies (Ire.)
Tablet
Theology
Third Way
Together
Universe
War Cry
West Africa
Woman Alive
*Word (Ire.)
Young Soldier

Rural Life and Country (*See also* Natural History)

Bedfordshire Magazine
Cheshire Life
Country
Country Life
Country Quest
Countryman
Country-Side
County
Coventry Evening Telegraph
Cumbria
Dalesman
Derbyshire Life and
  Countryside
Dorset Life – The Dorset
  Magazine
East Lothian Life

Eastern Daily Press
Essex Countryside
The Field
Green Magazine
Hampshire
Heritage
Hertfordshire Countryside
In Britain
Inverness Courier
*Ireland's Eye
Kent
Lady
Lancashire Evening Post
Lancashire Life
Lancashire Magazine
Lincolnshire Life

Local Historian
Manx Life
Rambling Today
Scots Magazine
Scottish Field
Scottish Home and Country
Shooting Times and Country
  Magazine
The Shropshire Magazine
Somerset Magazine
This England
Town and Country Planning
Waterways World
Yorkshire Life
Yorkshire Ridings Magazine

Sciences

Criminologist
*Equinox (Can.)
Geological Magazine

Heredity
Mind
Nature

New Scientist
Science Progress
*Technology Ireland

Services: Naval, Military, Air and Civil

Air International
Air Pictorial
Army Quarterly & Defence
  Journal

*Guns Australia
Jane's Defence Weekly

Red Tape
RUSI Journal

Sports, Games, Hobbies and Pastimes (*See also* **Motoring**)

Aeromodeller
Anglers' Mail
Angling Times
Astronomy Now
Athletics Weekly
*Australasian Sporting Shooter
*Australian Angler's Fishing
  World
*Australian Skiing
Bird Watching
Birdwatch
Boards
Bowls International
Bridge International
British Birds
British Chess Magazine
Camping Magazine
*Canadian Yachting
Classic Boat
Climber and Hill Walker
Cricketer International
Darts World
Eventing
Family Tree Magazine
The Field
Fly-Fishing & Fly-Tying

Gemmological Newsletter
Gibbons Stamp Monthly
Golf Monthly
Golf Weekly
Golf World
Great Outdoors
Guiding
*Guns Australia
Horse and Hound
Horse and Rider
In Britain
Military Modelling
Model Boats
Model Engineer
Model Railways
90 Minutes
Our Dogs
Outdoor
Popular Crafts
Radio Control Models
Rambling Today
Runner's World
Scale Models International
Scottish Field
Scouting
Sea Angler

Shooting Times
The Skier and
  The Snowboarder
Snooker Scene
*South African Yachting
Sport and Leisure
Sporting Life
Squash Player
Stamp Lover
Stamp Magazine
Steam Classic
Tennis World
Today's Golfer
Today's Runner
Trout and Salmon
Wisden Cricket Monthly
Woodworker
*Word (Ire.)
Workbox
World of Bowls
World Fishing
World Soccer
Yachting Monthly
Yachting World
Yachts and Yachting

Theatre, Drama and Dancing (*See also* **Cinema, Music**)

Amateur Stage
Ballroom Dancing Times
*Canadian Forum
Contemporary Review
DAM
Dance & Dancers
*Dance Australia
Dancing Times

Illustrated London News
In Britain
New Statesman & Society
New Theatre Quarterly
*Performing Arts &
  Entertainment in Canada
Plays & Players

Radio Times
*Reality (Ire.)
Speech and Drama
Stage and Television Today
*Theatre Ireland Magazine
Tribune
TV Times

Travel and Geography

*Australian Geographic
*Australian Skiing
BBC Holidays
La Brita Esperantisto
Bulletin of Hispanic Studies
Caravan Magazine
Contemporary Review
*Equinox (Can.)

Expression
Flightpath Magazine
France Magazine
*Geo (Aus.)
Geographical Journal
Geographical Magazine
Heritage
Illustrated London News

In Britain
*In Dublin (Ire.)
*Ireland of the Welcomes
Local Historian
*Natal Witness (SA)
Town and Country Planning
Traveller

Syndicates, News and Press Agencies

In their own interests writers and others are strongly advised to make preliminary enquiries before submitting MSS, and to ascertain terms of work. Commission varies. Strictly speaking, syndication is the selling and reselling of previously published work and the details given for agencies in the following list should be noted carefully. Some news and presss agencies may handle original material.

Academic File (1985), The Centre for Near East, Afro-Asia Research (NEAR), Acre House, 69-76 Long Acre, London WC2E 9AS   *tel* 071-379 3939/081-392 1122   *fax* 081-392 1422. *Managing editor:* Sajid Rizvi; *executive editor:* Shirley Rizvi. Feature and photo syndication with special reference to the developing world and immigrant communities in the West.

Advance Features, Clarendon House, Judges Terrace, East Grinstead, West Sussex RH19 3AD   *tel* (0342) 328562. *Managing editor:* Peter Norman. Supplies text and visual services to the national and regional press in Britain and newspapers overseas. Editorial for advertising supplements on consumer and commercial themes. Instructional graphic panels on a variety of subjects. Text services (weekly); 'agony' columns (teenagers and general), property, stars, nature, women's page editorial, daily, weekly and theme crosswords. Legal and business articles for the specialist press. Daily and weekly cartoons for the regional press (not single cartoons).

A.L.I. Press Agency Ltd (1948), Boulevard Anspach 111-115, Bte 9, B9-1000 Brussels, Belgium   *tel* 02 512 73 94   *fax* 02 512 03 30. *Director:* George Lans. All types of feature services except information and news: cartoons, puzzles, strips, comics, illustrations, picture stories, transparencies, articles of general interest, etc. for magazines, newspapers and books, especially illustrated books for children and adults. Syndication in all major countries. Commissions 35%, syndication 50%.

Ameuropress   *postal address* Clasificador 5, Tajamar, Providencia, Santiago, Chile   *located at* Darío Urzúa 1523, Santiago   *tel* (56 2) 235 2902/1584   *cables* Europress   *telex* 340260   *fax* (56-2) 2351731. Branch Office: PO Box 3535, Buenos Aires 1000, Argentina   *tel* 7777588, 7730339   *cables* Ameuropres   *fax* (54-1) 7777589. *Director:* José Gregorio Rios. Illustrated features to newspapers and magazines world-wide. Specialising in Latin American subjects including travel, human interest stories, hobbies, science, animal features. Regularly supplies women's material including cookery, beauty, fashion, interior decorating, glamour. Also stock colour library for advertising, calendars and illustrations. Undertakes special requirements and local assignments.

ANPS (Australasian News & Press Services) (D.J. Varney & Associates 1964), Box T 1834, GPO, Perth, W Australia 6001   *tel* (09) 293 1455   *fax* (09) 257 1558. Australian correspondents and representatives for the international media. Services provided: features and news for colour photo magazines; articles for consumer, trade, technical and professional journals; trade news summaries and newsletters. Full range of professional public relations and market research services available including film, television and stage writing, production and talent services.

The Associated Press Ltd (News Department), The Associated Press House, 12 Norwich Street, London EC4A 1BP   *tel* 071-353 1515   *telegraphic address* Associated Londonpsy   *fax* 071-353 8118.

Australian Associated Press (1935), 12 Norwich Street, London EC4A 1EJ *tel* 071-353 0153 *fax* 071-583 3563. News service to the Australian, New Zealand and Pacific Island press, radio and television.

BIPS—Bernsen's International Press Service Ltd, 9 Paradise Close, Eastbourne, East Sussex BN20 8BT *tel* (0323) 728760. *Editor:* Harry Gresty. Specialise in photo-features, both b&w and colour. Want human interest, oddity, glamour, pin-ups, scientific, medical, etc., material suitable for marketing through own branches in London, San Francisco, Paris, Hamburg, Milan, Stockholm, Amsterdam (for Benelux), Helsinki. Give full information, well researched. Willing to syndicate abroad material already sold in the UK, whether articles or photos. May buy outright or handle on commission. Query with ideas/suggestions.

Bulls Presstjänst AB, Tulegatan 39, Box 6519, S-11383 Stockholm, Sweden *tel* (08) 23 40 20 *cables* Pressbull *telex* 19 482 *fax* (08) 15 80 10; **Bulls Presse-dienst GmbH,** Eysseneckstrasse 50, D-6000 Frankfurt am Main 1, Germany *tel* (069) 59 04 18 *cables* Pressbull *telex* 412117 *fax* (069) 596 22 67; **Bulls Pressetjeneste A/S,** Ebbels Gate 3, N-0183 Oslo 1, Norway *tel* 22 20 56 01 *cables* Bullpress *fax* 22 20 49 78; **Bulls Pressetjene-ste,** Östbanegade 9, 1.th, DK-2100 Copenhagen Ö, Denmark *tel* 31 38 90 99 *cables* Pressbull *fax* 31 38 25 16; **Bulls Finska Försäljnings AB,** Ison-niitynkatu 7, SF-00520, Helsinki, Finland *tel* (90) 757 13 11 *fax* (90) 757 06 34; **Bulls Press,** ul. Chocimska 28, Pojok 509, Warszawa, 00-791 Poland *tel/ fax* (22) 49 80 18. *Market:* newspapers, magazines and weeklies in Sweden, Denmark, Norway, Finland, Iceland, Poland, Germany, Austria and German-speaking Switzerland. *Syndicates:* dramatic and human interest picture stories; topical and well-illustrated background articles and series; photographic fea-tures dealing with science, people, personalities, glamour; condensations and serialisations of best-selling fiction and non-fiction; cartoons, comic strips, film and TV rights, merchandising, newspaper graphics.

The Canadian Press (1919), Chief Correspondent: Stephen Ward, The Associ-ated Press House, 12 Norwich Street, London EC4A 1EJ *tel* 071-353 6355 *fax* 071-583 4238. London Bureau of the national news agency of Canada.

Capital Press Service, 2 Long Cottage, Church Street, Leatherhead, Surrey KT22 8EJ *tel* (0372) 377451. *Directors:* M. Stone, E.W. Stone; *news editor:* Nicholas Miller. Stories of trade, commerce and industry for trade papers in this country and abroad. Interested in air-cargo affairs and business travel (including hotels, luggage, guides, new routes via air, sea, road and train) for UK and US journals.

Caters News Agency Ltd, 42 Bartholomew Street, Digbeth, Birmingham B5 5QW *tel* 021-616 1100 *telegraphic address* Copy, Birmingham. *Managing director:* R.P. Blyth. Collection of news and pictures throughout Midlands. Representatives of overseas, national and provincial press.

Central Press Features, 20 Spectrum House, 32/34 Gordon House Road, London NW5 1LP *tel* 071-284 1433 *fax* 071-284 4494. Supplies every type of feature to newspapers and other publications in 50 countries. Included in over 100 daily and weekly services are columns on international affairs, politics, sports, medicine, law, finance, computers, video, motoring, science, gardening, fashion, house and home, health and beauty, women's and children's features, strips, crosswords, cartoons and regular 6-12 article illustrated series of interna-tional human interest; also editorial material for advertising features.

J.W. Crabtree and Son (1919), 36 Sunbridge Road, Bradford BD1 2AA   *tel* (0274) 732937 (office)/(0535) 655288 (home). News, general, trade and sport; information and research for features undertaken.

Daily & Sunday Telegraph Syndication, Ewan MacNaughton Associates, Alexandra Chambers, 6 Alexandra Road, Tonbridge, Kent TN9 2AA   *tel* (0732) 771116   *fax* (0732) 771160. News, features, photography; world-wide distribution and representation.

Europa-Press, Saltmätargatan 8, 1st Floor, Box 6410, S-113 82, Stockholm, Sweden *tel* 8-34 94 35   *cables* Europress   *fax* 8-34 80 79. *Managing director:* Sven Berlin. *Market:* newspapers, magazines and weeklies in Sweden, Denmark, Norway and Finland. *Syndicates:* high quality features of international appeal such as topical articles, photo-features – b&w and colour, women's features, short stories, serial novels, non-fiction stories and serials with strong human interest, crime articles, popular science, cartoons, comic strips.

Europress Features (UK), 18 St Chads Road, Didsbury, near Manchester M20 9WH   *tel* 061-445 2945. Representation of newspapers and magazines in Europe, Australia, United States. Syndication of top-flight features with exclusive illustrations – human interest stories – showbusiness personalities. 30-35% commission on sales of material successfully accepted; 40% on exclusive illustrations.

Express Enterprises, division of Express Newspapers plc, Ludgate House, 245 Blackfriars Road, London SE1 9UX   *tel* 071-922 7902   *cable* Lon Express   *telex* 21841   *fax* 071-922 7871. Text and pictures from all Express titles. Archive from 1900. Numerous strips and political cartoons. Material handled worldwide for freelance journalists.

Features International, Tolland, Lydeard St Lawrence, Taunton TA4 3PS   *tel* (0984) 623014   *fax* (0984) 623901. *Editorial director:* Anthony Sharrock. Syndicates features to magazines and newspapers throughout the world. The agency produces a wide range of material – mainly from freelance sources – including topical articles, women's features and weekly columns. Distributes directly to all English-language countries. Agents throughout the Common Market countries, Scandinavia, Japan, the Americas and Eastern Europe. Buys copy outright and welcomes story ideas. Sae essential.

Gemini News Service, 9 White Lion Street, London N1 9PD   *tel* 071-833 4141   *fax* 071-837 5118. *Editor:* Daniel Nelson; *managing director:* Bethel Njoku. Network of correspondents and specialist writers all over the world. Some opening for freelance. Specialists in news-features of international, topical and development interest. Preferred *length* 1000-1200 words.

Global Syndication & Literary Agency, Limited, 120 Westmont, Hemet, CA 92543, USA. *President:* A.D. Fowler. Interested in previously published books for possible syndication and placement of subsidiary rights. Our book reviewers always looking for non-fiction titles. US postage or International Reply Coupons required for return of material.

Graphic Syndication (1981), 2 Angel Meadows, Odiham, Hants RG25 1AR   *tel* (0256) 703004. *Manager:* M. Flanagan. Cartoon strips and single frames supplied to newspapers and magazines in Britain and overseas. *Terms:* 50%.

India-International News Service, *Head office:* Jute House, 12 India Exchange Place, Calcutta 700001, India   *tel* 2209563, 2206572, 4791009   *telegraphic address* Zeitgeist. *Proprietor:* Ing H. Kothari BSc, DWP(Lond), FIMechE, FIE, FVI, FInstD. 'Calcutta Letters' and Air Mail news service from Calcutta. Specialists in industrial and technical news. Public relations and publicity consultants. Publishes trade and professional journals.

INS (International News Service)/Irish International News Service, 7 King's Avenue, Minnis Bay, Birchington-on-Sea, East Kent CT7 9QL *tel* (0843) 845022. *Editor and managing director:* Barry J. Hardy PC; *photo editor:* Jan Vanek. News, sport, book reviews, TV, radio, photographic department; also equipment for TV films, etc.

International Fashion Press Agency, Mumford House, Mottram Road, Alderley Edge, Cheshire SK9 7JF *tel* (0625) 583537 *fax* (0625) 584344. *Directors:* P. Bentham (managing), P. Dyson, L.C. Bentham, S. Fagette, J. Fox. Monitors and photographs international fashion collections and developments in textile and fashion industry. Specialist writers on health, fitness, beauty and personalities. Undertakes individual commissioned features. Supplies syndicated columns and pages to press, radio and TV (NUJ staff writers and photographers). Associate companies specialise in management consultancy and PR.

International Feature Service, 104 rue de Laeken, 1000 Brussels, Belgium *tel* 217-03-42 *fax* 217-03-42. *Managing director:* Max S. Kleiter. Feature articles, serial rights, tests, cartoons, comic strips and illustrations. Handles English TV-features and books; also production of articles for merchandising.

International Media Association (1988), 1610B Belmont Street NW, Washington, DC 20009, USA *tel* 202-483-8645. *President:* Sheila O'Connor. World-wide syndication of previously published women's features, religious pieces and singles articles, humour pieces, travel and general interest. *Commission:* 50%.

The International Press Agency (Pty) Ltd (1934), PO Box 67, Howard Place 7450, South Africa *tel* (021) 531 1926 *fax* (021) 531 8789. *Manager:* Mrs T. Temple; *UK Office:* Mrs U.A. Barnett PhD (*managing editor*), 19 Avenue South, Surbiton, Surrey KT5 8PJ *tel/fax* 081-390 4414. South African agents for many leading British, American and continental press firms for the syndication of comic strips, cartoons, jokes, feature articles, short stories, serials, press photos for the South African market.

ITAR-Tass Agency, Suite 12-20, Morley House, 314-320 Regent Street, London W1R 5AB *tel* 071-580 5543 *fax* 071-580 5547. General, economic and commercial news service to Russia and the CIS.

Knight Features (1985), 20 Crescent Grove, London SW4 7AH *tel* 071-622 1467 *fax* 071-622 1522. *Director:* Peter Knight; *associates:* Ann King-Hall, Robin Mackay Miller, Caroline Figini. World-wide selling of strip cartoons and major features and serialisations. Exclusive agent in UK and Republic of Ireland for United Feature Syndicate and Newspaper Enterprise Association of New York.

London News Service, 68 Exmouth Market, London EC1R 4RA *tel* 071-278 5661 *fax* 071-278 8480 *telex* 94018004 FSNA G. *Editor:* John Rodgers. World-wide syndication of features and photos.

Maharaja Features Pvt. Ltd, 5/226 Sion Road East, Bombay 400022, India *tel* 22-4097951 *fax* 22-4097801. *Editor:* K.R.N. Swamy; *managing editor:* K.R. Padmanabhan. Syndicates feature and pictorial material, of interest to Asian readers, to newspapers and magazines in India, UK and abroad. Specialists in well-researched articles on India by eminent authorities for publication in prestige journals throughout the world. Also topical features 1000-1500 words. Represents PA NewsFeatures and Central Press Features of London in India. *Illustrations:* b&w prints and colour transparencies.

Mirror Syndication International, Unique House, 21-31 Woodfield Road, London W9 2BA *tel* 071-266 1133 *fax* 071-266 2563. Supplies publishing material and international rights for news text and pictures from Mirror Group Newspapers and other large publishing houses. Extensive picture library of all subjects.

New Blitz International, Via Cimabue 5, 00196 Rome, Italy *tel* 32 01 489, 32 00 620 *fax* 32 19 014. *President:* Vinicio Congiu; *sales manager:* Gianni Piccione; *graphic, literary and television depts:* Giovanni A. Congiu. Syndicates cartoons, comic strips, humorous books with drawings, general books, feature and pictorial material, environment, travels, throughout the world and Italy. Average rates of commission 60-40%, monthly report of sales, payments on receipt of invoice.

New Zealand Press Association, 85 Fleet Street, London EC4P 4AJ *tel* 071-353 7040 *fax* 071-583 3563.

North West News & Sports Agency Ltd (1956), 148 Meols Parade, Meols, Wirral L47 6AN *tel* 051-632 5261 *fax* 051-632 5484. News and sports coverage, Birkenhead, Bebington, Wallasey and Wirral.

Orion Press, 55 1-Chome, Kanda-Jimbocho, Chiyoda-ku, Tokyo 101, Japan *tel* (03) 3295-1402 *telegraphic address* Orionserv, Tokyo *fax* (03) 3295-1430. International press service.

PA NewsFeatures (the Feature Service of the Press Association Ltd), 85 Fleet Street, London EC4P 4BE *tel* 071-353 7440 *fax* 071-936 2400. *NewsFeatures editor:* Catharine Eccles. World-wide syndication to newspapers, magazines and trade journals of text and strip services.

Chandra S. Perera, Cinetra, 437 Pethiyagoda, Kelaniya, Sri Lanka *tel* 521885 *cables* 521885 Colombo *telex* 22973 VITHY-CE ATTN CHANDRA PERERA *fax* 449427/446045 VITHTHY COM ATTN CHANDRA PERERA. Press and TV news, news films on Sri Lanka and Maldives, colour and b&w photo news and features, photographic and film coverages, screenplays and scripts for TV and films, press clippings. Broadcasting, television and newspapers; journalistic features, news, broadcasting and TV interviews.

Pixfeatures, P.G. Wickman, 5 Latimer Road, Barnet, Herts. EN5 5NU *tel* 081-449 9946 *fax* 081-441 6246. Specialises in sale of picture features and news to British, European and South African press.

The Press Association Ltd (1868), 85 Fleet Street, London EC4P 4BE *tel* 071-353 7440 *telegraphic address* Press Association, London. *Chief executive:* R.B. Simpson; *editor-in-chief:* C.T. Webb; *finance director:* R.C. Henry. National news agency: screen teleprinter and viewdata news and sports, photos, features. Distributes world agencies' news in British Isles outside London.

Christopher Rann & Associates Pty Ltd (1977), 185 Melbourne Street, North Adelaide, South Australia 5006 *tel* (08) 267 2299 *fax* (08) 267 5524. *Proprietors:* C.F. Rann, J.M. Jose. Former BBC and CBS News foreign correspondents offering full range of professional PR, press releases, special newsletters, commercial intelligence, media monitoring. Major clients in Australia, Britain and Scandinavia. Welcomes approaches from organisations requiring PR representation or press release distribution.

Reportage Bureau RBL, Kalevankatu 14 C, 00100 Helsinki-10, Finland *tel* (0) 640 522 *cables* Reportage Helsinki *telex* 123949 RBL SF. Philip Laszlo.

Republican Press (London), Suite 15-17, The Outer Temple, 222-225 Strand, London WC2R 1BA   *tel* 071-353 2580   *fax* 071-353 2578. Acquire material for publication in South Africa.

Reuters Limited, 85 Fleet Street, London EC4P 4AJ   *tel* 071-250 1122   *telex* 28355/265952.

Anton Rippon Press Services, 20 Chain Lane, Mickleover, Derby DE3 5AJ   *tel* (0332) 512379   *fax* (0332) 292755. News, sport and feature coverage of East Midlands.

Singer Media Corporation, Seaview Business Park, 1030 Calle Cordillera, Unit 106, San Clemente, CA 92673   *tel* 714-498-7227   *fax* 714-498-2162. *President:* Dr Kurt Singer. Use 30 features every week which are distributed to publications in 35 countries. Current needs for reprint rights (no originals): profiles of famous people – 1-3 parts; women's fiction (high standard only); modern romance books; books published by reputable publishers. 'We accept only previously published material.' Interested in books for serial and book rights. Modern romance titles in demand; also business and computer books, mysteries and biographies. World-wide syndication of cartoons, strips and interviews with celebrities.

Solo Syndication & Literary Agency Ltd (1978), 49-53 Kensington High Street, London W8 5ED   *tel* 071-376 2166   *fax* 071-938 3165. *Chairman:* Don Short. World-wide syndication of newspaper features, photos, cartoons, strips and book serialisations. Professional journalists only. *Commission:* 50/50. Agency represents the international syndication of Associated Newspapers, IPC Magazines (*Woman, Woman's Own, Woman's Realm, Woman's Weekly*), News Ltd of Australia, *New Idea* and *TV Week,* Australia.

South Bedfordshire News Agency, 134 Marsh Road, Luton LU3 2NL   *tel* (0582) 572222   *fax* (0582) 493486.

Southern Media Services (division of Maximedia Pty Ltd), PO Box 268, Springwood, NSW 2777, Australia   *tel* (047) 514 967   *fax* (047) 515 545. *Directors:* Nic van Oudtshoorn, Daphne van Oudtshoorn. Illustrated features (colour and b&w) to newspapers and magazines in Australasia and many parts of the world. Also stock colour library. Assignments (news and feature stories, photos) accepted at moderate rates. Syndicates freelance features and photo features in Australia and abroad, but query before submitting. Commission 50% or by arrangement.

Swedish Features, Görwellsgatan 28B, 112 88 Stockholm, Sweden   *tel* 8-738 32 74   *telex* 17480   *fax* 8-618 28 72. *Managing director:* Herborg Ericson. *Market:* newspapers, magazines and weeklies in Sweden, Norway, Denmark and Finland. *Syndicates:* high quality features of international appeal such as topical articles, photo-features – b&w and colour, women's features, short stories, serial novels, non-fiction stories and serials with strong human interest, popular science, cartoons, comic strips and TV features and TV personalities.

Syndicated International Network (S.I.N.) (1984), Second Floor, 208-209 Upper Street, Islington, London N1 1RL   *tel* 071-359 0200   *fax* 071-359 2228. *Managing director:* Johnny Waller; *photo editor:* Liane Hentscher. World-wide syndication of interview texts and photos, primarily of music and cinema artists. Unsolicited material always considered. *Commission:* 40%.

Peter Tauber Press Agency (1950), 94 East End Road, London N3 2SX   *tel* 081-346 4165   *telegraphic address* Tauberpres N3. UK and world-wide syndication of exclusive big name celebrity interviews, especially interviews with their associates or ex-associates. Also unique human interest features. *Commission:* 25%.

TEXT Syndication (at Camera Press) (1993), 21 Queen Elizabeth Street, London SE1 2PD *tel* 071-378 1300 ext 232 *fax* 071-278 5126. *Contact:* Amanda Jackson. Syndicates freelance material to magazines and newspapers around the world. Please enquire before submitting manuscripts. *Terms:* 50%.

TransAtlantic News Service, 7100 Hillside Avenue, Suite 304, Hollywood, CA 90046, USA *tel* 213-874-1284. News and photo agency serving the British and foreign press. Staffed by former Fleet Street reporters, TANS supplies entertainment news, features and columns from Hollywood, and topical news in general from California. Covers all Hollywood events and undertakes commissions and assignments in all fields. Candid photos of stars at major Hollywood events a speciality.

United Press International, 408 Strand, London WC2R 1NG *tel* 071-333 0999 (news), 071-333 0990 (admin), 071-333 1666 (sports) *fax* 071-333 1690 (news), 071-333 1680 (admin).

Universal Pictorial Press & Agency Ltd (1929), New Bridge Street House, 30-34 New Bridge Street, London EC4V 6BN *tel* 071-248 6730 *fax* 071-489 8982. *Managing director:* T.R. Smith. Syndication of daily press and library photo service to the national and provincial press, periodicals and television companies in the British Isles and overseas.

Visual Humour (1984), 5 Greymouth Close, Stockton-on-Tees, Cleveland TS18 5LF *tel* (0642) 581847/021-429 5861 *fax* (0642) 581847. *Contact:* Peter Dodsworth. Daily and weekly humorous cartoon strips; also single panel cartoon features (not single cartoons) for possible syndication in the UK and abroad. Picture puzzles and humorous greetings card designs also considered. Submit photocopy samples only initially, with sae.

Wessex News (1981), Neate's Yard, 108 High Street, Hungerford, Berks. RG17 0NB *tel* (0488) 686810 *fax* (0488) 686900. *Proprietor:* Jim Hardy. News service for nationals, TV and radio from the South of England. Commission: NUJ rates.

Eric Whitehead, Picture Agency and Library (1984), PO Box 33, Kendal, Cumbria LA9 4SU *tel* (05396) 21002 *mobile* (0850) 713572. News coverage of Lancaster to Carlisle, Lake District.

Yaffa Newspaper Service of New Zealand, PO Box 509, 10 Spencer Street, Wellington 4, New Zealand *tel* (04) 793 531 *fax* (04) 797 221.

Books

Book Publishers

SUBMITTING MANUSCRIPTS

Care should be taken when submitting manuscripts to book publishers. A suitable publisher should be chosen either by examining publishers' lists of publications or by looking out for the names of suitable publishers in the relevant sections in libraries and bookshops. It is a waste of time and money to send the MS of a novel to a publisher who publishes no fiction, or poetry to one who publishes no verse, though all too often this is done. To assist the writer of fiction in particular, a classified list of publishers, by fiction genre, will be found on page 207.

A preliminary letter is appreciated by most publishers, and this should outline the nature and extent of the MS and enquire whether the publisher would be prepared to read it (writers have been known to send out such letters of enquiry in duplicated form, an approach not calculated to stimulate a publisher's interest). It is desirable to enclose the cost of return postage (International Reply Coupons if writing from outside the UK) when submitting the MS and finally it must be understood that although every reasonable care is taken of material in the publishers' possession, responsibility cannot be accepted for any loss or damage thereto.

Publishers are busy people, who collectively receive thousands of unsolicited MSS each year. Be patient, therefore, in awaiting a decision on your work. Most publishers acknowledge receipt of a MS: if you do not hear within a few days, it is permissible to check that your work has arrived safely. Some publishers – especially if your material is topical – will then decide fairly quickly, but a two months' wait is more usual. If you have not then heard, write politely asking for a decision.

Children's books

Submission of material – both text and illustrations – for children's books requires particular consideration. Attention is therefore drawn to the article on page 245 on advice for this market. A classified list of publishers and packagers of children's books follows on page 248.

For more on the submission of manuscripts, see *Typescripts* in the **Preparation of Material, Resources** section. See also the article *Writing for the European Community*, especially page 122.

EUROPEAN ENGLISH-LANGUAGE PUBLISHERS

With the advent of the European single market, and to assist writers in placing English-language works with European publishers, a list of European publishers in the English language, and the material they accept, will be found on page 211.

SMALL PRESSES

It is beyond the scope of the *Yearbook* to list all the many smaller publishers which have either a limited output, or who specialise in poetry, avant-garde or other fringe publishing. Details are given of some of the better-known small poetry houses, but for a comprehensive listing, the reader is referred to the *Small Press Yearbook*, published by Small Press Group, Middlesex University, White Hart Lane, London N7 8HR   *tel* 081-362 6058, and to *Small Presses & Little Magazines in the UK and Ireland*, available from Oriel, The Welsh Arts Council's Bookshop, The Friary, Cardiff CF1 4AA   *tel* (0222) 225855.

SELF-PUBLISHING

Authors are strongly advised not to pay for the publication of their work. If a MS is worth publishing, a reputable firm of publishers will undertake publication at its own expense, except possibly for works of an academic nature. In this connection attention is drawn to the articles on *Self-publishing* and *Vanity Publishing*, at the end of this section, and to Michael Legat's article on *Publishing Agreements* in the **Publishing Practice** section.

UNITED KINGDOM

(For Northern Ireland publishers, see under Irish listings on page 225.)

* Member of the Publishers Association

*AA Publishing (1979), Automobile Association, Fanum House, Basingstoke, Hants RG21 2EA   *tel* (0256) 20123   *telex* 858538 AABAS G   *fax* (0256) 22575. *Managing director:* John Howard, *marketing and international sales director:* S.J. Mesquita; *editorial manager:* Michael Buttler.
Travel, atlases, maps, leisure interests, including Baedeker, Essential, Thomas Cook and Explorer Travel Guides.

Abacus (1971)—see **Little, Brown and Company (UK) Ltd.**

ABC, All Books for Children (1990), 33 Museum Street, London WC1A 1LD   *tel* 071-436 6300   *telex* 21134 ABCDEF G   *fax* 071-240 6923. *Managing director/publisher:* Susan Tarsky; *chairman:* Timothy Chadwick; *financial director:* Michael Raine. Division of The All Children's Co. Ltd.
Children's picture books up to age seven; non-fiction for 7-11. All MSS to Carol Mackenzie.

Absolute Press (1979), 14 Widcombe Crescent, Bath, Avon BA2 6AH   *tel* (0225) 316013   *fax* (0225) 445836. *Director:* Jon Croft.
Food and wine, theatre/playscripts, travel guides.

*Abson Books (1970), 17 Fosseway Court, The Fosseway, Clifton, Bristol BS8 4EH   *tel/fax* (0272) 734486. *Partners:* Anthea Bickerton, Pat McCormack.
English speaking glossaries, guides, West Region; literary puzzle books. No fiction.

*Academic Press—see **Harcourt Brace and Co.**

*Academy Editions (1967), 42 Leinster Gardens, London W2 3AN   *tel* 071-402 2141   *fax* 071-723 9540. *Director:* J.V. Stoddart. Member of the Academy Group Ltd.
Art, architecture, crafts, design, photography, fashion, urbanism, philosophy. *Series include Architectural Design* Profiles, Architectural Monographs, *Art and Design* Profiles, Art Monographs, and *UIA Journal, Journal of Philosophy and the Visual Arts, What Is . . .?*.

*Access Press—see **HarperCollins Publishers.**

*Ace Books (1973), Age Concern England, 1268 London Road, London SW16 4ER *tel* 081-679 8000 *fax* 081-679 6069. *Manager:* David Moncrieff; *marketing:* Michael Addison.
Health and care, advice, leisure, finance, gerontology.

*Acorn Editions—see **James Clarke & Co. Ltd.**

Actinic Press—see **Cressrelles Publishing Co. Ltd.**

*Addison-Wesley Publishers Ltd (1970), Finchampstead Road, Wokingham, Berks. RG11 2NZ *tel* (0734) 794000 *telex* 846136 *fax* (0734) 794035. *Directors:* Derek Hall (managing), L. Jones, N.W. White.
Educational, pure and applied sciences, engineering, computing, software, business studies, economics.

*Adlard Coles Nautical—see **A. & C. Black (Publishers) Ltd.**

*Adlib—see **Scholastic Children's Books.**

Airlife Publishing Ltd (1976), 101 Longden Road, Shrewsbury, Shropshire SY3 9EB *tel* (0743) 235651 *fax* (0743) 232944. *Directors:* Alastair Simpson (chairman and managing), Robert Pooley, Andrew Johnston (sales), John Gibbs; *managing editor:* John Beaton.
Aviation, technical and general, military.
Swan Hill Press (imprint). *Managing editor:* John Beaton. Natural history, wildlife arts, travel, equestrian, fishing, country sports and pursuits.
Waterline Books (imprint). *Managing editor:* P. Coles. Sailing.

Alkin Books Ltd (1992), 28 Phillimore Walk, Kensington, London W8 7SA *tel/ fax* 071-937 2351. *Managing director:* Mrs Amber G. Moore.
General non-fiction.

Ian Allan Ltd, Coombelands House, Coombelands Lane, Addlestone, Surrey KT15 1HY *tel* (0932) 855909 *fax* (0932) 854750. *Publishing director:* Simon Forty.
Transport: railways, aircraft, shipping, road; naval and military history; reference books and magazines; no fiction.

*George Allen & Unwin Publishers Ltd—acquired by **HarperCollins Publishers.**

J.A. Allen & Co. Ltd (1926), 1 Lower Grosvenor Place, Buckingham Palace Road, London SW1W 0EL *tel* 071-834 0090/5606 *telegraphic address* Allenbooks, London *fax* 071-976 5836. *Chairman and managing director:* Joseph A. Allen; *publishing manager:* Caroline Burt.
Specialist publishers of books on the horse and equestrianism including bloodstock breeding, racing, polo, dressage, horse care, carriage driving, breeds, veterinary and farriery. Technical books usually commissioned but willing to consider any serious, specialist MSS on the horse and related subjects. Also willing to consider exceptionally well-written horse/pony related fiction suitable for young and teenage readers.

W.H. Allen—acquired by **Virgin Publishing Ltd.**

*Allen Lane The Penguin Press—see **Penguin Books Ltd.**

Allison & Busby, 5 The Lodge, Richmond Way, London W12 8LW *tel* 081-749 9441/3254 *fax* 081-749 9496. *Managing director:* Peter Day; *editors:* Petra Fergusson, Katherine Bright-Holmes; *rights:* Sarah Fulford.
Biography and memoirs, general, crime and international fiction, translations, writers' guides. Unsolicited MSS welcome but sae essential.

AN Publications (1980), PO Box 23, Sunderland SR4 6DG *tel* 091-567 3589 *fax* 091-564 1600. *Commissioning editor:* David Butler; *publisher:* Richard Padwick.
Information for the visual arts, including directories of galleries, setting up exhibitions, copyright, finance, health and safety, crafts.

Anaya Publishers Ltd (1988), 3rd Floor, Strode House, 44-50 Osnaburgh Street, London NW1 3ND *tel* 071-383 2997 *fax* 071-383 3076. *Chairman:* Germán Sánchez Ruipérez; *managing director:* Colin Ancliffe; *publishing director:* Carey Smith (craft and general).
Reference: cookery, up-market life style and interiors, arts and crafts, sports and leisure, biography.

Andersen Press Ltd (1976), 20 Vauxhall Bridge Road, London SW1V 2SA *tel* 071-973 9720 *telegraphic address* Literarius, London *telex* 261212 LITLDN G *fax* 071-233 6263. *Managing director/publisher:* Klaus Flugge; *directors:* Philip Durrance, Denise Johnstone-Burt (editorial), Joëlle Flugge (company secretary).
Children's picture books and fiction (send synopsis and sample chapter with sae); *no* short stories. International co-productions.

Antique Collectors' Club (1965), 5 Church Street, Woodbridge, Suffolk IP12 1DS *tel* (0394) 385501 *telex* 987271 ANTBOK G *fax* (0394) 384434. *Managing director:* Diana Steel.
Fine art, antiques, gardening and garden history, architecture.

Anvil Press Poetry (1968), 69 King George Street, London SE10 8PX *tel* 081-858 2946. *Directors:* Peter Jay, Nicole Lee.
Poetry. Submissions only with sae.

Apple Press (1984), The Old Brewery, 6 Blundell Street, London N7 9BH *tel* 071-700 6700 *fax* 071-700 4191. Imprint of **Quarto Publishing plc**, book packagers.
Leisure, domestic and craft pursuits; cookery, gardening, sport, transport, militaria, fine and decorative art.

*Aquarian Press—see **HarperCollins Publishers.**

Arc Publications (incorporating **Littlewood · Arc**), Nanholme Mill, Shaw Wood Road, Todmorden, Lancs. OL14 6DA *tel* (0706) 812338 *fax* (0706) 818948. *Partners:* Rosemary Jones, Tony Ward (general editor), Angela Jarman; *associate editors:* Michael Hulse (international), David Morley (UK).
Poetry.

Arena—see **Ashgate Publishing Ltd.**

Argus Books, Argus House, Boundary Way, Hemel Hempstead, Herts. HP2 7ST *tel* (0442) 66551 *fax* (0442) 66998. *Manager:* B. Laughlin.
Modelling, model engineering, woodworking, aviation, railways, military, crafts, electronics, home brewing and winemaking.

*Arkana—see **Penguin Books Ltd.**

*Armada—see **HarperCollins Publishers.**

*Arms & Armour Press—see **Cassell plc.**

*E.J. Arnold Publishing Division—see **Thomas Nelson & Sons Ltd.**

*Edward Arnold (1890)—see **Hodder Headline plc.**

*Arrow Books Ltd—see **Random House UK Ltd.**

Art Trade Press Ltd, 9 Brockhampton Road, Havant, Hants PO9 1NU *tel* (0705) 484943. *Editorial director:* J.M. Curley.
Publishers of *Who's Who in Art.*

Ashford, Buchan and Enright (1985), PO Box 20, Leatherhead, Surrey KT24 5HH *tel* (0483) 282991 *fax* (0483) 281121. *Managing director:* John Mole.
Travel, field sports, nautical, general and military history.

Ashgate Publishing Ltd (1987), Gower House, Croft Road, Aldershot, Hants GU11 3HR *tel* (0252) 331551 *fax* (0252) 344405. *Chairman:* Nigel Farrow.
Arena (imprint). *Editor:* Jo Gooderham. Social work and issues.
Avebury (imprint). *Editors:* Jo Gooderham, Sarah Markham. Social sciences research publications, including economics, business, organisational and development studies, regional science, social work and policy, ethnic studies, criminology; joint imprint with **Cranfield University Press** includes aviation and aeronautics, business studies, and agricultural and food sciences.
Scolar Press (imprint). *Editors:* Nigel Farrow, Alec MacAulay, Rachel Lynch.
Art history, print making, music studies, history of the book and other arts and humanities.
Variorum (imprint). *Editor:* John Smedley. Early and medieval history.

Ashmolean Museum Publications (1972), Beaumont Street, Oxford OX1 2PH *tel* (0865) 278009/278010 *fax* (0865) 278018. *Publications officer:* Ian Charlton.
Fine and applied art, archaeology, history, numismatics.

Aslib (The Association for Information Management) (1924), 20-24 Old Street, London EC1V 9AP *tel* 071-253 4488 *fax* 071-430 0514. For details see entry under **Societies, Associations and Clubs** on page 610.

Associated University Presses—see **Golden Cockerel Press.**

The Athlone Press Ltd (1949), 1 Park Drive, London NW11 7SG *tel* 081-458 0888. *Directors:* Brian Southam, Doris Southam, Clive Bingley.
Anthropology, archaeology, architecture, art, economics, history, Japan, language, law, literature, medical, music, oriental, philosophy, politics, psychology, religion, science, sociology, cultural studies.

Atlantic Europe Publishing Co. Ltd (1989), 86 Peppard Road, Sonning Common, Reading, Berks. RG4 9RP *tel* (0734) 723751 *fax* (0734) 724488. *Directors:* Dr B.J. Knapp, D.L.R. McCrae.
Children's colour information books: science, geography, history, design and technology. Associate company: Earthscape Editions (*see* Book Packagers).

Aurum Press Ltd (1977), 25 Bedford Avenue, London WC1B 3AT *tel* 071-637 3225 *fax* 071-580 2469. *Directors:* André Deutsch (chairman), Bill McCreadie (managing), Piers Burnett (editorial), Sheila Murphy (marketing and rights).
General, illustrated and non-illustrated adult non-fiction: biography and memoirs, visual arts, film, home interest, travel.

Avebury—see **Ashgate Publishing Ltd.**

Bernard Babani (Publishing) Ltd, The Grampians, Shepherds Bush Road, London W6 7NF *tel* 071-603 2581/7296 *fax* 071-603 8203. *Directors:* S. Babani, M.H. Babani BSc(Eng).
Practical handbooks on radio, electronics and computing.

*Baillière Tindall (1826)—see **Harcourt Brace and Co.**

*Bantam, Bantam Press, Bantam Young Adult—see **Transworld Publishers Ltd.**

Barefoot Books Ltd (1993), PO Box 95, Kingswood, Bristol BS15 5BH   *tel* (0272) 328885   *fax* (0272) 328881. *Publisher:* Tessa Strickland.
Children's picture books: myth, legend, fairytale.

*Barrie & Jenkins—see **Random House UK Ltd.**

*Bartholomew—see **HarperCollins Publishers.**

*B.T. Batsford Ltd (1843), 4 Fitzhardinge Street, London W1H 0AH   *tel* 071-486 8484   *fax* 071-487 4296. *President:* Peter Kemmis Betty; *chairman:* Stephen Quinn; *chief executive:* Bobby Cox; *deputy chairman:* Ian Moore; *directors:* Timothy Auger (editorial), A.N. Finlay (finance; company secretary), R.E. Huggins (production; US sales); David Kidd (sales and marketing).
Archaeology, architecture, building, art techniques, cinema, chess, costume, equestrian, country sports, craft, needlecraft, lace, horticulture, junior reference, technical/professional, graphic design.
Seaby (imprint). Numismatics.

*BBC Books, BBC Publishing, Woodlands, 80 Wood Lane, London W12 0TT   *tel* 081-576 2000   *telex* 934678 BBCENT G   *fax* 081-576 2858. *Editorial manager:* Caroline Plaisted.
Books related to BBC television and radio programmes of all subjects.
Network Books (imprint). Range of non-fiction titles tied into non-BBC television programmes.

*BBC Radio Collection, BBC Publishing, Woodlands, 80 Wood Lane, London W12 0TT   *tel* 081-576 2000   *telex* 934678 BBCENT G   *fax* 081-743 0393. *Head of spoken word:* Sue Anstruther.
Audio cassettes of BBC Radio and Television comedy, readings and dramatised serials for adults and children.

Bedford Square Press—see **NCVO Publications.**

Belitha Press Ltd (1980), 31 Newington Green, London N16 9PU   *tel* 071-241 5566   *fax* 071-254 5325. *Directors:* Richard Hayes (chairman), Peter Osborn (managing), Martin Pick, Erik Pordes (Austrian), Rachel Pick (non-executive).
Illustrated children's non-fiction for international co-editions: art, atlases, science, natural history, geography, history, picture books, humour.

*Bell & Hyman Ltd—acquired by **HarperCollins Publishers.**

Bellew Publishing Co. Ltd (1983), The Nightingale Centre, 8 Balham Hill, London SW12 9EA   *tel* 081-673 5611   *telex* 8951182 GECOMS G   *fax* 081-675 3542. *Chairman:* Anthony Rainbird; *managing director:* Ib Bellew.
Sociology of religion, art and art criticism, some fiction.

Benn Business Information Services, Riverbank House, Angel Lane, Tonbridge, Kent TN9 1SE   *tel* (0732) 362666   *telex* 95132 BENTON G   *fax* (0732) 367301.
Over 35 directories for business and industry.

David Bennett Books Ltd (1989), 94 Victoria Street, St Albans, Herts. AL1 3TG   *tel* (0727) 855878   *fax* (0727) 864085. *Managing director:* David Bennett.
Highly illustrated children's fiction and non-fiction; board books and gift books for the very young.

Berg Publishers (1983), 150 Cowley Road, Oxford OX4 1JJ   *tel* (0865) 245104   *fax* (0865) 791165. *Managing director:* Peter Cowell.
Social anthropology, European studies, politics and economics, literature.
Oswald Wolff Books (imprint), 8 Circus Lodge, Circus Road, London NW7

9JL *tel* 071-286 5654. *Director:* Mrs Ilse Wolff. German and European studies.

Berkswell Publishing Co. Ltd, PO Box 420, Warminster, Wilts. BA12 9XB *tel/fax* (0985) 40189. *Directors:* J.N.G. Stidolph, S.A. Abbott.
Books of local interest in Wessex, field sports, royalty. Ideas and MSS welcome.

Berlitz Publishing Co. Ltd (1960), Berlitz House, Peterley Road, Oxford OX4 2TX *tel* (0865) 747033 *fax* (0865) 779700. *Managing director:* Roger Kirkpatrick; *travel publisher:* Sarah Hudson; *language publisher:* Julian Parish. Travel and language.

Bible Society, Stonehill Green, Westlea, Swindon, Wilts. SN5 7DG *tel* (0793) 513713 *telex* 44283 BIBLES G *fax* (0793) 512539. *Bible Programmes director:* Julie Farrar.
Bibles, testaments, portions and selections in English and over 200 other languages; also books and audio-visual material on use of Bible for personal, education, church situations.

*Clive Bingley Ltd (1965)—see **Library Association Publishing Ltd.**

*Birnbaum—see **HarperCollins Publishers.**

*A. & C. Black plc (1807), 35 Bedford Row, London WC1R 4JH *tel* 071-242 0946 *fax* 071-831 8478. *Directors:* Charles Black (chairman and joint managing), David Gadsby (joint managing), Jill Coleman, Paul Langridge, Terry Rouelett. Proprietors of A. & C. Black (Publishers) Ltd, Nautical Publishing Co. Ltd, Christopher Helm (Publishers) Ltd, Adlard Coles Ltd.

*A. & C. Black (Publishers) Ltd (1978), 35 Bedford Row, London WC1R 4JH *tel* 071-242 0946 *fax* 071-831 8478. *Chairman:* Charles Black; *managing directors:* Charles Black, David Gadsby; *directors:* Jill Coleman (children's books), Paul Langridge (rights), Janet Murphy (Adlard Coles Nautical), Terry Rouelett (distribution), Oscar Heini (production). Subsidiary of **A. & C. Black plc.**
Children's and educational books (including music) for 3-15 years; arts and crafts, calligraphy, drama (*New Mermaid* series), fishing, reference (*Who's Who*), sport, theatre, travel (*Blue Guides*).
Adlard Coles Nautical (imprint). *Editorial director:* Janet Murphy. Nautical.
Christopher Helm (imprint). *Editor:* Robert Kirk. Ornithology.

Black Lace—see **Virgin Publishing Ltd.**

*Black Swan—see **Transworld Publishers Ltd.**

*Blackie Academic and Professional—see **Chapman & Hall Ltd.**

*Blackie Children's Books—see **Penguin Books Ltd.**

Blackstaff Press Ltd—see under Irish Book Publishers.

*Blackwell Publishers (Basil Blackwell Ltd) (1922), 108 Cowley Road, Oxford OX4 1JF *tel* (0865) 791100 *telex* 837022 *fax* (0865) 791347. *Directors:* Nigel Blackwell (chairman), René Olivieri (managing), Philip Carpenter, Sue Corbett, Mark Houlton, John Davey, Stephen Chambers.
Economics, education (academic), geography, history, industrial relations, linguistics, literature and criticism, politics, psychology, social anthropology, social policy and administration, sociology, theology, business studies, professional, law, reference, feminism, information technology, philosophy. **NCC-Blackwell**—joint venture company.
Shakespeare Head Press (imprint). Finely printed books; scholarly works.

*Blackwell Scientific Publications Ltd (1939), Osney Mead, Oxford OX2 0EL *tel* (0865) 206206 *cables* Research, Oxford *telex* 83355 MEDBOK G *fax* (0865)

721205. *Chairman:* Nigel Blackwell; *managing director:* Robert Campbell; *directors:* Jonathan Conibear, John Robson, Peter Saugman, Martin Wilkinson, John Strange, Bill Gibson (Boston).
Medicine, nursing, dentistry, veterinary medicine, life sciences, earth sciences, chemistry, professional, allied health.

Blake Publishing (1991), 158 Fulham Palace Road, London W6 9ER   *tel* 081-748 7606   *fax* 081-748 7613. *Chairman:* David Blake; *managing director:* John Blake; *assistant publisher:* Rosie Ries.
Popular fiction and non-fiction, including biographies and true crime.

*Blandford Press—see **Cassell plc.**

Bloodaxe Books Ltd (1978), PO Box 1SN, Newcastle upon Tyne NE99 1SN   *tel* 091-232 5988   *fax* 091-222 0020. *Directors:* Neil Astley, Simon Thirsk.
Poetry, literary criticism, literary biography.

*Bloomsbury Publishing plc (1986), 2 Soho Square, London W1V 5DE   *tel* 071-494 2111   *telex* 21323 BLOOMS G   *fax* 071-434 0151. *Chairman:* Nigel Newton; *directors:* Nigel Newton (managing), David Reynolds (deputy managing and publishing), Liz Calder (publishing), Alan Wherry (marketing), Kathy Rooney (editorial), Sarah Beal (sales), Florence Whyte (publicity), Ruth Logan (rights), Elizabeth Pitman (production).
Fiction, biography, illustrated, reference, travel in hardcover; trade paperback and mass market paperback.
Bloomsbury Children's Books (division). *Director:* Barry Cunningham. Picture books, fiction, novelty books.

*Blueprint—see **Chapman & Hall Ltd.**

Blueprint Monographs—see **Fourth Estate Ltd.**

*Bodley Head—see **Random House UK Ltd.**

*Bodley Head Children's—see **Random House UK Ltd.**

Bowker-Saur, Maypole House, Maypole Road, East Grinstead, West Sussex RH19 1HH   *tel* (0342) 330100   *fax* (0342) 330191. *Directors:* Ira Siegal (chairman), Charles Halpern (managing).
Bibliographies, trade and reference directories, library and information science, electronic publishing, abstracts and indexes.
Hans Zell Publishers (imprint), PO Box 56, Oxford OX1 2SJ   *tel* (0865) 511428   *fax* (0865) 311534/793298. Bibliographies, directories and other reference works; African studies, African literature (criticism only); development studies; studies on publishing and book development.

Boxtree Ltd (1986), Broadwall House, 21 Broadwall, London SE1 9PL   *tel* 071-928 9696   *fax* 071-928 5632. *Directors:* S. Mahaffy (managing), D. Inman, A. Sington, C. Brown, M. Alcock, P. Roche (non-executive chairman).
TV and film tie-ins (adult and children's non-fiction); illustrated and general non-fiction; mass market paperbacks linked to TV, film, rock and sporting events; humour.

*Marion Boyars Publishers Ltd, 24 Lacy Road, London SW15 1NL   *tel* 081-788 9522   *fax* 081-789 8122. *Directors:* Marion Boyars, Arthur Boyars.
Belles-lettres and criticism, fiction, sociology, psychology, Briefings series, feminism, history of ideas, ideas in progress series, music, travel, drama, cinema, dance, biography.

Boydell & Brewer Ltd (1969), PO Box 9, Woodbridge, Suffolk IP12 3DF.
Medieval studies, history, literature, archaeology, art history, country and sporting books. *No* unsolicited MSS.

Brassey's (UK) Ltd (1886), 33 John Street, London WC1N 2AT *tel* 071-753 7777 *fax* 071-753 7795. *Directors:* Major General A.J. Trythall CB, MA (executive deputy chairman and joint managing director), Jenny Shaw BSc(Econ), MA (joint managing director and publishing director).
Defence and national security, international relations, weapons technology, military affairs, military biography, military history, Soviet studies, reference. Publisher to the International Institute for Strategic Studies, Centre for European Policy Studies and Centre for Defence Studies.
Conway Maritime Press (imprint). *Contact:* Jenny Shaw. Maritime and naval history, ship modelling.
Putnam Aeronautical Books (imprint). *Publishing director:* Jenny Shaw. Technical and reference.

Nicholas Brealey Publishing Ltd (1992), 21 Bloomsbury Way, London WC1A 2TH *tel* 071-404 8330 *fax* 071-404 8311. *Managing director:* Nicholas Brealey.
Business, management training, Europe, law, reference, current affairs.

Breedon Books Publishing Co. Ltd (1981), 44 Friar Gate, Derby DE1 1DA *tel* (0332) 384235 *fax* (0332) 292755. *Directors:* Anton Rippon (chairman/editorial), John Grainger.
Sports, heritage, local history. *No* unsolicited MSS; preliminary letter essential.

Brimax Books Ltd—see **Reed Consumer Books.**

British Academic Press—see **I.B. Tauris & Co. Ltd.**

****The British Library (Publications)** (1973), Marketing & Publishing Office, Public Services, 41 Russell Square, London WC1B 3DG *tel* 071-323 7704 *telex* 21462 *fax* 071-323 7768. *Head of marketing and publishing:* Jane Carr; *managers:* David Way (publishing), Anne Young (product development), Karen Fermor (bookshop).
Bibliography, book arts, music, maps, oriental, manuscript studies, history, literature, facsimiles, audio-visual, and multimedia CD-ROM.

****British Museum Press** (1973), 46 Bloomsbury Street, London WC1B 3QQ *tel* 071-323 1234 *telex* 28592 BMPUBS G *fax* 071-436 7315. *Managing director:* H.J.F. Campbell; *publishing manager:* Emma Way.
Art history, archaeology, numismatics, history, oriental art and archaeology, horology.

James Brodie Ltd (1926), 15 Springfield Place, Lansdown, Bath BA1 5RA *tel* (0225) 317706. *Directors:* Corinne Wimpress (secretary), Jeremy Wimpress.
Educational (primary and secondary) books; literal classical translations.

Brown, Son & Ferguson, Ltd (1860), 4-10 Darnley Street, Glasgow G41 2SD *tel* 041-429 1234 (24 hours) *telegraphic address* Skipper, Glasgow *fax* 041-420 1694. *Editorial director:* L. Ingram-Brown.
Nautical books; Scottish poetry and plays; Scout, Cub Scout, Brownie Guide and Guide story books.

Burns & Oates Ltd (1847), Publishers to the Holy See, Wellwood, North Farm Road, Tunbridge Wells, Kent TN2 3DR *tel* (0892) 510850 *fax* (0892) 515903. *Directors:* Charlotte de la Bedoyere, Hans Küpfer.
Theology, philosophy, spirituality, church history, books of Catholic interest, craft books with religious themes and children's books with religious themes.

Burrows Publishing Ltd (1900), Publicity House, 106a Stafford Road, Wallington, Surrey SM6 9TD *tel* 081-773 9944 *fax* 081-773 8888. *Managing director:* Paul Dipre.
Guidebooks, street plans and maps, industrial and economic development handbooks, business and industrial directories.

Butterworth & Co. (Publishers) Ltd, Halsbury House, 35 Chancery Lane, London WC2A 1EL   *tel* 071-400 2500   *telex* 95678   *fax* 071-400 2842. *Chairman and chief executive:* Neville Cusworth. Division of **Reed International Books.** Law, tax and accountancy publishing.

Butterworth Architecture (imprint of Butterworth-Heinemann). *Editorial director:* Peter Dixon; *publisher:* Neil Warnock-Smith. Architecture, the environment, planning, townscape, building technology; general.

Butterworth Law Publishers   *fax* 071-405 1332. *Chief executive:* David Summers. Legal books, journals and loose leaf services.

Butterworth Tax Publishers   *fax* 071-405 1332. *Executive director:* Christine Durman. Tax and accountancy books, journals and loose leaf services.

Butterworth-Heinemann, Linacre House, Jordan Hill, Oxford OX2 8DP   *tel* (0865) 310366   *fax* (0865) 310898. *Managing director:* Douglas Fox. Academic, technical, medical and business books.

Focal Press (imprint of Butterworth-Heinemann)   *fax* (0865) 314572. *Publishing director:* Peter Dixon. Professional, technical and academic books on photography, broadcasting, film, television, radio, audio visual and communication media.

Cadogan Books Ltd, Letts House, Parkgate Road, London SW11 4NQ   *tel* 071-738 1961   *fax* 071-924 5491. *Chairman:* William Colegrave.
Travel (Cadogan Travel Guides), chess (Pergamon), bridge.

*Calder Publications Ltd, 9-15 Neal Street, London WC2H 9TU   *tel* 071-497 1741. *Director:* John Calder.
European, international and British fiction and plays, art, literary, music and social criticism, biography and autobiography, essays, humanities and social sciences, European classics. *No unsolicited typescripts. Letters of inquiry must include an sae.* Series include: New Paris Editions, Scottish Library, New Writing and Writers, Platform Books, Opera Library, Historical Perspectives.

*Cambridge University Press (1534), The Edinburgh Building, Shaftesbury Road, Cambridge CB2 2RU   *tel* (0223) 312393   *telex* 817256 CUPCAM G   *fax* (0223) 315052. *Chief executive of the Press and University printer:* Anthony K. Wilson MA; *deputy chief executive and managing director (publishing division) and Press editorial director:* Jeremy Mynott MA, PhD.
Anthropology and archaeology, art and architecture, classical studies, computer science, educational (primary, secondary, tertiary), educational software, English language teaching, history, journals (humanities, social sciences and sciences), language and literature, law, mathematics, medicine, music, oriental, philosophy, politics, psychology, reference, science (physical and biological), social sciences, theology, religion. The Bible and Prayer Book.

Canongate Press Ltd (1973), 14 Frederick Street, Edinburgh EH2 2HB   *tel* 031-220 3800   *fax* 031-220 3888. *Directors:* Andrew Haigh (managing), Stephanie Wolfe Murray, J. Ridge, J. Halpin, N. Moir, S. Snow.
Adult general non-fiction and fiction; children's fiction.

The Canterbury Press Norwich, St Mary's Works, St Mary's Plain, Norwich, Norfolk NR3 3BH   *tel* (0603) 616563/612914   *fax* (0603) 624483. *Publisher:* G.A. Knights. Book publishing imprint of **Hymns Ancient and Modern Ltd,** music publishers.
Church of England doctrine, theology, history and associated topics, music and liturgy.

*Jonathan Cape—see **Random House UK Ltd.**

*Jonathan Cape Children's Books—see **Random House UK Ltd.**

Carcanet Press Ltd (1969), 208 Corn Exchange Buildings, Manchester M4 3BQ　*tel* 061-834 8730　*fax* 061-832 0084. *Director:* Michael Schmidt.
Poetry, memoirs (literary), Fyfield Series, translations, biography.

Carlton Books (1992), 20 St Anne's Court, Wardour Street, London W1V 3AW　*tel* 071-734 7338　*fax* 071-434 1196. *Directors:* Jonathan Goodman (managing), John Maynard (operations), Piers Murray Hill (editorial), Russell Porter (design), Adrian Whitton (finance).
Popular music, sport, games, film, video, popular science, life style, New Age, TV tie-ins, criminology.

Frank Cass & Co. Ltd (1958), Newbury House, 890-900 Eastern Avenue, Newbury Park, Ilford, Essex IG2 7HH　*tel* 081-599 8866　*fax* 081-599 0984.
Directors: Frank Cass (managing), A.E. Cass, M.P. Zaidner.
History, African studies, Middle East studies, economic and social history, military and strategic studies, international affairs, development studies, academic journals.
Vallentine Mitchell (imprint). Jewish interest.
Woburn Press (imprint). Educational.

***Cassell plc** (1848), Villiers House, 41-47 Strand, London WC2N 5JE　*tel* 071-839 4900　*fax* 071-839 1804. *Chairman and managing director:* Philip Sturrock; *directors:* Stephen Butcher (trade sales and marketing), Clare Howell (general non-fiction), Stephen Lustig (academic), Alan Badger (UK trade sales).
Arms & Armour Press (imprint). *Director:* Rod Dymott. Military history (land, sea, air, weaponry), military reference, military adventure non-fiction, modern defence/intelligence.
Blandford Press (imprint). *Director:* Rod Dymott. Aviculture, history, hobbies, music, natural history, practical handbooks, sport, New Age/mind, body, spirit.
Cassell (general imprint). *Editorial director:* Clare Howell. Cookery, poetry, life style, gardening, word reference, art and craft, popular science, current affairs.
Cassell (academic imprint). *Editorial director:* Stephen Lustig. Education, hotel and catering management, psychology and counselling, business and professional reference.
Geoffrey Chapman (imprint). *Publisher:* Ruth McCurry. Religion and theology, particularly Roman Catholic.
Victor Gollancz Ltd (imprint). *Directors:* Richard Evans (science fiction and fantasy), Chris Kloet (children's), Liz Knights (publishing and general non-fiction). Biography and autobiography, children's books, current affairs, fiction, crime fiction, science fiction, fantasy and macabre, history, music, humour, sociology, travel. In association with Peter Crawley: Master Bridge Series, historical architecture, cookery, general. Synopsis, sample chapters and sae requested before submitting MSS.
Mansell Publishing (imprint). *Director:* Stephen Lustig. Bibliographies in all academic subject areas and monographs in urban and regional planning, Islamic studies, librarianship, history.
Mowbray (imprint). *Publisher:* Judith Longman. Religion and theology, both Anglican and non-denominational.
New Orchard Editions (imprint). *Director:* Alan Smith. Antiques and collecting, children's, cookery, wines and spirits, gardening, history and antiquarian, illustrated and fine editions, military and war, natural history, reference and dictionaries, transport, travel and topography.
Studio Vista (imprint). *Editorial director:* Clare Howell. Art, antiques and collecting, architecture and design, decorative arts, film books, practical art.

Cassell plc—*continued*
Tycooly Publishing (imprint). *Director:* Stephen Lustig. Natural resources, agriculture and environment, scientific policy for economy of tropical and developing world.
Ward Lock (imprint). *Director:* Alison McWilliam. Cookery, gardening, equestrian and outdoor pursuits, popular reference books, DIY, health.
Wisley Handbooks (imprint). *Trade publisher:* Barry Holmes. Gardening.
H.F. & G. Witherby Ltd (imprint). *Consultant:* Antony Witherby. Sport.

Castle House Publications Ltd (1973), 28-30 Church Road, Tunbridge Wells, Kent TN1 1JP   *tel* (0892) 539606   *fax* (0892) 517005. *Director:* D. Reinders. Medical.

Kyle Cathie Ltd (1990), 7/8 Hatherley Street, London SW1P 2QT   *tel* 071-834 8027   *fax* 071-821 9258. *Publisher and managing director:* Kyle Cathie.
History, natural history, health, biography, food and drink; craft; gardening; reference; poetry.

Catholic Truth Society (1868), 192 Vauxhall Bridge Road, London SW1V 1PD   *tel* 071-834 4392. *Chairman:* Rt Rev. Peter Smith DCL, LLB; *general secretary:* David Murphy MA.
General books of Roman Catholic and Christian interest, bibles, prayer books and pamphlets of doctrinal, historical, devotional or social interest. MSS of 4000 to 5000 words or 2500 to 3000 words with up to six illustrations considered for publication as pamphlets.

Causeway Press Ltd (1982), PO Box 13, 129 New Court Way, Ormskirk, Lancs. L39 5HP   *tel* (0695) 576048/577360   *fax* (0695) 570714. *Directors:* Mike Haralambos (chairman), Pauline Haralambos, Dave Gray (company secretary), David Alcorn.
School textbooks: mathematics, history, economics, business studies, sociology, politics, geography, technology.

CBD Research Ltd (1961), 15 Wickham Road, Beckenham, Kent BR3 2JS   *tel* 081-650 7745   *fax* 081-650 0768. *Directors:* G.P. Henderson, S.P.A. Henderson, C.A.P. Henderson, A.J.W. Henderson.
Directories, reference books, bibliographies, guides to business and statistical information.

Centaur Press (1954), Fontwell, Arundel, West Sussex BN18 0TA   *tel* Eastergate (0243) 543302. *Directors:* Jon Wynne-Tyson, Jennifer M. Wynne-Tyson, M.S. Cover, S.J. Cover, C.A. Vacher, C.G. Vacher.
Philosophy, environment, humane education, biography. Principal series: The Kinship Library. A preliminary letter should be sent before submitting MS.

*Century—see **Random House UK Ltd.**

*Chambers—imprint of **Larousse plc.**

Chansitor Publications Ltd, St Mary's Works, St Mary's Plain, Norwich, Norfolk NR3 3BH   *tel* (0603) 615995   *fax* (0603) 624483. *Publisher:* G.A. Knights. Church Pulpit Year Book.
Religious and Moral Education Press (RMEP) (imprint). Books for teachers, primary and secondary schools on religious, moral, personal and social education.

Chapman (1989)—see **The Orion Publishing Group Ltd.**

*Chapman & Hall Ltd, 2-6 Boundary Row, London SE1 8HN   *tel* 071-865 0066   *telex* 290164 CHAPMA G   *fax* 071-522 9623. *Directors:* D.S.B. Inglis (managing), A. Watkinson (publisher), J. Lavender (marketing), G. McDonald

(production), A. Davis (finance), P. Read (publisher, Spon), D. Recaldin (publisher), A. Graeme MacKintosh (publisher, Blackie), J. Buckingham (publisher), N. Dunton (publisher, medicine and life sciences).
Scientific, technical, medical and professional publishers.
Blackie Academic and Professional (imprint), Bishopbriggs, Glasgow G64 2NZ *tel* 041-762 2332 *fax* 041-772 7524. *Editorial director:* Dr A. Graeme MacKintosh. Academic and professional, books for chemistry and food science.
Blueprint (imprint). *Publisher:* Vivien James. Books for the publishing and printing industries.
H.K. Lewis & Co. Ltd (imprint). Science, medical.
E. & F.N. Spon Ltd (division). *Publisher:* P. Read. Architecture, building, surveying, civil engineering, landscape architecture, construction, planning, sports sciences, leisure and recreation management.

*Geoffrey Chapman—see **Cassell plc.**

Paul Chapman Publishing Ltd (1987), 144 Liverpool Road, London N1 1LA *tel* 071-609 5315/6 *fax* 071-700 1057. *Directors:* P.R. Chapman (managing), Marianne Lagrange (editorial).
Business, management, accounting, finance, economics, geography, environment, planning, education.

*Chatto & Windus—see **Random House UK Ltd.**

Child's Play (International) Ltd (1972), Ashworth Road, Bridgemead, Swindon, Wilts. SN5 7YD *tel* (0793) 616286 *fax* (0793) 512795. *Chairman and publishing director:* Michael Twinn.
Children's educational books: board, activity and play books, fiction and non-fiction.

Church of Scotland Board of Communication—see **The Saint Andrew Press.**

*Churchill Livingstone, Robert Stevenson House, 1-3 Baxter's Place, Leith Walk, Edinburgh EH1 3AF *tel* 031-556 2424 *telex* 262433 MONREF G *fax* 031-558 1278. *Managing director:* Andrew Stevenson; *directors:* Peter Shepherd (nursing and allied health), Peter Richardson (publishing), John Richardson (publishing services), Sally Morris (Churchill Livingstone journals), Mary Law (editorial), Timothy Wright (sales), Jane Grounsell (marketing). Medical division of **Longman Group Ltd.**
Medical books and journals for students, trainees and practitioners; books and journals in nursing, midwifery, physiotherapy, complementary medicine, and other allied health disciplines. Note – preliminary letter recommended before submitting MSS.

Cicerone Press (1969), 2 Police Square, Milnthorpe, Cumbria LA7 7PY *tel* (05395) 62069 *fax* (05395) 63417. *Managing and sales director:* Dorothy Unsworth; *editorial director:* Walt Unsworth; *production director:* R.B. Evans.
Guidebooks to the great outdoors – walking, climbing, etc. – Britain, Europe, and world-wide; general books about the North of England. *No* fiction or poetry.

*Clarendon Press—see **Oxford University Press.**

Robin Clark Ltd (1976), 27 Goodge Street, London W1P 1FD *tel* 071-636 3992 *fax* 071-637 1866. *Director:* N.I. Attallah (chairman); *managing editor:* G. de Chamberet. Member of the Namara Group.
Fiction, biography, social history in paperback.

T. & T. Clark (1821), 59 George Street, Edinburgh EH2 2LQ *tel* 031-225 4703 *fax* 031-220 4260. *Managing director:* Geoffrey F. Green MA, PhD. Law, philosophy, theology.

*James Clarke & Co. Ltd (1859), PO Box 60, Cambridge CB1 2NT *tel* (0223) 350865 *fax* (0223) 66951. *Managing director:* Adrian Brink.
Theology, academic, reference books.
Acorn Editions (imprint). Local books on East Anglia.
Patrick Hardy Books (imprint of Lutterworth Press). Children's fiction.
Lutterworth Press (subsidiary). The arts, biography, children's books (fiction, non-fiction, picture, rewards), educational, environmental, general, history, leisure, philosophy, science, sociology, theology and religion.

*Collins—see **HarperCollins Publishers.**

Collins & Brown (1989), Letts of London House, Great Eastern Wharf, Parkgate Road, London SW11 4NQ *tel* 071-924 2575 *fax* 071-924 7725. *Publisher:* Mark Collins; *chairman:* Cameron Brown; *director:* Roger Bristow (art).
Literature, history, practical photography, natural history, gardening, cookery, travel, DIY, crafts, music, biography, letters, art.

Condé Nast Books—see **Random House UK Ltd.**

Conran Octopus—see **Reed Consumer Books.**

Conservative Political Centre (1945), 32 Smith Square, London SW1P 3HH *tel* 071-222 9000 *fax* 071-233 2065. *Director:* Alistair B. Cooke OBE.
Politics, current affairs.

*Constable & Co. Ltd (1890), 3 The Lanchesters, 162 Fulham Palace Road, London W6 9ER *tel* 081-741 3663 *fax* 081-748 7562. *Chairman and joint managing director:* Benjamin Glazebrook; *directors:* Richard Dodman, Miles Huddleston, Richard Tomkins, Robin Baird-Smith (joint managing and publishing), Jeremy Potter, Yvette Evans-Foster.
Fiction: general, crime and suspense; general non-fiction: literature, biography, memoirs, history, politics, current affairs, food, travel and guidebooks, social sciences, psychology and psychiatry, counselling, social work, sociology, mass media.

*Consumers' Association (1957), 2 Marylebone Road, London NW1 4DF *tel* 071-830 6000 *fax* 071-830 7660. *Chief executive:* John Beishon; *assistant director (book publishing):* Kim Lavely; *head of book publishing:* Gill Rowley.
Travel, restaurant, hotel and wine guides, medicine, law and personal finance for the layman, gardening, education, DIY – all *Which?* branded titles.

Conway Maritime Press (1972)—see **Brassey's (UK) Ltd.**

Leo Cooper Ltd—see **Pen & Sword Books Ltd.**

*Corgi—see **Transworld Publishers Ltd.**

Cornwall Books—see **Golden Cockerel Press.**

*Coronet—see **Hodder Headline plc.**

Council for British Archaeology (1944), Bowes Morrell House, 111 Walmgate, York YO1 2UA *tel* (0904) 671417 *fax* (0904) 671384. *Director:* Richard Morris; *managing editor:* Christine Pietrowski.
British archaeology – academic; practical handbooks; no general books.

Countryside Books (1976), 2 Highfield Avenue, Newbury, Berks. RG14 5DS *tel* (0635) 43816 *fax* (0635) 551004. *Partners:* Nicholas Battle, Suzanne Battle.
Books of local or regional interest, usually on a county basis, walking, outdoor activity, local history; genealogy.

Cranfield University Press—see **Ashgate Publishing Ltd.**

Cressrelles Publishing Co. Ltd (1973), 311 Worcester Road, Malvern, Worcs. WR14 1AN *tel* (0684) 565045. *Directors:* Leslie Smith, Audrey Smith. General publishing.
Actinic Press (imprint). Chiropody.

*****Croom Helm Ltd**—incorporated in **Routledge.**

The Crowood Press (1982), The Stable Block, Ramsbury, Marlborough, Wilts. SN8 2HR *tel* (0672) 20320 *fax* (0672) 20280. *Directors:* John Dennis (chairman), Ken Hathaway (managing).
Sport, motoring, climbing and walking, fishing, country sports, farming, natural history, gardening, DIY, crafts, dogs, equestrian, games.
Helmsman (imprint). Nautical.

James Currey Ltd (1985), 54b Thornhill Square, London N1 1BE *tel* 071-609 9026 *fax* 071-609 9605. *Directors:* James Currey, Clare Currey, Keith Sambrook.
Academic studies of Africa, Caribbean, Third World: history, archaeology, economics, agriculture, politics, literary criticism, sociology.

Dalesman Publishing Co. Ltd (1939), Stable Courtyard, Broughton Hall, Skipton, North Yorkshire BD23 3AE *tel* (0756) 701381 *fax* (0756) 701326. *Chairman:* T.J. Benn; *managing director:* C.G. Benn; *publishing director:* T. Bennett.
Countryside books, walking, caving, humour, folklore, guides.

Terence Dalton Ltd (1966), Water Street, Lavenham, Sudbury, Suffolk CO10 9RN *tel* (0787) 247572 *fax* (0787) 248267. *Directors:* T.A.J. Dalton, E.H. Whitehair (managing).
Maritime and aeronautical history, East Anglian interest and history.

The C.W. Daniel Company Ltd (1902), 1 Church Path, Saffron Walden, Essex CB10 1JP *tel* (0799) 521909 *fax* (0799) 513462. *Directors:* Ian Miller, Jane Miller.
Natural healing, homoeopathy, aromatherapy, mysticism.
Health Science Press (imprint). *Directors:* Ian Miller, Jane Miller. Homeopathy.
Neville Spearman Publishers (imprint). *Editorial director:* Sebastian Hobnut. Mysticism.

Dartmouth Publishing Co. Ltd (1989), Gower House, Croft Road, Aldershot, Hants GU11 3HR *tel* (0252) 331551 *fax* (0252) 344405. *Managing director:* John Irwin.
International relations, law, management, politics.

*****Darton, Longman & Todd Ltd** (1959), 1 Spencer Court, 140-142 Wandsworth High Street, London SW18 4JJ *tel* 081-875 0155 *fax* 081-875 0133. *Editorial director:* Mary Jean Pritchard.
Religious books and bibles, including the following themes: bible study, spirituality, prayer and meditation, anthologies, daily readings, healing, counselling and pastoral care, bereavement, personal growth, mission, political, environmental and social issues, biography and autobiography, theological and historical studies.

Darwen Finlayson Ltd—see **Phillimore & Co. Ltd.**

*****David & Charles Publishers** (1960), Brunel House, Newton Abbot, Devon TQ12 4PU *tel* (0626) 61121 *telex* 42904 BOOKS G *fax* (0626) 331367. *Directors:* Terry Stubbs (managing), Piers Spence (publishing), John Allgrove (sales and marketing).

High quality illustrated non-fiction specialising in crafts and hobbies, art techniques, cookery, gardening, natural history, equestrian, nautical and DIY.

Christopher Davies Publishers Ltd (1949), PO Box 403, Swansea SA1 4YF *tel* (0792) 648825 *fax* (0792) 648825. *Directors:* Christopher Talfan Davies, K.E.T. Colayera, D.M. Davies.
History, leisure books, sport and general of Welsh interest, Welsh dictionaries, *Triskele Books.*

J.M. Dent (1888)—acquired by **The Orion Publishing Group Ltd.**

*****André Deutsch Ltd** (1950), 105-106 Great Russell Street, London WC1B 3LJ *tel* 071-580 2746 *fax* 071-631-3253. *Chairman and managing director:* T.G. Rosenthal; *directors:* Robin Baum, Gérard H. Boulanger, Julian Tobin; *literary adviser:* Anthony Thwaite.
Art, belles-lettres, biography and memoirs, fiction, general, history, humour, politics, travel, photography, cricket.

*****André Deutsch Children's Books**—see **Scholastic Children's Books.**

Dial—see **Reed Information Services Ltd.**

*****Dinosaur Publications**—see **HarperCollins Publishers.**

Eric Dobby Publishing Ltd (1992), 12 Warnford Road, Orpington, Kent BR6 6LW *tel/fax* (0689) 862855 *fax* (0689) 861256. *Managing director:* E.R. Dobby.
Biography, true crime, antiques (especially wristwatches).

Doctor Who—see **Virgin Publishing Ltd.**

John Donald Publishers Ltd (1973), 138 St Stephen Street, Edinburgh EH3 5AA *tel* 031-225 1146 *fax* 031-220 0567. *Directors:* Gordon Angus, D.L. Morrison.
British history, archaeology, ethnology, local history, vernacular architecture, general non-fiction.
Sportsprint (imprint). *Editorial director:* D.L. Morrison. Sports.

Dorling Kindersley Ltd (1974), 9 Henrietta Street, Covent Garden, London WC2E 8PS *tel* 071-836 5411 *telex* 8954527 DEEKAY G *fax* 071-836 7570. *Chairman:* Peter Kindersley; *deputy chairman and publisher:* Christopher Davis; *managing director:* Rod Hare; *directors:* Michael Devenish (international sales), David Lamb (adult), Linda Davis (children's), Stuart Jackman (art), John Adams (video), Alan Buckingham (multimedia), Martyn Longly (production), Peter Gill (finance), Ruth Sandys (education), David Holmes (UK sales), Louise Cavanagh (cartography), Peter Cartwright (DKFL), Giles Cunningham (legal).
High quality illustrated books on non-fiction subjects, including health, cookery, gardening, crafts and reference; also children's non-fiction and picture books. Specialists in international co-editions.

*****Doubleday (UK)** (1989)—see **Transworld Publishers Ltd.**

*****Doubleday Children's Books**—see **Transworld Publishers Ltd.**

Dragon's World Ltd, Paper Tiger Books (1975), 26 Warwick Way, London SW1V 1RX *tel* 071-976 5477 *fax* 071-976 5429. *Directors:* H.A. Schaafsma, C.M.A. Schaafsma, Pippa Rubinstein (editorial), Leslie Cramphorn (sales/marketing).
High quality illustrated books on fable and fantasy illustration and mythology, natural history, DIY and general interest subjects; children's illustrated classics, natural history and general non-fiction.

Gerald Duckworth & Co. Ltd (1898), 48 Hoxton Square, London N1 6PB *tel* 071-729 5986 *fax* 071-729 0015. *Directors:* D.C. Blake, R.J. Davies, C.B. Haycraft (chairman and managing), J. Earl, S. Hill.
Mainly academic; also general and fiction.

Martin Dunitz Ltd (1978), The Livery House, 7-9 Pratt Street, London NW1 0AE *tel* 071-482 2202 *fax* 071-267 0159. *Directors:* Martin Dunitz, Ruth Dunitz, John Slaytor, Rosemary Allen.
Radiology, orthopaedics, metabolic bone disease, dermatology, dentistry, oncology, cardiology, rheumatology, pathology, sports medicine, allied health and nursing.

*Earthscan Publications Ltd (1987)—see **Kogan Page Ltd.**

*East-West Publications (UK) Ltd (1977), 8 Caledonia Street, London N1 9DZ *tel* 071-837 5061 *fax* 071-278 4429. *Chairman:* L.W. Carp; *editor:* B. Thompson.
General non-fiction, travel, Eastern studies, sufism.
Gallery Children's Books (imprint). Quality children's books.

*Ebury Press—see **Random House UK Ltd.**

*Eclipse—see **HarperCollins Publishers.**

Edinburgh University Press, 22 George Square, Edinburgh EH8 9LF *tel* 031-650 4218 *telegraphic address* Edinpress *telex* 727442 UNIVED G *fax* 031-662 0053.
Academic and general publishers. Archaeology, botany, environment, Islamic studies, history, linguistics, literature (criticism), philosophy, Scottish studies, theology.
Polygon (imprint) *tel* 031-650 4689. New international fiction, including translations, oral history, general, Scottish, social and political (Determination series).

Educational Explorers (1962), 11 Crown Street, Reading, Berks. RG1 2TQ *tel* (0734) 873103. *Directors:* M.J. Hollyfield, D.M. Gattegno.
Educational, mathematics: *Numbers in colour with Cuisenaire Rods*, languages: *The Silent Way*, literacy, reading: *Words in Colour*; educational films.

Element Books (1978), The Old School House, The Courtyard, Bell Street, Shaftesbury, Dorset SP7 8BP *tel* (0747) 851448 *fax* (0747) 855721. *Directors:* Michael Mann (publisher), Annie Wilson (rights), David Alexander (managing), John Salkeld FCA.
Philosophy, religion, popular psychology, health, astrology and esoteric traditions.

Edward Elgar Publishing Ltd (1986), 8 Lansdown Place, Cheltenham, Glos GL50 2HU *tel* (0242) 226934 *fax* (0242) 262111. *Managing director:* Edward Elgar.
Economics and other social sciences.

Elliot Right Way Books (1946), Kingswood Buildings, Brighton Road, Lower Kingswood, Tadworth, Surrey KT20 6TD *tel* Mogador (0737) 832202. Clive Elliot, Malcolm Elliot.
Independent publishers of practical non-fiction 'how to' paperbacks. The low-price *Paperfronts* series includes games, pastimes, horses, pets, motoring, sport, health, business, public speaking and jokes, financial and legal, cookery, home and garden, popular education, family subjects and etiquette. Titles of a more specialist nature are covered in the larger-format *Right Way* series. Welcomes new ideas; editorial help provided.

ELM Publications (1977), Seaton House, Kings Ripton, Huntingdon, Cambs. PE17 2NJ   *tel* (048 73) 238   *fax* (048 73) 359. Sheila Ritchie.
Educational books and resources (especially history); books and training aids (tutor's packs and software) for business and management; software simulations; languages; library and information studies. Intending authors are invited to telephone in the first instance, rather than to send MSS. Please note: we publish mainly to curricula and course syllabi.

Elsevier Science Ltd, The Boulevard, Langford Lane, Kidlington, Oxford OX5 1GB   *tel* (0865) 843000   *fax* (0865) 843010. *Managing director:* M. Boswood; *publishing director (primary and reference):* P. Shepherd; *director, magazines and newsletters:* D. Bousfield.
Journal, magazine and book publishers in science, technology and medicine. Imprints: **Pergamon, Elsevier Applied Science, Elsevier Trends Journals.**

*****Encyclopaedia Britannica International Ltd,** Carew House, Station Approach, Wallington, Surrey SM6 0DA   *tel* 081-669 4355   *telex* 23866 ENBRI G   *fax* 081-773 3631. *Managing director:* Joe D. Adams.

Enitharmon Press (1969), 36 St George's Avenue, London N7 0HD   *tel* 071-607 7194   *fax* 071-607 8694. *Director:* Stephen Stuart-Smith.
Poetry, literary criticism, translations, art, photography. No unsolicited MSS.

Epworth Press, Hartley Victoria College, Luther King House, Brighton Grove, Manchester M14 5JP   *tel* 061-224 2215   *fax* 061-248 9201. *Editorial committee:* Dr Valerie Edden, Rev. Dr Ivor H. Jones, Dr Cyril S. Rodd (hon. sec.), Rev. Graham Slater (chairman), Rev. Michael J. Townsend.
Religion, theology, church history.

Ethnographica (1976), 19 Westbourne Road, London N7 8AN   *tel* 071-607 4074. *Directors:* Stuart Hamilton, Jane Hansom.
Ethnography, history, anthropology, social studies, arts and crafts; catalogues and books produced for museums, galleries and universities in UK and overseas.

Eurobook Ltd—see **Peter Lowe (Eurobook Ltd).**

Euromonitor plc (1972), 87-88 Turnmill Street, London EC1M 5QU   *tel* 071-251 8024   *telex* 262433   *fax* 071-608 3149. *Directors:* T.J. Fenwick (managing), R.N. Senior (chairman).
Business and commercial reference, marketing information, European and International Surveys, directories.

Europa Publications Ltd, 18 Bedford Square, London WC1B 3JN   *tel* 071-580 8236   *telex* 21540 EUROPA G   *fax* 071-636 1664. *Directors:* C.H. Martin (chairman), P.A. McGinley (managing), J.P. Desmond, R.M. Hughes, P.G.C. Jackson, M.R. Milton, A.G. Oliver, J. Quinney.
Directories, international relations, reference, year books.

Evangelical Press of Wales (1955), Bryntirion, Bridgend, Mid Glamorgan CF31 4DX   *tel* (0656) 655886   *fax* (0656) 656095. *Chief executive:* G. Wyn Davies.
Theology and religion (in English and Welsh).

*****Evans Brothers Ltd** (1905), 2A Portman Mansions, Chiltern Street, London W1M 1LE   *tel* 071-935 7160   *telegraphic address* Byronitic, London W1   *telex* 8811713 EVBOOK G   *fax* 071-487 5034. *Directors:* S.T. Pawley (managing), B.O. Bolodeoku (Nigeria), Brian D. Jones (international publishing), A.O. Ojora (Nigeria), M. Jackson, J.D. Solly.
Educational books, particularly pre-school, school library and teachers' books for the UK; primary and secondary for Africa, the Caribbean and Hong Kong.

Everyman—see **The Orion Publishing Group Ltd.**

Everyman's Library, 79 Berwick Street, London W1V 3PF *tel* 071-287 0035 *fax* 071-287 0038. *Managing director:* David Campbell.
Clothbound reprints of the classics; Everyman's Children's Classics; Everyman's Travel Guides.

Exley Publications Ltd (1976), 16 Chalk Hill, Watford, Herts. WD1 4BN *tel* (0923) 250505 *fax* (0923) 818733/800440. *Directors:* Richard Exley, Helen Exley, Lincoln Exley, Dalton Exley.
Humour series, cartoon series, gift books, children's biographies, children's activity books, anthologies for special occasions. Publish series *only*. Series proposals welcome. No unsolicited MSS; sae essential.

Eyre & Spottiswoode Publishers—list acquired by **Cambridge University Press.**

*Faber & Faber Ltd (1929), 3 Queen Square, London WC1N 3AU *tel* 071-465 0045 *telegraphic address* Fabbaf, London WC1 *telex* 299633 FABER G *fax* 071-465 0034. *Chairman and managing director:* Matthew Evans; *directors:* John Bodley, Dennis Crutcher, Patrick Curran, Giles de la Mare, Valerie Eliot, T.E. Faber, Tom Kelleher, Joanna Mackle, Robert McCrum, Peter Simpson (company secretary).
High quality general fiction and non-fiction; all forms of creative writing. For current lists, write to the above address.
Address all submissions (with sae or return postage) to the Editorial Department. In the case of MSS, preliminary letter required. For information on submission procedure ring 071-465 0189.

Fabian Society (1884), 11 Dartmouth Street, London SW1H 9BN *tel* 071-222 8877 *fax* 071-976 7153 (also controls **NCLC Publishing Society Ltd**). *Research and publications officer:* Stephen Tindale.
Current affairs, economics, educational, environment, political economy, social policy.

Facts on File, c/o Roundhouse Publishing, PO Box 140, Oxford OX2 7FF *tel* (0865) 512682 *fax* (0865) 59594. *Contact:* Alan Goodworth.
Arts, business, current affairs, dictionaries, general interest, history, literature and language, natural history, sciences, medical, sport, professional reference, politics, music, young adult.

*Fantail (1988)—see **Penguin Books Ltd.**

Farming Press Books (1951), Wharfedale Road, Ipswich, Suffolk IP1 4LG *tel* (0473) 241122 *fax* (0473) 240501. *Manager:* Roger Smith.
Agriculture, humour, veterinary; videos.

Fernhurst Books (1979), Duke's Path, High Street, Arundel, West Sussex BN19 9AJ *tel* (0903) 882277 *fax* (0903) 882715. *Publisher:* Tim Davison.
Sailing, watersports.

Financial Times/Pitman Publishing—see **Pitman Publishing.**

*Firefly Books—incorporated in **Wayland (Publishers) Ltd.**

First and Best in Education Ltd (1992; incorporating **Hamilton House Publishing**), 34 Nene Valley Business Park, Oundle, Peterborough PE8 4HL *tel* (0832) 275285 *fax* (0832) 275281. *Directors:* Tony Attwood, Philippa Attwood.
All schools related books, including books for further and higher education. Currently actively recruiting new writers for schools; ideas welcome (*contacts:* Keith Buckby and Sally Morgan, editors). Sae must accompany submissions.

Fishing News Books Ltd (1953), Osney Mead, Oxford OX2 0EL *tel* (0865) 240201 *telex* 83355 MEDBOK G *fax* (0865) 721205. *Manager:* Philip Saugman.
Commercial fisheries, aquaculture and allied subjects.

*Flamingo—see **HarperCollins Publishers.**

Flicks Books (1986), 29 Bradford Road, Trowbridge, Wilts. BA14 9AN   *tel* (0225) 767728   *fax* (0225) 760418. *Partners:* Matthew Stevens (publisher), Aletta Stevens.
Cinema, television, related media.

*Floris Books (1978), 15 Harrison Gardens, Edinburgh EH11 1SH   *tel* 031-337 2372   *fax* 031-346 7516. *Editor:* Christopher Moore.
Religion, science, Celtic studies, craft; children's books: picture and board books, fiction, activity books.

Focal Press—see **Butterworth & Co. (Publishers) Ltd.**

*Fodor Guides—see **Random House UK Ltd.**

*Folens Ltd (1987), Albert House, Apex Business Centre, Boscombe Road, Dunstable LU5 4RL   *tel* (0582) 472788   *fax* (0582) 472575. *Managing director:* Malcolm Watson.
Primary and secondary educational books, learn at home books.

*Fontana—now **HarperCollins Paperbacks.**

*Fontana Press—see **HarperCollins Publishers.**

Forest Books (1984), 20 Forest View, Chingford, London E4 7AY   *tel* 081-529 8470   *telex* 891182 GECOMS G   *fax* 081-524 7890. *Managing director:* Brenda Walker.
Only international literature in English translation; poetry, plays, novels and short stories, especially East European literature.

G.T. Foulis & Co.—see **Haynes Publishing.**

W. Foulsham & Co. Ltd (1819), 837 Yeovil Road, Slough, Berks. SL1 4JH   *tel* (0753) 526769   *telex* 849041 SHARET G   *fax* (0753) 811409. *Editorial director:* B.A.R. Belasco.
General manuals, children's activity, educational, school library, popular occult, DIY, hobbies and games, sport, travel, art directories, collectibles.
Quantum (imprint). *Editor:* Ian Fenton. Popular philosophy, practical psychology.

The Foundational Book Company, PO Box 659, London SW3 6SJ   *tel* 071-584 1053. *Editorial director:* Mrs Peggy M. Brook.
Spiritual science.

Foundery Press—see **Methodist Publishing House.**

*Fount—see **HarperCollins Publishers.**

Fourmat Publishing—see **Tolley Publishing Co. Ltd.**

Fourth Estate Ltd (1984), 289 Westbourne Grove, London W11 2QA   *tel* 071-727 8993   *fax* 071-792 3176. *Directors:* Victoria Barnsley (managing), Patric Duffy (financial), Jane Carr (editorial), Christopher Potter (editorial), Joanna Prior (publicity), Stephen Page (sales).
Current affairs, literature, guidebooks, popular culture, fiction, humour, architecture, design, self-help, business, science.
Blueprint Monographs (imprint). Design and architecture books co-published with *Blueprint Magazine.*
Fourth Estate Paperbacks (imprint). Publishes paperback editions of Fourth Estate hardback titles.
Guardian Books (imprint). *Editorial director:* Clive Priddle. Books stemming from *The Guardian* newspaper.

L.N. Fowler & Co. Ltd (1880), 1201-3 High Road, Chadwell Heath, Romford, Essex RM6 4DH   *tel* 081-597 2491   *fax* 081-598 2428. *Editorial director:* C.J. Nagle.
Astrology, healing, creative thinking.

Framework Press Educational Publishers Ltd (1983), Parkfield, Greaves Road, Lancaster, Lancs. LA1 4TZ   *tel* (0524) 39602   *fax* (0524) 841520. *Directors:* Brenda V. Abercrombie, Nicholas Abercrombie, David R. Green.
School and college management, staff development, vocational, English.

Free Association Books (1984), Omnibus Business Centre, 39-41 North Road, London N7 9DP   *tel* 071-609 5646/607 8868   *fax* 071-700 0330. *Directors:* T.E. Brown, G. Davies, R.M. Young.
Psychoanalysis, politics of science, cultural studies, social sciences.

W.H. Freeman & Co. Ltd (1959), 20 Beaumont Street, Oxford OX1 2NQ   *tel* (0865) 726975   *fax* (0865) 790391. *Directors:* R. Biewen (chairman), A. Degutis, E. Warner.
Science, technical, medicine, economics, psychology, archaeology.

Freeway—see **Transworld Publishers Ltd.**

*****Samuel French Ltd** (1830), 52 Fitzroy Street, London W1P 6JR   *tel* 071-387 9373   *fax* 071-387 2161. *Directors:* Charles Van Nostrand (chairman), John Bedding (managing), Neil Peters, Amanda Smith, Jerry Stalworth, Paul Taylor.
Publishers of plays and agents for the collection of royalties.

David Fulton Publishers Ltd (1987), 2 Barbon Close, Great Ormond Street, London WC1N 3JX   *tel* 071-405 5606   *fax* 071-831 4840. *Managing director:* David Fulton; *editorial director:* John Owens.
Education, educational psychology, special education, geography, psychiatry.

Gaia Books Ltd, 66 Charlotte Street, London W1P 1LR   *tel* 071-323 4010   *fax* 071-323 0435; and 20 High Street, Stroud, Glos. GL5 1AS   *tel* (0453) 752985   *fax* (0453) 752987. *Managing director:* Joss Pearson; *directors:* David Pearson, Lars Kjeldsen, Tor Svensson, Imogen Bright, Robin Hayfield FCA, Patrick Nugent, Susan Walby.
Illustrated reference books on ecology, natural living, health, mind.

Gairm Publications, incorporating Alex MacLaren & Sons (1875), 29 Waterloo Street, Glasgow G2 6BZ   *tel/fax* 041-221 1971. *Editorial director:* Derick Thomson.
(Gaelic and Gaelic-related only) dictionaries, language books, novels, poetry, music, children's books, quarterly magazine.

Gale Research International Ltd   *editorial office* Berkshire House, 168-173 High Holborn, London WC1V 7AA   *tel* 071-497 1423   *fax* 071-497 1424. *Managing director:* Ian Savage. Subsidiary of the Thomson Corporation.
Reference books for libraries, research and industry; literary and other biographical works; St James contemporary reference works on fine arts, performing arts and literature.

*****Gallery Children's Books**—see **East-West Publications (UK) Ltd.**

Garnet Publishing Ltd (1991), 8 Southern Court, South Street, Reading RG1 4QS   *tel* (0734) 597847   *fax* (0734) 597356. *Managing director:* Kenneth Banerji.
Art, architecture, photography, mainly on Middle and Far East, and Islam.
Ithaca Press (imprint). Post-graduate academic works, especially on the Middle East.

Gateway Books (1982), The Hollies, Wellow, Nr Bath, Avon BA2 8QJ   *tel* (0225) 835127   *fax* (0225) 840012. *Publisher:* Alick Bartholomew.
Popular psychology, spirituality, health and healing, earth mysteries, ecology, self help, metaphysics and alternative science. Please do not send unsolicited MSS – outline and sample welcome.

The Gay Men's Press—see **GMP Publishers Ltd.**

Geddes & Grosset Ltd (1988), David Dale House, New Lanark ML11 9DJ   *tel* (0555) 665000   *fax* (0555) 665694. *Directors:* Ron Grosset, Mike Miller, David Geddes.
Popular reference; children's non-fiction and activity books.

Gee & Son (Denbigh) Ltd (1808), Chapel Street, Denbigh, Clwyd LL16 3SW   *tel* (0745) 812020. *Directors:* E. Evans, E.M. Evans.
Oldest Welsh publishers. Books of interest to Wales, in Welsh and English.

*****Geographia**—now **Bartholomew**; see **HarperCollins Publishers.**

*****Stanley Gibbons Publications** (1856), Parkside, Christchurch Road, Ringwood, Hants BH24 3SH   *tel* (0425) 472363   *fax* (0425) 470247. *Chairman:* P.I. Fraser.
Philatelic handbooks, stamp catalogues and albums, *Gibbons Stamp Monthly*.

Robert Gibson & Sons Glasgow Ltd (1885), 17 Fitzroy Place, Glasgow G3 7SF   *tel* 041-248 5674   *fax* 041-221 8219. *Directors:* R.D.C. Gibson, R.G.C. Gibson, Dr J.S. McEwan, M. Pinkerton, H.C. Crawford, N.J. Crawford.
Bibliography and library science; educational and textbooks.

Ginn & Co.—see **Reed Consumer Books.**

*****Mary Glasgow Publications**—merged with **Stanley Thornes (Publishers) Ltd.**

GMP Publishers Ltd (1979), PO Box 247, London N17 9QR   *tel* 081-341 7818   *fax* 081-341 7467. *Directors:* Aubrey Walter, David Fernbach, James Sprague.
The Gay Men's Press (imprint). Modern, popular, historical/literary fiction, including translations from European languages, biography and memoir, history, drama, health, social and political questions, poetry, literary criticism; *Gay Modern Classics:* reprints of gay fiction/non-fiction from past 100 years; *Édition Aubrey Walter:* male photography both art and glamour, fine-art editions of gay artists.
Heretic Books (imprint). Ecology, animal liberation, green politics, third world.

Godfrey Cave Holdings Ltd (1975), 42 Bloomsbury Street, London WC1B 3QJ   *tel* 071-636 9177   *fax* 071-636 9091. *Directors:* Laura Bamford, Jack Cooper. Subsidiary of **Penguin Books Ltd.**
General non-fiction, reprints, remainders.

Golden Cockerel Press, 25 Sicilian Avenue, London WC1A 2QH   *tel/fax* 071-405 7979. *Directors:* Tamar Yoseloff, Thomas Yoseloff (USA).
Academic.
Associated University Presses (imprint). Literary criticism, art, music, history, film, theology, philosophy, Jewish studies, politics, sociology.
Cornwall Books (imprint). Antiques, history, film.

*****Victor Gollancz Ltd** (1927)—see **Cassell plc.**

Gomer Press (1892), Llandysul, Dyfed SA44 4BQ   *tel* (0559) 362371   *fax* (0559) 363758. *Directors:* J. Huw Lewis, John H. Lewis; *editor:* Dyfed Elis-Gruffydd.
Books in Welsh; biography, local history.

*Gower Publishing Ltd (1967), Gower House, Croft Road, Aldershot, Hants GU11 3HR *tel* (0252) 331551 *fax* (0252) 344405. *Managing director:* Christopher Simpson.
Practical management and business reference.

*Grafton—now **HarperCollins Paperbacks.**

Graham & Trotman Ltd (1972), Sterling House, 66 Wilton Road, London SW1V 1DE *tel* 071-821 1123 *telegraphic address* Infobooks, London *telex* 298878 GRAMCO G *fax* 071-630 5229. *Directors:* A.M.W. Graham, S. Willcox, A. Visser, H.A. Pabbruwe, P. le Bosquet.
International law, international business, finance and banking.

Granta Publications Ltd (1982), 2/3 Hanover Yard, Noel Road, Islington, London N1 8BE *tel* 071-704 9776 *fax* 071-704 0474. *Editor:* W.H. Buford; *managing director:* Catherine Eccles.
Fiction, autobiography, political non-fiction.

Green Books (1987), Foxhole, Dartington, Totnes, Devon TQ9 6EB *tel/fax* (0803) 863843. *Managing director:* John Elford.
Ecology, philosophy, the arts. *No* fiction or children's books. *No* MSS; synopsis and covering letter please.

Green Print—see **Merlin Press Ltd.**

Greenhill Books/Lionel Leventhal Ltd (1984), Park House, 1 Russell Gardens, London NW11 9NN *tel* 081-458 6314 *fax* 081-905 5245. *Managing director:* Lionel Leventhal.
Military history.

Gresham Books Ltd, The Gresham Press, PO Box 61, Henley-on-Thames, Oxon RG9 3LQ *tel/fax* (0734) 403789. *Chief executive:* Mrs M.V. Green.
Hymn books, prayer books, wood engraving.

Grisewood & Dempsey Ltd—merged into **Larousse plc.**

Grub Street (1981), The Basement, 10 Chivalry Road, London SW11 1HT *tel* 071-924 3966/738 1008 *fax* 071-738 1009. *Directors:* John B. Davies, Anne Dolamore.
Adult non-fiction: aviation history, cookery and health, gift books and cartoon humour.

Guardian Books—see **Fourth Estate Ltd.**

Guild of Master Craftsman Publications Ltd (1979), Castle Place, 166 High Street, Lewes, East Sussex BN7 1XU *tel* (0273) 477374/478449 *fax* (0273) 486300. *Chairman:* Alan E. Phillips.
Practical, illustrated woodworking and crafts.

*Guinness Publishing Ltd (1954), 33 London Road, Enfield, Middlesex EN2 6DJ *tel* 081-367 4567 *cables* Mostest, Enfield *telex* 23573 GBRLDN G *fax* 081-367 5912.
General and recreational reference books.

Gwasg Gee—see **Gee & Son (Denbigh) Ltd.**

Peter Halban Publishers Ltd (1986), 42 South Molton Street, London W1Y 1HB *tel* 071-491 1582 *fax* 071-629 5381. *Directors:* Martine Halban, Peter Halban.
General non-fiction; history and biography; Jewish subjects and Middle East. No unsolicited MSS considered; preliminary letter essential.

Robert Hale Ltd (1936), Clerkenwell House, 45-47 Clerkenwell Green, London EC1R 0HT *tel* 071-251 2661 *telegraphic address* Barabbas, London

EC1 *fax* 071-490 4958. *Managing director:* John Hale; *directors:* Eric Restall (production), Robert Kynaston (financial), Martin Kendall (marketing), Betty Weston (rights).
Adult general non-fiction and fiction.

*Hamish Hamilton Ltd (1931)—see Penguin Books Ltd.

*Hamish Hamilton Children's Books—see Penguin Books Ltd.

Hamilton House Publishing—see First and Best in Education Ltd.

Hamlyn—see Reed Consumer Books.

Hamlyn Children's Books—see Reed Consumer Books.

*Harcourt Brace and Co., 24-28 Oval Road, London NW1 7DX *tel* 071-267 4466 *telex* 25775 ACPRES G *fax* 071-482 2293/485 4752. *Managing director:* Bill M. Barnett.
Scientific and medical.
Academic Press (division). *Managing director:* Jan Velterop. Academic and reference.
Baillière Tindall (division). *Editorial director:* Sean Duggan. Medical, veterinary, nursing, pharmaceutical books and journals.
Holt, Rinehart & Winston (division). *Managing director:* Bill M. Barnett. Educational books (school, college, university) in all subjects.
W.B. Saunders Co. Ltd (division). *Editorial director:* Sean Duggan. Medical and scientific.

*Patrick Hardy Books—see James Clarke & Co. Ltd.

*HarperCollins—see HarperCollins Publishers.

*HarperCollins Publishers (1819), 77-85 Fulham Palace Road, Hammersmith, London W6 8JB *tel* 081-741 7070 *telex* 25611 COLINS G *fax* 081-307 4440. *Executive chairman and publisher:* Eddie Bell; *chief executive:* Peter Winslow; *managing directors:* David Young (Trade), Roy Davey (Children's and Education), Robert Williams (HarperCollins Cartographic), Eileen Campbell (Thorsons and Religious), Richard Thomas (Dictionaries), Robin Wood (General Reference), Simon Hulse (HarperCollins Enterprises); *publisher:* Stuart Proffitt (Trade).
Unsolicited submissions should be made in the form of a typewritten synopsis. MSS are not considered and can be returned only if accompanied by the cost of postage.
Access Press (imprint). *Managing director:* Robin Wood. Travel guides.
Aquarian Press (imprint). *Managing director:* Eileen Campbell. New Age subjects including astrology, tarot and divination, mythology and psychic awareness.
Armada (imprint). *Publishing director:* Gail Penston. Paperback children's books.
Birnbaum (imprint). *Managing director:* Robin Wood. Travel guides.
Collins (imprints). Collins Crime, Collins Classics, Collins English Library, Collins Educational, Collins Bibles, Collins Liturgical Books, Collins Dictionaries, Collins Cobuild, Collins Gems, Collins New Naturalist Library, Collins Willow, Collins Longman.
Dinosaur Publications (imprint). *Publishing director:* Gail Penston. Children's books.
Eclipse (imprint). *Publishing director:* Malcolm Edwards. Graphic novels.
Flamingo (imprint). Literary fiction; non-fiction.

HarperCollins Publishers—*continued*
Fontana Press (imprint). *Senior editor:* Philip Gwyn Jones. Paperback intellectual non-fiction.
Fount (imprint). *Managing director:* Eileen Campbell. Religious.
HarperCollins (imprints). Audiobooks, Hardbacks (fiction and non-fiction), Paperbacks (fiction and non-fiction), Religious.
HarperCollins Cartographic (imprint). *Managing director:* Robert Williams. Maps, atlases, guides, reference.
HarperCollins Science Fiction & Fantasy (imprint). *Editorial director:* Jane Johnson. Science fiction and fantasy fiction.
Harvill (imprint). *Editorial director:* Christopher MacLehose. Africana, quality illustrated books, literature, literature in translation (especially Russian, Italian, French), quality thrillers.
Jets (imprint). *Publishing director:* Gail Penston. Children's books.
Lions (imprint). *Publishing director:* Gail Penston. Children's books.
Marshall Pickering (imprint). *Managing director:* Eileen Campbell. Theology, music, popular religion, illustrated children's, wide range of Christian books.
Nicholson (imprint). *Publishing director:* Chris Moore. London maps, atlases and guidebooks. Waterways map and guidebooks.
Pandora Press (imprint). *Managing director:* Eileen Campbell. Feminist press publishing. General non-fiction: biography, arts, media, health, current affairs, reference and sexual politics.
Thorsons (imprint). *Managing director:* Eileen Campbell. Complementary medicine, health and nutrition, business and management, self-help and positive thinking, popular psychology, parenting and childcare, and environmental issues.
Tolkien (imprint). *Editorial director:* Mary Butler.
Tracks (imprint). *Publishing director:* Gail Penston. Children's books.

Harrap, 43-45 Annandale Street, Edinburgh EH7 4AZ *tel* 031-557 4571 *fax* 031-557 2936. *Chairman:* John Clement; *international sales:* Richard Drew; *UK marketing manager:* Liz Anderson; *publishing manager:* Katharine Boyd. Subsidiary of **Larousse plc.**
Bilingual dictionaries.

Harriman House Publishing (1991), Silverbeck, Churt, Nr Farnham, Surrey GU10 2HL *tel/fax* (0252) 792525. *Managing director:* Philip Jenks. Business, humour, 'The Official . . . Handbook' series.

*Harvester Wheatsheaf—see **Paramount Publishing Europe.**

*Harvill—see **HarperCollins Publishers.**

Hawk Books (1986), Suite 309, Canalot Studios, 222 Kensal Road, London W10 5BN *tel* 081-969 8091 *fax* 081-968 9012. *Director:* Patrick Hawkey. Comics, nostalgia, juveniles, art.

Haynes Publishing, Sparkford, Yeovil, Somerset BA22 7JJ *tel* North Cadbury (0963) 440635 *telex* 46212 HAYNES G *fax* (0963) 440023. *Directors:* J.H. Haynes (chairman), A.C. Haynes, I.P. Mauger, S.L. Reed, D.J. Reach (editorial), A.J. Sperring, K.C. Fullman, C. Davies.
Car and motorcycle owners workshop manuals, car handbooks/servicing guides, do-it-yourself books, aircraft, trains, nautical.
G.T. Foulis & Co. (imprint). *Editor:* Darryl Reach. Motoring/motorcycling, marque and model history, practical maintenance and renovation, related biographies, motor/motorcycle sport, aircraft, nautical, aviation.
Oxford Illustrated Press (imprint). *Editor:* Darryl Reach. Well-illustrated non-fiction books, sport, leisure and travel guides, car books, art books, general.

Oxford Publishing Company (OPC Railbooks) (imprint). *Editor:* Peter Nicholson. Railway transport.

Patrick Stephens Ltd (imprint). *Editorial director:* Darryl Reach. Aviation, biography, maritime, military and wargaming, model making, motorcycling, motoring and motor racing, railways and railway modelling.

Hazar Publishing Ltd (1992), 147 Chiswick High Road, London W4 2DT   *tel* 081-742 8578   *telex* 9419879 AREEN G   *fax* 081-994 1407. *Director:* Namir Cortas; *children's editor:* Rio Brown; *adult non-fiction editor:* Marie Clayton. Children's picture and novelty books; adult non-fiction: architecture and design.

Headland Publications (1970). *Editorial office:* Tŷ Coch, Galltegfa, Llanfwrog, Ruthin, Clwyd LL15 2AR, and 38 York Avenue, West Kirby, Wirral, Merseyside L48 3JF. *Director/editor:* Gladys Mary Coles.
Poetry, anthologies of poetry and prose. *No* unsolicited MSS.

*****Headline Book Publishing Ltd**—see **Hodder Headline plc.**

Health Education Authority (1987), Hamilton House, Mabledon Place, London WC1H 9TX   *tel* 071-413 1846   *fax* 071-413 0339. *Managing director:* Elisabeth Bolshaw.
Health promotion, disease prevention in areas of: alcohol, cancer, coronary heart disease, food and nutrition, HIV/AIDS and sexual health, smoking.

Health Science Press—see **The C.W. Daniel Company Ltd.**

William Heinemann—see **Reed Consumer Books.**

Heinemann Educational—see **Reed Educational Publishing.**

Heinemann English Language Teaching—see **Reed Educational Publishing.**

Heinemann Young Books—see **Reed Consumer Books.**

Helicon Publishing Ltd (1992), 42 Hythe Bridge Street, Oxford OX1 2EP   *tel* (0865) 204204   *fax* (0865) 204205. *Directors:* David Attwooll (managing), Michael Upshall (editorial), Anne-Lucie Norton (acquisitions), Tony Ballsdon (production), Bridget Macleod (sales and marketing).
General trade reference, hardback and paperback; electronic reference.

*****Christopher Helm**—see **A. & C. Black (Publishers) Ltd.**

Helmsman—see **The Crowood Press.**

Henderson Publishing Ltd (1990), Tide Mill Way, Woodbridge, Suffolk IP12 1BY   *tel* (0394) 380622   *fax* (0394) 380618. *Managing director:* Barrie Henderson; *editor:* Hazel Jones.
Children's books: activity, novelty, non-fiction.

*****Herbert Press Ltd** (1972), 46 Northchurch Road, London N1 4EJ   *tel* 071-254 4379   *fax* 071-254 4332. *Directors:* David Herbert, Brenda Herbert.
Art, architecture, design, crafts, art nostalgia, fashion and costume, natural history, archaeology, illustrated non-fiction.

Heretic Books (1982)—see **GMP Publishers Ltd.**

Nick Hern Books Ltd (1988), 14 Larden Road, London W3 7ST   *tel* 081-740 9539   *fax* 081-746 2006. *Publisher:* Nick Hern.
Theatre, plays.

Hilmarton Manor Press (1964), Calne, Wilts. SN11 8SB   *tel* Hilmarton (0249) 760208   *fax* (0249) 760379. *Editorial director:* Charles Baile de Laperriere.
Fine art, photography, antiques, visual arts.

*****Hippo** (1980)—see **Scholastic Children's Books.**

Hippopotamus Press (1974), 22 Whitewell Road, Frome, Somerset BA11 4EL *tel* (0373) 466653. *Editors:* Roland John, Anna Martin.
Poetry, essays, criticism. Publishes *Outposts Poetry Quarterly*. Poetry submissions from new writers welcome.

*****HMSO Books**. *Head Office:* St Crispins, Duke Street, Norwich NR3 1PD *tel* (0603) 622211 *telex* 97301 *fax* (0603) 695317; *distribution and order point:* HMSO Books Publication Centre, PO Box 276, London SW8 5DT *tel* 071-873 0011 *telex* 297138; *HMSO bookshops* (retail): 49 High Holborn, London WC1V 6HB *tel* 071-873 0011; 9-21 Princess Street, Manchester M60 8AS *tel* 061-834 7201; 71 Lothian Road, Edinburgh EH3 9AZ *tel* 031-228 4181; 258 Broad Street, Birmingham B1 2HE *tel* 021-643 3740; Southey House, Wine Street, Bristol BS1 2BQ *tel* (0272) 264306; 16 Arthur Street, Belfast BT1 4GD *tel* (0232) 238451; plus HMSO agents (see Yellow Pages).
Archaeology, architecture, art, current affairs, directories or guidebooks, educational (primary, secondary, technical, university), general, history, naval and military, practical handbooks, reference, science, sociology, year books. As the Government Publisher, **HMSO** publishes only material sponsored by Parliament, Government Departments and other official bodies. Consequently it cannot consider unsolicited work submitted by private citizens.

Hobsons Publishing plc (1974), Bateman Street, Cambridge CB2 1LZ *tel* (0223) 354551 *fax* (0223) 323154. *Directors:* Charles Sinclair (chairman), Martin Morgan (managing), Robert Baker (deputy managing), Roger Dalzell, David Hepburn, Andrew Round, Chris Letcher, Frances Halliwell; *company secretary:* Stuart Mott.
Careers guidance, PSE, science, business studies, leisure, *Johansens Guides*. Publishers under licence to CRAC – Careers Research & Advisory Centre.

*****Hodder Headline plc** (1993), 338 Euston Road, London NW1 3BH *tel* 071-873 6000 *fax* 071-873 6024. *Chairman:* The Earl of Donoughmore (non-executive); *deputy chairman:* Philip Attenborough CBE (non-executive); *group chief executive:* Tim Hely Hutchinson; *directors:* Paul Coley FCA (financial, company secretary), Martin Neild (managing, Hodder & Stoughton General), Sue Fletcher (deputy managing, Hodder & Stoughton General), Mary Tapissier (managing, children's, chairman, religious), Eric Major (managing, religious), Ken Pickett (managing, Bookpoint), Sian Thomas (managing, Headline), Malcolm Edwards (managing, Australia and New Zealand), Brian Steven (managing, Educational), Richard Stileman (managing, Edward Arnold), Jeremy Dawson (non-executive), Christopher Weston (non-executive).
Edward Arnold (division) *fax* 071-873 6325. *Directors:* Richard Stileman (managing), Philip Blackwell (sales and marketing), Chris Wheeler (publishing). Textbooks and advanced works in humanities, social sciences, pure and applied science, engineering and medicine; journals.
Coronet (imprint of Hodder & Stoughton Ltd). *Deputy managing director:* Sue Fletcher. Fiction and non-fiction paperbacks.
Headline Book Publishing Ltd (division). *Managing director:* Sian Thomas; *publishing directors:* Jane Morpeth (fiction), Alan Brooke (non-fiction). Fiction, biography, humour, food and wine, design, British heritage and countryside, military, history, art history, sport, music, cinema, TV and film tie-ins, hardbacks, and both trade and mass-market paperbacks.
Hodder & Stoughton Ltd (subsidiary). *Directors:* Martin Neild (managing, General), Sue Fletcher (deputy managing, General), Richard Stileman (managing, academic), Eric Major (managing, religious), Rod Ritchie (publishing,

Hodder Headline plc—*continued*
children's), Amanda Ridout (sales), Sue Beavan (production). Fiction (hardback and paperback), non-fiction, religious, children's, schoolbooks, further education, academic.
Knight (imprint of Hodder & Stoughton Ltd). *Joint managing directors:* Rod Ritchie, Fiona Kenshole. Children's paperbacks.
New English Library Ltd (imprint of Hodder & Stoughton Ltd). *Deputy managing director:* Sue Fletcher. Fiction and non-fiction paperbacks.
Sceptre (imprint of Hodder & Stoughton Ltd). *Editorial director:* Carole Welch; *publisher (non-fiction):* Roland Philipps. Fiction and non-fiction paperbacks.

*****Hodder & Stoughton Ltd** (1868)—see **Hodder Headline plc.**

*****Hogarth Press**—see **Random House UK Ltd.**

*****Holmes McDougall**—list acquired by **HarperCollins Publishers.**

*****Holt, Rinehart & Winston**—see **Harcourt Brace and Co.**

Ellis Horwood Ltd (1973)—see **Paramount Publishing Europe.**

How To Books Ltd (1991), Plymbridge House, Estover Road, Plymouth, Devon PL6 7PZ   *tel* (0752) 735251   *telex* 45635 HARDIS G   *fax* (0752) 695699. *Managing director:* R.E. Ferneyhough; *secretary:* M.W. Beevers FCA.
How To series of personal achievement paperbacks covering student life, careers, employment and expatriate topics, business skills, creative/media skills, education, parenting, community and life style development.

Hugo's Language Books (1864), Old Station Yard, Marlesford, Woodbridge, Suffolk IP13 0AG   *tel* (0728) 746546   *fax* (0728) 746236.
Hugo's language books and courses.

*****Hulton Educational Publications**—merged with **Stanley Thornes (Publishers) Ltd.**

Hunt & Thorpe (1989), Bowland House, off West Street, Alresford, Hants SO23 9AT   *tel* (0962) 735633   *fax* (0962) 735320. *Partners:* John Hunt, Debbie Thorpe.
Children's and religious.

*****C. Hurst & Co. (Publishers) Ltd** (1967), 38 King Street, London WC2E 8JT   *tel* 071-240 2666, (night) 081-852 9021   *fax* 071-240 2667. *Directors:* Christopher Hurst, Michael Dwyer.
Scholarly 'area studies' covering contemporary history, politics, political economy, social studies and comparative religion.

*****Hutchinson**—see **Random House UK Ltd.**

*****Hutchinson Children's**—see **Random House UK Ltd.**

*****Hutchinson Education**—list acquired by **Stanley Thornes (Publishers) Ltd.**

ICSA Publishing Ltd (1981), Campus 400, Maylands Avenue, Hemel Hempstead, Herts. HP2 7EZ   *tel* (0442) 881900   *fax* (0442) 257115. *Editorial director:* Susan Richards.
Official publishing company of The Institute of Chartered Secretaries and Administrators. Company administration and law, local government, non-profit organisation management.

Impact Books Ltd (1985), 151 Dulwich Road, London SE24 0NG   *tel* 071-924 0760   *fax* 071-924 0250. *Chairman:* Jean-Luc Barbanneau; *directors:* David Skinner, Tim Pearce, David Collins, Roy Greenslade, Nicholas Darton.
Travel writing, illustrated country books, practical guides, reference, fiction, children's books.

In Print Publishing Ltd (1990), 9 Beaufort Terrace, Brighton, East Sussex BN2 2SU *tel* (0273) 682836 *fax* (0273) 620958. *Directors:* Alastair Dingwall, John Edmondson.
Special interest travel (including literary guides), Japan, South-east Asia, guides to teaching English.

Institute of Personnel Management (1913), IPM House, 35 Camp Road, Wimbledon, London SW19 4UX *tel* 081-946 9100 *fax* 081-947 2570. *Head of publishing:* Judith Tabern.
Personnel management.

*Institute of Physics Publishing, Techno House, Redcliffe Way, Bristol BS1 6NX *tel* (0272) 297481 *telex* 449149 INSTP G *fax* (0272) 294318.
Monographs, graduate texts, conference proceedings, in physics and physics-related science and technology, and popular science titles.

*Inter-Varsity Press, 38 De Montfort Street, Leicester LE1 7GP *tel* (0533) 551700 *fax* (0533) 555672.
Theology and religion.

Ithaca Press—see **Garnet Publishing Ltd.**

Arthur James Ltd (1935), 1 Cranbourne Road, London N10 2BT *tel* 081-883 1831/2201/8307 and (0386) 446566 *fax* (0386) 446566/081-883 8307. *Directors:* D.M. Duncan, Jillian Tallon.
Religion, sociology, psychology.

Jane's Information Group, 163 Brighton Road, Coulsdon, Surrey CR5 2NH *tel* 081-763 1030 *telex* 916907 *fax* 081-763 1005. *Managing director:* Alfred Rolington.
Military, aviation, naval, defence, non-fiction, reference.

Jarrold Publishing (1770), Whitefriars, Norwich NR3 1TR *tel* (0603) 763300 *fax* (0603) 662748. *Managing director:* Antony Jarrold; *publishing director:* Caroline Jarrold. Division of Jarrold & Sons Ltd.
Guidebooks, travel, sport.

*Jets—see **HarperCollins Publishers.**

Jewish Chronicle Publications, 25 Furnival Street, London EC4A 1JT *tel* 071-405 9252 *fax* 071-405 9040. *Executive director:* M. Weinberg.
Theology and religion, reference; *Jewish Year Book*, *Jewish Travel Guide*.

*Johnson Publications Ltd (1946), 130 Wigmore Street, London W1H 0AT *tel* 071-486 6757 *fax* 071-487 5436. *Directors:* M.A. Murray-Pearce, Z.M. Pauncefort.
Perfume, cosmetics, beauty culture, aromatherapy and essential oils, including dictionaries, *objets d'art*, advertising, marketing, biography and memoirs. Return postage should be sent with unsolicited MSS.

Jordan Publishing Ltd (1863), 21 St Thomas Street, Bristol BS1 6JS *tel* (0272) 230600 *telex* 449119 *fax* (0272) 250486 *DX* 78161 Bristol. *Managing director:* Richard Hudson.
Law, particularly company and family (including the *Family Law Journal*), company administration, business, finance, looseleaf services.

*Michael Joseph Ltd (1935)—see **Penguin Books Ltd.**

The Journeyman Press—see **Pluto Publishing Ltd.**

Karnak House (1979), 300 Westbourne Park Road, London W11 1EH *tel/fax* 071-221 6490. *Directors:* Dada A. Imarogbe (chairman), Amon Saba Saakana (editorial), Vanessa Kansinally (administration).
Specialists in African/Caribbean studies world-wide: anthropology, education, Egyptology, fiction, history, language, linguistics, literary criticism, music, parapsychology, philosophy, prehistory.

Kelly's—see **Reed Information Services Ltd.**

The Kenilworth Press Ltd (1989; incorporates **Threshold Books**, 1970), Addington, Buckingham MK18 2JR *tel* (029 671) 5101 *fax* (029 671) 5148. *Directors:* David Blunt, Deirdre Blunt.
Equestrian, including official publications for the British Horse Society.

Kenyon-Deane Ltd, 311 Worcester Road, Malvern, Worcs. WR14 1AN *tel* (0684) 565045. *Directors:* Leslie Smith, Audrey Smith.
Plays and drama textbooks. Specialists in plays for women.

*****Laurence King Publishing** (1991), 71 Great Russell Street, London WC1B 3BN *tel* 071-831 6351 *fax* 071-831 8356. *Directors:* Robin Hyman (chairman), Laurence King (managing), Lesley Ripley Greenfield (editorial: college and fine arts), Donald Sommerville (editorial: reference and trade), David Lewis, Judith Rasmussen (production). Imprint of **Calmann and King Ltd.**
Art, design, decorative art.

Kingfisher Books—see **Larousse plc.**

Jessica Kingsley Publishers (1986), 116 Pentonville Road, London N1 9JB *tel* 071-833 2307 *fax* 071-837 2917. *Director:* Jessica Kingsley.
Psychology, psychotherapy, therapy, social work, higher education policy, regional studies, education.
Penton Press (imprint). Materials science, engineering.

*****Kingsway Publications Ltd,** Lottbridge Drove, Eastbourne, East Sussex BN23 6NT *tel* (0323) 410930 *fax* (0323) 411970. *Directors:* Phil Bacon, Ray Bodkin, Bob Clark, Richard Herkes, David Nickalls, William Owen, John Paculabo (chief executive officer).
Christian autobiographies, theology/doctrine for laymen, Christian children's books, church drama/humour, Christian fiction. No poetry. *All submissions must have Evangelical Christian content.* Please send synopsis/2 sample chapters only to the Editorial Department with return postage.

Kluwer Publishing (1972), Croner House, London Road, Kingston-upon-Thames, Surrey KT2 6SR *tel* 081-547 3333. *Directors:* Hans Staal (managing), Chris Hilton-Childs (finance). Subsidiary of Croner Publications Ltd.
Law, taxation, finance, insurance, business management, medicine, farming, looseleaf information services, books, databases, conferences.

*****Knight**—see **Hodder Headline plc.**

Charles Knight Publishing—see **Tolley Publishing Co. Ltd.**

Knockabout Comics (1975), 10 Acklam Road, London W10 5QZ *tel* 081-969 2945 *fax* 081-968 7614. *Editors:* Tony Bennett, Carol Bennett.
Humorous and satirical comic strips for an adult readership.

*****Kogan Page Ltd** (1967), 120 Pentonville Road, London N1 9JN *tel* 071-278 0433 *telex* 263088 KOGAN G *fax* 071-837 6348. *Managing director:* Philip Kogan; *directors:* Pauline Goodwin (editorial), Peter Chadwick (production), Praba Kan (financial), Kate Griffin (sales), Dolores Black, June Lines (associate, editorial), Noel McPherson (associate, marketing), Hamish McGibbon (non-executive), Jonathan Sinclair-Wilson (Earthscan, editorial).

Education, training, educational and training technology, journals, business and management, human resource management, transport and distribution, marketing, sales, advertising and PR, finance and accounting, directories, small business, careers and vocational, personal finance, environment.

Earthscan Publications Ltd (subsidiary). *Directors:* Philip Kogan, Jonathan Sinclair-Wilson (editorial), Kate Griffin. Third world and environmental issues including politics, sociology, feminism, cultural questions, environment, economics, current events, geography, health.

Kompass—see **Reed Information Services Ltd.**

*****Ladybird Books Ltd** (1924), Beeches Road, Loughborough, Leics. LE11 2NQ   *tel* (0509) 268021   *telex* 341347 LDBIRD G   *fax* (0509) 234672. *Chairman:* Paula Kahn; *managing director:* Anthony Forbes Watson; *directors:* A.T. Warren, J.D. Williamson.
Children's books, general and educational (infants, primary, junior and secondary).

Lampada Press—see **The University of Hull Press.**

*****Larousse plc.** London office: Elsley House, 24-30 Great Titchfield Street, London W1P 7AD   *tel* 071-631 0878   *fax* 071-323 4694; Edinburgh office: 43-45 Annandale Street, Edinburgh EH7 4AZ   *tel* 031-557 4571   *fax* 031-557 2936. *Chairman:* Daniel Grisewood; *directors:* John Clement (managing), Margaret Barrett (finance), Chris McLaren (UK sales), Richard Drew (international sales), David Swarbrick (marketing).
Chambers (imprint). *Publishing directors:* Robert Allen, Min Lee. Dictionaries, reference and local interest.
Kingfisher (imprint). *Publishing director:* Jacqui Bailey. Children's books.
Larousse (imprint). *Publishing directors:* Robert Allen, Min Lee, Jim Miles. Reference books and bilingual dictionaries.
See also **Harrap.**

Lawrence & Wishart Ltd, 144A Old South Lambeth Road, London SW8 1XX   *tel* 071-820 9281   *telegraphic address* Interbook, London SW8   *fax* 071-587 0469. *Directors:* J. Skelley, S. Davison, W. Norris, J. Rodrigues, B. Kirsch, M. Seaton, M. Perryman.
Cultural studies, current affairs, history, socialism and Marxism, philosophy, politics, popular culture.

*****Legend**—see **Random House UK Ltd.**

*****Leicester University Press** (1951)—see **Pinter Publishers Ltd.**

Lennard Publishing, Windmill Cottage, Mackerye End, Harpenden, Herts. AL5 5DR   *tel* (0582) 715866   *fax* (0582) 715121. *Directors:* K.A.A. Stephenson, R.H. Stephenson. Division of **Lennard Associates Ltd.**
General adult non-fiction.

Letts Educational (1979), Aldine House, Aldine Place, London W12 8AW   *tel* 081-743 7514   *fax* 081-743 8451. *Managing director:* Jonathan Harris; *publicity director:* Claire Wright.
Educational books for home study, ages 5-18.

*****H.K. Lewis & Co. Ltd** (1844)—see **Chapman & Hall Ltd.**

Lewis Masonic (1870), Coombelands House, Coombelands Lane, Addlestone, Surrey HT15 1HY   *tel* (0932) 820560   *fax* (0932) 821258. *Managing director:* C. Beach.
Masonic books; *Masonic Square Magazine.*

John Libbey & Co. Ltd (1979), 13 Smiths Yard, Summerley Street, London SW18 4HR *tel* 081-947 2777 *telex* 94013503 JOHN G *fax* 081-947 2664. *Directors:* John Libbey, G. Cahn.
Medical: nutrition, obesity, epilepsy, neurology, diabetes, biological psychiatry; media communications.

*****Library Association Publishing Ltd** (1981), 7 Ridgmount Street, London WC1E 7AE *tel* 071-636 7543 *telex* 9312134504 LA G *fax* 071-636 3627. *Managing director:* Janet Liebster.
Library and information science, reference works, directories, bibliographies.
Clive Bingley Ltd (imprint). Library and information science, reference works.

Frances Lincoln Ltd (1977), 4 Torriano Mews, Torriano Avenue, London NW5 2RZ *tel* 071-284 4009 *fax* 071-485 0490. *Directors:* Frances Lincoln (managing), Erica Hunningher (editorial, adult books), Janetta Otter-Barry (editorial, children's books).
Illustrated, international co-editions: gardening, interiors, health, crafts, cookery, children's books.

*****Lion Publishing plc** (1972), Peter's Way, Sandy Lane West, Oxford OX4 5HG *tel* (0865) 747550 *telex* 837161 LION G *fax* (0865) 747568. *Directors:* David Alexander, Pat Alexander, Tony Wales, Mark Beedell, Robin Keeley, Denis Cole, Rebecca Winter.
Reference, paperbacks, illustrated children's books, educational, gift books, religion and theology; all reflecting a Christian position.

*****Lions**—see **HarperCollins Publishers.**

Little, Brown and Company (UK) Ltd (1988), Brettenham House, Lancaster Place, London WC2E 7EN *tel* 071-911 8000 *fax* 071-911 8100. *Directors:* Philippa Harrison (managing), B. Boote (editorial), A. Samson (editorial), David Kent (home sales), Nigel Batt (financial), Charles Viney (export sales), Terry Jackson (marketing).
Hardback and paperback fiction, general non-fiction and illustrated books. *No unsolicited MSS.*
Abacus (division). *Editorial director:* Richard Beswick. Trade paperbacks.
Illustrated (division). *Editorial director:* Vivien Bowler. Hardback photographic and art books.
Optima (division). *Editorial director:* Hilary Foakes. Health, alternative medicine, women's studies, the environment, popular psychology, self-help.
Orbit (imprint). *Editor:* Colin Murray. Science fiction and fantasy paperbacks.
Warner (division). *Editorial directors:* Barbara Boote, Alan Samson, Hilary Hale. Paperbacks: original fiction and non-fiction; reprints.
Warner–Futura (imprint). *Editorial director:* Hilary Hale. British paperback crime fiction.

Littlewood · Arc—see **Arc Publications.**

*****Liverpool University Press** (1901), PO Box 147, Liverpool L69 3BX *tel* 051-794 2232/7 *telex* 627095 UNILPL G *fax* 051-708 6502. *Publisher:* Robin Bloxsidge.
Academic and scholarly books in a range of disciplines. Special interests: education, literature, social, political, economic and ancient history, archaeology, veterinary science, urban and regional planning.

Y Lolfa Cyf. (1967), Talybont, Dyfed SY24 5HE *tel* (0970) 832304 *fax* (0970) 832782. *Directors:* Robat Gruffudd, Enid Gruffudd.
Welsh-language popular fiction and non-fiction, music, children's books; Welsh-language tutors; English-language political books and a range of Welsh-interest books for the tourist market.

***Longman Group Ltd** (1724), Longman House, Burnt Mill, Harlow, Essex CM20 2JE　*tel* (0279) 426721　*telex* 81259 LONGMN G　*fax* (0279) 431059/451946. *Chairman:* P. Kahn; *directors:* P. Warwick (deputy chief executive), R.G.B. Duncan, J.D. Williamson (finance), J.M. Little, H. Reece, T. Davy, D. Feldman, A. Forbes Watson.

Atlases, audio-visual aids, children's, school, further education, university, scholarly, undergraduate, post-graduate, academic, scientific and technical, legal, financial, business education, dictionaries, reference, English language teaching, directories, learned journals; micro computer software, videos; Africana (including African studies and African and Caribbean literature).

Longman Education (imprint). *Managing director:* Jeff Andrew. Curriculum-related books on all subjects and interactive materials.

Longman ELT (imprint). *Managing director:* Rob Francis. English language teaching books and interactive materials in both British English and American English.

Longman GeoInformation (imprint). *Managing director:* Seppe Cassettari. Digital geographical information. Publishes *GIS Europe.*

Longman Higher Education (imprint). *Managing director:* Smuts Beyers. Books and journals for students, academics and practising engineers and scientists for colleges of further education and universities.

Longman Information & Reference (imprint). *Managing director:* Gillian Reid-Holden. Specialist management and reference books for managers in health, education, local and central government, housing, leisure and social services.

Longman International Education (imprint). *Managing director:* Graham Taylor. Educational material mainly for Africa, the Caribbean and the Middle East.

Longman Law Tax and Finance (imprint), 21-27 Lamb's Conduit Street, London WC1N 3NJ　*tel* 071-242 2548　*fax* 071-831 8119. *Directors:* L.W. Herbert (managing), A.R. Wells, S.R. Moncrieff, M. Staunton, J.D. Williamson, J.E. Robinson, P. Warwick. Books and professional journals on law, business, taxation, pensions, insurance, government contracting, finance and accountancy.

Longman Logotron (imprint). Computer software for schools, businesses and the home.

Longman Training (imprint). *Managing director:* Mike Smith. Video-based and technology-based training for use in business and industry.

Oliver & Boyd (imprint). *Divisional managing director:* Jeff Andrew. Educational material for primary and secondary schools; Scottish schoolbooks. See also **Churchill Livingstone, Pitman Publishing**.

Peter Lowe (Eurobook Ltd) (1968), PO Box 52, Wallingford, Oxon OX10 0XU *tel* (0865) 749033　*fax* (0865) 749044. *Directors:* P.S. Lowe, R. Lowe. Publishers of natural history and related subjects as illustrated non-fiction and as illustrated fiction with natural history/environmental background. All ages but no general or general teen fiction.

Lund Humphries Publishers Ltd, Park House, 1 Russell Gardens, London NW11 9NN　*tel* 081-458 6314　*fax* 081-905 5245. *Directors:* Clive Bingley, Lionel Leventhal. Art, architecture, graphic art and design, Arabic language.

***Lutterworth Press** (1799)—see **James Clarke & Co. Ltd.**

Macdonald Group—adult titles acquired by **Little, Brown and Company (UK) Ltd**, educational and children's book titles acquired by **Simon & Schuster Young Books.**

*McGraw-Hill Book Company Europe, McGraw-Hill House, Shoppenhangers Road, Maidenhead, Berks. SL6 2QL   *tel* (0628) 23432   *telegraphic address* McGraw-Hill, Maidenhead   *telex* 848484 MCHILL G   *fax* (0628) 770224. *Managing director:* Stephen White; *directors:* Roger Horton (editorial), Dan Jennings (financial).
Technical, scientific, professional reference, medical.

*Macmillan London—see Macmillan Publishers Ltd.

*The Macmillan Press Ltd—see Macmillan Publishers Ltd.

*Macmillan Publishers Ltd, 4 Little Essex Street, London WC2R 3LF   *tel* 071-836 6633   *fax* 071-379 4204. *Chairman:* N.G. Byam Shaw; *directors:* R. Barker, M. Barnard, I.K. Burns (managing), C.J. Paterson, A. Soar, A.J. Sutherland, G.R.U. Todd.
The Macmillan Press Ltd (division), Houndmills, Basingstoke, Hants RG21 2XS   *tel* (0256) 29242   *fax* (0256) 479476. *Managing director:* D. Knight; *publishing directors:* H. Holt (medical and scientific journals), T.M. Farmiloe (postgraduate and scholarly), S. O'Neill (reference and professional), D. Robertson (directories), S. Kennedy (university texts), J. Winkler (further education). Further and higher education textbooks, monographs, ELT, journals and reference books. Unsolicited MSS welcome, with return postage.
Macmillan General Books (division), 18-21 Cavaye Place, London SW10 9PG   *tel* 071-373 6070   *fax* 071-370 0746. *Managing director:* I.S. Chapman. Publishes under **Macmillan, Macmillan London, Pan, Papermac, Sidgwick & Jackson. Fiction**   *editorial directors:* Suzanne Baboneau, Maria Rejt. Novels, detective fiction, sci-fi, fantasy and horror. **Non-fiction**   *publisher:* William Armstrong; *editorial director:* Georgina Morley. Autobiography, biography, business and industry, cinema and video, crafts and hobbies, economics, gift books, health and beauty, history, humour, literature and criticism, medical, military and war, music, natural history, philosophy, politics and world affairs, pop and rock, psychology, sports and games, theatre and drama, travel, wines and spirits.
Macmillan Reference Books (division). *Publisher:* J. Ashby. General reference, including encyclopedias and dictionaries, gardening and cookery. MSS, synopses and ideas welcome; send to the submissions editor, with return postage.
Macmillan Children's Books Ltd (division). *Executive director:* Kate Wilson; *editorial director (fiction):* Marion Lloyd; *senior editor (non-fiction and poetry):* Susie Gibbs. Publishes under **Macmillan, Pan.** Picture books, fiction, poetry, non-fiction, pop-up, novelty. *No* unsolicited material.
Picador (imprint of Macmillan General Books). *Literary publisher:* Peter Straus; *deputy publishing director:* Jonathan Riley; *editorial director:* Georgia Garrett. Literary international fiction and non-fiction. MSS, synopses and ideas welcome; send to the submissions editor, with return postage.
Macmillan Education (division), Houndmills, Basingstoke, Hants RG21 2XS   *tel* (0256) 29242   *fax* (0256) 479985. *Managing director:* Christopher Harrison; *publishing director:* Alison Hubert; *marketing director:* John G. Watson; *Caribbean director:* G.W. Lennox. School and College books in all subjects for all ages, including English Language Teaching.

*Julia MacRae Books (1979)—see **Random House UK Ltd.**

Magi Publications (1987)   *postal address only* 55 Crowland Avenue, Hayes, Middlesex UB3 4JP   *editorial office* 112 Whitfield Street, London W1P 5RU   *tel* 071-387 0610   *fax* 071-383 5003. *Publisher:* Monty Bhatia; *editor:* Linda Jennings.
Quality children's picture books. New material will be considered from authors and illustrators, but please enquire first.

Mainstream Publishing Co. (Edinburgh) Ltd (1978), 7 Albany Street, Edinburgh EH1 3UG *tel* 031-557 2959 *fax* 031-556 8720. *Directors:* Bill Campbell, Peter MacKenzie.
Biography, autobiography, art, photography, sport, health, guidebooks, humour, literature, fiction, current affairs, history, politics.

Mammoth—see **Reed Consumer Books.**

Management Books 2000 Ltd (incorporating **Mercury Books**), 125A The Broadway, Didcot, Oxon OX11 8AW *tel* (0235) 815544 *fax* (0235) 817188. *Directors:* N. Dale-Harris, A. Finn, R.C. Postema.
Business books.

*****Manchester University Press** (1912), Oxford Road, Manchester M13 9PL *tel* 061-273 5530/5539 *telex* 666517 UNIMAN G *fax* 061-274 3346.
Works of academic scholarship: literary criticism, art, architecture, urban studies, cultural studies, history, politics, economics; general books on North of England; specialises in international law, Spanish, Italian, German and French texts; social anthropology, sociology, special education; sixth form/ student texts.

Mandarin—see **Reed Consumer Books.**

The Mandeville Press (1974), Old Hall, Norwich Road, South Burlingham, Norwich NR13 4EY *tel* (0493) 750804. *Editor/proprietor:* Peter Scupham; *editor:* John Mole.
Contemporary poetry.

Mandrake of Oxford (1986), PO Box 250, Oxford OX1 1AP *tel* (0865) 243671. *Directors:* Kris Morgan, Shantidevi Nath.
Occult and bizarre.

*****Mansell Publishing**—see **Cassell plc.**

*****Manson Publishing Ltd** (1992), 73 Corringham Road, London NW11 7DL *tel* 081-905 5150 *fax* 081-201 9233. *Managing director:* Michael Manson.
Medical, scientific, veterinary.

Mantra Publishing Ltd (1984), 5 Alexandra Grove, London N12 8NU *tel* 081-445 5123 *fax* 081-446 7745. *Managing director:* M. Chatterji.
Multicultural children's books/cassettes; dual language books/cassettes; South Asian literature – teenage fiction, translations.

*****Marshall Pickering**—see **HarperCollins Publishers.**

*****Martin Books,** Grafton House, 64 Maids Causeway, Cambridge CB5 8DD *tel* (0223) 66733 *fax* (0223) 461428. Imprint of Simon & Schuster Consumer Group.
Cookery, gardening, illustrated non-fiction and high quality sponsored publishing.

Martin Brian & O'Keeffe Ltd (1971), 78 Coleraine Road, Blackheath, London SE3 7PE *tel* 081-858 5164. *Director:* Timothy O'Keeffe.
General literature including biography, fiction, history, travel, science, economics and poetry.

*****Martin Robertson & Co. Ltd**—now merged with **Blackwell Publishers.**

*****Kenneth Mason Publications Ltd** (1958), Dudley House, 12 North Street, Emsworth, Hants PO10 7DQ *tel* (0243) 377977 *fax* (0243) 379136. *Directors:* Kenneth Mason (chairman), Piers Mason (managing), Michael Mason, Anthea Mason.
Nautical, slimming, health, fitness, family and women's topics; technical journals and high court law reports.

Meadowfield Press Ltd (1976), I.S.A. Building, Hackworth Industrial Park, Shildon, Co. Durham DL4 1LH *tel* Bishop Auckland (0388) 773065 *telex* 587188 *fax* (0388) 774888. *Directors:* Dr J.G. Cook, M. Cook, J.A. Verdon, A.M. Creasey.
Microbiology, zoology, archaeology, botany, biology.

Medici Society Ltd, 34-42 Pentonville Road, London N1 9HG *tel* 071-837 7099 *fax* 071-837 9152.
Publishers of Medici Prints, greetings cards and other colour reproductions. Art and children's books. Preliminary letter with brief details of the work requested.

Melrose Press Ltd (1969), 3 Regal Lane, Soham, Ely, Cambs. CB7 5BA *tel* (0353) 721091 *fax* (0353) 721839. *Directors:* Ernest Kay, R.A. Kay, J.M. Kay, B.J. Wilson, N.S. Law, C. Emmett FCA, V.A. Kay, J.E. Pearson.
International biographical reference works, including *International Authors & Writers Who's Who*.

*The Mercat Press (1970), James Thin Ltd, 53-59 South Bridge, Edinburgh EH1 1YS *tel* 031-556 6743 *fax* 031-557 8149. *Chairman:* D. Ainslie Thin; *editorial managers:* Tom Johnstone, Seán Costello.
Scottish books of general and academic interest. *No* fiction.

Mercury Books—acquired by **Management Books 2000 Ltd.**

Merehurst Ltd/J.B. Fairfax Press Ltd, Ferry House, 51/57 Lacy Road, London SW15 1PR *tel* 081-780 1177 *fax* 081-780 1714. *Directors:* Debbie Kent and Paul Mockett (sales), Shirley Patton (editorial), Kirsten Schlesinger (marketing), Roger Potter (finance).
Crafts and hobbies, cake decorating, cookery, floristry.

Merlin Press Ltd, 10 Malden Road, London NW5 3HR *tel* 071-267 3399 *fax* 071-284 3092. *Directors:* M.W. Eve, P.M. Eve.
Radical history and social studies. Letters/synopses only please.
Green Print (imprint). Green politics and the environment.
Seafarer Books (imprint). Traditional sailing.

*Mermaid—see **Penguin Books Ltd.**

Merrow Publishing Co. Ltd (1951), I.S.A. Building, Hackworth Industrial Park, Shildon, Co. Durham DL4 1LH *tel* Bishop Auckland (0388) 773065 *telex* 587188 *fax* (0388) 774888. *Directors:* Dr J.G. Cook, M. Cook, J.A. Verdon, A.M. Creasey.
Textiles, plastics, popular science, scientific.

Methodist Church, Division of Education and Youth, 2 Chester House, Pages Lane, Muswell Hill, London N10 1PR *tel* 081-444 9845 *fax* 081-365 2471.
Theology and religion.

Methodist Publishing House (1773), 20 Ivatt Way, Peterborough PE3 7PG *tel* (0733) 332202 *fax* (0733) 331201.
Hymn and service books, general religious titles, church supplies.
Foundery Press (imprint). Ecumenical titles.

Methuen—see **Reed Consumer Books.**

*Methuen Academic—incorporated in **Routledge.**

Methuen Children's Books—see **Reed Consumer Books.**

Michelin Tyre plc (1989), Tourism Department, The Edward Hyde Building, 38 Clarendon Road, Watford, Herts. WD1 1SX   *tel* (0923) 415000   *telex* 919071   *fax* (0923) 415250. *Head of tourism department:* D.C. Brown.
Tourist guides, maps and atlases, hotel and restaurant guides; children's activity books.

Milestone Publications (1967), Forestside House, Forestside, Rowlands Castle, Hants PO9 6EE   *tel* (0705) 631468   *fax* (0705) 591975. *Directors:* Nicholas J. Pine (managing), Philip G. Robinson (sales), Sarah H. Hushes (administration).
Heraldic china, antique porcelain, business, economics.

Millennium—see **The Orion Publishing Group Ltd.**

J. Garnet Miller Ltd (1951), 311 Worcester Road, Malvern, Worcs. WR14 1AN   *tel* (0684) 565045. *Directors:* Leslie Smith, Audrey Smith.
Drama, theatre, plays.

*****Harvey Miller Publishers** (1968), 20 Marryat Road, London SW19 5BD   *tel* 081-946 4426   *fax* 081-944 6082. *Directors:* H.I. Miller, E. Miller.
Art history, medical atlases.

*****Mills & Boon (Publishers) Ltd** (1908), Eton House, 18-24 Paradise Road, Richmond, Surrey TW9 1SR   *tel* 081-948 0444   *telex* 24420 MILBON G   *fax* 081-940 5899. *Chairman:* J.T. Boon CBE; *managing director:* A. Flynn; *directors:* A.W. Boon, M.J. Westwell (financial), M.N. Saraceno (production), R. Hedley (hardback and export sales), K. Stoecker (editorial), F. Fothergill (direct marketing), H. Walton (retail/corporate marketing), G. Howe (paperback sales).
Romantic fiction in paperback and hardback.
Silhouette (imprint). *Senior editor:* Linda Fildew. Popular romantic fiction.
Worldwide Books (imprint). *Senior editor:* Linda Fildew. Contemporary fiction, thriller, mystery, romance.

Minerva—see **Reed Consumer Books.**

Mitchell Beazley—see **Reed Consumer Books.**

Monarch Publications, Broadway House, The Broadway, Crowborough, East Sussex TN6 1HQ   *tel* (0892) 652364   *fax* (0892) 663329. *Publisher:* Tony Collins, Jane Collins.
Christian books: (Monarch) issues of faith and society; (MARC) leadership, mission, evangelism; (Mitre) Christian fiction, drama and humour. Submit synopsis/2 sample chapters *only* with return postage please.

Mondo—see **Titan Books Ltd.**

Moorland Publishing Co. Ltd (1972), Moor Farm Road, Ashbourne, Derbyshire DE6 1HD   *tel* (0335) 344486   *fax* (0335) 346397. *Directors:* Dr J.A. Robey (chairman and editorial director), C.L.M. Porter (managing), J. Angell.
Travel, gardening.

*****Mosby Wolfe Publishing**—see **Times Mirror International Publishers Ltd.**

The Mothers' Union (1876), 24 Tufton Street, London SW1P 3RB   *tel* 071-222 5533 *fax* 071-222 5533 ext 200.
Religious, educational and social subjects connected with marriage and the family; religious books for adults and children; quarterly magazine *Home and Family*.

*****Mowbray**—see **Cassell plc.**

Multimedia Books Ltd—see **PRION.**

*John Murray (Publishers) Ltd (1768) 50 Albemarle Street, London W1X 4BD *tel* 071-493 4361 *telegraphic address* Guidebook, London W1 *telex* 21312 MURRAY G *fax* 071-499 1792. *Chairman:* John R. Murray (general books marketing); *managing director:* Nicholas Perren; *directors:* Grant McIntyre (general editorial), Judith Reinhold (educational marketing); *company secretary:* John Roberts.
General: art and architecture, biography, autobiography, letters and diaries, travel, exploration and guidebooks, Middle East, Asia, India and sub-continent, general history, health education, aviation, craft and practical. *No* unsolicited MSS please.
Educational: biology, chemistry, physics, business studies, economics, management and law, English, geography and environmental studies, history and social studies, mathematics, modern languages, technical subjects. Also self teaching in all subjects in *Success Studybook* series.

*National Christian Education Council (incorporating **Hillside Publishing** and **International Bible Reading Association**), Robert Denholm House, Nutfield, Redhill RH1 4HW *tel* (0737) 82411 *fax* (0737) 822116.
Books on all aspects of Christian education. Material for children's work in the Church, also RE material for day schools. Activity, visual and resource material, religious drama and religious music.

The Natural History Museum Publications (1881), Cromwell Road, London SW7 5BD *tel* 071-938 8761 *fax* 071-938 8709.
Natural sciences; entomology, botany, geology, palaeontology, zoology.

*Nautical Books—now **Adlard Coles Nautical**; see **A. & C. Black (Publishers) Ltd.**

NCVO Publications (incorporating **Bedford Square Press**), Regent's Wharf, 8 All Saints Street, London N1 9RL *tel* 071-713 6161 *fax* 071-713 6300. *Managing editor:* Jacqueline Sallon. Imprint of the National Council for Voluntary Organisations.
Practical guides, reference books, directories and policy studies on voluntary sector concerns including management, legal, fundraising, self-help and community development.

*Thomas Nelson & Sons Ltd (1798), Nelson House, Mayfield Road, Walton-on-Thames, Surrey KT12 5PL *tel* (0932) 252211 *telegraphic address* Thonelson, Walton-on-Thames *fax* (0932) 246109. *Directors:* M.E. Thompson (managing), Phillip Blundell, John Tuttle, Barry Hinchmore, Pamela Hutchinson, Fred Grainger.
Educational (infant, primary, secondary), college and multimedia, English language teaching world-wide, educational books for Caribbean and SE Asia.

*Nelson-Blackie *editorial office* Bishopbriggs, Glasgow G64 2NZ *tel* 041-772 2311 *fax* 041-762 0897. *Commissioning editor:* Alison Payne.
Educational books.

*Network Books—see **BBC Books.**

New Beacon Books (1966), 76 Stroud Green Road, London N4 3EN *tel* 071-272 4889. *Directors:* John La Rose, Sarah White, Michael La Rose, Janice Durham.
Small specialist publishers: general non-fiction, fiction, poetry, critical writings, mainly concerning the Caribbean, Africa, Afro-America, Black Europe.

New Cavendish Books (1973), 3 Denbigh Road, London W11 2SJ *tel* 071-229 6765/792 9984 *telex* 8951182 GECOMS G *fax* 071-792 0027. **White Mouse Editions Ltd** (1979).
Specialist books for the collector; art reference books and Thai guidebooks.

*New English Library Ltd (1957)—see **Hodder Headline plc.**

*New Holland Publishers, 37 Connaught Street, London W2 2AZ *tel* 071-258 0204 *fax* 071-262 6184. *Managing director:* John Beaufoy; *publishing directors:* Charlotte Parry-Crooke, Yvonne McFarlane (home interest).
Illustrated books on natural history and travel, cookery, cake decoration, needlecrafts and handicrafts, gardening, DIY.

*New Orchard Editions—see **Cassell plc.**

Newpoint—see **Reed Information Services Ltd.**

Nexus (1988)—see **Virgin Publishing Ltd.**

*NFER-NELSON Publishing Co. Ltd (1981), Darville House, 2 Oxford Road East, Windsor, Berks. SL4 1DF *tel* (0753) 858961 *fax* (0753) 856830. *Editorial director:* Keith Nettle.
Testing, assessment and management publications and services for education, business and health care.

*Nicholson (1967)—see **HarperCollins Publishers.**

James Nisbet & Co. Ltd (1810), 78 Tilehouse Street, Hitchin, Herts. SG5 2DY *tel* (0462) 438331 *fax* (0462) 431528. *Directors:* Miss E.M. Mackenzie-Wood, Mrs A.A.C. Bierrum.
Dictionaries, educational (infants, primary, secondary).

The Nonesuch Press Ltd—see **Reinhardt Books Ltd.**

Northcote House Publishers Ltd (1985), Plymbridge House, Estover Road, Plymouth, Devon PL6 7PZ *tel* (0752) 735251 *telex* 45635 HARDIS G *fax* (0752) 695699. *Directors:* B.R.W. Hulme, M.W. Beevers FCA (secretary).
Careers and training, education management, educational dance and drama, English literature (*Writers and their Work*).

W.W. Norton & Company (1980), 10 Coptic Street, London WC1A 1PU *tel* 071-323 1579 *telegraphic address* Gavia, London WC1 *fax* 071-436 4553. *Directors:* Alan Cameron (managing), Donald Lamm (USA), Victor Schmalzer (USA), Edwin Barber (USA), Lord Bullock FBA, Robin Denniston
History, biography, current affairs, sailing, English and American literature, economics, music, psychology, science.

The Octagon Press Ltd (1972), PO Box 227, London N6 4EW *tel* 081-348 9392 *fax* 081-341 5971. *Managing director:* George R. Schrager.
Psychology, philosophy, Eastern religion.

The Oleander Press (1960), 17 Stansgate Avenue, Cambridge CB2 2QZ *tel* (0223) 244688 *telegraphic address* Oleander. *Managing director:* P. Ward.
Language, literature, Libya, Arabia and Middle East, Indonesia and Far East, Cambridgeshire, travel, medical history, reference. Preliminary letter required before submitting MSS; please send sae for reply.

*Oliver & Boyd—see **Longman Group Ltd.**

Michael O'Mara Books Ltd (1985), 9 Lion Yard, Tremadoc Road, London SW4 7NQ *tel* 071-720 8643 *fax* 071-627 8953. *Chairman:* Michael O'Mara; *managing director:* Lesley O'Mara; *editorial director:* David Roberts.
General non-fiction: Royal books, true crime, ancient history, anthologies and illustrated classics.

*Omnibus Press/Music Sales Ltd (1976), 8/9 Frith Street, London W1V 5TZ *tel* 071-434 0066 *fax* 071-439 2848. *Director:* Robert Wise.
Rock music biographies, books about music.

Oneworld Publications (1984), 185 Banbury Road, Oxford, Oxon OX2 7AR *tel* (0865) 310597 *fax* (0865) 310598. *Directors:* Juliet Mabey (editorial), Novin Doostdar (marketing).
Social issues, psychology, self-help, religion, inter-religious dialogue, philosophy.

Onlywomen Press Ltd (1974), 71 Great Russell Street, London WC1B 3BN *tel* 071-404 6227 *fax* 071-831 8356. *Managing director:* Lilian Mohin.
Lesbian feminist fiction, poetry and theory (cultural criticism).

Open Books Publishing Ltd (1974), Beaumont House, New Street, Wells, Somerset BA5 2LD *tel* (0749) 677276 *fax* (0749) 670760. *Directors:* P. Taylor (managing), C. Taylor.
Books on gardening.

***Open Eye Publishing** (1993), Unit 18, City Business Centre, Brighton Road, Horsham, West Sussex RH13 5BA *tel* (0403) 274598 *fax* (0403) 274599. *Publisher:* Barry O'Dwyer.
Books for the visual communications industry: advertising, design, illustration, graphics.

***Open University Press** (1977), Celtic Court, 22 Ballmoor, Buckingham MK18 1XW *tel* (0280) 823388 *fax* (0280) 823233. *Directors:* John Skelton (managing), Jacinta Evans (editorial), Sue Hadden (production), Barry Clarke (financial).
Education, management, politics, psychology, sociology, criminology, counselling, health and social welfare, women's studies.

Optima (1974)—see **Little, Brown and Company (UK) Ltd.**

Orbit (1989)—see **Little, Brown and Company (UK) Ltd.**

***Orchard Books** (1985)—see **The Watts Publishing Group.**

Orion Books Ltd (1992)—see **The Orion Publishing Group Ltd.**

Orion Children's Books Ltd (1993)—see **The Orion Publishing Group Ltd.**

The Orion Publishing Group Ltd (1992), Orion House, 5 Upper St Martin's Lane, London WC2H 9EA *tel* 071-240 3444 *fax* 071-240 4822. *Directors:* Sir John Cuckney (non-executive chairman), Anthony Cheetham (chief executive), Peter Roche (managing), Rosie Cheetham, Ion Trewin.
Chapman (imprint) *fax* 071-240 4822. Wide range of fiction and general nonfiction.
Everyman (imprint). *Contact:* Hilary Laurie. Paperbacks.
Millennium (imprint). *Contact:* Caroline Oakley. Science fiction and fantasy.
Orion Books Ltd (division). *Directors:* Rosie Cheetham, Susan Lamb, Jane Wood. Fiction and non-fiction.
Orion Children's Books Ltd (division) *fax* 071-240 4823. *Managing director and publisher:* Judith Elliott. Children's fiction, picture books and novelty books, in hardback and paperback.
Phoenix House (imprint). *Director:* Maggie McKernan. Quality hardbacks and paperbacks.
Weidenfeld & Nicolson (division). *Publishers:* Michael Dover, Ion Trewin. Architecture, art, biography and memoirs, business, current affairs, economics, fiction, general, history, politics, sport, humour, cookery, crime, crafts and hobbies, gardening, science, sociology, travel.

Osprey—see **Reed Consumer Books.**

***Peter Owen Ltd,** 73 Kenway Road, London SW5 0RE *tel* 071-373 5628/370 6093 *fax* 071-373 6760. *Managing director:* Peter L. Owen.
Art, belles-lettres, biography and memoirs, fiction, general, theatre.

Owl Press (1990), PO Box 315, Downton, Salisbury, Wilts. SP5 3YE *tel/fax*
(0243) 572988. *Managing editor:* Anne Musgrove, Marjorie Hewitt.
Adult humour and gift books.

Oxford Illustrated Press—see **Haynes Publishing.**

Oxford Publishing Company (OPC Railbooks)—see **Haynes Publishing.**

*****Oxford University Press** (1478), Walton Street, Oxford OX2 6DP *tel* (0865)
56767 *cables* Clarendon Press, Oxford *telex* 837330 CLARPRESS G *fax* (0865)
56646. *Chief executive and secretary to the delegates:* James Arnold-Baker;
deputy secretary and finance director: W.R. Andrewes; Art and Reference
Division: *managing director:* Ivon Asquith; Science, Medical and Journals
Division: *managing director:* John Manger; Education Division: *managing
director:* Fiona Clarke; ELT Division: *managing director:* Peter Mothersole.
Anthropology, archaeology, architecture, art, belles-lettres, bibles, bibliography, children's books (fiction, non-fiction, picture), commerce, current
affairs, dictionaries, drama, economics, educational (infants, primary, secondary, technical, university), English language teaching, electronic publishing,
essays, general history, hymn and service books, journals, law, maps and
atlases, medical, music, oriental, philosophy, poetry, political economy, prayer
books, reference, science, sociology, theology and religion, educational software. Academic books published under the imprint **Clarendon Press.** Trade
paperbacks published under the imprint of **Oxford Paperbacks.**

*****Paladin**—now merged with **Flamingo**; see **HarperCollins Publishers.**

*****Pan** (1944)—see **Macmillan Publishers Ltd.**

*****Pan Macmillan Ltd**—now **Macmillan General Books.**

*****Pan Macmillan Children's Books Ltd**—now **Macmillan Children's Books Ltd.**

*****Pandora Press**—see **HarperCollins Publishers.**

*****Papermac**—see **Macmillan Publishers Ltd.**

Paramount Publishing Europe, Campus 400, Maylands Avenue, Hemel
Hempstead, Herts. HP2 7EZ *tel* (0442) 881900 *telex* 82445 *fax* (0442)
882099. *President:* B. Scanlan.
Harvester Wheatsheaf (division) *fax* (0442) 252544. Literature, literary
theory, cultural studies, women's studies, psychology, cognitive science, economics, political science, policy studies, politics, sociology, social policy, social
studies.
Ellis Horwood (division) *fax* (0442) 252544. Chemistry, computer science,
environmental science, mathematics, physics, food science, biomedicine, geology.
Prentice Hall (division) *fax* (0442) 252544. Computer science, business and
economics, mathematics, physics.
Prentice Hall Macmillan (division) *fax* (0422) 252544. Computer science,
business and economics, mathematics, physics.
Simon & Schuster Young Books/Simon & Schuster Education (division) *fax*
(0442) 214467. *Publisher:* Philippa Stewart. Educational and reference books;
picture books and fiction for children from pre-school to teenage.
Woodhead-Faulkner (division) *fax* (0442) 252544. Finance and investment,
management, International Company Secretaries Association and Institute of
Directors publications.

*****Partridge Press** (1987)—see **Transworld Publishers Ltd.**

*****The Paternoster Press,** PO Box 300, Carlisle, Cumbria CA3 0QS *tel* (0228)
512512 *fax* (0228) 514949.
Biblical studies, Christian theology, philosophy, ethics, history, mission.

*Stanley Paul—see **Random House UK Ltd.**

Pavilion Books (1980), 26 Upper Ground, London SE1 9PD *tel* 071-620 1666 *fax* 071-620 1314. *Joint chairmen:* Sir Tim Rice, Michael Parkinson; *directors:* Colin Webb, Pamela Webb, Tim James, Rosanna Dickinson, Trevor Dolby, Nicky Granville, Terry Shaugnessy, Fiona Brownlee, David Grant. Cookery, gardening, travel, humour, sport, children's.

*Pelham Books (1959)—see **Penguin Books Ltd.**

Pen & Sword Books Ltd, 47 Church Street, Barnsley, South Yorkshire S70 2AS *tel* (0226) 734222 *fax* (0226) 734438. *Chairman:* Sir Nicholas Hewitt, Bt; *managing director:* Leo Cooper; *director/company secretary:* T.G. Hewitt. Military history.
   Leo Cooper Ltd (imprint), 190 Shaftesbury Avenue, London WC2H 8JL *tel* 071-836 3141 *fax* 071-240 9247. Specialist military publisher.

*Penguin Books Ltd, Bath Road, Harmondsworth, Middlesex UB7 0DA *tel* 081-899 4000 *telex* 933349 *fax* 081-899 4099. *London office* 27 Wrights Lane, W8 5TZ *tel* 071-416 3000 *telex* 917181/2 *fax* 071-416 3099. *Founder:* Sir Allen Lane; *chief executive:* Peter Mayer; *managing director:* Trevor Glover; *directors:* Elizabeth Attenborough, Peter Carson, Roger Clarke, Stephen Hall, Brenda Johnson, Tony Lacey, John Rolfe, John Webster, Nigel Williams, Jonathan Yglesias, Sally Floyer, Andrew Franklin, Susan Watt, Clare Alexander, Ros Barker, Patrick Hutchinson, Cecily Engle, Laura Bamford.
   Allen Lane The Penguin Press (imprint) *fax* 071-416 3193. *Contact:* Paul Keegan. Hardback non-fiction titles of academic and intellectual interest, principally but not exclusively the humanities. Unsolicited MSS and poetry discouraged.
   Arkana (imprint). *Contact:* Janice Brent. 'Mind, body and spirit' list. Please do not submit unsolicited proposals.
   Blackie Children's Books (imprint) *fax* 071-416 3086. *Editorial director:* Rosemary Stones. Children's fiction, poetry, picture books, novelties and gift books. Unsolicited MSS to be sent to the Children's Reader, enclosing an sae.
   Fantail (imprint) *fax* 071-416 3086. *Publishing manager:* Richard Scrivener. Children's media books, licensed character publishing, novelties, film and TV tie-ins, teenage and mass-market fiction.
   Hamish Hamilton Ltd (subsidiary) *tel* 071-416 3200 *fax* 071-416 3295. *Publishing director:* Andrew Franklin; *directors:* Trevor Glover, Kate McFarlan, Adrian Din, Karen Geary, Ruth Salazar, Bob Kelly, Joy Harrison, Anthony Moggach, Max Adam, Peter Carson, Kate Jones. Fiction, belles-lettres, biography and memoirs, current affairs, general, history, literature, politics, travel. Unsolicited MSS, synopses and ideas welcome.
   Hamish Hamilton Children's Books (imprint). *Editorial director:* Jane Nissen. Children's fiction and picture books.
   Michael Joseph Ltd (subsidiary) *tel* 071-416 3200 *fax* 071-416 3293. *Publishing director:* Susan Watt; *directors:* Jenny Dereham, Nellie Flexner, Trevor Glover, Ruth Salazar, Max Adam, Peter Carson, Adrian Din, Joy Harrison, Bob Kelly, Kate McFarlan, Anthony Moggach. Biography and memoirs, current affairs, fiction, history, humour, travel, crafts, sports, handbooks, general leisure, illustrated books. Unsolicited MSS discouraged; synopses and ideas welcome.
   Mermaid (imprint of Michael Joseph Ltd). Trade paperbacks.
   Pelham Books (imprint of Michael Joseph Ltd) *tel* 071-416 3200 *fax* 071-416 3293. *Contact:* Susan Watt. *Pears Cyclopaedia, Junior Pears Encyclopaedia.* Autobiographies of men and women in sport, sports handbooks, hobbies,

Penguin Books Ltd—*continued*
crafts and pastimes, practical handbooks on dogs and other pets, country pursuits.
Penguin (imprint) *fax* 071-416 3193. *Publishing director:* Tony Lacey. Adult paperback books – wide range of fiction, non-fiction, classics, TV and film tie-ins. No unsolicited fiction or poetry.
Puffin (imprint) *fax* 071-416 3086. *Editorial director:* Philippa Milnes-Smith. Children's paperback books – mainly reprints: fiction, poetry, picture books, limited non-fiction.
RoC (imprint). *Contact:* Luigi Bonomi. Science fiction, fantasy.
Signet (imprint). *Contact:* Luigi Bonomi. Mass market fiction and non-fiction paperbacks. Unsolicited MSS and synopses welcome.
Viking (imprint) *fax* 071-416 3274. *Publishing director:* Clare Alexander. Fiction, general non-fiction; history, literature, art, biography, autobiography, current affairs, popular science and travel. Please do not submit unsolicited MSS for fiction; approach in writing only.
Viking Children's Books (imprint) *fax* 071-416 3086. *Editorial director:* Rosemary Stones. Fiction, poetry, picture books. Unsolicited MSS discouraged; synopses and ideas welcome.
Frederick Warne & Co. Ltd (subsidiary) *fax* 071-416 3199. *Directors:* Sally Floyer (publisher), Trevor Glover, John Rolfe, Stephen Hall, John Webster. Beatrix Potter, Flower Fairies, Orlando, Spot.
Also: **Penguin Audiobooks.**

Penton Press—see **Jessica Kingsley Publishers.**

Pergamon—see **Elsevier Science Ltd.**

Peterloo Poets (1976), 2 Kelly Gardens, Calstock, Cornwall PL18 9SA *tel* (0822) 833473. *Publishing director:* Harry Chambers; *trustees:* Rosemarie Bailey, Linda Squire, David Selzer.
Poetry.

*Phaidon Press Ltd, 140 Kensington Church Street, London W8 4BN *tel* 071-221 5656 *fax* 071-221 8474. *Chairman and managing director:* Richard Schlagman; *directors:* Andrew Price (financial), Frances Johnson (production), Simon Littlewood (sales).
Fine arts, architecture, design and decorative arts, photography, practical art.

George Philip—see **Reed Consumer Books.**

Phillimore & Co. Ltd (incorporating **Darwen Finlayson Ltd**), Shopwyke Manor Barn, Chichester, West Sussex PO20 6BG *tel/fax* (0243) 787636. *Directors:* Philip Harris JP (chairman), Noel Osborne MA, FSA (managing), Ian Macfarlane FCA (financial), Hilary Clifford Brown (marketing).
Local and family history; architectural history, archaeology, genealogy and heraldry; also Darwen County History Series, *The Local Historian* (Q), Journal of the British Association for Local History.

Phoenix House—see **The Orion Publishing Group Ltd.**

Piatkus Books (1979), 5 Windmill Street, London W1P 1HF *tel* 071-631 0710 *fax* 071-436 7137. *Managing director:* Judy Piatkus; *directors:* Philip Cotterell (marketing), Gill Cormode (editorial).
Business, fiction, women's interest, self-help, health, mind, body and spirit, biography, how to and practical, popular psychology, cookery.

*Picador—see **Macmillan Publishers Ltd.**

Piccadilly Press (1983), 5 Castle Road, London NW1 8PR   *tel* 071-267 4492   *fax* 071-267 4493. *Directors:* Brenda Gardner (chairman and managing), Philip Durrance (secretary).
Children's hardback books and women's interest/self-help trade paperbacks; trade paperback adult and teenage humour and sports books.

*Piccolo—former imprint of **Macmillan Children's Books Ltd.**

*Picture Corgi—see **Transworld Publishers Ltd.**

*Pimlico (1991)—see **Random House UK Ltd.**

*Pinter Publishers Ltd (1973), 25 Floral Street, London WC2E 9DS   *tel* 071-240 9233   *fax* 071-379 5553. *Chairman:* Anne Weyman; *managing director:* Janet Joyce; *directors:* Frances Pinter, Robert Macleod, Christopher Conolly-Smith, Mark Hawksworth, Patrick Armstrong (production).
Academic and professional publishers specialising in social sciences including international relations, politics, economics, new technology, linguistics, communications and religious studies.
Leicester University Press (division). *Commissioning editor:* Nicola Viinikka.
Academic books, especially medieval history, museum studies, political theory.

*Piper—former imprint of **Macmillan Children's Books Ltd.**

Pitkin Pictorials—see **Reed Consumer Books.**

*Pitman Publishing (1845), 128 Long Acre, London WC2E 9AN   *tel* 071-379 7383   *telegraphic address* Ipandsons, London WC2   *telex* 261367 PITMAN G   *fax* 071-240 5771 Pitman Ldn. *Managing director:* Rod Bristow; *publishing directors:* Simon Lake (educational), Mark Allin (professional). Division of **Longman Group Ltd.**
Secretarial studies, business education, management, professional studies, M & E Handbooks.
Financial Times/Pitman Publishing (imprint). Books for business.

The Playwrights Publishing Company (1990), 70 Nottingham Road, Burton Joyce, Notts. NG14 5AL   *tel* (0602) 313356. *Proprietor:* Liz Breeze; *consultant:* Tony Breeze.
One-act and full-length drama. Reading fee and sae required.

Plexus Publishing Ltd (1973), 26 Dafforne Road, London SW17 8TZ   *tel* 081-672 6067   *fax* 081-672 1631. *Directors:* Terence Porter (managing), Sandra Wake (editorial). Also **Eel Pie Publishing.**
Film, music, biography, popular culture, fashion.

Pluto Publishing Ltd (1968), 345 Archway Road, London N6 5AA   *tel* 081-348 2724   *fax* 081-348 9133. *Directors:* Roger van Zwanenberg (managing), Anne Beech (editorial).
Social and political science including economics, history; cultural, international, women's studies.
The Journeyman Press (trade imprint). Feminist, biography, social history, media handbooks.

Pocket Books—see **Simon & Schuster Ltd.**

Poetry Wales Press—see under imprint name of **Seren Books.**

*Point—see **Scholastic Children's Books.**

Polity Press (1983), 65 Bridge Street, Cambridge CB2 1UR *tel* (0223) 324315 *fax* (0223) 461385. *Directors:* Anthony Giddens, David Held, John Thompson.
Social and political theory, politics, sociology, history, economics, psychology, media and cultural studies, philosophy, theology, literary theory, feminism, human geography, anthropology.

Polygon—see **Edinburgh University Press.**

Prentice Hall, Prentice Hall Macmillan—see **Paramount Publishing Europe.**

PRION–Multimedia Books Ltd (1986), Unit L, 32-34 Gordon House Road, London NW5 1LP *tel* 071-482 4248 *fax* 071-482 4203. *Managing director:* Arnon Orbach.
Psychology and health, food, environment, photography, animals, space and aviation.

Prism Press Book Publishers Ltd (1974), 2 South Street, Bridport, Dorset DT6 3NQ *tel* (0308) 427022 *fax* (0308) 421015. *Director:* Julian King.
Non-fiction, including health, food, New Age, politics, ecology. Synopses and ideas welcome, but *no* complete MSS.

P.S.I. Policy Studies Institute, 100 Park Village East, London NW1 3SR *tel* 071-387 2171 *fax* 071-388 0914. *Director:* Pamela Meadows; *head of external relations:* Nicholas Evans; *secretary:* Eileen M. Reid.
Economic, industrial and social policy, political institutions, social sciences, arts and cultural industries.

*Puffin—see **Penguin Books Ltd.**

Putnam Aeronautical Books—see **Brassey's (UK) Ltd.**

Quantum—see **W. Foulsham & Co. Ltd.**

Quartet Books Ltd (1972), 27 Goodge Street, London W1P 1FD *tel* 071-636 3992 *telex* 919034 NAMARA G *fax* 071-637 1866. *Chairman:* N.I. Attallah; *editorial director:* S. Pickles. Member of the Namara Group.
General fiction and non-fiction, foreign literature in translation, classical music, jazz, biography.

Queen Anne Press, Windmill Cottage, Mackerye End, Harpenden, Herts. AL5 5DR *tel* (0582) 715866 *fax* (0582) 715121. *Directors:* K.A.A. Stephenson, R.H. Stephenson. Division of **Lennard Associates Ltd.**
Sport and leisure activities.

Quiller Press Ltd, 46 Lillie Road, London SW6 1TN *tel* 071-499 6529 *telex* 21120 MONREF G *fax* 071-381 8941. *Directors:* J.J. Greenwood, A.E. Carlile.
Publishers of sponsored books: guidebooks, history, industry, humour, architecture, cookery, aviation, country sports.

*Random House UK Ltd, 20 Vauxhall Bridge Road, London SW1V 2SA *tel* 071-973 9670 *telex* 299080 RANDOM G *fax* 071-233 6058. *Chief executive:* Gail Rebuck; *directors:* Simon King, Simon Master, Piet Snyman, Amelia Thorpe, Mike Broderick, Anthony McConnell.
Arrow Books Ltd (imprint) *tel* 071-973 9700 *fax* 233 6127. *Directors:* Simon King (managing), Andy McKillop (publishing), Nicky Stonehill (publicity), Mark McCallum (marketing), Alison Wood (finance). Fiction, non-fiction, science fiction, fantasy, crime, humour, film tie-ins.
Barrie & Jenkins (imprint of Ebury Press) *tel* 071-973 9710/9670 *fax* 071-233 6057. *Managing director:* Julian Shuckburgh. Art, antiques and collecting, architecture, decorative and applied arts.

Random House UK Ltd—*continued*
Jonathan Cape (imprint)   *tel* 071-973 9730   *fax* 071-233 6117. *Directors:* Dan Franklin, Neil Belton, Robin Robertson, Tom Maschler, Tony Colwell. Archaeology, biography and memoirs, current affairs, drama, economics, fiction, history, philosophy, poetry, sociology, travel. Imprint: **Bodley Head.**
Century (imprint)   *tel* 071-973 9680   *fax* 071-233 6127. *Directors:* Simon King (managing), Kate Parkin (publishing), Mark Booth, Oliver Johnson, Liz Sich (publicity), Mark McCallum (marketing). Fiction, classics, romance, biography, autobiography, business, general non-fiction, film tie-ins.
Chatto & Windus (imprint)   *tel* 071-973 9740   *fax* 071-233 6123. *Directors:* Jonathan Burnham (publishing), Barry Featherstone (production). Art, belles-lettres, biography and memoirs, cookery, crime/thrillers, current affairs, drama, essays, fiction, history, illustrated books, poetry, politics, psycho-analysis, translations, travel, hardbacks and paperbacks. Imprint: **Hogarth Press.** No unsolicited MSS.
Condé Nast Books (imprint of Ebury Press). *Editorial director:* Julian Shuckburgh. Highly illustrated home interest books, fashion and beauty, food.
Ebury Press Special Books (division)   *tel* 071-973 9690   *fax* 071-233 6057. *Directors:* Amelia Thorpe (managing), Brenda Glover (production), Barry Milton (special sales), Robert Gwyn Palmer (rights/deputy managing), Nicola Cowen (publicity and marketing), Fiona MacIntyre (publishing), Julian Shuckburgh (associate publisher), Denise Lie (foreign rights), Denise Bates (editorial), Caroline Buckland (special sales). Cookery, health, beauty, photography, crafts, biography, antiques, hobbies, gardening, natural history, DIY, diaries, stationery. Publishes books from *Good Housekeeping, Cosmopolitan, Harpers & Queen, She, Esquire, Country Living, House Beautiful* magazines.
Fodor Guides (imprint). World-wide annual travel guides.
Hutchinson (imprint)   *tel* 071-973 9680   *fax* 071-233 6129. *Directors:* Simon King (managing), Sue Freestone (publishing), Anthony Whittome, Paul Sidey (editorial), Alex Hippisley-Cox (publicity). Belles-lettres, biography, memoirs, thrillers, crime, current affairs, general fiction, history, politics, translations, travel, film tie-ins.
Legend (imprint of Arrow Books Ltd). *Publishing director:* Andy McKillop; *editorial director:* John Jarrold. Science fiction and fantasy.
Stanley Paul (imprint of Ebury Press)   *tel* 071-973 9690   *fax* 071-233 6057. *Publishing director:* Julian Shuckburgh; *senior editor:* Marion Paull. Sport, games, hobbies and handicrafts, sporting biographies, practical books on breeding, care, training and general management of dogs.
Pimlico (imprint)   *tel* 071-973 9730   *fax* 071-828 7213. *Publishing director:* Will Sulkin. History, biography, literature.
Random House Children's Books (division)   *tel* 071-973 9750. *Directors:* Piet Snyman (chairman), Caroline Roberts (publishing), Margaret Conroy (publishing), Julia Macrae (publishing), Tom Maschler (publishing), Katharine Toseland (marketing and sales), Alan Lee (production), Linda Summers (rights). Publishes under **Bodley Head Children's, Jonathan Cape Children's Books, Hutchinson Children's, Julia MacRae Books, Red Fox, Riverswift, Tellastory.** Picture books, fiction, poetry, music, audio cassettes.
Rider (imprint of Ebury Press). *Publishing director:* Fiona MacIntyre; *editorial consultant:* Judith Kendra. Buddhism, religion and philosophy, psychology, ecology, health and healing, mysticism, meditation and yoga.
Vermilion (imprint of Ebury Press). *Publishing director:* Fiona MacIntyre; *senior editor:* Riona McNamara. Paperback practical self-help, health, fitness, guidebooks, practical parenting.

Random House UK Ltd—*continued*
Vintage (imprint). *Publisher:* Frances Coady; *editorial director:* Sarah Westcott. Quality fiction and non-fiction.
Also: **Random House Audio Books.**

*****The Reader's Digest Association Ltd,** Berkeley Square House, Berkeley Square, London W1X 6AB *tel* 071-629 8144 *telegraphic address* Readigest, London W1 *telex* 264631 *fax* 071-499 9751. *Directors:* S.N. McRae (managing), B.C. Gray, A.T. Lynam-Smith, R.G. Twisk, H. van Wyk, R.S. Hosie, F.K. Ross, H.K. Helenius.
Monthly magazine, condensed and series books; also DIY, car maintenance, gardening, medical, handicrafts, law, touring guides, encyclopedias, dictionaries, nature, folklore, atlases, cookery.

*****Red Fox**—see **Random House UK Ltd.**

Reed Academic Publishing, Linacre House, Jordan Hill, Oxford OX2 8EJ *tel* (0865) 310366 *fax* (0865) 310898. *Managing director:* Doug Fox. Academic books division of **Reed International Books.**

Reed Consumer Books, Michelin House, 81 Fulham Road, London SW3 6RB *tel* 071-581 9393 *fax* 071-225 9424. *Chief executive:* Richard Charkin. Consumer books division of **Reed International Books.**
Brimax Books (imprint), Units 4/5, Studland Park Industrial Estate, Exning Road, Newmarket, Suffolk CB8 7AU *tel* (0638) 664611 *fax* (0638) 665220. *Publisher:* Patricia Gillette. Mass market picture books for children.
Conran Octopus (imprint), 37 Shelton Street, London WC2H 9HN *tel* 071-240 6961 *fax* 071-836 9951. *Publishing director:* John Wallace. Quality illustrated books, particularly life style, cookery, gardening.
Hamlyn (imprint) *fax* 071-225 9458. *Publisher:* Robert Snuggs. Popular illustrated non-fiction, particularly cookery, gardening, craft, sport, film tie-ins, rock'n'roll, road atlases.
Hamlyn Children's Reference Books (imprint) *fax* 071-225 9731. *Publisher:* John Moulder. Illustrated non-fiction and reference books for children.
William Heinemann (imprint) *fax* 071-225 9095. *Publisher:* Tom Weldon. Fiction and general non-fiction. No unsolicited MSS and synopses considered.
Heinemann Young Books (imprint), 38 Hans Crescent, London SW1X 0LZ *tel* 071-581 9393 *fax* 071-225 9731. *Publisher:* Ingrid Selberg. Books for children including quality picture books, novels, anthologies, TV tie-ins.
Mammoth (imprint), 38 Hans Crescent, London SW1X 0LZ *tel* 071-581 9393 *fax* 071-225 9731. *Publisher:* Ingrid Selberg. Children's paperbacks.
Mandarin (imprint) *fax* 071-225 9095. *Publisher:* Tom Weldon. Paperback fiction and general non-fiction. No unsolicited MSS and synopses considered.
Methuen (imprint) *fax* 071-225 9095. *Publisher:* Geoffrey Strachan. Drama, humour, fiction, music, arts, plays. No unsolicited MSS or synopses considered.
Methuen Children's Books (imprint), 38 Hans Crescent, London SW1X 0LZ *tel* 071-581 9393 *fax* 071-225 9731. *Publisher:* Ingrid Selberg. Books for children including picture books and fiction for babies to early teens.
Minerva (imprint) *fax* 071-225 9095. *Publisher:* Max Eilenberg. Paperback literary fiction and non-fiction.
Mitchell Beazley (imprint) *fax* 071-225 9458. *Publisher:* Robert Snuggs. Illustrated encyclopedias, other quality illustrated books, wine.
Osprey (imprint) *fax* 071-225 9458. *Publisher:* Robert Snuggs. Militaria, aviation, automotive, natural history.
George Philip (imprint) *fax* 071-225 9458. *Publisher:* John Gaisford. Atlases, maps, travel guides, astronomy.

Reed Consumer Books—*continued*

Pitkin Pictorials (imprint), Healey House, Dene Road, Andover, Hants SP10 2AA *tel* (0264) 334303 *fax* (0264) 334110. *Publisher:* Ian Corsie. Illustrated souvenir guides.

Secker and Warburg (imprint) *fax* 071-225 9095. *Publisher:* Max Eilenberg. Literary fiction, general non-fiction, poetry. *No* unsolicited MSS/synopses.

Sinclair-Stevenson (imprint) *fax* 071-225 9095. *Publisher:* Christopher Sinclair-Stevenson. Fiction, general non-fiction and poetry. No unsolicited MSS or synopses considered.

Reed Educational Publishing, Halley Court, Jordan Hill, Oxford OX2 8EJ *tel* (0865) 311366 *fax* (0865) 310043. *Managing director:* William Shepherd. Educational books division of **Reed International Books.**

Ginn & Co. (imprint), Prebendal House, Parson's Fee, Aylesbury, Bucks. HP20 2QZ *tel* (0296) 394442 *fax* (0296) 393433. *Managing director:* Nigel Hall. Textbook/other educational resources for primary and secondary schools.

Heinemann Educational (imprint). *Managing director:* Bob Osborne. Textbooks/literature/other educational resources for all levels.

Heinemann English Language Teaching (imprint). *Managing director:* Mike Esplen. English language teaching books and materials.

Reed Information Services Ltd (1983), Windsor Court, East Grinstead House, East Grinstead, West Sussex RH19 1XA *tel* (0342) 326972 *telegraphic address* Infoservices, East Grinstead *telex* 95127 INFSER G *fax* (0342) 335612. *Directors:* R.J.E. Dangerfield (chief executive), J.R. Clayton, K. Burton (managing), D. Barr, G. Waller, J. Minch.

Publishers of commercial and industrial directories under the **Reed Information Services, Kompass, Dial, Kelly's** and **Newpoint** imprints.

Reed International Books, Michelin House, 81 Fulham Road, London SW3 6RB *tel* 071-581 9393 *fax* 071-225 9424. *Chairman:* Paul Hamlyn CBE; *chief executive:* Ian Irvine; *directors:* Richard Charkin (managing), Tony Bovill, Peter Cheeseman, Neville Cusworth, Doug Fox, Derek Freeman, Robert Osborne, Mark Radcliffe, William Shepherd, David Summers. Book publishing subsidiary of Reed Elsevier (UK) Ltd.

See main book publishing divisions: Butterworth & Co. (Publishers) Ltd, Reed Academic Publishing, Reed Consumer Books, Reed Educational Publishing.

Reinhardt Books Ltd, including **The Nonesuch Press Ltd,** Flat 2, 43 Onslow Square, London SW7 3LR *tel* 071-589 3751. *Directors:* Max Reinhardt (chairman), Joan Reinhardt, John R. Hews FCA.

Biography, fiction, essays, belles-lettres, children's books. *No* unsolicited MSS.

Religious and Moral Education Press (RMEP)—see **Chansitor Publications Ltd.**

*Rider—see **Random House UK Ltd.**

Rivelin Grapheme Press (1984), The Annexe, Kennet House, 19 High Street, Hungerford, Berks. RG17 0NL *tel* (0488) 684645 *fax* (0488) 683018. *Director:* Snowdon Barnett.

Poetry. Please do not send unsolicited MSS.

Riverswift—see **Random House UK Ltd.**

Robinson Publishing Ltd (1983), 7 Kensington Church Court, London W8 4SP *tel* 071-938 3830 *telex* 2622433 MONREF G REF 778 *fax* 071-938 4214. *Publisher:* Nicholas Robinson.

Fiction: anthologies, horror, fantasy; general non-fiction includes country, natural history, pets, health, self-help, true crime, puzzles. *No* MSS; letters/synopses only, please.

*Robson Books (1973), Bolsover House, 5-6 Clipstone Street, London W1P 7EB   *tel* 071-323 1223/637 5937   *telegraphic address* Robsobook, London W1   *fax* 071-636 0798. *Managing director:* Jeremy Robson.
General, biography, music, humour.

*RoC—see **Penguin Books Ltd.**

*George Ronald (1939), 46 High Street, Kidlington, Oxon OX5 2DN   *tel* (0865) 841515   *fax* (0865) 841230. *Managers:* W. Momen, E. Leith.
Religion, specialising in the Baha'i faith.

Barry Rose Law Publishers Ltd (1972), Little London, Chichester, West Sussex PO19 1PG   *tel* (0243) 783637   *fax* (0243) 779278.
Law, local government, police, legal history.

Roundhouse Publishing Ltd (1991), PO Box 140, Oxford OX2 7FF   *tel* (0865) 512682   *fax* (0865) 59594. *Publisher:* Alan T. Goodworth.
Film, cinema, theatre and performing arts, photography, reference books.

*Routledge, 11 New Fetter Lane, London EC4P 4EE   *tel* 071-583 9855   *cables* Elegiacs, London EC4   *telex* 263398 ROUT G   *fax* 071-583 0701. *Managing director:* Janice Price; *publishing director:* Peter Sowden; *financial director:* David Tebbutt; *publishers:* David Stonestreet (social and behavioural science), Wendy Morris (reference), Claire L'Enfant (humanities), Gordon Smith (social studies). Division of Routledge, Chapman & Hall.
Access, addiction, anthropology, archaeology, art, Asian studies, business and management, classical heritage and studies, counselling, criminology, development and environment, dictionaries, economics, education, geography, health, history, Japanese studies, library science, linguistics, literary criticism, media and culture, Middle East, philosophy and religion, politics, political economy, psychiatry, psychology, reference, social administration, social studies/sociology, women's studies; journals.

*Routledge & Kegan Paul—incorporated in **Routledge.**

Royal National Institute for the Blind (1868), PO Box 173, Peterborough, Cambs. PE2 6WS   *tel* (0733) 370777   *fax* (0733) 371555.
Magazines and books for blind people, in Braille and Moon embossed types. Also tape-recorded books (*Talking Books* and cassette library). For complete list of magazines see page 132.

*Sage Publications Ltd (1971), 6 Bonhill Street, London EC2A 4PU   *tel* 071-374 0645   *fax* 071-374 8741. *Directors:* David Hill (managing), Lynn Adams, Ian Eastment, Stephen Barr, Mike Birch, Matt Jackson, S. Jones, David F. McCune (USA), Sara Miller McCune (USA).
Sociology, psychology, political and social sciences.

The Saint Andrew Press, 121 George Street, Edinburgh EH2 4YN   *tel* 031-225 5722   *fax* 031-220 3113. *Publishing manager:* Lesley A. Taylor. Section of **Church of Scotland Board of Communication.**
Theology and religion, church and local history.

St James Press—merged with **Gale Research International Ltd.**

St Pauls (1948), St Pauls House, Middlegreen, Slough, Berks. SL3 6BT   *tel* (0753) 520621   *fax* (0753) 574240.
Theology, ethics, spirituality, biography, education, children's books with religious themes, general books of Roman Catholic and Christian interest.

St Paul's Bibliographies (1974), West End House, 1 Step Terrace, Winchester, Hants SO22 5BW   *tel* (0962) 860524   *fax* (0962) 842409. *Managing director:* Robert S. Cross.
Bibliography and scholarly books on books and the book trade.

Salamander Books Ltd (1973), 129-137 York Way, London N7 9LG   *tel* 071-267 4447   *cables* Salamander, London N7   *fax* 071-267 5112. *Directors:* Jef Proost (chairman), Ray Bonds (managing), David Spence, Philip Hughes.
Cookery, crafts, children's, military, natural history, music, gardening, hobbies, pets, transport, sports.

Salvationist Publishing and Supplies Ltd, 117-121 Judd Street, London WC1H 9NN   *tel* 071-387 1656   *fax* 071-383 3420.
Devotional books, theology, biography, world-wide Christian and social service, children's books, music.

*W.B. Saunders Co. Ltd—see Harcourt Brace and Co.

K.G. Saur—see Bowker-Saur.

SAUS Publications (1978), School for Advanced Urban Studies, University of Bristol, Rodney Lodge, Grange Road, Bristol BS8 4EA   *tel* (0272) 741117   *fax* (0272) 737308. *Directors:* Alison Shaw (managing), Jane Raistrick (editorial), Julia Mortimer (marketing and sales).
Public policy, social policy; health, housing, employment, social management and urban studies.

S.B. Publications (1987), c/o 19 Grove Road, Seaford, East Sussex BN25 1TP   *tel* (0323) 893498. *Proprietor:* Stephen Benz.
Local history (illustrated by postcards/old photographs), local themes (e.g. walking books, guides), maritime history, transport, specific themes.

Scarlet Press (1990), 5 Montague Road, London E8 2HN   *tel* 071-241 3702. *Editorial director:* Christine Considine.
Women's studies, lesbian, cultural studies, history, politics, health.

*Sceptre—see Hodder Headline plc.

Schofield & Sims Ltd (1901), Dogley Mill, Fenay Bridge, Huddersfield HD8 0NQ   *tel* (0484) 607080   *fax* (0484) 606815. *Directors:* John S. Nesbitt (chairman), J. Stephen Platts (managing), J. Brierley (sales).
Educational: infants, primary, secondary, technical, music for schools, children's books.

*Scholastic Children's Books, 7-9 Pratt Street, London NW1 0AE   *tel* 071-284 4474   *fax* 071-284 4234. *Editorial director:* David Fickling. Imprint of **Scholastic Publications Ltd.**
Adlib (imprint). *Editorial director:* David Fickling. Quality teenage fiction.
André Deutsch Children's Books (imprint). *Editorial director:* David Fickling. Children's fiction and non-fiction.
Hippo (imprint). *Managing editor:* Anne Finnis. Children's paperbacks – fiction and non-fiction. *No* unsolicited MSS.
Point (imprint). *Editor:* Julia Moffatt. Fiction for 11+: horror, crime, romance, fantasy, science fiction.

*Scholastic Publications Ltd (1964), Villiers House, Clarendon Avenue, Leamington Spa, Warks. CV32 5PR   *tel* (0926) 887799   *fax* (0926) 883331. *London office:* 7-9 Pratt Street, London NW1 0AE   *tel* 071-284 4474   *fax* 071-284 4234. *Directors:* D.M.R. Kewley (managing), M.R. Robinson (USA), R.M. Spaulding (USA), D.J. Walsh (USA).
Children's division—see **Scholastic Children's Books.**
Direct marketing. Children's book clubs and school book fairs.
Educational division. *Publishing director:* Anne Peel. Publishers of books for teachers (Bright Ideas and other series), primary classroom resources and magazines for teachers (*Child Education, Junior Education* and others).

Science Museum Publications, Science Museum, Exhibition Road, London SW7 2DD *tel* 071-938 8211 *telex* 21200 SCMLIB G *fax* 071-938 8213. *Publications assistant:* Victoria Smith.
History of science and technology, public understanding of science.

***SCM Press Ltd** (1929), 26-30 Tottenham Road, London N1 4BZ *tel* 071-249 7262 *fax* 071-249 3776. *Managing director and editor:* John Bowden; *directors:* Margaret Lydamore (associate editor and company secretary), Linda Foster (bookroom), Roger Pygram (finance).
Theological books with special emphasis on biblical, philosophical and modern theology; books on sociology of religion and religious aspects of current issues.

Scolar Press—see **Ashgate Publishing Ltd.**

Scottish Academic Press plc (1969), 56 Hanover Street, Edinburgh EH2 2DX *tel* 031-225 7483 *fax* 031-225 7662. *Editor:* Dr Douglas Grant.
All types of academic books and books of Scottish interest.

The Scout Association, Baden-Powell House, Queen's Gate, London SW7 5JS *tel* 071-584 7030 *fax* 071-581 9953. *General editor:* David Easton.
Technical books dealing with all subjects relevant to Scouting and monthly journal *Scouting.*

***Scripture Union Publishing** (1867), Scripture Union House, 130 City Road, London EC1V 2NJ *tel* 071-782 0013 *fax* 071-782 0014.
Christian books and Bible reading materials for people of all ages. Educational and worship resources for churches.

Seaby (1926)—see **B.T. Batsford Ltd.**

Seafarer Books—see **Merlin Press Ltd.**

Search Press Ltd (1962), Wellwood, North Farm Road, Tunbridge Wells, Kent TN2 3DR *tel* (0892) 510850 *fax* (0892) 515903. *Directors:* Charlotte de la Bedoyère, The Hon. G.E. Noel, Ruth B. Saunders.
Arts, crafts, leisure, cookery, organic gardening, philosophy.

Secker and Warburg—see **Reed Consumer Books.**

Seren Books (1981), Andmar House, Trewsfield Industrial Estate, Tondu Road, Bridgend, Mid Glamorgan CF31 4LJ *tel* (0656) 767834. *Director:* Mick Felton.
Poetry, fiction, drama, history, film, literary criticism, biography – mostly with relevance to Wales.

Serpent's Tail (1986), 4 Blackstock Mews, London N4 2BT *tel* 071-354 1949 *fax* 071-704 6467. *Director:* Peter Ayrton.
Modern fiction in paperback: literary and experimental work, first novels and work in translation. Approach with query letter please; do *not* send complete MSS.

Settle Press (1983), 10 Boyne Terrace Mews, London W11 3LR *tel* 071-243 0695. *Directors:* D. Settle (managing), M. Carter (editorial).
Travel guidebooks and general.

Severn House Publishers (1974), 1st Floor, 9/15 High Street, Sutton, Surrey SM1 1DF *tel* 081-770 3930 *fax* 081-770 3850. *Chairman:* Edwin Buckhalter.
Adult fiction: romances, thrillers, detective, adventure, war, western, science fiction; film and TV tie-ins. Accepts unsolicited MSS only through a literary agent.

Shakespeare Head Press (1904)—see **Blackwell Publishers.**

Sheed & Ward Ltd (1926), 14 Coopers Row, London EC3N 2BH   *tel* 071-702 9799   *fax* 071-702 3583. *Directors:* M.T. Redfern, K.G. Darke, A.M. Redfern.
Publishers of books, mostly by Catholics. History, philosophy, theology, catechetics, scripture and religion.

Sheldon Press—see **Society for Promoting Christian Knowledge.**

Sheldrake Press (1979), 188 Cavendish Road, London SW12 0DA   *tel* 081-675 1767   *fax* 081-675 7736. *Publisher:* J.S. Rigge.
History, travel, architecture, cookery, music; stationery.

Shepheard-Walwyn (Publishers) Ltd (1971), Suite 34, 26 Charing Cross Road, London WC2H 0DH   *tel* 071-240 5992   *fax* 071-379 5770. *Directors:* A.R.A. Werner, M.M. Werner.
History, political economy, philosophy, religion; illustrated gift books, some originated in calligraphy; Scottish interest.

John Sherratt & Son Ltd, Hotspur House, 2 Gloucester Street, Manchester M1 5QR   *tel* 061-236 9963   *fax* 061-236 2026.
Educational (primary, secondary, technical, university), medical, practical handbooks, collectors' books.

Shire Publications Ltd (1966), Cromwell House, Church Street, Princes Risborough, Bucks. HP27 9AJ   *tel* (0844) 344301   *fax* (0844) 347080. *Directors:* J.P. Rotheroe, J.W. Rotheroe.
Discovering paperbacks, Shire Albums, Shire Archaeology, Shire Natural History, Shire Ethnography, Shire Egyptology, Shire Garden History.

*Sidgwick & Jackson (1908)—see **Macmillan Publishers Ltd.**

Sigma Press (1979), 1 South Oak Lane, Wilmslow, Cheshire SK9 6AR   *tel* (0625) 531035   *fax* (0625) 536800. *Partners:* Graham Beech, Diana Beech.
Leisure, popular science, computing.

*Signet—see **Penguin Books Ltd.**

*Silhouette—see **Mills & Boon (Publishers) Ltd.**

*Simon & Schuster (1986), West Garden Place, Kendal Street, London W2 2AQ   *tel* 071-724 7577   *fax* 071-402 0639. *Directors:* Nick Webb (managing), Jo Frank (editorial, fiction), Martin Fletcher (editorial, mass-market fiction/Touchstone), Mary Pachnos (rights), Julian Clayton (sales and marketing).
Fiction; non-fiction: reference, music, travel, mass market paperbacks.
Pocket Books (imprint). Mass-market fiction and non-fiction paperbacks.
Touchstone (imprint). Quality upmarket fiction and non-fiction paperbacks.

*Simon & Schuster Young Books/Simon & Schuster Education—see **Paramount Publishing Europe.**

Sinclair-Stevenson—see **Reed Consumer Books.**

Skoob Books Publishing Ltd (1987), 25 Lowman Road, London N7 6DD   *tel/fax* 071-609 0699. *Directors:* I.K. Ong (managing), C. Johnson (editorial).
Poetry, literary autobiographies, esoterica/occult, oriental literature.

Slow Dancer Press (1977), Flat 2, 59 Parliament Hill, London NW3 2TB   *tel* 071-435 5964. *Director:* John Harvey.
Poetry.

Smith Gryphon Ltd (1990), Swallow House, 11-21 Northdown Street, London N1 9BN *tel* 071-278 2444 *fax* 071-833 5680. *Chairman and managing director:* Robert Smith.
Biography, autobiography, rock music, cinema, true crime, topical issues, finance and business, wine, food and cookery, illustrated, and personality-led fiction.

*Colin Smythe Ltd (1966), PO Box 6, Gerrards Cross, Bucks. SL9 8XA *tel* (0753) 886000 *fax* (0753) 886469. *Directors:* Colin Smythe (managing), Peter Bander van Duren, A. Norman Jeffares, Ann Saddlemyer, Leslie Hayward.
Biography, literary criticism, folklore, Irish interest and Anglo-Irish literature.

*Society for Promoting Christian Knowledge (1698), Holy Trinity Church, Marylebone Road, London NW1 4DU *tel* 071-387 5282 *fax* 071-388 2352. *Publishing director:* Simon Kingston.
Sheldon Press (imprint). *Publisher:* Joanna Moriarty. Popular medicine, health, self-help, psychology, psychoanalysis, business.
SPCK (imprint). *Publisher:* Philip Law. Theology and religion.
Triangle (imprint). *Editor:* Rachel Boulding. Popular Christian paperbacks.

Southside (Publishers) Ltd (1968)—subsidiary of **Canongate Press Ltd.**

*Souvenir Press Ltd, 43 Great Russell Street, London WC1B 3PA *tel* 071-580 9307-8 and 637 5711/2/3 *telegraphic address* Publisher, London *fax* 071-580 5064. *Managing director:* Ernest Hecht BSc(Econ), BCom; *executive director:* Jeanne Manchee.
Archaeology, biography and memoirs, children's books (non-fiction, rewards), educational (secondary, technical), fiction, general, humour, practical handbooks, psychiatry, psychology, sociology, sports, games and hobbies, travel, supernatural, parapsychology, illustrated books.

*SPCK—see **Society for Promoting Christian Knowledge.**

Neville Spearman Publishers—see **The C.W. Daniel Company Ltd.**

Specialist Crafts Ltd (formerly **Dryad**), PO Box 247, Leicester LE1 9QS *tel* (0533) 510405 *fax* (0533) 515015. *Joint managing director:* P.A. Crick.
'How to' booklets on various art and craft skills. *Specialist Crafts 500 series* full colour craft booklets and patterns. Suppliers of over 6000 art and craft items.

*Spindlewood (1980), 70 Lynhurst Avenue, Barnstaple, Devon EX31 2HY *tel* (0271) 71612 *fax* (0271) 25906. *Directors:* Michael Holloway, Anne Holloway.
Children's picture books; young adult and children's fiction.

*E. & F.N. Spon Ltd (1834)—see **Chapman & Hall Ltd.**

Sportsprint—see **John Donald Publishers Ltd.**

Stacey International (1974), 128 Kensington Church Street, London W8 4BH *tel* 071-221 7166 *telex* 298768 STACEY G *fax* 071-792 9288. *Directors:* Tom Stacey (managing), C.S. Stacey.
Illustrated non-fiction, encyclopedic books on regions and countries, Islamic and Arab subjects, world affairs, art.

Stainer & Bell Ltd (1906), PO Box 110, Victoria House, 23 Gruneisen Road, London N3 1DZ *tel* 081-343 3303 *fax* 081-343 3024. *Directors:* Bernard Braley ACIS (chairman), Keith Wakefield (joint managing), Carol Wakefield (joint managing/secretary), Joan Braley, John Hosier CBE, Antony Kearns, Robert Schuneman.
Books on music, religious communication.

*Harold Starke Publishers Ltd, Pixey Green, Stradbroke, Eye, Suffolk IP21 5NG   *tel* (0379) 388334   *fax* (0379) 388335; and 203 Bunyan Court, Barbican, London EC2Y 8DH   *tel* 071-588 5195. *Directors:* Harold K. Starke, Naomi Galinski.
Specialist, scientific, medical, reference.

Patrick Stephens Ltd (1967)—see **Haynes Publishing.**

The Sterling Publishing Group plc (1978), PO Box 839, 86-88 Edgware Road, London W2 2YW   *tel* 071-258 0066   *telex* 8953130 ESPEPE G   *fax* 071-723 5766. *Chairman:* R. Harrison; *managing director:* R.M. Summers; *directors:* D.M. Coughlan, R.G.B. Heller, V.L. Lewis, M.D. Preston, C.E. Whitley, D. Shorthouse.
Reference, management and technology directories, leisure, commemorative publishing, exhibition organising.

Stevens and Sons Ltd (founded 1799; incorporated 1889)—see **Sweet & Maxwell Ltd.**

Stride Publications (including **Taxus Press, Stride Conversation Pieces** and **Apparitions Press**) (1980), 11 Sylvan Road, Exeter, Devon EX4 6EW. *Proprietor:* Rupert M. Loydell.
Poetry, short stories, literary experimental novels, arts, theology of arts.

*Studio Vista—see **Cassell plc.**

Sunflower Books, 12 Kendrick Mews, London SW7 3HG   *tel* 071-589 1862   *telex* 269388 LONHAN G   *fax* 071-589 1862. *Directors:* P.A. Underwood (USA), J.G. Underwood, S.J. Seccombe.
Travel guidebooks.

Sussex University Press (1971)—publications distributed by **Scottish Academic Press plc.** Academic books.

Alan Sutton Publishing Ltd (1978), Phoenix Mill, Far Thrupp, Stroud, Glos. GL5 2BU   *tel* (0453) 731114   *fax* (0453) 731117. *Directors:* David Prigent, Peter Clifford, Richard Bryant, Christopher Sackett, Nicholas Mills, Alan Plank.
General and academic publishers of high quality fully illustrated books, including history, travel, military, countryside, topography, regional interest, local history, railways, literature, biography, archaeology.

Swan Hill Press—see **Airlife Publishing Ltd.**

Swedenborg Society, 20-21 Bloomsbury Way, London WC1A 2TH   *tel* 071-405 7986.
The writings of Swedenborg.

*Sweet & Maxwell Ltd (founded 1799; incorporated 1889), South Quay Plaza, 183 Marsh Wall, London E14 9FT   *tel* 071-538 8686   *fax* 071-538 8625. *Directors:* A. Kinahan, C. Tullo, I. Drane, P. Riddle, S. Harris, B. Grandage.
Law.
Stevens and Sons Ltd (imprint). Law.

Tamarind Ltd (1987), PO Box 296, Camberley, Surrey GU15 1QW   *tel* (0276) 683979   *fax* (0276) 685365. *Managing director:* Verna Wilkins.
Children's picture books and educational material. Publications give a high positive profile to black children. Unsolicited material welcome with return postage.

Tango Books—children's fiction and non-fiction imprint of **Sadie Fields Productions Ltd**, book packagers.

I.B. Tauris & Co. Ltd (1983), 45 Bloomsbury Square, London WC1A 2HY   *tel* 071-916 1069   *fax* 071-916 1068. *Directors:* I. Bagherzade (chairman and

managing), Anna Enayat (editorial), Jonathan McDonnell (sales and marketing).
Modern history, politics, international relations, economics, current affairs, Middle East.

British Academic Press (imprint). *Director:* Dr Lester Cook. Academic monographs on history, politics, international relations, economics, international law.

Tauris Parke Books (imprint). *Director:* Francesco Venturi. Illustrated books on architecture, design, cultural history and travel.

Tauris Parke Books—see **I.B. Tauris & Co. Ltd.**

*****Tavistock Publications Ltd**—incorporated in **Routledge.**

*****Taylor & Francis Ltd,** 4 John Street, London WC1N 2ET   *tel* 071-405 2237-9.
President: Professor Sir Nevill Mott MS, DSC, FInstP, FRS; *directors:* Professor B.R. Coles BSc, DPhil, FInstP, FRS (chairman), Professor K.W. Keohane CBE, BSc, PhD, FInstP, A.R. Selvey FCCA, FBIM (managing), E. Ferguson MA (vice-chairman), Professor H. Baum, K.R. Courtney, S.B. Neal BSc, Dr D.J. Banister BA, MCIT, A.M. Foye BA, ACA.
Educational (university), science: physics, and mathematics, chemistry, electronics, natural history, pharmacology and drug metabolism, medical science, astronomy, technology, history of science, ergonomics, production engineering, Falmer Press Ltd.

Telegraph Books (1920), The Daily Telegraph, 1 Canada Square, Canary Wharf, London E14 5DT   *tel* 071-538 6829   *fax* 071-538 6950. *Publishing director:* Marilyn Warnick.
Business, personal finance, crosswords, sport, travel and guides, cookery and wine, general, gardening, history – all by *Telegraph* journalists and contributors, and co-published with major publishing houses.

*****Tellastory**—see **Random House UK Ltd.**

*****Thames and Hudson Ltd,** 30-34 Bloomsbury Street, London WC1B 3QP   *tel* 071- 636 5488   *telegraphic address* Thameshuds, London WC1   *telex* 25992 THBOOK G   *fax* 071-636 4799. *Chairman:* E.U. Neurath; *managing director:* T.M. Neurath; *directors:* E. Bates (company secretary), J.R. Camplin (editorial), T.L. Evans (sales and marketing), C.A. Ferguson (production), W. Guttmann, S. Huntley, C.M. Kaine (design), I.H.B. Middleton (rights), N. Stangos (editorial), T.J. Flood (finance), P. Hughes CBE.
Art, archaeology and anthropology, architecture, photography, travel, social, classical history, fashion, literature and criticism, practical guides, design, cultural history, craft, mythology and religion, philosophy, music.

Thames Publishing (1970), 14 Barlby Road, London W10 6AR   *tel* 081-969 3579. *Publishing manager:* John Bishop.
Books about music, particularly by British composers. Preliminary letter essential.

D.C. Thomson & Co. Ltd – Publications, Dundee DD1 9QJ   *tel* (0382) 23131   *telegraphic address* Courier, Dundee   *telex* 76380   *fax* (0382) 22214.
London office: 185 Fleet Street, EC4A 2HS   *tel* 071-242 5086   *telegraphic address* Courier, London, EC4   *fax* 071-404 5694. Publishers of newspapers and periodicals.
Children's books (annuals), based on weekly magazine characters; fiction.

*****Stanley Thornes (Publishers) Ltd** (incorporating **Mary Glasgow Publications**), Ellenborough House, Wellington Street, Cheltenham, Glos. GL50 1YD   *tel* (0242) 228888   *fax* (0242) 221914. *Chairman:* Jean-Pierre Dubois; *managing*

director: David Smith; *directors:* Brian Carvell, Kevin Waterman, Paul Vinson, Oliver Gadsby.
Educational: primary, secondary, further education books, higher education, professional.

*Thorsons—see HarperCollins Publishers.

Threshold Books—acquired by The Kenilworth Press Ltd.

*Times Books—see HarperCollins Publishers.

*Times Mirror International Publishers Ltd (TMIP Ltd), Lynton House, 5th Floor, 7-12 Tavistock Square, London WC1H 9LB   *tel* 071-388 7676   *fax* 071-344 0020. *Chairman:* Tim Hailstone; *managing director:* John Hirst; *directors:* Peter Heilbrunn, Derrick Holman, Geoffrey Greenwood, Fiona Foley, Elizabeth Horne.
Mosby Wolfe Publishing (imprint). *Publishing director:* Fiona Foley. International colour atlases and texts in medicine, dentistry and veterinary science.

*Alec Tiranti Ltd—taken over by Academy Group Ltd.

Titan Books Ltd (1981), 42-44 Dolben Street, London SE1 0UP   *tel* 071-620 0200   *fax* 071-620 0032. *Publisher and managing director:* Nick Landau; *managing editor:* Katy Wild.
Graphic novels, including Aliens and Batman, featuring comic strip material; film and TV tie-ins and fact books, including Doctor Who and Star Trek; humour. Also true crime and the bizarre under the **Mondo** imprint. *No* unsolicited material without preliminary letter please; send large sae for current author guidelines.

*Tolkien—see HarperCollins Publishers.

Tolley Publishing Co. Ltd (1916), Tolley House, 2 Addiscombe Road, Croydon, Surrey CR9 5AF   *tel* 081-686 9141   *fax* 081-681 7986. *Directors:* Graham Wilson (chairman), Harry King (managing), Robert McKay (divisional chief executive), Kelvin Ladbrook (divisional chief executive), Robin Webb (production; sales), Nicholas Parmée (editorial), Peter Diggles (finance; administration).
Law, taxation, accountancy, business.
Fourmat Publishing (division). *Publisher:* Carol Doyle-Linden; *commissioning editor:* Irene Kaplan. Books and legal forms for lawyers, business and the professions.
Charles Knight Publishing (division). *Publisher:* Carol Doyle-Linden; *managing editor:* S.C. Cotter. Looseleaf legal works and periodicals on local government law, construction law and technical subjects.

Touchstone—see Simon & Schuster Ltd.

*Tracks—see HarperCollins Publishers.

*Transworld Publishers Ltd, 61-63 Uxbridge Road, London W5 5SA   *tel* 081-579 2652   *telex* 267974 TRNSPB G   *fax* 081-579 5479. *Managing director and chief executive:* Paul Scherer. Subsidiary of Bertelsmann AG.
Bantam (imprint). *Publisher:* Anthony Mott; *editorial director:* Francesca Liversidge. Paperback general fiction and non-fiction.
Bantam Press (imprint). *Directors:* Mark Barty-King, Ursula Mackenzie. Fiction, general, cookery, business, crime, health and diet, history, humour, military, music, paranormal, self-help, science, travel and adventure, biography and autobiography.
Bantam Young Adult (imprint). *Editorial director:* Philippa Dickinson. Paperback young adult books.

Transworld Publishers Ltd—*continued*
Black Swan (imprint). *Publisher:* Patrick Janson-Smith. Paperback quality fiction.
Corgi (imprint). *Publisher:* Patrick Janson-Smith. Paperback general fiction and non-fiction.
Doubleday (UK) (imprint). *Directors:* Mark Barty-King, Marianne Velmans, Sally Gaminara. General fiction and non-fiction.
Doubleday Children's Books (imprint). *Editorial director:* Philippa Dickinson. Hardback picture books, fiction and poetry for children.
Freeway (imprint). *Editorial director:* Philippa Dickinson. Paperback young adult books.
Partridge Press (division). *Director:* Mark Barty-King; *manager:* Debbie Beckerman. Sport and leisure.
Picture Corgi (imprint). *Editorial director:* Philippa Dickinson. Children's paperback picture books.
Yearling (imprint). *Editorial director:* Philippa Dickinson. Paperback fiction for ages 8-11.
Young Corgi (imprint). *Editorial director:* Philippa Dickinson. Paperback fiction for ages 5-9.
Also: **IDG Computer Books** and **Expert Gardening Books.**

***Trentham Books Ltd** (1968), Westview House, 734 London Road, Oakhill, Stoke-on-Trent, Staffs. ST4 5NP   *tel* (0782) 745567   *fax* (0782) 745553. *Directors:* Professor S.J. Eggleston (managing), Gillian Klein, Barbara Wiggins. *Editorial office:* 28 Hillside Gardens, London N6 5ST   *tel* 081-348 2174.
Education (including specialist fields – multicultural issues, equal opportunities, bullying, design and technology, early years), social policy, sociology of education, European education.

***Triangle**—see **Society for Promoting Christian Knowledge.**

Triton Publishing Company Ltd (1964), 1A Montagu Mews North, London W1H 1AJ   *tel* 071-706 0486. *Directors:* G. Golledge, Carolyn Whitaker.
Fiction and general non-fiction.

Trotman & Company Ltd (1970), 12 Hill Rise, Richmond, Surrey TW10 6UA   *tel* 081-940 5668   *fax* 081-948 9267. *Director:* A.F. Trotman; *publications manager:* Morfydd Jones.
Higher education guidance, careers, lifeskills.

Two Heads Publishing (1992), 12A Franklyn Suite, The Priory, Haywards Heath, West Sussex RH16 3LB   *tel/fax* (0444) 458090. *Publishers:* Charles Frewin, Derek Lubner.
London-based guides, sport, cycling books.

Two-Can Publishing (1987), 346 Old Street, London EC1V 9NQ   *tel* 071-613 3376   *fax* 071-613 3371. *Directors:* Andrew Jarvis (chairman), Ian Grant (marketing), Sara Lynn (creative).
Children's: reference and non-fiction books, magazines, multimedia products.

***Tycooly Publishing**—see **Cassell plc.**

Unicorn Books, 16 Laxton Gardens, Paddock Wood, Kent TN12 6BB   *tel* (0892) 833648   *fax* (0892) 833577. *Director:* R. Green.
Militaria, music, transport.

University of Exeter Press (1958), Reed Hall, Streatham Drive, Exeter, Devon EX4 4QR   *tel* (0392) 263066   *telex* 42894 EXUNIV G   *fax* (0392) 263064. *Secretary to the University Press:* Simon Baker.
History, local history (Exeter and the South West), archaeology, classical studies, English literature, medieval English, linguistics, modern languages,

American, Commonwealth and European literature and arts, maritime studies, mining history, economics, politics, sociology, Arabic studies.

The University of Hull Press & Lampada Press (1983/1991), Cottingham Road, Hull, North Humberside HU6 7RX *tel* (0482) 465322 *telex* 592592 KHMAIL G, FAO HULIB 375 *fax* (0482) 465936. *Assistant registrar:* Miss J.M. Smith.
General interest: economic and social history, history, local history, modern languages, English, geography, law, music.

University of Wales Press (1922), 6 Gwennyth Street, Cathays, Cardiff CF2 4YD *tel* (0222) 231919 *fax* (0222) 230908.
Academic and educational (Welsh and English). Publishers of *Bulletin of the Board of Celtic Studies*, *Welsh History Review*, *Studia Celtica*, *Llên Cymru*, *Delta*, *Y Gwyddonydd*, *Efrydiau Athronyddol*, *Contemporary Wales*, *Welsh Journal of Education*, *Journal of Celtic Linguistics*, *ALT-J (Association for Learning Technology Journal)*.

Merlin Unwin Books (1990), 21 Corve Street, Ludlow, Shropshire SY8 1DA *tel* (0584) 877456 *fax* (0584) 877457. *Proprietor:* Merlin Unwin.
Fishing.

*****Unwin Hyman Ltd**—acquired by **HarperCollins Publishers.**

*****Unwin Hyman Academic**—incorporated in **Routledge.**

Usborne Publishing (1973), Usborne House, 83-85 Saffron Hill, London EC1N 8RT *tel* 071-430 2800 *telex* 8953598 *fax* 071-430 1562. *Directors:* T.P. Usborne, Jenny Tyler, Robert Jones, David Lowe, Keith Ball, C. Rawson, D. Harte, L. Hunt.
Children's books: reference, practical, craft, natural history, science, languages, history, geography, fiction.

Vallentine Mitchell (1950)—see **Frank Cass & Co. Ltd.**

Variorum—see **Ashgate Publishing Ltd.**

*****Vermilion**—see **Random House UK Ltd.**

Verso Ltd (1970), 6 Meard Street, London W1V 3HR *tel* 071-437 3546/434 1704 *fax* 071-734 0059. *Directors:* Colin Robinson (managing), Robin Blackburn (chairman), Tariq Ali, Lucy Heller.
Politics, sociology, economics, history, philosophy, cultural studies.

Victoria & Albert Museum Publications, 38-40 Clareville Street, London SW7 5AJ *tel* 071-835 1715 *fax* 071-835 1785. *Contact:* Jennifer Blain.
Architecture, decorative arts, fashion and textiles.

Victoria House Publishing Ltd (1980), 4 North Parade, Bath BA1 1LF *tel* (0225) 463401 *fax* (0225) 460942. *Directors:* Michael J. Morris, Josh Gaspero. Fully owned subsidiary of The Reader's Digest Association Inc.
International children's co-editions.

*****Viking**—see **Penguin Books Ltd.**

*****Viking Children's Books**—see **Penguin Books Ltd.**

*****Vintage**—see **Random House UK Ltd.**

Virago Press (1973), First Floor, The Rotunda, 42/43 Gloucester Crescent, London NW1 7PD *tel* 071-916 6066 *fax* 071-916 6101. *Managing director:* Harriet Spicer; *directors:* Lennie Goodings, Gill McNeil, Anna Coen; *non-executive directors:* Carmen Callil, Ursula Owen.

Fiction, non-fiction and poetry books, for the general and educational market, which highlight all aspects of women's lives.

Virgin Books—see **Virgin Publishing Ltd.**

Virgin Publishing Ltd, 332 Ladbroke Grove, London W10 5AH   *tel* 081-968 7554   *fax* 081-968 0929. *Chairman:* Robert Devereux; *directors:* Robert Shreeve (managing), Peter Darvill-Evans (publisher, fiction), Philip Dodd (publisher, illustrated), Emma Worth (rights), Siobhan Flynn (marketing), Ray Mudie (sales), Michael Cohen (financial); Mal Peachey (senior editor, general).
Black Lace (imprint). *Publisher:* Peter Darvill-Evans. Erotic fiction.
Doctor Who (imprint). *Editorial director:* Peter Darvill-Evans. Novelisations and large format fan books based on the series under licence from the BBC.
Nexus (imprint). *Publisher:* Peter Darvill-Evans. Erotic fiction for women.
Virgin Books (imprint). *Editorial:* Mal Peachey (general), Philip Dodd (illustrated). Popular culture: entertainment, showbiz, arts, film and TV, music, humour, biography and autobiography, popular reference, true crime, children's books.

Virtue Books Ltd, Edward House, Tenter Street, Rotherham S60 1LB   *tel* (0709) 365005   *fax* (0709) 829982. *Directors:* Peter E. Russum, Margaret H. Russum, Michael G. Virtue.
Books for the professional chef, catering and drink.

Walker Books Ltd (1979), 87 Vauxhall Walk, London SE11 5HJ   *tel* 071-793 0909   *fax* 071-587 1123. *Directors:* David Ford, David Heatherwick, Wendy Boase, David Lloyd, Amelia Edwards, Judy Burdsall, Harold G. Gould OBE, Henryk Wesolowski.
Children's – mainly picture books; junior and teenage fiction.

Warburg Institute, University of London, Woburn Square, London WC1H 0AB   *tel* 071-580 9663   *fax* 071-436 2852.
Cultural and intellectual history, with special reference to the history of the classical tradition.

*****Ward Lock**—see **Cassell plc.**

Ward Lock Educational Co. Ltd (1952), 1 Christopher Road, East Grinstead, West Sussex RH19 3BT   *tel* (0342) 318980   *fax* (0342) 410980. *Directors:* Au Bak Ling (chairman, Hong Kong), Vincent Winter, Au King Kwok (Hong Kong), Au Wai Kwok (Hong Kong), Albert Kw Au (Hong Kong), Au Chun Kwok (Hong Kong); Andrew Thraves (publishing and sales), Quentin Hockliffe (overseas sales).
Primary and secondary pupil materials, Kent Mathematics Project, Reading Workshops, Take Part Series and Take Part Starters, teachers' books, music books, history, science, geography, religious education, environmental studies.

*****Frederick Warne & Co. Ltd**—see **Penguin Books Ltd.**

Warner (1992)—see **Little, Brown and Company (UK) Ltd.**

Warner–Futura (1992)—see **Little, Brown and Company (UK) Ltd.**

Waterline Books (1991)—see **Airlife Publishing Ltd.**

*****Watts Books** (1969)—see **The Watts Publishing Group.**

*****The Watts Publishing Group,** 96 Leonard Street, London EC2A 4RH   *tel* 071-739 2929   *fax* 071-739 2318. *Directors:* Francesca Dow (editorial: Orchard), Chester Fisher (editorial: Watts Books), Marlene Johnson (managing), Rita Ireland (production), George Spicer (sales), Sarah Odedina (rights). Division of Grolier Ltd.

Orchard Books (division). *Editorial director:* Francesca Dow. Children's picture books, fiction, poetry, novelty books, board books.
Watts Books (division). *Publishing director:* Chester Fisher. Children's illustrated non-fiction, reference, education.

*__Wayland (Publishers) Ltd__ (incorporating **Firefly Books**) (1969), 61-61A Western Road, Hove, East Sussex BN3 1JD *tel* (0273) 722561 *fax* (0273) 329314. *Chairman:* J.-P. Dubois; *managing director:* J.W. Lewis; *directors:* S. White-Thomson (editorial), F.M. Jane (finance), K. Lilley (international sales), B. Nevin (UK sales).
Children's information books for ages 4-18.

Weidenfeld & Nicolson Ltd (1948)—see **The Orion Publishing Group Ltd.**

*__Wheatsheaf Books Ltd__—see **Harvester Wheatsheaf.**

Wheldon & Wesley Ltd, Lytton Lodge, Codicote, Hitchin, Herts. SG4 8TE *tel* Stevenage (0438) 820370 *fax* (0438) 821478.
Natural history booksellers and publishers.

*__Which? Books__—see **Consumers' Association.**

*__J. Whitaker & Sons Ltd,__ 12 Dyott Street, London WC1A 1DF *tel* 071-836 8911 *fax* 071-836 2909. *Directors:* Peter Allsop, Louis Baum, Robin Baum, Alan Mollison, T.E. Sweetman, David Whitaker (chairman), Sally Whitaker (managing), Martin Whitaker (sales and marketing).
Reference including *Whitaker's Almanack* (1869), *The Bookseller* (1858), *Whitaker's Books in Print* (1874), *Whitaker's Book List* (1924), and other book trade directories.

Whittet Books Ltd (1976), 18 Anley Road, London W14 0BY *tel* 071-603 1139 *fax* 071-603 8154. *Directors:* Annabel Whittet, John Whittet.
Natural history, countryside, transport.

*__Whurr Publishers Ltd__ (1987), 19B Compton Terrace, London N1 2UN *tel* 071-359 5979 *fax* 071-226 5290. *Managing director:* Colin Whurr.
Disorders of human communication, medicine, psychology, psychiatry, business.

*__John Wiley & Sons Ltd__ (incorporating **Interscience Publishers**), Baffins Lane, Chichester, West Sussex PO19 1UD *tel* (0243) 779777 *telegraphic address/cables* Wilebook, Chichester *telex* 86290 WIBOOK G *fax* (0243) 775878 *BTG* 83 JWP001. *Chairman:* The Duke of Richmond; *managing director:* J.H. Jarvis; *directors:* P.W. Ferris, C.J. Dicks, M. Dixon, R. Long, M. Foyle, D. Roberts, C.R. Ellis, D.E. Wiley. Subsidiary of John Wiley & Sons Inc., New York.
Physics, chemistry, mathematics, statistics, engineering, computer science, biology, medicine, earth science, psychology, business, economics, finance, law.

*__Philip Wilson Publishers Ltd__ (1975), 26 Litchfield Street, London WC2H 9NJ *tel* 071-379 7886 *fax* 071-836 7049. *Directors:* Philip Wilson, Anne Jackson, Mary Osborne, Piers Russell-Cobb.
Art.

The Windrush Press (1987), Little Window, High Street, Moreton-in-Marsh, Glos. GL56 0LL *tel* (0608) 652012/652025 *fax* (0608) 652125. *Managing director:* Geoffrey Smith; *publishing director:* Victoria Huxley.
History, travel, biography, humour, local interest.

*__Wisley Handbooks__—see **Cassell plc.**

*__H.F. & G. Witherby Ltd__—see **Cassell plc.**

Woburn Press (1968)—see **Frank Cass & Co. Ltd.**

Oswald Wolff Books—see **Berg Publishers.**

The Women's Press (1978), 34 Great Sutton Street, London EC1V 0DX *tel* 071-251 3007 *fax* 071-608 1938. *Directors:* Kathy Gale (publishing), Mary Hemming (sales).
Books by women in the areas of fiction, autobiography, health, politics; Livewire Books for Teenagers.

Woodhead Publishing Ltd (1989), Abington Hall, Abington, Cambridge CB1 6AH *tel* (0223) 891358 *telex* 81883 WELDEX G *fax* (0223) 893694. *Managing director:* Martin Woodhead; *finance director:* Duncan Leeper.
Materials engineering, welding, finance, investment, business.

*****Woodhead-Faulkner** (1972)—see **Paramount Publishing Europe.**

World International Publishing Ltd, Egmont House, PO Box 111, 61 Great Ducie Street, Manchester M60 3BL *tel* 061-834 3110 *telegraphic address* World, Manchester *telex* 668609 WORLD G *fax* 061-834 0059. *Directors:* Ian Findley (managing), David Smith, Michael Herridge, David Sheldrake, Tony Pickup, Robin Rough.
Children's stories, early learning, activity, annuals, gift and novelty books.

*****Worldwide Books**—see **Mills & Boon (Publishers) Ltd.**

*****Yale University Press London** (1961), 23 Pond Street, London NW3 2PN *tel* 071-431 4422 *fax* 071-431 3755. *Managing director:* John Nicoll.
Art, architecture, history, economics, political science, literary criticism, Asian and African studies, religion, philosophy, psychology, history of science.

*****Yearling**—see **Transworld Publishers Ltd.**

Yorkshire Art Circus (1986), School Lane, Glass Houghton, Castleford, West Yorkshire WF10 4QH *tel* (0977) 550401. *Books co-ordinator:* Olive Fowler.
Fiction with Yorkshire/Humberside connection; non-fiction of Yorkshire interest; short stories (up to 5000 words) accepted for inclusion in occasional anthologies. Send for fact sheet first.

*****Young Corgi**—see **Transworld Publishers Ltd.**

Young Library Ltd (1982), 3 The Old Brushworks, 56 Pickwick Road, Corsham, Wilts. SN13 9BX *tel* (0249) 712025 *fax* (0249) 715558. *Director:* Roger Bonnett.
Highly illustrated non-fiction for children's libraries, including geography, history, natural history, social and urban studies, science and technology, and reference.

*****Zed Books Ltd** (1976), 7 Cynthia Street, London N1 9JF *tel* 071-837 4014 (general)/837 0384 (editorial) *fax* 071-833 3960. *Chief editor:* Robert Molteno.
Social sciences on international and Third World issues; women's studies, development and environmental studies; area studies (Africa, Asia, Caribbean, Latin America, Middle East and the Pacific).

Hans Zell Publishers—see **Bowker-Saur.**

A. Zwemmer Ltd (1951), 26 Litchfield Street, London WC2H 9NJ *tel* 071-379 7886 *fax* 071-836 7049.
Architecture, photography, fine art, decorative art.

Classified Index of UK Publishers of Fiction

Addresses for UK publishers start on page 146.

Adventure/Thrillers

Bantam
Bantam Press
Black Swan
Blake Publishing
Bloomsbury Publishing
Chapman
Chatto & Windus
Corgi
Coronet
André Deutsch
Doubleday (UK)
Fourth Estate

Gairm Publications
Victor Gollancz
HarperCollins Publishers
Headline Book Publishing
William Heinemann
Hodder & Stoughton
Hutchinson Books
Michael Joseph
Little, Brown
New English Library
Pan
Penguin Books

Piatkus Books
The Random Century Group
Sceptre
Severn House Publishers
Simon & Schuster
Sinclair-Stevenson
Souvenir Press
Vintage
Virago Press
Warner
Weidenfeld & Nicolson
The Women's Press

Crime/Mystery/Suspense

Allison & Busby
Arrow Books
Bantam
Bantam Press
Bellew
Black Swan
Blake Publishing
Bloomsbury Publishing
Chapman
Chatto & Windus
Constable & Co.
Corgi
Coronet
André Deutsch
Faber & Faber

Fourth Estate
Gairm Publications
Victor Gollancz
Hamish Hamilton
HarperCollins Publishers
Headline Book Publishing
William Heinemann
Hodder & Stoughton
Hutchinson Books
Michael Joseph
Little, Brown
Macmillan London
New English Library
Pan

Penguin Books
Piatkus Books
The Random Century Group
Sceptre
Serpent's Tail
Severn House Publishers
Sinclair-Stevenson
Souvenir Press
Viking
Vintage
Virago Press
Warner – Futura
Weidenfeld & Nicolson
The Women's Press

Gay/Lesbian

Bantam
Black Swan
Marion Boyars Publishers
Corgi
Faber & Faber
Fourth Estate

GMP Publishers
Victor Gollancz
Hamish Hamilton
Onlywomen Press
Peter Owen
Penguin Books

Polygon
Serpent's Tail
Vintage
Virago Press
The Women's Press

General

Allison & Busby
Bantam
Bantam Press
Bellew
Black Swan
Blake Publishing
Bloomsbury Publishing

Marion Boyars Publishers
Canongate Press
Jonathan Cape
Century
Chapman
Chatto & Windus
Constable & Co.

Corgi
André Deutsch
Doubleday (UK)
Gerald Duckworth & Co.
Faber & Faber
Fourth Estate
Gairm Publications

Victor Gollancz
Granta Publications
Robert Hale
Hamish Hamilton
HarperCollins Publishers
Headline Book Publishing
William Heinemann
Hodder & Stoughton
Hutchinson Books
Michael Joseph
Karnak House
Little, Brown
Y Lolfa Cyf. (Welsh language)
Macmillan London
Mainstream Publishing Co.

Martin Brian & O'Keeffe
Methuen
New English Library
Orion
Peter Owen
Pan Books
Penguin Books
Piatkus Books
Pimlico
Pocket Books
Quartet Books
The Random Century Group
Sceptre
Secker and Warburg

Serpent's Tail
Signet
Simon & Schuster
Sinclair-Stevenson
Souvenir Press
Touchstone
Triton Publishing Company
Viking
Vintage
Virago Press
Warner
Weidenfeld & Nicolson
Worldwide Books
Yorkshire Art Circus

Historical

Bantam
Bantam Press
Bellew
Marion Boyars Publishers
Canongate Press
Jonathan Cape
Chapman
Robin Clark
Constable & Co.
André Deutsch
Doubleday (UK)
Fourth Estate
Victor Gollancz

Robert Hale
HarperCollins Publishers
Headline Book Publishing
William Heinemann
Hodder & Stoughton
Hutchinson Books
Michael Joseph
Karnak House
Little, Brown
Mainstream Publishing Co.
Peter Owen
Pan

Penguin Books
Piatkus Books
Pimlico
The Random Century Group
Sceptre
Simon & Schuster
Sinclair-Stevenson
Souvenir Press
Vintage
Virago Press
Warner
Weidenfeld & Nicolson

Literary

Abacus
Bantam
Bantam Press
Black Swan
Bloomsbury Publishing
Marion Boyars Publishers
Calder Publications
Canongate Press
Jonathan Cape
Chapman
Chatto & Windus
Robin Clark
Constable & Co.
Corgi
J.M. Dent
André Deutsch
Doubleday (UK)
Faber & Faber
Flamingo

Forest Books
Fourth Estate
Gairm Publications
Victor Gollancz
Granta Publications
Robert Hale
Hamish Hamilton
HarperCollins Publishers
Harvill
William Heinemann
Hodder & Stoughton
Hutchinson Books
Impact Books
Karnak House
Little, Brown
Macmillan London
Mainstream Publishing Co.
Methuen
Peter Owen

Pan
Penguin Books
Picador
Pimlico
Polygon
The Random Century Group
Reinhardt Books
Sceptre
Secker and Warburg
Serpent's Tail
Sinclair-Stevenson
Skoob Books
Souvenir Press
Stride Publications
Viking
Vintage
Virago Press
Weidenfeld & Nicolson
The Women's Press

Romantic

Bantam
Bantam Press
Black Swan
Blake Publishing
Chapman

Corgi
Coronet
Doubleday (UK)
Robert Hale
Headline Book Publishing

William Heinemann
Hodder & Stoughton
Little, Brown
Macmillan London
Mills & Boon Publishers

Monarch Publications
Pan
Piatkus Books

The Random Century Group
Silhouette

Souvenir Press
Warner

Science Fiction/Fantasy

Arrow Books
Bantam
Bantam Press
Black Swan
Blake Publishing
Chapman
Corgi
Coronet
Victor Gollancz

HarperCollins Publishers
Headline Book Publishing
Hodder & Stoughton
Legend
Little, Brown
Millennium
New English Library
Orbit

Pan
Penguin Books
The Random Century Group
Robinson Publishing
RoC
Severn House Publishers
Weidenfeld & Nicolson
The Women's Press

Short Stories

Bantam
Bellew
Bloomsbury Publishing
Marion Boyars Publishers
Jonathan Cape
Chatto & Windus
Constable & Co.
Faber & Faber
Forest Books
Fourth Estate
Gairm Publications

Granta Publications
Hamish Hamilton
William Heinemann
Hodder & Stoughton
Karnak House
Little, Brown
Mainstream Publishing Co.
Peter Owen
Pan
Penguin Books

Polygon
The Random Century Group
Reinhardt Books
Robinson Publishing
Secker and Warburg
Serpent's Tail
Severn House Publishers
Sinclair-Stevenson
Stride Publications
Yorkshire Art Circus

Other

Christian

Kingsway Publications
Monarch Publications

Classic

Allison & Busby

Erotic

Black Lace
Nexus

Graphic

Eclipse
Titan Books

Horror

Chapman
Robinson Publishing
Warner

Humour

Black Swan
Corgi
Victor Gollancz
Warner

International

Allison & Busby

New/Experimental

Serpent's Tail
Stride Publications

Translations

Marion Boyars Publishers
Quartet Books
Serpent's Tail

War

Severn House Publishers

Westerns

Robert Hale
Severn House Publishers

Classified Index of UK Publishers of Poetry

Addresses for UK publishers start on page 146; see classified index on page 250 for publishers of poetry for children.

Anvil Press Poetry
Arc Publications
Bloodaxe Books
Jonathan Cape
Carcanet Press
Cassell plc
Kyle Cathie
Chatto & Windus
Enitharmon Press
Faber & Faber
Forest Books

Gairm Publications
GMP Publishers
Headland Publications
Hippopotamus Press
The Mandeville Press
Martin Brian & O'Keeffe
New Beacon Books
Onlywomen Press
Oxford University Press
Penguin Books

Peterloo Poets
Poetry Wales Press
Random House UK
Rivelin Grapheme Press
Secker and Warburg
Sinclair-Stevenson
Skoob Books Publishing
Slow Dancer Press
Stride Publications
Virago Press

Clues

Perhaps the best way of tricking readers into seeing but not seeing what you put in front of them is by stating your fact in a way that seems clearly to be doing so for a different purpose than that of playing the game. Let us assume that the give-away clue is that your murderer has dyed his moustache. You could provide an easy clue by having your detective remark to his Watson, 'There is the matter of the colour of Dr Demulch's moustache.' Or you could hover angel-like behind your detective and write, 'He saw that Dr Demulch's moustache was of a deep, homogenous brown colour.' But it would be less obvious to produce a whole description of Dr Demulch in perhaps a mildly humorous vein: 'Dr Demulch was a brown man. His suit was coffee-coloured. His shoes were of a brilliant and gleaming tan. His hair was made to look even browner by the liberal application of hair-oil. His moustache somehow was yet browner than his hair. Even his enormous spectacles were hornrims of spectacular chestnutery.' Your readers take in, probably without stopping to think much about it, that they are being treated to a rather over-the-top descriptive passage, and they then 'see without seeing' that dyed moustache.

from *Writing Crime Fiction* by H R F Keating (A & C Black, £7.99)

European English-language Publishers

BELGIUM

De Boeck-Weshael S.A., rue des Minimes 39, B-1000 Brussels *tel* (010) 48 25 11 *fax* (010) 48 26 50. *Directors:* Christian De Boeck (managing), Georges Hoyos. English as a second language.

Editions Haug International, Chausée de Ninove 1072, B-1080 Brussels *tel* 02 520 76 70 *fax* 02 521 17 43. *Managing director:* M. Rinchart. Homeopathy, acupuncture, manual medicine, dietetics, neural therapy.

Nauwelaerts Editions S.A., rue de l'Eglise St Sulpice 19, B-1320 Beauvechain *tel* (010) 86 67 37 *fax* (02) 751 74 08. *Directors:* Stephane Rouget (managing), Huguette Bo'sman (commercial). Periodical medicine; sciences, human sciences, philosophy.

Peeters, Bondgenotenlaan 153, B-3000 Leuven *tel* 016 123 51 70 *fax* 016 122 85 00. *Contact:* Emmanuel Peeters. Theology, philosophy, Orientalism, history, medieval and Renaissance studies, literature, linguistics, medicine.

La Renaissance du Livre, Fond Jean-Pâques 4, B-1348 Louvain-la-Neuve *tel* 10 48 25 11 *fax* 10 48 26 50. *Managing director:* Christian De Boeck; *publisher:* Michel de Grand Ry. Art, history, mentalities.

DENMARK

Gyldendalske Boghandel, Nordisk Forlag A/S, 3 Klareboderne, DK-1001 Copenhagen K *tel* 33 11 07 75 *cables* Gyldendalske *telex* 15887 GYLDAL DK *fax* 33 11 03 23. *Managing director:* Kurt Fromberg. Fiction, non-fiction, textbooks.

Munksgaard International Publishers Ltd, 35 Nørre Søgade, PO Box 2148, DK-1016 Copenhagen K *tel* 33 12 70 30 *cables* Bogotto *fax* 33 12 93 87. *Managing director:* Joachim Malling. Medicine, social sciences, reference, fiction.

Rhodos, International Science and Art Publishers, 36 Strandgade, DK-1401 Copenhagen K *tel* 31 54 30 20 *cables* Sciencebooks *telex* 31502 *fax* 31 95 47 42. *Managing director:* Niels Blädel. Art and science books.

Samlerens Forlag A/S, 4 Snaregade, DK-1205 Copenhagen K *tel* 33 13 10 23 *fax* 33 14 43 14. *Managing director:* Johannes Riis. Fiction, contemporary history, biography.

FRANCE

Editions Actes Sud, Le Mejan, F-13200 Arles *tel* 90 49 86 91 *fax* 90 96 95 25. *Editorial:* Hubert Nyssen, Bertrand Py, Marie-Catherine Vacher, Sabine Wespiesser. Literature, essays, biography, theatre, poetry.

Editions Arthaud SA, 26 rue Racine, 75278 Paris Cedex 06 *tel* (1) 40 51 31 00 *telex* 205641 FLAMEDI F *fax* (1) 43 29 21 48. *Director:* Charles-Henri Flammarion. Literature, arts.

Editions Aubier-Montaigne SA, 13 quai de Conti, F-75006 Paris *tel* (1) 40 51 31 00. *Editorial director:* Louis Audibert. Belles lettres, poetry, reference.

Editions Belin, 8 rue Férou, F-75278 Paris Cedex 06 *tel* (1) 46 34 21 42 *fax* (1) 43 25 18 29. *Editorial:* Marie-Claude Brossollet. Educational and textbooks.

Editions Bordas, 17 rue Remy Dumoncel – BP 50, F-75661 Paris Cedex 14 *tel* (1) 42 79 62 00 *fax* (1) 43 22 85 18. *President, general manager:* Jean Lissarrague. Educational.

Editions Casterman, 66 rue Bonaparte, F-75006 Paris *tel* (1) 40 51 28 00 *telex* 200001 EDICAST F *fax* (1) 43 54 54 24. *President:* Didier Platteau. Fine arts.

Editions Denoël, 9 rue du Cherche-Midi, F-75278 Paris Cedex 06 *tel* (1) 44 39 73 73 *fax* (1) 44 39 73 90. *Managing director:* Henry Marcellin. General fiction and non-fiction.

Editions Dis Voir, 3 rue Beautreillis, F-75004 Paris *tel* (1) 48 87 07 09 *fax* (1) 48 87 07 14. *Managing director:* Danièle Rivière. Literature, fine art and cinema.

Dunod Editeur, 15 rue Gossin, 92543 Montrouge Cedex *tel* (1) 40 92 65 00 *fax* (1) 40 92 65 97/40 92 65 50. *Managing director:* Geoffrey Staines. Subsidiary of Group de la Cité. Scientific, technical.

Librairie Arthème Fayard, 75 rue des Sts-Pères, F-75006 Paris *tel* (1) 45 44 38 45 *fax* (1) 42 22 40 14. *Managing director:* Claude Durand. Biography, history, sciences, music, essays, novels.

Flammarion, 26 rue Racine, F-75278 Paris Cedex 06 *tel* (1) 40 51 31 00 *fax* (1) 43 29 21 48. *President:* Charles-Henri Flammarion; *managing director:* Jean-Pierre Arbon. Art history, design, life style.

Editions Gallimard, 5 rue Sébastien-Bottin, F-75007 Paris *tel* (1) 45 44 39 19 *cables* Enerefene Paris 044 *telex* 204121 GALLIM F *fax* (1) 42 86 83 88. *Managing director:* Antoine Gallimard. Belles lettres, poetry, biography.

Société des Editions Grasset et Fasquelle, 61 rue des Sts-Pères, F-75006 Paris *tel* (1) 45 44 38 14 *fax* (1) 42 22 64 18. *Chairman:* Jean-Claude Fasquelle. General fiction and non-fiction.

Librairie Gründ, 60 rue Mazarine, F-75006 Paris 6 *tel* (1) 43 29 87 40 *cables* Gründ Paris *telex* 204926 F *fax* (1) 43 29 49 86. *President:* Alain Gründ. General non-fiction.

Hachette Livre, 79 blvd St-Germain, F-75288 Paris Cedex 06 *tel* (1) 46 34 86 34 *cables* Hachechi Paris 25 *telex* 204434 HACSI PARIS F. *Chairman and ceo:* Jean-Louis Lisimachio. Textbooks, history, bibliography, general non-fiction, education, how-to, youth.

Pierre Horay Editeur, 22 bis passage Dauphine, F-75006 Paris *tel* (1) 43 54 53 90 *fax* (1) 40 51 06 37. *Managing director:* Sophie Horay. General fiction and non-fiction.

Editions Robert Laffont, 6 pl St-Sulpice, F-75279 Paris Cedex 06 *tel* (1) 43 29 12 33 *cables* Edilaf Paris 110 *telex* 270607 *fax* (1) 43 29 64 35. *Chairman and managing director:* Bertrand Favreul. General fiction, non-fiction, biography, social sciences.

Larousse, 17 rue du Montparnasse, F-75298 Paris Cedex 06 *tel* (1) 44 39 44 00 *telex* 250828 LAROUS PARIS F *fax* (1) 44 39 43 43. *Chairman and managing director:* Patrice Maubourguet. Reference.

Editions Jean-Claude Lattès, 17 rue Jacob, F-75006 Paris *tel* (1) 44 41 74 00 *telex* 205652 *fax* (1) 43 25 30 47. *Managing director:* Daniel Radford; *foreign rights manager:* Hélène Morel. General fiction and non-fiction.

Les Editions Magnard S.A.R.L., 6 rue Lacépède, F-75005 Paris *tel* (1) 44 08 85 85 *fax* (1) 43 31 66 13. *Publishing director:* Isabelle Magnard. University, secondary and primary textbooks.

Masson SA, 120 blvd St-Germain, F-75280 Paris Cedex 06   *tel* (1) 40 46 60 00   *cables* Gemas Paris 025   *telex* 205986 MASSONED F   *fax* (1) 40 46 60 01. *Director:* Dr Jérôme Talamon. Medicine, scientific, technical, social sciences.

Editions A.M. Métailié, 5 rue de Savoie, F-75006 Paris   *tel* (1) 43 26 60 10   *fax* (1) 46 33 74 00. *Managing director:* Anne Marie Métailié. Foreign literature, social sciences.

Les Editions de Minuit SA, 7 rue Bernard-Palissy, F-75006 Paris   *tel* (1) 44 39 39 20. *Managing director:* Jérôme Lindon. Philosophy, social science, literature.

Paris-Musées, 31 rue des Francs-Bourgeois, F-75004 Paris   *tel* (1) 42 76 65 18   *fax* (1) 42 76 66 22. *Editorial manager:* Arnauld Pontier. Fine arts, contemporary arts, photography, fashion, exhibition catalogues and practical guides to Paris museums.

Editions du Seuil, 27 rue Jacob, F-75261 Paris Cedex 06   *tel* (1) 40 46 50 50   *cables* Ediseuil   *telex* 270024 F   *fax* (1) 43 29 08 29. *Chairman:* Claude Cherki. Novels, poetry, general literature, human sciences, history, political, economic and scientific essays, biography, accounts, religious literature, illustrated collections, co-editions, pocket books, books for children.

Editions Technip, 27 rue Ginoux, F-75737 Paris Cedex 15   *tel* (1) 45 78 33 80   *telex* 200375 F   *fax* (1) 45 75 37 11. *President:* Sylvie Haxaire. Transport, economics, geology, geophysics, geochemistry, drilling, refining, chemical engineering, petrochemistry, engines, energy conversion, statistics and computer science.

GERMANY

Verlagsgruppe Bertelsmann GmbH, Neumarkterstr 18, D-81673 (PF) Munich   *tel* (089) 431890   *cables* Bertelsmann Munchen   *telex* 529965 WGVMN D   *fax* (089) 43189440. *Chairman:* Frank Wössner. Tourism and maps.

Verlag Harri Deutsch, Gräfstr 47, D-60486 Frankfurt am Main   *tel* (069) 775021   *fax* (069) 7073739. *Publisher:* Harri Deutsch. Science, technical, textbooks, reference, dictionaries.

D T V-Deutscher Taschenbuch Verlag GmbH & Co. KG, Friedrichstr 1a, Postfach 400422, D-80704 Munich   *tel* (089) 381706-0   *telex* 05215396. *Managing director:* Dr Wolfram Göbel. General non-fiction, textbooks.

Prisma Verlag GmbH, Neumarkter Str 18, D-81664 Munich   *tel* (089) 431890   *telex* 931149   *fax* (089) 43189458. *Director:* Carlo Lauer. Travel, guidebooks, maps and atlases, geography reference books.

Springer-Verlag GmbH & Co. KG, Heidelberger Platz 3, D-14197 Berlin   *tel* (030) 8207-0/8214093   *telex* 183319   *fax* (030) 8214091. *Editorial:* Professor Dr Dietrich Götze. Scientific and technical.

Verlag Valentin Koerner GmbH, PO Box 304, D-76482 Baden-Baden   *tel* (07221) 22423   *fax* (07221) 38697. *Publisher:* Valentin Koerner. Bibliography, history of the printed book, humanism and Reformation (16th century), theology, musicology, art history.

Vogel-Verlag und Druck KG, Max-Planck-Str 7-9, D-97082 Würzburg   *tel* (0931) 4180   *cables* Vogelverlag Würzburg   *fax* (0931) 4182100. *Managing directors:* Dr Kurt Eckernkamp, Karl-Michael Mehnert. Technical media and computer magazines.

GREECE

Efstathiadis Group SA, Agiou Athanassiou Street, 14565 Anixi Attikis   *tel* (01) 8140602/8140702   *cables* Efbook Athens   *telex* 216176   *fax* (01) 8142915. *Contact:* Richard Flower. English language teaching books; books for tourists in various languages.

Denise Harvey (Publisher), Katounia, 340-05 Limni, Evia   *tel* (0227) 31921. *Managing director:* Denise Harvey. Modern Greek studies (literature, translations, music, anthropology, travel, etc.), metaphysics, belles-lettres, poetry.

ITALY

Gruppo Editoriale Fabbri SpA, Via Mecenate 91, I-20138 Milan   *tel* (02) 50951   *cables* Librifabbri Milan   *telex* 311321 FABBRI I   *fax* (02) 5095311. *Managing director:* Giovanni Cobolli Gigli. Reference, textbooks, general non-fiction.

THE NETHERLANDS

A.A. Balkema, Postbus 1675, 3000 BR Rotterdam   *tel* (010) 4145822   *fax* (010) 4135947. *Managing director:* A.T. Balkema. African studies, palaeontology, marine biology, aquaculture, botany, zoology, soil and rock mechanics, mining engineering, hydraulic research.

John Benjamins BV, Postbus 75577, 1070 AN Amsterdam   *tel* (020) 6738156   *cables* Benper, Amsterdam   *fax* (020) 6739773. *Managing director:* John L. Benjamins. Academic books and journals on linguistics, literature, philology, art, pragmatics, translation studies.

E.J. Brill, Postbus 9000, 2300 PA Leiden   *tel* (071) 312624   *fax* (071) 317532. *Editorial director:* Mrs M.G.E. Venekamp. Humanities, biology, Islam, medieval.

Elsevier Science BV, Postbus 2400, 1000 CK Amsterdam   *tel* (020) 5862911   *fax* (020) 5862843. *Chairman:* J.J.F. Kels. Academic.

Van Gorcum BV, Industrieweg 38, POB 43, 9403 AB Assen   *tel* (05920) 46846   *cables* Vangorcum   *fax* (05920) 72064. *Managing director:* G. Vlieghuis. Academic.

IOS Press, Van Diemenstraat 94, 1013 CN Amsterdam   *tel* (020) 6382189   *fax* (020) 6203419. *Managing director:* Dr Einar H. Fredriksson. Information technology, environmental sciences, medical engineering, medical research, mathematics.

Kluwer Law and Taxation Publishers, Staverenstr 15, Postbus 23, 7400 GA Deventer   *tel* (05700) 47261   *telex* 49295   *fax* (05700) 22244. *Publisher & chief executive:* Karel E. vander Linde. International law and taxation.

Kugler Publications BV, PO Box 11188, 1001 GD Amsterdam   *tel* (020) 6278070   *fax* (020) 6380524. *Managing director:* S.D. Bakker. Medicine, criminology, biology.

Pudoc Scientific Publishers, PO Box 4, 6700 AA Wageningen   *tel* (08370) 84440   *telex* 45015   *fax* (08370) 84761. *Managing director:* J.M. Schippers. Natural science, agriculture.

Swets en Zeitlinger BV, Heereweg 347, 2161 CA Lisse   *tel* (02521) 35111   *cables* Swezeit-Lisse   *telex* 41325 SZLIS NL   *fax* (02521) 15888. *Editorial:* R. Kohnstamm. Academic.

VSP, Godfried van Seystlaan 47, 3703 BR Zeist *tel* (03404) 25790 *fax* (03404) 32081. *Managing director:* Dr J.R.F.Th. Groesbeek. Science, technology, medicine.

VU University Press, De Boelelaan 1105, 1081 HV Amsterdam *tel* (020) 6444355 *fax* (020) 6462719. *Managing director & editorial:* P.J. Kans. Academic.

Wolters Kluwer Academic Publishers BV, PO Box 989, 3300 AZ Dordrecht *tel* (078) 334933 *fax* (078) 334254. *Managing director:* Dr H.A. Pabbruwe. Agriculture, business studies, economics, human rights, international law, linguistics, medicine, philosophy, science, transportation.

NORWAY

H. Aschehoug & Co (W. Nygaard), PO Box 363 Sentrum, 0102 Oslo *tel* (22) 40 04 00 *fax* (22) 20 63 95. *Publisher:* William Nygaard. Textbooks, books for tourists.

J.W. Cappelens Forlag A/S, PO Box 350 Sentrum, 0101 Oslo 1 *tel* (22) 36 50 00 *fax* (22) 36 50 40. *Publisher:* Sigmund Strømme. Non-fiction, fiction, facts, schoolbooks.

Det Norske Samlaget, PO Box 4672 Sofienberg, 0506 Oslo *tel* (22) 68 76 00 *fax* (22) 78 75 02. *Managing director:* Audun Heskestad. Education, dictionaries; occasionally general literature.

Gyldendal Norsk Forlag A/S, PO Box 6860 St Olavs Plass, 0130 Oslo 1 *tel* (22) 03 41 06 *fax* (22) 03 41 05. *Managing director:* Nils Kåre Jacobsen. Fiction and educational books.

NKS-Forlaget, PO Box 5853 Majorstua, 0308 Oslo 3 *tel* (22) 56 85 00 *fax* (02) 56 68 20. *Publisher:* Hallstein Laupsa. Educational books.

TANO A/S, Stortorvet 10, 0155 Oslo *tel* (22) 42 55 00 *fax* (22) 42 01 64. *Manager:* Astrid de Vibe. Educational books, textbooks, computing, non-fiction.

Universitetsforlaget (Scandinavian University Press), Kolstadgt 1, PO Box 2959 Tøyen, 0608 Oslo *tel* (22) 57 53 00 *fax* (22) 57 53 53. *Publisher:* Trygve Ramberg. Academic books and international journals.

PORTUGAL

Bertrand Editora Lda, Rua Anchieta 29-1°, 1200 Lisbon *tel* 3420084/5 *fax* 3479728. *Editorial:* Joaõ Carlos Aluim. Fiction, human sciences, business, juvenile, art books.

Livraria Civilizacão, Rua Alberto Aires de Gouveia 27, 4000 Porto *tel* (02) 2002286/2002287 *fax* (02) 2012382. *Managing director:* Arquitecto Moura Bessa. Social and political science, economics, history, art, children's books.

Frank Cook Publications Lda, Largo do Rato 14, 3° Esq., 1200 Lisbon *tel* (01) 3870866 *fax* (01) 3870571. *Managing director:* Christina Hippisley. Travel guides in English.

Edições Inapa, Campo Santa Clara 160 C/D, 1100 Lisbon *tel* 8885175 *fax* 8885167. *Managing director:* Dr Manuel de Bragança. History of the arts and religion.

Editorial Verbo, Rua Carlos Testa 1, 1000 Lisbon *tel* 3562131 *telex* 15177 *fax* 3562139. *Managing director:* Fernando Guedes. Reference books, encyclopedias, dictionaries, academic textbooks, history, beaux arts, children's and juvenile books, general science, education.

SPAIN

Alhambra Longman, SA, Fernández de la Hoz 9, 28010 Madrid *tel* (91) 594 00 20 *fax* (91) 594 12 20. *Editorial:* Isidro Moreno. School book publishing at infant, junior and senior levels; modern language teaching at infant, junior and senior levels; vocational and professional publishing; trade publishing.

Editorial Incafo SA, Castelló 59, Madrid E28001 *tel* (91) 4313460/ 4313519 *telex* 42459 ICF E *fax* (91) 4313589. *Managing director:* Luis Blas Aritio. Natural history, art, ecology, exploration.

SWEDEN

Almqvist & Wiksell International, Alsnögatan 7, Box 4627, S-116 91 Stockholm *tel* (08) 6408800 *fax* (08) 6411180. *Director:* Stefan Mellin. Scientific, technical.

Bonnier Alba, Box 3159, S-103 63 Stockholm *tel* (08) 6968660 *cables* Bonniers *fax* (08) 6968361. *Publishing director:* Kerstin Angelin. Fiction and non-fiction.

AUSTRALIA

*Member of the Australian Book Publishers Association

Access Press (1979), 282 Newcastle Street, Northbridge, Western Australia 6003 *postal address* PO Box 132, Northbridge, Western Australia 6865 *tel* (09) 328 9188 *fax* (09) 328 4605. *Managing editor:* Helen Weller. Australiana, fiction, poetry, children's, history, general. Privately financed books published and distributed.

*Allen & Unwin Pty Ltd, 9 Atchison Street, PO Box 8500, St Leonards, NSW 2065 *tel* (02) 901 4088 *fax* (02) 906 2218. General trade, including fiction and children's books, academic, especially social science and history.

Edward Arnold—imprint of **Hodder Headline Australia Pty Ltd.**

*The Australian Council for Educational Research Ltd, 19 Prospect Hill Road, Private Bag 55, Camberwell, Victoria 3124 *tel* (03) 277 5555 *fax* (03) 277 5500. Range of books and kits: for teachers, trainee teachers, parents, psychologists, counsellors, students of education, researchers.

Blackwell Scientific Publications Pty Ltd, 54 University Street, Carlton, Victoria 3053 *tel* (03) 347 0300 *telegraphic address* Blackwell, Melbourne *fax* (03) 347 5001. *Editorial director:* Mark Robertson. Medical, healthcare, life, earth sciences.

Brooks Waterloo Publishers—imprint of **Jacaranda Wiley Ltd.**

*Butterworths, 271-273 Lane Cove Road, North Ryde, NSW 2113 *tel* (02) 335 4444 *fax* (02) 335 4655. *Managing director:* D.J. Jackson; *editorial and deputy managing director:* J. Broadfoot. Division of Reed International Books Australia Pty Ltd. Legal, tax and commercial

*Cambridge University Press Australian Branch, 10 Stamford Road, Oakleigh, Melbourne, Victoria 3166 *tel* (03) 568 0322 *fax* (03) 563 1517; and 35 Sophia

Street, Surry Hills, Sydney, NSW 2010   *tel* (02) 211 0604. *Director:* Kim W. Harris. Academic, educational, reference, English as a second language.

Craftsman House (1981), 20 Barcoo Street, Roseville East, NSW 2069   *postal address* PO Box 480, Roseville, NSW 2069   *tel* (02) 417 1670   *fax* (02) 417 1501. *Directors:* Nevill Drury (managing), Martin Gordon; Nichola Dyson Walker (marketing manager). Australian and European fine arts.

Elephas Books (1989), 1/78 Mooney Street, Bayswater, WA 6053   *tel* (09) 370 1461   *fax* (09) 341 8952. *Principals:* Alan J. Falkson, Rune Karlson. How-to and informational subjects.

Samuel French Ltd, represented by Dominie Pty Ltd, Drama Department, 8 Cross Street, Brookvale, NSW 2100   *tel* (02) 905 0201   *fax* (02) 905 5209. Publishers of plays and agents for the collection of royalties for Samuel French Ltd, incorporating Evans Plays and Samuel French Inc., The Society of Authors, ACTAC, and Bakers Plays of Boston.

*****HarperCollins Publishers Pty Ltd,** 25-31 Ryde Road, Pymble, NSW 2073   *postal address* PO Box 321, Pymble, NSW 2073   *tel* (02) 952 5000   *fax* (02) 952 5555. *Managing director:* Barrie Hitchon. Division of **HarperCollins Publishers Australia**. Australiana, general, literature, fiction, non-fiction, reference, women's issues, biography, autobiography, politics, humour, history, popular health, stationery, natural history, children's books.

*****William Heinemann Australia**—see **Reed Publishing Australia.**

*****Hill of Content Publishing Co. Pty Ltd** (1965), 86 Bourke Street, Melbourne, Victoria 3000   *tel* (03) 654 3144   *fax* (03) 662 2527. *Directors:* M. Slamen, M.G. Zifcak, Michelle Anderson. Health, general, life style, children's.

*****Hodder Headline Australia Pty Ltd,** 10-16 South Street, (PO Box 386), Rydalmere, NSW 2116   *tel* (02) 638 5299   *fax* (02) 684 4942. *Directors:* Malcolm Edwards (managing), Tim Hely Hutchinson, Lisa Highton, Mary Howell, John Clarke. General, illustrated non-fiction, children's, hardback and paperback.

*****Jacaranda Wiley Ltd,** 33 Park Road, Milton, Queensland 4064   *tel* (07) 369 9755   *telex* AA 41845   *fax* (07) 369 9155; 184-186 Glenferrie Road, Malvern, Victoria 3144   *tel* (03) 576 1011   *fax* (03) 576 1132; Suite 4, Level 4, Building 1, 1 Thomas Holt Drive, North Ryde, NSW 2113   *tel* (02) 805 1100   *fax* (02) 805 1597. *Managing director:* P. Donoughue. Educational, technical, atlases, software, professional, reference, trade.

*****Kangaroo Press Pty Ltd** (1980), 3 Whitehall Road, Kenthurst, NSW 2156   *postal address* PO Box 6125 Dural Delivery Centre, Dural, NSW 2158   *tel* (02) 654 1502   *fax* (02) 654 1338. *Directors:* David Rosenberg, Priscilla Rosenberg. Gardening, craft, Australian history and natural history, collecting, fitness, transport, children's non-fiction.

*****Lansdowne Publishing**—division of **Weldon International Pty Ltd.** Non-fiction including gardening, cookery, Australiana, sport, natural history, health and life style, Aboriginal subjects.

*****The Law Book Company Ltd,** 44-50 Waterloo Road, North Ryde, NSW 2113   *tel* (02) 887 0177   *fax* (02) 888 9706.

*****Lonely Planet Publications** (1973), PO Box 617, Hawthorn, Victoria 3122   *tel* (03) 819 1877   *fax* (03) 819 6459. *Publisher:* Tony Wheeler. Travel guidebooks, trekking books and phrasebooks.

*****Longman Australia Pty Ltd,** Longman Cheshire House, Kings Gardens, 95 Coventry Street, South Melbourne, Victoria 3205   *tel* (03) 697 0666   *fax* (03)

699 2041. *Managing director:* Robert W. Fisher. Educational and professional publishers.

*****Lothian Publishing Co. Pty Ltd,** 11 Munro Street, Port Melbourne, Victoria 3207 *tel* (03) 645 1544 *fax* (03) 646 4882. *Directors:* P. Lothian (chairman and managing), E. McDonald, G. Matthews, B. Hilliard (sales). Juveniles, health, gardening, general literature, craft.

*****Macmillan Education Australia Pty Ltd,** 107 Moray Street, South Melbourne, Victoria 3205 *tel* (03) 699 8922 *telex* AA 34454 *fax* (03) 690 6938; Suite 310, Henry Lawson Business Centre, Birkenhead Point (Cary Street), Drummoyne, NSW 2047 *tel* (02) 719 8944 *fax* (02) 719 8613. *Directors:* Brian Stonier (executive chairman), John Rolfe (managing), N. Byam Shaw (UK), Margaret Brownie, Peter Huntley, Brian McCurdy, George Smith; *company secretary/financial controller:* Terry White. Educational books.

*****The Macquarie Library Pty Ltd,** Macquarie Dictionary, Macquarie University, NSW 2109 *tel* (02) 805 9800 *fax* (02) 888 2984. Division of **Weldon International Pty Ltd.** The *Macquarie Dictionary*; dictionaries with lexicons appropriate to Australia and South-East Asia; reference.

*****Melbourne University Press,** 268 Drummond Street, Carlton, Victoria 3053 *postal address* PO Box 278, Carlton South, Victoria 3053 *tel* (03) 347 3455 *fax* (03) 349 2527. *Chairman:* Professor J.R.V. Prescott; *director:* Brian Wilder. Academic, scholastic and cultural; educational textbooks and books of reference.

*****Thomas Nelson Australia,** 102 Dodds Street, South Melbourne, Victoria 3205 *tel* (03) 685 4111 *fax* (03) 685 4199. Educational books.

*****Oxford University Press, Australia,** 253 Normanby Road, South Melbourne, Victoria 3205 *postal address* GPO Box 2784Y, Melbourne, Victoria 3001 *tel* (03) 646 4200 *fax* (03) 646 3251. *Managing director:* Marek Palka. Australian history, biography, literary criticism, general, but excluding fiction; school books in all subjects.

*****Pan Macmillan Publishers Australia,** 63-71 Balfour Street, Chippendale, NSW 2008 *tel* (02) 318 0111 *fax* (02) 319 3438. *Directors:* Ross Gibb (managing), James Fraser (publishing). Siv Toigo (finance), Peter Phillips (sales). Fiction, non-fiction, children's.

*****Penguin Books Australia Ltd** (1946), (PO Box 257), 487 Maroondah Highway, Ringwood, Victoria 3134 *tel* (03) 871 2400 *telegraphic address* Penguinook, Melbourne *fax* (03) 870 9618. *Directors:* P.W. Dart (information services), P.J. Field (managing), R.E. Ford (trade services), T.D. Glover (chairman), P.M. Mayer, T.V. Moloney (sales), R.W. Fisher, J.C. Strike (finance and administration), J.W. Webster, R.P. Sessions (publishing). Fiction, general non-fiction, current affairs, sociology, economics, environmental, travel guides, anthropology, politics, children's.

*****Pitman Publishing**—imprint of **Longman Australia Pty Ltd.**

*****Random House Australia Pty Ltd,** 20 Alfred Street, Milsons Point, NSW 2061 *tel* (02) 954 9966 *fax* (02) 954 4562. *Directors:* S.M. Brockhoff, J.E. Bullivant, J.D. Cody, A.J. Davidson, R.J. Ford, M.J. Kelly, E.F. Mason (managing), M. Macleod, S. Master. General, non-fiction, fiction, children's.

*****Reed Books,** Level 9, North Tower, 1-5 Railway Street, Chatswood, NSW 2067 *tel* (02) 372 5252 *fax* (02) 419 6159. *Publisher:* Bill Templeman. Part of **William Heinemann Australia.** Natural history, natural science, prehistory.

*Reed Publishing Australia, 22 Salmon Street, Port Melbourne, Victoria 3207 *tel* (03) 646 6688 *fax* (03) 646 6925. *Managing director:* Sandy Grant. General fiction and non-fiction, children's books, reference.

Reeve Books (1987), 282 Newcastle Street, Northbridge, Western Australia 6003 *postal address* PO Box 132, Northbridge, Western Australia 6865 *tel* (09) 328 9188 *fax* (09) 328 4605. *Managing director/editor:* Helen Weller. Biography, local history, general non-fiction. Commissioned works only.

Sun Books Pty Ltd (1965), 107 Moray Street, South Melbourne, Victoria 3205 *tel* (03) 699 8922 *telegraphic address* Sunbooks. *Directors:* K.B. Stonier, J. Rolfe, N.G. Byam Shaw. Paperbacks – fiction, non-fiction, educational, especially Australian titles. Subsidiary of The Macmillan Company of Australia Pty Ltd.

*Transworld Publishers (Aust) Pty Ltd (1981), Ground Floor, 40 Yeo Street, Neutral Bay, NSW 2089 *tel* (02) 908 4366 *fax* (09) 953 8563. *Managing director:* Geoffrey Rumpf. Bio, self-help, personal awareness, health, parenting and childcare, sports, current affairs, social history.

University of Queensland Press (1948), PO Box 42, St Lucia, Queensland 4067 *tel* (07) 365 2127 *telex* UNIVQLD AA 40315 PRESS *fax* (07) 365 1988. *General manager:* L.C. Muller. Scholarly works, tertiary texts, Australian fiction, young adult fiction, poetry, history, general interest.

*Viking O'Neil (1987), 56 Claremont Street, South Yarra, Victoria 3141 *tel* (03) 827 9901 *fax* (03) 827 0913. *Associate publisher:* Helen Duffy. Imprint of **Penguin Books Australia Ltd.** Pictorial and general works relating to Australia, cartographic publications, craft, health, cookery, gardening, sport.

*Weldon International Pty Ltd, Level 5, 70 George Street, Sydney, NSW 2000 *postal address* PO Box 48, Millers Point, NSW 2000 *tel* (02) 240 9222 *fax* (02) 241 4818. *Chairman:* Kevin Weldon. Incorporates publishing divisions of Lansdowne Publishing, Weldon Russell, Weldon Owen, The Macquarie Library and Mimosa Publications.

*Weldon Owen—division of **Weldon International Pty Ltd.** Cookery, natural science, aerial photography, encyclopedic reference works, young readers' non-fiction.

*Weldon Russell—division of **Weldon International Pty Ltd.** Illustrated non-fiction including natural history, cookery, gardening, ancient history, general reference books and gift books.

*Wild & Woolley P (1974), PO Box 41, Glebe, NSW 2037 *tel* (02) 692 0166 *fax* (02) 552 4320. *Director:* Pat Woolley. Offers short-run paperback printing for self-publishing writers.

CANADA

*Member of the Canadian Book Publishers' Council
†Member of the Association of Canadian Publishers

Butterworths, 75 Clegg Road, Markham, Ontario L6G 1A1 *tel* 905-479-2665 *fax* 905-479-2826.

*Canada Publishing Corporation (1844), 164 Commander Boulevard, Agincourt, Ontario M1S 3C7 *tel* 416-293-8141 *fax* 416-293-9009. Publishers of elementary and secondary school textbooks; general trade/consumer publications including cookbooks, business, sport and fiction; professional and reference materials; annual publications, including *Canadian Global Almanac* and *Who's Who in Canada*.

Canadian Stage and Arts Publications Ltd, 263 Adelaide Street West, 5th Floor, Toronto, Ontario M5H 1Y2 *tel* 416-785-4300 *fax* 416-785-4329. *President and publisher:* George Hencz. Primarily interested in children's books of an educational nature, art books. Also publishes quarterly *Performing Arts & Entertainment in Canada* (*editor:* Karen Bell).

Carswell, Thomson Professional Publishing, Corporate Plaza, 2075 Kennedy Road, Scarborough, Ontario M1T 3V4 *tel* 416-609-8000 *fax* 416-298-5094. *President/ceo:* Ross M. Inkpen. Law, tax, business reference.

The Charlton Press (1952), 2010 Yonge Street, Toronto, Ontario M4S 1Z9 *tel* 416-488-4653 *fax* 416-488-4656. *President:* W.K. Cross. Collectibles, numismatics, Sportscard price catalogues.

Wm. Collins Sons & Co. (Canada) Ltd—see **HarperCollins Canada.**

***Copp Clark Pitman Ltd,** 2775 Matheson Boulevard East, Mississauga, Ontario L4W 4P7 *tel* 905-238-6074 *fax* 905-238-6075. *President:* Stephen J. Mills. Educational textbooks for elementary, secondary and college, technical and business education. Preliminary letter required before submitting MSS.

†**Douglas & McIntyre Ltd** (1964), 1615 Venables Street, Vancouver, BC V5L 2H1 *tel* 604-254-7191 *fax* 604-254-9099. General list including Canadian biography, art and architecture, natural history, history, North American anthropology/ethnology, Canadian fiction. Children's division (Groundwood Books) specialises in fiction and illustrated flats.

†**ECW Press** (1979), 1980 Queen Street E, Toronto, Ontario M4L 1J2 *tel* 416-694-3348 *fax* 416-698-9906. *President:* Jack David; *secretary-treasurer:* Robert Lecker. Literary criticism, indexes, bibliographies, biographies, guidebooks.

Fitzhenry & Whiteside Limited (1966), 195 Allstate Parkway, Markham, Ontario L3R 4T8 *tel* 416-477-9700 *fax* 416-477-9179 *toll free* 1-800-387-9776. *Directors:* R.I. Fitzhenry, Sharon Fitzhenry, Robert W. Read, Jim Sullivan. Trade, educational, college books.

***Gage Education**—see **Canada Publishing Corporation.**

***Harlequin Enterprises Ltd** (1949), 225 Duncan Mill Road, Don Mills, Ontario M3B 3K9 *tel* 416-445-5860 *fax* 416-445-8655. *President and ceo:* Brian E. Hickey. Romance, action adventure.

HarperCollins Canada, 1995 Markham Road, Scarborough, Ontario M1B 5M8 *tel* 416-321-2241 *fax* 416-321-3033; **HarperCollins Publishers Ltd,** Suite 2900, Hazelton Lanes, 55 Avenue Road, Toronto, Ontario M5R 3L2 *tel* 416-975-9334 *fax* 416-975-9884. Publishers of general literature, trade and reference, bibles, religious, mass market paperbacks, audio cassettes, children's books.

Holt, Rinehart & Winston of Canada Ltd, 55 Horner Avenue, Toronto, Ontario M8Z 4X6 *tel* 416-255-4491 *fax* 416-255-4046.

***Irwin Publishing,** division of General Publishing Co. Ltd, 1800 Steeles Avenue W, Concord, Ontario L4K 2P3 *tel* 905-660-0611 *fax* 905-660-0676. *President:* Brian O'Donnell; *chairman:* Jack Stoddart. Educational books at the elementary, high school and college levels.

†**Kids Can Press Ltd,** 29 Birch Avenue, Toronto, Ontario M4V 1E2 *tel* 416-925-5437 *fax* 416-960-5437. *Publisher:* Valerie Hussey. Juvenile/young adult books.

†**Lester Publishing Ltd** (1991), 56 The Esplanade, Suite 507A, Toronto, Ontario M5E 1A7 *tel* 416-362-1032 *fax* 416-362-1647. *President and publisher:* Malcolm Lester. Biography, history, fiction, children's.

†**Lone Pine Publishing** (1980), 206, 10426-81 Avenue, Edmonton, Alberta T6E 1X5 *tel* 403-433-9333 *fax* 403-433-9646. *Publisher and president:* Grant Kennedy; *editor-in-chief:* Glenn Rollans. Natural history, recreation and wildlife guidebooks, popular history.

*****McClelland & Stewart Inc.** (1906), 481 University Avenue, Suite 900, Toronto, Ontario M5G 2E9 *tel* 416-598-1114 *fax* 416-598-7764. *Chairman/president and ceo:* Avie Bennett. General and educational.

†**McGill-Queen's University Press** (1969), 3430 McTavish Street, Montreal, Quebec H3A 1X9 *tel* 514-398-3750 *telex* 05-268510 *fax* 514-398-4333; and Queen's University, Kingston, Ontario K7L 3N6 *tel* 613-545-2155 *fax* 613-545-6822. Academic.

*****McGraw-Hill Ryerson Ltd,** 300 Water Street, Whitby, Ontario L1N 9B6 *tel* 905-430-5000 *fax* 905-430-5020. Educational and trade books.

*****Macmillan Canada** (1905), division of **Canada Publishing Corporation,** 29 Birch Avenue, Toronto, Ontario M4V 1E2 *tel* 416-963-8830 *fax* 416-923-4821. Trade book publishers.

*****Maxwell Macmillan Canada** (1958), 1200 Eglinton Avenue East, Don Mills, Ontario M3C 3N1 *tel* 416-449-6030 *fax* 416-449-0068. *President:* Ray Lee. Academic, technical, educational, children's and adult, trade.

*****Nelson Canada** (1914), 1120 Birchmount Road, Scarborough, Ontario M1K 5G4 *tel* 416-752-9100 *telex* 06-963813 *fax* 416-752-9646. *Directors:* Alan G. Cobham (president), Martin Keast, Andrew Clowes, Dick Parkinson. Elementary, high school, college textbooks; measurement and guidance; children's library.

†**Oberon Press,** 400-350 Sparks Street, Ottawa, Ontario K1R 7S8 *tel* 613-238-3275. General.

*****Oxford University Press, Canada,** 70 Wynford Drive, Don Mills, Ontario M3C 1J9 *tel* 416-441-2941 *fax* 416-444-0427. *Managing director:* Susan Froud. General, educational, juvenile and academic.

*****Pippin Publishing Ltd,** 380 Esna Park Drive, Markham, Ontario L3R 1H5 *tel* 905-513-6966 *fax* 905-513-6977. *Editorial director:* Jonathan Lovat Dickson. ESL/EFL, teacher reference, adult basic education, school and university texts (all subjects).

*****Prentice-Hall Canada, Inc.** (1960), 1870 Birchmount Road, Scarborough, Ontario M1P 2J7 *tel* 416-293-3621 *telex* 065-25184 *fax* 416-299-2529. *Directors:* John C. Isley, Paling Y. Chu. Educational (elementary, secondary, post-secondary), business and personal finance.

†**Quarry Press** (1965), PO Box 1061, Kingston, Ontario K7L 4Y5 *tel* 613-548-8429 *fax* 613-548-1556. *Publisher:* Bob Hilderley. Fiction, poetry, children's, biography, historical non-fiction, travel, folk stories.

*****Stoddart Publishing Co. Ltd,** 34 Lesmill Road, Don Mills, Ontario M3B 2T6 *tel* 416-445-3333 *fax* 416-445-5967. Fiction and non-fiction.

Tundra Books Inc., 345 Victoria Avenue, Suite 604, Montreal, Quebec H3Z 2N2 *tel* 514-932-5434 *fax* 514-484-2152. *President:* May Cutler. General trade juvenile books; art books.

†**University of Toronto Press Inc.**, 10 St Mary Street, Suite 700, Toronto, Ontario M4Y 2W8 *tel* 416-978-5171 (editorial); 416-978-2239 (administration) *fax* 416-978-4738 (editorial/administration).

INDIA

*Member of the Federation of Indian Publishers

*Ajanta Books International** (1975), 1 UB Jawahar Nagar, Bungalow Road, Delhi 110007 *tel* 2926182, 7258630 *fax* 11-7249664. *Chief executive:* S. Balwant. Social sciences and humanities, specialising in: politics, sociology, management, history, literature (Indian and Western), education, linguistics, philosophy, archaeology, library science, fiction.

Allied Publishers Ltd, 15 J.N. Heredia Marg, Ballard Estate, Bombay 400038 *tel* 2617926 *telex* 011-86506 *fax* (92) 2617928. *Managing director:* S.M. Sachdev. School and general books on current affairs and Oriental art.

*Atma Ram & Sons** (1909), 1376 Kashmere Gate, Delhi 110006 *tel* 2523082 *cables* Books Delhi. *Managing proprietor:* Ish Kumar Puri; *senior director:* Sushil Puri. Art, literature, reference, biography, fiction, economics, politics, education, history, philosophy, psychology, science, technology. Books published in English and Hindi languages. Translations and reprints of foreign books undertaken.

*B.I. Publications Pvt Ltd,** 54 Janpath, New Delhi 110001 *tel* 3325313 *telex* 031 63352 BI IN *fax* 011-3323138. *Chairman:* R.D. Bhagat. Scientific, technical, medical, business and industrial management, educational, children's, reference and general; scientific and medical journals.

*S. Chand & Co. Ltd** (1917), Ram Nagar, New Delhi 110055 *tel* 7772080 *telegraphic address* Eschand, New Delhi *telex* 031-61310 *fax* 11-7777446. *Directors:* Rajendra Kumar Gupta, Ravindra Kumar Gupta. Science, technology, medicine, educational books, children's books.

Children's Book Trust (1957), Nehru House, 4 Bahadur Shah Zafar Marg, New Delhi 110002 *tel* 3316970 *telegraphic address* Childtrust, New Delhi. *Founder:* K. Shankar Pillai. Children's books.

*English Book Depot** (1923), 15 Rajpur Road, Dehra Dun (UP) 248001 *tel* 23792, 842159 *telex* 583 345 EBD IN *fax* 91-135-28392. *Directors:* Snehlata and Sandeep Dutt. Military science, agriculture, forestry, geology and petroleum.

HarperCollins Publishers India Pvt. Ltd, 7/16 Ansari Road, Daryaganj, New Delhi 110002 *tel* 011-3278586, 3270260, 3272161 *fax* 011-3277294. *Managing director:* R.K. Mehra. Literature, fiction, biography, autobiography, sports, cookery, sociology, management, philosophy and religion, politics, history, travel, dictionaries and reference, engineering and technology, children's fiction and non-fiction.

Heritage Publishers (1973), 5 Ansari Road, Daryaganj, New Delhi 110002 *tel* 3263050, 3266258. *Proprietor:* B.R. Chawla. Social science, Indology, humanities.

*Hind Pocket Books Pvt Ltd,** G.T. Road, Dilshad Garden, Delhi 110095 *tel* 2282467 *telegraphic address* Pocketbook Delhi *fax* 2282332. *Managing director:* Madhvi Malhotra. Paperbacks in Indian languages and English.

Indian Press (Publications) Private, Limited, 36 Pannalal Road, Allahabad 211002 *tel* 600858/9 *telegraphic address* Publikason. *Managing director:* D.P. Ghosh. Publishers of *Saraswati Hindi Monthly Magazine*, and school, college, university and general books in Hindi, Bengali, English, Gurumukhi, Urdu, Marathi, Nepali languages.

*Jaico Publishing House (1946), 121 Mahatma Gandhi Road, Bombay 400023 *tel* 276702 *telegraphic address* Jaico Books Bombay *telex* 118-6398 JAI IN *fax* 91-22-2041673. *Managing director:* Ashwin J. Shah. History, politics, sociology, management, computers, engineering, economics, psychology, philosophy, religion, law, crime.

Kothari Publications, Jute House, 12 India Exchange Place, Calcutta 700001 *tel* 2209563, 2206572, 4791009 *cables* Zeitgeist. *Proprietor:* Ing. H. Kothari of Sujangarh, Rajasthan. Technical, general and reference books. *Who's Who* series in India. Agents for many foreign publishers.

The Little Flower Co. (1929), Bhurangam Buildings, P.B. 1028, 43 Ranganathan Street, Thyagarayanagar, Madras 600017 *tel* 441538 *telegraphic address* Lifco, Madras. Lifco books. General, fiction, technical, dictionaries, astrology, medicine, legal, commercial, educational and religious.

*Macmillan India Ltd, 315/316 Raheja Chamber, 12 Museum Road, Bangalore 560001 *tel* 80-5587878 *telex* 0845 2615 MCHO IN *fax* 80-5588713. Publishers of educational, scientific, humanities, literature, technical, medical and general books.

Narosa Publishing House (1977), 6 Community Centre, Panchsheel Park, New Delhi 110017 *tel* 6433992, 6433818 *telex* 31-71298 NAR IN *fax* 11-6468717. *Directors:* N.K. Mehra (managing), Rosemarie Mehra, Sascha Mehra. Chemistry, computer science, earth science, engineering, mathematics, medicine and physics.

National Book Trust, India (1957), A-5 Green Park, New Delhi 110016 *tel* 664667, 664020, 664540 *telex* 031-73034 NBT IN. Publishes books for general readers on a variety of subjects, in 13 Indian languages, including English; provides assistance for the publication of textbooks, reference books for the diploma, undergraduate and postgraduate levels, and books for children and for neo-literates.

*Orient Longman Ltd, 3-6-272 Himayat Nagar, Hyderabad 500029 *tel* 240 305/306, 240 294/297/391 *telex* 425 6803 OLEX IN. Fiction and non-fiction, biography, history, philosophy, reference, children's literature, paperbacks, medicine, psychology, engineering, general and social science, technology, university, secondary and primary textbooks, educational materials.

*Oxford & IBH Publishing Co. Pvt Ltd (1964), 66 Janpath (2nd Floor), New Delhi 110001 *tel* 3324578, 3320518 *telegraphic address* Indamer *telex* 31-62492 TCP IN *fax* 011-3322639. Agricultural sciences, biology, zoology, civil engineering, mechanical engineering, botany, economics and management.

*Oxford University Press (Indian Branch). *Head office* Post Box 43, YMCA Library Building, Jai Singh Road, New Delhi 110001 *tel* 3732990, 3747124, 3747125, 3734769 *cables* Oxorient, Delhi *telex* 61108 OXON IN *fax* 91-11-351312. *General manager:* Neil O'Brien. Publishers in all subjects.

Penguin Books India (P) Ltd (1985), 210 Chiranjin Tower, Nehru Place, New Delhi 110048 *tel* 6446122, 6446097 *fax* 011-6420866, 011-6472522. *Directors:* Peter Mayer, Aveek Sarkar (managing), Peter Carson, Arup Sarkar, Trevor Glover, Max Adam, Shobha Subramaniam, V.S.T. Shankardass, Rani Shankardass; *publisher:* David Davidar. Fiction, non-fiction, history, biography, autobiography, belles-lettres, social sciences, management, humour, sports, classics, poetry, children's books.

*Prentice-Hall of India Pvt Ltd, M-97 Connaught Circus, New Delhi 110001 *tel* 332 1779 *cables* Prenhall, New Delhi *telex* 31-61808 PH IN *fax* 011-316 0818. *Chairman/managing director:* Asoke K. Ghosh. Textbooks.

*Rajpal & Sons, PO Box 1064, Delhi 110006 *tel* 2523904, 2519104 *telegraphic address* Rajpalsons, Delhi. *Managing partner:* Vishwanath. Literary criticism, social and general, humanities, textbooks, juvenile literature, Hindi and English; specialises in dictionaries and encyclopedias.

Rupa & Co., PO Box 12333, 15 Bankim Chatterjee Street, Calcutta 700073 *tel* 321291, 316597, 326335 *telegraphic address* Rupanco, Calcutta-73. Art, education, history, literature, fiction, philosophy, religion, sport pastimes.

*Sage Publications India Pvt Ltd, 32 M-Block Market, Greater Kailash-I, New Delhi 110048 *tel* 6419884, 6444958 *cables* Sagepub, New Delhi 110048. *Managing director:* Tejeshwar Singh. Social sciences.

Shiksha Bharati (1955), 1590 Madarsa Road, Kashmere Gate, Delhi 110006 *tel* 2523904. *Managing partner:* Veena Malhotra. Textbooks, popular science and children's books in Hindi and English; also juvenile literature.

*Sterling Publishers Pvt Ltd (1964), L-10 Green Park Extension, New Delhi 110016 *tel* 669560, 660904 *fax* 011-6851028. *Directors:* S.K. Ghai (chairman and managing), Mrs Vimla Ghai, Vikas Ghai, Gaurav Ghai. Biography, computer science, cookery, economics and commerce, education, history and Indology, language and literature, law, library science, management, military, philosophy and religion, politics, psychology and sociology.

*D.B. Taraporevala Sons & Co., Private, Ltd (original firm established 1864), 210 Dr Dadabhai Naoroji Road, Bombay 400001 *tel* 2041433. *Directors:* Mrs Manekbai J. Taraporevala and Miss Sooni J. Taraporevala; *chief executive:* Prof. Russi J. Taraporevala. Books on India and on Indian interest, fine arts, handicrafts, pictorial albums, business, economics, education, electronics, psychology, cookery, domestic economy, pets, hobbies, reference, languages, religion, philosophy, mysticism, occult sciences, law, history, culture, mythology, sociology, health, medical, sex, science, technology, self-improvement, self-instruction, sports, Indian classics.

*Tata McGraw-Hill Publishing Co. Ltd (1970), 4/12 Asaf Ali Road, New Delhi 110002 *tel* 278711, 273763 *telegraphic address* Corinthian, New Delhi *telex* 0361979 TMHD IN. *Director:* R. Radhakrishnan. Engineering, sciences, management, humanities, social sciences, computer science, electronics.

The Theosophical Publishing House, Adyar, Madras 600020 *tel* 4911338 *telegraphic address* Theotheca, Madras 600020 *fax* 044-4915552. Books and cassettes on philosophy, psychology, religion, yoga and occultism.

*Vikas Publishing House Pvt Ltd (1969), 576 Masjid Road, Jangpura, New Delhi 100014 *tel* 4624605, 4624902, 4615313 *cables* Vikasbooks, New Delhi *telex* 31-65106 UBS IN *fax* 011-3276593. *Chairman and managing director:* C.M. Chawla. Science and technology, humanities and social sciences, college level textbooks, school level textbooks, children's books, paperbacks.

*Vision Books Pvt Ltd (1975). Head Office: 1590 Madarsa Road, Kashmere Gate, Delhi 110006 *tel* 2517001, 2512267 *fax* 011-291-6315; Editorial Office: 24 Firoze Gandhi Road, Lajpat Nagar III, New Delhi 110 024 *tel* 6836470, 6836480 *telegraphic address* Visionbook, Delhi *fax* 011-3328898. *Directors:* Sudhir Malhotra (managing), Kapil Malhotra, Vishwanath. Fiction (including Indo-Anglian and translation from Indian languages and other languages), health care, alternative medicine, cookery, vocational skills, sports, Indian culture, politics, biography, travel, poetry, drama, management, military, religion, anthropology, mountaineering, education, international relations, DIY books, investment analysis and planning, stock market studies. *Imprints:* Vision Books, Orient Paperbacks, Anand Paperbacks, Naya Sahitya.

*Wiley Eastern Ltd (1966), 4835/24 Ansari Road, Daryaganj, New Delhi 110002 *tel* 3276802, 3261487, 3267996 *telegraphic address* Wileyeast *telex* 031-66507 WELIN *fax* 011-3267437. *Directors:* Deborah Wiley, Charles Ellis, E.B. Desai, A. Machwe, F.N. Mulla, A.R. Kundaji. Physics, chemistry, mathematics, engineering sciences, humanities and social sciences.

THE REPUBLIC OF IRELAND AND NORTHERN IRELAND

*Member of the Irish Book Publishers' Association

*Anvil Books/The Children's Press (1964), 45 Palmerston Road, Dublin 6 *tel* (01) 973628 *cables* Anvil, Dublin. *Directors:* Rena Dardis (managing), Margaret Dardis (editorial). Anvil: history, biography; Children's Press: adventure, humour, fantasy.

*Appletree Press Ltd (1974), 19-21 Alfred Street, Belfast BT2 8DL *tel* (0232) 243074 *telex* 9312100435 *fax* (0232) 246756. *Director:* John Murphy. Academic, biography, cookery, educational, guidebooks, history, Irish interest, literary criticism, music, photographic, social studies, sport, travel.

*Attic Press (1984), 4 Upper Mount Street, Dublin 2 *tel* (01) 6616128 *fax* (01) 6616176. *Directors:* Róisín Conroy, Maeve Kneafsey, Ann Harper, Gretchen Fitzgerald. Books by and about women in the areas of social and political comment, fiction, women's studies, humour, reference guides and handbooks. **Basement Press** (imprint). Fiction and non-fiction by men and women.

*Blackstaff Press Ltd (1971), 3 Galway Park, Dundonald BT16 0AN *tel* (0232) 487161 *fax* (0232) 489552. *Chairman:* Michael Burns; *managing director:* Anne Tannahill. Fiction, poetry, biography, history, art, academic, natural history, sport, politics, music, education, fine limited editions.

*The Blackwater Press—imprint of **Folens Publishing Company.** General non-fiction, Irish interest.

*Brandon Book Publishers Ltd (1982), Cooleen, Dingle, Co. Kerry *tel* (066) 51463 *fax* (066) 51234. *Directors:* Steve MacDonogh, Bernard Goggin. Biography, literature, politics, fiction, travel (Ireland), history, children's folklore.

Catholic Communications Institute of Ireland, Inc.—see **Veritas Publications.**

*Cló Iar-Chonnachta Teo. (1985), Indreabhán, Conamara, Co. Galway *tel* (091) 93307 *fax* (091) 93362. *Managing director:* Micheál Ó Conghaile. Mostly Irish-language publications – novels, short stories, plays, poetry, songs, history; cassettes (writers reading from their works in Irish and English).

Dolmen Press Ltd—stock acquired by **Colin Smythe Ltd**; see UK list.

The Educational Company of Ireland, PO Box 43a, Ballymount Road, Walkinstown, Dublin 12 *tel* (01) 4500611 *fax* (01) 4500993. *Executive directors:* F.J. Maguire (chief executive), J.F. O'Callaghan FCA, R. McLoughlin. Trading unit of Smurfit Services Ltd. Educational MSS on all subjects in English or Gaelic.

C.J. Fallon (1927), Lucan Road, Palmerstown, Dublin 20 *tel* (01) 6265777 *fax* (01) 6268225. *Directors:* M. Kavanagh (chairman), H.J. McNicholas (managing), P. Tolan (secretary), N. White (editorial), G. Brosnan, M. Kelly, E. Tighe. Educational text books.

Folens Publishing Company, Airton Road, Tallaght, Dublin 24 *tel* (01) 515519 *fax* (01) 515306. *Directors:* John O'Connor (managing), Anna O'Donovan (secondary), Deirdre Whelan (primary). Educational (primary, secondary, comprehensive, technical, in English and Irish), educational children's magazines.

*Four Courts Press (1969), Kill Lane, Blackrock, Co. Dublin *tel* (01) 2892922 *fax* (01) 2893072. *Managing director:* Michael Adams. Theology, church history.

The Gallery Press (1970), Loughcrew, Oldcastle, Co. Meath *tel/fax* (049) 41779. *Editor and publisher:* Peter Fallon. *Allied company:* Deerfield Publications Inc., Massachusetts. Poetry, drama, occasionally fiction, by Irish authors. Also, hand-printed limited editions poetry.

*Gill & Macmillan Ltd (1968), Goldenbridge, Inchicore, Dublin 8 *tel* (01) 4531005 *fax* (01) 4541688. Biography or memoirs, educational (secondary, university), history, sociology, theology and religion, literature, cookery, current affairs, guidebooks, professional (law, accountancy, tax).

The Goldsmith Press (1972), Newbridge, Co. Kildare *tel* (045) 33613 *fax* (045) 34648. *Directors:* D. Egan, V. Abbott, Peter Kavanagh; *secretary:* Peter Mulreid. Literature, art, Irish interest, poetry; *ERA Review* (occasional).

Government Supplies Agency, Publications Division, 4-5 Harcourt Road, Dublin 2 *tel* (01) 613111 *fax* (01) 780645. Parliamentary publications.

*Institute of Public Administration (1957), Vergemount Hall, Clonskeagh, Dublin 6 *tel* (01) 2697011 *fax* (01) 2698644. *Assistant director general and publisher for the Institute:* Jim D. O'Donnell. Government, economics, politics, law, social policy and administrative history.

*Irish Academic Press (1974), Kill Lane, Blackrock, Co. Dublin *tel* (01) 2892922 *fax* (01) 2893072. *Directors:* Michael Adams, Frank Cass, Gilbert Raff, Michael Philip Zaidner. Publishes under the imprints **Irish University Press, Irish Academic Press** and **Tara Books**. Scholarly books especially in history, law, art and literature.

The Kavanagh Press Ltd (1989), Newbridge, Co. Kildare *tel* (045) 33613 *fax* (045) 34648. *Directors:* Desmond Egan, Vivienne Abbott. Poetry, Irish interest, literary criticism, Irish history, art; cassettes.

The Lilliput Press Ltd (1984), 4 Rosemount Terrace, Arbour Hill, Dublin 7 *tel/fax* (01) 6711647. *Managing director:* Antony T. Farrell. General and Irish literature: essays, biography/autobiography, fiction, criticism; Irish history; nature and environment.

Longman, Browne & Nolan—now incorporated in **The Educational Company of Ireland.**

*The Mercier Press (1945), PO Box 5, 5 French Church Street, Cork *tel* (021) 275040 *fax* (021) 274969. *Directors:* G. Eaton (chairman), J.F. Spillane (managing), M.P. Feehan, D.J. Keily, M.L. McNamara. Irish literature, folklore, history, politics, humour, ballads, education, theology, law.

*Moytura Press (1988), 4 Arran Quay, Dublin 7 *tel* (01) 8722373/8723923 *fax* (01) 8723902. *Directors:* J.G. O'Connor, Brian O'Kane. Fiction.

*Oak Tree Press (1991), 4 Arran Quay, Dublin 7 *tel* (01) 8722373/8723923 *fax* (01) 8723902. *Directors:* J.G. O'Connor, Brian O'Kane. Law, accountancy, business management.

O'Brien Educational (1976), 20 Victoria Road, Rathgar, Dublin 6 *tel* (01) 4923333 *fax* (01) 4922777. *Directors:* Michael O'Brien, Bride Rosney.

Humanities, science, environmental studies, history, geography, English, Irish, art, commerce, music, careers, media studies.

*The O'Brien Press Ltd (1974), 20 Victoria Road, Rathgar, Dublin 6 *tel* (01) 4923333 *fax* (01) 4922777. *Directors:* Michael O'Brien, Ide Ni Laoghare, Ivan O'Brien. Folklore, nature, fiction, architecture, topography, history, general, illustrated books, sport, anthropology, children, biography; tapes for children. Series include *Lucky Tree Books*, *Junior Biography Library*, *Urban Heritage*, *Other World Series* (science fiction/fantasy/horror for juveniles).

*On Stream Publications Ltd (1986), Currabaha, Cloghroe, Blarney, Co. Cork *tel/fax* (021) 385798. *Owner:* Rosalind Crowley. Cookery, wine, travel, human interest non-fiction, local history and practical books.

*Poolbeg Press Ltd (1976), Knocksedan House, 123 Baldoyle Industrial Estate, Baldoyle, Dublin 13 *tel* (01) 8321477 *fax* (01) 8321430. *Directors:* Philip MacDermott (managing), Breda Purdue (marketing), Kate Cruise O'Brien (editorial), Kieran Devlin (finance). Fiction, public interest, women's interest, history, politics, current affairs, Children's Poolbeg, Beachwood, Business Poolbeg.
Salmon Publishing Ltd (imprint). *Editorial director:* Jessie Lendennie. Contemporary poetry, mostly Irish, especially women poets.
Torc Books Ltd (imprint). *Managing editor:* Zoë O'Connor. General fiction and non-fiction.

The Round Hall Press Ltd (1981), Kill Lane, Blackrock, Co. Dublin *tel* (01) 2892922 *fax* (01) 2893072. *Managing director:* Michael Adams. Law.

*Salmon Publishing Ltd—see **Poolbeg Press Ltd.**

School and College Publishing Ltd (1968), Taney Road, Dundrum, Dublin 14 *tel* (01) 2983544 *fax* (01) 2988554. *Directors:* William J. Connolly, Phyllis O'Brien, Gilbert Brosnan, Mark Kavanagh, Michael Kelly. Educational books for post-primary schools.

Stationery Office—see **Government Supplies Agency.**

*Torc Books Ltd—see **Poolbeg Press Ltd.**

*Town House and Country House (1981), 42 Morehampton Road, Donnybrook, Dublin 4 *tel* (01) 6683466/6683307 *fax* (01) 6607008. *Directors:* Treasa Coady, Jim Coady. Natural history, general illustrated non-fiction, popular fiction, art and archaeology.

*Veritas Publications, division of the **Catholic Communications Institute of Ireland, Inc.,** Veritas House, 7/8 Lower Abbey Street, Dublin 1 *tel* (01) 8788177 *fax* (01) 8786507. *UK:* Veritas Book & Video Distribution Ltd, Lower Avenue, Leamington Spa, Warks. CV31 3NP *tel* (0926) 451 730 *fax* (0926) 451 733. Religion, including social and educational works, and material relating to the media of communication.

*Wolfhound Press (1974), 68 Mountjoy Square, Dublin 1 *tel* (01) 740354. *Publisher:* Seamus Cashman; *publishing manager:* Siobhan Campbell. Literary studies and criticism, fiction, art, biography, history, young readers, children's and teenage fiction, law, gift titles, cookery, general non-fiction.

NEW ZEALAND

*Member of the New Zealand Book Publishers' Association

*Ashton Scholastic Ltd (1962), 165 Marua Road, Panmure, Auckland *postal address* Private Bag 92801, Penrose, Auckland *tel* (09) 579-6089 *fax* (09)

579-3860. *Managing director/publisher:* Graham Beattie; *company secretary/ operations manager:* David Peagram. Children's books.

*Auckland University Press (1966), University of Auckland, Private Bag 92019, Auckland *tel* (09) 373-7528 *fax* (09) 373-7465. *Chairman of University Press Committee:* J. Deeks; *managing editor:* Elizabeth Caffin. NZ history, NZ poetry, Maori and Pacific studies, politics, sociology, literary criticism, art history, biography, education.

*David Bateman Ltd (1979), 32-34 View Road, Glenfield *postal address* PO Box 100242 North Shore Mail Centre, Auckland 10 *tel* (09) 444-4680 *fax* (09) 444-0389. *Directors:* David L. Bateman (managing), Janet Bateman, Paul Bateman, Paul Parkinson. Natural history, gardening, encyclopedias, sport, art books, cookbooks, historical, juvenile, travel, motoring, maritime history, business.

Bush Press Communications Ltd (1979), 4 Bayview Road, Hauraki Corner, Takapuna, Auckland 1309 *postal address* PO Box 33-029, Takapuna, Auckland 1309 *tel/fax* (09) 486-2667. *Governing director and publisher:* Gordon Ell. NZ non-fiction, particularly outdoor, nature, travel, architecture, crafts, Maori, popular history; children's non-fiction.

*Butterworths of New Zealand Ltd, 203-207 Victoria Street, Wellington *tel* (04) 385-1479 *fax* (04) 385-1598. *Legal publishing director:* James Clarke. Law, accountancy, business management.

The Caxton Press, 113 Victoria Street, Christchurch, PO Box 25-088 *tel* (03) 366-8516 *fax* (03) 365-7840. *Directors:* B.C. Bascand, E.B. Bascand. Fine printers and publishers since 1935 of NZ books of many kinds, including verse, fiction, biography, history, natural history, travel, gardening.

Dunmore Press Ltd (1970), PO Box 5115, Palmerston North *tel* (06) 358-7169 *fax* (06) 357-9242. *Directors:* Murray R. Gatenby, Valerie K. Gatenby. Education, history, sociology, business studies.

Grantham House Publishing (1984), PO Box 17-256, Wellington 6033 *tel* (04) 476-4625 *fax* (04) 476-3048. *Publisher and chief executive:* Graham C. Stewart; *editorial:* Anna Rogers. Antiques and collecting, architecture and design, aviation, gardening, history and antiquarian, illustrated and fine editions, military and war, nautical, transport, railways, tramways.

*HarperCollins Publishers (New Zealand) Ltd, PO Box 1, Auckland *tel* (09) 444-3740 *fax* (09) 444-1086. Publishers of general literature, teen fiction, non-fiction, reference books, trade paperbacks.

*Hodder Headline New Zealand Ltd, PO Box 3858, Auckland 1 *tel* (09) 444-3640 *fax* (09) 444-3646.

*Longman Paul Ltd, Private Bag 102908, North Shore Mail Centre, Glenfield, Auckland 10 *tel* (09) 444-4968 *fax* (09) 444-4957. NZ educational books.

*McIndoe Publishers (1968), 51 Crawford Street, PO Box 694, Dunedin *tel* (03) 477-0355 *fax* (03) 477-1982. *Managing editor:* B. Larson. All categories.

Mallinson Rendel Publishers Ltd (1980), 7 Grass Street, PO Box 9409, Wellington *tel* (04) 385-7340 *fax* (04) 385-4235. *Directors:* Ann Mallinson, David Rendel. Children's, general NZ books, aviation.

*Moa Beckett Publishers Ltd, 28 Poland Road, Glenfield, Auckland *tel* (09) 444-8036 *fax* (09) 444-1967. *Managing director:* Richard Beckett; *publishing director:* John Blackwell. Sport, gardening, cooking, travel, atlases, general; no fiction or children's.

*Nelson Price Milburn Ltd, PO Box 38-945, Wellington Mail Centre, Wellington *located at* 1 Te Puni Street, Petone *tel* (04) 568-7179 *fax* (04) 568-2115. Children's fiction, primary school texts, especially school readers and social studies, secondary educational.

New Zealand Council for Educational Research (1933), Box 3237, Education House, 178-182 Willis Street, Wellington 1 *tel* (04) 384-7939 *fax* (04) 384-7933. *Art director:* Peter Ridder. Education, including educational administration and planning, vocational education and adult learning, special education, families, women and parents, rural education, early childhood education, higher education, Maori schooling, educational achievement tests, etc.

*Oxford University Press, PO Box 11-149, Ellerslie, Auckland 5 *tel* (09) 523-3134 *cables* Oxonian, Auckland *fax* (09) 524-6723. *NZ academic and trade publisher:* Linda Cassells.

*Pitman New Zealand—imprint of **Longman Paul Ltd.** Educational, commercial, legal.

*Random House New Zealand Ltd (1977), Private Bag 102950, North Shore Mail Centre, Auckland 10 *tel* (09) 444-7197 *fax* (09) 444-7524. *Directors:* J. Rogers (managing), S. Master. Fiction, junior books, sports and pastimes, general non-fiction, gardening.

*Reed Publishing (New Zealand) Ltd, incorporating **Reed Books, Octopus Books** and **Heinemann Education,** Private Bag 34901, Birkenhead, Auckland 10 *tel* (09) 480-6039 *fax* (09) 419-1212. *Chairman:* Richard Charkin; *managing director:* Alan Smith. NZ literature, specialist and general titles, primary, secondary and tertiary textbooks. *Imprints:* George Philip, Conran Octopus, Mitchell Beazley, Reed Publishing Group Australia Pty Ltd, Heinemann Young Books, Secker & Warburg, Hamlyn, Bounty, Dean, Buzz, Minerva, Mandarin, Cedar, Methuen Drama, Brimax, Budget Books, Octopus Publishing Group, Ginn & Company, Heinemann Education Books, Rigby Heinemann (Australia), Rigby (USA), Heinemann Education Books Inc. (USA).

*Ray Richards Publisher (1977), 3-49 Aberdeen Road, Castor Bay, Auckland *postal address* PO Box 31240, Milford, Auckland *tel* (09) 410-5681 *fax* (09) 410-6389. *Partners:* Ray Richards, Barbara Richards. Publishers for organisations; especially history, science, equestrian, agriculture.

*Shortland Publications Ltd (1984), 360 Dominion Road, Auckland *tel* (09) 638-7128 *fax* (09) 638-6422. *Managing director:* Avelyn Davidson. Children's books: reading material (ages 5-12), science/non-fiction (ages 5-14).

*University of Otago Press (1958), University of Otago, PO Box 56, Dunedin *tel/fax* (03) 479-8807 *fax* (03) 479-8385. *Managing editor:* Wendy Harrex. Student texts and scholarly works in all disciplines and general books, including Maori and women's studies, health and fiction.

*Victoria University Press (1974), Victoria University of Wellington, PO Box 600, Wellington *tel* (04) 495-5263 *fax* (04) 495-5199. *Chairman:* Professor G.R. Hawke; *editor:* Fergus Barrowman. Academic, scholarly books on NZ history, sociology, political history, architecture, economics, law, zoology, biology; also fiction, plays.

Viking Sevenseas Ltd, 23b Ihakara Street, Paraparaumu *tel* (04) 297-1990 *telegraphic address* Vikseven *fax* (04) 297-1990. *Managing director:* M.B. Riley. Factual books on New Zealand only.

Other Commonwealth Publishers

GHANA

Emmanuel Publishing Services, PO Box 5282, Accra-North *tel* 225238. *Director:* Adwoa Nsiah. Representing Oxford University Press, University Press plc, Ibadan, Nigeria.

Moxon Paperbacks (1967), PO Box M 160, Osu, Accra *fax* 021 774338 *telegraphic address* Moxon, Accra. *Partners:* James Moxon, Oliver Carruthers. Crime, current affairs, biography, travel, fiction. UK: c/o Tortoise Shell Press, 131 Corve Street, Ludlow SY8 2PG *tel* (0584) 874259.

Sam-Woode Ltd (1988), PO Box 12719, Accra-North *tel* 220257 *cables* Samwoode Accra *telex* 2687 GH *fax* 662210. *Executive chairman:* Kwesi Sam-Woode. Children's educational books (mathematics, science, English).

Sedco Publishing Ltd, Sedco House, Tabon Street, North Ridge, Accra *postal address* PO Box 2051, Accra *tel* 221332 *cables* Sedco, Accra *telex* 2456 SEDCO GH *fax* 220107. *Editorial director:* E.K. Sallah. Educational and children's.

HONG KONG

Jacaranda Wiley Ltd, 10A Causeway Bay Mansions, 42-48 Paterson Street, Causeway Bay, Hong Kong *tel* 8905738 *fax* 5761813.

Longman Asia Ltd, Cornwall House, 18th Floor, Taikoo Place, 979 King's Road, Quarry Bay, Hong Kong *tel* 8118168 *telex* 73051 LGHK HX *fax* 5657440.

Macmillan Publishers (China) Limited, Warwick House, East Wing, 19th Floor, Taikoo Trading Estate, 28 Tong Chong Street, Quarry Bay, Hong Kong *tel* 8118781 *telex* 85969 PENHK HX *fax* 8110743. *Publisher:* Deborah Veness. Educational and general books.

Oxford University Press, 18/F Warwick House, Taikoo Trading Estate, 28 Tong Chong Street, Quarry Bay, Hong Kong *tel* (852) 516 3222 *fax* (852) 565 8491.

KENYA

East African Educational Publishers Ltd (1965), PO Box 45314, Nairobi *tel* 444700/445260/1 *telegraphic address* Edpubs *fax* 448753. *Managing director:* Henry Chakava. Academic and educational books.

Longman Kenya Ltd, PO Box 18033, Nairobi *tel* 532579/80/81 *telex* 24101 *fax* 540037. *Chairman:* F.T. Nyammo; *managing director:* Frank Japheth Njagi. Primary and secondary school books; tertiary: languages, humanities, business education and technical, tourism; novels.

Macmillan Kenya Publishers Ltd (1970), PO Box 30797, Nairobi *tel* 220012/224485 *fax* 254 02 212179. *Managing director:* David Muita. Science and agriculture, education, health.

Oxford University Press (Eastern Africa), PO Box 72532, 2nd Floor, ABC Place, Waiyaki Way, Nairobi *tel* 440555/8 *fax* 443972. *Managing director:* Abdulla Ismaily.

MALAYSIA

Longman Malaysia Sdn. Berhad, 2nd Floor, 3 Jalan Kilang A, off Jalan Penchala, 46050 Petaling Jaya, Selangor *tel* 03-7920466 *telegraphic address* Freegrove, Kuala Lumpur *telex* 37600 LMSB MA *fax* 03-7918005.

Oxford University Press (South-East Asian Publishing Unit), 19-25 Jalan Kuchai Lama, 58200 Kuala Lumpur *postal address* PO Box 160 Jalan Kelang Lama, 58700 Kuala Lumpur *tel* 7839942, 7930551, 7837171, 7837522 *fax* 03-7812836. *Editorial manager:* Noor Azlina Yunus.

NIGERIA

African Universities Press. *Head office:* New Oluyole Industrial Estate, Phase II, Ibadan-Lagos Expressway, PMB 5617, Ibadan *tel* 022-317218 *cables* Pilgrim Ibadan *telex* 20311-BOX 078. *Directors:* Emmanuel A. Jaja, J.E. Leigh, Nicholas Perren. Educational, Africana.

Evans Brothers (Nigeria Publishers), Ltd, Jericho Road, PMB 5164, Ibadan *tel* 417570, 417601, 417626 *telex* 31104 EDBOOK NG *fax* 410757.

Fourth Dimension Publishing Co. Ltd (1977), 15 Fifth Avenue, City Layout-New Haven, PMB 01164 Enugu *tel* 042-339969 *telex* 51128 BONGS NG *fax* 234-42-334811. *Managing director:* Victor U. Nwankwo. Medicine, law, history and biography, business and management, fiction, school, children's.

Longman Nigeria, Ltd, 52 Oba Akran Avenue, PMB 21036, Ikeja, Lagos *tel/ fax* 901150-9 *telex* 2663 LNGMAN G *fax* 964370.

University Press plc (1978), Three Crowns Building, Eleyele Road, Jericho, PMB 5095, Ibadan, Oyo State *tel* 022-411356/412313/412386 *telex* 31121 OXONIA NG *fax* 412056. *Managing director:* W.A. Olajide. Educational books.

SINGAPORE

Butterworth Asia, 10 Anson Road, 32-01 International Plaza, Singapore 0207 *tel* 2203684 *telex* RS 42890 BGASIA *fax* 2255026.

Federal Publications (S) Pte Ltd (1957), Times Centre, 1 New Industrial Road, Singapore 1953 *tel* 2848844 *cables* Fedpubs, Singapore *telexmail* RS 24200 TM 6223 *fax* 2889254. *Vice president & general manager:* Y.H. Mew. Educational, children's, general reference and academic books.

Oxford University Press Pte Ltd, 37 Jalan Pemimpin #03-03, Union Industrial Building Block A, Singapore 2057 *tel* 2597122 *fax* 2598622.

Reed International (Singapore) Pte Ltd (1963), 37 Jalan Pemimpin, #07-04/05 Block B, Union Industrial Building, Singapore 2057 *tel* 2583255 *telex* RS 24299 HEBOOKS *fax* 2588279.

TANZANIA

Oxford University Press (East & Central Africa), POB 5299, Maktaba Street, Dar es Salaam *tel* 29209 *cables* Oxonian, Dar es Salaam.

ZIMBABWE

College Press Publishers (Pvt) Ltd, PO Box 3041, Harare *tel* 754145, 754255 *telex* 22558 *fax* 754256. *Production director:* Engelbert L. Luphahla.

HarperCollins Publishers (Zimbabwe) (Pvt) Ltd, PO Box UA 201, Union Avenue, Harare *tel* 727516/721413 *fax* 721413 ext 2.

Longman Zimbabwe (Pvt) Ltd, PO Box ST 125, Southerton, Harare *tel* Harare 62711, 65945 *telegraphic address* Longman, Harare *telex* 22566 LONZIM ZW *fax* 263-4-62716.

Oxford University Press—represented by College Press Publishers (Pvt) Ltd.

SOUTH AFRICA

*Member of the South African Publishers' Association

Ashanti Publishing (Pty) Ltd (1987)—acquired by **William Waterman Publications.**

Books of Africa (Pty) Ltd, 39 Atlantic Road, PO Box 10, Muizenberg 7951 *tel* (021) 888-316. *Directors:* T.V. Bulpin, M. Bulpin. Any subject about Africa.

Ad Donker (Pty) Ltd (1973), 25 Rudd Road, Illovo, Johannesburg 2196 *postal address* PO Box 2105, Parklands 2121 *tel* (011) 880-8150 *fax* (011) 880-7446. Africana, literature, history, academic, biography, socio-political.

HarperCollins Publishers (SA) (Pty) Ltd, 10-14 Watkins Street, Denver Ext. 4, Johannesburg *postal address* PO Box 33977, Jeppestown 2043 *tel* (011) 622-2900 *fax* (011) 622-3553. General publications, fiction, reference books, bibles, juveniles, school textbooks and paperbacks, tertiary books, prayer and hymn books.

*Juta & Company Ltd** (1853), PO Box 14373, Kenwyn 7790 *tel* (021) 797-5101 *fax* (021) 762-7424. Educational, academic, professional and legal publishers.

*Lovedale Press,** Private Bag X1346, PO Lovedale 5702, Alice Ciskei 5700 *tel* (0404) 31-135 *fax* (0404) 31-871. Educational, religious and general book publications for African market.

*Maskew Miller Longman (Pty) Ltd,** Howard Drive, Pinelands 7405 *postal address* PO Box 396, Cape Town 8000 *tel* (021) 531-7750 *telex* 526053 *fax* (021) 531-4049. Educational and general publishers.

*Oxford University Press (Southern African Branch),** 5th Floor, Harrington House, 37 Barrack Street, Cape Town 8001 *postal address* PO Box 1141, Cape Town 8000 *tel* (021) 457-266 *fax* (021) 457-265. *Managing director:* Kate McCallum.

David Philip Publishers (Pty) Ltd (1971), PO Box 23408, Claremont 7735, Cape Province *tel* (021) 644-136 *telegraphic address* Philipub, Capetown *fax* (021) 643-358. *Managing directors:* David Philip, Marie Philip; *directors:* Russell Martin, Bridget Impey. Academic, history, social sciences, politics, theology, biography, belles-lettres, reference books, fiction, learners' texts, children's books.

Ravan Press (Pty) Ltd (1972), 6th Floor, Randhill, Bordeaux Drive, Randburg *postal address* PO Box 145, Randburg 2125 *tel* (011) 789-7636 *fax* (011) 789-7653. *Manager:* Glenn Moss. African studies: history, politics, social studies; fiction, literature, children's, educational.

*Shuter and Shooter (Pty) Ltd** (1925), 230 Church Street and 199 Pietermaritz Street, Pietermaritzburg 3201, Natal *postal address* PO Box 109, Pietermaritzburg 3200 *tel* (0331) 946-830/948-881 *telegraphic address* Shushoo *fax* (0331) 943-096/427-419. *Publishing director:* D.F. Ryder. Primary and secondary educational, science, biology, history, maths, geography, English,

Afrikaans, biblical studies, music, teacher training, agriculture, accounting, school readiness, dictionaries, African languages.

*Southern Book Publishers (Pty) Ltd, PO Box 3103, Halfway House, Transvaal 1685 *tel* (011) 315-3633/7 *fax* (011) 315-3810. Publishers of academic and general non-fiction books, especially natural history, as well as those of South African interest.

*Struik Publishers, PO Box 1144, Cape Town 8000. Division of The Struik Publishing Group (Pty) Ltd *tel* (021) 462-4360 *fax* (021) 461-9378/462-4379. *Managing director:* Dick Wilkins. General non-fiction.

*Struik Winchester Publishers, PO Box 1144, Cape Town 8000. Division of Struik Publishers *tel* (021) 455-573 *fax* (021) 462-4379/461-9378. *Managing director:* Dick Wilkins. Natural history, cultural history, Africana.

*J.L. Van Schaik (1914), 1064 Arcadia Street, Hatfield, Pretoria 0083 *tel* (012) 342-2765 *fax* (012) 433-563. Publishers of books in English, Afrikaans and African languages. Specialists in Afrikaans non-fiction, dictionaries, textbooks and fiction in the African languages.

William Waterman Publications Pty Ltd (incorporating Ashanti Publishing, Justified Press, Justified Press for Juniors and Vlietman Agencies), PO Box 5091, Rivonia 2128 *tel* (011) 803-2506 *fax* (011) 803-5094. *Directors:* Murray J. Bolton, Nicholas W. Combrinck (managing), Debby de Groot. General non-fiction, military history, literature, poetry, children's educational.

Witwatersrand University Press, Private Bag 3, Wits 2050 *tel* (011) 716-2023 *telex* 4-27125 SA *fax* (011) 339-3559.

UNITED STATES OF AMERICA

*Member of the Association of American Publishers, Inc.

Abbeville Press (1977), 488 Madison Avenue, 23rd Floor, New York, NY 10022 *tel* 212-888-1969 *fax* 212-644-5085. *Publisher and president:* Robert Abrams. Art and illustrated books.

Abingdon Press, PO Box 801, Nashville, TN 37202-0801 *tel* 615-749-6404 *fax* 615-749-6512. Editorial offices for academic books: 2495 Lawrenceville Highway, Decatur, GA 30033-3240 *tel* 404-636-6001 *fax* 404-636-5894. *Editorial director:* Neil M. Alexander. General interest, professional, academic and reference – primarily directed to the religious market.

Academy Chicago Publishers (1975), 363 West Eric Street, Chicago, IL 60610 *tel* 312-751-7300 *fax* 312-751-7306. *Directors:* Anita Miller, Jordan Miller. Fiction, mystery, biography, travel, books of interest to women; quality reprints.

And/Or Books (1974), PO Box 2246, Berkeley, CA 94702 *tel* 510-548-2124. Imprint of **Ronin Publishing, Inc.** Health and nutrition, life styles. No unsolicited work.

Andrews & McMeel, 4900 Main Street, Kansas City, MO 64112 *tel* 816-932-6700 *fax* 816-932-6706. *Vice-president and editorial director:* Donna Martin. General trade publishing, with emphasis on humour and consumer reference.

Arcade Publishing, 141 Fifth Avenue, New York, NY 10010 *tel* 212-475-2633 *fax* 212-353-8148. *President and publisher:* Richard Seaver; *associate publisher:* Jeannette Seaver; *general manager:* Cal Barksdale. General, including adult hard cover and paperbacks.

Ashley Books Inc. (1971), 4600 W Commercial Blvd, Tamarac, FL 33319 *tel* 305-739-2221 *fax* 305-485-2287. *Directors:* Simeon Paget (managing), Billie Young (president); *associate editor:* Gwen Costa. Fiction, especially emotional page turners, but no erotica; medicine, health, vitamins, diet and natural foods; controversy, how-to, humour, reference, self-help and technical.

Atlantic Monthly Press—see **Grove/Atlantic, Inc.**

Avon Books (1941), The Hearst Corporation, 1350 Avenue of the Americas, New York, NY 10019 *tel* 212-261-6800 *fax* 212-261-6895. *Executive vp and general manager:* Michael Greenstein. All subjects, fiction and non-fiction.

Walter H. Baker Company (1845), 100 Chauncy Street, Boston, MA 02111 *tel* 617-482-1280 *fax* 617-482-7613. *President:* Charles Van Nostrand; *editor:* John B. Welch. Plays and books on the theatre. Also agents for plays. *UK agents:* Samuel French Ltd, 52 Fitzroy Street, London W1P 6JR.

*Bantam Doubleday Dell Publishing Group Inc., 1540 Broadway, New York, NY 10036 *tel* 212-354-6500 *telex* 7608009 *fax* 212-782-9597. *Chairman:* Bernard von Minckwitz; *president and ceo:* Jack Hoeft. Fiction, classics, biography, health, business, general non-fiction, social sciences, religion, sports, science, audio tapes.

Barron's Educational Series, Inc. (1941), 250 Wireless Boulevard, Hauppage, NY 11788 *tel* 516-434-3311 *fax* 516-434-3723. *President:* Manuel H. Barron; *executive vice president:* Ellen Sibley. Test preparation, juvenile, cookbooks, crafts, business, pets, gardening.

*Beacon Press, 25 Beacon Street, Boston, MA 02108 *tel* 617-742-2110 *fax* 617-723-3097. *Director:* Wendy Strothman. General non-fiction in fields of religion, ethics, philosophy, current affairs, gender studies, environmental concerns, African-American studies, anthropology and women's studies, nature.

Bergh Publishing, Inc. (1983), 20 East 53rd Street, Suite 7E, New York, NY 10022 *tel* 212-593-1040 *fax* 212-593-4638. *Chairman and ceo:* Sven-Erik Bergh MA(Oxon). Quality popular non-fiction, especially yearbooks, culinary and cook books. Query first with sase.

R.R. Bowker, 121 Chanlon Road, New Providence, NJ 07974 *tel* 908-464-6800 *fax* 908-464-3553. *President:* Ira T. Siegel. A Reed Reference Publishing company. Bibliographies and reference tools for the book trade and literary and library worlds, available in hardcopy, on microfiche, on-line and CD-ROM. Reference books for music, art, business, computer industry, cable industry and information industry.

Brassey's Inc. (1984), 8000 Westpark Drive, 1st Floor, McLean, VA 22102 *tel* 703-442-4535. *Publisher:* Franklin D. Margiotta PhD. Foreign policy, defence, national and international affairs, military history, intelligence, biography.

George Braziller Inc. (1954), 60 Madison Avenue, Suite 1001, New York, NY 10010 *tel* 212-889-0909 *fax* 212-689-5405. *Publisher:* George Braziller. Art, architecture, history, biography, fiction, poetry, science.

*Cambridge University Press (North American branch), 40 West 20th Street, New York, NY 10011 *tel* 212-924-3900 *fax* 212-691-3239. *Director:* Barbara Colson.

Candlewick Press (1991), 2067 Massachusetts Avenue, Cambridge, MA 02140 *tel* 617-661-3330 *fax* 617-661-0565. *Vice president/editor-in-chief:* Amy Ehrlich. Children's books – 6 months to 14 years: picture books, novels, non-fiction, novelty books.

Capra Press (1969), PO Box 2068, Santa Barbara, CA 93120 *tel* 805-966-4590 *fax* 805-965-8020. *Publisher:* Noel Young. Fiction, natural history, animals.

Carroll & Graf Publishers, Inc. (1983), 260 Fifth Avenue, New York, NY 10001 *tel* 212-889-8772. *President:* Herman Graf; *publisher:* Kent Carroll; *subrights:* Jennifer Prior. Mystery and science fiction, popular fiction, history, biography, literature, business, sports.

Chilton Book Company, Trade Division, 1 Chilton Way, Radnor, PA 19089-0230 *tel* 215-964-4100 *fax* 215-964-2926. *General manager:* Christopher J. Kuppig; *executive editor:* Jeff Day; *acquisitions editor:* Susan Clarey. Antiques and collectibles, sewing and crafts, consumer automotive, professional and technical.

Chronicle Books (1967), 275 Fifth Street, San Francisco, CA 94103 *tel* 415-777-7240 *fax* 415-777-2289. *Publisher:* Jack Jensen; *associate publisher:* Caroline Herter; *editor-in-chief:* Nion McEvoy. Cooking, art, fiction, general, children's.

Coffee House Press (1984), 27 N 4th Street, Suite 400, Minneapolis, MN 55401. *Publisher:* Allan Kornblum. Literary fiction and poetry.

*****Columbia University Press,** 562 West 113th Street, New York, NY 10025 *tel* 212-666-1000 *fax* 212-316-3100. *Editor-in-chief:* Kate Wittenberg; *UK:* 1 Oldlands Way, Bognor Regis, West Sussex PO22 9SA *tel* (0243) 842165 *fax* (0243) 842167. Scholarly work in all fields, translations and serious non-fiction of more general interest.

Concordia Publishing House (1869), 3558 S Jefferson Avenue, St Louis, MO 63118 *tel* 314-268-1000 *fax* 314-268-1329. *Executive vp, editorial:* Dr Stephen J. Carter; *chief editor, books:* The Rev. David V. Koch. Religious books, Lutheran perspective. Few freelance MSS accepted; query first.

Contemporary Books Inc., 180 North Stetson, Chicago, IL 60601 *tel* 312-540-4500 *fax* 312-782-2157. *President:* Harvey Plotnick; *vice president and editorial director:* Nancy Crossman; *subsidiary rights:* Christine Albritton. Non-fiction.

*****The Continuum Publishing Company, Inc.** (1980), 370 Lexington Avenue, New York, NY 10017-6503 *tel* 212-532-6006 *fax* 212-532-6039. *Chairman and publisher:* Werner Mark Linz. General non-fiction, education, literature, psychology, politics, sociology, literary criticism, religious studies.

*****Cornell University Press** (including **Comstock Publishing Associates**) (1869), Sage House, 512 East State Street, Ithaca, NY 14850 *tel* 607-277-2338 *fax* 607-277-2374. *Director:* John G. Ackerman. Scholarly books. *Agents overseas:* Trevor Brown Associates, First Floor, Dilke House, Malet Street, London WC1E 7JA *tel* 071-436 1874 *fax* 071-436 1868.

Council Oak Books (1984), 1350 East 15th Street, Tulsa, OK 74120-5801 *tel* 918-587-6454 *fax* 918-583-4995. *Publisher/president:* Michael Hightower; *publishers/vice presidents:* Sally Dennison PhD, Paulette Millichap. Non-fiction: native American, multicultural, life skills, life accounts, Earth awareness, meditation.

The Countryman Press, Inc. (1973), PO Box 175, Maxham Meadow, Woodstock, VT 05091 *tel* 802-457-1049. *Editor-in-chief:* Carl Taylor; *editor (mysteries):* Louis Kannenstine. Mysteries, outdoor recreation guides for anglers, hikers, cyclists, anglers, canoeists and skiers, US travel guides, New England non-fiction, how-to books, country living books, books on nature and the environment, classic reprints and general non-fiction. *No* unsolicited MSS.

Crown Publishing Group, 201 East 50th Street, New York, NY 10022 *tel* 212-572-6117 *fax* 212-572-6192. *President and publisher:* Michelle Sidrane. General fiction, non-fiction, illustrated books.

John Daniel and Company (1980), PO Box 21922, Santa Barbara, CA 93121 *tel* 805-962-1780. *Editor/publisher:* John Daniel; *editor/sales manager:* Susan Daniel. Memoir, short fiction, poetry.

Devin-Adair Publishers, Inc. (1911), 6 North Water Street, Greenwich, CT 06830 *tel* 203-531-7755. Conservative politics, health and ecology, Irish topics, gardening and travel topics, homeopathy and holistic health books.

*Doubleday, division of **Bantam Doubleday Dell Publishing Group Inc.,** 1540 Broadway, New York, NY 10036 *tel* 212-354-6500 *fax* 212-782-9597; *London:* 100 Wigmore Street, W1H 9DR *tel* 071-935 1269. Trade, general fiction and non-fiction. Anchor Books.

Dover Publications, Inc. (1941), 31 E 2nd Street, Mineola, NY 11501 *tel* 516-294-7000 *fax* 516-742-6953. *Vp, editorial:* Stanley Appelbaum. Art, architecture, antiques, crafts, juvenile, food, history, folklore, literary classics, mystery, language, music, math and science, nature, design and ready-to-use art.

Dryden Press, City Center Tower II, 301 Commerce Street, Suite 3700, Fort Worth, TX 76102 *tel* 817-334-7500 *fax* 817-334-0878. *Publisher:* Elizabeth Widdicombe. College textbooks.

*E.P. Dutton, division of Penguin USA, 375 Hudson Street, New York, NY 10014 *tel* 212-366-2000 *fax* 212-366-2666. General publishers. General non-fiction, including biographies, adventure, history, travel; fiction, mysteries, juveniles, quality paperbacks.

*Dutton Children's Books, 375 Hudson Street, 3rd Floor, New York, NY 10014 *tel* 212-366-2600 *fax* 212-366-2011. *President and publisher:* Christopher Franceschelli; *editor in chief:* Lucia Monfried; *executive editor:* Donna Brooks; *managing editor special projects:* Karen Lotz. Picture books, young adult novels, non-fiction photographic books.

Faber and Faber, Inc. (1976), 50 Cross Street, Winchester, MA 01890 *tel* 617-721-1427 *fax* 617-729-2783. *Publisher:* Tom Kelleher; *executive editor:* Fiona McCrae; *senior editor:* Betsy Uhrig. Adult non-fiction: film, popular music, ethnic and cultural works, travelogues, drama and poetry (mostly from London office), anthologies, literary novels.

Facts On File Inc. (1940), 460 Park Avenue South, New York, NY 10016 *tel* 212-683-2244 *cables* Factsfile New York *fax* 212-213-4578. *President:* Thomas C. Conoscenti; *executive vp and publisher:* Martin Greenwald. General reference books and services for colleges, libraries, schools and general public.

Farrar, Straus & Giroux Inc., 19 Union Square West, New York, NY 10003 *tel* 212-741-6900 *cables* Farrarcomp *fax* 212-633-9385. *Senior vp and editor-in-chief:* Jonathan Galassi. General publishers.

Fearon/Janus/Quercus, 500 Harbor Boulevard, Belmont, CA 94002 *tel* 415-592-7810. *Supervising editor:* Stephen Feinstein. Publisher of ESL and special education materials in all academic areas for junior and senior high students and adult basic education; fiction.

Firebrand Books (1986), 141 The Commons, Ithaca, NY 14850 *tel* 607-272-0000. *Editor/publisher:* Nancy K. Bereano. Feminist and lesbian fiction and non-fiction.

Four Walls Eight Windows (1987), 39 West 14th Street, Room 503, New York, NY 10011   *tel* 212-206-8965   *fax* 212-206-8799. *Co-publishers:* John Oakes, Dan Simon. Fiction, graphic works, novels, memoirs, art, African-American studies, current affairs, biography, environment, health.

Samuel French Inc., 45 West 25th Street, New York, NY 10010   *tel* 212-206-8990   *fax* 212-206-1429. Play publishers and authors' representatives (dramatic).

David R. Godine, Publisher Inc. (1970), Horticultural Hall, 300 Massachusetts Avenue, Boston, MA 02115   *tel* 617-536-0761   *fax* 617-421-0934. *President:* David R. Godine; *editorial director:* Mark Polizzotti. Fiction, photography, history, natural history, art, biography, children's.

Greenwillow Books, division of **William Morrow & Co., Inc.,** 1350 Avenue of the Americas, New York, NY 10019   *tel* 212-261-6500   *fax* 212-261-6619. *Senior vice-president/editor-in-chief:* Susan Hirschman. Children's books.

Grosset & Dunlap, Inc., 200 Madison Avenue, New York, NY 10016   *tel* 212-951-8700. *Vp and publisher:* Jane O'Connor. Children's mass market and picture books, series books, activity books.

Grove/Atlantic, Inc., 19 Union Square West, New York, NY 10003   *tel* 212-645-4462   *fax* 212-727-0180. *Publisher:* Morgan Entrekin. MSS of permanent interest, fiction, biography, autobiography, history, current affairs, social science, belles-lettres, natural history. *Imprints:* **Atlantic Monthly Press, Grove Press.**

Grove Press—see **Grove/Atlantic, Inc.**

****Harcourt Brace & Company,** 525 B Street, Suite 1900, San Diego, CA 92101   *tel* 619-231-6616. *President:* Rubin Pfeffer; *managing editor:* Marianna Lee; 15 East 26th Street, New York, NY 10010. General publishers. Fiction, history, biography, etc.; college and school textbooks of all kinds; children's; technical; reference; religious; dictionaries. Imprints: **Holt Rinehart and Winston, Dryden Press, Saunders College.**

****HarperCollins Publishers** (1817), 10 East 53rd Street, New York, NY 10022   *tel* 212-207-7000   *cables* Harpsam, NY   *telex* 12-5741(dom.), 6-2501(intl). *President and chief executive officer:* George Craig. Religious books division: 1160 Battery Street, San Francisco, CA 94111   *tel* 415-477-4400   *fax* 415-477-4444. *London:* HarperCollins Publishers, 77-85 Fulham Palace Road, Hammersmith, London W6 8JB. Fiction, history, biography, poetry, science, travel, juvenile, educational, business, technical, medical and religious. *No* unsolicited material; all submissions must come through a literary agent.

Hastings House, 141 Halstead Avenue, Mamaroneck, NY 10543   *tel* 914-835-4005   *fax* 914-835-1037. *Publisher:* Hy Steirman; *director of operations:* Richard Cadier. Non-fiction, general, consumer, travel, cooking, juveniles and how-to.

****D.C. Heath and Co.,** international division of Raytheon Co., 125 Spring Street, Lexington, MA 02173   *tel* 617-860-1340   *fax* 617-860-1508. *International office manager:* Ruth Thompson. Elementary, secondary, college textbooks.

Hill & Wang (1956), division of **Farrar, Straus & Giroux Inc.,** 19 Union Square West, New York, NY 10003   *tel* 212-741-6900   *telex* 667428   *fax* 212-633-9385. *Editor-in-chief:* Arthur W. Wang; *publisher:* Elisabeth Sifton. General non-fiction, drama, history.

Hippocrene Books, Inc. (1971), 171 Madison Avenue, New York, NY 10016   *tel* 212-685-4371   *fax* 212-779-9338. *President and editorial director:* George Blagowidow; *publisher and director of marketing:* Jacek Galazka. Foreign language books, foreign language dictionaries, travel, military history, Polonia, general trade.

Holiday House (1935), 425 Madison Avenue, New York, NY 10017 *tel* 212-688-0085 *fax* 212-421-6134. *President:* John Briggs; *vp and editor-in-chief:* Margery Cuyler. General children's books.

Holmes & Meier Publishers Inc. (1969), 160 Broadway, East Building, New York, NY 10038 *tel* 212-374-0100 *fax* 212-374-1313. *Executive editor:* Katharine Turok. History, biography, political science, art, costume, Jewish studies, international affairs, women's studies, fiction in translation, Africana publishing.

*****Henry Holt and Company, Inc.** (1866), 115 West 18th Street, New York, NY 10011 *tel* 212-886-9200 *fax* 212-633-0748. *Associate publisher, editor-in-chief adult books:* William Strachan; *associate publisher, editor-in-chief books for young readers:* Brenda Bowen; *editorial director reference books:* Ken Wright; *publisher, Twenty-First Century Books:* Jeanne Vestal; *vp and publisher MIS Press:* Steven Berkowitz. History, biography, nature, science, self-help, novels, mysteries; books for young readers; trade paperback line, computer books.

Holt, Rinehart and Winston, Inc., 1120 S Capital of Texas Highway, Austin, TX 78746 *tel* 512-314-6500. *President:* William A. Talkington.

*****Houghton Mifflin Company** (1832), 222 Berkeley Street, Boston, MA 02116 *tel* 617-351-5000 *telex* 4430255 HMHQ UI. *Executive vp and publisher, trade and reference division:* Joseph A. Kanon. Fiction, biography, history, works of general interest of all kinds, both adult and juvenile; also school and college textbooks in all departments, and standardised tests. Best length: 75,000-180,000 words; juveniles, any reasonable length.

Indiana University Press (1950), 601 North Morton Street, Bloomington, IN 47404-3797 *tel* 812-855-4203 *fax* 812-855-7931. *Director:* John Gallman. African studies, Russian and East European studies, semiotics, literary criticism, music, history, women's studies, Jewish studies, African-American studies, film, folklore, philosophy, medical ethics, archaeology, anthropology.

*****The Johns Hopkins University Press** (1878), 2715 North Charles Street, Baltimore, MD 21218-4319 *tel* 410-516-6971 *fax* 410-516-6968. *Director:* J.G. Goellner. History, literary criticism, classics, politics, economic development, environmental studies, biology, medical genetics, consumer health.

Keats Publishing Inc. (1971), 27 Pine Street, PO Box 876, New Canaan, CT 06840 *tel* 203-966-8721. *Directors:* Nathan Keats (president); Norman Goldfind (vice president, marketing). Natural health, nutrition and medical books.

Alfred A. Knopf Inc. (1915), division of **Random House, Inc.,** 201 East 50th Street, New York, NY 10022 *tel* 212-751-2600 *telegraphic address* Knopf, New York *fax* 212-572-2593. General literature, fiction, belles-lettres, sociology, politics, history, nature, science, etc.

David S. Lake Publishers—now Fearon/Janus/Quercus.

J.B. Lippincott Co. (1792), a Wolters Kluwer company, 227 East Washington Square, Philadelphia, PA 19106 *tel* 215-238-4200 *cables* Lippcot, Phila. *Publishers:* Richard Lampert (medical), Diana Intenzo (nursing). Medical and nursing books and journals.

Little, Brown & Company, 34 Beacon Street, Boston, MA 02108 *tel* 617-227-0730 *cables* Brownlit, Boston. General literature, especially fiction, nonfiction, biography, history, trade paperbacks, books for boys and girls, law, medical books. Art and photography books under the **Bulfinch Press/New York Graphic Society Books** imprint.

Lothrop, Lee & Shepard Books (1859), division of **William Morrow & Co., Inc.**, 1350 Avenue of the Americas, New York, NY 10019 *tel* 212-261-6641 *fax* 212-261-6648. *Vice-president/editor-in-chief:* Susan Pearson. Children's books only.

Lyons & Burford, 31 West 21st Street, New York, NY 10010 *tel* 212-620-9580 *fax* 212-929-1836. *Publishers:* Nick Lyons, Peter Burford. Outdoor sport, natural history, general sports, art.

*McGraw-Hill Book Co., 1221 Avenue of the Americas, New York, NY 10020 *tel* 212-512-2000. *College books:* Sieb Adams; *professional and reference books:* Theodore Nardin. Professional and reference: engineering, scientific, business, architecture, encyclopedias; college textbooks; high school and vocational textbooks: business, secretarial, career; trade books; microcomputer software; training courses for industry.

*Macmillan Publishing—now reference imprint of **Paramount Publishing**.

McPherson & Company (1974), PO Box 1126, 148 Smith Avenue, Kingston, NY 12401 *tel/fax* 914-331-5807. *Publisher:* Bruce R. McPherson. Literary fiction; non-fiction: art criticism, writings by artists, filmmaking, etc; occasional general titles (e.g. anthropology). No poetry. No unsolicited MSS; query first.

Mercury House (1985), Mercury House, 201 Filbert Street, Suite 400, San Francisco, CA 94133 *tel* 415-433-7042 *fax* 415-392-3041. *Publisher:* William Brinton; *executive editor:* Thomas Christensen. Fiction; non-fiction: performing arts, biography, political science, translations.

Milkweed Editions (1979), 528 Hennepin Avenue, Suite 505, Minneapolis, MN 55403 *tel* 612-332-3192 *fax* 612-332-6248. *Publisher/editor:* Emilie Buchwald; *art director:* R.W. Scholes. Fiction, poetry, essays, literature, images & words (collaborations).

*The MIT Press (1961), 55 Hayward Street, Cambridge, MA 02142 *tel* 617-253-5646 *fax* 617-258-6779. *Director:* Frank Urbanowski; *managing editor:* Laurence Cohen. *UK:* The MIT Press, Fitzroy House, 11 Chenies Street, London WC1E 7ET. Architecture and design, cognitive sciences, neuroscience, linguistics, computer science and artificial intelligence, economics and management sciences, aesthetic criticism, philosophy, environment and ecology, natural history.

Morehouse Publishing Co., PO Box 1321, Harrisburg, PA 17105 *tel* 717-541-8130 *fax* 717-541-8128. *President & publisher:* E. Allen Kelley; *vice-president:* Leslie Merrell. Religious books, religious education, texts, seminary texts, children's books.

Morrow Jr. Books, division of **William Morrow & Co., Inc.**, 1350 Avenue of the Americas, New York, NY 10019 *tel* 212-261-6500 *fax* 212-261-6689. *Vp/editor-in-chief:* David Reuther. Children's books only.

William Morrow & Co., Inc., 1350 Avenue of the Americas, New York, NY 10019 *tel* 212-261-6500 *fax* 212-261-6595. Adrian Zackheim (vp, editorial director). General literature, fiction and juveniles. *Imprints:* Greenwillow Books, Lothrop, Lee & Shepard, Morrow Jr Books, Tambourine Books, Mulberry/Beech Tree/Tupelo.

The Naiad Press, Inc. (1973), PO Box 10543, Tallahassee, FL 32302 *tel* 904-539-5965 *fax* 904-539-9731. *Ceo:* Barbara Grier. Lesbian fiction; non-fiction: bibliographies, biographies, essays.

Thomas Nelson, Inc. (1978), Nelson Place at Elm Hill Pike, PO Box 141000, Nashville, TN 37214-1000   *tel* 615-889-9000   *fax* 615-391-5225. *Vp of publishing:* Ken H. Stephens. Bibles, religious, non-fiction and fiction general trade, stationery gift items.

W.W. Norton & Company, Inc., 500 Fifth Avenue, New York, NY 10110   *tel* 212-354-5500   *fax* 212-869-0856. General fiction and non-fiction, music, boating, psychiatry, economics, family therapy, social work, reprints, college texts, science.

Orchard Books (1987), 95 Madison Avenue, New York, NY 10016   *tel* 212-686-7070   *fax* 212-213-6435. *President and publisher:* Neal Porter. Books for children and young adults; picture books, fiction and photo essays.

Ottenheimer Publishers Inc. (1890), 10 Church Lane, Baltimore, MD 21208   *tel* 410-484-2100   *fax* 410-486-8301. *Directors:* Allan T. Hirsh, Jr, Allan T. Hirsh, III. Juvenile and adult non-fiction, reference.

*The Overlook Press, 149 Wooster Street, 4th Floor, New York, NY 10012   *tel* 212-477-7162   *fax* 212-477-7525. *Editorial director:* Tracy Carns. Non-fiction, fiction, children's books.

*Oxford University Press, Inc., 200 Madison Avenue, New York, NY 10016   *tel* 212-679-7300   *fax* 212-725-2972. Scholarly, professional, reference, bibles, college textbooks, religion, medicals, music.

*Pantheon Books, division of **Random House, Inc.,** 201 East 50th Street, New York, NY 10022   *tel* 212-572-2564   *fax* 212-572-6030. Fiction, mysteries, belles-lettres, translations, philosophy, history and art, sociology, psychology, juvenile.

*Paramount Publishing, 1230 Avenue of the Americas, New York, NY 10020   *tel* 212-698-7000. *Chairman and chief executive officer:* Jonathan Newcomb. General fiction, non-fiction, children's and young adult books, multimedia products, travel guides, reference books; educational books, multimedia materials, services and integrated learning systems; English-as-a-Second Language and English Language Teaching materials; computer-use books, business and professional books, audio-visual products, newsletters, training programs and computer-based learning systems.

*Pelican Publishing Company (1926), PO Box 3110, Gretna, LA 70054   *tel* 504-368-1175   *fax* 504-368-1195. *Publisher & president:* Milburn Calhoun. Art and architecture, cookbooks, travel, music, children's.

*Penguin USA, 375 Hudson Street, New York, NY 10014   *tel* 212-366-2000   *fax* 212-366-2666. General books, fiction, non-fiction, biography, sociology, poetry, art, travel, children's books.

The Permanent Press and Second Chance Press (1978), RD 2, Noyac Road, Sag Harbor, NY 11963   *tel/fax* 516-725-1101. *Directors:* Martin Shepard, Judith Shepard. Quality fiction.

Clarkson N. Potter, Inc. (1962), 201 East 50th Street, Md 5-4, New York, NY 10022   *tel* 212-751-2600   *fax* 212-572-6181. *Editorial director:* Lauren Shakely; *art director:* Howard Klein. Life style, food, biography, travel, self-help, photography; quality fiction.

Praeger Publishers, Greenwood Publishing Group, Inc., 88 Post Road West, Westport, CT 06881   *tel* 203-226-3571   *fax* 203-222-1502. *Editor-in-chief:* James R. Dunton. Non-fiction on international relations, social sciences, economics, reference, contemporary issues, urban affairs, psychology, education.

*Prentice Hall—now imprint of **Paramount Publishing.**

Price Stern Sloan (1963), 11150 Olympic Boulevard, Los Angeles, CA 90064   *tel* 310-477-6100   *fax* 310-445-3933. *Publisher:* Tanni Tytel. Children's books: pop-ups, novelty/lift-flaps, activity books, board books.

*The Putnam Berkley Group Inc., 200 Madison Avenue, New York, NY 10016   *tel* 212-951-8400. All types of literature; history, economics, political science, natural science, and standard literature; fiction; children's books.

*Rand McNally, PO Box 7600, Chicago, IL 60680   *tel* 708-392-8100. *Chairman and ceo:* Andrew McNally IV; *executive editor:* Jon M. Leverenz. Maps, guides, atlases, educational publications, globes and children's geographical titles and atlases.

*Random House, Inc., 201 East 50th Street, New York, NY 10022   *tel* 212-751-2600. General publishers.

Rawson Associates, 866 Third Avenue, New York, NY 10022   *tel* 212-702-3436   *fax* 212-605-3099. *Vice-chairman, publications committee:* Eleanor S. Rawson. Adult non-fiction.

Rizzoli International Publications, Inc. (1976), 300 Park Avenue South, New York, NY 10010   *tel* 212-387-3400   *fax* 212-387-3535/3636. *President/ceo:* Judith R. Joseph. Art, architecture, photography, fashion, gardening, design, gift books, cookbooks; children's books.

Rodale Press, Inc. (1930), 33 East Minor Street, Emmaus, PA 18098   *tel* 610-967-5171   *fax* 610-967-8961. *President, book division:* Pat Corpora; *editor-in-chief, book division:* Bill Gottlieb. Health, women's health, men's health, fitness, gardening, woodworking, do-it-yourself, quilting, crafts, healthy cooking, psychological self-help.

Ronin Publishing Inc., Box 1035, Berkeley, CA 94701   *tel* 510-540 6278. New Age business, controlled substances, visionary, underground comix. Preliminary letter essential; no unsolicited MSS or artwork.

Routledge, Inc., 29 West 35th Street, New York, NY 10001   *tel* 212-244-3336   *telegraphic address* Algernon, New York   *telex* 6801368   *fax* 212-563-2269. *Directors:* John von Knorring (president), Edward R. Sands (secretary/treasurer), William P. Germano (editorial). Literary criticism, history, philosophy, psychology and psychiatry, politics, women's studies, education, anthropology, lesbian and gay studies, classical studies.

Rutledge Hill Press (1982), 211 Second Avenue North, Nashville, TN 37219   *tel* 615-244-2700   *fax* 615-244-2978. *President:* Lawrence M. Stone; *vice president:* Ronald E. Pitkin. Regional books, cookbooks, books on quilts, gift books.

*St Martin's Press, Inc., 175 Fifth Avenue, New York, NY 10010   *tel* 212-674-5151   *telegraphic address* Saintmart, New York   *fax* 212-420-9314. Trade, reference, college.

*Saunders College, The Public Ledger Building, 150 South Independence Mall West, Suite 1250, Philadelphia, PA 19106   *tel* 215-238-5500   *fax* 215-238-5660. College textbooks.

*Schocken Books Inc. (1945), imprint of **Random House, Inc.,** 201 East 50th Street, New York, NY 10022   *tel* 212-572-2564   *fax* 212-572-6030. Education, Judaica and holocaust studies, women's studies, social sciences, literature, literary criticism.

*Scribner's (1846)—now imprint of **Paramount Publishing.**

*Simon & Schuster—now trade imprint and children's imprint of **Paramount Publishing.**

Soho Press Inc. (1986), 853 Broadway, New York, NY 10003 *tel* 212-260-1900 *fax* 212-260-1902. *Publisher:* Juris Jurjevics; *associate publisher:* Laura Hruska. Literary fiction, commercial fiction, mystery, thrillers, travel, memoir, general non-fiction.

*Stanford University Press, Stanford, CA 94305-2235 *tel* 415-723-9434 *fax* 415-725-3457. *Acting director:* Norris Pope. Scholarly non-fiction.

Strawberry Hill Press (1973), 3848 SE Division Street, Portland, OR 97202 *tel* 503-235-5989. *President:* Jean-Louis Brindamour PhD; *executive vice-president and art director:* Ku Fu-Sheng; *treasurer:* Edward E. Serres. Health, self-help, cookbooks, philosophy, religion, history, drama, science and technology, biography, mystery, Third World. No unsolicited MSS; preliminary letter and return postage essential.

*Taplinger Publishing Co., Inc. (1955), PO Box 1324, New York, NY 10185 *tel* 201-432-3257 *telegraphic address* Taplinpub. *Vice president:* Theodore Rosenfeld. Calligraphy, literature (including translated works into English), music, art and art criticism, non-fiction.

Theatre Arts Books, division of **Routledge, Inc.,** 29 West 35th Street, New York, NY 10001 *tel* 212-244-3336. *President:* John von Knorring; *editorial director:* William Germano. Successor to the book publishing department of Theatre Arts (1921-1948). Theatre, performance, dance and allied books – acting techniques, costume, tailoring, etc.; a few plays.

*Ticknor & Fields (1980), 215 Park Avenue South, New York, NY 10003 *tel* 212-420-5800 *fax* 212-420-5850. *Editorial director:* John Herman. Subsidiary of **Houghton Mifflin Company.** Fiction, non-fiction, including history, current events, essays, biographies.

Tor Books (1980), 175 Fifth Avenue, 14th Floor, New York, NY 10010 *tel* 212-388-0100 *fax* 212-388-0191. *President and publisher:* Tom Doherty. Subsidiary of **St Martin's Press, Inc.** Fiction: general, historical, western, suspense, mystery, horror, science fiction, fantasy, humour, juvenile, classics (English language); non-fiction: adult and juvenile.

*Charles E. Tuttle Co., Inc. (1949), 28 South Main Street (PO Box 410), Rutland, VT 05701-0410 *tel* 802-773-8930/802-773-8229 *cables* Tuttbooks *fax* 802-773-6993. *President:* Peter Ackroyd; and Suido I-chome, 2-6 Bunkyo-ku, Tokyo 112, Japan *tel* 811-7106-9 *cables* Tuttbooks, Tokyo *telex* 0272-3170 TUTBKS J *fax* 811-6953. *President:* Nicholas J. Ingleton. Oriental art, culture, Eastern philosophy, martial arts, health.

The University of Alabama Press (1945), Box 870380, Tuscaloosa, AL 35487 *tel* 205-348-5180 *fax* 205-348-9201. *Director:* Malcolm M. MacDonald; *managing editor:* Elizabeth May. American and Southern history, rhetoric and speech communication, Judaic studies, linguistics, literary criticism, anthropology and archaeology, history of American science and technology.

The University of Arkansas Press (1980), The University of Arkansas, 201 Ozark Street, Fayetteville, AR 72701 *tel* 501-575-3246 *fax* 501-575-6044. *Director:* Miller Williams. History, literary criticism, biography, poetry, fiction.

University of California Press, 2120 Berkeley Way, Berkeley, CA 94720. *Director:* James H. Clark. Publishes scholarly books, books of general interest, series of scholarly monographs and scholarly journals. *UK:* University Presses of California, Columbia, and Princeton, 1 Oldlands Way, Bognor Regis, West Sussex PO22 9SA *tel* (0243) 842165 *fax* (0243) 842167.

*University of Chicago Press, 5801 South Ellis Avenue, Chicago, IL 60637 *tel* 312-702-7700 *fax* 312-702-9756. *Director:* Morris Philipson. Scholarly books and monographs, religious and scientific books, general trade books, and 54 scholarly journals.

University of Illinois Press (1918), 1325 South Oak Street, Champaign, IL 61820 *tel* 217-333-0950 *fax* 217-244-8082. *Director:* Richard L. Wentworth. American studies (history, music, literature), poetry, working-class and ethnic studies, communications, regional studies, art and photography, architecture, philosophy and women's studies.

The University of Massachussetts Press (1964), PO Box 429, Amherst, MA 01004-0429 *tel* 413-545-2217 *cables* Masspress *fax* 413-545-1226. *Director:* Bruce G. Wilcox. Scholarly books and works of general interest: American studies and history, black and ethnic studies, women's studies, cultural criticism, architecture and environmental design, literary criticism, poetry, philosophy, political science, sociology, books of regional interest.

The University of Michigan Press (1930), 839 Greene Street, PO Box 1104, Ann Arbor, MI 48106 *tel* 313-764-4388 *fax* 313-936-0456. *Director:* Colin Day; *assistant director:* Mary Erwin; *executive editor:* LeAnn Fields; *managing editor:* Christina Milton. Scholarly works in literature, classics, history, theatre, women's studies, political science, anthropology, economics, archaeology; textbooks in English as a second language; regional trade titles.

University of Missouri Press (1958), 2910 LeMone Boulevard, Columbia, MO 65201 *tel* 314-882-7641 *fax* 314-884-4498. *Director/editor-in-chief:* Beverly Jarrett; *poetry/fiction editor:* Clair Willcox. American and European history, American, British and Latin American literary criticism, journalism, political philosophy, art history, regional studies; poetry and short fiction.

University of New Mexico Press (1929), 1720 Lomas Boulevard NE, Albuquerque, NM 87131-1591 *tel* 505-277-2346 *fax* 505-277-9270. *Director:* Elizabeth C. Hadas. Western history, anthropology and archaeology, Latin American studies, photography, multicultural literature.

*The University of North Carolina Press (1922), PO Box 2288, 116 South Boundary Street, Chapel Hill, NC 27514 *tel* 919-966-3561 *fax* 919-966-3829. *Director:* Kate Douglas Torrey. American history, American studies, Southern studies, European history, women's studies, Latin American studies, political science, anthropology and folklore, classics, regional trade.

*University of Oklahoma Press (1928), 1005 Asp Avenue, Norman, OK 73019-0445 *tel* 405-325-5111 *fax* 405-325-4000. *Director:* George Bauer, History of American West, American Indian studies, Mesoamerican studies, classic studies, women's studies, natural history.

University of Pennsylvania Press (1869), Blockley Hall, 418 Service Drive, Philadelphia, PA 19104-6097 *tel* 215-898-6261 *telegraphic address* PNSYL PRESS *fax* 215-898-0404. *Director:* Thomas M. Rotell. American and British history, anthropology, art, architecture, biological sciences, business, computer science, cultural studies, economics, folklore, history of science, technology and medicine, human rights, law, linguistics, literature, medicine, music theory, Pennsylvania regional studies, women's studies.

*University of Washington Press (1909), PO Box 50096, Seattle, WA 98145-5096 *tel* 206-543-4050 *telex* 4740096 UWUI *fax* 206-543-3932. *Director:* Donald R. Ellegood; *editor-in-chief:* Naomi B. Pascal. Anthropology, Asian-American studies, Asian studies, art and art history, aviation history, environmental studies, forest history, literary criticism, marine sciences, music, regional studies, including history and culture of the Pacific Northwest and

Alaska, Native American studies, resource management and public policy, Scandinavian studies.

Van Nostrand Reinhold (1848), 115 Fifth Avenue, New York, NY 10003 *tel* 212-254-3232 *cables* Readbooks Newyork *telex* 272562 VNRC UR *fax* 212-254-9499, 212-475-2548. *President & ceo:* Brian Heer; *vp, editorial:* Marianne Russell. Reference, encyclopedias, handbooks: architecture, design, occupational health and safety, computer science and engineering, hospitality and tourism, and technology management.

*****Viking**—see **Penguin USA.**

Walker & Co. (1960), 435 Hudson Street, New York, NY 10014 *tel* 212-727-8300 *fax* 212-727-0984. *President:* Ramsey R. Walker; *mystery:* Michael Seidman; *juvenile:* Emily Easton. General publishers, biography, popular science, health, business, mystery/suspense, westerns, juveniles, early childhood education, parenting, self-help.

Warner Books Inc. (1973), 1271 Avenue of the Americas, 9th Floor, New York, NY 10020 *tel* 212-522-7200 *fax* 212-522-7991. *President:* Laurence J. Kirshbaum. Fiction and non-fiction, hardcovers, trade paperbacks, mass market paperbacks.

Franklin Watts, 95 Madison Avenue, New York, NY 10016 *tel* 212-951-2650 *fax* 212-689-7803. *Vp and editorial director:* John W. Selfridge. School and library books for grades K-12.

Westminster/John Knox Press, 100 Witherspoon Street, Louisville, KY 40202-1396 *tel* 502-569-5043 *fax* 502-569-5018. *Editorial manager:* Stephanie Egnotovich. Religious, academic, reference, general.

Whispering Coyote Press, Inc. (1989), 480 Newbury Street, Suite 104, Danvers, MA 01923 *tel* 508-922-7273 *fax* 508-921-7113. *President:* Lou Alpert. Children's picture books.

Workman Publishing Co. (1968), 708 Broadway, New York, NY 10003 *tel* 212-254-5900 *fax* 212-254-8098. *President:* Peter Workman. General non-fiction, calendars.

Writers and Readers Publishing Inc. (1974), PO Box 461, Village Station, New York, NY 10014 *tel* 212-982-3158 *fax* 212-777-4924. *Publisher:* Glenn Thompson; *associate publisher:* Deborah Dyson. For Beginners series, non-fiction, children's books, poetry.

Writer's Digest Books, 1507 Dana Avenue, Cincinnati, OH 45207 *tel* 513-531-2222 *fax* 513-531-4744. Market Directories, books for writers, photographers and songwriters. **North Light Books:** fine art and graphic arts instruction books; **Betterway Books:** how-to in home building, remodelling, woodworking, sports, home organisation, theatre.

*****Yale University Press,** 302 Temple Street, New Haven, CT 06511 *postal address* 92A Yale Station, New Haven, CT 06520 *tel* 203-432-0960 *telex* 963531 *fax* 203-432-0948/2394. *Director:* John G. Ryden; *London:* 23 Pond Street, Hampstead, NW3 2PN *tel* 071-431 4422 *fax* 071-431 3755. Scholarly books and art books.

Writing and Illustrating Children's Books

CAROLINE SHELDON

Sammy the Squirrel, Cyril the Slug, Teddy the Traffic Light . . . mention such titles to a group of children's book editors and they all recognise yesterday's pile of rejected manuscripts. To a man (or in fact generally to a woman) they are looking for something with more originality and punch. The best way to get a feel of what children's publishers are publishing today is to read a large range of children's books published now and over the last thirty years. They cover an enormous spectrum in length and content – from simple, highly-illustrated picture book stories to full length novels for teenagers, and most children's publishers' lists cover the whole range. The following is a brief *vade mecum* for the submission of children's manuscripts.

WRITING CHILDREN'S BOOKS

Observe all the rules of submission as for other work – a doubled-spaced, attractively presented manuscript; covering letter giving information about yourself and your writing; return postage; no bulky ring binders that burst open in the post. Mention any experience of working with children.

PICTURE BOOKS

There is limited opportunity for authors to get involved in bath books or board books, and therefore picture books are generally the youngest end of the age range for writers. The high cost of printing in full colour necessitates a long print run of copies to keep the unit cost down. To achieve this, collaboration with an American, European or other foreign publisher is essential. Thus a publisher has to believe a book is really going to make its mark in the international market before taking it on. It is a very competitive field, but ask most publishers what they are short of and they will say good picture book texts – which just proves how difficult they are to write successfully. Almost all picture books are 32 pages long with 12-14 spreads (i.e. double-pages) of full colour illustration. The number of words varies from none (it has been done; the author provided the storyline to which the artist worked) to a maximum of about 2500. The book has to encompass a big enough idea to make it something of an event, yet not deal with issues too wide to resolve within the limits of the page size and design. A narrative with a strong beginning, middle and end is needed to encourage the reader to turn the pages. Even some successful authors in the area find their publisher or agent may reject five stories before one magically slips into place. So be warned, it's tough . . .

Picture book manuscripts should be typed as a series of numbered pages each with its own text. Detailed descriptions of the illustrations and instructions to the illustrator are almost always a mistake. However, if there is something that should be included in the picture, but this is not clear from the text, this should be pointed out.

YOUNGER FICTION

This area of publishing is designed for children who are reading their first whole novels. Texts tend to be anything from 2000 to 7500 words long; in many cases the books will be illustrated with much line illustration breaking up the words on the page. Generally, publishers don't want a use of restricted vocabulary, but writers should remember that, particularly at the bottom end of the age range, they are writing for children who have just learnt to read. Novels for this age range can be published as individual books but often publishers put them out under an umbrella series name. It is an enormous step forward in getting your book placed to have investigated a series before approaching the publisher and checked that your book fits in to that series in terms of length and interest level. You can indicate in a covering letter that you have planned that it will be illustrated but don't give illustration notes in the manuscript.

The following are some currently published series with the approximate word length of the manuscript and the age group at which the books are aimed.

Publisher	Series name	Word length	Age group	Comments
Andersen Press	Tigers	3000-5000	6-9	B&w illustrations on every spread
A. & C. Black/ HarperCollins	Jets	2500	6-8	B&w illustrations on every page
	Jumbo Jets	4000-5000	7-9	B&w illustrations on every page
Blackie	Blackie Bears	2500	5-7	B&w illustrations on every page
	Story Factory	6000-8000	6-8	B&w illustrations
Corgi	Young Corgi	4000-6000	5-8	Extensively illustrated in b&w
Hutchinson	Tigers	3000-5000	6-9	B&w illustrations on every spread
Hamish Hamilton	Antelopes	7500	6-9	B&w illustrations throughout
	Gazelles	2500	5-8	B&w illustrations throughout
	Cartwheels	1000	4-8	Picture story books illustrated in full colour
HarperCollins	Beginner Readers	2000	6-8	Full colour illustrations
Heinemann	Bananas	3000	7-9	Full colour illustrations
	Superchamps	6000	9-11	Full colour illustrations
Hodder & Stoughton	Hedgehogs	1000	4-7	Full colour illustrations
Simon & Schuster	Storybooks	2000-3000	6-9	Full colour and b&w illustrations
	Dart	7000-10,000	8-10	B&w illustrations
Pan Macmillan	Flippers	2 × 1250-word stories	6-9	B&w throughout
Methuen	Read Aloud	8000	5-9	B&w line illustrations
Puffin Books	Ready, Steady, Read	1000-2000	5-7	Integrated b&w illustrations
Viking	Kites	7500-8000	7-9	B&w illustrations throughout
	Read Alone	2000-3000	6-8	B&w illustrations on every spread

GENERAL FICTION

Children's novels for 9 plus tend to be published as individual books. Generally, they are shorter than children's books read by previous generations. Any books over 40,000 words will have to face the problems of a higher price than the publisher would like. Each book stands on its own merits and publishers are looking for authors whose work they like and whom they believe will go on to write a number of books for their list.

NON-FICTION

Non-fiction is an area almost exclusively covered by specialists. Some publishers have much of their non-fiction written by their own staff. If you are interested in this area, nothing can replace a research trip to a good children's library or bookshop to establish who is publishing what, and how your work or field of interest could fit in.

ILLUSTRATING CHILDREN'S BOOKS

Illustrating children's books is a highly professional field but one in which there is always room for new talent. Most illustrators working in children's books have an art school background but there are also those who have come to it without formal training. The work available varies from illustrations for full colour picture books, to jackets and black-and-white line illustrations for novels, to non-fiction illustration.

Illustrators looking for work in this area should try to make appointments to show their portfolios to either the Art Director or Children's Book Editor at a publishing house and to show their work to suitable agents. A portfolio should show as wide a range of work as possible – it is well worth working up some line black-and-white illustrations for children's novels for the 7-10 age range since so much bread-and-butter work is commissioned in this area. Once you have achieved this, people are more likely to be interested in spending time with you developing your special picture book project. The main complaints of those who look at prospective illustrators' portfolios is that the work shown is too stylised and sophisticated, and there is not an obvious application to children's book illustration. If you find it difficult to get an appointment, send in a photocopied folder of samples of your work together with a letter outlining the type of work for which you are looking.

My advice would always be to send colour photocopies of work, never the original artwork; even if the photocopies don't do full justice to the colour, publishers are experienced at spotting the sort of quality that makes them want to see more. Another useful tool can be to put some sample slides of your illustration work into the Association of Illustrators' Image File slide bank (see page 627).

WHICH COMES FIRST – THE WRITER OR THE ILLUSTRATOR?

Unless you are best buddies with a best selling illustrator or writer, it is best to present your work individually. It is an unwanted complication to have wonderful artwork tied in to an amateurish text, or a nice text illustrated by an artist whose work won't stand up in the very competitive picture book market. Publishers are experienced in matching the work of writers and artists and my advice is that the individual work should stand on its own. Having said that, at the younger end of children's publishing, life is much simpler if you are a writer/illustrator.

Classified Index of UK Children's Book Publishers and Book Packagers

Addresses for UK book publishers start on page 146 and for book packagers on page 262.

Picture Books

Book publishers

ABC, All Books for Children
Andersen Press
Bantam
Barefoot Books
BBC Books
David Bennett Books
A. & C. Black
Blackie Children's Books
Bloomsbury Children's Books
Bodley Head Children's Books
Brimax Books
Jonathan Cape Children's Books
J.M. Dent
André Deutsch Children's Books
Dorling Kindersley
Dragon's World
Faber & Faber
Fantail
Floris Books
Gallery Children's Books
Victor Gollancz

Hamish Hamilton Children's Books
HarperCollins Publishers
Hawk Books
Hazar Publishing
Heinemann Young Books
Hippo Books
Hodder & Stoughton
Hunt & Thorpe
Hutchinson Children's Books
Kingfisher
Ladybird Books
Frances Lincoln
Lion Publishing
Little, Brown and Company (UK)
Peter Lowe (Eurobook Ltd)
Lutterworth Press
Macmillan Children's Books
Julia MacRae Books
Magi Publications
Mammoth
Mantra

Medici Society
Methuen Children's Books
Michael O'Mara Books
Orchard Books
Orion Children's Books
Oxford University Press
Pavilion Books
Piccadilly Press
Puffin
Red Fox
Reinhardt Books
Simon & Schuster Young Books
Spindlewood
Tamarind
Tango Books
Transworld Publishers
Usborne Publishing
Victoria House Publishing
Viking Children's Books
Walker Books
Frederick Warne
World International Publishing

Book packagers

Aladdin Books
Albion Press
Beanstalk Books
Breslich & Foss

Graham-Cameron Publishing
Angus Hudson
Mathew Price
Sadie Fields Productions

Teeney Books
The Templar Company
Tucker Slingsby
Zigzag Publishing

Fiction

Book publishers

Adlib
J.A. Allen (pony-related only)
Andersen Press
Bantam
Barefoot Books
BBC Books
David Bennett Books
A. & C. Black
Blackie Children's Books
Bloomsbury Children's Books

Bodley Head Children's Books
Brimax Books
Canongate Press
Jonathan Cape Children's Books
Child's Play (International)
J.M. Dent
André Deutsch Children's Books
Dorling Kindersley

Faber & Faber
Fantail
Floris Books
Victor Gollancz
Hamish Hamilton Children's Books
Patrick Hardy Books
HarperCollins Publishers
Hawk Books
Heinemann Young Books

Hippo
Hodder & Stoughton
Hutchinson Children's Books
Kingfisher
Frances Lincoln
Lion Publishing
Peter Lowe (Eurobook Ltd)
Lutterworth Press
Macmillan Children's Books
Julia MacRae Books
Mammoth

Mantra Publishing
Methuen Children's Books
Michael O'Mara Books
Orchard Books
Orion Children's Books
Oxford University Press
Piccadilly Press
Point
Puffin
Red Fox
Simon & Schuster Young Books

Spindlewood
Tango Books
Thomson-Leng Publications
Titan Books (graphic novels)
Transworld Publishers
Usborne Publishing
Victoria House Publishing
Viking Children's Books
Walker Books
The Women's Press
World International Publishing

Book packagers

Albion Press
Beanstalk Books

Oyster Books
Mathew Price

Signpost Books
Touchstone Publishing

Non-Fiction

Book publishers

ABC, All Books for Children
Atlantic Europe Publishing Co.
Bantam
BBC Books
Belitha Press
David Bennett Books
A. & C. Black
Boxtree
Brimax Books
Child's Play International
J.M. Dent
André Deutsch Children's
  Books
Dorling Kindersley
Dragon's World
Exley Publications
Fantail
Geddes & Grosset
Hamlyn Children's Books

HarperCollins Publishers
Heinemann Young Books
Henderson Publishing
Hippo
Hodder & Stoughton
Kingfisher
Ladybird Books
Frances Lincoln
Lion Publishing
Little, Brown and Company
  (UK)
Peter Lowe (Eurobook Ltd)
Lutterworth Press
Macmillan Children's Books
Mantra Publishing
Medici Society
Michelin Tyre
New Orchard Editions
Oxford University Press

Pavilion Books
Piccadilly Press
Puffin
Salamander Books
Simon & Schuster Young Books
Souvenir Press
Tango Books
Transworld Publishers
Two-Can Publishing
Usborne Publishing
Walker Books
Frederick Warne
Watts Books
Wayland
The Women's Press
World International Publishing
Young Library

Book packagers

Aladdin Books
Albion Press
Beanstalk Books
Bender Richardson White
Book Packaging and Marketing
Breslich & Foss
Brown Wells and Jacobs

Philip Clark
Earthscape Editions
Graham-Cameron Publishing
Lionheart Books
Marshall Editions
Oyster Books
Mathew Price

Signpost Books
The Templar Company
Touchstone Publishing
Tucker Slingsby
Zigzag Publishing
Zoe Books

Other
Activity and novelty
Book publishers

Andersen Press
Atlantic Europe Publishing Co.
BBC Books
Belitha Press

Blackie Children's Books
Bloomsbury Children's Books
Brimax Books
Child's Play International

Dorling Kindersley
Dragon's World
Exley Publications
Floris Books

W. Foulsham & Co.
Geddes & Grosset
Hamlyn Children's Books
Hazar Publishing
Heinemann Young Books
Henderson Publishing
Hippo
Impact Books
Kingfisher
Ladybird Books
Frances Lincoln

Lion Publishing
Macmillan Children's Books
Mammoth
Methuen Children's Books
Michelin Tyre
Michael O'Mara Books
Orchard Books
Orion Children's Books
Oxford University Press
Pavilion Books
Puffin

Salamander Books
Simon & Schuster Young Books
Tango Books
Transworld Publishers
Two-Can Publishing
Usborne Publishing
Victoria House Publishing
Walker Books
Frederick Warne
World International Publishing

Book packagers

Aladdin Books
Beanstalk Books
Bellew Publishing
Book Packaging and Marketing
Breslich & Foss
Brown Wells and Jacobs

Earthscape Editions
Graham-Cameron Publishing
Angus Hudson
Oyster Books
Mathew Price
Sadie Fields Productions

Signpost Books
Teeney Books
The Templar Company
Tucker Slingsby
Zigzag Publishing
Zoe Books

Poetry

Book publishers

Andersen Press
Bantam
A. & C. Black
Blackie Children's Books
Bodley Head Children's Books
Jonathan Cape Children's
  Books
André Deutsch Children's
  Books
Faber & Faber

HarperCollins Publishers
Heinemann Young Books
Hutchinson Children's Books
Kingfisher
Frances Lincoln
Lutterworth Press
Macmillan Children's Books
Mammoth
Methuen Children's Books
Orchard Books

Oxford University Press
Piccadilly Press
Puffin
Red Fox
Simon & Schuster Young Books
Transworld Publishers
Usborne Publishing
Viking Children's Books
Walker Books

Book packagers

Albion Press

Beanstalk Books

Religion

Book publishers

Burns & Oates
Gallery Children's Books
Hamlyn Children's Books
HarperCollins Publishers
Angus Hudson
Hunt & Thorpe

Kingsway Publications
Lion Publishing
Lutterworth Press
Marshall Pickering
Medici Society
The Mothers' Union

Oxford University Press
St Pauls
Salvationist Publishing and
  Supplies
Scripture Union Publishing
Victoria House Publishing

Book packagers

Albion Press
Graham-Cameron Publishing

Angus Hudson
Marshall Editions

Oyster Books

Miscellaneous

Book publishers

Boxtree (film/TV tie-ins)
Brown, Son & Ferguson
  (Scout/Guide)

Doctor Who (fan books)
Fantail (film/TV tie-ins)

Gairm Publications (Gaelic)
Y Lolfa Cyf. (Welsh)

Book packagers

Bender Richardson White
  (multi-media)

Ventura Publishing
  (*Spot* books by Eric Hill)

LITERARY AGENTS FOR CHILDREN'S BOOKS

The following literary agents are prepared to consider work suitable for children's book illustration, see listing on page 406; see also the art agents listing on page 339.

Greene & Heaton Ltd (Susan Elliott)
A.M. Heath & Co Ltd (Michael Thomas)
Lemon Unna & Durbridge Ltd (Hilary Delamere)
The Peters, Fraser & Dunlop Group Ltd (Rosemary Canter)
Murray Pollinger (Gina Pollinger)
Rosemary Sandberg Ltd
Caroline Sheldon Literary Agency
Ed Victor Ltd (Sophie Hicks)

Who are *you*?

You, as a writer, cannot keep your values hidden. As Peter Hollindale said, they will be revealed in everything you write. When you are starting on a book for children, it is worth spending time examining your values, knowing that these are what you are passing on to another generation whose circumstances may be very different from yours. If you have no doubts, then press ahead, concentrating on the words that will most exactly reproduce the scene and the characters that are in your mind. It is then up to your editor to make the first response, to say what impression has be transmitted to the *reader's* mind. Where the two don't match – that is where the editorial work begins, and at the same time it is the editor's responsibility to point out words that may be misunderstood, that are discriminatory or may cause offence, just as it is the editor's job to look out for any words that could be thought libellous and therefore the subject of legal action. (This is very unlikely to occur in a book for children, but your contract should include a clause which allows your publisher to carry insurance against any legal proceedings resulting from libellous statements.)

from *Writing for Children* by Margaret Clark (A & C Black, £7.99)

Pictures into Print

DAVID ASKHAM

Imagine completing a book-length manuscript, accompanied by a fine selection of your own photographs, only to discover that the publisher requires colour *transparencies*, whereas your illustrations are in the form of colour *prints*!

To an author such a set-back can be highly demoralising. Apart from the frustrations of lost time and opportunities, there is the daunting prospect of a major re-shoot of the photography, a costly conversion of negatives into transparencies, or facing up to hiring photographs from a picture library at a cost probably not included in the original budget.

Of course the street-wise photographer would probably not make such a fundamental mistake. Increasingly, however, more and more writers are undertaking the provision of their own photographs to illustrate their written work. And why not? Modern cameras are well-endowed with automatic features to simplify the task and are quite capable of yielding results perfectly acceptable for reproduction.

So this article is intended primarily for writers who wish to make a success of supplying their own photography. It will not transform them into multi-talented professional photographers. That would be wildly optimistic. Rather it will help them avoid basic mistakes, such as that mentioned earlier, and give some useful pointers to success.

It should be stressed, however, that an author should know and respect the upper limits of his or her photographic capabilities. A publisher will not thank you for second-rate results. If in doubt, consider engaging a talented colleague, though your agreement needs to take account of the ultimate division of labour. At all times be honest with your editor about the degree of confidence you have in providing acceptable photography.

On the positive side, many authors have acquired and developed photographic skills to the point where their work is highly accomplished in its own right. But first – back to basics.

BASIC REQUIREMENTS

Before embarking on any photography it is essential first to elicit a publisher's or editor's requirements. In the case of a book-length project the contract should set out, precisely, what the author accepts and is obliged to produce in terms of numbers of pictures and their breakdown, where appropriate, into colour or monochrome images. With illustrated features, it is less usual to have a written contract prior to production. Nevertheless, a letter should spell out the salient facts concerning the provision of pictures.

The question of fees and reproduction rights should also be addressed, not only for text but also for the illustrations. Publishers have budgets for their editorial needs and prior agreement on fees is essential if the contributing author is not to finish the commitment unwittingly well out of pocket. While photographic film may appear a relatively inexpensive item, travel to distant locations can inflate overall costs. Thought, therefore, must be given to the question of expenses.

Where colour is concerned, transparencies (derived from colour reversal or slide film) provide the better source for high quality reproduction than do colour prints. Gradually this situation may change as reproduction techniques continue to develop. To be safe, however, always check with your publisher before deviating from industry standards. If in any doubt when, for example, you are producing pilot material to form the basis of a book proposal, do use colour slide film. Then, if the proposal is accepted, you have already made a valuable start with your photography.

Editors rarely influence the choice of pictorial content of images produced by authors, provided the pictures offered meet certain criteria and accepted standards. So, while the author would appear to enjoy unbridled freedom in deciding what pictures to take and supply to the publisher, the editor will only be satisfied if your pictures are truly relevant to the manuscript and the aim of your work, and are also of a satisfactory quality. Let us now look at these aspects in more detail.

PICTURE RELEVANCE

Images should complement and help to clarify the text. Additionally they can beautify and add interest. Picture subjects often suggest themselves. However there is a potential trap in sacrificing relevance when the most appropriate pictures are unavailable or difficult to acquire.

Take an example of a non-fiction book about London Midland and Scottish Railway locomotives which would clearly require illustrations of some, if not all, of the models described. It would be quite misleading to intermix pictures of the London and North Western Railway locomotives unless a specific point of comparison or contrast was being made. Without such justification, readers could become confused, misled and eventually lose interest in the book. The author's credibility would suffer. Fortunately such lack of relevance should be spotted at the editorial stage and the author would be required to rectify the error.

A biographer seeking to illustrate the boyhood home environment of an historical figure would be lucky indeed to find the actual dwelling, let alone the atmosphere of the period, unless immortalised in a museum. In the absence of contemporary artwork, it becomes acceptable to show the current locale provided captions clearly account for the time-shift.

Occasionally a publisher will have preferences or fixed ideas on the need for certain illustrations. Provided these ideas are feasible and reasonable they should be respected and added to the author's list of picture requirements.

PICTURE QUALITY

Next to relevance comes picture quality which is vitally important. Photographs should be *sharp* and *clear*. Modern cameras are capable of yielding high definition results provided the lens is correctly focused on the principal subject and the camera is held steady at the time of exposure. The latter calls for practice and suggestions for success appear in instruction manuals and books.

Paradoxically, a photograph may appear to be sharp but at the same time suffer from lack of clarity. Why should this be?

Usually the cause of such obfuscation is conflict and confusion in the picture area, caused by lack of thought at the time of exposure. Remedies lie in isolating the main subject by using certain simple techniques such as careful framing, differential focus or employing contrasting tones or colour.

It should be realised that no amount of camera automation will substitute for skill on the part of the photographer. Only the photographer can compose the picture in such a way as to communicate his or her ideas clearly and unambiguously to the reader.

Quality results also depend on reliable equipment, films, processing and presentation. Avoid skimping in any of these areas. It is not necessary to invest a small fortune in photographic equipment. A modern 35mm camera of a reputable make will serve an author well. Choose wisely taking counsel from a learned colleague or trusted dealer. Use fresh films and have them processed by a professional laboratory rather than a cut-price corner shop.

While the emphasis has been on colour photography, most of the principles apply equally to monochrome pictures. Black and white photography will continue to be an important source of illustration in publishing.

It is becoming more difficult to find good processors of black and white films which is why many photographers set up a small darkroom to print their own 10″ × 8″ or whole plate enlargements. In extremis, however, publishers can derive impressive black and white illustrations from colour transparency originals, albeit at a cost.

ADMINISTRATION

Once you start producing your own pictures for publication, it is important to consider their administration.

Each picture should be presented in such a way that your name, address, telephone number, reference and caption is clearly related to the subject. Records should be kept of pictures stored in your library and of those held by publishers. Despite all reasonable care losses will occasionally occur. Depending on circumstances, compensation should be claimed.

Colour transparencies need to be mounted, handled, stored and transmitted with extreme care if damage is to be avoided. Never mount colour transparencies intended for publication in glass.

Depending on urgency, pictures can be dispatched by post or courier services. In all cases they should be carefully packed and insured, if so inclined, according to their value.

Questions of copyright are addressed in detail in a separate chapter of this book (see page 554). Normally an author retains copyright both of his or her literary and artistic works unless these are assigned to a publisher. It is customary to assign only limited rights (eg First British Serial Rights for an article, or Single Reproduction Rights (qualified by territory and time if appropriate)) for pictures unless special circumstances prevail.

Occasionally problems arise in the reproduction of historic photographs, such as those produced, for example, by Henry Fox Talbot and other pioneering practitioners. By any definition these old pictures would be out of copyright by virtue of the time elapsed since the photographer's death. However trustees or independent commercial libraries often levy hire charges if material in their possession is subsequently reproduced.

In summary, authors are well placed to produce their own photography to illustrate their literary works. With sensible understanding of publishers' requirements and thoughtful application with the camera, writers will derive extra pleasure and profit from seeing their pictures, as well as words, in print.

Top Hundred Chart of
1993 Paperback Fastsellers

ALEX HAMILTON

In the pages which follow this preamble readers will find a table of the 100 highest sales figures for paperbacks uttered during 1993 by British publishers. It is an annual survey, which I have compiled for *The Guardian* newspaper since 1979, but for readers encountering it for the first time it would perhaps be useful to describe its terms of reference and indicate certain limitations.

An important distinction has first to be made between 'bestsellers' and the term used here – 'fastsellers'. The former have the real commercial pedigree. Sometimes, but not always, they have made a very visible showing in the fastseller lane, but among bestselling authors there are hundreds whose books have made a slow start and only through the cumulative sales over many years demonstrate the faith of the original publisher. Among many examples of those whose sales in their lifetimes was modest but the posthumous interest spectacular, two obvious cases are D.H. Lawrence and George Orwell.

Again, while serious poets never repeat Lord Byron's success in becoming a bestseller and 'famous overnight', and the only two works with short lines in a decade of fastsellers were collections of comic verse, a poet like T.S. Eliot, not to mention Shakespeare and Chaucer, will over the long haul rack up sales in millions. In fact the bread and butter of the publishing trade, year in and year out, continues to be Bibles, classic authors, cookbooks, dictionaries and other reference books. Although the larger bulk of counter sales, and of library borrowings, consists of fiction, the topselling individual titles for this century, with figures over 20 million copies, include most of these categories.

However, it must also be said that the gross figures world-wide, hardcover and paperback, with translations, of prolific authors like Agatha Christie, Alistair MacLean, Mickey Spillane, Ed McBain and Catherine Cookson prompt claims between 50 million and 300 million copies. The individual titles of such popular authors would generally show up in topical bestseller lists, but not always. Dennis Wheatley, for instance, had a very big following in Britain, but the 'British' quality he prided himself on did not travel, and overseas he was hardly read. And as another instance, none of the romances of Barbara Cartland has ever sold enough in one year to qualify for my fastseller list, despite a figure of over 100 million copies for the totality of her oeuvre. The presumption must be that it is divided between over 400 titles in many translations.

The fastselling tank which follows consists of the outpourings of the parish pump. That is to say that it is limited to paperbacks which have appeared for the first time in that year from British publishers (regardless of their hardcover provenance) and which have sold over 100,000 copies by the end of the calendar year. (Since 1979 there had always been between 102 and 125 of these, until the 1990s recession.) Though one has a natural inclination to suspect a distortion for the titles published at the end of the period, one finds (checking some months later) that it has rarely made much difference. The significant sale of new paperpacks, particularly by authors with a regular following, takes place within a very few weeks of their appearance on the racks. This can be said though very few of them advance into the magic circle of bestsellers: during the eighties the highest cumulative sales were for books by Sue Townsend and Jeffrey Archer, each passing five million, which had sold 400,000 and a million respectively in their first year of publication.

It was never the intention behind this list to make it into a competition, and it would be a total misinterpretation to use it as a comparative index of the sales efficiency or business health of the publishers involved. It is possible to go broke with a runaway fastseller on your list – it may even be the cause of a failure if its success entails an unrealistic expansion – and on the other hand there are a number of attractive and profitable imprints which have never come within hailing distance of having a title in this list in the whole time of its collection. The best way to look at it is as a reflection of current popular taste.

As such it indicates a rather conservative attitude on the part of the public. It is very unusual for a book to appear in the top 20 (which earn between them much the same as the rest of the list put together) which has not appeared somewhere else on the list before. Once properly established on the list, an author has only to turn in a similar performance to stay on it year after year. The stalwarts and dominant figures of the eighties were Wilbur Smith (who has now 20 novels or so with a sale over a million), Barbara Taylor Bradford, Dick Francis, Len Deighton, Stephen King, Catherine Cookson, Jeffrey Archer, Danielle Steel and Victoria Holt, with Jilly Cooper in the later stages strengthening her hand, particularly in the UK market. There is as yet no significant shift in the 1990s; they will be among the dominant figures for as long as they produce new books. It is the author's name that has the most influence, for which good evidence lies in the fact that of a thousand titles only three have been volumes of short stories, two with sales over 750,000 copies, because they were by Frederick Forsyth and Jeffrey Archer (the other was by Rosamund Pilcher).

Some 80 per cent of the bulk is usually fiction, and the regular features of the non-fiction remainder are diet books, the horoscope division of astrology, movie exploitations, joke books, and showbiz lives. Of the fiction, genres take up most of the slots, particularly adventure yarns, thrillers, horror stories, family sagas and a mixed bag of romances, from historical to 'Gothic' to the now faded bodice-ripper, and a variety of 'shopping romances' and career conflict stories under the vague umbrella of 'women's fiction'. (There seems to be no overt category of 'men's fiction' that might perhaps once have included authors like Mickey Spillane and Harold Robbins.) It is curious, in view of the fact that more than half the buyers of paperbacks are said to be women, that hardly more than a quarter of the authors are women – at least, for the first eight years it remained a steady 25% and only in the last years has it risen a few points (to its new high of 39% in 1992). One should be asking if this figure corresponds to the percentages in publishing as a whole.

Science fantasy is more likely to appear in the list than science fiction of a harder, more experimental kind. Westerns never figure at all, despite the fame on the range of authors like Louis L'Amour and J.T. Edson. There are rarely more than ten or a dozen in any list that could count on reviews from serious book pages, and most of these appear some way down the list, though in recent years, broadly since the leverage given it by television focus, the Booker Prize has taken the winners into the fastseller list. At present the Booker seems to establish the book rather than the author, and the only winner who has kept a place with subsequent books is Anita Brookner. No other literary award has yet resulted in a 100,000 paperback sale for the author.

The highest selling title for the eighties happens to have been a juvenile, *The Secret Diary of Adrian Mole Aged 13¾*, whose author Sue Townsend is said to have been embarrassed when she heard that the publishers had a print of 70,000 in hand, and begged them to reduce it because she could not bear to think of their losing a lot of money on her behalf. With this and a sequel she very nearly equals the total sale for 11 titles of the best-known author in children's fiction, the late Roald Dahl, and in the long run probably the only one capable of an international sale rivalling that of Dr Seuss. Dahl's death left the role of natural market leader vacant, a position apparently now being filled by Terry Pratchett.

The most successful child author, and the youngest of the list so far registered, wrote a book about solving Rubik's Cube. In the juvenile field it should also be mentioned that a genre of Dungeons and Dragons books had a fairly extended vogue, though it has now lapsed.

Nevertheless books for children, important though they are as an element of general education, especially when some are favoured as a prescription by the Ministry, and whose rude health in the market place has been one of the few cheering factors in a generally depressed commercial sector, do not as a rule command many places in the fastseller list (unless you count their influence in the sale of horror books, which shrewd booksellers will rack at child eye-level).

Looking at the results of the list as a whole, few doubt that even blue-chip properties can be affected by recession. It is not merely that consumers shop less, but that breakdowns occur in the selling network. In 1993 the collapse of two wholesalers supplying non-traditional outlets (such as supermarkets), the consequent mergers and restructures and delays in filling orders seem to have reduced by up to 10% some of the best-known names on this list.

During the previous three years there had been a rise in the average price of a fastselling paperback from £4.25 to £5.30, but this was not believed to be the essential reason for a decline of some four million units in the sales graph (which had always moved upward through the 1980s) leaving it on a new plateau of some 22.5 million. The strategy seemingly worked up to a point, because the gross retail take actually moved up from £103.2m to £113.3m to £119.5m for 1992. (It may be an item of incidental interest that when the average cover price reached £5, it was 200 times the figure chosen by Allen Lane for his first list of Penguins in 1936.) In 1993, for the first time, the publishers reined in: the average price was £5.24. It was worth noting that the top 25, accounting for more than half the turnover, register a drop of 12p. All this recovered two million of the lost sales, to 24.4m, and lifted turnover to £128.4m.

Casting about for evidence of those genres which have been spoken of optimistically in recent times, it has to be said that few fulfil their promise. Those that do are new sub-divisions from the major categories of thriller, horror and romance. The Western has disappeared into the sunset; the modest flutter in travel writing subsided again, perhaps through overproduction; fantasy now does generally better than hardcore SF; and 'green books', after looking as if they would sell as well as sermons in the late 19th century, never expanded their original niche market.

But the main category themes of love, crime and the supernatural still generate new variations. Thus, while the 'bodice ripper' and the 'shopper' are now virtually obsolete, a more discreet type of romance the trade calls 'Aga sagas', characterised by middle-class manners, lower key language, and an absence of sex or violence, is well established.

Then there are hybrids. Two lead the chart for 1993. Three proven ingredients came together with thriller writer Michael Crichton, dinosaurs and Spielberg's animatronics. The other book delivered the 20th-century history of China in one easy read, allied to a regular feature of fastseller lists, the saga of three generations of one family: *Wild Swans*. It made more money than any paperback had ever done in one year in Britain.

No	Title	Genre	Author	Imprint
1	Jurassic Park	Dinosaur	Michael Crichton (US)	Arrow
2	Wild Swans	Autobiog	Jung Chang (Br)	Flamingo
3	The Firm	Thriller	John Grisham (US)	Arrow
4	1994 Horoscopes	Astrology	Anon (US)	Diamond
5	The Copper Beech	Novel	Maeve Binchy (Ire)	Orion
6	The Pelican Brief	Thriller	John Grisham (US)	Arrow
7	House of Women	Saga	Catherine Cookson (Br)	Corgi
8	Driving Force	Thriller	Dick Francis (Br)	Pan
9	Maltese Angel	Saga	Catherine Cookson (Br)	Corgi
10	Father Land	Thriller	Robert Harris (Br)	Arrow
11	Bridges of Madison County	Novel	Robert J. Waller (US)	Mandarin
12	Gerald's Game	Horror	Stephen King (US)	NEL
13	Mostly Harmless	SF	Douglas Adams (Br)	Pan
14	Scarlett	Saga	Alexandra Ripley (US)	Pan
15	The Stars Shine Down	Novel	Sidney Sheldon (US)	Fontana
16	Jewels	Romance	Danielle Steel (US)	Corgi
17	Dolores Claiborne	Horror	Stephen King (US)	NEL
18	Mixed Blessings	Romance	Danielle Steel (US)	Corgi
19	The Road to Omaha	Thriller	Robert Ludlum (US)	Grafton
20	The Men and the Girls	Aga Saga	Joanna Trollope (Br)	Black Swan
21	The Queen and I	Novel	Sue Townsend (Br)	Mandarin
22	Rising Sun	Thriller	Michael Crichton (US)	Arrow
23	Jurassic Park (Jr)	Dino Juv	Anon (US)	Red Fox
24	The Scorpio Illusion	Thriller	Robert Ludlum (US)	HarperCollins
25	City of Gold	Thriller	Len Deighton (Br)	Arrow
26	Every Living Thing	Autobiog	James Herriot (Br)	Pan
27	Eye of the Storm	Thriller	Jack Higgins (Br)	Signet
28	Wicked Pleasures	Novel	Penny Vicenzi (Br)	Orion
29	Sahara	Thriller	Clive Cussler (US)	Grafton
30	Lords and Ladies	Fantasy	Terry Pratchett (Br)	Corgi
31	This Other Eden	Novel	Ben Elton (Br)	Pocket Books
32	Portent	Horror	James Herbert (Br)	NEL
33	Small Gods	Fantasy	Terry Pratchett (Br)	Corgi
34	A Dubious Legacy	Saga	Mary Wesley (Br)	Black Swan
35	Cross of Fire	Thriller	Colin Forbes (Br)	Pan
36	Way Through the Woods	Crime	Colin Dexter (Br)	Pan
37	The Secret History	Novel	Donna Tartt (US)	Penguin
38	An Evil Cradling	Autobiog	Brian Keenan (Ire)	Vintage
39	The Journeyman Tailor	Thriller	Gerald Seymour (Br)	Fontana
40	All That Remains	Thriller	Patricia Cornwell (US)	Warner
41	Crimson	Novel	Shirley Conran (Br)	Penguin
42	Dragon Tears	Thriller	Dean Koontz (US)	Headline
43	Kissing...Gunner's Daughter	Crime	Ruth Rendell (Br)	Arrow
44	Secrets of the Morning	Saga	'Virginia Andrews' (US)	Pocket Books
45	What's It All About?	Autobiog	Michael Caine (Br)	Arrow
46	Red Square	Thriller	Martin Cruz Smith (US)	HarperCollins
47	The Hooded Crow	Thriller	Craig Thomas (Br)	Fontana
48	Rock & Water Garden Expert	Gardening	D.G. Hessayon (Br)	PBI
49	Love Over Gold	Romance	Susannah James (Br)	Corgi
50	Dawn	Saga	'Virginia Andrews' (US)	Pocket Books

Price £	Month	Home	Export	Total	Gross £	No
4.99	Jun	769,981	248,661	1,018,642	5,083,023	1
7.99	Jun	529,068	413,857	942,925	7,533,970	2
4.99	Aug	438,044	212,921	650,965	3,248,315	3
2.99	Apr	479,004	129,900	608,904	1,820,622	4
4.95	Jul	419,149	178,232	597,381	2,957,035	5
4.99	Jun	348,154	223,482	571,636	2,852,503	6
4.99	Mar	395,821	143,646	539,467	2,691,940	7
4.99	Dec	293,599	221,487	515,086	2,570,279	8
4.99	Oct	352,936	132,840	485,776	2,424,022	9
4.99	May	280,231	198,043	478,274	2,386,587	10
3.99	Sep	334,888	138,906	473,794	1,890,438	11
5.99	Apr	286,835	167,110	453,945	2,719,130	12
4.99	Oct	256,492	193,494	449,986	2,245,430	13
5.99	Mar	125,968	323,921	449,889	2,694,835	14
4.99	Jul	218,889	218,807	437,696	2,184,103	15
4.99	Aug	309,344	123,501	432,845	2,159,896	16
4.99	Oct	226,487	201,253	427,740	2,134,422	17
4.99	Dec	281,917	101,394	383,311	1,912,721	18
5.99	Apr	152,559	204,241	356,800	2,137,232	19
5.99	Jul	311,761	40,129	351,890	2,107,821	20
4.99	Sep	280,714	68,573	349,287	1,742,942	21
4.99	May	178,891	164,777	343,668	1,714,903	22
2.99	Jun	216,993	125,562	342,555	1,024,239	23
5.99	Dec	150,947	177,912	328,859	1,969,865	24
4.99	Sep	168,689	143,867	312,556	1,559,654	25
4.99	Sep	282,951	18,061	301,012	1,502,049	26
4.99	May	202,870	79,038	281,908	1,406,720	27
5.99	Aug	152,367	116,292	268,659	1,609,267	28
5.99	Mar	149,522	111,898	261,420	1,565,905	29
4.99	Nov	219,009	42,010	261,019	1,302,484	30
5.99	Oct	252,623	5,314	257,937	1,545,042	31
5.99	Jul	223,360	32,755	256,115	1,534,128	32
4.99	May	203,760	48,484	252,244	1,258,697	33
5.99	Feb	211,350	40,292	251,642	1,507,335	34
4.99	Jan	140,873	110,687	251,560	1,255,284	35
4.99	Jul	208,393	42,684	251,077	1,252,874	36
5.99	Jul	181,259	68,094	249,353	1,493,624	37
5.99	Apr	204,679	36,434	241,113	1,444,266	38
4.99	Jun	170,627	54,665	225,292	1,124,207	39
4.99	Jul	149,503	71,983	221,486	1,105,215	40
5.99	Jun	153,785	67,604	221,389	1,326,120	41
5.99	Dec	107,340	102,875	210,215	1,259,187	42
4.99	Apr	162,346	46,477	208,823	1,042,026	43
4.99	Sep	141,445	59,553	200,998	1,002,980	44
4.99	Jul	128,252	72,245	200,497	1,000,480	45
4.99	Aug	104,785	83,432	188,217	939,202	46
4.99	May	128,698	58,284	186,982	933,040	47
4.99	Apr	161,060	18,986	180,046	898,429	48
3.99	Feb	178,196	0	178,196	711,002	49
4.99	Feb	86,277	86,324	172,601	861,278	50

No	Title	Genre	Author	Imprint
51	The First Wives Club	Glitz	Olivia Goldsmith (US)	Mandarin
52	On Mother Brown's Doorstep	Saga	Mary Jane Staples (Br)	Corgi
53	Miami	Novel	Pat Booth (Br)	Arrow
54	Paperweight	Humour	Stephen Fry (Br)	Mandarin
55	Astral Horoscopes	Astrology	Teri King (Br)	Pan
56	Domes of Fire	Fantasy	David Eddings (US)	Grafton
57	Entwine	Novel	Lynda La Plante (Br)	Pan
58	Sleeping Beauty	Romance	Judith Michael (US)	Warner
59	The Funhouse	Thriller	Dean Koontz (US)	Headline
60	Stardust	Novel	Charlotte Bingham (Br)	Bantam
61	Fever Pitch	Sport	Nick Hornby (Br)	Gollancz
62	Raptor Attack	Juvenile	Anon (US)	Red Fox
63	Jurassic Park Film Book	Dino Juv	Anon (US)	Red Fox
64	The English Patient	Novel	Michael Ondaatje (Can)	Picador
65	The Minpins	Juvenile	Roald Dahl (Br)	Puffin
66	To Play the King	Novel	Michael Dobbs (Br)	Fontana
67	The Door to December	Thriller	Dean Koontz (US)	Headline
68	Elf Queen of Shannara	Fantasy	Terry Brooks (US)	Legend
69	Only You Can Save Mankind	Juvenile	Terry Pratchett (Br)	Corgi
70	The Food Combining Diet	Diet	Kathryn Marsden (Br)	Thorsons
71	The Chickens are Restless	Cartoons	Gary Larson (US)	Warner
72	Super Horoscopes 1994	Astrology	Anon	Arrow
73	Black Blade	Thriller	Eric Lustbader (US)	Grafton
74	The Original Sin	Romance	Marius Gabriel (Br)	Arrow
75	The Far Side Gallery 4	Cartoons	Gary Larson (US)	Warner
76	Don't Cry Alone	Saga	Josephine Cox (Br)	Headline
77	The Water Meadows	Saga	Emma Blair (Br)	Corgi
78	The Ladykiller	Novel	Marina Cole (Br)	Headline
79	The Days are Just Packed	Cartoons	Bill Watterson (US)	Warner
80	River God	Novel	Wilbur Smith (Br)	Macmillan
81	Backstreet Child	Thriller	Harry Bowling (Br)	Headline
82	All Around the Town	Thriller	Mary Higgins Clark (US)	Arrow
83	Samson and Delilah	Novel	Frances Edmonds (Br)	Pan
84	Mystical Paths	Novel	Susan Howatch (Br)	Fontana
85	Princess	Biog	Jean Sasson (US)	Bantam
86	Daughters of the Moon	Saga	Susan Sallis (Br)	Corgi
87	Bygones	Romance	LaVyrl Spencer (US)	Grafton
88	Jessica's Girl	Saga	Josephine Cox (Br)	Headline
89	The Crow Road	Novel	Iain Banks (Br)	Abacus
90	Rainbow Through the Rain	Saga	Elvi Rhodes (Br)	Corgi
91	Mistress of the Empire	Fantasy	Feist & Wurts (US)	Grafton
92	Spinning Jenny	Saga	Ruth Hamilton (Br)	Corgi
93	No Exit	Glitz	Julie Burchill (Br)	Mandarin
94	The Immortals	Novel	Michael Korda (US)	Pan
95	Arrivals & Departures	Novel	Leslie Thomas (Br)	Mandarin
96	Hand in Glove	Novel	Robert Goddard (Br)	Corgi
97	The General's Daughter	Thriller	Nelson DeMille (US)	HarperCollins
98	The Chinaman	Thriller	Stephen Leather (Br)	Coronet
99	The King's Buccaneer	Fantasy	Raymond Feist (US)	HarperCollins
100	In Still and Stormy Waters	Novel	Reay Tannahill (Br)	Penguin

Price £	Month	Home	Export	Total	Gross £	No
4.99	Mar	139,751	30,824	170,575	**851,169**	51
3.99	Jan	163,710	651	164,361	**655,800**	52
4.99	Mar	119,666	41,553	161,219	**804,482**	53
4.99	Oct	143,489	13,046	156,535	**781,109**	54
2.50	Jun	54,084	99,240	153,324	**383,310**	55
5.99	Jul	80,809	72,212	153,021	**916,595**	56
4.99	Jun	81,649	69,553	151,202	**754,497**	57
5.99	Apr	92,837	56,814	149,651	**896,409**	58
4.99	Aug	100,066	47,882	147,948	**738,260**	59
4.99	Jul	86,686	60,641	147,327	**735,161**	60
4.99	Aug	133,665	9,733	143,398	**715,556**	61
3.99	Jun	59,100	83,804	142,904	**570,186**	62
3.99	Jun	90,019	52,864	142,883	**570,103**	63
5.99	Jul	72,252	69,420	141,672	**848,615**	64
4.99	Apr	91,529	49,984	141,513	**706,149**	65
4.99	Jan	126,034	15,329	141,363	**705,401**	66
5.99	Apr	80,870	59,803	140,673	**842,631**	67
5.99	Mar	101,587	38,968	140,555	**841,924**	68
3.99	Sep	114,559	25,425	139,984	**558,536**	69
4.99	Jan	118,616	17,743	136,359	**680,431**	70
5.99	Nov	83,001	49,372	132,373	**792,914**	71
3.99	Jun	72,169	58,592	130,761	**521,736**	72
5.99	Jun	39,384	89,730	129,114	**773,392**	73
4.99	Feb	95,432	32,067	127,499	**636,220**	74
7.99	Oct	80,108	46,144	126,252	**1,008,753**	75
5.99	Mar	118,158	7,585	125,743	**753,200**	76
4.99	May	102,307	22,500	124,807	**622,786**	77
5.99	Jul	96,908	27,413	124,321	**744,682**	78
6.99	Oct	101,506	22,310	123,816	**865,473**	79
9.99	Nov	120,010	0	120,010	**1,198,899**	80
5.99	Nov	115,883	902	116,785	**699,542**	81
4.99	Jul	57,608	59,043	116,651	**582,088**	82
4.99	Aug	67,572	48,933	116,505	**581,359**	83
4.99	Feb	69,693	46,537	116,230	**579,987**	84
4.99	Aug	43,864	71,507	115,371	**575,701**	85
4.99	Apr	105,462	6,218	111,680	**557,283**	86
2.99	May	67,669	43,992	111,661	**333,866**	87
5.99	Sep	104,254	6,864	111,118	**665,596**	88
6.99	Apr	98,176	12,603	110,779	**774,345**	89
4.99	Nov	108,427	910	109,337	**545,591**	90
5.99	May	41,499	66,418	107,917	**646,422**	91
4.99	Jun	106,800	611	107,411	**535,980**	92
4.99	Nov	83,875	21,435	105,310	**525,496**	93
4.99	Nov	55,897	47,616	103,513	**516,529**	94
4.99	May	88,716	14,022	102,738	**512,662**	95
4.99	Jul	65,122	35,784	100,906	**503,520**	96
4.99	Nov	42,458	58,446	100,904	**503,510**	97
4.99	Feb	56,934	43,511	100,445	**501,220**	98
5.99	Dec	38,014	60,959	98,973	**592,848**	99
5.99	Jul	50,025	47,446	97,471	**583,851**	100

Book Packagers

Many modern illustrated books are created by book packagers, whose special skills are in the areas of book design and graphic content. Children's interests and informational how-to are the usual subject areas; such books match up the expertise of specialist writers, artists and photographers, usually freelances, with the craftsmanship of in-house desk editors and art editors.

Packaged books are often expensive to produce, beyond the cost parameters set by traditional publishers for their own markets; the packager recoups the expense by pre-selling titles to publishers in various countries. Thus packaged books are usually international in content and approach, avoiding local interests such as cricket or Cornish cream teas.

The working style in most packagers' offices is more akin to magazine publishing than to traditional book publishing, with creative groups concentrating on the complexities of integrating words and pictures for individual titles rather than merely manuscript editing for a broad publishing list.

The many opportunities for freelance writers, specialist contributors and consultants, photographers and illustrators will usually be short-term and high pressure; packagers rarely spend more than a year on any title. As packaged books are frequently the work of more than one 'author' and because of the complications of the overseas rights deals that will be made and the formulae for a packager's earnings, which are obviously only a proportion of a book's retail price, flat fees are often suggested rather than royalty agreements. Where royalties are appropriate, they will be based on the packager's receipts, but the expectation is that there will be more foreign language editions than a traditional publisher can achieve.

The Book Packagers Association (*Secretary:* Rosemary Pettit, 93a Blenheim Crescent, London W11 2EQ) is the forum for the exchange of creative and commercial experience in this branch of the publishing industry. The BPA has devised standard contracts to cover members' relationships with contributors and customers.

* Member of the Book Packagers Association

Aladdin Books Ltd (1980), 28 Percy Street, London W1P 9FF *tel* 071-323 3319 *telex* 21115 ALADIN G *fax* 071-323 4829. *Directors:* Charles Nicholas, Lynn Lockett. Full design and book packaging facility.

Albion Press Ltd (1984), Spring Hill, Idbury, Oxon OX7 6RU *tel* (0993) 831094 *fax* (0993) 831982. *Directors:* Emma Bradford, Neil Philip. Quality integrated illustrated titles specialising in literature, social history, fine and graphic arts, cookery, children's books. Supply finished books. Publishers' commissions undertaken.

***Alphabet & Image Ltd** (1972), Alpha House, South Street, Sherborne, Dorset DT9 3LU *tel* (0935) 814944 *fax* (0935) 816717. *Directors:* Anthony Birks-Hay, Leslie Birks-Hay. Complete editorial, picture research, photographic, design and production service for illustrated books on ceramics, beekeeping, horticulture, architecture, history, etc.

Andromeda Oxford Ltd (1986), 11-15 The Vineyard, Abingdon, Oxon OX14 3PX *tel* (0235) 550296 *fax* (0235) 550330. *Directors:* M. Ritchie (managing), M. Desebrock (group publishing), J. Taylor (group finance), J.G. Bateman,

L. Clarke, J. Ridgeway, C. Sparling, D. Hall, E. Glover. Illustrated reference titles for the international market.

BCS Publishing Ltd (1993), 1 Bignell Park Barns, Kirtlington Road, Chesterton, Bicester, Oxon OX6 8TD *tel* (0869) 324423 *fax* (0869) 324385. *Directors:* Ben Lenthall (chairman), Steve McCurdy (managing; art), Candida Hunt (publishing). Creation, editorial and design of highly illustrated general interest books for the co-edition market. Opportunities for freelances.

Beanstalk Books Ltd (1983), The Gardens House, Hever Castle Private Road, Threshersfield, Nr Chiddingstone, Kent TN8 7NE *editorial tel/fax* (0730) 825723 *production tel* (0892) 870912 *fax* (0435) 872850. *Directors:* Shona McKellar, Penny Kitchenham. Specialists in highly illustrated books for adults and children; novelties; editorial, design and production service.

***Bellew Publishing Co. Ltd** (1983), The Nightingale Centre, 8 Balham Hill, London SW12 9EA *tel* 081-673 5611 *telex* 8951182 GECOMS G *fax* 081-675 3542. *Chairman:* Anthony Rainbird; *managing director:* Ib Bellew. Adult and children's illustrated titles from origination of idea through concept and design to production. Opportunities for freelances.

Bender Richardson White (1990), PO Box 266, Uxbridge, Middlesex UB9 5NX *tel* (0895) 832444 *fax* (0895) 835213. *Partners:* Lionel Bender, Kim Richardson, Ben White. Book and multi-media packaging, specialising in children's natural history, science and family information. Opportunities for freelances.

Berkswell Publishing Co. Ltd (1974), PO Box 420, Warminster, Wilts. BA12 9XB *tel/fax* (0985) 40189. *Directors:* J.N.G. Stidolph, S.A. Abbott. Book packaging, editorial, design, research, picture research, exhibition organisation and design. Opportunities for freelances.

Bison Books Ltd (1974), Kimbolton House, 117a Fulham Road, London SW3 6RL *tel* 071-823 9222 *fax* 071-244 7139. *Managing director:* S.L. Mayer. Non-fiction illustrated titles principally history, military history, weaponry, natural history, transport, travel, sport, art, entertainment.

BLA Publishing Ltd (1981), Christopher Road, East Grinstead, West Sussex RH19 3BT *tel* (0342) 318980 *fax* (0342) 410980. *Directors:* Au Bak Ling (chairman, Hong Kong), Vincent Winter, Au King Kwok (Hong Kong), Au Chun Kwok (Hong Kong), Albert Kw Au (Hong Kong), Au Wai Kwok (Hong Kong); Quentin Hockliffe (sales). High quality illustrated reference books, particularly science dictionaries and encyclopedias, for the international market.

***Book Packaging and Marketing** (1990), 3 Murswell Lane, Silverstone, Towcester, Northants. NN12 8UT *tel/fax* (0327) 858380. *Proprietor:* Martin F. Marix Evans. Illustrated general and informational non-fiction and reference for adults and children. Product development and project management; editorial and marketing consultancy. Opportunities for freelances.

***Breslich & Foss** (1978), Golden House, 28-31 Great Pulteney Street, London W1R 3DD *tel* 071-734 0706 *fax* 071-494 0854. *Directors:* Paula G. Breslich, K.B. Dunning. Books produced from MS to bound copy stage from in-house ideas. Specialising in the arts, sport, health, crafts, gardening, children's.

Brown Wells and Jacobs Ltd (1981), 2 Vermont Road, London SE19 3SR *tel* 081-653 7670 *fax* 081-771 1765. *Director:* Graham Brown. Design, editorial, illustration and production of high quality non-fiction illustrated children's books. Specialities include pop-ups and novelties. Opportunities for freelances.

Calmann and King Ltd (1976), 71 Great Russell Street, London WC1B 3BN *tel* 071-831 6351 *fax* 071-831 8356. *Directors:* Robin Hyman, Laurence King, Judy Rasmussen, Lesley Ripley Greenfield, Donald Sommerville, David Lewis. Illustrated books on design, art, history, nature, architecture for international co-editions.

Cameron Books (1976), PO Box 1, Moffat, Dumfriesshire DG10 9SU *tel* (0683) 20808 *fax* (0683) 20012. *Directors:* Ian A. Cameron, Jill Hollis. Illustrated non-fiction including architecture, design, fine arts, the decorative arts and crafts, antiques, collecting, natural history, environmental studies, social history, films, food. **Edition** (1975). Design, editing, typesetting, production work from concept to finished book for other publishers.

Carroll & Brown Ltd (1989), 5 Lonsdale Road, London NW6 6RA *tel* 071-372 0900 *fax* 071-372 0460. *Directors:* Amy Carroll (managing), Denise Brown (creative). Editorial and design through to final film of cookery, health, crafts and life style titles. Opportunities for freelances.

*****Philip Clark Ltd** (1981), 53 Calton Avenue, Dulwich Village, London SE21 7DF *tel* 081-693 5605 *fax* 081-299 4647. *Director:* Philip Clark. Illustrated non-fiction for the international co-edition market, including books on wine, travel, natural history, windsurfing and other sports, children's reference and sponsored titles.

Diagram Visual Information Ltd (1967), 195 Kentish Town Road, London NW5 8SY *tel* 071-482 3633 *fax* 071-482 4932. *Director:* Bruce Robertson. Research, writing, design and illustration of reference books, supplied as film, computer disks or manufactured copies. Opportunities for freelances.

Earthscape Editions (1987), 86 Peppard Road, Sonning Common, Reading, Berks. RG4 9RP *tel* (0734) 723751 *fax* (0734) 724488. *Partners:* B.J. Knapp, D.L.R. McCrae. High quality, full colour, illustrated children's books, including co-editions, for education and library market. Sae with MSS essential. Opportunities for freelances. Associate company: Atlantic Europe Publishing (*see* UK Book Publishers).

*****Eddison Sadd Editions Ltd** (1982), St Chad's Court, 146B King's Cross Road, London WC1X 9DH *tel* 071-837 1968 *fax* 071-837 2025. *Directors:* Nick Eddison, Ian Jackson, Maria White, David Owen. Illustrated non-fiction books for the international co-edition market.

Elvendon Press (1978), The Old Bakehouse, High Street, Goring-on-Thames, Reading, Berks. RG8 9AR *tel* (0491) 875800 *fax* (0491) 874233. *Directors:* Ray Hurst, Bernice Hurst. Complete packaging service. Business, professional and popular consumer titles; magazines, directories and all types of publications for publishers, commercial companies and institutions.

Equinox (Oxford) Ltd—acquired by **Andromeda Oxford Ltd.**

*****Gardenhouse Editions** (1980), 15 Grafton Square, London SW4 0DQ *tel* 071-622 1720 *fax* 071-720 9114. *Managing director:* Lorraine Johnson. Practical and art-related books on gardening, cookery, interior design, fashion, architecture.

Graham-Cameron Publishing (1984), The Studio, 23 Holt Road, Sheringham, Norfolk NR26 8NB *tel* (0263) 821333 *fax* (0263) 821334. *Directors:* Mike Graham-Cameron, Helen Graham-Cameron. Children's books; biographies; sponsored publications. Illustration, editorial and production services. *No* unsolicited MSS please.

Angus Hudson Ltd (1971), Concorde House, Grenville Place, Mill Hill, London NW7 3SA *tel* 081-959 3668 *fax* 081-959 3678. *Directors:* Angus Hudson (managing), Stephen Price (production), Nicholas Jones (finance). Children's and religious international co-editions, from concept to finished copies.

Lennard Books, Windmill Cottage, Mackerye End, Harpenden, Herts. AL5 5DR *tel* (0582) 715866 *fax* (0582) 715121. *Directors:* K.A.A. Stephenson, R.H. Stephenson. Division of **Lennard Associates Ltd.** Sport, personalities, TV tie-ins, humour.

Lexus Ltd (1980), 205 Bath Street, Glasgow G2 4HZ *tel* 041-221 5266 *fax* 041-226 3139. *Director:* P.M. Terrell. Reference book publishing (especially bilingual dictionaries) as contractor, packager, consultant; translation.

Lionheart Books (1985), 10 Chelmsford Square, London NW10 3AR *tel* 081-459 0453 *fax* 081-451 3681. *Partners:* Lionel Bender (editorial), Madeleine Bender (editorial), Ben White (design). Handle all aspects of editorial and design packaging of, mostly, children's illustrated science, natural history and history projects.

*****Market House Books Ltd** (1981), 2 Market House, Market Square, Aylesbury, Bucks. HP20 1TN *tel* (0296) 84911 *fax* (0296) 437073. *Directors:* Dr Alan Isaacs, Dr John Daintith, P.C. Sapsed. Compilation of dictionaries, encyclopedias, and reference books.

Marshall Cavendish Books (1969), 119 Wardour Street, London W1V 3TD *tel* 071-734 6710 *telex* 23880 MARCAV G *fax* 071-439 1423. *Head of editorial:* Maggie Calmels; *head of marketing:* Duncan Crole. Cookery, crafts, gardening, do-it-yourself, general non-fiction.

*****Marshall Editions Ltd** (1977), 170 Piccadilly, London W1V 9DD *tel* 071-629 0079 *fax* 071-834 0785. *Directors:* Bruce Marshall, John Bigg, Barbara Anderson, Barry Baker. Highly illustrated non-fiction, for the adult and children's co-edition markets, including science and natural history, fitness, sports and leisure interests, management and photography.

Oyster Books (1985), Unit 4B, Kirklea Farm, Badgworth, Axbridge, Somerset BS26 2QH *tel* (0934) 732251 *fax* (0934) 732514. *Directors:* Jenny Wood, Tim Wood, Ali Brooks. Specialises in high-quality children's books and book/toy gift items.

*****Parke Sutton Ltd** (1982), Orchard House, Grange Farm, Ashwellthorpe, Norfolk NR16 1ET *tel/fax* (0508) 489212. *Directors:* Ian S. McIntyre, Cris de Boos (financial), Alan Boardman (chairman), Paul Boardman. Packagers of non-fiction books. Also publish newspapers, magazines and reference books for specific organisations.

Playne Books (1987), Trefin, Haverfordwest, Dyfed SA62 5AY *tel* (0348) 837073 *fax* (0348) 837063. *Director:* David Playne; *editor:* Gill Davies. Book packaging and production service. All stages of production undertaken from initial concept (editorial, design and manufacture) to delivery of completed books.

*****Mathew Price Ltd** (1983), The Old Glove Factory, Bristol Road, Sherborne, Dorset DT9 4HP *tel* (0935) 816010 *fax* (0935) 816310. *Chairman:* Mathew Price. Illustrated fiction and non-fiction children's books for all ages for the international market.

*****Quarto Publishing plc** (1976), **Quintet Publishing Ltd** (1984), The Old Brewery, 6 Blundell Street, London N7 9BH *tel* 071-700 6700 *fax* 071-700 4191. *Directors:* L.F. Orbach, R.J. Morley, M.J. Mousley. International co-editions.

Sadie Fields Productions Ltd (1983), 3D West Point, 36/37 Warple Way, London W3 0RQ *tel* 081-746 1171 *fax* 081-746 1170. *Directors:* Sheri Safran, David

Fielder. Creates and produces international co-productions of pop-up, novelty and picture and board books for children.

*Savitri Books Ltd (1983), 115 J Cleveland Street, London W1P 5PN   *tel* 071-436 9932   *fax* 071-580 6330. *Director:* Mrinalini S. Srivastava. Packaging, design, production.

Signpost Books Ltd (1988), 25 Eden Drive, Headington, Oxford OX3 0AB   *tel* (0865) 60444   *fax* (0865) 751399. *Directors:* Dorothy Wood, Sally Wood. Project development, editorial, design and production through to finished books, film or CRC. Specialises in children's fiction, non-fiction and novelty. Opportunities for freelances.

Sports Book Specialists, Grove Meadow, Jordans Way, Jordans, Bucks. HP9 2SP   *tel/fax* (0494) 873137. *Managing editor:* C. Plumridge. Division of **Lennard Associates Ltd.** Sports projects.

Teeney Books Ltd (1990), 24 Christchurch Street West, Frome, Somerset BA11 1EB   *tel* (0373) 452565   *fax* (0373) 452567. *Directors:* Martyn Lewis, Tiny de Vries. Creation of full colour children's picture books, 1-5 years. Opportunities for freelance artists; no opportunities for writers.

*The Templar Company plc, Pippbrook Mill, London Road, Dorking, Surrey RH4 1JE   *tel* (0306) 876361   *fax* (0306) 889097. *Directors:* Richard Carlisle (creative), Amanda Wood (managing), Co van Woerkom (production), Graeme East (financial). Children's picture and illustrated information books; most titles aimed at international co-edition market. Established links with major co-publishers in UK, USA, Australia and throughout Europe.

Thames Head, Christopher Road, East Grinstead, West Sussex RH19 3BT   *tel* (0342) 318980   *fax* (0342) 410980. *Sales:* Quentin Hockliffe. Division of **BLA Publishing Ltd.** Illustrated international co-editions: general non-fiction, militaria, history, travel guides and practical crafts.

*Toucan Books Ltd (1985), Albion Courtyard, Greenhills Rents, London EC1M 6BN   *tel* 071-251 3921   *fax* 071-251 1692. *Directors:* Robert Sackville West, Adam Nicolson, Jane MacAndrew. International co-editions; editorial, design and production services.

Touchstone Publishing Ltd (1989), 68 Florence Road, Brighton, East Sussex BN1 6DJ   *tel* (0273) 884179   *fax* (0273) 550415. *Directors:* Roger Coote (managing), Edwina Conner (publishing). High quality, illustrated children's fiction and non-fiction for trade and institutional markets world-wide. Supply CRC, film or finished books. Publishers' commissions undertaken.

Tucker Slingsby (1993), 27 Bockhampton Road, Kingston upon Thames, Surrey KT2 5JU   *tel/fax* 081-974 9526. *Directors:* Janet Slingsby, Del Tucker. Creation, editorial and design to CRC or film, of children's books and general interest adult books. Opportunities for freelances.

Ventura Publishing Ltd, 27 Wrights Lane, London W8 5TZ   *tel* 071-416 3000   *telex* 917181 PENGRP G   *fax* 071-416 3070. *Director:* Sally Floyer. Specialise in production of the *Spot* books by Eric Hill.

Webb & Bower (Publishers) Ltd (1975), 9 Duke Street, Dartmouth, Devon TQ6 9PY   *tel* (0803) 835525   *fax* (0803) 835552. *Director:* Richard Webb. Specialise in licensing illustrated non-fiction books.

*Wordwright (1987), 25 Oakford Road, London NW5 1AJ   *tel* 071-284 0056   *fax* 071-284 0041. *Directors:* Charles Perkins, Veronica Davis. Full packaging service – research, editorial, design and production. Produces illustrated non-fiction. Also assesses and prepares MSS for the US market.

Zigzag Publishing (1989), The Barn, Randolph's Farm, Brighton Road, Hurst-pierpoint, West Sussex BN6 9EL   *tel* (0273) 832777   *fax* (0273) 835511. *Directors:* Dr T.C. Potter, B. Austin, G. Sutton, B. Dancer. Children's books and multimedia. Opportunities for freelances.

Zoe Books Ltd (1990), 15 Worthy Lane, Winchester, Hants SO23 7AB   *tel* (0962) 851318   *fax* (0962) 843015. *Directors:* I.Z. Dawson (managing/publishing), A.R. Davidson. Children's information and reference books for the school and library markets world-wide; specialists in co-editions for world markets; publishing consultancy in school and library markets world-wide. Opportunities for freelances.

Structure

Each episode of *The Archers* lasts fifteen minutes, which means in practice a reading-out-loud time of about thirteen minutes. Each instalment usually contains five scenes, and not more than seven characters. The plotting is the longest and most demanding part of the process. Some writers actually do this on graph paper, ensuring that storylines peak at the right places in the week to keep listeners tuned in. Each writer should have been given a mix of plot-lines at the meeting — something funny, something romantic, something agricultural etc. Each should get a clear idea of what his main story is for the week, and his second story, and so on, otherwise the scripts can come in flat. What the Producer looks for is peaks and troughs in the right places.

Each 15-minute episode needs to be planned for a good mix. A writer should ask himself if there is a variety of tones. An echo-y barn interior might follow a breezy scene on Lakey Hill; a cosy slow-moving chat among the old folk of Ambridge might be followed by a snappy, funny scene with younger characters; an emotional scene might need a comic scene to pick the audience up again. Each scene needs to 'thicken' at its ending, and in some way signpost the listeners on: the momentum of a soap is always onwards. There might be three peaks in a week as the different storylines come to fruition, and the last scene on a Friday needs a good strong ending. It can just be a happy ending, or a mysterious one, or a funny one, but it certainly needs to be strong.

from *Writing for Radio* by Rosemary Horstmann (A & C Black, £9.99)

Doing It On Your Own

Self-publishing for Writers

PETER FINCH

Why bother?

You've tried all the usual channels and been turned down; your work is uncommercial, specialised, technical; you are concerned with art while everyone else is obsessed with cash; you need a book out quickly; you want to take up small publishing as a hobby; you've heard that publishers make a lot of money out of their authors and you'd like a slice – all reason enough. But be sure you understand what you are doing before you begin.

But isn't this cheating? It can't be real publishing – where is the critical judgement? Publishing is a respectable activity carried out by firms of specialists. Writers of any ability never get involved

But they do. Start self-publishing and you'll be in good historical company: Horace Walpole, Balzac, Walt Whitman, Virginia Woolf, Gertrude Stein, John Galsworthy, Rudyard Kipling, Beatrix Potter, Lord Byron, Thomas Paine, Mark Twain, Upton Sinclair, W.H. Davies, Zane Grey, Ezra Pound, D.H. Lawrence, William Carlos Williams, Alexander Pope, Robbie Burns, James Joyce, Anaïs Nin and Lawrence Stern. All these at some time in their careers dabbled in doing it themselves. William Blake did nothing else. He even made his own ink, handprinted his pages and got Mrs Blake to sew on the covers.

But today it's different

Not necessarily. This is not vanity publishing we're talking about although if all you want to do is produce a pamphlet of poems to give away to friends then self-publishing will be the cheapest way. Doing it yourself today can be a valid form of business enterprise. Look at the huge success of the late Aeron Clement with his story of badgers, *The Cold Moons*: 8000 self-produced hardbacks sold in three months, then brought out as a best-selling paperback by Penguin. Clement self-published with the help of his local publican from Llandeilo in West Wales – hardly a base from which to take the book world by storm but this is just what he did. More recently Jay de Leon took the trade by surprise with the runaway success of her self-produced *Love Talk in 5 Languages* – a phrase book which took over where others left off. 'Cela tombe mal, j'ai mes règles' it now says across the airport bookstalls of Europe, and the author-publisher gets all the money.

Can anyone do it?

Certainly. If you are a writer then a fair number of the required qualities will already be in hand. If, in addition, you can put up a shelf then the manufacture of the book to go on it will not be beyond you. The more able and practical you are then the cheaper the process will be. The utterly inept will need to pay others to help them, but it will still be self-publishing in the end.

Where do I start?

With research. Read up on the subject. Make sure you know what the parts of a book are. Terms like *verso, recto, prelims, dummy, typeface* and *point size* all have to lose their mystery. You will not need to become an expert but you will need a certain familiarity. Don't rush. Learn.

What about ISBN numbers?

International Standard Book Numbers – a standard bibliographic code, individual to each book published, are used by booksellers and librarians alike. They are issued free of charge by the Standard Book Numbering Agency, 12 Dyott Street, London WC1A 1DF. Write giving the basic details of your proposed book and, if appropriate, you will receive an ISBN by return.

Next?

Put your book together – be it the typed pages of your novel, your selected poems or your nature notes and drawings – and see how large a volume it will make. Follow the details on preparation of typescript given elsewhere in this yearbook. No real idea of what your book should look like? Anything will not do. Go to your local bookshop and hunt out a few contemporary examples of volumes produced in a style you would like to emulate. Ask the manager for advice. Take your typescript and your examples round to a number of local printers (find these through *Yellow Pages*) and ask for a quote. This costs nothing and will give you an idea of what the enterprise is likely to involve. Anthony Rowe Ltd (Bumper's Way, Bristol Road, Chippenham SN14 6LM) are specialists in low runs from camera ready copy, and will quote you a price. A number of others advertise their services in the writers' magazines. Many are worth a look but tread with care. Don't rush.

How much?

It depends. How long is a piece of string? You will not get a pamphlet of poems out for less than a few hundred pounds while a hardbacked work of prose will come in well above £3000. Unit cost is important. The larger the number of copies you have printed the less each will cost. Print too many and the total bill will be enormous. Books are no longer cheap; perhaps they never were.

Can I make it cost less?

Yes. Do some of the work yourself. If it's poems and you are prepared to manage with text set on a typewriter then that can make a considerable saving. Could you accept home production, run the pages off on an office photocopier, then staple the sheets? Text prepared on a word processor with a decent printer can be very presentable. Access to one running a desktop publishing program will give even better results. Home binding, if your abilities lie in that direction, can save a fair bit. What it all comes down to is the standard of production you want and indeed at whom your book is aimed. Books for the commercial market place need to look like their fellows, specialist publications can afford to be more eccentric.

Who decides how it looks?

You do. No one should ever ask a printer simply to produce a book. You should plan the design of your publication with as much care as you would a house extension. Books which sell are those which stand out in the bookshop. Spend as much time and money as you can on the cover. It is the part of the book your buyer will see first. Look at the volumes in bookshop displays especially those in the window. Imitate British paperback design, it's the best in the world.

How many copies should I produce?

Small press poetry pamphlets sell about 300 copies, new novels sometimes manage 1500, literary paperbacks 10,000, mass-market blockbusters over a million. But that is generally where there is a sales team and whole distribution organisation behind the book. You are an individual. You must do all yourself. Do not on the one hand end up with a prohibitively high unit cost by ordering too few copies. One hundred of anything is usually a waste of time. On the other hand can you really sell 3000? Will shops buy in dozens? They will probably only want twos and threes. Take care. Research your market first.

How do I sell it?

With all your might. This is perhaps the hardest part of publishing. It is certainly as time consuming as both the writing of the work and the printing of it put together. To succeed here you need a certain flair and you should definitely not be of a retiring nature. If you intend selling through the trade (and even if you don't you are bound to come into contact with bookshop orders at some stage) your costing must be correct and *worked out in advance*. Shops will want at least 33% of the selling price as discount. You'll need about the same again to cover your distribution, promotion and other overheads leaving the final third to cover production costs and any profit you may wish to make. Take your unit production cost and multiply by at least 4. Commerical publishers often multiply by as much as 9.

Do not expect the trade to pay your carriage costs. Your terms should be 33% post free on everything bar single copy orders. Penalise these by reducing your discount to 25%. Some shops will suggest that you sell copies to them on *sale or return*. This means that they only pay you for what they sell and then only after they've sold it. This is a common practice with certain categories of publications and often the only way to get independent books into certain shops; but from the self-publisher's point of view it should be avoided if at all possible. Cash in hand is best but expect to have your invoices paid by cheque at a later date. Buy a duplicate pad in order to keep track of what's going on. Phone the shops you have decided should take your book or turn up in person and ask to see the buyer. Letters and sample copies sent by post will get ignored. Get a freelance distributor to handle all of this for you if you can. Check the trade section of Cassell's *Directory of Publishing* or advertise for one in *The Bookseller*. They will want another 12% or so commission on top of the shops' discount – but expect to have to go it alone.

What about promotion?

A vital aspect often overlooked by beginners. Send out as many review copies as you can, all accompanied by slips quoting selling price and name and address of the publisher. Never admit to being that person yourself. Invent a name, it will give your operation a professional feel. Ring up newspapers and local radio stations ostensibly to check that your copy has arrived but really to see if they are prepared to give your book space. Try to think of an angle for them, anything around which they can write a story. Buying advertising space rarely pays for itself but good local promotion with 100% effort will generate dividends.

What about depositing copies at the British Library?

Under the Copyright Acts the British Library, the Bodleian Library, Oxford, The University Library, Cambridge, The National Library of Scotland, the Library of Trinity College Dublin and the National Library of Wales are all entitled to a free copy of your book which must be sent to them within one month of publication. One copy should go direct to the Legal Deposit Office at The British Library, Boston Spa, Wetherby, West Yorkshire LS23 7BY. The other libraries use an agent, Mr A.T. Smail, at 100 Euston Street, London NW1 2HQ *tel* 071-388 5061. Contact him directly to find out how many copies he requires. Many self-publishers object to sending books out for nothing but there are advantages. Data on your title will be used by the libraries as part of their bibliographic services and the book itself will eventually form part of a comprehensive national printed archive and be made available to the public.

What if I can't manage all this myself?

You can employ others to do it for you. If you are a novelist and you opt for a package covering everything, it could set you back more than £10,000. A number of publishers and associations advertise such services in writers' journals and in the Sunday classifieds. *Authors. Publish with us.* is a typical ploy. They will do a competent job for you, certainly, but you will still end up having to do the bulk of the selling yourself. It is a costly route, fraught with difficulty. Do the job on your own if you possibly can.

And what if it goes wrong?

Put all the unsolds under the bed or give them away. It has happened to lots of us. Even the big companies who are experienced at these things have their regular flops. It was an adventure and you did get your book published. On the other hand you may be so successful that you'll be at the London Book Fair selling the film rights and wondering if you've reprinted enough. Whichever way it goes – good luck.

Where to learn more

Finch, Peter, *How To Publish Yourself*, Allison & Busby, 1991
Foster, Charles, *Editing, Design and Book Production*, Journeyman, 1993
Godber, Bill, Webb, Robert, and Smith, Keith, *Marketing For Small Publishers*, Journeyman, 1992
Spicer, Robert, *How To Publish A Book*, How To Books, 1993
Zeitlyn, Jonathan, *Print: How You Can Do It Yourself!*, Journeyman, 1992

Organisations which can help

Association of Little Presses, 30 Greenhill, Hampstead High Street, London NW3 5UA   *tel* 071-435 1889. Membership £10. Offers advice, publishes a catalogue of small independent publications, produces a newsletter, organises book fairs.

Small Press Group, Middlesex University, White Hart Lane, London N7 8HR   *tel* 081-362 6058. Membership £17.50. Campaigns on behalf of small presses in Britain, publishes a yearbook (see page 147), a monthly magazine, organises book fairs. Also runs the Small Press Centre – a physical focus for British small publishers; send for their leaflet.

Password (Books) Ltd, 23 New Mount Street, Manchester M4 4DE   *tel* 061-953 4009. Runs publishing training courses for small and self-publishers; grants available.

Author-Publisher Enterprise, PO Box 1844, Colchester, Essex CO3 3SL   *tel* (0206) 752778. Membership £25. A self-publishers' self-help organisation. Runs courses, lectures; publishes a useful magazine.

See also the **Preparation of materials, resources** section for articles on word processing and desktop publishing, and for the list of editorial, literary and production services.

A Self-publishing Success Story
How *The Silver Tide* Came to be Published

MICHAEL TOD

> I had been duped by men whose greed
> Outweighed their honour . . .

These two lines are from my poem *Gypsy Mary*, written at the time I decided to write a novel. My business as a designer of Victorian-style conservatories had been reduced by the recession to the point where I was vulnerable to the promises of these 'greedy men', and it cost me my house. Not the best atmosphere in which to write a novel, and yet it was to avoid the negative thoughts of that period that I turned my mind to writing.

A year before I had met Aeron Clement, whose badger book *The Cold Moons* is the classic modern example of a book rejected by many agents and publishers but which, after self-publication, went on to earn a small fortune for the author. Unfortunately, Aeron Clement died soon after this happened. Could I write a book in the same genre? I thought I might be able to, and it did offer some hope of a way out and up.

So there I was, broke, tapping away at my word processor from 5am to 9am to banish negative thoughts, before going out to earn that day's bread.

Could I recover the family fortune?

I had been writing poetry for some years and had joined a writers' group to improve this work, but there was little money in poetry. If only I could emulate Aeron Clement there was a chance that I could recover the family fortune.

I have always been fascinated by the parallel between the way we arrogant Europeans went to such places as America and Australia and took the lands from the natives, and the way in which the grey squirrels, introduced into England at the end of the last century, did the same thing to our native reds. Here was a theme for the book but, as with most writers of a first novel, I tried to incorporate into the story large amounts of glamorised autobiography and personal fantasy, chapters alternating between squirrel activity and human activity. It did not work! The frequent change of viewpoint and culture was disconcerting, to say the least. My writing group was helpful; and one member suggested that I take out the humans and make it a squirrel-only book.

That was the point at which it started to work. Now I could envisage each scene as though it were happening in animated cartoon form so that I actually *heard* what the squirrels were saying to each other. All I had to do was to write it down. Each day was exciting: *I* wanted to know what was going to happen next!

After about six months of the rewrite I had a complete story, even if it was a bit raw: in essence, the peace-loving red squirrels who live at the Blue Pool in Dorset come under threat from the invading, colonising Greys and are driven from their homes to the safety of Brownsea Island in Poole Harbour from where some set out to reconquer their homeland.

A potential bestseller?

I sent the first three chapters with a synopsis to an agent in London expecting the delay of weeks or months that I had been warned was likely to follow. To my amazement and delight, he telephoned the next evening raving about the story, using such terms as 'potential bestseller', 'sure-fire winner', etc., and asking for the rest of the manuscript to be sent at once. Naturally I was over the moon, envisaging an immediate end to poverty with the substantial advances I expected to receive. But life is seldom that simple. On reading the rest of the manuscript the agent said it was 'Disappointing – the characters are not fully developed.' Even so, while I was working on the characters as suggested by him, he showed my manuscript to a senior editor of one of the largest publishing houses. It was not as well received as he and I had hoped, and shortly afterwards the agent's assistant told me that, if I sent the postage, my manuscripts would be returned to me.

I tried another agent with the revised version and received a letter using the words 'Delightful manuscript, I was enchanted', but shortly after this the parcel came back with the comment, 'My readers did not care for it as much as I did.'

The self-publishing option

Several agents and a couple of publishers later I was as frustrated as hell and kept thinking of Aeron Clement's experiences in self-publishing. But of course I had no money and no credit with the bank. I did however have some supportive friends and relatives. Thinking that if I had invented something physical and needed cash to develop and launch it I would sell shares in any future profits, I wrote a prospectus and offered 20 shares @ £250, each against one per cent of any profits earned by the book in its first five years after publication. The result of this, together with a direct loan from another member of the family, enabled me to spend time revising, polishing and preparing the manuscript for the printer. My wife and son did the final editing. I decided to use the same printers, the Dinefwr Press in South Wales, as Aeron Clement had used, though, in consultation with Donald Martin, the managing director, we produced 3000 paperback copies rather than the 5000 hardbacks that had launched *The Cold Moons*. Donald had boasted that he could deliver in ten weeks. He did this with a few days to spare.

Cadno Books

The cost of the 3000, including a full-colour laminated cover and sewn sections, was just under £4000, giving a cost per book of £1.32. I planned to sell at £4.99, so after deducting the bookseller's 35 per cent discount, the price to shops would be £3.25. This left me £1.93 to cover distribution and any profit, but by now I was not expecting a net profit from the first batch. My hope was that it would sell and so be recognised by a major publishing house, as had happened with the badger book.

It was necessary to set up a nominal publishing business which I did, Cadno Books. 'Cadno' is the Welsh word for fox as 'Tod' (my surname) is the Scots' name for that wily animal. Setting up the business was easy, no formal paperwork being involved, and I applied for an ISBN number for *The Silver Tide*, which was the title finally chosen.

While the book was being printed I did the preparatory work to ensure that I would sell at least the 3000 which were in production. Both the main settings for the book, the Blue Pool and Brownsea Island in Dorset, are popular with tourists and both have gift-shops selling books. The owners and managers agreed to take two cases (120 books) each and more if they sold, so I set up signing sessions at the Blue Pool, the Corfe Castle National Trust shop and at Brownsea Island. These were scheduled for the three days of the Spring Bank Holiday, trusting that the printer would not let me down. He did not and, with a car full of smart and surprisingly heavy books to sell by the case, I set out to visit all the bookshops of Dorset. In my innocence I did not know that shops seldom buy cases of books:

they usually buy in ones and twos, for modern logistics enable them to replace stock virtually overnight. However, in my enthusiasm I sold 1100 in the first three weeks!

The radio interview – and the contract

I also sent review copies to nearly every newspaper, radio and TV station from Swansea to Southampton, producing six reviews (favourable) and an invitation to be interviewed on three radio stations.

The key interview was recorded for BBC Wales's book programme *And Now Read On* where my interview was followed by another with Anthony Cheetham, the chief executive of Orion Books. He was saying that Orion were looking for new authors with something different to say, and I was saying that I had self-published to prove my book would sell. And it was selling, so now I was looking for a publisher to take it over. I sent a copy to Mr Cheetham and four days later he telephoned to ask 'How precious was my book?'

What he actually meant was, how much would I be prepared to alter it if necessary to suit their marketing requirements, should they take it up. A week or so later I was sitting in Orion's London office signing a contract for three squirrel books with Judith Elliot, the managing director of Orion Children's Books Ltd, who was to edit the trilogy. It had been agreed that *The Silver Tide* would be treated as a 'cross-over' book, that is one to be read by both children and adults, as with Richard Adams's *Watership Down* and William Horwood's *Duncton Wood* stories. I was very aware at that time that there were some 100,000 aspiring authors who would have given their right arms to be sitting where I was, signing such a contract.

The professional editor

Now, of course, I was exposed to professional editing. My wife and son had been properly hard on me, striking out my more fanciful (and irrelevant) passages and ruthlessly exposing weaknesses in the plot and the dialogue. Now Judith Elliot, keen to ensure that the book would attract the widest readership, went through my version, suggesting cuts and alterations and proposing additional scenes and details. She also wanted the book to appeal to librarians, seeing them as an important part of the potential market.

I was advised to amend 'Grey race' and 'Red race', when referring to the different squirrels, to 'Grey kind' and 'Red kind' respectively; the insulting shout of 'Grey bastards', became 'You flea-ridden tree-rats'. Some other scenes were amended and, overall, the word count increased by about 10 per cent. But that improved the book by more than 10 per cent.

I agreed with most of Judith's proposed amendments, bowing to her professional skills. Now that I know how much an editor contributes to a book, I am surprised that they do not have a credit on the title page. They deserve one.

Breaking even

It was a condition of Orion's contract that I stop selling my paperback edition by the end of October and on the 31st of that month, I shipped the last consignment. If I take into account my time selling, travelling costs and telephone calls I probably broke even and the selling was hard, if enjoyable, work. A crucial factor in the selling success was the location of the story in one real area so that I could focus the publicity there and capitalise on local interest. This enabled me to sell a notable number quickly – but a book does not become a bestseller by selling 1000 copies out of one, two or three shops. What makes a bestseller is 1000 shops selling just two books each week for a year. Work it out.

Is self-publishing for everyone?

Would I advise others to self-publish? 'Yes' for non-fiction, especially if it has a strong local connection. But a hitherto unrecognised novel? Almost certainly 'No' if you want to make money from it. Distribution and sales are just too expensive to organise. But if your plan is to prove that a book will actually sell so that you can then attract a commercial publisher, as Aeron Clement and I did, it might be worth a try. But only if you are prepared to go out and sell the books – and yourself.

Prizewinner – and the sequel

The original paperback edition of *The Silver Tide* won the David Thomas Charitable Trust Award for Self-Published Fiction. The hardback edition was published in January 1994. It has received a number of good reviews and has been accepted by two book clubs. Translation and publication rights have been sold in Germany, Holland and Denmark. The sequel, *The Second Wave*, has been delivered and, after the same severe editing, has been accepted by Orion who will publish it in October. The final book in the trilogy, *The Golden Flight*, also exists in draft form.

And yes, I have a great idea for a fourth book burning to be written. But that's another story.

Writing for older children and teenagers

As readers acquire increasing confidence and become more fluent, so their appetites grow for more and more stories of all kinds – adventure, family, fantasy, historical, mystery, school, thriller – and you can assume that the range of subject-matter you can consider is almost limitless. You are certainly not confined to what lies within a child's own experience, and when thinking about an idea that has come into your mind you can rely on common sense to decide whether it's a story to be written for children or adults. A mystery about insider dealing on the stock exchange might not interest children; a robbery in which children played a part in catching the criminals might make a cops-and-robbers story for them (and often has). A story in which a child was a thief, got away with it and showed no remorse – ah, there's the catch. *That*, I think, could only be told as a psychological thriller for adults. For most people would agree, I believe, that in a story for children justice should be seen to be done, and the challenge for the writer is to admit, and gradually introduce into realistic stories, the possibility that *in*justice, evil, wickedness – however you name it, whatever its origin – exists in similar measure to its opposite.

from *Writing for Children* by Margaret Clark (A & C Black, £7.99)

Vanity Publishing

A reputable publisher very rarely asks an author to pay for the production of his work, or to contribute to its cost, or to undertake to purchase copies. The only exception is in the case of a book of an extremely specialised nature, with a very limited market or perhaps the first book of poems by a new writer of some talent. In such instances, especially if the book is a good one making a contribution to its subject, an established and reliable publisher may be prepared to accept a subvention from the author to make publication possible, and such financial grants often come from scientific or other academic foundations or funds. This is a very different procedure from that of the *vanity publisher* who claims to perform, for a fee to be paid by the author, all the many functions involved in publishing a book.

In his efforts to secure business the vanity publisher will usually give exaggerated praise to an author's work and arouse equally unrealistic hopes of its commercial success. Those who pay for the publication of their books should realise that what they are paying for is simply the manufacture of copies. And if all that they want is a book which they can show with pride to their family and friends – then no harm may come of it. But they should not confuse 'manufacture' with 'publication'. The true publisher invests *his own* money in the whole publishing process: editorial, design, manufacturing, selling, distribution. The vanity publisher invests *the author's* money in but one part of this process: manufacture.

The distressing reports we have received from embittered victims of vanity publishers underline the importance of reading extremely carefully the contracts offered by such publishers. Often these will provide for the printing of, say, 2000 copies of the book, usually at a quite exorbitant cost to the author, but will leave the 'publisher' under no obligation to bind more than a very limited number. Frequently, too, the author will be expected to pay the cost of any effective advertising, while the 'publisher' makes little or no effort to promote the distribution and sale of the book. Again, the names and imprints of vanity publishers are well known to literary editors, and their productions therefore are rarely, if ever, reviewed or even noticed in any important periodical. Similarly, such books are hardly ever stocked by the booksellers.

We repeat, therefore: except in rare instances, never pay for 'publication', whether for a book, an article, a lyric, or a piece of music. If a work is worth publishing, sooner or later a publisher will be prepared to publish it at his own expense. But if a writer cannot resist the temptation of seeing his work in print, in book form, he should consider the possibility of self-publishing. If, after all, he decides to approach a vanity publisher, even though he has to pay a substantial sum, he should first discover just how much or how little the publisher will provide and will do in return for the payment demanded.

See also the **Agents** section for literary agents.

Poetry

Poetry into Print

JOHN WHITWORTH

I have never edited a poetry magazine nor worked in a publishing house. But I *have* submitted hundreds of poems and I have had dealings, most of them happy, with a number of publishers of poetry. My advice will therefore be from the handle end of the long spoon that poets use to sup with those they would persuade or bamboozle into printing, even paying for, their work.

There are two things to say at the outset. Do not expect to make more than pin money *directly* from publication of your work. You may, in the fullness of time, make quite a tidy sum *indirectly* – I mean you get work because you are a published poet: readings, workshops, reviewing and so forth, if you like any of that sort of thing. But if you get £40 for a poem from a national magazine you may feel very satisfied, and as for your published slim volumes – they will not sell in four figures, nor do the publishers, except in a very few instances, expect them to. In a sense nearly all poetry publishing is vanity publishing. Nobody is in it for the money.

And, secondly, as one poet put it to me, do not have too much respect for the taste of individual literary editors. She is right. An editor is not God (whatever he thinks). Remember that, though it can be hard if you are diffident (and most poets are). But this person is just like you; the fact that he or she (nearly always he) is warming an editorial chair may mean many things. It certainly does not mean papal infallibility. If Snooks of the *Review* sends back your work, despatch it immediately to Snurd of the *Supplement*. And if Snurd concurs with Snooks, they may both be wrong, indeed neither may actually have read through (or at all) what you sent. Grit your teeth and send to Snarl and then to Snivel. Do not be discouraged by rejection. If your poems are as good as you can make them and have been submitted in as professional a way as you can manage, then just keep on sending them out. I started writing poems in 1968, wrote my first good one in 1972, and was paid my first proper money (£40 from the Arts Council) in 1976. The first book was published in 1980. So patience and a thick skin are big advantages.

It does help, of course, to have read the magazine you are making submissions to. This will prevent your sending your bawdy ballad to *PN Review* or concrete poetry to *The Spectator*. And I am assuming that you actually are interested in the *craft* of poetry and the names of, say, Milton, Tennyson and Eliot mean something to you. You will also be interested to know what Heaney, Hughes,

Harrison, Carol Ann Duffy and Fiona Pitt-Kethley actually do. You don't have to like it, but you ought to want to know about it. If no one is writing anything remotely like your work, perhaps you should ask yourself why that might be. On the other hand, remember the words of Charlie Coburn, the old music-hall singer: 'I sang my song to them, and they didn't like it. So I sang it again, and they still didn't like it. So I sang it a third time and one of them thought he might just get to like it if I changed the tune and altered the words. So I sang it again, just exactly the same way, and after a bit they all liked it.'

SUBMITTING YOUR WORK TO MAGAZINES

I asked a number of poets about this. Some of them surprised me by saying they never submitted to magazines at all, because they disliked being rejected. I must say I think that a rather craven attitude, but you *can*, if you are talented enough, carve out a poetic reputation through workshops and readings. You must be good at putting yourself about in public and have the time and energy to expend on it.

All who did submit work regularly agreed on a number of basics:

1. Submit your poem on an A4 sheet (or the computer-paper rough equivalent), typed or printed out from a word processor. One poet, David Phillips, reckoned his percentage of successful submissions had gone up appreciably since he bought his word processor, and he assumed it was because his work now looked much more professional. It might be, of course, that it has just got better. Do not do it in italic, capitals or mock cursive. Keep it simple.

2. Put your name and address at the bottom of each poem. Editors, reasonably, do not keep your letters, only the poems that interest them. You might consider one of those rubber stamps. I know a number of poets who have them, though I don't myself.

3. Fold the poem once and put it into the sort of envelope designed to take A4 folded once. I don't know why poets like to scrunch their verses into tiny envelopes, but don't do it. Don't go to the other extreme either and send it decorated with admonitions not to bend, etcetera. Include a stamped, self-addressed envelope of the same size. This really is important. Shakespeare himself would be consigned to the wpb without an appropriate sae.

4. Do not send just one poem. Do not send 20 poems. Send enough to give a reasonable flavour of your work – say about four or five. Long poems are less likely to be accepted than short poems, for various obvious reasons. If you write different *kinds* of things, then make sure your selection covers a fair few of these kinds. Send what you think of as your best work, but do not be surprised if what is finally accepted is the one you put in at the last minute, 'to make the others look better' as Larkin lugubriously puts it. And if an editor says he likes your work and would like to see more, then *send* more as soon as possible. He wasn't just being polite. Editors aren't. He said it because he meant it.

5. At this point there is generally some po-faced stuff about *never* sending the same poem to more than one editor simultaneously. As it happens, I don't do this, but it appears that some well-known poets do. And indeed, if Snurd of the *Supplement* sits on your poems for six months, what are you supposed to do, since the polite follow-up letter recommended will, almost certainly, have no effect at all, except to waste your time and your stamps? The real reason for not making multiple submissions is the embarrassment of having to make grovelling noises when the same poem is accepted by two editors at once. I once, inadvertently, won two microscopic prizes in poetry competitions for the same poem. What did I do? I kept my mouth shut and cashed the cheques, that's what I did.

6. You wouldn't have been daft enough to send off your *only* copies of poems to Snurd, would you? *Of course* he lost them and it's all your own silly fault. No you can't sue him through the civil courts, but you'll know better next time. Send photocopies and keep your originals. No, editors don't mind photocopies. Why should they? They look a lot better than the original all covered in Tippex anyway.

7. Keep your covering letter short, but if you have been published in reputable places then it will do no harm to say so. This advice comes from Duncan Forbes. Selling poems is very like selling anything else, so blow your own trumpet, but don't blow for too long. Don't ask the editor for help in the advancement of your poetic career. He doesn't care, and anyway, what does he know? Being rude won't help either. I know artists are supposed to be rude and a lot of them are, too, but it hasn't actually helped them to anything except an ulcer or a punch on the nose.

WHICH MAGAZINES?

You *could* start with *The Times Literary Supplement* but I wouldn't advise it. One editor (not from the *TLS*) said honestly that he tended to reject, more or less unread, poems from anyone he had never heard of. Before you play with the big boys perhaps you ought to have some sort of a record in the little magazines. Some of these pay and some do not. The size of the cheque seems to depend on the size of the Arts Council grant rather than the quality of the magazine, though I suppose the two ought to have some sort of relationship. What matters is not the cash but whether you feel proud or ashamed to be seen in the thing. The Poetry Library at the South Bank Centre (Royal Festival Hall, London SE1 8XX) publishes a list of poetry magazines, and if you can get along there (very convenient for Waterloo Station and open 11-8 for seven days a week), you can nose around among the back numbers and see what is appealing to you. If you can't do that, then a letter with an sae will get you the list. The one I am looking at has well over a hundred titles, from photocopied and stapled compilations all the way up to *Poetry Review*, the magazine of the Poetry Society, to which I suggest you subscribe (for your own benefit, and not the Poetry Society's). They also have a list of American poetry magazines of which there are a great number. ('Anyone who cannot get poems published in America has simply run out of stamps,' Simon Rae.) There is another in preparation on Commonwealth magazines. Judge where you think you will fit in, and buy yourself a big sheet of second-class stamps. Send off your work and be prepared to be reasonably patient. Most editors reply in the end. Little magazines have a high mortality rate, so be prepared for a particularly crushing form of disappointment – having your work accepted by a magazine which promptly ceases publication. It happens to us all; it goes on happening to me.

Some inexperienced poets seem very worried that editors will filch their 'ideas' and pay them nothing, but poems are not made up of ideas; they are made up of words, and if anyone prints your poem without permission they are infringing your copyright and you can threaten them with all sorts of horrible things. But, honestly, this is a buyer's market, and even the editor of that badly photocopied rag has more material than he can use.

I have already recommended *Poetry Review*. *Poetry Wales* and *The New Welsh Review* are both beautifully produced, though they lack *PR*'s bite and attack, and there is a certain amount of relentless celticity. *The Honest Ulsterman* is unpretentious to look at, but consistently interesting and intelligent – you don't have to be at all Irish to contribute either. *Ambit* is lively with good artwork; the editors take ages to look at submissions though. *Iron* is run by a relic of the 60s (Peter Mortimer who has a little boy called Dylan), and mixes the very good and the very bad in an exhilarating cocktail. Mortimer is a most conscientious editor, and replies promptly and individually. A rare man! *Stand* has a wide distribution – a rather Guardian-y feel to the poems and opinions. *London Magazine* is as good as ever – Alan Ross scribbles cryptic encouragement on poems that don't quite make it. *PN Review* is a Leavisite dinosaur with very rude reviewers. It is an offshoot of the publisher Carcanet (or the other way around) and prints a wide range of poems. Auberon Waugh's *Literary Review* has competitions each month for poems that rhyme and scan. They are generally won by a chap called Frank McDonald, but if you can do better, then enter – the prizes are worth having. Unfortunately, these competitions are now open only to subscribers. This is a very personal list – these are the magazines I read from time to time. There are plenty of others, particularly from Scotland. Go to the Poetry Library and look. *Poetry Review* has been doing an excellent round-up of magazines.

The two literary heavyweights are *The Times Literary Supplement* and the *London Review of Books* who both publish poetry. Their difference may be that the *TLS* does not publish Fiona Pitt-Kethley. P.J. Kavanagh at *The Spectator* publishes poems every week. All worth trying once you are getting published in little magazines, probably not before.

BOOK PUBLICATION

Every poet wants to get a book out. How do you do it? One pretty sure way is to win a big prize in a competition, the National or the biennial Arvon or Harry Chambers' Peterloo, though a high proportion of the winners have published books already, which seems unfair of them. Otherwise, you wait until you have reached the stage of having had two or three dozen poems published in reputable places; then you type out enough poems for a collection, traditionally 64pp but collections seem to be getting longer, and send them out, keeping your own copy and including return postage. I suppose you do. I first got published by talking to Anthony Thwaite in a pub; everybody needs a slice of luck. I know some excellent poets who are still trying to place their first book and, contrariwise, there are books from big publishers that are complete disasters in every way. Poetry, like most things, goes in fashions. But don't be in a hurry. Wait until you have some sort of a reputation in the magazines and small presses. Neil Astley at Bloodaxe reckons more than 90 per cent of what comes through his letterbox he sends back, and he has usually had an eye on the successful ones before they got around to submitting.

Who do you send out to? Faber stand at the top of the tree (though they did turn down Larkin and the small press Marvell got *The Less Deceived*, the most influential book of English poems in the last 50 years. They have the rising star, Simon Armitage, though they now can't afford Craig Raine, who auctioned himself off to Penguin). They promote their poets too and sell their books. Everybody wants to be Fabered – you are in the company of Eliot and Larkin for a start. Sinclair-Stevenson now have a good list (though with very boring covers). Most big publishers have their poetry wing, as it were, waxing and waning with the person, often a poet, in the editorial chair. But being published by a household name does not necessarily mean selling a lot of copies. Publishers like to have poetry on their list as a kind of badge of virtue, but often they don't want to know much about it, they don't promote it and they don't persist with it. The book sinks or swims, and usually it sinks. Mine sank.

Specialist poetry presses (some, though not all of which, publish nothing but poetry) produce books that look every bit as good and, in most cases, sell every bit as well (or badly). Bloodaxe, Peterloo and Carcanet are probably leaders in the field, all a very long way from London, though they are not biased against poor South Easterners.

Carcanet publish both Elizabeth Jennings and John Ashberry, which indicates Michael Schmidt's catholicity and willingness to go outside this country. He sees them as extending the Wordsworthian tradition of the common voice and welcomes manuscripts, though he wishes people would read some of the books on his list first. This is good advice; every publisher has a style, just as every magazine has. Harry Chambers at Peterloo has Dana Gioia, the American 'new formalist' on his list, as well as U.A. (Ursula) Fanthorpe and me. Typically he goes for late flowerers rather than fresh faces. Bloodaxe sounds fearsomely dismissive, but the name is from a Viking who conquered Northumberland. They have Tony Harrison, Irina Ratushinskaya and Simon Rae's Guardian poems, 'from traditional formalists to post-modernists,' says Neil Astley. Bloodaxe is now the leading poetry publisher, certainly in terms of quantity, probably of quality also.

Anvil are London-based and do a lot of poetry in translation. Enitharmon have Duncan Forbes and Sebastian Barker, Headland Elizabeth Bartlett and Mainstream William McIlvanney. These may not be their best poets (how can you tell?) but they are the ones I like, and a few years ago most of them would have been with the big London names. But that was before the publishing revolution and the rise of the conglomerates who remainder most of their lists within a couple of years.

Most of these presses (not Carcanet or Bloodaxe) are represented by Password, a distribution network working for small literary presses (mostly, but not exclusively, poetry) in the UK and Eire. It has its own warehouse and deals with the Jiffy-bagging of books to bookshops and individual customers for most (though not all) of its members. It is expanding into Europe, with agencies in many EU countries (information from David Parrish on 061-953 4009). If this system works well, then there is little if any advantage to be gained from going with the big publishers.

There are a lot more excellent small presses and information on them is available from the following:

The Association of Little Presses (ALP), 30 Greenhill, Hampstead High Street, London NW3 5UA. They put out a newsletter and a catalogue for £3.00 + 75p p&p.
The Oriel Bookshop (Welsh Arts Council Bookshop, The Friary, Cardiff CF1 4AA) publishes *Small Presses and Little Magazines of the UK and Ireland.*
The *Small Press Yearbook* is available from The Small Press Group, Middlesex University, White Hart Lane, London N7 8HR *tel* 081-362 6058.
The Poetry Library (address earlier) has a Current Awareness List for Asian and Afro-Caribbean Poetry. Mine is 38pp of bookshops, competitions, libraries, magazines, organisations, UK publishers and workshops.

COMPETITIONS

Some poets are very snooty about these, though I can't think why. Of course they are popular because they make money for the organisers. Think of the numbers: a biggish competition may attract ten thousand entries paying £3 a time. That gives an income of £30,000, enough to pay for some good prizes, a fair bit of promotion, fees for the judges and running costs, and still leave a nice bit in the kitty. But, from the poet's end, it is a good deal too. Over the last ten years I have entered about 30 competitions, and won small prizes, £5 to £100, in half a dozen of them. I reckon I might be on the right side to the extent of £100. And though unknowns (everybody starts as an unknown, don't they?) only occasionally win the big prizes, they do pick up the smaller ones quite often, and that can be a great encouragement when you need it. The competitions (I have judged two big ones and a number of little ones) are organised fairly, and everyone does have an equal chance. So why *not* have a go? If you think you write as well as John Latham (a consistent winner), here's your chance to prove it. You can find details of current competitions on page 284.

VANITY PUBLISHING/SUBSIDY PUBLISHING

Never give a publisher money. That is what they give to you. If you want your work in print and nobody will do it for you without a cheque, then do it yourself. Self-publishers have made money before now, though not usually (I think) with poetry. You could probably buy yourself an Amstrad with the money you save by *not* answering that advertisement!

LISTINGS

I give no separate listings, not out of idleness, but because the Poetry Library (see below) does it much better. And the magazines are evanescent things; the Poetry Library updates its list monthly. (But see the classified list on page 136 for the poetry magazines listed in this *Yearbook*.)

A LAST WORD

Invest some time, invest some money. Buy yourself, if not a word processor, at least a decent typewriter and some nice paper. Buy some books of poetry and try to see how your favourites do it. If you're a joiner, join a local group. Your local Regional Arts Board will know who they are. The Muse chooses her favourites, but be a bit welcoming.

Poetry Organisations

MARY ENRIGHT
The Poetry Library

SOCIETIES

The Poetry Society, 22 Betterton Street, London WC2H 9BU   *tel* 071-240 4810   *fax* 071-240 4818. The Poetry Society has been operating for over 80 years and exists to promote poetry, to assist poets and to campaign for poetry and poets whenever the opportunity arises. Its principal activities include the publication of *Poetry Review*; the provision of an Advice and Information Service; the maintenance of a database of living UK poets, the Poets Register; the administration of the W.H. Smith-sponsored Poets-in-Schools Scheme; the running of the National Poetry Competition; and the provision of a Critical Service. Membership is available on an annual basis and details can be obtained from the above address.

Poetry Ireland, Bermingham Tower, Upper Yard, Dublin Castle, Dublin 2, Republic of Ireland   *tel* (01) 6714632   *fax* (01) 6714634. Poetry Ireland acts as the Irish Poetry Society and also runs the Austin Clarke Library, a reference library of over 6000 titles. It publishes *Poetry Ireland Review*, a quarterly magazine, and organises readings in Dublin and nationally.

European Association for the Promotion of Poetry, Blijde Inkomststraat 9, B-3000 Louvain, Belgium.

Regional Arts Boards. The officers responsible for literature in the Regional Arts Boards can provide information on local poetry groups, workshops and societies. Many Boards give grant aid to local publishers and magazines and help fund festivals and readings, etc.; some run critical services. A list of the relevant officers is available on receipt of an sae from the Information Service, The Arts Council of England, 14 Great Peter Street, London SW1P 3NQ.

LIBRARIES

The Poetry Library, Royal Festival Hall, South Bank Centre, London SE1 8XX *tel* 071-921 0943/0664. The Poetry Library was founded in 1953 by the Arts Council of Great Britain (now the Arts Council of England). It is now part of the Literature section of the South Bank Centre and can be found on Level 5 of the Royal Festival Hall. Its two principal roles are to collect and preserve all poetry published in the UK in this century, and to act as a public lending library. Two copies of all titles are purchased, allowing one to be available for consultation and the other to go out on loan. Books may be borrowed by those outside London through the national Inter-Library Lending network. The collection of about 30,000 titles is all in the English language, although it includes translations from all over the world. There is a large children's section, as well as poetry on cassette, record and video.

As well as the normal functions of all libraries, the Poetry Library also runs an active information service on all poetry-related activities, and offers advice to the new poet. Current awareness lists are produced and are available by post on receipt of a large sae. They include lists of magazines, competitions, bookshops, groups and workshops, evening classes, festivals, etc. and are updated regularly. The Library also stocks the full range of British poetry magazines as well as a large selection from abroad.

Membership of the Library is free, and is open to all on production of proof of identity and current address.

The Scottish Poetry Library, Tweeddale Court, 14 High Street, Edinburgh EH1 1TE *tel* 031-557 2876. Founded in 1984, the Scottish Poetry Library is run along similar lines to the Poetry Library in London, specialising in twentieth-century poetry written in Scotland, in Scots, Gaelic and English. It also collects pre-twentieth century Scottish poetry and contemporary poetry from all over the world. Information and advice on all poets is given and visits by individuals, groups and schools are welcome. It has branches in libraries and arts centres throughout Scotland and also runs a mobile library service. Readings and exhibitions are regularly organised, particularly during the Edinburgh Festival.

Northern Poetry Library, County Library, The Willows, Morpeth, Northumberland NE61 1TA *tel* (0670) 512385. Founded in 1968, the Northern Arts Poetry Library serves the area covered by the Northern Arts Regional Board, i.e. Tyne and Wear, Durham, Northumberland, Cumbria and Cleveland. Its collection contains over 6000 titles of mostly British material. It is run by Northumberland Public Library as one of its special services.

Public libraries. Public libraries can be an invaluable source of information on writing activities in the area in addition to having collections of modern poetry for loan. Some also have literature field workers or writers-in-residence, who can be very helpful to beginners.

COMPETITIONS

There are literally hundreds of poetry competitions going on throughout the year, varying widely in quality and quantity of entries and prizes. The two most important are the National Poetry Competition run by the Poetry Society and the biennial Arvon Foundation International Poetry Competition. Details of these, and the Bridport, Leek and Peterloo, competitions can be found under **Literary prizes and awards**. The Poetry Library produces a free list, updated monthly, of these and other competitions, and is available on receipt of a large sae.

AWARDS

There are several prestigious awards for poetry, most awarded annually to published poets, and therefore non-competitive. A complete list of all awards is included in the *Guide to Literary Prizes, Grants and Awards in Britain and Ireland*, published by Book Trust (45 East Hill, London SW18 2QZ) in 1992. A new edition is planned for late 1994.

BOOKSHOPS

Not all general bookshops have a strong modern poetry section but there are some which specialise in poetry. The principal ones are the following:

The Poetry Bookshop/Alan Halsey
22 Broad Street
Hay-on-Wye
Herefordshire HR3 5DB

Bernard Stone/Turret Books
36 Great Queen Street
London WC2B 5AA

Peter Riley
27 Sturton Street
Cambridge CB1 2QG

Oriel/The Welsh Arts Council
Bookshop
The Friary
Cardiff CF2 4AA

These and other good bookshops stocking a range of poetry are listed by the Poetry Library; this list is divided into London and outside London areas and can be obtained by sending a large sae. A separate list is available for suppliers of poetry on audio cassette and record.

FESTIVALS

Literature festivals have become increasingly popular and prestigious in the past few years and are now held in almost every part of the country. Again information on what is happening in your area should be readily available from your local library and Regional Arts Board. The British Council keeps lists of forthcoming Literature Festivals and Arts Festivals with Literature Events, which are available on receipt of a large sae from the Information Officer, Literature Department, British Council, 10 Spring Gardens, London SW1A 2BN.

PERFORMANCE VENUES

In London the best way to keep up to date with readings and poetry events is through the weekly listing magazine, *Time Out*, and *What's On in London*. Now that the Poetry Society has ceased to run regular events for the moment, the main London venues are the Voice Box in the South Bank Centre, Apples and Snakes Performance Poetry, the Blue Nose Cafe and Troubadour Coffee House.

Outside London, local listings magazines should be helpful and Regional Arts Boards and public libraries will have details of all literature events happening in their area.

POETRY GROUPS AND WORKSHOPS

Joining a poetry group can be an excellent way to get useful help and advice on writing and publishing. Groups vary enormously; if possible, try a few in your area to find the one most congenial to your style. Unfortunately there is no national list of groups and they tend to wax and wane, so again the first point of contact is your Regional Arts Board and your local library.

The Poetry Library compiles a list of groups and workshops for the Greater London area; this is updated regularly and available on receipt of a large sae.

WRITING COURSES

There is currently much more available than ever before in the area of short term creative writing courses, as writers-in-residence are appointed by Regional Arts Boards, and by libraries, colleges, prisons, etc. There is also a choice of residential writing courses of which the best are those run by the Arvon Foundation and the Tŷ Newydd. All areas of writing are covered, as well as poetry.

Arvon Foundation

The Arvon Foundation now runs three centres, in Yorkshire, Devon and Inverness-shire, and has wide experience of residential writing courses. Most last for about five days and offer tuition by working writers. Full details of annual courses may be obtained from the centres as follows:

The Arvon Foundation at Lumb Bank, Hebden Bridge, West Yorkshire HX7 6DF

The Arvon Foundation at Totleigh Barton, Sheepwash, Beaworthy, Devon EX21 5NS

The Arvon Foundation at Moniack Mhor, Teavarran, Kiltarlity, Beauly, Inverness-shire IV4 7HT.

Tŷ Newydd

Courses here are run along similar lines to the Arvon Houses with a wide variety of courses offered. Some of the tutors used are Welsh writers though there is a good mix. Full details can be obtained from Taliesin, Tŷ Newydd, Llanystumdwy, Cricieth, Gwynedd LL52 0LW.

Other courses

East Midlands Arts runs a number of residential writing courses from April to September and the 1994 programme was located at Leicester University. Again a variety of types of writing is covered and details for future courses are available from East Midlands Arts, Mountfields House, Epinal Way, Loughborough, Leics. LE11 0QE.

Information on other such courses can be obtained from the Regional Arts Boards, local libraries or the Poetry Library.

POETRY FOR CHILDREN AND YOUNG ADULTS

The Poetry Society Education Department

The Poetry Society Education Department promotes poetry through schools and educational organisations and offers a wide range of services and facilities to teachers, children and students. It runs activities such as the W.H. Smith-sponsored Poets-in-Schools scheme and publishes the *BP Teachers' Poetry Resources File* (available in primary and secondary versions at £10.95 each + £4.00 p&p), for which updates are available on an annual basis. The Department also produces a Teacher's Newsletter, a quarterly journal and teaching resource distributed through Teacher/Education membership of the Poetry Society; offers an Advice and Information Service which can help to put schools in touch with poets; and works to keep young writers informed about competitions, publications, and developing their creative writing. Full details can be obtained from the Education Officer, The Poetry Society, 22 Betterton Street, London WC2H 9BU *tel* 071-240 4810.

The Poetry Library

The Poetry Library has a large children's section of about 4000 books incorporating the SIGNAL Collection of Children's Poetry. It also runs an Education service for teachers and schools and welcomes class visits. There is a range of work packs for children's use while visiting the Library. A Teachers' Information Pack covering all aspects of poetry in education is available, as are selected reading lists for different age groups. Teachers Days are also arranged and children's events are included in the Literature programme. All services are free. Details from the Children's Section, The Poetry Library, Royal Festival Hall, London SE1 8XX.

Young Book Trust

Young Book Trust is the children's division of Book Trust. Its aims are to promote reading and offer advice and information on all aspects of children's reading and books. It runs a library of all children's books published over the last two years. It organises Children's Book Week, held usually in October, co-ordinating national activities throughout the week. It also offers an information service, including information on authors (Authorbank), and publishes a newsletter. A subscription service is available for schools, libraries, colleges, bookshops and publishers. Details from Young Book Trust, Book House, 45 East Hill, London SW18 2QZ.

National Association of Writers in Education

NAWE is a national organisation which aims to widen the scope of writing in education, and co-ordinate activities between writers, teachers and funding bodies. It publishes a magazine, *Writing in Education*, and a national directory of writers who work in schools, colleges and the community. Membership details and further information from NAWE, 49 Bryam Arcade, Huddersfield HD1 1ND *tel* (0484) 452070.

Competitions

The number of good poetry competitions for children are very limited, especially now that Shell Young Poet of the Year Award is no longer running.

W.H. Smith Young Writers Competition This is an annual open competition for original writing – poems, stories, plays or articles – by children aged 16 and under. Information is available from W.H. Smith Young Writers Competition, Strand House, 7 Holbein Place, Sloane Square, London SW1W 8NR.

Welsh Academy Young Writers Competition This is a national competition in which poetry and prose are acceptable in three categories, the upper limit being 18. The closing date is usually July. Information from Young Writers Competition, PO Box 328, Cardiff CF2 4XL.

FURTHER READING LIST

ALP, *Catalogue of Little Press Books in Print*, Association of Little Presses
Baldwin, Michael, *The Way to Write Poetry*, Hamish Hamilton, 1982
Bolton, Marjorie, *The Anatomy of Poetry*, Routledge, 1990
Chevalier, Tracy (ed.), *Contemporary Poets*, 5th edn, St James Press, 1991

Chisholm, Alison, *The Craft of Writing Poetry*, Allison & Busby, 1992
Clifford, Johnathon, *Metric Feet and Other Gang Members*, National Poetry Foundation, 1993
Dawe, Gerald, *How's the Poetry Going?*, Lagan Press, Ireland, 1991
Fergusson, Rosalind, *The Penguin Rhyming Dictionary*, Penguin Books, 1992
Finch, Peter, *How to Publish Your Poetry*, Allison & Busby, 1985
Finch, Peter, *Small Presses and Little Magazines of the UK and Ireland: an address list*, Oriel
Fulton, Len, *Directory of Poetry Publishers*, 8th edn, Dustbooks, USA
Fulton, Len, *The International Directory of Little Magazines and Small Presses*, 27th edn, Dustbooks, USA
Green, J.C.R., *Writers' Guidelines*, revised edn, Aquila Publishing
Hyland, Paul, *Getting into Poetry*, Bloodaxe, 1992
Jerome, Judson, *1994 Poet's Market: Where and How to Publish Your Poetry*, Writer's Digest Books, USA
Lendennie, Jessie, *The Salmon Guide to Poetry Publishing in Ireland*, Salmon Publishing, 1989
Livingstone, Dinah, *Poetry Handbook for Readers & Writers*, Macmillan, 1992
Myers, Jack & Simms, Michael, *Longman Dictionary and Handbook of Poetry*, Longman, 1989
PALPI Poetry and Little Press Information, Association of Little Presses
Preminger, Alex, *New Princeton Encyclopedia of Poetry and Poetics*, 3rd rev. edn, Princeton University Press, USA, 1993
Roberts, Philip Davies, *How Poetry Works: the Elements of English Poetry*, Penguin Books, 1991
Sansom, Peter, *Writing Poems*, Bloodaxe, 1994
Scannell, Vernon, *How to Enjoy Poetry*, Piatkus, 1987
SPG, *Small Press Yearbook*, The Small Press Group of Britain

See also the **Classified indexes** for poetry magazines and poetry book publishers; the **Illustration and design** section for verses in greetings cards; the **Societies and prizes** section.

Scripts for theatre, radio, tv and film

Marketing a Play

JULIA JONES
Society of Authors

As soon as a play is written, it is protected under the copyright laws of this country. No formalities are necessary here to secure copyright protection but it is a good plan to deposit a copy with the bank and take a dated receipt for it, so as to be able to prove the date of its completion, if this should be necessary at some time either, for example, to enforce a claim for infringement of copyright or to rebut such a claim. The copyright belongs to the author unless and until it is parted with; and this should never be done, since the copyright is in effect the sum total of all the author's rights in the work. An author should, so far as possible, deal separately with the component rights which go to make up the copyright and grant limited licences for the principal rights with, where customary or necessary, limited interests in the ancillary rights. A West End production agreement (see below) illustrates this principle.

The author can try to market the play personally, but once a play is accepted, it is wise to have professional assistance. All aspects of a contract are open for negotiation and the contractual complications are best handled by a reputable literary agent.

Although most ambitious young playwrights visualise a West End opening for their plays, the first step, except for the established dramatist, is usually to try to place the play with a company known to be interested in presenting new plays. It is wise to write to the company first, giving salient details, such as type of play, size of cast, number of sets, etc., and ask if the management would be willing to read it. This saves the frustration and expense of copies of the play being kept for long periods by managements who have no interest in it. (Do not send your only copy of the play away – this seems obvious, but many authors have suffered the torment of having to rewrite from memory when the only copy has been lost.) It is also possible to get a first production by entering the play for the various competitions which appear from time to time, but in this case great care should be taken to study the rules and ensure that the organisers of the competition do not acquire unreasonably wide rights and interests in the entries.

Many repertory companies will give a new play a try-out production in the hope that it will be seen by London managements and transfer to the West End. For the run at the repertory company's own theatre the company will receive a licence for a given period from a fixed date and pay the author a royalty of between 6 per cent and 10 per cent calculated on the gross box office receipts. In return for the risk involved in presenting a new play, the repertory company will expect a share in the author's earnings from subsequent professional stage productions of the play during a limited period (usually two years). Sometimes on transfer the West End management will agree to take over responsibility for part or all of this payment.

The contract, for repertory or West End production, or for the use of any other rights in the play, should specify precisely the rights to which it refers, the territory covered, the period of time covered, the payments involved and make it clear that all other rights remain the property of the author.

For a first-class production in the West End of London, usually preceded by a short provincial tour, the author's contract will include clauses dealing with the following main heads of agreement. The substance, as well as the phrasing of these clauses will vary considerably, but those given below probably represent the average, as do the figures in brackets, which must not be assumed to be standard:

1. UK option

In consideration of a specified minimum sum (between £500 and £1000) as a non-returnable advance against royalties, the Manager shall have the exclusive option for a specified period (usually six months) to produce the play in a first-class theatre in the West End of London (preceded possibly by a tour of a specified number of weeks) with an extension for a further period upon payment of a further similar sum.

2. UK licence

When the Manager exercises his option he shall have the UK licence for a specified period (three or five years) from the date of the first performance under the licence such licence to terminate before the expiry of the specified period if
(a) the play is not produced before a specified date;
(b) (i) less than a specified number (between 50 and 75) of consecutive professional performances are given and paid for in any year; or
(ii) the Manager has not paid at the beginning of any year a non-returnable advance against royalties. This variant on clause (b) (i) prevents the rights being tied up for a year while waiting to check if the qualifying performances have been given and is thus desirable from the author's point of view.

3. US option

If the Manager gives a specified number (usually 24) of consecutive performances in the West End he shall have an option exercisable within a specified period of the first West End performance (six weeks) to produce the play on Broadway on payment of a specified non-returnable advance on royalties (between £500 and £1000).

4. US licence

When the Manager exercises his option the Broadway licence shall be for a specified period (three years) on terms not less favourable than those specified in the Minimum Basic Agreement of the Dramatists' Guild of America.

5. Other rights

Provided the play has run for the qualifying period (usually 24 performances) the Manager acquires interests in some of the other rights as follows:
(i) *Repertory*. The author should reserve these rights paying the Manager a share (one-third) of his royalties for a specified period (two years after the end of the West End run or the expiry of the West End licence whichever is the shorter). The author agrees not to release these rights until after the end of the West End

run without the Manager's consent, this consent not to be unreasonably withheld. It is recommended that a play should be released to theatres on the A list immediately after the end of the West End run, and to theatres on the B list within three months from the end of the West End run, if an option for a tour has not been taken up by then, otherwise at the end of the tour. The theatres on these lists are those recommended by the Theatres' National Committee for immediate and early release of plays to repertory.

(ii) *Amateur*. The author should reserve these rights and pay the Manager no share in his royalties, but should undertake not to release these rights for an agreed period, to allow the repertory theatres to have maximum clear run.

(iii) *Radio, television and video*. The author should reserve these rights but it may well be in his interest not to release them until some time after the end of the West End run. During the run of the play in the West End, however, the Manager may arrange for an extract from the play to be broadcast or televised for publicity purposes, the author's fee for such broadcast or television performances being paid to him in full without any part of it going to the Manager.

(iv) *Film*. If the Manager has produced the play for the qualifying period it is expected that the author will pay him a percentage (often 20 per cent) of the author's net receipts from the disposal of the film rights, if these rights are disposed of within a specified period (one year) from the last West End performance. If the Manager has also produced the play on Broadway for the qualifying period the author is expected to allow him a further percentage (20 per cent) of the author's net receipts from the disposal of the film rights if the rights are disposed of within a specified time (one year) of the last Broadway performance. This is a field where the established dramatist can, not unnaturally, strike a much better bargain than the beginner. In no case, however, should the total percentage payable to the Manager exceed 40 per cent.

(v) *Foreign language*. These rights should be reserved to the author, the Manager receiving no share of the proceeds.

(vi) *Cassette*. These rights should be specifically reserved to the author.

Other clauses which should appear include:

(a) *A royalty clause* setting out the royalties which the author shall receive from West End and touring performances of the play – usually a scale rising from 5 per cent through 7½ per cent to 10 per cent. If the author is registered for VAT, provision for VAT should be included here.

(b) *Cast approval, etc*. The author should be consulted about the casting and the director of the play, and in some cases may be able to insist on approval of the casting of a particular part.

(c) *Rehearsals, scripts, etc*. The author should be entitled to attend all rehearsals of the play and no alteration in the title or script should be made without the author's consent. All approved alterations in or suggestions for the script should become the author's property. In this clause also should appear details about supply of tickets for the author for opening performances and any arrangements for tickets throughout the West End run.

(d) *Credits*. Details of billing of the author's name on posters, programmes and advertising matter should be included.

(e) *Lord Chamberlain's licence*. The Theatres Act 1968 abolishes the power of the Lord Chamberlain to censor stage plays and play licences are no longer required. However, it is obligatory for managers to deposit a copy of the script on which the public performance of any new play is based with the Keeper of Manuscripts, British Library, Great Russell Street, London WC1B 3DG, within one month of the performance.

(f) The author will normally warrant that the play contains nothing that is obscene or defamatory or that infringes copyright.

There must also be:

(g) An accounting clause giving details of payment and requiring a certified statement of box office receipts.

(h) A clause giving the conditions under which the agreement may be assigned or sub-leased.

(i) A termination clause, stating the conditions under which the agreement shall terminate.

ARRANGEMENTS FOR OTHER RIGHTS AFTER THE FIRST-CLASS RUN OF THE PLAY

Provincial or repertory

The author or his representative will license provincial or repertory performances for a fixed royalty on the gross box office receipts – usually 10 per cent for a new play immediately after its West End run, dropping perhaps to $7\frac{1}{2}$ per cent in later years.

Amateur

The author or his representative will license amateur performances of the play for a flat fee (normally between £20 and £30).

Publication

A firm specialising in acting editions of plays may offer to publish the play in which case it will expect to license amateur performances and collect the fees on a commission basis (20 per cent to 50 per cent). The publication contract will also usually provide for the author to receive a royalty of 10 per cent of the published price of every copy sold.

Radio and television

Careful negotiation is required and care should be taken that repeat fees for repeat performances are included in the contract in addition to the initial fee for the first broadcast.

Film rights

Professional advice is absolutely necessary when dealing with a film contract as there are many complications. The rights may be sold outright or licensed for a number of years – usually not less than 7 or 10 or more than 15. The film company normally acquires the right of distribution throughout the world in all languages and expects a completely free hand in making the adaptation of the play into a film.

Foreign rights

It is usual to grant exclusive foreign language rights for the professional stage to an agent or translator who will arrange for a translation to be prepared and produced – it is wise to ask for evidence of the quality of the translator's work unless the translator is very well known. The financial arrangement is usually an advance against royalties for a given period to enable a translation to be prepared and then a licence to exploit the translation for a further period after production (usually 5 years).

Markets for Stage Plays

It is not easy for a new or comparatively unknown writer to find a management willing to present his play. The English Stage Company at the Royal Court Theatre and some other similarly enterprising organisations present a number of plays by new authors. The new and inexperienced writer may find it easier to persuade amateur drama groups or provincial repertory theatres to present his work. A further possible market may be found in the smaller fringe theatre companies.

The Stage reports productions of most new plays first produced by repertory theatres and a study of this journal may reveal other potential new markets for plays.

The Arts Council of England publishes a brochure, *Schemes for Writers & Theatre Companies*, which gives details of various forms of assistance available to playwrights and to theatres wishing to commission new plays. The help given by the Arts Council includes Bursaries (including the John Whiting Award) and help to writers who are being commissioned or encouraged by a theatre company. There is a number of Resident Dramatists' Attachment Awards available. Copies of the brochure and further information may be obtained from The Drama Director, The Arts Council of England, 14 Great Peter Street, London SW1P 3NQ.

It is probable that competitions for full-length and one-act plays and other special opportunities for new plays will be announced after the *Yearbook* has gone to press, and writers with plays on the stocks would do well to watch carefully for announcements in the Press. *The Observer, The Author, Amateur Stage*, and *The Stage*, are the journals in which announcements are most likely to appear.

Sketches for revues and broadcasting and plays for youth organisations are in demand. Sketches are usually bought outright, but in any case authors should make quite certain of what rights they will be disposing before accepting any offer.

In every case it is advisable to send a preliminary letter before submitting a manuscript. Suggestions for the preparation of manuscripts will be found in the article **Typescripts**.

Writers of plays are also referred to **Marketing a Play** and to the sections on **Radio** and **Television**, media which also provide a market for the writers of plays.

LONDON

Bush Theatre, Shepherd's Bush Green, London W12 8QD   *tel* 071-602 3703   *fax* 071-602 7614. *Literary manager:* Nick Drake. Welcomes unsolicited full-length scripts (accompanied by 1 small and 1 large sae); commissions writers at an early stage in their career; produces six premieres a year.

Michael Codron Ltd, Aldwych Theatre Offices, Aldwych, London WC2B 4DF   *tel* 071-240 8291   *fax* 071-240 8467. *Contact:* Joe Scott Parkinson.

Ray Cooney Presentations Ltd, Hollowfield Cottage, Littleton, Surrey GU3 1HN   *tel* (0483) 440 443   *fax* (0483) 32068. *Contact:* H.S. Udwin.

English Stage Company Ltd, Royal Court Theatre, Sloane Square, London SW1W 8AS   *tel* 071-730 5174   *fax* 071-730 4705. *Literary manager:* Robin Hooper. New plays.

Greenwich Theatre Ltd, Greenwich Theatre, Crooms Hill, London SE10 8ES *tel* 081-858 4447. *Contact:* artistic director.

Hampstead Theatre, Swiss Cottage Centre, Avenue Road, London NW3 3EX *tel* 071-722 9224 *fax* 071-722 3860. *Contact:* Anna Koutelieri. New plays and the occasional modern classic. After initial assessment, promising scripts are then read by the literary manager and/or artistic director. It can therefore take 2-3 months to reach a decision.

Bill Kenwright Ltd, 59 Shaftesbury Avenue, London W1V 7AA *tel* 071-439 4466 *fax* 071-437 8370.

King's Head Theatre, 115 Upper Street, London N1 1QN *tel* 071-226 8561 *fax* 071-226 8507. *Contact:* general manager.

Brian Kirk Associates, 7 Wigton Place, London SE11 4AN *tel* 071-820 0077 *fax* 071-820 1237.

Knightsbridge Theatrical Productions Ltd, 21 New Fetter Lane, London EC4A 1JJ *tel* 071-583 8687 *fax* 071-583 1040. *Contact:* Mrs Sheila H. Gray.

Lyric Theatre Hammersmith, King Street, London W6 0QL *tel* 081-741 0824 *fax* 081-741 7694. *Chief executive:* Sue Storr; *artistic director:* Neil Bartlett. A producing theatre as well as a receiving venue for work by new writers.

Orange Tree Theatre, 1 Clarence Street, Richmond, Surrey TW9 2SA *tel* 081-940 0141.

Questors Theatre, Mattock Lane, Ealing, London W5 5BQ *tel* 081-567 0011. *Marketing manager:* Ms Sam Jennings.

Royal National Theatre, South Bank, London SE1 9PX *tel* 071-928 2033 *fax* 071-620 1197. Little opportunity for the production of unsolicited material, but submissions welcomed. Send to John Burgess, Literary Manager (New Writing), together with an sae.

Royal Shakespeare Company, Barbican Theatre, Barbican, London EC2Y 8BQ *tel* 071-628 3351 *fax* 071-374 0818. *Literary manager:* Colin Chambers.

Peter Saunders Ltd, Vaudeville Theatre Offices, 10 Maiden Lane, London WC2E 7NA *tel* 071-240 3177 *fax* 071-497 9505.

Soho Theatre Company, Cockpit Theatre, Gateforth Street, London NW8 8EH *tel* 071-262 7907 *fax* 071-723 8146. *Artistic director:* Abigail Morris; *literary manager:* Jack Bradley. Always on the look out for new plays and playwrights and welcome unsolicited scripts. These are read by a professional panel who write a detailed critical report. Also offer various levels of workshop facilities, including rehearsed reading and platform performances, for promising playwrights, and in-depth script development with the Artistic Director and Literary Manager. See also the Verity Bargate Award on page 660.

Tabard Theatre, 2 Bath Road, Turnham Green, Chiswick, London W4 1LW *tel* 081-995 6035. *Contact:* artistic director. Produces a number of shows each year, ranging from classic to contemporary world theatre.

Theatre Royal, Stratford East, Gerry Raffles Square, Newham, London E15 1BN *tel* 081-534 7374 *fax* 081-534 8381. *Assistant to the directors:* Paul Everitt.

The Tricycle Theatre Company, Tricycle Theatre, 269 Kilburn High Road, London NW6 7JR *tel* 071-372 6611 *fax* 071-328 0795. *Contact:* Nicolas Kent.

Triumph Proscenium Productions Ltd, Suite 4, Waldorf Chambers, 11 Aldwych, London WC2B 4DA   *tel* 071-836 0186   *fax* 071-240 7511.

Turnstyle, Duke of York's Theatre, St Martin's Lane, London WC2N 4BG   *tel* 071-240 9891   *fax* 071-379 5748. *General manager:* Meryl Faiers.

Unicorn Theatre for Children, Arts Theatre, 6-7 Great Newport Street, London WC2H 7JB   *tel* 071-379 3280   *fax* 071-836 5366. *Administrative director:* Patricia Mahoney; *artistic director:* Richard Williams. Six productions a year, in repertoire, for children aged 4-12 – new writing and adaptations.

Warehouse Theatre, Dingwall Road, Croydon CR0 2NF   *tel* 081-681 1257. *Artistic director:* Ted Craig. New playwriting theatre producing up to six in-house productions each year. New scripts usually accepted via the South London International Playwriting Festival held annually in November (see page 681).

Michael White, 13 Duke Street, St James's, London SW1Y 6DB   *tel* 071-839 3971   *fax* 071-839 3836.

PROVINCIAL

Abbey Theatre, Lower Abbey Street, Dublin 1, Republic of Ireland   *tel* (01) 8748741   *fax* (01) 8729177. *Artistic director:* Patrick Mason; *general manager:* Martin Fahy. Mainly produces plays written by Irish authors or on Irish subjects. Foreign plays are however regularly produced.

Yvonne Arnaud Theatre Management Ltd, Yvonne Arnaud Theatre, Millbrook, Guildford, Surrey GU1 3UX   *tel* (0483) 64571   *fax* (0483) 64071. Receives and produces Number One touring and pre-West End product.

Belgrade Theatre, Belgrade Square, Coventry CV1 1GS   *tel* (0203) 256431   *fax* (0203) 550680. Produces new plays both in the main house and studio. Scripts for consideration should be addressed to the Joint Artistic Directors. Please enclose sae.

Birmingham Repertory Theatre Ltd, Broad Street, Birmingham B1 2EP   *tel* 021-236 6771   *fax* 021-236 7883.

Bristol Old Vic Company, Theatre Royal, King Street, Bristol BS1 4ED   *tel* (0272) 277466   *fax* (0272) 225055. *Directors office:* Sheila Pearce.

The Byre Theatre of St Andrews Ltd, Abbey Street, St Andrews KY16 9LA   *tel* (0334) 76288   *fax* (0334) 75370. *Artistic director:* Ken Alexander. Open all year round, operating as a summer rep., and as a touring venue for the rest of the year. Producing five plays between June and October; also, touring with TIE productions. The company has a major commitment to new writing and is host to the Byre Writers' Group, Scotland's leading training ground for new playwrights.

Chester Gateway Theatre Trust Ltd, Chester Gateway Theatre, Hamilton Place, Chester CH1 2BH   *tel* (0244) 344238   *fax* (0244) 317277. *Administrative director:* Jane Dawson; *artistic director:* Jeremy Raison.

Chichester Festival Theatre Productions Company Ltd, Chichester Festival Theatre, Oaklands Park, Chichester, West Sussex PO19 4AP   *tel* (0243) 784437   *fax* (0243) 787288. *Artistic director:* Patrick Garland; *managing director:* Peter Stevens; *general manager:* Paul Rogerson. Festival season May-Oct in Festival Theatre and Minerva Theatre; rest of year seasons of touring plays, opera, ballet, dance, jazz and orchestral concerts.

Churchill Theatre Trust Ltd, High Street, Bromley, Kent BR1 1HA *tel* 081-464 7131 *fax* 081-290 6968. *Contact:* theatre director. Full-length plays; comedies, thrillers, dramas, new plays considered.

Theatr Clwyd, Mold, Clwyd CH7 1YA *tel* (0352) 756331 *fax* (0352) 758323.

Colchester Mercury Theatre Ltd, Balkerne Gate, Colchester, Essex CO1 1PT *tel* (0206) 577006 *fax* (0206) 769607. *Business manager:* Tony Hill.

The Coliseum Theatre, Fairbottom Street, Oldham OL1 3SW *tel* 061-624 1731 *fax* 061-624 5318. *Artistic director:* Warren Hooper. Special interest in musicals and comedies. Contact by letter initially.

Contact Theatre Company, Oxford Road, Manchester M15 6JA *tel* 061-274 3434 *fax* 061-273 6286. *Associate director:* Richard Gregory. Interested in non-naturalistic work aimed at under-30 audience.

Crucible Theatre, 55 Norfolk Street, Sheffield S1 1DA *tel* (0742) 760621 *fax* (0742) 701532. *Chief executive:* Stephen Barry. Large-scale producing house with smallish studio.

Derby Playhouse Ltd, Theatre Walk, Eagle Centre, Derby DE1 2NF *tel* (0332) 363271 *fax* (0332) 294412.

Druid Theatre Company, Druid Lane Theatre, Chapel Lane, Galway, Republic of Ireland *tel* (091) 68617/68660 *fax* (091) 63109. *General manager:* Jane Daly; *artistic director:* Maelíosa Stafford.

The Duke's Playhouse, Moor Lane, Lancaster LA1 1QE *tel* (0524) 67461 *fax* (0524) 846817. *Artistic director:* Han Duijvendak; *general manager:* Penny McPhillips.

Dundee Repertory Theatre, Tay Square, Dundee DD1 1PB *tel* (0382) 27684. *Artistic director:* Hamish Glen.

Everyman Theatre, Regent Street, Cheltenham, Glos. GL50 1HQ *tel* (0242) 512515 *fax* (0242) 224305. *Chief executive:* Bubble Lodge.

Everyman Theatre Company Ltd, 5-9 Hope Street, Liverpool L1 9BH *tel* 051-708 0338 *fax* 051-709 0398. *General manager:* Kevin Fearon.

Farnham Repertory Company Ltd, The Redgrave Theatre, Brightwells, Farnham, Surrey GU9 7SB *tel* (0252) 727000 *fax* (0252) 712350. *Administrator:* Keith Murray. Interested in new and innovative work.

Grand Theatre, Singleton Street, Swansea SA1 3QJ *tel* (0792) 475242 *fax* (0792) 475379. *General manager:* Gary Iles.

Harrogate Theatre, Oxford Street, Harrogate, North Yorkshire HG1 1QF *tel* (0423) 502710. *Theatre secretary:* Anne Kingsley.

Haymarket Theatre Company, The Haymarket Theatre, Wote Street, Basingstoke, Hants RG21 1NW *tel* (0256) 55844. *Artistic director:* Adrian Reynolds. Mounts seasons of plays, many of which are designed for co-production with London managements.

The Hornchurch Theatre Trust Ltd, The Queen's Theatre, Billet Lane, Hornchurch, Essex RM11 1QT *tel* (0708) 456118 *fax* (0708) 452348. *Administrative director:* Christopher Moxon; *artistic director:* Marina Caldarone. Regional theatre.

Leicester Haymarket Theatre, Belgrave Gate, Leicester LE1 3YQ *tel* (0533) 530021 *fax* (0533) 513310.

Liverpool Repertory Theatre Ltd, Liverpool Playhouse, Williamson Square, Liverpool L1 1EL *tel* 051-709 8478 *fax* 051-709 7113. *General manager:* David Redmayne.

New Victoria Theatre, Etruria Road, Newcastle under Lyme ST5 0JG   *tel* (0782) 717954 *fax* (0782) 712885. *Theatre director:* Peter Cheeseman. Europe's first purpose built theatre in the round, presenting new plays, major classics, adaptations, documentaries.

New Victoria Theatre, Peacocks Arts & Entertainment Centre, Woking, Surrey GU21 1GQ   *tel* (0483) 747422 *fax* (0483) 740477. *Contact:* Robert Cogo-Fawcett (Theatre Royal, Sawclose, Bath BA1 1ET). Large-scale touring house. Interested to co-produce or produce.

Northampton Repertory Players Ltd, The Royal Theatre, Guildhall Road, Northampton NN1 1EA   *tel* (0604) 38343 *fax* (0604) 602408. Presents plays for main house, studio, theatre-in-education, community touring and youth theatre. Please send scripts, indicating which area of work they are for, to Julie Martell, Director's Assistant.

Northcott Theatre, Stocker Road, Exeter, Devon EX4 4QB   *tel* (0392) 56182. *Artistic director:* John Durnin.

Northern Stage Company, Newcastle Playhouse, Barras Bridge, Newcastle upon Tyne NE1 1RH   *tel* 091-232 3366 *fax* 091-261 8093. *Artistic director:* Alan Lyddiard.

Nottingham Playhouse, Nottingham Theatre Trust Ltd, Wellington Circus, Nottingham NG1 5AF   *tel* (0602) 474361 *fax* (0602) 475759. *Executive director:* Ruth Mackenzie. Works closely with communities of Nottingham and Nottinghamshire; presents best of innovative and world theatre. Takes six months to read unsolicited MSS.

Nuffield Theatre, University Road, Southampton SO2 1TR   *tel* (0703) 315500 *fax* (0703) 315511. *Literary manager:* Penny Gold.

Octagon Theatre, Howell Croft South, Bolton BL1 1SB   *tel* (0204) 29407 *fax* (0204) 380110. *Administrative director:* Amanda Belcham; *artistic director:* Lawrence Till. Repertory season Sept-June, including new plays and contemporary theatre.

The Oxford Stage Company, 15-19 George Street, Oxford OX1 2AU   *tel* (0865) 723238 *fax* (0865) 790625. *Contact:* marketing manager.

Palace Theatre, Clarendon Road, Watford, Herts. WD1 1JZ   *tel* (0923) 235455 *fax* (0923) 819664. *Contact:* Lou Stein.

Palace Theatre Trust Ltd, London Road, Westcliff-on-Sea, Essex SS0 9LA   *tel* (0702) 347816. *Theatre secretary:* Iris Stewart. Subsidised repertory theatre producing a programme of predominantly modern British drama with some foreign writers, particularly American. Most new work is done in small, 100-seater studio.

Peacock Theatre, The Abbey Theatre, Lower Abbey Street, Dublin 1, Republic of Ireland   *tel* (01) 8748741 *fax* (01) 8729177. *Artistic director:* Patrick Mason; *general manager:* Martin Fahy. Experimental theatre associated with the Abbey Theatre; presents mostly new writing as well as exploring the entire canon of world drama.

Perth Theatre Ltd, 185 High Street, Perth PH1 5UW   *tel* (0738) 38123 *fax* (0738) 24576. *Artistic director:* Andrew McKinnon; *general manager:* David Bonnar. Three-weekly repertory programme Aug-May of plays, musicals, revivals and new writing; also studio and theatre-in-education work.

Plymouth Theatre Royal, Theatre Royal, Royal Parade, Plymouth, Devon PL1 2TR   *tel* (0752) 668282 *telex* 45115 TROYAL G *fax* (0752) 671179. *Artistic director:* Roger Redfarn.

Royal Exchange Theatre Company Ltd, St Ann's Square, Manchester M2 7DH   *tel* 061-833 9333   *fax* 061-832 0881. *General manager:* Patricia Weller. Provides a varied programme of major classics, new plays, musicals, contemporary British and European drama; also explores the creative work of diverse cultures.

Royal Lyceum Theatre Company Ltd, Royal Lyceum Theatre, Grindlay Street, Edinburgh EH3 9AX   *tel* 031-229 7404   *fax* 031-228 3955. *Artistic director:* Kenny Ireland; *associate literary director:* Tom McGrath.

Salisbury Playhouse, Malthouse Lane, Salisbury, Wilts. SP2 7RA   *tel* (0722) 320117   *fax* (0722) 421991. *Artistic director:* Deborah Paige. Regional repertory theatre producing a broad programme of classical and modern plays.

Scarborough Theatre Trust Ltd, Stephen Joseph Theatre in the Round, Valley Bridge Parade, Scarborough, North Yorkshire YO11 2PL   *tel* (0723) 370540   *fax* (0723) 360506. *Script assistant:* Gordon Townsend.

Sherman Theatre (1974), Senghennydd Road, Cardiff CF2 4YE   *tel* (0222) 396844. *General manager:* Jo Weston. Plays mainly for 15-25 age range.

Swan Theatre, The Moors, Worcester WR1 3EF   *tel* (0905) 726969   *fax* (0905) 723738. *Contact:* artistic director.

Thorndike Theatre, Church Street, Leatherhead, Surrey KT22 8DF   *tel* (0372) 376211   *fax* (0372) 362595. *Contact:* threatre controller.

Traverse Theatre, 10 Cambridge Street, Edinburgh EH1 2ED   *tel* 031-228 3223   *fax* 031-229 8443. *Dramaturge:* Ella Wildridge.

Watermill Theatre Ltd, Bagnor, Newbury, Berks. RG16 8AE   *tel* (0635) 45834. *Contact:* Jill Fraser.

The West Yorkshire Playhouse, Quarry Hill Mount, Leeds LS9 8AW   *tel* (0532) 442141   *fax* (0532) 448252. *Artistic director:* Jude Kelly; *administrative director:* Padraig Cusack. Twin auditoria complex – with a policy of encouraging new writing; community theatre; Young People's Theatre programme.

The Wilde Community Theatre Company (1985), The Wilde Theatre, South Hill Park, Bracknell, Berks. RG12 7PA   *tel* (0344) 427272   *fax* (0344) 411427. *Contact:* Community Theatre officer. Main house and experimental studio. Welcomes new writers.

Windsor Theatre Company (Capoco Ltd), Theatre Royal, Windsor, Berks. SL4 1PS   *tel* (0753) 863444   *fax* (0753) 831673. *Artistic director:* Mark Piper. Interested mainly in comedies and thrillers.

The Wolsey Theatre, Civic Drive, Ipswich, Suffolk IP1 2AS   *tel* (0473) 218911   *fax* (0473) 212946. *Executive director:* Moss Cooper.

York Citizens' Theatre Trust Ltd, Theatre Royal, St Leonard's Place, York YO1 2HD   *tel* (0904) 658162   *fax* (0904) 611534. *Executive director:* Elizabeth Jones; *artistic director:* John Doyle. Repertory productions, tours.

TOURING COMPANIES

Black Theatre Co-Operative Ltd, 8 Bradbury Street, London N16 8JN   *tel* 071-249 9150   *fax* 071-275 9440. *Artistic director:* Joan-Ann Maynard. Interested in Black plays, especially those that relate to the experiences of Black people both in Britain and outside Britain.

Compass Theatre Company, Carver Street Institute, 24 Rockingham Lane, Sheffield S1 4FW   *tel* (0742) 755328   *fax* (0742) 786931. *Administrator:* William Jones.

Gay Sweatshop, The Holborn Centre, Three Cups Yard, Sandland Street, London WC1R 4PZ *tel* 071-242 1168 *fax* 071-242 3143. *Joint artistic directors:* James Neal-Kennerley, Lois Weaver. Interested in developing (often commissioning) scripts into full production of new plays by lesbian and gay writers.

Hull Truck Theatre Co. Ltd, Hull Truck Theatre, Spring Street, Hull HU2 8RW *tel* (0482) 224800 *fax* (0482) 228546. *Executive producer:* Barry Nettleton.

Live Theatre, 8 Trinity Chare, Quayside, Newcastle upon Tyne NE1 3DF *tel* 091-261 2694. *Artistic director:* Max Roberts. Interested in new plays, by Northern writers, which relate to the history and/or present culture and concerns of the region and which are accessible to a wide audience.

The London Bubble (Bubble Theatre Company), 3/5 Elephant Lane, London SE16 4JD *tel* 071-237 4434 *fax* 071-231 2366.

M6 Theatre Company, Hamer C.P. School, Albert Royds Street, Rochdale, Lancs. OL16 2SU *tel* (0706) 355898 *fax* (0706) 711700. *Contact:* Les Hampson. Theatre-in-education and community theatre company providing high quality, educational, innovative and relevant live theatre for children and for audiences who may not normally have access to theatre.

Major Road Theatre Company, 29 Queens Road, Bradford, West Yorkshire BD8 7BS *tel* (0274) 480251 *fax* (0274) 548528. *Artistic director:* Graham Devlin.

New Perspectives Company, Mansfield Arts Centre, Leeming Street, Mansfield, Notts. NG18 1NG *tel* (0623) 635225. *Artistic director:* Gavin Stride. Has a policy of employing writers for new work. Regret unsolicited scripts returned, unless writers are local to the East Midlands region.

NTC Touring Theatre Company (formerly Northumberland Theatre Company), The Playhouse, Bondgate Without, Alnwick, Northumberland NE66 1PQ *tel* (0665) 602586. *Artistic director:* Gillian Hambleton. Performs a wide cross-section of work: new plays, extant scripts, classics and TIE. Particularly interested in non-naturalism and plays with direct relevance to rural audiences.

Orchard Theatre Company, 108 Newport Road, Barnstaple, North Devon EX32 9BA *tel* (0271) 71475 *fax* (0271) 71825. *Administrator:* Geof Keys.

Paines Plough, Interchange Studios, Dalby Street, London NW5 3NQ *tel* 071-284 4483 *fax* 071-284 4506. *Literary manager:* Tony Dinner. Welcomes scripts from new writers; provides a report on 95% of scripts submitted. Please enclose two saes for acknowledgement and return of script. Writers should expect to wait at least two months for their scripts to be considered.

Proteus Theatre Company (1981), Fairfields Arts Centre, Council Road, Basingstoke, Hants RG21 3DH *tel* (0256) 54541. *Administrative director:* Charlotte Donelan; *artistic director:* James Brining. Small-scale touring company. Presents three plays per year, at least one a new play; also 2-3 projects which may include commissioned written pieces of drama.

Quicksilver Theatre for Children (formerly Theatre of Thelema), 4 Enfield Road, London N1 5AZ *tel* 071-241 2942 *fax* 071-254 3119. *Artistic director:* Guy Holland. Tours schools and theatres London and nationwide. Produces three plays a year for specific age ranges: 3-5-year-olds, 5-9-year-olds and 7-11-year-olds. Particularly interested in visual, physical and music theatre.

Red Ladder Theatre Co., Cobden Avenue, Lower Wortley, Leeds LS12 5PB *tel* (0532) 792228 *fax* (0532) 310660. *Artistic director:* Kully Thiarai. Theatre performances for young people (14-25) in youth clubs and similar venues.

Commissions at least two new plays each year. Training/residentials for youth workers/young people.

Red Shift Theatre Company, BAC, Old Town Hall, Lavender Hill, London SW11 5TF   *tel* 071-223 3256   *fax* 071-978 5207.

Solent People's Theatre, The Heathfield Centre, Valentine Avenue, Sholing, Southampton SO2 8EQ   *tel* (0703) 443943   *fax* (0703) 440752. *Administrative director:* Fionn Peat.

The Sphinx (formerly **Women's Theatre Group**), Sadler's Wells, Rosebery Avenue, London EC1R 4TN   *tel* 071-713 0991/2. *Artistic director:* Sue Parrish. Women writers only.

Theatre Centre, Hanover School, Noel Road, Islington, London N1 8BD   *tel* 071-354 0110   *fax* 071-359 7562. *Contact:* Isobel Hawson. National touring theatre for young people.

PUBLISHERS SPECIALISING IN THE PUBLICATION OF PLAYS

Playwrights are reminded that it is unusual for a publisher of trade editions of plays to publish plays which have not had at least reasonably successful, usually professional, productions *on stage* first.

Walter H. Baker Company, 100 Chauncy Street, Boston, MA 02111, USA   *tel* 617-482-1280. *Editor:* John B. Welch. Plays and books on theatre.

Faber & Faber Ltd, 3 Queen Square, London WC1N 3AU   *tel* 071-465 0045   *fax* 071-465 0034.

Samuel French Ltd, 52 Fitzroy Street, London W1P 6JR   *tel* 071-387 9373   *fax* 071-387 2161.

Samuel French Inc., 45 West 25th Street, New York, NY 10010, USA   *tel* 212-206-8990   *fax* 212-206-1429.

Nick Hern Books Ltd, 14 Larden Road, London W3 7ST   *tel* 081-740 9539. *Publisher:* Nick Hern. Professionally produced plays only. Initial letter required.

Kenyon-Deane Ltd, 311 Worcester Road, Malvern, Worcs. WR14 1AN   *tel* (0864) 565045. *Contact:* L. Smith. Plays for amateur dramatic societies and Women's Institute groups, particularly all-women casts.

Methuen, Michelin House, 81 Fulham Road, London SW7 6RB   *tel* 071-581 9393   *fax* 071-225 9095. *Publisher:* Geoffrey Strachan. Full-length plays; comedy, modern and classic.

J. Garnet Miller Ltd, 311 Worcester Road, Malvern, Worcs. WR14 1AN   *tel* (0684) 565045. *Contact:* S. Smith. All types of plays for amateur dramatic groups. European agents for I.E. Clark Inc., American publishers of plays for all theatre groups.

New Playwrights' Network, 35 Sandringham Road, Macclesfield, Cheshire SK10 1QB   *tel/fax* (0625) 425312. *Publishing director:* J.C.F. Gray. General plays for the amateur stage, one-act and full length.

The Playwrights Publishing Company, 70 Nottingham Road, Burton Joyce, Notts. NG14 5AL   *tel* (0602) 313356. *Proprietor:* Liz Breeze; *consultant:* Tony Breeze. Serious work and comedies, for mixed cast, all women or schools. Reading fee: £10 one-act, £20 full-length.

Warner Chappell Plays Ltd, 129 Park Street, London W1Y 3FA   *tel* 071-629 7600   *fax* 071-499 9718. Stage plays only, in both acting and trade editions. Preliminary letter essential.

Writing for Broadcasting

JOCELYN HAY
Chairman, Voice of the Listener and Viewer

Writers for radio and television face a more uncertain future in Britain then ever before because of the lifting of former public service requirements on the nature and scheduling of programmes on commercial radio and television. Also, Channel 4, although still protected by its Trust status and remit to provide alternative programming, must now compete with ITV for its advertising revenue. And both channels are in competition with a rising number of satellite and cable channels leading to higher costs and a harder, leaner environment for all.

The requirement that ITV should commission 25 per cent of their programmes from independent production companies (contained in the 1990 Broadcasting Act) is being used as an excuse for even greater economies as the broadcasters seek to reduce the high overheads involved in maintaining studios and specialist facilities. New take-overs within the ITV network bring fears that more companies will operate as publishers rather than programme makers.

For writers this makes life difficult because instead of dealing directly with Drama Departments at the 15 ITV companies they must get to know the needs and specialities of dozens of different producers and commissioning editors working for small independent production companies. This means a huge amount of research; writers not prepared to make the effort should employ an agent. For information about independent producers, contact their professional body PACT (see entry on page 634).

This more competitive environment, coupled with the legacy of a recession in advertising revenue, means that all programme makers are careful about costs and many are looking for overseas sales and partners to help co-finance productions. Others want to take advantage of the relaxed rules on sponsorship of ITV and IR programmes. However, sponsorship and co-production often bring compromises over themes, storylines and locations which can limit the writer's freedom.

The BBC must also commission at least 25 per cent of its television programmes from independent producers as a result of the 1990 Act and, in the run-up to the renewal of its Royal Charter which expires in 1996, the BBC is anxious to impress government ministers that it is efficient and giving 'value-for-money'. A government White Paper on the future of the BBC was to be published in the early summer of 1994 and, although the general feeling is that the BBC's Charter will be renewed without drastic change, we cannot take it for granted. The most optimistic scenario is that the licence fee, linked to the RPI, will be kept as the BBC's main source of income. But this will not provide the BBC with an income that keeps pace with the faster rise in broadcasting inflation and the consequence could be less money for programmes.

Writers must therefore involve themselves in the debate about the future of the BBC. The BBC is Britain's biggest and most generous cultural patron, providing an irreplaceable market for writers and musicians. The cultural life of our nation depends on it and so do the livelihoods of many writers and musicians.

The BBC has committed itself to the continued production of a wide range of high quality drama, documentary, education, comedy and 'innovative' programmes. Managers have stated that the aim of the current restructuring is to release more money for programme making.

But it may be easier for radio writers to break in to the market than for screenwriters, because of the lower costs involved in radio – but the market is almost entirely with the BBC. Most IR stations have reduced their speech output in recent years and the first two national IR stations, Classic FM and Virgin 1215, are both music channels. A third national commercial network will come on air in late 1994. Its format must consist of at least 51 per cent speech. Six companies bid for the licence but most of the formats consist of news, sports, chat and phone-ins. Only one appears to offer the hope of large employment of writers. It is targeted at young people and will carry educational broadcasts. These are the well-crafted kinds of programmes where a writer is important. As this bid is the lowest, however, and the Radio Authority has little leeway not to accept the highest, its chances of success do not look good.

This, ironically, has been put together by the former editor of BBC Radio 5. Radio 5, created only three years ago, provided a marvellous range of stories, plays and magazine programmes for young people and a welcome new source of demand for writers. In addition to youth programmes it also carried most of BBC Radio's adult education and schools broadcasts. Radio 5, however, was axed at the end of March 1994 to make way for 'Five Live', BBC Radio's new controversial 24-hour sports and news station, a phillistine act which not only deprived Britain's young people of their only opportunity to hear specially designed speech radio, but put in jeopardy the future of BBC school radio, currently used by 1.5 million primary school children across the country, and put many of the BBC's adult education programmes under threat. Schools radio broadcasts have been cut by a third to fit a new slot on Radio 3 and Open University programmes have been cut by a fifth in their new place on long wave. Other adult education programmes will have to fight for a place on the other four networks.

Elsewhere, BBC managers say they want to raise the speech content on Radios 1 and 2 which may provide some openings for new writers but Radio 3 is not looking for more drama and there are rumours that Radio 4's drama output may be cut before long. BBC managers have set a target of 10 per cent for the purchase of independent radio productions, but it is hard to see how this will be achieved following the demise of Radio 5 which was the pioneer in this field.

Would-be radio drama writers should try to contact individual producers with ideas and scripts or contact Caroline Raphael, the new Head of BBC Radio Drama, who has said she is looking for new writers and innovative material. There is also a new Independent Association of Radio Producers and they can be contacted via Sarah Dickinson at Ladbroke Radio, Essel House, 29 Foley Street, London W1P 7LB tel 071-323 2770.

The broadcast market is changing more rapidly than ever before. There is a growing number of channels and an encouraging rise in advertising income, but the trend is towards easier listening and less crafted, scripted programmes. If writers are to benefit they must keep abreast of market trends and be flexible enough in their approach to suggest not only new programme ideas but often sources of finance and sponsorship. Perhaps the most promising trend is the growing use of non-broadcast tapes. Many businesses, charities and public services use video and audio tapes for training and, increasingly, for internal and external communication. It is a highly specialised market and well-paid.

British Broadcasting Corporation

Potential contributors to the BBC should be aware that the needs of television and radio are quite different. Writers should study in detail the possible outlets by watching and listening to programmes, and tailor their work to fit them.

TELEVISION

Drama

Original dramas for film (60, 75 and 90 minutes) and for studio (a few at 40 or 50 minutes) are sought. Plays and screenplays using few locations and small casts are advantageous. No standardised layout or technical instructions are required in any scripts. However, well-spaced presentation with dialogue and stage directions clearly distinguished is essential. Series and Serials represent the bulk of Drama output, but new writers should always present sample scripts with any submission of ideas for either form.

Since the BBC has opened its doors to national and international Independent drama markets, competition is very fierce indeed and all unsolicited scripts will therefore be rigorously sifted.

Scripts should be submitted to appropriate Editorial Heads, Executive Producers, Strand Editors and Development Executives at BBC Drama Group, BBC Television Centre, Wood Lane, London W12 7RJ.

Light Entertainment Television

The Comedy Department is looking for new narrative 30-minute series, preferably mainly studio based. Original formats are always in demand rather than variations on existing programmes.

All scripts and enquiries should be addressed to the Comedy Script Development Unit, Room 4127, Television Centre, Wood Lane, London W12 7RJ   *tel* 081-576 1900.

RADIO

Short stories

Short stories specially written for broadcasting will be considered. A short story written for a 15-minute broadcasting space should be between 2000 and 2300 words in length. Unsolicited material is considered but it has to compete with regularly commissioned work.

Drama Department

The Department broadcasts several hundred new plays and adaptations every year, in addition to series and serials, and readings. There is therefore a very large market regularly available to the freelance writer. A free leaflet, *Writing Plays for Radio*, giving basic guidance on the technique of radio writing and also on the market is available from the Literary Manager (Radio Drama), BBC, Broadcasting House, Portland Place, London W1A 1AA to whom all submissions should be addressed.

Music

At the heart of the BBC's music policy is a commitment to high-quality, live music-making in all its forms and across the full range of styles and periods. Audition sessions for professional soloists and ensembles are held every other week, except in July and August, with an outside professional assessor on the listening panel. The BBC also regularly commissions new works from a wide range of composers both nationally and internationally for all its house orchestras and the BBC Singers as well as for other groups and special occasions. These too have broadened their range in recent years to include jazz, electronic and radiophonic media.

The BBC makes best endeavours to consider all unsolicited scores and tapes for broadcast. This is carried out chiefly by the Music Department's New Music unit, and where further opinions are sought, they are put before the Readers on the New Music Panel, who provide objective advice to the production teams without bias or prejudice.

Light Entertainment

Light Entertainment Radio is interested in receiving scripts or ideas for series of half-hour sitcoms or panel games, principally for Radio 4. Before submitting material, please read the writers' guidelines – explaining such matters as length, layout, structure and so on – available (enclosing an A4 sae) from the Senior Producer Scripts (Light Entertainment Radio), BBC, Room 112, 16 Langham Street, London W1A 1AA, where the material should ultimately be sent.

Two programmes, *Week Ending* and *The News Huddlines*, are interested in using unsolicited topical sketches during the course of their run. *Week Ending* holds a weekly writers' meeting at which anyone is welcome, at the above address. Details (and times of deadlines) can be obtained by ringing 071-580 4468 and asking for the production office of the programme concerned. All fees are a matter for negotiation with the Corporation's Copyright Department.

BROADCASTING RIGHTS AND TERMS

Contributors are advised to check latest details of fees with the BBC.

Specially written dramatic material for television

From 1 August 1992 the rates for one performance of a 60-minute original television play were a minimum of £4310 for a play written by a beginner and a 'going rate' of £6790 for an established writer, or *pro rata* for shorter or longer timings. Fees for submitted material are paid on acceptance, and for commissioned material half on commissioning and half on acceptance as being suitable for television.

Fees for a 50-minute episode in a series during the same period were a minimum of £3555 for a beginner and a 'going rate' of £5135 for an established writer.

Fees for a 50-minute dramatisation were a minimum of £2480 for a beginner and a £3655 'going rate' for an established writer.

All fees were subject to negotiation above the minima.

Specially written light entertainment sketch material for television

From 1 August 1992 the rates for sketch material were a minimum of £31.31 per minute for beginners and a 'going rate' of £62.62 for established writers.

The fee for a quickie or news item is half the amount of the writer's per minute rate.

Fees for submitted material are payable on acceptance and for commissioned material half on signature and half on acceptance.

Published prose and poems for television

Prose works, £16.87 per minute.
Poems £19.58 per minute.

Stage plays and source material for television

Fees for stage plays are negotiable.

Specially written material for radio

Fees are assessed on the basis of the type of material, its length, the author's status and experience in writing for radio. From 29 June 1993 fees for two performances of specially written radio dramas in English (other than educational programmes) are £36.00 a minute for beginners and a 'going rate' of £54.80 a minute for established writers.

Fees for submitted material are paid on acceptance, and for commissioned material half on commissioning and half on acceptance as being suitable for broadcasting.

Short stories specially written for radio
Fees range from £110.00 for 15 minutes.

Published material for radio (from 10 August 1993)
Domestic service:
Dramatic works: £10.81 per minute.
Prose works: £10.81 per minute.
Prose works required for dramatisation: £8.43 per minute.
Poems: £10.81 per *half* minute.
World Service: English language services:
Dramatic works: £5.41 per minute for up to five broadcasts.
Prose works: £5.41 per minute for up to five broadcasts.
Prose works required for dramatisation: £4.22 per minute for up to five broadcasts.
Poems: £5.41 per *half* minute for up to five broadcasts.
For Foreign Language Services approximately one-fifth of the rate for English Language Services.

Repeats in BBC programmes
Further proportionate fees are payable for repeats.

Use abroad of recordings of BBC programmes
If the BBC sends abroad recordings of its programmes for use by overseas broadcasting organisations on their own networks or stations, further payments accrue to the author, usually in the form of additional percentages of the basic fee paid for the initial performance or a royalty based on a percentage of the distributors' receipts. This can apply to both sound and television programmes.

Value Added Tax
A self-billing system for VAT was introduced in January 1978 for programmes made in London. This now covers radio, external services and television.

TALKS FOR TELEVISION

Contributors to talks will be offered the standard Television talks contract which provides the BBC certain rights to broadcast the material in a complete, abridged and/or translated manner, and which provides for the payment of further fees for additional usage of the material whether by television, domestic radio or external broadcasting. The contract also covers the assignment of material and limited publication rights. Alternatively a contract taking all standard rights may be negotiated. Fees are arranged by the contract authorities in London and the Regions.

TALKS FOR RADIO

Contributors to talks for domestic Radio and World Service broadcasting may be offered either: the standard talks contract which takes rights and provides for residual payments, as does the Television standard contract above; or be offered an STC (Short Talks Contract) which takes all rights except print publication rights where the airtime of the contribution does not exceed five minutes and which has set fees or disturbance money payable; or an NFC (No Fee Contract) where no payment is made which provides an acknowledgement that a contribution may be used by the BBC.

ADDRESSES

Letters addressed to speakers c/o the BBC will be forwarded, but may be opened before being forwarded. Letters marked 'Personal' are forwarded unopened.

LONDON

BBC Corporate Headquarters and BBC Radio: Broadcasting House, London W1A 1AA *tel* 071-580 4468 *telegraphic address/cables* Broadcasts, London *telex* 265781.

BBC Television: Television Centre, Wood Lane, London W12 7RJ *tel* 081-743 8000 *telegraphic address/cables* Telecasts, London *telex* 265781.

BBC Books: Woodlands, 80 Wood Lane, London W12 0TT *tel* 081-743 5588 *telex* 934678 BBCENT G *fax* 081-749 8766.

BBC Magazines: Woodlands, 80 Wood Lane, London W12 0TT *tel* 081-743 5588 *telex* 934678 BBCENT G *fax* 081-749 8766.

BBC World Service: PO Box 76, Bush House, Strand, London WC2B 4PH *tel* 071-240 3456 *telegraphic address/cables* Broadbrit, London *telex* 265781.

BBC White City: 201 Wood Lane, London W12 7TS *tel* 081-752 5252 *fax* 081-752 4429.

ENGLAND

Birmingham: Broadcasting Centre, Pebble Mill, Birmingham B5 7QQ *tel* 021-414 8888.

Bristol: Broadcasting House, Whiteladies Road, Bristol BS8 2LR *tel* (0272) 732211.

Caversham: Caversham Park, Reading, Berks. RG4 8TZ *tel* (0734) 472742.

Norwich: St Catherine's Close, All Saints Green, Norwich, Norfolk NR1 3ND *tel* (0603) 619331.

Nottingham: East Midlands Broadcasting Centre, York House, Mansfield Road, Nottingham NG1 3JB *tel* (0602) 472395.

Manchester: New Broadcasting House, Oxford Road, Manchester M60 1SJ *tel* 061-200 2020.

Milton Keynes: OUPC, Walton Hall, Milton Keynes MK7 6BH *tel* (0908) 274033.

Newcastle: Broadcasting Centre, Barrack Road, Newcastle upon Tyne NE99 2NE *tel* 091-232 1313.

Leeds: Broadcasting Centre, Woodhouse Lane, Leeds LS2 9PX *tel* (0532) 441188.

Plymouth: Broadcasting House, Seymour Road, Mannamead, Plymouth PL3 5BD *tel* (0752) 229201.

Southampton: Broadcasting House, Havelock Road, Southampton SO1 0QX *tel* (0703) 226201.

NORTHERN IRELAND

Belfast: Broadcasting House, Ormeau Avenue, Belfast BT2 8HQ   *tel* (0232) 338000.

BBC Radio Foyle: 8 Northland Road, Londonderry BT48 7NE   *tel* (0504) 262244.

SCOTLAND

Glasgow: Broadcasting House, Queen Margaret Drive, Glasgow G12 8DG   *tel* 041-339 8844.

Edinburgh: Broadcasting House, 5 Queen Street, Edinburgh EH2 1JF   *tel* 031-225 3131.

Aberdeen: Broadcasting House, Beechgrove Terrace, Aberdeen AB9 2ZT   *tel* (0224) 625233.

Dundee: Nethergate Centre, 66 The Nethergate, Dundee DD1 4ER   *tel* (0382) 202481.

BBC Highland: 7 Culduthel Road, Inverness IV2 4AD   *tel* (0463) 221711.

BBC Radio Nan Gaidheal: Rosebank, Church Street, Stornoway, Isle of Lewis   *tel* (0851) 7050000.

BBC Orkney: Castle Street, Kirkwall, Orkney KW15 1DF   *tel* (0856) 873939.

BBC Shetland: Brentham House, Lerwick, Shetland ZE1 0LR   *tel* (0595) 4747.

BBC Solway: 'Elmbank', Lovers' Walk, Dumfries DG1 1NZ   *tel* (0387) 68008.

BBC Tweed: Municipal Buildings, High Street, Selkirk TD7 4BU   *tel* (0750) 21884.

WALES

Cardiff: Broadcasting House, Llantrisant Road, Llandaff, Cardiff CF5 2YQ   *tel* (0222) 572888.

Bangor: Broadcasting House, Meirion Road, Bangor, Gwynedd LL57 2BY   *tel* (0248) 370880.

Swansea: Broadcasting House, 32 Alexandra Road, Swansea SA1 5DT   *tel* (0792) 654986.

BBC Radio Clwyd: The Old School House, Glanrafon Road, Mold, Clwyd CH7 1PA   *tel* (0352) 700367.

OVERSEAS OFFICES

USA: 630 Fifth Avenue, New York, NY 10111   *tel* 212-581-7100   *cables* Broadcasts, New York City   *telex* 620150.
2030 M Street NW, Suite 607, Washington, DC 20036   *tel* 202-223-2050.

Cairo Bureau: PO Box 2642, Cairo, Egypt   *tel* Cairo 770040/741931   *telex* 94169 NYTIM UN.

South East Asia Bureau: PO Box 434, Maxwell Road Post Office, Singapore 9008   *tel* (65) 254 7878   *telex* RS 35414.

South American Office: Casilla de Correo, 1566 Buenos Aires, Argentina   *tel* Buenos Aires 3926439   *telex* FLORIDA 734.

Australia and New Zealand: Suite 101, 80 William Street, Sydney, NSW 2011, Australia *tel* (02) 957 3777.

India: 1 Nizamuddin East, New Delhi 110013 *tel* 616108/616102 *cables* Loncalling, Newdelhi *telex* 31 2927 BBC IN.

France: 155 rue du Faubourg Saint-Honoré, BP 487 08, 75366 Paris, Cedex 08 *tel* (1) 45 61 97 00 *cables* Broadbrit, Paris *telex* 650341.

Germany: BBC Buro, Savignyplatz 6, D-1 Berlin *tel* Berlin 316773/3133063.

Belgium: BBC Office, PO Box 50, International Press Centre, 1 Boulevard Charlemagne, Brussels 1040 *tel* 322 2302120 *telex* 25912 BBCBRU B.

BBC LOCAL RADIO STATIONS

Local Radio also affords opportunities for writers to submit short stories and plays. A number of stations hold play-writing or short story competitions where the winners have their work broadcast. Others consider original work from local writers. Material should be submitted to the Assistant Editor.

Bedfordshire: BBC Three Counties Radio, PO Box 3CR, Luton, Beds. LU1 5XL *tel* (0582) 441000.

Berkshire: BBC Radio Berkshire, Portman Road, Reading, Berks. RG3 1NB *tel* (0734) 567056.

Birmingham: BBC Radio WM, Pebble Mill Road, Birmingham B5 7SD *tel* 021-414 8484.

Bristol: BBC Radio Bristol, 3 Tyndalls Park Road, Bristol BS8 1PP *tel* (0272) 741111.

Cambridgeshire: BBC Radio Cambridgeshire, Broadcasting House, 104 Hills Road, Cambridge CB2 1LD *tel* (0223) 259696.

Cleveland: BBC Radio Cleveland, PO Box 1548, Newport Road, Middlesbrough, Cleveland TS1 5DG *tel* (0642) 225211.

Cornwall: BBC Radio Cornwall, Phoenix Wharf, Truro, Cornwall TR1 1UA *tel* (0872) 75421.

Coventry: BBC CWR, 25 Warwick Road, Coventry CV1 2WR *tel* (0203) 559911.

Cumbria: BBC Radio Cumbria, Annetwell Street, Carlisle, Cumbria CA3 8BB *tel* (0228) 592444.

Derby: BBC Radio Derby, 56 St Helen's Street, Derby DE1 3HY *tel* (0332) 361111.

Devon: BBC Radio Devon, PO Box 100, Exeter, Devon EX4 4DB *tel* (0392) 215651.

Essex: BBC Essex, 198 New London Road, Chelmsford, Essex CM2 9AB *tel* (0245) 262393.

Gloucestershire: BBC Radio Gloucestershire, London Road, Gloucester GL1 1SW *tel* (0452) 308585.

Guernsey: BBC Radio Guernsey, Commerce House, Les Banques, St Peter Port, Guernsey, CI *tel* (0481) 728977.

Hereford and Worcester: BBC Hereford and Worcester, 43 Broad Street, Hereford HR4 9HH *tel* (0432) 355252; Hylton Road, Worcester WR2 5WW *tel* (0905) 748485.

Humberside: BBC Radio Humberside, 9 Chapel Street, Hull HU1 3NU *tel* (0482) 23232.

Jersey: BBC Radio Jersey, 18 Parade Road, St Helier, Jersey, CI *tel* (0534) 70000.

Kent: BBC Radio Kent, Sun Pier, Chatham, Kent ME4 4EZ *tel* (0634) 830505.

Lancashire: BBC Radio Lancashire, 26 Darwen Street, Blackburn, Lancs. BB2 2EA *tel* (0254) 262411.

Leeds: BBC Radio Leeds, Broadcasting House, Woodhouse Lane, Leeds LS2 9PN *tel* (0532) 442131.

Leicester: BBC Radio Leicester, Epic House, Charles Street, Leicester LE1 3SH *tel* (0533) 516688.

Lincolnshire: BBC Radio Lincolnshire, Radio Buildings, Newport, Lincoln LN1 3XY *tel* (0522) 511411.

London: BBC GLR, 35c Marylebone High Street, London W1A 4LG *tel* 071-224 2424.

Manchester: BBC GMR, Oxford Road, Manchester M60 1SJ *tel* 061-200 2000.

Merseyside: BBC Radio Merseyside, 55 Paradise Street, Liverpool L1 3BP *tel* 051-708 5500.

Newcastle: BBC Radio Newcastle, Broadcasting Centre, Barrack Road, Newcastle upon Tyne NE99 1RN *tel* 091-232 4141.

Norfolk: BBC Radio Norfolk, Norfolk Tower, Surrey Street, Norwich, Norfolk NR1 3PA *tel* (0603) 617411.

Northampton: BBC Radio Northampton, Braodcasting House, Abington Street, Northampton NN1 2BE *tel* (0604) 239100.

Nottingham: BBC Radio Nottingham, York House, Mansfield Road, Nottingham NG1 3JB *tel* (0602) 415161.

Oxford: BBC Radio Oxford, 269 Banbury Road, Summertown, Oxford OX2 7DW *tel* (0865) 311444.

Sheffield: BBC Radio Sheffield, Ashdell Grove, 60 Westbourne Road, Sheffield S10 2QU *tel* (0742) 686185.

Shropshire: BBC Radio Shropshire, 2-4 Boscobel Drive, Shrewsbury, Shropshire SY1 3TT *tel* (0743) 248484.

Solent: BBC Radio Solent, Broadcasting House, Havelock Road, Southampton SO1 0XR *tel* (0703) 631311.

Stoke-on-Trent: BBC Radio Stoke, Cheapside, Hanley, Stoke-on-Trent, Staffs. ST1 1JJ *tel* (0782) 208080.

Suffolk: BBC Radio Suffolk, Broadcasting House, St Matthews Street, Ipswich IP1 3EP. *tel* (0473) 250000.

Sussex and Surrey: BBC Radio Sussex and Surrey, Broadcasting House, Guildford, Surrey GU2 5AP *tel* (0483) 306113.

Swindon: BBC Wiltshire Sound, Broadcasting House, Prospect Place, Swindon, Wilts. SN1 3RW *tel* (0793) 513626.

York: BBC Radio York, 20 Bootham Row, York YO3 7BR *tel* (0904) 641351.

Independent Broadcasting

NATIONAL AND SATELLITE TELEVISION

Channel Four Television Corporation, 124 Horseferry Road, London SW1P 2TX   *tel* 071-396 4444   *fax* 071-306 8347. Commissions and purchases programmes (does not make them) for broadcast during the whole week throughout the United Kingdom (except Wales).

GMTV, London Television Centre, Upper Ground, London SE1 9TT   *tel* 071-827 7000   *fax* 071-827 7001. ITV's national breakfast television service, 6.00-9.25 a.m., seven days a week.

Independent Television News Ltd, 200 Gray's Inn Road, London WC1X 8XZ   *tel* 071-833 3000. Provides the national and international news programmes for all ITV areas.

Teletext UK Ltd, 101 Farm Lane, London SW6 1QJ   *tel* 071-386 5000   *fax* 071-386 5002.

BSkyB, 6 Centaurs Business Park, Grant Way, Isleworth, Middlesex TW7 5QD   *tel* 071-705 3000   *fax* 071-705 3113.

ITV Network Centre, 4th Floor, 200 Gray's Inn Road, London WC1X 8HF   *tel* 071-843 8000   *fax* 071-843 8158.

Independent Television Commission (ITC), 33 Foley Street, London W1P 7LB   *tel* 071-255 3000   *fax* 071-306 7800. Licenses and regulates all commercially funded UK television services, including cable and satellite services as well as terrestrial services.

REGIONAL TELEVISION

It is advisable to check before submitting any ideas/material – in all cases, scripts are preferred to synopses. Programmes should be planned with natural breaks for the insertion of advertisements. These companies also provide some programmes for Channel 4.

Anglia Television Ltd, Anglia House, Norwich NR1 3JG   *tel* (0603) 615151   *fax* (0603) 631032; 48 Leicester Square, London WC2H 7FB   *tel* 071-321 0101   *fax* 071-930 8499. Provides programmes for the East of England, and drama and Survival natural history programmes for the ITV Network. Drama submissions only through an accredited agency or similar source.

Border Television plc, The Television Centre, Carlisle CA1 3NT   *tel* (0228) 25101. Provides programmes for The Borders and the Isle of Man, during the whole week. Ideas for programmes, but not drama programmes, are considered from outside sources. Suggestions should be sent to Neil Robinson, Manager, Production.

Carlton Television Ltd, 101 St Martin's Lane, London WC2N 4AZ   *tel* 071-240 4000   *fax* 071-240 4171. Provides ITV programmes for London and the South East from Monday to Friday.

Central Independent Television plc, Central House, Broad Street, Birmingham B1 2JP   *tel* 021-643 9898; East Midlands Television Centre, Nottingham NG7 2NA   *tel* (0602) 863322; Unit 9, Windrush Court, Abingdon Business Park, Abingdon, Oxon OX14 1SA   *tel* (0235) 554123. Provides programmes to the

ITV Network and the East and West and South Midlands seven days a week. Central's requirements are constantly changing, and interested professional writers should contact the relevant Development Departments.

Channel Television, The Television Centre, St Helier, Jersey, CI   *tel* (0534) 68999   *fax* (0534) 59446. Provides programmes for the Channel Islands during the whole week relating mainly to Channel Islands news and current affairs.

Grampian Television plc, Queens Cross, Aberdeen AB9 2XJ   *tel* (0224) 646464   *telex* 73151   *fax* (0224) 635127; Albany House, 68 Albany Road, West Ferry, Dundee DD5 1NW   *tel* (0382) 739363; 23-25 Huntly Street, Inverness IV3 5PR   *tel* (0463) 242624; Seaforth House, 54 Seaforth Road, Stornaway PH87 2SH   *tel* (0851) 704433   *fax* (0851) 706406. Provides programmes for North Scotland during the whole week.

Granada Television Ltd, Granada Television Centre, Manchester M60 9EA   *tel* 061-832 7211; 36 Golden Square, London W1R 4AH   *tel* 071-734 8080. The ITV franchise holder for the North West of England. Produces programmes across a broad range for both its region and the ITV Network. It is advisable for writers to make their approach through agents who would have some knowledge of Granada's current requirements.

HTV Ltd, HTV Wales, The Television Centre, Culverhouse Cross, Cardiff CF5 6XJ   *tel* (0222) 590590; HTV West, The Television Centre, Bristol BS4 3HG   *tel* (0272) 778366. Provides programmes for Wales and West of England during the whole week. Produces programmes for home and international sales.

LWT, The London Television Centre, London SE1 9LT   *tel* 071-620 1620. Provides programmes for Greater London and much of the Home Counties area from Friday 5.15 p.m. to Monday 6.00 a.m. (excluding 6.00-9.25 a.m. on Sat/Sun).

Meridian Broadcasting, Television Centre, Southampton, Hants SO2 0TA   *tel* (0703) 222555   *fax* (0703) 335050. The ITV franchise holder for the South and South East. Meridian is a publisher contractor and commissions independent production companies.

Scottish Television Enterprises, Cowcaddens, Glasgow G2 3PR   *tel* 041-332 9999   *telex* 77388   *fax* 041-332 6982. Wholly owned subsidiary of Scottish Television, making drama and other programmes for the ITV network. Material: ideas and formats for long-form series with or without a Scottish flavour. Approach in the first instance to the Controller of Drama, Robert Love.

Tyne Tees Television Ltd, The Television Centre, City Road, Newcastle upon Tyne NE1 2AL   *tel* 091-261 0181   *fax* 091-261 2302; 15 Bloomsbury Square, London WC1A 2LJ   *tel* 071-312 3700. Serving the North of England seven days a week, 24 hours a day.

Ulster Television plc, Havelock House, Ormeau Road, Belfast, Northern Ireland BT7 1EB   *tel* (0232) 328122   *fax* (0232) 246695. Provides programmes for Northern Ireland during the whole week.

Westcountry Television Ltd, Langage Science Park, Plymouth PL7 5BG   *tel* (0752) 333333   *fax* (0752) 333444. Provides programmes for South West England throughout the week. In-house production mainly news, regional current affairs and topical features; other regional features commissioned from independent producers. Conduit to the Network for independent production packages.

Yorkshire Television Ltd, The Television Centre, Leeds LS3 1JS   *tel* (0532) 438283   *fax* (0532) 445107; Television House, 15 Bloomsbury Square, London WC1A 2LJ   *tel* 071-312 3700. Yorkshire Television is a Network Company which produces many programmes for the ITV Network and the Yorkshire area seven days a week.

INDEPENDENT NATIONAL RADIO

Virgin Radio, 1 Golden Square, London W1R 4DJ   *tel* 071-434 1215   *fax* 071-434 1197.

Classic FM, Academic House, 24-28 Oval Road, London NW1 7DQ   *tel* 071-284 3000.

IRN (Independent Radio News), 1 Euston Centre, Euston Road, London NW1 3JG   *tel* 071-388 4558   *fax* 071-388 4449. National news provider to all UK commercial radio stations, including live news bulletins, sport and financial news, and coverage of the House of Commons.

The Radio Authority, Holbrook House, 14 Great Queen Street, London WC2B 5DG   *tel* 071-430 2724   *fax* 071-405 7062. Licenses and regulates Independent Radio. Plans frequencies, awards licences, regulates (as necessary) programming and radio advertising, and plays an active role in the discussion and formulation of policies which affect the Independent Radio industry and its listeners.

Association of Independent Radio Companies (AIRC), Radio House, 46 Westbourne Grove, London W2 5SH   *tel* 071-727 2646   fax 071-229 0352. AIRC is the trade association for Independent Radio companies.

INDEPENDENT LOCAL RADIO

Aberdeen: NorthSound Radio, 45 King's Gate, Aberdeen AB2 6BL   *tel* (0224) 632234.

Alton: Wey Valley Radio, Prospect Place, Mill Lane, Alton, Hants GU34 2SY   *tel* (0420) 544444.

Aylesbury: Mix 96, Friars Square Studios, 11 Bourbon Street, Aylesbury, Bucks. HP20 2PZ   *tel* (0296) 399393   *fax* (0296) 398988.

Ayr: West Sound, Radio House, 54 Holmston Road, Ayr KA7 3BE   *tel* (0292) 283662   *fax* (0292) 283665.

Barnstaple: Lantern FM, The Light House, 17 Market Place, Bideford, Devon EX39 2DR   *tel* (0237) 424444.

Belfast: 96.7 BCR, Russell Court, Claremont Street, Lisburn Road, Belfast, Northern Ireland BT9 6JX   *tel* (0232) 438500   *fax* (0232) 230505.

Belfast: Cool FM, PO Box 974, Belfast, Northern Ireland BT1 1RT   *tel* (0247) 817181   *fax* (0247) 814974.

Belfast: Downtown Radio, Kiltonga Industrial Estate, Newtownards, Co. Down, Northern Ireland BT23 4ES   *tel* (0247) 815555   *fax* (0247) 818913.

Birmingham: 96.4FM BRMB/XTRA-AM, Radio House, Aston Road North, Birmingham B6 4BX   *tel* 021-359 4481   *fax* 021-359 1117.

Birmingham: Choice FM, c/o 175 Hampstead Road, Handsworth Wood, Birmingham B20 2RL   *tel* 021-553 6199.

Blackpool: Radio Wave, 965 Mowbray Drive, Blackpool, Lancs. FY3 7JR *tel* (0253) 304965.

Borders: Radio Borders, Tweedside Park, Galashiels TD1 3TD *tel* (0896) 59444 *fax* (0896) 59494.

Bournemouth: Two Counties Radio, 5 Southcote Road, Bournemouth, Hants BH1 3LR *tel* (0202) 294881.

Bradford: Sunrise FM, 30 Chapel Street, Little Germany, Bradford BD1 5DN *tel* (0274) 735043.

Bradford/Huddersfield & Halifax: The Pulse, PO Box 3000, Bradford BD1 5NE *tel* (0274) 731521.

Brighton: South Coast Radio 'Light & Easy', Radio House, Fareham, Hants PO15 5SH *tel* (0489) 589911 *fax* (0489) 589453.

Brighton: Southern FM Classic Hits, Radio House, PO Box 2000, Brighton, East Sussex BN41 2SS *tel* (0273) 430111 *fax* (0273) 430098.

Bristol: Galaxy Radio, 25 Portland Square, Bristol BS2 8RZ *tel* (0272) 240111.

Bristol: GWR Radio, PO Box 2000, Bristol BS99 7SN *tel* (0272) 279900 *fax* (0272) 256098.

Bury St Edmunds: SGR-FM, PO Box 250, Bury St Edmunds, Suffolk IP33 1AD *tel* (0284) 701511.

Cambridge & Newmarket: CN.FM 103, PO Box 1000, The Vision Park, Chivers Way, Histon, Cambridge CB4 4WW *tel* (0223) 235255 *fax* (0223) 235161.

Cardiff: Red Dragon FM, West Canal Wharf, Cardiff CF1 5XJ *tel* (0222) 384041 *fax* (0222) 384014.

Carlisle: CRFM, PO Box 964, Carlisle, Cumbria CA1 3NG *tel* (0228) 818964.

Central Scotland: Scot FM, Grampian Television plc, Queen's Cross, Aberdeen AB9 2XJ *tel* (0224) 646464.

Ceredigion: Radio Ceredigion, PO Box 600, Aberystwyth, Dyfed SY23 1PE *tel* (0970) 627999.

Cheltenham: 603 Radio, Churchill Studios, Churchill Road, Cheltenham, Glos. GL53 7EP *tel* (0242) 255023.

Cleveland: TFM Radio, Yale Crescent, Stockton-on-Tees, Cleveland TS17 6AA *tel* (0642) 615111 *fax* (0642) 674402.

Colchester: SGR-FM, Abbeygate Two, 9 Whitewell Road, Colchester, Essex CO2 7DE *tel* (0206) 575859.

Cornwall: Pirate FM102, Carn Brea Studios, Wilson Way, Redruth, Cornwall TR15 3XX *tel* (0209) 314400.

Coventry: Mercia FM, Hertford Place, Coventry CV1 3TT *tel* (0203) 633933 *telex* 31413 MERCIA G *fax* (0203) 258206.

Coventry: Radio Harmony, Ringway House, Hill Street, Coventry CV1 4AN *tel* (0203) 525656 *fax* (0203) 551744.

Cross-Channel Travellers: Channel Travel Radio, Eurotunnel, Victoria Plaza, 111 Buckingham Palace Road, London SW1W 0ST *tel* 071-834 7575.

Dumfries: South West Sound, Campbell House, Bankend Road, Dumfries DG1 4TH *tel* (0387) 50999 *fax* (0387) 65629.

Dundee/Perth: Radio Tay, PO Box 123, 6 North Isla Street, Dundee DD1 9UF *tel* (0382) 200800.

Eastbourne/Hastings: Southern FM, PO Box 2000, Brighton, East Sussex BN41 2SS   *tel* (0273) 430111   *fax* (0273) 430098.

Edinburgh: Forth FM, Forth House, Forth Street, Edinburgh EH1 3LF   *tel* 031-556 9255.

Exeter/Torbay: DevonAir Radio, 35-37 St David's Hill, Exeter, Devon EX4 4DA   *tel* (0392) 430703   *fax* (0392) 411893; and Harbour Point, Victoria Parade, Torquay TQ1 2RA   *tel* (0803) 298241   *fax* (0803) 201099.

Exeter/Torbay: Gemini Radio, c/o Curzon House, Southernhay West, Exeter, Devon EX4 3LY. Launch: January 1995.

Fort William: Nevis Radio, 'Sol', Seafield Gardens, Fort William PH33 6RJ   *tel* (0397) 704129/705540   *fax* (0397) 706177.

Glasgow: Clyde 1 FM and Clyde 2, Clydebank Business Park, Clydebank, Glasgow G81 2RX   *tel* 041-306 2200   *fax* 041-306 2265.

Gloucester & Cheltenham: Severn Sound, Broadcast Centre, Southgate Street, Gloucester GL1 2DQ   *tel* (0452) 423791.

Guernsey: Island FM, 12 Westerbrook, St Sampson, Guernsey GY2 4QQ, Channel Islands   *tel* (0481) 42000   *fax* (0481) 49676.

Guildford & Crawley: Mercury Extra AM, Broadfield House, Brighton Road, Crawley, West Sussex RH11 9TT   *tel* (0293) 519161   *fax* (0293) 560927. Broadcasting to Surrey, Sussex and Hampshire.

Guildford & Crawley: Radio Mercury, Broadfield House, Brighton Road, Crawley, West Sussex RH11 9TT   *tel* (0293) 519161   *fax* (0293) 560927.

Harlow: Ten 17, Latton Bush Centre, Southern Way, Harlow, Essex CM18 7BU   *tel* (0279) 432415   *fax* (0279) 445289.

Harrogate: Stray FM, PO Box 972, Harrogate HG1 5YF   *tel* (0423) 522972   *fax* (0423) 522922.

Hereford/Worcester: Radio Wyvern, Barbourne Terrace, Worcester WR1 3JZ   *tel* (0905) 612212.

Humberside: Viking, Commercial Road, Hull HU1 2SG   *tel* (0482) 25141   *fax* (0482) 587067.

Inverness, Moray Firth Radio, PO Box 271, Inverness IV3 6SF   *tel* (0463) 224433   *fax* (0463) 243224.

Inverurie: North East Community Radio, Little Couchercairn, St. Katherines, Inverurie, Aberdeenshire AB51 8QT   *tel* (0651) 891605.

Ipswich: SGR·FM, Radio House, Alpha Business Park, Whitehouse Road, Ipswich IP1 5LT   *tel* (0473) 461000.

Isle of Wight: Isle of Wight Radio, Dodnor Park, Newport, Isle of Wight PO30 5XE   *tel* (0983) 822557   *news tel* (0933) 821777   *fax* (0983) 821690.

Jersey: Channel 103, 6 Tunnell Street, St Helier, Jersey, CI JE2 4LU   *tel* (0534) 888103.

Kent: Invicta FM, Radio House, John Wilson Business Park, Whitstable, Kent CT5 3QX   *tel* (0227) 772004   *fax* (0227) 771558.

Kettering: KCBC Radio, PO Box 1584, Kettering, Northants. NN16 8PU   *tel* (0536) 412413   *fax* (0536) 517390.

King's Lynn: KL·FM96·7 Radio, PO Box 77, 18 Blackfriars Street, King's Lynn, Norfolk PE30 1NN   *tel* (0553) 772777   *fax* (0553) 767200.

Leeds: Radio Aire FM/Magic 828, PO Box 2000, Leeds LS3 1LR   *tel* (0532) 452299   *fax* (0532) 421830   *news fax* (0532) 343985.

Leicester: Leicester Sound FM, Granville House, Granville Road, Leicester LE1 7RW   *tel* (0533) 551616.

Leicester: Sunrise East Midlands, Granville House, Granville Road, Leicester LE1 7RW   *tel* (0533) 543002.

Lincoln: Lincs FM, Witham Park, Waterside South, Lincoln LN5 7JN   *tel* (0522) 549900.

Liverpool: Radio City, 8/10 Stanley Street, Liverpool L1 6AF   *tel* 051-227 5100.

London (General and Entertainment Service): Capital Radio, Euston Tower, London NW1 3DR   *tel* 071-608 6080.

London (Brixton): Choice FM, 16-18 Trinity Gardens, London SW9 8DP   *tel* 071-738 7969.

London (Haringey): London Greek Radio, Florentia Village, Vale Road, London N4 1TD   *tel* 081-800 8001.

London (West): Sunrise Radio, Sunrise House, Sunrise Road, Southall, Middlesex UB2 4AU   *tel* 081-574 6666   *fax* 081-813 9700.

London, Greater: County 1035, 3 Park Gate, London N2 8DJ   *tel* (0293) 562020.

London, Greater: J-FM, 26/27 Castlereagh Street, London W1H 5YR   *tel* 071-706 4100   *fax* 071-723 9742.

London, Greater: London News Radio, 72 Hammersmith Road, London W14 8YE   *tel* 071-603 2400.

London, Greater: Spectrum Radio, Endeavour House, Brent Cross, London NW2 1JT   *tel* 081-905 5000   *fax* 081-209 1029.

Londonderry: Q102.9, The Old Waterside, Railway Station, Duke Street, Waterside, Londonderry, Northern Ireland   *tel* (0504) 46666.

Ludlow: Sunshine 855, Sunshine House, Waterside, Ludlow, Shropshire SY8 1PE   *tel* (0584) 873795.

Luton/Bedford: Chiltern Radio, Chiltern Road, Dunstable, Beds. LU6 1HQ   *tel* (0582) 666001.

Manchester: Faze FM, c/o 6b Steine Gardens, Brighton BN2 1WB.

Manchester: Fortune 1458, PO Box 1458, Quay West, Trafford Park, Manchester M17 1FL   *tel* 061-872 1458   *fax* 061-872 0206.

Manchester: Piccadilly Radio, 127-131 The Piazza, Piccadilly Plaza, Manchester M1 4AW   *tel* 061-236 9913.

Milton Keynes: Horizon Radio, Broadcast Centre, Crownhill, Milton Keynes MK8 0AB   *tel* (0908) 269111.

Montgomeryshire: Radio Maldwyn, The Studios, The Park, Newtown, Powys SY16 2NZ   *tel* (0686) 624756.

Morecambe Bay: The Bay, PO Box 969, St George's Quay, Lancaster LA1 3LD   *tel* (0524) 848747.

Newport (Gwent): Red Dragon FM, West Canal Wharf, Cardiff CF1 5XJ   *tel* (0222) 384041   *fax* (0222) 384014.

North East: Century Radio, PO Box 100, Gateshead NE8 2YY   *tel* 091-477 6666   *fax* 091-477 5660.

North Wales Coast: Marcher Coast FM, 41 Conwy Road, Colwyn Bay, Clwyd LL28 5AB   *tel* (0492) 534555   *fax* (0492) 535248.

North West: J-FM, The World Trade Centre, Exchange Quay, Manchester M5 3EQ   *tel* 061-877 1004   *fax* 061-877 1005.

Northampton: Northants Radio, Broadcast Centre, The Enterprise Park, Boughton Green Road, Northampton NN2 7AH   *tel* (0604) 792411.

Norwich & Great Yarmouth: Broadland FM, St George's Plain, 47-49 Colegate, Norwich NR3 1DB   *tel* (0603) 630621   *fax* (0603) 666353.

Nottingham/Derby: Trent FM, 29-31 Castle Gate, Nottingham NG1 7AP   *tel* (0602) 581731.

Oxford/Banbury: Fox FM, Brush House, Pony Road, Horspath Estate, Cowley, Oxford OX4 2XR   *tel* (0865) 748787.

Paisley: Q96, 26 Lady Lane, Paisley PA1 2LG   *tel* 041-887 9630   *fax* 041-887 0963.

Perthshire: Heartland FM, Lower Oakfield, Pitlochry, Perthshire PH16 5DS   *tel* (0796) 474040.

Peterborough: 1332 AM The World's Greatest Music Station, PO Box 225, Queensgate Centre, Peterborough PE1 1XJ   *tel* (0733) 346225   *fax* (0733) 896400.

Peterborough: Hereward Radio, PO Box 225, Queensgate Centre, Peterborough, Cambs. PE1 1XJ   *tel* (0733) 346225   *fax* (0733) 342714.

Plymouth: Plymouth Sound, Earl's Acre, Plymouth PL3 4HX   *tel* (0752) 227272   *fax* (0752) 670730.

Portsmouth/Southampton: Ocean FM, Radio House, Fareham, Hants PO15 5TA   *tel* (0489) 589911.

Portsmouth/Southampton: Power FM, Radio House, Fareham, Hants PO15 5TL   *tel* (0489) 589911.

Portsmouth/Southampton/Brighton: South Coast Radio, Radio House, Fareham, Hants PO15 5SH   *tel* (0489) 589911.

Preston & Blackpool: Red Rose Radio, PO Box 301, St Paul's Square, Preston, Lancs. PR1 1YE   *tel* (0772) 556301.

Reading/Basingstoke: 210 Classic Gold, PO Box 2020, Reading, Berks. RG3 5RZ   *tel* (0734) 413131   *fax* (0734) 431215.

Reading/Basingstoke & Andover: 2-TEN FM, PO Box 210, Reading, Berks. RG3 5RZ   *tel* (0734) 413131   *fax* (0734) 431215.

St Albans/Watford: Oasis Radio, c/o Chiltern Road, Dunstable, Beds. LU6 1HQ   *tel* (0582) 666001.

Salisbury: Spire FM, City Hall Studios, Malthouse Lane, Salisbury, Wilts. SP2 7QQ   *tel* (0722) 416644.

Scarborough: Yorkshire Coast Radio, 62 Falsgrave Road, Scarborough, North Yorkshire YO12 5AX   *tel* (0723) 500962   *fax* (0723) 501050.

Severn Estuary: Galaxy Radio, Broadcast Centre, 25 Portland Square, Bristol BS2 8RZ   *tel* (0272) 240111.

Sheffield & Rotherham/Barnsley/Doncaster: Hallam FM and Great Yorkshire Gold, Radio House, 900 Herries Road, Hillsborough, Sheffield S6 1RH   *tel* (0742) 853333/852121   *fax* (0742) 853159.

Shetland Islands: SIBC, Market Street, Lerwick, Shetland ZE1 0JN.

Slough, Maidenhead and Windsor: Star FM, The Observatory Shopping Centre, Slough, Berks. SL1 1LH   *tel* (0753) 551016.

Somerset & South Avon: Orchard FM, Haygrove House, Shoreditch, Taunton, Somerset TA3 7BT   *tel* (0823) 338448.

South Buckinghamshire: elevenSEVENTY, PO Box 1170, High Wycombe, Bucks HP13 6YT   *tel* (0494) 446611   *fax* (0494) 445400   *news fax* (0494) 447272.

Southend/Chelmsford: Essex FM, Radio House, Clifftown Road, Southend-on-Sea, Essex SS1 1SX   *tel* (0702) 333711.

Stirling: Central FM Radio, PO Box 967, Stirling FK7 7RP   *tel* (0786) 451188   *fax* (0786) 461883.

Stockport: Signal Radio Cheshire, Regent House, Heaton Lane, Stockport, Cheshire SK4 1BX   *tel* 061-480 5445.

Stoke-on-Trent: Signal Radio, Stoke Road, Stoke-on-Trent, Staffs. ST4 2SR   *tel* (0782) 747047   *fax* (0782) 744110.

Sunderland: Wear FM, The Forster Building, Chester Road, Sunderland, Tyne and Wear SR1 3SD   *tel* 091-515 2103   *fax* 091-515 2270.

Swansea: Swansea Sound, Victoria Road, Gowerton, Swansea, West Glamorgan SA4 3AB   *tel* (0792) 893751   *fax* (0792) 898841.

Swindon/West Wiltshire: GWR Radio, PO Box 2000, Swindon, Wilts. SN4 7EX   *tel* (0793) 853222.

Tendring: Mellow 1557, 21-23 Walton Road, Frinton-on-Sea, Essex CO13 0AA   *tel* (0255) 675303   *fax* (0255) 678585.

Thamesmead: RTM (Independent Radio Thamesmead), 17-20 Tavy Bridge, Thamesmead, London SE2 9UG   *tel* 081-311 3112   *fax* 081-312 1930.

Tyne and Wear: Metro FM, Long Rigg, Swalwell, Newcastle upon Tyne NE99 1BB   *tel* 091-488 3131   *fax* 091-488 9222.

West Midlands: Heart FM, Chrysalis Group plc, The Chrysalis Building, 13 Bramley Road, London W10 6SP   *tel* 071-221 2213.

Weymouth and Dorchester: Wessex FM, Trinity Street, Dorchester, Dorset DT1 1DJ   *tel* (0305) 250333.

Whitstable: Invicta Radio, PO Box 100, Whitstable, Kent CT5 3YR   *tel* (0227) 772004.

Wolverhampton & Black Country/Shrewsbury & Telford: Beacon Radio, 267 Tettenhall Road, Wolverhampton WV6 0DQ   *tel* (0902) 757211; 28 Castle Street, Shrewsbury SY1 2BQ   *tel* (0743) 232271.

Wrexham & Deeside: Marcher Sound/Sain-Y-Gororau, The Studios, Mold Road, Wrexham, Clwyd LL11 4AF   *tel* (0978) 752202.

Markets for Radio Programmes

Almondell Productions (1993), 14 Mansefield, East Calder, West Lothian EH53 0JQ   *tel/fax* (0506) 881483. *Contact:* David Calder. Scripts for docs and speech-based programmes; no plays.

Boom Media Ltd (1993), 25 Market Place, Halesworth, Suffolk IP19 8DA   *tel* (0986) 875000   *fax* (0986) 875050. *Director:* Nick Patrick. Features and docs with an East Anglian bias, sports' features, popular culture, East Anglian drama.

Business Sound Ltd (1989), Unit 9, Bramley Business Centre, Station Road, Bramley, Surrey GU5 0AZ   *tel* (0483) 898868   *fax* (0483) 894056. *Managing director:* Michael Bartlett. Ideas and synopses for packages for the corporate training market; docs. No unsolicited material; initial approach by phone, please.

Features Unlimited (1992), Studio A132, The Riverside Business Centre, Bendon Valley, London SW18 4LZ   *tel* 081-875 9999. *Producer:* Louise Armitage. Drama, comedy and light entertainment.

The Flying Dutchman Company (1988), Units 5 & 6, 143 Chatham Road, London SW11 6HJ   *tel* 071-223 9067   *fax* 071-585 0459. *Partner:* Michael Cameron. Plays, docs and other programmes on all topics.

GRF Christian Radio (1948), 342 Argyle Street, Glasgow G2 8LY   *tel* 041-221 9447   *fax* 041-332 9187. *Programme controller:* Brian W. Muir. Docs on ethical/moral/religious issues; mini-dramas (up to four minutes) on religious themes; one-minute scripts; children's programmes (religious/educational).

Heavy Entertainment Ltd (1992), 208 Canalot Studios, 222 Kensal Road, London W10 5BN   *tel* 081-960 9001/2   *fax* 081-960 9003. *Company director:* David Roper. Full-length plays, docs and comedy programmes.

Mike Hopwood Productions Ltd (1991), Conway House, Cheapside, Hanley, Stoke-on-Trent, Staffs. ST1 1JJ   *tel* (0782) 201319   *fax* (0782) 289115. *Editor:* Mike Hopwood. Plays, docs, comedy, soaps, light entertainment.

Independent Productions Ltd (1990), 4 Eaton Road, Bowdon, Altrincham, Cheshire WA14 3EH   *tel* 061-928 6105   *fax* 061-926 8652. *Director:* Tony Hawkins. Scripts and ideas for commercials and promotions for independent radio.

IRDP, Box 518, Manningtree, Essex CO11 1XD   *tel* (0206) 299088. *Directors:* Tim Crook, Richard Shannon. Dramatisations, serialisations and adaptations.

London Hispanic Foundation (1993), PO Box 3281, London NW9 5EW   *tel* 081-905 5000. *Head of Hispanic service:* Bruno Giorgi. Short plays and docs suitable for broadcasting in Spanish, so material translated into Spanish an advantage.

Mediatracks (1987), 93 Columbia Way, Blackburn, Lancs. BB2 7EA   *tel* (0254) 691197. *Contact:* Steve Johnson. Pop-music and general interest docs for BBC local radio network.

Partners in Sound Ltd (1993), 14 Highwood Road, London N19 4PN   *tel* 071-281 1555/071-485 0873   *mobile* (0973) 221479   *fax* 071-272 4147. *Director:* Ian Willox. Scripts for plays, docs and other programmes.

Planet 24 (1991), Norex Court, Thames Quay, 195 Marsh Wall, London E14 9SG   *tel* 071-712 9300   *fax* 071-712 9400. *Development producer:* Alex Connock. Scripts, synopses and ideas for plays, docs and other programmes.

Radio Lynx (1985), Unit 4, Chelsea Studios, 92 Lots Road, London SW10 0RN   *tel* 071-351 4895   *fax* 071-352 0771. *Sales and marketing director:* Simon Hughes. Scripts for docs and other programmes, particularly short form comedy sketches.

Saffron Productions Ltd (1985), Craigs End, Stambourne, Halstead, Essex CO9 4NQ   *tel* (0440) 785200   *fax* (0440) 785775. *Managing director/executive producer:* Victor Pemberton; *director programmes:* David Spenser. Scripts and ideas for 1-hour plays, and drama series, serials, docs and other programmes.

ScreenPlay Ltd (1987), 104 George Crescent, Muswell Hill, London N10 1AJ   *tel* 081-444 7196. *Managing director:* Robert J. Shepherd. Scripts for drama and comedy, particularly series and serials. Unsolicited material occasionally considered. Send synopsis and sample dialogue in first instance; sae essential for return of material.

SH Radio (1988), Robert Symes, Green Dene Cottage, Honeysuckle Bottom, East Horsley, Surrey KT24 5TD   *tel/fax* (0483) 283223;   Mary-Jean Hasler, 22 Carew Road, Ealing, London W13 9QL   *tel* 081-567 2100. Music series, documentary features and broadcast/non-broadcast commercial material.

Smooth Operations (1992), PO Box 286, Cambridge CB1 4TW   *tel* (0223) 880835   *fax* (0223) 881647. *Executive producer:* Nick Barraclough. Scripts and ideas for docs and series with popular music theme.

Soundbite Productions Ltd (1991), 55 Tasman Road, Stockwell, London SW9 9LZ   *tel/fax* 071-274 1349. *Managing director:* Lizzie Jackson. Well-thought-out ideas and research for series and programmes for BBC Radio and World Service. Material only accepted from those with a proven track record in radio or TV.

Splash Sound Productions (1982), 1 Mossley Hill Drive, Liverpool L17 1AJ   *tel/fax* 051-724 5813. Ideas for plays, serials, musical drama and comedy.

Testbed Productions (1992), 3 Richmond Avenue, London SW20 8LA   *tel* 081-542 2602   *fax* 081-715 7264. *Directors:* Nick Baker, Viv Black. Docs and other programmes; ideas for interview and feature series and panel games; no plays.

Overseas Radio and Television Companies

AUSTRALIA

Australian Broadcasting Corporation, Box 9994, GPO, Sydney, NSW 2001. Manager for Europe: Australian Broadcasting Corporation, 54 Portland Place, London W1N 4DY. The Australian Broadcasting Corporation is a statutory authority established by Act of Parliament and responsible to Parliament. It provides television and radio programmes in the national broadcasting service and operates Radio Australia. It operates six symphony orchestras and stages concerts throughout Australia.

ABC television restricts its production resources to work closely related to the Australian environment. For this reason scripts submitted from outside Australia in the field of television drama and short stories have little chance of success. ABC radio also looks principally to Australian writers for the basis of its drama output. However, ABC radio is interested in reading or auditioning new creative material of a high quality from overseas sources and this may be submitted in script or taped form. No journalistic material is required. Talks on international affairs are commissioned.

ATN Channel 7, Australian Television Network, Amalgamated Television Services Pty Ltd, Television Centre, Epping, NSW 2121   *tel* (02) 877 7777   *telegraphic address* Telecentre, Sydney   *telex* AA 20250   *fax* (02) 877 7886. Willing to consider original television material of all types, especially drama series/serials, situation-comedy series and children's drama series/serials that have received a 'C' classification as well as 2 × 2 mini-series format. Material should have an *Australian* background and deal with *Australian* characters. Unsolicited material not accepted.

BTQ Channel 7, Brisbane TV Limited, Sir Samuel Griffith Drive, Mt Coot-tha, GPO Box 604, Brisbane 4001   *tel* (07) 369 7777   *fax* (07) 368 2970. Children's educational-type series, children's entertainment programmes. Writers should have a thorough understanding of Australian culture.

HSV Channel 7, HSV Channel 7 Pty Ltd, 119 Wells Street, South Melbourne, Victoria 3205 *tel* (03) 697 7777. For requirements see ATN Channel 7.

National Nine Network (TCN-9 Sydney, GTV-9 Melbourne, QTQ-9 Brisbane, NWS-9 Adelaide, STW-9 Perth), c/o 24 Artarmon Road, Willoughby, NSW 2068 *tel* (02) 906 9999 *fax* (02) 958 2279. *Network program director:* John Stephens; *network director of drama:* Kris Noble; *network director program development:* David Lyle. Interested in receiving material from freelance writers strictly on the basis of payment for material or ideas used. No necessity for writers to be Australian-based, but membership of the Australian Writers' Guild helpful.

CANADA

Canadian Broadcasting Corporation, PO Box 8478, Ottawa, Ontario K1G 3J5 *tel* 613-724-1200.

Canadian Radio-television and Telecommunications Commission, Ottawa, Ontario K1A 0N2. *General information tel* 819-997-0313 *fax* 819-994-0218; *Visual Ear* 819-994-0423. The federal authority which regulates telecommunications and the broadcasting system in Canada.

INDIA

All India Radio, Akashvani Bhavan, Parliament Street, New Delhi 110001 (*telex* 031-65585 Dair IN) is part of the Ministry of Information and Broadcasting of the Government of India which operates the broadcasting network in the country. There are 164 stations covering almost the entire area of the country and catering to the various social, cultural and linguistic needs of the people. Programmes consist of news, music, talks, plays, discussions, documentary features and special audience programmes for women, children, industrial workers and rural audiences.
External Services Division of All India Radio broadcasts programmes in 24 languages. The object of these programmes is to entertain Indians abroad and keep them in touch with the events and developments in India.
The Commercial Service is broadcast over 30 AIR stations.
The National Channel commenced in May 1988.

Television: Director General, Doordarshan India (Television), Mandi House, Copernicus Marg, New Delhi 110001 *tel* 382094 *telex* 3166143. Covers most of India, providing a wide variety of programmes, both educational and for entertainment. Some commercial advertising.

REPUBLIC OF IRELAND

Radio Telefis Eireann, Donnybrook, Dublin 4 *tel* (01) 643111 *telex* 93700 *fax* (01) 643080. The Irish national broadcasting service operating radio and television.

Television: script requirements: original television plays, length 52 minutes, preferably set in Ireland or of strong Irish interest. Plays should be sent to the Head of Drama. Guidelines on writing plays for television are available from the Head of Television Drama. Before submitting material to Current Affairs, Drama, Features or Young People's programmes, authors are advised to write to the department in question.

Radio: talks and short stories (length 14 minutes) in Irish or English suitable for broadcasting: features, dramatic or narrative and plays are welcomed and paid for according to merit. Plays should run 30, 60 or 90 minutes. Guidelines on writing for radio are available from the RTE Radio Drama Department, Radio Centre, Donnybrook, Dublin 4, Republic of Ireland.

Independent Radio and Television Commission, Marine House, Clanwilliam Place, Dublin 2 *tel* (01) 6760966 *fax* (01) 6760948. Statutory body with responsibility for independent broadcasting. At present there are 21 local radio stations operating, with further stations in the Dublin area covering community and special interests, and the Irish language.

NEW ZEALAND

Radio New Zealand Ltd, PO Box 2092, Wellington, C1 *tel* (04) 474-1555 *telex* NZ 31031 *fax* (04) 474-1340. *Chief executive:* Nigel Milan. A 24-hour state-owned radio enterprise, with editorial and programming independence, controlling a NZ-wide group of over 30 commercial community stations and three public service non-commercial networks, and a shortwave service directed primarily to the Pacific area.

Television New Zealand Ltd, PO Box 3819, Auckland *tel* (09) 377-0630 *telex* NZ 60056 TVNZAC Q *fax* (09) 375-0918. *Chairman:* Norman Geary; *group chief executive:* Brent Harman.

Auckland Television Centre *tel* (09) 377-0630. TVNZ is a state-owned enterprise with production facilities in all four main centres. It owns and operates Television One, Channel 2 and four subsidiary companies, South Pacific Pictures Ltd, Avalon Studios Ltd, Broadcast Communications Ltd and Moving Pictures.

Avalon Studios Ltd, PO Box 30945, Lower Hutt, Wellington *tel* (04) 619-0600 *fax* (04) 619-0888. *Managing director:* Gary Mollard.

TVNZ Christchurch, PO Box 1945, Christchurch *tel* (03) 379-2680 *fax* (03) 365-7882.

TVNZ Dunedin & TVNZ Natural History Unit, PO Box 474, Dunedin *tel* (03) 479-9799 *fax* (03) 479-9916.

South Pacific Pictures Ltd, PO Box 35 656, Browns Bay, Auckland 10 *tel* (09) 444-3000 *fax* (09) 443-5900. *Managing director:* John Barnett.

Broadcast Communications Ltd, PO Box 98, Wellington *tel* (04) 382-6000 *fax* (04) 382-6066. *Managing director:* John Chellingworth.

SOUTH AFRICA

South African Broadcasting Corporation, Private Bag XI, Auckland Park 2006 *tel* (011) 714-9111 *fax* (011) 714-3106. Operates five national networks: Radio South Africa, Afrikaans Stereo, Radio 5, Radio Metro, Radio 2000, and eight regional services, Highveld Stereo, Port Natal Stereo, Good Hope Stereo, Radio Lotus, Jacaranda Stereo, Algoa Stereo, Radio Oranje, Radio Komtrei. The nine radio services in Nguni and Sotho languages broadcast in Zulu, Xhosa, Southern Sotho, Northern Sotho, Tswana, Venda, Tsonga, Swazi and Ndebele. The External Service, known as Channel Africa, transmits radio and television programmes to Africa and the India Ocean islands.

The service which makes the greatest use of written material in English is Radio South Africa.

Drama. One-hour plays of all kinds are welcomed, both original works and adaptations/dramatisations – comedies, domestic dramas, thrillers, 'social' plays, etc. Half-hour plays are occasionally broadcast in a 'double bill' format, and about five 90-minute plays are broadcast annually. A series of weekly half-hour self-contained episodes (about 13 per series) is also broadcast. Serials (up to 65 15-minute episodes) are broadcast daily. These may be dramatisations or originals.

Afrikaans Stereo also accepts quality material for translation into Afrikaans.

Short Stories. Short stories of all kinds, of between 1500 and 1800 words, are welcomed.

Children's Programmes. Short stories, plays and serials (maximum 15 minutes) may be submitted.

Talks. Most are locally commissioned, but outstanding material of particular interest may be submitted (3-10 minutes).

Television. There are three television services in nine languages.

TV1 broadcasts in English and Afrikaans; CCV-TV broadcasts in English, Afrikaans, Zulu, Xhosa, South Sotho, North Sotho and Tswana, as well as Hindi and Tamil. NNTV is a non-commercial channel broadcasting programmes of a public service nature. Both TV1 and CCV accept scripts for drama and comedy, either for one-off programmes or series.

Writing for Television

BILL CRAIG
Past-President of The Writers' Guild of Great Britain

'Television drama' is a generic term which covers several varied and specialist areas of writing for the domestic screen. Since each differs from the others in terms of requirements and rewards and since each is definable in copyright terms, let's start by identifying them.

The television play is a one-off creation of a single mind and talent and absolutely the property of its author. As a form it is the vehicle for the talents of newest and least-experienced writers in the medium and also for those who are held in the highest regard. It is (for practical reasons) the traditional point of entry for the tyro. There has been some reduction in the number of plays produced annually but the BBC and certain ITV companies are still in the market for 30, 60 and 90 minute slot-length works. If the bad news is that they get several thousand unsolicited manuscripts every year, the good news is that they are all read. No script-unit will risk missing out on an undiscovered genius.

The same observations (with some modification) would apply to the original series or serial: that is, a multi-part work of sole authorship and of finite length. They tend to be written by established television writers who have a proven ability to go the necessary distance, but a new writer with an attractive idea can come in through this door.

What's the procedure? Invest some time and talent and write the play. A commission on a synopsis is unlikely without some evidence that you can write interesting action, dialogue and characters. With the finite series/serial – write the first episode and synopsise the rest.

The situation-comedy is the most highly paid area of television writing – and understandably so. It calls for a quirky and idiosyncratic mind, and its overriding imperative – to make the viewer laugh – subordinates all of the other dramatic tools to this end. If it's difficult to play Beethoven's *Ninth* on a one-stringed fiddle, then it's Hell to do it for a run of six episodes. The sit-com is unique in screen drama in so far as most of them are played before live studio audiences.

Once upon a time, they were constructed around individual comedians. Some still are, but for several years now the practice has been to cast according to the script with actors who can play comedy. And that's not a bad thing, is it?

Again, this form is an original in copyright terms, though dual authorships are not uncommon. A synopsis is pretty useless (ever tried to explain a joke?), so write the pilot-script and briefly indicate where you can go with other episodes.

We now come to a significant point of departure and go into those areas where the copyright is split with another party.

First, the drama-series: *Lovejoy, The Bill, Casualty*, et al. These are definable as a series of original and self-contained scripts using the same characters and backgrounds throughout. The format – that is, the characters and general ambience – will be owned or leased by the production organisation. They represent a substantial part of television drama, but it is rare for a writer without previous screen experience to be commissioned to write for them. It is quite pointless to submit a speculative script or synopsis: the series you are seeing now was recorded months ago.

Serials, such as *Coronation Street, Brookside, Take the High Road* and *Emmerdale*, will occasionally try out new writers, but the production pressures on reliability and deadline delivery dates don't allow for too many risks to be taken outside what is usually an established and pretty permanent writing team.

Dramatisation and Adaptation are terms which are interchanged in an ignorantly casual manner; they are not the same thing. A dramatisation is the conversion of a prose-work to a screenplay. An adaptation is a similar conversion of a dramatic work. The difference is considerable, and the screen credit should reflect this fact.

There has been a great increase in the number of dramatisations made from novels. Again, these are usually written by writers with a track record in television, but occasionally the author of the book to be dramatised will be approached to write the screenplay. If you don't come under either of those headings, then you probably wouldn't get very far by simply suggesting that you'd like to dramatise this or that novel. Adaptations are usually 'in-house' works.

All of this leaves uncovered an odd and often lucrative area – the format. It is possible to sell an idea for a series without ever having written a script. But make sure that your submission is as detailed as it possibly can be in terms of background, main characters and development. Doing it the simple way in this instance can mean finding out that fifty other people have had the same simple idea. And selling an idea carries no guarantee that you'll be asked to write the scripts.

Script layout and presentation. Use A4. Type it or have it typed. Blank margin about four inches on the left hand side. Directions and character names in capitals, dialogue in capitals and lower case, double spaced. Don't go mad with directions; keep them functional and indicative. Don't be intimidated by camera directions; use them only when they make a dramatic point you want to get across.

Number and head the scenes thus: 1. INT. JOE'S ROOM. DAY

Avoid nonsense action directions such as 'Her inner resilience manifests itself in a way reminiscent of the wind howling across her native moors'. If you mean she's from Yorkshire, just say it.

There are several books on the subject of layout and technique. Two which come to mind are *Writing for Television* by Gerald Kelsey (Black) and *The Way to Write for Television* by Eric Paice (Elm Tree Books) (new editions Spring 1995). Another on scriptwriting is *Writing Comedy* by Ronald Wolfe (Hale).

Given success to your efforts, you will be contracted under the terms of the relevant agreement between the British Broadcasting Corporation or the ITV Network Centre and the Writers' Guild of Great Britain, 430 Edgware Road,

London W2 1EH. The Guild has sole bargaining rights in the television drama rates, its agreements are complex and comprehensive and several of the rights and benefits contained in them are available to Guild members only.

Payments are made in stages: BBC – half on commission, half on acceptance; ITV Network Centre – half on commission, a quarter on delivery, a quarter on acceptance.

The foregoing comments apply mainly to programmes produced by the British Broadcasting Corporation or the ITV companies. The increasingly important independent production sector should not, however, be ignored, since many of their productions are primarily intended for television screening.

These programmes are made by either entirely independent production organisations or subsidiaries of the ITV companies (e.g. *Between the Lines*, Island World/BBC).

Generally speaking, the scripts are laid out in film format (see **Screenplays for Films** on page 329) although some, since they produce on tape, might prefer the television format. The procedures described above for submitting unsolicited work should be observed.

Contracts should conform to the terms laid down by the agreement between the Writers' Guild of Great Britain and the Producers Alliance for Cinema and Television (PACT). Again, the agreement is comprehensive and covers all forms and aspects of screen drama. Payment is made in four stages: treatment, first draft, second draft and principal photography. Further exploitation is also covered.

Further useful information and addresses may be found in a booklet called *Contacts*. The 1994-95 edition is available from November from *The Spotlight*, 7 Leicester Place, London WC2H 7BP   *tel* 071-437 7631.

Naming your characters

One final point. Names are important. First names, in particular, can in themselves be clichés. At this point in time Agnes and Agatha suggest an elderly woman, Susan and Samantha someone much younger. Fred and Bert are almost certainly manual workers while Frederick and Bertram are not. Names go in and out of fashion and they carry with then an association of class and time and geography. Unimportant as it may seem names must be chosen with care.

from *Writing for Television* by Gerald Kelsey (A & C Black, £9.99)

Markets for Screenplays

JEAN McCONNELL

There have been setbacks for the British film industry recently. Nevertheless, a market still exists – particularly material being made for television or for videograms, with which many film companies are now very actively engaged.

The recommended approach is through a recognised literary agent, but most film companies have a story department to whom material can be sent for consideration. But it is a good idea to check with the company first to make sure it is worth your while.

It is a fact that many of the feature films these days are based on already best-selling books, but there are some companies, particularly those with a television outlet, which will sometimes accept unsolicited material if it seems to be exceptionally original. It is obviously sensible to try to sell your work to a company which is currently in active production, such as those listed below. *But again remember the best way to achieve success is through the knowledge and efforts of a literary agent.*

When a writer submits material direct to a company, some of the larger ones, usually those American based, may request that a Release Form be signed before they are prepared to read it. This document is ostensibly designed to absolve the company from any charge of plagiarism if they should be working on a similar idea; also to limit their liability in the event of any legal action. Writers must make up their own minds whether they wish to sign this but, in principle, it is not highly recommended.

Markets for Screenplays and Television Programmes

Aardman Animations (1972), Gas Ferry Road, Bristol BS1 6UN   *tel* (0272) 227227   *fax* (0272) 227225. *Contact:* producer, broadcast/features. Specialists in model animation, looking for screenplays for adults for cinema and TV.

Anglia Television Entertainment (1988), 48 Leicester Square, London WC2H 7FB   *tel* 071-321 0101   *fax* 071-930 8499. *Chief executive:* Chris Pye. Synopses for television drama or mini-series, non-factual programme ideas.

British Lion Screen Entertainment (1927), Pinewood Studios, Iver, Bucks. SL0 0NH   *tel* (0753) 651700   *fax* (0753) 656391. *Contact:* Peter Snell. Screenplays and treatments for cinema; TV drama and sitcoms. No unsolicited material.

Brook Associates Ltd, 21-24 Bruges Place, Randolph Street, London NW1 0TF   *tel* 071-482 6111   *fax* 071-284 0626. *Development executives:* Anne Lapping, Phillip Whitehead. Screenplays for TV; TV documentaries, current affairs and drama.

Celador Productions Ltd (1983), 39 Long Acre, London WC2E 9JT   *tel* 071-240 8101   *fax* 071-836 1117. *Contacts:* Paul Smith, Nic Phillips. Popular entertainment TV programmes: comedy, entertainment, game show productions, 'people show' ideas, drama serials and series.

Chatsworth Television Ltd (1980), 97-99 Dean Street, London W1V 5RA   *tel* 071-734 4302   *fax* 071-437 3301. *Contact:* Stephen Jeffery-Poulter. Screenplays for television drama; light entertainment.

Children's Film and Television Foundation Ltd, Elstree Studios, Borehamwood, Herts. WD6 1JG *tel* 081-953 0844 *fax* 081-207 0860. Not a production company; finances script development, especially for feature films (principally television) aimed at children between 5 and 12 years old.

Childsplay Productions Ltd (1984), 8 Lonsdale Road, London NW6 6RD *tel* 071-328 1429 *fax* 071-328 1416. *Contact:* Kim Burke. Treatments for children's (not pre-school) and family TV programming. Chiefly drama; also comedy, entertainment and education.

The Comic Strip Ltd (1980), 43A Berwick Street, London W1V 3RE *tel* 071-439 9509 *fax* 071-734 2793. *Contact:* Nira Park. Screenplays for cinema and TV; ½-hour comedy and drama series.

Compass Film Productions Ltd (1974), 1st Floor, 175 Wardour Street, London W1V 3FB *tel* 071-734 8115 *fax* 071-439 6456. *Contact:* Simon Heaven. Screenplays for TV; cultural, educational and sponsored TV programmes.

The Walt Disney Company Ltd, Beaumont House, Kensington Village, Avonmore, London W14 8TS *tel* 071-605 2400 *fax* 071-605 2593. Screenplays not accepted by London office. *Must be submitted by an agent* to The Walt Disney Studios in Burbank, California.

Diverse Production Ltd (1982), Gorleston Street, London W14 8XS *tel* 071-603 4567 *fax* 071-603 2148. *Drama producer:* Laurence Bowen. Film and TV drama.

Domino Films (1988), 8 Stockwell Terrace, London SW9 0QD *tel* 071-582 0393 *fax* 071-582 0437. *Contact:* Joanna Mack. Documentaries.

Fairwater Films Ltd (1982), North Chambers, Castle Arcade, Cardiff CF1 2BX *tel* (0222) 640140 *fax* (0222) 230482. *Managing director:* Tony Barnes. Animation for cinema and TV; live action entertainment. All material should be submitted through an agent.

The First Film Company Ltd (1984), 38 Great Windmill Street, London W1V 7PA *tel* 071-439 1640 *fax* 071-437 2062. *Producer:* Roger Randall-Cutler; *head of development:* Aysha Rafaele. Screenplays for cinema. All material should be submitted through an agent.

Focus Films (1982), The Rotunda Studios, rear of 116-118 Finchley Road, London NW3 5HT *tel* 071-435 9004 *fax* 071-431 3562. *Contact:* head of development. Screenplays for cinema; TV features, and TV production and financing.

Mark Forstater Productions Ltd, Unit 66, Pall Mall Deposit, 124-126 Barlby Road, London W10 6BL *tel* 081-964 1888 *fax* 081-960 9819. *Contact:* Nicky Lund. Film and TV production. No unsolicited scripts, please.

Fourth Wall Productions (1988), 1 Little Argyll Street, London W1R 5DB *tel* 071-437 2222 *fax* 071-734 0663. *Director:* Lino Ferrari. Documentaries (single/series): current affairs, religion, arts and education; new formats for talks programmes.

Front Page Films (1985), 23 West Smithfield, London EC1A 9HY *tel* 071-329 6866 *fax* 071-329 6844. *Contact:* script editor. Screenplays for cinema. Material only accepted through agents.

Noel Gay Television (1987), 6th Floor, 76 Oxford Street, London W1N 0AT *tel* 071-412 0400 *fax* 071-412 0300. *Contact:* head of development. Screenplays for cinema and TV; light entertainment and documentaries.

The Grade Company (1985), 8 Queen Street, London W1X 7PH　*tel* 071-409 1925　*fax* 071-408 2042. *Script department:* John Hough. Screenplays for cinema and TV; dramatisation of novels.

Granada Film (1989), 36 Golden Square, London W1R 4AH　*tel* 071-494 6388　*fax* 071-494 6360. *Head of film:* Pippa Cross. Screenplays for cinema and TV: major commercial feature films, smaller UK-based films, internationally financeable TV movies.

Hammer Film Production Ltd, Elstree Studios, Borehamwood, Herts. WD6 1JG　*tel* 081-207 4011　*fax* 081-905 1127. *Contact:* Jane Herd. Completed screenplays and published books for cinema and TV development: drama/ mystery/horror/ghost.

HandMade Films (1978), 26 Cadogan Square, London SW1X 0JP　*tel* 071-581 1265. Screenplays for cinema (will only consider material submitted through an agent known to the company).

Hartswood Films (1981), Shepperton Studios, Studios Road, Shepperton, Middlesex TW17 0QD　*tel* (0932) 572294　*fax* (0932) 572299. *Producer:* Beryl Vertue; *development:* Elaine Cameron. Screenplays for cinema and TV; comedy and drama. No unsolicited material.

Hat Trick Productions Ltd (1986), 10 Livonia Street, London W1V 3PH　*tel* 071-434 2451　*fax* 071-287 9791. *Contact:* Denise O'Donoghue. Comedy TV programmes and sit-coms.

Jim Henson Productions Ltd (1979), 1(b) Downshire Hill, Hampstead, London NW3 1NR　*tel* 071-431 2818　*fax* 071-431 3737. *Contact:* director of development. Screenplays for cinema and TV; fantasy, family and children's programmes – usually involving puppetry or animatronics. All material should be submitted through an agent.

Hightimes Productions (1981), 5 Anglers Lane, Kentish Town, London NW5 3DG　*tel* 071-482 5202　*fax* 071-485 4254. *Production executive:* Tony Humphreys. Screenplays for TV; light entertainment, comedy and drama.

Illuminations (1982), 19-20 Rheidol Mews, Rheidol Terrace, London N1 8NU　*tel* 071-226 0266　*fax* 071-359 1151. *Contact:* Linda Zuck. Screenplays for TV; cultural documentaries, arts and entertainment for broadcast TV. All material should be submitted through an agent.

Island World Productions (1990), 12-14 Argyll Street, London W1V 1AB　*tel* 071-734 3536　*fax* 071-734 3585. *Head of development:* Carolann Docherty. Screenplays for TV; TV drama series and serials.

Brian Lapping Associates (1988), 21 Bruges Place, Randolph Street, London NW1 0TF　*tel* 071-482 5855　*fax* 071-284 0626. *Contact:* Brian Lapping. Screenplays for TV; documentary series, dramas, studio programmes.

Little Bird Company Ltd (1982), 91 Regent Street, London W1R 7TA　*tel* 071-434 1131　*fax* 071-434 1803. *Development executives:* J. Cavendish, A. Gavin. Screenplays for cinema and TV.

Little Dancer Ltd (1992), Avonway, 3 Naseby Road, Crystal Palace, London SE19 3JJ　*tel* 081-653 9343. *Producer:* Robert Smith. Screenplays for cinema and TV; drama.

London Film Productions Ltd, Kent House, 14-17 Market Place, Great Titchfield Street, London W1N 8AR　*tel* 071-323 5251　*telex* 896805　*fax* 071-436 2834. *Chairman:* J. Eliasch. No unsolicited material considered.

Malone Gill Productions Ltd (1978), Canaletto House, 39 Beak Street, London W1R 3LD   *tel* 071-287 3970   *telex* 262433 ref W6701   *fax* 071-287 8146. *Contact:* Georgina Denison. TV programmes.

Maya Vision Ltd (1982/3), 43 New Oxford Street, London WC1A 1BH   *tel* 071-836 1113   *fax* 071-838 5169. *Producer/director:* Rebecca Dobbs. Screenplays for cinema and TV; drama and documentaries.

Meditel Productions Ltd (1978), Bedford Chambers, The Piazza, Covent Garden, London WC2E 8HA   *tel* 071-836 9216   *fax* 071-240 3818. *Director:* Joan Shenton. Screenplays for TV; science, medicine and health series; documentaries on education and social issues; drama and animation projects.

New Blitz TV, Via Cimabue 5, 00196 Rome, Italy   *tel* 32 01 489, 32 00 620   *fax* 32 19 014. *Television department:* Giovanni A. Congiu. Importation and dubbing TV series, documentaries, educational films and video for schools. Material from freelance sources required.

Oxford Scientific Films Ltd (1968), Lower Road, Long Hanborough, Oxon OX8 8LL   *tel* (0993) 881881   *fax* (0993) 882808. *Managing director:* Karen Goldie-Morrison. Natural history and science based programmes for broadcast, corporate, multimedia and advertising. See also entry in picture agencies and libraries section.

Paramount Pictures (UK) Ltd, Paramount House, 162-170 Wardour Street, London W1V 4AB   *tel* 071-287 6767   *fax* 071-734 0387. Screenplays for cinema. Material only accepted through agents.

Paravision (UK) Ltd (1989), 114 The Chambers, Chelsea Harbour, London SW10 0XF   *tel* 071-351 7070   *fax* 071-352 3645. *Contacts:* Linda Agran, Nick Barton. Screenplays for cinema; drama and factual TV programmes.

Picture Palace Films Ltd (1971), 53a Brewer Street, Soho, London W1R 3FD   *tel* 071-734 6630   *fax* 071-734 8574. *Contact:* Malcolm Craddock. Screenplays for cinema and TV; low budget films; TV drama series. Material only considered if submitted through an agent.

Picture Parade Ltd (1983), Suite 106, Canalot Production Studios, 222 Kensal Road, London W10 5BN   *tel* 081-964 1500   *fax* 081-964 4907. *Contacts:* David Capey, Claire Rawcliffe. TV documentaries and animation. Material only considered if submitted through an agent.

Portman Productions Ltd (1970), 43-45 Dorset Street, London W1H 4AB   *tel* 071-224 3344   *fax* 071-224 1057. *Head of development:* Steve Matthews. Cinema and TV.

Portobello Pictures Ltd (1987), 42 Tavistock Road, London W11 1AW   *tel* 071-379 5566   *fax* 071-379 5599. *Contacts:* Eric Abraham, Vanessa Lees. Screenplays for cinema and TV; drama.

Primetime Television (1968), Seymour Mews House, Seymour Mews, Wigmore Street, London W1H 9PE   *tel* 071-935 9000   *telex* 22872 TVFILM G   *fax* 071-487 3975. *Contacts:* Ian Gordon, Judy Craymer. Screenplays for TV and TV programmes of international interest, especially drama and documentary series. One-page synopsis *must* accompany any unsolicited script.

Red Rooster Film & Television Entertainment Ltd (1982), 29 Floral Street, London WC2E 9DP   *tel* 071-379 7727   *fax* 071-379 5766. *Contacts:* Stephen Bayly (films), Jenny Reeks (drama), Jill Green (children/family), Sue Birbeck (comedy). Screenplays for cinema and TV; long-running series: drama, children and entertainment. All material should be submitted through an agent.

Regent Productions Ltd (1982), The Mews, 6 Putney Common, London SW15 1HL *tel* 081-789 5350 *fax* 081-789 5332. *Contact:* William G. Stewart. Screenplays for TV; drama, situation comedies.

RM Associates Ltd (1982), 46 Great Marlborough Street, London W1V 1DB *tel* 071-439 2637 *telex* 24549 RMALTD G *fax* 071-439 2316. *Contact:* Meckie Offermanns. Music and arts programmes: opera, dance, music, arts features and documentary series.

Specific Ltd/Midnight Films Ltd, 25 Rathbone Street, London W1P 1AG *tel* 071-580 7476 *fax* 071-494 2676. *Contact:* Clare Wise. Comedy screenplays for cinema.

Spitting Image Productions Ltd (1983), 17-19 Plumbers Row, Aldgate, London E1 1EQ *tel* 071-375 1561 *fax* 071-375 2492. *Head of development:* Jenny Landreth. Screenplays for film and TV; TV programmes, including 'live action' areas of comedy.

Talisman Films Ltd (1991), 5 Addison Place, London W11 4RJ *tel* 071-603 7474 *fax* 071-602 7422. *Contact:* Alan Smallcross. Screenplays for cinema and TV. Material only considered if submitted through an agent.

TalkBack Productions (1989), 33 Percy Street, London W1P 9FG *tel* 071-631 3940 *fax* 071-631 4273. TV situation comedies and comedy dramas. Send unsolicited material to Sally Macdougall; material through an agent to Peter Fincham or Sophie Clarke-Jervoise.

Tiger Aspect Productions Ltd (1993), 5 Soho Square, London W1V 5DE *tel* 071-434 0672 *fax* 071-287 1448. *Contact:* Colette Blair. Screenplays for TV; TV comedy drama.

Triple Vision Ltd (1983), 36A Greenwood Road, London E8 1AB *tel/fax* 071-254 4377. *Contact:* Penny Dedman. Screenplays for cinema and TV; arts/drama and documentaries, plays. Material only accepted through agents.

Twentieth Century Fox Productions Ltd, Twentieth Century House, 31-32 Soho Square, London W1V 6AP *tel* 071-437 7766 *fax* 071-434 2170. Will not consider unsolicited material.

Twenty Twenty Television (1982), 10 Stucley Place, London NW1 8NS *tel* 071-284 2020 *telex* 914951 ZOZOTV G *fax* 071-284 1810. *Executive producer:* Claudia Milne. Current affairs, documentaries, travel films, science and educational programmes, drama documentaries.

Tyburn Productions Ltd, Pinewood Studios, Iver Heath, Bucks. SL0 0NH *tel* (0753) 651700 *telex* 847505 *fax* (0753) 656844. Submissions (TV movies, TV drama series and, very occasionally, cinema screenplays) to Gillian Garrow, Director of Research and Development.

UBA Ltd (1983), 32 Porchester Terrace, London W2 3TP *tel* 071-402 6313 *fax* 071-724 5825. *Contact:* Peter Shaw. Screenplays for cinema and TV of international interest; TV drama and mini series. All material should be submitted through an agent.

Warner Bros. Productions Ltd, 20 Broadwick Street, London W1V 4AP *tel* 071-437 5600. Screenplays for cinema. Will only consider material submitted through an agent.

Warner Sisters Film & TV Ltd (1984), 21 Russell Street, London WC2B 5HP *tel* 071-836 0134 *fax* 071-836 6559. Screenplays for cinema and TV; TV programmes. All material should be submitted through an agent.

Michael White Productions Ltd (1963), 13 Duke Street, St James's, London SW1Y 6DB   *tel* 071-839 3971   *fax* 071-839 3836. *Contact:* Louise Craig. Screenplays for cinema and TV.

Working Title Films and Television (1984), 1 Water Lane, Kentish Town Road, London NW1 8NZ   *tel* 071-911 6100   *fax* 071-911 6150. *Head of development, feature films:* Debra Hayward; *drama, TV:* Grainne Marmion; *comedy, TV:* Simon Wright. Screenplays for cinema and TV; TV drama and comedy.

ZED Ltd (1985), 29 Heddon Street, London W1R 7LL   *tel* 071-494 3181   *fax* 071-434 1203. *Contacts:* Sophie Balhetchet, Glenn Wilhide, Ruth Walsh. Screenplays for cinema and TV; drama.

Zenith Productions Ltd, 43-45 Dorset Street, London W1H 4AB   *tel* 071-224 2440   *fax* 071-224 3194. Screenplays for cinema; TV drama. No unsolicited scripts.

Screenplays for Films

JEAN McCONNELL

Despite the old saying that the plot of the best movie can be written on a postcard, film companies do not actually welcome a plot on a postcard. Nor is it enough simply to send a story in narrative form. You should be prepared to write your idea into a full screenplay. In consequence, it is advisable to check as far as possible in case a company is already working on a similar idea and your efforts are likely to be wasted.

LAYOUT

1. Use A4 size typing paper.
2. It is not necessary to put in elaborate camera directions. A shooting script will be made later. Your job is to write the master scenes, clearly broken down into each incident and location.
3. Your screenplay will tell your story in terms of visual action and dialogue spoken by your characters. If you intend it to be a full-length feature film, running about 1½ hours, your script will be about 100-130 pages long.
4. The general layout of a page of screenplay can be seen from the specimen on page 331. The following points should be noted.
(a) Each scene should be numbered on the left and given a title which indicates whether the scene is an interior or an exterior, where it takes place, and the lighting conditions, i.e. Day or Night. The situation of each scene should be standardised; don't call your 'sitting room' a 'lounge' the next time you come to it, or people will think you mean a different place.
(b) Note that the dialogue is spaced out, with the qualifying directions such as '(frowning)' on a separate line, slightly inset from the dialogue. Double space each speech from the previous one.
(c) Always put the names of the characters in CAPITALS, except when they occur in the actual dialogue. Double space the stage directions from the dialogue, but single space the lines of the stage directions themselves.
(d) Leave at least a 1½ inch margin on the left hand and a reasonably wide right-hand margin. It is false economy to cram the page. You will, of course, type on one side of the sheet only.

(e) If you have to make a correction, cross it out neatly and type the whole section out again. But don't irritate your reader with too many corrections. Better to re-type the page.

(f) Only give the camera directions when you feel it to be essential. For instance, if you want to show something from a particular character's point of view, or if you think you need it to make a point, i.e. 'HARRY approaches the cliff edge and looks down. LONG SHOT – HARRY'S POINT OF VIEW. ALICE fully-clad is walking into the sea. CUT TO: CLOSE UP OF HARRY'S HORRIFIED FACE.' Note the camera directions are put in capital letters on a separate line, as in the specimen page.

PREPARATION OF MANUSCRIPT

1. Make at least two copies, and never send your very last copy out to anyone. It will invariably be lost.
2. The length of your manuscript will depend on whether you are submitting a feature film, a short film for children, say, or a documentary. But it is better to present a version which is too short rather than too long.
3. Prepare the title page in the same way as for a story or article to an editor, except that it is not necessary to state the number of words.
4. If you give a list of characters, do not suggest the actor or actress you would like to play it. This is a decision to be made elsewhere and relies on many factors about which you cannot know. Don't attach character sketches, as these should appear in the body of the screenplay.
5. Bind your screenplay, giving it a front and back cover, and securing the pages firmly.

SUBMISSION

Attach a stamped, addressed envelope to your manuscript whether sending it through an agent or direct. But do remember that if film companies state that they will only consider material sent through an agent, they definitely mean it.

Most companies have Story Departments to which you should address your material. As Story Editors are very busy people, you can make their life easier by complying with the following rules.

1. If you have based your screenplay on someone else's published work you should make the fact clear in a covering letter, stating *(a)* that the material is no longer in copyright, or *(b)* that you yourself own the copyright, or at least an option on it, or *(c)* that you have not obtained the copyright but have reason to believe that there would be no difficulty in doing so.
2. Apart from a note of any relevant credits you may already possess, do not regale the Editor with your personal details, unless they bear a direct relation to the material submitted. For instance, if your story concerns a brain surgeon, then it would be relevant for the Editor to know that you actually are one. Otherwise, trust your work to stand on its own merit.
3. There is no need to mention if your work has been turned down by other companies, however regretfully. The comments of others will not influence a Story Editor one way or the other.
4. Don't pester the company if you don't get a reply, or even an acknowledgement, for some weeks. Most companies will formally acknowledge receipt and then leave you in limbo for at least six weeks. However, after a passage of three months or more, a brief letter asking politely what has happened is in order. A telephone call is unlikely to be helpful. It is possible the company may have liked your work enough to have sent it to America, or to be getting further

13 (continued)

She moves across the barn to the door, where she turns.

ELIZABETH
I still think the police ought to know.

She goes out. ALAN stands immobile until her
footsteps retreat, and then he sighs with relief.
He darts quickly to the large wine vat, climbs
up and begins heaving at the lid.

CUT TO:

14 EXT. FARMYARD DAY

DONALD intercepts ELIZABETH as she crosses yard.

DONALD
What does he say?

ELIZABETH
Nothing.

DONALD
(frowning)

Right! Now it's my turn.

He starts for the barn. ELIZABETH watches him
anxiously.

CUT TO:

15 INT. BARN DAY

DONALD's shadow falls across the threshold.
He hesitates while his eyes get used to the gloom.

DONALD
Alan?

ALAN lets the lid of the vat fall and jumps down.
He stands quite still as DONALD crosses the barn
and stands staring at him. The two men are silent
a moment.

DONALD
(then, with realisation)
You knew it was there, didn't you?

CLOSE SHOT — DONALD'S POINT OF VIEW
ALAN'S face is haggard.

ALAN
I hoped to God it wouldn't be.
Nobody will ever understand.

readers' opinions on it. This all takes time. If they don't like it, you will certainly get it back in due course.

5. Accept that this is really a tough market; for this there are at least three reasons. One, films cost so much to make these days that the decision to go ahead is only taken after a great many important factors have been satisfied and an even greater number of important people are happy about it. Two, the number of films made is small in relation to, say, books published or TV plays produced. Three, writing a screenplay calls for knowledge and appreciation of the technicalities of film-making, as well as the ability to combine dialogue, action and pictures, visualising the story throughout in the language of the cinema.

6. Try to get an agent. A good agent will give you a fair opinion of your work and, if your work is worthwhile, then the agent is the one who will know the particular film company to whom it can be sold.

(A list of agents who handle film material appears opposite.)

Transmission and reception

Some ideas, of course, are better than others. Steeped in enthusiasm for one's current obsession, it can be difficult to see your idea as others will see it. In this sense all creative ideas are somewhat arcane. By virtue of their originality they will present a challenge to their audience and initially, perhaps, be difficult to grasp.

However, theatre is very much a medium of the present tense, an immediate and social experience. It is a waste of its opportunities if a play is so obscure that the widest possible audience cannot appreciate it. Unlike a novel, you can't go back a few pages and reread. A careful balance has to be struck between the familiar and unfamiliar, between accessibility and innovation.

Recognising this balancing act is the first stage in the process of transmission and reception which writing for live theatre represents. What signals is this play putting out, and how will they be received? How will this look to others? Have I got the presentation of my idea such that an audience will see the same things in it as I do? With all these questions in mind, tentative consideration of the possible outlets for a play become meaningful right from the beginning.

from *Writing a Play* by Steve Gooch (A & C Black, £5.95)

Literary Agents Specialising in Plays, Films, Television and Radio

Full particulars about these and other agents will be found in the section beginning on page 406.

*US Literary Agent

A & B Personal Management Ltd
*American Play Company Inc.
Yvonne Baker Associates
*Lois Berman
Blake Friedman Literary,
  TV & Film Agency Ltd
Rosemary Bromley Literary
  Agency
Peter Bryant (Writers)
Casarotto Ramsay Ltd
Jonathan Clowes
Elspeth Cochrane Agency
Rosica Colin Ltd
Jane Conway-Gordon
Cruickshank Cazenove Ltd
Curtis Brown
*Curtis Brown Ltd
Judy Daish Associates Ltd
Felix De Wolfe
*Ann Elmo Agency
Fact & Fiction Agency Ltd
Film Rights Ltd
Laurence Fitch Ltd
Jill Foster Ltd
*Robert A. Freedman Dramatic
  Agency, Inc.
French's
Jüri Gabriel
Kerry Gardner Management
Eric Glass
David Higham Associates Ltd
Valerie Hoskins
ICM Ltd
Michael Imison Playwrights Ltd
International Copyright Bureau Ltd
Harry Joyce Ltd
Juvenilia
*Ben F. Kamsler Ltd
*The Lazear Agency Inc.
Lemon Unna & Durbridge Ltd

*Ellen Levine Literary Agency, Inc.
Barbara Levy Literary Agency
Christopher Little Literary Agent
Andrew Mann Ltd
*The Evan Marshall Agency
Judy Martin
*Elisabeth Marton Agency
Blanche Marvin
MBA Literary Agents
*Scott Meredith Literary Agency
  Inc.
Richard Milne
William Morris Agency (UK)
  Ltd
*Fifi Oscard Associates, Inc.
*Pegasus International Inc.
The Peters Fraser & Dunlop
  Group Ltd
*PMA Literary and Film Management,
  Inc.
PVA Management Ltd
Radala & Associates
Tessa Sayle Agency
*Susan F. Schulman Literary &
  Dramatic Agents Inc.
The Sharland Organisation Ltd
Sheil Land Associates Ltd
*The Shukat Company Ltd
*Singer Media Corporation
Micheline Steinberg Playwrights' Agent
*Sterling Lord Literistic, Inc.
*Gloria Stern Agency
*H.N. Swanson, Inc.
Jon Thurley
*Austin Wahl Agency, Inc.
*Wallace Literary Agency, Inc.
Warner Chappell Plays Ltd
A.P. Watt Ltd
*Sandra Watt and Associates

Illustration and design

Opportunities for Freelance Artists

CAMILLA BRYDEN-BROWN

FINE ART

Opportunities for freelance artists are more numerous than is generally supposed. For fine art such as painting, it is best to contact galleries, of which there are many in this country, particularly in London. It is worth remembering, though, that they have the choice of a large market and specialise in a fairly limited field. If you want to exhibit at these galleries, perhaps to have a one-man show, it is advisable to find out about the type of exhibitions they hold. This you can do by visiting each gallery yourself and assessing the current work. It is best to visit likely galleries frequently in order to get to know their work and how they function. *The Art Review Yearbook* (£19.95, plus £2.00 postage and packing), published by Art Review, 20 Prescott Place, London SW4 6BT *tel* 071-978 1000, contains a guide to London and regional galleries – including a description of the type of work in which they specialise – and also a list of art organisations. *London Art and Artists Guide* (6th edn, £8.95, UK free p&p) is another comprehensive guide to art in London. Obtainable at bookshops or from 27 Holland Park Avenue, London W11 3RW *tel* 071-221 6983.

If you decide to approach a gallery, it is usual to write to the director with a short description, and photographs of some of your work, with an sae for their return. The photographs should be clear, but not necessarily up to reproduction quality. It is possible to take the photographs yourself, but most towns have commercial photographers who work freelance for industry. Ask for an estimate first. The photocopying shops are worth investigating; many can produce photocopies in colour, too. Some of the greetings-card manufacturers listed in this book are interested in paintings for reproduction. It would be wiser to write to them, if possible enclosing good colour transparencies of your work, before becoming involved in the expense of packing and sending paintings by post or carrier.

One of the best methods of displaying and selling paintings is at the annual Summer Exhibition at the Royal Academy in London. Anyone can submit work, which is put to the Selection Committee and the Hanging Committee. Artists considering entering work are advised in the first instance to contact the Royal Academy in January or early February. Sending in days are in late March and early April and these dates must be strictly adhered to. A handling fee allows artists to enter up to three pieces of work at currently £10.00 per entry. Should any subsequently be hung and sold the Royal Academy charges commission at

30% plus VAT. Full details will be found in the leaflet of regulations entitled *Notice to Artists* which is obtainable from early February each year by sending an sae to The Registry, 'Summer Exhibition', The Royal Academy of Arts, Piccadilly, London W1V 0DS   *tel* 071-439 7438. This leaflet refers to the exhibition of the coming summer of that year. If requests for it are sent at other times of the year the Royal Academy can only send the leaflet from the previous February. Other exhibitions are listed in *Art Review* (£3.50 monthly), which has a comprehensive exhibition guide for the whole of Great Britain, and *Artists & Illustrators* (£2.25 monthly).

ILLUSTRATION AND DESIGN

For a career in the field of illustration and design it is advisable to have a training in illustration, and also in typography if possible. Although the latter is not absolutely essential, it is helpful to the artist and to the publisher. Now that desktop publishing and illustration software programs are available on personal computers the possibility of producing work with integrated type and drawing is fact. These programs and the printers and scanners are being improved at such speed that in the near future it will be practicable for an illustrator to present some work ready for press. Artists who launch into freelance work often do so gradually from the security of full-time employment, probably in the same field. It is useful to have the experience of working with a publisher or in an advertising agency or a studio first, as this gives the artist valuable background knowledge of suppliers and sources of work. Training in illustration can be obtained through a recognised course at art school, or through employment in a studio. Either method is an advantage, for even the most brilliantly gifted illustrator should know how to think in terms of printed work and to realise how work will reduce and reproduce.

Once an artist feels competent to accept commissions it is important to be available and reliable. Both these attributes are essential, and busy clients will not be bothered with artists who say vaguely that they had to go away or that the children were ill. Freelance work is a business, and will stand or fall by the competence or otherwise of the staff – you.

THE FOLIO

Artists who have already been in full-time employment in an advertising agency or publishing house will know of clients who are prepared to give them commissions, and if one commission is a success it will very often lead to another. For all artists, but particularly those with no connections, it is essential to make up a professional folio of work, spending some time and money on it, and showing as versatile a range of work as possible. For instance, it should include work in line, pencil, ink, line and tone, two or more colour line and full colour, and be on a variety of subjects. There are excellent folders, plastic envelopes or elaborate specimen books or cases containing plastic folders, for sale at most shops which stock equipment for designers. An overall colour scheme for your presentation helps to make your work look well-organised and professional. Designs or samples should be neatly trimmed and mounted on coloured cover paper (use black if in doubt) of a size to fit the folder or envelope. Paste the specimens of work on the cover paper, but do not use petroleum-based rubber solution if the sample of work is to be enclosed in a plastic envelope.

Gradually you will collect together printed specimens as the commissions increase, and your folio of work should be brought up to date all the time. Always get as many samples as you can beg, although if it is a book you may receive only one copy. In this case, see if you can get some extra dust-jackets so that should the first one become worn you can replace it; if necessary buy more copies of the book if that should also become worn. The publisher may well give you a discount on books on which you have worked. Any book specimens should be kept separately in plastic bags, but it would be expedient to ask for colour proofs of your illustrations early on in the proceedings, and they should be mounted up in your specimen book. Try to keep your specimens immaculate.

PUBLISHERS

When the specimen folder is complete it is time to type letters to the production manager or art director of as many publishing houses as practicable, asking for an interview in order to show your work, whether for illustrations or for book-jackets, or both. It would be wise to design an attractive personal stationery range which can be an excellent advertisement of your work. There are print shops that will produce your design very well and advise you if you are not skilled in typography or finished artwork. Usually they print by lithography quickly and at a reasonable price. A letterheading, preferably A4 because this is the most popular size and therefore is easily filed, can also be used as a compliment slip, invoice and estimate if necessary. A business card can be very useful. Space these letters out, or you may find yourself with too many appointments in one week. The production managers will usually grant you interviews (be on time), since they are interested in seeing new work, and they will probably be helpful about prices too, if you have no experience in this field. Book-publishing houses as a rule are not able to pay as highly as advertising agencies or popular magazines but they are usually fair. Do not overlook educational departments of publishing houses for there is considerable scope for illustrating school textbooks. You may have to accept low fees to begin with until you know your market and your worth, but you will be gaining valuable knowledge and experience. Newspapers and magazines are another source of work, as are publishers of greetings cards and other stationery.

At each interview it would be a good idea to ask if there is anyone else in the firm who would be interested in seeing your work, such as editors, who occasionally commission artists. Do not expect to be seen by other people in the firm at the same time as your first interview, but be prepared to come back another time. It would be better not to leave your samples to be seen by other people, particularly if you have only one folio. You will be needing your folio for other interviews, and there is a very real danger that it will go astray, or that specimens will be damaged beyond use, with no redress. If your work is liked and your first commission is satisfactory, you will often find that you will be recommended to other people in similar fields.

You would be very wise to make a contract with the publisher when commissioned. Some of the well-known illustrators have fought hard and long for fair conditions. The Association of Illustrators has produced a Standard Form of Contract. It is important for illustrators to realise that the artwork remains the property of the artist, and so does the copyright, and this includes commissioned work. You should make clear from the outset that the work belongs to you and that definitely you want it returned. Publishers have a sad history of losing artwork.

ARTISTS' AGENTS

Advertising agencies frequently use the services of artists' agents, who can be good or bad, but if you are accepted on the books of a good one life will be much easier for you. Agents generally work very hard on behalf of both clients and artists: they take the brief, negotiate the price and commission you to do the work, usually taking about 30 per cent of the fee. Although this percentage may seem high, you should remember that they do a lot of work on your behalf and invariably manage to get a more professional fee for you than you can obtain for yourself, even after the percentage has been deducted.

FEES

There is no definite rule in assessing fees. A simple method of calculation is to decide upon a weekly salary and the number of hours of work for a normal week. This salary is then divided by the number of hours, which gives a basic hourly rate. Rent, Council Tax, heating, telephone and other general studio costs should be considered, materials bought especially for a commission have to be added to the invoice concerned. As a rough guide one third of a fee will be payable to the Inland Revenue. Time spent at meetings with clients and the travelling time and cost involved should be added to the time sheet.

This solution may appear to be simple but it will be seen that the hourly rate is high. Many clients offer low fees and it is sometimes necessary to choose between accepting work at little or no return when the result is a good specimen of work, or to do without work. One of the greatest problems to the freelance artist is the artist in full-time employment who is prepared to accept commissions out of hours for a lower fee. With no studio overheads and a regular salary the market is spoilt for the serious professional.

ADVERTISING AGENCIES

Advertising agencies employ art buyers who are very skilled and capable people and should be approached by a letter similar to that previously described, giving details of the type of work at which you are best. Here again, once you have obtained the interview and shown your work, you might ask if there is anyone else who would be interested, not necessarily at that moment.

STUDIOS

Studios exist in most cities, and the type of their work varies; some specialise in purely commercial work in finished lettering and finished artwork, and they employ highly skilled and extremely able artists. Often their work involves the use of airbrushes and photographic skills, but they do sometimes employ freelance artists for specific commissions, and may well like to have photocopies of your work on file in case they need drawings or diagrams for catalogues or similar uses. Technical drawing is called technical drawing with good reason and requires specific training. If you feel your work would be of interest to a studio, write to the studio manager and ask for an interview. Should they ask for photographs of your work, a commercial photographic studio will prepare these for you. If you wish to have photographs made, the photographic studio will help you with the details and give you prices before they take on the work. Photocopies may be acceptable, especially now that colour copying is available. The studio might offer to photocopy work which they might like to keep for future reference.

GRAPHIC DESIGNERS

A graphic designer, who may be running a studio on their own and doing freelance design and typography (designing for printing), may also use illustrators from time to time. They will not be able to use your work all the time, even if they like it, as not all their commissions require drawings. The more versatile you are the more opportunities are available to you, and artists skilled only in very specialised fields, such as lettering and illumination, usually know where to offer their work.

IMPORTANCE OF RELIABILITY

Remember also that once you have started to get commissions, you must be accurate and reliable, as well as available. If you are given a date for the work, it must be presented on time, even if this means sitting up half the night before. Do not, for example, fall back on the excuse of mild illness or you will lose sympathy and understanding should you have the misfortune to be more seriously ill. Once you have received the commission you are part of a team, even though you may not know the other members of it. There are often unforeseen events which hold up production anyway, and it is as well to see that you do not come to be considered one. It is wise to take trouble over the presentation, and you have only yourself to blame if you have not protected your finished work adequately. It is distressing to have one's precious work destroyed or damaged, the more so if it means doing it all again.

You will discover that once you have started freelance work your commissions will build up gradually, although most artists have some periods when there is little work available. Use these 'rests' advantageously to prepare more specimen drawings and to experiment with new techniques and equipment, and to make sure your folio is ready to show again. At such times you should be looking for new outlets, visiting more agencies and publishers, or checking with the ones you have visited in the past.

Above all decide whether or not you really want to do this work: are you sure it is not just a pleasant day-dream with the appeal of being called an artist. It is hard work, but if you have ability and are consistent, reliable, enthusiastic and optimistic, even at those times when there is a lull, then you will be happy and successful.

See also Writing and Illustrating
Children's Books in the
Books section.

Markets for Artists

ART AGENTS AND COMMERCIAL ART STUDIOS

In their own interests, artists are advised to make preliminary enquiries before submitting work, and to ascertain terms of work. Commission varies but averages 25-30 per cent. **The Association of Illustrators** (full details on page 627) provides a valuable service for illustrators, agents and clients.

A.L.I. Press Agency Ltd, Boulevard Anspach 111-115, B9–1000 Brussels, Belgium *tel* 02 512 73 94 *fax* 02 512 03 30. *Director:* G. Lans. Cartoons, comics, strips, puzzles, entertainment features, illustrations for covers. All feature material for newspapers and magazines. Large choice of picture stories for children and adults. Market for transparencies: paintings, portraits, nudes, landscapes, handicrafts. Interest in video productions.

Allied Artists Ltd, 31 Harcourt Street, London W1H 1DT *tel* 071-724 8809 *fax* 071-262 8526. *Director:* Gary Mills. Represents over 30 artists specialising in highly finished realistic figure illustration for magazines, books, video, plates, prints and advertising. Also offers extensive library of second rights illustrations for syndication.

Arena (1970), 144 Royal College Street, London NW1 0TA *tel* 071-267 9661 *fax* 071-284 0486. *Contacts:* Liane Payne, Valerie Paine and Alison Eldred. Variety of artists working in traditional and progressive styles. *Average commission:* 30%.

Associated Freelance Artists Ltd, 124 Elm Park Mansions, Park Walk, Chelsea, London SW10 0AR *tel* 071-352 6890 *fax* 071-352 8125. *Directors:* Eva Morris, Doug FitzMaurice. Freelance illustrators mainly in children's and educational fields; and lots of greetings cards.

Bardon Art, S.L. (1957), Gran Via de los Corts Catalanes 806, Barcelona E-08013, Spain *tel* (3) 245 56 84 *fax* (3) 246 30 19. *Directors:* Jordi Macabich, Barry Coker, Mercè Biadiu, Montserrat Serra. Picture strips for newspapers and comic magazines, cartoons, illustrations for juvenile books.

Becker! (1985), Lerchenstr. 100, D-2000 Hamburg 50, Germany *tel* (040) 43 70 91 *fax* (040) 43 20 18. *Director:* Hartmut Becker. Comics, cartoons, illustrations. *Commission:* 25%.

Sarah Brown Agency (1977), 10 The Avenue, Ealing, London W13 8PH *tel* 081-998 0390 *fax* 081-843 1175. *Director:* Carol Butfoy. Specialises in science fiction and fantasy, but includes most other imaginative illustration for book jackets, computer games, video and advertising. *Commission:* 25%.

Beint & Beint (1976), 3 Richborne Terrace, London SW8 1AR *tel* 071-793 7000 *fax* 071-735 2565. Illustrations in a variety of styles for advertising, design groups and publishing.

Central Illustration Agency (1983), 36 Wellington Street, London WC2E 7BD *tel* 071-240 8925/836 1106 *fax* 071-836 1177. *Director:* Brian Grimwood. Illustrations for design, publishing and advertising. *Commission:* 30%.

Barry Everitt Associates, April Cottage, Mill Road, Stock, Essex CM4 9LJ *tel* (0277) 840639 *fax* (0277) 841223. *Director:* Barry M. Everitt. UK/international representation for artists, illustrators and designers seeking high quality markets for their work. Greetings cards, fine art prints, calendars, collectors' ceramics, jigsaws, books, character merchandise, etc. *Commission:* negotiable.

Ian Fleming Associates Ltd (1970), 4 Wedgwood Mews, 12-13 Greek Street, London W1V 5LW *tel* 071-734 8701 *fax* 071-439 3400. *Managing director:* Ian Fleming. Illustration and lettering for advertising and publishing. *Commission:* 33⅓%.

Folio Illustrators' & Designers' Agents (1976), 10 Gate Street, Lincoln's Inn Fields, London WC2A 3HP *tel* 071-242 9562 *fax* 071-242 1816. All areas of illustration.

Garden Studio (1929), 23 Ganton Street, Soho, London W1V 1LA *tel* 071-287 9191 *fax* 071-287 9131. *Agents:* John Havergal, Harry Lyon-Smith. Worldwide all-round coverage. *Commission:* 33⅓% (publishing 25%).

Simon Girling & Associates (1985), 61B High Street, Hadleigh, Suffolk IP7 5DY *tel* (0473) 824083 *fax* (0473) 827846. Illustrations for book publishing (children's and adult), encyclopedias, magazines, dust jackets, greetings cards. *Commission:* 28%.

Graham-Cameron Illustration (1988), The Studio, 23 Holt Road, Sheringham, Norfolk NR26 8NB *tel* (0263) 821333 *fax* (0263) 821334. *Partners:* Mike Graham-Cameron, Helen Graham-Cameron. All forms of illustration for book publishers and communications and advertising agencies. Specialises in children's and educational markets.

The Guild of Aviation Artists (1971), Bondway Business Centre, 71 Bondway, London SW8 1SQ *tel/fax* 071-735 0634. *President:* Michael Turner PGAvA; *secretary:* Hugo Trotter DFC. Professional body of 300 artists specialising in aviation art in all mediums. The Guild sells, commissions and exhibits members' work. *Commission:* 25%.

Hambleside Design and Marketing Ltd (1990), Winton Road, Petersfield, Hants GU32 3HA *tel* (0730) 231010 *telex* 86166 HAMBLE G *fax* (0730) 231117. *Directors:* D.R. Yellop, R.A. Jeffery, R.B. Gamble (USA). Design studio specialising in all forms of promotional graphics, advertising and marketing. Enquiries from freelance illustrators and photographers welcome.

John Hodgson Agency (1965), 38 Westminster Palace Gardens, Artillery Row, London SW1P 1RR *tel* 071-580 3773 *fax* 071-222 4468. Illustrations for advertising, publishing, design, editorial. Sae with samples please. *Commission:* 25%.

Image by Design (1987), Lydford Farm, Highbury Street, Coleford, Bath BA3 5NS *tel/fax* (0373) 812393. *Partners:* John R. Brown, Burniece M. Brown. Artwork for prints, greetings cards, calendars, posters, stationery, book publishing, jigsaw puzzles, tableware, ceramics. *Commission:* negotiable.

The Impressionists (1991), Bushwood House, Wood Lane, Fressingfield, Nr Eye, Suffolk IP21 5SF *tel* (0379) 86637 *fax* (0379) 868189. *Contact:* Lyn Ellis. Illustrations for greetings cards, giftwrap, calendars and magazines; children's and adult book illustrations. Enclose sae for return of samples. *Commission:* 30%.

David Lewis Illustration Agency (1974), Worlds End Studios, 134 Lots Road, Chelsea, London SW10 0RJ *tel* 071-351 4333 *fax* 071-351 5044. *Contact:* David Lewis. All types of illustration for a variety of applications but mostly suitable for book publishing purposes. Sae with samples essential. *Average commission:* 30%.

Libba Jones Associates (1983), Hopton Manor, Hopton, Nr Wirksworth, Derbyshire DE4 4DF *tel* (062 985) 353 *fax* (062 985) 577. *Contacts:* Libba Jones,

Ieuan Jones. High quality artwork and design for china, greetings cards and gift wrap, jigsaw puzzles, calendars, prints, posters, stationery, book illustration, fabric design. Submission of samples required for consideration.

John Martin Artists Ltd, 26 Danbury Street, Islington, London N1 8JU   *tel* 071-734 9000   *fax* 071-226 6069. *Directors:* W. Bowen-Davies, C.M. Bowen-Davies, B.L. Bowen-Davies. Illustrations for children (educational and fictional), dust jackets, paperbacks, magazines, encyclopedias, advertising. Return postage for any artwork sent please.

Meiklejohn Illustration (1971), 28 Shelton Street, Covent Garden, London WC2H 9JN   *tel* 071-240 2077   *fax* 071-836 0199. *Contacts:* Chris Meiklejohn, Paul Meiklejohn. All types of illustration.

N.E. Middleton Ltd, 20 Trefoil Road, Wandsworth, London SW18 2EQ   *tel*/*fax* 081-875 9525. Designs for greetings cards, stationery, prints, calendars and china. Sae with samples, please.

Maggie Mundy Illustrators' Agency, Britannia House, 1-11 Glenthorpe Road, London W6 0LF   *tel* 081-741 5862   *fax* 081-748 5532. Represents 25 artists in varying styles of illustration for children's books.

Oxford Illustrators Ltd (1968), Aristotle Lane, Oxford OX2 6TR   *tel* (0865) 512331   *fax* (0865) 512408. Studio of 30 full-time illustrators working for publishers, business and industry – science, technical, airbrush, graphic, medical, biological, botanical, figure, cartoon, maps, diagrams, graphs. Macintosh generated artwork with Linotronic 300 output. (Not an agency.)

Pennant Illustration (1992), Yukon Court, 6 Yukon Road, London SW12 9PU   *tel* 081-673 8008   *fax* 081-673 4227. *Director:* Matthew Doyle. Illustrations for publishing, design and advertising. Samples *must* be accompanied by an sae. *Commission:* 30%.

Rogers & Co., Artists' Agents—now Temple Rogers Artists' Agency.

Linda Rogers Associates (1975), PO Box 330, 1 Bloomsbury House, 9 Guilford Street, London WC1N 1PX   *tel* 071-242 0975   *fax* 071-405 0876. *Partners:* Linda Rogers, Helen Mighell. Represent a group of artists and designers covering all fields of illustration.

Specs Art Agency (1982), 93 London Road, Cheltenham, Glos. GL52 6HL   *tel* (0242) 515951   *fax* (0242) 518862. *Director:* Roland Berry. High quality illustration work for advertisers, publishers and all other forms of visual communication.

Sharp Practice (1985), Unit 30 Waterside, 44-48 Wharf Road, London N1 7UX   *tel* 071-490 1712   *fax* 071-490 0545. *Directors:* Sarah Culshaw, Jane Hartley, Jacqui Figgis. Illustrations for advertising, design, publishing and editorial. *Commission:* 30%.

Summer Lane Pictures (1993), Lower Tower Street, Birmingham B19 3NE   *tel* 021-359 6269   *fax* 021-333 5366. *Directors:* Trevor Jones (managing), Sue Hammond (sales and marketing). Licensing agency offering a wide variety of images, linking artists and illustrators with manufacturers in many product areas; in-house design and reproduction facilities available.

Guitty Talberg Illustration Agents (1985), 142 Greenwich High Road, London SE10 8NN   *tel* 081-293 1304   *fax* 081-293 1268. *Directors:* Guitty Talberg, Anne Magill. Contemporary illustrations for advertising, publishing and editorial, for UK and overseas markets. *Commission:* 33% UK, 40% overseas.

Temple Rogers Artists' Agency, 120 Crofton Road, Orpington, Kent BR6 8HZ   *tel* (0689) 826249   *fax* (0689) 896312. *Contact:* Patrick Kelleher. Illustrations for children's educational books, picture strips and magazine illustrations. *Commission:* by arrangement.

2D Illustration Agency (1986), 19 All Saints Road, Notting Hill, London W11 1HE   *tel* 071-727 5243/8685   *fax* 071-727 9680. *Proprietor:* Tim Morris. Stylised, contemporary and traditional illustrations for advertising, design and publishing, Europe-wide. Sae with samples please. *Commission:* 25% UK, 30% overseas.

Vicki Thomas Associates (1985), 19 Hickman Close, Fulmer Road, London E16 3TA   *tel* 071-511 5767   *fax* 071-473 5177. *Consultant:* Vicki Thomas. Considers the work of illustrators and designers working in greetings and gift industries, and promotes such work to gift, toy, publishing and related industries. Written application and b&w photocopies required. *Commission:* from 25%.

Wildlife Art Agency (1992), Studio 2 Muspole Workshops, 25-27 Muspole Street, Norwich, Norfolk NR3 1DJ   *tel* (0603) 617868   *fax* (0603) 219017. *Contact:* Sarah Whittley. All forms of natural history illustration for book publishing, greetings cards/calendar design and advertising agencies, ranging from children's books to scientific, cartoons, realistic, etc. Sae with samples essential. *Commission:* 30%.

Michael Woodward Licensing (1980), Parlington Hall, Aberford, West Yorkshire LS25 3EG   *tel* (0532) 813913   *fax* (0532) 813911. *Proprietor:* Michael R. Woodward. International art agency with subsidiary offices overseas. Specialists in greetings cards, stationery, posters, prints, calendars and gift products. Character merchandising division. Freelance artists please send samples with sae. *Terms:* on application.

DRAWINGS, DESIGNS AND VERSES FOR GREETINGS CARDS AND SOCIAL STATIONERY

In their own interest, artists are advised to write giving details of the work which they have to offer, and asking for requirements before submitting the work.

*Member of the Greeting Card and Calendar Association

Arnold Barton Cards—see **Hambledon Studios Ltd.**

Athena International, PO Box 918, Harlow, Essex CM20 2DU   *tel* (0279) 641125. *Art directors:* R. Watt, T. Jones. Designs for greetings cards. Paintings and illustrations of a professional standard for reproduction as prints and posters. Sae essential for return of work.

The Andrew Brownsword Collection (1975), James Street West, Bath BA1 2BS. *Sales director:* John Curtis. Contemporary and traditional imagery for greetings cards, giftwrap and social stationery. Submit 5 × 4 in transparencies of original artwork. Will consider verses.

The Bucentaur Gallery Ltd (1977), Bucentaur House, Travellers Close, Welham Green, Herts. AL9 7NT   *tel* (0707) 251757   *fax* (0707) 251401. *Contact:* production editor (art). Fine art, traditional greetings cards: florals, animals, wildlife, cottages, etc., plus Christmas subjects. All submissions to be accompanied by an sae; original artwork, or minimum 5 × 4 in transparencies or photographs or laser copies of originals. No verses please.

Card Connection Ltd (1992), Park House, South Street, Farnham, Surrey GU9 7QQ   *tel* (0252) 733177   *fax* (0252) 735644. *Directors:* Simon Hulme (managing), Chris Drew. Cute, humour, traditional, floral, contemporary, sport. Submit artwork, or 5 × 4 in transparencies of originals. No verses.

Carlton Cards Ltd, Mill Street East, Dewsbury, West Yorkshire WF12 9AW   *tel* (0924) 465200. *Marketing director:* Keith Auty. All types of artwork, any size; submit as colour roughs, colour copies or transparencies.

C.C.A. Stationery Ltd, Eastway, Fulwood, Preston PR2 4WS   *tel* (0772) 662800. Publishers of personalised wedding stationery and Christmas cards. Pleased to consider original artwork, preferably of relevant subject matter, but verses not required.

Elgin Court (1964), Shepherd Road, Gloucester GL2 6EL   *tel* (0452) 423451   *fax* (0452) 410312. *Product director:* Neil Holliday. Contemporary, fine art greetings cards ('Elgin Court', 'Tapestry Collection', 'Youngsters'). Submit original artwork or transparencies of originals.

Fine Art Graphics Ltd (incorporating **Raphael Tuck & Sons Ltd**), Dawson Lane, Dudley Hill, Bradford BD4 6HW   *tel* (0274) 689514   *telex* 517669   *fax* (0274) 651218. *Managing director:* D.B. Roxburgh; *creative director:* D. Nicholls. Greetings card and calendar publishers.

Gibson Greetings International Ltd (1991), Gibson House, Hortonwood 30, Telford, Shropshire TF1 4ET   *tel* (0952) 608333   *fax* (0952) 608363. *Product director:* Jan Duncan. Everyday, wedding and all seasonal illustrations: cute, humorous, juvenile age, traditional landscapes and subjects; giftwrap and calendars. Humorous verse.

Giesen & Wolff Ltd (1908), Kaygee House, Rothersthorpe Crescent, Northampton NN4 9JD   *tel* (0604) 709499   *fax* (0604) 709399. *Art director:* D. Falconer. Illustrations: cute characters, wedding, sympathy, juvenile age subjects, traditional landscapes, humour – anything suitable for everyday and all seasonal occasions. Will consider verses.

Graphic Humour (1984), 4 Britannia Centre, Point Pleasant, Wallsend, Tyne and Wear NE28 6HQ   *tel* 091-295 4200   *fax* 091-295 3916. Risqué, off-beat and zany artwork ideas for greetings cards; short, humorous copy.

Greetings Cards By Noel Tatt Ltd (1954/1988), Appledown House, Barton Business Park, Appledown Way, New Dover Road, Canterbury, Kent CT1 3AA   *tel* (0227) 455540   *fax* (0227) 458976. *Directors:* Noel Tatt, Vencke Tatt, Jarle Tatt, Diane Tatt. Greetings cards and giftwrap.

*Hallmark Cards Ltd, Hallmark House, Station Road, Henley-on-Thames, Oxon   RG9 1LQ   *tel* (0491) 578383   *fax* (0491) 578817. *Chairman and chief executive:* A. Brownsword; *managing director UK:* Trish Davies. Humorous editorial ideas considered, including short jokes and punchlines. Submit all ideas to the Editorial Department. *No* traditional verse.

Hambledon Studios Ltd, Hambledon House, Marlborough Road, Accrington, Lancs. BB5 6BX   *tel* (0254) 872266   *telex* 635169 CARDAC G   *fax* (0254) 872079. *Art managers:* D. Jaundrell, J. Ashton, D. Fuller, N. Harrison; *creative director:* M. Smith. Designs suitable for reproduction as greetings cards. *Brands:* Arnold Barton, Donny Mac, Reflections, New Image.

Hanson White—Accord (1958), 9th Floor, Wettern House, 56 Dingwall Road, Croydon, Surrey CR0 0XH   *tel* 081-680 1885   *fax* 081-760 0093. *Product development director:* A. Emmett. Artwork for greetings cards, giftwrap and related stationery items: cute, humorous (including strip cartoons), contemporary, fine art. Humorous copy lines, including short jokes and punchlines; occasional non-humorous verses.

Images & Editions (1984), Bourne Road, Essendine, Nr Stamford, Lincs. PE9 4UW   *tel* (0780) 57118   *fax* (0780) 54629. *Directors:* Lesley Forrow, Maurice Miller. Greetings card artwork: cute, floral, animals. Will consider short, humorous verses.

*Jarrold Publishing (1770), Whitefriars, Norwich NR3 1TR   *tel* (0603) 763300   *fax* (0603) 662748. *Managing director:* Antony Jarrold; *publishing director:* Caroline Jarrold. Drawings for calendars and guidebooks. Verses not required.

Jooles Ltd (1988), Unit 5, St Margaret's Business Centre, Drummond Place, Moor Mead Road, Twickenham, Middlesex TW1 1JN   *tel* 081-744 1333   *fax* 081-891 4295. *Contact:* write to F. McMahon, Art Co-ordinator, with sae for submission of artwork. Artwork for greetings cards: humorous, traditional, cute. Will consider verses.

Kardonia Ltd, Farrier Street, Worcester WR1 3BH   *tel* (0905) 611294   *fax* (0905) 724792. *Contact:* the art editor.

Thomas Leach Ltd, 54 Ock Street, Abingdon, Oxon OX14 5DE   *tel* (0235) 520444   *fax* (0235) 554270. *Contact:* David J. Leach. Line drawings of religious subjects suitable for reproduction as Christmas or Easter cards.

Leeds Postcards (1979), PO Box 84, Leeds LS1 1HU   *tel* (0532) 468649   *fax* (0532) 436730. Workers co-operative. Publishers and producers of campaign postcards (and greetings cards) for left wing political campaigns, the women's movement, environmental and campaigns for international justice. Joint publishers of Women Artists Cards. No verses.

*Henry Ling & Son (London) Ltd, Chiddingstone Causeway, Nr Tonbridge, Kent TN11 8JP   *tel* (0892) 870333   *telex* 8813271 GECOMS G REF H087   *fax* (0892) 870466. *Contact:* Product manager – greetings cards. Artwork for greetings cards; no verses.

Medici Society Ltd, 34-42 Pentonville Road, London N1 9HG   *tel* 071-837 7099   *fax* 071-837 9152. Requirements: full colour paintings suitable for reproduction as greetings cards. Preliminary letter with brief details of work requested.

New Concept Cards Ltd (1989), 3 Heathfield, Stacey Bushes, Milton Keynes MK12 6HP   *tel* (0908) 312366   *fax* (0908) 225323. *Directors:* N. Patel, H.Y. Patel, Y. Patel. Illustrations for greetings cards, including Christmas, and giftwrap. Will consider verses.

*Panache Studio Ltd (1985)—now **Hallmark Cards Ltd.**

Paperlink Ltd (1986), 346-348 Kennington Road, London SE11 4LD   *tel* 071-582 8244   *fax* 071-587 5212. *Directors:* Louise Tighe, Jo Townsend, Tim Porte. Specialise in own brand products for charities and retail traders, including greetings cards, calendars, notelets, mugs, t-shirts, prints.

Parnassus Gallery, Shepherd Road, Gloucester GL2 6EL   *tel* (0452) 423451   *fax* (0452) 410312. *Product director:* Neil Holliday. 'Classics' fine art greetings cards: Christmas, seasons, everyday. Submit original artwork or transparencies of originals.

*Nigel Quiney Publications Ltd (1988), Cloudesley House, Shire Hill, Saffron Walden, Essex CB11 3FB   *tel* (0799) 520200   *fax* (0799) 520100. *Director:* Stewart F.E. Stott. Everyday and seasonal greetings cards (sizes: 7 × 5, 9 × 6 and 12 × 9 in) and giftwrap. Submit original artwork or 5 × 4 in transparencies of originals.

Rainbow Cards Ltd (1977), Albrighton Business Park, Albrighton By-pass, Albrighton, Wolverhampton, West Midlands WV7 3QH   *tel* (0902) 374347. *Directors:* M. Whitehouse, R. Fellows, J. Whitehouse, I. Mackintosh. Artwork for greetings cards. No verses.

Felix Rosenstiel's Widow & Son Ltd, Fine Art Publishers, 33-35 Markham Street, London SW3 3NR   *tel* 071-352 3551. Invite offers of original oil paintings and strong watercolours of a professional standard for reproduction as picture prints for the picture framing trade. Any type of subject considered.

*Royle Publications Ltd, Royle House, Wenlock Road, London N1 7ST   *tel* 071-253 7654. Greetings cards, calendars, fine art reproductions and social stationery. Only accept work in colour.

Scandecor Ltd (1967), 3 The Ermine Centre, Hurricane Close, Huntingdon, Cambs. PE18 6XX   *tel* (0480) 456395   *telex* 32365   *fax* (0480) 456269. *Director:* G. Huldtgren. Drawings all sizes.

Second Nature Ltd (1981), 10 Malton Road, London W10 5UP   *tel* 081-960 0212   *fax* 081-960 8700. *Marketing/publishing director:* David Roxburgh. Contemporary artwork for greetings cards; jokes for humorous range.

*W.N. Sharpe/Classic Cards, Creative Department, Bingley Road, Bradford, West Yorkshire BD9 6SD   *tel* (0274) 542244   *fax* (0274) 772395. Greetings cards for all occasions; gift wrap, artwork in colour; sentimental and humorous editorial verses considered.

Solomon & Whitehead (Guild Prints) Ltd, Lynn Lane, Shenstone, Staffs. WS14 0DX   *tel* (0543) 480696   *fax* (0543) 481619. Fine art prints and limited editions, framed and unframed.

SP Publishing (1986), Lower Tower Street, Birmingham B19 3NE   *tel* 021-359 7088   *fax* 021-333 5366. *Managing director:* Trevor Jones; *sales and marketing director:* Sue Hammond. Commercial decorative art with broad appeal – especially classic and contemporary floral imagery, William Morris designs, fine art – for greetings cards and gift stationery.

Noel Tatt Ltd (1954), Coombe House, Coombe Valley Road, Dover, Kent CT17 0EU   *tel* (0304) 211644   *fax* (0304) 240470. *Directors:* Noel Tatt, Vencke Tatt, Derek Bates, Anthony Sharpe, Paul Tatt, Robert Dixon. Greetings cards, prints, postcards.

United Greeting Card Co. (UK) Ltd (1969), River Park, Billet Lane, Berkhamsted, Herts. HP4 1EL   *tel* (0442) 871381. *Directors:* R.H. Seddon, M. Howard. Ideas and artwork for humorous, cute and general greetings cards.

*Valentines of Dundee Ltd—see **W.N. Sharpe Ltd.**

*Verkerke Ltd (1965), Cedar Court, 9/11 Fairmile, Henley-on-Thames, Oxon RG9 2JR   *tel* (0491) 412300   *fax* (0491) 411977. *Director:* K. Taylor. Greetings cards and posters of juvenile and teenage appeal, especially wild and sea life.

Webb Ivory (Burton) Ltd, Queen Street, Burton-on-Trent, Staffs. DE14 3LP *tel*
(0283) 66311. High quality Christmas cards and paper products.

See also **Newspapers and magazines, Book
publishers** and **Book packagers**; and **Literary
agents** (particularly for children's books).

It is recommended that artists read the article
on copyright in the **Law and regulations**
section; the **Publishing practice** section for
information about formal agreements.

Story in a local newspaper

Never turn away a commission or a chance to work on a story
because you don't know anything about the subject. An editor asked
me to fill in for another writer who had been taken ill and write
about a band of duck-devotees holding up the traffic to let squads of
ducks cross the road in safety from one part of a country park to
another. Many times I'd seen ducks gathering at a particular spot by
the side of the road and had prayed they would stay there. But I had
no idea they were trained to wait until their personal crossing war-
dens arrived to see them to the other side. Adopting one of the tenets
of a journalist's craft and never being afraid to ask anyone for information, I discovered the local police could not grant official permission to the kindly patrols when they wanted to hold up traffic but
had promised they would only take action against them if motorists
complained about being asked to stop. The duck-devotees had done
their teaching job well; so impeccably behaved were their quacking
charges in waddling across that motorists were only amused and
intrigued. My story (and some pix) in the local paper (and further
afield) ensured everyone in the area knew about the web-footed
crossing patrols. Extra volunteers joined the others in shepherding
the ducks and someone suggested there should be a crossing sign
showing a little green duck when it was safe to cross. It was all harm-
less fun which everyone enjoyed as much as I did.

from *Freelance Writing for Newspapers* by Jill Dick (A & C Black, £9.99)

Classified Index of UK Markets for Cartoons in Newspapers and Magazines

Listed below are newspapers and magazines which take cartoons – either occasionally, or on a regular basis. Approach *in writing* in first instance (see listing starting on page 5 for addresses) to ascertain the editor's requirements.

Newspapers and Colour Supplements

Aberdeen Evening Express
Athletics Weekly
Birmingham Evening Mail
Daily Mail
Daily Mirror
Daily Sport
Daily Star
Eastern Evening News
The European
Evening Echo
Evening Gazette (Teesside)
Express and Star
Glasgow Evening Times
Grimsby Evening Telegraph
Hartlepool Mail
The Herald

The Independent Magazine
The Independent on Sunday
Inverness Courier
The Journal
Lancashire Evening Post
Liverpool Echo
Mail on Sunday
The News, Portsmouth
Nottingham Evening Post
The Scotsman
Shropshire Star
South Wales Echo
The Star
The Sun
Sunday Mail
Sunday Mercury

Sunday Mirror Magazine
The Sunday Sun
The Sunday Times
Telegraph Magazine
The Times
Wales on Sunday
Weekend Guardian
The Weekly Journal
The Weekly News
Western Daily Press
Western Mail
The Western Morning News
You
Young Telegraph
Yorkshire Evening Post
Yorkshire Evening Press

Consumer and Special Interest Magazines

Aeroplane Monthly
Air International
Amateur Photographer
Annabel
The Aquarist and Pondkeeper
The Author
Back Street Heroes
Bad Attitude
Baptist Times
BBC Holidays
BBC Vegetarian GoodFood
Bella
Best
Bird Watching
Boards
Bowls International
British Chess Magazine
Bunty
Buster
Cage and Aviary Birds
Cat World
Catch
Catholic Gazette
Catholic Herald
Catholic Pictorial
Chapman
Chat
Christian Herald
Church of England Newspaper

Classic Cars
Classic CD
Computer Weekly
Computing
Country Life
Countryman
Country-Side
The Cricketer International
Cycling Weekly
DAM
The Dandy
Dandy Cartoon Library
Darts World
Dirt Bike Rider
Disability Now
East Lothian Life
The Economist
Edinburgh Review
Essentials
Euromoney
Everyday with Practical
 Electronics
Everywoman
Financial Adviser
Fly-Fishing & Fly-Tying
Football Picture Story Library
Fortean Times
Fourth World Review
France

Freelance Writing &
 Photography
Garden News
Gay Times
Geographical Magazine
Golf Monthly
Golf World
The Great Outdoors
Greenscene
Guiding
Health & Efficiency
 International
Here's Health
Hertfordshire Countryside
HIM Magazine
Home and Country
Home Words
Horse and Hound
Horse & Pony
The Illustrated London News
Index on Censorship
i-to-i
Jewish Telegraph
Just Seventeen
Life and Work
Mandy/Judy
Men Only
Methodist Recorder
Mobile & Holiday Homes

Modus
Money Week
Motor Boat and Yachting
Motor Caravan Magazine
Musical Opinion
My Weekly Puzzle Time
New Internationalist
New Musical Express
New Scientist
New Statesman & Society
The New Welsh Review
New World
Office Secretary
The Oldie
Opera Now
Organic Gardening
Penthouse
Performance Car
Pilot
Planet
Poetry Review
Pony
Practical Fishkeeping
Practical Householder

Practical Motorist
Practical Photography
Priests & People
Private Eye
Reform
Risqué
Runner's World
Scootering
The Scots Magazine
Scottish Homes and Country
Scouting
She
The Short Wave Magazine
Sight and Sound
Smallholder
The Spectator
Squash Player
Stage and Television Today
The Tablet
Take a Break
The Times Educational
 Supplement
Titbits

Today
Today's Runner
Tribune
Trout and Salmon
Twinkle
The Universe
The Vegan
Vegetarian Living
Viz
The Voice
Vox
War Cry
Weight Watchers Magazine
What's on TV
Woman
Woman Alive
Woodworker
World Soccer
Yachting Monthly
Yachting World
Young Soldier
Yours
YX

Business and Professional Magazines

Accountancy
Art Business Today
British Printer
Broadcast
Buses
Carers World
Certified Accountant
Child Education
Control and Instrumentation
CTN
Drapers Record
Education
Electrical Review

The Electrical Times
Gifts International
Hospitality
House Builder
International Construction
Journalist
Liberal Democrat News
Local Government Chronicle
Marketing Week
Media Week
Museums Journal
Music Teacher

Nursing Times and Nursing
 Mirror
Pig Farming
PR Week
Printing World
Publishing News
Red Tape
The Scottish Farmer
Solicitors Journal
Therapy Weekly
Toy Trader
Waterways World

Photography

The Freelance Photographer and the Agent

BRUCE COLEMAN

Photographic agencies and libraries have a dual role in the service they provide. They meet the needs and demands of picture editors, picture researchers and art buyers and, at the same time, provide a service to the freelance photographer. The enterprising photographer, wishing to penetrate the publishing market, would do well to consider employing the services of an agent whose knowledge of current trends and client contact will gear the photographer's output to the requirements of the markets. The complexities of reproduction rights are best left to an agent – that's if you wish to protect the copyright of your work!

Selecting the right agent very much depends on your type of work and you should, therefore, take a look at several agencies before choosing the one you think will be of advantage to you. Some agents, for example, work in the syndication area, selling news and topical pictures to the world's press; others are in the stock business maintaining a library of photographers' work orientated to the editorial market. Agents normally do not sell pictures outright but lease them for a specific use and fee from which they deduct a commission. A good photograph in the hands of a good agent can be published several times over and bring in royalties for many years.

Before submitting your work to an agent, a preliminary letter is recommended enquiring whether the agent is accepting new photographers and asking for details of their specific needs.

The agent will wish to see an initial presentation of at least two hundred photographs and any photographer should indicate the number of photographs they plan to submit in the course of a year. Agents are keen to encourage the active photographer who can supply a regular stream of good quality work. Serious attention should be given to the caption of every picture as this can often mean the difference between a sale or a rejection. A caption should be brief and legible and an example of a good nature caption would be:

> Spotted Hyena (*C. crocuta*)
> Serengeti
> Aggressive behaviour

or, a geographical caption:

> Canada: Northwest Territories
> Inuit fur trappers and dogsled

Some time spent on the presentation of your work, editing for composition, content, sharpness and, in the case of transparencies, colour saturation, will create a favourable impression. When submitting original colour transparencies, to ensure they are protected from damage and also to facilitate easy examination, place them in clear plastic sleeves, never between glass. Do not submit transparencies which you may require for personal use as it is quite impossible for an agent to recall pictures at short notice from his client.

One final point, never supply similar photographs to more than one agent as the problems created by almost identical pictures appearing, say, on a calendar or a greetings card can be embarrassing and costly to rectify. Indeed, for this reason, many agents insist on an exclusive arrangement between themselves and their photographers.

How to run your own Picture Library

JOHN FELTWELL

Photographers seeking to have someone else place their work should consider the possibilities of engaging a photographic agency (*see* Bruce Coleman's piece above). Photographers wishing to market their work themselves, either as specialist libraries listed below, or those wishing to establish a library, might find useful the following guidelines and tips.

It is important to draw up strict terms of business to cover items such as search fee, holding fee, and particularly loss or damage to original transparencies (£300 to £500 or more per transparency. See also *Picture Research* article.) Remember that the loss/damage fee may be subject to tax as earnings. A month is a reasonable time for transparencies to be reviewed, thereafter a weekly holding fee per transparency is recommended, unless stated otherwise. Search fees may or may not be waived if transparencies are accepted. Reproduction rights should be calculated according to territorial limitations, whether non-exclusive UK only, English speaking countries, world rights, etc., as well as size (small 'editorial' size to front cover). Sliding scales are required and bulk discounts. Agree fees, including future fees, before publication; restrict all electronic rights.

Beware of and budget for use of transparencies by editors, and especially design studios, for preparation of 'dummies'; pictures used may not be accounted for in-house by the resident picture researcher if acquired by editors, subeditors, etc. Forbid any slide projection of transparencies. Be wary of the use of transparencies from which artists can derive ideas, unless arranged, and of publicity/advertising companies who generate computer models and logos and bill accordingly. Beware of supplying private individuals who are naive to procedures. Some libraries ask for an official letter of request from the publisher.

The photographer's transparencies are treasured possessions. Unfortunately *some* publishers and magazines do not see it like that and treat them as dispensable and with some irreverence. You can be sure that picture researchers who are members of SPREd (full details at end of *Picture Research* article) know all about looking after transparencies and they are safe in their hands.

Make sure that dispatched transparencies (all sleeved) are well packed by whatever means and sent (by messenger/courier or by Registered Plus post with Consequential Loss Insurance) and are properly insured – and that the recipient knows when his or her liability starts and finishes. This includes transit to printers away from publishers' premises. Once accepted, transparencies may lie up for several months waiting to be used. This can run on to a year, unless strictly controlled. Arrange for payment six months after acceptance or on publication, whichever happens first, otherwise it might be on publication, some time off, or never. Specify that transparencies are returned from printers in a clean condition without any printers' solvents, but with original mounts.

The British Association of Picture Libraries and Agencies (BAPLA) (13 Woodberry Crescent, London N10 1PJ   *tel* 081-444 7913) mostly represents commercial and institutional libraries. Smaller libraries, who are perhaps more vulnerable to disputes, can only be assisted (the right is reserved) by BAPLA after first year membership (currently (1994) £275 + initial joining fee of £75 + VAT).

Picture Agencies and Libraries

For a **classified index** of picture agencies and libraries, see page 375.

Before submitting examples of work, photographers are advised to write a preliminary letter to ascertain terms and conditions. Usually, colour transparencies are required: medium and large format (minimum of 56 mm sq) are preferred to 35 mm. Only top quality transparencies should be submitted; inferior work is never accepted. *Postage for return material should be enclosed.*

Photographers are also referred to the markets for greetings cards and calendars on page 383, and to the children's book publishers and packagers classified index on page 248; also to the main Newspapers and Magazines, and Book Publishers, listings.

*Member of the British Association of Picture Libraries and Agencies

*A.A. & A. Ancient Art & Architecture Collection, 6 Kenton Road, Harrow-on-the-Hill, Middlesex HA1 2BL   *tel* 081-422 1214   *fax* 081-426 9479. Specialises in the history of civilisations of the Middle East, Mediterranean countries, Europe, Asia, Americas, from ancient times to recent past, their arts, architecture, beliefs and peoples.

*A-Z Botanical Collection Ltd, Bedwell Lodge, Cucumber Lane, Essendon, Hatfield, Herts. AL9 6JB   *tel* (0707) 649091   *fax* (0707) 649091. Colour transparencies of plant life world-wide, 5 × 4, 6 × 6, 35 mm.

Academic File News Photos (1985), The Centre for Near East, Afro-Asia Research (NEAR), Acre House, 69-76 Long Acre, London WC2E 9AS   *tel* 071-379 3939/081-392 1122   *fax* 081-392 1422. *Director:* Sajid Rizvi. Daily news coverage in UK and general library of people and places, with special reference to the Middle East, North Africa and Asia. New photographers welcomed to cover UK and abroad.

*Ace Photo Agency (1980), 22 Maddox Street, London W1R 9PG   *tel* 071-629 0303   *fax* 071-495 6100. General library: people, industry, business, travel, commerce, skies, sport, music and natural history. World-wide syndication. Sae for enquiries. Portfolio – standard work only. *Terms:* 50%.

*Action Plus (1986), 54-58 Tanner Street, London SE1 3LL   *tel* 071-403 1558   *fax* 071-403 1526. Comprehensive and creative coverage of action, venues and personalities in over 120 sports and leisure activities, world-wide. Extensive colour and b&w library of high quality work from staff and contributing photographers. *Terms:* 50%.

Lesley and Roy Adkins Picture Library (1989), Longstone Lodge, Aller, Langport, Somerset TA10 0QT   *tel* (0458) 250075   *fax* (0458) 250858. Colour library covering archaeology and heritage; prehistoric, Roman and medieval sites and monuments; landscape, countryside, architecture, towns, villages and religious monuments.

Aerofilms (1919), Hunting Aerofilms Ltd, Gate Studios, Station Road, Borehamwood, Herts. WD6 1EJ *tel* 081-207 0666 *fax* 081-207 5433. Comprehensive library – over 1½ million photos going back to 1919 – of vertical and oblique aerial photographs of UK; large areas with complete cover.

Air Photo Supply (1963), 42 Sunningvale Avenue, Biggin Hill, Kent TN16 3BX *tel* (0959) 574872. Aircraft and associated subjects, South-East England, colour and monochrome. No other photographers' material required.

Al Ahram (1983), Barry Davies, Dyffryn, Bolahaul Road, Cwmffrwd, Carmarthen, Dyfed SA31 2LP *tel* (0267) 233625. Natural history, landscape (especially waterfalls), Egypt, children, outdoor activities and general subjects. Formats 35 mm, 6 × 6 cm, 6 × 7 cm, 5 × 4 in. Other photographers' work not accepted.

*Bryan and Cherry Alexander Photography (1973), Higher Cottage, Manston, Sturminster Newton, Dorset DT10 1EZ *tel* (0258) 473006 *fax* (0258) 473333. Polar regions with emphasis on Eskimos, Lapps and the modern Arctic.

Rev. J. Catling Allen, St Giles House, Little Torrington, Devon EX38 8PS *tel* (0805) 22497. Library of colour transparencies (35 mm) and b&w photos of Bible Lands, including archaeological sites and the religions of Christianity, Islam and Judaism. Medieval abbeys and priories, cathedrals and churches in Britain. Also historic, rural and scenic Britain. (Not an agent or buyer.)

Allied Artists Ltd (1983), 31 Harcourt Street, London W1H 1DT *tel* 071-724 8809 *fax* 071-262 8526. *Contact:* Gary Mills. Agency for illustrators, with colour library of realistic figurative illustrations available for syndication.

*Allsport Photographic Ltd (1972), 3 Greenlea Park, Prince George's Road, London SW19 2JD *tel* 081-685 1010 *telex* 8955022 *fax* 081-648 5240. International sport and leisure.

American History Picture Library, 3 Barton Buildings, Bath BA1 2JR *tel* (0225) 334213. Photographs, engravings, colour transparencies covering the exploration, social, political and military history of North America from 15th to 20th century. Conquistadores, Civil War, gangsters, Moon landings, etc. Prints and photos purchased.

*Andes Press Agency (1983), 26 Padbury Court, London E2 7EH *tel/fax* 071-739 3159. *Director:* Carlos Reyes. Social, political and economic aspects of Latin America, Africa, Asia, Middle East, Europe and Britain; specialises in Latin America and contemporary world religions.

*Heather Angel, Highways, 6 Vicarage Hill, Farnham, Surrey GU9 8HJ *tel* (0252) 716700 *fax* (0252) 727464. Colour transparencies (35 mm and 2¼ in square) with world-wide coverage of natural history and biological subjects including animals, plants, natural habitats (deserts, polar regions, rainforests, wetlands, etc.), landscapes, gardens, close-ups and underwater images; also man's impact on the environment – pollution, acid rain, urban wildlife, etc. Large China file. Detailed catalogues on request by *bona fide* picture researchers.

*Animal Photography (1955), 4 Marylebone Mews, New Cavendish Street, London W1M 7LF *tel* 071-935 0503 *fax* 071-487 3038. Horses, dogs, cats, East Africa, Galapagos.

*Aquarius Picture Library (1977 in UK), PO Box 5, Hastings, East Sussex TN34 1HR *tel* (0424) 721196 *fax* (0424) 717704. *Contact:* David Corkill. Colour and b&w library specialising in showbusiness: film stills, candids, portraiture, archive material to present. Also television, pop, opera, ballet and stage. World-wide representation and direct sales. Collections considered, either outright purchase or 50%-50% marketing.

*Aquila Photographics, Haydon House, Alcester Road, Studley, Warks. B80 7AN *tel* (052 785) 2357 *fax* (052 785) 7507. Specialists in ornithological subjects, but covering all aspects of natural history, also pets and landscapes, in both colour and b&w.

*ARCAID Architectural Photography and Picture Library, The Factory, 2 Acre Road, Kingston, Surrey KT2 6EF *tel* 081-546 4352 *fax* 081-541 5230. 'The built environment' – international collection: architecture, interior design, gardens, travel, museums, historic and contemporary. *Terms:* 50%.

*Archivio Veneziano (formerly **Venice Picture Library**) (1990), c/o Unesco, Piazza San Marco 63, 30124 Venice, Italy *tel/fax* (041) 520 2119. *Curator:* Sarah Quill. Specialises in Venice, covering most aspects of the city, islands and lagoon, especially their architecture, conservation and the environment. Commissions undertaken; visitors are welcome by appointment.

Arctic Camera, Derek Fordham (1978), 66 Ashburnham Grove, Greenwich, London SE10 8UJ *tel/fax* 081-692 7651. Colour transparencies of all aspects of Arctic life and environment.

*Ardea London Ltd, 35 Brodrick Road, London SW17 7DX *tel* 081-672 2067 *fax* 081-672 8787. Su Gooders. Specialist world-wide natural history photographic library of animals, birds, plants, fish, insects, reptiles, world-wide scenics.

*Aspect Picture Library Ltd (1971), 40 Rostrevor Road, London SW6 5AD *tel* 071-736 1998/731 7362 *fax* 071-731 7362. General library including wildlife, tribes, cities, industry, science, Space.

The Associated Press Ltd, News Photo Department, The Associated Press House, 12 Norwich Street, London EC4A 1BP *tel* 071-353 1390 (colour and b&w request), 071-353 0354 (colour department), 071-353 1515 ext 3264 (library manager) *fax* 071-353 0836. News, features, sports.

Attard Lifestyle Photolibrary (1992), 5 Brewer Street, London W1R 3FN *tel* 071-287 2866 *fax* 071-287 3977. *Director:* Nigel Attard. Specialises in people: lifestyle, romance, contemporary themes. *Terms:* 50%.

Australia Pictures (1988), 28 Sheen Common Drive, Richmond, London TW10 5BN *tel* 081-876 3637 *fax* 081-332 7739. *Contact:* John Miles. Comprehensive library covering Australia, Aboriginals and their art, indigenous peoples, underwater, Tibet, Peru, Bolivia, Iran, Irian Jaya, Pakistan.

*Aviation Photographs International (1970), 15 Downs View Road, Swindon, Wilts. SN3 1NS *tel* (0793) 497179 *fax* (0793) 497179. All types of aviation and military subjects. Assignments undertaken.

*Aviation Picture Library (Austin J. Brown) (1970), 35 Kingsley Avenue, West Ealing, London W13 0EQ *tel* 081-566 7712 *fax* 081-566 7714 *cellphone* (0860) 292661. World-wide aviation photographic library, including dynamic views of aircraft. Aerial and travel library including Europe, Caribbean, USA, and East and West Africa. Material taken since 1960. Specialising in air-to-air and air-to-ground commissions.

B. & B. Photographs (1974), Prospect House, Clifford Chambers, Stratford upon Avon, Warks. CV37 8HX *tel* (0789) 298106 *fax* (0789) 292450. 35 mm colour library of horticulture (especially pests and diseases) and biogeography (world-wide), natural history (especially Britain) and biological education. Other photographers' work not represented.

Bandphoto Agency (division of **UPPA Ltd**), 30-34 New Bridge Street, London EC4V 6BN *tel* 071-329 8649 *fax* 071-489 8982. International news and feature picture service for British and overseas publishers.

*****Barnaby's Picture Library,** 19 Rathbone Street, London W1P 1AF *tel* 071-636 6128/9 *fax* 071-637 4317. General library of 4 million photos, colour and b&w, illustrating yesterday, today and tomorrow. Requires photographs for advertising and editorial publication. Photographs not purchased, sender retains copyright.

*****BBC Hulton Picture Library**—see **Hulton Deutsch Collection.**

Dr Alan Beaumont, 52 Squires Walk, Lowestoft, Suffolk NR32 4LA *tel* (0502) 560126. World-wide collection of monochrome prints and colour transparencies (35 mm and 6 × 7 cm) of natural history, countryside, windmills and aircraft. Subject lists available. No other photographers required.

Bee Photographs—see **Heritage & Natural History Photography.**

Stephen Benson Slide Bureau, 45 Sugden Road, London SW11 5EB *tel* 071-223 8635. World: agriculture, archaeology, architecture, commerce, everyday life, culture, environment, geography, science, tourism. Speciality: South America, the Caribbean, Australasia, Nepal, Turkey, Israel and Egypt. Assignments undertaken.

BIPS-Bernsen's International Press Service Ltd, 9 Paradise Close, Eastbourne, East Sussex BN20 8BT *tel* (0323) 728760. (For full details see page 140.)

Bird Images (1989), 28 Carousel Walk, Sherburn in Elmet, North Yorkshire LS25 6LP *tel* (0977) 684666. *Principal:* P. Doherty. Specialist in the birds of Britain and Europe. Expert captioning service available.

*****John Birdsall Photography** (1980), 75 Raleigh Street, Nottingham NG7 4DL *tel* (0602) 782645 *fax* (0602) 785546. *Contact:* Clare Marsh. Contemporary social documentary library covering children, youth, old age, health, disability, education, housing, work; also Nottingham and surrounding area; Spain – commissions and stock pictures.

*****The Anthony Blake Photo Library,** 54 Hill Rise, Richmond, Surrey TW10 6UB *tel* 081-940 7583 *fax* 081-948 1224. Food and wine around the world, including shops, restaurants, markets, agriculture and viticulture. Commissions undertaken. Contributors welcome.

*****John Blake Picture Library** (1975), The Georgian House, 6 The Plain, Thornbury, Bristol BS12 2AG *tel* (0454) 418321 *fax* (0454) 416636. General topography of England, Europe and the rest of the world. Landscapes, architecture, churches, gardens, countryside, towns and villages. Horse trials covered including Badminton and Gatcombe Park. *Terms: 50%.*

Blitz International News & Photo Agency (1988), Stubcroft Studios, Stubcroft Farm, Stubcroft Lane, East Wittering, Nr Chichester, West Sussex PO20 8PJ *tel* (0243) 671469. *Contact:* Simon Green. Comprehensive library of colour transparencies and monochrome prints (35 mm, medium and large formats). Action and sports photography (especially yachting and motorsport, including Le Mans 24hr race), travel, natural history, landscapes and aerial, reportage, personalities, news, advertising shots, general. Commissions undertaken and photographers accepted. Catalogue on request. *Terms: 50%.*

Bodleian Library, Oxford OX1 3BG   *tel* (0865) 277153/277214   *fax* (0865) 277182. Photographic library of 32,000 35 mm colour transparencies, of subjects mostly from medieval manuscripts with iconographical index to illuminations; 35 mm filmstrips available for immediate sale (not hire); other formats to order.

Bookart Architecture Picture Library (1991), 1 Woodcock Lodge, Epping Green, Hertford SG13 8ND   *tel* (0707) 875253   *fax* (0707) 875286. Modern and historic buildings, landscapes, works of named architects in Great Britain, Europe, Scandinavia, North America, India, South-East Asia, Japan, North and East Africa; modern sculpture. Listed under style, place and personality.

Boxing Picture Library, 3 Barton Buildings, Bath BA1 2JR   *tel* (0225) 334213. Prints, engravings and photos of famous boxers, boxing personalities and famous fights from 18th century to recent years.

*Bridgeman Art Library, 19 Chepstow Road, London W2 5BP   *tel* 071-727 4065   *fax* 071-792 8509. Large source of fine art images: paintings, sculpture, prints, manuscripts, antiquities and the decorative arts from 15,000 BC to the present day on large format colour transparencies. Represent many major museums, art galleries and private collections around the world.

Britain on View Photographic Library, official photographic library for British Tourist Authority and English Tourist Board. Colour library operated on their behalf by **Syndication International.** Encompasses all aspects of Britain: coast, countryside, villages, towns, pageantry, landmarks, historic houses and the British people. For details of b&w, contact Manager, Design, BTA, Thames Tower, Black's Road, London W6 9EL   *tel* 081-846 9000   *fax* 081-563 0302.

David Broadbent/Derbyshire Scene (1989), 66 Norfolk Street, Glossop, Derbyshire SK13 9RA   *tel* (0457) 862997. The Derbyshire County and all its aspects: people, places and life; also natural history, birds a speciality. Lists available. Commissions undertaken. *Terms:* 50%.

Hamish Brown, 21 Carlin Craig, Kinghorn, Fife KY3 9RX   *tel* (0592) 890422. Photographs and 35 mm transparencies of Scottish sites and topographical, Morocco, mountain ranges of Europe, Africa, India and South America. Commissions undertaken. No pictures purchased.

Butterflies (1990), 27 Lucastes Lane, Haywards Heath, West Sussex RH16 1LE   *tel* (0444) 454254. *Proprietors:* Dr J. Tampion, Mrs M.D. Tampion. World-wide: butterflies, silkmoths, hawkmoths, adults, larvae, pupae, their foodplants, poisonous plants, wild, garden and greenhouse plants, botanical and gardening science, ecology, environment. Articles and line illustrations also available; commissions undertaken. *Terms:* 50%.

*Camera Press Ltd (1947), 21 Queen Elizabeth Street, London SE1 2PD   *tel* 071-378 1300   *fax* 071-278 5126. B&w prints and colour transparencies covering British Royalty, portraits of world statesmen, politicians, entertainers, reportage, humour, nature, pop, features. *Terms:* 50%.

Camerapix—see **C.P.L. (Camerapix Picture Library).**

*J. Allan Cash Photolibrary (J. Allan Cash Ltd), 74 South Ealing Road, London W5 4QB   *tel* 081-840 4141   *fax* 081-566 2568. World-wide photographic library: travel, landscape, natural history, sport, industry, agriculture. Details available for photographers interested in contributing.

Celtic Picture Library (1985), 5 Llys Llannerch, Trefnant, St Asaph, Clwyd LL17 0AZ   *tel/fax* (0745) 730395. All subjects relating to Wales: ancient monuments, crafts and customs, conservation, farming, industry, landscapes, tourism, environment, wildlife.

*The Central Press Photos Ltd—see **Hulton Deutsch Collection.**

*Cephas Picture Library, 20 Bedster Gardens, West Molesey, Surrey KT8 1SZ *tel/fax* 081-979 8647. People, places, agriculture, industry, religion, architecture, travel, food and wine, crafts; wine industry and vineyards. *Terms: 50%.*

*City Syndication Ltd—see **Monitor Syndication.**

Bruce Coleman Inc., 117 East 24th Street, New York, NY 10010-2919, USA *tel* 212-979-6252 *fax* 212-979-5468. *President:* Norman Owen Tomalin. Specialising exclusively in colour transparencies. All formats from 35 mm acceptable. All subjects required.

*Bruce Coleman Ltd, 16 Chiltern Business Village, Arundel Road, Uxbridge, Middlesex UB8 2SN *tel* (0895) 257094 *fax* (0895) 272357. Colour transparencies on natural history, ecology, environment, geography, archaeology, anthropology, agriculture, science, scenics and travel.

*Collections (1990), 13 Woodberry Crescent, London N10 1PJ *tel* 081-883 0083 *fax* 081-883 9215. Traditional British customs, bridges, castles, horticulture, landscape, steam trains, family life, and lots of other British things.

*Colorific Photo Library, The Innovation Centre, 225 Marsh Wall, London E14 9FX *tel* 071-515 3000 *fax* 071-538 3555. Handles the work of top international photographers, most subjects currently on file, upwards of 250,000 images. Represents the following agencies: Black Star (New York), Contact Press Images (New York/Paris), Visages (Los Angeles/New York), GLMR (Paris), Regards (Paris), ANA Press (Paris). Also represents *Sports Illustrated.*

*Sylvia Cordaiy Photo Library (1990), 72 East Ham Road, Littlehampton, West Sussex BN17 7BQ *tel* (0903) 715297 *fax* (0903) 731605. World-wide travel and architecture, global environmental topics, wildlife and domestic animals, veterinary, comprehensive UK files, ocean racing. *Terms: 50%.*

C.P.L. (Camerapix Picture Library), 8 Ruston Mews, London W11 1RB *tel* 071-221-0077 *telex* 263996 *fax* 071-792 8105; and PO Box 45048 Nairobi, Kenya *tel* 223511/334398 *telex* 22576 *fax* 217244. Kenya, Tanzania, Pakistan, Jordan, Namibia, Nepal, Maldives, Mauritius, Seychelles, Zimbabwe; portraits, agriculture, industry, tribal cultures, landscapes; wildlife including rare species; extensive collection on Aldabra Island; Islamic portfolio: Mecca, Medina, Muslim pilgrimage. News material available and special assignments arranged. Further material available from collection held in Nairobi.

Crafts Council (1973), 44a Pentonville Road, Islington, London N1 9BY *tel* 071-278 7700 *fax* 071-837 6891. Picture library holds large, medium and small format transparencies available for reproduction and an extensive collection of slides available for loan only. Subjects covered include ceramics, jewellery, textiles, metal and silver, furniture, wood, glass, knitting, weaving, bookbinding, fashion accessories, toys and musical instruments. Reference Library and Information Service available. Publisher of *Crafts* magazine (Bi-M, *editor:* Geraldine Rudge), full colour features and reviews on all crafts.

*Cumbria Picture Library (1990), PO Box 33, Kendal, Cumbria LA9 4SU *tel* (05396) 21002. *Contact:* Eric Whitehead. Specialist picture library with over 20,000 images covering every aspect of Cumbria and The Lake District. Subjects include: places, people, events, customs, outdoor pursuits and landscapes; snooker photos by Eric Whitehead. The library holds work from many photographers and commissions are accepted.

*Lupe Cunha (1987), 2nd Floor, 887 Green Lanes, London N21 2QS *tel* 081-360 0144 *fax* 081-364 0420. Specialist library on all aspects of childhood from pregnancy to school age, also women's interest and health/medical with focus on the patient and nursing care. Commissioned photography undertaken. Also represents collection on Brazil for Brazil Photo Agency. *Terms:* 50%.

*Sue Cunningham Photographic, 56 Chatham Road, Kingston upon Thames, Surrey KT1 3AA *tel* 081-541 3024 *fax* 081-541 5388. All aspects of Brazil; Africa: Tanzania, Burundi, Zambia and Gambia. Travel: Chile, Guatemala, Portugal, Spain, UK.

The Dance Library (1983), 18 Conduit Mews, London W2 3RE *tel* 071-262 6300 *fax* 071-262 6400. Contemporary and historical dance: classical ballet, jazz, tap, disco, popping, ice dancing, musicals, variety, folk, tribal rites and rituals.

Das Photo (1975), c/o Cherry Trees, 1 Chatton Row, Bisley, Surrey GU24 9AP *tel* Brookwood (0483) 473395; and Chalet le Pin, Domaine de Bellevue 181, 6940 Septon, Belgium *tel* (086) 32 24 26. Arab countries, Americas, Europe, SE Asia, Amazon, world festivals, archaeology, people, biblical, motor bikes, education, schools, modern languages.

Dennis Davis Photography (1984), 9 Great Burrow Rise, Northam, Bideford, Devon EX39 1TB *tel* (0237) 475165. Gardens, wild and garden flowers, domestic livestock including rare breeds and poultry, agricultural landscapes, architecture – interiors and exteriors, landscape, coastal, rural life. Commissions welcomed. No other photographers required.

*James Davis Travel Photography, 30 Hengistbury Road, New Milton, Hants BH25 7LU *tel* (0425) 610328 *fax* (0425) 638402. *Proprietor:* James Davis. Stock transparency library specialising in world-wide travel photos. Supply publishers, advertising agents, etc. Submissions only considered from photographers experienced in travel photography, particularly professionals. 6 × 6 cm or larger preferred. *Terms:* 50%.

*Peter Dazeley, The Studios, 5 Heathmans Road, Parsons Green, London SW6 4TJ *tel* 071-736 3171 *fax* 071-371 8876. Extensive golf library dating from 1970. Colour and b&w coverage of major tournaments. Constantly updated, with over 250,000 images of players (male and female), courses world-wide, action shots, portraits, trophies, including miscellaneous images: clubs, balls and teaching shots.

George A. Dey (1986), 'Drumcairn', Aberdeen Road, Laurencekirk, Kincardineshire AB30 1AJ *tel* (0561 37) 8845. Scottish Highland landscapes, Highland Games, forestry, castles of NE Scotland, gardens, spring, autumn, winter scenes, veteran cars, North Holland.

*Douglas Dickins Photo Library (1946), 2 Wessex Gardens, Golders Green, London NW11 9RT *tel* 081-455 6221. World-wide collection of colour transparencies (mostly 6 × 6 cm, some 35 mm) and b&w prints (10 × 8 in originals), specialising in Asia, particularly India and Indonesia; also, USA, Canada, France, Austria and Switzerland.

Gordon Dickson (1975) Flagstones, 72 Catisfield Lane, Fareham, Hants PO15 5NS *tel* (0329) 842131. Colour transparencies of fungi, in natural habitat; also butterflies, moths, beetles. No other photographers required.

*C.M. Dixon, The Orchard, Marley Lane, Kingston, Canterbury, Kent CT4 6JH *tel* (0227) 830075 *fax* (0227) 831135. Europe and Ethiopia, Iceland, Sri Lanka, Tunisia, Turkey, former USSR. Main subjects include agriculture, ancient art, archaeology, architecture, clouds, geography, geology, history, horses, industry, meteorology, mosaics, mountains, mythology, occupations, people.

*Ecoscene (1987), Sally Morgan, The Oasts, Headley Road, Passfield, Liphook, Hants GU30 7RX *tel* (0428) 751056 *fax* (0428) 751057. Natural history, specialising in the environment and ecology. Subjects include animal and plant species, habitats, conservation, energy, industry, all forms of pollution; world-wide coverage. *Terms:* 55% to photographer.

T. Malcolm English BA, LRPS, MRAeS, 3 The Bakery, Silver Street, Stevington, Beds. MK43 7QN *tel* (0234) 824150. Aviation photographic library specialising in military, historic and air weapons.

*English Heritage Photographic Library (1984), Room 517, 23 Savile Row, London W1X 1AB *tel* 071-973 3338/3339 *fax* 071-973 3001. Wide range of large format colour transparencies ranging from ancient monuments to artefacts, legendary castles to stone circles, elegant interiors to industrial architecture.

*Environmental Investigation Agency (1985), 2 Pear Tree Court, London EC1R 0DS *tel* 071-490 7040 *fax* 071-490 0436. *Photograph co-ordinator:* Tamara Gray. Specialist library covering animal abuse, trade in endangered species, abuse of the environment; also animals in their natural environment.

Euro-Parly Services (News Pix) (1974), 2 Denbigh Place, Westminster, London SW1V 2HB *tel* 071-730 8976 (24-hour). *Contact:* Myles Sweeney. News, current affairs, conferences, London tourism and leisure subjects. Dark room and picture transmission facilities available. Advertorial assignments undertaken. *Terms:* 50%.

*Greg Evans International Photo Library (1979), 91 Charlotte Street, London W1P 1LB *tel* 071-636 8238 *fax* 071-637 1439. Comprehensive, general colour library with over 300,000 transparencies. Subjects include: abstract, aircraft, arts, animals, beaches, business, children, computers, couples, families, food/restaurant, women, industry, skies, sports (action and leisure), UK scenics, world-wide travel. Visitors welcome; combined commissions undertaken; first search fee. Photographers' submissions welcome. Please phone for free brochure.

*Mary Evans Picture Library, 59 Tranquil Vale, Blackheath, London SE3 0BS *tel* 081-318 0034 *fax* 081-852 7211. Millions of historical illustrations in colour and b&w covering all aspects of the past, emphasis on social conditions and cultural activities. Portraits, topography, science and many specialist subjects, notably women's rights, psychical research, psychology (Freud). Many special collections including individual photographers 1930s to 1960s.

Eyeline Photography (1979), 259 London Road, Cheltenham, Glos. GL52 6YG *tel/fax* (0242) 513567. Watersports, particularly sailing and powerboating, world-wide; equestrian events; windvanes; scenics.

*Feature-Pix Colour Library—see World Pictures.

*Fogden Natural History Photographs (1980), Mid Cambushinnie Cottage, Kinbuck, Dunblane, Perthshire FK15 9JU *tel/fax* (0786) 822069. *Library manager:* Susan Fogden. Wide natural history coverage, including camouflage, warning coloration, mimicry, breeding strategies, feeding, animal/plant relationships, environmental studies, especially in rain forests and deserts.

Ron and Christine Foord, 155b City Way, Rochester, Kent ME1 2BE *tel* (0634) 847348. Colour picture library of 1000 species of wild flowers; British insects, garden flowers, pests and diseases, indoor plants, cacti, countryside views.

*Footprints Colour Picture Library (1991), Goldfin Cottage, Maidlands Farm, Broad Oak, Rye, East Sussex TN31 6BJ *tel/fax* (0424) 883078. *Proprietor:* Paula Leaver. Specialises in underwater and above water coverage of holiday destinations in the tropics; also food and flowers by Debbie Patterson.

*Forest Life Picture Library (1983), Forestry Commission, 231 Corstorphine Road, Edinburgh EH12 7AT *tel* 031-334 0303 *fax* 031-334 4473. *Head of photographic department:* Douglas M.B. Green. Tree species, forest and woodland management, harvesting, marketing, conservation, wildlife and recreation, general views.

*Werner Forman Archive (1975), 36 Camden Square, London NW1 9XA *tel* 071-267 1034 *fax* 071-267 6026. Art, architecture, archaeology, history and peoples of ancient, oriental and primitive cultures.

*Fortean Picture Library, Melysfan, Llangwm, Corwen, Clwyd LL21 0RD *tel* (0490) 420472 *fax* (0490) 420321. Library of colour and b&w pictures covering all strange phenomena: UFOs, Loch Ness Monster, ghosts, Bigfoot, witchcraft, etc.; also antiquities (especially in Britain – prehistoric and Roman sites, castles, churches).

Fotoccompli–The Picture Library (1989), 11 Ampton Road, Edgbaston, Birmingham B15 2UH *tel* 021-454 3305 *fax* 021-454 9257. Comprehensive library, ranging from abstracts to zoology, serving all of Britain, especially the Birmingham and West Midlands areas. *Terms:* 50%; minimum retention period – two years.

*Fotomas Index, 12 Pickhurst Rise, West Wickham, Kent BR4 0AL *tel/fax* 081-776 2772. Specialises in supplying pre-20th century (mostly pre-Victorian) illustrative material to publishing and academic worlds, and for television and advertising. Complete production back-up for interior décor, exhibitions and locations.

*Fox Photos—see **Hulton Deutsch Collection.**

Freelance Focus (1988), 7 King Edward Terrace, Brough, North Humberside HU15 1EE *tel/fax* (0482) 666036. *Contact:* Gary Hicks. UK/international network of photographers. Over two million stock pictures available, covering all subjects, world-wide, at competitive rates. Assignments undertaken for all types of clients. Further details/subject list available on request.

Frontline Photo Press Agency (1988), 18 Wall Street, Norwood, Australia 5067 *postal address* PO Box 162, Kent Town, Australia 5071 *tel* (08) 333 2691 *fax* (08) 364 0604. *Director:* Carlo Irlitti. Sports photo press agency and general photo library, covering sport, people, personalities, travel, scenics, environmental, natural history, social documentary and press images. Contributors welcomed; assignments undertaken. Write or fax for details. *Terms:* 60%.

Frost Historical Newspaper Collection, 8 Monks Avenue, New Barnet, Herts. EN5 1DB *tel* 081-440 3159. Headline stories from 50,000 British and overseas newspapers reporting major events since 1850.

Brian Gadsby Picture Library, Route de Maubourguet, Labatut-Riviere 65700, Hautes Pyrenees, France *tel* 62 96 38 44. Colour (2¼ in sq, 6 × 4.5 cm, 35 mm) and b&w prints. Wide range of subjects but emphasis on travel, natural history, children. Catalogue on request by picture researchers. No other photographers' material required.

Galaxy Picture Library (1992), 1 Milverton Drive, Ickenham, Uxbridge, Middlesex UB10 8PP *tel* (0895) 637463 *fax* (0895) 623277 *e-mail* CompuServe 100014,2426. *Contact:* Robin Scagell. Astronomy: specialities include the night sky, amateur astronomy, astronomers and observatories.

*Garden Matters Photographic Library (1993), Dr John Feltwell, Marlham, Henley's Down, Battle, East Sussex TN33 9BN *tel* (0424) 830566 *fax* (0424) 830224. **Plants 4000:** over 4000 scientifically named species of garden flowers, wild plants, trees (over 550 species), grasses, crops, herbs, spices, house plants, carnivorous plants, climbers and roses. **General gardening** and how-to, gardening techniques, garden design and embellishments, cottage gardens, USA designer-gardens, 200 garden portfolios from 16 states in the USA, 100 portfolios from ten European countries.

*Leslie Garland Picture Library (1985), 69 Fern Avenue, Jesmond, Newcastle upon Tyne NE2 2QU   *tel* 091-281 3442   *fax* 091-281 3442. Colour library of all subjects in the geographic areas of Northumberland, Durham, Tyne and Wear, Cleveland, Cumbria, Lancashire and Yorkshire. Details available for photographers interested in contributing – send sae. *Terms:* 50%.

*Colin Garratt—see **Railways – Milepost 92½.**

*Genesis Space Photo Library (1990), Peppercombe Lodge, Horns Cross, Bideford, Devon EX39 5DH   *tel* (0237) 451 756   *fax* (0237) 451 600. *Contact:* Tim Furniss. Specialises in rockets, spacecraft, spacemen, Earth, Moon, planets.

Geo Aerial Photography (1992), 4 Christian Fields, London SW16 3JZ   *tel/fax* 081-764 6292 or (0602) 815474. *Director:* J.F.J. Douglas. Air-to-air and air-to-ground colour library: natural and cultural/man-made landscapes and individual features. Commissions undertaken. *Terms:* 50%.

*GeoScience Features, 6 Orchard Drive, Wye, Kent TN25 5AU   *tel* (0233) 812707   *fax* (0233) 812707. *Director:* Dr Basil Booth. Colour library (35 mm to 5 × 4 in). Animals, biology, birds, botany, chemistry, earth science, ecology, environment, geology, geography, habitats, landscapes, macro/micro, peoples, plants, travel, sky, weather, wildlife and zoology; Americas, Africa, Australasia, Europe, India, SE Asia. Incorporates K.S.F. colour library.

Geoslides (1968), 4 Christian Fields, London SW16 3JZ   *tel/fax* 081-764 6292. *Library director:* John Douglas. Geographical and general interest subjects from Africa, Asia, Antarctic, Arctic and sub-Arctic areas. Interested only in large recent collections of relevant colour transparencies, regionally based. Photographs for all types of publications, television, advertising. *Terms:* 50% on UK sales.

Mark Gerson Photography, 3 Regal Lane, Regents Park Road, London NW1 7TH   *tel* 071-286 5894   *fax* 071-267 9246. Portrait photographs of personalities, mainly literary, in colour and b&w from 1950 to the present. No other photographers' material required.

Global Syndications (1990), Chartwood Towers, Punchbowl Lane, Dorking, Surrey RH5 4ED   *tel* (0306) 741213   *fax* (0306) 875347. *Managing editor:* Sam Hall. Colour transparencies of all aspects of Arctic life and environment, particularly Eskimo (Inuit) and Lapps (Sami); Scandinavia and UK (landscapes, people, etc.). Assignments undertaken. No other photographers required.

John Glover Photography (1979), Fairfield, Hale House Lane, Churt, Farnham, Surrey GU10 2NQ   *tel* (0428) 717196   *fax* (0428) 717129. Gardens and gardening, from overall views of gardens to plant portraits with Latin names; UK landscapes including ancient sites, Stonehenge, etc.

*Martin and Dorothy Grace (1984), 40 Clipstone Avenue, Mapperley, Nottingham NG3 5JZ   *tel* (0602) 208248   *fax* (0602) 626802. General British natural history, specialising in native trees, shrubs, flowers, habitats and ecology.

Tim Graham (1970), 31 Ferncroft Avenue, London NW3 7PG   *tel* 071-435 7693   *fax* 071-431 4312. Royal Family in this country and on tours; background pictures on royal homes, staff, hobbies, sports, cars, etc.; English and foreign country scenes; international heads of state and VIPs.

Greater London Photograph Library, 40 Northampton Road, London EC1R 0HB *tel* 071-332 3823 *fax* 071-833 9136. Over 350,000 photos of London and the London area from *c.*1860 to 1986. Especially strong on local authority projects – schools, housing, open spaces, etc.

Robert Haas Photo Library (1978), 11 Cormont Road, Camberwell, London SE5 9RA *tel* 071-326 1510. Holland, Greek Islands, Morocco, Scottish oil industry, Notting Hill Carnival, skies. *Specialities:* people; New York City, Lloyd's of London, Docklands.

*Robert Harding Picture Library, 58-59 Great Marlborough Street, London W1V 1DD *tel* 071-287 5414 *fax* 071-631 1070. Photographic library. Require photographs of outstanding quality for advertising and editorial use, all subjects considered particularly life style.

Harper Horticultural Slide Library, 219 Robanna Shores, Seaford, VA 23696, USA *tel* 804-898-6453. 160,000 35 mm slides of plants, gardens and native habitats.

Heritage & Natural History Photography, Dr John B. Free, 37 Plainwood Close, Summersdale, Chichester, West Sussex PO19 4YB *tel* (0243) 533822. Archaeology, history, agriculture: Mexico, Mediterranean countries, Oman, Iran, USSR, India, Nepal, Thailand, Japan, UK. Bees and bee keeping, insects and small invertebrates, tropical crops and flowers.

Historical Picture Service, 3 Barton Buildings, Bath BA1 2JR *tel* (0225) 334213. Engravings, prints and photos on all aspects of history from ancient times to 1920. Special collection Old London: buildings, inns, theatres, many of which no longer exist.

Pat Hodgson Library & Picture Research Agency, Jasmine Cottage, Spring Grove Road, Richmond, Surrey TW10 6EH *tel* 081-940 5986. Small collection of b&w historical engravings, book illustrations, ephemera, etc.; some colour and modern photos. Subjects include history, Victoriana, ancient civilisations, occult, travel. Text written and research undertaken on any subject. Of special interest to educational publishers, film makers and exhibition designers.

*Holt Studios International (Agriculture, Horticulture, Environment) (1981), The Courtyard, 24 High Street, Hungerford, Berks. RG17 0NF *tel* (0488) 683523 *fax* (0488) 683511. World-wide agriculture, horticulture, crops and associated pests (and their predators), diseases and deficiencies, farming people and practices, livestock, machinery, landscapes and diverse environments.

Horizon International Creative Images (1978). Photographer enquiries: Horizon International, Horizon House, Route de Picaterre, Alderney, Channel Islands *fax* (0481) 823880; picture research and UK sales enquiries: Images-Horizon International London, 12-14 Argyll Street, London W1V 1AB *tel* 071-734 7344 *fax* 071-287 3933. Transparencies: comprehensive collection of the work of several photo libraries in London. Network of international companies specialising in marketing of distinctive quality images, both illustration and photography.

David Hosking FRPS, Pages Green House, Wetheringsett, Stowmarket, Suffolk IP14 5QA *tel* (0728) 861113 *fax* (0728) 860222. Natural history subjects, especially birds covering whole world. Also Dr D.P. Wilson's unique collection of marine photos.

*Houses & Interiors Photographic Features Agency (1987), Warwick House, 7 Nevill Street, Tunbridge Wells, Kent TN2 5RU *tel* (0892) 524404 *fax* (0892) 523785. *Contact:* Richard Wiles. Stylish house interiors and exteriors, home dossiers, renovations, architectural details, interior design, gardens, houseplants and cookery. Also step-by-step photographic sequences of DIY subjects and gardening techniques. Colour and b&w. Commissions undertaken. *Commission:* Library 50%, Agency negotiable.

***Hulton Deutsch Collection,** Unique House, 21-31 Woodfield Road, London W9 2BA *tel* 071-266 2662 *fax* 071-289 6392. One of the largest picture resources in Europe, with over 15 million b&w and colour images. Specialises in social history, Royalty, transport, war, fashion, sport, entertainment, people, places and early photography. Collections include *Picture Post, Express, Evening Standard,* Keystone, Fox and Topical Press. Manages Syndication International; only London agents for the Reuter News Picture Service; publisher of CD-ROMS for creative image access.

***The Hutchison Library** (1976), 118b Holland Park Avenue, London W11 4UA *tel* 071-229 2743 *fax* 071-792 0259. General colour library; world-wide subjects: agriculture, environments, festivals, human relationships, industry, landscape, peoples, religion, towns, travel.

***The Illustrated London News Picture Library,** 20 Upper Ground, London SE1 9PF *tel* 071-928 2111 *fax* 071-928 1469. Engravings, photos, illustrations in b&w and colour from 1842 to present day, especially 19th and 20th century social history, wars, portraits, Royalty. Travel archive including The Thomas Cook collection.

***The Image Bank** (1979), 7 Langley Street, London WC2H 9JA *tel* 071-240 9621 *fax* 071-831 1489. Hi-tech, special effects, food, still life, sports, scenic, people, industry, medical, business and concepts. Free catalogue featuring 1200 images from 450 photographers available on request.

***Images of Africa Photobank** (1983), 11 The Windings, Lichfield, Staffs. WS13 7EX *tel* (0543) 262898 *fax* (0543) 417154. *Contact:* David Keith Jones. Colour and b&w covering wildlife, traditional and modern people, land, resources, beauty, tourist attractions, hotels and lodges, National Parks and Reserves. *Terms:* 50%.

Images-Horizon International London—see **Horizon International Creative Images.**

Images of India (1991), 33 Greyhound Road, London W6 8NH *tel* 071-386 9060 *fax* 071-385 6244. Comprehensive library of all aspects of Indian and Nepalese life, scenery and culture.

***Imperial War Museum** (1917), Department of Photographs, Lambeth Road, London SE1 6HZ *tel* 071-416 5000 *fax* 071-416 5379. National archive of over five million photos, dealing with war in the 20th century involving the armed forces of Britain and the Commonwealth countries. Visitors' Room (IWM All Saints Annexe, Austral Street, SE11 – five minutes walk from main building) open by appointment Mon-Fri. Enquiries should be as specific as possible; prints made to order.

International Press Agency (Pty) Ltd (1934), PO Box 67, Howard Place 7450, South Africa *tel* (021) 531 1926 *fax* (021) 531 8789. Press photos for South African market.

Isle of Wight Pictures (1985), 60 York Street, Cowes, Isle of Wight PO31 7BS *tel* (0983) 290366 *fax* (0983) 297282. *Proprietor:* Patrick Eden. Covers all aspects of the Isle of Wight, including Cowes Week, sailing events, nautical aspects. Any picture not on file can be shot on request.

Jazz Index (1979), 26 Fosse Way, London W13 0BZ *tel* 081-998 1232 *fax* 081-991 2565. Photo library of jazz and blues musicians and anything connected with music. Pictures sold on behalf of photographers. *Terms:* 50%.

Joe Filmbase (1991), 107 Oakfield Road, Walthamstow, London E17 5RL *tel/ fax* 081-531 6686. General library specialising in Africa and Europe. *Terms:* 3-year contract.

JS Library International (1979) 101A Brondesbury Park, London NW2 5JL *tel* 081-451 2668 *fax* 081-459 0223. The Royal Family, world-wide travel pictures, particularly the African continent, stage and screen celebrities, authors, world-wide general material. New material on any subject, in any quantity, always urgently required. Assignments undertaken.

Just Europe (1989), 50 Basingfield Road, Thames Ditton, Surrey KT7 0PD *tel/ fax* 081-398 2468. Specialises in Europe – major cities, towns, people and customs. Assignments undertaken; background information available; advice and research service.

*Keystone Collection—see Hulton Deutsch Collection.

Lakeland Life Picture Library (1979), Langsett, Lyndene Drive, Grange-over-Sands, Cumbria LA11 6QP *tel* (05395) 33565 (answer phone). English Lake District: industries, crafts, sports, shows, customs, architecture, people. Not an agency. Catalogue available on request.

*Landscape Only (1986), 12-14 Argyll Street, London W1V 1AB *tel* 071-734 7344 *fax* 071-287 3933. Outdoor subjects: villages, countryside, places, landscape, countries, travel, towns, cities. *Terms:* 50%.

*Frank Lane Picture Agency Ltd, Pages Green House, Wetheringsett, Stowmarket, Suffolk IP14 5QA *tel* (0728) 860789 *fax* (0728) 860222. Natural history and meteorology.

Michael Leach, Brookside, Kinnerley, Oswestry, Shropshire SY10 8DB *tel* (0691) 682639. Specialist in high-speed photography of wildlife: general wildlife and natural history subjects, with particular emphasis on mammals and urban wildlife; very comprehensive collection of owls from all over the world. No other photographers required.

Lears Magical Lanterns Museum, Spa Road, Llandrindod Wells, Powys D1 5EJ *tel* (0597) 824737. 10,000 lantern slides, mainly Victorian, some Edwardian; all subjects.

The Billie Love Historical Collection (1969), Reflections, 3 Winton Street, Ryde, Isle of Wight PO33 2BX *tel* (0983) 812572 *fax* (0983) 568388. *Proprietor:* Billie Love. Photos (late 19th century-1930s), engravings, coloured lithographs, covering people, places and events up to the Second World War; also more recent material.

*Ludvigsen Library Ltd (1984), 73 Collier Street, London N1 7JU *tel* 071-837 1700 *fax* 071-837 1776. *Photographic resources:* Christine Lalla. Vintage, antique and classic cars; cars of all countries; historical motor sports events (Formula 1, Le Mans, US racing, motor shows).

*The MacQuitty International Collection, 7 Elm Lodge, River Gardens, Stevenage Road, London SW6 6NZ *tel* 071-385 6031 *tel/fax* 071-384 1781. 300,000 photos covering aspects of life in 70 countries: archaeology, art, buildings, flora and fauna, gardens, museums, people and occupations, scenery, religions, methods of transport, surgery, acupuncture, funeral customs, fishing, farming, dancing, music, crafts, sports, weddings, carnivals, food, drink, jewellery and oriental subjects. Period: 1920 to present day.

*Mander & Mitchenson Theatre Collection, The Mansion, Beckenham Place Park, Beckenham, Kent BR3 2BP *tel* 081-658 7725 *fax* 081-663 0313. Prints, drawings, photos, programmes, etc., theatre, opera, ballet, music hall, and other allied subjects including composers, playwrights, etc. All periods. Available for books, magazines, TV.

Mansell Collection Ltd, 42 Linden Gardens, London W2 4ER *tel* 071-229 5475. General historical material up to the 1920s, 1930s.

John Massey Stewart, 20 Hillway, Highgate, London N6 6QA *tel* 081-341 3544 *fax* 081-341 5292. Large collection Russia, including topography, people, culture, Siberia, plus Russian and Soviet history, 3000 pre-revolutionary PCs, etc. Also Britain, Europe, Asia (including Mongolia and South Korea), Alaska, USA, Israel, Sinai desert, etc.

*S. & O. Mathews, Stitches Farm House, Eridge, East Sussex TN3 9JB *tel* (0892) 852848 *fax* (0892) 853314. Country life, landscapes, gardens and flowers.

Chris Mattison, 138 Dalewood Road, Beauchief, Sheffield S8 0EF *tel* (0742) 364433. Colour library specialising in reptiles and amphibians; other natural history subjects; habitats and landscapes in SE Asia, South America, USA, Mexico, Mediterranean. Captions or detailed copy supplied if required. No other photographers' material required.

Robin May Collection, 23 Malcolm Road, London SW19 4AS *tel* 081-946 8965. Library specialising in Western Americana and the theatrical arts.

Merseyside Photo Library (1989), 65 Woodside Business Park, Woodside, Birkenhead, Wirral L41 1EH *tel* 051-647 6898 *fax* 051-649 8501 (operated by Ron Jones Associates). Library specialising in images of Liverpool and Merseyside; now being expanded to include NW England, other destinations and general stock photos.

Microscopix (1986), Middle Travelly, Beguildy, Nr Knighton, Powys LD7 1UW *tel/fax* (0547) 510242. Scientific photo library specialising in scanning electron micrographs and photomicrographs for technical and aesthetic purposes. Commissioned work, both biological and non-biological, undertaken offering a wide variety of applicable microscopical techniques.

Military History Picture Library, 3 Barton Buildings, Bath BA1 2JR *tel* (0225) 334213. Prints, engravings, photos, colour transparencies covering all aspects of warfare and uniforms from ancient times to present.

Mirror Syndication International, Unique House, 21-31 Woodfield Road, London W9 2BA *tel* 071-266 1133 *fax* 071-266 2563. Photo library specialising in pop, Royalty and personalities. Agents for Mirror Group Newspapers, The British Tourist Authority and other leading magazine publishers.

*Monitor Syndication (1960), 17 Old Street, London EC1V 9HL *tel* 071-253 7071 *fax* 071-251 4405. *Contact:* Ian Hendry. Specialists in portrait photos of leading national and international personalities from politics, trade unions, entertainment, sport, Royalty and well-known buildings in London. Incorporates the **City Syndication** library.

Motorcycles Unlimited (1993), 106 Wilberforce Road, Finsbury Park, London N4 2SU *tel* 071-354 1229 *fax* 071-704 0646. *Owner:* Roland Brown. Bikes of all kinds, from latest roadsters to classics, racers to tourers. Detailed information available on all machines pictured.

Mountain Dynamics (1990), Heathcourt, Morven Way, Monaltrie, Ballater AB35 5SF *tel* (03397) 55081 *fax* (03397) 55526. *Proprietor:* Graham P. Adams. Scottish and European mountains – from ground to summits – in panoramic

(6 × 17 cm), 5 × 4 in and medium format. Commissions undertaken. *Terms:* 50%.

Mountain Visions (1984), Graham and Roslyn Elson, 25 The Mallards, Langstone, Havant, Hants PO9 1SS   *tel* (0705) 478441. Colour transparencies of mountaineering, skiing, and associated travel, in Europe, Africa, Himalayas, Arctic, Far East and Australia. Do not act as agents for other photographers.

*****David Muscroft Snooker Photography** and **David Muscroft Picture Library** (1977), 16 Broadfield Road, Heeley, Sheffield S8 0XJ   *tel* (0742) 589299   *fax* (0742) 550113. Snooker; most other sports, Northern England news, personalities, features, events; Falkland Islands from 1880.

The Mustograph Agency, 19 Rathbone Street, London W1P 1AF   *tel* 071-636 6128/9   *fax* 071-637 4317. Britain only: b&w general subjects of countryside life, work, history and scenery.

National Motor Museum, Beaulieu, Photographic Library, Beaulieu, Hants SO42 7ZN   *tel* (0590) 612345   *fax* (0590) 612655. All aspects of motoring, cars, commercial vehicles, motor cycles, traction engines, etc. Illustrations of period scenes and motor sport. Also large library of 5 × 4 in and smaller colour transparencies of veteran, vintage and modern cars, commercial vehicles and motor cycles.

*****Natural History Photographic Agency**—see **NHPA.**

Natural Image, Dr Bob Gibbons (1982), 49 Bickerley Road, Ringwood, Hants BH24 1EG   *tel/fax* (0425) 478742. Colour library covering natural history, habitats, countryside and gardening (UK and world-wide); special emphasis on conservation. Commissions undertaken. *Terms:* 50%.

News Blitz International, Via Cimabue 5, 00196 Rome, Italy   *tel* 32 01 489, 32 00 620   *fax* 32 19 014. *Contact:* Giovanni A. Congiu. News and general library.

*****Newsfocus Press Photograph Agency Ltd** (1989), 18 Rosebery Avenue, London EC1R 4TD   *tel* 071-328 8759. *Contact:* David Fowler. Specialises in colour and b&w portrait photos of leading British and international personalities, especially politics, entertainment, Royalty, trade unions, media. No search/service fees to clients. *Terms:* 50%; occasional outright purchase.

*****NHPA** (Natural History Photographic Agency), Little Tye, 57 High Street, Ardingly, West Sussex RH17 6TB   *tel* (0444) 892514   *fax* (0444) 892168. Represents more than 100 of the world's leading natural history photographers covering a wide range of fauna and flora, landscapes and environmental subjects. Specialisations include high-speed photography, a large Kalahari Bushmen collection, and the wildlife of North America and southern Africa. Recent additions to the files include strong coverage on Arctic wildlife and underwater photography, plus the work of new contributors in Poland, France, Germany, East Africa and the USA. UK agents for Australasian Nature Transparencies.

*****The Northern Picture Library,** Greenheys Business Centre, 10 Pencroft Way, Manchester M15 6JJ   *tel* 061-226 2007   *fax* 061-226 2022. *Proprietor:* Roy Conchie. General library covering Britain, the world, industry, sport, leisure, etc. Submissions considered from other photographers. Assignments undertaken.

*****Operation Raleigh**—see **Raleigh International.**

Orion Press, 1-13 Kanda Jimbocho, Chiyoda-ku, Tokyo 101, Japan   *tel* (03) 3295-1400   *telex* J2 4447 ORIONPRS   *fax* (03) 3295-0227. All subjects in all formats.

*Christine Osborne Pictures/MEP (1984), 53A Crimsworth Road, London SW8 4RJ *tel/fax* 071-720 6951. Colour and b&w. Middle East and North Africa; South-East Asia and Australia; Indian sub-continent; long-haul travel; tourism; environment; people and way-of-life; religions, vanishing cultures, ethnic minorities, EU.

*Oxford Scientific Films Ltd, Photo Library, Long Hanborough, Oxon OX8 8LL *tel* (0993) 881881 *fax* (0993) 882808. Comprehensive collection of colour transparencies and film footage of wildlife and scenics world-wide; special effects; illustrated articles on natural history topics. UK agents for *Animals Animals* and Photo Researchers (Nature Source), New York and *Okapia*, Frankfurt. Representatives in New York, Tokyo, Milan, Barcelona, Frankfurt, Copenhagen, Paris, Amsterdam, Buenos Aires.

*PA Photo Library (1902), The Press Association, 85 Fleet Street, London EC4P 4BE *tel* 071-353 7440 *fax* 071-353 0784. Over five million news and feature photos from 1902 to present day. International material includes photos from AFP, DPA and EPA.

*Panos Pictures (1986), 9 White Lion Street, London N1 9PD *tel* 071-837 7505 (direct line)/278 1111 *fax* 071-278 0345. Third World and Eastern European documentary photos focusing on social, political and economic issues with a special emphasis on environment and development. Files on agriculture, education, energy, environment, family life, festivals, food, health, industry, landscape, people, politics, pollution, refugees, religions, rural life, transport, urban life, water, weather. *Terms:* 50%.

*Papilio Natural History Library (1988), 44 Palestine Grove, Merton, London SW19 2QN *tel/fax* 081-687 2202. *Contacts:* Robert Pickett, Justine Bowler. World-wide coverage of natural history and environmental subjects; travel commissions undertaken.

*Ann & Bury Peerless, 22 King's Avenue, Minnis Bay, Birchington-on-Sea, Kent CT7 9QL *tel* (0843) 841428 *fax* (0843) 848321. Art, architecture, geography, history, social and cultural aspects in India, Pakistan, Bangladesh, Sri Lanka, Thailand, Malaysia and parts of the Middle East, Egypt and Africa. Specialist material on world religions: Hinduism, Buddhism, Jainism, Christianity, Islam, Sikhism. Recent additions: Morocco, Russia: St Petersburg and Moscow, Samarkand and Bukhara, Taiwan and Beijing.

Chandra S. Perera Cinetra (1958), 437 Pethiyagoda, Kelaniya, Sri Lanka *tel* 521885 *telex* 21193/21213 CE *fax* 541414 OTS ATTN CHANDRA PERERA. B&w and colour library including news, wildlife, religious, social, political, sports, adventure, environmental, forestry, nature and tourism. Photographic and journalistic features on any subject.

*Photo Flora (1982), 46 Jacoby Place, Priory Road, Birmingham B5 7UN *tel* 021-471 3300. Comprehensive collection of British wild plants; Mediterranean wild plants and travel; Egypt, India, Tibet, China, Nepal.

*Photo Library International, PO Box 75, Leeds LS7 3NZ *tel* (0532) 623005 *fax* (0532) 625366. Colour transparencies only. Most subjects. New material always welcome.

Photo Link (1990), 126 Quarry Lane, Northfield, Birmingham B31 2QD *tel/ fax* 021-475 8712. *Contact:* Mike Vines. Colour and b&w aviation library, covering subjects from 1909 to the present day. Specialises in air-to-air photography. Assignments undertaken.

Photo Resources, The Orchard, Marley Lane, Kingston, Canterbury, Kent CT4 6JH *tel* (0227) 830075 *fax* (0227) 831135. Ancient civilisations, art, archaeology, world religions, myth, and museum objects covering the period from 30,000 BC to AD 1900. European birds, butterflies, trees.

*Photofusion, 17A Electric Lane, Brixton, London SW9 8LA *tel* 071-738 5774 *fax* 071-738 5509. Collection of 50,000 b&w photos and 15,000 colour transparencies on contemporary social issues, including disability, education, family, health, homelessness and work.

*The Photographers' Library (1978), 81A Endell Street, Covent Garden, London WC2H 9AJ *tel* 071-836 5591. Requires transparency material on world-wide travel, industry, agriculture, commerce, sport, people, leisure, girls, scenic. Colour only. *Terms:* 50%.

*Pictor International Ltd, Lymehouse Studios, 30-31 Lyme Street, London NW1 0EE *tel* 071-482 0478 *fax* 071-267 1396. Offices in 17 countries. All subjects. *Rates:* 50%.

*Picturepoint Ltd, 94B Dedworth Road, Windsor, Berks. SL4 5AY *tel* (0753) 833680 *fax* (0753) 833681. Have ready world-wide markets for high quality colour transparencies. Any subject other than *news*. Minimum of 250 pictures in first submission. Send by Registered Mail enclosing stamps or IRC for returns. *Terms:* 5-year contract, 50% commission.

Sylvia Pitcher (1968), 75 Bristol Road, Forest Gate, London E7 8HG *tel* 081-552 8308. Specialist in blues, jazz and old-time country musicians, etc., including cities and landscapes relevant to the music.

Pixfeatures (Mr P.G. Wickman), 5 Latimer Road, Barnet, Herts. EN5 5NU *tel* 081-449 9946 *fax* 081-441 6246. Picture-features, preferably topical. Especially for sale to British, German, South African, Spanish and American magazines. *Terms:* 35% of all sales, unless otherwise arranged.

*Planet Earth Pictures: Seaphot Ltd (1969), 4 Harcourt Street, London W1H 1DS *tel* 071-262 4427 *fax* 071-706 4042. All aspects of natural history and the natural environment, farming, fishing, pollution and conservation.

*Popperfoto (Paul Popper Ltd), The Old Mill, Overstone Farm, Overstone, Northampton NN6 0AB *tel* (0604) 670670 *fax* (0604) 670635. Offer documentary and feature photos (b&w and colour) from all countries of the world. Collection includes Exclusive News Agency, Odhams Periodicals Photo Library, Conway Picture Library, Reuters, United Press International (UPI) Library, Planet, Agence-France Presse and European Pressphoto Agency.

Power Pix International Picture Library—see **S. & I. Williams, Power Pix International Picture Library.**

*Premaphotos Wildlife, Amberstone, 1 Kirland Road, Bodmin, Cornwall PL30 5JQ *tel/fax* (0208) 72302. Library of 35 mm transparencies of own work only by K.G. Preston-Mafham and Dr R.A. Preston-Mafham. Wide range of natural history subjects from around the world. All work done in the field.

*Press Association Photos (news picture service of The Press Association)—see **PA Photo Library.**

Pro-file Photo Library (1982), 2B Winner Commercial Building, 401-403 Lockhart Road, Hong Kong *tel* (852) 5747788 *fax* (852) 5748884; 460 North Bridge Road, 04–01, Singapore 0718 *tel* (65) 336-5322 *fax* (65) 338-4493. *Director:* Neil Farrin. General photo library. *Terms:* 50%.

*Punch Cartoon Library (1841), 245 Blackfriars Road, London SE1 9UZ *tel* 071-921 5900 *fax* 071-928 5158. Comprehensive collection of cartoons and illustrations, indexed under subject categories: humour, historical events, politics, fashion, sport, personalities, etc.

*Railways – Milepost 92½ (1969), Milepost 92½, Newton Harcourt, Leics. LE8 0FH *tel* (0533) 592068 *fax* (0533) 593001. Comprehensive collection of railway photos, including British Rail's library of railway and scenic pictures of the UK and abroad, Colin Garratt's collection of world steam trains and thousands of other professional railway photos.

*Raleigh International Picture Library (1978), Raleigh House, 27 Parson's Green Lane, London SW6 4HS *tel* 071-371 8585 *fax* 071-371 5116. *Contacts:* Mark Bainbridge, Roger Askew. Source of stock colour images from locations around the world: the 50,000+ images are updated eight times a year. Also, a Directory of International Travel and Location Photographers, containing the catalogues of various editorial and location photography specialists, plus a wide range of photo-features from world-wide locations, which are available as exclusives for national and international publication. Free research for first-time users, and open to researchers by appointment, 9.30-5.30 weekdays.

*Retna Pictures Ltd (1984), 1 Fitzroy Mews, Cleveland Street, London W1P 5DQ *tel* 071-388 3444 *fax* 071-383 7151. Library of colour transparencies and b&w prints of rock and pop performers, show business personalities, celebrities, actors and actresses, travel and general stock library.

*Retrograph Nostalgia Archive (1984), 164 Kensington Park Road, London W11 2ER *tel* 071-727 9378/9426 *fax* 071-229 3395. Specialising in world-wide advertising, packaging, posters, fashion and fine art illustrations from 1870-1970. Research service and presentations on request.

Rich Research (1978), 1 Bradby House, Carlton Hill, St John's Wood, London NW8 9XE *tel* 071-624 7755. *Director:* Diane Rich. Speedy and innovative picture research service. Visuals found for all sectors of publishing and the media. Stock images, commissioned photography and artwork. Negotiations of rights and fees.

*Ann Ronan at Image Select, Suite H1, Kebbell House, Delta Gain, Carpenders Park, Watford, Herts. WD1 5BE *tel* 081-421 3131/863 4882 *fax* 081-861 4755. Woodcuts, engravings, etc., social and political history plus history of science and technology, including military and space.

Roundhouse Ornithology Collection (1991), Roundhouse Publishing Ltd, PO Box 140, Oxford OX2 7FF *tel* (0865) 512682 *fax* (0865) 59594. *Director:* Alan T. Goodworth. Colour library specialising in birds of UK, Europe, Middle East (especially), North Africa, Far East and South America.

*Royal Geographical Society Picture Library (1830), 1 Kensington Gore, London SW7 2AR *tel/fax* 071-584 4381 (direct line) *tel* 071-589 5466 ext 152 *fax* 071-584 4447. *Contact:* picture library manager. World-wide coverage of geography, travel, exploration, expeditions and cultural environment from 1870s to the present.

*The Royal Photographic Society (1853), The Octagon, Milsom Street, Bath BA1 1DN *tel* (0225) 462841 *fax* (0225) 448688. Exhibitions; library of books, photos and photographic equipment.

Royal Society for Asian Affairs, 2 Belgrave Square, London SW1X 8PJ *tel* 071-235 5122. Archive library of original 19th and 20th century b&w photos, glass slides, etc., of Asia. Publishes *Asian Affairs* 3 p.a.

Dawn Runnals Photographic Library (1985), 5 St Marys Terrace, Kenwyn Road, Truro, Cornwall TR1 3SW *tel* (0872) 79353. General library: land and sea-scapes, flora and fauna, sport, animals, people, buildings, boats, harbours, miscellaneous section and some specialised subjects – details on application. Other photographers' work not accepted. Sae appreciated with enquiries.

*The Russia and Republics Photo Library (1988), Conifers House, Cheapside Lane, Denham, Uxbridge, Middlesex UB9 5AE *tel* (0895) 834814 *fax* (0895) 834028. *Library manager:* Mark Wadlow. Colour photo library specialising in cities, towns, famous landmarks and people. Do not accept other photographers' work.

*Peter Sanders Photography (1987), 9 Meades Lane, Chesham, Bucks. HP5 1ND *tel/fax* (0494) 773674. Specialises in Islamic world, but now expanding into other world religions, beliefs and cultures.

Steffi Schubert, Wildlife Conservation Collection Photographic Library (1990), Avondale Farm, Southwold Road, Holton, nr Halesworth, Suffolk IP19 8PW *tel/fax* (0986) 872777. All aspects of British wildlife and fauna.

*Science Photo Library (1979), 112 Westbourne Grove, London W2 5RU *tel* 071-727 4712 *fax* 071-727 6041. Scientific photography of all kinds – medicine, technology, Space, nature.

Scotland in Focus Picture Library (1988), 22 Fleming Place, Fountainhall, Galashiels, Selkirkshire TD1 2TA *tel/fax* (0578 760) 256. Library specialising in all aspects of Scotland, including British wildlife and natural history subjects. All Scottish material required on 35 mm and upwards, medium format preferred. Photographers must enclose return postage. *Commission: 50%.*

SCR Photo Library (1943), Society for Co-operation in Russian and Soviet Studies, 320 Brixton Road, London SW9 6AB *tel* 071-274 2282. Russian and Soviet life and history. Comprehensive coverage of cultural subjects: art, theatre, folk art, costume, music; agriculture and industry, architecture, armed forces, education, history, places, politics, science, sport. Also posters and theatre props, artistic reference and advice. Research by appointment only.

*Sealand Aerial Photography (1976), Goodwood Airfield, Goodwood, Chichester, West Sussex PO18 0PH *tel* (0243) 781025 *fax* (0243) 531422. Aerial photo coverage of any subject that can be photographed from the air in the UK. Most stock on 2¼ in format colour negative/transparency. Subjects constantly updated from new flying.

*S & G Press Agency Ltd, 68 Exmouth Market, London EC1R 4RA *tel* 071-278 1223. Press photos and vast photo library. Send photos, but negatives preferred.

Mick Sharp (1981), Eithinog, Waun, Penisarwaun, Caernarfon, Gwynedd LL55 3PW *tel/fax* Llanberis (0286) 872425. Archaeology, ancient monuments, architecture, churches, countryside, environment, history, landscape, travel and tourism. Emphasis on British Isles, but material from many other countries including France, Iraq, Morocco and USA. Access to other similar photo collections. B&w prints from 5 × 4 in negatives, and 35 mm and 6 × 4.5 cm colour transparencies.

*Brian and Sal Shuel—see Collections.

Sites, Sights and Cities (1990), PO Box 92, Penzance, Cornwall TR18 2XL *tel/fax* (0736) 65790. *Director:* Paul Devereux. Ancient monuments, mainly in Britain, Egypt and USA; city features in UK, Europe and USA; general nature shots.

*Skishoot – Offshoot (1986), 28 Dalebury Road, London SW17 7HH *tel* 081-767 0059 *fax* 081-767 6680. *Partner:* Felice Eyston. Library specialising in all aspects of skiing and travel. Assignments undertaken. *Terms: 50%.*

Skyscan Balloon Photography (1984), Oak House, Toddington, Cheltenham, Glos. GL54 5BY   *tel* (0242) 621357   *fax* (0242) 621343. Unique aerial views of British landscapes, cities, heritage sites, etc., taken from remotely controlled cameras suspended beneath a tethered balloon, which produce unusual viewpoints and very high definition photos.

The Slide File (1978), 79 Merrion Square South, Dublin 2, Republic of Ireland   *tel* (01) 6766850   *fax* (01) 6608332. Specialise in Eire and Northern Ireland: landscapes, Irish natural history, agriculture and industry, Irish people and their traditions, Celtic heritage.

Patrick Smith Associates (1964), Gloucester House, High Street, Borth, Dyfed SY24 5HZ   *tel* (0970) 871296. South London 1950-1977, mid-Wales, aviation; also The Patrick Smith Collection of London photos, now in The Museum of London.

Society for Anglo-Chinese Understanding (1965), Sally & Richard Greenhill Photo Library, 357a Liverpool Road, London N1 1NL   *tel* 071-607 8549   *fax* 071-607 7151. Colour and b&w prints of China, late 1960s-1989.

Society for Co-operation in Russian and Soviet Studies—see **SCR Photo Library.**

Source Photographic Archives (1974), 66 Claremont Road, Sandymount, Dublin 4, Republic of Ireland   *tel* (01) 6607090. *Director:* Thomas Kennedy. Mostly recent photos by living photographers on many different subjects.

Southern Media Services, division of Maximedia Pty Ltd, PO Box 268, Springwood, NSW 2777, Australia   *tel* (018) 211232. *Directors:* Nic van Oudtshoorn, Daphne van Oudtshoorn. Stock colour library; also illustrated features.

Spectrum Colour Library, 41-42 Berners Street, London W1P 3AA   *tel* 071-637 1587   *fax* 071-637 3681. Extensive general library of high-quality transparencies, for world-wide marketing, including electronically. Photographer's information pack available. Purchases photos and collections of photos.

Sporting Pictures (UK) Ltd, 7A Lambs Conduit Passage, Holborn, London WC1R 4RG   *tel* 071-405 4500   *fax* 071-831 7991. *Director:* Crispin J. Thruston; *librarian:* Mark Whitmore. Specialises in sports, sporting events, sportsmen.

Peter Stiles Picture Library, 4 Rockingham Close, Durrington, Worthing, West Sussex BN13 2NU   *tel* (0903) 690764   *fax* (0903) 503147. Specialises in horticulture, plus natural history, pictorial views. Sequences and illustrated features. Own pictures only. Commissions undertaken.

The Still Moving Picture Company (1991), 67A Logie Green Road, Edinburgh EH7 4HF   *tel* 031-557 9697   *fax* 031-557 9699. 250,000 pictures of Scotland and all things Scottish; sport (Allsport agent for Scotland).

Stockphotos, 7 Langley Street, London WC2H 9JA   *tel* 071-240 7361   *fax* 071-831 1489. Stock colour library covering travel, people, business, industry, scenics, sport and leisure. Free catalogue available on request.

Tony Stone Images, Worldwide House, 116 Bayham Street, London NW1 0BA   *tel* 071-267 8988   *fax* 071-722 9305. International photo library. Subjects required: travel, people, natural history, commerce, industry, technology, sport, etc. Check first with Creative Department. *Terms:* 50%.

Survival Anglia Photo Library (1960), 48 Leicester Square, London WC2H 7FB   *tel* 071-321 0101   *fax* 071-493 2598. Outstanding natural history collection, by some of world's top wildlife photographers, the result of over 30 years of the award-winning ITV programme 'Survival'. *Terms:* 50%.

Sutcliffe Gallery, 1 Flowergate, Whitby, North Yorkshire YO21 3BA   *tel* (0947) 602239   *fax* (0947) 820287. Collection of 19th century photography, all by Frank M. Sutcliffe Hon. FRPS (1853-1941), especially inshore fishing boats and fishing community; also farming interests. Period covered 1872 to 1910.

Charles Tait Photo Library (1978), Kelton, St Ola, Orkney KW15 1TR   *tel* (0856) 873738/875003   *fax* (0856) 875313. Colour photo library specialising in islands: coverage includes Orkney, Shetland and Western Isles, as well as many parts of Scotland and France. Subjects include archaeology, landscapes, transport, industry, seascapes, events, people and wildlife, especially seabirds and seals. Panoramic landscapes using Alpa Rotocam a speciality. Publisher of postcards, calendars and guidebooks.

The Tank Museum Photo Library & Archive (c.1946), The Tank Museum, Bovington Camp, Wareham, Dorset BH20 6JG   *tel* (0929) 403463   *fax* (0929) 405360. International collection, from 1900 to present, of armoured fighting vehicles and military transport, including tanks, armoured cars, personnel carriers, self-propelled artillery carriers, missile launchers, cars, lorries and tractors.

*Telegraph Colour Library, The Innovation Centre, 225 Marsh Wall, London E14 9FX   *tel* 071-987 1212   *fax* 071-538 3309. Stock photography agency covering a wide subject range: business, sport, people, industry, animals, medical, nature, space, travel and graphics. Sameday service for all UK clients. Free catalogues available upon request.

Theatre Museum, National Museum of the Performing Arts, 1ᴇ Tavistock Street, Covent Garden, London WC2E 7PA   *tel* 071-836 7891   *fax* 071-836 5148. In addition to extensive public displays on live entertainment, the Museum has an unrivalled collection of programmes, playbills, prints, photos, plays, books and press cuttings relating to performers and productions from the 17th century onwards. Available by appointment, free of charge through the Study Room, open Tues-Fri, 1030-1630. Reprographic services available.

*Three Lions—see **Hulton Deutsch Collection.**

*Topham Picture Source (1928), PO Box 33, Edenbridge, Kent TN8 5PB   *tel* Cowden (0342) 850313   *fax* (0342) 850244. Historic library: personalities, warfare, Royalty, topography, France, natural history. World news file from original sources: UPI, INP, Press Association, Central News, Planet News, Alfieri, Pictorial Press, Syndicated Features Ltd, etc.

*B.M. Totterdell Photography (1989), Constable Cottage, Burlings Lane, Knockholt, Kent TN14 7PE   *tel* (0959) 532001. Specialist volleyball library, covering all aspects of the sport.

Transworld Feature Syndicate (UK) Ltd, Scope Features, 26 St Cross Street, London EC1N 8UH   *tel* 071-831 0013. *Contact:* Valerie Dobson. Colour: situations/beauty pictures.

*Travel Images (1990), The Penthouse, 6 Princes Buildings, Clifton, Bristol BS8 4LB   *tel* (0272) 706196   *fax* (0272) 706115. *Sales and marketing manager:* Frances Allen. Comprehensive travel library, covering over 80 countries.

Travel Photo International, 8 Delph Common Road, Aughton, Ormskirk, Lancs. L39 5DW   *tel/fax* (0695) 423720. Touristic interest including scenery, towns, monuments, historic buildings, archaeological sites, local people. Specialises in travel brochures and books. *Terms:* 50%.

Travel Trade Photography, Colour Library, 22 Princedale Road, London W11 4NJ   *tel* 071-727 5471. *Principal:* Teddy Schwarz. Landscapes, townscapes, ancient monuments and buildings of historical interest in England and foreign countries, peoples, and their customs. Return postage essential. *Terms: 50%*.

*Tropix Photographic Library (1973), 156 Meols Parade, Meols, Wirral, Merseyside L47 6AN   *tel/fax* 051-632 1698. All human and environmental aspects of tropics, sub-tropics and non-tropical developing countries. Environmental issues are accepted from locations world-wide. New collections welcome but preliminary enquiry in writing essential; send sae for details. *Terms: 50%*.

Ulster Photographic Agency (1985), 22 Casaeldona Park, Belfast, Northern Ireland BT6 9RB   *tel* (0232) 795738. Motoring and motorsport. *Terms: 50% or outright purchase*.

*Universal Pictorial Press & Agency Ltd (UPPA) (1929), New Bridge Street House, 30-34 New Bridge Street, London EC4V 6BN   *tel* 071-248 6730   *telex* 8952718 UNIPIX G   *fax* 071-489 8982. Notable Royal, political, company, academic, legal, diplomatic, church, military, pop, arts, entertainment and sports personalities and well-known views and buildings. Commercial, industrial, corporate and public relations photo assignments undertaken.

John Vickers Theatre Collection, 27 Shorrolds Road, London SW6 7TR   *tel* 071-385 5774. Archives of British theatre and portraits of actors, writers and musicians by John Vickers from 1938-1974.

Vidocq Photo Library (1983), 162 Burwell Meadow, Witney, Oxon OX8 7GD   *tel/fax* (0993) 778518. Extensive coverage of wide range of subjects. Register of Photographers includes many specialists who market their work exclusively through the library. New photographers welcome. *Terms: 60%* to photographer.

*Viewfinder Colour Photo Library (1984), 90 Whiteladies Road, Bristol BS8 2QN   *tel* (0272) 237268/239449   *fax* (0272) 239198. Colour library covering industry, agriculture, transport, people, world-wide travel; detailed sections on South West England and Wales. *Terms: 50%*.

Simon Warner, Whitestone Farm, Stanbury, Keighley, West Yorkshire BD22 0JW   *tel* Haworth (0535) 644644. Landscape photographer with own stock pictures of northern England, North Wales and NW Scotland.

*Waterways Photo Library (1976), 39 Manor Court Road, London W7 3EJ   *tel* 081-840 1659   *fax* 081-567 0605. *Contact:* Derek Pratt. British inland waterways; canals and rivers; bridges, aqueducts, locks and all waterside architectural features; waterway holidays, boats, fishing; town and countryside scenes. No other photographers' work required.

*Weimar Archive (1983), 8-9 The Incline, Coalport, Telford, Shropshire TF8 7HR   *tel* (0952) 680050   *fax* (0952) 587184. Germany, specialising in World War I, Weimar Republic and Third Reich; but all aspects of social, political and cultural life in central Europe from Middle Ages until 1945; plus a comprehensive collection of German painting and sculpture, Soviet posters and cartoons 1917-1945, and German Democratic Republic.

Welfare History Picture Library (1975), Heatherbank Museum of Social Work, 163 Mugdock Road, Milngavie, Glasgow G62 8ND   *tel* 041-956 5923. Social history and social work, especially child welfare, workhouses, prisons, hospitals, slum clearance, women's movement, social reformers and their work. Catalogue on request.

Westcountry Pictures (1989), 23 Southernhay West, Exeter, Devon EX1 1PR   *tel* (0392) 71937   *fax* (0392) 51745. *Contact:* Peter Cooper. All aspects of Devon and Cornwall.

Western Americana Picture Library, 3 Barton Buildings, Bath BA1 2JR *tel* (0225) 334213. Prints, engravings, photos and colour transparencies on the American West, cowboys, gunfighters, Indians, including pictures by Frederic Remington and Charles Russell, etc. Interested in buying pictures on American West.

Roy J. Westlake ARPS, Photo Library, 31 Redwood Drive, Plympton, Plymouth PL7 3FS *tel* (0752) 336444. Britain, especially the West Country. Landscapes, seascapes, communications, leisure activities, etc., suitable for holiday brochures, advertising, book illustrations, etc. Also camping, caravanning and inland waterways subjects in Britain, including rivers and canals. Other photographers' work not accepted.

*Eric Whitehead Picture Agency and Library—see **Cumbria Picture Library.**

Derek G. Widdicombe, Worldwide Photographic Library, 'Oldfield', High Street, Clayton West, Huddersfield HD8 9NS *tel/fax* (0484) 862638. Landscapes, seascapes, architecture, human interest of Britain and abroad. Moods and seasons, buildings and natural features. Holds copyright of Noel Habgood FRPS Collection.

*Wilderness Photographic Library, Mill Barn, Broad Raine, Sedbergh, Cumbria LA10 5ED *tel* (05396) 20196 *fax* (05396) 21293. *Director:* John Noble FRGS. Specialist library in mountain and wilderness regions, especially polar. Associated aspects of people, places, natural history, geographical features, exploration and mountaineering, adventure sports, travel.

*Wildlife Matters Photographic Library (1980), Dr John Feltwell, Marlham, Henley Down, Battle, East Sussex TN33 9BN *tel* (0424) 830566 *fax* (0424) 830224. 56 mm sq and 6 × 4 cm colour transparencies: ecology, conservation and environment; habitats and pollution; agriculture and horticulture; general natural history, entomology; Mediterranean wildlife; rainforests; aerial pics of countryside UK, Europe, USA.

*David Williams Picture Library (1989), 50 Burlington Avenue, Glasgow G12 0LH *tel* 041-339 7823 *fax* 041-337 3031. Specialises in colour transparencies of Scotland and Iceland (2¼ in and 35 mm). Subjects include landscapes, towns, villages, buildings and antiquities. Catalogue available. Commissions undertaken.

S. & I. Williams, Power Pix International Picture Library (1968), Castle Lodge, Wenvoe, Cardiff CF5 6AD *tel* (0222) 595163 *fax* (0222) 593905. Worldwide travel, people and views, girl and 'mood-pix', sub-aqua, aircraft, flora, fauna, agriculture, children. Agents world-wide.

Timothy Woodcock (1983), 45 Lyewater, Crewkerne, Somerset TA18 8BB *tel* (0460) 74488 *fax* (0460) 74988. British and Eire landscape, seascape, architecture and heritage; children, parenthood, adults and education; gardens and containers; mountain biking. Location commissions undertaken. *Terms:* 50%.

*Woodmansterne Ltd, Watford Business Park, Watford, Herts. WD1 8RD *tel* (0923) 228236 *fax* (0923) 245788. Britain, Europe, Holy Land; architecture, cathedral and stately home interiors; general art subjects; museum collections; natural history, butterflies, geography, volcanoes, transport, Space; opera and ballet; major state occasions; British heritage.

*World Pictures (formerly **Feature-Pix Colour Library**), 85a Great Portland Street, London W1N 5RA *tel* 071-437 2121/436 0440 *fax* 071-439 1307. *Directors:* Gerry Brenes, Joan Brenes, David Brenes. Over 600,000 medium and large format colour transparencies aimed at travel and travel-related markets. Extensive coverage of cities, countries and specific resort areas, together with material of an emotive nature, i.e. children, couples and families on holiday, all types of winter and summer sporting activities, motoring abroad, etc. *Terms:* 50%; major contributing photographers 60%.

Murray Wren Picture Library, 3 Hallgate, London SE3 9SG   *tel* 081-852 7556. Outdoor nudes; nudist holiday resorts and activities in Europe and elsewhere; historic and erotic art of the nude through the ages.

The Allan Wright Photo Library (1986), The Stables, Parton, Castle Douglas, Kirkcudbrightshire, Scotland DG7 3NB   *tel* (06447) 260   *fax* (06447) 202. North Sea oil – offshore activities; all aspects of Dumfries and Galloway region; Argyll and general Scottish landscape.

Yorkshire in Focus, 75A Selby Road, Garforth, Leeds LS25 1LR   *tel* (0532) 863016. Transparencies, 35 mm/6 × 9 cm. Landscapes, rivers, buildings, tourist attractions in Yorkshire and the north. Camping and caravanning subjects: sites, caravans, motor caravans, tents and all equipment. Large collection of touristy stock subjects. Assignments undertaken.

Picture researchers are referred to
the list of government offices in the
Preparation of material, resources
section.

The how-dun-it

Suppose some little physical fact has struck you; for instance, a green dress seen under a red light can look black. So you devise a situation where an absolutely unimpeachable witness sees the murderer in black leaving the scene of the crime. Then you tell the story of the murder and the subsequent investigation, adroitly working in the fact that there was a red light shining at the vital time and place, using one of the ways of tricking your reader into 'noticing and not noticing' this that we looked at in the previous chapter, and you also harp like mad on the impossibility of a person in a black dress or suit having been on hand at the moment the murder was committed. (You had better find a cleverer central device for a book than my example, though.)

from *Writing Crime Fiction* by H R F Keating (A & C Black, £7.99)

Classified Index of Picture Agencies and Libraries

This index gives the major subject area(s) only of each entry in the main listing which begins on p. 351, and should be used with discrimination.

Aerial Photography

Aerofilms Ltd
Aviation Picture Library

Geo Aerial Photography
Sealand Aerial Photography

Skyscan Balloon Photography

Africa

Animal Photography
Hamish Brown
Sue Cunningham
  Photographic

David Hosking (Animals)
Images of Africa Photobank
Joe Filmbase

Panos Pictures
Tropix Photographic Library

Agriculture and Farming

The Anthony Blake Photo
  Library
Blitz International News &
  Photo Agency
Dennis Davis Photography

Frontline Photo Press Agency
Heritage & Natural History
  Photography
Frank Lane Picture Agency
  Ltd

Holt Studios International
Planet Earth Pictures
Sutcliffe Gallery

Aircraft and Aviation

Air Photo Supply
Aviation Photographs
  International

Aviation Picture Library
Dr Alan Beaumont
T. Malcolm English

Photo Link
Patrick Smith Associates

Archaeology, Antiquities, Ancient Monuments and Heritage

A.A. and A. Ancient Art &
  Architecture Collection
Lesley and Roy Adkins
  Picture Library
Rev. J. Catling Allen
C.M. Dixon

English Heritage Photo
  Library
Werner Forman Archive
Fortean Picture Library
Heritage & Natural History
  Photography

Pat Hodgson Library
Chandra S. Perera Cinetra
Mick Sharp
Sites, Sights and Cities
Skyscan Balloon Photography
Woodmansterne Ltd

Architecture, Houses and Interiors

A.A. & A. Ancient Art and
  Architecture Collection
ARCAID Architectural
  Photography and Picture
  Library
Archivio Veneziano

Bookart Architecture Picture
  Library
Dennis Davis Photography
English Heritage Photo
  Library

Houses & Interiors
  Photographic Features
  Agency
Woodmansterne Ltd

Art, Sculpture and Crafts

A.A. & A. Ancient Art and
  Architecture Collection
Archivio Veneziano
Bodleian Library

Bookart Architecture Picture
  Library
Bridgeman Art Library
Crafts Council

Werner Forman Archive
Photo Resources
Retrograph Nostalgia Archive

Asia

Douglas Dickins Photo
 Library
Images of India
Ann & Bury Peerless

Photo Flora
Royal Society for Asian
 Affairs

Society for Anglo-Chinese
 Understanding

Australia

Australia Pictures

Britain (*See also* **Ireland, Scotland, Wales**)

Rev. J. Catling Allen
John Blake Picture Library
Britain on View Photographic
 Library
David Broadbent/Derbyshire
 Scene
Collections
Cumbria Picture Library
English Heritage Photo
 Library
Fotoccompli—The Picture
 Library
Leslie Garland Picture Library
 (North England)
Global Syndications

Isle of Wight Pictures
Just Europe
Lakeland Life Picture Library
 (Lake District)
Landscape Only
Merseyside Photo Library
David Muscroft Picture
 Library (North England)
The Mustograph Agency
Spectrum Colour Library
Vidocq Photo Library
Viewfinder Colour Photo
 Library (South West
 England)

Simon Warner (North
 England)
Westcountry Pictures (Devon,
 Cornwall)
Roy J. Westlake (West
 Country)
Derek G. Widdicombe
Timothy Woodcock
Woodmansterne Ltd
Yorkshire in Focus

Camping and Caravanning

Roy J. Westlake

Yorkshire in Focus

Children and People (*See also* **Social Issues**)

Attard Lifestyle Photolibrary
Collections
Lupe Cunha

Brian Gadsby Picture Library
Robert Haas Photo Library
The Hutchinson Library

Photofusion
Telegraph Colour Library
Timothy Woodcock

Cities and Towns (*See also* **London**)

Lesley and Roy Adkins
 Picture Library

Robert Haas Photo Library
Sites, Sights and Cities

Waterways Photo Library

Civilisations, Cultures and Way of Life

Bryan and Cherry Alexander
 Photography
Werner Forman Archive

Christine Osborne Pictures/
 MEP

Photo Resources

Countryside and Rural Life (*See also* **Landscapes**)

Dr Alan Beaumont
Ron and Christine Foord
Forest Life Picture Library
Tim Graham

Isle of Wight Pictures
Lakeland Life Picture Library
S. & O. Mathews
Sutcliffe Gallery

Waterways Photo Library
Wildlife Matters Photographic
 Library

Developing Countries

Geoslides
Christine Osborne Pictures/
 MEP

Panos Pictures

Tropix Photographic Library

Entertainment (Theatre, Dance, Music)

Aquarius Picture Library
Camera Press Ltd
The Dance Library
Jazz Index

Mander & Mitchenson
  Theatre Collection
Robin May Collection
Sylvia Pitcher

Theatre Museum
John Vickers Theatre
  Collection

Environment, Conservation, Ecology and Habitats

Heather Angel
Aquila Photographics
Ardea London Ltd
Dr Alan Beaumont
Butterflies
Bruce Coleman Ltd
George A. Dey (forestry,
  natural history)
Ecoscene
Environmental Investigation
  Agency

Fogden Natural History
  Photographs
Forest Life Picture Library
Martin and Dorothy Grace
Harper Horticultural Slide
  Library
Holt Studios International
Frank Lane Picture Agency
  Ltd
Chris Mattison

Natural Image
NHPA
Papilio Natural History
  Library
Planet Earth Pictures
Premaphotos Wildlife
Tropix Photographic Library
Wildlife Matters Photographic
  Library

Europe and Eastern Europe (*excluding* UK/Ireland)

Archivio Veneziano (Venice)
Das Photo
James Davis Travel
  Photography
Douglas Dickins Photo
  Library
C.M. Dixon

Global Syndications
  (Scandinavia)
Joe Filmbase
Just Europe
Panos Pictures (Eastern
  Europe)

Russia & Republics
  Photolibrary
Vidocq Photo Library
Weimar Archive (Germany)
David Williams Picture
  Library (Iceland)

Food

The Anthony Blake Photo
  Library
Cephas Picture Library

Footprints Colour Picture
  Library

Retrograph Nostalgia Archive

Gardens, Gardening and Horticulture (*See also* Plant Life)

A-Z Botanical Collection
Ardea London Ltd
B. & B. Photographs
Butterflies
Collections
Dennis Davis Photography
Forest Life Picture Library

Garden Matters Photographic
  Library
John Glover Photography
Harper Horticultural Slide
  Library
Holt Studios
  International

Houses & Interiors
  Photographic Features
  Agency
S. & O. Mathews
Natural Image
Peter Stiles Picture Library
Timothy Woodcock

General and Stock Libraries

Ace Photo Agency
Al Ahram
Aspect Picture Library Ltd
Bandphoto Agency
Barnaby's Picture Library
Stephen Benson Slide Bureau
Blitz International News &
  Photo Agency
J. Allan Cash Photolibrary
Cephas Picture Library
Bruce Coleman Inc.
Bruce Coleman Ltd
Colorific Photo Library

Sylvia Cordaiy Photo Library
C.P.L. (Camerapix Picture
  Library)
C.M. Dixon
Greg Evans International
  Photo Library
Fotocompli—The Picture
  Library
Freelance Focus
Frontline Photo Press Agency
Geo Aerial Photography
GeoScience Features
Geoslides

Robert Harding Picture
  Library
Horizon International
  Creative Images
Hulton Deutsch Collection
The Hutchison Library
The Image Bank
Joe Filmbase
Lears Magical Lanterns
  Museum
The MacQuitty International
  Collection
Merseyside Photo Library

News Blitz International
The Northern Picture Library
Orion Press
Photo Library International
Photofusion
The Photographers' Library
Pictor International Ltd
Picturepoint Ltd
Popperfoto (Paul Popper Ltd)
Pro-file Photo Library
Raleigh International Picture
	Library
Retna Pictures Ltd

Rich Research
Royal Geographical Society
	Picture Library
The Royal Photographic
	Society
Dawn Runnals Photographic
	Library
S & G Press Agency Ltd
Source Photographic Archives
Southern Media Services
Spectrum Colour Library
Stockphotos

Tony Stone Images
Telegraph Colour Library
Universal Pictorial Press &
	Agency Ltd (UPPA)
Vidocq Photo Library
Viewfinder Colour Photo
	Library
Derek G. Widdicombe
S. & I. Williams, Power Pix
	International Picture
	Library
Yorkshire in Focus

Geography, Biogeography and Topography

Arctic Camera
B. & B. Photographs

John Blake Picture Library

Geoslides

Glamour, Moods and Nudes

Attard Lifestyle Photolibrary
The Photographers' Library
Transworld Feature Syndicate
	(UK) Ltd

S. & I. Williams, Power Pix
	International Picture
	Library

Murray Wren Picture Library

Health and Medicine

Lupe Cunha

High-Tech, High-Speed, Macro/Micro, Special Effects and Step-by-Step

Houses & Interiors
	Photographic Features
	Agency (step-by-step)
The Image Bank (high-tech,
	special effects)

Michael Leach (high-speed)
Microscopix
NHPA (high-speed)

Oxford Scientific Films Ltd,
	Photo Library (special
	effects)

History

Bodleian Library
Mary Evans Picture Library
Frost Historical Newspaper
	Collection
Historical Picture Service

Pat Hodgson Library
The Billie Love Historical
	Collection
Mansell Collection Ltd
Pixfeatures

The Royal Photographic
	Society
Topham Picture Source
Weimar Archive (Europe)

Ireland

Picturepoint

The Slide File

Source Photographic Archives

Landscapes and Scenics

Al Ahram
Bookart Architecture Picture
	Library
Cumbria Picture Library
James Davis Travel
	Photography
George A. Dey (Scottish)
Eyeline Photography
Geo Aerial Photography

John Glover Photography
Isle of Wight Pictures
Landscape Only
S. & O. Mathews
Chris Mattison
Picturepoint
Scotland in Focus Picture
	Library
Mick Sharp

Peter Stiles Picture Library
The Still Moving Picture
	Company
Charles Tait Photo Library
Simon Warner
Roy J. Westlake
Derek G. Widdicombe
The Allan Wright Photo
	Library

Latin America

Andes Press Agency
Das Photo

Fogden Natural History
Photographs

London

ARCAID Architectural
Photographic and Picture
Library
Greater London Photograph
Library

Historical Picture Service
The Illustrated London News
Picture Library
Monitor Syndication

Skyscan Balloon Photography
Patrick Smith Associates

Middle East

Stephen Benson Slide Bureau
Das Photo

Christine Osborne Pictures/
MEP

Ann & Bury Peerless

Military and Armed Forces

Air Photo Supply
Aviation Photographs
International
T. Malcolm English

Imperial War Museum
Military History Picture
Library

The Tank Museum Photo
Library & Archive

Mountains

Hamish Brown
Mountain Dynamics
Mountain Visions

Royal Geographical Society
Picture Library

Wilderness Photographic
Library

Natural History (*See also* Environment, Plant life)

A-Z Botanical Collection
Al Ahram
Heather Angel
Animal Photography
Aquila Photographics
Ardea London Ltd
B. & B. Photographs
Dr Alan Beaumont
Bird Images
David Broadbent/Derbyshire
Scene (birds)
Butterflies
Bruce Coleman Ltd
Sylvia Cordaiy Photo Library
Gordon Dickson (fungi,
insects)
Ecoscene
Environmental Investigation
Agency

Fogden Natural History
Photographs
Ron and Christine Foord
(insects)
Footprints Colour Picture
Library
Brian Gadsby Picture Library
Geoscience Features
Martin and Dorothy Grace
Heritage & Natural History
Photography (insects,
especially bees)
David Hosking (birds)
Michael Leach (owls)
Chris Mattison (reptiles,
amphibians)
Natural Image
NHPA

Oxford Scientific Films Ltd,
Photo Library
Papilio Natural History
Library
Planet Earth Pictures
Premaphotos Wildlife
Roundhouse Ornithology
Collection
Steffi Schubert, Wildlife
Conservation Collection
Photographic Library
Scotland in Focus Picture
Library
Peter Stiles Picture Library
Survival Anglia Photo Library
Wildlife Matters Photographic
Agency

News, Features and Photo Features

Academic File News Photos
The Associated Press Ltd
Bandphoto Agency
BIPS
Blitz International News &
Photo Agency

Euro-Parly Services (News
Pix)
Frost Historical Newspaper
Collection
International Press Agency
(Pty) Ltd

News Blitz International
PA Photo Library
Chandra S. Perera Cinetra
Pixfeatures
S & G Press Agency Ltd
Topham Picture Source

North America

American History Picture
Library
Douglas Dickins Photo
Library

Robin May Collection
Western Americana Picture
Library

Nostalgia, Illustrations, Engravings and Cartoons

Allied Artists Ltd
Bodleian Library
Mary Evans Picture Library
Fotomas Index

The Illustrated London News
Picture Library
Lears Magical Lanterns
Museum

The Billie Love Historical
Collection
Punch Cartoon Library
Retrograph Nostalgia Archive

Personalities and Portraits (*See also* **Royalty**)

Aquarius Picture Library
Camera Press Ltd
Mark Gerson Photography
Tim Graham
Pat Hodgson Library
(historical)
JS Library International

Mander & Mitchenson
Theatre Collection
Monitor Syndication
Newsfocus Press Photograph
Agency Ltd
Punch Cartoon Library
Retna Pictures Ltd

The Royal Photographic
Society
Syndication International Ltd
Topham Picture Source
Universal Pictorial Press &
Agency Ltd (UPPA)
John Vickers Theatre
Collection

Plant Life (*See also* **Gardens**)

A-Z Botanical Collection Ltd
Heather Angel
Aquila Photographics
Ron and Christine Foord
Garden Matters Photographic
Library

John Glover Photography
Martin and Dorothy Grace
Harper Horiticultural Slide
Library

Photo Flora
Premaphotos Wildlife
Source Photographic Archives

Polar and Arctic

Bryan and Cherry Alexander
Photography
Arctic Camera

Global Syndications
Royal Geographical Society
Picture Library

Wilderness Photographic
Library

Religions and Religious Monuments

Lesley and Roy Adkins
Picture Library
Rev. J. Catling Allen

Andes Press Agency
Ann & Bury Peerless

Photo Resources
Peter Sanders Photography

Royalty

Camera Press Ltd
Tim Graham
JS Library International

Monitor Syndication
Newsfocus Press Photograph
Agency Ltd

Syndication International Ltd

Russia

John Massey Stewart
The Russia and Republics
Photo Library

SCR Photo Library

Science, Technology and Meteorology

Ace Photo Agency
Leslie Garland Picture Library
GeoScience Features

Frank Lane Picture Agency
Ltd
Microscopix

Ann Ronan at Image Select
Science Photo Library

Scotland

Hamish Brown
George A. Dey (castles,
    Highland Games)
Scotland in Focus Picture
    Library

The Still Moving Picture
    Company
Charles Tait Photo Library
Simon Warner

David Williams Picture
    Library
The Allan Wright Photo
    Library

Social Issues and Social History

Andes Press Agency
John Birdsall Photography
Mary Evans Picture
    Library

Greater London Photograph
    Library
Imperial War Museum
Photofusion

Ann Ronan at Image Select
Welfare History Picture
    Library

South America

Animal Photography
    (Galapagos)
Australia Pictures
Stephen Benson Slide Bureau

Lupe Cunha (Brazil)
Sue Cunningham
    Photographic (Brazil)

David Hosking (Falklands)
David Muscroft Picture
    Library (Falklands)

Space and Astronomy

Aspect Picture Library
Galaxy Picture Library

Genesis Space Photo Library

Science Photo Library

Sport and Leisure

Action Plus
Allsport Photographic Ltd
The Associated Press Ltd
John Blake Photo Library
    (equestrian)
Boxing Picture Library
Cumbria Picture Library
    (snooker)
Peter Dazeley (golf)
Eyeline Photography
    (watersports, equestrian)

Frontline Photo Press Agency
Mountain Visions (skiing)
David Muscroft Snooker
    Photography
Skishoot – Offshoot
Sporting Pictures (UK) Ltd
The Still Moving Picture
    Company

B.M. Totterdell Photography
    (volleyball)
Ulster Photography Agency
    (motorsport)
Universal Pictorial Press &
    Agency Ltd (UPPA)
World Pictures

Strange Phenomena

Fortean Picture Library

Sites, Sights and Cities

Transport (Cars and Motoring, Railways)

Ludvigsen Library
Motorcycles Unlimited

National Motor Museum,
    Beaulieu

Railways—Milepost 92½
Ulster Photographic Agency

Travel

Ace Photo Agency
Air Photo Supply
ARCAID Architectural
    Photography and Picture
    Library
Aspect Picture Library
Aviation Picture Library
Bandphoto Agency
The Anthony Blake Photo
    Library

Britain on View Photographic
    Library
Cephas Picture Library
Sylvia Cordaiy Picture
    Library
Sue Cunningham
    Photographic
James Davis Travel
    Photography
Ecoscene

Greg Evans International
    Photo Library
Footprints Colour Picture
    Library
Fotoccompli—The Picture
    Library
Brian Gadsby Picture Library
The Hutchinson Library
The Illustrated London News
    Picture Library

JS Library International
Just Europe
Landscape Only
Mountain Visions
Papilio Natural History
    Library
Photo Flora
The Photographers' Library
Raleigh International Picture
    Library

Retna Pictures Ltd
Peter Sanders Photography
Mick Sharp
Skishoot – Offshoot
Spectrum Colour Library
Charles Tait Photo Library
Telegraph Colour Library
Travel Images

Travel Photo International
Travel Trade Photography
Viewfinder Colour Photo
    Library
Wilderness Photographic
    Library
World Pictures

Wales

Celtic Picture Library

Patrick Smith Associates

Waterways

Waterways Photo Library

Roy J. Westlake

You don't need to jet to faraway places

Not least of the attractions of writing about travel is that it can take you to strange and exotic places, lead you into rare experiences. It can also lead you into bus journeys through Australia of mind-dulling monotony, tedious train journeys across New Mexico, wasted hours waiting for the rain to go off, and listening to interminable speeches in a language you can't begin to comprehend. That side of travel writing, though, is rarely emphasised, even though the result may be an empty notebook. The illusion persists that travel writing is only for those who travel adventurously or to faraway places, for those who can offer travel experiences out of reach of the writer who never travels beyond the British Isles.

But the same principles apply whether you are writing about York or New York, Dunoon or Delhi. The British Isles encompass not only famous cities and towns and villages of enormous character but great tracts of unpopulated countryside; hundreds of islands waiting to be explored from the Shetlands to the Scilly Isles; gardens such as Inverewe and Sissinghurst famed for their interest; ancient and unusual parish churches; stately homes and even pubs which were standing long before our great great-grandparents were born. A good and perceptive travel writer can make readers just as keen and curious to visit his own particular corner of Britain as they are to visit, say, Bali or Bangkok.

from *Writing about Travel* by Morag Campbell (A & C Black, £5.95)

Markets for Photographers

TRANSPARENCIES AND PHOTOGRAPHS FOR GREETINGS CARDS, CALENDARS AND VIEWCARDS

Before submitting examples of work, in their own interest, photographers are advised to write a preliminary letter to ascertain requirements, including terms and conditions. Only top quality material should be submitted; inferior work is never accepted. *Postage for return of material should be enclosed.*

*Member of the Greeting Card and Calendar Association

Arnold Barton Cards—see **Hambledon Studios Ltd.**

Athena International, PO Box 918, Harlow, Essex CM20 2DU *tel* (0279) 641125. *Art directors:* Roger Watt, Ben Wilson, Sarah Finney, Trevor Jones. Photos and illustrations of a professional standard for reproduction as prints, posters, greetings cards and postcards. Sae essential for return of work.

C.C.A. Stationery Ltd, Eastway, Fulwood, Preston PR2 4WS *tel* (0772) 662800. Personalised wedding stationery, Christmas cards.

Dennis Print and Publishing, Printing House Square, Melrose Street, Scarborough, North Yorkshire YO12 7SJ *tel* (0723) 500555 *fax* (0723) 501488/500545. Interested in first-class transparencies for reproduction as local view postcards and calendars. $3\frac{1}{4} \times 2\frac{1}{4}$ in or 35 mm transparencies ideal for postcard reproduction.

Giesen & Wolff Ltd (1908), Kaygee House, Rothersthorpe Crescent, Northampton NN4 9JD *tel* (0604) 709499 *fax* (0604) 709399. *Art director:* D. Falconer. Transparencies, $2\frac{1}{4}$ in sq minimum: floral studies, still life.

Hambledon Studios Ltd, Hambledon House, Marlborough Road, Accrington, Lancs. BB5 6BX *tel* (0254) 872266 *telex* 635169 CARDAC G *fax* (0254) 872079. *Art managers:* D. Jaundrell, J. Ashton, D. Fuller, N. Harrison; *creative director:* M. Smith. Photos for reproduction as greetings cards. *Brands:* Arnold Barton, Donny Mac, Reflections, New Image.

Images & Editions (1984), Bourne Road, Essendine, Nr Stamford, Lincs. PE9 4UW *tel* (0780) 57118 *fax* (0780) 54629. *Directors:* Lesley Forrow, Maurice Miller. Greetings cards, giftwrap, gift products and social stationery: flowers, gardens and landscape, animals, especially cats and teddy bears. Any format accepted; transparencies preferred.

Jane's Information Group, Sentinel House, 163 Brighton Road, Coulsdon, Surrey CR5 2NH *tel* 081-763 1030 *telex* 916907 JANES G *fax* 081-763 1005. Considers defence, aerospace and transportation transparencies.

*****Jarrold Publishing** (1770), Whitefriars, Norwich NR3 1TR *tel* (0603) 763300 *fax* (0603) 662748. *Managing director:* Antony Jarrold; *publishing director:* Caroline Jarrold. Transparencies (35 mm or larger) for guidebooks, calendars and postcards.

Leeds Postcards (1979), PO Box 84, Leeds LS1 1HU *tel* (0532) 468649 *fax* (0532) 436730. Workers co-operative. Publishers and producers of campaign postcards for left wing political campaigns, the women's movement, environmental and campaigns for international justice. Joint publishers of Women Artists Cards.

New Concept Cards Ltd (1989), 3 Heathfield, Stacey Bushes, Milton Keynes MK12 6HP   *tel* (0908) 312366   *fax* (0908) 225323. *Directors:* N. Patel, H.Y. Patel, Y. Patel. Transparencies for greetings cards, including Christmas, and giftwrap. Will consider verses.

*Royle Publications Ltd, Royle House, Wenlock Road, London N1 7ST   *tel* 071-253 7654. Colour transparencies required for two calendars, *Beautiful Britain* and *Gardens of Britain*. Natural landscape photography and pictures of ornate flower gardens in Britain. Submissions end of November through to February only.

J. Salmon Ltd, 100 London Road, Sevenoaks, Kent TN13 1BB   *tel* (0732) 452381   *fax* (0732) 450951. Picture postcards, calendars and greeting cards.

Scandecor Ltd (1967), 3 The Ermine Centre, Hurricane Close, Huntingdon, Cambs. PE18 6XX   *tel* (0480) 456395   *telex* 32365   *fax* (0480) 456269. *Director:* G. Huldtgren. Transparencies all sizes.

Noel Tatt Ltd (1954), Coombe House, Coombe Valley Road, Dover, Kent CT17 0EU   *tel* (0304) 211644   *fax* (0304) 240470. *Directors:* Noel Tatt, Vencke Tatt, Derek Bates, Anthony Sharpe, Paul Tatt, Robert Dixon. Greetings cards, prints and postcards.

> See also the **Articles, reports and short stories** and the **Books** sections for lists of magazines and publishers.

Picture research

Picture Research

JENNIE KARRACH

Picture research is the art of obtaining pictures – photos and illustrations – suitable for reproduction, which suit the project's brief, budget and deadline. It also includes the clearance of permissions, copyright, the negotiation of rights and fees, and the eventual return of pictures to their owners at the end of the project. Given the incidence of pictures in daily life it can be appreciated that picture researchers are responsible for supplying a vast range of clients, in the book and magazine industry, both publishers and packagers, advertising agencies, film, television and video companies, newspapers and exhibition organisers. Although the skills involved in picture research are relevant in all these contexts, the type of pictures required varies enormously. As a result researchers tend to specialise in the type of work they undertake, and they may well have a specialist knowledge of one particular area, such as science and technology.

Picture researchers are employed either as staff members or freelance by the hour, day, for the duration of the project, as appropriate. An employee working full time on a long-running project may have time to carry out extensive research, but freelance work is often constrained by the client's budget and schedule. It is here that experience counts. Knowing where to find material quickly to suit the brief saves time and therefore money. The researcher's fees are often included in the total budget, so that although the final deadline for delivery of pictures to the client may be a month away, the total allowed for picture research amounts to three days' work. It may be that this is unrealistic, and that the job will require five days. These details all need to be clarified at the outset and some sort of agreement listing the picture brief, deadlines, budget and invoicing particulars needs to be drawn up. It is important to put everything in writing so that in the event of dispute both parties can refer back to the agreement. Pictures themselves are often worth large amounts of money, and in the event of loss it will become difficult to agree who will pay compensation unless this has been pre-arranged. It can also prove difficult to collect payment for work completed, so it may be advisable to agree upon regular payments and an advance to cover expenses such as travel, postage and telephone, etc.

THE BRIEF

It is important to clarify the brief so that both parties, the picture researcher and the editor/design team, are agreed upon the image required. It may be that the picture requested needs no further description – a work of art, by a well-known artist, e.g. *The Mona Lisa* by Leonardo da Vinci, to be used in colour. Or it may be that the picture is to depict an historical event which occurred long before the advent of photography. What is required? A photo of a contemporary manuscript which describes the incident, or perhaps a contemporary illumination exists. Or does the client have in mind an illustration executed by a more recent artist, perhaps a nineteenth-century engraving? Or perhaps a photograph of the remains of an historic site? It may be that the client has no one image in mind, but rather needs to evoke a specific mood, or provoke a reaction. This is often the case in advertising campaigns. Pictures are highly subjective, and what is evocative to some will appear bleak to others. A good picture researcher is able to capture the image conjured up in a picture meeting, responding to the ideas of an art director or editor.

It may be that the picture required must be a specific shape – portrait (upright) or landscape (horizontal), or it may need to have an area lacking in detail, such as sky, into which text can fit. Or a dark area suitable for text reversal. If there are too many design constraints it may be cost effective to commission a photographer, rather than to search for a non-existent 'existing' photo.

THE BUDGET, RIGHTS AND DEADLINE

Once the brief has been agreed, the budget, rights and deadline must be confirmed. These are interdependent. Picture fees increase according to the size and use made of the image; for instance, a picture used at quarter-page size in a school textbook will cost less than one used quarter-page size in a glossy, adult non-fiction book. Fees are calculated also according to the rights requested. The larger the territory, the larger the fee, although the percentage increase between the various categories will vary from agency to agency. The territories sold are usually: UK only; UK and first foreign edition; English language, world rights, excluding US; English language, world rights, including US; world rights, all languages. It may well be that, as the European Union attempts to remove trade barriers, the rights available will change. The print run will also have an effect on the fees charged.

Other fees will need to be budgeted for. Many commercial picture agencies charge 'research' or 'service' fees. These may be linked to the amount of material they are loaning or there may be a fixed charge levied. In both cases the source should advise of this at the initial enquiry stage. Some will only charge if a personal visit is not possible and pictures are despatched by a member of their staff. The levying of these fees can erode the total picture budget quickly. It is not unusual to receive a service fee of £30, which may be acceptable if this is the only source used, and the pictures obtained are accepted by the client. However, on projects where a selection of pictures to cover a wider range of topics is required, many sources will have to be approached. It is worth discussing service fees at the outset. It is not unknown for agencies to waive or reduce them if it increases the likelihood of a sale. Some only charge the service fee if all pictures are returned and none selected for use. Other sources do not loan out material but instead sell copy transparencies or prints. This is usually the case with museums who can supply a transparency of a particular object or manuscript, but are unable to respond to a vague request for a selection of pictures for possible use. A transparency of reproduction quality may cost £20, or more, if a 'rush job' surcharge is added on.

Most commercial picture libraries or agencies operate on a loan system. Pictures are selected and loaned for an agreed period, usually a month. After this time material not required should be returned and some indication given as to the fate of the pictures still held. Is a subsequent picture selection to be made, or are those retained going to be used? If material is kept longer than the agreed loan period, then holding fees may be charged. These should only be levied if a reminder sent fails to elicit news of the pictures or return. (Freelance picture researchers need to make sure that such reminders are forwarded to them either by the source or sent on by the client.) Holding fees are charged per picture, per week over the deadline, and are usually waived if a reasonable extension to the free loan period is requested.

PICTURE SOURCES

Sources are many and various. They include government departments, institutions, companies, libraries, commercial picture libraries and agencies, individual collectors, and individual photographers. Some of these sources supply pictures without charge, but that is not to say that they are necessarily easy to obtain, or that no copyright pertains. Many sources are not primarily concerned with the supply of pictures and give it low priority. Access to the collection may be limited to research students and those who hold readers' cards. Enquiries may have to be made in writing, and the idea of urgency is an alien one. Or lack of resources may prevent an efficient service.

There is no one source book which lists all picture sources and if one existed it would run to many volumes and be in need of constant updating. Commercial libraries and agencies maintain a high profile, advertising by mail shots to prospective clients. The larger ones produce glossy catalogues, usually free, which include a selection of their images, enough to give a flavour of the type of stock held. 'General stock libraries' hold pictures which fall into the following broad categories: travel, architecture, food, business, science/medicine, people, sport, nature, animals, transport, etc. They would almost certainly hold pictures of famous foreign landmarks, e.g. the Eiffel Tower, photographed from the ground, the air, by night, by day, with lovers . . . It is much more difficult to find pictures of less glamorous sites. Street furniture, cars and pedestrians date quickly, and some agencies, keen to keep pictures saleable for as long as possible, will attempt to keep such features to a minimum. The result is strange; London, peopled only by bobbies and red buses, Venice reduced to St Mark's Square and gondoliers on the Grand Canal, Los Angeles depicted by traffic on freeways. This problem extends to the 'people' pictures, which tend to be stereotypes posed by models. It is not impossible to find pictures of 'real' people going about everyday activities, but it can be time-consuming. Directories cannot hope to express the nuances of photographic collections, and it is only over time, after visits to many sources, that an overview of the range available will emerge. Specialist picture libraries are usually one-subject libraries, and cover the whole range of picture needs. The level of captioning is usually higher in specialist sources as the photographer has expert knowledge. It can be the case that a good quality photograph badly captioned is rendered useless. A photo filed in the 'elderly people' category of a general stock agency showed a woman standing in a slight depression in the desert somewhere. The woman was actually a famous anthropologist, but her name meant nothing to the library so she had been miscaptioned and then wrongly filed. It may be that for certain purposes any train, boat, car, etc. will be acceptable, but if the picture required is of a specific model then it is frustrating to find insubstantial captions and undated pictures.

USE OF PHOTOS

Once pictures have been found which fit the brief, the next stage is clearance for use. Permission must be sought from the copyright holder for use of particular photos in set contexts. The supply of photos does not automatically guarantee permission to reproduce. It may be that the agency or picture source is not the copyright holder, and permission has to be sought elsewhere. This is often the case with photos of works of art still in copyright. The artist, or the artist's estate, may be represented by a copyright protection society such as DACS (Design and Artists Copyright Society – see page 621), which will approach the estate or artist on behalf of a picture researcher and, if permission is granted, often subject to conditions, issue a licence. Conditions could include the right to approve colour proofs. The production department or designer of the project would therefore need to be informed to allow time in the schedule. DACS have reciprocal representation agreements with similar copyright protection societies in some 26 countries. This simplifies a copyright enquiry considerably but sufficient time should be allowed for clearance. It may take a day or several weeks. If the copyright holder and the supplier of the photograph are not one and the same, then a fee may be due to both parties.

It may be that the context in which the photo is to appear is a sensitive one, perhaps an article about child abuse, divorce, AIDS, or that the caption is to make some derogatory statement about the subject. If this is the case it is important to be honest about the context with the supplier of the photo. If the article is educational and positive in its approach, then the photo will play a different role from one appearing in an exposé of shameful goings on. It is prudent to enquire whether the photographer has obtained 'model release' from the subject in the photo. In return for a sum of money the model grants the photographer the right to sell the photos taken. This is standard procedure at photo sessions, where a particular shot has been commissioned by a client, or a personality has granted a shoot. The release may have certain riders attached as to use, precisely to avoid certain contexts.

It may be that the agency grants permission to use the photo in a sensitive area, but insists on a declaration appearing with it or with the photo credits 'all photos posed by models'. Or it may be that the agency or photographer do not have model release for the photo. At present in the UK, if a person is photographed in public they cannot prevent that photo being published. Hence the breed of paparazzi photographers. There is as yet no law protecting against the invasion of privacy. (The situation is different in the USA.) As a result many British photo libraries hold photos of members of the public, taken 'in the public domain' for which they hold no model release. Most agencies reproduce the following or similar statement in their Terms & Conditions: 'although the agency takes all reasonable care, the agency shall not be liable for any loss or damage suffered by the client or by any third party arising from any defect in the picture or its caption, or in any way from its reproduction.' The onus is put onto the picture user. It is fair to say that if the context of the photo is an innocent one, most members of the public are pleased to be in the spotlight, and require no more than a complimentary copy of the book, magazine, or whatever.

CAPTIONS

It is important for picture researchers to make caption writers aware that litigation may result from derogatory or inappropriate captions. Staff researchers should attempt to prevent pictures which were obtained for one project, e.g. a book on health care, being transferred to another, such as a booklet on safe sex. Freelance researchers would be well advised to include a paragraph in the agreement mentioned above which would disclaim responsibility for use by the client of pictures supplied in any use other than that stated in the brief, and any subsequent copyright infringement by the client. It is not unknown for clients to withhold information or mislead picture researchers as to the length of the print run, or the production of foreign language editions.

Picture researchers do not generally write captions themselves but may be asked to provide information for captions. This can be very time-consuming if the pictures do not already have a reasonable amount of caption information attached, supplied by the source or photographer.

CREDITS AND COPYRIGHT

Once pictures have been selected, captioned, and sized for the project in hand, the credit or acknowledgement list will need to be drawn up. This usually includes a courtesy line thanking the various picture sources for permission to reproduce photographs. Sources are either listed alphabetically, with page numbers as to where their pictures appear, or the name of the source appears next to the picture.

Under the provisions of the Copyright, Designs and Patents Act 1988, photographers have 'moral rights' which include the right to be identified as the author of a photograph (see page 561). Newspapers, magazines, encyclopedias, and other works of reference, are exempt from crediting contributors, but most will include credits as a matter of course. Under the terms of the 1988 Act photography is now copyright for the same duration and in the same way as other works of art. At present this is for 50 years after the death of the photographer. However, harmonisation of EU legislation may bring about an extension of this period in line with other EU countries such as Germany, where the duration is 70 years. Commissioned work, where previously the copyright belonged to the commissioner, is now the property of the photographer. This means that photos can only be kept for a limited period after a photo session, and rights must be agreed in the same way as for stock library images. All photos, used and unused, must be returned to the photographer. Staff photographers as employees do not own copyright on their photos.

A short booklet, *The Photographer's Guide to the 1988 Copyright Act*, has been produced by the British Photographers Liaison Committee (BPLC) which summarises the changes in copyright relevant to photographers brought about by the 1988 Act. Currently out of print; a new edition is in preparation and details may be obtained from the Association of Photographers (address below).

LAST STAGES

The pictures are now ready to go off to the printers. A final check should be made to see that they have not been damaged by any of the people who have handled them – editors, designers, etc. If the printer returns photos damaged it will be easier to refute claims that pictures were already scratched if everything is checked as a matter of course. If prints or transparencies are damaged, a fee to compensate the agency or photographer is due. This will vary in amount according to whether the picture was an original or a duplicate. Some photographs are irreplaceable. The amount due for loss is stated in the Terms & Conditions listed on the reverse of most delivery notes. This may be in the region of £400 for an original. Sometimes pictures are not damaged irreparably but are returned by the printer with torn mounts, or still sticky from origination. It is best to return such pictures to the printer for cleaning, in case any damage occurs during a DIY cleaning session. Pictures should then be returned to their owners and one or two copies of the book or proofs supplied as evidence of use, as stated in the Terms & Conditions of the source.

GETTING INTO PICTURE RESEARCH

This can be difficult as employers are loath to employ people without experience, and some picture sources are nervous about loaning pictures. A job with a picture library would give an insight into that particular source and might lead into a job as a picture researcher. Jobs in picture libraries, and picture research work, are advertised in the Arts/Media section of *The Guardian* on Saturdays and Mondays. Sometimes such ads appear in *The Bookseller*, the weekly publishing journal, and *Campaign*, the weekly advertising magazine. These may all be available at the local library. Salaries tend to be low initially as one learns the skills involved. The idea of working freelance may appeal but it is difficult to obtain enough freelance work without the contacts amassed over a period of time. Many picture researchers build up experience working for an employer full time, and then go freelance. This is not without risks. Getting enough work; getting paid for work completed; sorting out tax; National Insurance; motivation; and loneliness are some of the problems which may arise.

USEFUL DIRECTORIES

Picture Sources UK, Rosemary Eakins, Macdonald, 1985. Now out of print but may be available through a library.

Picture Researcher's Handbook, Hilary & Mary Evans, 5th edition, Blueprint, £39.00 (£42.50 inc. p&p). Also available from The Mary Evans Picture Library, 59 Tranquil Vale, London SE3 0BS   *tel* 081-318 0034   *fax* 081-852 7211.

BAPLA Directory, £10. This lists all the current members of the British Association of Picture Libraries and Agencies (BAPLA), at present totalling around 300. Copies available from Sal Shuel, BAPLA Administrator, 13 Woodberry Crescent, London N10 1PJ   *tel* 081-444 7913   *fax* 081-883 9215.

USEFUL ORGANISATIONS

BAPLA – see above.

DACS (Design and Artists Copyright Society), St Mary's Clergy House, 2 Whitechurch Lane, London E1 7QR   *tel* 071-247 1650   *fax* 071-377 5855.

Association of Photographers, 9-10 Domingo Street, London EC1Y 0TA   *tel* 071-608 1441   *fax* 071-253 3007. Includes fashion and advertising photographers amongst its members.

SPREd (The Society of Picture Researchers and Editors) – see opposite.

Picture Research Course

The Book House Training Centre offers training in picture research in the form of a two-day course designed for those working in book publishing. The objective of the course is to give a professional approach to the search for and use of suitable sources; to make picture researchers aware of all the implications of their task: suitability for reproduction, legal and financial aspects, efficient administration.

Details of the course, with the outline of the programme, may be obtained from Book House Training Centre, 45 East Hill, Wandsworth, London SW18 2QZ   *tel* 081-874 2718/4608   *fax* 081-870 8985.

The London School of Publishing offers a course in picture research twice a year – spring and autumn. Each course lasts eight weeks and there is one lecture a week. Further details may be obtained from John Dalton, 8 Herbrand Street, London WC1N 1HZ   *tel* 071-713 0043.

SPREd (Society of Picture Researchers and Editors)

SPREd was formed in 1977 as a professional body for picture researchers and picture editors. It is not a trade union but a society for people who work in similar fields, and who wish to share problems and exchange information on all aspects of dealing with illustrations.

Its main aims are:

1. To promote the recognition of picture research as a profession, requiring particular skills and knowledge.
2. To promote and maintain professional standards and ethics within the profession.
3. To bring together those involved in the research and publication of visual material and to provide a forum for the exchange of information.
4. To encourage the use of trained researchers throughout publishing and other media, and to ensure common professional standards in all areas of picture use.
5. To provide guidance and advice to its members.

All picture researchers need a wide circle of contacts and a good knowledge of sources. Picture researchers tend to encounter the same problems and have the same need for up-to-date information, but they tend to work in isolation from each other. SPREd sets out to be a clearing house for information. More importantly, it provides an opportunity for researchers to meet each other informally and to exchange ideas and discuss problems. It can be a great relief to discover that others have already met and overcome the very difficulties that are worrying you.

To this end SPREd runs meetings for members, and publishes a quarterly magazine to which non-members may subscribe. Advertising space may be purchased in this magazine.

SPREd members sign a Code of Practice which sets out the professional standards expected from a SPREd member and states the responsibilities of a picture researcher.

For further details about SPREd write, enclosing an sae, to The Secretary, BM Box 259, London WC1N 3XX   *tel* 071-404 5011.

See also the **Books** section for lists of publishers; the **Classified list of picture agencies and libraries**.

Music

Introduction to Music Publishing

PETER DADSWELL
The Music Publishers' Association Ltd

Although we live in an age in which music is everywhere and is taken for granted, aspiring composers and songwriters abound. Some desperately seek instant fame and fortune firmly convinced that they are gifted with creative talent; others harbour more modest ambitions and are content to see their work in print in the hope that it will eventually gain recognition and critical acclaim. It is the music publisher's lot to try and serve such individuals at a time when new music is competing on an unprecedented scale with other forms of leisure-time occupation and entertainment.

This brief introduction to a few aspects of music publishing will help those interested in making their compositions available to a wider audience, be it educational or the public at large, and tries to dispel a little of the mystique which unfortunately still surrounds music publishing activity.

The role of the music publisher is to find, nurture, promote and protect the original creative output of composers, authors and songwriters by administering their business interests so that they are properly rewarded for the use of their works. Creativity and the commercial acumen required to exploit fully the music produced are seldom to be found in the same person although some do possess the necessary entrepreneurial skills to do both! In most cases, however, it is not possible to be a prolific writer and take care of the fairly demanding degree of promotion or administration needed in professional, and dynamic, modern music publishing.

SUBMISSIONS OF COMPOSITIONS TO MUSIC PUBLISHERS

The first hurdle to be overcome in the music publishing process is obtaining acceptance of a work by a music publisher. Thorough research is worthwhile as it is important to establish the kinds of works already in a particular publisher's catalogue, since it is patently foolish to submit a choral work to a brass or wind band specialist!

Popular music

Most publishers will listen to unsolicited material submitted on cassettes although there are now some who no longer do so because they will only deal with writers

392

with a known track record. There have been a number of cases where music publishers, record companies and major artists have been frivolously accused of stealing musical works from unknown writers; some music publishers who have been involved in time-wasting litigation have therefore made it their policy not to deal with anyone who is not strongly recommended or referred by reputable colleagues in the industry. All tapes or discs (some creators now produce demonstration compact discs) in this field should be sent in clearly marked with the title, author's name and a short covering letter giving full details of the address and telephone number. A stamped addressed envelope must be enclosed. Only the best items should be submitted and a selection of the two or three most representative works from the songwriter's output will suffice for assessment. Bear in mind that publishers listen to vast quantities of material and the response will rarely be immediate; delays must not be unreasonable, however, and reputable publishers should give an initial indication fairly promptly but it is important to be patient with them. Beware of any company asking for a fee to listen to new music – such a practice is most unusual and ought to be treated with the utmost caution.

The British Academy of Songwriters, Composers and Authors (BASCA; 34 Hanway Street, London W1P 9DE) gives guidance to its members in regular workshops where the work of songwriters is independently assessed for potential by industry professionals.

Although artists who do not write music are looking for material to record it is not generally a good idea to send it to them direct; they are busy people and are usually recording or touring. It puts them in a difficult position if they are constantly receiving cassettes, which will probably be passed on to a manager, agent, record producer or record company, and adds to the possibility of the material going astray.

These days many writers regularly perform their own material in pubs, halls and clubs either as individual performers or as members of a band; like record companies many publishers use talent scouts hunting for new creative sounds and publishing projects are frequently begun as a result of seeing and hearing a live performance. In fact it is probably more common for songwriters to become published through these encounters than as a consequence of a music publisher signing a writer from hearing a demonstration tape. There is now a London Songwriters' Showcase, also supported by BASCA and which can be contacted through the BASCA office, enabling songwriters to present material live and music publishers have been encouraged to attend these events.

It is not normally possible to market song lyrics on their own. Music publishers prefer listening to complete works – songs with words and music. It is therefore important for someone who is unable to compose music, or who recognises that their strength is in writing lyrics, to team up with a person who can produce music prior to approaching a music publisher. If a person who writes words only is unable to display sufficient initiative or enterprise in finding a collaborator, it is unlikely that a publisher will consider lyrics in isolation. Enthusiastic popular song lyricists can normally find partners through music contacts or through friends, or by advertising in the music or local press, and they may also find co-writers by joining BASCA. If, however, a composer or lyricist has already managed to establish a music industry reputation as a specialist in either discipline, a music publisher will be happy to provide a matching service.

Music primarily intended for print and performance by orchestras, bands and choirs

Other genres of music in a 'serious' or 'classical' style or form require a different approach. It is most unlikely that a work sent in by someone without reasonably advanced formal musical training or knowledge of compositional techniques will be of a sufficient standard to be accepted. Many talented composers attract the attention of publishers whilst they are still at music college, university or taking a specialist further education course although there are very well-known exceptions who did not follow the established routes. Principals, professors of music and tutors will often be familiar with publishing staff and refer their most talented protégés to them. Promotional staff are also constantly attending concerts to hear new works. The Society for the Promotion of New Music (West Heath Studios, 174 Mill Lane, London NW6 1TB) plays an important role in launching the careers of young composers and does much to encourage them in a variety of ways.

Anyone interested in publication of educational or classical music should submit their material in a similar fashion to that required for popular music for editorial scrutiny, except that the music publisher needs to assess the manuscript or, if it is an opera or musical, a synopsis of the work. Tutorial or instructional works should be submitted in full. Taped extracts of vocal, instrumental, orchestral or band works accompanying the manuscripts are also acceptable.

COMPETITIONS AND CONTESTS AS A ROUTE FOR SUCCESS

Competitions and contests are events which are monitored by music publishers and the most prestigious of these in the popular music world is the Eurovision Song Contest and its UK preliminary 'Song for Europe'. In recent years the Vivian Ellis Prize sponsored by the Performing Right Society (PRS) has been recognised as a major national competition to encourage composers and librettists to write for the musical stage. Various bodies such as music colleges, commercial sponsors, professional orchestras, trusts and foundations offer prizes to young composers or run competitions for composition. Such events are useful for music publishers.

A publisher expressing positive interest in a musical work should be prepared to explain the basics of any proposed business relationship at the outset. The administrative aspects cannot be overlooked as, whilst creative matters are likely to be discussed in some detail, the aspiring composer or songwriter may not be aware of such matters as normal recommended usage values, accounting time scales and the role of the music industry collecting societies. It is desirable that a composer should be advised to obtain expert independent advice from either a lawyer with experience in the music business or one of the established composer organisations, such as the Association of Professional Composers (APC), BASCA (previously mentioned), Composers' Guild (all at 34 Hanway Street, London W1P 9DE) or the Incorporated Society of Musicians (ISM; 10 Stratford Place, London W1N 9AE), prior to signing any legally binding document.

DO IT YOURSELF?

As competition is so intense and music publishers are currently minimising their risks in what is essentially a very risky operation anyway, with the advent of desktop music publishing and origination in the classical world and the use of sequencers or MIDI recorders in the pop sphere, some composers consider this to be the preferable route for them to take, particularly if their work has been rejected by established publisher houses. There are royalty and tax advantages in opting to self-publish, but there are also considerable drawbacks as much work is involved if the promotion and administration is to be really effective. Investment money to start up is required and sufficient capital must be available to print and distribute the works or make recordings for promotional purposes. It is recommended that very careful consideration is given to the self-publishing option.

MUSIC PUBLISHING CONTRACTS

Quite simply the publishing contract will say that the publisher will promote the writer's music and look after his business interests in return for a share in the income it generates. The rights granted under copyright law in the musical works are transferred by the creator to the music publisher and a share of any resultant income is agreed; the more the music is used, the greater the income. The creator and music publisher have other clearly specified obligations to each other and the interests of each should be fairly balanced.

The publishing contract must be clear, unambiguous, comprehensive and should be honoured in both the letter and the spirit showing the obligations of creator and music publisher. Lawyers make a living by using complex language to express basic facts. Ideally agreements should be short, easy to understand and drawn up in plain English. Too many words and lengthy documents can cause problems and it is to be hoped the day will come when less money will be spent on legal costs because contracts are drawn up on a simple basis.

Matters which particularly need to be defined include:

- a title which identifies the musical work(s) and, where appropriate, the nature, agreed length and scope of the work(s).
- the nature of the rights conferred – the ownership of the copyright (an assignment or an exclusive licence), territories and duration. The term (period) of an exclusive agreement should not be excessive.
- the timescale for delivery of the work or manuscript (where appropriate) and for publication of the printed music.
- the payments, royalties and advances (if any) to be paid, what they are for and when they are due.
- the provisions for sub-publishing (licensing); these should not 'erode' income in the publisher's favour.
- the termination and reversion (where appropriate) provisions of the contract.

Even allowing for the wide diversity of musical genres and of music publishing, whether classical, educational, popular, media or background music, it is possible broadly to define the areas of exploitation and administration carried out by the music publisher. Generally speaking the exploitation or promotion of a musical work will involve one or more of the following activities: the release of a commercial sound recording; the issue of a synchronisation licence for an audio-visual use of the work (the incorporation of songs or music in a film soundtrack or television programme); the publication of the work in print for sale or hire; the public performance; the broadcast.

On commercial sound recordings a royalty of 8.5% of the dealer price of each sound carrier, exclusive of VAT, is shared between the music publisher and the composer(s)/authors(s), and, if appropriate, the other copyright musical works on the record. The composer and publisher divisions are always specified in the publishing agreement. The percentages to be received by the composer and music publisher for public performances and broadcasts of the musical work will also be detailed. These rights are, for the majority of compositions, traditionally assigned to the Performing Right Society and the royalties arising from the exercise of these rights are paid directly to each party.

Royalties for the sales of printed music are generally expressed as a percentage of the retail selling price of the music and the normal royalty is 10% of this amount.

Composers will, if successful, earn royalties on virtually every conceivable use of their music and these days it plays an integral part in feature films, advertising campaigns, television productions and commercial videos, plus all kinds of miscellaneous use such as in computer games, telephone lines, musical greetings cards and even underwear! These too must be properly licensed and paid for, but at a time when publishing is exploding into multi-media and many other startling new areas, the proper control of such usage is becoming increasingly difficult. Music publishing is rapidly becoming even more complex as the music is no longer bound to a particular medium as information and entertainment can be accessed with no regard for the media upon which it is delivered. Digital information transmission has effectively separated the content from the carrier.

Music publishers may offer contracts on a work by work basis or an exclusive contract to accept a number of works over a specified period. Exclusive agreements normally state that if a work is not exploited within a reasonable period of time, the composer/writer should have the option to call for the work to be reassigned.

The publishing contract, in dealing with administration, should undertake to protect the copyright in the work and preserve the moral rights of the composer. The music publisher should also register the works with appropriate collecting societies such as the Performing Right Society Ltd and the Mechanical-Copyright Protection Society Ltd. Reasonable requests for additional information should receive favourable consideration.

The creator in return will need to guarantee that works created are original and do not contain substantial portions or copies of other material. Delivery times for all works must be adhered to.

Most music publishers will still ask for a full assignment of all rights for the life of copyright for all works to enable them to generate enough income to carry on the publishing process, and use the money to reinvest in the composer they wish to sign and the others on their books.

ARRANGING

Copyright in a musical work lasts for the life of the composer plus 50 years from the end of the year of that person's death. This period of copyright 'protection' will soon be increased to 70 years in line with a European Commission directive to harmonise further copyright laws in the European Union. If it is a vocal work and the words have been written by someone else they too cannot be tampered with without the author's permission. Under copyright law the arrangement of any copyright musical work in printed or manuscript form requires the prior written permission of the original copyright owner of that work, who is usually the music publisher. Arrangers must contact the original publisher prior to undertaking any arrangement since it is that publisher's responsibility either to permit the arrangement to proceed or, for contractual or other reasons, to prohibit such an arrangement. Permissions to make arrangements of copyright works may be subject to a written licence requiring the payment of a fee or royalty to the original publisher or composer. Other terms and conditions may also be appropriate and these will be notified when the approach to the original publisher is made. It is dangerous to submit or offer an arrangement to a music publisher for publication without evidence from the original publisher that all necessary clearances have been made. Any difficulties in tracing the copyright owners of musical works should be referred to the PRS, MCPS or the Music Publishers' Association, 3rd Floor, Strandgate, 18-20 York Buildings, London WC2N 6JU   *tel* 071-839 7779.

THE PHOTOCOPYING DILEMMA

Part of the role of the music publisher is to protect composers against copyright infringement by any means. Apart from the commercial piracy of sound recordings, videos, printed music and home taping, which have deprived composers of income, indiscriminate unauthorised photocopying over the last 25 years or so has seriously threatened the livelihood of many composers who have been published. Such infringement has narrowed the repertoire of works available. The use and availability of unsupervised, high-speed, photocopying machines has also harmed the 'consumers' of musical works whether amateur or professional. As printed music is the catalyst for many live, broadcast and recorded performances of copyright music, photocopying has stifled additional exploitation on behalf of creators by music publishers, depriving them both of further income. In the UK, an equitable solution to the problem has been found. It is the Code of Fair Practice whose contents have been agreed between publishers and users. It is also available from the Music Publishers' Association and attempts to define 'fair dealing for printed music' enshrining two general principles as follows:

a) Copyright owners (composers and their publishers) recognise the need of musicians and students for reasonable access to copyright material so that their music may be widely performed and studied.
b) At the same time, composers and their publishers must be properly compensated for their work so that the economic incentive and means for the creation and publication of music continue to exist. It follows that copying to evade purchase or hire will always be wrong.

Voluntary blanket licensing schemes are felt by music publishers to be appropriate for some types of copyright works but not for printed music which is specifically excluded from these arrangements. Such blanket licensing schemes administered by the Copyright Licensing Agency Ltd are dealt with on page 548. Such arrangements are considered unsuitable for music as it is virtually impossible to specify clear parameters to permit photocopying which would not conflict with the normal method of exploitation, publishing the music. As yet, there is no standard numbering system for all printed musical works which would assist collective licensing, collection and distribution. There are also other important reasons why printed music has to be treated separately. Reading music is a specialist matter for initiates and it is published in very much smaller units than textbooks and other literary works so that in most cases the copying of entire works is quick and easy. With music, the infringer generally wishes to copy the whole work, whereas it is rare for a student or researcher to need to copy a complete novel or textbook.

THE COLLECTING SOCIETIES

Part of the administrative role of the music publisher is to know precisely how the activities, practices, rules and regulations of these organisations (PRS and MCPS) affect the operation of the business; see pages 553 and 552 for more details.

FURTHER READING

Bagehot, R., *Music Business Agreements*, Waterlow, 1989
British Music Education Yearbook, Rhinegold Publishing
British Music Yearbook, Rhinegold Publishing
Copying Music – A Code of Fair Practice agreed between composers, publishers and users, rev. edn, Music Publishers' Association, 1992
Copyright, Designs & Patents Act 1988, HMSO
The Creative Role of the Music Publisher, International Publishers Copyright Council for the IPA (available from MPA)

Dann, Allan and Underwood, John, *How to Succeed in the Music Business*, Wise Publications, 1948

de Freitas, Denis, *The British Copyright Council's Guide to Copyright and Rights in Performances in the United Kingdom*, British Copyright Council, 1990

Ehrlich, Cyril, *Harmonious Alliance – A History of the Performing Right Society*, Performing Right Society, 1989

Gibson, James, *Getting Noticed: A Musician's Guide to Publicity and Self-promotion*, 2nd rev. edn, Omnibus Press, 1990

Homewood, Susan and Matthews, Colin, *The Essentials of Music Copying – A Manual for Composers, Copyists and Processors*, Music Publishers' Association

Lester, David and Mitchell, Paul, *Joynson-Hicks on UK Copyright Law*, Sweet & Maxwell, 1989

Music Week Directory (annual published by *Music Week*)

Rachlin, Harvey, *The Songwriter's and Musician's Guide to Making Successful Demos*, 2nd rev. edn, Omnibus Press, 1989

Music Publishers

UNITED KINGDOM

The publishers in the following list are all members of the Performing Right Society except those marked †. The list does not include all publisher-members of the Performing Right Society.

Lyrics without a musical setting are not accepted unless stated by individual firms

†**Baker Music** (1984), Unit 2, Crown Close Business Centre, 2-4 Crown Close, Wick Lane, London E3 2JQ   *tel* 081-983 0947   *fax* 081-983 0970. *Managing director:* Bernard Baker. European music – all instruments; books on and about music. Welcomes submissions and ideas from new composers.

Banks Music Publications (Ramsay Silver), The Old Forge, Sand Hutton, York YO4 1LB   *tel* (0904) 468472   *fax* (0904) 468679. Publishers of choral and instrumental music.

Bardic Edition UK (1987), 6 Fairfax Crescent, Aylesbury, Bucks. HP20 2ES   *tel/fax* (0296) 28609. Piano, vocal, chamber, choral, educational, orchestral, Grainger Society Edition, Copperplate Music.

†**Bärenreiter** (1925), Burnt Mill, Elizabeth Way, Harlow, Essex CM20 2HX   *tel* (0279) 417134 ext 224/236   *fax* (0279) 429401. *Director:* Christopher Jackson. Music for strings, wind, piano, organ, choral, solo voice, chamber, orchestral; collected editions, scores, books on music.

A. & C. Black (Publishers) Ltd (1978), 35 Bedford Row, London WC1R 4JH   *tel* 071-242 0946   *fax* 071-831 8478. *Editor:* Sheena Roberts. Song books and instrumental books for children.

Boosey & Hawkes Music Publishers Ltd, 295 Regent Street, London W1R 8JH   *tel* 071-580 2060   *telex* 8954613 BOOSEY G   *fax* 071-436 5675. General and educational.

Bosworth & Co. Ltd (1889), 14-18 Heddon Street, London W1R 8DP   *tel* 071-734 4961   *fax* 071-734 0475. Orchestral, chamber, instrumental, operetta, church, educational, piano, string, recorder and recorder ensemble, and part-songs.

Bourne Music Ltd, 34-36 Maddox Street, London W1R 9PD *tel* 071-493 6412 *fax* 071-493 6583. Popular and educational music.

Brampton Music International Ltd (1970), 3rd Floor, 9 Carnaby Street, London W1V 1PG *tel* 071-437 1958 *fax* 071-437 3852. *Managing director:* Tony Hall. Pop, soul, dance.

Breitkopf & Härtel (1719), Castle House, Ivychurch, Romney Marsh, Kent TN29 0AL *tel/fax* (0797) 344011. *Contact:* Robin Winter. Baroque, classical, romantic and contemporary music.

Bugle Songs Ltd (1979), Bugle House, 21A Noel Street, London W1V 3PD *tel* 071-439 2282 *fax* 071-439 7649. *Directors:* Miles Copeland III, Torquil Creevy. Popular. Will consider tapes, demo discs, etc.

Cambridge University Press (1534), The Edinburgh Building, Shaftesbury Road, Cambridge CB2 2RU *tel* (0223) 312393 *telex* 817256 CUPCAM G *fax* (0223) 315052. *Music editor:* Penny Souster BA, ARCM. Books on music and history of music; music books and music for schools.

Cathedral Music (1977), Maudlin House, Westhampnett, Chichester, West Sussex PO18 0PB *tel* (0243) 776325. *Managing director:* Richard Barnes. All classical music, but weighted towards choral.

Chester Music (1860), 8-9 Frith Street, London W1V 5TZ *tel* 071-434 0066 *fax* 071-287 6329. Classical, contemporary and educational music.

CMA Publications (1987), 10 Avenue Road, Kingston, Surrey KT1 2RB *tel* 081-541 0857 *fax* 081-974 8120. *Proprietor:* Geraldine Russell-Price. Contemporary music: instrumental, solo, ensemble, band, orchestral, Grade 4 – professional.

Complete Music Ltd, 3rd Floor, Bishops Park House, 25-29 Fulham High Street, London SW6 3JH *tel* 071-731 8595 *fax* 071-384 1854. *Chairman:* Iain McNay; *managing director:* Martin Costello. Modern/pop music of all kinds; vocal and instrumental.

Con Moto Publications UK (1984 as Mostyn Music), 17 Mostyn Street, Dukinfield, Cheshire SK16 5JS *tel* 061-303 0963. *Partners:* Maureen Cresswell, Tony Cresswell. Brass band, wind band, ensembles and solos, junior band (brass and wind), the John Golland and Thomas Pitfield collections.

†**Cramer Music** (1824), 23 Garrick Street, London WC2E 9AX *tel* 071-240 1612. General and educational.

De Wolfe Ltd, 80-88 Wardour Street, London W1V 3LF *tel* 071-439 8481-6 *fax* 071-437 2744. Symphonic recorded orchestral (English and foreign); comprehensive library of recorded music on CD and tape; extensive effects library; original film scores; recording studio.

†**East-West Publications (UK) Ltd** (1977), 8 Caledonia Street, London N1 9DZ *tel* 071-837 5061 *fax* 071-278 4429. *Chairman:* L.W. Carp; *editor:* B. Thompson. Piano, guitar, recorder and vocal music.

Emerson Edition Ltd (1972), Windmill Farm, Ampleforth, North Yorkshire YO6 4HF *tel* (043 93) 324 *fax* (043 93) 715. *Managing director:* June Emerson. Music for wind instruments, and music from Albania.

EMI Music Publishing Ltd, 127 Charing Cross Road, London WC2H 0EA *tel* 071-434 2131 *telemessages/cables* Emimus *telex* 269189 *fax* 071-434 3531. Popular and standard.

Comprising Dix Ltd, EMI Songs Ltd, EMI United Partnership Ltd, B. Feldman & Co. Ltd, Francis, Day & Hunter Ltd, KPM Music Group, The Peter Maurice Music Co. Ltd, Keith Prowse Ltd, Reynolds Music, Robbins Music

Corp. Ltd, Screen Gems-EMI Music Ltd, Lawrence Wright Music Ltd, Virgin Music Publishers Ltd, ATV Music Ltd.

Faber Music Ltd (1966), 3 Queen Square, London WC1N 3AU *tel* 071-278 7436 *telegraphic address* Fabbaf, London WC1 *telex* 299633 FABER G *fax* 071-278 3817. *Directors:* Donald Mitchell (president), Robin Boyle (chairman & chief executive), Martin Kingsbury (vice-chairman & director of publishing), Sally Cavender, Piers Hembry, Thomas H. Pasteur. A general list of the highest quality, comprising both old and new music, and music books.

Fentone Music Ltd, Fleming Road, Earlstrees, Corby, Northants. NN17 4SN *tel* (0536) 260981 *fax* (0536) 401075. Educational and classical music.
Agents for Fenette Music, Earlham Press, Mimram Music, Edizioni Bèrben, Ancona, Italy, F & R. Walsh Publications, London, Notaset, Wiesbaden, London Orchestral Series, Luck's Music Library, Detroit, Norsk Musikforlag, Oslo, XYZ International, Amsterdam.

First Time Music (Publishing) UK Ltd (1986), Sovereign House, 12 Trewartha Road, Praa Sands, Penzance, Cornwall TR20 9ST *tel* (0736) 762826 *fax* (0736) 763328. *Managing director:* Roderick G. Jones. Popular, country, folk, gospel music; music for choirs – in all styles.

Forsyth Bros. Ltd (1857), 126 Deansgate, Manchester M3 2GR *tel* 061-834 3281 *fax* 061-834 0630. Educational piano and instrumental music; modern teaching material. UK distributors of *Music Minus One* and *Pocket Songs*.

Glocken Verlag Ltd (1946), 12-14 Mortimer Street, London W1N 7RD *tel* 071-580 2827 *fax* 071-436 9616. *Directors:* R.M. Toeman, R.G. Holt. Musical works by Franz Lehar.

†**Gresham Books Ltd,** The Gresham Press, PO Box 61, Henley-on-Thames, Oxon RG9 3LQ *tel/fax* (0734) 403789. *Chief executive:* Mrs M.V. Green. Hymn books and prayer books for churches and schools.

Cwmni Cyhoeddi Gwynn Cyf., Y Gerlan, Heol Y Dŵr, Penygroes, Gwynedd LL54 6LR *tel* (0286) 881797. Publishers of Welsh educational and international choral music. Official music publishers to the Welsh Folk Song Society, The Welsh Folk Dance Society, The Court of the National Eisteddfod.

Hughes & Son, Publishers (1820), Parc Tŷ Glas, Llanishen, Cardiff CF4 5DU *tel* (0222) 747444 *telex* 94017032 SIAN G *fax* (0222) 741474. Welsh music, Welsh language, television related material, educational publications, novels.

Hymns Ancient and Modern Ltd, trading under the imprint of **The Canterbury Press Norwich,** St Mary's Works, St Mary's Plain, Norwich, Norfolk NR3 3BH *tel* (0603) 612914/616563 *fax* (0603) 624483. *Directors:* The Very Revd Professor Henry Chadwick KBE (chairman), Dr Allan Wicks, Dr Lionel Dakers, Sir Richard O'Brien; *publisher:* Gordon Knights. The leading hymn book publisher in the UK for churches, schools and other institutions.

†**International Music Publications Ltd,** Woodford Trading Estate, Southend Road, Woodford Green, Essex IG8 8HN *tel* 081-551 6131 *fax* 081-551 3919. Standard and popular, educational, instrumental tutors.

Janus Music (1978), Flat 11, 100 Friars Avenue, Roehampton, London SW15 3DU. *Proprietor:* C.J. Gordon. Recorder music, contemporary wind music, contemporary piano music; woodwind ensembles for schools/amateurs; duets for equal/mixed wind instruments; orchestral music for school/youth orchestras.

Alfred A. Kalmus Ltd, 48 Great Marlborough Street, London W1V 2BN *tel* 071-437 5203/4 *fax* 071-437 6115. Sole representatives of Universal Edition AG, Vienna, Universal Edition (London) Ltd; Theodore Presser Co, Lea

Pocket Scores, International Music Co, Boelke-Bomart Inc., European American Music Corp., Helicon Inc., Bourne Music, Belmont Music, Trio Associates, all USA; Doblinger Edition, Vienna, PWM Editions, Cracow (complete Chopin-Paderewski), Harmonia, Hilversum, Panton, Prague, Berandol, Canada, Boccaccini and Spada, Italy, Aldo Bruzzichelli, Italy, Musikwissenschaftlicher Verlag, Austria, Musica Rara, France, Fraser-Enoch, Kent; Olivan Press, London; Broekmans & Van Poppel, Amsterdam; Power Music, West Yorkshire, Virgo Music, West Midlands, Itchy Fingers Publications, London, Thames Publishing, London, Hug Musikverlag/Foetisch, Zürich.

Edward Kassner Music Co. Ltd (1939), Exmouth House, 11 Pine Street, London EC1R 0JH   *tel* 071-837 5020   *fax* 071-837 4795. *Directors:* Edward Kassner (chairman), David Kassner (managing), Victoria Haslam (copyright manager). Pop music, including rock 'n' roll, country, jazz, ballads, rock and film music.

†**Alfred Lengnick & Co. Ltd** (1893), Pigeon House Meadow, 27 Grove Road, Beaconsfield, Bucks. HP9 1UR   *tel* (0494) 681216   *fax* (0494) 670443. *General manager:* Sally Willison; *creative director:* David Willison. Division of **Complete Music Ltd.** Specialise in educational music; also English contemporary music. Always ready to consider MSS of any type.

MCA Music Ltd, West 6, 77 Fulham Palace Road, London W6 8JA   *tel/fax* 081-741 8646. *Managing director:* Paul Connolly; *creative director:* Kees Van der Hoeven. General and popular vocal music. Includes ATV Music Ltd and Northern Songs.

Maecenas Music, 5 Bushey Close, Old Barn Lane, Kenley, Surrey CR8 5AU   *tel* 081-660 4766/1349   *fax* 081-668 5273. *Directors:* Malcolm Binney, Maggie Barton. Classical, including educational, choral, keyboard and other instrumental.

Momentum Music Ltd (1983), 17-19 Alma Road, Wandsworth, London SW18 1AA   *tel* 081-871 2121   *fax* 081-871 2745. *Directors:* A. Heath, M. Mills. Indie. Welcomes tapes.

M.S.M. Music Publishers (incorporating **Leonard, Gould & Bolttler**), Gilbert House, 406 Roding Lane South (off Woodford Avenue), Woodford Green, Essex IG8 8EY   *tel* 081-551 1282   *fax* 081-550 8377. General and educational.

Music Exchange (Manchester) Ltd (1965), Claverton Road, Manchester M23 9ZA   *tel* 061-946 1234   *fax* 061-946 1195. *Directors:* S.W. Taylor (managing), W. Taylor, A. Osborn, G. Burns. Educational, all grades: instrumental, vocal, tutors.

Music Sales Ltd, 8-9 Frith Street, London W1V 5TZ   *tel* 071-434 0066   *fax* 071-439 2848/734 2246/287 6329. General, popular, classical and educational. Handles copyright, sale and rental of sheet music and other print-related media for: Associated Music Publishers Inc., Chester Music Ltd, Campbell Connelly & Co. Ltd, Cinephonic Music Co. Ltd, Cross Music Ltd, Dash Music Ltd, Dorsey Brothers Music Ltd, Edwin Ashdown Limited, Emergency Music Ltd, Evergreen Music Ltd, Glad Music Ltd, Glendale Music Ltd, Golden Apple Productions, G. Schirmer Inc., Harrison Music Co. Ltd, High-Fye Music Ltd, Hournew Music Ltd, Ivy Music Ltd, J. Curwen & Sons Ltd, Montclare Music Co. Ltd, Noel Gay Music Publishing Ltd, Novello & Company Ltd, Shapiro Bernstein & Co. Ltd, Shawnee Press Inc., Skidmore Music Ltd, Twangy Music Ltd, Union Musical Ediciones, Veronica Music Ltd, Edition Wilhelm Hansen.

Novello & Co. Ltd (1811), 8/9 Frith Street, London W1V 5TZ   *tel* 071-434 0066   *fax* 071-287 6329. Classical and modern orchestral, instrumental, vocal and choral music, church music, school and educational music books.

Octava Music Co. Ltd (1938), 12-14 Mortimer Street, London W1N 7RD   *tel* 071-580 2827   *fax* 071-436 9616. *Contact:* R.M. Toeman. Theatrical and music publishers.

Orestes Music Publishing Ltd (1986), 112 Gunnersbury Avenue, Ealing, London W5 4HB   *tel* 081-993 7441   *fax* 081-992 9993. *Directors:* Dee O'Reilly, Hazel Hemmings. Pop, New Age, dance, musicals.

Oxford University Press, Music Department, Walton Street, Oxford OX2 6DP   *tel* (0865) 56767   *telex* 837330   *fax* (0865) 56646. Orchestral, instrumental, operatic, choral, vocal works, church and organ music by early and modern composers, educational music, courses, and books on music.

Paterson's Publications Ltd—acquired by **Novello & Co. Ltd.**

Peters Edition Ltd (1938), 10-12 Baches Street, London N1 6DN   *tel* 071-253 1638. Copyright/Hire: *tel* 071-251 5094; Promotion/Editorial: *tel* 071-251 6732   *fax* 071-490 4921. Classical and modern music (piano, organ, other instrumental, vocal, choir and brass band). Peters Edition, Hinrichsen Edition, Collection Litolff.

G. Ricordi & Co. (London) Ltd (1808), The Bury, Church Street, Chesham, Bucks. HP5 1JG   *tel* (0494) 783311   *telegraphic address* Ricordi, Chesham   *fax* (0494) 784427. Publishers of Italian opera, music for piano, classical and contemporary, operatic arias, songs, choral large scale works and part songs for all voices, orchestral works, classical and contemporary, instrumental, string, woodwind, brass tutors, exercises, etc., guitar music of all types.

Roberton Publications, The Windmill, Wendover, Aylesbury, Bucks. HP22 6JJ   *tel* (0296) 623107. *Partners:* Kenneth Roberton, Margaret Roberton. Choral and educational; also piano, chamber, orchestral, and music for all instruments. Represent Leslie Music Supply, Oakville, Ontario; Swingle Music, New Jersey.

Schott & Co. Ltd (1835), 48 Great Marlborough Street, London W1V 2BN   *tel* 071-437 1246   *fax* 071-437 0263. Classical/contemporary/educational music/books.

Sea Dream Music (1976), 236 Sebert Road, Forest Gate, London E7 0NP   *tel* 081-534 8500. *Senior partner:* S.A. Law. Christian-based rock, blues and folk.

R. Smith & Co. Ltd (1857), c/o Campbell Connelly & Co. Ltd, 8-9 Frith Street, London W1V 5TZ. Wind/brass band, wind/brass ensemble, educational.

Spartan Press Ltd (1989), Old Brewery House, Redbrook, Monmouth NP5 4LU   *tel* (0600) 712482   *fax* (0600) 712483. *Directors:* M.T.R. Goddard, P.D. Goddard. Educational music for teachers/students; choral/church music.

†**Sphemusations,** Gramercy House, 12 Northfield Road, Onehouse, Stowmarket, Suffolk IP14 3HF   *tel* (0449 61) 3388. Serious music, brass band, choral, keyboard music, instrumental and educational; records of modern works; tapes.

Stainer & Bell Ltd, PO Box 110, Victoria House, 23 Gruneisen Road, London N3 1DZ   *tel* 081-343 3303   *fax* 081-343 3024. Serious music of all kinds: instrumental, choral, songs, educational and religious; tutors.
Book and music publishers including the imprints of Augener, Belton Books, Galliard, Stainer & Bell, A. Weekes, Joseph Williams.

Sylvester Music Co. Ltd, 80-82 Wardour Street, London W1V 3LF   *tel* 071-437 4933/4   *fax* 071-437 2744. Popular and orchestral music. Comprehensive library of recorded music on CD and tape; extensive effects library; specially composed scores; transfers to tape and film.

Thames Publishing (1970), 14 Barlby Road, London W10 6AR   *tel* 081-969 3579. Serious music of all types, particularly vocal, choral and instrumental. MSS welcome *but should always be preceded by a letter.*

United Music Publishers Ltd (1932), 42 Rivington Street, London EC2A 3BN   *tel* 071-729 4700   *fax* 071-739 6549. Contemporary English works. Agents for the principal French music publishing houses and specialists in the distribution of French, Spanish and other foreign music.

Universal Edition (London) Ltd, 48 Great Marlborough Street, London W1V 2BN   *tel* 071-437 5203   *fax* 071-437 6115. Serious music of all types.

Vanderbeek & Imrie Ltd (1983), 15 Marvig, Lochs, Isle of Lewis PA86 9QP   *tel/ fax* (0851) 88216. *Directors:* Martyn Imrie, M.E.H. Hunter OBE, J.M. Imrie. 20th century serious contemporary music; 15th and 16th century Latin church music.

Warner Chappell Music Ltd, 129 Park Street, London W1Y 3FA   *tel* 071-629 7600   *fax* 071-499 9718. Popular, standard and show music.
Brussels, Munich, Johannesburg, Los Angeles, Madrid, Milan, Bussum, Nashville, New York, Paris, Stockholm, Sydney, Tokyo, Toronto, Buenos Aires, Vienna, Rio de Janeiro, Copenhagen, Hamburg, Athens, Hong Kong, Tel-Aviv, Kuala Lumpur, Mexico, Oslo, Lima, Lisbon, Singapore, Caracas.

†**Warren & Phillips** (1906), 126 Deansgate, Manchester M3 2GR   *tel* 061-834 3281   *fax* 061-834 0630. Educational piano and instrumental music; modern teaching material.

Josef Weinberger Ltd (1885), 12-14 Mortimer Street, London W1N 7RD   *tel* 071-580 2827 (4 lines)   *fax* 071-436 9616. *Directors:* R.G. Holt, R.M. Toeman; *executive directors:* G. Barker, K. Dixon, G. Kingsley, J. Schofield. Musical theatre, contemporary classical, educational and religious music.

Workers' Music Association (1936), 240 Perry Rise, Forest Hill, London SE23 2QT   *tel* 081-699 2250. General music organisation with emphasis on the social aspects of music. Publications; Music courses.

UNITED STATES OF AMERICA

Boosey & Hawkes, Inc., 24 East 21st Street, New York, NY 10010-7200   *tel* 212-228-3300   *fax* 212-473-5730. Symphonic, opera, ballet, concert and educational music.

Bourne Co., 5 West 37th Street, New York, NY 10018   *tel* 212-391-4300   *fax* 212-391-4306; *London office:* 34-36 Maddox Street, W1R 9PD   *tel* 071-493 6412   *fax* 071-493 6583. Popular, standard, choral, educational wind band, instrumental, production and film music.

Hinrichsen Edition—part of **C.F. Peters Corporation.** Classical and contemporary music.

International Music Company, 5 West 37th Street, New York, NY 10018   *tel* 212-391-4200   *fax* 212-391-4306. Subsidiary of **Bourne Co.** Performing editions of classical, romantic and modern chamber music for piano, instrumental solo, duet, trio, quartet, quintet, large ensembles, voice; study scores, opera scores; concerto and aria orchestral parts on hire.

The Lorenz Corporation, 501 East Third Street, PO Box 802, Dayton, OH 45401-0802   *tel* 1-800-444-1144/513-228-6118   *fax* 513-223-2042.
Roger Dean Publishing (division). *Editor:* Scott Foss. MSS for schools, colleges and churches.

Heritage Music Press (division). *Editors:* Mary Lynn Lightfoot (choral), Barbara Meeks (instrumental). Choral and concert band MSS for elementary, junior-high and high schools (secondary schools).

Kirkland House (division). *Editor:* Terry Kirkland. Sacred choral music for children's choirs.

Laurel Press (division). Gospel music.

Lorenz Publishing Co. (division). *Editors:* Gil Martin, Hugh S. Livingston, Dorothy Wells. Anthems and church keyboard voluntaries.

The Sacred Music Press (division). *Editor:* Dale Wood. Church choral and organ music.

Sonshine Productions (division). Contemporary sacred music.

Triune Music Inc. (division). *Editor:* Terry Kirkland. Sacred choral music.

Unity Music Press (division). *Editor:* Mark Barnard. Sacred contemporary choral and keyboard music for liturgical churches.

Music Sales Corp., 257 Park Avenue South, New York, NY 10010 *tel* 212-254-2100 *telex* 428351 *fax* 212-254-2013. Popular music.

C.F. Peters Corporation, 373 Park Avenue South, New York, NY 10016 *tel* 212-686-4147. (Edition Peters, Hinrichsen Edition, and other European music publications, in USA.)

Theodore Presser Co. (1783), Bryn Mawr, PA 19010 *tel* 610-525-3636 *fax* 610-527-7841. *Contact:* editor-in-chief. Serious and educational music. Considers suitable MSS from composers. Does not use or buy songs or lyrics unless with a musical setting. Publication at the firm's expense only.

Publishes under: **John Church Company, Oliver Ditson Company, Elkan-Vogel, Inc., Mercury Music Corporation, Merion Music, Inc.**

G. Schirmer Inc., 257 Park Avenue South, New York, NY 10010 *tel* 212-254-2100 *fax* 212-254-2013 *Internet* 71360.3514 @compuserv.com. Subsidiary of **Music Sales Corp.** Classical and contemporary music.

Associated Music Publishers, Inc. (subsidiary). Classical and contemporary music.

Warner/Chappell Music Inc., 10585 Santa Monica Boulevard, Los Angeles, CA 90025-4950 *tel* 310-441-8600. Popular, standard and show music.

Includes, among others, the following companies: WB Music Corp., Warner-Tamerlane Publishing Corp., Harms Inc., M. Witmark, Remick, Advanced, New World Music Corp., Pepamar Music Corp., Schubert Music Publishing Corp., Weill-Brecht-Harms Company Inc., Viva Music Inc., Zapata Music Inc., Curtom Publishing Co. Inc., Rodart Music Corp., Jalynne Corp., Twentieth Century Fox Music Corp., House of Gold Music, Foster Frees Music Inc., Pendulum Music, Chappell Music, Unichappell, Rightsongs, Ricks Music, Delightful Music, Summy Birchard, Mighty Three Music, Bellboy Music.

Agents

Literary Agents

Literary agents exist to look after the commercial interests of their authors and to sell saleable material. In addition to placing work with a British publisher, a literary agent will negotiate on behalf of the author – either directly or via associates – the sale of US, translation, dramatic, film and all other rights in a copyright work. While they are looking for new writers and are prepared to take pains with a writer whose work shows quality or promise, agents do not exist to teach people how to write. Writers must not expect agents, publishers or editors to comment at length on unsuitable work submitted to them. Every writer must expect disappointments, especially at the outset, but if he has something to say and knows how to say it, then eventually (if he is patient) he will learn how to satisfy an editor's requirements. Alternatively he will learn that he should give up attempting to write and turn to some other form of activity.

If a writer of proven ability is contemplating using an agent, he is advised in his own interests *to write a preliminary letter* to ascertain whether the agent will consider him as a potential client. He should also enquire the agent's terms if they are not given in the entry in the following pages. Reputable agents do not accept work unless they consider it to be of a marketable standard and an author submitting work to an agent for the first time *should therefore enclose return postage*. Most agents prefer a synopsis and specimen chapters to be sent in the first instance. It is not advisable for a writer to send work to more than one agent at the same time. It is discourteous and wastes the agent's time.

The Association of Authors' Agents (see page 612) is the trade association of British agents. Members, designated with an asterisk in the following list, meet regularly and commit themselves to observe a code of practice in the conduct of their business. Association members do not charge a reading fee, but some firms do, whether or not they agree to take the author on. Usually the reading fee (for a report and advice on a MS) is refunded on acceptance of the material. It is not to be confused with commission which is a percentage charge on monies earned for the author.

All agents listed below were circulated with a questionnaire with a view to providing pertinent information and are asked to keep this information up to date. The list does not purport to be exhaustive. If any who are not included would like to receive a copy of the questionnaire and to be considered for inclusion, application should be made to the publishers.

UNITED KINGDOM

*Full member of the Association of Authors' Agents

A & B Personal Management Ltd (1982), 5th Floor, Plaza Suite, 114 Jermyn Street, London SW1Y 6HJ   *tel* 071-839 4433   *fax* 071-930 5738. *Directors:* R.W. Ellis, R. Ellis.
Full-length MSS. Scripts for TV, theatre, cinema; also novels, fiction and non-fiction (home 12½%, overseas 15%), performance rights (12½%). Synopsis required initially from writers submitting work for first time. No reading fee for synopsis, plays or screenplays, but fee charged for full-length MSS. Return postage required.

Aitken, Stone & Wylie Ltd, incorporating **Hughes Massie Ltd,** 29 Fernshaw Road, London SW10 0TG   *tel* 071-351 7561   *fax* 071-376 3594. *Directors:* Gillon Aitken, Brian Stone, Sally Riley, David Godwin, Andrew Wylie (USA).
Full-length MSS (home 10%, USA 15%, translations 20%). USA associates: Wylie, Aitken & Stone Inc., Suite 2106, 250 West 57th Street, New York, NY 10107   *tel* 212-246-0069. Preliminary letter and return postage essential.

Jacintha Alexander Associates (1981), 47 Emperor's Gate, London SW7 4HJ   *tel* 071-373 9258   *fax* 071-373 4374. *Directors:* Jacintha Alexander, Julian Alexander.
Full length MSS. General fiction and non-fiction (home 15%, overseas 20%). No poetry, plays, textbooks or science fiction. Film or TV scripts handled for established clients only. Works with agents world-wide. No reading fee but preliminary letter, synopsis and sae essential.

Darley Anderson Literary Agency, Estelle House, 11 Eustace Road, London SW6 1JB   *tel* 071-385 6652   *fax* 071-386 5571. *Proprietor:* Darley Anderson; *associates:* Pippa Dyson (film/TV), Tara Lawrence (crime).
Full-length MSS. Popular, commercial fiction and non-fiction. Special fiction interests: all types of women's novels including contemporary, 20th century romantic sagas, sexy novels and 'women in jeopardy' stories; thrillers; crime (cosy/hard boiled); historical crime; horror; fantasy; comedy; and Irish novels. Special non-fiction interests: celebrity biography and autobiography, diet, beauty, health, cookery, popular psychology, self-help, popular religion and supernatural (home 15%, US/translation 20%, film, TV, radio 20%). No poetry, plays or academic books. Can arrange PR and author publicity and specialist financial advice; editorial guidance on selected MSS. Preliminary letter, synopsis and first three chapters. Return postage/sae essential. Overseas associates: Mitchell Rose Agency (New York), H.N. Swanson Film Agency (LA/Hollywood) and leading foreign agents world-wide.

Aquarius Literary Agency & Picture Library (1973 in UK), PO Box 5, Hastings, East Sussex TN34 1HR   *tel* (0424) 721 196   *fax* (0424) 717 704. *Directors:* David P. Corkill, Gilbert Gibson (SA).
Showbusiness only, including biography and autobiography. No fiction. Full-length and short MSS (home 10-15%, overseas 20-30%); performance rights (home 10%, overseas 20%). Works in conjunction with overseas agents. Will suggest revision. Preliminary letter; no unsolicited material. No reading fee.

Yvonne Baker Associates (1987), 8 Temple Fortune Lane, London NW11 7UD   *tel* 081-455 8687   *fax* 081-458 3143.
Television, film (12½%), theatre, radio (10%). Particularly interested in contemporary drama and TV comedy drama series. No books, short stories, articles, poetry. No reading fee but preliminary letter essential with full information and sae.

*Blake Friedmann Literary, TV & Film Agency Ltd (1977), 37-41 Gower Street, London WC1E 6HH   *tel* 071-631 4331   *fax* 071-323 1274. *Directors:* Carole Blake, Julian Friedmann, Barbara Jones, Conrad Williams.
Full-length MSS. Fiction: thrillers, contemporary and historical women's novels and literary fiction; non-fiction: investigative books, biography, travel; no poetry or plays (home 15%, overseas 20%). Specialise in film and television rights; place journalism and short stories for existing clients only. Represented world-wide; in USA by Writers House Inc. Preliminary letter, synopsis and first two chapters preferred. No reading fee.

David Bolt Associates, 12 Heath Drive, Send, Surrey GU23 7EP   *tel* Woking (0483) 721118   *fax* (0483) 222878.
Specialises in biography, fiction, theology. Full-length MSS (home 10%, overseas 19%; all other rights including film, video and television 10%). No unsolicited short stories or play scripts. Will sometimes suggest revision. Works in association with overseas agencies world-wide. Preliminary letter essential. Reading fee terms on application.

Rosemary Bromley Literary Agency, Avington, Winchester, Hants SO21 1DB   *tel/fax* (0962) 779656.
Specialises in biography, travel, leisure, cookery (home 10%, overseas from 15%.) No poetry. No reading fee. *No* unsolicited MSS; enquiries unaccompanied by return postage will not be answered. For children's books see **Juvenilia.**

*Felicity Bryan, 2A North Parade, Banbury Road, Oxford OX2 6PE   *tel* (0865) 513816   *fax* (0865) 310055.
Fiction and general non-fiction; no light romance, science fiction, short stories, plays or children's (home 10%, overseas 20%). Performance rights handled by Curtis Brown; translation rights handled by Andrew Nurnberg Associates; works in conjunction with US agents. Return postage essential.

Peter Bryant (Writers) (1980), 94 Adelaide Avenue, London SE4 1YR   *tel* 081-691 9085   *fax* 081-692 9107.
Special interests: children's fiction and TV comedy; also handles drama scripts for theatre, radio and television (home/USA 10%). Overseas associate: Hartmann and Stauffacher, Germany. No reading fee for the above categories, but sae essential for all submissions.

Diane Burston (1984), 46 Cromwell Avenue, Highgate, London N6 5HL   *tel* 081-340 6130.
General fiction and non-fiction, full-length MSS (home 10%, overseas 20%, USA 15%), short stories (15%). No unsolicited MSS; preliminary enquiry and sae essential. Reading service available on request.

Bycornute Books, 76a Ashford Road, Eastbourne, East Sussex BN21 3TE   *tel* (0323) 726819   *fax* (0323) 649053 Bycorn/Cresc. *Director:* Ayeshah Abdel-Haleem.
Specialises in illustrated books on sacred art, comparative religion, mythology, cosmology, astrology, iconography, symbolism, metaphysics and spiritual development (*not* fiction, children's, psychic studies or psychology); associated cardboard novelties. Full-length and short MSS (10%). Will suggest revision; fee by arrangement.

*Campbell Thomson & McLaughlin Ltd, 1 King's Mews, London WC1N 2JA   *tel* 071-242 0958   *fax* 071-242 2408. *Directors:* John McLaughlin, Charlotte Bruton, Hal Cheetham.
Full-length book MSS (home 10%, overseas up to 20% including commission to foreign agent). No poetry, plays or television scripts, short stories or

children's books. USA agents represented: Raines & Raines, The Fox Chase Agency, Inc. Representatives in most European countries. Preliminary letter with sae first, please. No reading fee, but return postage required. Subsidiary company: **Peter Janson-Smith Ltd.**

Carnell Literary Agency (1951), Danes Croft, Goose Lane, Little Hallingbury, Herts. CM22 7RG *tel* (0279) 723626. *Proprietor:* Pamela Buckmaster.
All MSS except poetry. Specialises in science/fantasy fiction. Works in conjunction with many foreign agents (home 10%, overseas 10% or 19% through sub-agent). Outline plus first two chapters initially – return postage essential.

Casarotto Ramsay Ltd (1992; formerly **Margaret Ramsay Ltd,** 1953), National House, 60-66 Wardour Street, London W1V 3HP *tel* 071-287 4450 *fax* 071-287 9128. *Directors:* Tom Erhardt, Jenne Casarotto.
MSS – theatre, films, television, sound broadcasting only (10%). Works in conjuction with agents in USA and in all foreign countries. Preliminary letter essential. No reading fee.

Judith Chilcote (1990), 8 Wentworth Mansions, Keats Grove, London NW3 2RL *tel* 071-794 3717 *fax* 071-794 7431.
Commercial fiction, non-fiction – celebrity, Royal books, health and beauty, self-help, alternative medicine, cinema, current affairs, TV tie-ins (home 15%, overseas 20-25%). *No* short stories, children's, poetry. Works in conjunction with overseas agents and New York affiliate. UK representative for Jonathon Lazear Agency, The Miller Agency and Cader Books. No reading fee but preliminary letter with CV and sae essential.

Teresa Chris Literary Agency (1988), 16 Castellain Mansions, Castellain Road, London W9 1HA *tel* 071-289 0653. *Director:* Teresa Chris.
Crime, women's general and literary fiction; all non-fiction, especially health, cooking, business, arts and crafts. *No* science fiction, horror, short stories, poetry, academic books (home 10%, USA 15%, rest 20%). Own US office: Thompson & Chris Literary Agency. No reading fee. No unsolicited MSS accepted without introductory letter describing work and enclosing return postage.

Christy & Moore Ltd—see **Sheil Land Associates Ltd.**

Serafina Clarke (1980), 98 Tunis Road, London W12 7EY *tel* 081-749 6979 *fax* 081-740 6862.
Full-length MSS (home 15%, overseas 20%). Works in conjunction with agents overseas. No reading fee, but preliminary letter and return postage essential.

Robert Clarson-Leach (1985), Downlands, Jevington Road, Wannock, East Sussex BN26 5NX *tel/fax* given only to accepted clients.
Biography, finance, humour, adventure; full-length fiction occasionally handled (home 12½%, overseas 25%); will suggest revision where appropriate. Initial letter and sae essential; correct postage required for return of MSS. Modest reading fee.

Mary Clemmey (1992), 6 Dunollie Road, London NW5 2XP *tel/fax* 071-267 1290.
Full-length MSS. Fiction and non-fiction (home 10%, overseas 20%), performance rights (15%). *No* children's books. Works in conjunction with US agent. No reading fee.

Jonathan Clowes Ltd (1960), 10 Iron Bridge House, Bridge Approach, London NW1 8BD *tel* 071-722 7674 *fax* 071-722 7677. *Directors:* Jonathan Clowes, Ann Evans, Brie Burkeman.

Full-length MSS fiction and non-fiction; no academic or text books (home/ USA 15%, translation 19%). Television, film, theatre and radio. Works in association with agents in most foreign countries.

Elspeth Cochrane Agency (1967), 11-13 Orlando Road, London SW4 0LE *tel* 071-622 0314 *fax* 071-622 0314. *Director:* Miss Elspeth Cochrane. Full-length MSS (home and overseas 12½%), performance rights (12½%). No reading fee.

Dianne Coles Agency (1980), The Old Forge House, Sulgrave, Banbury, Oxon OX17 2RP *tel/fax* (0295) 760692. *Contact:* Dianne Coles, Philip Gosling. Small, select, non-fiction agency (home 15%, overseas 20%). Own US office. No phone calls, scripts or unsolicited MSS; preliminary letter and return postage essential.

Rosica Colin Ltd (1949), 1 Clareville Grove Mews, London SW7 5AH *tel* 071-370 1080 *telegraphic address* Colrep, London SW7 *fax* 071-244 6441. *Directors:* Sylvie Marston, Joanna Marston. All full-length MSS (excluding sci-fi and poetry); also theatre, film and sound broadcasting (home 10%, overseas 10-20%). No reading fee, but may take 3-4 months to consider full MSS. Send synopsis only in first instance, with letter outlining writing credits and whether MS has been previously submitted, plus return postage.

*Jane Conway-Gordon (1982), in association with Andrew Mann Ltd, 1 Old Compton Street, London W1V 5PH *tel* 071-494 0148 *fax* 071-287 9264. Full length MSS, performance rights (home 10%, overseas 20%). Represented in all foreign countries. No reading fee but preliminary letter and return postage essential.

*Rupert Crew Ltd (founded by F. Rupert Crew, 1927), King's Mews, London WC1N 2JA *tel* 071-242 8586 *telegraphic address* Authorship, Holb., London *fax* 071-831 7914. *Directors:* Kathleen A. Crew, Doreen Montgomery, Shirley Russell, Caroline Montgomery. International business management, available to a limited clientele, for authors seeking world representation: the agency specialises in promoting major book projects – non-fiction, general and women's fiction – especially those having serialisation potential. Preliminary letter and sae. Commission 10-20% by arrangement. No reading fees. Also acts independently as publishers' consultants.

Cruickshank Cazenove Ltd (1983), 97 Old South Lambeth Road, London SW8 1XU *tel* 071-735 2933 *fax* 071-820 1081. *Director:* Harriet Cruickshank. Fiction, film, television, theatre and radio scripts (home 10%, overseas varies). Works with agents abroad. No reading fee but preliminary letter essential with sae. Also agent for directors and designers.

Curtis Brown, 162-168 Regent Street, London W1R 5TB *tel* 071-872 0331 *cables* Browncurt, London W1 *telex* 920379 *fax* 071-872 0332. *Chairman:* Robert Loder; *managing director:* Peter Murphy; *directors:* Diana Baring, Sebastian Born, Tim Curnow (Australia), Sue Freathy, Antony Harwood, Julia Kreitman, Jonathan Lloyd, Diana Mackay, Anne McDermid, Anthea Morton-Saner, Peter Robinson, Leah Schmidt, Vivienne Schuster, Michael Shaw, Elizabeth Stevens. Agents for the negotiation in all markets of novels, general non-fiction, children's books and associated rights (home 10%, USA 15-20%, Canada and foreign 20%). Preliminary letter required; no reading fee. MSS for films, theatre, television and radio. Also agents for directors and designers.

Judy Daish Associates Ltd (1978), 83 Eastbourne Mews, London W2 6LQ *tel*
071-262 1101 *fax* 071-706 1027. *Agents:* Judy Daish, Sara Stroud, Deborah
Harwood.
Theatre, film, television, radio (rates by negotiation). No reading fee.

The Caroline Davidson and Robert Ducas Literary Agency (1988), 5 Queen
Anne's Gardens, London W4 1TU *tel* 081-995 5768 *fax* 081-994 2770.
Specialises in literary fiction and all kinds of non-fiction, including highly
illustrated books, academic and reference works ($12\frac{1}{2}$%); will suggest revision.
Works with Robert Ducas in New York and overseas agents, if necessary. No
reading fee, but preliminary letter with book proposal, CV and sae required.

Merric Davidson Literary Agency (1990), Oakwood, Ashley Park, Tunbridge
Wells, Kent TN4 8UA *tel/fax* (0892) 514282.
Fiction and general non-fiction; popular music (home 10%, overseas 20%).
No unsolicited MSS. Preliminary letter with synopsis, author information and
sae essential. No initial reading fee, may suggest revision, subsequent editorial
advice by arrangement.

Felix De Wolfe (1946), Manfield House, 376 Strand, London WC2R 0LR *tel*
071-379 5767 *fax* 071-836 0337.
Theatre, films, television, sound broadcasting, fiction (home $12\frac{1}{2}$%, overseas
20%). Works in conjunction with many foreign agencies.

Dorian Literary Agency (1986), Upper Thornehill, 27 Church Road, St Mary-
church, Torquay, Devon TQ1 4QY *tel* (0803) 312095. *Proprietor:* Mrs D.
Lumley.
Full-length MSS. Specialises in women's writing, SF, fantasy and horror, crime
and thrillers (home 10%, USA 15%, translations 20-25%), performance rights
(10%). No poetry, children's or short stories. Works in conjunction with
agencies in most countries; negotiates direct with USA. No reading fee;
preliminary letter with sample material essential; return postage essential.

Anne Drexl (1988), 8 Roland Gardens, London SW7 3PH *tel* 071-244 9645.
Special interest in women's fiction, glitzy, family sagas and crime fiction.
Inclusive short stories for both genres. Also illustrated books for young readers,
activity titles, and juvenile fiction generally (home $12\frac{1}{2}$%, overseas 20-23%).
Works in conjunction with foreign agencies and negotiates direct with foreign
publishers. No reading fee, but no unsolicited MSS; return postage and preliminary letter essential.

Toby Eady Associates Ltd (1968), in association with Xandra Hardie, 18 Park
Walk, London SW10 0AQ *tel* 071-352 4450 *fax* 071-352 3627. *Directors:*
Toby Eady, M.A. Siepmann; *associates:* Xandra Hardie, Herta Ryder.
Books on Africa, the Middle East, India, China, fishing, fiction, non-fiction
and poetry (home 10%, overseas 20%), performance rights (10%). Works
with overseas associates. No reading fee, but return postage essential.

Faith Evans Associates (1987), Clerkenwell House, 45 Clerkenwell Green, Lon-
don EC1R 0EB *tel* 071-490 2535 *fax* 071-490 4958.
Small select agency (home 15%, overseas 20%). Sub-agents in most countries.
No phone calls, scripts or unsolicited MSS; preliminary letter and sae essential.
No reading fee.

Fact & Fiction Agency Ltd, 16 Greenway Close, London NW9 5AZ *tel* 081-
205 5716. *Directors:* Roy Lomax, Vera Lomax.
Television, radio (home 10%, overseas 15%). By introduction only.

*****John Farquharson Ltd**—see **Curtis Brown.**

Film Rights Ltd (1932), 483 Southbank House, Black Prince Road, Albert Embankment, London SE1 7SJ   *tel* 071-735 8171. *Directors:* D.M. Sims, Maurice Lambert, Laurence Fitch.
Theatre, films, television and sound broadcasting (10%). Represented in USA and abroad.

Laurence Fitch Ltd (1952) (incorporating The London Play Company; 1922), 483 Southbank House, Black Prince Road, Albert Embankment, London SE1 7SJ   *tel* 071-735 8171. *Directors:* F.H.L. Fitch, Joan Potts, Brendan Davis.
Theatre, films, television and sound broadcasting. Also works with several agencies in New York and in Europe.

Jill Foster Ltd (1978), 3 Lonsdale Road, London SW13 9ED   *tel* 081-741 9410 *fax* 081-741 2916.
Theatre, films, television, sound broadcasting (12½%). Particularly interested in film and television comedy and drama. No novels or short stories. No reading fee. Preliminary letter essential.

Fox & Howard Literary Agency (1992), 4 Bramerton Street, Chelsea, London SW3 5JX   *tel* 071-352 0561   *fax* 071-352 8691. *Partners:* Chelsey Fox, Charlotte Howard.
Full-length MSS. General non-fiction: biography, health, sport, naval and military history, business, humour, self-help, true crime, travel; educational and reference: GCSE and A level (home 10%, overseas 20%); will suggest revision where appropriate. *No* poetry, plays, short stories, children's, science fiction, fantasy or horror. No reading fee, but preliminary letter and synopsis with sae essential.

*****Fraser & Dunlop Ltd**—see **The Peters Fraser & Dunlop Group Ltd.**

*****Fraser & Dunlop Scripts Ltd**—see **The Peters Fraser & Dunlop Group Ltd.**

French's, 9 Elgin Mews South, London W9 1JZ   *tel* 071-266 3321   *fax* 071-286 6716. *Director:* John French.
All MSS; specialises in novels and screenplays (home/overseas 10%); theatre, films, television, radio (10%). Reading service available, details on application. Sae must be enclosed with all MSS.

Vernon Futerman Associates (1984), 159A Goldhurst Terrace, London NW6 3EU   *tel* 071-625 9601   *fax* 071-372 1282. *Directors:* Vernon Futerman (managing), Guy Rose, Wendy Futerman.
Specialises in academic (science, humanities), art, education, politics, current affairs, literary criticism, showbusiness, travel and business books. Full-length MSS (home 12½-17½%, overseas 17½-22½%), performance rights (12½-17½%). Works in conjunction with overseas agents. Will suggest revision. No reading fee; preliminary letter with synopsis and sae essential. No unsolicited MSS.

Jüri Gabriel, 35 Camberwell Grove, London SE5 8JA   *tel/fax* 071-703 6186.
Quality fiction and non-fiction (current specialisations: medical, military, practical art, popular academic); radio, television and film. Full-length MSS (home 10%, overseas 20%), performance rights (10%); will suggest revision where appropriate. No short stories, articles, verse or books for children. No reading fee; return postage essential.

Kerry Gardner Management (1975), 15 Kensington High Street, London W8 5NP   *tel* 071-937 4478   *fax* 071-376 2587.
Specialises in performance rights – represents playwrights, and film, TV and radio scriptwriters (10%). Works in conjunction with overseas agents. No reading fee.

Eric Glass Ltd (1932), 28 Berkeley Square, London W1X 6HD *tel* 071-629 7162 *telegraphic address* Blancheric, London W1 *fax* 071-499 6780. *Directors:* Eric Glass, Janet Glass.
Full-length MSS only; also theatre, films, television, and sound broadcasting. No unsolicited MSS. No reading fee. Sole representatives of the French Society of Authors (Societé des Auteurs et Compositeurs Dramatiques).

*Christine Green Author's Agent (1984), 2 Barbon Close, London WC1N 3JX *tel* 071-831 4956 *fax* 071-831 4840.
Fiction and general non-fiction. Full-length MSS (home 10%, overseas 20%). Works in conjunction with agencies in Europe and Scandinavia. No reading fee, but preliminary letter and return postage essential.

*Greene & Heaton Ltd (1962), 37 Goldhawk Road, London W12 8QQ *tel* 081-749 0315 *fax* 081-749 0318. *Directors:* Elaine Greene (USA), Carol Heaton, Timothy Webb.
Full-length MSS, fiction and non-fiction (home 10%, overseas 20%, translation 20%); Susan Elliott (children's) – writers and illustrators. *No* plays, TV or film scripts. Works in conjunction with agencies in most countries. No reading fee. Preliminary letter and return postage required.

*The Jane Gregory Agency (1982)—see **Gregory & Radice Authors' Agents.**

*Gregory & Radice Authors' Agents (1982), Riverside Studios, Crisp Road, Hammersmith, London W6 9RL *tel* 081-741 3646 *fax* 081-846 9039. *Partners:* Jane Gregory, Dr Lisanne Radice.
Full-length MSS; fiction and non-fiction. Specialise in crime fiction, thrillers and politics (home 15%, articles, USA and translation 20%, film/TV rights 15%). No short stories, plays, film scripts, science fiction, fantasy, poetry, academic or children's books. No reading fee, editorial advice given to own authors. No unsolicited MSS: preliminary letter, synopsis and first three chapters essential plus return postage.

David Grossman Literary Agency Ltd (1976), 110-114 Clerkenwell Road, London EC1M 5SA *tel* 071-251 5046/7 *fax* 071-490 2702.
Full-length MSS (home 10-15%, overseas 20% including foreign agent's commission), performance rights (15%). Works in conjunction with agents in New York, Europe, Japan. No reading fee, but preliminary letter required.

The Guidelines Partnership (1986), 18 Pretoria Road, Cambridge CB4 1HE *tel* (0223) 314668 *fax* (0223) 64619. *Partners:* Geoff Black, Stuart Wall, Linda Black, Eleanor Wall.
Specialises in educational texts and exam-related study guides for all ages and all subject areas (home 15%, overseas 20%); will suggest revision where appropriate. Works with overseas educational publishers. No reading fee.

*A.M. Heath & Co. Ltd (1919), 79 St Martin's Lane, London WC2N 4AA *tel* 071-836 4271 *cables* Script, London *telegraphic address* Script, London WC2 *fax* 071-497 2561. *Directors:* Mark Hamilton, Michael Thomas, William Hamilton, Sara Fisher, Sarah Molloy.
Full-length MSS (home 10-15%, USA 20%, translation 20%), performance rights (15%). Agents in USA and all European countries and Japan. No reading fee.

Duncan Heath Associates Ltd—see **ICM Ltd.**

*David Higham Associates Ltd (1935), 5-8 Lower John Street, Golden Square, London W1R 4HA *tel* 071-437 7888 *fax* 071-437 1072. *Directors:* Bruce Hunter, Jacqueline Korn, Anthony Crouch, John Rush, Elizabeth Cree, Anthony Goff, Ania Corless.

Agents for the negotiation of all rights in fiction, general non-fiction, plays, film and television scripts (home 10%, USA/translation 20%). USA associate agency: Harold Ober Associates Inc. Represented in all foreign markets. Preliminary letter and return postage essential. No reading fee.

Pamela Hodgson Agency (1990), 38 Westminster Palace Gardens, Artillery Row, London SW1P 1RR *tel/fax* 071-222 4468.
Picture story books for young children (home 15%). Preliminary phone call or letter essential. Sae for return of MS.

*Vanessa Holt Associates Ltd (1989), 59 Crescent Road, Leigh-on-Sea, Essex SS9 2PF *tel* (0702) 73787 *fax* (0702) 471890.
General adult fiction and non-fiction (home 10%, overseas 20%). Works in conjunction with many foreign agencies. No reading fee, but preliminary letter essential.

Valerie Hoskins Associates, 20 Charlotte Street, London W1P 1HJ *tel* 071-637 4490 *fax* 071-436 9618. *Proprietor:* Valerie Hoskins.
Film, television, theatre and radio only (12.5% home and maximum 20% overseas). No reading fee, but sae appreciated. Works in conjunction with overseas agents. *No* unsolicited MSS; preliminary letter essential.

Howard Seddon Associates (1988), BM Box 1129, London WC1N 3XX *tel* (0923) 229784 *fax* (0923) 229784. *Partners:* Dr Keith H. Seddon, Sarah J. Howard.
Full-length MSS. Fiction: fantasy, gothic, horror, literary; non-fiction: folklore, New Age, occult, philosophy, religion, social issues (home 15%, overseas 20%); will suggest revision where appropriate (will also undertake revision; fees variable). Reading fee may be charged.

*Tanja Howarth Literary Agency (1970), 19 New Row, London WC2N 4LA *tel* 071-240 5553/836 4142 *fax* 071-379 0969.
Full-length MSS, fiction and non-fiction (home 10%, USA 15%, translation 20%). No reading fee.

Hughes Massie Ltd—see Aitken, Stone & Wylie Ltd.

ICM Ltd, Oxford House, 76 Oxford Street, London W1R 1RB *tel* 071-636 6565 *fax* 071-323 0101. *Directors:* Duncan Heath, Susan Rodgers, Michael Foster, Ian Amos, Amanda Davis, Serena Cullen.
Specialises in scripts for film, theatre, TV, radio (home 10%, overseas 10%). Part of International Creative Management Inc., Los Angeles and New York. No reading fee.

Michael Imison Playwrights Ltd (formerly Dr Jan Van Loewen Ltd), 28 Almeida Street, London N1 1TD *tel* 071-354 3174 *fax* 071-359 6273. *Directors:* Michael Imison MA, Tamsyn Imison BSc.
Specialises in stage plays, also cover radio, TV, film (home 10%, overseas 15%), no fiction or general MSS. Represented in all major countries. No reading fee. No unsolicited scripts; recommendation from known theatre professional required.

*Intercontinental Literary Agency (1965), The Chambers, Chelsea Harbour, Lots Road, London SW10 0XF *tel* 071-351 4763 *fax* 071-351 4809. Anthony Guest Gornall and Nicki Kennedy.
Concerned only with translation rights for The Peters Fraser & Dunlop Group Ltd, London and Harold Matson Company, Inc., New York.

International Copyright Bureau Ltd (1905), 22A Aubrey House, Maida Avenue, London W2 1TQ *tel* 071-724 8034 *telegraphic address* Volscius, London *fax* 071-724 7662. *Directors:* Joy Westendarp, J.C.H. Hadfield (secretary).

Theatre, films, television, radio (home 10%, overseas 19%). Works in conjunction with agents in New York and most foreign countries. Preliminary letter essential.

International Management Group, Pier House, Strand on the Green, Chiswick, London W4 3NN   *tel* 081-994 1444   *fax* 081-994 9606. *Chairman:* Mark H. McCormack; *agents:* Jean Sewell, Michael Attenborough (UK), Julian Bach, Trish Lande, Mark Reiter (US), Fumiko Matsuki (Japan).
Represents UK authors and, in US, Julian Bach/IMG authors. Also represents sports celebrities, classical musicians and broadcasting personalities (home/ US 15%, elsewhere 25%); will suggest revision. No reading fee.

International Scripts (1979), 1 Norland Square, Holland Park, London W11 4PX   *tel* 071-229 0736   *fax* 071-792 3287. *Directors:* H.P. Tanner, J. Lawson.
Specialises in full-length contemporary and women's fiction, horror, general non-fiction; no poetry (home 15%, overseas 20%), first works (15%), performance rights (10-20%). Works with overseas agents world-wide. Return postage required for MSS plus a £25.00 reading fee (for which a report will be provided).

Mary Irvine (1974), 11 Upland Park Road, Oxford OX2 7RU   *tel* (0865) 513570.
Specialises in women's fiction and family sagas. No plays, scripts, children's books, short stories or poetry (home 10%, USA 15%, translations 20%). Works with agents in USA, Europe, Japan. No unsolicited MSS. Preliminary letter essential and return postage required. No reading fee.

Gordon Jarvie Editorial (1990), 81 Comiston Drive, Edinburgh EH10 5QT   *tel* 031-447 3417   *fax* 031-452 8595. *Directors:* Gordon Jarvie, Frances Jarvie.
Full-length MSS. Fiction and non-fiction; Scottish interest; educational, reference and ELT (home 15%, overseas 15%). No reading fee. Preliminary letter and return postage essential.

*****Heather Jeeves Literary Agency**, 9 Dryden Place, Edinburgh EH9 1RP   *tel/ fax* 031-668 3859; London (open first seven days each month):   *tel* 071-723 2973   *fax* 071-262 4566. Specialises in crime, cookery, bestseller fiction (home 10%, overseas 20%); will suggest revision. No short stories or poetry. Represented world-wide. No reading fee.

*****John Johnson (Authors' Agent) Ltd** (1956), Clerkenwell House, 45-47 Clerkenwell Green, London EC1R 0HT   *tel* 071-251 0125   *fax* 071-251 2172.
Full-length MSS (home 10%, overseas direct 15%, with subagent maximum of 20%). Works in conjunction with agents in USA and many European countries. Strictly no MSS without preliminary letter and sae first.

Harry Joyce Ltd, 67 Underhill Road, South Benfleet, Essex SS7 1ER   *tel* (0268) 755755.
Scripts for theatre, films, TV (home 10%, overseas 15%); will suggest revision. No reading fee.

*****Jane Judd Literary Agency** (1986), 18 Belitha Villas, London N1 1PD   *tel* 071-607 0273   *fax* 071-607 0623.
Full-length MSS only (home 10%, overseas 20%). Works with agents in USA and most foreign countries. No reading fee, but preliminary letter with synopsis and sae essential.

Juvenilia (1973), Avington, Winchester, Hants SO21 1DB   *tel/fax* (0962) 779656. *Proprietor:* Mrs Rosemary Bromley.
Full-length MSS for the children's market, fiction and non-fiction (home 10%, overseas from 15%), performance rights (10%). Short stories only if specifically for picture books, radio or TV. No verse. No unsolicited MSS; preliminary

letter with sae and full details essential. No reading fee. Postage for acknowledgement and return of material imperative.

Michelle Kass Associates (1991), 12 Moor Street, London W1V 5LH   *tel* 071-
439 1624   *fax* 071-734 3394. *Proprietor:* Michelle Kass.
Full-length MSS. Fiction and drama (screen and stage) (home 10%, overseas
15-20%), performance rights (10%); will suggest revision where appropriate.
Works with agents overseas. No reading fee. Preliminary letter and return
postage required.

*Frances Kelly Agency (1978), 111 Clifton Road, Kingston upon Thames, Surrey
KT2 6PL   *tel* 081-549 7830   *fax* 081-547 0051.
Full-length MSS. Non-fiction: general and academic, reference and pro-
fessional books, all subjects (home 10%, overseas 20%), television, radio
(10%). *US associate:* The Balkin Agency. No reading fee, but no unsolicited
MSS; return postage and preliminary letter requested.

Peter Knight Agency (1985), 20 Crescent Grove, London SW4 7AH   *tel* 071-
622 1467   *fax* 071-622 1522. *Director:* Peter Knight; *associates:* Ann King-
Hall, Robin Mackay Miller, Caroline Figini, Gaby Martin.
Motor sports, cartoon books for both adults and children, and factual and
biographical material (commission dependent upon authors and territories).
No poetry, science fiction or cookery. Overseas associates: United Media
(USA), Auspac Media (Australia). No unsolicited MSS. Send letter
accompanied by CV and sae with synopsis of proposed work.

*Lemon Unna & Durbridge Ltd, 24 Pottery Lane, Holland Park, London W11
4LZ   *tel* 071-727 1346   *fax* 071-727 9037. *Directors:* Stephen Durbridge,
Sheila Lemon, Girsha Reid, Wendy Gresser, Bethan Evans, Hilary Delamere.
Represents writers for theatre, film, television, radio and children's writers
and illustrators for all media. Adult novels represented only for existing clients.
Commission 10% unless sub-agents employed overseas; works in conjunction
with agents in USA and all foreign countries. No reading fee, but preliminary
letter and return postage essential.

*Barbara Levy Literary Agency (1986), 16 Jeffreys Place, London NW1 9PP   *tel*
071-485 6037   *fax* 071-267 3024. *Director:* Barbara Levy; *associate:* John Selby
(solicitor).
Full-length MSS only; also films, television and radio (home 10%, overseas by
arrangement). No reading fee, but informative preliminary letter and return
postage essential.

Limelight Management (1991), 9 Coptic Street, London WC1A 1NH   *tel* 071-
436 6949   *fax* 071-323 6791. *Directors:* Fiona Lindsay, Linda Shanks.
Full-length and short MSS. Food, wine, health, crafts, gardening (home 10%,
overseas 20%), TV and radio rights (10-20%); will suggest revision where
appropriate. No reading fee.

*The Christopher Little Literary Agency (1979), 49 Queen Victoria Street, London
EC4N 4SA   *tel* 071-236 5881   *fax* 071-236 7625. *Contacts:* Christopher Little,
Patrick Walsh, Janine Quick, Sarah Gorman.
Handles commercial and literary full-length fiction, non-fiction and film/TV
scripts. Special interests: crime, thrillers, science fiction, fantasy, horror,
romance, children's, narrative and investigative non-fiction, sport, biography,
New Age. No reading fee. Send detailed letter and sae in first instance.

London Independent Books Ltd (1971), 1A Montagu Mews North, London
W1H 1AJ   *tel* 071-706 0486   *fax* 071-486 3470. *Directors:* Carolyn Whitaker,
Patrick Whitaker.

Specialises in commercial and fantasy fiction, cinema, jazz, show business, travel. Full-length MSS (home 15%, overseas 20%), films, television and sound broadcasting (15%). Will suggest revision of promising MSS. No reading fee.

Jennifer Luithlen Agency (1986), The Rowans, 88 Holmfield Road, Leicester LE2 1SB *tel* (0533) 738863 *fax* (0533) 735697. *Agent:* Jennifer Luithlen.
Children's books – in particular pony/horse series; adult fiction: crime, historical, saga (home 10%, overseas 20%), performance rights (15%); will suggest revision where appropriate. Handles translation sales direct. No reading fee, but *no unsolicited MSS* without prior telephone call; sae essential.

Lutyens & Rubinstein (1993), 231 Westbourne Park Road, London W11 1EB *tel* 071-792 4855 *fax* 071-792 4833. *Directors:* Sarah Lutyens, Felicity Rubinstein.
Fiction and non-fiction, commercial and literary (home 10%, overseas 20%). Send outline/2 sample chapters and sae. No reading fee.

Duncan McAra (1988), 30 Craighall Crescent, Edinburgh EH6 4RZ *tel* 031-552 1558. Thrillers and literary fiction; non-fiction: art, architecture, archaeology, biography, film, military, travel (home 10%, overseas by arrangement). Preliminary letter with sae essential. No reading fee.

Maclean Dubois (Writers & Agents) (1977), Hillend House, Hillend, Edinburgh EH10 7DX *tel* 031-445 5885 *fax* 031-445 5898. *Directors:* Charles Maclean, Ross Leckie, Geraldine Coates, James Hardie, P.B. Maguire.
Full-length MSS and proposals. Scottish literature, history and topography; food and drink, especially Scotch whisky (home 10%, overseas 15%); will suggest revision, fee payable. Reading fee.

Eunice McMullen Children's Literary Agent Ltd (1992), 38 Clewer Hill Road, Windsor, Berks. SL4 4BW *tel* (0753) 830348 *fax* (0753) 833459. *Directors:* Eunice McMullen, Mark Jenner (Pentos plc).
All types of children's books, particularly picture books (home 10%, overseas 15%). No unsolicited scripts without prior letter.

*****Andrew Mann Ltd** (1974), in association with Jane Conway-Gordon, 1 Old Compton Street, London W1V 5PH *tel* 071-734 4751 *fax* 071-287 9264. *Directors:* Anne Dewe, Tina Betts.
Full-length MSS (home 10%, USA 19%, Europe 19%), performance rights (10%). Associated with agents in Europe and USA. No reading fee, but no unsolicited MSS without preliminary enquiry and sae.

Manuscript ReSearch (1988), PO Box 33, Bicester, Oxon OX6 7PP *tel* (0869) 252992 *fax* (0869) 324096. *Proprietor:* T.G. Jenkins.
Full-length MSS. Specialises in crime/thrillers, historical romance, biographies (home 10%, overseas 20%), performance rights (15%); short MSS only from established clients. Professional line by line editing and laser printing £3.00 per A4 page. No reading fee, but sae for script return essential.

The Marsh Agency (1994), 138 Buckingham Palace Road, London SW1W 9SA *tel* 071-730 1124 *fax* 071-730 0037. *Partners:* Paul Marsh, Susanna Nicklin.
Translation rights only (10%).

Marsh & Sheil Ltd (1985), 19 John Street, London WC1N 2DL *tel* 071-405 7473 *fax* 071-405 5239. Benita Edzard, Emilia Bulman, Anthony Sheil, Sonia Land.
Translation rights only. Also operates under Sheil Land Associates Ltd.

Judy Martin (1990), 138 Buckingham Palace Road, London SW1W 9SA   *tel* 071-730 3779   *fax* 071-730 3801.
Fiction, non-fiction, film and TV tie-ins, film and TV scripts; *no* plays, poetry or children's stories (home 15%, overseas 20%), performance rights (15%). Translation rights handled by Marsh & Sheil. No reading fee, but sae required for all unsolicited MSS, together with details of publishing history.

M.C. Martinez Literary Agency (1988), 60 Oakwood Avenue, Southgate, London N14 6QL   *tel* 081-886 5829. *Proprietor:* Mary Caroline Martinez.
Fiction, children's books, arts and crafts, DIY, cookery, travel, business books, educational books (home 15%, overseas 20%), performance rights (20%); will suggest revision where appropriate. Works in conjunction with foreign agencies. Preliminary letter and sae required; no reading fee. Full desktop publishing service using Ventura is offered to both publishers and authors.

Blanche Marvin, 21A St John's Wood High Street, London NW8 7NG   *tel/fax* 071-722 2313.
Full-length MSS (home 12½% + 12½% overseas), performance rights. No reading fee but return postage essential.

*****MBA Literary Agents Ltd** (1971), 45 Fitzroy Street, London W1P 5HR   *tel* 071-387 2076/4785   *fax* 071-387 2042. *Directors:* Diana Tyler, John Richard Parker, Meg Davis, Ruth Needham, Timothy Webb.
Full-length MSS; no poetry (home 10%, overseas 20%), theatre, television, radio (10%), films (10-15%). No reading fee. Works in conjunction with agents in most countries.

Millstone Lit (1991), 17 Broombank, Birkby Park, Huddersfield, West Yorkshire HD2 2DJ   *tel* (0484) 512817. *Director:* R.S. Byram.
Adult fiction and non-fiction only (home 10%, overseas 15%); may suggest revision. Small fee may be asked for appraisal. Send synopsis and return postage first.

Richard Milne Ltd (1956), 15 Summerlee Gardens, London N2 9QN   *tel* 081-883 3987. *Directors:* R.M. Sharples, K.N. Sharples.
Specialises in scripts for films, television, sound broadcasting (10%). Unable to represent any additional authors at present.

*****William Morris Agency (UK) Ltd** (1965), 31/32 Soho Square, London W1V 5DG   *tel* 071-434 2191   *fax* 071-437 0238. *Contacts:* Stephen M. Kenis (films), Jane Annakin (television and theatre), Sappho Clissitt (books).
World-wide theatrical and literary agency with offices in New York, Beverly Hills and Nashville, and associates in Rome, Munich and Sydney. Represents theatre, television, film and radio scripts; fiction and general non-fiction (television, theatre, film and UK book 10%, US book and translation 20%). No unsolicited material or MSS.

Judith Murdoch Literary Agency (1993), 19 Chalcot Square, London NW1 8YA   *tel* 071-722 4197.
Full-length adult fiction only (home 15%, overseas 20%). No science fiction/ fantasy, poetry, short stories, academic or children's. Must send first two chapters and synopsis with preliminary letter. Return postage/sae essential. Editorial advice given; no reading fee. Translation rights handled by The Marsh Agency.

*****Maggie Noach Literary Agency** (1982), 21 Redan Street, London W14 0AB   *tel* 071-602 2451   *fax* 071-603 4712.
General fiction and non-fiction; non-illustrated children's books. Full-length MSS (home 15%, US/translation 20%). No scientific, academic or specialist non-fiction; no romantic fiction, poetry, plays, short stories or books for the

very young. Encourages promising young writers but *very* few new clients taken on as it is considered vital to give individual attention to each author's work. Unsolicited MSS not welcome. Approach by letter (*not by telephone*), giving a brief description of the book and enclosing a few sample pages. Return postage essential. No reading fee.

*Andrew Nurnberg Associates Ltd, Clerkenwell House, 45-47 Clerkenwell Green, London EC1R 0HT   *tel* 071-417 8800   *fax* 071-417 8812.
Specialises in the sale of translation rights of English and American authors into European languages.

Alexandra Nye, Writers & Agents (1991), 45 Blackheath Road, Greenwich, London SE10 8PE   *tel* 081-691 9532. *Director:* Alexandra Nye.
Literary fiction, historical, biographies; no poetry or plays (home 10%, overseas 20%, translation 15%). Will suggest revision where appropriate. Unsolicited MSS welcome if accompanied by return postage. No reading fee. Critical service available at a charge.

David O'Leary Literary Agency (1988), 10 Lansdowne Court, Lansdowne Rise, London W11 2NR   *tel* 071-229 1623   *telex* 27636 AEZRA G   *fax* 071-727 9624.
Popular general fiction and non-fiction: special interests Russia, Ireland, history, science (home 10%, overseas 20%), performance rights (15%). Will suggest revision; no reading fee. Write or call before submitting MSS.

*Deborah Owen Ltd (1971), 78 Narrow Street, Limehouse, London E14 8BP   *tel* 071-987 5119/5441   *fax* 071-538 4004. Deborah Owen, Rosemary Scoular.
Full-length MSS (home 10%, overseas 15%). All types of literary material except plays, scripts, children's books, short stories or poetry. No unsolicited MSS. No new authors at present.

*Mark Paterson & Associates (1955), 10 Brook Street, Wivenhoe, Colchester, Essex CO7 9DS   *tel* (0206) 825433/4   *fax* (0206) 822990.
Book-length MSS; general but little fiction. Specialise in psychoanalysis, psychotherapy and clinical psychology representing five US publishers in same field for translation rights, history and copyright (20% including sub-agents' commission). No articles or short stories except for existing clients. Preliminary letter with synopsis, sample material and sae essential.

John Pawsey (1981), 60 High Street, Tarring, Worthing, West Sussex BN14 7NR   *tel* (0903) 205167   *fax* (0903) 205167.
Full-length popular fiction and non-fiction MSS (home 10-15%, overseas 19%). No unsolicited material, poetry, short stories, journalism or original film and stage scripts. Preliminary letter and return postage with all correspondence essential. Works in association with agencies in the USA, Europe and the Far East. Will suggest revision if MS sufficiently promising. No reading fee.

Maggie Pearlstine (1989), 31 Ashley Gardens, Ambrosden Avenue, Westminster, London SW1P 1QE   *tel* 071-828 4212   *fax* 071-834 5546.
Full-length MSS, fiction and non-fiction. Special interests: commercial fiction, illustrated non-fiction, home and leisure, health, biography, history and politics (home 10-12½%, overseas 20%). No children's or poetry; only deals with scripts and short stories by authors already on its books. No unsolicited MSS. Preliminary letter required and sae. No reading fee.

*A.D. Peters & Co. Ltd—see **The Peters Fraser & Dunlop Group Ltd.**

*The Peters Fraser & Dunlop Group Ltd, 503/4 The Chambers, Chelsea Harbour, Lots Road, London SW10 0XF   *tel* 071-344 1000   *fax* 071-352 7356/351 1756.
Directors: Michael Sissons (joint chairman and managing director), Anthony Jones (joint chairman), Kenneth Ewing, Pat Kavanagh, Tim Corrie, Maureen Vincent, Norman North, Anthony Baring, Mark Lucas, Caroline Dawnay.

Incorporating A.D. Peters & Co. Ltd, Fraser & Dunlop Scripts Ltd, Fraser & Dunlop Ltd, June Hall Literary Agency Ltd. *Associated agencies:* Intercontinental Literary Agency, Sterling Lord Literistic (New York).
Specialists in the negotiation of all rights in general fiction and non-fiction, film and television scripts, plays, and certain specialist and academic works. Children's MSS and illustrations to Peters Fraser & Dunlop Children's List, Rosemary Canter (home/overseas 10-20%). No unsolicited MSS accepted. We ask for an introductory letter from the author describing the work offered, with sae. No reading fee.

Laurence Pollinger Ltd, 18 Maddox Street, London W1R 0EU *tel* 071-629 9761 *telegraphic address* Laupoll, London W1 *fax* 071-629 9765. *Directors:* Gerald J. Pollinger, Margaret Pepper, Lesley Hadcroft, Juliet Burton; *secretary:* Denzil De Silva.
Authors' agents for all material with the exception of original film stories, poetry and freelance journalistic articles. Dramatic associate, Micheline Steinberg. Terms are a commission of 15% of the amounts obtained, except on translation sales, where the total commission of 20% may include the commission to the associate in the territory concerned. No reading fee. An editorial contribution may be requested.

*Murray Pollinger (1969), 222 Old Brompton Road, London SW5 0BZ *tel* 071-373 4711 *telegraphic address/cables* Chopper, London SW5 *fax* 071-373 3775.
Agents for the negotiation in all markets of adult fiction and non-fiction, children's fiction and picture books (home 10%, overseas 20%). Preliminary letter with synopsis required, together with return postage; also names of agents and publishers previously contacted. No reading fee.

*Shelley Power Literary Agency Ltd (1976), Le Montaud, 24220 Berbiguières, France *tel* 53 29 62 52 *fax* 53 29 62 54. Also based in the UK.
General fiction and non-fiction. Full-length MSS (home 10%, USA and translations 19%). No children's books, poetry or plays. Works in conjunction with agents abroad. No reading fee, but preliminary letter with sae for return from UK essential.

PVA Management Ltd, Hallow Park, Worcester WR2 6PG *tel* (0905) 640663 *fax* (0905) 640633. *Managing director:* Paul Vaughan.
Full-length MSS (home 15%, overseas 20%), performance rights (15%).

Radala & Associates (1970), 17 Avenue Mansions, Finchley Road, London NW3 7AX *tel* 071-794 4495 *fax* 071-431 7636. *Director:* Richard Gollner; *associates:* Neil Hornick, Anna Swan.
Full-length MSS (home 10%, overseas 15%). Fiction and non-fiction. Books, television, sound broadcasting. Electronic publishing division, including video, audio tape, computer program packages for multi-media publishing production companies.

Margaret Ramsay Ltd—now **Casarotto Ramsay Ltd.**

Jim Reynolds Associates (1988), 7 Banbury Lane, Byfield, Daventry, Northants. NN11 6UX *tel/fax* (0327) 61542. *Director:* Ann Reynolds.
Full-length MSS – biography, social, political and military history, current affairs, investigative journalism, cricket (home 10%, overseas 19%); will suggest revision where appropriate. Works in conjunction with foreign agencies. No reading fee.

*Rogers, Coleridge & White Ltd (1967), 20 Powis Mews, London W11 1JN *tel* 071-221 3717 *telegraphic address* Debrogers, London W11 *fax* 071-229

9084. *Directors:* Deborah Rogers, Gill Coleridge, Patricia White (USA); *consultant:* Ann Warnford-Davis.

Full-length book MSS, including children's books (home 10%, USA 15%, translations 20%). *USA associate:* International Creative Management, Inc. No unsolicited MSS please, and no submissions by fax. No reading fee.

Elizabeth Roy Literary Agency (1990), White Cottage, Greatford, Nr Stamford, Lincs. PE9 4PR *tel/fax* (0778) 560672.

Women's fiction, general non-fiction, including gardening, natural history, music, children's books (home 10%, overseas 20%). Will suggest revision. Preliminary letter, synopsis and sample chapters preferred. Return postage essential. No reading fee.

***Hilary Rubinstein Books** (1992), 61 Clarendon Road, London W11 4JE *tel* 071-792 4282 *fax* 071-221 5291. *Directors:* Hilary Rubinstein, Helge Rubinstein.

Full-length MSS. Fiction and non-fiction (home 10%, overseas 20%); will suggest revision where appropriate. *No* plays, scripts or poetry. No reading fee, but *no* unsolicited MSS without preliminary letter or call.

Herta Ryder (1984), c/o Toby Eady Associates Ltd, 18 Park Walk, London SW10 0AQ *tel* 081-948 1010.

Specialises in novels for older children, adult fiction and non-fiction. Full-length MSS (home 10%, USA 15%, overseas 20%). Represented by agents in all major foreign countries. No reading fee. Preliminary letter essential.

Sheri Safran Literary Agency Ltd (1979), 3D Westpoint, 36/37 Warple Way, London W3 0RQ *tel* 081-746 1171 *fax* 081-746 1170.

Non-fiction titles for, by and about women; and children's books (home 15%, overseas 20%). Preliminary letter with outline or partial MSS together with return postage and sae essential. No reading fee. See also: **Sadie Fields Productions Ltd (Book Packagers).**

Rosemary Sandberg Ltd (1991), 6 Bayley Street, London WC1B 3HB *tel* 071-304 4110 fax 071-304 4109. *Directors:* Rosemary Sandberg, Ed Victor, Graham Greene CBE.

Children's – writers and illustrators, general fiction, women's fiction and non-fiction (home 10-15%, overseas 20%). Negotiates direct with USA. No reading fee but no unsolicited MSS; preliminary letter and sae essential.

***Tessa Sayle Agency,** 11 Jubilee Place, London SW3 3TE *tel* 071-823 3883 (5 lines) *fax* 071-823 3363. *Proprietor:* Rachel Calder.

Full-length MSS (home 10%, overseas 20%), film, TV, theatre (home 10%, overseas 15-20%). USA Associates: Darhansoff & Verrill, 1220 Park Avenue, New York, NY 10028. Represented in all foreign countries. No reading fee, but preliminary letter and return postage essential.

The Sharland Organisation Ltd (1988), 9 Marlborough Crescent, Bedford Park, London W4 1HE *tel* 081-742 1919 *fax* 081-995 7688. *Directors:* Mike Sharland, Alice Sharland.

Specialises in film, television, stage and radio rights throughout the world (home 15%, overseas 20%); also negotiates multimedia, interactive TV deals and computer game contracts. Works in conjunction with overseas agents. Sae required.

***Sheil Land Associates Ltd** (1962), incorporating Christy & Moore Ltd (1912) and Richard Scott Simon Ltd (1971), 43 Doughty Street, London WC1N 2LF *tel* 071-405 9351 *fax* 071-831 2127. *Agents:* Anthony Sheil, Sonia Land, Giles Gordon, Vivien Green, Robert Kirby, Simon Trewin, Jane Villiers (film/

drama/TV), Lynda Myles (film/drama/TV consultant), Benita Edzard, Emilia Bulman (foreign/Marsh & Sheil).
Handles full-length general and literary fiction, biography, travel, cookery, humour (home 10%, USA/translations 20%). Also theatre, film, radio and TV scripts (home 10%, overseas 20%). Preliminary letter and return postage essential. Translations: also see **Marsh & Sheil Ltd.**

*Caroline Sheldon Literary Agency (1985), 71 Hillgate Place, London W8 7SS   *tel* 071-727 9102.
Full-length MSS. General fiction, women's fiction, and children's books (home 10%, overseas 20%). No reading fee. Synopsis and first three chapters with return postage required initially.

Jeffrey Simmons, 10 Lowndes Square, London SW1X 9HA   *tel* 071-235 8852   *fax* 071-235 9733.
Specialises in adult fiction, biography, autobiography, show business, law, crime, politics, world affairs. Full-length MSS (home from 10%, overseas from 15%). Will suggest revision. No reading fee, but preliminary letter essential.

*Richard Scott Simon Ltd—see Sheil Land Associates Ltd.

Carol Smith (1976), 25 Hornton Court, Kensington High Street, London W8 7RT   *tel* 071-937 4874   *fax* 071-938 5323.
Full-length MSS, mainly new fiction (home 10%, USA/translation 20%). Will suggest revision of promising MSS. Works in conjunction with many foreign agencies. No reading fee, but preliminary letter essential. Please enclose return postage.

Solo Literary Agency Ltd (1978), 49-53 Kensington High Street, London W8 5ED   *tel* 071-376 2166   *fax* 071-938 3165. *Directors:* Don Short (managing), Wendy Short (secretary).
Specialises in celebrity and autobiographical books. Fiction from established authors only (home 15%, overseas 20%).

Spokesmen—see Curtis Brown.

*Abner Stein, 10 Roland Gardens, London SW7 3PH   *tel* 071-373 0456   *fax* 071-370 6316.
Full-length and short MSS (home 10%, overseas 20%). No reading fee, but no unsolicited MSS; preliminary letter and return postage required.

Micheline Steinberg Playwrights' Agent (1987), 110 Frognal, London NW3 6XU   *tel* 071-433 3980   *fax* 071-794 8355.
Full-length MSS – theatre, films, television, radio (home 10%, overseas 15%). Dramatic Associate for Laurence Pollinger Ltd; works in conjunction with agents in USA and other countries. No reading fee, but preliminary letter essential and return postage with MSS.

Rochelle Stevens & Co. (1984), 2 Terretts Place, Upper Street, London N1 1QZ   *tel* 071-359 3900   *fax* 071-354 5729. *Proprietor:* Rochelle Stevens.
Drama scripts for film, television, theatre and radio (10%); will suggest revision where appropriate. No reading fee.

Peter Tauber Press Agency (1950), 94 East End Road, London N3 2SX   *tel* 081-346 4165. *Directors:* Peter Tauber, Martha Tauber, Robert Tauber.
Women's fiction, especially sagas and glitz, thrillers, crime, horror and fantasy; non-fiction primarily celebrity auto/biographies (20% worldwide). No poetry, short stories, plays, children's or foreign books. Please send synopsis, first three chapters, copies of all previous rejections, a non-returnable submission fee of £50 and an sae. Failure to comply with these exact terms will result in no reply.

Jon Thurley MA (1976), 213 Linen Hall, 162-168 Regent Street, London W1R 5TA	*tel* 071-437 9545/6	*fax* 071-287 9208. Patricia Preece BA.
Literary and dramatic work for all media (home 10%, overseas 20%). American and European representation arranged geared to specific projects. No reading fee.

Jane Turnbull (1986), 13 Wendell Road, London W12 9RS	*tel* 081-743 9580	*fax* 081-749 6079.
Fiction and non-fiction (home 10%, USA/translation 20%), performance rights (15%). No children's or short stories. Works in conjunction with Aitken, Stone & Wylie for sale of translation rights. No reading fee but preliminary letter and sae essential.

*Harvey Unna & Stephen Durbridge (1975) Ltd—see **Lemon Unna & Durbridge Ltd.**

Dr Jan Van Loewen Ltd—see **Michael Imison Playwrights Ltd.**

*Ed Victor Ltd (1976), 6 Bayley Street, Bedford Square, London WC1B 3HB	*tel* 071-304 4100	*telegraphic address* Victorious, London W1	*fax* 071-304 4111.
Directors: Ed Victor, Graham C. Greene CBE, Carol Ryan, Leon Morgan, Margaret Phillips, Sophie Hicks.
Full-length MSS, fiction and non-fiction, but no short stories, film/TV scripts, poetry or plays (home 15%, USA 15%, translation 20%), performance rights (15%). Represented in all foreign markets. No unsolicited MSS. Sophie Hicks (children's) – writers and illustrators.

S. Walker Literary Agency (1939), 96 Church Lane, Goldington, Bedford MK41 0AS	*tel* (0234) 216229. *Partners:* Alan Oldfield, Cora-Louise Oldfield; *consultant:* E.K. Walker.
Full-length novels only (home 10%, overseas 20% including 10% to overseas agent). Do not handle short topical articles, poetry or fictional short stories. Works in conjunction with agencies in most European countries, and also negotiates directly with foreign publishers. No reading fee but preliminary letter and return postage essential.

Warner Chappell Plays Ltd (formerly **English Theatre Guild Ltd**) (1938), part of **Warner Chappell Music Ltd,** 129 Park Street, London W1Y 3FA	*tel* 071-629 7600	*fax* 071-499 9718.
Specialises in stage plays. Works in conjunction with overseas agents. Preliminary letter essential.

*Watson, Little Ltd, 12 Egbert Street, London NW1 8LJ	*tel* 071-722 9514	*fax* 071-586 7649. *Directors:* Sheila Watson, Amanda Little.
Full-length MSS. Special interests: business books, popular science, military, psychology, all leisure activities, fiction; no short stories or play scripts (home 10%, overseas 19%; electronic rights 20%; all other rights including film, video and television 10%). Will sometimes suggest revision. Works in association with US agency and many foreign agencies. Preliminary letter please.

*A.P. Watt Ltd (1875), 20 John Street, London WC1N 2DR	*tel* 071-405 6774	*fax* 071-831 2154. *Directors:* Caradoc King, Linda Shaughnessy, Rod Hall, Lisa Eveleigh, Nick Marston, Derek Johns.
Full-length MSS; dramatic works for all media (home 10%, US and foreign 20% including commission to US or foreign agent). No poetry. Works in conjunction with agents in USA and most European countries and Japan. No reading fee. No unsolicited MSS without preliminary letter.

*Dinah Wiener Ltd, 27 Arlington Road, London NW1 7ER	*tel* 071-388 2577	*fax* 071-388 7559.

Full-length MSS only, fiction and general non-fiction; no plays, scripts, poetry, short stories or children's books (home 15%, overseas 20%), film and television in association (15%). No reading fee, but preliminary letter and return postage essential.

Elisabeth Wilson (1979), 24 Thornhill Square, London N1 1BQ   *tel* 071-609 1965   *fax* 071-863 6460.
Rights agent and consultant on illustrated books (home/overseas 10%).

UNITED STATES OF AMERICA

*Member of the Association of Authors' Representatives

In all cases, and in their own interests, writers are advised to send a preliminary letter with a self-addressed, stamped envelope (or an International Reply Coupon if writing from outside the USA) and to ascertain terms before submitting MSS.

*Acton, Dystel, Leone & Jaffe (1975), 79 Fifth Avenue, New York, NY 10003   *tel* 212-647-9500   *fax* 212-647-9512. *Directors:* Edward J. Acton, Jane D. Dystel, Adele Leone, Marc Jaffe.
Full-length and short MSS. Women's romance, mysteries, sports, history, biography, true crime, health, women's issues, cookbooks, parenting, travel (home 15%, overseas 19%), film, television and radio (15%); may suggest revision. Works with overseas agents. No reading fee.

American Play Company Inc., 19 West 44th Street, Suite 1204, New York, NY 10036   *tel* 212-921-0545   *fax* 212-869-4032. *President:* Sheldon Abend.

*The Axelrod Agency (1983), 54 Church Street, Lenox, MA 01240   *tel* 413-637-2000   *fax* 413-637-4725. *President:* Steven Axelrod.
Full-length MSS. Fiction and non-fiction, software (home 10%, overseas 20%), film and TV rights (10%); will suggest revision where appropriate. Works with overseas agents. No reading fee.

*The Balkin Agency Inc., PO Box 222, Amherst, MA 01004   *tel* 413-548-9835   *fax* 413-548-9836. *Director:* Richard Balkin.
Full-length MSS – adult non-fiction only (home 15%, overseas 20%). Query first. May suggest revision. Agents in all major countries. *British representative:* Barbara Levy. No reading fee.

*Virginia Barber Literary Agency, Inc. (1974), 353 West 21st Street, New York, NY 10011   *tel* 212-255-6515   *fax* 212-691-9418. *Directors:* Virginia Barber, Mary Evans, Jennifer Rudolph Walsh.
General fiction and non-fiction (home 10-15%, overseas 20% for new authors), performance rights (10-15% for new authors); will suggest revision. Has co-agents in all major countries; Abner Stein handles UK rights. No reading fee.

*Lois Berman · Judy Boals Writers Representatives, 21 West 26th Street, New York, NY 10010   *tel* 212-684-1835   *fax* 212-684-6563.
Dramatic writing only (and only by recommendation).

*Georges Borchardt Inc. (1967), 136 East 57th Street, New York, NY 10022   *tel* 212-753-5785   *fax* 212-838-6518. *Directors:* Georges Borchardt, Anne Borchardt.
Full-length and short MSS (home 10%, British 15%, translations 20%), performance rights (10%). Agents in most foreign countries. No unsolicited MSS. No reading fee.

*Brandt & Brandt Literary Agents Inc., 1501 Broadway, New York, NY 10036   *tel* 212-840-5760   *fax* 212-840-5776.

Full-length and short MSS (home 10%, overseas 15-20%), performance rights (10%). *British representative:* A.M. Heath & Co. Ltd. No reading fee.

*The Helen Brann Agency Inc., 94 Curtis Road, Bridgewater, CT 06752   *tel* 203-354-9580   *fax* 203-355-2572.

*James Brown Associates Inc.—see Curtis Brown Ltd.

*Maria Carvainis Agency, Inc., 235 West End Avenue, New York, NY 10023   *tel* 212-580-1559   *fax* 212-877-3486. *President:* Maria Carvainis.
Fiction: all categories (except science fiction), especially general fiction/literary and mainstream; mystery, thrillers and suspense; fantasy; historical, Regency and category romance. Non-fiction: young adult and children's; political and film biographies; medicine and women's health; business, finance, psychology and popular science (home 15%, overseas 20%). Maria Carvainis views the author's editorial needs and career development as integral components of the literary agent's role, in addition to the negotiation of intricate contracts. Works in conjunction with foreign, TV and movie agents. No reading fee. Query first; no unsolicited MSS.

*Martha Casselman, Literary Agent (1978), PO Box 342, Calistoga, CA 94515   *tel* 707-942-4341   *fax* 707-942-4358.
Full-length MSS. Food and cookbook, non-fiction, limited fiction, some children's (home/overseas 15%); will suggest revision where appropriate. *No* poetry or textbooks. Works with overseas agents. No reading fee.

Faith Childs Literary Agency (1990), 275 West 96th Street, New York, NY 10025   *tel* 212-662-1232   *fax* 212-662-1456. *Director:* Faith Hampton Childs.
Literary fiction; non-fiction (home 15%, overseas 20%). Works in conjunction with overseas agents. Will suggest revision. No reading fee.

*Ruth Cohen, Inc. Literary Agency (1982), PO Box 7626, Menlo Park, CA 94025   *tel* 415-854-2054.
Requires quality writing: women's contemporary fiction, Regencies, historical romances; mysteries; juvenile – picture books to middle grade novels and young adult novels (home 15%, overseas 20%), film, TV rights (15%); will suggest revision. Works in conjunction with overseas agents. Send query letter and 25 opening pages plus sase. No reading fee.

*Frances Collin Literary Agent (successor to **Marie Rodell-Frances Collin Literary Agency,** 1948), PO Box 33, Wayne, PA 19087-0033   *tel* 610-254-0555.
Full-length MSS (specialisations of interest to UK writers: mysteries, women's fiction, history, biography, science fiction, fantasy) (home 15%, overseas 20%), performance rights (20%). No screenplays. Works in conjunction with agents world-wide. No reading fee. No unsolicited MSS please. Letter queries should include sufficient return postage.

*Don Congdon Associates, Inc. (1983), 156 Fifth Avenue, Suite 625, New York, NY 10010   *tel* 212-645-1229. *Agents:* Don Congdon, Michael Congdon, Susan Ramer.
Full-length and short MSS. General fiction and non-fiction (home 10%, overseas 19%), performance rights (10%); will sometimes suggest revision. Works with co-agents overseas. No reading fee, but *no* unsolicited MSS – query first.

*Richard Curtis Associates Inc. (1970), 171 East 74th Street, New York, NY 10021   *tel* 212-772-7363   *fax* 212-772-7393. *President:* Richard Curtis; *associates:* Rob Cohen, Richard Henshaw.
All types of commercial fiction; also non-fiction (home 15%, overseas 20%), multimedia, film, TV rights (15%). Works in conjunction with overseas agents. Will suggest revision. No reading fee.

*Curtis Brown Ltd, 10 Astor Place, New York, NY 10003 *tel* 212-473-5400. *Chairman:* Perry Knowlton; 1750 Montgomery Street, San Francisco, CA 94111 *tel* 415-954-8566. *Contact:* Peter Ginsberg.
Fiction and non-fiction, juvenile, film and TV rights. No unsolicited MSS; query first with sase. No reading fee; handling fees.

*Joan Daves Literary Agency (founded in 1952 by Joan Daves), 21 West 26th Street, New York, NY 10010 *tel* 212-685-2663 *fax* 212-685-1781. *Director:* Jennifer Lyons. Subsidiary of **Writers House Inc.**
Full-length MSS or a detailed outline of n-f projects (home 15%, overseas 20%). No reading fee. No unpublished writers.

Elaine Davie Literary Agency (1986), Village Gate Square, 274 N Goodman Street, Rochester, NY 14607 *tel* 716-442-0830. *President:* Elaine Davie.
Full-length MSS. Specialises in books by and for women, especially genre romance (home 15%, overseas 20%); will sometimes suggest revision. Works with overseas agents. No reading fee, but preliminary letter with sase essential.

*Anita Diamant, 310 Madison Avenue, New York, NY 10017 *tel* 212-687-1122.
Fiction, non-technical non-fiction, young adult.

*Sandra Dijkstra Literary Agency (1981), 1155 Camino del Mar, Suite 515, Del Mar, CA 92014 *tel* 619-755-3115. *President:* Sandra Dijkstra.
Adult fiction, especially literary/contemporary, mystery/suspense; non-fiction: current affairs, memoir/biography, science, health, history and psychology/self-help, business, how-to; selected children's projects (home 15%, overseas 20%). Works in conjunction with foreign agents. Will suggest revision. No reading fee. Send first 50 pages and sase for response/return. No faxed queries accepted. Response period 2-8 weeks; do not call to inquire.

*Donadio & Ashworth, Inc., 231 West 22nd Street, New York, NY 10011 *tel* 212-691-8077.
Literary book agents, fiction and non-fiction.

Dorese Agency, 37965 Palo Verde Drive, Cathedral City, CA 92234 *tel* 619-321-1115 *fax* 619-321-1049. Alyss Barlow Dorese.
Specialises in true crime, non-fiction.

Peter Elek Associates (1979), PO Box 223, Canal Street Station, New York, NY 10013 *tel* 212-431-9368/9371 *fax* 212-966-5768 *e-mail* 73174,2515 COM-PUSERVE. *Directors:* Peter Elek, Helene W. Elek.
Full-length and short MSS. Adult and illustrated adult non-fiction: style, culture, popular history, popular science, current affairs; juvenile picture books (home 15%, overseas 20%), performance rights (20%); will sometimes suggest revision. Works with overseas agents. No reading fee. Experienced in licensing for multimedia, on-line and off-line.

The Ethan Ellenberg Literary Agency (1983), 548 Broadway, 5-c, New York, NY 10012 *tel* 212-431-4554 *fax* 212-941-4652. *President:* Ethan Ellenberg.
Thrillers, mysteries, quality fiction; non-fiction: biography, history. Full-length and short MSS (home 15%, overseas 10%), performance rights (15%); will suggest revision. Works in conjunction with overseas agents. Published authors only. Submit one-page outline and first three sample chapters, plus self-addressed envelope and return postage (US stamps or US$ international money order). No reading fee.

*Ann Elmo Agency, Inc., 60 East 42nd Street, New York, NY 10165 *tel* 212-661-2880 *fax* 212-661-2883. *Directors:* Ann Elmo, Lettie Lee.

Full-length fiction and non-fiction MSS (home 15%, overseas 20%), theatre, films, television (15%). Will suggest revision when MSS is promising. Works with foreign agencies. No reading fee.

Frieda Fishbein Ltd, 2556 Hubbard Street, Brooklyn, NY 11235 *tel* 212-247-4398.

Forthwrite Literary Agency (1988), 3579 E Foothill Boulevard, Suite 327, Pasadena, CA 91107 *tel* 818-365-3400. *Owner:* Wendy L. Zhörne.
How-to, self-help and general non-fiction. Subjects include: animals, art, horticulture/gardening, archaeology, European history (especially English), biography, health (especially homeopathy and alternative medicines), parenting, coffee table (illustrated) books, crafts (bobbin lace, handicrafts, etc.), nature, psychology, juvenile and young adult fiction and non-fiction; religious. Send IRC with query. Response in 8 weeks.

*The Fox Chase Agency Inc., The Public Ledger Building, Room 930, Independence Square, Philadelphia, PA 19106 *tel* 215-625-2450 *fax* 215-574-9190.

*Robert A. Freedman Dramatic Agency, Inc. (formerly **Harold Freedman Brandt & Brandt Dramatic Dept., Inc.**), 1501 Broadway, Suite 2310, New York, NY 10036 *tel* 212-840-5760.
Plays, motion picture and TV scripts. Send letter of inquiry first, with sase.

*Samuel French Inc., 45 West 25th Street, New York, NY 10010 *tel* 212-206-8990 *fax* 212-206-1429. *President:* Charles R. Van Nostrand.

*Jay Garon-Brooke Associates Inc., 101 West 55th Street, Suite 5ᴋ, New York, NY 10019 *tel* 212-581-8300 *fax* 212-581-8397.
Specialises in fiction. Writer must be referred by an editor or a client. Will not read unsolicited MSS. *London:* Abner Stein *tel* 071-373 0456.

*Gelfman Schneider Literary Agents, Inc., 250 West 57th Street, Suite 2515, New York, NY 10107 *tel* 212-245-1993 *fax* 212-245-8678. *Directors:* Jane Gelfman, Deborah Schneider.
General adult fiction and non-fiction (home 15%, overseas 20%). Works in conjunction with Curtis Brown, London. Will suggest revision. No reading fee.

*Goodman Associates, Literary Agents (1976), 500 West End Avenue, New York, NY 10024 *tel* 212-873-4806 *fax* 212-580-3278. *Partners:* Arnold P. Goodman, Elise Simon Goodman.
Adult book length fiction and non-fiction (home 15%, overseas 20%). No reading fee.

*Sanford J. Greenburger Associates, Inc., 55 Fifth Avenue, New York, NY 10003 *tel* 212-206-5600 *fax* 212-463-8718.

*John Hawkins & Associates, Inc. (formerly **Paul R. Reynolds, Inc.**) (1893), 71 West 23rd Street, Suite 1600, New York, NY 10010 *tel* 212-807-7040 *fax* 212-807-9555. *President:* John Hawkins; *vice-president:* William Reiss; *foreign rights:* Moses Cardona; *permissions:* Gladys Guadalupe; *other agents:* Sharon Friedman, J. Warren Frazier.
Fiction, non-fiction, juvenile.

*Heacock Literary Agency, Inc. (1978), 1523 6th Street, Suite 14, Santa Monica, CA 90401 *tel* 310-393-6277. *President:* James B. Heacock; *vice president:* Rosalie G. Heacock.
Adult non-fiction, including diet, nutrition, exercise, popular psychology, women's studies, celebrity bios, arts, crafts, parenting, childbirth (home 15%, overseas 15%-25%). Works in conjunction with overseas agents. Will suggest

revision; no reading fee but charge for expenses. No unsolicited MSS; send bio, outline, 2 sample chapters and sase.

*The Jeff Herman Agency (1986), 500 Greenwich Street, Suite 501c, New York, NY 10013   *tel* 212-940-0540   *fax* 212-941-0614.
Business, reference, popular psychology, computers, health and beauty, spirituality, general non-fiction (home/overseas 15%); will suggest revision where appropriate. Works with overseas agents. No reading fee.

Frederick Hill Associates (1979), 1842 Union Street, San Francisco, CA 94123   *tel* 415-921-2910   *fax* 415-921-2802; *branch office:* 8446½ Melrose Place, Los Angeles, CA 90069   *tel* 213-852-0830   *fax* 213-852-0426.
Full-length fiction and non-fiction (home 15%, overseas 20%). Will suggest revision. Works in conjunction with agents in Scandinavia, France, Germany, Holland, Japan, Spain. No reading fee.

*IMG-Julian Bach Agency Inc., 22 East 71st Street, New York, NY 10021   *tel* 212-772-8900   *fax* 212-772-2617.
Fiction (no science fiction) and non-fiction. Send query letter with sase for response.

InterLicense, Ltd (1982), 200 Gate Five Road, Suite 207, Sausalito, CA 94965   *tel* 415-331-7460   *fax* 415-331-6940. *Executive director:* Manfred Mroczkowski.
International administration of creative rights in non-fiction, self-help and esoterica, children's books (home/overseas 15%-33%). No reading fee.

*International Creative Management, Inc., 40 West 57th Street, New York, NY 10019   *tel* 212-556-5600   *telex* 125422/661562 ICMNYK   *fax* 212-556-5665.
No unsolicited MSS, please; send query letters.

*JCA Literary Agency Inc., Suite 1103, 27 West 20th Street, New York, NY 10011   *tel* 212-807-0888.

Ben F. Kamsler Ltd (1990), 5501 Noble Avenue, Van Nuys, CA 91411   *tel* 818-785-4167   *fax* 818-988-8304. *Directors:* Ben Kamsler, Irene Kamsler.
Full-length novel MSS, plays, TV specials, screenplays (home 10%, overseas 20%), performance rights (10%). Will suggest revision on promising MSS. No reading fee, but preliminary letter with sase essential.

*Barbara S. Kouts, Literary Agent (1980), PO Box 558, Bellport, NY 11713   *tel* 516-286-1278   *fax* 516-286-1538.
Full-length MSS. Fiction and non-fiction, children's and adult (home 10%, overseas 20%); will suggest revision. Works with overseas agents. No reading fee. Query first.

*Lucy Kroll Agency, 390 West End Avenue, New York, NY 10024   *tel* 212-877-0627   *fax* 212-769-2832.

*The Robert Lantz-Joy Harris Literary Agency, 156 Fifth Avenue, Suite 617, New York, NY 10010   *tel* 212-924-6249   *fax* 212-924-6609. *President:* Joy Harris.

*Michael Larsen-Elizabeth Pomada Literary Agents (1972), 1029 Jones Street, San Francisco, CA 94109   *tel* 415-673-0939. *Partners:* Michael Larsen and Elizabeth Pomada.
Full-length MSS (home 15%, overseas 20%). Works in conjunction with agents in Hollywood, Europe, Israel, Japan, South America. Preliminary letter and first 30 pages, with sase, essential.

The Lazear Agency Inc. (1984), 430 First Avenue North, Suite 416, Minneapolis, MN 55401   *tel* 612-332-8640   *fax* 612-332-4648. *Directors:* Jonathon Lazear, Eric Vrooman, Dennis Cass, Susanne Moncur.
Full-length MSS. Adult/young adult fiction and non-fiction; juvenile; film and

TV rights/software; syndication (home 15%, overseas 20%); will suggest revision. Works with overseas agents. No reading fee.

*Lescher & Lescher Ltd (1966), 67 Irving Place, New York, NY 10003 *tel* 212-529-1790 *telegraphic address* Micawber *fax* 212-529-2716. *Directors:* Robert Lescher, Susan Lescher.
Full-length and short MSS (home 15%, overseas 20%). No unsolicited MSS; query first with sase. No reading fee.

*Ellen Levine Literary Agency (1980), Suite 1801, 15 East 26th Street, New York, NY 10010 *tel* 212-899-0620 *fax* 212-725-4501.
Full-length MSS: biography, contemporary affairs, women's issues, history, science, literary and commercial fiction (home 15%, overseas 20%); in conjunction with co-agents, theatre, films, television (15%). Will suggest revision. Works in conjunction with agents in Europe, Japan, Israel, Brazil, Argentina. *UK representative:* A.P. Watt. No reading fee; preliminary letter and sase essential.

Literistic Ltd—see **Sterling Lord Literistic, Inc.**

*Gerard McCauley Agency, Inc., PO Box 844, Katonah, NY 10536 *tel* 914-232-5700.
Specialises in history, biography, science for general reader.

Kirby McCauley/The Pimlico Agency Inc., Box 20447, 1539 First Avenue, New York, NY 10028 *tel* 212-628-9729 *fax* 212-535-7861. *Contact:* Christopher Shepard; *directors:* Kirby McCauley, Kay McCauley.
Specialise in science fiction, horror, fantasy and true crime.

*Anita D. McClellan Associates, 50 Stearns Street, Cambridge, MA 02138 *tel* 617-576-6950. *Director:* Anita D. McClellan.
General fiction and non-fiction. Full-length MSS (home 15%, overseas 20%). Will suggest revision for agency clients. No unsolicited MSS. Send preliminary letter and sase bearing US postage or International Reply Coupon.

McIntosh, McKee & Dodds, Inc., 276 Fifth Avenue, New York, NY 10001 *tel* 212-679-4490 *cables* Halmatson *fax* 212-545-1224.

*McIntosh & Otis Inc. (1928), 310 Madison Avenue, New York, NY 10017 *tel* 212-687-7400 *fax* 212-687-6894.

*Carol Mann Agency (1977), 55 Fifth Avenue, New York, NY 10003 *tel* 212-206-5635 *fax* 212-463-8718. *Associates:* Carol Mann, Gareth Esersky.
Psychology, popular history, biography, general non-fiction; fiction (home 15%, overseas 20%). Works in conjunction with foreign agents. No reading fee.

*Elaine Markson Literary Agency (1973), 44 Greenwich Avenue, New York, NY 10011 *tel* 212-243-8480 *fax* 212-691-9014. *Directors:* Elaine Markson, Geri Thoma, Sally Wofford-Girand.
Full-length MSS. Literary and mainstream commercial fiction (no genre); biography, sociology, history, popular culture, feminism (home 15%, overseas 20%), performance rights (10%); will suggest revision. Works with overseas agents. No reading fee.

*Mildred Marmur Associates Ltd (1987), 310 Madison Avenue, Suite 724, New York, NY 10017 *tel* 212-949-6055 *fax* 212-949-0329. *President:* Mildred Marmur; *associate agent:* Jennie Dunham.
Serious non-fiction, literary fiction, juveniles. Full-length and short MSS (home licences 15%, overseas licences 20%), performance rights (15%). Works with co-agents in all major countries. No reading fee. Queries must include sase or International Reply Coupons.

*The Evan Marshall Agency (1987), 22 South Park Street, Suite 216, Montclair, NJ 07042-2744 *tel* 201-744-1661 *fax* 201-744-6312. *President:* Evan Marshall. General fiction and non-fiction (home 15%, overseas 20%); screenplays, teleplays (20%). Works in conjunction with overseas agents. Will suggest revision; no reading fee but $28 handling fee for unpublished writers.

*Elisabeth Marton Agency, 1 Union Square West, Room 612, New York, NY 10003 *tel* 212-255-1908 *fax* 212-691-9061. *Owner:* Tonda Marton. Stage plays only.

*Harold Matson Company, Inc. (1937), 276 Fifth Avenue, New York, NY 10001 *tel* 212-679-4490 *cables* Halmatson *fax* 212-545-1224. Full-length MSS (home 10%, UK 19%, translation 19%). No unsolicited MSS. No reading fee.

*Claudia Menza Literary Agency (1983), 1170 Broadway, Suite 807, New York, NY 10001 *tel* 212-889-6850. *President:* Claudia Menza; *partner:* Richard M. Derus.
Full-length MSS. Serious non-fiction, photographic books, books by and about Black Americans, avant-garde fiction; limited number of screenplays (home 15%, overseas 20%); will suggest revision. Works with overseas agents. No reading fee.

Scott Meredith Literary Agency Inc. (1946), 845 Third Avenue, New York, NY 10022 *tel* 212-751-4545 *fax* 212-755-2972. *President:* Arthur Klebanoff; *vice-presidents:* Mark Joly, Joshua Bilmes; *senior vice-president and director of foreign rights:* William T. Haas.
Full-length and short MSS. General fiction and non-fiction, books and magazines, juveniles, plays, TV scripts, motion picture rights and properties (home 10%, overseas 20%), performance rights (10%). Will read unsolicited MSS, queries, outlines. Single fee charged for readings, criticism and assistance in revision. *London:* Mark Hamilton, A.M. Heath & Co. Ltd.

*Helen Merrill Ltd, 435 West 23rd Street, Suite 1A, New York, NY 10011 *tel* 212-691-5326 *fax* 212-727-0545.

Peter Miller Agency Inc.—see PMA Literary and Film Management, Inc.

Robert P. Mills Ltd, c/o Richard Curtis Associates, 171 East 74th Street, New York, NY 10021 *tel* 212-772-7363 *fax* 212-772-7393.

*William Morris Agency Inc., 1350 Avenue of the Americas, New York, NY 10019 *tel* 212-586-5100.

*Multimedia Product Development Inc. (1971), 410 South Michigan Avenue, Suite 724, Chicago, IL 60605 *tel* 312-922-3063 *fax* 312-922-1905. *Contact:* Jane Jordan Browne.
General fiction and non-fiction (home 15%, overseas 20%), performance rights (15%). Works in conjunction with foreign agents. Will suggest revision; no reading fee.

*Jean V. Naggar Literary Agency (1979), 216 East 75th Street, Suite 1E, New York, NY 10021 *tel* 212-794-1082. *President:* Jean V. Naggar.
Mainstream commercial and literary fiction (no formula fiction); non-fiction: psychology, science, biography (home 15%, overseas 20%), performance rights (15%). Works in conjunction with foreign agents. No reading fee.

*Ruth Nathan Agency (1981), 80 Fifth Avenue, Suite 706, New York, NY 10011 *tel/fax* 212-675-6063. *Director:* Ruth Nathan.
Fine art, decorative arts, show biz, biographies pertaining to those areas; occasional fiction and true crime (home 15%, overseas 10%-15%). No reading fee.

*New England Publishing Associates, Inc. (1982), PO Box 5, Chester, CT 06412 *tel* 203-345-READ *fax* 203-345-3660. *Directors:* Elizabeth Frost Knappman, Edward W. Knappman.
Serious non-fiction for the adult market (home 15%, overseas varies), performance rights (varies). Works in conjunction with foreign publishers. No reading fee; will suggest revision – if undertaken, 15% fee; 15% fee for placing MSS.

*Harold Ober Associates Inc., 425 Madison Avenue, New York, NY 10017 *tel* 212-759-8600 *fax* 212-759-9428. *Directors:* Claire M. Smith, Phyllis Westberg.
Full-length MSS (home 15%, British 15%, overseas 20%), performance rights (10%). Will suggest revision. *London representative:* David Higham Associates. No reading fee.

*Fifi Oscard Agency Inc., 24 West 40th Street, New York, NY 10018 *tel* 212-764-1100 *fax* 212-840 5019. *President:* Fifi Oscard; *agents:* Ivy Fischer Stone, Kevin McShane, Nancy Murray.
Full-length MSS (home 15%, overseas 20%), performance rights (10%). Will suggest revision. Works in conjunction with many foreign agencies. No reading fee, but no unsolicited submissions.

Pegasus International Inc. (1987), literary and film agents. PO Box 5470, Winter Park, FL 32793-5470 *tel* 407-699-1299 *fax* 407-699-1299. *Director:* Gene Lovitz.
All non-fiction/fiction genres. Specialises in: regency and historical romances, gothic, horror, mystery, mainstream, science fiction, juveniles, medicine and health; TV/film scripts (home 10%, overseas 15%). Literary assistance to unpublished authors. Evaluation fee charged (returned when published). MSS with high film potential need not be submitted in screenplay form. Personal telephone calls returned anywhere in the world (call at any hour).

Perkins' Literary Agency, PO Box 48, Childs, MD 21916 *tel* 410-398-2647.
Full-length MSS (home 15%, overseas 20%), film/television (20%); will suggest revision. Reading fee. Query first.

*James Peter Associates, Inc. (1981), 151 Sunset Lane, PO Box 772, Tenafly, NJ 07670 *tel* 201-568-0760 *fax* 201-568 2959. *Contact:* Bert Holtje.
Non-fiction, especially history, politics, popular culture, health, psychology, reference, biography (home 15%, overseas 20%). Foreign rights handled by: Bobbe Siegel, 41 West 83rd Street, New York, NY 10024. Will suggest revision. No reading fee.

PMA Literary and Film Management, Inc. (1976), 220 West 19th Street, Suite 501, New York, NY 10011 *tel* 212-929-1222 *fax* 212-206-0238. *President:* Peter Miller.
Full-length MSS, specialising in commercial fiction, true crime, biography, Hollywood history and all books with film and television production potential (home 15%, overseas 25%), films, television (10-20%). Works in conjunction with agents world-wide. Preliminary enquiry with synopsis and resumé essential.

*Raines & Raines (1961), 71 Park Avenue, New York, NY 10016 *tel* 212-684-5160. *Directors:* Theron Raines, Joan Raines, Keith Korman.
Full-length MSS (home 15%, overseas 20%). Works in conjunction with overseas agents. No unsolicited MSS.

*Helen Rees Literary Agency (1982), 308 Commonwealth Avenue, Boston, MA 02115 *tel/fax* 617-262-2401.

Full-length MSS. Business books, self-help, biography, autobiography, political, literary fiction (home 15%); will suggest revision. Works with foreign agent. No reading fee.

*Flora Roberts Inc., 157 West 57th Street, Penthouse A, New York, NY 10019 *tel* 212-355-4165.

*Rosenstone/Wender, 3 East 48th Street, 4th Floor, New York, NY 10017 *tel* 212-832-8330 *fax* 212-759-4524.

*Russell & Volkening Inc., 50 West 29th Street, New York, NY 10001 *tel* 212-684-6050 *fax* 212-889-3206.

Schaffner Agency (1948), 6625 Casas Adobes Road, Tucson, AZ 85704 *tel* 602-797-8000 *fax* 602-797-8271. *Director:* Timothy Schaffner.
Full-length MSS (home 15%, foreign 15-20%). British/translation representatives: A.M. Heath & Co. Ltd. No reading fee.

*Susan F. Schulman Literary & Dramatic Agents Inc., 454 West 44th Street, New York, NY 10036 *tel* 212-713-1633 *fax* 212-581-8830.
Agents for negotiation in all markets (with co-agents) of fiction, general nonfiction, children's books, academic and professional works, and associated subsidiary rights including plays, film and television (home 15%, UK 7½%, overseas 20%). Return postage required.

*Charlotte Sheedy Literary Agency, Inc., 611 Broadway, Suite 428, New York, NY 10012 *tel* 212-780-9800 *fax* 212-780-0308.

*The Shukat Company Ltd, 340 West 55th Street, Suite 1A, New York, NY 10019 *tel* 212-582-7614 *telex* 6502224600 MC1 UW *fax* 212-315-3752. Scott Shukat.
Theatre, films, novels, television, radio (15%). No reading fee. No unsolicited material accepted.

Singer Media Corporation, Seaview Business Park, 1030 Calle Cordillera, Unit 106, San Clemente, CA 92673 *tel* 714-498-7227 *fax* 714-498-2162. *Directors:* Katherine Han (executive vice-president), Kurt Singer (president), Janis Hawkridge (editor), Helen J. Lee (treasurer).
Full-length MSS, including romance, mysteries, horror, biography; also teen-age romance (age 12-16) (home 15%, overseas 20%); short MSS (home 10%, overseas 15%); films, television, radio, merchandising, audio (15%, overseas 20%), video (20%). Interested in reprint rights of published non-fiction books for foreign publishers. Represented in most countries abroad. Published authors only.

The Spieler Agency (1982), 154 West 57th Street, Room 135, New York, NY 10019 *tel* 212-757-4439 *fax* 212-333-2019. *Directors:* F. Joseph Spieler, Lisa M. Ross.
Full- and short-length MSS. History, politics, ecology, business, some fiction (home 15%, overseas 20%). No reading fee.

*Philip G. Spitzer Literary Agency, 50 Talmage Farm Lane, East Hampton, NY 11937 *tel* 516-329-3650 *fax* 516-329-3651.
General fiction and non-fiction; specialises in mystery/suspense, sports, politics, biography, social issues.

*Stepping Stone Literary Agency (1974), 59 West 71st Street, Suite 9B, New York, NY 10023 *tel* 212-362-9277 *fax* 212-362-1998. *President:* Sarah Jane Freymann; *associate:* Katharine Sands.
Fiction and non-fiction, especially commercial and mainstream fiction (home/overseas 15%). Works in conjunction with Abner Stein and Marsh & Sheil in London. No reading fee.

Sterling Lord Literistic, Inc., One Madison Avenue, New York, NY 10010 *tel* 212-696-2800 *cables* Literistic New York *fax* 212-686-6976. *Directors:* Peter Matson, Sterling Lord, Michael Sissons, Anthony Jones.
Full-length and short MSS (home 15%, overseas 19%), performance rights (15%). Will suggest revision. UK representative: The Peters Fraser & Dunlop Group Ltd. No reading fee.

*Gloria Stern Agency (1984), 12535 Chandler Boulevard, Suite 3, North Hollywood, CA 91607-1934 *tel* 818-508-6296 *fax* 818-508-6296. *Director:* Gloria Stern.
Fiction and films (home 10%, overseas 15%). Reading fee; consultation fee for revisions; some author expenses for placing MSS.

H.N. Swanson, Inc. (1934), 8523 Sunset Boulevard, Los Angeles, CA 90069 *tel* 310-652-5385 *fax* 310-652-3690. *Owner:* N.V. Swanson; *president:* Thomas J. Shanks; *agents:* James Anderson, Gail Barrick, Larry Kennar, Steve Fisher.
Full-length MSS. Fiction novels, plays (home 15%, overseas 20%), film and TV rights (home 10%, overseas 20%), performance rights. No unsolicited MSS; query first, submit outline. No reading fee.

*Roslyn Targ Literary Agency, Inc., 105 West 13th Street, New York, NY 10011 *tel* 212-206-9390 *fax* 212-989-6233.
Full-length MSS. Affiliates in most foreign countries. No reading fee; preliminary letter with sase essential.

*Susan P. Urstadt, Inc., Writers and Artists Agency (1975), PO Box 1676, New Canaan, CT 06840 *tel* 203-966-6111. *Director:* Susan P. Urstadt.
All quality non-fiction, especially biography, decorative arts, gardening, history, natural history and popular reference (home 15%, overseas 20%). No reading fee. Query first, enclosing an sase.

*Ralph Vicinanza Ltd, 111 8th Avenue, Suite 1501, New York, NY 10011 *tel* 212-924-7090.
No unsolicited MSS (home 10%, overseas 20%).

Austin Wahl Agency, Ltd (1935), 1820 North 76th Court, Elmwood Park, IL 60635-3631 *tel* 312-922-3331. *President:* Thomas Wahl.
Full-length and short MSS (home 15%, overseas 20%), theatre, films, television (10%). No reading fee; professional writers only.

*Wallace Literary Agency, Inc. (1988), 177 East 70th Street, New York, NY 10021 *tel* 212-570-9090 *fax* 212-772-8979. *Directors:* Lois Wallace, Thomas C. Wallace.
Full-length MSS; no cookery, humour, how-to; film, television, theatre for agency clients. Will suggest revision. No unsolicited MSS; no faxed queries.

Watkins/Loomis Agency, Inc., 133 East 35th Street, New York, NY 10016 *tel* 212-532-0080 *cables* Anwat, Newyork *fax* 212-889-0506. *London:* Abner Stein (UK), The Marsh Agency (foreign).

Sandra Watt and Associates (1978), 8033 Sunset Boulevard, Suite 4053, Hollywood, CA 90046 *tel* 213-653-2339. *Owner:* Sandra Watt.
Lead women's fiction, suspense, mysteries, New Age, cyber-punk; psychological self-help, gardening, single-volume reference works; screenplays (home 15%, overseas 25%), films (10%). Works in conjunction with foreign agents. Will suggest revision; no reading fee; $100 marketing fee for unpublished authors.

Wecksler-Incomco (1971), 170 West End Avenue, New York, NY 10023 *tel* 212-787-2239 *fax* 212-496-7035. *President:* Sally Wecksler; *associate:* Joann Amparan.

Illustrated books, non-fiction (home 12-15%, overseas 20%); will suggest revision where appropriate. No reading fee.

*Rhoda Weyr Agency (1983), 151 Bergen Street, Brooklyn, NY 11217   *tel* 718-522-0480   *fax* 718-522-0410.
General non-fiction and fiction with particular interest in science, history, biography. Full-length MSS for fiction; proposal for n-f (home 15%, overseas 20%), performance rights (15%). Co-agents in all foreign markets. Sase required.

*Writers House Inc. (1974), 21 West 26th Street, New York, NY 10010   *tel* 212-685-2400   *fax* 212-685-1781. *President:* Albert Zuckerman; *executive vice-president:* Amy Berkower.
Full-length MSS. Popular and literary fiction, novels for children and young adults, history, biography, popular science, how-to books in business, health, nutrition and popular psychology (home 15%, overseas 20%). No reading fee.

Wylie, Aitken & Stone, Inc., 250 West 57th Street, Suite 2114, New York, NY 10107   *tel* 212-246-0069   *fax* 212-586-8953. *Directors:* Andrew Wylie (president), Deborah Karl, Sarah Chalfant, Bridget Love.
Full-length and short MSS. Literary fiction/non-fiction (home 10%, overseas 20%); will suggest revision. Own London office. No reading fee.

*Mary Yost Associates, Inc. (1958), 59 East 54th Street, Suite 73, New York, NY 10022   *tel* 212-980-4988   *telegraphic address* Mybooks.
Full-length and short MSS (home and overseas 10%). Works with individual agents in all foreign countries. Will suggest revision. No reading fee.

*Susan Zeckendorf Associates Inc. (1978), 171 West 57th Street, New York, NY 10019   *tel* 212-245-2928. *President:* Susan Zeckendorf
Literary fiction, women's commercial fiction, mysteries, thrillers, science, music (home 15%, overseas 20%), film, TV rights (15%). Works in conjunction with overseas agents. Will suggest revision. No reading fee.

Other Literary Agents

Most of the agents whose names and addresses are given below work in association with an agent in London.

In all cases, and in their own interests, writers are advised to send a preliminary letter and to ascertain terms before submitting MSS or books.

ARGENTINA

International Editors Co., Avenida Cabildo 1156, 1426 Buenos Aires   *tel* 786-0888/788-2992   *fax* 541-786-0888/552-5832.

Lawrence Smith BA (1938), Avenida de los Incas 3110, 1426 Buenos Aires   *tel* 552-5012   *cables* Litagent, Baires   *fax* 54-1-8045508/54-1-5525012.

AUSTRALIA

Curtis Brown (Australia) Pty Ltd, 27 Union Street, Paddington, Sydney, NSW 2021   *tel* (02) 331 5301/361 6161   *fax* (02) 360 3935.

Literary Resources (1992), PO Box 540, North Adelaide, South Australia 5006   *tel/fax* (08) 332 8341. *Principal:* Doug Nancarrow. Full-length and short MSS, adult fiction and non-fiction (home 10%, overseas 20%), performance rights (10%); will suggest revision. Works with overseas agents. One-off reading fee for unpublished authors only.

BRAZIL

Agencia Literária Balcells Mello e Souza Riff, Rua Visconde de Pirajá, 414 s1 1108 Ipanema, 22410-002 Rio de Janeiro, RJ   *tel* (55-21) 287-6299   *fax* (55-21) 267-6393. Lucia de Mello e Souza Riff.

Karin Schindler, Rights Representative (formerly **Dr J.E. Bloch Literary Agency**), Caixa Postal 19051, 04599-970 São Paulo, SP   *tel* 241-9177   *fax* 241-9077.

CANADA

Acacia House Publishing Services Ltd (1985), 51 Acacia Road, Toronto, Ontario M4S 2K6   *tel/fax* 416-484-8356. *Managing director:* Mrs Frances A. Hanna. Literary fiction and non-fiction, quality commercial fiction, most non-fiction, except business books; selective quality children's list, mainly fiction (15% English language world-wide, 30% translation), performance rights (15-30%). *No* science fiction, horror or occult. Works with overseas agents. Reading fee on MS over 200pp, where an evaluation is also provided.

Curtis Brown Canada Ltd, Janet Turnbull Irving, Dean Cooke, 200 First Avenue, Toronto, Ontario M4M 1X1   *tel* 416-406-3390.

CZECH REPUBLIC

Aura-Pont, Theatrical and Literary Agency Ltd (1990), Radlická 99, Prague 5   *tel/fax* (0422) 53 99 09, 53 63 51. *Director:* Dr Alexander Jerie. Handles authors' rights in books, theatre, film, TV, radio software – both Czech and foreign, literary scouting for Czech publishers (home 10%, overseas 15%); will suggest revision.

Dilia Theatrical and Literary Agency, Polská 1, 120 00 Prague 2   *tel* (02) 25 22 07   *fax* (0422) 25 22 07.

Interlit Services Ltd (1993), PO Box 125, 130 00 Prague 3   *tel* (02) 78 19 324, 78 10 327   *fax* (02) 24 224 114. *Directors:* Klaus Flugge, Otakar Bozejowski; *manager:* Alena Šmídová. Sells rights to Czech and Slovak publishers, including fiction, literature, popular science and esoteric (home 10%).

FRANCE

Bureau Littéraire International Marguerite Scialtiel, 14 rue Chanoinesse, 75004 Paris   *tel* (1) 43 54 71 16. Geneviéve Ulmann.

Robert Fouques Duparc (1986), Van Beuningenstraat 23, 2582 KG Den Haag, Netherlands   *tel* (070) 358 64 48   *fax* (070) 358 65 68.

Agence Hoffman, 77 boulevard Saint-Michel, 75005 Paris   *tel* (1) 43 26 56 94   *cables* Aghoff   *telex* 203605   *fax* (1) 43 26 34 07.

Mme Michelle Lapautre, 6 rue Jean Carriès, 75007 Paris   *tel* (1) 47 34 82 41   *fax* (1) 47 34 00 90.

Donine Mouche, Agent Littéraire (formerly **McKee & Mouche**), 12 rue du Regard, 75006 Paris   *tel* (1) 45 48 45 03/42 22 42 33.

La Nouvelle Agence, 7 rue Corneille, 75006 Paris   *tel* (1) 43 25 85 60   *fax* (1) 43 25 47 98. Mary Kling.

GERMANY (*See also* SWITZERLAND)

Brigitte Axster, Dreieichstr. 43, D-60594 Frankfurt/Main   *tel* 069-629856   *fax* 069-623526.

Geisenheyner & Crone, Gymnasiumstrasse 31B, 70174 Stuttgart   *tel* 0711-293738   *fax* 0711-2261748.

Agence Hoffman, Bechsteinstrasse 2, 80804 Munich   *tel* 089-308 48 07   *fax* 089-308 21 08.

Michael Meller Literary Agency (1988), PO Box 400 323, 80703 Munich   *tel* (089) 366371   *fax* (089) 366372. Full-length MSS. Fiction and non-fiction, screenplays for films and television (home 15%, overseas 20%). Own US office. No reading fee.

Thomas Schlück, Literary Agency, Hinter der Worth 12, 30827 Garbsen   *tel* 05131-93053   *fax* 05131-93045.

HONG KONG

Holmes Literary Agency (1989), 341 Shek O Village, Shek O, Hong Kong   *tel* 852 809 2745   *fax* 852 809 2743. *Directors;* Stephanie Holmes, Christopher Holmes. General fiction and non-fiction. Full-length and short MSS (overseas 15%); performance rights (15%). Will suggest revision; no reading fee.

HUNGARY

Artisjus. Agency for Literature and Theatre of the Hungarian Bureau for the Protection of authors' rights, Mészáros u. 15-17, 1016 Budapest   *postal address* H-1538 Budapest, Pf. 593   *tel* 1-212-15-53   *fax* 1-212-15-50.

INDIA

Ajanta Books International (1975), 1 U.B. Jawahar Nagar, Bungalow Road, Delhi 110007   *tel* 2926182, 7258630   *telegraphic address* AJANTA BOOKS INT   *telex* 03179032 TCS IN   *fax* 91-11-7249664. *Proprietor:* S. Balwant. Full-length MSS in social sciences and humanities (commission varies according to market – Indian books in Indian and foreign languages, foreign books into Indian languages). Will suggest revision; charges made if agency undertakes revision; reading fee.

IRELAND

Jonathan Williams Literary Agency (1981), 2 Mews, 10 Sandycove Avenue West, Sandycove, Co. Dublin, Republic of Ireland   *tel/fax* (01) 2803482. *Director:* Jonathan Williams. General fiction and non-fiction, preferably by Irish authors (home 10%). Will suggest revision; usually no reading fee.

ISRAEL

I. Pikarski Ltd Literary Agency (1977), 200 Hayarkon Street, PO Box 4006, Tel Aviv 61040   *tel* 03-5270159/5231880   *fax* 03-5270160. *Director:* Ilana Pikarski. General trade publishing and merchandising rights.

ITALY

Eulama SRL (1962), Via Guido de Ruggiero 28, 00142 Rome *tel* (06) 540 73 09 *fax* (06) 540 87 72. *Directors:* Harald Kahnemann, Karin von Prellwitz, Norbert von Prellwitz, Maria G. Ocello von Prellwitz. Quality fiction and non-fiction, social sciences, politics, philosophy, religion, psychology, education, linguistics, architecture, urban studies (home 15%, overseas 20%); will suggest revision where appropriate. Works with overseas agents. No reading fee.

Grandi & Vitali Associati SRL (1988), Via Caradosso 12, 20123 Milan *tel* (02) 469 55 41/481 89 62 *fax* (02) 481 951 08. *Directors:* Laura Grandi, Mara Vitali. Provides publicity and foreign rights consultation for publishers and authors as well as sub-agent services; will suggest revision where appropriate. Reading fee.

ILA–International Literary Agency–USA (1969), I-18010 Terzorio-IM *tel* (0184) 48 40 48 *fax* (0184) 48 72 92. Publishers' and authors' agent, interested in bestsellers and mass market books. *Speciality:* books on collecting and antiques.

Agenzia Letteraria Internazionale SRL, Via Fratelli Gabba 3, 20121 Milan *tel* (02) 86 54 45/86 46 34 18/86 15 72 *telex* 323574 Linali I *fax* (02) 87 62 22.

News Blitz International, Via Cimabue 5, 00196 Rome *tel* (06) 32 01 489/32 00 620 *fax* (06) 32 19 014. *Literary department:* Giovanni A. Congiu.

Irina Reylander Literary Agency (1989), Viale Monza 167/A, 20125 Milan *tel/ fax* (02) 28 47 828. *Director:* Dr Irina Reylander. Full-length MSS (15%). Marketing fee.

JAPAN

The English Agency (Japan) Ltd (1979), 305 Azabu Empire Mansion, 4-11-28 Nishi Azabu, Minato-ku, Tokyo 106 *tel* 03-3406 5385 *fax* 03-3406 5387. *Managing director:* William Miller. Handles work by English-language writers living in Japan; arranges Japanese translations (home/overseas 10%), performance rights (10%); will suggest revision where appropriate. Works with overseas agents. No reading fee.

Orion Literary Agency, Popyrus Building, 1-58 Kanda-Jimbocho, Chiyoda-ku, Tokyo 101 *tel* 03-3295-1405 *telegraphic address* Orionagy, Tokyo *telex* J24408 Orionagy *fax* 03-3295-4366.

NETHERLANDS

Auteursbureau Greta Baars-Jelgersma (1951), Bovensteweg 46, NL-6585 KD Mook *tel* 8896-1470/85-635017 *fax* 8896-2439. Literature; illustrated co-productions, including children's, art, handicraft, hobby and nature (home/ overseas 20%). Works with overseas agents. Occasionally charges a reading fee.

Robert Fouques Duparc (1986), Van Beuningenstraat 23, 2582 KG Den Haag *tel* (070) 358 64 48 *fax* (070) 358 65 68.

International Drama Agency, Ilperveldstraat 82, 1024 PJ Amsterdam *tel* (020) 636 77 54/634 08 04 *fax* (020) 636 73 55. Francis Lonnee.

Internationaal Literatuur Bureau B.V., Postbus 10014, 1201 DA, Hilversum *tel* (035) 21 35 00 *fax* (035) 21 57 71. Menno Kohn.

NEW ZEALAND

Glenys Bean Literary Agency (1989), PO Box 47-098, Auckland 2 *tel/fax* (09) 378-6287. Adult and children's fiction, educational, non-fiction, film, TV, radio (home 10%, overseas 20%). Represented by Diane Cleaver (USA); translations – Sheil Land (UK). Preliminary letter, synopsis and sae required.

Richards Literary Agency (1977), 3-49 Aberdeen Road, Castor Bay, Auckland 9 *postal address* PO Box 31240, Milford, Auckland 9 *tel* (09) 410-5681 *fax* (09) 410-6389. *Partners:* Ray Richards, Barbara Richards. Full-length MSS, fiction, non-fiction, juvenile, educational, academic books; films, television, radio (home 10%, overseas 10-20%). Preliminary letter, synopsis with sae required. No reading fee.

NIGERIA

Joe–Tolalu & Associates (Nigeria) Ltd (1983), Plot 14, Block A, Surulere Industrial Road, Ogba,. PO Box 7031, Ikeja, Lagos *tel* 01-932929, 01-931505, 034-233031. *Directors:* Joseph Omosade Awolalu, Tosin Awolalu, Foluke Awolalu, Dimeji Popoola. Full-length MSS: fiction and non-fiction; short MSS: picture books only (home 10-15%, overseas 15-20%; translation 15%, performance, film/TV 10%). Will suggest revision. Works in conjunction with overseas agents. Preliminary letter essential; no reading fee. Also acts as publishing consultant.

PORTUGAL

Ilidio da Fonseca Matos, Avenida Gomes Pereira, 105-3°-B, 1500 Lisbon *tel* 716 29 88 *fax* 715 44 45.

SCANDINAVIA, including FINLAND and ICELAND

A/S Bookman, Nørregade 45, DK-1165 Copenhagen K, Denmark *tel* 33 14 57 20 *fax* 33 12 00 07. Handles rights in Denmark, Sweden, Norway, Finland and Iceland for foreign authors.

Gösta Dahl & Son, AB, Aladdinsvägan 14, S-161 38 Bromma, Sweden *tel* 08 25 62 35 *fax* 08 25 11 18.

Lennart Sane Agency AB (1969), Holländareplan 9, S-374 34 Karlshamm, Sweden *tel* 0454 123 56 *fax* 0454 149 20. *Directors:* Lennart Sane, Elisabeth Sane, Ulf Töregård. Fiction, non-fiction, children's books, film and TV scripts; will suggest revision where appropriate. No reading fee.

Leonhardt Literary Agency aps, Studiestraede 35, DK-1455 Copenhagen K, Denmark *tel* 33 13 25 23 *cables* Leolitag *fax* 33 13 49 92.

Licht & Licht, Maglemosevej 46, DK-2920 Charlottenlund, Denmark *tel* 31 61 09 08 *cables* Literagent *fax* 31 61 11 05. Represents foreign agents and publishers in Denmark, Finland, Iceland, Norway and Sweden.

Gustaf von Sydow (1988), Lorensbergsvägen 76, S 136 69 Haninge, Sweden *tel/ fax* 08 776 10 54. *Directors:* Gustaf von Sydow, Elizabeth von Sydow. Handles television, film, celebrity and news features in Sweden, Norway, Denmark and Finland. Literary agent working in Sweden, Norway, Denmark and Finland.

SLOVAKIA

Lita Slovak Literary Agency, Partizánska 21, 815 30 Bratislava *tel/fax* 42 7
313645 *telegraphic address* Lita, Bratislava.

SOUTH AFRICA

Frances Bond Literary Services (1985), 32B Stanley Teale Road, Westville North
3630, Natal *postal address* PO Box 223, Westville 3630 *tel* (031)
824532 *fax* (031) 822620. *Managing editor:* Frances Bond; *editor:* Eileen
Molver.

Isabel Cooke Literary Agency (1985), PO Box 22477, Glenashley 4022 *tel*
(031) 524635 *fax* (031) 835187. Full-length MSS, fiction and non-fiction,
screenplays; public speaking consultant and writing tuition offered.

International Press Agency (Pty) Ltd, PO Box 67, Howard Place 7450 *tel* (021)
5311926 *fax* (021) 5318789. *Manager:* Terry Temple. *UK office:* Ursula A.
Barnett, 19 Avenue South, Surbiton, Surrey KT5 8PJ *tel* 081-390 4414 *fax*
081-390 4414.

Sandton Literary Agency (1982), PO Box 785799, Sandton 2146 *tel* (011)
4428624. *Directors:* J. Victoria Canning, M. Sutherland. Full-length MSS and
screenplays; lecture agents. Letter or telephone call first, please. Works in
conjunction with: (*UK*) Joan Beakbane, Jacob's Ladder, Low Habberley,
Kidderminster, Worcs. DY11 5RF, (*USA*) H.N. Swanson, Inc., Los Angeles.

SPAIN

A.C.E.R. Literary Agency (1959), San Bernardo 16, 28015 Madrid *tel* 1-522-
5157/522-9803 *fax* 1-522-8722. *Directors:* Elizabeth Atkins, Laure Merle
d'Aubigné. Represents UK, US, French and German publishers for Spanish
and Portuguese translation rights; represents Spanish- and Portuguese-lan-
guage authors (home/overseas 10%); will suggest revision where appropriate.
£20 reading fee.

Miss Carmen Balcells, Agencia Literaria Carmen Balcells, Diagonal 580, Barcelona 08021 *tel* 200-89-33, 200-85-65 *cables* Copyright, Barcelona *telex*
50459 COPY E *fax* 200-70-41.

Mercedes Casanovas Literary Agency (1980), Teodora Lamadrid 29, 08022
Barcelona *tel* 212-47-91 *fax* 417-90-37. Literature, non-fiction, children's
books (home 10%, overseas 20%). Works with overseas agents. No reading
fee.

International Editors Co., S.A., Rambla Cataluña 63, 3º-1ª, 08007 Barcelona *tel*
215-88-12 *fax* 487-35-83.

N.A.L.I. (1983), Maldonadas 9, E-28005 Madrid *tel* 365-25-16/366-57-02 *fax*
364-07-00. *Directors:* Raquel de la Concha, Anne Marie Vallat. Fiction, non-
fiction, children's books; will suggest revision where appropriate. No reading
fee.

Lennart Sane Agency AB (1965), Paseo de Mejico 65, Las Cumbres-Elviria,
E-29600 Marbella (Malaga) *tel* (9) 52 83 41 80 *fax* (9) 52 83 31 96. Fiction,
non-fiction, children's books, film and TV scripts; will suggest revision where
appropriate. No reading fee.

Julio F. Yañez, Agencia Literaria, Via Augusta 139, 6º-2ª, 08021 Barcelona *tel*
200-71-07 *fax* 209-48-65.

SWITZERLAND

Paul & Peter Fritz AG Literary Agency, Jupiterstrasse 1, CH-8032 Zürich   *postal address* Postfach, CH-8032 Zürich   *tel* (01) 381 41 40   *fax* (01) 381 20 35. Represents authors, agents and publishers in German-language areas.

Liepman AG, Maienburgweg 23, CH-8044 Zürich   *tel* (01) 261 76 60   *cables* Litagent   *fax* (01) 261 01 24. Dr Ruth Liepman, Eva Koralnik, Ruth Weibel. Represents authors, agents and publishers from all over the world for German translation rights, and authors from MSS on for world rights.

Mohrbooks Literary Agency, Klosbachstrasse 110, CH-8032 Zürich   *tel* (01) 251 16 10   *fax* (01) 262 52 13. Rainer Heumann, Sabine Ibach.

Niedieck Linder AG, Wehrenbachhalde 34, Postbox 153, CH-8053 Zürich   *tel* (01) 381 65 92   *fax* (01) 381 65 92. Represents German-language authors.

See also **Scripts for theatre, radio, tv and film** section for agents specialising in these fields.

Character before plot!

There are two reasons for doing your detailed plotting *after* you have given your characters life. The first is that, as we have seen, plot flows most easily and genuinely from character. The second is that, unless your characters live and breathe on that page, the finest plot in the world will not save your book – and every editor and publisher in the world knows this.

You might ask, 'Why not first work out the plot and then simply people it with characters designed expressly for executing the plot?' The short answer is that it doesn't work. I don't know of any exception. This procedure merely delivers wooden characters to well-deserved ridicule and – because the characters lack credibility – laughable plots. Quite literally, and inescapably, dull characters can only be an argument for applying euthanasia to the whole novel. On the other hand, a dud plot can often be fixed without any tears at all, even in none too-expert hands, while an experienced writer will turn the most unpromising plot into a thing of glittering excitement.

from *Writing a Thriller* by André Jute (A & C Black, £9.99)

Merchandising Rights

What are they? – As a writer or artist should merchandising rights concern you?

NICHOLAS DURBRIDGE
Managing Director, The Copyrights Group Ltd

Most writers and artists have, from early experience, a basic understanding of film, television and publishing rights, but ask that same writer or artist about the merchandising rights that they own and a much vaguer response will normally be received. Merchandising rights – the very term is elastic and can mean many different things to different people. Often in publishing contracts a grant of merchandising rights is to be found towards the end of the subsidiary rights clause as a sort of sweeping-up provision to catch anything which might remotely be commercial and which, perhaps, the person drafting the contract hasn't given specific thought to covering earlier on. The purpose of this article is to shed a little light, albeit briefly, on what merchandising rights are, their value and the broad commercial terms of a merchandising licence.

There is no agreed-upon definition of merchandising rights that I am aware of, nor any legal case which has sought to define the term. But for the purposes of this article, I will try and set some parameters. Essentially, merchandising rights centre around the commercial exploitation of copyrights, trademarks and other intellectual property rights through their association with products and services. The huge variety of goods and services that can be associated with a well-known character or trademark is enormous, hence the elasticity of the term 'merchandising rights'. Toys, games, clothing, bedding, nursery accessories, ceramics, glassware, melamine, silverware, confectionery, food, garden equipment, etc.; the list of products is endless. Promotions for banking services, travel, airlines, breakfast cereals, hamburger restaurants, magazines and insurance. The possibilities are without limit. As a merchandising agency which specialises in representing writers and artists, we have been involved in licensing all of the above and more. Over the years, we have licensed some very strange products and promotions. Paddington Bear has appeared on Visa credit cards in Japan, and a Japanese airline used Paddington to promote their ski tours. Silver-plated Mrs Tiggy-Winkle car mascots was one product range with perhaps a limited appeal, but the Peter Rabbit cucumber frames recently marketed, along with other gardening equipment, have a broader market. A Paddington party book packaged with family packs of frozen sausage rolls springs to mind not so much for the royalties that were earned, but for the difficult problem that had first to be solved as to whether the glue in the book-binding would break up when frozen. Variety certainly is the name of the game.

Many people immediately equate merchandising with huge extra income, but before any author or artist gets excited about the untapped source of income awaiting him or her from merchandising rights, it is necessary to examine what, in practice, can be merchandised. Any manufacturer of a product or provider of a service is not going to pay royalties nor spend their hard earned cash developing products or advertising campaigns unless you bring something to the table. That something is fame or recognition or popularity; something unique which they cannot obtain anywhere else, and is, therefore, worth paying for. It is something which makes the manufacturer believe that if he associates your character or copyright with his product then there will be an audience out there wanting to purchase it or the ensuing product would be so attractive that it will be purchased by consumers for its aesthetic appeal. The higher the recognition or popularity of the character or copyright, or the more unique the aesthetic appeal of a picture, the more valuable it becomes to the manufacturer and it is not surprising, therefore, that the majority of licensed characters and concepts stem from film and television. James Bond, The Magic Roundabout, Teenage Mutant Ninja Turtles have each, at different points in time, given rise to large and successful merchandising programmes based on their film or television following.

Whilst film and television perhaps account for the majority of merchandise licensing, other sources of material for merchandising should not be overlooked. Merchandising is not a new phenomena. Kate Greenaway successfully merchandised her illustrations in the nineteenth century and Beatrix Potter was busy designing soft toys, games, slippers and other products before the First World War. Merchandising rights can, therefore, be valuable if they come from a publishing success. Of particular recent note has been the enormous programme derived from *The Country Diary of an Edwardian Lady*, with ranges of fabrics, clothing, household textiles, ceramics, food, kitchenware and other items marketed, not only in the United Kingdom, but also in the United States, Japan and other countries.

What all merchandising programmes have in common, however, is their requirement of a visual image. Whilst it is certainly possible to merchandise an idea that stems from a non-visual medium, think, for example, of The Ambridge merchandise based upon The Archers, before a product is produced a visual image is required to go on it. That visual image has to be appealing and adapt well onto a product so as to make that product appealing when sitting on the shelf in your local Boots, Marks and Spencer or department store. As an agency, the majority of our properties originate as books, and we look at hundreds of successful books each year. Sadly, very few of these, even when successful as books, have potential for successful merchandising programmes. Often the illustrations may be ideal as book illustrations but would not translate well onto product or packaging. The style may be too sketchy, or the illustration too specific to the events in the book, so when separated from the text it becomes meaningless. Merchandising is a distinctive medium, and in the same way that a television adaptation of a novel must adapt to the television medium, so the development of a product as a spin-off to a successful TV programme or publishing programme must adapt to the merchandise itself. The product must symbolise and represent in perhaps a very small space – the side of a box or the top of a bar of chocolate – everything that the consumer liked about the original television series, book or illustration. That can be very hard to achieve on occasion.

The artist who works already in a visual medium has an obvious advantage over a writer who does not when it comes to merchandising; however, there are still constraints that they work under. Companies in the greetings card and stationery industries consume large quantities of artwork and to control costs will often not work on a royalty basis, but merely for a flat fee. To secure a royalty-based licence the artwork must have some unique quality either through recognition and fame of the artist or through a unique quality which a manufacturer will not be able to replicate elsewhere. *The Country Diary of an Edwardian Lady* is a good example of what is required. On its own, floral artwork is hard to license for a royalty. There are hundreds of good natural history artists in the UK producing attractive studies. Add support from a successful book marketing programme and those same pictures become more desirable to manufacturers for their products and ones for which they will pay a royalty and not a mere fee.

Let us move ahead. Assume that you have written or illustrated a successful series of books featuring a character who has become a household name, or have scripted that successful film or television programme which has achieved high ratings. Manufacturers want to associate their products with your creation but on what basis should they do so? First of all, do you have the merchandising rights? Most publishing contracts and film and television contracts provide for these to be assigned to the publisher or film or television producer. Normally in publishing contracts you would expect to share the royalties derived from the merchandising rights with the publisher perhaps on a 50/50 basis. On a film or television contract they will be less generous and you may receive very little as the income will be submerged in a profit share once elastic production 'costs' have been recouped. If you can retain the merchandising rights, then it is obviously to your advantage to do so. Publishing contracts frequently require a red pen through many of the clauses, but ultimately whether you can retain the merchandising rights comes down to negotiation and the strength of your position. The employment of a film or literary agent to negotiate these contracts is usually advisable as the expertise and clout they can bring to a negotiation will usually enable you to improve a deal substantially beyond the commission such an agent will cost. If you do retain the merchandising rights and find yourself dealing with a manufacturer who wants to take a licence from you, the structure of a royalty-based merchandising deal is fairly standard, although more complicated than a publishing contract, with many more eventualities to be covered.

ROYALTIES

Merchandising royalties normally are between 5% and 10%. Mass market food products tend to attract lower royalty rates, perhaps as low as 1% due to the small margins on which manufacturers in that industry work, but the low royalty rate is compensated by higher volumes. Royalties are normally calculated on the manufacturer's selling price, not the retail price as in publishing, and the manufacturer will normally deduct trade discounts and returns. He may try also to deduct cash discounts, i.e. a discount which he gives his customer if they pay their bills early or within 30 days, but this should not be allowed as a deduction because the royalty is payable to the copyright-owner regardless of when or whether the manufacturer ultimately collects the money at all. As an author or artist you cannot be responsible for bad debts which are a risk that a manufacturer must assume.

Normally, there is an advance payable upon signature of the licence agreement. This may be a nominal £1000 or a substantial sum depending on the nature of the rights being granted and the product or services being licensed. There may also be a guarantee that the royalties payable under the licence agreement will amount to a certain sum over a period of time.

ROYALTY ACCOUNTING

Unlike publishing, the normal accounting period is quarterly with manufacturers rendering statements 30 days after the end of the quarter. Six-monthly accounting should be avoided unless it makes specific sense in the context of the product being licensed, e.g. it is seasonal, such as Christmas decorations, when all the royalties will arise within one six-month period.

PERIOD OF THE LICENCE

The normal licence period is two or three years, although certain manufacturers may try to negotiate longer periods, especially if their investment is particularly large or if it will take them a long period of time to bring their product to market. A prudent manufacturer will want an option to renew the licence agreement on the same financial terms so that upon the expiry of the licence he cannot be held to ransom if the product range is a success and he wishes to continue it.

TERRITORY

Manufacturers frequently seek world rights, but as an agency we usually resist this as our experience shows that rarely is a manufacturer effective throughout all the world's markets, and rights could be tied up and not fully exploited. We tend to license, therefore, by individual country, although with the current changes to Common Market Law it is no longer possible to grant an exclusive licence to a manufacturer just for the UK market. Our policy now within the Common Market is to grant non-exclusive licences, but to undertake with a manufacturer that we will not license another manufacturer in the same line of business who is based in the licensee's home market. If we are granting a licence to a UK manufacturer for placemats, for example, we give that UK manufacturer the right to sell throughout the whole Common Market and undertake that we will not license another UK-based placemat manufacturer to produce the same product. We may, however, license a French manufacturer to produce placemats for the French market and similarly that French manufacturer will have the freedom to sell their placemats throughout the whole of the Common Market which includes the UK. Otherwise giving just one manufacturer an exclusive EU licence may effectively cut off sales throughout large segments of the Common Market if that manufacturer is not an efficient exporter or if his products are too highly priced when competing against a locally made product.

QUALITY APPROVAL

It is essential in any merchandise licence that the copyright- or trademark-owner retains absolute approval of the product being manufactured. That approval should be strictly enforced and should call upon the product to be seen for approval at rough design stage, artwork stage and proof stage. Manufacturers will always tell you that they know what is best for their market and will frequently try to impose changes or compromises which the copyright-owner may be unhappy about. You should stick to your guns. Many manufacturers, who operate outside recognised 'aesthetic' industries such as ceramics or greetings cards, are visually illiterate and often they will try and cut corners and shave expense, thereby cheapening the appearance of a product and ultimately decreasing its appeal and commercial success.

COPYRIGHT ASSIGNMENT

As part of the copyright design process, a manufacturer may create new images that appear on the product which are original and which, whilst based upon the book or television programme that is being licensed, are not actual images taken from the book or television programme. It is important that the original copyright-owner controls all visual images that are created including those subsequently created for the product. Merchandise licences, therefore, always contain a copyright assignment from the manufacturer in favour of the owner of all derivative and new copyrights, trademarks and other intellectual property rights that come into existence through the design, creation and marketing of the product. On no account should you as the writer or artist assign the copyright in your creation to the manufacturer, as to do so will obviously deprive you of all future exploitation of your creation.

Other terms normally contained within a merchandising licence that you would expect to see are: termination for breach and insolvency, notice provisions on termination, best endeavours by the manufacturer – these are all standard. Also often clauses are contained providing for the destruction of printing films, plates and moulds by a manufacturer once the licence is ended and a manufacturer will normally have a sell-off period within which to dispose of any surplus stock. It is also important to understand and approve of how any surplus stock will be sold. To walk into a store and find a range of products marked as '50% off, discontinued line' will do nothing for you when trying to interest another manufacturer to take a licence for the same concept for a different range of products!

The above thumb-nail sketch may encourage you to deal with a particular licensing opportunity that comes your way. Alternatively, it may make you decide that you need specialist advice. There are a number of merchandising agencies who specialise in this area and who work on a commission basis. Merchandising commissions, however, are much higher than literary agents' commissions because of the amount of continuing work and expense that a merchandising agent is involved in. Merchandising commissions range from 25% to 60% as a percentage of royalties earned. Frequently your publisher (if they control merchandising rights) may decide to engage the services of a specialist agency, in which case it is worth sorting out early on how the agent's commission is paid. If you have decided to leave your merchandising rights with your publisher on a 50/50 split, does the merchandising agent's commission come out of the publisher's 50%, or yours, or is the 50/50 split net of commission? It can make a significant difference to the amount of income that you earn.

For a major successful merchandising property, the royalties to be derived can be astronomical. A film and television property such as Ninja Turtles will have earned millions of dollars worldwide in merchandising royalties. On a more modest scale, however, the royalties to be earned from the occasional deal can also make an attractive extra to an author's or artist's income. The potential is there and you are only really limited by your imagination.

This article is based on material which first appeared in *The Author*.

Merchandising Agents

A number of agents specialise in the handling of rights connected with the promotion of characters from books, television programmes, etc., or with the books and programmes themselves. This is a selective listing, both of agents and of properties handled.

BBC Licensing, BBC Worldwide, Room A2106, Woodlands, 80 Wood Lane, London W12 0TT *tel* 081-576 2550 *telex* 934678 *fax* 081-743 0393. Representing BBC TV and Radio and a selection of copyright owners.
Properties: *'Allo 'Allo, Animals of Farthing Wood, Antiques Roadshow, Archers, BBC, BBC Sport, Blinky Bill, Byker Grove, Chronicles of Narnia, Clothes Show, Crimewatch, Doctor Who, EastEnders, Edd the Duck, Every Second Counts, Fireman Sam, Food and Drink, Forget me not Farm, Funny Bones, Gardeners World, Generation Game, Give us a Break, Going Live, Mastermind, Match of the Day, Noddy, Only Fools and Horses, Pingu, Playdays, Question of Sport, Radio One, Spider, Telly Addicts, Top of the Pops, Watch with Mother, Mr Blobby, Noel's House Party, Albert: The Fifth Musketeer, Arabel and Mortimer, Hairy Jeremy, House of Elliot, Wallace and Gromit.*

Copyright Promotions Ltd, 12th Floor, Metropolis House, 22 Percy Street, London W1P 0DN *tel* 071-580 7431 *telex* 28992 Cpl Ldn *fax* 071-631 1147.

Properties include *Brockum, Elvis Presley, Dan Dare, Judge Dredd, Roy of the Rovers, Mr Men* and *Little Miss, GI Joe, My Little Pony, Playskool, Tonka, Thunderbirds, Pink Panther, Teenage Mutant Hero Turtles, Dennis the Menace, Desperate Dan, Minnie the Minx, Beryl the Peril, The Bash Street Kids, Toxic Crusaders, Tom and Jerry, Captain Scarlet, Stingray, The Prisoner, Sonic the Hedgehog, WCW, Mad Gadget, Zig & Zag,* Turner movies, *Monopoly, Cluedo,* Hanna-Barbera characters including: *The Flintstones, Yogi Bear, Scooby Doo, Top Cat, Wacky Races.*

The Copyrights Company (UK) Ltd, Manor Barn, Milton, Nr Banbury, Oxon OX15 4HH   *tel* (0295) 721188   *fax* (0295) 720145; *London office:* 14 Cinnamon Row, Plantation Wharf, York Road, London SW11 3TW   *tel* 071-924 3292   *fax* 071-924 3208. *Directors:* Nicholas Durbridge (managing), Linda Pooley, Mark Robinson, Julie Nellthorp, Karen Addison.
Properties include *Beatrix Potter, Paddington Bear, Brambly Hedge, Flower Fairies,* and other book-related properties for merchandise licensing.

Hawk Books, 309 Canalot, 222 Kensal Road, London W10 5BN   *tel* 081-969 8091   *fax* 081-968 9012. *Director:* Patrick Hawkey.
Properties: *Billy Bunter, Dolphinman, Dopey Dinosaur.*

Link Licensing Ltd (1986), 7 Baron's Gate, 33/35 Rothschild Road, Chiswick, London W4 5HT   *tel* 081-995 5080   *fax* 081-747 9452. *Directors:* Claire L. Derry, David A. Hamilton.
Properties: *Barney, Count Duckula, Barbie, Magic Roundabout, Victor & Hugo,* Gerry Anderson's *GFI, Creature Comforts, Avenger Penguins,* Natural History Museum, *Asterix,* NSPCC The Happy Kids, Jane Hissey's Old Bear & Friends.

Marvel Licensing, Arundel House, 13-15 Arundel Street, London WC2R 3DX   *tel* 071-497 2121   *fax* 071-497 8844.
Properties include *The Marvel Super-Heroes, Sesame Street, James Bond Junior.*

Patrick, Sinfield (PSL) (1980), 95 White Lion Street, London N1 9PF   *tel* 071-837 5440   *fax* 071-837 5334. *Directors:* Christopher Patrick, John Sinfield.
Represent properties of: Nikelodeon (*Ren and Stimpy, Rugrats*), Viacom International (*Mighty Mouse, Deputy Dawg*), MTV (MTV, *Beavis & Butt-Head*), Leisure Concepts Inc. (*Nintendo: Super Mario Bros, Crash Dummies*), Twentieth Century Fox (*Aliens, Operations: Aliens, Alien War*), United Feature Syndicate (*Garfield, Snoopy, Fido Dido*), Capcom (*Street Fighter II*), Gremlin Graphics (*Zool*), MGM (*Grimmy,* the MGM lion), Carolco Inc. (inc. *Terminator 2, James Cameron/Lightstorm*), Gresham Marketing (*Foxwood Tales*), Zodiac Entertainment (*Widget, Mr Bogus*), Hamilton Projects Inc. (*Beverley Hills 90210*), NHL (National Hockey League), Turner Broadcasting (*Captain Planet*), Zorro Productions (*Zorro*), Hallmark Group (Crayola).

Michael Woodward Creations Ltd (1990), Parlington Hall, Aberford, West Yorkshire LS25 3EG   *tel* (0532) 813913   *fax* (0532) 813911. *Directors:* Michael R. Woodward, John Millington.
International licensing company with own in-house studio. Worldwide representation. Current properties include *Teddy Tum Tum, Railway Children, Purrfect Partners, Zolan, Kit'n'Kin.* New concepts considered. Please forward synopsis and sae, with sample illustrations. Scripts or stories not accepted without illustration/design or concept mock-up.

PART TWO

General Information

Preparation of materials, resources

Books, Research and Reference Sources for Writers

MARGARET PAYNE ALA

Almost every writing project will involve the use of books or research at some stage. Some references are quickly found; others require accumulating numerous books or information files on a specific topic and visits to specialist libraries or other relevant places or people. Although research can be an interest or pleasure in itself, it can also be time-consuming, cutting into writing or earning time. Even checking a single fact can take hours or days if you ask the wrong question or check the wrong source first. No article or book can hope to solve all problems – sometimes there are no answers, or the lack of information is itself the answer – but a few guidelines as to routines and sources may save much time and money. The following is an introduction to printed sources. For a more detailed approach, including guides to original and unpublished material, it is recommended you consult Ann Hoffmann's *Research for Writers*, Black, revised edition 1992, £10.99, a most useful book which covers methods, sources, specific organisations and specialist libraries.

Suggestions for a core collection of reference books to own are given below under 'A writer's reference bookshelf'. The final choice of title often depends on personal preference and interests, space, the frequency with which it needs to be consulted, its cost and the proximity of your nearest public reference library. Anyone living in or near a large city has an advantage over the country dweller. Those living within easy reach of London have the best advantage of all: a choice of major reference libraries; a variety of specialist sources such as headquarters of various societies, companies and organisations; academic and other specialist libraries and the government. Often a question can be answered much nearer home, but you may find the further back in time you go, or the more detailed your research, the further afield you need to travel.

CHECKING A FACT

What do you really want to know?

Clarifying your question in advance can save much work for you or your researcher. If you want to check someone's date of birth and know the person is alive or very recently dead and in *Who's Who*, then ask for that book, or phrase your telephone request so that the librarian goes straight to that source. Do not start with general questions such as 'Where are the biographies?' In a branch library you may be shown sections of individual lives; on the telephone you are adding to British Telecom's profits and your telephone bill, as well as wasting time. If the person is dead, did he or she die recently enough to have a newspaper obituary – it often mentions the date of birth – or long enough ago to be in a volume of *Who Was Who* or the *Dictionary of National Biography*? Never assume that information that you know is necessarily common knowledge; it needs to be specified.

Go straight to the index.

Most reference books are arranged in alphabetical order but, if not, they should have an index. Some indexes may seem inadequate, but have you used the right key word? A good index should refer you from the one not used. For example, some will use carpentry and ignore woodwork as an entry. Others will ignore both and go straight to the object to be made or repaired. If there is no index, turn first to the contents page, as in some books the index is at the front rather than the back.

Is it important to be up to date?

Most books have the date of publication on the back of the title page. Is the answer given one which may be surpassed or superseded? Despite some instant publishing, when dealing with statistics most books have a built in obsolescence. There is a cut off date when the text goes to the printer and the updating must wait for the next edition. Some current events are too recent to be found in books at all, although well documented at the time in newspapers and magazines (see below).

If in doubt, re-check your answer.

If the answer is of importance, try not to depend on one source. Mistakes can occur in print or in transcribing. Sometimes it is necessary to check another source for verification or to obtain another point of view. In all cases you should . . .

Note your source.

Even if you think you will remember, always note where you find your information, preferably next to the answer, or in a card file or book where it can be easily found. Note the title, author, publisher and date of publication as well as the page number. Nothing is more annoying than having to undertake the same search twice.

RESEARCHING A SUBJECT

Reference has already been made to Ann Hoffmann's book for detail, but Kipling's six honest serving men can still be the basis for any subject: What? Why? When? How? Where? Who? cover aspects of most enquiries. The starting point depends on the writer's personal knowledge of the subject. Where it is unfamiliar always start from the general and go on to the particular. An article in an encyclopedia can fill in the background and often recommend bibliographies or other references. If an article in the *Encyclopaedia Britannica* is too detailed or too complex, try *The World Book*. The latter may be in the children's library, but because it has to appeal to a wider readership, the text and illustrations are clearer. Avoid a detailed book on the subject until you need it; it may tell you more than you want to know.

The following sources are suggestions as sources of information, but not all will be relevant to your subject.

Reference libraries. Use the largest one in your vicinity for encylopedias, specialised reference books, annuals and for back numbers of newspapers and periodicals. Ask for *Walford's Guide to Reference Material*. The three volumes list the standard reference works of subjects, most of which should be available for consultation.

Lending libraries. Find the class number of the books you want, and see what is available.

Special libraries. *The Aslib Directory of Information Sources in the United Kingdom* should be available in your reference library. It gives details of special libraries of industries, organisations and societies.

Catalogues, bibliographies and subject guides. Some libraries publish their catalogues, but this is becoming less frequent. There is a series of subject catalogues to the British Library (formerly the British Museum Library) up to 1975 and the *British National Bibliography* updates this (*see* 'Compiling a bibliography' below).

Newspapers and bibliographies. There is a monthly index to *The Times*, cumulated annually, which often provides the date of an event. The index also includes the *The Times Supplements*. For periodical articles, begin with the *British Humanities Index*, and, if necessary, check also the specialist indexes and abstracting journals such as *Current Technology Index*. Your public library can often locate runs of periodicals and magazines, and the interloan service can obtain specific periodical articles if you have the details. *Profile*, an on line index to quality newspapers, is the most up to date available, but retrospective only to 1985 and few libraries have the facility as yet.

COMPILING A BIBLIOGRAPHY

Checking what books are already available may reveal both the range of titles already in print and the potential market for your work. If yours is to be the tenth book on the subject published in the last two years, saturation point may be near. On the other hand, if you know the books and believe you can do better, or have evolved a different approach, you can mention this in a covering letter to a potential publisher. A quick way to evaluate what is available is by checking the shelves of a public library or bookstore, but it should be remembered that in a library, many of the best books will be on loan. This practice also makes one aware of publishers' interests.

A more comprehensive and systematic list of recent books can be compiled by consulting the *British National Bibliography*, a cumulating list based on the copyright books in the British Library, with advance notice (up to three months) of new books through the Cataloguing in Publication scheme. The arrangement is by the Dewey Decimal Classification used in all public libraries. Other subject lists are less satisfactory to consult. The British Museum (now British Library) has a series of subject indexes up to 1975, and many British books are included in the American *Cumulative Book Index* (1928 on). *Whitaker's Books in Print* is predominantly an author-title list, but does index some books under the key word of a subtitle; as its name implies, out of print books are excluded.

Facilities now exist to obtain a bibliography on any subject by using one of the computer data banks based on the British Library, the Library of Congress or commercial firms. The difficulties are expense (£25.00 per hour) and finding local access points.

OBTAINING BOOKS

Books in print. In 1993 82,322 different books were published in the United Kingdom alone, joining the many thousands of other titles still in print from previous years. The number of books available means that the chances of finding a copy of what you want on your bookseller's shelf, when you want it, may be slim. But if it is in print it can be ordered for you, although delivery times vary with each publisher. Most large bookshops and libraries now have the monthly microfiche editions of *Whitaker's Books in Print* giving details of author, publisher, price, number of pages and international standard book number (ISBN). The latter is often useful for speeding the order.

Out of print books present more difficulty. Generally the older the book, the more difficult it may be to obtain. Such books are no longer available from the publishers, who retain only a file copy, all other stocks having been sold. Therefore unless you are lucky enough to find an unsold copy on a bookseller's shelves, it must be sought in the second-hand market or through a library loan. There are many specialist second-hand and antiquarian booksellers, and a number of directories listing them and their interests. The most well known are *Sheppard's Book Dealers in the British Isles*, now published by R. Joseph, and Peter Marcan's *Directory of Specialist Book Dealers in the United Kingdom*. Copies of these should be in your local reference library. Many advertise in *Book and Magazine Collector*, a monthly magazine, which has an extensive 'wants' column.

Public libraries should be able to obtain books for you, whether or not they are in print, either from their own stock, from other libraries in the system or through the interloan scheme. This operates through the British Lending Library, but all requests must go through your library as you cannot apply direct. Your local library tickets may sometimes be used in other libraries, but different issuing systems have discouraged this in recent years.

A WRITER'S REFERENCE BOOKSHELF

However good and accessible a public library may be, there are some books required for constant or instant consultation, which should be within easy reach of the desk or typewriter. The choice of title may vary, but the following list is offered as suggestions for a core collection.

1. **Dictionaries.** With the use of word processor packages, a dictionary is no longer quite so essential for spelling checks, although still needed to clarify definitions and meanings. A book is often easier to consult, and portable. The complete *Oxford English Dictionary* is not, and although the definitive work, neither the full nor the compact edition with its magnifying glass, nor the two volume *Shorter Oxford Dictionary* is easy to handle for quick reference, so a one volume dictionary is more practical. The number of new words and meanings coming into vogue suggests a replacement every five years or so, or supplementing your choice by a good paperback edition. If you use an old copy, you will be surprised by the improved format and readability of the new editions.

The most popular one volume dictionaries are the *Concise Oxford Dictionary* (8th edn 1991, £12.95 – 80,000 definitions), *Chambers' English Dictionary* (5th edn 1991, £19.99 – 150,000 entries, appealing to crossword addicts), *The Collins English Dictionary* (£19.99 – 110,000 entries). A recommended paperback dictionary is *Oxford Paperback Dictionary* (1988, £4.99 – 50,000 entries). If you write for the American market, it is advisable also to have an American dictionary to check variant spellings and meanings. The equivalent of the Oxford family of dictionaries is Webster's, the most popular one volume edition being *Webster's New World Dictionary* (Prentice-Hall, 3rd edn 1988, £14.50).

2. **Roget's Thesaurus.** When the exact word or meaning eludes you, the thesaurus may help clear a mental block. There are many versions of Roget available, both in hardback and paperback, including a revision by E.M. Kirkpatrick (Longman, 1987, £15.99) and a paperback edition from Penguin (1984, £4.99).

3. **Grammar and English usage.** A wide choice is available but Fowler's *Modern English Usage* remains a standard work (2nd edn revised Sir Ernest Gowers, Oxford UP, £13.95 and £5.99 paperback). Many prefer Sir Ernest Gowers' *Complete Plain Words* (3rd edn 1986 revised Sidney Greenbaum and Jane Whitcut, Penguin 1987, £6.99). More recent works are *The Oxford Guide to English Language* (Oxford UP, 1984, £19.50 and £6.99) and *Bloomsbury Guide to Better English* (Bloomsbury, 1993, paperback £5.99), and Michael Legat's *The Nuts and Bolts of Writing* (Hale, 1989, £9.95 and £5.99).

4. **Encyclopedias and annuals.** Multi-volume encyclopedias are both expensive and space consuming. They are best left for consultation at the nearest reference library, where the most up-to-date versions should be available, unless your need justifies ownership. Of the single volumes, *Pears Cyclopaedia* contains a surprising amount of general information and a new edition is issued annually (Pelham Books, 103rd edn 1994, £14.99). For those concerned with current affairs, the complete edition of *Whitaker's Almanack* has valuable statistics and information on government and countries, as well as many miscellaneous facts not found elsewhere. For annual replacement if constantly used.

5. **Atlases, gazetteers and road maps.** These also need replacing with updated editions from time to time. An old edition can be misleading with recent changes of placenames and metrication. The *The Times Atlas of the World* is the definitive work, but it is expensive and bulky for quick reference. The *The Times Concise Atlas of the World* (Times Books, 1986, £35.00) has the most comprehensive gazetteer-index. It is a little more manageable but still requires special shelving.

With the building of the M25 and other motorways, many existing road atlases of Britain may be out of date and need replacing. There are many paperback editions at 3 miles to 1 inch (1:190,080) for less than £5.00, but most detailed is *A-Z Great Britain Road Atlas* (Geographers A-Z, 1994, £6.95; 1:250,000) with 31,000 place names and 56 town maps. Hardbacks recommended by *Which?* magazine are *A-Z Great Britain Road Atlas* (1993, £12.95; and £5.95 paperback; 1:152,064) and *Ordnance Survey Touring Atlas of Great Britain* (Hamlyn, 1993, £16.99 and £9.99). The *Reader's Digest Atlas of the British Isles* (1992, £21.95) includes Ireland. For London and environs *Greater London Street Atlas* (Nicholson, 7th edn 1991, £25.99 and £14.99) is a detailed 3.17 miles to 1 inch, 1:20,000 street map for the whole M25 area.

6. **Literary companions and dictionaries.** There are many to choose from, and frequency of consultation will determine whether all or some of the following are desirable. *Brewer's Dictionary of Phrase and Fable* (Cassell, 14th edn 1991, £18.99) and its companion volume *Brewer's Twentieth Century Dictionary of Phrase and Fable* (Cassell, 1991, £16.95 and £10.99 paperback) avoid many distractions by settling queries, as does *The Oxford Companion to English Literature* (5th edn edited by Margaret Drabble, Oxford UP, 1985, £25.00). This new edition complements rather than replaces Sir Paul Harvey's earlier editions. Either can be used for checking an author's work, but the definitive and exhaustive lists are to be found in the *New Cambridge Bibliography of English Literature*. The four volumes and the index volume can be found in major reference libraries.

7. Books of quotations. Once divorced from their text and unattributed, quotations are not easy to trace. This should be a warning to any writer or researcher to note author, title and page number to any item copied. Tracing quotations often needs resort to more than one collection, but the most popular anthologies are *The Oxford Dictionary of Quotations* (4th edn, Oxford UP, 1992, £25.00) and the *Bloomsbury Dictionary of Quotations* (Bloomsbury, 2nd edn 1991, £17.99 and paperback, £12.99) and *The New Penguin Dictionary of Quotations* (Penguin, 1993, £6.99).

8. Biographical dictionaries. *Pears Cyclopaedia* contains a brief but useful section, but for a fuller working tool the standard works are *Chambers' Biographical Dictionary* (Chambers, 5th edn 1990, £35.00, paperback £19.99 – 15,000 entries) or the American-biased *Webster's New Biographical Dictionary* (Merriam-Webster Inc, 1990, £17.95 – 150,000 entries). Frequency of consultation will determine whether you need a personal copy of *Who's Who* or the *Concise Dictionary of National Biography*, which are available in most libraries.

9. Dates, anniversaries and names. A brief guide to anniversaries is included in the Journalists' Calendar section of this book (see p. 456). *Everyman's Dictionary of Dates* (Dent, 7th rev. edn, 1987, £7.95) and *The Independent Book of Anniversaries* (Headline, 1993, £20.00 and £8.99) are useful. Leslie Dunkling's *Guinness Book of Names* (Guinness, 5th edn 1993, £9.99) is an encyclopedic source on its subject from first names to places and pubs, with a comprehensive index.

10. Working directories for writers. A current copy of *Writers' & Artists' Yearbook* is essential, as recent moves and mergers have made so many publishers' details out of date. It is useful for very much more information besides that found in the first section. Browse through, or use the index, in spare moments to familiarise yourself with its contents for future reference.

Frequency of consultation will determine whether you also need *Willings Press Guide* (annual, British Media Publications). *Benn's Media Directory* (Benn, 2 vols. annual) is expensive; both are very comprehensive in their coverage of British and overseas newspapers, magazines and other media information. *Cassell's Directory of Publishing* complements all the above, but gives more information about publishing personnel not found elsewhere.

SOME BOOKS ABOUT WRITING AND THE BOOK TRADE

The book trade has changed considerably in the last decades. The paperback explosion of the seventies appears to have settled down, as has the bookshop chain development. In publishing, computerisation has affected a great many aspects and recent mergers and takeovers of publishing companies large and small are now leading to many staff changes, though not as yet reducing the number of titles published annually. Partly for that reason, much material in older books is inapplicable, although a few remain important for historical reasons. The following is a selection from recent publications. It does not include any of the many books on writing specific types of novels or articles which are best examined in a library or book shop before purchase.

Bolt, David, *The Author's Handbook*, Piatkus Books, 1986, £9.95 and £5.95.
    Written to fill some of the gaps in the author's search for information.
Bonham-Carter, Victor, *Authors by Profession, volume 2: From the Copyright Act 1911 until the End of 1981*, Bodley Head, 1984, o.p. Volume 1 published by the Society of Authors covered the history of authorship up to 1911; the present volume brings it closer to date.

Clark, Giles N., *Inside Book Publishing: a career builder's guide*, Blueprint, 1988, £9.99. Intended to give an overview to young publishers, it describes the processes and business of modern publishing.

Legat, Michael, *An Author's Guide to Publishing*, Robert Hale, 2nd edn 1991, £7.50. Assumes no experience of publishing; a useful, clear introduction with a glossary.

Legat, Michael, *Writing for Pleasure and Profit*, Robert Hale, 2nd edn 1993, paperback £5.95. The best of the recent introductions to writing, covering novels, non-fiction and other topics briefly but clearly.

Mumby, F.A., *Publishing and Bookselling in the Twentieth Century*, Unwin Hyman, 6th edn, paperback 1984, o.p. Revised by Ian Norrie to include events up to 1970, this is the best historical survey.

Owen, Peter (ed.), *Publishing – the Future*, Peter Owen, 1988, £6.95 and *Publishing Now*, Peter Owen, 1993, £12.95. Collections of articles by leading figures on various aspects of the book trade today and tomorrow.

Waterhouse, Keith, *Waterhouse on Newspaper Style*, Viking, 1989, £11.99, Penguin, 1993, £5.99. Based on the *Daily Mirror* house style, it contains much information on writing succinctly and clearly.

Not many people know this . . .

Not all magazines open to freelance contributors fall into the 'consumer' bracket and see their circulation figures recorded by the Audit Bureau of Circulation. In a separate category, for assessment purposes, lie the large number of business magazines, whose success is measured by the value of the display advertising carried on their pages. You may be surprised to find which magazines fall into this classification, including some you had hardly thought of as being 'different' from consumer titles on sale to the general public. On the current list of the Media Monitoring Service (the ABC equivalent for business magazines) come *Farmers Weekly*, *Computer Shopper*, *Commercial Motor*, *Music Week* and *Bathrooms*. From the writer's point of view there is virtually no difference between studying the pages of business titles and poring over consumer magazines: if either want freelance contributors, that's the only spur we need. There's just one extra point: I said they are virtually the same but there is one important difference. Because business magazines are less obvious targets freelance writers submitting to their pages often face little competition.

from *Writing for Magazines* by Jill Dick (A & C Black, £9.99)

Journalists' Calendar
1995

SELECTED ANNIVERSARIES

On page 461, there is a list of anniversaries and centenaries, by year rather than by individual date, of notable events, first publication of books and plays, and the founding of charities, societies and institutions.

JANUARY

1 Amalgamation of the British Foreign and Commonwealth Services as the Diplomatic Service, 1965

 J. Edgar Hoover, director of the FBI between 1924 and 1972, born 1895

 The League of Nations came into being, 1920

2 11th Duke of Devonshire, owner of Chatsworth House, born 1920

3 Victoria Principal, American actress, born 1945

 Clement Attlee became Prime Minister, 1945

 Josiah Wedgwood, potter, died 1795

6 Barry John, former Wales and British Lions fly-half, born 1945

8 Elvis Presley, singer and film actor, born 1935

10 Sir Clive Sinclair launched the Sinclair C5 (battery/pedal-powered three-wheeler), 1985

12 National Trust founded, 1895

13 Harry Worth, comedian, born 1920

15 HRH Princess Michael of Kent born, 1945

16 Prohibition began in the US, 1920

18 Rocco Forte, chairman of Forte plc (formerly Trusthouse Forte), born, 1945

19 Javier Pérez de Cuéllar, former Secretary-General of the United Nations, born 1920

20 Federico Fellini, Italian film director, born 1920

21 Martin Shaw, actor, born 1945

23 Charles Kingsley, author and cleric, died 1875

24 Lord Randolph Churchill, statesman, died 1895

 Sir Winston Churchill, statesman, died 1965

25 The first hockey international was played: Ireland v Wales, 1895

 Death of Amedo Modigliani, Italian artist

26 Marti Caine, singer-comedienne, born 1945

26 Jacqueline du Pré, cellist, born 1945

27 The Red Army liberated Auschwitz, 1945

28 Iceland became the first country to introduce legalised abortion within the first 28 weeks of pregnancy on medico-social grounds, 1935

30 Patrick Heron, painter, born 1920

FEBRUARY

2 Bertrand Russell, philosopher, died 1970

4 Norman Wisdom, comedian, born 1920

 Joseph Stalin, Franklin D. Roosevelt and Winston Churchill met at the start of the Yalta Conference to discuss the future of Poland, surrender of Germany and arrangements for the United Nations conference, 1945

5 RAF Cranwell took its first intake of trainees, 1920

 Frank Muir, writer and broadcaster, born 1920

7 The US first bombed North Vietnam, 1965

9 Mia Farrow, actress, born 1945

10 Dr Alex Comfort, sex expert and author of *The Joy of Sex*, born 1920

11 Margaret Thatcher became Britain's first woman leader of a political party, 1975

 Civil servant, Clive Ponting, cleared of breaking the Official Secrets Act, 1985

14 Dresden bombed by the Allies, 1945

15 Nat 'King' Cole, popular singer and jazz pianist, died 1965

16 Publication of the New English Bible, 1970

18 Gambia became independent within the Commonwealth, 1965

21 Malcolm X, black nationalist leader, shot dead 1965

22 The world's first greyhound-racing stadium opened in California, 1920

23 Stan Laurel, comedian, died 1965

24 Nancy Astor became the first woman to speak in Parliament, 1920

Coronation of King Birendra of Nepal, 1975

25 Elkie Brooks, singer, born 1945

28 43 people died in Moorgate tube station disaster, 1975

MARCH

1 Roger Daltrey, singer, born 1945

2 Sir Thomas Bodley, after whom the Bodleian Library at Oxford is named, born 1545

3 Ronald Searle, artist and cartoonist, born 1920

Seretse Khama became the first premier of Bechuanaland, 1965

Florida became the 27th US state, 1845

End of the year-long miners' strike in Britain, 1985

10 Charles Worth, couturier, died 1895

11 Bank of Canada founded, 1935

Mikhail Gorbachev became leader of the Soviet Union, 1985

14 Jasper Carrott, comedian, born 1945

16 Leo McKern, actor, born 1920

17 The elastic band patented by Stephen Perry of Perry & Co. of London, 1845

18 Aleksey Leonov, Soviet cosmonaut, made the first space walk, 1965

19 Nicolae Ceaușescu elected Communist Party Secretary in Romania, 1965

20 Tim Yeo, MP, born 1945

21 Peter Brook, theatre producer, born 1925

22 In Paris, Auguste and Louis Lumière gave the first public showing of a film on a screen, 1895

23 Paul Schockemohle, show jumper, born 1945

Britain's first woman coroner was appointed, 1965

26 David Lloyd George, Liberal Prime Minister, died 1945

27 Wilhelm Röntgen, physicist who discovered X-rays, born 1845

James I, King of England and Scotland, died 1625

28 Marc Chagall, artist, died 1985

29 Julie Goodyear, actress, born 1945

30 Eric Clapton, guitarist, born 1945

APRIL

1 The Greater London Council came into being, 1965

London County Council Green Belt Scheme came into force, 1935

6 Capital Gains Tax introduced in Britain, 1965

7 Ravi Shankar, musician and composer, born 1920

9 Nikolai Lenin, Russian revolutionary leader, born 1870

10 Norman Vaughan, comedian, born 1925

12 Franklin D. Roosevelt, 32nd US President, died 1945

The Scottish Nationalists won their first Parliamentary seat, 1945

14 Rod Steiger, US actor, born 1925

17 Cambodia fell to Khmer Rouge forces on the surrender of Phnom Penh, 1975

19 Dudley Moore, actor, born 1935

22 George Cole, actor, born 1925

23 Henry Vaughan, poet, died 1695

Mike Smith, disc jockey, born 1955

25 'Buster' Mottram, former British tennis player, born 1955

26 Gypsy Rose Lee, striptease artist, died 1970

28 Benito Mussolini, Italian dictator, executed 1945

30 Adolf Hitler, German dictator, died 1945

In South Vietnam, President Minh surrendered to the Viet Cong as the Americans withdrew from Saigon, 1975

MAY

2 The first transatlantic programme relay was transmitted via the communications satellite *Early Bird*, linking 300 million viewers in nine countries, 1965

3 Rhodesia named by proclamation, 1895

Thomas Hood, poet, died 1845

4 Four students shot dead during peace march at Kent State University, USA, 1970

5 René Lalique, glass engraver and designer, died 1945

The Paddington to Weston-super-Mare service became the first British Rail high speed train in scheduled service, 1975

6 Rudolph Valentino, star of the silent screen, born 1895

7 Germany surrendered to the Allies, 1945

8 50th anniversary of VE (Victory in Europe) Day, 1945

Jack Charlton, football manager, born 1935

11 Bradford City football stadium fire disaster, 1985

Dr Rhodes Boyson, MP, born 1925

12 Alcoholics Anonymous founded in Ohio, USA, 1935

14 Francesca Annis, actress, born 1945

Warsaw Pact signed by Eastern Bloc nations, 1955

15 Ted Dexter, former England cricketer, born 1935

16 Olga Korbut, Russian gymnast, born 1955

Junko Tabei of Japan became the first woman to scale Everest, 1975

17 Dennis Potter, playwright, born 1935

19 James Boswell, Dr Johnson's biographer, died 1795

T.E. Lawrence, scholar, author and soldier, died 1935

Pete Townsend, singer, born 1945

20 Cher, actress and singer, born 1945

Barbara Hepworth, sculptress, died in St Ives, Cornwall, 1975

24 Jan Smuts, South African statesman, born 1870

25 Dave Lee Travis, disc jockey, born 1945

29 The Epsom Derby became the first horse race to be filmed, 1895

Heysel football stadium disaster, 1985

JUNE

1 Driving tests and 'L' plates became compulsory in Britain, 1935

2 Index-linked National Savings Certificates ('Granny Bonds') introduced, 1975

3 Tony Curtis, US actor, born 1925

Hale Irwin, golfer, born 1945

5 First national referendum took place in Britain. The nation voted to stay in the EEC, 1975

8 Andrew Jackson, 7th US President, died 1845

Derek Underwood, cricketer, born 1945

9 Charles Dickens, author, died 1870

First Parliamentary transmission from the House of Commons by the BBC and LBC, 1975

10 Miss C.V. Ward joined the Sheffield Stock Exchange, becoming the first woman to be elected to a stock exchange trading floor in Britain, 1965

11 82 spectators killed at Le Mans 24-hour race, 1955

12 Pat Jennings, goal-keeper, born 1945

The Beatles awarded the MBE in the Birthday Honours list, 1965

13 Thomas Arnold, headmaster of Rugby, immortalised in *Tom Brown's Schooldays*, born 1795

14 Battle of Naseby at which the Royalists were defeated by Oliver Cromwell, 1645

15 Richard Baker, broadcaster, born 1925

The Family Allowance was introduced in Britain, 1945

17 Ken Livingstone, MP, born 1945

Beryl Reid, actress, born 1920

20 The first news-film (other than a sporting event) depicted the opening of the Kiel Canal by Kaiser Wilhelm II, 1895

21 Françoise Sagan, author, born 1935

The West Indies won the first Cricket World Cup, 1975

23 Maggie Philbin, television presenter, born 1955

24 Betty Stove, tennis player and coach, born 1945

25 Carly Simon, singer, born 1945

The Hague selected as seat of the International Court of Justice, 1920

29 Thomas Huxley, natural historian, died 1895

JULY

3 The RAF performed its first air display at Hendon, 1920

4 Dr Thomas Barnado, founder of Dr Barnardo's, born 1845

6 Dalai Lama, spiritual leader of Tibet, born 1935

7 Unseeded Boris Becker won his first Wimbledon singles title at the age of seventeen, 1985

9 Steve Coppell, footballer, born 1955

9 National Film Archive founded, 1935

Michael Williams, actor, born 1935

10 John Motson, sports commentator, born 1945

Virginia Wade, British tennis player, born 1945

12 Oscar Hammerstein II, US songwriter, born 1895

The first recorded motor journey of any length in Britain was made by The Hon Evelyn Ellis and Frederick Simms. They travelled 56 miles in about five and a half hours, contravening the 4 mph speed limit, 1895

13 Ruth Ellis hanged, 1955
Live Aid charity concert, 1985

15 'La Marseillaise' officially adopted as the French national anthem, 1795

16 First atomic bomb exploded in New Mexico, 1945
The first parking meters came into service in Oklahoma, USA, 1935

18 Disneyland opened near Los Angeles, California, 1955

19 Henry VIII's flag-ship, *Mary Rose*, sank in the Solent, 1545
Start of the Franco–Prussian War, 1870

20 Paul Valéry, French poet, died 1945

28 Edward Heath elected Leader of the British Conservative Party, 1965
Britain's first woman jurors sat in Bristol, 1920

29 The BBC Light Programme was broadcast for the first time, 1945

30 The first Penguin book, *Ariel*, by André Maurois, published, 1935

AUGUST

1 Jim Clark, Scottish racing driver, won the world motor racing championships, 1965
Ban on cigarette advertising on commercial television in Britain, 1965

2 Alan Whicker, broadcaster, born 1925

3 P.D. James, author, born 1920

4 British Red Cross founded, 1870

6 US dropped first atomic bomb on Hiroshima, 1945

7 Daylight Saving Act established, 1925

8 First America's Cup contest, 1870

9 Atomic bomb dropped on Nagasaki, 1945
W.E. Forster's state education system instituted under the Education Act, 1870

10 First Sir Henry Wood Promenade concert, 1895

12 Norris McWhirter, founder editor (with late Ross McWhirter; killed 27 November 1985) and compiler of *The Guinness Book of Records*, born 1925

12 Elizabeth Lane appointed Britain's first woman High Court judge, 1965
Thomas Mann, German writer, died 1955

14 The Japanese surrendered to the Allies (VJ Day), 1945
Marshal Henri Pétain sentenced to death (later commuted to a life sentence) for collaboration, 1945

15 Oscar Peterson, jazz musician, born 1925

19 The Third Test between England and Australia was abandoned after protesters for the 'Free George Davis Campaign' dug up the pitch at Headingley, 1975

22 Boeing 737 burst into flames on the runway at Manchester Airport killing 54 passengers, 1985

23 Sir Roy Strong, former director of the Victoria and Albert Museum, born 1935

27 Foundation of Rugby League, 1895
Le Corbusier, architect, died 1965

28 The first motion picture film to involve the use of actors, *The Execution of Mary Queen of Scots*, was shot in the US, 1895

SEPTEMBER

3 Sir Malcolm Cambell set a land-speed record of 301.13 mph in *Bluebird*, becoming the first person to break the 300 mph barrier, 1935

4 Albert Schweitzer, medical missionary and philosopher, died 1965

9 Chaim Topol, Israeli actor, born 1935

12 Percy Sinclair Pilcher was the first Briton to make a successful controlled glider flight, 1895

13 First baseball club, the Knickerbocker Club, founded in New York, 1845

15 Jessye Norman, opera and concert singer, born 1945

16 Charles Haughey, former Irish Prime Minister, born 1925
BB King, blues singer, born 1925

17 Laura Ashley, founder of Laura Ashley empire/fashion chain, died 1985

21 Battle of Prestonpans, victory for Bonnie Prince Charlie, 1745
BP struck oil in the North Sea, 1965

22 Fay Weldon, author, born 1935
Commercial television began in Britain, 1955

23 Mickey Rooney, Thirties child star, born 1920
Prosper Mérimée, author, died 1870
Prestel was first publicly demonstrated by the Post Office, 1975

24 Douglas Haston and Doug Scott climbed Everest, 1975

27 Béla Bartók, Hungarian composer, died 1945

28 Louis Pasteur, scientist, died 1895

29 Jerry Lee-Lewis, singer, born 1935

30 James Dean, American film actor, killed in car-crash, 1955

OCTOBER

1 Julie Andrews, actress and singer, born 1935

The Post Office issued the first postcard, 1870

Walter Matthau, American actor, born 1920

2 Budd Abbot, of Abbot and Costello, born 1895

The first installation of fluorescent lighting, Piccadilly Circus underground, 1945

3 End of six-day IRA seige of the Spaghetti House restaurant in London, 1975

4 Buster Keaton, comedian, born 1895

Janis Joplin, rock star, died 1970

7 Post Office Tower opened in London, 1965

9 Don McCullin, photographer, born 1935

Nobel Peace Prize awarded to Soviet dissident, Dr Andrei Sakharov, 1975

Steve Ovett, athlete, born 1955

10/ Foundation of London School of
11 Economics, 1895

12 Elizabeth Fry, prison reformer, died 1845

Luciano Pavarotti, operatic tenor, born 1935

13 Margaret Thatcher, former Prime Minister, born 1925

16 Angela Lansbury, actress, born 1925

17 John Henry Knight and James Pullinger of Farnham became the first people in Britain to be charged with motor offences, 1895

Harry Carpenter, sports commentator, born 1925

18 Surrey County Cricket Club founded, 1845

19 Jonathan Swift, author, died 1745

22 Robert Rauschenberg, American artist, born 1925

23 Johnnie Carson, American television host, born 1925

Sarah Bernhardt, actress, born 1845

24 United Nations Charter came into force, 1945

25 Sir Charles Hallé, pianist and conductor, died 1895

28 Ian Brady and Myra Hindley charged with Moors Murders, 1965

University of Exeter founded, 1955

29 Robert Hardy, actor, born 1925

30 Michael Winner, film producer, born 1935

31 John Keats, poet, born 1795

NOVEMBER

1 Gary Player, South African golfer, born 1935

2 The first British motoring journal, *Autocar*, was published, 1895

3 HM The Queen inaugurated the first flow of North Sea oil in Britain at the BP Forties oil field, 1975

5 Lester Piggott, jockey, born 1935

8 X-rays discovered by Wilhelm Röntgen, 1895

9 Capital punishment abolished in Britain, 1965

10 Angola became independent of Portugal after 500 years of colonial rule, 1975

11 Rhodesian Prime Minister, Ian Smith, signed Declaration of Independence. Britain declared regime illegal, introducing trade restrictions, 1965

12 Neil Young, rock singer, born 1945

14 King Hussein of Jordan born 1935

20 Nuremberg Trial opened to try Nazi war criminals, 1945

In Spain, Francisco Franco died and was succeeded by King Juan Carlos, 1975

21 Goldie Horn, American actress, born 1945

Henry Purcell, English composer, died 1695

24 Ian Botham, cricketer, born 1955

27 Ernie Wise, comedian, born 1925

29 Federal People's Republic of Yugoslavia founded, 1945

First ever air–sea rescue by helicopter took place near an oil rig off Long Island, USA 1945

Mrs Mary Whitehouse launched The National Viewers' and Listeners' Association, 1965

Graham Hill, British motor racing champion, killed in air crash, 1975

DECEMBER

1 Woody Allen, American actor and film director, born 1935

Bette Midler, American actress, born 1945

Henry Williamson, author of *Tarka the Otter*, born 1895

Friedrich Engels, philosopher, died 1895

2 Philip Larkin, poet, died 1985

3 Sir Rowland Hill, inventor of the postage stamp, born 1795

4 Thomas Carlyle, historian, born 1795

5 Alexandre Dumas, French novelist and playwright, died 1870

7 Robert Graves, poet and novelist, died 1985

8 Sammy Davis Jr, entertainer, born 1925

10 Nobel Prize for Literature presented to Alexander Solzhenitsyn, 1970

14 King George VI born, 1895

Four of the eight occupants of an aeroplane died in the first disaster involving a scheduled passenger flight, Golders Green, London, 1920

17 Christopher Cazenove, actor, born 1945

18 Rosemary Leach, actress, born 1935

27 The World Bank and the International Monetary Fund (IMF) were established, 1945

29 The Sex Discrimination and Equal Pay Acts came into force in Britain, 1975

Texas became the 28th US state, 1845

30 L.P. Hartley, author of *The Go Between*, born 1895

ANNIVERSARIES AND CENTENARIES

EVENTS

1595 Warsaw became the capital of Poland

Sir Walter Raleigh voyaged to Orinoco in South America in search of El Dorado and explored the Orinoco River

Dutch traders colonised the East Indies

Spanish explorer, Mendana, discovered the Marquesas Islands

Robert Southwell, Jesuit poet, hanged for treason

Death of Torquato Tasso, Italian poet

1695 Death of Juana Inés de la Cruz, South American feminist poet

Death of Jean de la Fontaine, author of *Contes et Fables*

1745 House in Cumberland, in which the poet Wordsworth was born, built. Now known as Wordsworth House

Fort George in Inverness-shire built

Admiral Edward Vernon introduced the Navy rum ration or 'grog'

1795 The British landed in Cape Town, South Africa, and took the colony from the Dutch

Mungo Park explored West Africa

France was the first country to introduce the metric system

1845 The British army in India began the conquest of Kashmir and the Punjab

John Henry Newman, a leading force in the Oxford Movement since 1833, converted to Catholicism

Parliament passed a law permitting Jews to stand for election

Hong Kong linked to Britain by a regular shipping line

Hona-Heka, a Maori tribal chieftain, led an attack on Kororareka in New Zealand, in protest at settlers settling land

The Oxford *v* Cambridge boat race transferred from Henley to Putney

1870 Outbreak of the Franco–Prussian War

Siege of Paris followed by the end of the Second Empire and proclamation of the Third Republic

First books published in Braille in the UK

The press agencies, Havas, Reuter and Wolff, signed an agreement to form an agency covering the whole world

First negro member entered the US House of Representatives

Diamonds discovered in the Orange Free State, South Africa

1895 Cardinal Vaughan laid the foundation stone of Westminster Abbey

First main-line passenger railway electrified, the Baltimore & Ohio Railroad, USA

China concluded a deal with Russia allowing Russia to build the Trans-Siberian Railway through Manchuria to the port of Vladivostok

French trade unions amalgamated to form the CGT (Confédération Générale du Travail)

The first-ever film of a regularly scheduled sporting event, the Oxford *v* Cambridge boat race, was made. The Derby was also filmed for the first time

First official staging of the US Open Golf Tournament

The British Ladies Football Club, the first women's football team, founded by Lady Florence Dixie in Crouch End, London

Volleyball was developed in the US

Trial of Oscar Wilde

1920 The first 'Black and Tans' arrived in Ireland. The IRA killed 14 soldiers on Bloody Sunday. Martial law declared

Burial of the unknown soldier in Westminster Abbey on Armistice Day. An unknown soldier was also buried in France under the Arc de Triomphe

France announced the creation of the state of Lebanon

British Board of Film Censors founded

Welwyn Garden City founded

First public broadcasting station in Britain opened by Guglielmo Marconi in Writtle

1935 New Deal Social Security legislation in the US introduced unemployment schemes and old-age pensions

Persia changed its name to Iran

Bruno Hauptmann found guilty in the US of the abduction and murder of aviator Charles Lindbergh's baby

The Saar coal region was returned to Germany

Adolf Hitler introduced conscription in Germany

Jews banned from public life in Germany

20,000 people died in an earthquake which wrecked the Indian hill station of Quetta

In China, Mao-Tse Tung and the Communists completed 'The Long March'

Benito Mussolini invaded Abyssinia

The Richter Scale was devised by C.F. Richter

Early developments in radar in Britain by Robert Watson-Watt

First chimpanzee born at London Zoo

Joseph Stalin opened the 50-mile-long Moscow underground railway

Cats' eyes, invented by Percy Shaw, were first used on British roads

Leicester Square underground station opened with the world's longest escalator

The prototype of the Hawker Hurricane fighter made its maiden flight

Death of Andre Citroën, French engineer and motor manufacturer

Surrey and England cricketer, Jack Hobbs, retired

Jesse Owens broke five world athletics records (long jump and hurdles) in 45 minutes at the Big Ten Championships in Alabama

1945 New Waterloo Bridge over the Thames opened

1970 First decimal postage stamps went on sale in Britain

Kevin Murphy of Kenton, Middlesex, was the first Briton to swim the English Channel both ways

Introduction of trans-Atlantic telephone direct-dialling, London–New York

Completion of the Aswan Dam

First inter-racial wedding in Mississippi

Edward Heath created the Department of the Environment and the Department of Trade and Industry

THE ARTS

1745 William Hogarth completed his series *Marriage à la Mode*

God Save the King was performed for the first time (at Drury Lane Theatre)

1845 Premiere of the opera *Tannhauser* by Richard Wagner

Benjamin Disraeli wrote *Sybil* or *The Two Nations*, his second political novel

Carmen, novel by Prosper Mérimée

Condition of the Working Class in England published by Frederick Engels

Tales of Mystery and Imagination published by Edgar Allen Poe

Piano Concerto in A Minor by Robert Schumann

1870 *Poems* by Gabriel Rossetti

1895 *The Importance of Being Earnest*, play by Oscar Wilde

The Time Machine, novel by H.G. Wells

Le Bateau ivre, poem by A. Rimbaud

Volume Three of *Das Kapital* by Karl Marx

Jude the Obscure, novel by Thomas Hardy

Poems by W.B. Yeats

1920 *Women in Love*, novel by D.H. Lawrence

The Mysterious Affair at Styles, first published detective story by Agatha Christie

Poems by Wilfred Owen

Six Characters in Search of an Author, play by Luigi Pirandello

International Dada Art Fair in Berlin

1935 *Murder in the Cathedral*, play by T.S. Eliot

Greta Garbo starred in the film *Anna Karenina*

The jazz term 'swing' was coined

Porgy and Bess, opera by George Gershwin

Song hits of the year included *Blue Moon*, *Red Sails in the Sunset* and *Cheek to Cheek*

1945 *Brideshead Revisited*, novel by Evelyn Waugh

The Age of Reason, philosophical work by Jean-Paul Sartre

The Family Group, sculpture by Henry Moore

The *Resurrection* series painted by Stanley Spencer

Peter Grimes, opera by Benjamin Britten

Animal Farm, novel by George Orwell

Celia Johnson and Trevor Howard starred in the film *Brief Encounter*

1955 Commercial television launched in the UK

Waiting for Godot, play by Samuel Beckett

The Quiet American, novel by Grahame Greene

This is Your Life, *Dixon of Dock Green* and *Crackerjack* series began on British television

Films *The Dambusters*, *Rebel Without a Cause* and *Rock Around the Clock* released

1970 *M*A*S*H* released, which won first prize at the Cannes Film Festival

Films *Love Story*, *Butch Cassidy and the Sundance Kid* released

Film *Woodstock* released

Oh Calcutta!, musical, opened in London

First episode of *The Goodies* and first showing of *A Question of Sport* on British television

Breath, play lasting only one minute, by Samuel Beckett

The magazines *Harper's Bazaar* and *Queen* merged

Slaughterhouse 5, novel, by Kurt Vonnegut

The Female Eunuch, by Germaine Greer

INSTITUTIONS AND CHARITIES

1695 Morden College, Blackheath, founded (designed by Sir Christopher Wren)

1745 Foundation of the Middlesex Hospital

1845 Queen's University, Belfast, founded

British Museum designed by Robert Smirke

The Madeleine in Paris completed

Restoration of Notre Dame in Paris and revival of the Gothic style

The Sisters of Mercy founded in London

1870 W.G. Grace and his brothers founded Gloucestershire Cricket Club

Keble College, Oxford, founded

1920 Royal Institute of International Affairs founded in London

King George V opened the Imperial War Museum, housed at Crystal Palace

The 'Flying Squad' of the Metropolitan Police formed

1935 National Federation of Music Societies founded

Ramblers Association founded

Montessori Society founded

Cromwell Association founded

1945 Harwell Atomic Research Station established

1965 University of Warwick founded

1970 Down's Syndrome Association founded

Gingerbread founded

Schizophrenia Association of Great Britain founded

Conservation Trust founded

The Young Vic founded

COMPANIES AND INVENTIONS

1845 Tarmac laid for the first time (in Nottingham)

The first glass paperweight manufactured in Venice

Self-raising flour marketed for the first time by Henry Jones of Bristol

The ball-valve for use in lavatory cisterns invented by Edward Chrimes of Rotherham

1870 Standard Oil Company founded by J.D. Rockefeller

1895 Armand Peugeot founded the French motor company, Peugeot

Guglielmo Marconi invented wireless telegraphy

King C. Gillette of the US invented the safety razor

First flaked breakfast cereal, Granose Flakes, announced by Dr John Kellogg of Michigan. (Corn Flakes introduced in 1898 by Dr Kellogg's brother, William.)

Milking machine developed in Glasgow

1905 Cadbury's Dairy Milk launched

1920 Sir Geoffrey de Havilland founded his aircraft company

J. de la Cierva invented the autogyro, precursor of the helicopter

Fox's Glacier Mints launched

Frank Smith founded Smith's Crisps

The trade name Almay originated

Cadbury's Flake launched

1935 Hawker Siddeley founded

Kit Kat first launched as 'Chocolate Crisp' by Rowntree

Milky Way introduced by Mars

The SS Jaguar car launched (became Jaguar Cars in 1945)

Perspex first exhibited in Britain

35mm Kodachrome film devised

1945 The Biro, the first ballpoint pen, marketed in the UK by the Miles Martin Pen Co.

Lurex fabric manufactured by Dobecknum Co., Cleveland, Ohio

J.C. Bamford (JCB) founded, manufacturer of mechanical excavators

Bantam Books, US paperback publishers, established by Ian Ballentine, formerly of Penguin

Earl Tupper founded the Tupperware company in the US

First microwave oven patented in the US by Percy Spencer

1955 Dorothy Hodgkin discovered the composition of Vitamin B_{12}

Jonas E. Salk prepared a new vaccine against polio

F. Sanger established the structure of insulin

Luncheon Vouchers introduced

Tefal manufactured the first non-stick pan

First Wimpy Bar opened at Lyons Corner House, Coventry Street, London

Bird's Eye introduced fish fingers

1965 First domestic video recorder marketed by Sony

Dolby Sound Recording developed and demonstrated to Decca in London

Gold Blend launched

1970 World's first pocket calculator announced in Tokyo by Canon Business Machines

First car cassette player marketed by Philips

The first Boeing 747 'Jumbo' jet, owned by Pan Am, flew from New York to Heathrow

Concorde first landed at Heathrow

Compiled by The Information Bureau.

This list has been compiled from a variety of sources and is designed as a guideline only. As some anniversary dates are open to discussion, all dates should be checked further before embarking on any major undertaking involving their use.

Typescripts

PREPARATION

Many publishers refuse even to consider handwritten manuscripts. No publisher will accept them as final copy. If you cannot afford to have the whole script typed before acceptance, there are ways round the problem; see below under Preliminary Letter.

NEATNESS

The first impression made on a publisher and a publisher's reader may be vital. They will try to discount the physical appearance of your typescript, but a tatty typescript covered with handwritten corrections, on different sizes of paper and with inadequate margins and spacing, will perhaps not receive benign consideration first thing on a Monday morning.

Even if you have followed the advice below and have a signed contract in your pocket, and the publisher is awaiting the final manuscript with impatience, there are other reasons for neatness. The publisher's copy editor needs a 'clean' manuscript in order to avoid spending an unnecessary amount of time on marking it up for the printer. The manuscript then has to go to a typesetter or printer for setting. Typesetting keyboard operators have to work a complicated and expensive set of equipment. They must be able to read your typescript quickly and accurately, and at the same time must interpret a code of marks which the copy editor or designer will have made all over it.

TYPING

Authors are increasingly using word processors for the advantages they have to offer over the traditional typewriter (see **Word Processing** article on page 481). For ordinary typescripts, use the black ribbon. For plays, use red for names of characters, stage directions, etc., and black for dialogue. If a two-colour ribbon is not available use capitals for character names and underline stage directions in red by hand. Keep a fairly new ribbon in the typewriter so that it is black but not splodgy. Remember that typewriter maintenance is a tax-deductible expense!

The paper used should be uniform in size, preferably the standard size A4, which has replaced the old foolscap and quarto sizes. Neither flimsy paper nor very thick paper should be used. If in doubt, ask the stationer for a standard A4 typewriter paper. Use one side of the paper only. It is helpful but not essential if manuscripts are typed to a width of sixty characters per line. This makes it easier for printers and publishers to calculate the extent of a work and so – using copyfitting tables – to work out the space occupied when it is printed.

Margins

Good margins are essential, especially on the left hand side. This enables the copy editor to include instructions to the printer. On A4 paper a left hand margin of 3 cm allows sufficient space.

Double spacing

This is necessary if you are to make any corrections to the typescript, and there are always some improvements which you will want to make; they can only be made clear to the printer if there is space available between the lines. The copy editor too needs this extra space. Double spacing means a *full* line of space between two lines of copy – not half a line of space.

Consistency

Be as consistent as possible in your choice of variant spellings, use of sub-headings, etc.

Authors who want to know more about the technicalities of preparing a manuscript for the printer should consult *Copy-editing* by Judith Butcher, Cambridge University Press, 3rd edn 1992, £22.95. Much of this is outside the author's scope, but dipping into this book will make you aware of points of style and consistency, particularly on the use of inverted commas, roman and arabic numerals, italic and roman, rendering of foreign words, etc.

Numbering

Pages (or folios as publishers prefer to call them to distinguish them from the pages of the final book) should be numbered throughout. If you need to include an extra folio after, say, folio 27, call it 27a and write at the foot of folio 27: 'Folio 27a follows'. Then write at the foot of 27a: 'Folio 28 follows'. Don't do this too often or you will confuse and irritate your readers.

CORRECTIONS TO TYPESCRIPT

Corrections to the final typescript should be kept to a minimum. Often the publisher's editor will want to suggest a few additional changes – this happens even to the best authors – and once all or some of these are included, the typescript may have become very messy. If the publishers then feel it is not in a fit state for the printer they may well ask you to have it retyped.

BINDING

Printers prefer to handle each folio separately, so do not use a binder which will make this impossible. Ring binders are acceptable. Alternatively you can use a cardboard envelope folder. In this case it will help if you can clip the pages of each chapter together, but never staple them.

PROTECTION OF TYPESCRIPTS

This can be achieved by placing a stiffer piece of paper at front and back. On the first folio of the typescript itself, give the title, your name and, most important of all, your address. It is worth including your address on the last page also, just in case the first folio becomes detached.

SUBMISSION

The terms 'manuscript' and 'typescript' are interchangeable in present usage, though different editors may favour one or the other.

CHOOSING YOUR PUBLISHER

It will save you time and postage if you check first that you are sending your typescript to a firm that will consider it. Publishers specialise. It is no use sending a work of romantic fiction to a firm that specialises in high-brow novels translated from obscure languages. It is still less use to send it to a firm which publishes no fiction at all. (For fiction publishers, see the classified index on page 207.)

The way to avoid the more obvious mistakes is to look in your library or bookshop for books which are in some way similar to yours, and find out who publishes them. Remember, though, that paperbacks are often editions of books published first in cased editions.

PRELIMINARY LETTER

This again will save you time, money and probably frustration. The letter by itself will tell the publisher very little; what he or she would in most cases prefer to see is a brief preliminary letter together with a synopsis of the book and the first couple of chapters from it. From this material the publisher will be able to judge whether the book would perhaps fit the list, in which case you will be asked to send the complete manuscript. This is one way of avoiding paying a typing bill until it looks as though the investment in the manuscript may be worthwhile.

There is no point whatsoever in asking for a personal interview. The publisher will prefer to consider the manuscript on its own merits, and will not want to be influenced by a personal meeting.

POSTAGE OF MANUSCRIPTS

Always send postage to cover the return of your manuscript or, if you prefer, explain that you will arrange to pick it up from the publisher's office. (Again, if your manuscript has been rejected the publisher will not be willing to discuss the reasons in person.)

Manuscripts are best sent by recorded delivery. Registered post is not recommended. You are unlikely to agree with the Post Office on the value of your lost manuscript, and if anyone does rob the mail, they head for the registered packets first. Recorded delivery is useful because you can check that the publisher has received the manuscript. Whether you send it first or second class depends entirely on how fast you want it to arrive. A properly packed parcel almost always arrives by either rate.

Packing is important. It is not enough to put the manuscript in an envelope. Padded bags are a good idea and are available in several sizes from many stationers and Postshops.

At all costs, *keep a duplicate*, with all the latest changes to the text included on it.

ESTIMATING

To estimate the length or *extent* of a manuscript, calculate the average number of words per page over, say, eight pages. Multiply the average by the number of pages in the manuscript, making allowances for half-pages at the end of chapters, etc.

WHAT IS THE PUBLISHER DOING WITH YOUR MANUSCRIPT?

Whether or not the publisher finally accepts or rejects the manuscript, there is usually a considerable interval between submission and the publisher's decision. Most publishers acknowledge receipt of manuscript, and if you do not receive an acknowledgement it is advisable to check that the manuscript has arrived. Apart from that, it is not worth chasing the publisher for a quick decision: if pressed, the publisher will probably reject, purely because this is the safer decision.

You should hear from the publisher within about two months. During this time the manuscript will either have been read 'in-house' or it will have been sent to one or more advisers whose opinions the publisher respects. Favourable readers' reports may mean that the publisher will immediately accept the manuscript, particularly if it fits easily into the current publishing programme.

On the other hand, a reader's report may be glowing, but the publisher may still hesitate. He knows he has a good book, but he wants to be sure he will be able to sell it. He is, after all, considering an investment of at least £5000 and frequently more. He may need time to obtain further opinions, and also to obtain estimates from printers, to judge whether the book could be produced at a reasonable price. The worst delays occur when the publisher is attracted to a manuscript but cannot see how he can publish it successfully.

If you have not had a decision after two months, write either a tactful letter saying 'I don't want to rush you, but . . . . .' or alternatively request an immediate decision and be prepared to start again with another publisher.

If your book is topical you have a right to a speedy decision, but it is as well to establish this early on.

ILLUSTRATIONS

If illustrations form a large part of your proposed book and you expect to provide them yourself, then they should be included with the manuscript. If you are sending specimen pages you should include also some sample illustrations. This applies largely to children's picture books and to travel and technical books. It is prudent to send duplicate photographs, photocopies of line drawings and so on so that little harm is done if illustrations go astray.

In the case of a children's book, if you intend to illustrate it yourself, obviously one finished piece of artwork is essential, plus photocopies of roughs for the rest (one must bear in mind that the final artwork may have to be drawn to a particular size and the number of illustrations fixed according to the format chosen by the publisher). If you have written a children's story, or the text for a picture book, do *not* ask a friend to provide the illustrations. The publisher who likes your story may well not like your friend's artwork: you will have considerably lengthened the odds against the story being accepted. Of course this does not apply when an artist and author work closely together to develop an idea, but in that case it is best to start by finding a publisher who likes the artist's work before submitting the story.

Travel manuscripts should be accompanied by a sketch map to show the area you are writing about. The publisher will have an atlas in his reference shelves, but it may not have sufficient detail with which to follow your manuscript. Irreplaceable material should not be sent speculatively.

Many illustrated books these days have illustrations collected by the publishers. If your proposed book is to be illustrated, it is best to establish early on who is responsible for the illustration costs: an attractive royalty offer might be less attractive if you have to gather the pictures, obtain permission for use, and foot the bills.

QUOTATIONS

It is normally the author's responsibility to obtain (and pay for) permission to quote written material which is still in copyright. Permission should always be sought from the publisher of the quoted work, not from the author. Fees for quotation vary enormously: for fashionable modern writers permission may be costly, but in other cases only a nominal fee of a few pounds is charged. There is no standard scale of fees. It is permissible to quote up to about 200 words for the purpose of criticism or review, but this does not apply to use in anthologies, nor does it apply to poetry. And it is a concession, not a right. Even though this is your area of responsibility, your publisher will be able to give you some advice.

PROOF READING

CORRECTIONS TO PROOFS

There are many ways of producing books, especially with the advent of modern printing processes, but they all have certain points in common from the author's point of view, and it is as well to be forewarned.

As author you will see either one or two stages of proofs. Sometimes you will be shown the finalised copy of the typescript immediately before it goes to the printer. If so, this is really your last chance to make changes which will not tend to sour relations with your publisher! (See also **Correcting Proofs.**) Take the opportunity to comb through the manuscript, and if there are changes which you suspect you will want to make in proof, make them now. There was a time when authors could virtually rewrite their books in galley proof, and revise them again at page. Do not be seduced by biographies of Victorian writers into thinking this is the way the professional writer works!

Modern printing is highly mechanised, but corrections are time-consuming and may involve extensive handwork. This makes corrections far more costly than the original setting. You will probably have signed a contract undertaking to pay the cost of corrections (other than printer's errors) over say 10 per cent or 15 per cent of the cost of composition. This does not mean that you can change ten or fifteen lines in every hundred.

The cost of adding a comma at galley stage, in modern processes, is insignificant. But if you add a word in one line of a paragraph, it will probably mean resetting down to the end of the paragraph. If you add a word at page stage, and this results in the paragraph being longer, many pages may have to be adjusted by one line until the end of the chapter is reached. What to you seemed a simple improvement may take an hour's work on expensive equipment.

STAGES OF PROOFS

Increasingly often only one stage of proofs is used in book production, and there is rarely any need for the author to see more than one stage. The proofs may be in several forms. Ask your editor how many stages of proofs you will see. It could be that you will be asked to check computer print-outs which bear no resemblance to the finished book but which do contain everything that will appear in that book!

Galley proofs hold columns of continuous text. They were originally a rough print taken from metal type. Modern typesetting methods most often produce proofs from a master print or direct from computer data by the Laserprint process.

Page proofs have been made up into pages, including page numbers, headlines, and so on. It is prohibitively expensive to make corrections at this stage, except to the printer's own errors.

It is worth noting that during the production of some books which have illustrations in the text, such as children's or 'coffee table' books, the editor or designer has to do a scissors and paste job to put the whole thing together. This may require some minor modifications to the text to make the final result come together happily.

Correcting Proofs

The following notes and table are extracted from BS 5261: Part 2: 1976 and are reproduced by permission of the British Standards Institution, 2 Park Street, London W1A 2BS, from whom copies of the complete Standard may be obtained.

NOTES ON COPY PREPARATION AND PROOF CORRECTION

The marks to be used for marking-up copy for composition and for the correction of printers' proofs shall be as shown in table 1.

The marks in table 1 are classified in three groups as follows.

(a) Group A: general.

(b) Group B: deletion, insertion and substitution.

(c) Group C: positioning and spacing.

Each item in table 1 is given a simple alpha-numeric serial number denoting the classification group to which it belongs and its position within the group.

The marks have been drawn keeping the shapes as simple as possible and using sizes which relate to normal practice. The shapes of the marks should be followed exactly by all who make use of them.

For each marking-up or proof correction instruction a distinct mark is to be made:

(a) in the text: to indicate the exact place to which the instruction refers;

(b) in the margin: to signify or amplify the meaning of the instruction.

It should be noted that some instructions have a combined textual and marginal mark.

Where a number of instructions occur in one line, the marginal marks are to be divided between the left and right margins where possible, the order being from left to right in both margins.

Specification details, comments and instructions may be written on the copy or proof to complement the textual and marginal marks. Such written matter is to be clearly distinguishable from the copy and from any corrections made to the proof. Normally this is done by encircling the matter and/or by the appropriate use of colour (see below).

Proof corrections shall be made in coloured ink thus:

(a) printer's literal errors marked by the printer for correction: green;

(b) printer's literal errors marked by the customer and his agents for correction: red;

(c) alterations and instructions made by the customer and his agents: black or dark blue.

Table 1. Classified list of marks

NOTE. The letters M and P in the notes column indicate marks for
marking-up copy and for correcting proofs respectively.

Group A General

Number	Instruction	Textual mark	Marginal mark	Notes
A1	Correction is concluded	None	/	P Make after each correction
A2	Leave unchanged	— — — — — under characters to remain	Ⓙ	M P
A3	Remove extraneous marks	Encircle marks to be removed	✕	P e.g. film or paper edges visible between lines on bromide or diazo proofs
A3.1	Push down risen spacing material	Encircle blemish	⊥	P
A4	Refer to appropriate authority anything of doubtful accuracy	Encircle word(s) affected	(?)	P

Group B Deletion, insertion and substitution

Number	Instruction	Textual mark	Marginal mark	Notes
B1	Insert in text the matter indicated in the margin	⋏	New matter followed by ⋏	M P Indentical to B2
B2	Insert additional matter identified by a letter in a diamond	⋏	⋏ Followed by for example ◈A	M P The relevant section of the copy should be supplied with the corresponding letter marked on it in a diamond e.g. ◈A
B3	Delete	/ through character(s) or ⊢——⊣ through words to be deleted	♌	M P
B4	Delete and close up	⌢/ through character or ⊢——⊣ through characters e.g. char̂acter charâcter	♌̂	M P

Table 1 *(continued)*

Number	Instruction	Textual mark	Marginal mark	Notes
B5	Substitute character or substitute part of one or more word(s)	/ through character or ⊢———⊣ through word(s)	New character or new word(s)	M P
B6	Wrong fount. Replace by character(s) of correct fount	Encircle character(s) to be changed	⊗	P
B6.1	Change damaged character(s)	Encircle character(s) to be changed	✕	P This mark is identical to A3
B7	Set in or change to italic	————— under character(s) to be set or changed	⊔⌋	M P Where space does not permit textual marks encircle the affected area instead
B8	Set in or change to capital letters	═══ under character(s) to be set or changed	≡	
B9	Set in or change to small capital letters	═══ under character(s) to be set or changed	=	
B9.1	Set in or change to capital letters for initial letters and small capital letters for the rest of the words	═══ under initial letters and ═══ under rest of the word(s)	═	
B10	Set in or change to bold type	∿∿∿∿ under character(s) to be set or changed	∿	
B11	Set in or change to bold italic type	∿∿∿∿ under character(s) to be set or changed	⊔⌋∿	
B12	Change capital letters to lower case letters	Encircle character(s) to be changed	⧧	P For use when B5 is inappropriate

Table 1 *(continued)*

Number	Instruction	Textual mark	Marginal mark	Notes
B12.1	Change small capital letters to lower case letters	Encircle character(s) to be changed	≠	P For use when B5 is inappropriate
B13	Change italic to upright type	Encircle character(s) to be changed	ЩJ	P
B14	Invert type	Encircle character to be inverted	Ω	P
B15	Substitute or insert character in 'superior' position	/ through character or ∧ where required	⌐ under character e.g. 2	P
B16	Substitute or insert character in 'inferior' position	/ through character or ∧ where required	L over character e.g. 2	P
B17	Substitute ligature e.g. ffi for separate letters	⊢————⊣ through characters affected	⌣ e.g. ffi	P
B17.1	Substitute separate letters for ligature	⊢————⊣	Write out separate letters	P
B18	Substitute or insert full stop or decimal point	/ through character or ∧ where required	⊙	M P
B18.1	Substitute or insert colon	/ through character or ∧ where required	⊙	M P
B18.2	Substitute or insert semi-colon	/ through character or ∧ where required	;	M P

Table 1 *(continued)*

Number	Instruction	Textual mark		Marginal mark	Notes
B18.3	Substitute or insert comma	/	through character	,	M P
		or ⋋	where required		
B18.4	Substitute or insert apostrophe	/	through character	⁊	M P
		or ⋋	where required		
B18.5	Substitute or insert single quotation marks	/	through character	⁊ and/or ⁊	M P
		or ⋋	where required		
B18.6	Substitute or insert double quotation marks	/	through character	⁊ and/or ⁊	M P
		or ⋋	where required		
B19	Substitute or insert ellipsis	/	through character	. . .	M P
		or ⋋	where required		
B20	Substitute or insert leader dots	/	through character	⊙	M P Give the measure of the leader when necessary
		or ⋋	where required		
B21	Substitute or insert hyphen	/	through character	⊢–⊣	M P
		or ⋋	where required		
B22	Substitute or insert rule	/	through character	⊢—⊣	M P Give the size of the rule in the marginal mark e.g. ⊢1 em⊣ ⊢4 mm⊣
		⋋	where required		

Table 1 *(continued)*

Number	Instruction	Textual mark	Marginal mark	Notes
B23	Substitute or insert oblique	/ through character or ⅄ where required	Ⓘ	M P

Group C Positioning and spacing

Number	Instruction	Textual mark	Marginal mark	Notes
C1	Start new paragraph			M P
C2	Run on (no new paragraph)			M P
C3	Transpose characters or words	between characters or words, numbered when necessary		M P
C4	Transpose a number of characters or words	3 2 1	1 2 3	M P To be used when the sequence cannot be clearly indicated by the use of C3. The vertical strokes are made through the characters or words to be transposed and numbered in the correct sequence
C5	Transpose lines			M P
C6	Transpose a number of lines		——— 3 ——— 2 ——— 1	P To be used when the sequence cannot be clearly indicated by C5. Rules extend from the margin into the text with each line to be transposed and numbered in the correct sequence
C7	Centre	enclosing matter to be centred		M P
C8	Indent			P Give the amount of the indent in the marginal mark

Table 1 *(continued)*

Number	Instruction	Textual mark	Marginal mark	Notes
C9	Cancel indent			P
C10	Set line justified to specified measure	and/or		P Give the exact dimensions when necessary
C11	Set column justified to specified measure			M P Give the exact dimensions when necessary
C12	Move matter specified distance to the right	enclosing matter to be moved to the right		P Give the exact dimensions when necessary
C13	Move matter specified distance to the left	enclosing matter to be moved to the left		P Give the exact dimensions when necessary
C14	Take over character(s), word(s) or line to next line, column or page			P The textual mark surrounds the matter to be taken over and extends into the margin
C15	Take back character(s), word(s), or line to previous line, column or page			P The textual mark surrounds the matter to be taken back and extends into the margin
C16	Raise matter	over matter to be raised under matter to be raised		P Give the exact dimensions when necessary. (Use C28 for insertion of space between lines or paragraphs in text)
C17	Lower matter	over matter to be lowered under matter to be lowered		P Give the exact dimensions when necessary. (Use C29 for reduction of space between lines or paragraphs in text)
C18	Move matter to position indicated	Enclose matter to be moved and indicate new position		P Give the exact dimensions when necessary

Table 1 *(continued)*

Number	Instruction	Textual mark	Marginal mark	Notes
C19	Correct vertical alignment			P
C20	Correct horizontal alignment	Single line above and below misaligned matter e.g. mi$_s$aligned		P The marginal mark is placed level with the head and foot of the relevant line
C21	Close up. Delete space between characters or words	linking ⌢⌣ characters	⌢⌣	M P
C22	Insert space between characters	| between characters affected	Y	M P Give the size of the space to be inserted when necessary
C23	Insert space between words	Y between words affected	Y	M P Give the size of the space to be inserted when necessary
C24	Reduce space between characters	| between characters affected	⌃	M P Give the amount by which the space is to be reduced when necessary
C25	Reduce space between words	⌃ between words affected	⌃	M P Give amount by which the space is to be reduced when necessary
C26	Make space appear equal between characters or words	| between characters or words affected	⋎⋏	M P
C27	Close up to normal interline spacing	(each side of column linking lines)		M P The textual marks extend into the margin

Marked galley proof of text

(B9.1) =/

(B13) 41/

(C7) []/

(C9) ⅃/

At the sign of the red pale

(C22) Y/

The Life and Work of William Caxton, by H W Larken

[An Extract]

(B10) w/

(B9) =/

Few people, even in the field of printing, have any clear conception of what William Caxton did or, indeed, of what he was. Much of this lack of knowledge is due to the absence of information that can be counted as factual and the consequent tendency to vague generalisation.

(B12) ≠/

(B1) i,l/

Though it is well known that Caxton was born in the county of Kent, there is no information as to the precise place. In his prologue to the *History of Troy*, William Caxton wrote 'for in France I was never and was born and learned my English in Kent in the Weald where I doubt not is spoken as broad and rude English as in any place of England.' During the fifteenth century there were a great number of Flemish cloth weavers in Kent; most of them had come to England at the instigation of Edward III with the object of teaching their craft to the English. So successful was this venture that the English cloth trade flourished and the agents who sold the cloth (the mercers) became very wealthy people. There have been speculations concerning the origin of the Caxton family and much research has been carried out. It is assumed often that Caxton's family must have been connected with the wool trade in order to have secured his apprenticeship to an influential merchant.

(A2) ⊘/

(B19) .../

(C23) Y/

(C1) ⌐/

(B6) Ⓚ/

(B5) t/

(B3) ∂n/

(B17) t̂i/

(C8) ⅃/

(C3) ⊔⌐/

(B14) Ω/

(A4) ⑦/

(B7) ⊔⊔/

W. Blyth Crotch (*Prologues and Epilogues of William Caxton*) suggests that the origin of the name Caxton (of which there are several variations in spelling) may be traced to Cambridgeshire but notes that many writers have suggested that Caxton was connected with a family at Hadlow or alternatively a family in Canterbury.

(B7) ⊔⊔/

(A3.1) ⊥/

(B18.1) ⊙/

Of the Canterbury connection a William Caxton became freeman of the City in 1431 and William Pratt, a mercer who was the printer's friend, was born there. H. R. Plomer suggests that Pratt and Caxton might possibly have been schoolboys together, perhaps at the school St. Alphege. In this parish there lived a John Caxton who used as his mark three cakes over a barrel (or tun) and who is mentioned in an inscription on a monument in the church of St. Alphege.

(C20) =/

(B15) ⅃/

(C26) χ/

(B2) ⋋Ⓐ/

In 1941, Alan Keen (an authority on manuscripts) secured some documents concerning Caxton; these are now in the BRITISH MUSEUM. Discovered in the library of Earl Winterton at Shillinglee Park by Richard Holworthy, the documents cover the period 1420 to 1467. One of Winterton's ancestors purchased the manor of West Wratting from a family named Caxton, the property being situated in the Weald of Kent.

(A3) χ/

(B12.1) ≠/

(B8) ≡/

(B6) Ⓚ/

(C27)

There is also record of a property mentioning Philip Caxton and his wife Dennis who had two sons, Philip (born in 1413) and William.

(C2) ⌐/

(B4) ∂l/

(B18) ⊙/

(C27)

Particularly interesting in these documents is one recording that Philip Caxton junior sold the manor of Little Wratting to John Christemasse of London in 1436, the deed having been witnessed by two aldermen, one of whom was Robert Large, the printer's employer. Further, in 1439 the other son, William Caxton, conveyed this property mentions one William Caxton conveyed his rights in the manor Bluntes Hall at Little alias Causton. It is an interesting coincidence to note that the lord of the manor of Little Wratting was the father of Margaret, Duchess of Burgundy.

(B22) 1e ⊢/

(C14)

(B21) ⊢/

(C6) ⊢/

(B18.3) '/

(C21) ⊂/

(C19) |||/

In 1420, a Thomas Caxton of Tenterden witnessed the will of a fellow townsman; he owned property in Kent and appears to have been a person of some importance.

(C25) T/

(C28) (+1pt

(C29))−1pt

¹ See 'William Caxton'.

Ⓐ *attached to Christchurch Monastery in the parish of*

Revised galley proof of text incorporating corrections

At the Sign of the Red Pale

The Life and Work of William Caxton, *by H W Larken*

An Extract

FEW PEOPLE, even in the field of printing, have any clear
conception of what William Caxton did or, indeed, of
what he was. Much of this lack of knowledge is due to the
absence of information that can be counted as factual
and the consequent tendency to vague generalisation.

Though it is well known that Caxton was born in the
county of Kent, there is no information as to the precise
place. In his prologue to the *History of Troy*, William Caxton
wrote '. . . for in France I was never and was born and
learned my English in Kent in the Weald where I doubt
not is spoken as broad and rude English as in any place
of England.'

During the fifteenth century there were a great number
of Flemish cloth weavers in Kent; most of them had come
to England at the instigation of Edward III with the
object of teaching their craft to the English. So successful
was this venture that the English cloth trade flourished
and the agents who sold the cloth (the mercers) became
very wealthy people.

There have been many speculations concerning the
origin of the Caxton family and much research has been
carried out. It is often assumed that Caxton's family must
have been connected with the wool trade in order to have
secured his apprenticeship to an influential merchant.

W. Blyth Crotch (*Prologues and Epilogues of William
Caxton*) suggests that the origin of the name Caxton (of
which there are several variations in spelling) may be
traced to Cambridgeshire but notes that many writers
have suggested that Caxton was connected with a family
at Hadlow or alternatively a family in Canterbury.

Of the Canterbury connection: a William Caxton
became freeman of the City in 1431 and William Pratt,
a mercer who was the printer's friend, was born there.
H. R. Plomer[1] suggests that Pratt and Caxton might possibly
have been schoolboys together, perhaps at the school
attached to Christchurch Monastery in the parish of St.
Alphege. In this parish there lived a John Caxton who
used as his mark three cakes over a barrel (or tun) and
who is mentioned in an inscription on a monument in
the church of St. Alphege.

In 1941, Alan Keen (an authority on manuscripts)
secured some documents concerning Caxton; these are
now in the British Museum. Discovered in the library of
Earl Winterton at Shillinglee Park by Richard Holworthy,
the documents cover the period 1420 to 1467. One of
Winterton's ancestors purchased the manor of West
Wratting from a family named Caxton, the property
being situated in the Weald of Kent. There is also record
of a property mentioning Philip Caxton and his wife
Dennis who had two sons, Philip (born in 1413) and
William.

Particularly interesting in these documents is one
recording that Philip Caxton junior sold the manor of
Little Wratting to John Christemasse of London in 1436—
the deed having been witnessed by two aldermen, one
of whom was Robert Large, the printer's employer.
Further, in 1439, the other son, William Caxton, conveyed his rights in the manor Bluntes Hall at Little
Wratting to John Christemasse, and an indenture of 1457
concerning this property mentions one William Caxton
alias Causton. It is an interesting coincidence to note that
the lord of the manor of Little Wratting was the father of
Margaret, Duchess of Burgundy.

In 1420, a Thomas Caxton of Tenterden witnessed the
will of a fellow townsman; he owned property in Kent
and appears to have been a person of some importance.

[1] See 'William Caxton'.

Table 1 *(continued)*

Number	Instruction	Textual mark	Marginal mark	Notes
C28	Insert space between lines or paragraphs	or		M P The marginal mark extends between the lines of text. Give the size of the space to be inserted when necessary
C29	Reduce space between lines or paragraphs	or		M P The marginal mark extends between the lines of text. Give the amount by which the space is to be reduced when necessary

The importance of age

Make particular note of birth dates so that, when writing, you can maintain consistency. This is particularly important when writing a story spanning a number of years, when it is essential that a character should remain at the right age throughout and not be, for instance twenty-one at the start and thirty-one only five years later.

Noting birth dates will also help you to visualise their growth from childhood and through the progression of time. Even though you may not write of them retrospectively, or refer much to their childhood or youth, you will have a greater depth of feeling for them if you know exactly when they were born and what life was like throughout their formative years, all of which has inevitably left its mark on them.

Remember the importance of age in depicting behaviour. In this it plays as vital a part as physical growth or physical deterioration. (Notice how the voices of older people can become gruffer or more highly pitched, or quavering and breathless.) Remember too that age can influence a person's attitudes, not only to younger people but to life and morals and politics and religion, and that in the young, particularly in teenagers, age can demonstrate itself in boisterous behaviour or shyness, impudence or sulkiness, gaucheness or bravado, defiance or apparently overweening self-confidence. In the very young it can reveal a touching dependence on, or trust in, their elders or, in disturbed children, sometimes a fear of them.

from *Writing Popular Fiction* by Rona Randall (A & C Black, £7.99)

Word Processing
A Guide for Authors

RANDALL McMULLAN

Writers never used to read much about typewriters, let alone pens and pencils, so perhaps it is a pity that we need an article about word processors for writers. Approach this knowledge with a similar attitude to collecting information about a new car. You don't wish to be a mechanic but there are certain automotive ideas and terms that you accept in order to make an appropriate choice of car and to get use from it.

Acquiring a word processor and learning to 'drive' the device is an investment of effort comparable to using a car and word processing offers similar gains in productivity, and convenience. If you do happen to enjoy extra technical features like power steering or central locking then you will find the equivalent in extra features associated with word processors, but they are not essential.

WRITING WITH A WORD PROCESSOR

A word processor should have a benign effect on your writing habits because the system encourages a fundamental rule of writing – to keep going. You do not stop typing at the end of a line because the word processor does that sort of housekeeping for you. You do not stop for any typing mistakes during 'text input' (writing) because the errors on screen are only transient until you decide to make them permanent. It is more efficient to fix mistakes during a separate editing pass over the screen. Indeed, you should learn to let the computer dictionary pick up the typos and automatically correct them, with a watchful eye from yourself. If you can't spell a word then you just need to make a best guess.

Initially you may miss the act of ripping pages from the typewriter and hurling them at the wastepaper basket but you can learn new and equally satisfying ways of savaging your text. Once the text is fixed then it need never be keyed again. Most publishers will be happy to accept your disk fresh from the word processor without further work from you, and you will be saved proofreading for typesetting mistakes. For some authors the electronic file from the word processor is the starting point for desktop publishing or for self-publishing, as described in the companion articles on pages 487 and 268 respectively.

WHAT EQUIPMENT IS NEEDED?

A word processor is essentially a device which accepts the input of text from a keyboard and displays it on screen for you to change and move about as you please. This text is then electronically stored for reuse and transport, like a cassette in a tape recorder, and the text can be printed on to paper at any time.

Being loath to lose sight of their paper, even temporarily, authors are often drawn towards new generations of electronic typewriters which can store some text and show it on a small screen for correction. At the most, you can only view a few lines at one time and it becomes difficult and discouraging to process pages of text. Electronic typewriters have their uses, especially if cheap, but they also run the risk of giving word processors a bad name.

Modern word processors are actually desktop computers for which a 'program' of word processing instructions is just one of many 'software' packages. The computer 'hardware' is neutral about what it does and can run other programs such as databases, accounts or even games. This ability can be regarded as a bonus but should not distract a writer while choosing a word processor. It is usually more satisfactory for all parties if children, for example, are given separate games machines to use in another room!

Most computers for word processing are various models of the 'PC' or 'Personal Computer' range which are produced by a large number of manufacturers, small and large. Although IBM originally set the standards for this family of computers, IBM now produce machines which are not especially compatible with the *de facto* standards used by the rest of the industry. The importance of the PC standard is that you can read and write your disks on other machines, like a tape cassette, or you can plug-in parts from other people's machines, such as keyboards or display screens. Some ranges of computer, such as the Apple Macintosh or Amstrad PCW, are less compatible with PC computers but have a moderate-sized base of users.

Word processing packages

Hundreds of different brands of word processing software have been produced for PC computers. As with the hardware, there are great advantages in choosing from the half dozen word processing packages which are established as standards. You will then have access to the training and general community help associated with a widely used product.

Like different models of cars, word processors are perhaps 90 per cent identical in their word processing capabilities although manufacturers, and some users, will declare that the difference or the extra features are of great importance. Without becoming too partisan however, you may certainly wish to observe different styles of word processor and look ahead to any desktop publishing ambitions.

The 'text editor' style, used in a traditional word processor, allows you to input and edit your text while you view a screen which shows the correct arrangements of lines on the page. The characters seen on screen are neutral in matters of style, although special text such as bold, superscript or subscript will be highlighted. But in such editing mode you will not expect to see the exact size and style of the type fonts.

The 'graphical interface' of some later word processors takes the concept of WYSIWIG (What You See Is What You Get) further, in that your text is displayed on screen in the same size and style of type that will be used by your current printer. The characters are usually shown as black on a white screen. If your printer can produce the appropriate varieties of size and style then you will be able to achieve a simple form of desktop publishing.

The graphical display of text will not necessarily replace the use of a simpler text editor screen. For intensive processing of words, rather than arrangement of print style, the 'clean' screen can be more efficient. If the text is to be used later by a desktop publishing program, or by a typesetter, then it should *not* be formatted with print styles. This difference in screen styles is not necessarily crucial in the later versions of well-known word processors, such as WordPerfect and WordStar, because they offer the option of previewing your text in graphical form.

Word processors also differ in the style by which you give them 'commands'. Learners and casual users often appreciate visible menus of options on screen which are activiated by moving arrow keys on the keyboard, or even by moving a mouse. As a constant keyboardist you may soon find such selection methods tedious and probably need keyboard commands. Fortunately, the mainstream packages offer a choice of command methods and screen clutter which can be reset at any time.

Other features of modern word processors include large dictionaries used for checking spelling and supplying an instant Thesaurus. The dictionaries are usually in 'British English' and you can add your own lists of specialised words. Remember that the spellchecker can not check for context although it should be smart enough to recognise and suggest automatic corrections for well-known typos such as 'hte' or 'the the'.

Most word processors have the ability to generate 'mailshots' of apparently personalised letters, like those promoting unique and unrepeatable timeshare offers. 'Indexing' and 'Footnoting' features sound alluring to authors but all of them rely on systematic coding by the writer before they spring into action. Such features are often optimised for technical publications and can never replace the skills of a good indexer.

If you choose a word processing program from outside the well-known names then you will be on your own. A minority of writing tasks may be better handled by programs which specialise in the layout of mathematical and scientific symbols. Foreign languages are another special area and there are word processors which can be set to display non-Roman scripts. You must expect the use of such a specialised package to be more of a lonely challenge.

Computers

The word processing 'computer' is usually a metal or plastic box connected by cables to the keyboard and display screen. Some of the components in the box can be varied to suit the requirements of the software that you wish to run. Typical decisions involve the speed of the processor chip, the amount of memory (RAM), the type of disk drives, and the type of display screen to be used. Some minimum technicalities are given in the later section about purchasing your word processor.

The computer will come with an *operating system*, the software which co-ordinates the tasks of the computer such as interpreting keystrokes, displaying characters on screen and storing them on disk in magnetic 'files'. A reasonable minimum knowledge of the operating system is needed to name the files, which contain your precious work, and to make backups of them.

The *keyboard* of a standard modern desktop computer is attached to the computer box by cable and can therefore be used in any convenient position. Good keyboards are constructed with springs beneath each key and an escapement mechanism to give a 'positive' feel. The keyboard works in the same way as a QWERTY typewriter keyboard and has some special keys such as the Control and Alt keys which give special effects. Computer keyboards have also gained some extra keys such as arrows to move the cursor about on screen, duplicate numeral keys, and 'function' keys for shortcut commands within programs.

Disks

Your writing is electronically stored on to a disk covered with a magnetic coating, like an audio or video tape. Yes, it is usually spelt 'disk' rather than disc. A 'floppy' disk can be taken in and out of a slot in the computer and the contents can be copied on to a blank disk. Unlike a tape recorder, you don't need two floppy disk drives to duplicate a floppy disk. Several sagas of text can easily be stored on a single floppy disk and they cost around £1.00 each. Like most information, writing is best stored and organised as separate 'files' of data, usually no longer than a chapter per file.

One advantage of accepted technical standards for computers is that the floppy disk, containing your work, written by one computer can be read by another computer. There are some variations in 'standards' but in general you should aim to be able to use your disk in other computers. For example, you may wish to use a portable computer, or to produce a printout on another style of printer at another site.

A 'hard disk' or 'fixed disk' can not be removed from the computer but holds much more information than a floppy disk and works more quickly. A hard disk is not an essential requirement for the storage of text and you should always keep a recent copy of your text on a floppy disk; stored in a safe place away from the computer. But hard disks are now relatively cheap and are needed to store the complex files of modern programs. The latest versions of word processors have so many features, like large dictionaries, that they are difficult or impossible to run from floppy disks.

Display screens

The display screen or 'monitor' on which you view your text work has some electronics in common with a TV but produces a higher resolution of dots in order to display at least 80 characters across the screen. It is expensive to have a monitor which can display the full length of an A4 page on screen, and it is not usually necessary as you can easily pan the screen over your text.

There are continuing investigations into possible radiation hazards from display screens which are either as significant or as negligible as sitting close to a TV set. Regular rest periods are the recommended methods of avoiding visual strain or muscular strain from word processing or from any other desk activities, such as handwriting.

Printers

The product of your word processing is the 'hard copy' on paper. The same text stored on disk can be printed out many times in different styles and on different printers. You will be generating a lot of paper so printers need to be fast, more robust than the average typewriter, and be able to feed paper automatically. Fortunately modern printers can offer these features at reasonable prices.

PURCHASING

The simple guideline for choosing your word processor is to buy what everyone else is using. If you do have any difficulties help will be available quickly and cheaply. Friends or colleagues, for example, may be able to loan equipment in an emergency or to provide a printout. The common makes of word processing equipment are accompanied by abundant training, help and advice available from books, magazines and acquaintances.

The following technical considerations are centred around the 'PC' standard of desktop computers which occupies over 90 per cent of the business market. National and local newspapers carry regular computer advertisements from well-known chains of retailers and you will find that they also use this jargon to describe their offers.

Computers

Although IBM set the original standard for modern desktop personal computers, most people now buy IBM-compatible machines or 'clones' offered under a variety of brand names over a range of prices. The particular brand name on the computer box is not as important as you might think. The electronic components are all made in countries far away and, fortunately, are usually interchangeable.

Apple has introduced a range of *PowerPC* computers which offer the possibility of running both Macintosh programs and PC programs on the same machine. Apple parts are not interchangeable with PCs.

A minimum choice for a modern professional word processing system is a machine based on the '386' processing chip running at a clockrate of 16 MHz (megahertz). The later and more powerful '486' chip has become cheaper and runs programs faster. These speed considerations will not trouble simple word processing programs but do have a noticeable effect on the speed of desktop publishing and the latest word processing programs which run inside the Windows environment.

The typical modern PC will have 1 to 4 MB (megabytes) of RAM (Random Access Memory) and most designs allow you to add more memory later if programs require it. The storage capacity of an average hard disk is 80 to 200 MB and modern programs need this capacity. You need at least one floppy disk drive, and the format (size) of the disks for this drive is now usually 3.25 inch. The 5.25 inch disk was used throughout the 1980s and will also be with us for some time. For about £50 extra you can have a second floppy disk drive of either format built into the computer box and many vendors offer this option. One floppy disk drive is all you need to make duplicate copies of disks in order to backup your work.

Display systems

A display system consists of a video monitor (screen) accompanied by a matching video adaptor card which plugs into a slot inside the computer. You pay more money for increased resolution (fineness) on screen, especially in colour. VGA and SVGA (Super VGA) are currently the leading colour standard while the EGA standard is adequate for word processing. Monochrome VGA or Mono-chrome Graphics (Hercules) are also adequate for simple word processing and a lot cheaper.

Word processing software

There are around half a dozen major brands of professional word processing programs for the PC. WordPerfect, WordStar and Word are found in general use. Word for Windows, WordPerfect for Windows and Ami Professional are from a newer generation of graphical word processors which run under the Windows operating system and need the power of later models of PC such as 386 and 486 machines.

Most of these word processors have evolved during the last ten years and later versions are often significantly different from earlier versions although the transitions between them are easy. Locoscript is a program which started life on the Amstrad PCW machines and is now also available on the PC. There are many other worthy word processors with enthusiastic users but they are not as widespread as the 'majors'. If you receive any word processor program 'bundled' free with your computer then it will be suitable for learning.

Printers

Dot-matrix printers are cheap, reasonably quiet, and can produce a variety of type styles ranging between fast dotty styles and slower NLQ (near-letter-quality) where the dot structure is hard to detect. Most dot-matrix printers use continuous paper with perforated 'tractor' margins but they will also print single sheets.

Laser printers and inkjet printers have replaced daisy-wheel printers for the production of office-quality text and both types of printer quietly feed on plain A4 paper. These printers can also produce different styles and sizes of text (fonts) when driven by an appropriate desktop publishing program. The prices of inkjet printers and laser printers have become attractive in price. An A4 page of dense text or graphics may use several pence worth of toner or ink and these costs should be considered when buying a laser printer or inkjet printer.

Portables

Writers have some good reasons for being tempted to buy a portable PC which will run any of the well-known word processing programs. The portables range in size from 'luggable' suitcases, through 'laptops' for people with strong knees, to 'notebooks' for large briefcases. All of the portables make various compromises in the size of memory and storage, the quality of keyboard and the display. None of them runs on batteries for extended periods, if at all, but they may fit a special need such as travel in places with unreliable electricity supplies.

Costs

It is possible to acquire a professional word processing setup, including printer, for between £700 and £1200, depending on its technical specification and your shopping acumen. You can buy the same equipment from well-known stores or from reputable discount warehouses. Computer equipment is as reliable as any consumer electronics and most likely to show a fault in the early hours when it is under warranty.

Unless you are spending corporate money it will not be sensible to take a maintenance contract. If continuous use of a word processor becomes really important to you then it is usually more economic to buy a standby machine, such as a portable or second-hand computer. Another common strategy is to have plenty of friends or neighbours who can oblige with a printout on their computers with the same ease as they can give you a lift in their cars.

Dead wood

Many more scripts are overwritten than underwritten. Many I've come across, both in teaching and script-reading for theatres and other organisations, could be cut by a quarter. Sometimes, if you're writing for radio or television, you discover your script is grossly over length. Cutting it back ruthlessly can be an educational experience. Things come into much sharper relief through having to be shorter. Dead wood flies away. Try it as an exercise. Say to yourself 'This script has to be fifteen pages shorter' and be really savage with it. Chances are you'll see the improvement.

The great enemy of disciplined revision is resignation. Something may be almost right and, your will waning, you think to yourself 'That'll do'. A good way of facing up to the fact that it won't do – especially if, by now, your first draft is covered in scribbled corrections – is to write it all out again. The tedium of the task is such that the sheer effort of writing stuff again which repeats or wanders or delays getting to the point helps you to cut it. An advantage of working in longhand first is that much can be weeded out when typing. Word-processors are, I suspect, the enemy of economic dialogue.

from *Writing a Play* by Steve Gooch (A & C Black, £5.95)

Desktop Publishing

RICHARD WILLIAMS

WHAT IS DESKTOP PUBLISHING?

Most writers will have heard of word processing, even if they do not use a word processor themselves, but desktop publishing (dtp) is a less familiar concept. It is important not to confuse it with self-publishing, which is dealt with elsewhere in this book (see page 268). Desktop publishing is a misnomer since a desktop publishing computer program does the work, not so much of a publisher, but of the specialists who prepare books or magazines for printing. Perhaps the best way to explain what it does is to look at the stages in producing a book or magazine by conventional methods, and then to see how desktop publishing can take over some of these.

Using conventional methods, manuscripts for books or magazines are delivered by the author as typewritten sheets. Before being sent to the typesetter these sheets have first to be marked up to indicate the different sizes and styles of type to be used. The typeset text comes back in the form of galleys, long strips of paper with the type in its final width.

When they have been proofread and revised the galleys are supplied as prints on photographic paper. They are then pasted up on boards by a graphics designer or layout artist to produce the page layout – a comparatively simple task for some books, but more complex for illustrated books and magazines. It is then known as camera ready copy, since the next stage is to photograph the boards, and use the resulting film to produce the plates from which the book or magazine is printed.

Desktop publishing programs can take over most of these stages. Instead of specialists setting type from the manuscript, a file from a word processor is transferred to a computer disk, and fed into the desktop publishing program. From this it emerges as the instructions from which camera ready copy can be produced. All the processes can be carried out by a desktop computer (hence the name) and indeed by a single operator.

So what does desktop publishing offer authors and illustrators? At the most, effectively the ability to control their own books, right from the original idea through to the final printed version. Even for those who do not want to go to these lengths, the ability of these programs to cut out the rekeying of text by accepting manuscripts on disk, and to integrate typesetting and layout, should cut publishing costs, and hopefully some of this saving will accrue to the author. Magazines are increasingly being produced by desktop publishing, and graphic designers, after initial suspicion of the new method, are adopting it for their work.

HOW DOES IT WORK?

Although desktop publishing programs differ in their features, most work in basically the same way. Instead of being marked up manually, and then typeset, the text is given invisible 'tags'. These specify the typeface, including its style and size, the letter, word and line spacing, and the alignment of the text. The program uses this information to format the text automatically in the equivalent of galleys. Some programs also have facilities for setting complicated tables, or mathematical equations.

Simultaneously the program lays out the text on the page (the equivalent of pasting up) in accordance with the instructions it has been given for page size, margins and number of columns. Illustrations can be positioned wherever required, and the text can be made to flow automatically around them. The other information needed on the page, such as headers, footers and page numbers, can be specified once and is then added automatically to each page. Some programs go further, and will automatically number sections as well as pages, and produce the index and table of contents for a book.

The end result is a complete page layout which can be viewed on-screen. The great advantage of this is that anything can be changed quickly and with immediate feedback. The change can be as simple as rewriting a few words so that the text fits a particular space, or as complex as changing the whole page layout with a different typeface, or a different number of columns. Various possibilities can be quickly tried out, and any obvious non-starters discarded as quickly, without needing to print out a page.

In practice it is necessary to print out a certain number of drafts, if only for proofreading, because the screen cannot show as much detail as the printed page – except for the most expensive systems the choice is between readable text on part of the page, or a full page view which only gives a general impression. These proofs can be produced relatively quickly, even on an inexpensive computer printer.

Once satisfied with the appearance of the document, the final printed version can be produced. If only a small number of copies are required, these can be produced on a laser printer. For larger print runs, such a printer can also be used to produce camera ready copy. This can then be reproduced by a photocopier, or photographed for platemaking and conventional printing. For the highest quality the camera ready copy can be produced on a special version of the normal typesetter which can take files direct from a desktop publishing program.

WHAT SORT OF EQUIPMENT IS NEEDED?

Anyone with a personal computer used for word processing can probably use it to make a start in desktop publishing, since there are now programs available for most machines. (If you do not already have a computer, and need some explanation of how they work, then turn to the article on word processing on page 481.) The three essentials are a screen which can display the page in sufficient detail for the text to be read easily, a printer to produce draft copies of the documents, and a mouse to operate the program.

Some screens such as the low resolution colour types found in cheaper computers are not suitable for desktop publishing, but higher resolution monochrome screens give quite acceptable results. The absence of colour is often no disadvantage since a great deal of printed matter is in black and white.

Although a laser printer is normally the minimum needed for high quality finished work, a surprising number of cheaper printers can produce draft versions which give a reasonable impression of the final result. You can then send a disk to a service bureau to have this run off on a laser printer or typesetter.

Most desktop publishing programs can be used with some dot matrix printers, and often with other types such as inkjets. As you might expect, inexpensive programs are more likely to cater for inexpensive printers, and vice versa.

Nowadays many computers are already equipped with a mouse (a small device which can be moved around the desktop to control an on-screen pointer). If not, models are now available to suit most types of computer and can be added relatively easily and cheaply.

Using your existing equipment with a relatively cheap program allows you to try your hand at dtp at little cost and if your requirements are simple this may well be all you need. If your requirements are more complex then it may well be worth spending more to allow work to be done more easily and quickly.

Updating a desktop publishing document on-screen is much more demanding than updating the text screen of an ordinary word processor. It will therefore be slower on a basic computer than on a more powerful machine. More expensive displays can also show more detail, and allow you to see more of the page on-screen while keeping the text readable.

Similarly non-laser printers usually take longer to print than lasers and their quality is not normally good enough for final prints. An inkjet printer like the HP Deskjet can give quality approaching a laser, at lower cost, but is still significantly slower. You may decide that the convenience of having your own laser justifies the cost.

Another piece of equipment which may be useful is a scanner. These convert photographs or drawings into electronic form for inclusion in desktop published documents. (This is not essential, since these can be pasted into camera ready copy in the conventional way, but it may be more convenient.) With special software, scanners can also convert typed or printed text into word processor files. Full page scanners are relatively expensive, but handheld versions covering a smaller area are much cheaper.

IS A SPECIAL PROGRAM NECESSARY?

When desktop publishing programs were first introduced word processing software was still producing much the same sort of output as an electric typewriter. Since then heavyweight word processors have added more and more desktop publishing-type features, such as multiple columns, headers and footers, the ability to include graphics, and to use a wide range of typefaces and sizes.

It is now claimed that it is possible to achieve much the same results with one of these programs as with true desktop publishing software. Is this true? The answer depends on what sort of work is to be done. The new generation of word processors is probably best suited to the business world, where there is a relatively narrow range of documents each with a standard format.

These programs tend not to have the flexibility in page layout needed for newsletters or magazines, or the more specialised features for longer documents which desktop publishing programs offer.

A DETAILED LOOK AT PARTICULAR COMPUTERS

This section looks at the main types of computer, and the desktop publishing programs which are available for them. Printers can normally be used with any type of computer, and so are considered separately at the end. A certain amount of knowledge about the technicalities of computers is assumed – if you are unsure about some of the terms used these are explained in the article on word processing (see page 481).

IBM personal computers and compatibles

These are the predominant type of machine, at least in the business sector, and have the widest selection of hardware and software. As a guide to prices, a basic machine with a 386 chip, 1 MB of memory, a monochrome monitor and a 40 MB hard disk can be bought for under £500. Faster machines based on the 486 SX chip with more memory, a colour monitor and a bigger hard disk can be bought for less than £900 and the even more powerful machines based on the 486 DX chip can cost less than £1200.

To a considerable extent the choice of machine will determine the choice of desktop publishing program since the heavyweight programs require a hard disk and at least four megabytes of machine memory. The leading contenders in this category are PC Pagemaker, Ventura Publisher and the IBM version of Quark Express. Their latest editions offer a wide range of facilities for producing complex page layouts and large books, with detailed and precise control over the size and positioning of print and illustrations, and also, apart from Quark Express, include index and table of contents compilation. Less well known but similarly heavyweight programs are 3B2 by Advent and Framemaker.

In the past there has been a clear distinction between the heavyweight programs which tended to cost as much as a basic machine, and a group of much cheaper alternatives. These used to be correspondingly limited in the features they offered, but now, with a combination of added functionality and price reductions, programs such as PressWorks, Microsoft Publisher and Page Plus offer very strong competition to the heavyweights. Although probably still not suitable for intensive book or magazine production, these programs are now capable of professional looking results.

Faced with this competition, two of the existing heavyweights have fought back with price reductions. Corel has now taken over Ventura, and combined it with their own graphics programs at a similar price to Ventura alone, whilst Aldus have introduced Pagemaker Classic, effectively the previous version of the program, but for a similar price to PagePlus. In terms of value for money the customer is much better off than before.

With one or two exceptions, all programs now run require the Windows program, but this is often supplied with machines, and most other programs like wordprocessors, spreadsheets and database programs will require it too.

There are a variety of display standards for IBM machines, but Hercules and EGA are now obsolete, and monochrome VGA is only found on the cheapest machines. Colour VGA is now effectively the standard for lower priced machines. Whilst this gives acceptable results, Super VGA, which allows more of a page to be shown on screen with readable characters, is better suited to dtp work and is increasingly the standard for more expensive machines.

Beyond this there are large screen displays which can show a whole page or a two-page spread at actual size. These are intended for professional users for whom the time saved justifies the price of £1500 or more for a colour screen.

The Apple Macintosh (Mac)

Although selling in smaller numbers than IBM compatibles, these are the only other machine to make a significant impact on the business sector. Because the standard machine has all the necessary features they are particularly popular for graphic design and desktop publishing work.

Besides Pagemaker, which originated on the Mac, the other established heavyweight dtp program is Quark Express. Recent additions in this category are the Mac versions of Ventura and Framemaker. All of these programs require a hard disk and at least 2 MB of RAM. At about a third of the price but with fewer features there are Personal Press from the same stable as Pagemaker and Publish-It, which can both be used on basic machines. The machines themselves have tended in the past to be more expensive than IBM compatibles, but relatively cheap new basic models have changed that.

Macs offer a choice of monochrome or colour screens in different resolutions. Unlike IBM even the cheapest Mac provides a satisfactory display for desktop publishing, but large screen displays are available at a price for professional work.

Other machines

All the other machines suitable for this purpose have at least one desktop publishing program available. Programs for the Acorn and Amiga are offered by the makers of these machines. The Atari has a wide choice, with heavyweight programs such as Calamus, Fleet Street Publisher and Pagestream. There is also a version of Timeworks for this machine.

PRINTERS

There are three basic types of printer to choose from: dot matrix, ink jet and laser. Dot matrix printers are cheap, but some ink jets, after their recent fall in price, are comparable in price and all offer higher quality combined with a much lower noise level. The best ink jets can produce quality almost as good as a laser (though rather more slowly). They can also print in colour; this can be useful for proofing pages with coloured text or graphics, but the quality is not high enough for full-colour work.

Laser printers have fallen in price as dramatically as ink jets, and it is now possible to buy a basic model for around £500. There are two main types, Postscript or Postscript compatibles, and PCL and PCL compatibles.

The difference between them is in the language used to send the information for a page from the computer to the printer. Postscript gives greater flexibility, and a closer match to the screen image, but at a higher price. With many printers you can buy either PCL or Postscript versions, and you can often upgrade a PCL printer to Postscript at a later date.

As well as the standard 300 dots per inch resolution that has been available for some years, many manufacturers are now offering higher resolution (600 dots per inch or more). This produces results of satisfactory quality for use as camera ready copy in text (but not half tone) work.

A laser printer with Postscript, high resolution and high speed, such as the HP Laserjet 4M, is around three times the price of a basic model, but smaller and slower versions would be some £250 cheaper.

With all types of printer make sure that you can connect them to the computer. Printers have both serial and parallel connections, which need different types of cable, and some types of computer will require different plugs to IBM machines. For this reason cables are not usually supplied with the machine – where you have a choice, use the parallel connection, since this gives faster printing and fewer compatability problems.

FURTHER READING

Inevitably in a short article such as this it is only possible to give a brief introduction to the subject. There are too many books dealing with individual programs or topics to list individually, but the following books on general topics may be useful:

Jones, Robert, *DTP The Complete Guide to Corporate Desktop Publishing*, Cambridge University Press, 1988
Miles, John, *Design for Desktop Publishing*, John Taylor Book Ventures, 1989

Writing Courses in Higher Education

DYMPHNA CALLERY

Why study writing? What's to be gained?

If you want to act or play the flute, you'll jump at the chance to train. And whether you've been writing for years or have just discovered an interest in it, you'll find that a course in writing offers a great deal, not least the impetus to write. Goals are set and you learn to produce to a deadline. A course promotes a disciplined approach to crafting for anyone who has been exploring writing on their own and the advice of experienced tutors and professionals can help to focus a direction in your writing that's hard to find on one's own. And it doesn't matter how old you are either, for courses in Higher Education these days welcome students of all ages and backgrounds. Studying writing, either as part of a degree or at postgraduate level, can enhance your writing skills and augment your chances in the publishing world or the workplace. But above all, it gives you the opportunity to improve and enrich your work.

What's available: BA degrees

At undergraduate level, several institutions have developed opportunities for Creative Writing to be taken as part of a degree in English, such as Sheffield Hallam University, one of the pioneers in this field. Others recognise that there is a place for writing courses within the broader context of the Creative Arts, Cultural Studies or Film Studies, and therefore writing courses are offered within those programmes. Some, such as Liverpool John Moores University, offer the opportunity to study Imaginative Writing as one half of a two subject degree. Currently, Bournemouth University is the only one offering a full programme – in Scriptwriting for Film and Television. But more and more institutions are developing courses in writing, so check with your local institution to see what's on offer.

What's available: MA degrees

Postgraduate courses are for those who already have a degree or the equivalent. Some focus on specific genres – such as the novel at East Anglia and Manchester, play-writing at Birmingham, or screen-writing at the Northern Film School – but most emphasise the process of discovery and re-discovery through writing practice. Students are usually assessed on a mixture of original creative work and critical writing. The study of critical theory is a component of all MA courses, but don't let that put you off, for although initially some of it can seem difficult or challenging, there are payoffs – you'll find yourself stretched intellectually as well as creatively. The basic assumption is that developing critical and analytical skills both enhances intellectual development and helps you to evaluate your own work. Through analysing narrative structure, for example, you can improve your storylining and plotting. You may even find yourself writing in genres or styles that you had never before considered.

Why have these courses developed?

Creative Writing has been a growth area in the Higher Education sector during the last ten years. This trend follows the American system where undergraduate options and Masters Degrees in Writing have been common for some time, producing a wealth of successful writers. The basis of this increasing trend in Britain is not that writing *ought* to be taught, but that it *can* be. If you haven't already got a degree, then now may be the time to consider developing your writing and gaining a qualification at the same time. If you already have a degree than why not consider following a full- or part-time writing course at postgraduate level?

How do these courses work? How can you 'study' writing? Surely it's better to 'do' it?

The main principle of these courses is that you learn by 'doing'. Just as an art student produces work in a studio, so writing students produce portfolio material. Most courses offer a framework of group workshops where material is generated and discussed. This is the principle of the 'writers' group'. However, the aim is not just to provide a supportive atmosphere in which writers can air their work, but to create a forum for critical debate. As someone who has experienced this workshop process (I recently completed the MA in Writing Studies at Edge Hill College) I can vouch for the success of this mode of study from the participating point of view. As someone who now teaches on the degree programme at Liverpool John Moores University, I find that this method of working nurtures talent and encourages experimentation.

In many instances, students are expected to read past and contemporary literature as well as critical theory. This not only invokes the old adage that the more you read the better you write, but that viewing these works from a critical standpoint facilitates the ability to read your own and others' work with more insight. By the end of such a course you will probably find yourself far better read than you were at the beginning, more aware of your own potential, and probably more critical too.

Who does the teaching? What qualifications do they have?

The majority of tutors on these programmes are themselves practising and published writers, some – e.g. Malcolm Bradbury, David Edgar – more well known than others, e.g. Jenny Newman, Jeremy Hooker. Whilst committed to their own writing they are keen to share their ideas and encourage new writers. They recognise that writing can be a lonely pursuit and that there's a great deal to be gained in an environment where creative problems and ideas are openly discussed. Any course worth its salt will incorporate visits from professional writers which means that your work may be read and commented upon by someone with a proven track record in the 'business'. Don't expect the course to offer contacts with publishers, editors or agents unless they specifically mention this in their information. But, tutors may be able to suggest the kind of publisher who might be interested in your work and many universities have their own writing magazines for which students' work is welcomed.

Being a student

There are benefits to be gained from becoming a student, not least of which is access to libraries and, in some institutions, access to IT and DTP machines and training. Whether part-time or full-time, you automatically become a member of your university or college library, and postgraduate students may apply for membership of the British Library. University libraries have, like those in the public sector, been hit by reductions in funding yet they are still often repositories of considerable excellence. And they frequently take periodicals, including some poetry titles, which are not available elsewhere.

Believe it or not, there are perks associated with being a student. Whether part-time or full-time, under forty or over fifty, you are entitled to join the Student Union and thereby gain access to such benefits as cheap travel, reduced price cinema and theatre tickets, etc. Most universities these days have postgraduate societies and mature student organisations. Many have cheap catering and bar facilities, and some of the more enlightened ones have crèches for those with small children (although there are normally charges for this service).

Who is eligible?

Although most of the undergraduate courses which include Creative Writing will expect English Literature at A level (generally with two other subjects), the majority of universities now welcome applications from those who have undertaken a BTEC or an Access to Higher Education course. Admissions policies in many institutions are flexible when dealing with mature applicants (for these purposes mature means those over 21), particularly those candidates who have work/life experience.

MA courses in all aspects of Creative Writing will usually expect applicants to have a degree, but not necessarily in a related field such as English Literature. They positively welcome applications from mature students, who make up the majority of students on these courses. Some will accept work experience in a related field, such as teaching, television production, journalism or publishing, as an equivalent entry qualification. All will require the submission of a portfolio of writing on which they base their assessment of your potential for the programme they offer. Some institutions will accept candidates purely on the basis of this, while others prefer to interview selected candidates.

How and when should I apply?

First contact the institutions that interest you. Follow their instructions for application procedures for courses. Visit the campus (some colleges may even let you sit in on a class or lecture). However, lecturing staff are notoriously under pressure these days, so don't expect individual attention. At this stage you are a potential applicant, not a student.

Although these courses usually begin in September/October, applications are considered much earlier in the year, for example the closing date for the MA in Playwriting Studies at Birmingham is mid-January. Applications for BA degrees are normally processed during November–March for the subsequent year. Check with the institution first and make sure you apply early as places tend to be filled on a first-come first-served basis.

How much does it cost?

Providing you have not previously been in receipt of a grant, you should be eligible for a full maintenance grant, which includes tuition fees, for an undergraduate degree. Your local authority will give you information. Some institutions with modular programming allow students to register for certain courses on a part-time basis, paying as they go. Check with the institution to see what is offered in this respect.

Fees for MA degrees vary but are generally in the region of £1200-£2000 for a full-time MA (nearer £6000 for foreign students). Most will allow payment in termly instalments. Part-time courses are usually considerably cheaper and of course the cost is spread over two years. Their fees range from £200-£500 (approx.) per year. Few grants are awarded for postgraduate courses, especially in the Arts, unless the first degree is exceptional. However, if you are accepted for a full-time MA you are eligible to apply for funding to the British Academy. Further information is available from: The British Academy, Postgraduate Studentships Office, Block 1, Spur 15, Government Buildings, Honeypot Lane, Stanmore, Middlesex HA7 1AX.

Many students support themselves by part-time work, and since most courses require two to four attendances a week during term time, this is not too difficult. Beware of trying to marry a full-time job with a full-time course as this is virtually impossible given the amount of reading and *writing* you will be expected to do.

And afterwards?

The major benefit of a writing course in Higher Education comes in improving your writing, but you may also find it moves you further towards that goal of 'being a writer'. Remember that Ian McEwan was a graduate of UEA's course and, although you may not be the next Booker prizewinner, there is little doubt that graduates of these courses succeed in getting published in a variety of ways, from magazines to children's books. It is also worth noting that having a higher qualification may open up opportunities for you to make use of your skills in related work, such as teaching creative writing or undertaking residencies for writers.

BA courses with components in creative writing

BA Combined Studies
Manchester Metropolitan University, All Saints, Manchester M15 6BH   *tel* 061-247 2000.

BA Creative Arts
Bath College of Higher Education, Newton Park, Bath BA2 9BN   *tel* (0225) 873701.
Crewe and Alsager Faculty, All Saints, Manchester M15 6BH   *tel* 061-247 2000.
University of Glamorgan, Pontypridd, Mid Glamorgan CF37 1DL   *tel* (0443) 480480.
Lancaster University, Lancaster LA1 4YW   *tel* (0524) 65201.

BA Creative Arts Studies
University of Sunderland, Langham Tower, Ryhope Road, Sunderland SR2 7EE   *tel* 091-515 2000.

BA Cultural Studies
Norfolk Institute of Art and Design, St George Street, Norwich, Norfolk NR3 1BB   *tel* (0603) 610561.

BA English
University of Wolverhampton, Wulfruna Street, Wolverhampton WV1 1SB   *tel* (0902) 321000.

BA English Studies
Sheffield Hallam University, Pond Street, Sheffield S1 1WB   *tel* (0742) 720911.

BA English and Creative Studies
University of Portsmouth, University House, Winston Churchill Avenue, Portsmouth PO1 2UP   *tel* (0705) 843082.

BA English Literature with Creative Writing
University of East Anglia, Norwich NR4 7TJ   *tel* (0603) 56161.

BA Imaginative Writing (Joint Hons)
Liverpool John Moores University, St Nicholas Centre, Great Orford Street, Liverpool L3 5YD   *tel* 051-231 2121.

BA Modular Scheme
University of Derby, Kedleston Road, Derby DE22 1GB   *tel* (0332) 62222.

BA Multidisciplinary Programme
Middlesex University, All Saints, White Hart Lane, London N17 8HR   *tel* 081-362 5000.

BA Performance Writings
Dartington College of Arts, Totnes, Devon TQ9 6EJ   *tel* (0803) 863234.

BA Related Arts and English
West Sussex Institute of Higher Education, The Dome, Upper Bognor Road, Bognor Regis, West Sussex PO21 1HR   *tel* (0243) 865581.

BA Scriptwriting for Film and Television
Bournemouth University, Talbot Campus, Fern Barrow, Poole, Dorset BH12 5BB   *tel* (0202) 314144.

MA courses in creative writing

Many of these programmes also offer a Postgraduate Diploma in Writing – please check with individual institutions.

All courses begin in October and run through an academic year unless otherwise indicated.

MA in Creative Writing (1yr FT   2yr PT)

A combination of taught courses and workshops led by tutors who are practising and published writers with intervention from professionals, e.g. Gillian Clark and Fay Weldon. *Contact:* Jeremy Hooker, Bath College of Higher Education, Newton Park, Newton St Loe, Bath BA2 9BN   *tel* (0225) 873701.

MA in Creative Writing: 1 Fiction, 2 Script and Screen (1yr FT)

Founded by Malcolm Bradbury and taught by him and Rose Tremain, this is the premiere course for aspiring novelists and is geared to 'those who are already writing seriously'. *Contact:* Professor Christopher Bigsby, School of English and American Studies, University of East Anglia, Norwich NR4 7TJ   *tel* (0603) 56161.

MA in Creative Writing (1yr FT   2yr PT)

Open to people already able to produce publishable work, students on this course write a book: a novel, collection of stories or poems, a film/play script. Visits from major authors. *Contact:* Professor David Craig, Bowland College, Lancaster University, Lancaster LA1 4YN   *tel* (0524) 65201 ext 4590.

MA in Creative Writing (1yr FT)

This course examines the crafting techniques of major writers of the novel, short story or poetry, and includes written three-hour examinations on these as well as original writing. *Contact:* Professor Douglas Dunn, School of English, University of St Andrews, Fife KY16 9AL   *tel* (0334) 62666.

MA in Film & Television Scriptwriting (Fiction) (1yr FT Jan.-Dec.)

Designed for those who have already achieved a body of writing, or those with appropriate professional experience. Focuses on original scriptwriting and contextual studies. *Contact:* Ian Macdonald, Head of Northern School of Film and Television, Leeds Metropolitan University, 2-8 Merrion Way, Leeds LS2 8BT   *tel* (0532) 832600.

MA in Novel Writing (1yr FT plus 1yr writing)

This new course is unique in offering a twelve-month taught course, followed by the writing of a novel under tutor supervision during the following year. Taught by published writers. *Contact:* Dr Richard Francis, The Postgraduate Admissions Secretary, Department of American Studies, University of Manchester, Oxford Road, Manchester M13 9PL   *tel* 061-275 3054.

MA in Playwriting Studies (1yr FT)

This course is led by David Edgar and features input from several major playwrights, e.g. Alan Bennett, Charlotte Keatley, as well as theatre directors such as Max Stafford Clark. *Contact:* Dr Brian Crow, Department of Drama and Theatre Arts, The University of Birmingham, Edgbaston B15 2TT   *tel* 021-414 5993.

MA in Screenwriting and Screen Research (2yr PT Jan.-Dec.)

The course prepares students to pursue careers as writers and researchers in film and television via a workshop and portfolio programme. Also useful for script editing. *Contact:* Phil Parker, School of Media, London College of Printing and Distributive Trades, Back Hill, Clerkenwell, London EC1R 5EN   *tel* 071-735 8484.

MA in Teaching & Practice of Creative Writing (1yr FT)

For writers with an interest in teaching Creative Writing as well as teachers interested in creative writing practice. The experienced group of tutors include Anne Cluysenaar. *Contact:* Norman Schwenk, School of English Studies, Journalism & Philosophy, University of Wales College of Cardiff, PO Box 94, Cardiff CF1 3XE *tel* (0222) 874241.

MA in Writing (2yr PT)
A unique flexible-learning scheme which offers students the opportunity to develop their book-length manuscript under the guidance of university tutors and prize-winning writers. *Contact:* Tony Curtis, School of Humanities and Social Sciences, University of Glamorgan, Treforest, Pontypridd, Mid Glamorgan CF37 1DL *tel* (0443) 482551.

MA in Writing (1yr FT)
After general workshops, students can specialise in fiction, scriptwriting, poetry or teaching in the classroom. Taught by working writers including Jane Rogers and Barry Hines. *Contact:* Robert Miles, English Department, Sheffield Hallam University, 32 Collegiate Crescent, Sheffield S10 2BP *tel* (0742) 720911.

MA in Writing Studies (2yr PT)
A course which combines advanced level writers' workshops with closely related courses in critical theory and contemporary writing. *Contact:* Jenny Newman, Edge Hill College of Higher Education, St Helens Road, Ormskirk, Lancs. L39 4QP *tel* (0695) 575171.

Editorial, Literary and Production Services

For a **classified list** of editorial, literary and production services, see page 511.

The following specialists offer a wide variety of services to writers (both new and established), to publishers, journalists and others. Services include advice on MSS, editing and book production, indexing, translation, research and writing.

'A Feature Factory' Editorial Services (incorporating **Academic Projects**), 25 Watlings Court, Upper St Giles, Norwich NR2 1HA   *tel* (0603) 615416/ 765909. *Editors:* Dr Dennis Chaplin, Leigh-Anne Perryman. Produces company magazines/newspapers, brochures, company histories, press releases/ features (including same-day turnaround), advertisement features, promotorials, celebrity ghostwriting, desktop publishing (design, typesetting, layouts, training), typing theses/books, research briefs for press/broadcasting, backgrounders, features, writing and research tuition. New specialist researchers always considered (CVs/sae only).

Abbey Writing Services (1989), Portsmouth Cottage, St Mary Bourne, Andover, Hants SP11 8BP   *tel/fax* (0264) 738556. *Director:* John McIlwain. Comprehensive project management and editorial service. Writing of most non-fiction types: areas of expertise include guidebooks, dictionaries and education.

Academic File (The Centre for Near East Afro-Asia Research) (NEAR) (1985), Acre House, 69-76 Long Acre, London WC2E 9AS   *tel* 081-392 1122   *fax* 081-392 1422. *Director:* Sajid Rizvi. Research, advisory and consultancy services related to politics, economics and societies of the Near and Middle East, Asia and North Africa and related issues in Europe. Risk analysis, editorial assessment, editing and publishing design and production.

Alpha Word Power (1985), 3 Bluecoat Buildings, Claypath, Durham DH1 1RF   *tel* 091-384 7219   *fax* 091-384 3767   *modem* 091-384 3767. Publishing services: camera-ready copy, word processing, text from and/or to disk, desk editing, proof-reading, liaison with printers/binders/graphic design; full secretarial services; business services. Specialise in versatility and speed of turnaround.

Lucia Alvarez de Toledo (1979), 138B Melrose Avenue, London NW2 4JX   *tel* 081-450 5344   *fax* 081-452 9005. Research, interpreting, translation, subtitles, voice overs, proof-reading, editing, copy-writing, into/from English, Spanish, French, Italian.

Anvil Editorial Associates (1966), Lleifior, Malltraeth, Bodorgan, Anglesey, Gwynedd LL62 5AF   *tel/fax* Bodorgan (0407) 840688. *Director:* Dr H. Bernard-Smith. Comprehensive editorial service, including editing, indexing, copy-editing, and proof-reading. Planning, preparation, writing and editing of books, house journals, company histories, reports, brochures, promotional literature, pamphlets, and scripts. Full MS service.

Archaeological Consultants, Lesley and Roy Adkins, Longstone Lodge, Aller, Langport, Somerset TA10 0QT   *tel* (0458) 250075   *fax* (0458) 250858. Work with an archaeological, historical and heritage theme undertaken, including all types of research, critical assessment of MSS, contract writing for publishers, copy-editing, indexing, some illustration, and picture research.

Arioma Editorial Services, Gloucester House, High Street, Borth, Dyfed SY24 5HZ   *tel* (0970) 871 296. *Partners:* Moira Smith, Patrick Smith. Research, co-writing, ghost-writing, dtp, complete book production service. *Specialities:* military aviation history and autobiography.

Aspect (1984), PO Box 43, Thatcham, Newbury, Berks. RG13 4WH   *tel* (0635) 871802   *fax* (0635) 871803. *Proprietor:* Graham Jones. Writing, editing, copy-editing, production of newspapers, magazines and books.

Auteursbureau Greta Baars Jelgersma (1951), Bovensteweg 46, NL-6585 KD Mook, The Netherlands   *tel* 8896-1470/85-635017   *fax* 8896-2439. Specialises in international co-printing of illustrated books; translations from German, English, French and Scandinavian languages.

Authors' Advisory Service (1972), 21 Campden Grove, Kensington, London W8 4JG   *tel* 071-937 5583. All typescripts professionally evaluated in depth and edited by long-established publishers' reader specialising in constructive advice to new writers and with wide experience of current literary requirements. Critic and reader for literary awards. Lecture service on the craft and technique of writing for publication.

Authors in Science Consultancy (1987), Sally Crawford, 112 Great Titchfield Street, London W1P 7AJ   *tel* 071-637 1759. Medical editor, publishers' reader and health writer offers general/technical editing and advice service to writers and publishers, and workshop/tutorial services for authors.

Authors' Research Services (1966), Richard Wright, 32 Oak Village, London NW5 4QN   *tel* 071-284 4316. Offers comprehensive research service to writers, academics and business people world-wide, including fact checking, bibliographical references and document supply. Specialises in English history, social sciences, business.

Ayrshire Business Services (1989), 84 Main Street, Monkton, Ayrshire KA9 2QL   *tel/fax* (0292) 77339. *Owner/manager:* Janet Spufford. Full manuscript service – word processing or desktop publishing; assists new authors with placement of book and liaises with agent/publisher on behalf of author; also tutorial service in Word Perfect 5.1 available for authors new to word processing.

Laraine Bamrah, 61 rue de Parmain, 95430 Butry sur Oise, Auvers sur Oise, France   *tel* (1) 34 73 09 75   *fax* (1) 34 08 81 36. British freelance writer and researcher resident in France's 'Impressionist' valley. Editorial, commercial picture and script research, especially EFL, tourism. Production assistant and liaison for radio, TV and film. Translations from French.

Richard A. Beck (1991), 49 Curzon Avenue, Stanmore, Middlesex HA7 2AL   *tel* 081-427 0480. Editing, proof-reading and indexing, especially scientific and environmental topics. Reduced rates for new authors, senior citizens, the unemployed, etc.

Beswick Writing Services (1988), Francis Beswick, 19 Haig Road, Stretford M32 0DS   *tel* 061-865 1259. Manuscript criticism/advice, editing, research, information books. Special interests: religious, ecology, outdoor activities, philosophical and educational. Expertise in correspondence courses.

Black Ace Book Production (1990), Ellemford Farmhouse, Duns, Berwickshire TD11 3SG   *tel* (0361) 890370   *fax* (0361) 890287. *Directors:* Hunter Steele, Boo Wood. Book production and text processing, including text capture (or scanning), editing, proofing to camera-ready/film, printing and binding, jacket artwork and design.

Book Production Consultants (1973), 25-27 High Street, Chesterton, Cambridge CB4 1ND   *tel* (0223) 352790   *fax* (0223) 460718. *Directors:* A.P. Littlechild, C.S. Walsh. Complete publishing service: editing, designing, illustrating, translating, indexing, artwork; production management of printing and binding; specialised sales and distribution; advertising sales. For books, journals, manuals, reports, magazines, catalogues.

Booksprint (1992; incorporating **Laserbacks,** 1987), Ann Kritzinger Ltd, 20 Shepherds Hill, London N6 5AH   *tel/fax* 081-341 7650. Ann Kritzinger (managing), Kim Spanoghe (technical), Amanda Little (secretary). Fast high-tech production of cost-effective short-run books for self-publishers, from typescript (or disk) to bound copies (hardbacks or paperbacks, sewn or unsewn).

Bookwatch Ltd (1982), 15-up, East Street, Lewin's Yard, Chesham, Bucks. HP5 1HQ   *tel* (0494) 792269   *fax* (0494) 784850. *Directors:* Peter Harland, Jennifer Harland. Market research, bestseller lists, syndicated reviews, features. Publishers of *Books in the Media*, weekly for booksellers and librarians.

Brooke Associates (Manchester) Ltd (1979, incorporated 1987), 21 Barnfield, Urmston, Manchester M41 9EW   *tel* 061-746 8140   *fax* 061-746 8132. Research, editing and contract writing. Specialises in business, management, tourism, history, biography, social science.

Lionel and Janet Browne – Editorial and Publishing Services (1991), 36 Albion Road, Sandhurst, Camberley, Surrey GU17 8BP   *tel* (0252) 877645   *fax* (0252) 890508. Editing, proof-reading, commissioning, technical writing/ rewriting, editorial development, text processing/keying to disk, editorial project management. Specialists in technical, professional and reference work; also religious manuscripts.

Mrs D. Buckmaster (1966), 51 Chatsworth Road, Torquay, Devon TQ1 3BJ   *tel* (0803) 294663. General editing of MSS, specialising in traditional themes in religious, metaphysical and esoteric subjects; also success and inspirational books or articles.

Bucks Literary Services (1983), 73 Vicarage Road, Marsworth, Nr Tring, Herts. HP23 4LU   *tel* Cheddington (0296) 668630. *Partners:* J.L.N. Stobbs, A.M.B. Stobbs. Authors' advisory, editorial and typing service.

John Button (1991), 14 Manor House Way, Brightlingsea, Colchester, Essex CO7 0QN   *tel/fax* (0206) 302769. Copy-editing and proof-reading, specialising in legal, financial, taxation, business education and corporate identity publications; Legal Reference Library series.

Cambridge Language Services Ltd (Book Machine) (1982), 64 Baldock Street, Ware, Herts. SG12 9DT   *tel/fax* (0920) 465890. *Director:* Paul Procter BA. Originator of a word-processing and page-make-up system (the **Book Machine**) specifically designed for the author, publisher's editor and designer, and the typesetter, running on standard IBM compatible microcomputers.

Causeway Resources (1989), 8 The Causeway, Teddington, Middlesex TW11 0HE   *tel/fax* 081-977 8797. *Director:* Keith Skinner. Genealogical, biographical and historical research, specialising in police history and true crime research.

Central Office of Information, Hercules Road, London SE1 7DU   *tel* 071-928 2345. The Government executive agency which provides publicity and information services to government departments, other executive agencies and public sector bodies. Commissions feature articles on British affairs for publication in overseas newspapers, magazines and trade press. Commissions photography, illustrations, artwork and design as well as translations into more than 30 foreign languages. In-house Copy Editorial Unit supplies copy editing and a proof-reading service.

Vanessa Charles (1975), 38 Ham Common, Richmond, Surrey TW10 7JG *tel/ fax* 081-940 9225. Design and book production services.

Karyn Claridge Book Production (1989), 244 Bromham Road, Biddenham, Bedford MK40 4AA *tel* (0234) 347909. Complete book production management service offered to publishers from MS to bound copies; graphic services also available.

Ingrid Cranfield (1972), 16 Myddelton Gardens, Winchmore Hill, London N21 2PA *tel* 081-360 2433/081-836 6633 ext 2573. Advisory and editorial services for authors and media, including critical assessment, rewriting, proof-reading, copy-editing, writing of marketing copy, indexing, research, interviews and transcripts. Special interests: geography, travel, exploration, adventure (own archives), language, education, youth training. Translations from German and French.

Creative Comics, Denis Gifford, 80 Silverdale, Sydenham, London SE26 4SJ *tel* 081-699 7725. Specialises in strip cartoons and comics for both adults and children, custom-tailored to clients' requirements. Everything from jokes, puzzles, and single strips to serials and complete comics, books, supplements and giveaways.

David A. Cross, West Wing, Isel Hall, Cockermouth, Cumbria CA13 0QG *tel* 0900-827555. Research and information service; editing texts, specialising in art history, English literature, biography and genealogy; creative writing tutorials; lectures on artists and writers of the Lake District.

Margaret Crush (1980), Moonfleet, Burney Road, West Humble, Dorking, Surrey RH5 6AU *tel* (0306) 884347. Editing, copy-editing, writing, rewriting and proof-reading for publishers, especially illustrated books.

D & N Publishing (1991), The Stable Block, Crowood Lane, Ramsbury, Marlborough, Wilts. SN8 2HR *tel* (0672) 21211 *fax* (0672) 21322. *Partners:* David and Namrita Price-Goodfellow. Complete project management including commissioning, editing, picture research, illustration and design, page layout and indexing. All stages managed in-house and produced on Apple Macintoshes running QuarkXPress and Freehand.

Meg and Stephen Davies, 31 Egerton Road, Ashton, Preston, Lancs. PR2 1AJ *tel* (0772) 725120 *fax* (0772) 723853. Indexing to general and postgraduate level in the arts and humanities. Can offer indexes on PC disk. Also proof-reading and copy-editing. Registered indexer with Society of Indexers since 1971; founder member of Society of Freelance Editors and Proofreaders.

DD Editorial Services (1983), Gosford House, Gosford Road, Beccles, Suffolk NR34 9QX *tel* (0502) 717735. *Partners:* D. Derbyshire, J. Nicholls. Proofreading, copy-editing, indexing, index repagination, compilation of diaries.

DOLPHIN ECS (1987), 38 Gyles Park, Stanmore, Middlesex HA7 1AW *tel* 081-952 8329 *fax* 081-952 5075. *Directors:* Ray and Yael Dennerstein. Translation, editing and typesetting services to publishing, commerce, industry and government.

Rosemary Dooley (1973), Crag House, Witherslack, Grange-over-Sands, Cumbria LA11 6RW *tel* (05395) 52286 *fax* (05395) 52013. Editorial advice, editing, copy-editing, specialising in books about music.

Dr Andrew Duncan (1986), 19 Rainham Road, London NW10 5DL   *tel/fax* 081-969 8332. Professional researcher working in historical and contemporary sources.

EditHelp (1993), 5 Wells Mount, Upper Cumberworth, Huddersfield HD8 8XQ   *tel/fax* (0484) 604749. *Principal:* Wendy Adamson. Indexing, copy writing, proof-reading, copy-editing, original research for journals/magazines.

Editorial/Visual Research (1973), Angela Murphy, 21 Leamington Road Villas, London W11 1HS   *tel* 071-727 4920   *fax* 071-221 1429. Comprehensive research service including historical, literary, film and picture research for writers, publishers, film and television companies. Services also include copy-writing, editing, and travel and feature writing.

Dr Martin Edwards (1985), 2 Highbury Hall, 22 Highbury Road, Weston-super-Mare, Avon BS23 2DN   *tel* (0934) 621261. Specialist editorial and research service in the medico-scientific field: including copy-editing, co-editorial/-authorship, proof-reading, abstracting and conference productions. Special interest in the improvement of foreign texts.

Lewis Esson Publishing (1989), 27 Elgin Crescent, London W11 2JD   *tel* 071-727-4248   *fax* 071-792 2894. Project management of illustrated books in areas of food, art and interior design; editing and writing of food books.

etr (Edward Twentyman Resources) (1992), 4 Little Green, Cheveley, Nr New-market, Suffolk CB8 9RG   *tel* (0638) 731332   *fax* (0638) 731152. *Proprietor:* Edward Twentyman. Employment agency specialising solely in freelance people in publishing.

First Edition Translations Ltd (1981), 6 Wellington Court, Wellington Street, Cambridge CB1 1HZ   *tel* (0223) 356733   *fax* (0223) 321488. *Directors:* Judy Boothroyd, Sarah Walsh. Translation, editing, proof-reading, indexing, dtp; books, manuals, reports, journals and promotional material. Also interpreting.

James Wilson Flegg (1970), via Paolini 11, 10138 Turin, Italy   *tel* (011) 4331192. Language consultant; writing, ghosting, copy-editing, translation, abstracting; projects and commissions undertaken.

Brian J. Ford, Rothay House, 6 Mayfield Road, Eastrea, Cambs. PE7 2AY   *tel/ fax* (0733) 350888. Scientist and adviser on scientific matters; author, producer/ director scientific films and programmes in addition to editor/contributor to many leading books and journals. Has hosted many leading BBC television and radio programmes, and overseas documentaries.

Freelance Editorial Services (1975), Bill Houston BSc, DipLib, MPhil, 45 Bridge Street, Musselburgh, Midlothian EH21 6AA   *tel* 031-665 7825. Editing, proof-reading, indexing, abstracting, translations, bibliographies; particularly scientific and medical.

Freelance Press Services (1967), Cumberland House, Lissadel Street, Salford M6 6GG   *tel* 061-745 8850   *fax* 061-745 8865. Market Research Department for the freelance writer and photographer issues a monthly Market News service the *Freelance Market News*; £24.50 p.a. A good rate of pay made for news of editorial requirements (small amounts are credited until a worthwhile payment is reached). Agents for the UK for the books of the American Writer Inc. and Writer's Digest Books, including *The Writer's Handbook*; also the American *Writer's Market*. Writers' market guides for Canada and Australia.

Geo Group & Associates, 4 Christian Fields, London SW16 3JZ   *tel/fax* 081-764 6292. Visual aid production services: slide packs; filmstrips; colour to monochrome processing; packaging. Photo library. Commission photography (including aerial photography). Specialist work for educational publishing. Audio tape production.

C.N. Gilmore (1987), 6c St Michael's Road, Bedford MK40 2LT   *tel* (0234) 346142. Sub-editing, copy-editing, slush-pile reading, reviewing. Will also collaborate. Undertakes work in all scholarly and academic fields as well as fiction and practical writing.

Global Syndications (1988), Chartwood Towers, Punchbowl Lane, Dorking, Surrey RH5 4ED   *tel* (0306) 741213   *fax* (0306) 875347. *Managing director:* Sam Hall. Research, editing, design, layout, proof-reading and print liaison; picture research and photo library – also preparation of artwork; will compile magazines, books, etc. from start to finish; brochures, newsletters and annual reports a speciality.

Grahame & Grahame Editorial (1989), 18 Chichester Place, Brighton, East Sussex BN2 1FF   *tel* (0273) 699533   *fax* (0273) 621262. *Directors:* Tony and Anita Grahame. Copy-editing; complete book production service, specialising in complicated table, figure and equation work; consultancy on all aspects of non-fiction publishing.

Guildford Reading Services (1978), 31 Southway, Guildford, Surrey GU2 6DA   *tel* (0483) 504325/(0252) 317950. *Director:* B.V. Varney. Proof-reading, press revision, copy preparation, sub-editing.

Bernard Hawton, 137 Park Road, Chandler's Ford, Hants SO5 1HT   *tel* (0703) 267400. Proof-reading, copy-editing.

Heath Associates (1988), Garden Flat, 15 South Hill Park Gardens, London NW3 2TD   *tel/fax* 071-435 4059. *Proprietor:* Richard Williams. Consultancy on desktop publishing, word processing and graphics programs for IBM PC; design and illustration specialising in academic and technical works; writing and editing for computing and related topics.

Antony Hemans (1981), Maranatha, 1 Nettles Terrace, Guildford, Surrey GU1 4PA   *tel* (0483) 574511. Biographical and historical research, specialising in industrial archaeology – railways, canals, shipping, etc.

Historica Consultancy (1986), 8-9 The Incline, Coalport, Telford, Shropshire TF8 7HR   *tel* (0952) 680050   *fax* (0952) 587184. Consultants for drama, documentary and fiction, specialising in European history and culture.

Robert Holland-Ford Associates, 103 Lydyett Lane, Barnton, Northwich, Cheshire CW8 4JT   *tel* (0606) 76960. *Director:* Robert Holland-Ford. Impresarios, concert/lecture agents.

Rosemary Horstmann, 34 Leicester Street, Leamington Spa CV32 4TE   *tel* (0926) 883689. Broadcasting scripts evaluated; general consultancy on editorial and marketing matters; tuition in interviewing and tape-recording, lectures, writing workshops. Send sae for brochure.

Howard Seddon Associates (1988), BM Box 1129, London WC1N 3XX   *tel/fax* (0923) 229784. *Partners:* Dr Keith Seddon, Sarah Howard. Copy-editing, proof-reading, blurb copy, ghost writing, copy-writing, indexing; reading and appraisal services for authors; report services for publishers.

E.J. Hunter, 6 Dorset Road, London N22 4SL   *tel* 081-889 0370. Editing, copy-editing, proof-reading; appraisal of MSS. Special interests: novels, short stories, drama, children's stories; primary education, alternative medicine, New Age.

Hurst Village Publishing (1989), Henry and Elizabeth Farrar, High Chimneys, Davis Street, Hurst, Reading RG10 0TH   *tel* (0734) 345211   *fax* (0734)

320348. Offers design, photography, typesetting, printing and binding services, using the latest desktop publishing programs, photographic equipment and high resolution colour and laser printers.

Society of Indexers, 38 Rochester Road, London NW1 9JJ   *tel* 071-916 7809 (see pages 514 and 627 for further details).

Indexing Specialists (1965), 202 Church Road, Hove, East Sussex BN3 2DJ   *tel/fax* (0273) 323309. *Director:* Richard Raper BSc, DTA. Indexes for books, journals and reference publications on professional, scientific and general subjects; copy-editing, proof-reading services; consultancy on indexing and training projects.

The Information Bureau (formerly **Daily Telegraph Information Bureau**), 51 The Business Centre, 103 Lavender Hill, London SW11 5QL   *tel* 071-924 4414   *fax* 071-924 4456. *Contacts:* Jane Hall, Emma Morfey. Offers an on-demand research service on a variety of subjects including current affairs, business, marketing, history, the arts, media and politics. Resources include range of cuttings amassed by the bureau since 1948.

Ken Jackson (1985), 30 The Boundary, Langton Green, Tunbridge Wells, Kent TN3 0YB   *tel* (0892) 545198. Copy-editing, proof-reading, indexing, particularly of technical, historical or religious MSS.

Hugh Lamb (1983), 10 The Crescent, Westmead Road, Sutton, Surrey SM1 4HU   *tel* 081-661 1936. Experienced journalist, proof-reader and anthologist offers proof-reading for publishers and typesetters; experienced in book, magazine and institution work.

Leeds Postcards (Northern Trading Co-operative Ltd) (1979), PO Box 84, Leeds, West Yorkshire LS1 4HT   *tel* (0532) 468649   *fax* (0532) 436730. *Directors:* Richard Honey, Christine Hankinson, Alison Sheldon, Stephen Edwards, Dinah Clark. Publishing, printing and distribution service for artists, campaigns and unions, specialising in postcards and greeting cards.

Library Research Agency (1974), Burberry, Devon Road, Salcombe, Devon TQ8 8HJ   *tel* (0548 84) 2769. *Directors:* D.J. Langford MA, B. Langford. Research and information service for writers, journalists, artists, businessmen from libraries, archives, museums, record offices and newspapers in UK, USA and Europe. Sources may be in English, French, German, Russian, Serbo-Croat, Bulgarian, and translations made if required.

Miles Litvinoff (1984), 104 Doyle Gardens, London NW10 3SR   *tel* 081-965 3427   *fax* 081-969 3550. Writer on environment, development and history. Editing, commissioning, co-authorship, rewriting, editorial advice; especially environment, Third World, human rights, history and biography, social science, current affairs, popular science and natural history, education.

London Media Workshops (1978), 101 King's Drive, Gravesend, Kent DA12 5BQ   *tel* (0474) 564676. *Booking secretary:* Linda Forbes. Short courses run in central London by top working professionals in writing for radio, television, video and the press. Plus mail order bookshop and mobile workshop service.

Leonie Luzak Ltd (1989), 22B Aldebert Terrace, London SW8 1BJ   *tel* 071-820 9548   *fax* 071-735 8194. *Directors:* Leonie Luzak (secretarial services), Catherine Batt (editorial services). Advice on MSS, editing services, literary research, complete word processing and presentation services.

Kenneth Lysons MA, MEd, DPA, DMS, FCIS, FInstPS, FBIM (1986), Lathom, Scotchbarn Lane, Whiston, Nr Prescot, Merseyside L35 7JB   *tel* 051-426 5513. Company and institutional histories, support material for organisational management and supervisory training, house journals, research and reports service. Full secretarial support.

Duncan McAra (1988), 30 Craighall Crescent, Edinburgh EH6 4RZ *tel* 031-552 1558. Consultancy on all aspects of general trade publishing; editing; proof correction. Main subjects include art, architecture, archaeology, biography, film, military and travel.

McText (1986), Denmill, Tough, By Alford, Aberdeenshire AB33 8EP *tel/fax* (09755) 62582. *Partners:* K. and Duncan McArdle. Editing, copy-editing, proof-reading. Specialist interests: archaeology, equestrian.

Manuscript Appraisals (1984), 95 Bramble Road, Eastwood, Leigh-on-Sea, Essex SS9 5HA *tel* (0437) 563822. *Proprietor:* Raymond J. Price; *consultants:* N.L. Price MBIM, Mary Hunt. Independent appraisal of authors' MSS (fiction and non-fiction, but no poetry) with full editorial guidance and advice. In-house editing, copy-editing, rewriting and proof-reading if required. Interested in the work of new writers.

Marlinoak (1984), 22 Eve's Croft, Birmingham B32 3QL *tel/fax* 021-475 6139. *Proprietors:* Alan L. Billing MIM, Hazel J. Billing JP. BA. DipEd. Preparation of scripts, plays, books, MSS service, ghostwriting, proof reading, research; also audio-transcription, word processing and full secretarial facilities.

M.C. Martinez (1988), 60 Oakwood Avenue, Southgate, London N14 6QL *tel* 081-886 5829. *Partners:* Mary Martinez, Françoise Budd. Advice and evaluation of MSS; critical assessment of MSS specialising in fiction and children's books; full desktop publishing service using VENTURA; translation in French and Spanish.

James Moore Associates (1975), 51 Firs Chase, West Mersea, Essex CO5 8NN *tel* (0206) 382073 *fax* (0206) 382326. *Partners:* James Moore BCom, Inge Moore. Editorial and rewriting of MSS, picture research, organises artwork and photography, proof-reading, translation from/into German, from French. Special subjects: educational (especially language courses), music, travel, sailing, ships and the sea.

Susan Moore Editorial Services (1994), 65 Albion Road, London N16 9PP *tel/ fax* 071-923 2480. Troubleshooting service for publishers, packagers and agents: co-authorship with specialists, ghostwriting, re-writing, translation fine tuning, re-drafting.

Morley Adams (1917), 20 Spectrum House, 32/34 Gordon House Road, London NW5 1LP *tel* 071-284 1433 *fax* 071-284 4494. *Editor:* Mike Hutchinson. Specialists in the production of crosswords and other puzzles, quizzes, etc.

Elizabeth Murray (1975), 3 Gower Mews Mansions, Gower Mews, London WC1E 6HR *tel/fax* 071-636 3761. Literary, biographical, historical, crime, military, cinema, genealogy research for authors, journalists, radio and television from UK, European and USA sources.

Paul H. Niekirk (1976), 40 Rectory Avenue, High Wycombe, Bucks. HP13 6HW *tel* (0494) 527200. Text editing for works of reference and professional and management publications, particularly texts on law; freelance writing; editorial consultancy and training; marketing consultancy and research.

Northern Writers Advisory Services (1986), 77 Marford Crescent, Sale, Cheshire M33 4DN *tel* 061-969 1573. *Proprietor:* Jill Groves. Offers word processing, copy-editing, proof-reading and desktop publishing to small publishers, societies and authors.

Northgate Training (1978), Scarborough House, 29 James Street West, Bath BA1 2BT *tel* (0225) 339733 *fax* (0225) 429151. *Directors:* M.R. Lynch,

J.M. Bayley. Writing and design of management games and training exercises. Specialists in distance and open learning training packages.

Oriental Languages Bureau, Lakshmi Building, Sir P. Mehta Road, Fort, Bombay 400001, India *tel* 2661258/2665640/2664598 *telegraphic address* Orientclip. *Proprietor:* Rajan K. Shah. Undertakes translations and printing in all Indian languages and a few foreign languages.

Ormrod Research Services (1982), Weeping Birch, Burwash, East Sussex TN19 7HG *tel* (0435) 882541. Comprehensive research service; literary, historical, academic, biographical, commercial. Critical reading with report, editing, indexing, proof-reading, ghosting.

Oxprint (1974), Aristotle House, Aristotle Lane, Oxford OX2 6TR *tel* (0865) 512331 *fax* (0865) 512408. *Directors:* Per Saugman, John Webb (managing), Peter Lawrence BA(Hons), Andrew King (company secretary). Design, typesetting, editorial, illustrating scientific, educational and general books. Specialists in project management. Macintosh desktop and bureau facilities, computer aided design and illustration.

Pageant Publishing (1978), 5 Turners Wood, London NW11 6TD *tel* 081-455 3703 *fax* 081-209 0726. *Director:* Gillian Page. Consultancy on all aspects of academic publishing: publication of academic journals.

Geoffrey D. Palmer (1987), 47 Burton Fields Road, Stamford Bridge, York YO4 1JJ *tel/fax* (0759) 372874. Editorial and production services, including STM and general copy-editing, artwork editing, proof-reading and indexing. Prepress project management.

Christopher Pick, 41 Chestnut Road, London SE27 9EZ *tel* 081-761 2585 *fax* 081-761 6388. Publishing consultancy advice, project management, writing and editing for companies and commercial and voluntary organisations including training manuals, strategy documents, company histories. Author and editor of non-fiction books and articles for all popular markets. Special interests: modern social and political history, travel, heritage and current affairs. Non-fiction title and series planning and development projects undertaken; rewriting, but only for publishers on already contracted MSS. Production and design services if required.

Picture Research Agency, Pat Hodgson, Jasmine Cottage, Spring Grove Road, Richmond, Surrey TW10 6EH *tel* 081-940 5986. Illustrations found for books, films and television. Written research also undertaken particularly on historical subjects, including photographic and film history. Small picture library.

Reginald Piggott (1962), Decoy Lodge, Decoy Road, Potter Heigham, Norfolk NR29 5LX *tel* (0692) 670384. Cartographer to the University Presses and academic publishers in Britain and overseas. Maps and diagrams for academic and educational books.

Keith Povey Editorial Services (1980), North Burrow, Bratton Clovelly, Okehampton, Devon EX20 4JJ *tel* (083 787) 296 *fax* (083 787) 369. Copyediting, indexing, proof-reading, publisher/author liaison. Partnership with T & A Typesetting Services, Unit 13, Rochdale Enterprise Generation Centre, Dane Street, Rochdale, Lancs. OL12 6XB *tel* (0706) 861662 *fax* (0706) 861673. Specialist book-typesetting to CRC and negs, graphic design.

Leigh Priest (1987), 32 Elphinstone Road, Hastings, East Sussex TN34 2EQ *tel* (0424) 720457 *fax* (0424) 719739. Accredited indexer: biography/memoirs, English literature, fashion and dressmaking, government, health and medical (layman), history, North American studies, philosophy, politics, photography, social sciences, travel (UK, USA).

Victoria Ramsay (1981), Abbots Rest, Chilbolton, Stockbridge, Hants SO20 6BE   *tel* (0264) 860251. Freelance editing, copy-editing and proof-reading; non-fiction research and writing of promotional literature and pamphlets. Any non-scientific subject undertaken. Special interests include education, cookery, travel, African and Caribbean works and works in translation.

Reading and Righting (Robert Lambolle Services) (1987), 618B Finchley Road, London NW11 7RR   *tel* 081-455 4564   *fax* 071-431 7636. MSS and script evaluation service: fiction, non-fiction, stage plays and screenplays; editorial services; one-to-one tutorials, creative writing courses, lectures; and research.

S. Ribeiro Editorial and Literary Services (1986), 42 West Heath Court, North End Road, London NW11 7RG   *tel* 081-458 9082. Editor and creative writing tutor offers detailed analysis and critical review, rewriting and editing, of unpublished MSS including advice on presentation and preparation for submission to publishers. New writers are welcome, but please write or telephone with your initial enquiry. Special interests and experience include: novels and short-stories, autobiography, travel and academic articles, newsletters and journals.

Rich Research (1978), 1 Bradby House, Carlton Hill, St John's Wood, London NW8 9XE   *tel* 071-624 7755. *Director:* Diane Rich. Speedy and innovative picture research service. Visuals found for all sectors of publishing and the media. Stock images, commissioned photography and artwork. Negotiation of rights and fees.

Anton Rippon Press Services, 20 Chain Lane, Mickleover, Derby DE3 5AJ   *tel* (0332) 512379/384235   *fax* (0332) 292755. Writer and researcher on historical, sociological and sporting topics. Features, programmes, brochures produced; ghost writing.

Vernon Robinson Editorial Services (1973), 114 Blinco Grove, Cambridge CB1 4TT   *tel* (0223) 244414. Copy-editing and proof-reading of all educational books, specialising in science, maths, engineering, economics, computer science, biology, etc. Also English correction of technical MSS translated into English for European publishers.

Roger Smithells Ltd, Editorial Services, Garth Cottage, 26 High Street, Buriton, Petersfield, Hants GU31 5RX   *tel* (0730) 262369   *fax* (0730) 260722. Journalistic specialists in everything relating to travel and holidays; newspaper and magazine articles; TV and radio scripts; compilers of travel books.

Sandton Literary Agency (1972), PO Box 785799, Sandton 2146, South Africa   *tel* (011) 4428624. *Directors:* J. Victoria Canning, M. Sutherland. Lecture agents.

Sarratt Information Services (1986), 68 St Andrews Road, Henley-on-Thames, Oxon RG9 1JE   *tel* 081-422 4384. *Directors:* D.M. Brandl MIInfSci, G.H. Kay BSc, CEng, MIChemE, MBCS. Research bibliographies compiled, references checked, indexes compiled. Specialists in bioengineering, bio materials and disability information research.

Science Unit, Rothay House, 6 Mayfield Road, Eastrea, Cambs. PE7 2AY   *tel/fax* (0733) 350888. Independent scientific consultancy specialising in microscopical matters and new directions in science. Advises on programmes and publications in general scientific field. Activities are world-wide, with publications in many overseas and foreign-language editions.

Scriptmate (1985), 20 Shepherd's Hill, London N6 5AH   *tel/fax* 081-341 7650. Ann Kritzinger. Reports and revision suggestions given on unpublished work in the fields of fiction, non-fiction and drama by freelance team of 46 specialist readers.

Mrs Ellen Seager, 3 Hereford Court, Hereford Road, Harrogate, North Yorkshire HG1 2PX   *tel* (0423) 509770. Critical assessment of fiction and non-fiction work with helpful direction, tuition and advice; creative writing tutor; ghost writing; publishing and market information.

SeaStar Editorial Services, 17 Hillcrest Avenue, Kettering, Northants NN15 7NG   *tel* (0536) 414949. *Proprietor:* Terry Scott. MSS revision and rewriting; compilation, keying-in for floppy disk, disk conversion; desktop publishing services; setting for printer.

Joan Shannon – Freelance Services (1991), 41A Newal Road, Ballymoney, Co. Antrim, Northern Ireland BT53 6HB   *tel* (02656) 62953   *fax* (02656) 65019. Writing, photography and desktop design, specialising in disability and geographical/historical subjects, including transport, tourism, etc., particularly in a Northern Ireland context. Full or part book production service and word processing.

Christine Shuttleworth (1981), Flat 1, 25 St Stephen's Avenue, London W12 8JB   *tel* 081-749 8797. Indexing (with MACREX program), copy-editing, proof-reading, non-technical translation from German. Registered Indexer and Council member, Society of Indexers; member, Society of Freelance Editors and Proofreaders, Translators' Association.

Small Print (1986), The Old School House, 74 High Street, Swavesey, Cambridge CB4 5QU   *tel* (0954) 231713   *fax* (0954) 232777. *Proprietor:* Naomi Laredo. Editorial, production and audio production services, specialising in ELT and foreign language courses for secondary schools and home study; also phrase books, travel guides, general humanities. Translation from/to and editing in many European and Asian languages.

Robert and Jane Songhurst (1976), 3 Yew Tree Cottages, Grange Lane, Sandling, Nr Maidstone, Kent ME14 3BY   *tel* Maidstone (0622) 757635. Literary consultants, authors' works advised upon (fees by agreement), literary and historical research, feature writing, reviewing, editing.

Mrs Gene M. Spencer (1970), 63 Castle Street, Melbourne, Derbyshire DE73 1DY   *tel* (0332) 862133. Editing, copy-editing and proof-reading; feature writing; theatrical profiles; book reviews; freelance writing.

Strand Editorial Services (1974), 16 Mitchley View, South Croydon, Surrey CR2 9HQ   *tel/fax* 081-657 1247. *Joint principals:* Derek and Irene Bradley. Provides a comprehensive service to publishers, editorial departments, and public relations and advertising agencies.

Streetwise Town Plans Ltd, 3 Rayleigh Road, Basingstoke, Hants. RG21 1TJ   *tel* (0256) 28186. *Contacts:* P.J. Corcoran, Rosemary Corcoran. Top quality computer-generated maps of almost every town in Europe, plus major towns and cities throughout the world. All maps personalised to order.

Tamar Literary Services (1988), 18 Barton Close, Landrake, Saltash, Cornwall PL12 5BA   *tel* (0752) 851451. Dr Brian Gee. Proof-reading; general and specialist editing in science, technology and the history of science; editing on disc (MS WORD/SPELLCHECK).

Hans Tasiemka Archives (1950), 80 Temple Fortune Lane, London NW11 7TU   *tel* 081-455 2485   *fax* 081-455 0231. *Proprietor:* Mrs Edda Tasiemka. Comprehensive newspaper cuttings library from 1850s to the present day on all subjects for writers, publishers, picture researchers, film and TV companies.

Lyn M. Taylor, 1 Eglinton Crescent, Edinburgh EH12 5DH   *tel* 031-225 6152. Comprehensive editorial service: copy-editing and proof-reading in all subjects. Specialises in scientific and medical.

Teamwork (1973), Unit 5, Spurlings Yard, Spurlings Road, Fareham PO17 6AB   *tel* (0329) 829135   *fax* (0329) 829136. *Proprietors:* Mrs D. Emmerson, N. Emmerson. Typesetting, paste-up, camera-ready artwork, design and preparation of books to print stage, illustration, proof-reading, indexing, general editing and research services.

Tecmedia Ltd (1972), Unit 4, The Courtyard, Whitwick Business Park, Stenson Road, Coalville LE67 4JP   *tel* (0530) 815800   *fax* (0530) 813452. *Managing director:* J.D. Baxter. Specialists in the design, development and production of mixed media training and information packages, newsletters and brochures.

Teral Research Services (1980), Alan C. Wood, 111 The Avenue, Bournemouth, Dorset BN9 2UX   *tel* (0202) 519220 and Terry C. Treadwell, 45 Forest View Road, Bournemouth, Dorset BH9 3BN   *tel/fax* (0202) 516834. Research and consultancy on military aviation, army, navy, defence, space, weapons (new and antique), police, intelligence, medals, uniforms and armour.

Hilary Thomas (1974), 27 Grasvenor Avenue, Barnet, Herts. EN5 2BY   *tel* 081-440 5662. Genealogical, literary and historical research.

3 & 5 Promotion (1985), Crag House, Witherslack, Grange-over-Sands, Cumbria LA11 6RW   *tel* (05395) 52286   *fax* (05395) 52013. *Proprietor:* Rosemary Dooley. Publicity services for publishers, specialising in music, health care, travel, including collaborative publishers' exhibitions.

Carolina Tucker BA, ALA (1986), Ford Cottage, Lymore Valley, Milford-on-Sea, Nr Lymington, Hants SO41 0TW   *tel* (0202) 472380, (0590) 642441 (evening). MSS reading and evaluation for publishers; advisory and editorial service for authors; re-typing of MSS if required; research and writing of travel brochures (UK).

John Vickers, 27 Shorrolds Road, London SW6 7TR   *tel* 071-385 5774. Archives of British Theatre photographs by John Vickers, from 1938-1974.

Gordon R. Wainwright, 22 Hawes Court, Sunderland SR6 8NU   *tel* 091-548 9342. Criticism, advice, revision and all other editorial work for publishers, especially those concerned with educational and how-to books. Articles on education and training matters supplied to newspapers, journals and magazines. Training in report writing, rapid reading, effective meetings, etc. Lecture service. Consultancy service in all aspects of communication. Travel writing assignments undertaken.

Caroline White (1985), 78 Howard Road, Walthamstow, London E17 4SQ   *tel/ fax* 081-521 5791. Project management of illustrated books, particularly medicine, natural history, travel. Research and writing of features for newspapers, magazines and radio, specialising in health and social issues. Corporate literature and reports. Written and spoken Italian, Spanish and French.

David Winpenny (1991), 17 Newlands Drive, York YO2 5PQ   *tel/fax* (0904) 784616. Writer and editor, including research and writing of features, news stories, brochures, speeches, advertising copy. Special interest in architectural history, the arts, music, landscape, heritage, business and the North.

Rita Winter, Translation and Editorial Services (1988), 'Kilrubie', Eddleston, Peeblesshire, Scotland EH45 8QS   *tel* (0721) 730353. Copy-editing and proof-reading (English and Dutch). Subjects: current affairs, sociology, philosophy, law, economics, education, theology, history, classics, African and European studies, general non-fiction. Special interests: reference works, dictionaries and academic material.

Working Press (1987), 85 St Agnes Place, Kennington, London SE11 4BB   *tel* 071-735 6221   *fax* 071-582 7021. *Directors:* Stefan Szczelkun, Graham Harwood, Mathew Fuller. Research, consultancy, training, educational workshops.

Richard M. Wright (1977), 32 Oak Village, London NW5 4QN   *tel* 071-284 4316. Indexing, copy-editing, specialising in politics, history, business, social sciences.

Write Line Critical Service (1988), 130 Morton Way, Southgate, London N14 7AL   *tel* 081-886 1329. Criticism and assessment of poetry and fiction (including short stories). Suggestions for revision/development of work, advice about publication outlets. Special interest: poetry. Enquiries by phone or write. Sae essential.

Write on. . . (1989), Yvonne Newman, 62 Kiln Lane, Headington, Oxford OX3 8EY   *tel* (0865) 61169   *fax* (0865) 69216. Specialists in writing, designing and publishing open learning materials; general writing and editing assignments; workshops and training courses in business communication.

Writerlink Ltd (1984), Bolsover House, 5 Clipstone Street, London W1P 7EB   *tel* 071-323 4323   *fax* 071-323 0286. *Directors:* Charles Dawes, John Hare, John Bennett, Sally Cartwright. Expert individual reports made and issued to authors by a team of readers widely experienced in publishing.

The Writers' Exchange (1977), 14 Yewdale, Clifton Green, Swinton, Manchester M27 2GN   *tel* 061-793 4606. *Directors:* Peter Collins, John Michael Wright. Reading and appraisal service for writers preparing to submit material to, or having had material rejected by, literary agents and/or publishers. We offer a constructive, objective evaluation service, particularly for those who cannot get past the standard rejection slip barrier or who have had an MS rejected by publishers and need an impartial view on why it did not sell. Novels, short stories, film and TV, radio and stage plays; sae for details.

Hans Zell, Publishing Consultant (1987), 11 Richmond Road, PO Box 56, Oxford OX1 2SJ   *tel* (0865) 511428   *fax* (0865) 311534. Consultancies, project evaluations, market assessments, feasibility studies, research and surveys, funding proposals, freelance editorial work, commissioning, journals management, exhibition services. Specialises in services to publishers and the book community in Third World countries and provides specific expertise in these areas.

Classified Index of Editorial, Literary and Production Services

Addresses for editorial, literary and production services start on page 498.

Complete Editorial, Literary and Book Production Services

'A Feature Factory' Editorial Services
Academic File
Book Production Consultants
Central Office of Information
Karyn Claridge Book Production

D & N Publishing
Global Syndications
Grahame & Grahame
Northern Writers Advisory Services

Oxprint
Christopher Pick
Keith Povey Editorial Services
Small Print
Teamwork

Advisory and Consultancy Services, Critical Assessments, Reports

Archaeological Consultants
Authors' Advisory Service
Authors in Science Consultancy
Ayrshire Business Services
Beswick Writing Services
Bookwatch Ltd
Bucks Literary Services
Ingrid Cranfield
Lewis Esson Publishing
James Wilson Flegg
C.N. Gilmore
Heath Associates
Historica Consultancy
Rosemary Horstmann
Howard Seddon Associates

E.J. Hunter
Indexing Specialists
Miles Litvinoff
Leonie Luzak Ltd
Duncan McAra
Manuscript Appraisals
M.C. Martinez
Susan Moore Editorial Services
Paul H. Niekirk
Pageant Publishing
Christopher Pick
Reading and Righting
S. Ribeiro Editorial and Literary Services
Science Unit

Scriptmate
Mrs Ellen Seager
Robert and Jane Songhurst
Teral Research Services
Carolina Tucker
Gordon R. Wainwright
Caroline White
Joan Wilkins Associates
Rita Winter, Translation and Editorial Services
Working Press
Write Line Critical Service
Writerlink Ltd
The Writers' Exchange
Hans Zell, Publishing Consultant

Editing, Copy-editing, Proof-reading

Abbey Writing Services
Alpha Word Power
Lucia Alvarez de Toledo
Anvil Editorial Associates
Aspect
Authors' Advisory Service
Authors in Science Consultancy
Richard A. Beck
Beswick Writing Services
Black Ace Book Production
Brooke Associates (Manchester) Ltd
Lionel and Janet Browne
Mrs D. Buckmaster
Bucks Literary Services
John Button
Ingrid Cranfield
David A. Cross
Margaret Crush
Meg and Stephen Davies
DD Editorial Services
DOLPHIN ECS
Rosemary Dooley
EditHelp

Editorial/Visual Research
Dr Martin Edwards
Lewis Esson Publishing
First Edition Translations Ltd
James Wilson Flegg
Freelance Editorial Services
C.N. Gilmore
Guildford Reading Services
Bernard Hawton
Heath Associates
Howard Seddon Associates
E.J. Hunter
Indexing Specialists
Ken Jackson
Hugh Lamb
Miles Litvinoff
Leonie Luzak Ltd
Duncan McAra
McText
Manuscript Appraisals
Marlinoak
James Moore Associates
Paul H. Niekirk
Geoffrey D. Palmer

Christopher Pick
Victoria Ramsay
Reading and Righting
S. Ribeiro Editorial and Literary Services
Vernon Robinson Editorial Services
Joan Shannon
Christine Shuttleworth
Roger Smithells Ltd, Editorial Services
Robert and Jane Songhurst
Mrs Gene M. Spencer
Strand Editorial Services
Tamar Literary Services
Lyn M. Taylor
Gordon R. Wainwright
Caroline White
David Winpenny
Rita Winter, Translation and Editorial Services
Richard M. Wright
Hans Zell, Publishing Consultant

Design, Typing, Word Processing, DTP, Book Production

'A Feature Factory' Editorial Services
Alpha Word Power
Arioma Editorial Services
Aspect
Auteursbureau
Ayrshire Business Services
Black Ace Book Production
Booksprint

Lionel and Janet Browne
Bucks Literary Services
Cambridge Language Services
Vanessa Charles
DOLPHIN ECS
First Edition Translations Ltd
Heath Associates
Hurst Village Publishing
Leeds Postcards

Leonie Luzak Ltd
Marlinoak
M.C. Martinez
Oriental Languages Bureau
Pageant Publishing
SeaStar Editorial Services
Joan Shannon
Tecmedia Ltd

Research and/or Writing, Rewriting, Picture Research

'A Feature Factory' Editorial Services
Abbey Writing Services
Lucia Alvarez de Toledo
Anvil Editorial Associates
Archaeological Consultants
Arioma Editorial Services
Aspect
Authors in Science Consultancy
Authors' Research Services
Laraine Bamrah
Beswick Writing Services
Bookwatch Ltd
Brooke Associates (Manchester) Ltd
Lionel and Janet Browne
Causeway Resources
Ingrid Cranfield
David A. Cross
Margaret Crush
Andrew Duncan

EditHelp
Editorial/Visual Research
Dr Martin Edwards
Lewis Esson Publishing
First Edition Translations Ltd
James Wilson Flegg
Global Syndications
Heath Associates
Antony Hemans
Howard Seddon Associates
The Information Bureau
Library Research Agency
Miles Litvinoff
Leonie Luzak Ltd
Kenneth Lysons
Manuscript Appraisals
Marlinoak
Susan Moore Editorial Services
Elizabeth Murray
Paul H. Niekirk
Ormrod Research Services

Christopher Pick
Picture Research Agency
Victoria Ramsay
Rich Research
Anton Rippon Press Services
Sarratt Information Services
SeaStar Editorial Services
Joan Shannon
Roger Smithells Ltd, Editorial Services
Robert and Jane Songhurst
Mrs Gene M. Spencer
Teral Research Services
Hilary Thomas
Carolina Tucker
Caroline White
David Winpenny
Working Press
Write on . . .
Hans Zell, Publishing Consultant

Indexing

Anvil Editorial Associates
Archaeological Consultants
Richard A. Beck
Ingrid Cranfield
Meg and Stephen Davies
DD Editorial Services

EditHelp
First Edition Translations Ltd
Freelance Editorial Services
Howard Seddon Associates
Society of Indexers
Indexing Specialists

Ken Jackson
Geoffrey D. Palmer
Leigh Priest
Sarratt Information Services
Christine Shuttleworth
Richard M. Wright

Translations

Lucia Alvarez de Toledo
Auteursbureau
Laraine Bamrah
Central Office of Information
Ingrid Cranfield
DOLPHIN ECS

First Edition Translations Ltd
James Wilson Flegg
Freelance Editorial Services
Library Research Agency
M.C. Martinez

James Moore Associates
Oriental Languages Bureau
Christine Shuttleworth
Small Print
Caroline White

Specialist Services

Archives
Hans Tasiemka Archives   John Vickers

Cartography, artwork, cartoons, puzzles
Creative Comics   Reginald Piggott   Streetwise Town Plans Ltd
Morley Adams

Cassettes, visual aids
Geo Group & Associates   Small Print   Write on . . .

Freelance employment agency
etr

Interpreting
First Edition Translations Ltd

Lecture agents
Holland-Ford Associates   Sandton Literary Agency

Media and publicity services
Central Office of Information   Freelance Press Services   3 & 5 Promotion

Tuition, lectures, conference services
Authors' Advisory Service   London Media Workshops   Mrs Ellen Seager
Authors in Science   Northgate Training   Gordon R. Wainwright
 Consultancy   Reading and Righting   Joan Wilkins Associates
Ayrshire Business Services   S. Ribeiro Editorial and   Working Press
David A. Cross   Literary Services   Write on . . .
Rosemary Horstmann

Voice overs, subtitles
Lucia Alvarez de Toledo

Creative writing

Creative writing, unlike journalism or sociology or essay writing, is rooted in the senses. It begins with the concrete. The reason isn't hard to see. After all, we experience your daily lives through our senses, and through our emotions. Creative writing attempts to recapture that vitality, the feel of life as it is lived, not how it is thought about when held at arm's length. How it does this, and to what end, is of course the business of the individual writer. We return to a favourite poem or story with enjoyment, because even if the emotions it produces are sad, what we read is in some way alive. What we respond to, with our senses as well as our minds, is a dramatic reconstruction of reality than an essay about it.

from *Word Power* by Julian Birkett (A & C Black, £9.99)

Indexing

INDEXES – DEFINITION AND FUNCTION

An index is a detailed key to the contents of a document, in contrast to a contents list, which gives only the titles of the parts into which the document is divided (chapters, for example).

Precisely, an index is 'A systematic arrangement of entries designed to enable users to locate information in a document'. The document may be a book, a series of books, an issue of a periodical, a run of several volumes of a periodical, an audiotape, a map, a film, a picture, a computer disk, an object, or any other information-carrying artefact in print or non-print form.

The objective of an index is to guide enquirers to information on given subjects in a document by providing the terms of their choice (single words, phrases, abbreviations, acronyms, dates, names, and so on) in an appropriately organised list which refers them to specific locations using page, column, section, frame, figure, table, paragraph, line or other appropriate numbers.

An index differs from a catalogue, which is a record of the documents held in a particular collection, such as a library; though a catalogue may require an index, for example to guide searchers from subject words to class numbers.

A document may have separate indexes for different classes of heading, so that personal names are distinguished from subjects, for example, or a single index in which all classes of heading are interfiled.

INDEXERS – THE PEOPLE

An index compiler requires:

(1) the ability to analyse the text on behalf of a wide range of users who may want to
   – locate information on a particular topic
   – scan the index to assess the scope of the book
   – find out how particular themes or ideas are developed
   – return to passages they remember reading
(2) a good knowledge of the subject matter
(3) the ability to devise suitable terms expressing the concepts in the text concisely and precisely
(4) the ability to organise the entries in the index in the most appropriate and retrievable fashion
(5) a passion for accuracy.

Indexing training aims to impart skills in

   – distinguishing the chief concepts contained in a document
   – devising the necessary index terms for those concepts
   – dealing with synonyms, homonyms and related terms
   – assessing any need for multiple indexes to the document
   – distinguishing between major and minor references
   – indicating differences between references to text and illustrations
   – preparing copy to a high standard of accuracy in terms of spelling, word forms, punctuation, order, and structure of headings, subheadings and sub-subheadings
   – presenting results in the physical form specified by the publisher.

Authors and other originators of documents sometimes compile their own indexes, but do so effectively only if they can combine their subject knowledge with the other abilities and skills listed above.

THE SOCIETY OF INDEXERS

The Society of Indexers is a non-profit organisation founded in 1957 and is the only autonomous professional body for indexers in the UK. It is affiliated with the American Society of Indexers, the Australian Society of Indexers and the Indexing and Abstracting Society of Canada, and has close ties with The Library Association and the Society of Freelance Editors and Proofreaders.

The main objectives of the Society are to promote all types of indexing standards and techniques and the role of indexers in the organisation of knowledge; to provide, promote and recognise facilities for both the initial and the further training of indexers; to establish criteria for assessing indexing standards; and to conduct research and publish guidance, ideas and information about indexing. It seeks to establish good relationships between indexers, librarians, publishers and authors both to advance good indexing and to improve the role and well-being of indexers.

Services to indexers

The Society publishes a learned journal *The Indexer*, a newsletter and *Occasional Papers in Indexing*. Meetings are held regularly on a wide range of subjects while local and special interest groups provide the chance for members to meet to discuss common interests. A weekend conference is held every two years. All levels of training are supported by regular workshops held at various venues throughout the country.

Professional competence is recognised in two stages by the Society. Accredited Indexers who have completed the open-learning course qualification (see Training in indexing below) have shown theoretical competence in indexing while Registered Indexers have proved their experience and competence in practical indexing through an assessment procedure and admission to the Register of Indexers. The services of Registered Indexers are actively promoted by the Society while all trained and experienced members have the opportunity of an annual entry in *Indexers Available*, a directory published by the Society and distributed without charge to over 1000 publishers to help them find an indexer.

The Society sets annually a minimum recommended indexing rate (£10.50 per hour in 1994) and provides advice on the business side of indexing to its members.

Services to publishers and authors

Anyone who commissions indexes needs to be certain of engaging a professional indexer working to the highest standards and able to meet deadlines.

Indexers Available only lists members of the Society and gives basic contact details (name, address, etc.) and subject specialisms. Those accepted for listing need to fall into the following categories: Registered Indexers who have had their competence in practical indexing recognised by the Society; Accredited Indexers who have passed the Society's tests of technical competence; and others with training and/or experience whose competence has not yet been established.

Advice on the selection of indexers is available from the Registrar, who may also be able to suggest names of professionals able to undertake related tasks such as thesaurus construction, terminology control or database indexing. The Registrar will also advise on relations with indexers.

The Society co-operates with The Library Association in the award of the Wheatley Medal for an outstanding index.

Training in indexing

The Society's course is based on the principle of open learning with Units, tutorial support and formal tests all available separately so that individuals can learn in their own way and at their own pace. A member of the Society who has successfully completed five formal tests will be entitled to the status of Accredited Indexer.

The Units cover five core subjects and contain practical exercises and self-administered tests. Members of the Society receive a substantial discount on the cost although anyone can purchase the Units. Only members of the Society can apply for the formal tests or for tutorial support.

Further information on the Society may be obtained by writing to The Secretary, Society of Indexers, 38 Rochester Road, London NW1 9JJ. Enquiries from publishers and authors seeking to commission an indexer should be made to The Registrar on 081-940 4771.

FURTHER READING

British Standards Institution, *Recommendations for the preparation of indexes to books, periodicals and other documents*, BSI, 1988 (BS3700:1988)
British Standards Institution, *British Standard recommendations for examining documents, determining their subjects and selecting indexing terms*, BSI, 1984 (BS6529:1984)

Putting words into mouths

One of the criticisms levelled sometimes at dramatists is that of 'putting words into character's mouths' – an odd comment because, in reality, that is exactly what dramatists do. What people mean, of course, is that their sense of what the dramatist is saying with the play outweighs their sense of the play's or the characters' autonomous reality.

Whatever the merits or demerits of realism, the comment isn't fundamentally about realism or characterisation but about the persuasiveness of the illusion a playwright has put on the stage. The most passionate, subjective and tendentious speech can become acceptable if it is somehow 'justified'. This is another curious term – justified by whom or what? In a different kind of play the most arcane speech and abstract characters can be quite acceptable. Everything depends on 'the main thrust of the work' (Arthur Miller), the consistency of the 'world of the play'. Dramatists can, of course, fail to find the 'art that conceals the art' of putting words into characters' mouths, but finally it is the vitality and conviction of the total world of the play which counts, more than notions of character or realism.

from *Writing a Play* by Steve Gooch (A & C Black, £5.95)

Translation

The role of the translator in enabling books, plays, etc. to pass beyond national frontiers is receiving growing recognition. In view of the general increase of activity in this field, it is not surprising that many people with writing ability and a knowledge of languages should think of adopting freelance translating as a full- or part-time occupation. Some advice may be usefully given to such would-be translators.

The first difficulty the beginner will encounter is the unwillingness of publishers to entrust a translation to anyone who has not already established a reputation for sound work. The least the publisher will demand before commissioning a translation is a fairly lengthy specimen of the applicant's work, even if unpublished. The publisher cannot be expected to pay for a specimen sent in by a translator seeking work. If, on the other hand, a publisher specifically asks for a lengthy specimen of a commissioned book the firm will usually pay for this specimen at the current rate. Perhaps the best way would-be translators can begin is to select some book of the type which they feel competent and anxious to translate, ascertain from the foreign author or publisher that the English-language rights are still free, translate a substantial section of the book and then submit the book and their specimen translation to an appropriate publisher. If they are extremely lucky, this may result in a commission to translate the book. More probably, however – since publishers are generally very well informed about foreign books likely to interest them and are rarely open to a chance introduction – the publisher will reject the book as such. But publishers who are favourably impressed may very possibly commission a translation of some other book of a similar nature which they already have in mind.

In this connection it is important to stress that translators should confine themselves to subjects of which they possess an expert knowledge. In the case of non-fiction, they may have to cope with technical expressions not to be found in the dictionary and disaster may ensue if they are not fully conversant with the subject. The translation of fiction, on the other hand, demands different skills (e.g. in the writing of dialogue) and translators would be wise to ask themselves whether they possess these skills before taking steps to secure work of this nature.

Having obtained a commission to translate a book, the translator will be faced with negotiating terms. These vary considerably from publisher to publisher but for the commoner languages the advance payment should range from £45.00 upwards per thousand words. Translators should be able to arrange that the advance is on account of a royalty of $2\frac{1}{2}\%$ and a small share of the proceeds from secondary uses such as paperback reprint and American rights. However, some publishers avoid paying royalties to the translator even after reducing the royalties they pay to the original author. In the past it was common practice for translators to assign their copyright to the publisher outright, but this is no longer the rule. Most reputable publishers will now sign agreements specifying the rights they require in the translation and leaving the copyright in the translator's hands.

Advice regarding contracts for full-length works, copyright, Public Lending Right and other matters may be obtained from the Translators Association of the Society of Authors (see page 645).

Translators of shorter technical and commercial material are catered for by the Institute of Translation and Interpreting (see page 645). Annual prizes are awarded for translations from German, Italian and French (see page 652). There are also prizes for translations from Swedish and Portuguese.

Press-cutting Agencies

UNITED KINGDOM

In the following section it should be noted that no agency can check every periodical, local paper, etc., and that some agencies cover more than others. Special attention should be given to the time limit specified by certain agencies.

Durrant's Press Cuttings Ltd (1880), 103 Whitecross Street, London EC1Y 8QT *tel* 071-588 3671 *fax* 071-374 8171. *Directors:* A.M. Kennedy, T.W. Lorenzen. Press-cutting service for publishers and art galleries from a guaranteed comprehensive reading list. *Subscription rates:* from £140.

Euro-Parly Services (News Indexing & Cuttings) (1967), 2 Denbigh Place, Westminster, London SW1V 2HB *tel* 071-730 8976 (24-hour). *Director:* Myles Sweeney. Press cuttings and pictures on European Community and small business start-ups, etc. No fixed fee and one-offs considered.

Historical Newspaper Loan Service (1972), 8 Monks Avenue, New Barnet, Herts. EN5 1DB *tel* 081-440 3159. *Proprietor:* John Frost. Headline stories from 50,000 British and overseas newspapers reporting major events since 1850.

International Press-Cutting Bureau (1920), 224-236 Walworth Road, London SE17 1JE *tel* 071-708 2113 *telegraphic address* Adverburo, London SE1 *fax* 071-701 4489. *Subscription rates:* on application. *Representatives:* Brussels, Copenhagen, Geneva, Madrid, Milan, Paris, Lisbon, Stockholm, Berlin, Helsinki, The Hague.

Newsclip (incorporating **Apcut Ltd**), 26 Aylmer Road, London N2 0BX *tel* 081-341 0091 *fax* 081-348 3927. *Subscription rates:* on application.

PA News Library (1928), The Press Association, 85 Fleet Street, London EC4P 4BE *tel* 071-353 7440 *fax* 071-936 2400. *News librarian:* Eugene Weber. National news agency offering public access to over 14 million cuttings covering every subject, from 1926 onwards. Customers can use the files themselves for a facilities fee, or members of staff will carry out research for a research fee.

Press Information (Scotland) Ltd, Virginia House, 62 Virginia Street, Glasgow G1 1TX *tel* 041-552 6767. Comprehensive Scottish cuttings service. *Subscription rates:* on application.

Romeike & Curtice Ltd (1852), Hale House, 290-296 Green Lanes, London N13 5TP *tel* 081-882 0155 *freephone* 0800 289543 *fax* 081-882 6716. *Directors:* Paul J. Morgan, Simon H. Lanyon, John F. Colleran, Ian A. Duncan, Stephen D. George. Provides a media monitoring service to over 5500 clients in different industries, covering more than 3000 newspapers and magazines as well as national radio and TV. *Subscription rates:* on application.

We Find It Press Clippings, 103 South Parade, Belfast, Northern Ireland BT7 2GN *tel* (0232) 646008. Northern Ireland press coverage; fast, up-to-date, accurate feedback. *Subscription rates:* on application.

Overseas

AUSTRALIA

Media Monitors Australia Pty Ltd, PO Box 2110, Strawberry Hills, Sydney, NSW 2012 *tel* (02) 310 3155 *fax* (02) 310 2833; PO Box 304, Richmond,

Melbourne, Victoria 3121 *tel* (03) 429 8388 *fax* (03) 429 9229. Comprehensive media monitoring bureau. Fast and extensive press clipping services, national television and radio monitoring, fast telephone and fax alerts, monthly media directory and database, press release distribution to all Australia media, archival research of Australian press, advertising monitoring services.

CANADA

Canadian Press Clipping Services, 2206 Eglinton Avenue East, Suite 190, Scarborough, Ontario M1L 4T5 *tel* 416-750-2220 *fax* 416-750-2233. *Manager:* Susan Petrykewycz.

INDIA

International Clipping Service, Lakshmi Building, Sir P. Mehta Road, Fort, Bombay 400001 *tel* 2661258, 2665640, 2664598 *telegraphic address* Orientclip. *Proprietor:* Rajan K. Shah. Supplies press cuttings of news, editorials, articles, advertisements, press releases, etc., from all India papers. Undertakes compilation of statistical reports on competitive press advertising pertaining to all products and TV monitoring all over India.

NEW ZEALAND

Chong Press Clippings Bureau, PO Box 13330, Onehunga, Auckland *tel* (09) 634-0463 *fax* (09) 636-7607. All NZ newspapers and most magazines read and clipped for subscribers on any topic; metro papers only from $60 per month. Information consultants. Data searches.

SOUTH AFRICA

S.A. Press Cutting Agency, 54/55 Mitrie House, 110 Stanger Street, Durban 4001, Natal *tel* (031) 370403 *fax* (031) 374307. English and Afrikaans newspapers and trade journals from Zambia to the Cape. *Minimum rates:* R.120.00 per 100 cuttings plus reading fee R.20.00 per month plus postage.

SPAIN

Express Mail (1961), Apartado 14762, 28080 Madrid *tel* 881 58 23. Comprehensive Spanish and Portuguese cuttings service. Individual attention. Undertakes full investigations.

SRI LANKA

Chandra S. Perera Cinetra (1958), 437 Pethiyagoda, Kelaniya *tel* 521885 *telex* 21193/21213 CE *fax* 541414 OTS ATTN CHANDRA PERERA. Supply of press cuttings of Sri Lanka newspapers and journals.

UNITED STATES OF AMERICA

Burrelle's Press Clipping Service (1888), 75 East Northfield Avenue, Livingston, NJ 07039 *tel* 201-992-6600.

Luce Press Clippings, Inc., 420 Lexington Avenue, New York, NY 10170 *tel* 212-889-6711/1-800-628-0376 *fax* 212-481-0105.

Government Offices and Public Services

Enquiries, accompanied by a stamped addressed envelope, should be sent to the Public Relations Officer.

AEA Technology, Harwell, Didcot, Oxon OX11 0RA   *tel* (0235) 821111   *telex* 83135 ATOMHA G   *fax* (0235) 432916.

Agriculture, Fisheries and Food, Ministry of, 3-8 Whitehall Place, London SW1A 2HH   *tel* 071-270 3000   *telex* 01-889351   *fax* 071-270 8125.

Arts Council of England, 14 Great Peter Street, London SW1P 3NQ   *tel* 071-333 0100   *fax* 071-973 6590.

Arts Council of Northern Ireland, 185 Stranmillis Road, Belfast BT9 5DU   *tel* (0232) 381591   *fax* (0232) 661715.

Arts Council of Wales, 9 Museum Place, Cardiff CF1 3NX   *tel* (0222) 394711   *fax* (0222) 221447.

Australian High Commission, Australia House, Strand, London WC2B 4LA   *tel* 071-379 4334   *telex* 27565   *fax* 071-240 5333.

Austrian Embassy, 18 Belgrave Mews West, London SW1X 8HU   *tel* 071-235 3731   *telex* 28327   *fax* 071-235 8025.

Bahamas High Commission, Bahamas House, 10 Chesterfield Street, London W1X 8AH   *tel* 071-408 4488   *fax* 071-499 9937.

Bangladesh High Commission, 28 Queen's Gate, London SW7 5JA   *tel* 071-584 0081-4   *fax* 071-225 2130.

The Bank of England, Threadneedle Street, London EC2R 8AH   *tel* 071-601 4444.

Barbados High Commission, 1 Great Russell Street, London WC1B 3JY   *tel* 071-631 4975   *fax* 071-323 6872.

Royal Belgian Embassy, 103 Eaton Square, London SW1W 9AB   *tel* 071-235 5422   *telex* 22823   *fax* 071-259 6213.

Bodleian Library, Oxford OX1 3BG   *tel* (0865) 277000   *telex* 83656   *fax* (0865) 277182   *e-mail* Bodley@UK.AC.OX.VAX.

Botswana High Commission, 6 Stratford Place, London W1N 9AE   *tel* 071-499 0031.

British Broadcasting Corporation, Broadcasting House, London W1A 1AA   *tel* 071-580 4468.

British Coal, Hobart House, Grosvenor Place, London SW1X 7AE   *tel* 071-201 4141   *telex* 882161 CBHOB G   *fax* 071-201 4141 ext 34682.

The British Council, 10 Spring Gardens, London SW1A 2BN   *tel* 071-930 8466   *telex* 895220 BRICON G   *fax* 071-839 6347.

British Film Institute, 21 Stephen Street, London W1P 1PL   *tel* 071-255 1444   *telex* 27624 BFILDN G   *fax* 071-436 7950.

The British Library, 96 Euston Road, London NW1 2DB   *tel* 071-323 7111   *telex* 21462 BLREF G   *fax* 071-323 7268.

British Library, Document Supply Centre, Boston Spa, Wetherby, West Yorkshire LS23 7BQ *tel* Boston Spa (0937) 546000 *telex* 557381 *fax* (0937) 546333.

British Library Newspaper Library, Colindale Avenue, London NW9 5HE *tel* 071-323 7353 *fax* 071-323 7379.

British Museum, Great Russell Street, London WC1B 3DG *tel* 071-636 1555 *fax* 071-323 8480.

British Railways Board, Euston House, 24 Eversholt Street, PO Box 100, London NW1 1DZ *tel* 071-928 5151 *telex* 299431 BRHQLN G *fax* 071-922 6545.

British Standards Institution, Customer Information, Linford Wood, Milton Keynes, Bucks. MK14 6LE *tel* (0908) 226888 *telex* 825777 BSIMK G *fax* (0908) 320856. *Head office:* 2 Park Street, London W1A 2BS *tel* 071-629 9000.

British Tourist Authority/English Tourist Board, Thames Tower, Black's Road, London W6 9EL *tel* 081-846 9000 *telex* 21231 *fax* 081-563 0302.

The Broadcasting Complaints Commission, Grosvenor Gardens House, 35-37 Grosvenor Gardens, London SW1W 0BS *tel* 071-630 1966.

Broadcasting Standards Council, 7 The Sanctuary, London SW1P 3JS *tel* 071-233 0544 *fax* 071-233 0397.

Bulgaria, Embassy of the Republic of, 186-188 Queen's Gate, London SW7 5HL *tel* 071-584 9400/9433, 071-581 3144 (5 lines) *fax* 071-584 4948.

The Cabinet Office, Secretariat, 70 Whitehall, London SW1A 2AS *tel* 071-270 3000.

Cadw: Welsh Historic Monuments, Brunel House, 2 Fitzalan Road, Cardiff CF2 1UY *tel* (0222) 465511 *fax* (0222) 450859.

Canadian High Commission, Cultural Affairs Section, MacDonald House, 1 Grosvenor Square, London W1X 0AB *tel* 071-258 6366 *telex* 261592 CDALDN G *fax* 071-258 6322.

Central Office of Information, Hercules Road, London SE1 7DU *tel* 071-928 2345. In the UK conducts press, television, radio and poster advertising; produces booklets, leaflets, films, radio and television material, exhibitions and other visual material. It also prepares for publication by HMSO the annual *Britain: An Official Handbook* and the Aspects of Britain series of factual books on British affairs. For the Foreign and Commonwealth Office, COI supplies British information posts overseas with press, radio and television material, publications and briefing material, films, exhibitions and display and reading-room material.

Central Statistical Office, Great George Street, London SW1P 3AQ *tel* 071-270 6363/6364.

Centre for Information on Language Teaching and Research (CILT), 20 Bedfordbury, Covent Garden, London WC2N 4LB *tel* 071-379 5101 *fax* 071-379 5082. Supports the work of all professionals concerned with language teaching and learning throughout the UK, across every sector and stage of education. Offers a full conference programme, plus *free* on-site INSET for teachers, a complete range of publications and a new Teaching Resources Library with extensive IT and AV facilities. CILT also provides a comprehensive information service and knowledge of research and developmental activity.

College of Arms or Heralds' College, Queen Victoria Street, London EC4V 4BT *tel* 071-248 2762 *fax* 071-248 6448.

The Commonwealth Institute, Kensington High Street, London W8 6NQ   *tel* 071-603 4535   *fax* 071-602 7374. For full details, see page 620.

Copyright Tribunal, Room 4/6, Hazlitt House, 45 Southampton Buildings, London WC2A 1AR   *tel* 071-438 4776   *fax* 071-438 4780.

Countryside Commission, John Dower House, Crescent Place, Cheltenham, Glos. GL50 3RA   *tel* (0242) 521381   *fax* (0242) 584270.

Court of the Lord Lyon, HM New Register House, Edinburgh EH1 3YT   *tel* 031-556 7255   *fax* 031-557 2148.

Crafts Council, 44a Pentonville Road, Islington, London N1 9BY   *tel* 071-278 7700   *fax* 071-837 6891. Exhibition Galleries, Picture Library, Reference Library, Information Centre, Shop, Education Workshop, Cafe.

Croatia, Embassy of the Republic of, 18-21 Jermyn Street, London SW1Y 6HP   *tel* 071-434 2946   *fax* 071-434 2953.

Cyprus High Commission, 93 Park Street, London W1Y 4ET   *tel* 071-499 8272   *telex* 263343   *fax* 071-491 0691

Czech Republic, Embassy of the, 26-30 Kensington Palace Gardens, London W8 4QY   *tel* 071-243 1115   *fax* 071-727 9654.

Royal Danish Embassy, 55 Sloane Street, London SW1X 9SR   *tel* 071-333 0200   *fax* 071-333 0270.

Data Protection Registrar, Office of the, Wycliffe House, Water Lane, Wilmslow, Cheshire SK9 5AF   *tel (enquiries)* (0625) 535777   *(administration)* (0625) 535711   *fax* (0625) 524510.

Defence, Ministry of, Main Building, Whitehall, London SW1A 2HB   *tel* 071-218 9000.

The Design Council, 28 Haymarket, London SW1Y 4SU   *tel* 071-839 8000   *telex* 8812963   *fax* 071-925 2130.

DTI: Department of Trade and Industry, Ashdown House, 123 Victoria Street, London SW1E 6RB   *tel (general enquiries)* 071-215 5000   *telex* 8813148 DTHQ G   *fax* 071-828 3258   *other tel Enterprise Initiative* 0800 500 200   *Business in Europe* 0272 444888   *The Innovation Enquiry Line* 0800 44 2001.

Economic and Social Research Council, Polaris House, North Star Avenue, Swindon, Wilts. SN2 1UJ   *tel* (0793) 413000.

Education, Department for, Sanctuary Buildings, Great Smith Street, London SW1P 3BT   *tel* 071-925 5000   *fax* 071-925 6000.

Electricity Regulation Northern Ireland, Office of (OFFER NI), Brookmount Buildings, 42 Fountain Street, Belfast, Northern Ireland BT1 5EE   *tel* (0232) 311575   *fax* (0232) 311740.

Electricity Regulation, Office of, Hagley House, Hagley Road, Edgbaston, Birmingham B16 8QG   *tel* 021-456 2100   *fax* 021-456 4664.

Employment, Department of, Information Branch, Caxton House, Tothill Street, London SW1H 9NF   *tel* 071-273 3000 (main switchboard)   *public enquiries* 071-273 6969.

Engineering and Physical Sciences Research Council, Polaris House, North Star Avenue, Swindon, Wilts. SN2 1ET   *tel* (0793) 444000   *fax* (0793) 444010.

English Heritage, 23 Savile Row, London W1X 1AB   *tel* 071-973 3000   *fax* 071-973 3001.

English Regional Arts Boards, 5 City Road, Winchester, Hants SO23 8SD *tel* (0962) 851063 *fax* (0962) 842033. See page 638 for full details of the various Regional Arts Boards.

Environment, Department of the, 2 Marsham Street, London SW1P 3EB *tel* 071-276 3000.

Equal Opportunities Commission, Overseas House, Quay Street, Manchester M3 3HN *tel* 061-833 9244 *fax* 061-835 1657.

The European Commission, Jean Monnet House, 8 Storey's Gate, London SW1P 3AT *tel* 071-973 1992.

European Parliament, UK Office, 2 Queen Anne's Gate, London SW1H 9AA *tel* 071-222 0411 *fax* 071-222 2713.

Fair Trading, Office of, Field House, 15-25 Bream's Buildings, London EC4A 1PR *tel* 071-242 2858 *telex* 269009 OFTRIN G *fax* 071-269 8800.

Foreign and Commonwealth Office, King Charles Street, London SW1A 2AH *tel* 071-270 1500 *telex* 297711 PRDRME G.

Forestry Commission, 231 Corstorphine Road, Edinburgh EH12 7AT *tel* 031-334 0303 *fax* 031-334 3047.

French Embassy, 58 Knightsbridge, London SW1X 7JT *tel* 071-235 8080; *Cultural department:* 23 Cromwell Road, London SW7 2EL *tel* 071-581 5292.

Gambia High Commission, 57 Kensington Court, London W8 5DG *tel* 071-937 6316/7/8 *telex* 857911 GAMEXT G *fax* 071-937 9095.

Gas Supply, Office of, Stockley House, 130 Wilton Road, London SW1V 1LQ *tel* 071-828 0898 *fax* 071-630 8164.

General Register Office, now part of the **Population Censuses and Surveys, Office of.**

Germany, Embassy of the Federal Republic of, 23 Belgrave Square, London SW1X 8PZ *tel* 071-235 5033 *fax* 071-235 0609.

Ghana, High Commission for, 104 Highgate Hill, London N6 5HE *tel* 081-342 8686 *fax* 081-342 8566.

Greece, Embassy of, Press and Information Office, 1A Holland Park, London W11 3TP *tel* 071-727 3071 *fax* 071-727 8960.

Guyana High Commission, 3 Palace Court, Bayswater Road, London W2 4LP *tel* 071-229 7684 *fax* 071-727 9809.

Hayward Gallery, South Bank Centre, Belvedere Road, London SE1 8XZ *tel* 071-928 3144.

Health, Department of, Richmond House, 79 Whitehall, London SW1A 2NS *tel* 071-210 3000.

Historic Scotland, 20 Brandon Street, Edinburgh EH3 5RA *tel* 031-244 3101 *fax* 031-244 3030.

HMSO Books, St Crispins, Duke Street, Norwich NR3 1PD *tel* (0603) 622211 *fax* (0603) 695317.

Home Office, Queen Anne's Gate, London SW1H 9AT *tel* 071-273 3000. *Public relations branch:* Director of information services: A.E. Moorey.

Housing Corporation, 149 Tottenham Court Road, London W1P 0BN *tel* 071-393 2000 *fax* 071-393 2111.

Hungary, Embassy of the Republic of, 35 Eaton Place, London SW1X 8BY *tel* 071-235 4048/7191 *fax* 071-823 1348.

Independent Television Commission, 33 Foley Street, London W1P 7LB *tel* 071-255 3000 *fax* 071-306 7800.

India, High Commission of, Press & Information Wing, India House, Aldwych, London WC2B 4NA *tel* 071-836 8484 ext 147, 286 *fax* 071-836 4331.

Inland Revenue, Board of, Somerset House, London WC2R 1LB *tel* 071-438 6622.

Ireland, Embassy of, 17 Grosvenor Place, London SW1X 7HR *tel* 071-235 2171 *telex* 916104 IVERNA G *fax* 071-245 6961.

Israel, Embassy of, 2 Palace Green, Kensington, London W8 4QB *tel* 071-957 9500 *fax* 071-957 9555.

Italian Embassy, 14 Three Kings Yard, Davies Street, London W1Y 2EH *tel/ fax* 071-629 8200.

Jamaican High Commission, 1-2 Prince Consort Road, London SW7 2BZ *tel* 071-823 9911 *telex* 263304 JAMCOM G *fax* 071-589 5154.

Japan, Embassy of, 101-104 Piccadilly, London W1V 9FN *tel* 071-465 6500.

Kenya High Commission, 45 Portland Place, London W1N 4AS *tel* 071-636 2371/5 *telex* 262551 *fax* 071-323 6717.

HM Land Registry, Lincoln's Inn Fields, London WC2A 3PH *tel* 071-917 8888 *fax* 071-955 0110. *Head of information:* Eric Davies.

Law Commission, Conquest House, 37-38 John Street, Theobalds Road, London WC1N 2BQ *tel* 071-411 1220. Covers England and Wales.

Law Commission, Scottish, 140 Causewayside, Edinburgh EH9 1PR *tel* 031-668 2131 *fax* 031-662 4900.

The Legal Deposit Office, The British Library, Boston Spa, Wetherby, West Yorkshire LS23 7BY *tel* (0937) 546267/546268 *fax* (0937) 546176.

Legal Services Ombudsman, Office of the, 22 Oxford Court, Oxford Street, Manchester M2 3WQ *tel* 061-236 9532 *fax* 061-236 2651 *dx* 18569 MAN-CHESTER 7.

Lesotho, High Commission of the Kingdom of, 7 Chesham Place, Belgravia, London SW1 8HN *tel* 071-235 5686 *fax* 071-235 5023.

London Museum—see Museum of London.

London Records Office, Corporation of, Guildhall, London EC2P 2EJ *tel* 071-332 1251 *fax* 071-332 1119.

London Transport, 55 Broadway, London SW1H 0BD *tel* 071-222 5600 (administration), 071-222 1234 (travel information) *telex* 893633 LRTBDY G *fax* 071-222 5719.

Luxembourg, Embassy of, 27 Wilton Crescent, London SW1X 8SD *tel* 071-235 6961 *fax* 071-235 9734.

Malawi High Commission, 33 Grosvenor Street, London W1X 0DE *tel* 071-491 4172/7 *telex* 263308 *fax* 071-491 9916.

Malaysian High Commission, 45 Belgrave Square, London SW1X 8QT *tel* 071-235 8033 *telex* 262550 *fax* 071-235 5161.

Malta High Commission, 16 Kensington Square, London W8 5HH *tel* 071-938 1712 *fax* 071-937 0979.

Mauritius, High Commission for the Republic of, 32-3 Elvaston Place, London SW7 5NW *tel* 071-581 0294/6 *commercial section* 071-225 3331 *tourist information* 071-584 3666 *fax* 071-823 8437.

Medical Research Council, 20 Park Crescent, London W1N 4AL   *tel* 071-636 5422.

Monopolies and Mergers Commission, New Court, 48 Carey Street, London WC2A 2JT   *tel* 071-324 1467/8   *fax* 071-324 1400.

Museum of London, London Wall, London EC2Y 5HN   *tel* 071-600 3699   *fax* 071-600 1058. Comprises the collections of the London Museum and the Guildhall Museum.

Museum of Mankind (Ethnography Department of the British Museum), Burlington Gardens, London W1X 2EX   *tel* 071-323 8043 (information)   *fax* 071-323 8013.

National Audit Office, 157-197 Buckingham Palace Road, London SW1W 9SP   *tel* 071-798 7000   *fax* 071-828 3774.

National Gallery, Trafalgar Square, London WC2N 5DN   *tel* 071-839 3321   *general information tel* 071-389 1785   *press office fax* 071-930 4764.

National Maritime Museum, Greenwich, London SE10 9NF, including the Queen's House and the Old Royal Observatory   *tel* 081-858 4422   *fax* 081-312 6632.

National Savings, Department for, Marketing and Information Division, Charles House, 375 Kensington High Street, London W14 8SD   *tel* 071-605 9300   *fax* 071-605 9432/9438.

The National Trust for Scotland, 5 Charlotte Square, Edinburgh EH2 4DU   *tel* 031-226 5922   *fax* 031-243 9501.

Natural Environment Research Council, Polaris House, North Star Avenue, Swindon, Wilts. SN2 1EU   *tel* (0793) 411500   *fax* (0793) 411501.

The Natural History Museum, Cromwell Road, London SW7 5BD   *tel* 071-938 9123   *fax* 071-938 8754.

Royal Netherlands Embassy, 38 Hyde Park Gate, London SW7 5DP   *tel* 071-584 5040   *fax* 071-581 3450; press and cultural affairs   *tel* 071-581 7962   *fax* 071-581 0053.

New Zealand High Commission, New Zealand House, Haymarket, London SW1Y 4TQ   *tel* 071-930 8422   *telex* 24368   *fax* 071-839 4580.

Nigeria High Commission, Nigeria House, 9 Northumberland Avenue, London WC2N 5BX   *tel* 071-839 1244   *fax* 071-839 8746.

Northern Ireland Office, Whitehall, London SW1A 2AZ   *tel* 071-210 3000; also Stormont Castle, Belfast, Northern Ireland BT4 3ST   *tel* (0232) 520700.

Northern Ireland Tourist Board, 59 North Street, Belfast, Northern Ireland BT1 1NB   *tel* (0232) 231221   *fax* (0232) 240960.

Royal Norwegian Embassy, 25 Belgrave Square, London SW1X 8QD   *tel* 071-235 7151   *fax* 071-245 6993.

Oftel—see **Telecommunications, Office of.**

OFWAT—see **Water Services, Office of.**

Ordnance Survey, Romsey Road, Maybush, Southampton SO9 4DH   *tel* (0703) 792000   *press officer tel* (0703) 792635   *fax* (0703) 792660.

Particle Physics and Astronomy Research Council, Polaris House, North Star Avenue, Swindon, Wilts. SN2 1SZ   *tel* (0793) 442000   *fax* (0793) 442002.

Patent Office (An Executive Agency of the Department of Trade and Industry), Cardiff Road, Newport, Gwent NP9 1RH   *tel* (0633) 814000. *Copyright enquiries:* Industrial Property and Policy Directorate, The Patent Office,

Hazlitt House, 45 Southampton Buildings, Chancery Lane, London WC2A 1AR   *tel* 071-438 4777.

Pensions Ombudsman, The, 11 Belgrave Road, London SW1V 1RB   *tel* 071-834 9144.

PLR Office, Bayheath House, Prince Regent Street, Stockton-on-Tees, Cleveland TS18 1DF   *tel* (0642) 604699   *fax* (0642) 615641. Address enquiries to the Registrar of Public Lending Right.

Poland, Embassy of the Republic of, 47 Portland Place, London W1N 3AG   *tel* 071-580 4324   *telex* 265691   *fax* 071-323 4018.

Police Complaints Authority, 10 Great George Street, London SW1P 3AE   *tel* 071-273 6450   *fax* 071-273 6401.

Population Censuses and Surveys, Office of, St Catherine's House, 10 Kingsway, London WC2B 6JP   *tel* 071-242 0262   *fax* 071-430 1779.

Portuguese Embassy, 11 Belgrave Square, London SW1X 8PP   *tel* 071-235 5331   *fax* 071-245 1287.

Post Office Headquarters, 5th Floor, 148 Old Street, London EC1V 9HQ   *tel* 071-250 2888.

Privy Council Office, Whitehall, London SW1A 2AT   *tel* 071-270 3000.

Public Record Office, *Records of Modern Government Departments:* Ruskin Avenue, Kew, Richmond, Surrey TW9 4DU   *tel* 081-876 3444   *fax* 081-878 8905; *Medieval, Early Modern and Legal Records* and the *Census Returns:* Chancery Lane, London WC2A 1LR   *tel* 081-876 3444   *fax* 081-878 7231.

Public Service and Science, Office of (OPSS), Horse Guards Road, London SW1P 3AL; 70 Whitehall, London SW1A 2AS   *tel* 071-270 5811.

Public Trust Office, Stewart House, 24 Kingsway, London WC2B 6JX   *tel* 071-269 7000   *fax* 071-831 0060.

Racial Equality, Commission for, Elliot House, 10-12 Allington Street, London SW1E 5EH   *tel* 071-828 7022   *fax* 071-931 0429.

The Radio Authority, Holbrook House, 14 Great Queen Street, Holborn, London WC2B 5DG   *tel* 071-430 2724   *fax* 071-405 7062.

Romania, Embassy of, 4 Palace Green, London W8 4QD   *tel* 071-937 9666   *telex* 22232 ROMCOM G   *fax* 071-937 8069.

Royal Commission on the Ancient and Historical Monuments of Scotland, John Sinclair House, 16 Bernard Terrace, Edinburgh EH8 9NX   *tel* 031-662 1456   *fax* 031-662 1477/1499.

Royal Commission on the Ancient and Historical Monuments of Wales, Crown Building, Plas Crug, Aberystwyth, Dyfed SY23 1NJ   *tel* (0970) 624381-2   *fax* (0970) 627701.

Royal Commission on Historical Manuscripts, Quality House, Quality Court, Chancery Lane, London WC2A 1HP   *tel* 071-242 1198   *fax* 071-831 3550.

Royal Commission on the Historical Monuments of England, National Monuments Record Centre, Kemble Drive, Swindon, Wilts. SN2 2GZ   *tel* (0793) 414600   *fax* (0793) 414707.

Royal Fine Art Commission, 7 St James's Square, London SW1Y 4JU   *tel* 071-839 6537.

Royal Fine Art Commission for Scotland, 9 Atholl Crescent, Edinburgh EH3 8HA   *tel* 031-229 1109   *fax* 031-229 6031.

Royal Mint, Llantrisant, Pontyclun, Mid-Glamorgan CF7 8YT *tel* Llantrisant (0443) 222111.

Royal National Theatre Board, South Bank, London SE1 9PX *tel* 071-928 2033.

Russian Federation, Embassy of the, 13 Kensington Palace Gardens, London W8 4QX *tel* 071-229 3628 *fax* 071-727 8625.

Science and Technology, Office of, Cabinet Office, Albany House, 84-86 Petty France, London SW1H 9ST *tel* 071-270 1234.

Science Museum, Exhibition Road, South Kensington, London SW7 2DD *tel* 071-938 8000 *fax* 071 938 8118. *Enquiries: Information Desk* 071-938 8080/8008; *Press Office tel* 071-938 8181 *fax* 071-938 8112.

Scotland, National Galleries of: National Gallery of Scotland, The Mound, Edinburgh EH2 2EL; Scottish National Portrait Gallery, 1 Queen Street, Edinburgh EH2 1JD; Scottish National Gallery of Modern Art, Belford Road, Edinburgh EH4 3DR *information tel* 031-556 8921.

Scotland, National Library of, George IV Bridge, Edinburgh EH1 1EW *tel* 031-226 4531 *fax* 031-220 6662.

Scottish Natural Heritage, 12 Hope Terrace, Edinburgh EH9 2AS *tel* 031-447 4784 *press office fax* 031-446 2279.

The Scottish Office, Dover House, Whitehall, London SW1A 2AU *tel* 071-270 6755.

The Scottish Office Information Directorate, New St Andrew's House, Edinburgh EH1 3TG *tel* 031-244 1111; and Dover House, Whitehall, London SW1A 2AU *tel* 071-270 6744.

Scottish Record Office, HM General Register House, Edinburgh EH1 3YY *tel* 031-556 6585 *fax* 031-557 9569.

Scottish Tourist Board, 23 Ravelston Terrace, Edinburgh EH4 3EU *tel* 031-332 2433 *telex* 72272 *fax* 031-343 1513.

Serpentine Gallery, Kensington Gardens, London W2 3XA *tel* 071-402 6075 *fax* 071-402 4103 *recorded information* 071-723 9072. International exhibitions of modern and contemporary art.

Seychelles High Commission, 111 Baker Street, 2nd Floor, Eros House, London W1M 1FE *tel* 071-224 1660 *fax* 071-487 5756.

Sierra Leone High Commission, 33 Portland Place, London W1N 3AG *tel* 071-636 6483-5 *fax* 071-323 3159.

Singapore High Commission, 9 Wilton Crescent, London SW1X 8SA *tel* 071-235 8315 *telex* 51-262564 SHCIUK G *fax* 071-245 6583.

Slovak Republic, Embassy of the, 25 Kensington Palace Gardens, London W8 4QY *tel* 071-243 0803 *fax* 071-727 5824.

Slovenia, Embassy of, Suite One, Cavendish Court, 11-15 Wigmore Street, London W1H 9LA *tel* 071-495 7775 *fax* 071-495 7776.

Social Security, Department of, Richmond House, 79 Whitehall, London SW1A 2NS *tel* 071-210 3000. Contact Benefits Agency Overseas Benefits Directorate (OBD) for a query about benefits being paid abroad, and Overseas Contributions (OSC) for queries about writing abroad and paying National Insurance contributions. Both OBD and OSC are at: Department of Social Security, Longbenton, Newcastle upon Tyne NE98 1YX *tel* 091-213 5000.

South Africa, Republic of, South African Embassy, Trafalgar Square, London WC2N 5DP *tel* 071-930 4488 *fax* 071-321 0835.

Spanish Embassy, 24 Belgrave Square, London SW1X 8QA   *tel* 071-235 5555.

Sri Lanka, High Commission of the Democratic Socialist Republic of, 13 Hyde Park Gardens, London W2 2LU   *tel* 071-262 1841   *fax* 071-262 7970.

Swaziland High Commission, 58 Pont Street, London SW1X 0AE   *tel* 071-581 4976   *telex* 28853   *fax* 071-589 5332.

Sweden, Embassy of, 11 Montagu Place, London W1H 2AL   *tel* 071-724 2101   *fax* 071-724 4174   *cultural section fax* 071-917 6477.

Switzerland, Embassy of, 16-18 Montagu Place, London W1H 2BQ   *tel* 071-723 0701   *telex* 28212 AMSWIS G   *fax* 071-724 7001.

Tanzania High Commission, 43 Hertford Street, London W1Y 8DB   *tel* 071-499 8951   *telex* 262504 TANLON G   *fax* 071-491 9321.

Tate Gallery, Millbank, London SW1P 4RG   *tel* 071-887 8000   *fax* 071-887 8007; Albert Dock, Liverpool L3 4BB   *tel* 051-709 3223; Porthmeor Beach, St Ives, Cornwall TR26 1TG   *tel* (0736) 796226.

Telecommunications, Office of, 50 Ludgate Hill, London EC4M 7JJ   *tel* 071-634 8700   *telex* 883584   *fax* 071-634 8943.

Theatre Museum, National Museum of the Performing Arts, 1E Tavistock Street, London WC2E 7PA   *tel* 071-836 7891   *fax* 071-836 5148. See page 371 for reprographic services.

Transport, Department of, 2 Marsham Street, London SW1P 3EB   *tel* 071-276 3000   *telex* 22221   *fax* 071-276 0818.

HM Treasury, Treasury Chambers, Parliament Street, London SW1P 3AG   *tel* 071-270 3000.

Trinidad and Tobago High Commission, 42 Belgrave Square, London SW1X 8NT   *tel* 071-245 9351   *fax* 071-823 1065.

Trinity House, Corporation of, Tower Hill, London EC3N 4DH   *tel* 071-480 6601   *telex* 987526 NAVAID G   *fax* 071-480 7662. The General Lighthouse Authority for England, Wales and the Channel Islands, a Charitable Organisation for the relief of Mariners and a Deep Sea Pilotage Authority.

Turkish Embassy, 43 Belgrave Square, London SW1X 8PA   *tel* 071-235 5252   *telex* 884236 TURKEL G   *fax* 071-235 8093; Information Counsellor's Office, 170 Piccadilly, London W1V 9DD   *tel* 071-355 4207   *fax* 071-431 0773.

Uganda High Commission, Uganda House, 58-59 Trafalgar Square, London WC2N 5DX   *tel* 071-839 5783   *fax* 071-839 8925.

United States Embassy, 24 Grosvenor Square, London W1A 1AE   *tel* 071-499 9000.

Victoria and Albert Museum, South Kensington, London SW7 2RL   *tel* 071-938 8500   *telex* 268831 VICART G   *fax* 071-938 8458.

Vocational Qualifications, National Council for, 222 Euston Road, London NW1 2BZ   *tel* 071-387 9898.

Wales, The National Library of, Aberystwyth, Dyfed SY23 3BU   *tel* (0970) 623816   *fax* (0970) 615709.

Wales Tourist Board, Brunel House, 2 Fitzalan Road, Cardiff CF2 1UY   *tel* (0222) 475252   *fax* (0222) 498151.

Water Services, Office of (OFWAT), Centre City Tower, 7 Hill Street, Birmingham B5 4UA   *tel* 021-625 1300   *fax* 021-625 1400.

Wellington Museum, Apsley House, 149 Piccadilly, Hyde Park Corner, London W1V 9FA   *tel* 071-499 5676   *fax* 071-493 6576. Closed for major works until mid 1995.

Welsh Office, Gwydyr House, Whitehall, London SW1A 2ER   *tel* 071-270 0564   *fax* 071-270 0586; and Cathays Park, Cardiff, CF1 3NQ   *tel* (0222) 825111   *fax* (0222) 823036.

West India Committee (The Caribbean), Nelson House, 8/9 Northumberland Street, London WC2N 5RA   *tel* 071-976 1493   *fax* 071-976 1541.

Yugoslavia, Embassy of the Federal Republic of, 5-7 Lexham Gardens, London W8 5JJ   *tel* 071-370 6105   *telex* 928542   *fax* 071-370 3838.

Zambia High Commission, 2 Palace Gate, Kensington, London W8 5NG   *tel* 071-589 6655   *telex* 263544   *fax* 071-581 1353.

Zimbabwe, High Commission of the Republic of, Zimbabwe House, 429 Strand, London WC2R 0SA   *tel* 071-836 7755.

The names and addresses of many other public bodies can be found in *Whitaker's Almanack*.

See also the **Picture research** section.

How to study markets

Market study is rather like trying to unbake a cake. There are all the ingredients, mixed to perfection by an expert; to discover the recipe the cake must be unbaked, i.e. reduced to its constituent parts. But doing that will reveal the ingredients only of that particular cake. And here our allegory ends: many cakes are baked to a single recipe, as we all know, but no periodicals are the same week after week or month after month.

Research into the market guides listed later in this chapter is a beginning and will provide outline information about magazines, but true market study means studying the magazines themselves. There is no substitute for purposeful, thorough and organised appraisal of the contents of your potential market over a period of time. For monthly magazines a study of at least four issues is advisable, including the most recent, and paying close attention to at least six editions of a weekly magazine is likely to yield the best results.

from *Writing for Magazines* by Jill Dick (A & C Black, £9.99)

Publishing practice

Publishing Agreements

MICHAEL LEGAT

Any author, presented with so complex a document as a publisher's agreement, should read it carefully before signing, making sure that every clause is understood, and not taking anything for granted. Bear in mind that there is no such thing as a standard form. A given publisher's 'standard' contract may not only differ substantially from those of other publishers, but will often vary from author to author and from book to book. Don't be fooled into believing that it is a standard form because it appears to have been printed – each agreement can be individually produced on a word processor to give exactly that effect.

MAKE SURE THE AGREEMENT IS FAIR AND REASONABLE

You should be able to rely on your agent, if you have one, to check the agreement for you, or – if you are a member – you can get it vetted by the Society of Authors or the Writers' Guild of Great Britain. But if you are on your own, you must either go to one of the solicitors who specialise in publishing business (probably expensive) or Do It Yourself. In the latter case it will help to compare the contract you have been offered, clause by clause, with a typical Minimum Terms Agreement such as those printed in my own books, *An Author's Guide to Publishing* and *Understanding Publishers' Contracts*.

THE MINIMUM TERMS AGREEMENT

The MTA, developed jointly by the Society of Authors and the Writers' Guild, is signed by a publisher on the one hand and the Society and the Guild on the other. It is not an agreement between a publisher and an individual author. It commits the publisher to offering his or her authors terms which are at least as good as those in the MTA. The intention is that only members of the Society and Guild should be eligible for this special treatment, but in practice publishers who sign the agreement tend to offer its terms to all their authors. There is no standard MTA, and most signatory publishers have insisted on certain variations in the agreement; nevertheless, the more important basic principles have always been accepted. It must be pointed out that the MTA does not usually apply to books in which illustrations take up 40 per cent or more of the space, to specialist works on the visual arts in which illustrations fill 25 per cent or more of the space, to books involving three or more participants in royalties, or to technical books, manuals and reference books.

Since its origins in 1980 comparatively few publishers have signed a Minimum Terms Agreement, although the signatories include several major publishing houses. Some publishers have refused, claiming to treat their authors quite well enough already, while others say that each author and each book is so different that standard terms cannot be laid down. Nonetheless, the MTA has been a resounding success. Almost all non-signatory publishers have adopted some or all of its provisions, and even in the case of the excluded books mentioned above, the terms have tended to improve. All authors can now argue, from a position of some strength, that their own agreements should meet the MTA's standards.

THE PROVISIONS OF THE MTA

The MTA is a royalty agreement (usually the most satisfactory form for an author), and it lays down the minimum acceptable royalties on sales, and the levels at which the rate should rise. These royalties are expressed as percentages of the book's retail price, but can easily be adjusted to apply to royalties based on price received, a system to which a number of publishers are changing, increasing the percentages so that the author's earnings are not adversely affected. The MTA also covers the size of the advance (calculated in accordance with the expected initial print quantity and retail price), and recommended splits between publisher and author of moneys from the sale of subsidiary rights (including US and translation rights). However, it is not by any means concerned solely with money, but with fairness to the author in all clauses of a publishing agreement, special attention being paid to provisions designed to make the author/publisher relationship more of a partnership than it has often been in the past. While recognising the publisher's right to take final decisions on such matters as print quantity, publication date, retail price, jacket or cover design, wording of the blurb, promotion and publicity, and remaindering, the MTA insists that the author has a right to consultation (which should not be an empty formality, but should mean that serious consideration is given to his or her views), in all such cases. Also the author's approval must be sought for the sale of any subsidiary rights.

SOME ESSENTIAL CLAUSES IN A PUBLISHER'S AGREEMENT

Any publisher's agreement you sign should contain, in addition to acceptable financial terms, clauses covering the following points:

- clear definition of which rights you are licensing to the publisher. The publisher will normally require volume rights, but the agreement must specify whether such rights will apply in all languages (or perhaps only in English) and through-out the world (or only in an agreed list of territories). The duration of the publisher's licence should be spelt out; commonly this is for the period of copyright (presently the author's lifetime plus 50 years, but to be increased by harmonisation within the European Union to the author's lifetime plus 70 years), although some publishers now accept a shorter term. A list of those subsidiary rights of which control is granted to the publisher must be included (make sure that the splits of moneys earned from these rights are in accordance with, or approximate reasonably to, those in the MTA, especially in the currently growing areas of merchandising and electronic and multimedia pub-lishing).
- commitment by the publisher to publication of the book by a specific date

(usually within a year or eighteen months from the delivery of the typescript). Avoid signing an agreement which is vague on this point, saying, for instance, only that the book will be published 'within a reasonable period'.

- confirmation that in all copies of the book the publisher will print a copyright notice in the author's name and a statement that the author has asserted his or her 'Right of Paternity' (the right to be identified as the author in future exploitation of the material in any form), and that a similar commitment will be required from any subsidiary licensee.
- clarification, if the book is to include a professionally prepared index or material the copyright of which does not belong to the author, of whether the author or the publisher will be responsible for the fees (or if costs are to be shared, in what proportions) and the clearance of permissions.
- acceptable accounting procedures. Most publishers divide the year into two six-month periods, accounting to the author, and paying any sums due, three months after the end of each period. Look askance at any less frequent accounting or longer delay after the royalty period. The publisher should also agree to pay the author the due share of any subsidiary moneys promptly on receipt, provided that the advance on the book has been earned.
- clear definition of the various conditions under which the agreement shall be terminated, with reversion of rights to the author.

CLAUSES TO QUESTION

You can question anything in a publisher's agreement before you sign it. Provided that you do so politely and are not just being difficult, the publisher should be prepared to answer every query, to explain, and where possible to meet your objections. Most publishing contracts are not designed to exploit the author unfairly, but you should watch out for the following points:

- it is unwise to accept a clause which allows the publisher to assign the rights in your book to another firm or person without your approval.
- the contract for a commissioned book often includes wording which alludes to the publisher's acceptance of the work, implying that there is no obligation to publish it if he or she deems it unacceptable. It may be understandable that the publisher wants an escape route in case the author turns in an inferior work, but he or she should be obliged to justify the rejection, and to give the author an opportunity to revise the work to bring it up to standard.
- some agreements prohibit the author from writing similar material for any other publisher. This may clearly affect the author's earning ability.
- don't agree to the publisher's right to edit your work without any requirement for him or her to obtain your approval of any changes made.
- the Society of Authors and the Writers' Guild are generally opposed to clauses giving the publisher the right to publish the author's next work, feeling that this privilege should be earned by the publisher's handling of the earlier book. If you accept an option clause, at least make sure that it leaves all terms for a future book to be agreed.

AGREEMENTS FOR JOINT AND MULTIPLE AUTHORSHIP

In the case of joint authorship (a work so written that the individual contributions of the authors cannot be readily separated), the first written agreement should be between the authors themselves, setting out the proportions in which any moneys earned by the book will be split, specifying how the authors' responsibilities are to be shared, and especially laying down the procedure to be adopted should the authors ever find themselves in dispute. The terms of any publishing agreement which they sign (each author having an identical copy) should reflect their joint understanding. The total earnings should not be less than would be paid were the book by a single author, and the authors should have normal rights of consultation.

In the case of multiple authorship (when the work of each contributor can be clearly separated), each author is likely to have an individual contract, and may not be aware of what terms are offered to the others involved. Because of the possibility of disagreement between the authors, the publisher will probably offer little in the way of consultation. All the individual author can do is to ensure that the agreement appears to be fair in relation to the amount of work contributed, and that the author's responsibilities indicated by the contract refer only to his or her work.

OUTRIGHT SALE

As a general rule no author should agree to surrender his or her copyright to the publisher, although this may be unavoidable in the case of a book with many contributors, such as an encyclopaedia. Even then, give up your copyright with great reluctance and only after an adequate explanation from the publisher of why you should (and probably a substantial financial inducement). The agreement itself will probably be no more than a brief and unequivocal letter.

SUBSIDIES AND VANITY PUBLISHING

Few commercial publishers will be interested in publishing your book on a subsidy basis (i.e. with a contribution from you towards costs), unless perhaps it is of a serious, highly specialised nature, such as an academic monograph, when a publisher who is well-established within that particular field will certainly behave with probity and offer a fair contract. Vanity publishers, on the other hand, will accept your book with enthusiasm, ask for 'a small contribution to production costs' (which turns out to be a very substantial sum, not a penny of which you are likely to see again), and will fail to achieve any sales for your book apart from the copies which you yourself buy. If you want to put your own money into the publication of your book, try self-publishing – you will be far better off than going to a vanity house. How do you tell which are the vanity publishers? That's easy – they're the ones who put advertisements in the papers saying things like, 'Authors Wanted!'. Regular publishers don't need to do that.

FURTHER READING

Clark, Charles (ed.), *Publishing Agreements: A Book of Precedents*, 4th edn, Butterworths, 1993

Flint, Michael F., *A User's Guide to Copyright*, 3rd edn, Butterworths, 1990

Legat, Michael, *An Authors' Guide to Publishing*, 3rd edn, Robert Hale, 1991

Legat, Michael, *Understanding Publishers' Contracts*, Robert Hale, 1992

Society of Authors, *Quick Guide: Publishing Contracts*, free to members or £3.00, including postage

Unwin, Sir Stanley, *The Truth About Publishing*, 8th edn, Unwin Hyman, 1976, O.P.

Net Book Agreement

The Net Book Agreement is an arrangement, approved by the Restrictive Practices Court as operating in the public interest, designed to improve the availability of a wide range of books to the public through a wide range of outlets. The Agreement, operated by The Publishers Association, enables (but does not require) any publishers who are signatories (whether or not in membership of the PA) to enforce a minimum retail price (the net price) for individual titles, then known as 'net books'. In this way, booksellers are encouraged to hold wide-ranging stocks, secure in the knowledge that the prices of their books, and the value of their stocks, will not be undermined by other retailers who do not provide similar levels of stock or customer-service, such as handling special orders. The Restrictive Practices Court held that, without such a system, the availability of books and the number of booksellers would be reduced, book prices would overall be higher, and fewer titles would be published, with particular loss to those of literary and scholastic value.

Under the arrangement, libraries open to the public, schools and school and church book agencies may be supplied by booksellers at permitted discounts on the net price. School books are normally sold non-net (not subject to the Agreement).

Following a decision of the European Commission relating to the application of the NBA in trade between Member States (which is the subject of an appeal to the European Court of Justice), the application of the NBA to the Republic of Ireland and to books imported into the UK from other Member States of the European Union has been suspended.

Book Clubs

Book clubs provide their members with selected books (offered either as a main choice or alternative choice) at book club prices, usually through the mail on a regular basis. In order to acquire selected books at special prices book club members are required to commit to the purchase of a number of selections over a given period.

Book clubs can enjoy relatively secure sales and offer savings to their members by buying or printing considerable numbers of copies and offering them to members who have indicated their interest in the type of books offered. These sales can provide valuable revenues to the authors and the publishers of the selected books.

In the case of books otherwise sold as 'net books' through booksellers (see **Net Book Agreement**), the conduct of book clubs is regulated by Book Club Regulations administered by The Publishers Association. These regulations are designed to ensure fairness between book clubs and booksellers offering the same titles.

Sales to book clubs are usually made by the original publisher under the terms of the contract between publisher and author – usually providing a royalty on the number of copies sold.

Artists' Choice (Quarterly), Artists' Choice Ltd, PO Box 3, Huntingdon, Cambs. PE18 0QX *tel* (0832) 710201 *fax* (0832) 710488.

BCA, 87 Newman Street, London W1P 4EN *tel* 071-637 0341 *fax* 071-631 3262.

Ancient & Medieval History Book Club
Arts Guild
Children's Book of the Month Club
Classical Music Direct
Executive World
Fantasy & SF
History Guild
Home Computer Club
The Literary Guild
Military and Aviation Book Society
Music Direct
Mystery & Thriller Guild
Quality Paperbacks Direct
Railway Book Club
World Books

Bookmarx Club (Quarterly), IS Books Ltd, 265 Seven Sisters Road, London N4 2DE *tel* 081-802 6145 *fax* 081-802 3835.

Books for Children (Monthly), BFC Limited, Whiteway Court, The Whiteway, Cirencester, Glos. GL7 7BA *tel* (0285) 657081 *fax* (0285) 657086.

The Bookworm Club, Children's Club in Schools (6 p.a.), Heffers Booksellers, 20 Trinity Street, Cambridge CB2 3NG *tel* (0223) 358351 *fax* (0223) 410464.

The British Psycho-Analytical Society Book Club (3 p.a.), The Institute of Psycho-Analysis, 63 New Cavendish Street, London W1M 7RD *tel* 071-580 4952 *fax* 071-323 5312.

Cygnus Book Club (Monthly), PO Box 15, Llandeilo, Dyfed SA19 9DB *tel* (0550) 777693/777701 *fax* (0550) 777569. Includes: psychology and self-help, diet, health and exercise, world religions, new economics and education, green issues, mythology.

The Folio Society, 202 Great Suffolk Street, London SE1 1PR   *tel* 071-407 7411   *fax* 071-378 6684. *Showroom:* The Folio Gallery at Henry Sotheran, 2 Sackville Street, London W1X 2DP.

Letterbox Library (Quarterly), Children's Books Co-operative, 2nd Floor, Leroy House, 436 Essex Road, London N1 3QP   *tel* 071-226 1633   *fax* 071-226 1768.

New Left Review Editions, 6 Meard Street, London W1V 3HR   *tel* 071-734 8839   *fax* 071-734 0059.

Poetry Book Society, Book House, 45 East Hill, London SW18 2QZ   *tel* 081-870 8403.

Pooh Corner Book Club, For all things Pooh, High Street, Hartfield, East Sussex TN7 4AE   *tel* (0892) 770453.

Readers Union Ltd, PO Box 6, Brunel House, Newton Abbot, Devon TQ12 2DW   *tel* (0626) 336424   *telex* 42904 BOOKS G   *fax* (0626) 664463/331374.

Birds and Natural History Book Society	Gardeners Book Society
	Maritime Book Society
Country Sports Book Society	Needlecraft Book Society
Craft Book Society	Photographic Book Society
Craftsman Book Society	Practical Art & Crafts
Creative Living Book Club	Ramblers and Climbers Book Society
Equestrian Book Society	

Red House Children's Book Club (13 p.a.), Windrush Park, Witney, Oxon OX8 5YF   *tel* (0993) 771144   *fax* (0993) 776813.

The Red House School Book Club (2 per term), Windrush Park, Witney, Oxon OX8 5YF   *tel* (0993) 771144   *fax* (0993) 776813.

The Royal Society of Chemistry Book Club (2 p.a.), Membership Development, The Royal Society of Chemistry, Thomas Graham House, Science Park, Cambridge CB4 4WF   *tel* (0223) 420066   *telex* 818293   *fax* (0223) 423623.

Scholastic Publications Ltd, Villiers House, Clarendon Avenue, Leamington Spa, Warks. CV32 5PR   *tel* (0926) 887799   *fax* (0926) 883331.

The Women's Book Club (Quarterly), Ground Floor, 45/46 Poland Street, London W1V 4AU   *tel* 071-437 1019   *fax* 071-437 4117.

International Standard Book Numbering (ISBN)

The Standard Book Numbering (SBN) system was introduced in this country in 1967. It became the International Standard Book Numbering (ISBN) system three years later.

The overall administration of the international system is done from Berlin, by the International ISBN-Agentur, Staatsbibliothek Preussicher Kulturbesitz, Potsdamer Str 33, 10785 Berlin, Germany.

In this country the system is administered by the Standard Book Numbering Agency Ltd, 12 Dyott Street, London WC1A 1DF. The Agency was set up before the scheme became international, which is why that word does not appear in its title.

Over the years a number of misconceptions have grown up about ISBNs, and this article endeavours to put right some of these.

The Standard Book Numbering Agency gets a large number of telephone calls, many of which follow a common pattern. For instance:

Are they legal? Do we have to have them?

There is no legal requirement for a book to carry an ISBN. But it is useful to educational authorities, certain library suppliers, public libraries and some computer using distributors, and is now essential to booksellers using the tele-ordering system. The introduction of Public Lending Right has also made ISBNs of importance to authors.

I am about to publish a book. Must I deposit a copy with the ISBN Agency to obtain copyright?

No. Copyright is obtained by the simple act of publication. However, by law, a copy of every new book must be deposited at the Legal Deposit Office of the British Library, Boston Spa, Wetherby, West Yorkshire LS23 7BY. The Legal Deposit Office issues a receipt, and this has, in the past, proved useful when a dispute has arisen over the date of publication.

Titles deposited are catalogued by the British National Bibliography, which records ISBNs where available. Perhaps a confusion about copyright and ISBNs arises from this, but the ISBN, of itself, has nothing to do with copyright.

What are the fees for ISBNs?

No charge is made for the allocation of a publisher prefix. Publishers may ask the Agency to supply a computer print out of all the ISBNs available to the publisher, with check digits calculated. A small charge is made for this print out.

Are you a Government Department?

No. Our parent company pays taxes; we get no subsidy from anyone. In most other countries the costs *are* borne by the state, through the national library system which frequently administers the scheme overseas.

Do I need an ISBN for a Church Magazine?

No. But you may need an ISSN (International Standard Serial Number). These are obtainable from the UK National Serials Data Centre, The British Library, Boston Spa, Wetherby, West Yorkshire LS23 7BY.

Incidentally, a yearbook can have both an ISBN and an ISSN.

Should we have our own identifier? We do not consider ourselves within the English speaking group.

This comes from publishers with devolution in mind. Usually Welsh, less often Irish. The group system within the ISBN scheme is not quite so categoric as to be dictated by language considerations only. A group is defined as a 'language, geographic or other convenient area'. There is no strict logic applied, just pragmatism as to what is most *convenient* for trading purposes.

I want my book to reach as wide a market as possible. Should I have an ISBN?

The ISBN will not automatically sell a book. If the book, like that famous mousetrap, is a better one, the world will beat a path to its door. However, the ISBN will oil the wheels of distribution and it is therefore advisable to have one.

Will you supply an ISBN for a carton of assorted painting books?

No. In the words of the ISBN manual (available from the SBN agency at £4.50, cash with order), 'an ISBN identifies one title, or edition of a title, from one specific publisher, and is unique to that title or edition'. It is now additionally used to identify computer software and maps. It is not designed for a carton of assorted painting books.

How does a publisher get an ISBN?

If they have not had ISBNs before, publishers should contact the SBN Agency. Written answers are required to some basic questions.

Reproduced by kind permission of the Standard Book Numbering Agency Ltd.

Start writing now

Thrillers come in all shapes and sizes and convolutions: they are distinguished from other narratives not by format but by a greater endowment of tension. Aspirants are sometimes told that the thriller writer *plots* for tension but that advice does him great disservice. You cannot plan or plot for tension, you *write* for tension. A plot is merely a sequence of events selected to illustrate some concept or idea you have. True, the events have a certain inherent edge-of-the-chair potential but that is all it is, until you realize the potential on the page.

Tension is a function of the reader's identification with the character in jeopardy – to state the obvious, you must present the character for that identification before the reader will thrill to his danger. I shall therefore assume, in the discussion of the tension building methods and devices, that you have sorted your notes and perhaps retyped them and are now in the process of writing your novel, stopping every so often to turn to me for help because you feel the tension lagging.

from *Writing a Thriller* by André Jute (A & C Black, £9.99)

Public Lending Right

FOR WRITERS AND ILLUSTRATORS OF BOOKS

Outline

Under the PLR system, payment is made from public funds to authors (writers, translators, illustrators and some editors/compilers) whose books are lent out from public libraries. Payment is made once a year, in February, and the amount authors receive is proportionate to the number of times (established from a sample) that their books were borrowed during the previous year (July to June).

The legislation

PLR was created, and its principles established, by the Public Lending Right Act 1979 (HMSO, 30p). The Act required the rules for the administration of PLR to be laid down by a scheme. That was done in the Public Lending Right Scheme 1982 (HMSO, £2.95), which includes details of transfer (assignment), transmission after death, renunciation, trusteeship, bankruptcy, etc. Amending orders made in 1983, 1984, 1988, 1989 and 1990 were consolidated in December 1990 (S.I. 2360, £3.90). Some further amendments affecting author eligibility came into effect in December 1991 (S.I. 2618, £1.00).

How the system works

From the applications he receives, the Registrar of PLR compiles a register of authors and books which is held on computer. A representative sample of book issues is recorded, consisting of all loans from selected public libraries. This is then multiplied in proportion to total library lending to produce, for each book, an estimate of its total annual loans throughout the country. Each year the computer compares the register with the estimated loans to discover how many loans are credited to each registered book for the calculation of PLR payments. The computer does this using code numbers – in most cases the ISBN printed in the book.

Parliament allocates a sum each year (£4,936,000 for 1994-95) for PLR. This Fund pays the administrative costs of PLR and reimburses local authorities for recording loans in the sample libraries. The remaining money is then divided by the total registered loan figure in order to work out how much can be paid for each estimated loan of a registered book.

Limits on payments

(1) *Bottom limit*. If all the registered interests in an author's books score so few loans that they would earn less than £1 in a year, no payment is due.

(2) *Top limit*. If the books of one registered author score so high that the author's PLR earnings for the year would exceed £6000, then only £6000 is paid. No author can earn more than £6000 in PLR in any one year.

Money that is not paid out because of these limits belongs to the Fund and increases the amounts paid that year to other authors.

The sample

The basic sample represents only public libraries (no academic, school, private or commercial libraries are included) and only loans made over the counter (not consultations of books on library premises). It follows that only those books which are loaned from public libraries can earn PLR and make an application worthwhile. However, the feasibility of extending PLR to reference books is currently under review.

The sample consists of the entire loans records for a year from libraries in thirty public library authorities spread through England, Scotland, Wales and Northern Ireland. Sample loans are about 3% of the national total. It is intended to change to a situation where all computerised sampling points in an authority contribute loans data ('multi-site' sampling). This change is being introduced gradually, and began in July 1991. The aim is to increase the sample without any significant increase in costs. In order to counteract sampling error, libraries in the sample change every two to three years. Loans are totalled every twelve months for the period 1 July to 30 June.

An author's entitlement to PLR depends, under the 1979 Act, on the loans accrued by his or her books in the sample. This figure is multiplied to produce regional and national estimated loans.

ISBNs

PLR depends on the use of code numbers to identify books lent and to correlate loans with entries on the register so that payment can be made. Principally the system uses the International Standard Book Number – the ISBN – which consists of ten digits and is usually printed with the publishing information on the back of the title page; it may also be on the back flap or back of the jacket or cover. Examples are: 0 10 541079 9 and 185036110x.

From July 1991 an ISBN was required for all new registrations. Different editions (for example, 1st, 2nd, hardcover, paperback, large print) of the same book have different ISBNs.

Authorship

In the PLR system the author of a book is the writer, illustrator, translator, compiler, editor or reviser. Authors must be named on the book's title page, or be able to prove authorship by some other means (e.g. receipt of royalties). The ownership of copyright (apart from crown copyright for which see below) has no bearing on PLR eligibility.

Co-authorship/illustrators

In the PLR system the authors of a book are those writers, translators, editors, compilers and illustrators as defined above. Authors must apply for registration before their books can earn PLR. There is no restriction on the number of authors who can register shares in any one book as long as they satisfy the eligibility criteria.

Applications from writers and/or illustrators

At least one must be eligible and they must jointly agree what share of PLR each will take. This agreement is necessary even if one or two are ineligible or do not wish to register for PLR. If they are not all eligible, those who are will receive a share(s) specified in the application. PLR can be any whole percentage. Illustrators and joint writers may only register more than 50% if justified by their actual contribution to the book. Detailed advice is available from the PLR office.

Applications from translators

Translators may apply, without reference to other authors, for a 30% fixed share (to be divided equally between joint translators).

Applications from editors and compilers

An editor or compiler may apply, either with others or without reference to them, to register a 20% share. Unless in receipt of royalties an editor must have written at least 10% of the book's contents or more than 10 pages of text in addition to normal editorial work. The share of joint editors/compilers is 20% in total to be divided equally. An application from an editor or compiler to register a greater percentage share must be accompanied by supporting documentary evidence of actual contribution.

Dead or missing co-authors

Where it is impossible to agree shares with a co-author because that person is dead or untraceable, then the surviving co-author or co-authors may submit an application without the dead or missing co-author, but must name the co-author and provide supporting evidence as to why that co-author has not agreed shares. The living co-author(s) will then be able to register a share in the book which will be 20% for the illustrator (or illustrators) and the residual percentage for writer (or writers).

If this percentage is to be divided between more than one writer or illustrator, then this will be in equal shares unless some other apportionment is requested and agreed by the Registrar.

Writers or illustrators may apply for a different percentage apportionment, and the Registrar will register different percentage shares if it is reasonable in relation to the authors' contribution to the particular book. Detailed advice and forms are available from the PLR Office.

The PLR Office keeps a file of missing authors (mostly illustrators) to help applicants locate co-authors. Help is also available from publishers, the writers' organisations, and The Association of Illustrators, 1 Colville Place, London W1P 1HN.

Life and death

Authors can only be registered for PLR during their lifetime. However, for authors so registered, books can later be registered if first published within one year before their death or ten years afterwards. New versions of titles registered by the author can be registered posthumously.

Residential qualifications

Eligibility for PLR is restricted to authors who are resident in the United Kingdom or Germany. A resident in these countries (for PLR purposes) has his or her only or principal home there. The United Kingdom does not include the Channel Islands or the Isle of Man.

Eligible books

In the PLR system each separate edition of a book is registered and treated as a separate book.

A book is eligible for PLR registration provided that:
(1) it has an eligible author (or co-author);
(2) it is printed and bound (paperbacks counting as bound);
(3) copies of it have been put on sale (i.e. it is not a free handout and it has already been published);
(4) it is not a newspaper, magazine, journal or periodical;
(5) the authorship is personal (i.e. not a company or association) and the book is not crown copyright;
(6) it is not wholly or mainly a musical score;
(7) it has an ISBN.

Notification and payment

Every registered author receives from the Registrar an annual statement of estimated loans for each book and the PLR due.

SAMPLING ARRANGEMENTS

Libraries

To help minimise the unfairnesses that arise inevitably from a sampling system, the Scheme specifies the eight regions within which authorities and sampling points have to be designated and makes provision for the inclusion of libraries of varying size. Part of the sample drops out by rotation each year to allow fresh libraries to be included.

The following library authorities have been designated for the year beginning 1 July 1994. (M) indicates a multi-site authority. *Wales*: Gwent (M), Clwyd (M), Llanelli (M); *Scotland*: Angus (M), Edinburgh, Kyle and Carrick (M); *Northern Ireland*: W Education & Library Board (M), SE Education & Library Board; *London*: Wandsworth (M), City of London, Haringey (M), Lewisham (M); *Metropolitan Districts*: Manchester (M), Sandwell (M), Gateshead (M), Bradford, Walsall; *Counties S&E*: Buckinghamshire (M), Kent, Surrey, Norfolk, Cambridge (M); *Counties S&W*: Gloucestershire (M), Hereford & Worcs. (M), Dorset, Wiltshire (M); *Counties N*: North Yorkshire (M), Leicestershire (M), Durham (M), Derbyshire (M).

Participating local authorities are reimbursed on an actual cost basis for additional expenditure incurred in providing loans data to the PLR Office. The extra PLR work mostly consists of modifications to computer programs to accumulate data already held in the local authority computer and to produce a monthly magnetic tape to be sent to the PLR Office at Stockton-on-Tees.

SUMMARY OF THE ELEVENTH YEAR'S RESULTS

Registration: authors

When registration closed for the eleventh year (30 June 1993) the number of books registered was 212,668 for 23,132 authors. This included 654 German authors.

Eligible loans

Of the 576 million estimated loans from UK libraries, 251 million belong to books on the PLR register. The loans credited to registered books – 43.5% of all library borrowings – qualify for payment. The remaining 56.5% of loans relate to books that are ineligible for various reasons, to books written by dead or foreign authors, and to books that have simply not been applied for.

Money and payments

PLR's administrative costs are deducted from the fund allocated to the Registrar annually by Parliament.

Operating the Scheme this year cost £628,000 representing some 13% of the PLR fund. The Rate per Loan for 1993-94 was set at 2.00 pence and calculated to distribute all the £4,372,000 available. The total of PLR distribution and costs is therefore the full £5.00 million which the Government provided in 1993-94.

The numbers of authors in various payment categories are as follows:

		£
116	payments at	6,000 maximum
43	payments at	5,000-5,999
217	payments between	2,500-4,999
609	payments between	1,000-2,499
754	payments between	500-999
3,849	payments between	100-499
13,064	payments between	1-99
18,652	TOTAL	

There were also 4480 registered authors whose books earned them *nil* payment.

As a result of the £6000 maximum payment rule some £646,503 became available for redistribution to other authors.

MOST BORROWED AUTHORS IN UK PUBLIC LIBRARIES

Based on PLR sample loans July 1992-June 1993. Includes all writers, both registered and unregistered, but not illustrators where the book has a separate writer. Writing names are used; pseudonyms have not been combined. (C) indicates a children's book author.

Authors with loans over 1 million (6% of national loans)

Allan & Janet Ahlberg (C)	Len Deighton	Penny Jordan	Rosamunde Pilcher
Virginia Andrews	Elizabeth Ferrars	Lena Kennedy	Ruth Rendell
Enid Blyton (C)	Dick Francis	Stephen King	Wilbur Smith
Agatha Christie	René Goscinny (C)	Ed McBain	Danielle Steel
Catherine Cookson	Jack Higgins	Ellis Peters	Kate William (C)
Roald Dahl (C)	Victoria Holt		

Authors with loans over 500,000 (8% of national loans)

Ted Allbeury	Janet Dailey	P.D. James	Jean Plaidy
Evelyn Anthony	Colin Dexter	Marie Joseph	Belva Plain
Jeffrey Archer	Daphne Du Maurier	Carolyn Keene (C)	Terry Pratchett
Tessa Barclay	Colin Forbes	Dick King-Smith (C)	Claire Rayner
Maeve Binchy	Helen Forrester	Dean R. Koontz	Miss Read
Emma Blair	Christine Marion Fraser	Charlotte Lamb	Douglas Reeman
Judy Blume (C)	Catherine Gaskin	Robert Ludlum	Harold Robbins
Barbara Taylor Bradford	Iris Gower	Alistair MacLean	Gerald Seymour
Tony Bradman (C)	Winston Graham	Ngaio Marsh	Sarah Shears
Philippa Carr	James Herbert	Graham Masterton	Sidney Sheldon
Barbara Cartland	Hergé (C)	Anne Mather	Jessica Stirling
Jon Cleary	Georgette Heyer	Philip McCutchan	Jamie Suzanne (C)
Virginia Coffman	Eric Hill (C)	Carole Mortimer	Leslie Thomas
Jackie Collins	Susan Howatch	Maisie Mosco	E.V. Thompson
Jilly Cooper	Shirley Hughes (C)	Betty Neels	Mary Wesley
Bernard Cornwell	Pat Hutchins	Christopher Nicole	Phyllis A. Whitney
John Cunliffe (C)	Hammond Innes	Pamela Oldfield	Margaret Yorke

RECIPROCAL ARRANGEMENTS

In 1981-1982 reciprocal arrangements with West Germany were sought by British writers to help ensure that they did not lose the German PLR they had enjoyed since 1974. The German Scheme, although loan based, is very different in most other respects. Reciprocity was brought into effect in January 1985. Authors can apply for German PLR through the Authors' Licensing and Collecting Society. (Comparison of PLR schemes internationally and consideration of prospects for reciprocity are covered in *PLR in Practice*, John Sumsion, 2nd edn, 1991, £14.50 inc. UK postage, from the PLR Office.)

ADVISORY COMMITTEE

The PLR Advisory Committee advises the Secretary of State for National Heritage and the Registrar on matters concerning PLR. Its present chairman is Philip Ziegler.

FURTHER INFORMATION

PLR application forms, information and publications can be obtained from The Registrar, PLR Office, Bayheath House, Prince Regent Street, Stockton-on-Tees, Cleveland TS18 1DF   *tel* (0642) 604699   *fax* (0642) 615641. The Registrar publishes an Annual Review which may also be obtained from the PLR Office.

Getting hold of experts

You may often find yourself at a loss as to how to get in touch with experts on particular subjects when there is no one in your immediate circle who can help. Here the best advice to be given is, 'Do not by shy. Go straight to the horse's mouth – in other words, look up the professional or trade association concerned (or it may be an international company, a bank, or almost any other kind of group), and either write or telephone to the general secretary, press or public relations officer. Remember that all these people have a vested interest in being portrayed correctly, and also that the expert is always flattered to be consulted. If the person you approach is too busy or unable for some other reason to give you what you want, he will usually be able to suggest an alternative contact.

The best way to find out if there is a relevant association is to look in an up-to-date *Directory of British Associations and Associations in Ireland* or the equivalent volumes for Europe, the *Directory of European Industrial and Trade Associations* and the *Directory of European Professional and Learned Societies*. Another goldmine of information of this nature, and fully up to date, is the *Hollis Press & Public Relations Annual*, which lists an enormous number of press contacts (with addresses and telephone numbers) in virtually every field of professional, industrial and commercial life, as well as official and public information sources, PR consultancies and much other invaluable data. The same firm now publishes a similar directory for Europe, *Hollis Europe*. There is also a list of societies and institutions in *Whitaker's Almanack*, but this is not so informative, nor is it as comprehensive as the two publications mentioned above. Lastly, do not overlook your local 'yellow pages' directory, in case there is some contact on your own doorstep.

from *Research for Writers* by Ann Hoffmann (A & C Black, £10.99)

The Florence Agreement and its Nairobi Protocol

This Agreement, on the Importation of Educational, Scientific and Cultural Materials, generally known as the Florence Agreement, was adopted by the Unesco General Conference in Florence in 1950 and came into force on 21 May 1952. It is concerned with the free flow of a wide variety of articles including books and the removal of tariff and trade obstacles. The principal undertaking of the contracting states is the exemption of books and other educational, scientific and cultural imports from customs duties, and the granting of licences and foreign exchange as far as possible for their importation. Books of every sort are included in the Agreement, not exempting those printed abroad from the work of an author in the importing country. Unbound sheets do not come under the Agreement.

The following is an up-to-date list of the States parties to the Agreement: Afghanistan, Australia, Austria, Barbados, Belgium, Bolivia, Bosnia-Herzegovina, Burkina-Faso, Cameroon, Congo, Côte d'Ivoire, Croatia, Cuba, Cyprus, Democratic Kampuchea, Denmark, Egypt, El Salvador, Fiji, Finland, France, Gabon, Germany, Ghana, Greece, Guatemala, Haiti, Holy See, Hungary, Iran, Iraq, Ireland, Israel, Italy, Japan, Jordan, Kenya, Lao People's Democratic Republic, Liechtenstein, Luxembourg, Madagascar, Malawi, Malaysia, Malta, Mauritius, Monaco, Morocco, Netherlands, New Zealand, Nicaragua, Niger, Nigeria, Norway, Oman, Pakistan, Philippines, Poland, Portugal, Romania, Rwanda, San Marino, Sierra Leone, Singapore, Slovenia, Socialist People's Libyan Arab Jamahiriya, Solomon Islands, Spain, Sri Lanka, Sweden, Switzerland, Syrian Arab Republic, Tanzania (United Republic of), Thailand, Tonga, Trinidad and Tobago, Tunisia, Uganda, United Kingdom, United States of America, Venezuela, Viet-Nam (Socialist Republic of), Zaire, Zambia.

A Protocol to the Florence Agreement or Nairobi Protocol adopted by the Unesco General Conference in Nairobi in 1976 came into force on 2 January 1982. It is open only to states which are parties to the Agreement. The Protocol broadens the scope of the Agreement by extending the benefits it offers to additional objects and by granting further benefits to a number of materials. The following States adhere to the Protocol: Australia, Barbados, Belgium, Bosnia-Herzegovina, Croatia, Cuba, Denmark, Egypt, Finland, France, Germany, Greece, Holy See, Iraq, Ireland, Italy, Luxembourg, Netherlands, Portugal, San Marino, Slovenia, Spain, United Kingdom, United States of America, Venezuela.

The Authors' Licensing and Collecting Society Ltd

ALCS was set up in 1977 to collect and distribute money to writers for payments which authors and other copyright holders are unable to collect individually.

ALCS is a company limited by guarantee (i.e. not having a share capital). It is run by members through a Council of Management on which the Society of Authors and Writers' Guild of Great Britain are represented.

ALCS is a member of CISAC (International Confederation of Authors and Composers Societies) and IFRRO (International Federation of Reprographic Rights Organisation) and through them maintains constant links with continental European and other overseas collecting societies.

ADMINISTRATION

The Council of Management has twelve members, all of whom are active writers. Four are elected by and from the Ordinary Members of ALCS, four are nominated by the Society of Authors and four by the Writers' Guild. The ALCS is served by the Secretary General and a small staff who manage the office and arrange the regular distributions.

POWER

On joining, members transfer to the Society the power to administer on their behalf specific rights which they are unable to exercise as individuals. Under the Society's constitution ALCS may administer (a) in the United Kingdom and the Republic of Ireland and (b) in other Countries:

lending right (not British PLR);
reprographic (photocopying) right;
cable transmission right;
private recording right;
off-air recording right;
right of public reception of broadcasts.

Where such a right can be exercised by an individual, the Society does not normally intervene.

From time to time ALCS may add other rights by special Resolution of a General Meeting to reflect the development of technology.

DISTRIBUTIONS

Foreign PLR

ALCS makes annual distributions from the collecting society, VG WORT, in Germany. Further money is held in Germany on behalf of British writers who have not yet joined ALCS. Those eligible to receive German PLR through ALCS are:

living British authors resident anywhere;
heirs of British authors through successor membership;
foreign writers resident in Britain.

Reprography

Set up in 1983 by ALCS together with the Publishers Licensing Society, the Copyright Licensing Agency (CLA) is now well-established and offers licences for reprography. ALCS is responsible for paying writers their share in any fees collected from such licences. (See the following article.)

Cable retransmission

ALCS collects fees for the retransmission of BBC 1 and 2 and BBC radio stations to Belgium and Holland and of BBC World Service Television to other European countries. ALCS also collect fees in Switzerland and other countries for British writers whose work is cabled from neighbouring countries.

Educational off-air recording

ALCS is part of the Educational Recording Agency Ltd (ERA) set up to license educational establishments to record off-air under the provisions of the 1988 Copyright Act.

GENERAL

ALCS is represented on the British Copyright Council and the Secretary General is a member of the PLR Advisory Committee. ALCS maintains a watching brief on all matters affecting copyright both in Great Britain and abroad and is recognised internationally as expert on writers' collective rights. ALCS increasingly operates as a central international information exchange.

TO JOIN

The current subscription is £5.00 (excl. VAT), £7.00 overseas. Application forms from: The Administration Manager, The Authors' Licensing and Collecting Society Ltd, 33/34 Alfred Place, London WC1E 7DP *tel* 071-255 2034.

Members of the Society of Authors and the Writers' Guild have free membership of ALCS.

The Copyright Licensing Agency Ltd
CLA

Over twenty years have passed since 1973, when interest groups in the UK started to prepare submissions to the government-appointed committee under the Hon. Mr Justice Whitford about ways of regulating copying from books, journals and periodicals. These interest groups, representing owners of copyright, were seeking both a mechanism of control and just recompense for authors and publishers while at the same time continuing to satisfy the reasonable demands of a modern information-driven society.

When it was eventually published in 1977, the Whitford Report on Copyright and Designs Law suggested, as the best likely solution to the problem, a collective administration system for copying rights organised by the rightsholders themselves.

This recommendation spawned first the Wolfenden Committee that brought together representatives of authors' societies and publishers' associations, and then the de Freitas committee that hammered out and fashioned, with these two sometimes antagonistic groups, a mutually acceptable constitution for such a licensing body. The outcome was the formation of the Copyright Licensing Agency, CLA, in April 1982 and its incorporation in January 1983 as a non-profit making company limited by guarantee. The Agency, which is primarily concerned with licensing 'heavy user' groups, issued its first licence in May 1984.

CLA is 'owned' by the Authors' Licensing and Collecting Society (ALCS) and the Publishers Licensing Society (PLS) in that they are its members. ALCS's members are members of the Society of Authors (SoA) and the Writers' Guild of Great Britain (WGoGB) and several thousand individual members; and PLS's members are the Publishers Association (PA), the Periodical Publishers Association (PPA) and the Association of Learned and Professional Society Publishers (ALPSP). All are represented on CLA's board of twelve directors, six being ALCS nominations and six PLS nominations.

CLA has six main functions and these are:

- to obtain mandates from publishers and authors in association with ALCS and PLS
- to license users for copying extracts from books, journals and periodicals
- to collect fees from licensed users for such copying
- to implement a system of record-keeping sufficient to provide statistically acceptable information on which to calculate a fair apportionment of the distributable income
- to pay ALCS and PLS their correct shares of the distributable income and provide sufficient data to enable these societies to pay individual authors and publishers
- to institute such legal proceedings as may be necessary for the enforcement of the rights entrusted to the Agency

CLA sees its principal licensing areas in the UK as being *education, government* and *industry*. Each of these broad categories has three or four sub-groups. In company with nearly all other Reprographic Rights Organisations (RROs) around the world, CLA started licensing in the general education sector. The first major development occurred in April 1986, when three-year voluntary licensing agreements with the country's local education authorities (LEAs) came into effect; in April 1989 these licences were extended for a further three years;

copying in all thirty thousand or so state colleges and schools is now covered by
such licences. The Agency also licenses the independent education sector through
its licensing scheme for independent schools.

With the general education sector (5 to 16 years) covered, CLA next turned
its attention to higher and further education (HE & FE) and during 1989,
after several years of negotiating, finalised arrangements whereby universities,
polytechnics, independent colleges and language schools, etc. all became licensed
from 1 January 1990. Three-year licences once again were agreed.

Having successfully negotiated the local education authority licences with
a joint committee of representatives appointed by the Association of County
Councils (ACC), the Association of Metropolitan Authorities (AMA) and the
Convention of Scottish Local Authorities (CoSLA), CLA will try to license the
non-LEA parts of local government in one fell swoop with a similar committee
but expanded to include representatives of the Association of District Councils
(ADC) and the Association of London Authorities (ALA).

It is the Agency's intention to deal with central government on a ministry by
ministry basis, starting with the Department of Trade & Industry (DTI) as the
sponsors of the Copyright, Designs and Patents Act 1988; the Department
for Education (DfE), as educational institutions are already licensed; and the
National Health Service (NHS) which, with 1.25 million employees, is the largest
employer in Europe.

Public bodies, i.e. those organisations for which government ministers have
some accountability (e.g. The British Council), may have to be dealt with in
some non-collective manner.

Trade, industry, commerce and the professions present CLA with its greatest
challenge because of their size and diversity. A first step has already been taken,
however, with the setting up of a joint task force with the Confederation of
British Industry (CBI). This CBI/CLA working party, chaired by an industrialist,
is examining the best way or ways forward, concentrating initially on manufacturing industry, with particular emphasis on R&D-driven sectors such as
pharmaceuticals, chemicals, engineering, electronics, aerospace and oil fuel.

Basically, CLA is a banking operation with legal overtones: it collects fees
from licensed users in respect of acts of photocopying from books and serials and
other copying such as microfiche printing and, after deducting its administration
costs and any reserves or provisions the Board may decide, distributes the balance
to ALCS and PLS for them to pay to authors and publishers.

CLA currently offers two basic services, that is, licences to copy, authorised
by many individual owners of copyright, both of which offer the collective
repertoire of copyright works mandated to CLA by those owners:

- a *collective user* service such as that made with the associations representing
  local education authorities for state colleges and schools
- a *transactional user* service for those institutions where a suitable representative organisation, such as an LEA, is unable or unwilling to provide
  the level of administrative support that a collective user scheme requires,
  e.g. implementation and supervision of a sampling system, single cheque
  payment, etc.

Both types of licence are valid for a specific period, usually two or three years.

Under a collective user arrangement the level of copying for a group of
institutions is mutually agreed and a global fee set; this fee total is then
apportioned by the organising body amongst its constituents and paid by them
to CLA on presentation of the agency's invoice. With the transactional user
scheme, fees are paid on a straight cost per copy-page basis; returns to CLA are
made at regular, agreed intervals, and a self-billing system is used.

Importantly, from the user community's standpoint, CLA indemnifies all licensees against any inadvertent infringement of copyright.

Right from the outset, the authors' representatives insisted first that writers should benefit individually and directly from the copying of their works and that the money should not go to authors' societies for 'social benefit' purposes, as is the case in some parts of the world. Secondly, they insisted that the individual authors' shares should be paid to them directly, and not through the accounting systems of their publishers.

In order to fulfil these requirements CLA had to devise a title-based distribution system and a form of record-keeping suitable for a geographically spread, stratified and statistically sound sample of the licensees. Some form of itemised record-keeping, therefore, is necessary on the part of both categories of licence holders. With *collective user* licensing, a rotating sample of about 5% of institutions in each broad category is required to maintain records of their copying, which are returned to CLA at agreed intervals, where they are checked and analysed. *Transactional user* licensees are required to keep records of all their copying.

Controlled record-keeping is crucial to CLA because the statistical information extracted from these records of copying is used as the basis for making payments to copyright owners whose works have been copied.

Once a licence has been issued, it has been relatively simple, so far, to collect fees. It is quite another matter, however, to edit, process and analyse the returns of copying, and to calculate the correct amounts due to copyright owners.

On return to the Agency, the record-keeping forms, which are regarded and treated as strictly confidential documents, some of which are deemed to be personal data under the Data Protection Act 1984, are:

- checked by the licensing officer responsible to ensure that the conditions of the licence are being adhered to
- scrutinised by the data preparation department to validate the information being submitted, e.g. missing ISBN/ISSNs etc. are searched for
- keyed for computer analysis
- subjected to a final edit for data quality

The results are analysed and summaries produced showing pages copied, by ISBN/ISSN and by title, by author and by publisher. Apportionments are then calculated, statements produced and cheques drawn.

The existence of the International Standard Book Number (ISBN) and the International Standard Serial Number (ISSN) systems is a great benefit to CLA and makes the Agency's task that much easier than it would otherwise be.

The CLA Board decided that the first distribution to members would be £1.4 million (US$2.3 million) and would be paid in two parts: the first tranche of just over £500,000 in October 1987, and the balance of around £900,000 in March/April 1988. Thereafter, payments to rights owners would be made every six months. At the time of writing CLA has distributed around £15.6 million to members.

It must be emphasised that a CLA licence is not a carte blanche to copy without restrictions. The conditions are clearly set down and are required to be displayed alongside every copying machine within the control of the licensee. The wording of the notices may vary slightly depending on the category of the licensee, but the core message is always the same! CLA also produces various user guides for issue to employees, and there is a warning sticker that goes on top of machines to act as a reminder to copier users.

For CLA there is comfort in knowing that it is not alone in pioneering the collective administration of copying rights. Counterpart organisations to CLA now exist in nineteen other countries – Australia, Austria, Canada, Denmark,

Finland, France, Germany, Iceland, Ireland, Italy, Japan, the Netherlands, New Zealand, Norway, South Africa, Spain, Sweden, Switzerland and the United States – nearly all of them in membership of IFRRO, the International Federation of Reproduction Rights Organisations. RROs are also presently being formed in Belgium and Israel.

Finally, the broader the repertoire an RRO can offer its licensees the better, and it is a priority of CLA to secure reciprocal agreements with counterpart organisations overseas, particularly those in English-speaking countries where UK books, journals and periodicals are being widely and extensively copied, and, equally, where much publishing in the English language takes place.

Critics of collecting societies say that they spend pounds to distribute pennies. From the start, this is a potential criticism of which the CLA directors were acutely conscious. As far back as November 1982 the board designate set down in its minutes that on no account were CLA's administration costs to exceed 20% of the fee income. The Agency has done much better than that: CLA's overhead is working out at about 12½% of the fee income, and the Agency continually strives to reduce that level where possible. It is, however, in the business of handling large numbers of documents and processing a great deal of information, and to do so efficiently in this day and age a high degree of office automation is required and technological wizardry does not come cheap.

CLA's aim is to distribute as much as it can, as fast as it can, and as efficiently as it can. It believes that £15.6 million, distributed between October 1987 and March 1994, speaks louder than any words, and demonstrates better than anything else the Agency's resolve to achieve its objectives.

Further information from The Secretary, The Copyright Licensing Agency Ltd, 90 Tottenham Court Road, London W1P 9HE *tel* 071-436 5931 *fax* 071-436 3986.

Borrowing, copying or stealing?

On the principle that there is nothing new in the universe, decide to write about, for instance, pollution in Britain and of course you won't be the first person to do so. But you are not guilty of borrowing, copying or stealing someone else's idea. What matters is the imagination and enthusiasm the idea plants in your head, coupled with your unique way of writing about it. The ideas in a previous section may be no help to you because they ignite no spark; if that is so, it is because they are not *your* ideas. Use other people's to find your own, to set you reflecting, contrasting, developing and generally giving your imagination room to expand in the way only you can. When I first understood what pundits meant by such 'lateral thinking' I realised I had been doing it instinctively all my life. Ideas float about by the million but the best *for you* are fed by a natural individuality that will show through the written words and breathe life into your work.

from *Writing for Magazines* by Jill Dick (A & C Black, £9.99)

Mechanical-Copyright Protection Society Ltd

The Society was formed in 1910 by a group of music publishers in anticipation of the introduction of new legislation which for the first time would provide for the protection of copyright material by mechanical reproduction.

This became effective on the introduction of the Copyright Act 1911 when only the music box, piano roll, cylinder and disc recordings were known.

Since those days the Society has grown with the technical advances into sound, film, radio and television recordings, magnetic tape and videocassettes, and now grants licences in all matters affecting recording rights, both in the UK and throughout the world by virtue of its affiliation with other similar organisations and agencies.

Membership of the Society is open to all music copyright owners, composers, lyric writers and publishers. There is no entrance fee or subscription. General information concerning the work of the Society is available from the Corporate Communications Department.

Enquiries for membership should be addressed to the Membership Department, Elgar House, 41 Streatham High Road, London SW16 1ER   *tel* 081-769 4400   *fax* 081-769 8792.

Morals and taboos

Find ways of balancing realism with discretion. If and when you feel that your young lovers have reached the stage of a sexual relationship, proceed with caution and avoid going into explicit, step-by-step details. You are writing a story, remember, not a manual on the delights of sex.

It's also worth remembering that publishers – and book club selectors, too – with reputations to safeguard, are on the whole reluctant to consider novels for young adults which delve into matters as controversial as AIDS, promiscuity, under-age sex and homosexuality. Readers avidly interested in themes such as these will find them aplenty on the adult book and magazine shelves.

It might be helpful, when writing your novel, to ask yourself if you would be happy for your own and your friends' children to read it. Think, too, whether you would feel in any way embarrassed or guilty if they happened to discover that it had been written by you.

from *Writing for the Teenage Market* by Ann de Gale (A & C Black, £8.99)

The Performing Right Society Ltd

The Performing Right Society is an Association of Composers, Authors and Publishers of copyright musical works, established in 1914 to collect royalties for the public performance, broadcasting and diffusion by cable of such works and their use by diffusion services; also to restrain unauthorised use thereof.

Licences are granted which convey the necessary permission for the public performance of any of the works of its members and those of the affiliated national societies of more than 30 other countries. The combined membership thus represented by the Society is about 500,000. Over 200,000 places of entertainment are covered by the Society's licence in the British Isles alone.

The Society does not control the performance of non-musical works (plays, sketches, etc.), but its licence is required for the use of its international repertoire in variety, as overture, entr'acte or exit music, or for any other form of live or mechanical performances (excluding operas, operettas, musical plays, specially written music for plays, revues or pantomimes (apart from interpolations therein of independent items) and ballets).

The constitution of the Society is that of a Company limited by guarantee having no share capital. The General Council consists of twelve composers and authors and twelve music publishers elected by the members from among their own number. The Society is not a profit-making organisation, the whole of the royalties it collects being distributed amongst its members and the affiliated societies after deduction of administration expenses and contributions to the PRS Members' Fund, established for the benefit of necessitous members and their dependants.

There are two distributions of general performing fees each year, and two distributions of broadcasting fees.

Applicants for membership are required to pay an initial admission fee, but no further subscriptions or fees are charged. All composers of musical works and authors of lyrics or poems which have been set to music are eligible for membership, provided that they satisfy the current membership criteria.

The Society has available for free loan a film entitled *PRS – The Movie*. For details of this and for further information contact the Public Affairs Department at PRS, 29-33 Berners Street, London W1P 4AA   *tel* 071-580 5544.

Copyright and libel

British Copyright Law

AMANDA L. MICHAELS MA
Barrister

INTRODUCTION

Copyright is a creature of statute. There have been a series of Copyright Acts over the years, gradually extending the scope of this area of the law so as to offer protection to the widening range of media used by writers and artists of all types.

On 1 August 1989, the Copyright Act 1956, previously the major Act in this field, was replaced by the Copyright, Designs and Patents Act 1988 ('the Act'). The Act sets out to restate the law of copyright. Much of the law in it is a true restatement of the pre-existing law, especially in so far as it relates to the essentials of what may be a copyright work and how they may be protected. To this end, section 172 of the Act in particular provides that mere changes of expression from the old law do not denote a substantive change in the law, whilst prior decisions may be referred to as an aid to the construction of the Act.

However, there is a good deal in the Act which is innovatory (see, for instance, the comments below on the new design right, and the repercussions upon infringement actions of section 51), as well as a number of provisions where one might well ask whether all that is intended is a change of expression from the old law, or whether a change of words implies a change of substance.

The general reader should therefore be aware that the old law, and old texts on the subject, may not apply to new copyright works. There are complicated transitional provisions (in Schedule 1 to the Act) relating to pre-existing works and infringements, and reference will need to be made to these and to the old law for some years to come, as well as to the numerous Orders in Council made under the Act. Users of this handbook particularly need to note that forms of publishing and licensing agreements suitable for use under the old law may need revision in the light of the Act.

Moreover, European Council Directive 93/98 requires certain changes to be made to English copyright law by 1 July 1995. No English draft is currently available, but the major change will be the extension of the term of copyright protection for most works to 70 years after the author's death.

In an article of this length, it is not possible to deal fully with all the changes in the law effected by the Act, nor indeed with all the complexities of this technical area of the law. The purpose of the article is rather to set out the basic principles of copyright protection, and to identify topics which may be of particular interest to readers of this handbook.

WORKS CAPABLE OF COPYRIGHT PROTECTION

Copyright protection has always protected the *form* in which the artist/author has set out his inspiration, not the underlying idea. So, plots, artistic ideas, systems and themes cannot be protected by copyright. Whilst an idea remains no more than that, it can be protected only by the law relating to confidential information (contrast the cases of *Green* v. *Broadcasting Corp. of New Zealand* [1989] RPC 700: no copyright in 'format' of *Opportunity Knocks*, and *Fraser* v. *Thames TV Ltd* [1984] QB 44: plot of a projected TV series protected by law of confidence). The law of copyright prevents the copying of the material form in which the idea has been presented, or of a substantial part of it, measured in terms of quality, not quantity.

The Act therefore starts out, in section 1, by setting out a number of different categories of works which can be the subject of copyright protection. These are:
 (a) original literary, dramatic, musical or artistic works,
 (b) sound recordings, films, broadcasts or cable programmes, and
 (c) typographical arrangements of published editions.

These works are further defined in sections 3 to 8. The definitions are not identical to those in the 1956 Act. A literary work, for instance, is defined as: 'any work, other than a dramatic or musical work, which is written, spoken or sung, and accordingly includes: (a) a table or compilation, and (b) a computer program.' A musical work means: 'a work consisting of music, exclusive of any words or action intended to be sung, spoken or performed with the music.' An artistic work means: '(a) a graphic work, photograph, sculpture or collage, irrespective of artistic quality, (b) a work of architecture being a building or model for a building, or (c) a work of artistic craftsmanship.'

The definitions of literary and musical works do not, however, contradict the basic rule that copyright protects the form and not the idea; works are not protected *before* being reduced into tangible form. Section 3 (2) specifically provides that no copyright shall subsist in a literary, musical or artistic work until it has been recorded in writing or otherwise.

On the other hand, all that is required to achieve copyright protection is to record the original work in any appropriate medium. Once that has been done copyright will subsist in the work (assuming that the qualifying features set out below are present) without any formality of registration or otherwise. As long as the work is produced in some tangible form there is, for instance, no need for it to be published in any way for the protection to attach to it. (Please note, however, that although this lack of formality applies here and in most European countries, the law of the USA does differ – see article: **US Copyright**). The common idea that one must register a work at Stationers Hall, or send it to oneself or to, say, a bank, in a sealed envelope so as to obtain copyright protection is incorrect. All that this precaution may do is provide some proof in an infringement action (whether as plaintiff or defendant) of the date of creation and content of one's work.

ORIGINALITY

Section 1 provides that in order to gain copyright protection, literary, dramatic, artistic and musical works must be original. Similarly, there are provisions which exclude from copyright protection sound recordings or films which are mere copies of pre-existing sound recordings and films, broadcasts which infringe rights in another broadcast or cable programmes which consist of immediate retransmissions of broadcasts.

The test of originality may not be quite that expected by the layman. Just as the law protects the form, rather than the idea, originality relates to the 'expression of the thought', rather than to the thought itself. Thus, over a number of years, the courts have held that a work need not be original in the sense of showing innovative or cultural merit, but that it needs only to have been the product of skill and labour on the part of the author. This can be seen from various sections in the Act, for instance in the definition of certain artistic works, and in the fact that it offers copyright protection to works such as compilations (like football pools coupons or directories) and tables (including mathematical tables).

There may be considerable difficulty, at times, in deciding whether a work is of sufficient originality, or has original features, where there have been a series of similar designs or amendments of existing works. See *L.A. Gear Inc* v. *Hi-Tec Sports Plc* [1992] FSR 121. What is clear, though, is that merely making a 'slavish copy' of a drawing will not create an original work: see *Interlego AG* v. *Tyco Industries* [1989] AC 217.

On the other hand, 'works' comprising the titles of books or periodicals, or advertising slogans, which may have required a good deal of original thought, generally are not accorded copyright protection, because they are too short to be deemed literary works.

See, too, the limited protection given to drawings of a functional or engineering type in the sections on infringement and design right below.

QUALIFICATION

The Act is limited in its effects to the UK (and to colonies to which it may be extended by Order in Council). It is aimed primarily at protecting the works of British citizens, or works which were first published here. However, in line with the requirements of various international conventions to which the UK is a party, copyright protection in the UK is also accorded to the works of nationals of many foreign states which are also party to these conventions, as well as to works first published in those states.

The importance of these rules (which largely repeat similar provisions of the 1956 Act) mainly arises when one is trying to find out whether a pre-existing foreign work is protected by copyright here, for instance, if one wishes to make a film based upon a foreign novel. Within the confines of this article, all that can be said is that there have been numerous different Orders in Council regulating the position for most of the major countries of the world, including the other member states of the EU and the USA, and further Orders continue to be made, but that in every case it will be wise to check the position.

OWNERSHIP

The general rule is that a work will initially be owned by its author, the author being the creator of the work, or in the case of a film or sound recording, the person who makes the arrangements necessary for it to be made.

One essential exception to the general rule is that the copyright in a work made by an employee in the course of his employment will belong to his employer, subject to any agreement to the contrary.

There can be joint authorship of a work where the work is produced by several people in such collaboration that the contribution of one is not distinct from the contribution of the other. Where two people collaborate to write a song, one producing the lyrics and the other the music, there will be two separate copyright works, the copyright in which will be owned by each of the authors separately. But where two people write a play, each rewriting what the other produces, there will be a joint work. The importance of knowing whether the work is joint or not arises firstly in working out the duration of the copyright (see below) and secondly from the fact that joint works can only be exploited with the agreement of all the joint authors, so that all of them have to join in any licence, although each of them can sue for infringement without joining the other author(s) in the proceedings.

DURATION OF COPYRIGHT

Copyright in a literary, dramatic, artistic or musical work expires fifty years after the end of the calendar year in which the author dies. If there were joint authors, the fifty-year period will run from the end of the year in which the last of them dies. However, there is an important exception to this general rule in the case of artistic works which have been industrially exploited, limiting the length of copyright protection to twenty-five years from the date of first marketing of articles made according to the design (see section 52).

If the author is unknown, the copyright will expire fifty years after the work is first made available to the public, by being performed, broadcast, exhibited, etc., depending upon the nature of the work (see section 12(2) of the Act).

If the work is 'computer-generated', copyright will expire fifty years from the date when the work was made. Copyright in a typeface runs for only twenty-five years from when it was first published.

Sound recordings will lose their copyright fifty years from the end of the year in which they are made, unless they have been released during that period, when they will enjoy copyright protection for fifty years after release. Similarly, copyright in broadcasts will expire fifty years after the end of the year in which they are made and that in cable programmes, fifty years after they are included in a cable programme.

These provisions are not identical with those under earlier Acts. Where one is dealing with a work made before the Act came into force, one needs to look at the law in force when it was made, as well as at the transitional provisions of the 1956 Act (for pre-1957 works) and/or of the Act (for pre-1989 works).

DEALING WITH COPYRIGHT WORKS: ASSIGNMENT AND LICENSING

As will be seen below, ownership of the copyright in a work confers upon the owner the exclusive right to deal with the work in a number of ways, and essentially stops all unauthorised exploitation of the work. Ownership of the copyright is capable of being separated from ownership of the material form in which the work is embodied, whether the transfer of the latter includes the former will depend upon the terms of any agreement or the circumstances. The sale of a copy of a book usually implies no sale of the copyright but a sale of a piece of sculpture might do so.

Copyright works can be exploited by their owners in two ways: the whole right in the work may be sold, with the owner retaining no interest in it (except, possibly, for payment by way of royalties); this is what is known as assignment. Alternatively, the owner may grant a licence to another to exploit the right, whilst retaining overall ownership. Agreements dealing with copyright should make it clear whether an assignment or a licence is being granted, and should clearly define the scope of any assignment or licence. The question of moral rights (see below) will also have to be considered by parties negotiating an assignment or licence.

An assignment must be in writing, signed by or on behalf of the assignor, but no other formality is required. One can make an assignment of future copyright (under section 91). Where the author of a projected work agrees in writing that he will assign the rights in a future work to another, the copyright vests in the assignee immediately upon the creation of the work, without further formalities.

This facility may be used where works are commissioned from the author, as the specific provisions as to ownership of commissioned works which existed in the 1956 Act are not reproduced as such in the new Act, save in respect of works protected by the new design right (see below).

These rules do not, apparently, affect the common law as to beneficial interests in copyright. Essentially, where someone has been commissioned to create a work for another, in circumstances in which copyright will not vest automatically in the latter, and the court finds that it was the parties' mutual intention that the copyright should belong to the 'commissioner', it will hold that the 'commissioner' is the equitable or beneficial owner of the copyright, and the author will be obliged to assign the copyright to him. 'Commission' in this context means only to order a particular piece of work to be done.

Licences do not need to take any form in particular, and may indeed be granted orally. However, an exclusive licence (i.e. one which excludes even the copyright owner himself from exploiting the work in the manner authorised by the licence) must be in writing, if the licensee is to enjoy rights in respect of infringements concurrent with those of the copyright owner.

Both assignments and licences can, and frequently do, split up the various rights contained within the copyright. So, for instance, a licence might be granted to one person to publish a novel in hardback and to another to publish in softback, a third person might be granted the film, television and video rights, and yet a fourth the right to translate the novel into other languages.

In practice, assignments may, and licences usually do, confer rights according to territory, dividing the USA from the EU or different EU countries one from the other. Two comments must be made about this. Firstly, it must be appreciated that any such agreement would be dealing with a bundle of different national copyrights, as each country's law extends only to its own borders; it must be noted that each country's law on copyright protection, on licensing and on infringement may differ and will continue to do so even once Directive 93/98 takes effect. Secondly, when purporting to divide rights between different territories of the EU there is a danger that one will infringe the competition rules of the EU (in the main Articles 30-36 and 85-86 of the Treaty of Rome), and professional advice should be taken to ensure that one is not in breach of these rules, which would render the parties liable to be fined, as well as making the agreement void in whole or in part.

Licences can also, of course, be of varying lengths. There is no need for a licence to be granted for the whole term of copyright; indeed this would be unusual, if not foolish. Well-drafted licences will provide for termination on breach, including the failure of the licensee to exploit the work properly, and on the bankruptcy or winding up of the licensee.

Copyright may be assigned by will, and where a bequest is given of an original document, etc. embodying an unpublished copyright work, the bequest will carry the copyright.

INFRINGEMENT

Copyright is infringed by doing any of a number of specified acts in relation to the copyright work, without the authority of the owner. In all forms of infringement, it suffices if a substantial part of the original is used, and the question is one to be judged according to quality not quantity (see, e.g., *Ravenscroft* v. *Herbert* [1980] RPC 193).

The form of infringement common to all forms of copyright works is that of copying. This means reproducing the work in any material form. It is important to note that primary infringement, such as copying, can be done innocently of any intention to infringe.

Infringement may occur where an existing work provides the inspiration for a later one, if copying results, e.g. by including edited extracts from a history book in a novel (*Ravenscroft* v. *Herbert*, see above) or using a photograph as the inspiration for a painting (*Baumann* v. *Fussell* [1978] RPC 485). Infringement will not necessarily be prevented merely by the application of significant new skill and labour by the infringer, nor by a change of medium.

In the case of a two-dimensional artistic work, reproduction can mean making a copy in three dimensions, and vice versa, although there is an important limitation on this general rule in section 51 of the Act, which provides that in the case of a 'design document or model' (defined as a record of a design of any aspect of the shape or configuration, internal or external, of the whole or part of an article, other than surface decoration) for something which is not itself an artistic work, it is no infringement to make an article to that design. This would appear to mean that whilst it would be an infringement to make an article from a design drawing for, say, a sculpture, it will not be an infringement of *copyright* to make a handbag from a copy of the design drawing therefor, or from a handbag which one has purchased. In order to protect such designs one will have to rely upon design right or upon a registered design (for both see below). However, under the transitional provisions, the right to rely upon copyright protection for any such designs made before the commencement of the new Act will continue until 1 August 1999 (see Schedule 1, para. 19) and see *Entec (Pollution Control) Ltd* v. *Abacus Mouldings* [1992] FSR 332.

Copying of a film, broadcast or cable programme can include making a copy of the whole or a substantial part of any one image from it (see section 17(4)). This means that copying one frame of the film would be an infringement, as it was under the previous law (see *Spelling Goldberg Productions* v. *BPC* [1981] RPC 283).

Copying is generally proved by showing substantial similarities between the original and the alleged copy, plus an opportunity to copy. Surprisingly often, minor errors in the original are reproduced by an infringer.

Copying need not be direct, so that, for instance, where the copyright is in a fabric design, copying the material, without ever having seen the original drawing, will still be an infringement, as will 'reverse engineering' of industrial designs e.g. to make unlicensed spare parts (subject to any defence of implied licence: see *British Leyland Motor Corp* v. *Armstrong Patents Co Ltd* [1984] FSR 591).

Issuing copies of a work to the public when it has not previously been put into circulation in the UK is also an infringement of all types of work.

Other acts which may amount to an infringement depend upon the nature of the work. It will be an infringement of the copyright in a literary, dramatic or musical work to perform it in public, whether by live performance or by playing recordings. Similarly, it is an infringement of the copyright in a sound recording, film, broadcast or cable programme to play or show it in public.

One rather different form of infringement is to make an adaptation of a literary, dramatic or musical work. An adaptation includes, in the case of a literary work, a translation, in the case of a non-dramatic work, making a dramatic work of it, and in the case of a dramatic work, making a non-dramatic work of it. An adaptation of a musical work is a transcription or arrangement of it.

There are also a number of 'secondary' infringements. These consist not of making the infringing copies, but of dealing with them in some way. So, it is an infringement to import an infringing copy into the UK, and to possess in the course of business, or to sell, hire, offer for sale or hire, or distribute in the course of trade an infringing copy. However, none of these acts will be an infringement unless the alleged infringer knew or had reason to believe that the articles were infringing copies.

Other secondary infringements consist of permitting a place to be used for a public performance in which copyright is infringed and supplying apparatus to be used for infringing public performance, again, in each case, with safeguards for innocent acts.

EXCEPTIONS TO INFRINGEMENT

The Act provides a large number of exceptions to the rules on infringement, many of which are innovatory. They are far too numerous to be dealt with here in full, but they include:
- fair dealing with literary, dramatic, musical or artistic works for the purpose of research or private study;
- fair dealing for the purpose of criticism or review or reporting current events;
- incidental inclusion of a work in an artistic work, sound recording, film, broadcast or cable programme;
- various educational exceptions (see sections 32-36);
- various exceptions for libraries (see sections 37-44);
- various exceptions for public administration (see sections 45-50);
- dealing with a work where the author cannot be identified and the work seems likely to be out of copyright;
- public recitation, if accompanied by a sufficient acknowledgement;
- recording broadcasts or cable programmes at home for viewing at a more convenient time.

REMEDIES FOR INFRINGEMENT

The copyright owner has all the remedies offered to other owners of property. Usually the owner will want one or both of two things: firstly, to prevent the repetition or continuation of the infringement, and, secondly, compensation.

In almost all cases an injunction will be sought at trial, stopping the continuation of the infringement. A very useful remedy offered by the courts is the 'interlocutory injunction'. This is a form of interim relief, applied for at short notice, with a view to stopping damaging infringement at an early stage, without having to await the outcome of a full trial. Interlocutory injunctions are not always granted in copyright cases, but it is always worth considering the matter as soon as an infringement comes to notice, for delay in bringing an interlocutory application may be fatal to its success. Where an infringement is threatened, the courts will in appropriate cases make a 'quia timet' injunction to prevent the infringement ever taking place.

Financial compensation may be sought in one of two forms. Firstly, damages may be granted for infringement. These will usually be calculated upon evidence of the loss caused to the plaintiff, sometimes based upon loss of business, at others upon the basis of what would have been a proper licence fee had the defendant sought a licence for the acts complained of. Additional damages may be awarded in rare cases for flagrant infringements.

Under the old law, a plaintiff could also claim conversion damages, which were often assessed at a much higher level than infringement damages. However, these cannot be claimed under the Act.

Damages will not be awarded for infringements where the infringer did not know, and had no reason to believe, that copyright subsisted in the work. This exception is of limited use to a defendant, though, in the usual situation where he had no actual knowledge of the copyright, but the work was of such a nature that he should have known that copyright would subsist in it.

The alternative to a claim for damages is a claim for an account of profits, that is, the profits made by the infringer by virtue of his illicit exploitation of the copyright. This is an equitable remedy, however, and is therefore discretionary.

A copyright owner may also apply for delivery up of infringing copies of his work (sections 99 and 113-15).

Finally, there are various criminal offences relating to the making, importation, possession, sale, hire, distribution, etc. of infringing copies (see sections 107-110).

DESIGN RIGHT

Many industrial designs will now effectively be excluded from copyright protection, by reason of the provisions of section 51 of the Act, described above. However, they may instead be protected by the new 'design right' created by sections 213-64 of the Act.

The protection of the new right will be given to original designs consisting of the shape or configuration (internal or external) of the whole or part of an article and not being merely 'surface decoration'. A design is not to be considered original if it was commonplace in the design field in question at the time of its creation. Nor will designs be protected if they consist of a method or principle of construction, or are dictated by the shape, etc. of an article to which the new article is to be connected or of which it is to form part, the so-called 'must-fit' and 'must-match' exclusions.

The new right will be granted to designs made by qualifying persons (in this part of the Act meaning UK and EU citizens or residents or others to whom the right may be extended) or commissioned by a qualifying person, or first marketed in the UK, another EU state or any other country to which the provision may be extended by Order in Council.

The design right lasts only fifteen years from the end of the year in which it was first recorded or an article made to the design, or (if shorter) ten years from the end of the year in which articles made according to the design were first sold or hired out.

The designer will be the owner of the right, unless he made it in pursuance of a commission, in which case the commissioner will be the first owner of the right. The same rule applies as in copyright, that an employee's designs made in the course of his employment will belong to the employer.

The right given to the owner of a design right is the exclusive right to reproduce the design for commercial purposes. The rules as to assignments and licensing and as to infringement, both primary and secondary, are substantially similar to those described above in relation to copyright, as are the remedies available.

This new design right will co-exist with the scheme of registered designs of the *Registered Designs Act* 1949 (as amended by the Act), which provides a monopoly right renewable for up to twenty-five years in respect of designs which have been accepted on to a register. Registered designs must contain features which appeal to and are judged by the eye, unlike designs protected by the design right.

MORAL RIGHTS

Another new departure in the Act is the provision of 'moral rights', commonly known as the rights of 'paternity' and 'integrity'.

The right of 'paternity' is for the author of a copyright literary, dramatic, musical or artistic work, and the director of a copyright film, to be identified as the author/director in a number of different situations, largely whenever the work is published, performed or otherwise commercially exploited (section 77).

However, the right does not arise unless it has been 'asserted' by the author or director, by appropriate words in an assignment, or otherwise by an instrument in writing (section 78), or in the case of an artistic work by ensuring that the artist's name appears on the frame, etc. Writers should therefore aim to ensure that all copies of their works carry a clear assertion of their rights under this provision, so that all who read their works are bound thereby (see end).

There are exceptions to the right, in particular where the first ownership of the copyright vested in the author's or director's employer.

The right of 'integrity' is not to have one's work subjected to 'derogatory treatment'. This is defined as meaning an addition to, deletion from, alteration to or adaptation of a work (save for a translation of a literary or dramatic work or an arrangement of a musical work involving no more than a change of key or register) which amounts to distortion or mutilation of the work or is otherwise prejudicial to the honour or reputation of the author/director.

Again, infringement of the right takes place when the maltreated work is published commercially or performed or exhibited in public. There are various exceptions set out in section 81 of the Act, in particular where the publication is in a newspaper, etc., and the work was made for inclusion therein or made available with the author's consent.

Where the copyright in the work vested first in the author's or director's employer, he has no right to 'integrity' unless he was identified at the time of the relevant act or was previously identified on published copies of the work.

These rights subsist for as long as the copyright in the work subsists.

A third moral right conferred by the Act is not to have a literary, dramatic, musical or artistic work falsely attributed to one as author, or to have a film falsely attributed to one as director, again where the work in question is published, publicly performed, etc. This right subsists until twenty years after a person's death.

None of these rights can be assigned during the person's lifetime, but all of them either pass on the person's death as directed by his will or fall into his residuary estate.

A fourth but rather different moral right is conferred by section 85. It gives a person who has commissioned the taking of photographs for private purposes a right to prevent copies of the work being issued to the public, etc.

The remedies for breach of these moral rights may again include damages and an injunction, although section 103(2) specifically foresees the granting of an injunction qualified by a right to the defendant to do the acts complained of, albeit subject to a suitable disclaimer.

NOTICE

I, AMANDA LOUISE MICHAELS, hereby assert and give notice of my right under section 77 of the Copyright, Designs and Patents Act 1988 to be identified as the author of the foregoing article.

AMANDA MICHAELS

US Copyright

GAVIN McFARLANE LLM, PhD
Barrister at Titmuss Sainer & Webb

THE SYSTEM OF INTERNATIONAL COPYRIGHT

The international copyright conventions

There is no general principle of international copyright which provides a uniform code for the protection of right owners throughout the world. There are however two major international copyright conventions which lay down certain minimum standards for member states, in particular requiring member states to accord to right owners of other member states the same protection which is granted to their own nationals. One is the higher standard Berne Convention of 1886, the most recent revision of which was signed in Paris in 1971. The other is the Universal Copyright Convention signed in 1952 with lower minimum standards, and sponsored by Unesco. This also was most recently revised in Paris in 1971, jointly with the Berne Convention. To this latter Convention the United States has belonged since 1955. On 16 November 1988, the Government of the United States deposited its instrument of accession to the Paris Revision of the Berne Convention. The Convention entered into force as regards the United States on 1 March 1989. Together with certain new statutory provisions made in consequence of accession to Berne, this advances substantially the process of overhaul and modernisation of US copyright law which was begun in the 1970s.

Summary of the Universal Copyright Convention

(1) The fundamental intent is to accord reciprocally in each member state to nationals of all other member states the same protection as that member grants to its own nationals.

(2) The minimum term of protection is the life of the author and twenty-five years after his death (by contrast with the Berne Convention which demands a term of the life of the author and a post-mortem period of fifty years).

(3) Any national requirement as a condition of copyright of such formalities as deposit, registration, notice, payment, or manufacture or publication within that state shall be satisfied for all works first published outside its territory and of which the author is not one of its nationals if all copies bear the symbol © accompanied by the name of the copyright owner and the year of first publication.

(4) Publication for the purposes of the Universal Copyright Convention means the reproduction in tangible form and the general distribution to the public of copies of a work from which it can be read or otherwise visually perceived.

(5) The effect of American ratification of the Universal Copyright Convention on 16 September 1955 was to alter completely the nature of the protection granted by the United States to copyright works originating abroad. The previous policy of American domestic law had been extremely restrictive for foreign authors, particularly those writing in the English language. But in consequence of ratification American law was amended to exempt from many of these restrictions works published in other member states, or by nationals of other member states. Recent amendments have relaxed the position even further.

Effect on British copyright owners

The copyright statute of the United States having been brought into line with the requirements of the Universal Copyright Convention, compliance with the formalities required by American law is all that is needed to acquire protection for the work of a British author first published outside the United States. Even these formality requirements have been largely removed now that the United States has joined the Berne Convention, although caution is still required. The Berne Convention Implementation Act of 1988 makes statutory amendments to the way foreign works are now treated in US law. These are now inserted in the US codified law as Title 17 – The Copyright Act. 'Foreign works' are works having a country of origin other than the United States. The formalities which were for so long a considerable handicap for foreign copyright owners in the American system have now become optional, though not removed altogether. Indeed the new system provides incentives to encourage such foreign right owners to continue to comply with formalities on a voluntary basis.

SUMMARY OF UNITED STATES COPYRIGHT LAW

Introduction of new law

After many years of debate, the new Copyright Statute of the United States was passed on 19 October 1976. The greater part of its relevant provisions came into force on 1 January 1978. It has extended the range of copyright protection, and further eased the requirements whereby British authors can obtain copyright protection in America. New Public Law 100-568 of 31 October 1988 has made further amendments to the Copyright Statute which were necessary to enable ratification of the Berne Convention to take place. The problems which derived from the old system of common law copyright no longer now exist.

Works protected in American law

Works of authorship include the following categories:
(1) literary works;
Note: Computer programs are classified as literary works for the purposes of United States copyright. In *Whelan Associates Inc.* v. *Jaslow Dental Laboratory Inc.* (1987) F.S.R.1, it was held that the copyright of a computer program could be infringed even in the absence of copying of the literal code if the structure was part of the expression of the idea behind a program rather than the idea itself.
(2) musical works, including any accompanying words;
(3) dramatic works, including any accompanying music;
(4) pantomimes and choreographic works;
(5) pictorial, graphic and sculptural works;
(6) motion pictures and other audiovisual works;
(7) sound recordings, but copyright in sound recordings is not to include a right of public performance.
(8) architectural works: the design of a building as embodied in any tangible medium of expression, including a building, architectural plans or drawings. The Architectural Works Copyright Protections Act applies this protection to works created on or after 1 December 1990.

The rights of a copyright owner

(1) To reproduce the copyrighted work in copies or phonorecords;
(2) to prepare derivative works based upon the copyrighted work;
(3) to distribute copies or phonorecords of the copyrighted work to the public by sale or other transfer of ownership, or by rental, lease or lending;
(4) in the case of literary, musical, dramatic and choreographic works, pantomimes, and motion pictures and other audiovisual works, but NOT sound recordings, to perform the copyrighted work publicly;
(5) in the case of literary, musical, dramatic, and choreographic works, pantomimes, and pictorial, graphic, or sculptural works, including the individual images

of a motion picture or other audiovisual work, to display the copyrighted work publicly.

(6) By the Record Rental Amendment Act 1984, s.109 of the Copyright Statute is amended. Now, unless authorised by the owners of copyright in the sound recording and the musical works thereon, the owner of a phonorecord may not, for direct or indirect commercial advantage, rent, lease or lend the phonorecord. A compulsory licence under s.115(c) includes the right of a maker of a phonorecord of non-dramatic musical work to distribute or authorise the distribution of the phonorecord by rental, lease, or lending, and an additional royalty is payable in respect of that. This modifies the 'first sale doctrine', which otherwise permits someone buying a copyright work to hire or sell a lawfully purchased copy to third parties without compensating the copyright owners, and without his consent.

(7) A further exception to the 'first sale doctrine' and s.109 of the Copyright Act is made by the Computer Software Rental Amendments Act. A similar restriction has been placed on the unauthorised rental, lease or lending of software, subject to certain limited exceptions. Both the phonecard and software exceptions to the first sale doctrine terminate on 1 October 1997.

(8) The Semiconductor Chip Protection Act 1984 adds to the Copyright Statute a new chapter on the protection of semiconductor chip products.

(9) The Visual Artists Rights Act 1990 has added moral rights to the various economic rights listed above. These moral rights are the right of integrity, and the right of attribution or paternity. A new category of 'work of visual art' is created, broadly paintings, drawings, prints and sculptures, with an upper limit of 200 copies. Works generally exploited in mass market copies such as books, newspapers, motion pictures and electronic information services are specifically excluded from these new moral rights provisions. Where they apply, they do so only in respect of works created on or after 1 June 1991, and to certain works previously created where title has not already been transferred by the author.

Manufacturing requirements

With effect from 1 July 1982, these ceased to have effect. Prior to 1 July 1982, the importation into or public distribution in the United States of a work consisting preponderantly of non-dramatic literary material that was in the English language and protected under American law was prohibited unless the portions consisting of such material had been manufactured in the United States or Canada. This provision did not apply where, on the date when importation was sought or public distribution in the United States was made, the author of any substantial part of such material was not a national of the United States or, if a national, had been domiciled outside the United States for a continuous period of at least one year immediately preceding that date.

Thus since 1 July 1982, there is no manufacturing requirement in respect of works of British authors. Certain interested groups in the United States still lobby for the restoration of the manufacturing clause in American law. Countries such as Britain will no doubt oppose this vigorously through diplomatic channels. With American ratification of the Berne Convention, the formalities previously required in relation to copyright notice, deposit and registration have been greatly modified.

Formalities: notice, deposit and registration

(1) Notice of copyright

Whenever a work protected by the American Copyright Statute is published in the United States or elsewhere by authority of the copyright owner, a notice of copyright should be placed on all publicly distributed copies. This should consist of (i) either the symbol © or the word 'Copyright' or the abbreviation 'Copr.'

plus (ii) the year of first publication of the work, plus (iii) the name of the copyright owner. Since the Berne Amendments, both US and works of foreign origin which were first published in the US after 1 March 1989 without having notice of copyright placed on them will no longer be unprotected. However, notice will allow a right owner to bring an infringement action. In general, authors are advised to place copyright notices on their works, as this is a considerable deterrent to plagiarism. Damages may well be lower in a case where no notice of copyright was placed on the work.

(2) Deposit

The owner of copyright or the exclusive right of publication in a work published with notice of copyright in the United States should within three months of such publication deposit in the Copyright Office for the use or disposition of the Library of Congress two complete copies of the best edition of the work (or two records, if the work is a sound recording). Deposit is part of the administrative procedure of registration, and no longer mandatory.

(3) Registration

Registration for copyright in the United States is optional. However, any owner of copyright in a work first published outside the United States may register a work by making application to the Copyright Office with the appropriate fee, and by depositing one complete copy of the work. This requirement of deposit may be satisfied by using copies deposited for the Library of Congress. Whilst registration is still a requirement for works of US origin and from non-Berne countries, it is no longer necessary for foreign works from Berne countries. But as a matter of practice there are considerable advantages in any litigation where there has been registration. On the whole, it is advisable. The United States has interpreted the Berne Convention as allowing formalities which are not in themselves conditions for obtaining copyright protection, but which lead to improved protection.

Duration of copyright

An important change in the new American law is that in general, copyright in a work created on or after 1 January 1978 endures for a term of the life of the author, and a period of fifty years after the author's death. This brings the United States into line with most other advanced countries, and with the further amendments made by Public Law 100-568 of 31 October 1988 has enabled her government to ratify the higher standard Berne Convention. Copyright in a work created before 1 January 1978, but not published or copyrighted before then, subsists from 1 January 1978, and lasts for the life of the author and a post-mortem period of fifty years.

Any copyright, the first term of which under the previous law was still subsisting on 1 January 1978, shall endure for twenty-eight years from the date when it was originally secured, and the copyright proprietor or his representative may apply for a further term of forty-seven years within one year prior to the expiry of the original term. Until 1992, application for renewal and extension was required. Failure to do so produced disastrous results with some material of great merit passing into the public domain in error. However, by Public Law 102-307 enacted on 26 June 1992, there is no longer necessity to make a renewal registration in order to obtain the longer period of protection. Now renewal copyright vests automatically in the person entitled to renewal at the end of the 28th year of the original term of copyright.

The duration of any copyright, the renewal term of which was subsisting at any time between 31 December 1976 and 31 December 1977, or for which renewal registration was made between those dates, is extended to endure for a term of seventy-five years from the date copyright was originally secured.

These alterations are of great importance for owners of existing American copyrights.

All terms of copyright provided for by the sections referred to above run to the end of the calendar year in which they would otherwise expire.

Public performance

Under the previous American law the provisions relating to performance in public were less generous to right owners than those existing in the copyright law of the United Kingdom. In particular, performance of a musical work was formerly only an infringement if it was 'for profit'. Moreover, the considerable American coin-operated record-playing machine industry (juke boxes) had obtained an exemption from being regarded as instruments of profit, and accordingly their owners did not have to pay royalties for the use of copyright musical works.

Now by the new law one of the exclusive rights of the copyright owner is, in the case of literary, musical, dramatic and choreographic works, pantomimes, and motion pictures and other audiovisual works, to perform the work publicly, without any requirement of such performance being 'for profit'. By Section 114 however, the exclusive rights of the owner of copyright in a sound recording are specifically stated not to include any right of public performance.

The position of coin-operated record players (juke boxes) is governed by the new Section 116A, inserted by Public Law 100-568 of 31 October 1988. It covers the position of negotiated licences. Limitations are placed on the exclusive right if licences are not negotiated.

These extensions of the scope of the right of public performance should augment the royalty income of authors, composers and publishers of musical works widely performed in the United States. All such right owners should ensure that their American interests are properly taken care of.

Mechanical right – alteration of the rate of royalty

Where sound recordings of a non-dramatic musical work have been distributed to the public in the United States with the authority of the copyright owner, any other person may, by following the provisions of the law, obtain a compulsory licence to make and distribute sound recordings of the work. This right is known in the United Kingdom as 'the mechanical right'. Notice must be served on the copyright owner, who is entitled to a royalty in respect of each of his works recorded of either two and three fourths cents or one half of one cent per minute of playing time or fraction thereof, whichever amount is the larger. Failure to serve or file the required notice forecloses the possibility of a compulsory licence and, in the absence of a negotiated licence, renders the making and distribution of such records actionable as acts of infringement.

Transfer of copyright

Under the previous American law copyright was regarded as indivisible, which meant that on the transfer of copyright, where it was intended that only film rights or some other such limited right be transferred, the entire copyright nevertheless had to be passed. This led to a cumbersome procedure whereby the author would assign the whole copyright to his publisher, who would return to the author by means of an exclusive licence those rights which it was not meant to transfer.

Now it is provided by Section 201(d) of the Copyright Statute that (1) the ownership of a copyright may be transferred in whole or in part by any means of conveyance or by operation of law, and may be bequeathed by will or pass as personal property by the applicable laws of intestate succession and (2) any of the exclusive rights comprised in a copyright (including any subdivision of any of the rights set out in *The rights of a copyright owner* above) may be transferred as provided in (1) above and owned separately. The owner of any particular exclusive right is entitled, to the extent of that right, to all the protection and remedies accorded to the copyright owner by that Statute. This removes the difficulties which existed under the previous law, and brings the position much closer to that existing in the copyright law of the United Kingdom.

Copyright Royalty Tribunal

A feature of the new United States law is the establishment of a Copyright Royalty Tribunal, with the purpose of making adjustments of reasonable copyright royalty rates in respect of the exercise of certain rights, mainly affecting the musical interests. The Tribunal consists of five commissioners appointed by the President with the advice and consent of the Senate for a term of seven years each. This body performs in the United States a function similar to the new Copyright Tribunal in the United Kingdom.

The new American law spells out the economic objectives which its Copyright Tribunal is to apply in calculating the relevant rates. These are:

(1) to maximise the availability of creative works to the public;
(2) to afford the copyright owner a fair return for his creative work and the copyright user a fair income under existing economic conditions;
(3) to reflect the relative roles of the copyright owner and the copyright user in the product made available to the public with respect to relative creative contribution, technological contribution, capital investment, cost, risk, and contribution to the opening of new markets for creative expression and media for their communication.
(4) to minimise any disruptive impact on the structure of the industries involved and on generally prevailing industry practices.

Every final determination of the Tribunal shall be published in the Federal Register. It shall state in detail the criteria that the Tribunal determined to be applicable to the particular proceeding, the various facts that it found relevant to its determination in that proceeding, and the specific reasons for its determination. Any final decision of the Tribunal in a proceeding may be appealed to the United States Court of Appeals by an aggrieved party, within thirty days after its publication in the Federal Register.

Fair use

One of the most controversial factors which held up the introduction of the new American copyright law for at least a decade was the extent to which a balance should be struck between the desire of copyright owners to benefit from their works by extending copyright protection as far as possible, and the pressure from users of copyright to obtain access to copyright material as cheaply as possible – if not completely freely.

The new law provides by Section 107 that the fair use of a copyright work, including such use by reproduction in copies or on records, for purposes such as criticism, comment, news reporting, teaching (including multiple copies for classroom use), scholarship or research is not an infringement of copyright. In determining whether the use made of a work in any particular case is a fair use, the factors to be considered shall include:

(1) the purpose and character of the use, including whether such use is of a commercial nature or is for non-profit educational purposes;
(2) the nature of the copyrighted work;
(3) the amount and substantiality of the portion used in relation to the copyrighted work as a whole; and

(4) the effect of the use upon the potential market for or value of the copyrighted work.

It is not an infringement of copyright for a library or archive, or any of its employees acting within the scope of their employment, to reproduce or distribute no more than one copy of a work, if:

(1) the reproduction or distribution is made without any purpose of direct or indirect commercial advantage;
(2) the collections of the library or archive are either open to the public or available not only to researchers affiliated with the library or archive or with the institution of which it is a part, but also to other persons doing research in a specialised field; and
(3) the reproduction or distribution of the work includes a notice of copyright.

It is not generally an infringement of copyright if a performance or display of a work is given by instructors or pupils in the course of face to face teaching activities of a non-profit educational institution, in a classroom or similar place devoted to instruction.

Nor is it an infringement of copyright to give a performance of a non-dramatic literary or musical work or a dramatico-musical work of a religious nature in the course of services at a place of worship or other religious assembly.

It is also not an infringement of copyright to give a performance of a non-dramatic literary or musical work other than in a transmission to the public, without any purpose of direct or indirect commercial advantage and without payment of any fee for the performance to any of the performing artists, promoters or organisers if either (i) there is no direct or indirect admission charge or (ii) the proceeds, after deducting the reasonable costs of producing the performance, are used exclusively for educational, religious or charitable purposes and not for private financial gain. In this case the copyright owner has the right to serve notice of objection to the performance in a prescribed form.

Note the important decision of the Supreme Court in *Sony Corporation of America* v. *Universal City Studios*. (No. 81-1687, 52 USLW 4090.) This decided that the sale of video-recorders to the public does not amount to contributory infringement of the rights in films which are copied as a result of television broadcasts of them. (The practice known as time-switching.) Among other reasons for their decision advanced by the majority of the judges was their opinion that even unauthorised time-switching is legitimate fair use.

REMEDIES FOR COPYRIGHT OWNERS

Infringement of copyright

Copyright is infringed by anyone who violates any of the exclusive rights referred to in *The rights of a copyright owner* above, or who imports copies or records into the United States in violation of the law. The owner of copyright is entitled to institute an action for infringement so long as that infringement is committed while he or she is the owner of the right infringed. Previously, no action for infringement of copyright could be instituted until registration of the copyright claim had been made, but this requirement has been modified now that the United States has ratified the Berne Convention.

Injunctions

Any court having civil jurisdiction under the copyright law may grant interim and final injunctions on such terms as it may deem reasonable to prevent or restrain infringement of copyright. Such injunction may be served anywhere in the United States on the person named. An injunction is operative throughout the whole of the United States, and can be enforced by proceedings in contempt or otherwise by any American court which has jurisdiction over the infringer.

Impounding and disposition of infringing articles

At any time while a copyright action under American law is pending, the court may order the impounding on such terms as it considers reasonable of all copies or records claimed to have been made or used in violation of the copyright owner's exclusive rights; it may also order the impounding of all plates, moulds, matrices, masters, tapes, film negatives or other articles by means of which infringing copies or records may be reproduced. A court may order as part of a final judgement or decree the destruction or other disposition of all copies or records found to have been made or used in violation of the copyright owner's exclusive rights. It also has the power to order the destruction of all articles by means of which infringing copies or records were reproduced.

Damages and profits

An infringer of copyright is generally liable either for the copyright owner's actual damage and any additional profits made by the infringer, or for statutory damages.

(1) The copyright owner is entitled to recover the actual damages suffered by him as a result of the infringement, and in addition any profits of the infringer which are attributed to the infringement and are not taken into account in computing the actual damages. In establishing the infringer's profits, the copyright owner is only required to present proof of the infringer's gross revenue, and it is for the infringer to prove his or her deductible expenses and the elements of profit attributable to factors other than the copyright work.

(2) Except where the copyright owner has persuaded the court that the infringement was committed wilfully, the copyright owner may elect, at any time before final judgement is given, to recover, instead of actual damages and profits, an award of statutory damages for all infringements involved in the action in respect of any one work, which may be between $250 and $10,000 according to what the court considers justified.

(3) However, where the copyright owner satisfies the court that the infringement was committed wilfully, the court has the discretion to increase the award of statutory damages to not more than $50,000. Where the infringer succeeds in proving that he was not aware that and had no reason to believe that his acts constituted an infringement of copyright, the court has the discretion to reduce the award of statutory damages to not less than $100.

Costs: time limits

In any civil proceedings under American copyright law, the court has the discretion to allow the recovery of full costs by or against any party except the Government of the United States. It may also award a reasonable sum in respect of an attorney's fee.

No civil or criminal proceedings in respect of copyright law shall be permitted unless begun within three years after the claim or cause of action arose.

Criminal proceedings in respect of copyright

(1) Anyone who infringes a copyright wilfully and for purposes of commercial advantage and private financial gain shall be fined not more than $10,000 or imprisoned for not more than one year, or both. However, if the infringement relates to copyright in a sound recording or a film, the infringer is liable to a fine of not more than $25,000 or imprisonment for not more than one year or both

on a first offence, which can be increased to a fine of up to $50,000 or imprisonment for not more than two years or both for a subsequent offence.

(2) Following a conviction for criminal infringement a court may in addition to these penalties order the forfeiture and destruction of all infringing copies and records, together with implements and equipment used in their manufacture.

(3) It is also an offence knowingly and with fraudulent intent to place on any article a notice of copyright or words of the same purport, or to import or distribute such copies. A fine is provided for this offence of not more than $2500. The fraudulent removal of a copyright notice also attracts the same maximum fine, as does the false representation of a material particular on an application for copyright representation.

Counterfeiting

By the Piracy and Counterfeiting Amendment Act 1982, pirates and counterfeiters of sound recordings and of motion pictures now face maximum penalties of up to five years imprisonment or fines of up to $250,000.

Colouring films

The United States Copyright Office has decided that adding colour to a black and white film may qualify for copyright protection whenever it amounts to more than a trivial change.

Satellite home viewers

The position of satellite home viewers is now controlled by the Satellite Home Viewer Act of 1988. (Title II of Public Law 100-667 of 16 November 1988.)

The Copyright Remedy Clarification Act has created s.511 of the Copyright Act, in order to rectify a situation which had developed in case law. By this, the component States of the Union, their agencies and employees are placed in the same position as private individuals and entities in relation to their liability for copyright infringement.

GENERAL OBSERVATIONS

The copyright law of the United States has been very greatly improved as a result of the new statute passed by Congress on 19 October 1976. (Title 17, United States Code.) Apart from lifting the general standards of protection for copyright owners to a much higher level than that which previously existed, it has on the whole shifted the balance of copyright protection in favour of the copyright owner and away from the copyright user in many of the areas where controversy existed. But most important for British and other non-American authors and publishers, it has gone a long way towards bringing American copyright law up to the same standards of international protection for non-national copyright proprietors which have long been offered by the United Kingdom and the other major countries, both in Europe and elsewhere in the English-speaking world. The ratification by the United States of the Berne Convention with effect from 1 March 1989 is an action which finally puts American copyright law on par with the protection offered by other major countries.

Libel

ANTONY WHITAKER

Legal Manager, Times Newspapers Ltd

What follows is an outline of the main principles of the law of libel, with special reference to points which appear most frequently to be misunderstood. But it is no more than that, and specific legal advice should be taken when practical problems arise. The law discussed is the law of England and Wales. Scotland has its own, albeit somewhat similar, rules.

LIBEL: LIABILITY TO PAY DAMAGES

English law draws a distinction between defamation published in permanent form and that which is not. The former is libel, the latter slander. 'Permanent form' includes writing, printing, drawings and photographs and radio and television broadcasts. It follows that it is the law of libel rather than slander which most concerns writers and artists professionally, and the slightly differing rules applicable to slander will not be mentioned in this article.

Publication of a libel can result in a civil action for damages, an injunction to prevent repetition and/or in certain cases a criminal prosecution against those responsible, who include the writer (or artist or photographer), the printers, the publishers, and the editor, if any, of the publication in which the libel appeared. Prosecutions are rare. Certain special rules apply to them and these will be explained below after a discussion of the question of civil liability, which in practice arises much more frequently.

Civil libel cases, for which legal aid is not available, are usually heard by a judge and jury, and it is the jury who decide the amount of any award, which is tax-free. It is not necessary for the plaintiff to prove that he has actually suffered any loss, because the law presumes damage. While the main purpose of a libel claim is to compensate the plaintiff for the injury to his reputation, a jury may give additional sums either as 'aggravated' damages, if it appears a defendant has behaved malevolently or spitefully, or as 'exemplary', or 'punitive', damages where a defendant hopes the economic advantages of publication will outweigh any sum awarded against him. Damages can also be 'nominal' if the libel complained of is trivial. It is generally very difficult to forecast the amounts juries are likely to award, though recent awards against newspapers have disclosed a tendency towards considerable generosity. The Court of Appeal now has power to reduce excessive awards of damages.

In an action for damages for libel, it is for the plaintiff to establish that the matter he complains of (1) has been published by the defendant, (2) refers to himself, (3) is defamatory. If he does so, the plaintiff establishes a *prima facie* case. However, the defendant will escape liability if he can show he has a good defence. There are five defences to a libel action. They are Justification, Fair Comment, Privilege, S.4 of the Defamation Act, 1952, Apology, etc., under the Libel Acts, 1843 and 1845. A libel claim can also become barred under the Limitation Acts, as explained below. These matters must now be examined in detail.

THE PLAINTIFF'S CASE

(1) 'Published' in the legal sense means communicated to a person other than the plaintiff. Thus the legal sense is wider than the lay sense but includes it. It

follows that the content of a book is published in the legal sense when the manuscript is first sent to the publishing firm just as much as it is when the book is later placed on sale to the public. Both types of publication are sufficient for the purpose of establishing liability for libel, but the law differentiates between them, since the scope of publication can properly be taken into account by the jury in considering the actual amount of damages to award.

(2) The plaintiff must also establish that the matter complained of refers to himself. It is of course by no means necessary to mention a person's name before it is clear that he is referred to. Nicknames by which he is known or corruptions of his name are just two ways in which his identity can be indicated. There are more subtle methods. The sole question is whether the plaintiff is indicated to those who read the matter complained of. In some cases he will not be unless it is read in the light of facts known to the reader from other sources, but this is sufficient for the plaintiff's purpose. The test is purely objective and does not depend at all on whether the writer intended to refer to the plaintiff.

It is because it is impossible to establish reference to any individual that generalisations, broadly speaking, are not successfully actionable. To say boldly 'All lawyers are crooks' does not give any single lawyer a cause of action, because the statement does not point a finger at any individual. However, if anyone is named in conjunction with a generalisation, then it may lose its general character and become particular from the context. Again if one says 'One of the X Committee has been convicted of murder' and the X Committee consists of, say, four persons, it cannot be said that the statement is not actionable because no individual is indicated and it could be referring to any of the committee. This is precisely why it is actionable at the suit of each of them as suspicion has been cast on all.

(3) It is for the plaintiff to show that the matter complained of is defamatory. What is defamatory is decided by the jury except in the extreme cases where the judge rules that the words cannot bear a defamatory meaning. Various tests have been laid down for determining this. It is sufficient that any one test is satisfied. The basic tests are: (i) Does the matter complained of tend to lower the plaintiff in the estimation of society? (ii) Does it tend to bring him into hatred, ridicule, contempt, dislike or disesteem with society? (iii) Does it tend to make him shunned or avoided or cut off from society? The mere fact that what is published is inaccurate is not enough to involve liability; it is the adverse impact on the plaintiff's reputation that matters. For example, merely to overstate a person's income is not defamatory; but it will be if the context implies he has not fully declared it to the tax authorities.

'Society' means right-thinking members of society generally. It is by reference to such people that the above tests must be applied. A libel action against a newspaper which had stated that the police had taken a statement from the plaintiff failed, notwithstanding that the plaintiff gave evidence that his apparent assistance to the police (which he denied) had brought him into grave disrepute with the underworld. It was not by their wrongheaded standards that the matter fell to be judged.

Further, it is not necessary to imply that the plaintiff is at fault in some way in order to defame him. To say of a woman that she has been raped or of someone that he is insane imputes to them no degree of blame, but nonetheless both statements are defamatory.

Sometimes a defamatory meaning is conveyed by words which on the face of them have no such meaning. 'But Brutus is an honourable man' is an example. If a jury finds that words are meant ironically they will consider this ironical sense when determining whether the words are defamatory. In deciding therefore whether or not the words are defamatory, the jury seek to discover what, without straining the words or putting a perverse construction on them, they will be understood to mean. In some cases this may differ substantially from their literal meaning.

Matter may also be defamatory by innuendo. Strictly so called, an innuendo is a meaning that words acquire by virtue of facts known to the reader but not stated in the passage complained of. Words, quite innocent on the face of them, may acquire a defamatory meaning when read in the light of these facts. For example, where a newspaper published a photograph of a man and a woman, with the caption that they had just announced their engagement, it was held to be defamatory of the man's wife since those who knew that she had cohabited with him were led to the belief that she had done so only as his mistress. The newspaper was unaware that the man was already married, but some of its readers were not.

DEFENCES TO A LIBEL ACTION

Justification

English law does not protect the reputation that a person either does not or should not possess. Stating the truth therefore does not incur liability, and the plea of justification – namely, that what is complained of is true in substance and in fact – is a complete answer to an action for damages. However, this defence is by no means to be undertaken lightly. For instance, to prove one instance of using bad language will be insufficient to justify the allegation that a person is 'foulmouthed'. It would be necessary to prove several instances, and the defendant is obliged in most cases to particularise in his pleadings giving details, dates and places. However, the requirement that the truth of every allegation must be proved is not absolute, and is qualified by the 'multiple charge – no worse off' defence. This applies where two or more distinct charges are levelled against a plaintiff, and some of what is said turns out to be inaccurate. If his reputation in the light of what is shown to be true is made no worse by the unprovable defamatory allegations – for example, mistaken accusations that a convicted pickpocket and car thief is also a shoplifter – the publisher will be safe. This is the extent of the law's recognition that some individuals are so disreputable as to be beyond redemption by awards of damages regardless of what is said about them. Subject to this, however, it is for the defendant to prove that what he has published is true, not for the plaintiff to disprove it, though if he can do so, so much the better for him.

One point requires special mention. It is insufficient for the defendant to prove that he has accurately repeated what a third person has written or said or that such statements have gone uncontradicted when made on occasions in the past. If X writes 'Y told me that Z is a liar', it is no defence to an action against X merely to prove that Y did say that. X has given currency to a defamatory statement concerning Z and has so made it his own. His only defence is to prove that Z is a liar by establishing a number of instances of Z's untruthfulness. Nor is it a defence to prove that the defendant genuinely believed what he published to be true. This might well be a complete answer in an action, other than a libel action, based on a false but non-defamatory statement. For such statements do not incur liability in the absence of fraud or malice, which, in this context, means a dishonest or otherwise improper motive. Bona fide belief, however, may be relevant to the assessment of damages, even in a libel action.

Special care should be taken in relation to references to a person's convictions, however accurately described. Since the Rehabilitation of Offenders Act, 1974, a person's convictions may become 'spent' and thereafter it may involve liability to refer to them. Reference to the Act and orders thereunder must be made in order to determine the position in any particular case.

Fair comment

It is a defence to prove that what is complained of is fair comment made in good faith and without malice on a matter of public interest.

'Fair' in this context means 'honest'. 'Fair comment' means therefore the expression of the writer's genuinely held opinion. It does not necessarily mean opinion with which the jury agree. Comment may therefore be quite extreme and still be 'fair' in the legal sense. However, if it is utterly perverse the jury may be led to think that no one could have genuinely held such views. In such a case the defence would fail, for the comment could not be honest. 'Malice' here includes the popular sense of personal spite, but covers any dishonest or improper motive.

The defence only applies when what is complained of is comment as distinct from a statement of fact. The line between comment and fact is notoriously difficult to draw in some cases. Comment means a statement of opinion. The facts on which comment is made must be stated together with the comment or be sufficiently indicated with it. This is merely another way of saying that it must be clear that the defamatory statement is one of opinion and not of fact, for which the only defence would be the onerous one of justification. The exact extent to which the facts commented on must be stated or referred to is a difficult question, but some help may be derived in answering it by considering the purpose of the rule, which is to enable the reader to exercise his own judgement and to agree or disagree with the comment. It is quite plain that it is not necessary to state every single detail of the facts. In one case it was sufficient merely to mention the name of one of the Press lords in an article about a newspaper though not one owned by him. He was so well known that to mention his name indicated the substratum of fact commented upon, namely his control of his group of newspapers. No universal rule can be laid down, except that, in general, the fuller the facts set out or referred to with the comment, the better. All these facts must be proved to be true subject, however, to the flexibility of the 'proportionate truth' rule. This means that the defence remains available even if, for example, only three out of five factual claims can be proved true, provided that these three are by themselves sufficient to sustain, and are proportionate to, the fairness of the comment. The impact of the two unproven claims would probably fall to be assessed in accordance with the 'multiple charge – no worse off' rule in justification, set out above.

The defence only applies where the matters commented on are of public interest, i.e. of legitimate concern to the public or a substantial section of it. Thus the conduct of national and local government, international affairs, the administration of justice, etc., are all matters of public interest, whereas other people's private affairs may very well not be, although they undoubtedly interest the public, or provoke curiosity.

In addition, matters of which criticism has been expressly or impliedly invited, such as publicly performed plays and published books, are a legitimate subject of comment. Criticism need not be confined merely to their artistic merit but equally may deal with the attitudes to life and the opinions therein expressed.

It is sometimes said that a man's moral character is never a proper subject of comment for the purpose of this defence. This is certainly true where it is a private individual who is concerned, and some authorities say it is the same in the case of a public figure even though his character may be relevant to his public life. Again, it may in some cases be exceeding the bounds of fair comment to impute a dishonourable motive to a person, as is frequently done by way of inference from facts. In general, the imputation is a dangerous and potentially expensive practice.

Privilege

In the public interest, certain occasions are privileged so that to make defamatory statements upon them does not incur liability. The following are privileged in any event: (i) fair, accurate, and contemporaneous reports of public judicial proceedings in England published in a newspaper, (ii) Parliamentary papers published by the direction of either House, or full republications thereof. The following are privileged provided publication is made only for the reason that the privilege is given and not for some wrongful or indirect motive: (i) fair and accurate but non-contemporaneous reports of public judicial proceedings in England, whether in a newspaper or not, (ii) extracts of Parliamentary papers, (iii) fair and accurate reports of Parliamentary proceedings, (iv) a fair and accurate report in a newspaper of the proceedings at any public meeting held in the United Kingdom. The meeting must be bona fide and lawfully held for a lawful purpose and for the furtherance or discussion of any matter of public concern. Admission to the meeting may be general or restricted. In the case of public meetings, the defence is not available, if it is proved that the defendant has been requested by the plaintiff to publish in the newspaper in which the original publication was made a reasonable letter or statement by way of explanation or contradiction, and has refused or neglected to do so, or has done so in a manner not adequate or not reasonable having regard to all the circumstances. This list of privileged occasions is by no means exhaustive, but they are those most commonly utilised.

S.4 of the Defamation Act, 1952

The defence provided by the above section is only available where the defamation is 'innocent'. As has been seen, liability for libel is in no way dependent on the existence of an intention to defame on the part of the defendant and the absence of such an intention does not mean that the defamation is 'innocent'.

Defamation is innocent if the publisher did not intend to publish the matter complained of about the plaintiff and did not know of circumstances by virtue of which it might be understood to refer to him, or, if the matter published was not defamatory on the face of it, if the publisher did not know of circumstances by virtue of which it might be understood to be defamatory. Further the publisher must have exercised all reasonable care in relation to the publication. If the publisher has published matter innocently, he should make an 'offer of amends' to the party aggrieved. This consists of an offer to publish a correction and apology and as far as practicable to inform others to whom the alleged libel has been distributed that the matter is said to be defamatory. If the offer of amends is accepted, it is a bar to further proceedings against the person making the offer. If rejected, the making of the offer affords a defence provided the defendant can prove that he did publish innocently and made the offer as soon as practicable after learning that the matter published was or might be defamatory. The offer must not have been withdrawn and must have been expressed to be for the purposes of the defence under S.4 and have been accompanied by an affidavit. It is vital that the offer should be made swiftly, but it is inadvisable to make it without professional advice owing to its technicality.

An example of the first type of innocent publication is where a reference to a person by name has been understood to refer to another person of the same name and this could not reasonably have been foreseen.

An example of the other type of innocent publication is the case referred to earlier in this article of the man pictured with 'his fiancée'. The publishers did not know that he was already married and that accordingly the picture and caption could be understood to be defamatory of his wife.

In practice all the conditions for a successful defence under this section are infrequently fulfilled.

Apology under the Libel Acts, 1843 and 1845

This defence is rarely utilised, since if any condition of it is not fulfilled, the plaintiff must succeed and the only question is the actual amount of damages. It only applies to actions in respect of libels in newspapers and periodicals. The defendant pleads that the libel was inserted without actual malice and without gross negligence and that before the action commenced or as soon afterwards as possible he inserted a full apology in the same newspaper, etc., or had offered to publish it in a newspaper, etc., of the plaintiff's choice, where the original newspaper is published at intervals greater than a week. Further a sum must be paid into court with this defence to compensate the plaintiff.

Apologies in general

Quite apart from the provisions concerning statutory apologies mentioned above, a swift and well publicised apology will always go some way towards assuaging injured feelings and help reduce an award of damages.

Limitation and death

In general, unless an action is started within three years of publication, a libel claim becomes 'statute-barred' through lapse of time. But successive and subsequent publications, such as the issue of later editions of the same book, or the sale of surplus copies of an old newspaper, can give rise to fresh claims.

Civil claims for libel cannot be brought on behalf of the dead. If an individual living plaintiff or defendant in a libel case dies before the jury gives their verdict, the action 'abates', i.e. comes to an end, so far as their involvement is concerned, and no rights arising out of it survive either for or against their personal representatives.

Insurance

For an author, the importance of at least an awareness of this branch of law lies first, in the fact that most book contracts contain a clause enabling the publisher to look to him should any libel claims result; and second, in the increasingly large awards of damages. It is therefore advisable to check what libel insurance a publisher carries, and whether it also covers the author who, if he is to have the benefit of it, should always alert the publisher to any potential risk. One company which offers libel insurance for authors is the Sun Alliance of 1 Leadenhall Street, London EC3V 1PP. Premiums start at £1000, and can be substantially higher if the book is tendentious or likely to be controversial. The company generally insists on the author obtaining, and paying for, a legal opinion first. Indemnity limits vary between £50,000 and £1 million, and the author is required to bear at least the first £5000, and 10 per cent of the remainder, of any loss. It is worth remembering that 'losses' include legal costs as well as damages, which they can often exceed. Libel insurance can also be obtained through a Lloyds broker.

CRIMINAL LIABILITY IN LIBEL AND RELATED AREAS

Whereas the object of a civil action is to obtain compensation for the wrong done or to prevent repetition, the object of criminal proceedings is to punish the wrongdoer by fine or imprisonment or both. There are four main types of writing which may provoke a prosecution:

(1) defamatory libel
(2) obscene publications
(3) sedition and incitement to racial hatred
(4) blasphemous libel

(1) The publication of defamatory matter is in certain circumstances a crime as well as a civil wrong. But whereas the principal object of civil proceedings will normally be to obtain compensation, the principal object of a criminal prosecution will be to secure punishment of the accused, for example by way of a fine.

Prosecutions are not frequent, but there have been signs of late of a revival of interest. There are important differences between the rules applicable to criminal libel and its civil counterpart. For example, a criminal libel may be 'published' even though only communicated to the person defamed and may be found to have occurred even where the person defamed is dead, or where only a group of persons but no particular individual has been maligned. During election campaigns, it is an 'illegal practice' to publish false statements about the personal character or conduct of a candidate irrespective of whether they are also defamatory.

(2) It is an offence to publish obscene matter. By the Obscene Publications Act, 1959, matter is obscene if its effect is such as to tend to deprave and corrupt persons who are likely, having regard to all relevant circumstances, to read, see or hear it. 'To deprave and corrupt' is to be distinguished from 'to shock and disgust'. It is a defence to a prosecution to prove that publication of the matter in question is justified as being for the public good, on the ground that it is in the interests of science, literature, art or learning, or of other objects of general concern. Expert evidence may be given as to its literary, artistic, scientific or other merits. Playwrights, directors and producers should note that the Theatres Act, 1968, though designed to afford similar protection to stage productions, does not necessarily prevent prosecutions for indecency under other statutes.

(3) Writings which tend to destroy the peace of the realm may be prosecuted as being seditious or as amounting to incitement to racial hatred. Seditious writings include those which advocate reform by unconstitutional or violent means or incite contempt or hatred for the monarch or Parliament. These institutions may be criticised stringently, but not in a manner which is likely to lead to insurrection or civil commotion or indeed any physical force. Prosecutions are a rarity, but it should be remembered that writers of matter contemptuous of the House of Commons, though not prosecuted for seditious libel are, from time to time, punished by that House for breach of its privileges, although, if a full apology is made, it is often an end of the matter. The Public Order Act 1986 makes it an offence, irrespective of the author's or publisher's intention, to publish, or put on plays containing, threatening, abusive or insulting matter if hatred is likely to be stirred up against any racial group in Great Britain.

(4) Blasphemous libel consists in the vilification of the Christian religion or its ceremonies. Other religions are not protected. The offence lies essentially in the impact of what is said concerning, for instance, God, Christ, the Bible, the Book of Common Prayer, etc.; it is irrelevant that the publisher does not intend to shock or arouse resentment. While temperate and sober writings on religious topics however anti-Christian in sentiment will not involve liability, if the discussion is 'so scurrilous and offensive as to pass the limit of decent controversy and to outrage any Christian feeling', it will.

Finance

Income Tax for Writers and Artists

PETER VAINES FCA, ATII, *Barrister*
Partner, Brebner, Allen & Trapp
Chartered Accountants

This article is intended to explain the impact of taxation on writers and others engaged in similar activities. Despite attempts by many Governments to simplify our taxation system, the subject has become increasingly complicated and the following is an attempt to give a broad outline of the position. At the time of writing the proposals in the November 1993 Budget have been announced and these are reflected in this article.

HOW INCOME IS TAXED

(a) Generally

Authors are usually treated for tax purposes as carrying on a profession and are taxed in a similar fashion to other professional persons, i.e. as self-employed persons assessable under Schedule D. This article is directed to self-employed persons only, because if a writer is employed he will be subject to the rules of Schedule E where different considerations apply – substantially to his disadvantage. Attempts are often made by employed persons to shake off the status of 'employee' and to attain 'freelance' status so as to qualify for the advantages of Schedule D, such attempts meeting with varying degrees of success. The problems involved in making this transition are considerable and space does not permit a detailed explanation to be made here – proper advice is necessary if the difficulties are to be avoided.

Particular attention has been paid by the Inland Revenue to journalists and to those engaged in the TV and film industry with a view to reclassifying them as employees so that PAYE is deducted from their earnings. This blanket treatment has been extended to other areas and, although it is obviously open to challenge by individual taxpayers, it is always difficult to persuade the Inland Revenue to change their views.

There is no reason why an employed person cannot carry on a freelance business in his spare time. Indeed, aspiring authors, painters, musicians, etc., often derive so little income from their craft that the financial security of an employment, perhaps in a different sphere of activity, is necessary. The existence of the employment is irrelevant to the taxation of the freelance earnings although it is most important not to confuse the income or expenditure of the employment with the income or expenditure of the self-employed activity. The Inland Revenue are aware of the advantages which can be derived by an individual having 'freelance' income from an organisation of which he is also an employee, and where such circumstances are contrived, it can be extremely difficult to convince an Inspector of Taxes that a genuine freelance activity is being carried on.

For those starting in business or commencing work on a freelance basis the Inland Revenue produce a very useful booklet entitled 'Starting in Business (IR28)', which is available from any tax office.

(b) Income

For income to be taxable it need not be substantial, nor even the author's only source of income; earnings from casual writing are also taxable but this can be an advantage, because occasional writers do not often make a profit from their writing. The expenses incurred in connection with writing may well exceed any income receivable and the resultant loss may then be used to reclaim tax paid on other income. There may be deducted from the income certain allowable expenses and capital allowances which are set out in more detail below. The possibility of a loss being used as a basis for a tax repayment is fully appreciated by the Inland Revenue who sometimes attempt to treat casual writing as a hobby so that any losses incurred cannot be used to reclaim tax; of course by the same token any income receivable would not be chargeable to tax. This treatment may sound attractive but it should be resisted vigorously because the Inland Revenue do not hesitate to change their mind when profits begin to arise. However, in the case of exceptional or non-recurring writing, such as the autobiography of a sports personality or the memoirs of a politician, it could be better to be treated as pursuing a hobby and not as a professional author. Sales of copyright can only be charged to capital gains tax (if at all) if the recipient is a professional author.

(c) Royalties

Where the recipient is a professional author, a series of cases has laid down a clear principle that sales of copyright are taxable as income and not as capital receipts. Similarly, lump sums on account of, or in advance of royalties are also taxable as income in the year of receipt, subject to a claim for spreading relief (see below).

Copyright royalties are generally paid without deduction of Income Tax. However, if royalties are paid to a person who normally lives abroad, tax will be deducted by the payer or his agent at the time the payment is made unless arrangements are made with the Inland Revenue for payments to be made gross.

(d) Arts Council Grants

Persons in receipt of grants from the Arts Council or similar bodies have been concerned for some time whether or not such grants were liable to Income Tax. In 1979, the Arts Council and other interested bodies engaged in detailed discussions with the Inland Revenue which culminated in the issue of a Statement of Practice regarding the tax treatment of those awards. Grants and other receipts of a similar nature have now been divided into two categories – those which are to be treated by the Inland Revenue as chargeable to tax and those which are not. Category A awards are considered to be taxable and arise from the following:
(1) Direct or indirect musical, design or choreographic commissions and direct or indirect commission of sculpture and paintings for public sites.
(2) The Royalty Supplement Guarantee Scheme.
(3) The contract writers' scheme.
(4) Jazz bursaries.
(5) Translators' grants.

(6) Photographic awards and bursaries.
(7) Film and video awards and bursaries.
(8) Performance Art Awards.
(9) Art Publishing Grants.
(10) Grants to assist with a specific project or projects (such as the writing of a book) or to meet specific professional expenses such as a contribution towards copying expenses made to a composer or to an artist's studio expenses.

Awards made under category B are not chargeable to tax and are as follows:
(1) Bursaries to trainee directors.
(2) In-service bursaries for theatre directors.
(3) Bursaries for associate directors.
(4) Bursaries to people attending full time courses in arts administration (the practical training course).
(5) In-service bursaries to theatre designers and bursaries to trainees on the theatre designers' scheme.
(6) In-service bursaries for administrators.
(7) Bursaries for actors and actresses.
(8) Bursaries for technicians and stage managers.
(9) Bursaries made to students attending the City University Arts Administration courses.
(10) Awards, known as the Buying Time Awards, made not to assist with a specific project or professional expenses but to maintain the recipient to enable him to take time off to develop his personal talents. These at present include the awards and bursaries known as the Theatre Writing Bursaries, awards and bursaries to composers, awards and bursaries to painters, sculptures and print makers, literature awards and bursaries.

This Statement of Practice has no legal force and is used merely to ease the administration of the tax system. It is open to anyone in receipt of a grant or award to disregard the agreed statement and challenge the Inland Revenue view on the merits of their particular case. However, it must be recognised that the Inland Revenue do not issue such statements lightly and any challenge to their view would almost certainly involve a lengthy and expensive action through the Courts.

The tax position of persons in receipt of literary prizes will generally follow a decision by the Special Commissioners in connection with the Whitbread Literary Award. In that case it was held that the prize was not part of the author's professional income and accordingly not chargeable to tax. The precise details are not available because decisions of the Special Commissioners are not reported unless an appeal is made to the High Court and the Inland Revenue chose not to appeal against this decision. Elsewhere in this *Yearbook* will be found details of the many literary awards which are given each year and this decision is of considerable significance to the winners of each of these prizes. It would be unwise to assume that all such awards will be free of tax as the precise facts which were present in the case of the Whitbread award may not be repeated in another case; however it is clear that an author winning a prize has some very powerful arguments in his favour, should the Inland Revenue seek to charge tax on the award.

ALLOWABLE EXPENSES

To qualify as an allowable business expense, expenditure has to be laid out wholly and exclusively for business purposes. Strictly there must be no 'duality of purpose', which means that expenditure cannot be apportioned to reflect the private and business usage, e.g. food, clothing, telephone, travelling expenses, etc. However, the Inland Revenue do not usually interpret this principle strictly and are prepared to allow all reasonable expenses (including apportioned sums) where the amounts can be commercially justified. It should be noted carefully that the expenditure does not have to be 'necessary', it merely has to be incurred 'wholly and exclusively' for business purposes; naturally, however, expenditure of an outrageous and wholly unnecessary character might well give rise to a presumption that it was not really for business purposes. As with all things, some expenses are unquestionably allowable and some expenses are equally unquestionably not allowable – it is the grey area in between which gives rise to all the difficulties and the outcome invariably depends on negotiation with the Inland Revenue.

Great care should be taken when claiming a deduction for items where there is a 'duality of purpose' and negotiations should be conducted with more than usual care and courtesy – if provoked the Inspector of Taxes may well choose to allow nothing. An appeal is always possible although unlikely to succeed as a string of cases in the Courts has clearly demonstrated. An example is the case of *Caillebotte* v. *Quinn* where the taxpayer (who normally had lunch at home) sought to claim the excess cost of meals incurred because he was working a long way from his home. The taxpayer's arguments failed because he did not eat only in order to work, one of the reasons for his eating was in order to sustain his life; a duality of purpose therefore existed and no tax relief was due. Other cases have shown that expenditure on clothing can also be disallowed if it is the kind of clothing which is in everyday use, because clothing is worn not only to assist the pursuit of one's profession but also to accord with public decency. This duality of purpose may be sufficient to deny relief – even where the particular type of clothing is of a kind not otherwise worn by the taxpayer. In the case of *Mallalieu* v. *Drummond* a lady barrister failed to obtain a tax deduction for items of sombre clothing purchased specifically for wearing in Court. The House of Lords decided that a duality of purpose existed because clothing represented part of her needs as a human being.

Despite the above Inspectors of Taxes are not usually inflexible and the following expenses are among those generally allowed:

(a) Cost of all materials used up in the course of preparation of the work.

(b) Cost of typewriting and secretarial assistance, etc.; if this or other help is obtained from one's spouse then it is entirely proper for a deduction to be claimed for the amounts paid for the work. The amounts claimed must actually be paid to the spouse and should be at the market rate although some uplift can be made for unsocial hours, etc. Payments to a wife (or husband) are of course taxable in her (or his) hands and should therefore be most carefully considered. The wife's earnings may also be liable for National Insurance contributions and if care is not taken these contributions can more than outweigh the tax savings.

(c) All expenditure on normal business items such as postage, stationery, telephone, fax and answering machines, agent's fees, accountancy charges, photography, subscriptions, periodicals, magazines, etc., may be claimed. The cost of daily papers should not be overlooked if these form part of research material. Visits to theatres, cinemas, etc., for research purposes may also be permissible (but not the cost relating to guests). Unfortunately expenditure on all types of business entertaining is specifically denied tax relief.

(d) If work is conducted at home, a deduction for 'use of home' is usually allowed providing the amount claimed is reasonable. If the claim is based on an appropriate proportion of the total costs of rent, light and heat, cleaning and maintenance, insurance, etc. (but not the Council Tax), care should be taken to ensure that no single room is used '*exclusively*' for business purposes, because this may result in the Capital Gains Tax exemption on the house as the only or main residence being partially forfeited. However, it would be a strange household where one room was in fact used exclusively for business purposes and for no other purpose whatsoever (e.g. storing personal bank statements and other private papers); the usual formula is to claim a deduction on the basis that most or all of the rooms in the house are used at one time or another for business purposes, thereby avoiding any suggestion that any part was used exclusively for business purposes.

(e) The appropriate business proportion of motor running expenses may also be claimed although what is the appropriate proportion will naturally depend on the particular circumstances of each case; it should be mentioned that the well-known scale benefits, whereby one is taxed according to the size and cost of the car, do not apply to self-employed persons.

(f) It has been long established that the cost of travelling from home to work (whether employed or self-employed) is not an allowable expense. However, if home is one's place of work then no expenditure under this heading is likely to be incurred and difficulties are unlikely to arise.

(g) Travelling and hotel expenses incurred for business purposes will normally be allowed but if any part could be construed as disguised holiday or pleasure expenditure, considerable thought would need to be given to the commercial reasons for the journey in order to justify the claim. The principle of 'duality of purpose' will always be a difficult hurdle in this connection – although not insurmountable.

(h) If a separate business bank account is maintained, any overdraft interest thereon will be an allowable expense. This is the *only* circumstance in which overdraft interest is allowed for tax purposes and care should be taken to avoid overdrafts in all other circumstances.

(i) Where capital allowances (see below) are claimed for a personal computer, television, video, CD or tape player, etc., used for business purposes an appropriate proportion of the costs of maintenance and repair of the equipment may also be claimed.

Clearly many other allowable items may be claimed in addition to those mentioned above. Wherever there is any reasonable business motive for some expenditure it should be claimed as a deduction although one should avoid an excess of imagination as this would naturally cause the Inspector of Taxes to doubt the genuineness of other expenses claimed.

The question is often raised whether the whole amount of an expense may be deducted or whether the VAT content must be excluded. Where VAT is reclaimed from the Customs and Excise (on the quarterly returns made by a registered person), the VAT element of the expense cannot be treated as an allowable deduction. Where the VAT is not reclaimed, the whole expense (inclusive of VAT) is allowable for Income Tax purposes.

CAPITAL ALLOWANCES

(a) Allowances

Where expenditure of a capital nature is incurred, it cannot be deducted from income as an expense – a separate and sometimes more valuable capital allowance being available instead. Capital allowances are given for many different types of expenditure, but authors and similar professional people are likely to claim only for 'plant and machinery'; this is a very wide expression which may include motor cars, computers and other business machines, televisions, CD, video and cassette players used for business purposes, books – and even a horse! Plant and machinery generally qualify for a 25% allowance in the year of purchase and 25% of the reducing balance in subsequent years. Exceptionally, during the period 1

November 1992 to 31 October 1993 a first year allowance of 40% was available but this has now been withdrawn, with no indication that any replacement relief will be introduced.

The reason these allowances can be more valuable than allowable expenses is that they may be wholly or partly disclaimed in any year that full benefit cannot be obtained – ordinary business expenses cannot be similarly disclaimed. Where, for example, the income of an author does not exceed his personal allowances, he would not be liable to tax and a claim for capital allowances would be wasted. If the capital allowances were to be disclaimed their benefit would be carried forward for use in subsequent years.

Careful planning with claims for capital allowances is therefore essential if maximum benefit is to be obtained.

As an alternative to capital allowances claims can be made on the 'renewals' basis whereby all renewals are treated as allowable deductions in the year; no allowance is obtained for the initial purchase, but the cost of replacement (excluding any improvement element) is allowed in full. This basis is no longer widely used, as it is considerably less advantageous than claiming capital allowances as described above.

Leasing is a popular method of acquiring fixed assets, and where cash is not available to enable an outright purchase to be made, assets may be leased over a period of time. Whilst leasing may have financial benefits in certain circumstances, in normal cases there is likely to be no *tax* advantage in leasing an asset where the alternative of outright purchase is available. Indeed, leasing can be a positive disadvantage in the case of motor cars with a new retail price of more than £12,000. If such a car is leased, only a proportion of the leasing charges will be tax deductible.

(b) Books

The question of whether the cost of books is eligible for tax relief has long been a source of difficulty. The annual cost of replacing books used for the purposes of one's professional activities (e.g. the annual cost of a new *Writers' & Artists' Yearbook*) has always been an allowable expense; the difficulty arose because the initial cost of reference books, etc. (for example when commencing one's profession) was treated as capital expenditure but no allowances were due as the books were not considered to be 'plant'. However, the matter was clarified by the case of *Munby* v. *Furlong* in which the Court of Appeal decided that the initial cost of law books purchased by a barrister was expenditure on 'plant' and eligible for capital allowances. This is clearly a most important decision, particularly relevant to any person who uses expensive books in the course of exercising his profession.

PENSION CONTRIBUTIONS

(a) Personal pensions

Where a self-employed person pays annual premiums under an approved personal pension policy, tax relief may now be obtained each year for the following amounts:

Age at 6/4/94	Maximum %	
35 and under	17.5% (max)	£13,440
36 – 45	20% (max)	£15,360
46 – 50	25% (max)	£19,200
51 – 55	30% (max)	£23,040
56 – 60	35% (max)	£26,880
61 and over	40% (max)	£30,720

These figures do not apply to existing retirement annuity policies; these remain subject to the old limits which are unchanged.

These arrangements can be extremely advantageous in providing for a pension as premiums are usually paid when the income is high (and the tax relief is also high) and the pension (taxed as earned income when received) usually arises when the income is low and little tax is payable. The reduction in the rates of income tax to a maximum of 40% makes this decision a little more difficult because the tax advantages could go into reverse. When the pension is paid it could, if rates rise again, be taxed at a higher rate than the rate of tax relief at the moment. One would be deferring income in order to pay more tax on it later. However, this involves a large element of guesswork, and many people will be content simply with the long-term pension benefits.

(b) Class 4 National Insurance contributions

Allied to pensions is the payment of Class 4 National Insurance contributions, although no pension or other benefit is obtained by the contributions; the Class 4 contributions are designed solely to extract additional amounts from self-employed persons and are payable in addition to the normal Class 2 (self-employed) contributions. The rates are changed each year and for 1994/95 self-employed persons will be obliged to contribute 7.3% of their profits between the range £6490-£22,360 per annum, a maximum liability of £1158.51 for 1994/95. This amount is collected in conjunction with the Schedule D Income Tax liability and appears on the same assessment; the comments below regarding assessments, appeals and postponement apply equally to Class 4 contributions. Tax relief is available for one half of the Class 4 contributions.

SPREADING RELIEF

(a) Relief for copyright payments

Special provisions enable authors and similar persons who have been engaged on a literary, dramatic, musical or artistic work for a period of more than twelve months, to spread certain amounts received over two or three years depending on the time spent in preparing the work. If the author was engaged on the work for a period exceeding twelve months, the receipt may be spread backwards over two years; if the author was engaged on the work for more than 24 months, the receipt may be spread backwards over three years. (Analogous provisions apply to sums received for the sale of a painting, sculpture or other work of art.)
The relief applies to:
a. lump sums received on the assignment of copyright, in whole or in part;
b. sums received on the grant of any interest in the copyright by licence;
c. non-returnable advances on account of royalties;
d. any receipts of or on account of royalties or any periodical sums received within two years of first publication.

A claim for spreading relief has to be made within eight years from 5 April following the date of first publication.

(b) Relief where copyright sold after ten years

Where copyright is assigned (or a licence in it is granted) more than ten years after the first publication of the work, then the amounts received can qualify for a different spreading relief. The assignment (or licence) must be for a period of more than two years and the receipt will be spread forward over the number of years for which the assignment (or licence) is granted – but with a maximum of six years. The relief is terminated by death, but there are provisions enabling the deceased author's personal representatives to re-spread the amounts if it is to the beneficiaries' advantage.

The above rules are arbitrary and cumbersome, only providing a limited measure of relief in special circumstances. The provisions can sometimes be helpful to repair matters when consideration of the tax position has been neglected, but invariably a better solution is found if the likely tax implications are considered fully in advance.

COLLECTION OF TAX

Assessments

In order to collect the tax which is due on the profits of authorship the Inland Revenue issue an assessment based on the income for the relevant period. Normally the income to be assessed will be that for the previous year (e.g. the 1994/95 assessment will be based on the accounts made up to some date in 1993/94 – perhaps 31 December 1993 or 5 April 1994). However, there are complicated rules for determining the income to be assessed in the years immediately after commencement, and in the years immediately prior to the discontinuance of the profession, and if for any reason there is a change in the date to which accounts are made up.

A new system for taxing the self-employed will come into effect for the tax year 1997/98. Under the new system, profits will not be taxed on the previous year basis but on the actual basis – that is to say, the profits for the accounting period ending in the year. This may seem a long way off but there has to be a transition from the old system to the new which can create advantages. One area where attention should be directed is the position for 1996/97. The taxable profits for that year will be the average of the profits for the accounts that end in 1994/95 and 1995/96. This means that half of those profits will not be taxed. As the accounts which end in the year 1994/95 may have already commenced, some early consideration to the position is recommended.

When an assessment is received it should be examined carefully.

(a) If it is correct, the tax should be paid on the dates specified. Usually the tax is payable in two equal instalments, on 1 January in the year of assessment and on the following 1 July. If payment is delayed then interest may arise – see below.

(b) If the assessment is incorrect (for example, if it is estimated), then prompt action is required. An appeal must be lodged within 30 days of the date of issue of the assessment specifying the grounds of the appeal. An appeal form usually accompanies the notice of assessment. (If for some reason an appeal cannot be lodged within the 30 days the Inland Revenue are often prepared to accept a late appeal, but this is at their discretion and acceptance cannot be guaranteed.) If there is any tax charged on an incorrect assessment it cannot simply be forgotten, because it will become payable despite any appeal, unless an application for 'postponement' is also made. (This may be done by completing the other half of the appeal form.) Tax can be postponed only where there are grounds for believing that too much tax has been charged, and the Inspector of Taxes will agree to postpone tax only if these grounds are reasonable. The tax which is not postponed will usually be payable on the normal due dates. It is necessary to consider claims for postponement most carefully to ensure that approximately the correct amount of tax remains payable; otherwise an unfortunate (and expensive) charge to interest could arise. It is important to recognise that 'postponement' does not mean elimination; it simply means that payment of tax may be deferred, and after six months interest will start to run on any tax which has been postponed but which is ultimately found to be payable. As agreement of the final liability may take a long time, a large amount of interest can arise unless a reasonably accurate amount has been paid on time.

Interest

Interest is chargeable on overdue tax at a variable rate, which at the time of writing is 5.5% per annum. It does not rank for any tax relief, which can make the Inland Revenue an expensive source of credit. It can be very difficult to persuade the Inland Revenue to withdraw a charge to interest – even where the delay is their fault.

However, the Inland Revenue can also be obliged to pay interest at the same rate (known as repayment supplement) tax-free where repayments are delayed. The rules relating to repayment supplement are less beneficial and even more complicated than the rules for interest payable but they do exist and can be very welcome if a large repayment has been delayed for a long time.

Example

Author's accounts made up to 30 April 1993 showing profits of £10,000 giving rise to tax of (say) £1500.

Assessment issued in September 1994 for 1994/95 in an estimated figure of £15,000 – showing tax payable of £2500.

Appeal must be made within 30 days of issue.

Application for postponement must also be made within 30 days to postpone £1000 of the tax charged.

Tax therefore becomes payable thus:

1 Jan 1995	£750
1 July 1995	£750

(If no application for postponement were to be made £1250 would become payable on each of these dates. When the final liability is agreed the excess of £1000 would be refunded but that could take some time, and repayment supplement might not apply.)

Unfortunately life is never as simple as the above illustration would suggest, but it serves to demonstrate the principle.

VALUE ADDED TAX

The activities of writers, painters, composers, etc., are all 'taxable supplies' within the scope of VAT and chargeable at the standard rate. (Zero rating which applies to publishers, booksellers, etc. on the supply of books does not extend to the work performed by writers.) Accordingly, authors are obliged to register for VAT if their income for the past twelve months exceeds £45,000 or if their income for the coming month will exceed that figure.

Delay in registering can be a most serious matter because if registration is not effected at the proper time, the Customs and Excise can (and invariably do) claim VAT from all the income received since the date on which registration should have been made. As no VAT would have been included in the amounts received during this period the amount claimed by the Customs and Excise must inevitably come straight from the pocket of the author.

He may be entitled to seek reimbursement of the VAT from those whom he ought to have charged VAT but this is obviously a matter of some difficulty and may indeed damage his commercial relationships. Apart from these disadvantages there is also a penalty for late registration. The rules are extremely harsh and are imposed automatically even in cases of innocent error. It is therefore extremely important to monitor the income very carefully because if in any period of twelve months the income exceeds the £45,000 limit, the Customs and Excise must be notified within 30 days of the end of the period. Failure to do so will give rise to an automatic penalty. It should be emphasised that this is a penalty for failing to submit a form and has nothing to do with any real or potential loss of tax. Furthermore, whether the failure was innocent or deliberate will not matter. Only the existence of a 'reasonable excuse' will be a defence to the penalty. However, a reasonable excuse does not include ignorance, error, a lack of funds or reliance on any third party.

However it is possible to regard VAT registration as a privilege and not a penalty, because only VAT registered persons can reclaim VAT paid on their expenses such as stationery, telephone, professional fees, etc., even typewriters and other plant and machinery (excluding cars). However, many find that the administrative inconvenience – the cost of maintaining the necessary records and completing the necessary forms – more than outweighs the benefits to be gained from registration and prefer to stay outside the scope of VAT for as long as possible.

OVERSEAS MATTERS

The general observation may be made that self-employed persons resident and domiciled in the United Kingdom are not well treated with regard to their overseas work, being taxable on their world-wide income. It is important to emphasise that if fees are earned abroad, no tax saving can be achieved merely by keeping the money outside the country. Although exchange control regulations no longer exist to require repatriation of foreign earnings, such income remains taxable in the UK and must be disclosed to the Inland Revenue; the same applies to interest or other income arising on any investment of these earnings overseas. Accordingly whenever foreign earnings are likely to become substantial, prompt and effective action is required to limit the impact of UK and foreign taxation. In the case of non resident authors it is important that arrangements concerning writing for publication in the UK, e.g. in newspapers, are undertaken with great care. A case concerning the wife of one of the great train robbers who provided detailed information for a series of articles in a Sunday newspaper is most instructive. Although she was acknowledged to be resident in Canada for all the relevant years, the income from the articles was treated as arising in this country and fully chargeable to UK tax.

The United Kingdom has double taxation agreements with many other countries and these agreements are designed to ensure that income arising in a foreign country is taxed either in that country or in the United Kingdom. Where a withholding tax is deducted from payments received from another country (or where tax is paid in full in the absence of a double taxation agreement), the amount of foreign tax paid can usually be set off against the related UK tax liability. Many successful authors can be found living in Eire because of the complete exemption from tax which attaches to works of cultural or artistic merit by persons who are resident there. However, such a step should only be contemplated having careful regard to all the other domestic and commercial considerations and specialist advice is essential if the exemption is to be obtained and kept; a careless breach of the conditions could cause the exemption to be withdrawn with catastrophic consequences.

COMPANIES

When an author becomes successful the prospect of paying tax at the higher rate may drive him to take hasty action such as the formation of companies, etc., which may not always be to his advantage. Indeed some authors seeing the exodus into tax exile of their more successful colleagues even form companies in low tax areas in the naive expectation of saving large amounts of tax. The Inland Revenue are fully aware of the opportunities and have extensive powers to charge tax and combat avoidance. Accordingly such action is just as likely to *increase* tax liabilities and generate other costs and should never be contemplated without expert advice; some very expensive mistakes are often made in this area which are not always able to be remedied.

To conduct one's business through the medium of a company can be a most effective method of mitigating tax liabilities, and providing it is done at the right time and under the right circumstances very substantial advantages can be derived. However, if done without due care and attention the intended advantages will simply evaporate. At the very least it is essential to ensure that the company's business is genuine and conducted properly with regard to the realities of the situation. If the author continues his activities unchanged, simply paying all the receipts from his work into a company's bank account, he cannot expect to persuade the Inland Revenue that it is the company and not himself who is entitled to, and should be assessed to tax on, that income. It must be strongly emphasised that many pitfalls exist which can easily eliminate all the tax benefits expected to arise by the formation of the company. For example, company directors are employees of the company and will be liable to pay much higher National Insurance contributions; the company must also pay the employer's proportion of the contribution and a total liability of over 20% of gross salary may arise. This compares most unfavourably with the position of a self-employed person. Moreover on the commencement of the company's business the individual's profession will cease and the Inland Revenue have the power to re-open earlier years' assessments to increase the liabilities for previous years; this is always a crucial factor in determining the best moment when the changeover to a company should take place.

No mention has been made above of personal reliefs and allowances (for example the single and married couples allowances, etc.); this is because these allowances and the rates of tax are subject to constant change and are always set out in detail in the explanatory notes which accompany the Tax Return. The annual Tax Return is an important document and should not be ignored because it is crucial to one's tax position. Indeed, it should be completed promptly with extreme care because the Inland Revenue treat failures to disclose income very harshly, invariably exacting interest and penalties – sometimes of substantial amounts. If filling in the Return is a source of difficulty or anxiety, comfort may be found in the Consumer Association's publication *Money Which? – Tax Saving Guide*; this is published in March of each year and includes much which is likely to be of interest and assistance.

Social Security Contributions

PETER ARROWSMITH FCA
Tax Manager, Grant Thornton

INTRODUCTION

In general, every individual who works in Great Britain either as an employee or as a self-employed person is liable to pay social security contributions. The law governing this subject is complicated and the following should only be regarded as a summary of the position.

All contributions are payable in respect of years ending on 5 April, the classes of contributions being as follows:

Class 1 These are payable by employees (primary contributions) and their employers (secondary contributions) and are based on earnings.

Class 1A Use of company car, and fuel, for private purposes.

Class 2 These are weekly flat rate contributions, payable by the self-employed.

Class 3 These are weekly flat rate contributions, payable on a voluntary basis in order to provide, or make up entitlement to, certain social security benefits.

Class 4 These are payable by the self-employed in respect of their trading or professional income and are based on earnings.

EMPLOYED OR SELF-EMPLOYED?

The question as to whether a person is employed under a contract *of* service and is thereby an employee liable to Class 1 contributions, or performs services (either solely or in partnership) under a contract *for* service and is thereby self-employed liable to Class 2 and Class 4 contributions, often has to be decided in practice. One of the best guides can be found in the case of *Market Investigations Limited* v. *Minister of Social Security* (1969 2 WLR 1) when Cooke J. remarked as follows:

'. . . the fundamental test to be applied is this: "Is the person who has engaged himself to perform these services performing them as a person in business on his own account?" If the answer to that question is "yes", then the contract is a contract for services. If the answer is "no", then the contract is a contract of service. No exhaustive list has been compiled and perhaps no exhaustive list can be compiled of the considerations which are relevant in determining that question, nor can strict rules be laid down as to the relative weight which the various considerations should carry in particular cases. The most that can be said is that control will no doubt always have to be considered, although it can no longer be regarded as the sole determining factor; and that factors which may be of importance are such matters as
—whether the man performing the services provides his own equipment,
—whether he hires his own helpers,
—what degree of financial risk he takes,
—what degree of responsibility for investment and management he has, and
—whether and how far he has an opportunity of profiting from sound management in the performance of his task.'

The above case was also considered as recently as November 1993 by the Court of Appeal in the case of *Hall* v. *Lorimer*. In this case a vis on mixer with around

20 clients and with around 120-150 separate engagements per annum was held to be self-employed. This follows the, perhaps surprising, contention of the Inland Revenue that the taxpayer was an employee. It is understood that the Inland Revenue are not appealing further against this decision.

There have been three cases dealing with musicians, in recent years, which provide further guidance on the question as to whether an individual is employed or self-employed.

Midland Sinfonia Concert Society Ltd v. *Secretary of State for Social Services* (1981 ICR 454)

A musician, employed to play in an orchestra by separate invitation at irregular intervals and remunerated solely in respect of each occasion upon which he does play, is employed under a contract for services. He is therefore self-employed, not an employed earner, for the purposes of the Social Security Act 1975, and the orchestra which engages him is not liable to pay National Insurance contributions in respect of his earnings.

Addison v. *London Philharmonic Orchestra Limited* (1981 ICR 261)

This was an appeal to determine whether certain individuals were employees for the purposes of section 11(1) of the Employment Protection (Consolidation) Act 1978.

The Employment Appeal Tribunal upheld the decision of an industrial tribunal that an associate player and three additional or extra players of the London Philharmonic Orchestra were not employees under a contract of service, but were essentially freelance musicians carrying on their own business.

The facts found by the industrial tribunal showed that, when playing for the orchestra, each appellant remained essentially a freelance musician, pursuing his or her own profession as an instrumentalist, with an individual reputation, and carrying on his or her own business, and they contributed their own skills and interpretative powers to the orchestra's performances as independent contractors.

Winfield v. *London Philharmonic Orchestra Limited* (ICR 1979, page 726)

This case dealt with the question as to whether an individual was an employee within the meaning of section 30 of the Trade Union and Labour Relations Act 1974.

The following remarks by the appeal tribunal are of interest in relation to the status of musicians:

'. . . making music is an art, and the co-operation required for a performance of Berlioz's *Requiem* is dissimilar to that required between the manufacturer of concrete and the truck driver who takes the concrete where it is needed. . . It took the view, as we think it was entitled on the material before it to do, that the company was simply machinery through which the members of the orchestra managed and controlled the orchestra's operation . . . In deciding whether you are in the presence of a contract of service or not, you look at the whole of the picture. This picture looks to us, as it looked to the industrial tribunal, like a co-operative of distinguished musicians running themselves with self and mutual discipline, and in no sense like a boss and his musician employees.'

Other recent cases have concerned a professional dancer and holiday camp entertainers (all of whom were regarded as employees), and there are special arrangements for workers in the film industry. In two recent cases income from part-time lecturing was held to be from an employment.

Accordingly, if a person is regarded as an employee under the above rules, he will be liable to pay contributions even if his employment is casual, part time or temporary.

Furthermore, if a person is an employee and also carries on a trade or profession either solely or in partnership, there will be a liability to more than one class of contributions (subject to certain maxima – see below).

Exceptions

There are certain exceptions to the above rules, those most relevant to artists and writers being:

(a) The employment of a wife by her husband, or vice versa, is disregarded for social security purposes unless it is for the purposes of a trade or profession (for example, the employment of his wife by an author would not be disregarded and would result in a liability for contributions if her salary reached the minimum levels).

(b) The employment of certain relatives in a private dwelling house in which both employee and employer reside is disregarded for social security purposes provided the employment is not for the purposes of a trade or business carried on at those premises by the employer. This would cover the employment of a relative (as defined) as a housekeeper in a private residence.

(c) In general, lecturers, teachers and instructors engaged by an educational establishment to teach on at least four days in three consecutive months are regarded as employees, although this rule does not apply to fees received by persons giving public lectures.

Freelance film workers

As regards the status of workers in the film and allied industries, the Inland Revenue made the following announcement on 30 March 1983:

'The Inland Revenue has recently carried out a review of the employment status of workers engaged on "freelance" terms within the industry. Following this review there has been an extensive series of discussions with representative bodies in the industry, including Independent Programme Producers Association, British Film and Television Producers Association, Advertising Film and Video Tape Producers Association, National Association of Theatrical and Kine Employees, and Association of Cinematograph, Television and Allied Technicians.

'As a result of that review and the subsequent discussions, the Inland Revenue consider that a number of workers engaged on "freelance" terms within the industry are engaged as employees under contracts of service, either written or oral, and should be assessed under Schedule E. Many workers in the industry already pay employee's National Insurance contributions.

'The Inland Revenue, however, accept that a number of "freelance" workers in certain types of work within the industry are likely to be engaged under contracts for services, as people in self-employment, and should therefore be assessed under Schedule D. Any individual who does not agree with the Revenue's determination of his position has the normal right of appeal to the independent Income Tax Commissioners.'

There is a list of grades in the film industry in respect of which PAYE need not be deducted and who are regarded as self-employed for tax purposes.

Further information can be obtained from the March 1992 edition of the Inland Revenue guidance notes on the application of PAYE to casual and freelance staff in the film industry. In view of the Inland Revenue announcement that the same status will apply for PAYE and DSS purposes, no liability for employee's and employer's contributions should arise in the case of any of the grades mentioned above. However, in the film and TV industry this general rule has not always been followed in practice. Early in 1993, after a long review, the DSS agreed that individuals working behind the camera and who have jobs on the Inland Revenue Schedule D list are self-employed for social security purposes. There are also special rules for, inter alia, personnel appearing before the camera, short engagements, payments to limited companies and payments to overseas personalities.

Artistes, performers and non-performers

From 6 April 1990 artistes and performers (excluding established performers with 'reserved Schedule D status' and guest artistes engaged by opera companies) working under standard Equity contracts are treated as employees for income tax purposes so far as earnings from such employments are concerned. This will bring the income tax treatment into line with that for social security, as it has been the view of the DSS for many years that the vast majority of performers are employees for social security contribution purposes because of the general conditions under which they usually work. The DSS has always acknowledged, however, that there is some scope for self-employment for performers (especially 'act as known' engagements), and specific claims to self-employment are looked into in detail. Accordingly, 'act as known' engagements will normally be treated as self-employment for both social security and income tax purposes.

The DSS does, however, permit subsistence allowances to be paid without liability to contributions, and special rules apply to travelling expenses.

The industry also uses standard agreements for the engagement of non-performers. The Inland Revenue has looked at some of these and concluded that some are normally contracts *for* services (self-employed) and others contracts *of* service (employed).

CLASS 1 CONTRIBUTIONS BY EMPLOYEES AND EMPLOYERS

As mentioned above, these are related to earnings, the amount payable depending upon whether the employer has applied for his employees to be 'contracted-out' of the State earnings-related pension scheme; such application can be made where the employer's own pension scheme provides a requisite level of benefits for his employees and their dependents.

Contributions are only payable once earnings exceed the lower earnings limit but are then due on *all* such earnings up to the upper earnings limit by employees ('primary contributions') but without an upper limit for employers ('secondary contributions').

Contributions are normally collected via the PAYE tax deduction machinery, and there are penalties for late submission of returns and for errors therein. From 19 April 1993, interest will be charged automatically on unpaid PAYE and social security contributions.

Employees liable to pay contributions

These are payable by any employee who is aged 16 years and over (even though he may still be at school) and who is paid an amount equal to, or exceeding, the lower earnings limit (see below).

Nationality is irrelevant for contribution purposes and, subject to special rules covering employees not normally resident in Great Britain, Northern Ireland or the Isle of Man, or resident in EU countries or those with which there are reciprocal agreements, contributions must be paid whether the employee concerned is a British subject or not provided he is gainfully employed in Great Britain.

Employees exempt from liability to pay contributions

Persons over pensionable age (65 for men and 60 for women) are exempt from liability to pay primary contributions, even if they have not retired.

However, the fact that an employee may be exempt from liability does not relieve an employer from liability to pay secondary contributions in respect of that employee.

Rate of employees' contributions

From 6 April 1994, the rate of employees' contributions, where the earnings are not less than the lower earnings limit, is 2% of earnings to the lower earnings limit and 10% of earnings between the lower and upper earnings limits (8.2% for contracted-out employments).

Certain married women who made appropriate elections before 12 May 1977 may be entitled to pay a reduced rate of 3.85%. However, they will have no entitlement to benefits in respect of these contributions.

Employers' contributions

All employers are liable to pay contributions on the gross earnings of employees. As mentioned above, an employer's liability is not reduced as a result of employees being exempted from, or being liable to pay only the (3.85%) reduced rate of, contributions.

For earnings paid on or after 6 April 1994 employers are liable at rates of 3.6%, 5.6%, 7.6% or 10.2% on earnings paid (without any upper earnings limit) depending upon the particular band into which the earnings fall (see below). The rate of contributions attributable to the band into which the earnings fall is applied to *all* those earnings and not merely to the earnings falling into that band. The above four rates of secondary contributions are reduced to 0.6%, 2.6%, 4.6% and 7.2% in respect of earnings above the lower earnings limit and up to and including the upper earnings limit for contracted-out employments from 6 April 1994.

The employer is responsible for the payment of both employees' and employer's contributions, but is entitled to deduct the employees' contributions from the earnings on which they are calculated. Effectively, therefore, the employee suffers a deduction in respect of his social security contributions in arriving at his weekly or monthly wage or salary.

Special rules apply to company directors and persons employed through agencies.

Rates of Class 1 contributions and earnings limits from 6 April 1994

	Rates payable on all earnings			
Earnings per week	Not Contracted-out		Contracted-out	
	Employee	Employer	Employee	Employer
£		%		%
Below 57.00	—	—	—	—
57.00 – 99.99	2% to lower	3.6	2% to lower	*3.6/0.6
100.00 – 144.99	earnings limit,	5.6	earnings limit,	*5.6/2.6
145.00 – 199.99	10% between	7.6	8.2% between	*7.6/4.6
200.00 – 430.00	lower and	10.2	lower and	*10.2/7.2
Over £430.00	upper earnings limits	10.2	upper earnings limits	†10.2/7.2

* The first figure is the rate to the lower earnings limit and the second is to all the excess.
† 10.2% to lower earnings limit and above upper earnings limit; 7.2% between these limits.

Items included in, or excluded from, earnings

Contributions are calculated on the basis of a person's gross earnings from his employment. This will normally be the figure shown on the tax deduction card, except where the employee pays superannuation contributions and, from 6 April 1987, charitable gifts – these must be added back for the purposes of calculating Class 1 liability. Profit-related pay exempt from income tax is not exempt from social security contributions.

Earnings include salary, wages, overtime pay, commissions, bonuses, holiday pay, payments made while the employee is sick or absent from work, payments to cover travel between home and office, and payments under the statutory sick pay and maternity pay schemes.

However, certain payments, some of which may be regarded as taxable income for income tax purposes, are ignored for social security purposes. These include certain gratuities paid other than by the employer, redundancy payments and most payments in lieu of notice, certain payments in kind, reimbursement of specific expenses incurred in the carrying out of the employment, benefits given on an individual basis for personal reasons (e.g. wedding and birthday presents), compensation for loss of office, and meal vouchers which can only be redeemed for food or drink.

DSS booklet NI 269 (April 1993), together with its April 1994 supplement, gives a list of items to include in or exclude from earnings for Class 1 contribution purposes.

Maximum contributions

There is a limit to the total liability for social security contributions payable by a person who is employed in more than one employment, or is also self-employed or a partner.

Where only not contracted-out Class 1 contributions, or not contracted-out Class 1 and Class 2 contributions, are payable, the maximum contribution is limited to 53 primary Class 1 contributions at the maximum weekly non-contracted-out standard rate. For 1994/95 the maximum will thus be £2037.32.

However, where contracted-out Class 1 contributions are payable, the maximum primary Class 1 contributions payable for 1994/95 where all employments are contracted-out are £1681.48.

Where Class 4 contributions are payable in addition to Class 1 and/or Class 2 contributions, *the Class 4 contributions are restricted* so that they shall not exceed the excess of £1457.96 (i.e. 53 Class 2 contributions plus maximum Class 4 contributions) over the aggregate of the Class 1 and Class 2 contributions.

Miscellaneous rules

There are detailed rules covering a person with two or more employments; where a person receives a bonus or commission in addition to a regular wage or salary; and where a person is in receipt of holiday pay. From 6 April 1991 employers' social security contributions arise under Class 1A in respect of the private use of a company car, and of fuel provided for private use therein. The rate was 10.4% to 5 April 1994 and is now 10.2%.

CLASS 2 CONTRIBUTIONS BY THE SELF-EMPLOYED

Rate

Class 2 contributions are payable at the weekly rate of £5.65 as from 6 April 1994.

Exemptions from Class 2 liability

These are as follows:
(1) A man over 65 or a woman over 60.
(2) A person who has not attained the age of 16.

(3) A married woman or, in certain cases, a widow who elected prior to 12 May 1977 not to pay Class 2 contributions.
(4) Persons with small earnings (see below).
(5) Persons not ordinarily self-employed (see below).

Small earnings

Any person who can show that his net self-employed earnings per his profit and loss account (as opposed to taxable profits):
(1) for the year of application are expected to be less than a specified limit (£3200 in the 1994/95 tax year); or
(2) for the year preceding the application were less than the limit specified for that year (£3140 for 1993/94) and there has been no material change of circumstances;
may apply for a certificate of exception from Class 2 contributions. Certificates of exception must be renewed in accordance with the instructions stated thereon. At the Secretary of State's discretion the certificate may commence up to 13 weeks before the date on which the application is made. Despite a certificate of exception being in force, a person who is self-employed is still entitled to pay Class 2 contributions if he wishes, in order to maintain entitlement to social security benefits.

Persons not ordinarily self-employed

Part-time self-employed activities as a writer or artist are disregarded for contribution purposes if the person concerned is not ordinarily employed in such activities and has a full-time job as an employee. There is no definition of 'ordinarily employed' for this purpose but the DSS regard a person who has a regular job and whose earnings from spare-time occupation are not expected to be more than £800 per annum as falling within this category. Persons qualifying for this relief do not require certificates of exception. It should be noted that many activities covered by this relief would probably also be eligible for relief under the small earnings rule (see above).

Method of payment

From April 1993, Class 2 contributions may be paid by monthly direct debit in arrears or by cheque, bank giro, etc. following receipt of a quarterly (in arrears) bill from DSS.

Overpaid contributions

If, following the payment of Class 2 contributions, it is found that the earnings are below the exception limit (e.g. the relevant accounts are prepared late), the Class 2 contributions that have been overpaid can be reclaimed for tax years 1988/89 onwards, provided a claim is made between 6 April and 31 December immediately following the end of the tax year.

CLASS 3 CONTRIBUTIONS

These are payable voluntarily, at the rate of £5.55 per week from 6 April 1994, by persons aged 16 or over with a view to enabling them to qualify for a limited range of benefits if their contribution record is not otherwise sufficient. In general, Class 3 contributions can be paid by employees, the self-employed and the non employed.

Broadly speaking, no more than 52 Class 3 contributions are payable for any one tax year, and contributions are not payable after the end of the tax year in which the individual concerned reaches the age of 64 (59 for women).

Class 3 contributions may be paid in the same manner as Class 2 (see above) or by annual cheque in arrears.

CLASS 4 CONTRIBUTIONS BY THE SELF-EMPLOYED

Rate

In addition to Class 2 contributions, self-employed persons are liable to pay Class 4 contributions. These are calculated at the rate of 7.3% on the amount of profits or gains chargeable to income tax under Schedule D Case I or II which exceed £6490 per annum but which do not exceed £22,360 per annum for 1994/95. Thus the maximum Class 4 contribution is 7.3% of £15,870 – i.e. £1158.51 for 1994/95.

For the tax year 1994/95, Class 4 contributions are based on the income tax assessment for 1994/95 (for example, the profits of the year ended 31 December 1993) and so on for subsequent years.

The income tax assessment on which Class 4 contributions are calculated is after deducting capital allowances and losses, but before deducting personal tax allowances or retirement annuity or personal pension plan premiums.

Class 4 contributions produce no additional benefits, but were introduced to ensure that self-employed persons as a whole pay a fair share of the cost of pensions and other social security benefits without the self-employed who make only small profits having to pay excessively high flat rate contributions.

Currently, one half of the Class 4 contributions (as finally settled) is deductible in computing total income. It should be noted that this deduction is given in arriving at total income for income tax purposes and not in arriving at the profits assessable under Schedule D. Although the legislation states that a claim is necessary, in practice the deduction will be given automatically. This deduction is broadly equivalent to that available to employers for tax purposes in respect of their secondary contributions, and was introduced to rectify the previous anomaly in that employers, but not the self-employed, were eligible for tax relief for the contributions they bore. Where deferment of Class 2 and 4 contributions has been obtained, it should be ensured that the eventually assessed Class 4 contributions, if any, are allowed for income tax purposes.

Payment of contributions

In general, contributions are calculated and collected by the Inland Revenue together with the income tax under Schedule D Case I or II, and accordingly the contributions are due and payable at the same time as the income tax liability on the relevant profits.

Persons exempt from Class 4 contributions

The following persons are exempt from Class 4 contributions:

(1) Men over 65 and women over 60 at the commencement of the year of assessment (i.e. on 6 April).

(2) An individual not resident in the United Kingdom for income tax purposes in the year of assessment.

(3) Persons whose earnings are not 'immediately derived' from carrying on a trade, profession or vocation (for example, sleeping partners and, possibly, limited partners).

(4) A child under 16 on 6 April of the year of assessment.

(5) Persons not ordinarily self-employed (see above as for Class 2 contributions).

Calculation of liability for married persons and partnerships

Under independent taxation of husband and wife from 1990/91 onwards, each spouse is responsible for his or her Class 4 liability.

In partnerships, each partner's liability is calculated separately, and the Inland Revenue will normally collect each partner's Class 4 liability in the partnership name as is the case with the income tax liability of the partnership under Schedule D. If a partner also carries on another trade or profession, the profits of all such businesses are aggregated for the purposes of calculating his Class 4 liability; in these circumstances the Class 4 liability in respect of his share of partnership profits may be assessed separately and not in the partnership name.

When an assessment has become final and conclusive for the purposes of income tax, it is also final and conclusive for the purposes of calculating Class 4 liability.

SOURCES OF FURTHER INFORMATION

Further information can be obtained from the many booklets published by the Department of Social Security.These can be obtained from local offices – refer to telephone directory under 'Contributions Agency' in the first instance. Individuals resident abroad should address their enquiries to Contributions Agency, Overseas Contributions, Newcastle upon Tyne NE98 1YX.

'A proper story'

Clearly-drawn characters, a strong story line and a satisfying conclusion appeal to many writers and readers. Bill Naughton, one of Britain's most popular short story writers, locates his stories firmly in a well-defined social setting, usually the North of his early life, exploits his intimacy with local speech to give his stories vitality and a strong realistic feel, and generally builds his stories round one incident of a dramatic or humours nature. In 'Seeing a Beauty Queen Home', a young man who obviously fancies himself with women, escorts a girl back to her grandmother's house late at night. The girl pretends to her gran upstairs that she is alone, but the old lady soon comes down to see for herself. Quick as a flash the young man hits upon the idea of pretending to be a neighbour's son who has of course grown up a bit since she last saw him. He exploits the old lady's failing eyesight and the dim light, and his quick-wittedness pulls him through the interrogation. When the couple are left alone, he turns to the girl in triumph. She responds however by kicking him out of the house, disgusted by his skill at impersonation which to her suggests long practice. The table turned on the crafty hero, the story ends.

from *Word Power* by Julian Birkett (A & C Black, £9.99)

Social Security Benefits

K.D. BARTLETT FCA
Partner, Clark Whitehill

Social security benefits are quite difficult to understand. There are many leaflets produced by the Department of Social Security and this article is written to try to simplify some of the more usual benefits that are available under the Social Security Acts. It deliberately does not cover every aspect of the legislation but the references given should enable the relevant information to be easily traced. These references are to the leaflets issued by the Department of Social Security.

It is usual for only one periodical benefit to be payable at any one time. If the contribution conditions are satisfied for more than one benefit it is the larger benefit that is payable. Benefit rates shown below were those payable from week commencing 6 April 1994.

Employed persons (Category A or D contributors) are covered for all benefits. Certain married women and widows (Category B and E contributors) who elected to pay at the reduced rate receive only attendance allowance, guardian's allowance and industrial injuries benefits. Other benefits may be available dependent on their husbands' contributions.

Self-employed persons (Class 2 and Class 4 contributors) are covered for all benefits except earnings-related supplements, unemployment benefit, widow's and invalidity pensions, widowed mother's allowance and industrial injury benefits.

The major changes, which took place from the week beginning 6 April 1994, were:

- Benefit rates rose by at least 1.8% in April 1994.
- Retirement pension was increased by £1.50 and by £2.30 a week for couples.
- Unemployed benefit for a single person increased by 80p a week. Family credit would also increase in line with prices.

FAMILY BENEFITS

Child Benefits (CH 1)

Child benefit is payable for all children who are either under 16 or under 19 and receiving full-time education at a recognised educational establishment. The rate is £10.20 for the first or eldest child and £8.25 a week for each subsequent child. It is payable to the person who is responsible for the child but excludes foster parents or people exempt from UK tax. A higher benefit (£6.15 a week more) is payable for the first or only child in a one parent family.

Maternity Benefits

Help with maternity expenses is given to selected people from the social fund. To be eligible the claimant must be receiving income support or family credit. £100 is paid for each new or adopted baby reduced by the amount of any savings over £500 held by the claimant or his or her family. A payment can be obtained from the social fund for an adopted baby provided the child is not more than 12 months old when application is made. The claimant has three months to make the claim from when adoption has taken place.

Maternity Pay (NI 17A)

Statutory maternity pay (SMP) was introduced for female employees who leave employment because of pregnancy.

SMP is applicable to those who have worked for 26 weeks by the 15th week before the expected date of confinement. This 15th week is known as the qualifying week (QW). The other qualifying conditions are that the woman must:
(1) be pregnant at the 11th week before the expected week of confinement, or already have been confined;
(2) have stopped working for her employer wholly or partly because of pregnancy or confinement;
(3) have average earnings of not less than the lower earnings limit for the payment of National Insurance contributions which is in force during her QW;
(4) provide her employer with evidence of her expected week of confinement;
(5) provide her employer with notice of her maternity absence.

Rates of SMP

There is a higher and a lower rate. The higher rate of SMP is 90% of an employee's weekly earnings and is paid for the first six weeks for which there is entitlement to SMP. To be eligible for the higher rate, a woman must meet all the qualifying conditions and have been employed by the employer for a continuous period of at least two years if she worked for more than 16 hours a week. Her service must continue into the QW.

The lower rate of SMP is a set rate reviewed each year. The rate for the tax year beginning 6 April 1994 is £48.80 per week. It is paid for 18 weeks to those not entitled to the higher amount and for up to 12 weeks to those who receive the higher rate for the first six weeks.

SMP is taxable and also subject to National Insurance contributions. The gross amount of SMP and the employer's portion of National Insurance payable on the SMP can be recovered from the State by deducting the amounts from the amount normally due for PAYE and National Insurance deductions payable to the Collector of Taxes.

Guardian's Allowance (NI 14)

This is paid at the rate of £11.00 a week for each child and for each child to people who have taken orphans into their own family. Usually both of the child's parents must be dead and at least one of them must have satisfied a residence condition.

The allowance can only be paid to the person who is entitled to child benefit for the child (or to that person's spouse). It is not necessary to be the legal guardian. The claim should be made within three months of the date of entitlement.

DISABILITY LIVING ALLOWANCE

Disability living allowance (DLA) was introduced on 6 April 1992 and replaces attendance allowance for disabled people before they reach the age of 65. It has also replaced mobility allowance. Those who are disabled after reaching 65 may be able to claim attendance allowance. The case component is divided into three rates whereas the mobility allowance has two rates. The rate of benefit from 6 April 1994 is as follows:

Care Component	Per week £
Higher rate (day and night, or terminally ill)	45.70
Middle rate (day or night)	30.55
Lower rate (if need some help during day, or over 16 and need help preparing a meal)	12.15

Mobility Component

Higher rate (unable or virtually unable to walk)	31.95
Lower rate (can walk but needs help when outside)	12.15

Attendance Allowance

Attendance allowance has been replaced by DLA from 6 April 1992 for those aged under 65. For those aged 65 or over, attendance allowance will continue to be paid.

The rate of benefit from 6 April 1994 is as follows:

	Per week £
Higher rate (day and night)	45.70
Lower rate (day or night)	30.55

The attendance allowance board decide whether, and for how long, a person is eligible for this allowance. Attendance allowance is not taxable.

BENEFITS FOR THE ILL OR UNEMPLOYED

Statutory Sick Pay (NI 27, NI 16, NI 244)

In the majority of cases the employer now has the responsibility of paying sick pay to its employees. The payment is dependent on satisfying various conditions in respect of periods of incapacity, periods of entitlement, qualifying days and rules on notification of absence. The rules are quite complicated and reference should be made to the relevant booklets for further clarification but the key points are:

(1) Payment is made by the employer.
(2) There is a possibility of two rates of payment dependent on the employee's gross average earnings.
(3) The employee must not be capable of work and must do no work on the day concerned.
(4) SSP is not usually payable for the first three working days.
(5) The maximum entitlement is 28 weeks in any period of incapacity.
(6) Notification must be made by the employer but this procedure must be within statutory guidelines.
(7) Payment can be withheld if notification of sickness is not given in due time.

The employer can only recover 80% of all SSP payments made in respect of 1993/94, as compensation for their share of National Insurance contributiors paid on SSP.

Sickness Benefit (DSS Leaflet NI 16)

The majority of illnesses are now covered by statutory sick pay and sickness benefit now only applies to those employees who are excluded from statutory sickness pay and the self-employed.

Sickness benefit is paid for up to 28 weeks for those who are off work. If a claimant is still ill after 28 weeks he is transferred to the long term benefit, invalidity benefit.

To be eligible for sickness benefit the claimant must have paid, in any one tax year ending before the calendar year in which he makes the claim, Class I contributions on an amount of earnings at least 25 times the weekly lower earnings limit for that tax year (or the equivalent of Class 2 contributions for self employed people).

There is another condition which must be satisfied in that the claimant must have paid, or been credited with, in the tax year ending before the benefit year in which he or she makes the claim, Class 1 contributions on an amount of earnings at least 50 times the weekly lower earnings limit for both the last two tax years (or the equivalent number of Class 2 contributions for self-employed people).

Invalidity Benefit (NI 16A)

An invalidity pension is substituted for sickness benefit or SSP after this has been paid for 168 days of incapacity. To qualify one must be unable to work and have been entitled to sickness benefit for 168 days in a period of interruption of employment. This pension is currently £56.10 a week.

An invalidity allowance is payable with invalidity pension to those who are more than five years away from retirement age. The rates are as follows:

Standard rate of invalidity pension:

	£
Single person	57.60
Spouse or adult dependant	34.50

Invalidity allowance:

(i) Higher rate	12.15
(ii) Middle rate	7.60
(iii) Lower rate	3.80

Child dependency increases amounting to £11.00 are available.

Severe Disablement Allowance (NI 252)

This is a benefit for people under pensionable age who cannot work because of physical or mental ill health and do not have sufficient NI contributions to qualify for sickness or invalidity benefit. The basic allowance is £34.30 a week. There are increases of £20.65 a week for adult dependants and £11.00 for each child.

Invalid Care Allowance (NI 212)

This is a taxable benefit paid to people of working age who cannot take a job because they have to stay at home to look after a severely disabled person. The basic allowance is £34.50 per week. An extra £20.65 is paid for each adult dependant and £11.00 for each child.

Unemployment Benefit (NI 12)

Unemployment benefit is payable for a maximum period of one year in any period of interruption of employment. Once this year's unemployment pay is reached a claimant cannot qualify again until he has worked as an employee for at least 13 weeks in the period of 26 weeks immediately before the claim, each week being work of at least 16 hours.

To be eligible the claimant must be unemployed but available for work but can be disqualified from receiving benefit for a period of up to 26 weeks if he lost his employment without just cause or failed to accept suitable employment offered or if he loses his job voluntarily without just cause or dismissed for misconduct.

Unemployment benefit is not payable for the first three days of a period of interruption of employment, in the same way as for sickness benefit.

Persons over 18 should register for work at their local Employment Office or Job Centre and should go to their local unemployment benefit office to claim benefit. Either a P45 or a note of their national insurance number should be produced. Persons under 18 should register for work at their local Youth Employment Office. Unemployment benefit is reduced, pound for pound, for those claimants over 55 years of age, whose pensions exceed £35.00 per week.

The standard rate of unemployment benefit is £45.45 for a single person and £28.05 for a wife or other adult dependant.

PENSIONS AND WIDOW'S BENEFITS (NP 23, NP 35, NP 31)

The state pension is divided into two parts – the basic pension, presently £57.60 per week for a single person or £92.10 per week for a married couple, and the State Earnings Related Pension Scheme, which will after it matures on the present basis pay a pension of 25% of revalued earnings between the lower and upper earnings limits.

The cost of the State Earnings Related Pension Scheme (SERPS) has been a major political consideration for some time. In order to reduce the long-term cost of the scheme, benefits will be reduced for those retiring or widowed after the year 2000. The benefits will be reduced as follows:

(1) The pension will be based on lifetime average earnings rather than the best 20 years as at present.

(2) The pension will be calculated on the basis of 20% of earnings between the lower and upper earnings limit rather than 25%. This will be phased in over ten years from the tax year 2000/2001.

(3) Presently all of a member's state earnings related benefit is inherited by a surviving spouse. For deaths occurring after April 2000 this will be reduced to 50%.

Women paying standard rate contributions into the scheme are eligible for the same amount of pension as men but five years earlier, from age 60. If a woman stays at home to bring up her children or to look after a person receiving attendance allowance she can have her basic pension rights protected without paying contributions.

The widow's pension and widowed mother's allowance also consists of a basic pension and an additional earnings related pension. The full amount of the additional pension applies only if the husband has contributed to the new scheme for at least 20 years.

Widow's Benefits

From 11 April 1988 there are three main widow's benefits:

(1) Widow's payment, which has replaced the widow's allowance which has been abolished;

(2) Widowed mother's allowance;

(3) Widow's pension.

Widow's payment

This is a new allowance, currently a lump sum payment of £1000 payable to widows who were bereaved on or after 11 April 1988. It is payable immediately on the death of the husband. Entitlement to this benefit is based on the late husband's contribution record but no payment will be made if the widow is living with another man as husband and wife at the date of death. The late husband must have actually paid contributions on earnings of at least 25 times the weekly or lower earnings limit for a given tax year in any tax year ending before his death (or ending before he reached pensionable age if he was over 65 when he died). The equivalent number of Class 2 or voluntary Class 3 contributions will be sufficient.

When claiming, the widow should complete the form on the back of the death certificate and send it to the local social security office. On receipt of this information the DSS will send the claimant a more detailed form (BD8) which, once completed, has to go back to the social security office. It is important to claim the benefit within twelve months of the husband's death.

Widowed mother's allowance (NP 45)

If a widow is left with children to look after she is entitled to a widowed mother's allowance provided that her late husband had paid sufficient national insurance contributions. These contributions are:

(a) 25 Class 1, 2 or 3 contributions before age 65 and before 6 April 1975; or
(b) contributions in any one tax year after 6 April 1975 on earnings of at least 25 times the weekly lower earnings limit for that year.

It is important that the widow is looking after either her own child or her husband's child and that the child is under 16 or, if between the age of 16 and 19, is continuing in full-time education.

The allowance stops immediately if the widow remarries and will be suspended if she lives with a man as his wife. From April 1994 the amounts payable are as follows:

	£
Basic allowance	57.60
Increase for each child	11.00

Where a husband's contributions only satisfied the first test above, the basic allowance may be payable at a reduced rate. This reduction does not alter the rate of an increase for a child.

Widow's pension (NP 45)

A widow who is over the age of 45 when her husband dies may be eligible for a widow's pension unless she is eligible for the widowed mother's allowance. In this situation the widow's pension becomes payable when the widowed mother's allowance ends, provided she is still under the age of 65. However, where a woman had been receiving widowed mother's allowance, she becomes entitled to a widow's pension if she is between the ages of 45 and 65 when the allowance ends, no matter what her age may have been when her husband died. Before 11 April 1988 a widow aged 40 or over could qualify for a widow's pension.

Qualification conditions

(a) The contributions conditions must be satisfied and these conditions are the same as those for the widowed mother's allowance above.
(b) The widow must not be receiving the widowed mother's allowance.
(c) When her husband died she was aged between 45 and 65 or she was entitled to widowed mother's allowance and is aged between 45 and 65 when her widowed mother's allowance finished.

Cessation of Widow's Pension

(a) Entitlement finishes if the widowed mother's allowance stops because she has remarried.
(b) Widow's pension must not be claimed when the payment of the widowed mother's allowance has been suspended because the widow is in pension or is living with a man as his wife.

From 11 April 1988 both the basic and additional pension are paid at a reduced rate if the widow was aged under 55:

(a) when her husband died, if she did not subsequently become entitled to widowed mother's allowance; or
(b) when her widowed mother's allowance ceased to be paid. The relevant rates from 6 April 1994 are as follows (the ages given in parentheses apply to women for whom widow's pension was payable before 11 April 1988):

Age related	£
Age 54 (49)	53.57
53 (48)	49.54
52 (47)	45.50
51 (46)	41.47
50 (45)	37.44
49 (44)	33.41
48 (43)	29.38
47 (42)	25.34
46 (41)	21.31
45 (40)	17.28

Funeral Expenses

The death grant was abolished from 6 April 1987. It has been replaced by a payment from the social fund where the claimant is in receipt of income support, family credit or housing benefit. The full cost of a reasonable funeral is paid, reduced by any savings over £500 held by the claimant or his family (£1000 for couples over 60).

FAMILY CREDIT

Family credit replaced family income supplement (FIS) with effect from 11 April 1988. Family credit is a tax-free benefit payable to families in Great Britain where:

(1) the claimant or partner is engaged in remunerative work for 16 hours or more per week; and

(2) there is at least one child under 16 in the family (or under 19 if in full-time education up to and including A level or OND standard) for whom the claimant and/or partner is responsible.

Entitlement to family credit is determined by comparing the family's normal income with a prescribed amount, known as the 'applicable amount'. The current applicable amount is £71.70. Eligible families fall into two income groups:
(i) those whose total income does not exceed the applicable amount. Such families will be entitled to the appropriate maximum amount of family credit payable; and
(ii) those whose total income does exceed the applicable amount but by an amount which still allows some entitlement. To determine eligibility, a prescribed percentage (currently 70%) of the excess income (over and above the applicable amount) is deducted from the appropriate maximum family credit. If there is an amount left (i.e. the figure is a plus sum of at least 50p) the family will be able to receive family credit equal to this amount, rounded to the nearest penny.

Maximum family credit benefit rates (from 6 April 1994)

Adult	£44.30
Child	
aged less than 11 years	£11.20
aged 11 to 15 years	£18.55
Young Person	
aged 16 to 17 years	£23.05
aged 18 years	£32.20

An award is normally made for a period of 26 weeks. Changes of circumstances during this period will not usually affect the award.

Capital and income

Families where the claimant and partner together hold capital in excess of £8000 will not be entitled to family credit. The resources of a family taken into account as income for family credit are the aggregate of their normal net earnings and other income plus any tariff income. Certain payments are disregarded in the calculation of income. For those with capital of between £3000 and £8000, the rate of benefit will be affected. For every £250 (or part of £250) held in excess of £3000, a 'tariff' income of £1.00 will be added to the family's other income.

INCOME SUPPORT (SBI, SB20)

Income support has replaced supplementary benefit. It is usually only payable to eligible persons who are unemployed or people who work less than 16 hours a week. If a person or partner works for 16 hours or more on average per week in 'remunerative' work, then no income support is payable.

Income support gives financial assistance towards regular weekly needs only. Claimants with exceptional needs will now have to apply for payments (in the form of a loan or grant) from the social fund.

The person's income must be insufficient to bring him up to the designated minimum level of income, known as the 'applicable amount'. The applicable amount is made up of a 'basic' personal allowance plus 'additional' premiums for those with additional needs, e.g. pensioners. People who are entitled to income support and who have no income at all will be entitled to the appropriate applicable amount in full. Those who have an income will receive income support equal to the difference between their income and the appropriate applicable amount.

As with supplementary benefit, there is a limit to the amount of capital a person can hold before income support is affected. Those who have capital above £8000 are disqualified from receiving income support altogether. Capital up to £3000 is disregarded but savings between £3000 and £8000 affect income support in the same way as for family credit.

As in the case of supplementary benefit, eligibility for income support is, in most instances, dependent on the claimant being 'available for work'. Where a person is disqualified from receiving unemployment benefit (or would be if it were otherwise payable), for such reasons as being dismissed from his or her former job because of misconduct, entitlement to income support will also be affected.

GRANTS FROM LOCAL AUTHORITIES

Council Tax Benefit

Those who will be able to claim benefit are those who:

(1) are on a low income, or
(2) are in receipt of income support
(3) share the house with certain other persons who are receiving income support.

The maximum benefit entitlement for a liable person claiming will be 100% of the liability.

The above does not set out to cover every aspect of the Social Security Acts legislation.

Further information can be obtained from the local office of the Department of Social Security or from Accountants Digest No. 280 published by the Institute of Chartered Accountants in England and Wales. Readers resident abroad who have queries should write to the Department's Overseas Branch, Newcastle upon Tyne NE98 1YX.

Societies and prizes

Societies, Associations and Clubs

Yr Academi Gymreig. *President:* Professor J.E. Caerwyn Williams; *chairman:* Harri Pritchard Jones; *treasurer:* Professor Dafydd Jenkins; *administrator:* Dafydd Rogers, 3rd Floor, Mount Stuart House, Mount Stuart Square, The Docks, Cardiff CF1 6DQ   *tel* (0222) 492064. The society was founded in 1959 to promote creative writing in the Welsh language. Existing members elect new members on the basis of their contribution to Welsh literature or criticism. The society publishes a literary magazine, *Taliesin*, books on Welsh literature, and translations of modern European classics into Welsh. It is currently engaged in the production of a new English/Welsh Dictionary. The society's activities are open to all.

Yr Academi Gymreig: English Language Section. *President:* Roland Mathias; *chairman:* Sally Roberts Jones; *director:* Kevin Thomas, 3rd Floor, Mount Stuart House, Mount Stuart Square, The Docks, Cardiff CF1 6DQ   *tel* (0222) 492025   *fax* (0222) 492930. This section was founded in 1968 to provide a meeting-point for writers in the English language who are of Welsh origin and/or take Wales as a main theme of their work. Membership open to all those who are deemed to have made a contribution to the literature of Wales, whether as writers, editors or critics. Associate membership is open to all interested individuals or organisations. Although it is an autonomous body, members of the English Language Section co-operate with members of the parent body for joint conferences and similar activities.

Acrylic Painters' Association, National (1985). *President:* Alwyn Crawshaw; *vice-president:* Dr Sally A. Bulgin; *founder and executive co-ordinator:* Kenneth J. Hodgson, 134 Rake Lane, Wallasey, Wirral, Merseyside L45 1JW   *tel* 051-639 2980. Promotes interest in, and encourages excellence and innovation in, the work of painters in acrylic. Holds an annual exhibition at the Royal Birmingham Society of Artists Gallery, 69A New Street, Birmingham B2 4DU; publishes an annual newsletter. *Full membership:* £16.00 p.a.; *associate membership:* £8 p.a.

Agricultural Journalists, Guild of. *President:* Lord Carter; *chairman:* David Lloyd; *hon. general secretary:* Don Gomery, Charmwood, 47 Court Meadow, Rotherfield, East Sussex TN6 3LQ   *tel* (0892) 853187. Established to promote a high standard among journalists who specialise in agricultural matters and to assist them to increase their sources of information and technical knowledge. Membership is open to those earning their livelihood wholly or mainly from agricultural journalism.

Amateur Press Association, British (1890), Michaelmas, Cimarron Close, South Woodham Ferrers, Essex CM3 5PB. To promote the fellowship of amateur writers, artists, editors, printers, publishers and other craftsmen/women, and to encourage them to contribute to, edit, print or publish, *as a hobby*, magazines and literary works produced by letterpress and other processes. All enquiries by post only; send sae for details of membership and subscription rates.

American Correspondents, Association of. *President:* David Feingold, c/o Secretary, Sandra Marshall, Associated Press, 12 Norwich Street, London EC4A 1BP *tel* 071-353 1515 ext 3202 *fax* 071-936 2229.

American Publishers, Association of, Inc. (1970). *President:* Nicholas A. Veliotes; *executive vice president:* Thomas D. McKee, 71 Fifth Avenue, New York, NY 10003, USA *tel* 212-255-0200 *fax* 212-255-7007. Confederation of approximately 230 member houses, nationwide, who publish the great majority of printed materials sold to American schools, colleges and libraries, bookstores, and by direct mail to homes. Members' interests cover all aspects of the publishing industry – books, journals, educational materials, multimedia, etc.

American Society of Composers, Authors and Publishers (1914), One Lincoln Plaza, New York, NY 10023 *tel* 212-593-3050 *fax* 212-721-0955. *President:* Morton Gould. ASCAP is a membership association of over 50,000 writers and publishers, which protects its members' rights and those of affiliated foreign societies. It licenses and collects royalties for public performance of copyrighted music. *Annual membership fees:* writers $10.00, publishers $50.00.

American Society of Indexers (1968), PO Box 386, Port Aransas, TX 78373, USA *tel* 512-749-4052 *fax* 512-749-6334. Aims to improve the quality and standards of indexing and related areas of information science; act as an advisory board on renumeration and qualifications of indexers and abstractors; defend and safeguard the professional interests of indexers. Holds meetings, seminars and workshops; provides free the bi-annual *The Indexer* and the 6 p.a. *ASI Newsletter. Annual membership fee:* $50.00, student $35.00, corporate $150.00.

Art and Design, National Society for Education in (1888), The Gatehouse, Corsham Court, Corsham, Wilts. SN13 0BZ *tel* (0249) 714825 *fax* (0249) 716138. *General secretary:* John Steers NDD, ATC, DAE. Professional association of principals and lecturers in colleges and schools of art and of specialist art, craft and design teachers in other schools and colleges. Has representatives on National and Regional Committees which are the concern of those engaged in Art and Design Education. Publishes *Journal of Art and Design Education* (3 p.a.).

Art Club, New English, 17 Carlton House Terrace, London SW1Y 5BD *tel* 071-930 6844 *fax* 071-839 7830. *Hon. secretary:* William Bowyer RA, RWS, RP. For all those interested in the art of painting, and the promotion of fine arts. Open Annual Exhibition at Mall Galleries.

Artists, Federation of British, 17 Carlton House Terrace, London SW1Y 5BD *tel* 071-930 6844 *fax* 071-839 7830. Administers nine major National Art Societies at The Mall Galleries, The Mall, London SW1.

Artists, International Guild of, Ralston House, 41 Lister Street, Riverside Gardens, Ilkley, West Yorkshire LS29 9ET *tel* (0943) 609075. *Director:* Leslie Simpson FRSA. Organises four seasonal exhibitions per year for three national societies: Society of Miniaturists, British Society of Painters in Oils, Pastels & Acrylics and British Watercolour Society. Promotes these three societies in countries outside the British Isles.

Artists, Royal Birmingham Society of, 69A New Street, Birmingham B2 4DU *tel* 021-643 3768. *President:* Ernest Horton; *hon. secretary:* James Davies RBSA. Society has its own galleries and rooms in the city centre. Members (RBSA) and Associates (ARBSA) are elected annually. There are two annual Spring Exhibitions open to all artists and an Autumn Exhibition of Members' and Associates' works. *Annual Subscription* (Friends of the RBSA): £10.00 entitles subscribers to attend painting days, criticisms and lectures organised by the Society and to submit work for the Annual Friends' Exhibition in February and July. Further details from the Hon. Secretary. Schedules for the Open Oil exhibition are available in February, and for the Open Watercolour exhibition in April. Please include sae with request for Schedule.

Artists, Royal Society of British, 17 Carlton House Terrace, London SW1Y 5BD *tel* 071-930 6844 *fax* 071-839 7830. *President:* Colin Hayes RA; *keeper:* Alfred Daniels. Incorporated by Royal Charter for the purpose of encouraging the study and practice of the arts of painting, sculpture and architectural designs. Annual Open Exhibition at the Mall Galleries, The Mall, London SW1.

Arts Club (1863), 40 Dover Street, London W1X 3RB *tel* 071-499 8581 *fax* 071-409 0913. *Secretary:* Jackie Downing. For all those connected with or interested in the arts.

The Arts Council/An Chomhairle Ealáion (1951), Literature Officer, 70 Merrion Square, Dublin 2, Republic of Ireland *tel* (01) 6611840 *fax* (01) 6761302. The national agency which promotes the arts in Ireland, including literature in English and Irish.

Arts Council of England, 14 Great Peter Street, London SW1P 3NQ *tel* 071-333 0100. *Chairman:* Lord Gowrie; *secretary-general:* Mary Allen; *director of literature:* Alastair Niven. To develop and improve the knowledge, understanding and practice of the arts, and to increase their accessibility to the public throughout England. The arts with which the Council is mainly concerned are dance, drama, mime, literature, music and opera, the visual arts, including photography and documentary films and videos on the arts. Within literature, 15 annual writers' awards are awarded competitively (see also page 658). Subsidies are provided to literary organisations and magazines, and schemes include support for translation, writers' residencies in prisons, tours by authors and the promotion of literature in libraries and education.

Arts Council of Northern Ireland, 185 Stranmillis Road, Belfast BT9 5DU *tel* (0232) 381591 *fax* (0232) 661715. *Chief executive:* Brian Ferran; *literature officer:* Ciaran Carson. Promotes and encourages the arts throughout Northern Ireland. Also owns the Grand Opera House in Belfast and uses this as a forum for ballet, operas and classical drama.

Arts Council of Wales, 9 Museum Place, Cardiff CF1 3NX *tel* (0222) 394711 *fax* (0222) 221447. *Chairman:* Sir Richard Lloyd Jones KCB; *chief executive:* Emyr Jenkins; *literature director:* Tony Bianchi; *art director:* Peter Jones; *craft director:* Roger Lefevre; *drama director:* Michael Baker; *dance director:* Maldwyn Pate; *music director:* Roy Bohana. The Arts Council of Wales was created by Royal Charter effective from 1 April 1994. Its objects are to promote and develop the practice and understanding of and access to the arts in Wales. It undertakes this work in both the English and Welsh languages. It has departments for Music, Art, Literature, Drama, Craft and Dance, and also runs the Oriel Bookshop and Gallery in Cardiff.
North East Wales Regional Office, Daniel Owen Centre, Earl Road, Mold, Clwyd CH7 1AP *tel* (0352) 758403 *fax* (0352) 700236. *Director:* Sandra Wynne.

North Wales Regional Office, 10 Wellfield House, Bangor, Gwynedd LL57 1ER   *tel* (0248) 353248   *fax* (0248) 351077. *Director:* Sandra Wynne.

South East Wales Regional Office, Victoria Street, Cwmbran, Gwent NP44 3YT   *tel* (0633) 875075   *fax* (0633) 875389. *Acting director:* Nigel Emery.

West Wales Regional Office, 3 Red Street, Carmarthen, Dyfed SA31 1QL   *tel* (0267) 234248   *fax* (0267) 233084. *Director:* Carwyn Rogers.

Arts, Manufactures and Commerce, Royal Society for the encouragement of (RSA) (1754), 8 John Adam Street, London WC2N 6EZ   *tel* 071-930 5115   *fax* 071-839 5805. *Chairman of council:* Richard Martineau MA; *director:* Christopher Lucas. The RSA sustains a forum for people from all walks of life to come together to address issues, shape new ideas and stimulate action. It works through conferences, projects, award schemes and its lecture programme, the proceedings of which are recorded in the monthly *RSA Journal.* There are 16,500 Fellows of the RSA. The Fellowship is open to accomplished men and women who support the society's aims. Fellows may use the Library, Fellows' Room and Fellows' Dining Room, Bar.

Asian Affairs, Royal Society for (1901), 2 Belgrave Square, London SW1X 8PJ   *tel* 071-235 5122. *President:* The Lord Denman CBE. MC. TD; *chairman of council:* Sir Michael Wilford GCMG; *secretary:* Miss M. FitzSimons MBE. For the study of all Asia past and present; fortnightly lectures, etc.; library. Publishes *Asian Affairs,* 3 p.a., free to members. *Subscription:* £45 London, £35 more than 60 miles from London; other rates on application.

Aslib, The Association for Information Management (1924), Information House, 20-24 Old Street, London EC1V 9AP   *tel* 071-253 4488   *fax* 071-430 0514. Promotes the effective management and use of information in industry, central and local government, education and the professions; provides publications, training, independent advice and recruitment and consultancy services to the information sector. For particulars of membership apply: Lascelles Lawrence, Membership Manager.

The Jane Austen Society. *Secretary:* Mrs Susan McCartan, Carton House, Redwood Lane, Medstead, Alton, Hants GU34 5PE. Founded in 1940 to promote interest in, and enjoyment of, Jane Austen's novels and letters. Eight branches in UK, and four overseas. *Membership:* £6.00 p.a., £60.00 life.

Australia Council, PO Box 788, Strawberry Hills, NSW 2012, Australia   *located at* 181 Lawson Street, Redfern, NSW 2016, Australia   *tel* (02) 950 9000   *fax* (02) 950 9111. *Chairperson:* Hilary McPhee AM. The Australia Council is a statutory authority which provides a broad range of support for the arts in Australia. Established in 1968 as the Australian Council for the Arts (supporting mainly the performing arts), it was restructured in 1973 to embrace music, theatre, film/radio/television, literature, visual arts, crafts. Aboriginal arts and community arts. (In June 1976 the activities of the film/radio/television Board were transferred to the Australian Film Commission.) In March 1975, by Act of Parliament, the Australia Council was established as an independent authority. It has five major Boards: Literature, Visual Arts/Craft, Performing Arts (music, theatre and dance), Aboriginal and Torres Strait Islander Arts and Community Cultural Development.

The Council is involved in the administration of grants, public information services, policy development, research, international activities, and advisory services to many other arts organisations including government bodies. A wide range of projects and activities, both individual and group, receive Australia Council funds. Support includes grants made to enable artists to study, and living allowances to permit others (notably writers) to 'buy time' to follow their creative pursuits. Some of the major initiatives of the Council in past years, include: negotiation with international bodies for the touring of exhibitions, a Public Lending Right scheme for Australian authors; copyright protection; moral rights for artists; art and working life; women in the arts; Arts Law Centre; Artist-in-Residence schemes at tertiary institutions; and increased employment for Australian artists in all fields. Australia Council publications include information booklets, directories, research reports, newsletters, program reviews and an Annual Report.

The Literature Board, Australia Council, PO Box 788, Strawberry Hills, NSW 2012, Australia *tel* (02) 950 9000 *fax* (02) 950 9111. Because of its size and isolation and the competition its literature meets from other English-speaking countries, Australia has always needed to subsidise writing of creative and cultural significance. The Literature Board, one of the Boards of the Australia Council, was created in 1973, taking over the duties of the earlier Commonwealth Literary Fund, established in 1908.

The Board's chief objective is the support of the writing of all forms of creative literature – novels, short stories, poetry, plays and literary non-fiction. The Board also assists with the publication of literary magazines. It has a publishing subsidies programme and it initiates and supports projects of many kinds designed to promote Australian literature both within Australia and abroad.

About 50 per cent of the Board's expenditure in recent years has gone to writers in the form of direct grants including Fellowships and Writers' Project Grants (living allowances), and Emeritus Fellowships. Category A Fellowships (valued at $30,000 per year) are living allowances to assist published writers of substantial achievement to complete a major project or projects. Category B Fellowships (valued at $24,000 per year) are living allowances for developing writers of potential who have had one or two full-length works published or performed. Writers' Project Grants ($5000-$15,000) are to assist writers who have achieved some publication or performance of their work to meet living expenses, travel and/or research costs while writing a particular literary work. Emeritus Awards are made to senior writers of distinction.

Australian Book Publishers Association, 89 Jones Street, Ultimo, NSW 2007, Australia *tel* (02) 281 9788 *fax* (02) 281 1073. Aims to foster original and licensed publishing in Australia, to help improve the Australian book industry as a whole. Has over 140 member firms.

Australian Library and Information Association, PO Box E441, Queen Victoria Terrace, ACT 2600, Australia *tel* (06) 285 1877 *fax* (06) 282 2249. *Executive director:* Virginia Walsh. Australia-wide organisation first incorporated by Royal Charter in 1964 and supplemented in 1988, with about 7500 members, of whom about 5500 are professional members. The objects of the association are to promote and improve the services of libraries and other information agencies; to improve the standard of library and information personnel and foster their professional interests; to represent the interests of members to governments, other organisations and the community; and to encourage people to contribute to the improvement of library and information services by supporting the association. It publishes the *Australian Library Journal* 3-4 p.a. and the newsletter *InCite* 12 p.a., as well as a range of specialist publications to cater for the interests of members in different types of library and information services.

The Australian Society of Authors, PO Box 1566, Strawberry Hills, NSW 2012, Australia *located at* 98 Pitt Street, Redfern, NSW 2016, Australia *tel* (02) 318 0877 *fax* (02) 318 0530. *Executive officer:* Lynne Spender; *chairman:* Robert Pullan. Aims to represent and enhance author rights and interests, through providing information, contract advice, publications (newsletters and journals), representation in disputes. Also seminars, research and information on new issues and new directions in writing and publishing. *Joining fee:* $20; *annual membership:* full/associate $95, affiliate $55.

Australian Writers' Guild Ltd (1962), 60 Kellett Street, Kings Cross, NSW 2011, Australia   *tel* (02) 357 7888   *fax* (02) 357 7776. *Executive officer:* Ms Chris Sharp. Trade union and professional association dedicated to promoting and protecting the professional interests of writers for stage, screen, television and radio. *Subscription:* full members: entrance fee $140, annual fee $140-$550 dependent on income from writing; associate members: entrance fee $70, annual fee $70.

Authors, The Society of, 84 Drayton Gardens, London SW10 9SB   *tel* 071-373 6642. *Chairman:* Anthony Sampson; *general secretary:* Mark Le Fanu OBE. Founded in 1884 by Sir Walter Besant with the object of representing, assisting and protecting authors. It is a limited company and an independent trade union. The Society's scope has been continuously extended; specialist associations have been created for translators, broadcasters, educational, medical, technical and children's writers and illustrators (details are elsewhere in this Yearbook). Members are entitled to legal as well as general advice in connection with the marketing of their work, their contracts, their choice of a publisher, problems with publishers, broadcasting organisations, etc. *Subscription:* £65 (£60 by direct debit) p.a. with certain reductions available to authors under 35 or over 65. Full particulars of membership from the Society's offices. (See also article on page 650.)

Authors' Agents, The Association of (1974), 5th Floor, The Chambers, Chelsea Harbour, London SW10 0XF   *tel* 071-351 4763. *President:* Caroline Dawnay; *secretary:* Nicki Kennedy; *treasurer:* Carolyn Brunton. Maintains a code of professional practice to which all members of the association commit themselves; holds regular meetings to discuss matters of common professional interest; and provides a vehicle for representing the view of authors' agents in discussion of matters of common interest with other professional bodies.

Authors' Club (1891) (at the Arts Club), 40 Dover Street, London W1X 3RB   *tel* 071-499 8581. *Secretary:* Ann Carter. For those interested in writing, or published authors. *Membership fee:* variable.

The Authors League of America, Inc. (1912), 330 West 42nd Street, New York, NY 10036, USA   *tel* 212-564-8350   *fax* 212-564-8363. National membership organisation to promote the professional interest of authors and dramatists, procure satisfactory copyright legislation and treaties, guard freedom of expression and support fair tax treatment for writers.

Authors' Licensing and Collecting Society Ltd (ALCS), 33/34 Alfred Place, London WC1E 7DP   *tel* 071-255 2034. Independent collecting society for the collective administration of literary and dramatic rights in the spheres of reprography, lending right, off-air and private recording and cable television. *Membership:* £5.88 p.a. (inc. VAT), £7.00 overseas residents; open to authors, successor membership to authors' heirs. See **ALCS** article on page 546.

Authors' Representatives, Inc., Association of (1991), Ten Astor Place, 3rd Floor, New York, NY 10003, USA   *tel* 212-353 3709. Voluntary association of agents, whose individual members subscribe to a strict code of ethical practices.

Aviation Artists, The Guild of (incorporating the Society of Aviation Artists), The Bondway Business Centre, 71 Bondway, Vauxhall Cross, London SW8 1SQ   *tel* 071-735 0634. *President:* Michael Turner PGAvA; *secretary:* Hugo Trotter DFC. Guild of artists formed in 1971 to promote all forms of aviation art through the organisation of exhibitions and meetings. Holds annual open exhibition in July in London; £1000 prize for 'The Aviation Painting of the Year'. Quarterly members' journal. Associates £30. Members £40 (by invitation). Non-exhibiting artists and friends £15.

BAPLA (British Association of Picture Libraries and Agencies) (1975). *Administrator:* Sal Shuel, BAPLA, 13 Woodberry Crescent, London N10 1PJ *tel* 081-444 7913 *fax* 081-883 9215. Trade association formed to promote fair and honest trading within the profession, and between members and their clients. Publishes a Code of Professional Standards and Fair Practice and a set of Recommended Terms and Conditions for the Submission and Reproduction of Photographs. BAPLA makes a constant effort to promote the fact that photographs, prints and drawings have a copyright and that this copyright has a commercial value, that if any picture has the impact to promote a product, sell a book, it also has a market value for being so used. Publishes an annual Directory of Members and an irregularly published Journal.

The E.F. Benson Society (1984), 88 Tollington Park, London N4 3RA *tel* 071-272 3375. *Secretary:* Allan Downend. To promote interest in the author E.F. Benson and the Benson family. The Society arranges a literary evening each year and has an annual outing to Rye in July. Holder of an Archive, including the Austin Seckersen Collection, transcriptions of the Benson diaries and letters. Publishes postcards, anthologies of Benson's works and an annual journal, *The Dodo. Annual subscription:* £7.50 single, £8.50 two people at same address; £12.50 overseas. Affiliated to the Alliance of Literary Societies.

E.F. Benson: The Tilling Society (1982), Martello Bookshop, 26 High Street, Rye, East Sussex TN31 7JJ *tel* (0797) 222242. *Secretaries:* Cynthia and Tony Reavell. To bring together enthusiasts for E.F. Benson and his Mapp & Lucia novels. News and information is exchanged through two lengthy annual newsletters. Annual gathering in Rye. *Annual subscription:* £7, overseas £9; full starters membership (including all back newsletters) £17, overseas £22.

Bibliographical Society (1892), British Library, Collections and Preservation, Great Russell Street, London WC1B 3DG. *President:* P. Davison; *hon. secretary:* Mrs M.M. Foot. Acquisition and dissemination of information upon subjects connected with historical bibliography.

The Blackpool Art Society (1884). *President:* Mrs Margaret Shepherd; *hon. secretary:* Denise Fergyson, 29 Stafford Avenue, Poulton-le-Fylde, Lancs. FY6 8BJ *tel* (0253) 884645. *Studio:* Wilkinson Avenue, Blackpool FY3 9HB. Summer and autumn exhibition (members' work only). Studio meetings, practicals, lectures, etc., out-of-door sketching.

Book Packagers Association (1985), 93a Blenheim Crescent, London W11 2EQ *tel* 071-221 9089. *Secretary:* Rosemary Pettit. Aims to represent the interests of book packagers; to exchange information at meetings and seminars; to provide services such as standard contracts and display/meeting facilities at book fairs. *Subscription:* £150.00 p.a.

Book Trust (1925, as the National Book Council), Book House, 45 East Hill, Wandsworth, London SW18 2QZ *tel* 081-870 9055 *fax* 081-874-4790. *Patron:* HRH Prince Philip, Duke of Edinburgh; *chairman:* Martyn Goff; *director:* Brian Perman. Book Trust exists to open up the world of books and reading to people of all ages and cultures. Its services include the Book Information Service, a unique, specialist information and research service for all queries on books and reading. Details about subscription rates and research charges are available on request.

Book Trust's Prizes and Publicity Department administers a number of literary prizes including the £20,000 Booker Prize. The Publications and Exhibitions Department produces a wide range of books, pamphlets and leaflets designed to make books more easily accessible to the public. A number of touring book exhibitions are available for hire. Contact the Publicity Office. **Young Book Trust** provides practical help and advice on all aspects of children's books and reading. The Children's Library houses a unique collection of every children's title published in the UK during the last two years. On joining, subscribers receive Bookfax, a folder full of information, regularly updated, on book prizes, costume characters, exhibitions, etc., plus author information, book week material and booklists. Young Book Trust produces a termly newsletter for its subscribers who include publishers, schools, libraries and booksellers. *Subscription:* £40 + VAT on joining; £30 + VAT p.a.

Book Trust Scotland (1960), The Scottish Book Centre, 137 Dundee Street, Edinburgh EH11 1BG   *tel* 031-229 3663   *fax* 031-228 4293. With a particular responsibility towards Scottish writing, and especially active in the field of children's writing, Book Trust Scotland exists to promote literature and reading, and aims to reach (and create) a wider reading public than has existed before. It also organises exhibitions, readings and storytellings, operates an extensive children's reference library available to everyone and administers literary prizes such as the Kathleen Fidler Award. Book Trust Scotland also publishes short biographies, literary guides and directories and advises other relevant art organisations.

Books Across the Sea, The English-Speaking Union of the Commonwealth, Dartmouth House, 37 Charles Street, London W1X 8AB   *tel* 071-493 3328   *fax* 071-495 6108; The English Speaking Union of the United States, 16 East 69th Street, New York, NY 10021, USA   *tel* 212-879-6800   *fax* 212-772-2886. World voluntary organisation devoted to the promotion of international understanding and friendship. Exchanges books regularly with its corresponding BAS Committees in New York, occasionally with Australia, Canada and New Zealand and has recently begun small presentations to its new branches in Eastern Europe. The books are selected to reflect the life and culture of each country and the best of its recent publishing and writing. The books are placed on exhibition and circulated among members and accredited borrowers, bulk loans are made to affiliated schools and public libraries. New selections are announced by bulletin, *The Ambassador Booklist.*

Booksellers Association of Great Britain and Ireland (1895), 272 Vauxhall Bridge Road, London SW1V 1BA   *tel* 071-834 5477   *fax* 071-834 8812. *Chief executive:* T.E. Godfray. To protect and promote the interests of booksellers engaged in selling new books.

The George Borrow Society (1991). *Hon. secretary:* Richard Burleigh, The Old George, The Square, Broadwindsor, Beaminster, Dorset DT8 3QD   *tel* (0308) 868966. To promote knowledge of the life and works of George Borrow (1803-81), traveller and author. Bi-annual *Bulletin. Annual membership fee:* £7.00. Affiliated to the Alliance of Literary Societies.

Botanical Artists, Society of (1985). *Founder president:* Suzanne Lucas FLS. PRMS. FPSBA; *hon. treasurer:* Pamela Davis; *hon. secretary:* Christine Hart-Davies; *executive secretary:* Mrs S.M. Burton, Burwood House, 15 Union Street, Wells, Somerset BA5 2PU   *tel* (0749) 674472 (during exhibitions 071-222 2723)   *fax* (0749) 672918. Aims to honour and strive to continue in the great tradition of talent, beauty and infinite care apparent in the art of botanical painting through the ages. Membership through selection. Annual Exhibition held, around Easter time, at The Westminster Gallery, Westminster Central

Hall, Storey's Gate, London SW1H 9NU. Open to non-members. Information and entrance forms available from the Executive Secretary from October, on receipt of sae. *Membership fee:* £35; lay members £15.

British Academy, 20-21 Cornwall Terrace, London NW1 4QP *tel* 071-487 5966 *telex* 2631947 *fax* 071-224 3807. *President:* Sir Keith Thomas; *foreign secretary:* Professor J.B. Trapp; *treasurer:* Dr E.A. Wrigley; *publications secretary:* Professor D.E. Luscombe; *secretary for postgraduate studies:* Professor T.J. Smiley; *secretary:* P.W.H. Brown.

British American Arts Association (UK), 116 Commercial Street, London E1 6NF *tel* 071-247 5385 *fax* 071-247 5256. *Director:* Jennifer Williams. Acts as an information service and clearing house for exchange between Britain and the United States in all the arts fields – literature, poetry, theatre, dance, music, visual arts. Counsels artists, administrators and organisations on opportunities to promote, perform, show and tour their work; does not run programmes or give funds.

The British Council, 10 Spring Gardens, London SW1A 2BN *tel* 071-930 8466 *telex* 8952201 BRICON G *fax* 071-839 6347. *Chairman:* Sir Martin Jacomb; *director-general:* John Hanson CBE. The British Council promotes Britain abroad. It provides access to British ideas, talents and experience in education and training, books and the English language, information, the arts, the sciences and technology.

The Council is represented in 101 countries where it runs 130 offices, 150 libraries, 75 English language schools and 29 Resource Centres. It employs 1600 staff in the UK and 4900 (including 1500 teachers of English) overseas.

The Council's lending and reference libraries throughout the world stock material appropriate to the Council's priorities in individual countries. Where appropriate the libraries act as showcases for the latest British publications. They vary in size from small reference collections and information centres to comprehensive libraries equipped with reference works, CD-ROM, on-line facilities and a selection of British periodicals. Bibliographies of British books on special subjects are prepared on request.

Working in close collaboration with book trade associations, the British Council organises book and electronic publishing exhibitions for showing overseas. These exhibitions range from small specialist displays of 100 or so titles to a big trade exhibit of 3000 titles representing 500 British publishers which is mounted annually at Frankfurt and elsewhere.

The Council publishes a series of literary bibliographies, including *The Novel in Britain since 1970* and *Shakespeare; Contemporary Writers,* a series of over 30 pamphlets on modern British writers; and exhibitions on literary topics such as *Writers Abroad: British Travel Writing* (a catalogue of these and other literature publications is available on request).

A catalogue of other publications, covering the arts, books, libraries and publishing, education and training, English language teaching and information for and about overseas students, is also available on request.

The Council acts as an agent of the Overseas Development Administration for book aid projects for developing countries.

In 1992/93 the Council also supported over 1000 events in the visual arts, film and television, drama, dance and music, ranging from the classical to the contemporary.

The Council is an authority on teaching English as a second or foreign language and gives advice and information on curriculum, methodology, materials and testing through its English Language Division. It also promotes British literature overseas through writers' tours, academic visits, seminars and exhibitions.

Further information about the work of the British Council is available from the Press and Public Relations Department at the headquarters in London or from British Council offices and libraries overseas.

British Film Institute, 21 Stephen Street, London W1P 1PL　*tel* 071-255 1444　*telex* 27624　*fax* 071-436 7950. *Director:* Wilf Stevenson; *press officer:* Gill Harrison. The British Film Institute (BFI) was established in 1933 and its aims, as outlined in its Royal Charter, are 'to encourage the development of the art of film in Great Britain, to promote its use as a record of contemporary life and manners, to foster study and appreciation of it from these points of view, to foster study and appreciation of films for television and television programmes generally and to encourage the best use of television in Great Britain'.

Its divisions include the National Film and Television Archive including Stills, Posters and Designs (with almost 6 million black and white stills and colour transparencies), the National Film Theatre which houses the annual London Film Festival and Museum of the Moving Image on London's South Bank. The Institute also helps to support a network of 46 regional film theatres across the UK. Its Library and Information service contains the world's largest collection of published and unpublished material relating to film and television. The BFI also publishes education materials relating to film and TV and the magazine, *Sight and Sound* (with credits and reviews of all films released in the UK). Annual membership of the BFI is £11.95 including the *BFI Film and Television Handbook* and NFT monthly programmes. Library passes are £10 for members and £25.00 for non-members. Concessionary rates are available for students, senior citizens, people with special needs and unemployed people.

Broadcasting Entertainment Cinematograph and Theatre Union, Writers Section (1946), 111 Wardour Street, London W1V 4AY　*tel* 071-437 8506　*fax* 071-437 8268. *Supervisory official:* Marilyn Goodman; *general secretary:* R. Bolton. To defend the interests of writers in film, television and radio. By virtue of its industrial strength, the union is able to help its writer members to secure favourable terms and conditions. In cases of disputes with employers, the union can intervene in order to ensure an equitable settlement. Its production agreement with PACT lays down minimum terms for writers working in the documentary area.

Broadcasting Group, 84 Drayton Gardens, London SW10 9SB　*tel* 071-373 6642. Specialist unit within the Society of Authors for radio and television writers and others involved in broadcasting.

The Brontë Society, Brontë Parsonage Museum, Haworth, Keighley, West Yorkshire BD22 8DR　*tel* Haworth (0535) 642323　*fax* (0535) 647131. *President:* Lord Briggs of Lewes MA, BSc, FBA; *chairman of the council:* Dudley E.C. Green MA(Oxon); *hon. council secretary:* Mrs Ruth M. Battye. Examination, preservation, illustration of the memoirs and literary remains of the Brontë family; exhibitions of MSS and other subjects. Publishes: *The Transactions of the Brontë Society* (bi-annual) and *The Brontë Gazette* (bi-annual). Enquiries to Executive Secretary. Affiliated to the Alliance of Literary Societies.

The Browning Society (1881, refounded 1969), 8 Church Close, Eton, Windsor, Berks. SL4 6AP. *Secretary:* Howard Moseley. Aims to widen the appreciation and understanding of the lives and poetry of Robert Browning and Elizabeth Barrett Browning, and other Victorian writers and poets. *Membership fee:* £10. Affiliated to the Alliance of Literary Societies.

The John Buchan Society (1979). *Hon. secretary:* Russell Paterson, Limpsfield, 16 Ranfurly Road, Bridge of Weir, Renfrewshire PA11 3EL　*tel* (0505)

613116. Promotes a wider understanding and appreciation of the life and works of John Buchan. Encourages publication of a complete annotated edition of Buchan's works, and supports the John Buchan Centre and Museum at Broughton, Borders. Holds regular meetings and social gatherings; produces a Newsletter and a Journal. *Subscription:* £10.00 p.a. full/overseas; other rates on application. Affiliated to the Alliance of Literary Societies.

Byron Society (International) (1971), Byron House, 6 Gertrude Street, London SW10 0JN *tel* 071-352 5112. *Hon. director:* Mrs Elma Dangerfield OBE. To promote research into the life and works of Lord Byron by seminars, discussions, lectures and readings. Publishes *The Byron Journal* (annual, £5.00). *Subscription:* £15.00 p.a. Affiliated to the Alliance of Literary Societies.

Cable Television Association (1934), The Fifth Floor, Artillery House, Artillery Row, London SW1P 1RT *tel* 071-222 2900 *fax* 071-799 1471. Trade body representing the interests of companies involved in the provision of cable television and telecommunications in the UK.

Randolph Caldecott Society (1983). *Secretary:* Kenn Oultram, Clatterwick Hall, Little Leigh, Northwich, Cheshire CW8 4RJ *tel* (0606) 891303 (office hours). To encourage an interest in the life and works of Randolph Caldecott, the Victorian artist, illustrator and sculptor. Meetings: Chester. *Subscription:* £5.00-£8.00 p.a. Newsletter (*Caldecott Sketch*) bi-annually. Affiliated to the Alliance of Literary Societies.

Canada, Periodical Writers Association of (1976), 54 Wolseley Street, Toronto, Ontario M5T 1A5, Canada *tel* 416-504-1645 *fax* 416-947-0159. To protect and promote the interests of periodical writers in Canada.

Canada, Writers Guild of, 24 Ryerson Avenue, Toronto, Ontario M5T 2P3, Canada *tel* 416-868-6914 *fax* 416-860-0826. *Executive director:* Penny Dickens. To further the professional, creative and economic rights and interests of writers in radio, television, film, video and all recorded media; to promote full freedom of expression and communication, and to oppose censorship unequivocally. *Annual membership fee:* $150, plus 2% of fees earned in the Guild's jurisdiction.

Canada, The Writers' Union of, 24 Ryerson Avenue, Toronto, Ontario M5T 2P3, Canada *tel* 416-868-6914 *fax* 416-860-0826. *Chair:* Myrna Kostash.

Canadian Authors Association, 275 Slater Street, Suite 500, Ottawa, Ontario K1P 5H9, Canada *tel* 613-233-2846 *fax* 613-235-8237. *President:* Mary E. Dawe.

Canadian Book Publishers' Council, 250 Merton Street, Suite 203, Toronto, Ontario M4S 1B1, Canada *tel* 416-322-7011 *fax* 416-322-6999. *Executive director:* Jacqueline Hushion. Consists of 44 educational and trade publishers. Interested in advancing the cause of the publishing business by co-operative effort and encouragement of high standards of workmanship and service. Co-operates with other organisations interested in the promotion and distribution of books. The Council has three divisions: the School Group concerned with primary and secondary school instructional materials, the College Group concerned with post-secondary materials, and the Trade Group concerned with general interest adult and children's books.

Canadian Magazine Publishers Association (1989), 2 Stewart Street, Toronto, Ontario M5V 1H6, Canada *tel* 416-362-2546 *fax* 416-362-2547. *Executive director:* Catherine Keachie. Trade association representing members' interests to provincial and federal governments, and providing services to Canadian magazines, including retail distribution. Resource centre for information about Canadian magazines.

Canadian Poets, League of (1966), 24 Ryerson Avenue, Toronto, Ontario M5T 2P3, Canada *tel* 416-363-5047 *fax* 416-860-0826. *Executive director:* Edita Petrauskaite; *executive assistant:* Emanuel Gonçalves. To promote the interests of poets and to advance Canadian poetry in Canada and abroad. Administer two annual awards: The Pat Lowther Award, for best book of poetry by a Canadian woman, and The Gerald Lampert Award, for the best first book of poetry by a Canadian. Also run an annual poetry competition, publish a newsletter and the books *Poetry Markets for Canadians*, *Who's Who in The League of Canadian Poets*, *When Is A Poem* (teaching guide), *Vintage 93* (contest anthology).

Canadian Publishers, Association of (1976; formerly Independent Publishers Association 1971), 2 Gloucester Street, Suite 301, Toronto, Ontario M4Y 1L5, Canada. *Director:* Garry Neil. Represents the interests of Canadian publishers in Canada and abroad; facilitates the exchange of information and professional expertise among its members.

Careers Writers' Association (1980). *Chairman:* Kieran Duignan, 84 Alderton Road, Croydon, Surrey CR0 6HJ *tel* 081-654 0808. Society for established writers on the inter-related topics of education, training and careers. Holds occasional meetings on subjects of interest to members, and circulates details of members to information providers. *Annual membership fee:* £10.00.

(Daresbury) Lewis Carroll Society (1970). *Secretary:* Kenn Oultram, Clatterwick Hall, Little Leigh, Northwich, Cheshire CW8 4RJ *tel* (0606) 891303 (office hours). To encourage an interest in the life and works of Lewis Carroll, author of *Alice's Adventures*. Meetings at Carroll's birth village (Daresbury). *Subscription:* £5.00 p.a. Newsletter (*Stuff & Nonsense*) bi-annually. Affiliated to the Alliance of Literary Societies.

The Lewis Carroll Society (1969), 16 Parkfields Avenue, London NW9 7PE. *Secretary:* Anne Clark Amor. To promote interest in the life and works of Lewis Carroll (Revd Charles Lutwidge Dodgson) and to encourage research. Activities include regular meetings and publication of *Jabberwocky* quarterly and newsletter *Bandersnatch*. *Annual subscription:* ordinary £8.00 ($20.00); institutions £10.00 ($23.00); students and retired £5.00 ($15.00). Affiliated to the Alliance of Literary Societies.

Cartoonists Club of Great Britain. *Secretary:* Terry Christien, Strawberry Vale, Twickenham TW1 4SE *tel* 081-892 3621 *fax* 081-891 5946. Aims to encourage social contact between members and endeavours to promote the professional standing and prestige of cartoonists. Fee on joining: provisional, full or associate £30; thereafter annual fee £20.

The Chesterton Society (1974), 11 Lawrence Leys, Bloxham, Nr Banbury, Oxon OX15 4NU *tel* (0295) 720869. To promote interest in the life and work of G.K. Chesterton and those associated with him or influenced by his writings. *Subscription:* £15 p.a., includes journal *The Chesterton Review* (Q.) and newsletters. Affiliated to the Alliance of Literary Societies.

Children's Book Foundation—now **Young Book Trust**; see entry under **Book Trust.**

Children's Writers and Illustrators Group, 84 Drayton Gardens, London SW10 9SB *tel* 071-373 6642. *Secretary:* Diana Shine. Subsidiary organisation for writers and illustrators of children's books, who are members of the Society of Authors.

Christian Literature, United Society for (1799), Robertson House, Leas Road, Guildford, Surrey GU1 4QW *tel* (0483) 577877 *fax* (0483) 301387. *President:* Lord Luke; *chairman:* Alan Brown; *general secretary:* Dr Alwyn

Marriage. To aid Christian literature principally in developing countries and Eastern Europe.

Agatha Christie Society (1993). *Secretary:* Elaine Z. Wiltshire, PO Box 985, London SW1X 9XA. To promote communication between the fans of Agatha Christie and the various media who bring her works to the public. Publishes four newsletters p.a. *Annual subscription:* UK/Europe £10, USA $20, rest of world £15.

Civil Service Authors, Society of. *Secretary:* Mrs J.M. Hykin, 21 Fontarabia Road, London SW11 5PE. Aims to encourage authorship by present and past members of the Civil Service (and some other public service bodies). There are annual competitions for poetry, short stories, etc., open to members only, and an annual 'Writer of the Year' award. The Society's magazine, *The Civil Service Author*, is free to members. *Annual subscription:* £10.00. Sae for enquiries.

The John Clare Society (1981), The Stables, 1a West Street, Helpston, Peterborough PE6 7DU *tel* (0733) 252678. Promotes a wider appreciation of the life and works of the poet John Clare. *Annual subscription:* ordinary/libraries/institutions £7.50, joint £10.00, retired £6.00, student (no voting rights) £3.00; overseas rates on application. Affiliated to the Alliance of Literary Societies.

Classical Association. *Secretary (branches):* Mrs Ann Hunt, 5 Grove Avenue, London N10 2AS; *secretary (council):* Dr M. Schofield, St John's College, Cambridge CB2 1TP. To promote and sustain interest in classical studies, to maintain their rightful position in universities and schools, and to give scholars and teachers opportunities of meeting and discussing their problems. Organises an annual conference lasting 3/4 days, in a university centre, and sponsors over 30 branches, which arrange programmes and lectures and discussions and many of which hold Greek and Latin Reading Competitions for Schools. Publishes *Classical Review*, *Classical Quarterly* and *Proceedings of the Classical Association*. Present membership of the Association is approximately 4000; membership is open both to individuals and to institutions. *Annual subscription:* £3.00; life membership, for individuals only, £63.00.

The William Cobbett Society (1976). *Chairman:* J. Wheater, 19A The Fairfield, Farnham, Surrey GU9 8AJ *tel/fax* (0252) 711165. To make the life and work of William Cobbett better known. *Subscription:* £5.00 p.a. Affiliated to the Alliance of Literary Societies.

The Wilkie Collins Society (1981). *Secretary:* Andrew Gasson, 3 Merton House, 36 Belsize Park, London NW3 4EA. To promote interest in the life and works of Wilkie Collins. Publishes a newsletter, an occasional scholarly journal and reprints of Collins's lesser known works. *Annual subscription:* £7.50, USA $10.

Comedy Writers Association of Great Britain (1981). Ken Rock, 61 Parry Road, Wolverhampton WV11 2PS *tel* (0902) 722729. Aims to develop and promote comedy writing in a professional and friendly way. *Membership:* £40 p.a.

Comhairle nan Leabhraichean (The Gaelic Books Council) (1968), Department of Celtic, University of Glasgow, Glasgow G12 8QQ *tel* 041-330 5190. *Chairman:* Professor Donald MacAulay. Stimulates Scottish Gaelic publishing by awarding publication grants for new books, commissioning authors and providing editorial services and general assistance to writers and readers. Also publishes a catalogue of all Scottish Gaelic books in print and an occasional magazine of book news. Runs a bookselling service and supports, and sometimes organises, literary evenings. Enquiries to the Chief Executive.

Comics Creators Guild (formerly **Society for Strip Illustration**), 7 Dilke Street, London SW3 4JE. Since 1977, the Guild has offered a service to professional comics creators, and is open to artists, writers, editors, colourists, publishers, journalists and comics retailers, and anyone professionally concerned with comics, newspaper strips and strip illustration; also welcomes enthusiasts and those working in the 'small' or 'independent' press who publish comics. Holds monthly meetings and publishes a monthly newsletter, *Comics Forum*, a Directory of Members' Work, Submission Guidelines for the major comics publishers, sample scripts for artists, a 'Guide to Contracts' and 'Getting Started in Comics', a beginners' guide to working in the industry.

The Commonwealth Institute (1893), Kensington High Street, London W8 6NQ *tel* 071-603 4535 *fax* 071-602 7374. *Director general:* Stephen Cox. Promotes Commonwealth education and culture in Britain. The Institute houses three floors of permanent exhibition galleries, designed to show the history, landscape, wildlife, arts, crafts and cultures of the 50 Commonwealth countries. Also promotes a range of programmes including special exhibitions, live events, cultural festivals, educational workshops and conferences. The Institute's galleries and conference facilities are available for commercial hire.

The Composers' Guild of Great Britain, 34 Hanway Street, London W1P 9DE *tel* 071-436 0007 *fax* 071-436 1913. Aims to represent and protect the interests of composers of music and to advise and assist its members on professional matters. *Annual subscription:* £30.00, associate membership £22.50. Further particulars obtainable from the General Secretary of the Guild.

The Joseph Conrad Society (UK) (1973). *Chairman:* Keith Carabine; *president:* Philip Conrad; *secretary:* Hugh Epstein; *editor of The Conradian:* R.G. Hampson, The English Dept., Royal Holloway, University of London, Egham Hill, Egham, Surrey TW20 0EX. Maintains close and friendly links with the Conrad family. Activities include an annual international conference, with lectures and discussions; publication of *The Conradian* and a series of pamphlets; and maintenance of a study centre in London at the Polish Cultural Centre, 238-246 King Street, W6 0RF. Affiliated to the Alliance of Literary Societies.

Contemporary Arts, Institute of, The Mall, London SW1Y 5AH *tel* 071-930 3647. Encourages collaboration between artforms, promotes experimental work and the mutual interchange of ideas and cultural practice at a national and international level. Produces a diverse monthly programme of exhibitions, theatre, dance, music, literature, cinema, video, lectures, conferences and discussions. Open 1200-0100 Mon-Sat, 1200-2300 Sun.

Copyright Clearance Center, Inc. (1978), 222 Rosewood Drive, Danvers, MA 01923, USA *tel* 508-750-8400 *fax* 508-750-4250. Operates a centralised photocopy authorisations and payment system in the US, serving photocopy users in their efforts to comply with the law, and foreign and domestic copyright owners in their efforts to protect their printed works. *Free registration* to rights holders.

Copyright Council, The British, Copyright House, 29-33 Berners Street, London W1P 4AA. *Chairman:* Maureen Duffy; *vice chairmen:* Anne Bolt, Mark Le Fanu, Robert Montgomery; *secretary:* Geoffrey Adams; *treasurer:* Lord Brain. Aims to defend and foster the true principles of creators' copyright and their acceptance throughout the world, to bring together bodies representing all who are interested in the protection of such copyright, and to keep watch on any legal or other changes which may require an amendment of the law.

The Copyright Licensing Agency Ltd (1983), 90 Tottenham Court Road, London W1P 9HE *tel* 071-436 5931 *fax* 071-436 3986. *Secretary:* Colin P. Hadley.

Formed by the Authors' Licensing & Collecting Society (ALCS) and the Publishers Licensing Society (PLS) in 1982, CLA administers collectively photocopying and other copying rights that it is uneconomic for writers and publishers to administer for themselves. The Agency issues collective and transactional licences, and the fees it collects, after the deduction of its operating costs, are distributed at regular intervals to authors and publishers via their respective societies. Since 1987 CLA has distributed over £15.6m. See article on page 548.

Crime Writers' Association (1953), PO Box 172, Tring, Herts. HP23 5LP. For professional writers of crime novels, short stories, plays for stage, television and sound radio, or of serious works on crime. Associate membership open to publishers, journalists, booksellers specialising in crime literature. Publishes *Red Herrings* monthly (for members only).

The Critics' Circle (1913). *President:* Jack Tinker; *vice-president:* Stephen Pettitt; *hon. general secretary:* Peter Hepple, 47 Bermondsey Street, London SE1 3XT *tel* 071-403 1818. Aims to promote the art of criticism, to uphold its integrity in practice, to foster and safeguard the professional interests of its members, to provide opportunities for social intercourse among them, and to support the advancement of the arts. Membership is by invitation of the Council. Such invitations are issued only to persons engaged professionally, regularly and substantially in the writing or broadcasting of criticism of drama, music, films or ballet.

The Cromwell Association (1935), *Press liaison officer:* B. Denton, 10 Melrose Avenue, off Bants Lane, Northampton NN5 5PB *tel/fax* (0604) 582516 during normal office hours, Mon.-Fri. Encourages the study of Oliver Cromwell and his times, holds academic lectures and meetings, publishes annual journal *Cromwelliana*, erects memorials at Cromwellian sites. *Subscription:* £10.00 p.a.

Cyngor Llyfrau Cymraeg—see **Welsh Books Council.**

The Danish Publishers Association (Den Danske Forlaeggerforening) (1837), Købmagergade 11, DK 1150, Copenhagen K, Denmark *tel* 33 15 66 88 *fax* 33 15 65 88. *Secretary:* Erik V. Krustrup. Aims to take care of publishers' interests related to the government, parliament, booksellers and authors' associations, among others.

Design and Artists Copyright Society (1983), St Mary's Clergy House, 2 Whitechurch Lane, London E1 7QR *tel* 071-247 1650 *telex* 885130 FABRIX G *fax* 071-377 5855. *Chief executive:* Rachel Duffield; *deputy chief executive:* Janet Ibbotson; *administrator:* Janet Tod. DACS is the British copyright and collecting society for the visual arts. It aims to protect and administer visual artists' copyright both nationally and internationally. DACS provides individual and blanket licences to users of artistic works in the UK. The Society also advises about copyright for visual creators, and pursues copyright infringements where appropriate. *Life membership:* £17.63 (inc. VAT).

Designers, The Chartered Society of, 29 Bedford Square, London WC1B 3EG *tel* 071-631 1510 *fax* 071-580 2338. *Director:* Brian Lymbery. Represents 8000 designers in 17 categories under the main sections of product design, fashion and textiles, interiors, graphics, design management and design education. It provides a range of services to members including general information, guidance on copyright and other professional issues, access to professional indemnity insurance, a credit-checking/debt collection service, etc. Members may use the rooms available at the Society's headquarters. Activities in the regions are included in an extensive annual programme of events and training courses. As the representative association for designers, the Society works to promote and regulate standards of competence, professional conduct and integrity. This includes representation on government and official bodies, design education and competitions. The Society's Code of Conduct was recently revised and republished. The Society has developed a new Business Design Programme to strengthen the links between designers and clients in business and industry.

Designers in Ireland, Society of (1972), 8 Merrion Square, Dublin 2, Republic of Ireland *tel/fax* (01) 2841477. *Executive officer:* Carainn Davies. Irish design profession's representative body, covering every field of design. *Full member:* £100 p.a.; *licentiate:* £45 p.a.

Dickens Fellowship (1902), The Dickens House, 48 Doughty Street, London WC1N 2LF *tel* 071-405 2127 *fax* 071-831 5175. *Hon. secretary:* Edward G. Preston. Based in house occupied by Dickens 1837-9; publishes *The Dickensian*, 3 p.a. Membership rates and particulars on application. Affiliated to the Alliance of Literary Societies.

Directory Publishers Association (1970). *Secretary:* Rosemary Pettit, 93a Blenheim Crescent, London W11 2EQ *tel* 071-221 9089. Maintains a code of professional practice; aims to raise the standard and professional status of UK directory publishing and to protect (and promote) the legal, statutory and common interests of directory publishers; provides for the exchange of technical, commercial and management information between members. *Subscription:* £100-£600 p.a.

Sean Dorman Manuscript Society (1957), Cherry Trees, Crosemere Road, Cockshutt, Ellesmere, Shropshire SY12 0JP *tel* (0939 270) 293. *Director:* Mary Driver. Aims to provide mutual help among part-time writers in England, Scotland and Wales. Members regularly receive circulating manuscript parcels affording constructive criticism of their work and providing opportunities for technical and general discussion. *Subscription:* £6.50 p.a. Full details available on receipt of sae.

The Arthur Conan Doyle Society (1989). *Joint organisers:* Christopher Roden and Barbara Roden, Ashcroft, 2 Abbottsford Drive, Penyffordd, Chester CH4 0JG *tel* (0244) 545210. Promotes the study of the life and works of Sir Arthur Conan Doyle. Publishes *ACD*, annual journal, and *The Parish Magazine*, biannual newsletter. Occasional reprints of Conan Doyle material. Major annual convention. *Subscription:* £12.50 p.a., overseas £15.00 p.a. (airmail extra).

Royal Dutch Publishers' Association (Koninklijke Nederlandse Uitgeversbond), Keizersgracht 391, 1016 EJ Amsterdam, The Netherlands *tel* (020) 626 77 36. *Secretary general:* R. M. Vrij.

Early English Text Society (1864). *Executive secretary:* R.F.S. Hamer, Christ Church, Oxford OX1 1DP; *hon. director:* Professor John Burrow. To bring unprinted early English literature within the reach of students in sound texts. *Annual subscription:* £15.00.

Editors, Association of British (1985). *Hon. secretary:* Nicholas Herbert, Westminster Press, Newspaper House, 8-16 Great New Street, London EC4P 4ER *tel* (0480) 492133 *fax* (0480) 492805. Independent organisation set up to study and enhance the practice of journalism in all media; to protect and promote the freedom of the media, both in the UK and throughout the world; and to consider common problems independent of any individual, group or interest. Publishes a quarterly journal, *British Editor. Annual subscription:* £50.

Edinburgh Bibliographical Society (1890), c/o New College Library, Mound Place, Edinburgh EH1 2LU *tel* 031-650 8956. *Secretary:* M.C.T. Simpson; *treasurer:* E.D. Yeo. Encourages bibliographical activity through organising talks for members, particularly on bibliographical topics relating to Scotland, and visits to libraries. Also publishes *Transactions* (bi-annual, free to members) and other occasional publications. *Membership:* £7.00 p.a. (£5.00 p.a. for full-time students).

Educational Writers Group, 84 Drayton Gardens, London SW10 9SB *tel* 071-373 6642. Specialist unit within the membership of the Society of Authors.

The Eighteen Nineties Society, 17 Merton Hall Road, Wimbledon, London SW19 3PP. *Patron:* HRH Princess Michael of Kent; *president:* Countess of Longford CBE; *chairman:* Martyn Goff OBE; *secretary:* Dr G. Krishnamurti. Founded in 1963 as The Francis Thompson Society, it widened its scope in 1972 to embrace the entire artistic and literary scene of the 1890 decade. Its activities include exhibitions, lectures, poetry readings. Publishes biographies of neglected authors and artists of the period; also check lists, bibliographies, etc. Its Journal appears periodically, and includes biographical, bibliographical and critical articles and book reviews. The Journal is free to members, and is not for public sale. All correspondence to the *hon. secretary,* 97-D Brixton Road, London SW9 6EE *tel* 071-582 4690. Affiliated to the Alliance of Literary Societies.

The George Eliot Fellowship (1930). *President:* Jonathan G. Ouvry; *secretary:* Mrs K.M. Adams, 71 Stepping Stones Road, Coventry CV5 8JT *tel* (0203) 592231. Promotes an interest in the life and work of George Eliot and helps to extend her influence; arranges meetings; produces an annual magazine and a quarterly newsletter. *Annual subscription:* £8.00. Affiliated to the Alliance of Literary Societies.

English Association, University of Leicester, 128 Regent Road, Leicester LE1 7PA *tel* (0533) 525927 *fax* (0533) 525928. *Chairman:* Dr Gordon Campbell; *secretary:* Helen Lucas. Aims to further knowledge, understanding and enjoyment of English literature and the English language, by working towards a fuller recognition of English as an essential element in education and in the community at large; by encouraging the study of English literature and language by means of conferences, lectures and publications; by fostering the discussion of methods of teaching English of all kinds; and by the establishment of local groups for the exchange of views and to work to further the status of English literature and language in the community.

English Speaking Board (International) Ltd, 26A Princes Street, Southport PR8 1EQ *tel* (0704) 501730. *President:* Christabel Burniston, MBE; *chairman:* Richard Ellis. Aims to foster all activities concerned with oral communication. The Board conducts examinations and training courses for teachers and students in schools and colleges where stress is on individual oral expression; also for those engaged in technical or industrial concerns, and for those using English as an acquired language. Members receive the journal *Spoken English* in Mar/Sept. Articles are invited by the editor on any special aspect of spoken English. Members can also purchase other ESB publications at reduced rates. Residential summer conference held annually at the end of July; AGM in the spring. *Membership:* individuals, £15.00 p.a., corporate £20.00 p.a.

The English-Speaking Union (1918), Dartmouth House, 37 Charles Street, London W1X 8AB *tel* 071-493 3328 *fax* 071-495 6108. *Director-general:* Mrs Valerie Mitchell. Promotes international understanding through the English language. The ESU is an educational charity which sponsors scholarships and exchanges, educational programmes promoting the effective use of English, and a wide range of international and cultural events. Members contribute to our work across the world. *Annual membership fee:* various categories. See also **Books Across the Sea.**

European Broadcasting Union (1950), Ancienne Route 17, Case Postale 67, CH-1218 Grand Saconnex (Geneva), Switzerland *tel* (22) 7172111 *telex* 415700 EBU CH *fax* (22) 7172481. *Secretary-general:* Dr Jean-Bernard Münch. Supports and promotes co-operation between its members and broadcasting organisations world-wide; represents the interests of its members in programme, legal, technical and other fields. *Annual membership fee:* according to number of broadcasting licences or households equipped with radio and/or TV receivers.

European Publishers, Federation of (1967). *President:* Volker Schwarz; *secretary:* Paul Cerf, 92 avenue de Tervuren, 1040 Brussels, Belgium *tel* (2) 736 36 16 *fax* (2) 736 19 87. Represents the interests of European publishers on EU affairs; informs members on the development of EU policies which could affect the publishing industry; lobbies the Commission and the European Parliament on behalf of European publishers.

Fabian Society, 11 Dartmouth Street, London SW1H 9BN *tel* 071-222 8877 *fax* 071-976 7153. Membership organisation which serves as a forum for the discussion of democratic socialist ideas. Holds conferences and publishes pamphlets and *Fabian Review*, a bi-monthly journal. Individual membership £24 (£10.50 unwaged), Library subscription £55.

Fantasy Society, The British (1971), 2 Harwood Street, Heaton Norris, Stockport SK4 1JJ *tel* 061-476 5368. *President:* Ramsey Campbell; *secretary:* Robert Parkinson. The Society was formed for devotees of fantasy, horror and related fields, in literature, art and the cinema. Publications include *British Fantasy Newsletter* (Q.) featuring news and reviews and approx. four annual booklets, including: *Dark Horizons*; *Winter Chills*, an all-fiction publication; *Masters of Fantasy* on individual authors; and *Mystique*, containing fiction and non-fiction. There is a small-press library and an annual convention and fantasy awards sponsored by the Society. *Membership:* £15.00 p.a.

The Fine Art Trade Guild (1910), 16-18 Empress Place, London SW6 1TT *tel* 071-381 6616 *fax* 071-381 2596. *Chief executive:* Scott Siemers. Promotes the sale of fine art prints and picture framing in the UK and overseas markets; establishes and raises standards amongst members and communicates these to the buying public. The Guild publishes a number of directories and guides, and *Art Business Today*, the trade's longest established magazine.

The Folklore Society (1878), c/o University College, Gower Street, London WC1E 6BT *tel* 071-387 5894. *Hon. secretary:* Tom Brown. Collection, recording and study of folklore.

Foreign Press Association in London (1888). *President:* Mustapha Karkouti; *secretary:* Davina Crole and Catherine Flury. *Registered office:* 11 Carlton House Terrace, London SW1Y 5AJ *tel* 071-930 0445 *fax* 071-925 0469. Aims to promote the professional interests of its members. Full Membership open to overseas professional journalists residing in the UK; Associate Membership available for British press and freelance journalists. *Entrance fee:* £110.45; *annual subscription:* £89.30.

Français, Syndicat des Conseils Littéraires, c/o Agence Hoffman, 77 bd Saint-Michel, 75005 Paris, France *tel* (1) 43-26-56-94 *telex* 203605 Aghoff *fax* (1) 43-26-34-07.

Free Painters & Sculptors, Loggia Gallery and Sculpture Garden, 15 Buckingham Gate, London SW1E 6LB *tel* 071-828 5963. Gallery hours: Mon.-Fri. 6-8 p.m., Sat.-Sun. 2-6 p.m. *Hon. secretary:* Philip Worth. Exhibits progressive work of all artistic allegiances and provides opportunities for FPS members to meet and discuss their work in either one-person or group shows.

Freelance Editors and Proofreaders, Society of (1988). *Office:* SFEP, 38 Rochester Road, London NW1 9JJ *tel* 071-813 3113. Aims to promote high editorial standards and to achieve recognition of its members' professional status. These aims are furthered through the dissemination of information, advice and training; the provision of a network of contacts; the fostering of good relations between members and their clients; and advice on how to overcome the sense of isolation often experienced by freelances. The SFEP meets these aims through local and national meetings, a yearly conference, a monthly newsletter and a programme of workshops/training sessions provided at reasonable rates. These sessions help newcomers to acquire basic skills, and provide experienced editors (whether in-house or freelance) with the opportunity to update, and/ or improve, their skills and develop or broaden their competence. They also cover aspects of professional practice or business matters for the self-employed. The SFEP also provides other services, including a yearly directory, which is made available to publishers, and the opportunity to buy reference books at publishers' discount prices. In addition, the Society is working towards recognised standards and accreditation for editors and proofreaders. Publishers and individuals interested in learning more about the Society should send an sae to the Office.

Freelance Photographers, Bureau of (1965), Focus House, 497 Green Lanes, London N13 4BP *tel* 081-882 3315 *fax* 081-886 5174. *Head of administration:* John Tracy. To help the freelance photographer by providing information on markets, and free advisory service. Publishes monthly *Market Newsletter*. *Membership:* £36 p.a.

French Publishers' Association (Syndicat National de l'Edition), 35 rue Grégoire de Tours, 75279 Paris 06, France *tel* (1) 43-29-75-75/44-41-28-00 *fax* (1) 43-25-35-01.

The Gaelic Books Council—see **Comhairle nan Leabhraichean.**

The Gaskell Society (1985). *Hon. secretary:* Mrs Joan Leach, Far Yew Tree House, Over Tabley, Knutsford, Cheshire WA16 0HN *tel* (0565) 634668. Promotes and encourages the study and appreciation of the work and life of Elizabeth Cleghorn Gaskell. Holds regular meetings and visits; produces an annual Journal and bi-annual Newsletters. *Subscription:* £7.50 p.a. Affiliated to the Alliance of Literary Societies.

Gay Authors Workshop (1978), Kathryn Byrd, BM Box 5700, London WC1N 3XX *tel* 081-520 5223. To encourage writers who are lesbian, gay or bisexual. Quarterly newsletter. *Membership:* £5.00; unwaged £2.00.

General Practitioners Writers Association (1985). *President:* Dr Robin Hull, Jasmine Cottage, Hampton Lucy, Warwick CV35 8BE *tel* (0789) 840509. Aims to improve the writing by, for, from or about general medical practice. Publishes own journal, *The GP Writer* (2 p.a.), with a register of members' writing interests which is sent to medical editors and publishers.

German Publishers' and Booksellers' Association (Börsenverein des Deutschen Buchhandels e. V.), Postfach 100442, 60549 Frankfurt am Main, Germany *tel* (069) 13060 *telex* 413573 BUCHV D *fax* (069) 1306201. *General manager:* Dr Hans-Karl von Kupsch.

The Ghost Story Society (1988), *Organisers:* Barbara Roden and Christopher Roden, Ashcroft, 2 Abbottsford Drive, Penyffordd, Chester CH4 0JG *tel* (0244) 545210. Devoted mainly to supernatural fiction in the literary tradition of M.R. James, Walter de la Mare, Arthur Machen, Algernon Blackwood, etc. Thrice-yearly magazine. *Membership:* £12 (£14/$22 overseas).

The Gothic Society (1990), Chatham House, Gosshill Road, Chislehurst, Kent BR7 5NS *tel* 081-467 8475 *fax* 081-295 1967. For the study of morbid, macabre and black-hued themes: Mrs Radcliffe, Monk Lewis, Mary Shelley, Sheridan Le Fanu, the Brontës, Bram Stoker, and many other writers and artists in the horror romance genre. Also publish new art and literature in the same mood. Books, monographs and a quarterly magazine, *Udolpho. Annual subscription:* £18.00, overseas £21.00 (£24.00 airmail).

Graphic Fine Art, Society of (1919), 75 Athenaeum Road, Whetstone, London N20 9AL. *President:* Mrs Lorna B. Kell FSBA, FRSA. A fine art society holding an annual open exhibition. Membership by election, requires work of high quality with an emphasis on good drawing, whether by pen, pencil (with our without wash), watercolour, pastel or any of the forms of print making.

Graphical, Paper & Media Union (amalgamation of NGA and SOGAT), Keys House, 63-67 Bromham Road, Bedford MK40 2AG *tel* (0234) 351521 *fax* (0234) 270580. Trade union representing the interests of employees in the printing and allied industries.

The Greeting Card and Calendar Association, 6 Wimpole Street, London W1M 8AS *tel* 071-637 7692 *fax* 071-436 3137. Publishes *Greetings* bi-monthly.

Guernsey Arts Council (1981), St James Concert and Assembly Hall, St Peter Port, Guernsey, CI *tel* (0481) 721902. *Secretary:* Angela Simon. Co-ordinates the organisations under the council's umbrella, presents artistic events, sponsors reports, aims to bring about the creation of an arts centre in Guernsey and to encourage all the arts in Guernsey, Alderney and Sark. *Membership fee:* £5, under 18 £2.

The Neil Gunn Society (1985). *Secretary:* Mrs J. Campbell, 25 Newton Avenue, Wick, Caithness KW1 5LJ *tel* (0955) 2607. To promote the works of the Scottish novelist, Neil Gunn; to research into the background of, and to encourage discussion on and evaluation of, Gunn's work; to collect material related to his life and work; to provide a focal point for and help with any Gunn-related activity. *Annual membership fee:* £5.00 (students £2.00).

Hakluyt Society (1846), c/o The Map Library, The British Library, Great Russell Street, London WC1B 3DG *tel* (0986) 86359. *President:* Professor P.E.H. Hair; *hon. secretaries:* Mrs Sarah Tyacke and Dr W.F. Ryan. Publication of original narratives of voyages, travels, naval expeditions, and other geographical records.

The Thomas Hardy Society Ltd (1967). *Secretary:* Mrs Helen Gibson, PO Box 1438, Dorchester, Dorset DT1 1YH *tel* (0305) 251501. Publishes *The Thomas Hardy Journal* (3 p.a.). Biennial conference in Dorchester, 1994. *Subscription:* £12.00 (£15.00 overseas) p.a. Affiliated to the Alliance of Literary Societies.

Harleian Society (1869), College of Arms, Queen Victoria Street, London EC4V 4BT. *Chairman:* J. Brooke-Little CVO, MA, FSA, Norroy and Ulster King of Arms; *secretary:* P. Ll. Gwynn-Jones MA, Lancaster Herald of Arms. Instituted for transcribing, printing and publishing the heraldic visitations of Counties, Parish Registers and any manuscripts relating to genealogy, family history and heraldry.

Heraldic Arts, Society of (1987), 46 Reigate Road, Reigate, Surrey RH2 0QN *tel* (0737) 242945. *Secretary:* John Ferguson ARCA, SHA, FRSA. Aims to serve the interests of heraldic artists, craftsmen, designers and writers, to provide a 'shop window' for their work, to obtain commissions on their behalf and to act as a forum for the exchange of information and ideas. The society also offers an information service to the public. Candidates for admission as craft members should be artists or craftsmen whose work comprises a substantial element of heraldry and is of a sufficiently high standard to satisfy the requirements of the society's advisory council. *Associate membership:* £12.00 p.a.; *craft membership:* £17.00 p.a.

The Sherlock Holmes Society of London (1951). *President:* A.D. Howlett MA, LLB; *chairman:* Philip H. Porter; *hon. secretary:* Cdr G.S. Stavert MBE, MA, RN (ret'd), 3 Outram Road, Southsea, Hants PO5 1QP   *tel* (0705) 812104. Aims to bring together those who have a common interest as readers and students of the literature of Sherlock Holmes; to encourage the pursuit of knowledge of the public and private lives of Sherlock Holmes and Dr Watson; to organise meetings and lectures for the discussion of these topics; to co-operate with other bodies at home and abroad that are in sympathy with the aims and activities of the Society. *Subscription,* including two issues of *The Sherlock Holmes Journal:* £12.50 p.a. UK, £12.50 Europe, £16.50 Far East, US$27.50 Americas.

Hopkins Society (1990), c/o Regional Officer, Arts Council of Wales, Daniel Owen Centre, Earl Road, Mold CH7 1AP   *tel* (0352) 758403   *fax* (0352) 700236. To promote and celebrate the work of the poet, Gerard Manley Hopkins, to inform members about the latest publications about Hopkins and to support educational projects concerning Hopkins' work. Annual lecture held in North Wales in the spring; two Newsletters per year. *Annual subscription:* £5.00. Affiliated to the Alliance of Literary Societies.

Hesketh Hubbard Art Society, 17 Carlton House Terrace, London SW1Y 5BD   *tel* 071-930 6844   *fax* 071-839 7830. *President:* Simon Whittle. Weekly drawing workshops open to all.

Illustrators, The Association of (1973), 29 Bedford Square, London WC1B 3EG   *tel* 071-636 4100. Non-partisan, non-profitmaking trade association established in order to support illustrators, and to promote illustration and to encourage professional standards in the industry. Membership open to all involved with illustration. Monthly magazine, and exhibiting space available for hire. All services give maximum support and assistance to members. Also holds the Image File slide bank, a large collection of slides submitted by illustrator members of the association. Each slide bears the illustrator's name and contact number. Most submit several slides into several categories at once. These categories are decided by style, i.e. cartoon, decorative and stylised, historical, children's book illustration, portrait, natural history and botanical, fashion and figure, architectural. *Contact:* Gina Morley.

Illustrators, Society of Architectural and Industrial (1975), PO Box 22, Stroud, Glos. GL5 3DH   *tel* (0453) 882563. *Administrator:* Eric Monk. Professional body to represent all who practise architectural, industrial and technical illustration, including the related fields of model making and photography.

Independent Literary Agents Association, Inc.—now Authors' Representatives, Association of.

Independent Programme Producers Association—see PACT.

Indexers, Society of. *Secretary:* Mrs H.C. Troughton, 38 Rochester Road, London NW1 9JJ   *tel* 071-916 7809. Objects: (1) to improve the standard of indexing; (2) to maintain a Register of Indexers (for details see article on page 514); (3) to act as an advisory body on the qualifications and remuneration of indexers; (4) to publish or communicate books, papers and notes on the subject of indexing; (5) to raise the status of indexers and to safeguard their interests; (6)

to publish and run an open-learning indexing course, 'Training in Indexing'. The Society's journal, *The Indexer*, is sent free to members. *Annual subscription:* £25 (£30 overseas), corporate £35 (£40 overseas).

Indian Publishers, The Federation of, 18/1-C Institutional Area, J.N.U. Road, New Delhi 110067, India   *tel* 654847, 6852263   *fax* 91-11-6864054.

Industrial Editors, The British Association of (1949), 3 Locks Yard, High Street, Sevenoaks, Kent TN13 1LT   *tel* (0732) 459331   *fax* (0732) 461757. Main aim is the development of the qualifications of those engaged in the management, editing and production of corporate communication media – defined by the BAIE to include such audiences as employees, customers, suppliers and shareholders. Membership is open to those engaged in, or have a valid interest in, corporate communication.

Irish Book Publishers Association (Clé), Irish Writers' Centre, 19 Parnell Square, Dublin 1, Republic of Ireland   *tel* (01) 8729090   *fax* (01) 8722035. *President:* John Spillane.

Irish Playwrights, Society of (Cumann Drámadóirí na hÉireann) (1969), Irish Writers' Centre, 19 Parnell Square, Dublin 1, Republic of Ireland   *tel* (01) 8721302   *fax* (01) 8726282. *Secretary:* Patricia Martin. To safeguard the rights of Irish playwrights and to foster and promote Irish playwriting. *Annual subscription:* IR£25.

Irish Writers' Union (Comhar na Scríbhneoirí) (1986), Irish Writers' Centre, 19 Parnell Square, Dublin 1, Republic of Ireland   *tel* (01) 8721302   *fax* (01) 8726282. *Secretary:* Clairr O'Connor. The Union aims to advance the cause of writing as a profession, to achieve better remuneration and more favourable conditions for writers and to provide a means for the expression of the collective opinion of writers on matters affecting their profession.

The Richard Jefferies Society (1950), 45 Kemerton Walk, Swindon, Wilts. SN3 2EA   *tel* (0793) 521512. *President:* Andrew Rossabi BA (Cantab); *hon. secretary:* Cyril Wright. World-wide membership. Promotes interest in the life, works and associations of the naturalist and novelist, Richard Jefferies; helps to preserve buildings and memorials, and co-operates in the development of a Museum in his birthplace; provides a service to students, lecturers, readers and writers. The society arranges regular meetings in Swindon, and occasionally elsewhere, organises outings and displays and publishes a Journal each spring and a Newsletter/Annual Report each September. *Annual subscription:* £5.00. Affiliated to the Alliance of Literary Societies.

The Johnson Society, Johnson Birthplace Museum, Breadmarket Street, Lichfield, Staffs. WS13 6LG   *tel* (0543) 264972. *Hon. general secretary:* Rita M. Willard. To encourage the study of the life and works of Dr Samuel Johnson; to preserve the memorials, associations, books, manuscripts, letters of Dr Johnson and his contemporaries; preservation of his birthplace. Affiliated to the Alliance of Literary Societies.

Johnson Society of London (1928). *President:* The Revd Dr E.F. Carpenter KCVO; *secretary:* Mrs Zandra O'Donnell MA, 255 Baring Road, Grove Park, London SE12 0BQ   *tel* 081-851 0173. To study the life and works of Dr Johnson, and to perpetuate his memory in the city of his adoption. Affiliated to the Alliance of Literary Societies.

Journalists, The Chartered Institute of. *General secretary:* Christopher Underwood FCIJ, 2 Dock Offices, Surrey Quays Road, London SE16 2XL   *tel* 071-252 1187   *fax* 071-232 2302. The senior organisation of the profession, founded in 1884 and incorporated by Royal Charter in 1890. The Chartered Institute maintains an employment register and has accumulated funds for the assistance of members. A Freelance Division links editors and publishers with freelances and a Directory is published of freelance writers, with their specialisations. There are special sections for broadcasters, motoring correspondents and public relations practitioners. Occasional contributors to the media may qualify for election as Affiliates. *Subscription:* related to earnings – maximum £160, minimum £50; Affiliate £75.

Keats-Shelley Memorial Association (1903). *Chairman:* K.V. Prichard-Jones; *patron:* HM Queen Elizabeth the Queen Mother; *hon. secretary:* D.R. Leigh-Hunt; enquiries to *hon. treasurer:* R.E. Cavaliero, 10 Lansdowne Road, Tunbridge Wells, Kent TN1 2NJ *tel* (0892) 533452 *fax* (0892) 519142. Occasional meetings; annual *Review* and progress reports. Owns and supports house in Rome where John Keats died, and celebrates the poets Keats, Shelley and Leigh Hunt. Subscription to 'Friends of the Keats-Shelley Memorial', minimum £10.00 p.a.

Kent and Sussex Poetry Society. *President:* Laurence Lerner; *chairman:* Clive Eastwood; *hon. secretary:* Mrs Doriel Hulse, Costens, Carpenters Lane, Hadlow, Kent TN11 0EY *tel* (0732) 851404. Based in Tunbridge Wells, the society was formed in 1946 to create a greater interest in Poetry. Well-known poets address the society, a Folio of members' work is produced and a full programme of recitals, discussions, competitions and readings is provided. See page 670 for details of Open Poetry Competition. *Annual subscription:* attending members £5.00; country members £3.00; students £1.00.

Kinematograph, Sound and Television Society, British (founded 1931, incorporated 1946), M6-14 Victoria House, Vernon Place, London WC1B 4DF *tel* 071-242 8400 *fax* 071-405 3560. *Hon. secretary:* Ray Clipson. Aims to encourage technical and scientific progress in the industries of its title. Publishes technical information, arranges international conferences and exhibitions, lectures and demonstrations, and encourages the exchange of ideas. Monthly journal: *Image Technology*.

The Kipling Society. *Secretary:* Norman Entract, PO Box 68, Haslemere, Surrey GU27 2YR *tel* (0428) 652709. Aims to honour and extend the influence of Kipling, to assist in the study of Kipling's writings, to hold discussion-meetings, to publish a quarterly journal and to maintain a Kipling Reference Library. Membership details on application. Affiliated to the Alliance of Literary Societies.

The Lancashire Authors' Association (1909). *President:* G.A. Wormleighton MBE, FCA; *general secretary:* Eric Holt, 5 Quakerfields, Westhoughton, Bolton BL5 2BJ *tel* (0942) 816785. 'For writers and lovers of Lancashire literature and history.' Publishes *The Record* (Q.). *Subscription:* £7.00 p.a.

The T.E. Lawrence Society (1985). *Secretary:* S.H.T. Johnson, 17 Norham End, Norham Road, Oxford OX2 6SG *tel* (0865) 511166. Promotes the memory of T.E. Lawrence and furthers knowledge by research into his life. Publishes bi-annual *Journal* and quarterly *Newsletter. Subscription:* £12.50 p.a., overseas £16.50 p.a. Affiliated to the Alliance of Literary Societies.

Learned and Professional Society Publishers, The Association of (1972). Aims to promote and develop the publishing activities of learned and professional organisations. Membership is open to professional and learned societies and to individuals with publishing interests, whose experience may contribute to the work of the association: details are available from the Secretary, Professor B.T. Donovan, 48 Kelsey Lane, Beckenham, Kent BR3 3NE *tel* 081-658 0459.

Librarians, Association of Assistant (1895), c/o The Library Association, 7 Ridgmount Street, London WC1E 7AE. *President:* Nigel Ward BA. MA. DMS. ALA; *hon. secretary:* Jane Dwyer BA, DipLib. ALA. Publishes bibliographical aids, the journal *Assistant Librarian*, works on librarianship; and runs educational courses.

The Library Association (1877), 7 Ridgmount Street, London WC1E 7AE *tel* 071-636 7543 *telex* 9312134504 LA G *fax* 071-436 7218. *Chief executive:* R. Shimmon FLA. For over a century, the Library Association has promoted and defended the interests of the Library and Information Service profession, those working within it and the people who use the services. The monthly journal, *The Library Association Record*, is distributed free to all members. *Subscription* varies according to income.

Limners, The Society of (1986). *Executive secretary:* Mrs C. Melmore, 104 Poverest Road, Orpington, Kent BR5 2DQ. *Founder/president:* Elizabeth Davys Wood PSLM, SWA. Aims to promote an interest in miniature painting (in any medium), calligraphy and heraldry and encourage their development to a high standard. New members are elected after the submission of four works of acceptable standard and guidelines are provided for new artists. Members receive four newsletters a year and two annual exhibitions are arranged. *Membership:* £16.50. Friends membership is open to non-exhibitors (£12 p.a.); Friends receive newsletters and invitations to exhibitions and seminar.

Linguists, Institute of, 24A Highbury Grove, London N5 2EA *tel* 071-359 7445 *fax* 071-354 0202. To provide language qualifications; to encourage Government and industry to develop the use of modern languages and encourage recognition of the status of professonal linguists in all occupations; to promote the exchange and dissemination of information on matters of concern to linguists.

Literary Societies, Alliance of. *Secretary:* Philip Fisher, Birmingham & Midland Institute, 3 Margaret Street, Birmingham B3 3BS *tel* 021-236 3591. Any literary society may affiliate, whether with 30 or 3000 members. Affiliated societies may use the ALS logo, attend the annual convention and receive an allocation of the official publication *Chapter One* (editor: Kenn Oultram, Clatterwick Hall, Little Leigh, Northwich, Cheshire CW8 4RJ *tel* (0606) 891303 office hours). *Subscription:* graded dependent upon membership.

Literature, Royal Society of (1823), 1 Hyde Park Gardens, London W2 2LT *tel* 071-723 5104 *fax* 071-402 0199. *Chairman of Council:* John Mortimer CBE. QC. FRSL; *secretary:* Maggie Parham. For the advancement of literature by the holding of lectures, discussions, readings, and by publications. Administrators of the Dr Richards' Fund and the Royal Society of Literature Award, under the W.H. Heinemann Bequest and the Winifred Holtby Memorial Prize. Membership open to anyone interested in literature, subscription fee £25.00 p.a.

Little Presses, Association of (1966). *Chairman:* Stanley Trevor, 30 Greenhill, Hampstead High Street, London NW3 5UA *tel* 071-435 1889. Loosely-knit association of individuals running little presses who have grouped together for mutual self-help, while retaining their right to operate autonomously. Publications include: *Poetry and Little Press Information*, *Catalogue of Little Press Books in Print*, *Getting Your Poetry Published*, *Publishing Yourself*. *Membership fee:* £10.00 p.a.

Little Theatre Guild of Great Britain. *Public relations officer:* Marjorie Havard, 19 Abbey Park Road, Great Grimsby DN32 0HJ *tel* (0472) 343424. Aims to promote closer co-operation amongst the little theatres constituting its membership; to act as co-ordinating and representative body on behalf of the little theatres; to maintain and advance the highest standards in the art of theatre; and to assist in encouraging the establishment of other little theatres. The LTG is non-political and non-sectarian. Yearbook available to non-members.

The Arthur Machen Society (1986), 19 Cross Street, Caerleon, Gwent NP6 1AF *tel* (0633) 422520 *fax* (0633) 420309 'Machen Society'. *President:* Barry Humphries; *secretary:* Rita Tait. To honour the life and work of Arthur Machen, novelist. Provides a forum for the exchange of ideas and information and aims to bring Machen's work before a new generation of readers. Publishes bi-annual journal *Avallaunius* and biannual newsletter *The Silurist*. Also publishes hardback books, by and about Machen and his circle, and an audio-cassette tape, under its Green Round Press imprint. Relevant second-hand and small press booklist available. *Annual subscription:* £12.00; £18.00 libraries; overseas, please enquire. Affiliated to the Alliance of Literary Societies.

Marine Artists, Royal Society of, 17 Carlton House Terrace, London SW1Y 5BD *tel* 071-930 6844 *fax* 071-839 7830. *President:* Mark Myers. To promote and encourage marine painting. Open Annual Exhibition.

The Marlowe Society (1955). *Secretary:* Leo McDonald, 26 Horace Road, Barkingside, Ilford, Essex IG6 2BG *tel* 081-550 5173. To extend appreciation and widen recognition of Christopher Marlowe (1564-93) as the foremost poet and dramatist preceding Shakespeare, whose development he influenced. Holds meetings, and visits Tudor stately homes, yeomen houses and farms, etc. *Annual subscription:* £5.

Mechanical-Copyright Protection Society Ltd (MCPS), Elgar House, 41 Streatham High Road, London SW16 1ER *tel* 081-769 4400 *telex* 946792 MCPS G *fax* 081-769 8792. *Chief executive:* Frans De Wit. Contact: Corporate Communications Department. See also article on page 552.

The Media Society (1973). *Secretary:* Rodney Bennett-England, Church Cottage, East Rudham, Norfolk PE31 8QZ *tel* (0485) 528664 *fax* (0485) 528155. To promote and encourage collective and independent research into the standards, performance, organisation and economics of the media and hold regular discussions, debates, etc. on subjects of topical or special interest and concern to print and broadcast journalists and others working in or with the media. *Subscription:* £25.00 p.a.

Medical Journalists Association (1966), Old Barley Mow, 185 High Street, Stony Stratford, Milton Keynes MK11 1AP *tel* (0908) 564623. *Chairman:* Michael Jeffries; *hon. secretary:* Gwen Yates. Formed by journalist/broadcasters specialising in medicine and the health services. Aims to improve the quality and practice of medical journalism. Administers major awards for medical journalism and broadcasting. Publishes *Directory of Full Members, Affiliate Members and Freelances* and a newsletter, *MJA News. Membership fee:* £20.00 p.a.

Medical Writers Group, 84 Drayton Gardens, London SW10 9SB *tel* 071-373 6642. *Secretary:* Jacqueline Granger-Taylor. Specialist unit within the membership of the Society of Authors giving contractual and legal advice. Also organises talks and day seminars covering many aspects of medical writing.

Miniature Painters, Sculptors and Gravers, Royal Society of (1895). *President:* Suzanne Lucas FLS, PRMS, FPSBA; *treasurer:* Alastair MacDonald; *hon. secretary:* Pauline Gyles. Membership is by selection and standard of work over a period of years (ARMS associate, RMS full member). Annual Exhibition in November in London. Open to non-members. Hand-in Sept/Oct, schedules available in July (send sae). Applications and enquiries to the *executive secretary:* Mrs S.M. Burton, 15 Union Street, Wells, Somerset BA5 2PU   *tel* (0749) 674472   *fax* (0749) 672918.

Miniaturists, The Hilliard Society of (1982). *President:* Mrs S.M. Burton, 15 Union Street, Wells, Somerset BA5 2PU   *tel* (0749) 674472   *fax* (0749) 672918. International society with approx. 300 members. Founded to increase knowledge and promote the art of miniature painting. Annual Exhibition held in May/June at Wells. Encourages Patron membership to keep collectors in touch with artists. Informative Newsletter includes news from miniature societies around the world.

Miniaturists, Society of (1895), *Director:* Leslie Simpson FRSA, Ralston House, 41 Lister Street, Riverside Gardens, Ilkley, West Yorkshire LS29 9ET   *tel* (0943) 609075. The oldest miniature society in existence. Holds two open exhibitions p.a. Membership by selection.

William Morris Society (1955), Kelmscott House, 26 Upper Mall, London W6 9TA   *tel* 081-741 3735. *Secretary:* Derek Baker. To spread knowledge of the life, work and ideas of William Morris. Publishes a *Newsletter* (Q.), and a *Journal* (2 p.a.). Library and collections open to the public Thu and Sat, 2-5 p.m. Affiliated to the Alliance of Literary Societies.

Motoring Artists, The Guild of (1986). *Administrator:* Roy Gardner FIMI, MIMgt, Woodlands, Welford Hill, Welford-on-Avon, Warwicks. CV37 8AE   *tel* (0789) 750618. To promote, publicise and develop motoring fine art; to build a recognised group of artists interested in motoring art, holding events and exchanging ideas and support; to hold motoring art exhibitions. *Annual membership fee:* £25.00, associate £20.00.

Motoring Writers, The Guild of. General Secretary, 30 The Cravens, Smallfield, Surrey RH6 9QS   *tel* (0342) 843294   *fax* (0342) 844093. To raise the standard of motoring journalism. For writers, broadcasters, photographers on matters of motoring, but who are not connected with the motor industry.

Music Publishers Association Ltd (1881), 3rd Floor, Strandgate, 18/20 York Buildings, London WC2N 6JU   *tel* 071-839 7779   *fax* 071-839 7776. *Secretary:* P.J. Dadswell. The only trade organisation representing the UK music publishing industry; protects and promotes its members' interests in copyright, trade and related matters. A number of sub-committees and groups deal with particular interests. Details of subscriptions available on written request.

Musical Association, The Royal, Dr Ewan West, Faculty of Music, St Aldates, Oxford OX1 1DB   *tel* (0865) 276125   *fax* (0865) 276128.

Musicians, Incorporated Society of, 10 Stratford Place, London W1N 9AE   *tel* 071-629 4413   *fax* 071-408 1538. *President:* 1994-5: Dr Philip Ledger CBE; *chief executive:* Neil Hoyle. Professional association for musicians. Aims to promote the art of music; protect the interests of the musical profession; represent, support and provide membership services for all professional musicians. Publishes *Music Journal*, 12 p.a. *Subscription:* £72.50 p.a.

Musicians, The Worshipful Company of (1500), The Irish Chamber, Guildhall, London EC2P 2EJ   *tel* 071-606 7269. *Clerk:* S.F.N. Waley.

Name Studies in Britain and Ireland, Society for. *Hon. secretary:* Miss Jennifer Scherr, c/o Queen's Building Library, University of Bristol, University Walk, Bristol BS8 1TR. Aims to advance, promote and support research into the place-names and personal names of Britain and Ireland and related regions by the collection, documentation and interpretation of such names; the publication of the material and the results of such research; the exchange of information between the various regions. Acts as a consultative body on Name Studies. Publishes an annual journal, *Nomina*, and an occasional newsletter. Membership is by subscription and is open to all interested individuals: £15 p.a. (1994). *Membership secretary:* Dr M. Higham, 22 Peel Park Avenue, Clitheroe, Lancs. BB7 1ET.

National Union of Journalists. Head Office: Acorn House, 314 Gray's Inn Road, London WC1X 8DP *tel* 071-278 7916 *telex* 892384 *fax* 071-837 8143. Trade union for working journalists with 28,000 members and 147 branches throughout the UK and the Republic of Ireland, and in Paris, Brussels and Geneva. Its wages and conditions agreements cover the newspaper press, news agencies and broadcasting, the major part of periodical and book publishing, and a number of public relations departments and consultancies, information services and Prestel-Viewdata services. Administers disputes, unemployment, benevolent and provident benefits. Official publications: *The Journalist, Freelance Directory, Freelance Fees Guide* and policy pamphlets.

New Zealand, Book Publishers Association of, Inc., Box 386, Auckland 1, New Zealand *tel* (09) 309 2561 *fax* (09) 309 7798. *President:* Tony Harkins.

New Zealand Copyright Council Inc., PO Box 5028, Wellington, New Zealand *tel* (04) 472-4430 *fax* (04) 471-0765. *Chairman:* Bernard Darby; *secretary:* Tony Chance.

Newspaper Press Fund, Dickens House, 35 Wathen Road, Dorking, Surrey RH4 1JY *tel* (0306) 887511. *Secretary:* P.W. Evans. For the relief of hardship amongst member journalists, their widows and dependants. Limited help is available for non-member journalists and their dependants. Financial assistance and retirement housing are provided.

The Newspaper Publishers Association Ltd, 34 Southwark Bridge Road, London SE1 9EU *tel* 071-928 6928 *fax* 071-928 2067.

Newspaper Society, Bloomsbury House, 74-77 Great Russell Street, London WC1B 3DA *tel* 071-636 7014 *fax* 071-631 5119 AdDoc DX35701 Bloomsbury. *Director:* Dugal Nisbet-Smith; *deputy director:* David Newell.

NGA—now **Graphical, Paper & Media Union.**

Oil Painters, Royal Institute of, 17 Carlton House Terrace, London SW1Y 5BD *tel* 071-930 6844 *fax* 071-839 7830. *President:* Brian Bennett. Promotes and encourages the art of painting in oils. Open Annual Exhibition.

Oils, Pastels and Acrylics, British Society of Painters in (1988), Ralston House, 41 Lister Street, Riverside Gardens, Ilkley, West Yorkshire LS29 9ET *tel* (0943) 609075. *Director:* Leslie Simpson FRSA. Promotes interest and encourages high quality in the work of painters in these media. Holds two open exhibitions per annum. *Membership:* by selection.

Outdoor Writers' Guild (1980). *Hon. secretary:* Terry Marsh, 27 Camwood, Clayton Green, Bamber Bridge, Preston, Lancs. PR5 8LA *tel/fax* (0772) 321243. Aims to promote a high professional standard among writers who specialise in outdoor activities; represents members' interests to representative bodies in the outdoor leisure industry; circulates members with news of media opportunities; provides a forum for members to meet colleagues and others in the outdoor leisure industry. *Membership:* £20.00 p.a. plus £15.00 joining fee.

Wilfred Owen Association (1989), 10 College Hill, Shrewsbury SY1 1LZ *tel* (0743) 235904. To commemorate the life and work of Wilfred Owen, and to encourage and enhance appreciation of his work. *Annual subscription:* £4.00

(£6.00 overseas); £10.00 groups/institutions; £2.00 senior citizens/students/ unemployed. Affiliated to the Alliance of Literary Societies.

PACT (Producers Alliance for Cinema and Television), Gordon House, Greencoat Place, London SW1P 1PH   *tel* 071-233 6000   *fax* 071-233 8935. *Contacts:* John Woodward (chief executive), Susan Finlayson-Sitch (membership officer). PACT serves the feature film and independent television production sector and is the UK contact point for co-production, co-finance partners and distributors. PACT works for participants in the industry at every level and operates a members' regional network throughout the UK with divisional offices in Scotland and the North. It lobbies actively with broadcasters, financiers and governments to ensure that the producer's voice is heard and understood in Britain and Europe on all matters affecting the film and television industry. Membership services include a dedicated industrial relations unit, legal documentation and back-up, a varied calendar of events, courses and business advice, representation at international film and television markets, a comprehensive research programme, publication of a monthly newsletter (*The PACT Magazine*), an annual members' directory, and a number of specialist guidebooks, affiliation with European and international producers' organisations, plus extensive information and production advice.

Painter-Printmakers, Royal Society of (1880), Bankside Gallery, 48 Hopton Street, London SE1 9JH   *tel* 071-928 7521. *President:* Joseph Winkelman. Membership (RE) open to British and overseas artists. An election of Associates is held annually, and applications for the necesssary forms and particulars should be addressed to the Secretary. Open exhibition held in early spring. One members' exhibition per year. Friends of the RE open to all those interested in artists' original printmaking.

Painters, Sculptors & Printmakers, National Society of (1930). *Hon. secretary:* Gwen Spencer NS, 122 Copse Hill, Wimbledon, London SW20 0NL; *president:* Denis Baxter PNS, UA, FRSA. An annual exhibition in London representing all aspects of art for artists of every creed and outlook.

Partners in Crime (1991). Stella A. Milner, 17 Eton Road, Burton-on-Trent, Staffs. DE14 2SP. Postal workshop for serious novelists specialising in the entire spectrum of crime (mystery/suspense/thrillers/murder). Aims to assist members with technique and presentation with a view to eventual publication. Three groups are in current circulation in manuscript form. Send sae for details; no subscription charged.

The Pastel Society (1899), 17 Carlton House Terrace, London SW1Y 5BD   *tel* 071-930 6844   *fax* 071-839 7830. *President:* Thomas Coates. Pastel and drawings in pencil or chalk. Annual Exhibition open to all artists working in dry media. Members elected from approved candidates' list.

The Mervyn Peake Society (1975). *Hon. president:* Sebastian Peake; *chairman:* Brian Sibley; *secretary:* Frank Surry, 2 Mount Park Road, Ealing, London W5 2RP. Devoted to recording the life and works of Mervyn Peake; publishes a journal and newsletter. *Annual subscription:* £10 (UK and Europe): £8 students; £12 all other countries. Affiliated to the Alliance of Literary Societies.

P.E.N., International. A world association of writers. *International president:* Ronald Harwood; *international secretary:* Alexandre Blokh, 9/10 Charterhouse Buildings, Goswell Road, London EC1M 7AT   *tel* 071-253 4308   *telegrams/cables* Lonpenclub, London EC1   *fax* 071-253 5711; *president of English Centre:* Josephine Pullein-Thompson MBE; *general secretary of English Centre:* Gillian Vincent, 7 Dilke Street, London SW3 4JE   *tel* 071-352 6303   *fax* 071-351 0220.

P.E.N. was founded in 1921 by C.A. Dawson Scott under the presidency of John Galsworthy, to promote friendship and understanding between writers and to defend freedom of expression within and between all nations. The initials P.E.N. stand for Poets, Playwrights, Editors, Essayists, Novelists – but membership is open to all writers of standing (including translators), whether men or women, without distinction of creed or race, who subscribe to these fundamental principles. P.E.N. takes no part in state or party politics. The International and English P.E.N. Writers in Prison Committees work on behalf of writers imprisoned for exercising their right to freedom of expression, a right implicit in the P.E.N. Charter to which all members subscribe. The International P.E.N. Translations and Linguistic Rights Committee strives to promote the translations of works by writers in the lesser-known languages and to defend those languages. The Writers for Peace Committee exists to find ways in which writers can work for peaceful co-existence in the world. The Women Writers' Committee works to promote women's writing and publishing in developing countries. International Congresses are held most years. The 60th Congress was held in Santiago de Compostela, Spain, in September 1993.

Membership of the English Centre is £25.00 p.a. for country and overseas members, £30.00 for London members. Associate membership is available for writers not yet eligible for full membership and for persons connected with literature. Membership of any one Centre implies membership of all Centres; at present 119 autonomous Centres exist throughout the world. The English Centre has a programme of literary lectures, discussion, dinners and parties. A yearly *Writers' Day* is open to the public as are some literary lectures.

Performing Right Society Ltd (1914), 29-33 Berners Street, London W1P 4AA   *tel* 071-580 5544   *fax* 071-631 4138. See article on page 553.

Periodical Publishers Association, Imperial House, 15-19 Kingsway, London WC2B 6UN   *tel* 071-379 6268   *fax* 071-379 5661. *Chief executive:* Ian Locks.

The Personal Managers' Association Ltd. *Liaison secretary:* Angela Adler, 1 Summer Road, East Molesey, Surrey KT8 9LX   *tel/fax* 081-398 9796. Association of personal managers in the theatre, film and entertainment world generally.

Photographers, The Association of (1969). *Co-secretary:* Gwen Thomas, 9-10 Domingo Street, London EC1Y 0TA   *tel* 071-608 1441   *fax* 071-253 3007. To protect and promote the interests of fashion advertising and editorial photographers. *Annual subscription:* £60.00-£345.00, depending on turnover.

Photographers Association, Master, Hallmark House, 2 Beaumont Street, Darlington, Co. Durham DL1 5SZ   *tel* (0325) 356555   *fax* (0325) 357813. To promote and protect professional photographers. Members can qualify for awards of Licentiate, Associate and Fellowship. *Subscription:* £85.00 p.a.

Photographic Society, The Royal (1853), The Octagon, Milsom Street, Bath BA1 1DN   *tel* (0225) 462841. Aims to promote the general advancement of photography and its applications. Publish *The Photographic Journal* monthly, £60.00 p.a., overseas £65.00 p.a. and *The Journal of Photographic Science*, bimonthly £89.00 p.a., overseas £99.00.

Photography, British Institute of Professional (founded 1901, incorporated 1921), Amwell End, Ware, Herts. SG12 9HN   *tel* (0920) 464011. *Principal objects:* Professional Qualifying Association; to represent all who practise photography as a profession in any field; to improve the quality of photography; establish recognised examination qualifications and a high standard of conduct; to safeguard the interests of the public and the profession. *Membership:* approx. 5000. Admission can be obtained either via the Institute's examinations, or by submission of work and other information to the appropriate examining board. Fellows, Associates and Licentiates are entitled to the designation Incorporated Photographer or Incorporated Photographic Technician. Organises numerous meetings and conferences in various parts of the country throughout the year; publishes a monthly journal, *The Photographer* and an annual Register of Members and *guide to buyers of photography*, plus various pamphlets and leaflets on professional photography.

Player-Playwrights (1948), St Augustine's Church Hall, Queen's Gate, London SW1. *Secretary:* Peter Thompson, 9 Hillfield Park, London N10 3QT   *tel* 081-883 0371. The society reads, performs and discusses plays and scripts submitted by members, with a view to assisting the writers in improving and marketing their work. *Annual membership:* £5.00 (and £1.00 per attendance).

The Playwrights' Co-operative (1978). *Administrator:* Gordon Monsen, 61-71 Collier Street, London N1 9BE   *tel* 071-713 7125. Supports and encourages London playwrights who, having already written at least one script, want to move forward but need professional advice and contact. Offers story conferences, workshops, rehearsed readings and criticism; publishes plays. *Membership:* £15.00 p.a.

Playwrights Trust, New, Interchange Studios, Dalby Street, London NW5 3NQ   *tel* 071-284 2818   *fax* 071-482 5292. *Director:* Polly Thomas; *administrator:* Ben Payne. Support and development organisation for playwrights and aspiring playwrights, and those interested in developing and producing new work. Services include script-reading. Workshops, writer/company Link Service. Issues *Newsletter* monthly. *Subscription:* rates on application.

Playwrights Workshop (1949). A meeting place where those people in the Manchester area interested in drama can meet to discuss playwriting in general and their own plays in particular. Details of places and times of meetings from *Hon. secretary:* Robert Coupland, 22 Brown Street, Altrincham, Cheshire WA14 2EU   *tel* 061-928 3095. Plays read privately by experienced playwright and detailed assessments made. Details from above with sae.

Poetry Foundation, National (1981), 27 Mill Road, Fareham, Hants PO16 0TH   *tel* (0329) 822218. Aims to provide a truly national poetry organisation which in turn provides advice, information and a magazine, all for a single low-cost fee, and to help poets have a book of their own poetry published at no additional cost, once they have sufficient poetry of a high enough standard. The Foundation also gives grants to deserving causes directly related to poetry.

The Poetry Society (1909), 22 Betterton Street, London WC2H 9BU   *tel* 071-240 4810   *fax* 071-240 4818. *Chairman:* Richard Tyrrell; *director:* Chris Meade. National membership body, open to all, to help poets and poetry thrive in Britain today. Publishes *Poetry Review* and *Poetry News* quarterly, has an information and imagination service, runs promotions and educational projects, and administers the annual National Poetry Competition and the biennial European Poetry Translation Prize.

The Polidori Society (1990). *President:* Franklin Bishop, Ebenezer House, 31 Ebenezer Street, Langley Mill, Notts. NG16 4DA. To promote appreciation of the life and works of John William Polidori MD (1795-1821), novelist, poet, philosopher, essayist and tragedian. Author of the seminal *The Vampyre – A tale* (1819), thereby introducing into English literature the icon of the vampyre as an aristocrat and seducer. The Society celebrates the life of Polidori by way of an annual dinner at various gothic locations, and members receive newsletters, book offers and field trips.

Portrait Painters, Royal Society of (1891), 17 Carlton House Terrace, London SW1Y 5BD *tel* 071-930 6844 *fax* 071-839 7830. *President:* George J.D. Bruce. Annual Exhibition when work may be submitted by non-members with a view to exhibition.

Portuguese Association of Publishers and Booksellers (Associação Portuguesa de Editores e Livreiros) (1939), Av. Estados Unidos da América, 97-6° Esq., Lisboa 1700, Portugal (1) *tel* 8489136 *telex* 62735 APEL P *fax* (1) 8489377. Represents the interests of those active in the fields of publishing, bookselling, distribution and second-hand bookselling in Portugal.

Beatrix Potter Society (1980). *Chairman:* Judy Taylor; *secretary:* Anne Poulter, 120 Aldwick Road, Bognor Regis, West Sussex PO21 2PB. Promotes the study and appreciation of the life and works of Beatrix Potter as author, artist, diarist, farmer and conservationist. *Subscription:* UK £7.00, overseas $US25, $Can27.50, $Aus30.

Press Agencies, National Association of (1983). *Administrator:* Jan Chambers, 41 Lansdowne Crescent, Leamington Spa, Warks. CV32 4PR *tel* (0926) 424181 *fax* (0926) 424760. Trade association representing the interests of regional news and photographic agencies. *Annual subscription:* £250.

The Press Complaints Commission (1991), *Chairman:* Lord McGregor of Durris; *director:* Mark Bolland, 1 Salisbury Square, London EC4Y 8AE *tel* 071-353 1248 *Help-Line tel* 071-353 3732 *fax* 071-353 8355. Independent body founded to oversee self-regulation of the Press. Deals with complaints by the public about the contents and conduct of British newspapers and magazines and advises editors on journalistic ethics. Complaints must be about the failure of newspapers or magazines to follow the letter or spirit of a Code of Practice, drafted by newspaper and magazine editors, adopted by the industry and supervised by the Commission.

Private Libraries Association (1956), Ravelston, South View Road, Pinner, Middlesex HA5 3YD. *President:* Iain Bain; *hon. editor:* David Chambers; *hon. secretary:* Frank Broomhead. International society of book collectors and private libraries. Publications include the quarterly *Private Library*, annual *Private Press Books*, and other books on book collecting. *Subscription:* £25.00 p.a.

The Producers Association—see **PACT**.

The Publishers Association (1896), 19 Bedford Square, London WC1B 3HJ *tel* 071-580 6321/5 and 7761 *telex* 267160 PUBASS G *fax* 071-636 5375. *Chief executive:* Clive Bradley; *director of International Division (BDC):* Ian Taylor; *director of educational and academic and professional publishing:* John Davies; *director of management services:* Peter Kilborn. Association of British publishers whose overall membership embraces some 180 companies.

Publishers Association, International (1896), 3 avenue de Miremont, CH-1206 Geneva, Switzerland *tel* (022) 346-30-18 *fax* (022) 347-57-17. *President:* Fernando Guedes; *secretary-general:* J. Alexis Koutchoumow.

Publishers Guild, Independent (1962), 25 Cambridge Road, Hampton, Middlesex TW12 2JL *tel/fax* 081-979 0250. Full membership is open to new and established publishers and book packagers; supplier membership is available to specialists in fields allied to publishing (but not printers and binders). The Guild offers a forum for the exchange of ideas and information and represents the interests of its members. *Membership:* £60.00 (+ VAT) p.a.

Publishers Licensing Society Limited (1981), 90 Tottenham Court Road, London W1P 9HE *tel* 071-436 5931 *fax* 071-436 3986. *Chairman:* Nicolas Thompson; *secretary:* Antony Henton. Aims to exercise and enforce on behalf of publishers the rights of copyright and other rights of a similar nature, to authorise the granting of licences for, *inter alia*, the making of reprographic copies of copyright works, and to receive and distribute to the relevant publisher copyright proprietors the sums accruing from such licensed use.

Publishers Publicity Circle (c. 1955). *Secretary:* Christina Thomas, 48 Crabtree Lane, London SW6 6LW *tel/fax* 071-385 3708. Enables book publicists – from both publishing houses and freelance PR agencies – to meet and share information on a regular basis. Monthly meetings provide a forum for press journalists, television and radio researchers and producers to meet publicists collectively. In conjunction with *Publishing News*, a quarterly award is presented for the best PR campaign; annual prizes are also awarded for the best campaigns of the year. A monthly newsletter summarises the proceedings of the previous meeting and gives details of forthcoming events and meetings. Jobs and positions sought can be advertised in the newsletter, as well as information given about or from the media.

The Radclyffe International Philosophical Association (1955), BM-RIPhA, Old Gloucester Street, London WC1N 3XX. *President:* William Mann FRIPhA; *secretary general:* John Khasseyan FRIPhA. Aims to dignify those achievements which might otherwise escape formal recognition; to promote the interests and talent of its members; to encourage their good fellowship and to form a medium of exchange of ideas between members. *Annual subscription:* £25.00 (Fellows, Members and Associates). Published authors and artists usually enter at Fellowship level.

The Radio Academy, PO Box 4SZ, London W1A 4SZ *tel* 071-323 3837 *fax* 071-765 4992. *Administrator:* Ann James. The Radio Academy is the UK's only membership association exclusively for those in the radio broadcasting industry. The Academy has over 800 individual members and 25 corporate patrons. Its principal patrons are the BBC and The Radio Authority. It organises conferences, seminars, debates and social events for members; publishes a monthly newsletter *Off Air*, and a twice-yearly magazine *Radio*. The UK Radio Festival, which takes place each July is the Academy's largest event, bringing together 350-400 delegates from BBC and independent radio throughout the UK. The Academy also has a number of Collegiate members and offers some practical training opportunities for students of radio.

Radio Producers, Independent Association of (1993), Essel House, 29 Foley Street, London W1P 7LB *tel* 071-323 2770 *fax* 071-436 0132. *Chair:* Sarah Dickinson; *secretary*: Tim Crook. To protect and promote the interests of independent radio and audio producers and to promote the interests and advancement of the industry. *Annual membership fee:* £50.

Railway Artists, Guild of (1979). *Hon. administrator:* F.P. Hodges, 45 Dickins Road, Warwick CV34 5NS *tel* (0926) 499246. Aims to forge a link between artists depicting railway subjects and to give members a corporate identity; also stages railway art exhibitions and members' meetings.

Regional Arts Boards (RABs). Following a process of restructuring in 1990/91, a network of ten Regional Arts Boards now covers England. The RABs are autonomous, strategic bodies which work in partnership with local authorities and a wide variety of other sectors and organisations and are policy led. Legally, they are limited companies with charitable status. They are concerned with all the arts and crafts – visual, performing, media and published – and work at regional level as partners of the three national agencies which provide most of their funds: the Arts Council, the British Film Institute and the Crafts Council.

The Arts Council retains the national responsibility for funding and assessing the 'national companies', the symphony orchestras and a handful of other high profile clients. The building-based companies are funded by the RABs. The overall planning system is becoming more 'integrated' with the principle of subsidiarity being increasingly applied to project and development work. The resources available to the RABs during 1994/95 total over £50 million.

English Regional Arts Boards is the representative body for the ten Regional Arts Boards in England. Its secretariat provides project management, services and information for the members and acts on their behalf in appropriate circumstances: 5 City Road, Winchester, Hants SO23 8SD *tel* (0962) 851063 *fax* (0962) 842033. *Chief executive:* Christopher Gordon; *assistant:* Carolyn Nixson. The Welsh Regional Arts Associations work in close partnership with the Arts Council of Wales (see page 609).

There are no regional arts boards in Scotland and all enquiries should be addressed to the Scottish Arts Council, 12 Manor Place, Edinburgh EH3 7DD *tel* 031-226 6051 *fax* 031-225 9833.

East Midlands Arts (1969), Mountfields House, Epinal Way, Loughborough, Leics. LE11 0QE *tel* (0509) 218292 *fax* (0509) 262214. *Chief executive:* John Buston; *literature officer:* Debbie Hicks. Derbyshire (excluding High Peak District), Leicestershire, Northamptonshire and Nottinghamshire.

Eastern Arts Board (1971), Cherry Hinton Hall, Cherry Hinton Road, Cambridge CB1 4DW *tel* (0223) 215355 *fax* (0223) 248075. *Chief executive:* Jeremy Newton. Specialist officers for each art form. Bedfordshire, Cambridgeshire, Essex, Hertfordshire, Lincolnshire, Norfolk and Suffolk.

London Arts Board (1991), Elme House, 133 Long Acre, Covent Garden, London WC2E 9AF *tel* 071-240 1313 *fax* 071-240 4580. *Chief executive:* Timothy Mason; *literature officer:* Lavinia Greenlaw; *principal visual arts and crafts officer:* Amanda King. The area of the 32 London Boroughs and the Corporation of London.

North West Arts Board (1966), 12 Harter Street, Manchester M1 6HY *tel* 061-228 3062 *fax* 061-236 5361. *Chief executive:* Brian Matcham. Greater Manchester, Merseyside, High Peak District of Derbyshire, Lancashire and Cheshire.

Northern Arts (1961), 9-10 Osborne Terrace, Newcastle upon Tyne NE2 1NZ *tel* 091-281 6334 *fax* 091-281 3276. *Chief executive:* Peter Hewitt; *head of published and broadcast arts:* John Bradshaw. Cumbria, Cleveland, Tyne and Wear, Northumberland and Durham.

South East Arts Board (1973), 10 Mount Ephraim, Tunbridge Wells, Kent TN4 8AS *tel* (0892) 515210 *information dept. ext.* 205/206 *fax* (0892) 549383. *Chief executive:* Christopher Cooper; *literature officer:* Celia Hunt (*ext.* 210/211). Covers Kent, Surrey, East Sussex and West Sussex. Information and publications list available.

South West Arts (1956), Bradninch Place, Gandy Street, Exeter, Devon EX4 3LS *tel* (0392) 218188 *fax* (0392) 413554. *Chief executive:* Christopher Bates. Avon, Cornwall, Devon, Dorset (except Districts of Bournemouth, Christchurch and Poole), Gloucestershire, Somerset.

Southern Arts Board (1968), 13 St Clement Street, Winchester, Hants SO23 9DQ *tel* (0962) 855099 *fax* (0962) 861186. *Executive director:* Sue Robertson; *literature officer:* Kieran Phelan. The arts development agency for Berkshire, Buckinghamshire, Hampshire, Isle of Wight, Oxfordshire, Wiltshire and South East Dorset.

West Midlands Regional Arts Board (1971), 82 Granville Street, Birmingham B1 2LH   *tel* 021-631 3121   *fax* 021 643 7239. *Chief executive:* Michael Elliott. County of Hereford and Worcester, West Midlands Metropolitan Area, Shropshire, Staffordshire, Warwickshire.

Yorkshire and Humberside Arts (1991), 21 Bond Street, Dewsbury, West Yorkshire WF13 1AX   *tel* (0924) 455555   *fax* (0924) 466522. *Literature and cultural industries officer:* Steve Dearden. North, South and West Yorkshire and Humberside. Funds schemes and projects for the promotion of contemporary literature and writing activities. Provides grants for festivals, events, courses, residencies, publishing. Offers advice and information on various aspects of literature. Preliminary enquiry advised.

Ridley Art Society (1889), 69 Sterndale Road, London W14 0HU   *tel* 071-603 4371. *President:* Carel Weight CBE. RA; *chairman:* Brian Robinson. Represents a wide variety of attitudes towards the making of art. In recent years has sought to encourage young artists. At least one central London exhibition annually.

The Romantic Novelists' Association. *Chairman:* Jean Saunders, The Hayes, 23 Hobbiton Road, Worle, Weston-Super-Mare BS22 0HP; *hon. secretary:* Joyce Bell, Cobble Cottage, 129 New Street, Baddesley Ensor, Nr Atherstone, Warwickshire CV9 2DL. To raise the prestige of Romantic Authorship. Open to romantic and historical novelists. See also under **Literary Awards.**

Royal Academy of Arts, Piccadilly, London W1V 0DS   *tel* 071-439 7438   *fax* 071-434 0837. *President:* Sir Philip Dowson CBE; *keeper:* Norman Adams RA; *treasurer:* Sir Philip Powell RA; *secretary:* Piers Rodgers. Academicians (RA) are elected from the most distinguished artists in the UK. Major loan exhibitions throughout the year with the Annual Summer Exhibition, June to August. Also runs art schools for 60 post-graduate students in painting and sculpture.

The Royal Literary Fund, 144 Temple Chambers, Temple Avenue, London EC4Y 0DA   *tel* 071-353 7150. *President:* His Honour Judge Stephen Tumim; *secretary:* Fiona Clark. Founded in 1790, the Fund is the oldest and largest charity serving literature. The object of the Fund is to help writers and their families who face hardship. It does not offer grants to writers who can earn their living in other ways, nor does it provide financial support for writing projects. But it sustains authors who have for one reason or another fallen on hard times – illness, family misfortune, or sheer loss of writing form, all of which can afflict established authors and deprive them of that peace of mind so necessary for work.

Applicants must have published work of approved literary merit, which may include important contributions to periodicals. The literary claim of every new applicant must be accepted by the General Committee before the question of need can be considered.

The Fund has never received a subsidy from the Government nor has the Welfare State replaced its function. It is supported by the investment of legacies, subscriptions and donations. The principal contributors are authors themselves, publishers and others in the book trade.

The Royal Society (1660), 6 Carlton House Terrace, London SW1Y 5AG   *tel* 071-839 5561   *telex* 917876   *fax* 071-930 2170. *President:* Sir Michael Atiyah OM. PRS; *treasurer:* Professor J.H. Horlock FRS; *biological secretary:* Professor

P. Lachmann FRS; *physical secretary:* Sir Francis Graham-Smith; *foreign secretary:* Dr Anne L. McLaren FRS; *executive secretary:* Dr P.T. Warren. Promotion of the natural sciences (pure and applied).

The Ruskin Society of London (1985). *Hon. secretary:* Miss O.E. Madden, 351 Woodstock Road, Oxford OX2 7NX   *tel* (0865) 310987. To promote literary and biographical interest in John Ruskin and his contemporaries. *Annual subscription:* £10.00. Affiliated to the Alliance of Literary Societies.

The Dorothy L. Sayers Society (1976). *Chairman:* Christopher J. Dean, Rose Cottage, Malthouse Lane, Hurstpierpoint, West Sussex BN6 9JY   *tel* (0273) 833444; *secretaries:* Lenelle Davis and Jasmine Simeone. To promote and encourage the study of the works of Dorothy L. Sayers; to collect relics and reminiscences about her and make them available to students and biographers; to hold an annual seminar; to publish proceedings and pamphlets and a bi-monthly bulletin. *Annual subscription:* £7.00.

Science Fiction Association Ltd, The British (1958). *President:* Arthur C. Clarke; *membership secretaries:* Alison Cook and Brian Stovold, 27 Albermarle Drive, Grove, Oxon OX12 0BN. For authors, publishers, booksellers and readers of science fiction, fantasy and allied genres. Publishes informal magazine, *Matrix*, of news and information, *Focus*, an amateur writers' magazine, *Vector*, a critical magazine and The Orbiter Service, a network of postal writers workshops (all enquiries to membership secretaries).

Science Writers, Association of British, c/o British Association for the Advancement of Science, Fortress House, 23 Savile Row, London W1X 1AB   *tel* 071-439 1205   *fax* 071-734 1658. *Chairman:* Wendy Barnaby; *secretary:* Dr Peter Briggs. Association of science writers, editors, and radio, film and television producers concerned with the presentation and communication of science, technology and medicine. Aims to improve the standard of science writing and to assist its members in their work. Activities include visits to research establishments, luncheon meetings for those concerned with scientific policy, and receptions for scientific attachés and Parliamentarians.

Scientific and Technical Communicators, The Institute of (1972), Kings Court, 2/ 16 Goodge Street, London W1P 1FF   *tel* 071-436 4425   *fax* 071-580 0747. *President:* Peter Greenfield; *executive secretary:* Jeannette Hobart. Professional body for those engaged in the communication of scientific and technical information. Aims to establish and maintain professional standards, to encourage and co-operate in professional training and to provide a source of information on, and to encourage research and development in, all aspects of scientific and technical communication. Publishes *The Communicator*, the official journal of the Institute, 4 p.a.

Scottish Academy, Royal (1826), The Mound, Edinburgh EH2 2EL   *tel* 031-225 6671   *fax* 031-225 2349. *President:* William J.L. Baillie PRSA; *secretary:* Ian McKenzie Smith RSA; *treasurer:* James Morris RSA; *administrative secretary:* W.T. Meikle. Academicians (RSA) and Associates (ARSA) and non-members may exhibit in the Annual Exhibition of Painting, Sculpture and Architecture, held approximately mid April to August; Festival Exhibition August/September. Other artists' societies' annual exhibitions, normally between October and January. Royal Scottish Academy Student Competition held in March.

Scottish Arts, 24 Rutland Square, Edinburgh EH1 2BW   *tel* 031-229 1076. *Hon. secretary:* D.J. Pickering   *tel* 031-229 8157. Art, literature, music. *Annual subscription:* Full £250.00, but various reductions.

Scottish Arts Council, 12 Manor Place, Edinburgh EH3 7DD   *tel* 031-226 6051. *Chairman:* Dr William Brown; *director:* Seona Reid; *literature director:* Walter

Cairns. Principal channel for government funding of the arts in Scotland, the Scottish Arts Council is funded by the Scottish Office. It aims to develop and improve the knowledge, understanding and practice of the arts, and to increase their accessibility throughout Scotland. It offers about 1300 grants a year to artists and arts organisations concerned with the visual arts, drama, dance and mime, literature, music, festivals, traditional and ethnic arts and community arts.

Scottish History Society (1886), Department of Scottish History, University of Edinburgh, 17 Buccleuch Place, Edinburgh EH8 9LN   *tel* 031-650 4030. *Hon. secretary:* Elizabeth P.D. Torrie PhD. The Society exists to publish documents illustrating the history of Scotland.

Scottish Newspaper Publishers' Association, 48 Palmerston Place, Edinburgh EH12 5DE   *tel* 031-220 4353   *fax* 031-220 4344. *President:* W. Laidlaw; *director:* J.B. Raeburn FCIS. To promote and represent local newspaper interests.

Scottish Publishers Association (1974), Scottish Book Centre, 137 Dundee Street, Edinburgh EH11 1BG   *tel* 031-228 6866   *fax* 031-228 3220. *Director:* Lorraine Fannin; *administrator:* Neil Gouans; *marketing manager:* Susanne Dickson. To assist Scottish trade publishers primarily in the publicity, promotion and marketing of their books.

Screenwriters Workshop, London (1983), 84 Wardour Street, London W1V 3LF   *tel* 071-434 0942/081-551 5570   *fax* 081-550 7537. *Contact:* Andy Fish. Founded in 1983 by writers as a forum for contact, information and tuition. The LSW helps new and established writers work successfully in the film and TV industry, and organises a continuous programme of activities, events, courses and seminars, many of which non-members can attend. Membership open to anyone interested in writing for film and television, and to anyone working in these and related media. *Annual subscription:* £18.

SCRIBO (1971), K. & P. Sylvester, Flat 1, 31 Hamilton Road, Boscombe, Bournemouth BH1 4EQ. A postal forum for novelists (published and unpublished), SCRIBO aims to give friendly, informal encouragement and help, to discuss all matters of interest to novelists and to offer criticism via MSS folios. Due to expansion, three specialist folios have been introduced: crime, fantasy/ sci-fi, saga/aga-saga/romance, and more recently a literary MSS folio (members are mostly graduates, writing serious novels). Send sae for details. No subscription.

Sculptors, Royal Society of British (1904), 108 Old Brompton Road, London SW7 3RA   *tel* 071-373 5554   *fax* 071-373 9202. *President:* Philomena Davidson Davis. Established 'to Promote and advance the art and practice of Sculpture'. The Society offers advice and services to sculptors; advice on commissions to corporations, developers and individuals; organises a number of national bursaries and competitions in the field of sculpture.

Shakespearean Authorship Trust. *Hon. secretary:* Dr D.W. Thomson Vessey, 26 Ouse Walk, Huntingdon, Cambs. PE18 6QL; *hon. treasurer:* John Silberrad, Dryads' Hall, Woodbury Hill, Loughton, Essex IG10 1JB. Promotes the advancement of learning with particular reference to the social, political and literary history of England in the sixteenth century and the authorship of the plays and poems commonly attributed to William Shakespeare. Subscribers receive copies of the Trust's publications, and are entitled to use its library. *Annual subscription:* £10.00.

The Shaw Society, 6 Stanstead Grove, Catford, London SE6 4UD   *tel* 081-690 2325. *Secretary:* Barbara Smoker. Improvement and diffusion of knowledge of the life and works of Bernard Shaw and his circle. Meetings in London, annual festival at Ayot St Lawrence; publication: *The Shavian. Annual membership:* £7.00 ($12.00). Affiliated to the Alliance of Literary Societies.

Singapore Book Publishers Association, c/o Chomen Publishers, 865 Mountbatten Road, 05-28/29 Katong Shopping Centre, Singapore 1543 *tel* (65) 3441495 *fax* (65) 3440180. *President:* N.T.S. Chopra; *hon. secretary:* Tan Wu Cheng.

The Small Press Group of Britain Ltd, The Small Press Centre, Middlesex University, White Hart Lane, London N7 8HR *tel* 081-362 6058. *Chair:* Don Jarvis. Organises exhibitions, an annual small press fair and events; runs courses of interest to the independent and novice publisher; supplies quarterly magazine *Small Press World* to members; publishes annual *The Small Press Yearbook. Annual subscription:* £17.50.

Society of Authors—see **Authors, The Society of.**

Songwriters & Composers, The Guild of International, Sovereign House, 12 Trewartha Road, Praa Sands, Penzance, Cornwall TR20 9ST *tel* (0736) 762826 *fax* (0736) 763328. *Secretary:* Carole Ann Jones. Gives advice to members on contractual and copyright matters; assists with protection of members rights; assists with analysis of members' works; international collaboration register free to members; outlines requirements to record companies, publishers, artists. *Subscription:* £25 p.a. UK, £35 p.a. EU/overseas. Publishers of quarterly magazine, *Songwriting & Composing.*

Songwriters, Composers and Authors, British Academy of (1947), 34 Hanway Street, London W1P 9DE *tel* 071-436 2261. *General secretary:* Amanda Harcourt. To give advice and guidance to its songwriter members and look after their interests within the industry. Presents the annual Ivor Novello Awards.

South Africa, Publishers' Association of, c/o Oxford University Press, PO Box 1141, Cape Town 8000, South Africa *tel* (021) 457-266 *fax* (021) 457-265.

South African Writers' Circle (1960). *Secretary:* Pat Lister, PO Box 10558, Marine Parade, Durban 4056, South Africa *tel* (031) 307-5668. Aims to help and encourage all writers, new and experienced, in the art of writing. Publishes a monthly magazine, *Newsletter. Annual subscription:* R50.

Spanish Publishers' Association, Federation of (Federación de Gremios de Editores de España), Juan Ramón Jiménez 45 9° Izda., 28036 Madrid, Spain *tel* 350 91 05/03 *telex* 48457 FGEE E *fax* 345 43 51. *President:* D. Fermín Vargas Lázaro; *secretary:* Dña. Ana Moltó Blasco.

SPREd – Society of Picture Researchers and Editors, BM Box 259, London WC1N 3XX *tel* 071-404 5011. Professional organisation of picture researchers and picture editors. Operates a freelance register service – details from Ruth Smith *tel* (0727) 833676. See article on page 391.

Stationers and Newspaper Makers, Worshipful Company of (1557), Stationers' Hall, London EC4M 7DD *tel* 071-248 2934. *Master:* R.K. Haselden; *clerk:* Captain P. Hames RN. One of the Livery Companies of the City of London. Connected with the printing, publishing, bookselling, newspaper and allied trades.

Strip Illustration, Society for—now **Comics Creators Guild.**

Sussex Playwrights' Club (1935). Members' plays are read by local actors before an audience of Club members. The Club from time to time sponsors productions of members' plays by local drama companies. Non-writing members welcome. Details: Hon. Secretary, Sussex Playwrights' Club, 2 Princes Avenue, Hove, East Sussex BN3 4GD.

Swedish Publishers Association (Svenska Bokförläggareföreningen) (1843), Drottninggaten 97, 2 tr., 113 60 Stockholm, Sweden *tel* 08-736 19 40 *fax* 08-736 19 44. *Secretary:* Kenth Muldin. Represents the Swedish book publishing industry and looks after the joint interests of its members; negotiates and has current contacts with ministries, public authorities, institutions and organisations; gives a wide range of service and information to members and to the general public.

Television Society, Royal (1927), Holborn Hall, 100 Gray's Inn Road, London WC1X 8AL *tel* 071-430 1000 *fax* 071-430 0924. *Membership services manager:* Deborah Halls; *publications manager:* Louise Bishop. The Society is a unique, central, independent forum to debate the art, science and politics of television. Holds awards, conferences, dinners, lectures and workshops. *Annual membership:* £47.

Theatre Exchange, International. *Secretariat:* 19 Abbey Park Road, Grimsby DN32 0HJ *tel* (0472) 343424. To encourage, foster and promote exchanges of theatre; student, educational, adult, puppet theatre activities at international level. To organise international seminars, workshops, courses and conferences, and to collect and collate information of all types for national and international dissemination.

Theatre Research, The Society for. *Hon. secretaries:* Mrs Eileen Cottis and Miss Frances Dann, c/o The Theatre Museum, 1E Tavistock Street, London WC2E 7PA. Publishes annual volumes and journal, *Theatre Notebook*, holds lectures, runs enquiry service and makes research grants annually.

Theatre Writers' Union, Actors Centre, 4 Chenies Street, London WC1E 7EP or telephone the Administrator on 081-883 7520. Formed in the mid 1970s. Specialises in the concerns of all who write for live performance, also radio and TV drama. Responsible, with the Writers' Guild of Great Britain, for the very first standard agreements on minimum pay and conditions for playwrights in British theatre. Actively seeks a membership which reflects the rich cultural diversity of playwriting today. Has national branch network. Membership open to every playwright who has written a play, whether performed or not performed. Members receive legal and professional advice, copies of standard contracts and regular newsletters. *Annual subscription* is related to income from writing; discount for members of other writers' organisations.

The Edward Thomas Fellowship (1980), Butler's Cottage, Halswell House, Goathurst, Nr Bridgwater, Somerset TA5 2DH *tel* (0278) 662856. *Hon. secretary:* Richard N. Emeny. To perpetuate the memory of Edward Thomas, poet and nature writer, foster an interest in his life and work, to assist in the preservation of places associated with him and to arrange events which extend fellowship amongst his admirers. *Annual subscription:* £5.00. Affiliated to the Alliance of Literary Societies.

The Francis Thompson Society, now incorporated in **The Eighteen Nineties Society.**

The Tolkien Society (1969). *Secretary:* Annie Haward, Flat 6, 8 Staverton Road, Oxford, Oxon OX2 6XJ; *membership secretary:* Alan Reynolds, 40 Hunters Hill, High Wycombe, Bucks. HP13 7EW. Dedicated to promoting research into and educating the public in the life and works of Professor J.R.R. Tolkien. *Subscription:* UK £15; overseas rates on application. Affiliated to the Alliance of Literary Societies.

Translation & Interpreting, The Institute of, 377 City Road, London EC1V 1NA *tel* 071-713 7600 *fax* 071-713 7650. All correspondence to be addressed to the *Secretary*. Professional association for translators and interpreters which restricts its qualified entry to those who have either passed translation or interpreting examinations in technical, scientific, commercial or social science fields, or can provide evidence of a similar degree of competence and experience gained by other specified means. Subscriber membership (non-qualified) and student membership are also possible. Details of members capable of handling particular language and subject combinations are available from the Institute office.

Translations Centre, International (1961), Schuttersveld 2, 2611 WE Delft, Netherlands *tel* (015) 14-22-42 *fax* (015) 15-85-35. *Director:* M. Risseeuw. A non-profit-making international awareness centre facilitating access to existing translations of scientific and technical literature in Western and other languages. ITC does not translate or commission translations of documents.

The Translators Association (1958), 84 Drayton Gardens, London SW10 9SB *tel* 071-373 6642. *Secretary:* Gordon Fielden. Specialist unit within the membership of the Society of Authors, exclusively concerned with the interests and special problems of translators into English whose work is published or performed commercially in Great Britain and English-speaking countries overseas. Members are entitled to general and legal advice on all questions connected with the marketing of their work, such as rates of remuneration, contractual arrangements with publishers, editors, broadcasting organisations, etc. *Annual subscription:* £60 by direct debit, £65 by cheque – includes membership of the Society of Authors. Full particulars may be obtained from the offices of the Association.

Travel Writers, The British Guild of. *Hon. secretary:* Lucy Koserski, 7 Lady Street, Lavenham, Suffolk CO10 9RA *tel* (0787) 248114. Arranges meetings, discussions and visits for its members (who are all professional travel writers) to help them encourage the public's interest in travel.

The Trollope Society (1987), 9A North Street, London SW4 0HN *tel* 071-720 6789. *Chairman:* John Letts. Aims to produce the first ever complete edition of the novels of Anthony Trollope (24 vols now available). *Membership fee:* ordinary (one year) £15.00, life £150. Affiliated to the Alliance of Literary Societies.

The Turner Society (1975), BCM Box Turner, London WC1N 3XX. *Chairman:* Eric Shanes. To foster a wider appreciation of all facets of Turner's work; to encourage exhibitions of his paintings, drawings and engravings. Publishes: *Turner Society News. Subscriptions:* £10 p.a. (other rates on application).

Typographic Designers, Society of (1928). *President:* René Kerfante FSTD; *chair:* John Harrison FSTD, FCSD; *hon. secretary:* Marilyn Sturgeon BA. FSTD. FCSD, 21-27 Seagrave Road, London SW6 1RP *tel* 071-381 4258 *fax* 071-385 8726. Recognised as the authoritative organisation for the typographic profession in the UK. Advises and acts on matters of professional practice, provides a better understanding of the craft and the rapidly changing technology in the graphic industries by lectures, discussions and through the journal *Typographic* and the Newsletter. Typographic students are encouraged to first gain Licentiateship of the Society, by an annual assessment of submitted work to a sponsored professional brief, as this is regarded as the accepted yardstick by employers. The STD is a full member of The International Council of Graphic Design Associations, ICOGRADA, which brings professionals together for a General Assembly, Congress and exhibition of work, every three years.

Undeb Awduron Cymru (Union of Welsh Writers) (1975), Cynfelin, Lôn Talwrn, Llangefni, Ynys Môn, Gwynedd LL77 7RP *tel* (0248) 724155. Aims to provide practical and inspirational help to writers in the Welsh language. Produces a newsletter/magazine (3 p.a.); holds meetings at Aberystwyth (2 or 3 p.a.); meets annually at the National Eisteddfod. *Annual subscription:* £5.00.

Visual Communication Association, International (IVCA) (1987), Bolsover House, 5-6 Clipstone Street, London W1P 7EB *tel* 071-580 0962 *fax* 071-436 2606. *Membership secretary:* Bridget Conneely. Professional association for those who use or supply visual communication. Aims to promote the industry and provide a collective voice; provides a range of services, publications and events to help existing and potential users to make the most of what film, video and live events can offer their business. *Annual membership fee:* from £150.00.

Voice of the Listener & Viewer (1983), 101 King's Drive, Gravesend, Kent DA12 5BQ *tel* (0474) 352835. *Chairman:* Jocelyn Hay; *administrative secretary:* Ann Leek. Independent association working to ensure the maintenance of high standards in broadcasting in the UK. Membership open to all concerned about the future of public service broadcasting.

Wales, Arts Council of—see **Arts Council of Wales.**

Edgar Wallace Society (1969), 9 Hurst Rise Road, North Hinksey, Oxford OX2 9HE *tel* (0865) 863655. *Organiser:* Neil Clark. To promote an interest in the life and work of Edgar Wallace through the *Crimson Circle* magazine (Q.). *Subscription:* £9.00 p.a. Affiliated to the Alliance of Literary Societies.

The Walmsley Society (1985). *Secretary:* Fred Lane, 23 Lennard Road, Dunton Green, Sevenoaks, Kent TN13 2UU; *records and archives:* Jack L.W. Hazell; *membership secretary:* Mrs Elizabeth Buckley, 21 The Crescent, Hipperholm, Halifax, West Yorkshire HX3 8NQ. Aims to promote and encourage an appreciation of the literary and artistic heritage left to us by Leo and J. Ulric Walmsley. Affiliated to the Alliance of Literary Societies.

Water Colours, Royal Institute of Painters in (1831), 17 Carlton House Terrace, London SW1Y 5BD *tel* 071-930 6844 *fax* 071-839 7830. *President:* Ronald Maddox. The Institute promotes the appreciation of watercolour painting in its traditional and contemporary forms, primarily by means of an annual exhibition at the Mall Galleries, London SW1 of members' and non-members' work and also by members' exhibitions at selected venues in Britain and abroad. Members elected from approved candidates' list.

Watercolour Society, British (1830). *Director:* Leslie Simpson, Ralston House, 41 Lister Street, Riverside Gardens, Ilkley, West Yorkshire LS29 9ET *tel* (0943) 609075. Promotes the best in traditional watercolour painting. Holds two open exhibitions p.a. *Membership:* by selection.

Watercolour Society, Royal (1804), Bankside Gallery, 48 Hopton Street, London SE1 9JH *tel* 071-928 7521. *President:* Leslie Worth. Membership (RWS) open to British and overseas artists. An election of Associates is held annually, and applications for the necessary forms and particulars should be addressed to the Secretary. Open Exhibition held in summer. Exhibitions: spring and autumn. Friends of the RWS open to all those interested in watercolour painting.

Mary Webb Society (1972). *Secretary:* Mrs F. Jones, 18 Russell Square, Madeley, Telford TF7 5BB *tel* (0952) 587640. To further an interest in the life and works of Mary Webb by meetings, lectures and excursions. Affiliated to the Alliance of Literary Societies.

The H.G. Wells Society (1960), Hon. General Secretary, English Department, Nene College, Moulton Park, Northampton NN2 7AL *tel* (0604) 735500 *fax* (0604) 720636. *Secretary:* Sylvia Hardy. Promotion of an active interest in and encouragement of an appreciation of the life, work and thought of H.G. Wells. Publishes *The Wellsian* (annually) and *The Newsletter* (bi-annually). *Subscription:* £10 p.a., corporate £15 p.a.

Welsh Books Council/Cyngor Llyfrau Cymraeg, Castell Brychan, Aberystwyth, Dyfed SY23 2JB *tel* (0970) 624151 *fax* (0970) 625385. *Director:* Gwerfyl Pierce Jones. Founded in 1961 to encourage and increase the interest of the public in Welsh literature and to support authors of popular books in the Welsh language. With the establishment of Editorial, Design, Marketing, Children's Books and Wholesale Distribution Departments, the Council promotes all aspects of book production in Wales and provides a service for Welsh-language books and English-language books of Welsh interest. Also distributes the government grant for Welsh-language publications.

Welsh Union of Writers (1982). *Secretary:* John Harrison, 13 Richmond Road, Roath, Cardiff CF2 3AQ *tel* (0222) 490303. Independent union open to persons born or working in Wales with at least one publication in a quality outlet, fiction, non-fiction or poetry. Lobbies for writing in Wales; represents members in disputes; annual conference; occasional events and publications. *Annual subscription:* £10 plus £5 joining fee.

Welsh Writers, Union of—see Undeb Awduron Cymru.

The West Country Writers' Association. *President:* Christopher Fry FRSL, DLitt; *chair:* John Paxton; *hon. secretary:* Anne Double, Malvern View, Garway Hill, Orcop, Hereford HR2 8EZ *tel* (0981) 580495. Founded in 1951 by Waveney Girvan for the purpose of fostering the love of literature in the West Country and to give authors an opportunity of meeting to exchange news and views. An Annual Weekend Congress is held in a West Country town and there are Regional Meetings. Newsletter (2 p.a.). Membership is open to published authors. *Annual subscription:* £10.

West of England Academy, Royal (1844), Queens Road, Clifton, Bristol BS8 1PX *tel* (0272) 735129 *fax* (0272) 237874. *President:* Leonard Manasseh OBE, RA, PRWA, AADipl, FRIBA, FCSD; *Academy secretary:* Jean McKinney. Aims to further the interests of practising painters and sculptors. Holds art exhibitions and is a meeting place for artists and their work.

Wildlife Artists, Society of, 17 Carlton House Terrace, London SW1Y 5BD *tel* 071-930 6844 *fax* 071-839 7830. *President:* Robert Gillmor. To promote and encourage the art of wildlife painting and sculpture. Open Annual Exhibition.

Charles Williams Society (1975), 26 Village Road, Finchley, London N3 1TL *Secretary:* Mrs Gillian Lunn. To promote interest in Charles Williams' life and work and to make his writings more easily available. Affiliated to the Alliance of Literary Societies.

The Henry Williamson Society (1980). *Secretary:* Will Harris. All correspondence to *membership secretary:* Mrs Margaret Murphy, 16 Doran Drive, Redhill, Surrey RH1 6AX *tel* (0737) 763228. Aims to encourage a wider readership and greater understanding of the literary heritage left by Henry Williamson. Two meetings annually; also weekend activities. Publishes journal 2 p.a. *Annual subscription:* £8.00; family, student and overseas rates available.

Women Artists, Society of (1855), Westminster Gallery, Westminster Central Hall, Storey's Gate, London SW1H 9NU. *President:* Barbara Tate. Annual Exhibition of painting, sculpture, etc. Open to all women.

Women in Publishing (1977), c/o J. Whitaker, 12 Dyott Street, London WC1A 1DF. Promotes the status of women within publishing; encourages networking and mutual support among women; provides a forum for the discussion of ideas, trends and subjects to women in the trade; offers practical training for career and personal development; supports and publicises women's achievements and successes. *Subscription:* £15.00 p.a.

Women Writers and Journalists, Society of (1894). *Secretary:* Jean Hawkes, 110 Whitehall Road, Chingford, London E4 6DW   *tel* 081-529 0886. For women writers: lectures, monthly lunch-time meetings; free literary advice for members. *The Woman Journalist* (3 p.a.) *Subscription:* town £21.00; country £18.00; overseas £12.00; joining fee £10.

Women Writers Network (1985), c/o Susan Kerr (information), 55 Burlington Lane, London W4 3ET   *tel* 081-994 0598; *membership secretary:* Cathy Smith, 23 Prospect Road, London NW2 2JU   *tel* 071-794 5861. London-based network serving both salaried and independent women writers from all disciplines, and providing a forum for the exchange of information, support and networking opportunities. Holds monthly meetings and publishes a newsletter. Enclose sae. *Annual membership:* £20.00.

Writers' Circles. The *Directory of Writers' Circles*, containing addresses of several hundred writers' circles, guilds, workshops and literary clubs, is published regularly. Copies of the latest edition (£4 post free) are available from compiler/ editor Jill Dick, Oldacre, Horderns Park Road, Chapel-en-le-Frith, Derbyshire SK12 6SY.

Writers' Guild of America, East (1954). *Executive director:* Mona Mangan, 555 West 57 Street, Suite 1230, New York, NY 10019, USA   *tel* 212-245-6180. Represents writers in screen and television for collective bargaining. It oversees member services (pension and health) as well as educational and professional activities. *Membership:* 1½% of covered earnings p.a.

Writers' Guild of America, West (1933). *Executive director:* Brian Walton, 8955 Beverly Boulevard, West Hollywood, CA 90048, USA   *tel* 310-550-1000   *fax* 310-550-8185. Union representing writers in film and broadcast industries for purposes of collective bargaining. *Membership:* initiation $2500, quarterly $25, annually 1½% of income.

The Writers' Guild of Great Britain, 430 Edgware Road, London W2 1EH   *tel* 071-723 8074   *fax* 071-706 2413. *General secretary:* Alison V. Gray. Founded in 1959 as the Screenwriters' Guild, now a trade union affiliated to the TUC, representing writers' interests in film, radio, television, theatre and publishing. Its scope extends into all areas of freelance writing and copyright protection and, where necessary, discusses at Government level policies on legislative matters affecting writers. The Guild's basic function is to negotiate minimum terms in those areas in which its members work. The Guild, by constitution non-political, employs a permanent secretariat and staff and is administered by an Executive Council of 26 members. There are also Regional Committees representing Scotland, Wales, the North and West of England. Full details of membership on request. (See also article on page 653.)

Writers' Postal Workshops and Folios. Writers' postal workshops and folios provide criticism, guidance, encouragement and support to both published and unpublished writers and enable regular contact to be made by post with others of similar interests. *The Cottage Guide to Writers' Postal Workshops* contains full details of postal workshops, folios and similar organisations and is published and updated regularly by Croftspun Publications. Price £1.50 from the compiler, Catherine M. Gill, Drakemyre Croft, Cairnorrie, Methlick, Ellon, Aberdeenshire AB41 0JN.

The Yorkshire Dialect Society (1897). *Hon. secretary:* Stanley Ellis, Farfields, Weeton, Leeds LS17 0AN. Aims to encourage interest in: (1) dialect speech; (2) the writing of dialect verse, prose and drama; (3) the publication and circulation of dialect literature and the performance of dialect plays; (4) the study of the origins and the history of dialect and kindred subjects – all dialects, not only of Yorkshire origin. Organises a number of meetings during the year – details from the Hon. Secretary; publishes annually *Transactions* and *The Summer Bulletin* free to members, list of other publications on request. *Annual subscription (1994):* £6.

Young Book Trust—see **Book Trust.**

Young Publishers, Society of (1949). The Secretary, c/o 12 Dyott Street, London WC1A 1DF *tel* 071-836 8911. Provides a lively forum for discussion on subjects relevant to its members in publishing. Membership open to anyone under 35 years of age employed in publishing, printing, bookselling or allied trades. Meetings held at the Publishers Association, on the last Wednesday of the month at 6.30 p.m. Associate membership available to those over 35.

Francis Brett Young Society (1979). *Secretary:* Mrs J. Pritchard, 52 Park Road, Hagley, Stourbridge, West Midlands DY9 0QF *tel* (0562) 882973. To provide opportunities for members to meet, correspond, and to share the enjoyment of the author's works. Journal published 2 p.a. *Annual subscription:* £5.00 (individual), life membership £45 (other rates on application). Affiliated to the Alliance of Literary Societies.

Keep a note book

Everything that comes within a writer's own experience is grist to the mill and should be stored away, ideally in note form or on tape or computer, for future use. Ideas, an unusual turn of phrase, a gesture, a conversation overheard, brief descriptions of people or places, on-the-spot reports of events, even pain suffered (you think at the time you will always remember how it felt, but you rarely do): these will be of immense value, provided that they are kept in such a way that they can be turned up quickly when required.

from *Research for Writers* by Ann Hoffmann (A & C Black, £10.99)

The Society of Authors

The Society of Authors is an independent trade union, representing writers' interests in all aspects of the writing profession, including publishing, broadcasting, TV and films, theatre and translation. Founded over a hundred years ago by Walter Besant, the Society now has more than 5500 members. It has a professional staff, responsible to a Management Committee of 12 authors and a Council (an advisory body meeting twice a year) consisting of 60 eminent writers. There are specialist groups within the Society to serve the particular needs of broadcasters, literary translators, educational writers, medical writers, children's writers and illustrators, and scientific and technical writers. There are also regional groups representing Scotland, the North of Engand and the Isle of Man.

WHAT THE SOCIETY DOES FOR MEMBERS

Through its permanent staff (including a solicitor), the Society is able to give its members a comprehensive personal and professional service covering the business aspects of authorship, including:

providing information about agents, publishers, and others concerned with the book trade, journalism, broadcasting and the performing arts;

advising on negotiations, including the individual vetting of contracts, clause by clause, and assessing their terms both financial and otherwise;

taking up complaints on behalf of members on any issue concerned with the business of authorship;

pursuing legal actions for breach of contract, copyright infringement, and the non-payment of royalties and fees, when the risk and cost preclude individual action by a member and issues of general concern to the profession are at stake;

holding weekend conferences, seminars, meetings and social occasions;

producing a comprehensive range of publications, free of charge to members, including the Society's quarterly journal, *The Author*, which has a twice yearly supplement, *The Electronic Author*. *Quick Guides* cover many aspects of the profession such as: copyright, publishing contracts, libel, income tax, VAT, authors' agents, permissions and the protection of titles. The Society also publishes a model translator/publisher agreement, *Guidelines for Academic Authors*, *Guidelines for Educational Writers*, *Guidelines for Medical Writers* and *Sell Your Writing*.

Members have access to:

- the Retirement Benefit Scheme
- Group Medical Insurance Schemes with both BUPA and the Bristol Contributory Welfare Association
- the Pension Fund (which offers discretionary pensions to a number of members)
- the Contingency Fund (which provides financial relief for authors or their dependents in sudden financial difficulties)
- automatic free membership of the Authors' Licensing and Collecting Society
- books at special rates
- membership of the Royal Over-Seas League at a discount
- use of the Society's photocopying machine at special rates.

The Society frequently secures improved conditions and better returns for members. It is common for members to report that, through the help and facilities offered, they have saved more, and sometimes substantially more, than their annual subscriptions (which are an allowable expense against income tax).

WHAT THE SOCIETY DOES FOR AUTHORS IN GENERAL

The Society lobbies Members of Parliament, Ministers and Government Departments on all issues of concern to writers. Recent issues have included the operation and funding of Public Lending Right, the threat of VAT on books, copyright legislation and European Community initiatives. Concessions have also been obtained under various Finance Acts.

The Society litigates in matters of importance to authors. For example, the Society backed Andrew Boyle when he won his appeal against the Inland Revenue's attempt to tax the Whitbread Award. It backed a number of members in proceedings against the BBC and Desmond Wilcox in connection with the publication of a book, *The Explorers*, and also in a High Court action over copyright infringement by *Coles Notes*.

The Society campaigns for better terms for writers. With the Writers' Guild, it has negotiated agreements with BBC Publications, Bloomsbury, Bodley Head, Jonathan Cape, Century, Chapmans, André Deutsch, Faber & Faber, Hamish Hamilton, HarperCollins, Hodder Headline, Hutchinson, Michael Joseph, Methuen, Penguin Books, Sinclair-Stevenson and Viking. Other publishers are now being approached, and the campaign is active. The translators' section of the Society has also drawn up a minimum terms agreement for translators which has been adopted by Faber & Faber, and has been used on an individual basis by a number of other publishers.

The Society is recognised by the BBC for the purpose of negotiating rates for writers' contributions to radio drama, talks and features, as well as for the broadcasting of published material. It was instrumental in setting up the Authors' Licensing and Collecting Society (ALCS), which collects and distributes fees from reprography and other methods whereby copyright material is exploited without direct payment to the originators.

The Society keeps in close touch with the Arts Council of Great Britain, the Association of Authors' Agents, the British Council, the Broadcasting Entertainment Cinematograph and Theatre Union, the Institute of Translation and Interpreting, the Secretary of State for National Heritage, the National Union of Journalists, the Publishers Association and the Writers' Guild of Great Britain.

The Society is a member of the European Writers Congress, the British Copyright Council, the National Book Committee and the International Confederation of Societies of Authors and Composers (CISAC).

AWARDS ADMINISTERED BY THE SOCIETY

- two travel awards: the Somerset Maugham Awards and the Travelling Scholarships
- four prizes for novels: the Betty Trask Awards, the Encore Award, the McKitterick Prize and the Sagittarius Prize
- two poetry awards: the Eric Gregory Awards and the Cholmondeley Awards
- the Tom-Gallon Award for short story writers
- the Crompton Bequest for aiding financially the publication of selected original work
- the Authors' Foundation and Kathleen Blundell Trust, which are endowed with wide powers to support work in progress
- the Margaret Rhondda Award for women journalists

- the Scott Moncrieff Prize for translations from French
- the Schlegel-Tieck Prize for translations from German books published in Germany
- the Bernard Shaw Prize for translations from Swedish
- the Portuguese Prize for translations from Portuguese
- the John Florio Prize for translations from Italian
- the Francis Head Bequest for assisting authors who, through physical mishap, are temporarily unable to maintain themselves or their families.

HOW TO JOIN

There are two categories of membership (admission to each being at the discretion of the Committee of Management):

Full Membership – those authors who have had a full-length work published, broadcast or performed commercially in the UK or have an established reputation in another medium.

Associate Membership – those authors who have had a full-length work accepted for publication, but not yet published; and those authors who have had occasional items broadcast or performed, or translations, articles, illustrations or short stories published.

Associate members pay the same annual subscription and are entitled to the same benefits as full members. The owner or administrator of a deceased author's copyrights can become a member on behalf of the author's estate.

The annual subscription (which is tax deductible under Schedule D) for full or associate membership of the Society is £65 (£60 by direct debit after the first year), and there are special joint membership terms for husband and wife. Authors under 35, who are not yet earning a significant income from their writing, may apply for membership at a lower subscription of £47. Authors over 65 may apply to pay at the reduced rate after their first year of membership.

Further information from The Society of Authors, 84 Drayton Gardens, London SW10 9SB *tel* 071-373 6642.

IN CONCLUSION

'When we begin working, we are so poor and so busy that we have neither the time nor the means to defend ourselves against the commercial organisations which exploit us. When we become famous, we become famous suddenly, passing at one bound from the state in which we are, as I have said, too poor to fight our own battles, to a state in which our time is so valuable that it is not worth our while wasting any of it on lawsuits and bad debts. We all, eminent and obscure alike, need the Authors' Society. We all owe it a share of our time, our means, our influence' *Bernard Shaw*

The Writers' Guild of Great Britain

The Writers' Guild of Great Britain is the writers' trade union, affiliated to the TUC, and representing writers' interests in film, radio, television, theatre and publishing. Formed in 1959 as the Screenwriters' Guild, the union gradually extended into all areas of freelance writing activity and copyright protection. In 1974 when book authors and stage dramatists became eligible for membership substantial numbers joined, and their interests are represented on the Executive Council. Apart from necessary dealings with Government and policies on legis- lative matters affecting writers, the Guild is, by constitution, non-political, has no involvement with any political party, and pays no political levy. The Guild employs a permanent secretariat and staff and is administered by an Executive Council of 26 members. There are also Regional Committees representing Scotland, Wales, the North and West of England.

The Guild comprises practising professional writers in all media, united in common concern for one another and regulating the conditions under which they work.

WHAT IT DOES

The Guild's basic function is to negotiate minimum terms in those areas in which its members work. Those agreements form the basis of the individual contracts signed by members. Further details are given below. It should also be noted that the Guild gives individual advice to its members on contracts and many of those matters which the writer encounters in his or her professional life.

Television

The Guild has national agreements with the BBC and the commercial companies regulating minimum fees and going rates, copyright licence, credit terms and conditions for television plays, series and serials, dramatisations and adaptations. One of the most important achievements in recent years has been the estab- lishment of pension rights for Guild members only. The BBC pay an additional 7.5% of the going rate on the understanding that the Guild member pays 5% of his or her fee. ITV companies now pay an additional 8% and the writer 5%. The Guild Pension Fund amounts to well over £3 million at present.

In 1985, a comprehensive agreement was negotiated with the BBC to cover cable sales. In addition, a special agreement was negotiated to cover the very successful serial *EastEnders*. In 1991, the first ever Light Entertainment Agree- ment was signed with the BBC. Most children's and educational drama has been similarly protected within the above industrial agreements. Rates of payment are updated from time to time.

Film

On 11 March 1985, an important agreement was signed with the two producer organisations: The British Film and Television Producers' Association and The Independent Programme Producers Association (now known as PACT, the Producers' Alliance for Cinema and Television). For the first time, there exists an industrial agreement which covers both independent television productions and independent film productions. Pension fund contributions have been nego- tiated for Guild members in the same way as for the BBC and ITV. The Agreement was comprehensively renegotiated and concluded in February 1992.

The areas of participation have been improved and the money paid upfront is considerably more than it was in the past.

Radio

The Guild has fought for and obtained a standard agreement with the BBC, establishing a fee structure which is annually reviewed. The current agreement includes a Code of Practice which is important for establishing good working conditions for the writer working for the BBC. In December 1985 the BBC agreed to extend the pension scheme already established for television writers to include radio writers. It was also agreed that all radio writers would be entitled to at least one attendance payment as of right. Again this brings the radio agreements more into line with the television agreements. In 1991 a comprehensive revision of the Agreement was undertaken and has been concluded.

In 1990/91 small independent radio companies came into being producing drama for the networks. Agreements have been concluded with the Guild and the Society of Authors to cover these new ventures. Both unions will be watching the development in the independent radio field with interest. In the past there has been little opportunity for dramatic writing in the independent sector. At the time of writing the Guild has been approached by the Independent Association of Radio Producers to negotiate an agreement with that organisation.

Books

The Guild fought long, hard and successfully for the loans-based Public Lending Right to reimburse authors for books lent in libraries. This is now law and the Guild is constantly in touch with the Registrar of the scheme which is administered from offices in Stockton-on-Tees.

The Guild, together with its sister union the Society of Authors, has drawn up a draft Minimum Terms Book Agreement which has been widely circulated amongst publishers. In 1984, the unions achieved a significant breakthrough by signing agreements with two major publishers; negotiations were also opened with other publishers. The publishing agreements will, it is hoped, improve the relationship between writers and publishers and help to clarify what writers might reasonably expect from the exploitation of copyright in their works.

Agreements have now been signed with BBC Publications, Bloomsbury, Bodley Head, Jonathan Cape, Century, Chapmans, André Deutsch, Faber & Faber, Hamish Hamilton, HarperCollins, Hodder Headline, Hutchinson, Michael Joseph, Methuen, Penguin Books, Sinclair-Stevenson and Viking. Negotiations are currently taking place with other leading publishers.

Theatre

In 1979, the Guild with its fellow union, the Theatre Writers' Union, negotiated the first ever industrial agreement for theatre writers. The Theatre National Committee Agreement covers the Royal Shakespeare Company, the Royal National Theatre Company and the English Stage Company. A new Agreement was concluded in April 1993.

On 2 June 1986, a new Agreement was signed with the Theatrical Management Association, covering some 95 provincial theatres. In 1991, negotiations opened for a comprehensive review of that agreement. The Agreement has now been concluded.

In 1991, after many years of negotiation, an Agreement was concluded between the Guild and Theatre Writers' Union, and the Independent Theatre Council, which represents some 200 of the smaller and fringe theatres as well as educational, touring companies. The Agreement breaks new ground.

Only the West End is not covered by a union agreement.

Copies of all the above agreements are available to members and non-members. There is a small charge to non-members.

Miscellaneous

The Guild is in constant touch with Government and national institutions wherever and whenever the interests of writers are in question or are being discussed. The Guild has been holding cross party Parliamentary lobbies since 1989 with its fellow arts unions, Equity and the Musicians Union. Further lobbies have been held in January 1991, February 1992, June 1993 and February 1994. The Guild and its fellow unions believe that it is important to keep in constant touch with all parties to ensure that the various art forms they represent are properly cared for.

Censorship is a matter for constant vigilance as far as the Guild is concerned. In the past the Guild has lobbied Parliament where attempts have been made to impose fairly draconian censorship Bills. There have been some successes in that area. Freedom of expression, of course, is vital as far as the Writers' Guild is concerned.

Proposals for changes in the law on copyright were published in a draft Bill in August 1986. The Guild along with other organisations made important submissions on behalf of the Guild and writers in general. The new Act came into effect in 1989. Moral rights have been granted to writers for the first time.

Working with the Federation of Entertainment Unions, the Guild makes its views known to Government bodies on a broader basis. It is constantly in touch with the Arts Council of England, the Independent Television Commission and other national bodies.

Perhaps one of the closest working relationships the Guild has established is with its fellow arts unions, Equity and the Musicians Union. The three unions have agreed to work much more closely together where they share a common interest. Representatives of the three governing bodies meet on a quarterly basis.

Regular Craft Meetings are held by all the Guild's specialist committees. This gives Guild members the opportunity of meeting those who control, work within, or affect the sphere of writing within which they work.

Internationally, the Guild plays a leading role in the International Affiliation of Writers' Guilds, which includes the American Guilds East and West, the Canadian Guilds (French and English) and the Australian and New Zealand Guilds. When it is possible to make common cause, then the Guilds act accordingly.

The Guild takes a leading role in the European Writers' Congress. It has been represented at every Congress since 1981. That body is becoming increasingly important and successful. An initiative from the Writers' Guild of Great Britain saw the setting up of a Copyright Committee to protect writers' interests within the EU in particular and throughout Europe in general. With the harmonisation of Copyright Law, an opportunity has been seized to make representation directly to Brussels which could lead to an improvement for British writers.

The Guild in its day-to-day work takes up problems on behalf of individual members, gives advice on contracts, and helps with any problems which affect the lives of its members as professional writers.

The Guild publishes two kinds of newsletters for its members. The first, published about six times a year, is the 'From the Office' newsletter which gives general advice and information about opportunities for Guild members. The second, which is the official newsletter of the Guild, is published four times a year. This carries articles, letters and reports written by members.

MEMBERSHIP

Membership is by a points system. One major piece of work (a full-length book, an hour-long television or radio play, a feature film, etc.) entitles the author to Full Membership; lesser work helps to accumulate enough points for Full Membership, while Temporary Membership may be enjoyed in the meantime. Importantly, previously unpublished, broadcast or performed writers can apply for membership when they receive their first contracts. The Guild's advice before signature can often be vital. Affiliate Membership is enjoyed by agents and publishers.

The minimum subscription is £60 plus 1% of that part of an author's income earned from professional writing sources in the previous calendar year.

IN CONCLUSION

The writer is an isolated individual in a world in which individual voices are not always heard. The Guild brings together those individual writers in order to make common cause of those many vitally important matters which are susceptible to influence only from the position of collective strength which the Guild enjoys. The writer properly cherishes his or her individuality; it will not be lost within a union run by other writers.

The Writers' Guild of Great Britain, 430 Edgware Road, London W2 1EH *tel* 071-723 8074.

Prizes and Awards

The following list provides details of many British prizes, competitions and awards, including grants, bursaries and fellowships, as well as details of major international prizes. In the UK, details of awards for novels, short stories and works of non-fiction, as they are offered, will be found in such journals as *The Author*. Book Trust publish a useful *Guide to Literary Prizes, Grants and Awards* (details available from Book Trust, Book House, 45 East Hill, Wandsworth, London SW18 2QZ   *tel* 081-870 9055).

J.R. Ackerley Prize for Autobiography
This £2000 prize, first awarded in 1982, is given annually for an outstanding work of literary autobiography written in English and published during the previous year by an author of British nationality or an author who has been a long-term resident in the UK. Books are nominated by the judges. Information from P.E.N., 7 Dilke Street, Chelsea, London SW3 4JE   *tel* 071-352 6303   *fax* 071-351 0220.

Acorn Award
Founded in 1989, this is an annual award of £250 to an author/illustrator who has published a book for younger children, fiction or poetry, in the preceding year. No application necessary; details from Nottinghamshire County Library Service, Glaisdale Parkway, Nottingham NG8 4GP   *tel* (0602) 854203 or Dillons The Bookstore, 25 Wheelergate, Nottingham NG1 2NF   *tel* (0602) 473531.

Air Canada Award
Award, two tickets to any destination served by the airline, given annually to a Canadian writer, in any genre, who is younger than 30 and shows promise. Nominations by governing executive of any CAA Branch or other writers' organisation. Administered by the Canadian Authors Association. Further details from the CAA, 275 Slater Street, Suite 500, Ottawa, Ontario K1P 5H9, Canada   *tel* 613-233-2846.

The Alexander Prize
Candidates for the Alexander Prize, who must either be under the age of 35 or be registered for a higher degree now or within the last three years, may choose their own subject for an Essay, but they must submit their choice for approval to the Literary Director, Royal Historical Society, University College London, Gower Street, London WC1E 6BT   *tel/fax* 071-387 7532.

The Hans Christian Andersen Medals
The Hans Christian Andersen Medals are awarded every two years to an author and an illustrator who by the outstanding value of their work are judged to have made a lasting contribution to literature for children and young people. Details from International Board on Books for Young People, Nonnenweg 12, Postfach, CH-4003 Basel, Switzerland   *tel* 272 29 17   *fax* 272 27 57.

Aristeion Prizes
European Literary Prize
Founded in 1990, this annual award of 20,000 ecus is awarded for a single work, which may belong to any literary genre.

European Translation Prize
Founded in 1990, this annual award of 20,000 ecus is awarded to a translator for an outstanding translation of a significant work of contemporary European literature; the work may belong to any literary genre.

Candidates must be nationals of a member state of the European Community; nationals of European countries which are not members of the Community, but signatories of the European Cultural Convention, are also eligible. Applications are not sought in these awards. Nominations are made by an appointed authority from each member state and the winning titles are selected by a specially appointed jury of experts. Further details may be obtained from Mrs Patricia Canellis, DGX, C1 Cultural Action, 120 rue de Trèves, 1040 Brussels, Belgium   *tel* (32) 2-299 94 10   *fax* (32) 2-299 92 83.

Rosemary Arthur Award

Founded in 1989, this is an annual award for a first book of poetry. The prize consists of the full cost of publishing the winner's book, £100 and an engraved clock. Full details from the National Poetry Foundation, 27 Mill Road, Fareham, Hants PO16 0TH   *tel* (0329) 822218.

The Arts Council/An Chomhairle Ealaíon, Ireland

Bursaries for Creative Writers
In 1993 awards totalling IR£50,000 were offered to creative writers of poetry, fiction and drama to enable them to concentrate on or complete writing projects. At least the same amount will be distributed in 1994.

Denis Devlin Memorial Award for Poetry
This award, value IR£1500, is made triennially for the best book of poetry in the English language by an Irish citizen published in the preceding three years. The next award will be made in 1994.

Macaulay Fellowship
Fellowships, value IR£4000, are awarded once every three years to writers under 30 years of age (or in exceptional circumstances under 35 years) in order to help them to further their liberal education and careers. The cycle of awards is: Visual Arts (1994), Music (1995), Literature (1996).

The Marten Toonder Award
This award is given to an artist of recognised and established achievement on a rotating cycle as follows: Music (1994), Literature (1995), Visual Arts (1996). Candidates must be Irish-born (Northern Ireland is included). Value IR£3500.

Prize for Poetry in Irish
This is Ireland's major award to Irish-language poetry; it is given triennially for the best book of Irish-language poetry published in the preceding three years. The next award will be made in 1996. Value IR£1500.

Travel Grants
Creative artists (including writers) may apply at any time of the year for assistance with travel grants to attend seminars, conferences, workshops, etc. Applications are assessed four times each year.

Please note that these literary awards are available only to Irish citizens, or to those who have been resident in Ireland for the previous five years. Further details may be obtained from The Arts Council (An Chomhairle Ealaíon), 70 Merrion Square, Dublin 2, Republic of Ireland   *tel* (01) 6611840   *fax* (01) 6761302.

Arts Council of England

Writers' Awards
The Arts Council gives annual bursaries to writers whose work is of outstanding quality. In 1994-95 there will be fifteen such awards. They will be offered only to already published authors who are writing works of poetry, fiction, autobiography or biography. The value of each bursary is £7000. The closing

date for applications is 30 September each year. Details are available from July onwards from the Literature Department, Arts Council of England, 14 Great Peter Street, London SW1P 3NQ *tel* 071-333 0100.

Translation Fund
The Arts Council has created a fund to support the publication of translated work. This is enhanced by a supplementation from the British Council. Any text suggested for support should already have secured a publisher by whom nominations should be made. Grants may be given for specimen chapters of a work in progress. The budget for 1994-95 stands at just over £100,000 and there are two deadline dates each year. Further information may be obtained from Jilly Paver, Assistant Literature Officer, Arts Council of England, 14 Great Peter Street, London SW1P 3NQ *tel* 071-333 0100.

The Arts Council of Wales Awards to Writers
Book of the Year Award
£3000 prize awarded to winners, in Welsh and English, and £1000 to four other short-listed authors for works of exceptional merit by Welsh authors (by birth or residence) published during the previous calendar year in the categories of poetry, fiction and creative non-fiction.

Bursaries and competitions
Bursaries totalling about £73,000 are awarded annually to authors writing in both Welsh and English. The Council also organises competitions from time to time.

For further details of the Arts Council of Wales' policies, write to the Literature Department, The Arts Council of Wales, Museum Place, Cardiff CF1 3NX *tel* (0222) 394711 *fax* (0222) 221447.

Arvon Foundation International Poetry Competition
This competition, founded in 1980, is awarded biennially for previously unpublished poems written in English. First prize £5000, plus at least £5000 in other cash prizes. Full details from Arvon Foundation Poetry Competition, Kilnhurst, Kilnhurst Road, Todmorden, Lancs. OL14 6AX *tel* (0706) 816582 *fax* (0706) 816359.

Author of the Year Award
Founded in 1993, £1000 is awarded annually, by vote of the members of the Booksellers Association, to the British or Irish author considered to have had the most impact during the previous year. Nomination takes place during November/December; forms available from Meryl Halls or Susannah Dann, Booksellers Association, 272 Vauxhall Bridge Road, London SW1V 1BA *tel* 071-834 5477.

Authors' Club Best First Novel Award
The award was instituted in 1954 by Lawrence Meynell and is made to the author of the most promising first novel published in the UK during each year. The award of £750 is presented to the winner at a dinner held in the Club at 40 Dover Street, London W1X 3RB. Entries for the award (one from each publisher) are accepted during October and November and must be full-length novels – short stories are not eligible.

Authors' Club Sir Banister Fletcher Award
The late Sir Banister Fletcher, who was President of the Authors' Club for many years, left the Authors' Club a sum of money to be held upon trust: 'to apply the income thereof in or towards the provision of an annual prize for the book on architecture or the arts most deserving.' The Committee of the Club present a prize of £750 at a dinner held in the Club. Details from the Authors' Club, 40 Dover Street, London W1X 3RB.

Authors' Club Marsh Christian Trust
Introduced for the years 1985-86, this major national biography prize of £3000 plus a trophy is presented every two years. Entries must be serious biographies written by British authors and published in the UK. Details from the Authors' Club, 40 Dover Street, London W1X 3RB.

The Authors' Foundation
The Foundation, which was founded in 1984 to mark the centenary of the Society of Authors, provides grants to published authors working on their next book. The aim is to provide funding (in addition to a proper advance) for research, travel or other necessary expenditure. Grants are available to novelists, poets and writers of non-fiction.

The closing date for applications is 30 April. An information sheet is available from the Society of Authors (84 Drayton Gardens, London SW10 9SB).

The Foundation hopes to provide grants totalling at least £70,000 in 1995, helped by support from the Arts Council, Mrs Isobel Dalziel and the Esmée Fairbairn Charitable Trust.

Verity Bargate Award
Created as a memorial to the founder of the Soho Theatre Company, each year this award is made to the writer of a new and previously unperformed full length play. In addition to the cash prize, the winning play has normally gone on to a full production by the Soho Theatre Company. Accordingly, the chosen playwright is required to offer first option to produce the winning play to the Soho Theatre Company. It is also intended that emerging writers of interest – such as those whose plays are shortlisted – will also be provided with workshop facilities to assist in their further development.

Each submitted play should have a title page stating the author's name and address alongside the name of the play, and be accompanied by two saes, one for an acknowledgement letter and the other for the return of the script. Details of the closing date for this award are available on submission of an sae in the New Year to Verity Bargate Award, c/o The Soho Theatre Company, The Cockpit Theatre, Gateforth Street, London NW8 8EH.

H.E. Bates Short Story Competition
This annual prize is awarded for a short story – maximum length 2000 words – to anyone resident in Great Britain. The first prize is for £100, other prizes to a total value of £150. Further details from the Events Team Office, Directorate of Environment Services, Cliftonville House, Bedford Road, Northampton NN4 7NR   *tel* (0604) 233500 ext 4243.

BBC Wildlife Magazine Award for Nature Writing
BBC Wildlife Magazine awards prizes annually with the aim of reviving the art of nature writing, discovering and encouraging new essayists and focusing attention on those writers whose skills might otherwise be neglected. Entries may be from professional or amateur writers and there are prizes of £1000, £400 for the runner up and £200 and £100 for writers aged 17 and under. For further information see the July issue of *BBC Wildlife Magazine*, or send an sae to: BBC Wildlife Magazine, Broadcasting House, Whiteladies Road, Bristol BS8 2LR.

The Samuel Beckett Award
Founded in 1983, this award is open to residents of the UK and the Republic of Ireland for new dramatic writing, professionally performed. The provisions of the award are currently under review. Further information from: Editorial Department, Faber and Faber, 3 Queen Square, London WC1N 3AU.

The David Berry Prize
Candidates for the David Berry Prize may select any subject dealing with

Scottish history within the reigns of James I to James VI inclusive, provided such subject has been previously submitted to and approved by the Council of the Royal Historical Society, University College London, Gower Street, London WC1E 6BT tel/fax 071-387 7532. Next closing date: 31 October 1997. Value of prize: £250.

The James Tait Black Memorial Prizes

Founded in memory of a partner in the publishing house of A. & C. Black, these prizes were instituted in 1918 and since 1979 have been supplemented by the Scottish Arts Council. Two prizes, of £1500 each, are awarded annually: one for the best biography or work of that nature, the other for the best novel, published during the calendar year. The adjudicator is the Professor of English Literature in the University of Edinburgh.

By the terms of the bequest, and by tradition, eligible novels and biographies are those written in English, originating with a British publisher, and first published in Britain in the year of the award; but technical publication elsewhere, simultaneously or even a little earlier, does not disqualify. Both prizes may go to the same author; but neither to the same author a second time.

Publishers are invited to submit a copy of any biography, or work of fiction, that in their judgement may merit consideration for the award. Copies, marked 'James Tait Black Prize', should be sent to the Department of English Literature, David Hume Tower, George Square, Edinburgh EH8 9JX tel 031-650 3619 fax 031-650 6898. They should be submitted as early as possible, with a note of the exact date of publication. Co-operation on this point is essential to the work of the adjudicator.

The Kathleen Blundell Trust

The Trust provides awards to published writers under the age of 40 to assist them with their next book. Applications should be in the form of a letter sent to the Kathleen Blundell Trust at the Society of Authors (84 Drayton Gardens, London SW10 9SB), giving reasons for the application. The application must be accompanied by a copy of the author's latest book and the author's work must 'contribute to the greater understanding of existing social and economic organisation'. The closing date for applications is 30 April. An information sheet is available from the Society of Authors.

The Boardman Tasker Prize

This annual prize of £2000, founded in 1983, is given for a work of fiction, non-fiction or poetry, the central theme of which is concerned with the mountain environment. Authors of any nationality are eligible but the work must be published or distributed in the UK. Entries from publishers only. Further details from Mrs Dorothy Boardman, 14 Pine Lodge, Dairyground Road, Bramhall, Stockport, Cheshire SK7 2HS.

Book of the Year

Founded in 1990, an annual award (1st IR£1500 + 3 at IR£500) to a writer or illustrator of children's books, born or currently living in Ireland. Details from: Irish Children's Book Trust, Irish Writers' Centre, 19 Parnell Square, Dublin 1, Republic of Ireland tel (01) 8721302 fax (01) 8726282.

The Booker Prize

This annual prize for fiction of £20,000 is sponsored by Booker plc, and administered by Book Trust. The prize is awarded to the best novel published each year. The Prize is open to novels written in English by citizens of the British Commonwealth, Republic of Ireland and South Africa and published for the first time in the UK by a British publisher. Entries are to be submitted only by UK publishers who may each submit not more than three novels with scheduled publication dates between 1 October of the previous year and 30 September of the current year, but the judges may also ask for other eligible novels to be submitted to them. In addition, publishers may submit eligible titles by authors who have been shortlisted or won the Booker Prize previously. Entry forms and further information are available from Book Trust, Book House, 45 East Hill, London SW18 2QZ *tel* 081-870 9055.

The Bridport Prize

Founded in 1980 (as the Bridport Arts Centre Creative Writing Competition), annual prizes are awarded for poetry and short stories – 1st £1000, 2nd £500, 3rd £250 in both categories. Entries should be in English, original work, typed or clearly written, and never published, read on radio/television/stage or entered for any other current competition. Closing date: 30 June each year. Winning stories are read by leading London literary agent, without obligation. Details from the Competition Secretary, Arts Centre, South Street, Bridport, Dorset DT6 3NR *tel* (0308) 427183.

Katharine Briggs Folklore Award

An award of £50 and an engraved goblet is given annually for a book in English, having its first, original and initial publication in the UK, which has made the most distinguished contribution to folklore studies. The term folklore studies is interpreted broadly to include all aspects of traditional and popular culture, narrative, belief, customs and folk arts. Details from the Convenor, The Folklore Society, University College London, Gower Street, London WC1E 6BT *tel* 071-387 5894.

The British Academy Research Awards

These are made annually (in the case of Learned Societies or group research applications) and quarterly (in the case of individual applications) to scholars conducting advanced academic research in the humanities and normally resident in the UK. The main headings under which an application would be eligible are: (a) travel and maintenance expenses in connection with an approved programme of research; (b) archaeology fieldwork; (c) costs of preparation of research for publication; (d) in special cases, aid to the publication of research. Details and application forms from The British Academy, 20-21 Cornwall Terrace, London NW1 4QP *tel* 071-487 5966.

British Book Awards

These awards, founded in 1989, are presented annually. Major categories include Author of the Year, Publisher of the Year, Bookseller of the Year, Children's Author and Illustrator of the Year and Book of the Year. Further information from Merric Davidson, British Book Awards, Publishing News, 43 Museum Street, London WC1A 1LY *tel* 071-404 0304 *fax* 071-242 0762.

British Fantasy Awards

Founded in 1972, the members of the British Fantasy Society vote annually for the best novel, short fiction, artist, small press and anthology of the preceding year. A further award, the Committee Award, is decided separately. The awards take the form of a statuette. Closing date for nominations: end August each year. Details from Robert Parkinson, Secretary, The British Fantasy Society, 2 Harwood Street, Stockport SK4 1JJ.

The British Film Institute Michael Powell Book Award

The Award highlights the importance of film and television literature and is presented for books published in the UK dealing with film and television by a UK author. Details from Wayne Drew, Head of Press and Promotions, British Film Institute, 21 Stephen Street, London W1P 1PL *tel* 071-255 1444.

Canadian Authors Association Literary Awards
The awards consist of a silver medal and $5000 and apply in (a) fiction, (b) non-fiction, (c) poetry, (d) drama (for any medium). These annual awards are to honour writing that achieves literary excellence without sacrificing popular appeal and are given to works by Canadian authors (citizens or landed immigrants). Further details from the Canadian Authors Association, 275 Slater Street, Suite 500, Ottawa, Ontario K1P 5H9, Canada   *tel* 613-233-2846   *fax* 613-235-8237.

Children's Book Award
Founded in 1980 by the Federation of Children's Book Groups, this award is given annually to authors of works of fiction for children published in the UK. Children participate in the judging of the award. 'Pick of the Year' booklist is published in conjunction with the award. Details from Jenny Blanch, 30 Senneleys Park Road, Northfield, Birmingham B31 1AL   *tel* 021-427 4860   *fax* 021-643 3152.

Cholmondeley Awards
In 1965, the then Dowager Marchioness of Cholmondeley established these non-competitive awards, for which submissions are not required, for the benefit and encouragement of poets of any age, sex or nationality. Total value of awards about £8000. The scheme is administered by the Society of Authors.

Arthur C. Clarke Award
Founded in 1985, an annual award of £1000 (+ engraved bookend) is given for the best science fiction novel with first UK publication during the previous calendar year. Titles are submitted by publishers. Details from The Administrator, David V. Barrett, 23 Oakfield Road, Croydon, Surrey CR0 2UD   *tel/ fax* 081-688 6081.

The David Cohen British Literature Prize
This prize of £30,000, launched in 1992 by the Arts Council of Great Britain (now the Arts Council of England) in association with Coutts & Co. and currently the largest in the UK, will be awarded every two years from spring 1993 to a living writer, novelist, short story writer, poet, essayist or dramatist in recognition of a lifetime's achievement. Work must be written primarily in English and the writer must be a British citizen. In addition, the Arts Council will make available an extra £10,000 to enable the winner to encourage reading or writing among younger people. No application is needed, since the choice of the winner is made by a distinguished jury on the basis of its collective reading, but further information may be obtained from The Literature Department, Arts Council of England, 14 Great Peter Street, London SW1P 3NQ   *tel* 071-333 0100.

Collins Biennial Religious Book Award
This £5000 prize was founded in 1969 to commemorate the 150th anniversary of the founding of Wm. Collins Sons & Co. Ltd. It is given biennially. The text can be in any style of writing, about Christianity or another religion, but by a professing Christian. Two categories of prize are awarded, of £2500 each: an academic work, and a spirituality/devotional work. The author can be of any nationality and resident in any part of the world, but the title must have been published in English by a British publisher since the date of the last award. Books 'bought in' are not accepted but translations and co-editions are eligible provided the English edition is published in Britain by a British publisher; a British publisher wholly or partly owned by an overseas organisation is eligible to participate. Details from Lesley Walmsley, HarperCollins Publishers, 77-85 Fulham Palace Road, London W6 8JB   *tel* 081-741 7070.

Commonwealth Writers Prize

Funded by the Commonwealth Foundation, this annual award is for the best work of fiction in English by a citizen of the Commonwealth published in the year prior to the award. A prize of £10,000 is awarded for best entry and a prize of £3000 for best first published book, selected from eight regional winners who each receive prizes of £1000. The award is currently administered in Singapore. Details and entry form available from Commonwealth Foundation, Marlborough House, Pall Mall, London SW1Y 5HY *tel* 071-930 3783 *fax* 071-839 8157.

The Constable Trophy

A biennial competition supported by the three Northern-based Regional Arts Boards for fiction writers living in the North of England (Northern Arts, North West Arts Board, Yorkshire and Humberside Arts), for a previously unpublished novel. The winning entry will receive a prize of £1000 and will be considered for publication by Constable & Co. Ltd, as may up to two runners-up. The winning novel may also receive an advance of £1000 against royalties on publication; next award to be presented in 1994. Full details from Constable & Co. Ltd, 3 The Lanchesters, 162 Fulham Palace Road, London W6 9ER *tel* 081-741 3663 *fax* 081-748 7562.

The Catherine Cookson Fiction Prize

Instituted in 1992, this annual award of £10,000 is given for an unpublished novel (which is free of commitment), of at least 70,000 words in length, and which has some of the distinctive qualities of Catherine Cookson. Next closing date: 31 May. For further details, send an sae to The Catherine Cookson Fiction Prize, Transworld Publishers Ltd, 61-63 Uxbridge Road, London W5 5SA *tel* 081-579 2652.

The Duff Cooper Prize

Friends and admirers of Duff Cooper, first Viscount Norwich (1890-1954), contributed a sum of money which has been invested in a Trust Fund. The interest is devoted to an annual prize for a literary work in the field of biography or history published in English by a recognised publisher during the previous twelve months. There are two permanent judges (Artemis Cooper, and the Warden of New College, Oxford) and three others who change every five years. All communications should be sent to Artemis Cooper, 54 St Maur Road, London SW6 4DP *tel* 071-736 3729 *fax* 071-731 7638.

The Rose Mary Crawshay Prizes

One or more Rose Mary Crawshay prizes are awarded each year. The Prizes, which were originally founded by Rose Mary Crawshay in 1888, are awarded to women of any nationality who, in the judgement of the Council of the British Academy, have written or published within the three calendar years immediately preceding the date of the award an historical or critical work of sufficient value on any subject connected with English literature, preference being given to a work regarding Byron, Shelley or Keats. Applications are not sought in this competition.

CWA Cartier Diamond Dagger Award

This award was first given in 1986 and is for outstanding contribution to the genre. Nominations not required. It is sponsored by Cartier in conjunction with the Crime Writers' Association, PO Box 172, Tring, Herts. HP23 5LP.

CWA John Creasey Memorial Award

The award was founded in 1973 following the death of John Creasey, to commemorate his foundation of the Crime Writers' Association. It is given annually, for the best crime novel by an author who has not previously published a full-length work of fiction, by the Crime Writers' Association.

Nominations by publishers only. PO Box 172, Tring, Herts. HP23 5LP. Award sponsored by Chivers Press.

CWA Gold Dagger Award and Silver Dagger Award
Founded in 1955 and awarded annually for a crime novel published in the UK. Nominations by publishers only. The panel of five judges are reviewers of crime fiction. Given by the Crime Writers' Association, PO Box 172, Tring, Herts. HP23 5LP.

CWA Gold Dagger Award for Non-Fiction
Founded in 1977 and awarded annually for a non-fiction crime book to an author published in the UK. Nominations by publishers only. Chosen by four judges of different professions. Given by the Crime Writers' Association, PO Box 172, Tring, Herts. HP23 5LP.

CWA Last Laugh Award
Founded in 1989 and awarded annually for the most amusing crime novel of the year. Nominations by publishers only. The judges are reviewers of crime fiction.

CWA Silver Dagger Award—for details see under CWA Gold Dagger Award.

The Rhys Davies Trust
The Trust aims to foster Welsh writing in English and offers financial assistance to English-language literary projects in Wales (e.g. competitions, bursaries, grants to publishers), directly or in association with other bodies. The Trust also supports the annual Rhys Davies Lecture. Details from Meic Stephens, The Secretary, The Rhys Davies Trust, 10 Heol Don, Whitchurch, Cardiff CF4 2AU   *tel* (0222) 623359.

The Earthworm Award
The Earthworm Award was set up by Friends of the Earth to promote and reward environmental awareness and sensitivity in literature for children of all ages. The award is given in September each year for children's books, of all types, published in the UK between May and April of the preceding year. There is a first prize of £2000 and the five shortlisted authors each receive £200. The Earthworm Award has been sponsored by the Save and Prosper Educational Trust. Applications to The Earthworm Award, The Events Department, Friends of the Earth, 26-28 Underwood Street, London N1 7JQ   *tel* 071-490 4734/1555.

Encore Award
This annual award of £7500 is for the best second novel of the year. The work submitted must be (a) a novel by one author who has had one (and only one) novel published previously, and (b) in the English language, first published in the UK. Closing date: 30 November. The Society of Authors, 84 Drayton Gardens, London SW10 9SB   *tel* 071-373 6642.

Esquire/Volvo/Waterstone's Non Fiction Award
Established in 1993, this award is given for the best non-fiction title published in the UK in the preceding year. The award (winner £5000, 5 runners up of £1000 each) is open to writers of all nationalities. Details from The Administrator, Esquire/Volvo/Waterstone's Non Fiction Award, Esquire, 72 Broadwick Street, London W1V 2BP.

The European Poetry Translation Prize
Founded in 1983 a prize of £500 is given every two years for a published volume of poetry which has been translated into English from a European language. It is part-funded by the Arts Council of England and administered by the Poetry Society, 22 Betterton Street, London WC2H 9BU.

Christopher Ewart-Biggs Memorial Prize
This prize of £4000 is awarded once every two years to the writer, of any nationality, whose work contributes most, in the opinion of the judges, to peace and understanding in Ireland; to closer ties between the peoples of Britain and Ireland; or to co-operation between the partners of the European Union. Eligible works must be published during the two years to 31 December 1994. Information from Secretary, Memorial Prize, Flat 3, 149 Hamilton Terrace, London NW8 9QS *tel* 071-624 1863.

The Geoffrey Faber Memorial Prize
This prize was established in 1963 by Faber and Faber Ltd, as a memorial to the founder and first Chairman of the firm.

An annual prize of £1000, it is awarded in alternate years for a volume of verse and for a volume of prose fiction. It is given to that volume of verse or prose fiction first published originally in the UK during the two years preceding the year in which the award is given which is, in the opinion of the judges, of the greatest literary merit.

To be eligible for the prize the volume of verse or prose fiction must be by a writer who is: (a) not more than 40 years old at the date of publication of the book; (b) a citizen of the UK and Colonies, of any other Commonwealth state, of the Republic of Ireland or of the Republic of South Africa.

There are three judges who are reviewers of poetry or of fiction as the case may be; and they are nominated each year by the editors or literary editors of newspapers and magazines which regularly publish such reviews.

Faber and Faber invite nominations from such editors and literary editors. No submissions for the prize are to be made.

The Eleanor Farjeon Award
In 1965 the Children's Book Circle instituted an annual award to be given for distinguished services to children's books and to be known as the Eleanor Farjeon Award in memory of the much-loved children's writer. A prize of (minimum) £750 may be given to a librarian, teacher, author, artist, publisher, reviewer, television producer or any other person working with or for children through books. The award is sponsored by Books for Children.

Prudence Farmer Poetry Prize
This poetry prize was founded in 1974 and is awarded annually for the best poem printed during the previous year in the *New Statesman & Society*, Foundation House, Perseverance Works, 38 Kingsland Road, London E2 8DQ *tel* 071-739 3211 *telex* 28449 *fax* 071-739 9307.

FAW National Literary Awards
Administered by the Fellowship of Australian Writers, these awards are open to any Australian or bona fide resident of Australia or its Territories. Part 1. Book Awards are given for a work of quality on an Australian theme, auto/biography or memoir, and poetry; Part 2. Manuscript Awards cover unpublished novels, short stories, non-fiction, children's literature and poetry; Part 3. Young Writers Awards cover scripts, poetry and short stories by writers aged 10 upwards. Dates for submission: 19 September-30 November 1994. Full details of the various awards, and entry forms, may be obtained from Adrian Peniston-Bird, President, Fellowship of Australian Writers (Vic) Inc., PO Box 528, Camberwell, Victoria 3124, Australia.

The Fawcett Bookprize—'New Light on Women's Lives'
Founded in 1982, the Fawcett Bookprize is awarded annually to the book which does most to further our understanding of women's lives and experiences. The prize is awarded during mid-May, in London, with a linked debate during early June. Entries to be submitted by 31 December, for titles published in the

previous year in Britain and the Commonwealth. Details from the Administrative Officer, The Fawcett Society, 46 Harleyford Road, London SE11 5AY   *tel* 071-587 1287   *fax* 071-793 0451.

The Kathleen Fidler Award
An annual award for an unpublished novel for children aged 8-12 years, to encourage authors new to writing for this age group. The work should be the author's first attempt to write for this age range. The winner will receive a cash prize of £1000 and the winning entry will be published by Blackie Children's Books. The award is sponsored by Blackie Children's Books and administered by Book Trust Scotland. For details, send an sae to Book Trust Scotland, The Scottish Book Centre, 137 Dundee Street, Edinburgh EH11 1BG.

The John Florio Prize
This prize was established in 1963 under the auspices of the Society of Authors and its Translators Association to be awarded biennially for the best translation into English published by a British publisher during the previous two years. Only translations of Italian 20th-century works of literary merit and general interest will be considered. The work should be entered by the publisher and not by the individual translator. Details from the Secretary, The Translators Association, 84 Drayton Gardens, London SW10 9SB.

E.M. Forster Award
The distinguished English author, E.M. Forster, bequeathed the American publication rights and royalties of his posthumous novel *Maurice* to Christopher Isherwood, who transferred them to the American Academy of Arts and Letters (633 West 155th Street, New York, NY 10032, USA), for the establishment of an E.M. Forster Award, currently $12,500, to be given annually to an English writer for a stay in the United States. *Applications for this award are not accepted.*

Forward Poetry Prizes
Established in 1992, three prizes are awarded annually: 1) best collection of poetry published between 1 August and 31 July (£10,000); 2) best first collection of poetry published between 1 August and 31 July (£5000); and 3) best individual poem, published but not as part of a collection (£1000). All poems entered are also considered for inclusion in the *Forward Book of Poetry*, an annual anthology. Details from Prize Administrator, Book Trust, Book House, 45 East Hill, London SW18 2QZ   *tel* 081-870 9055.

Miles Franklin Literary Award
Founded in 1957, this annual award of $25,000 is for a novel or play first published in the preceding year, which presents Australian life in any of its phases. More than one entry may be submitted by each author; collaborations between two or more authors are eligible. Biographies, collections of short stories or children's books are not eligible. Closing date: approx. 31 January each year. Details from Arts Management, 180 Goulburn Street, Darlinghurst, NSW 2010, Australia   *tel* (02) 283 2066.

The Lionel Gelber Prize
Established in 1989, this prize of $50,000 is given annually to the author of the best book on the subject of international relations published in English or in English translation. Details from the Manager, The Lionel Gelber Prize, 410 Queens Quay West, Suite 100, Toronto, Ontario M5V 2Z3, Canada   *tel* 416-973-4760   *fax* 416-954-4323.

The Glenfiddich Awards
Founded in 1970, awards are given annually to recognise excellence in writing, publishing and broadcasting relating to the subjects of food and drink. £800 is

given per category (12 in all), together with a case of Glenfiddich Pure Malt Scotch Whisky and an engraved quaich. The overall winner receives The Glenfiddich Trophy and an additional £3000. Details from The Glenfiddich Awards, 10 Stukeley Street, London WC2B 5LQ *tel* 071-405 8638.

The Gooding Award for Short Story Writing
Prizes (first £500, two runners up £250 each) are awarded annually in this open competition for original short stories in English of not more than 2500 words. Adjudication is organised in May each year by the South and Mid Wales Association of Writers. Next closing date: 1 March 1995. Details from The Competition Secretary, The Gooding Award, 95 Celyn Avenue, Lakeside, Cardiff CF2 6EL, on receipt of an sae.

GPA Book Award
This prize, to the value of IR£50,000, is awarded every three years for a work of fiction or poetry or a general work (autobiography, biography, history, essays, belles-lettres and criticism) by an author born on the island of Ireland or, if born elsewhere, resident on the island of Ireland since October 1992. Five copies of eligible books to be submitted to: Award Administrator, GPA House, Shannon, Co. Clare, Republic of Ireland *tel* (061) 360000.

E.C. Gregory Trust Fund
A number of substantial awards are made annually from this Fund for the encouragement of young poets who can show that they are likely to benefit from an opportunity to give more time to writing. A candidate for an Award must: (a) be a British subject by birth but *not* a national of Eire or any of the British dominions or colonies and be ordinarily resident in the UK or Northern Ireland; (b) be under the age of thirty at 31 March in the year of the Award (i.e. the year following submission); (c) submit for the consideration of the judges a published or unpublished work of belles-lettres, poetry or drama poems (not more than 30 poems). Entries for the Award should be sent not later than 31 October to the Society of Authors, 84 Drayton Gardens, London SW10 9SB.

The Guardian Children's Fiction Prize
The *Guardian*'s annual prize of £1000 for a work of children's fiction (usually for children over eight), published by a British or Commonwealth writer. The winning book is chosen by the Children's Book Editor together with a team of three or four other authors of children's books.

The Guardian Fiction Prize
The *Guardian*'s annual prize of £2000 for a work of fiction showing originality and promise published by a British or Commonwealth writer. The winning book will be chosen by the Literary Editor in conjunction with the *Guardian*'s regular reviewers of new fiction.

Guild Awards
Eighteen awards, reinstituted in 1991, covering radio, theatre, books, film and television, are awarded annually by the Writers' Guild of Great Britain. Nominations are made from works which have been published, performed or broadcast during the period 1 July to 30 June. The awards, in the form of a mounted glass inkwell, are presented in September each year. No nominations are required from the public.

The Hawthornden Prize
The Hawthornden Prize, for which books do not have to be specially submitted, is awarded annually to the author of what, in the opinion of the Committee, is the best work of imaginative literature published during the preceding calendar year by a British author. Details of this, and writers' fellowships, from

The Administrator, Hawthornden Castle International Retreat for Writers, Hawthornden Castle, Lasswade, Midlothian EH18 1EG   *tel* 031-440 2180.

The Felicia Hemans Prize for Lyrical Poetry
The Felicia Hemans Prize of books or money is awarded annually for a lyrical poem, the subject of which may be chosen by the competitor. Open to past and present members and students of the University of Liverpool only. The prize shall not be awarded more than once to the same competitor. Poems, endorsed 'Hemans Prize', must be sent in to the Registrar, The University of Liverpool, PO Box 147, Liverpool L69 3BX   (*tel* 051-794 2458   *fax* 051-708 6502), on or before 1 May. Competitors may submit either published or unpublished verse, but no competitor may submit more than one poem.

David Higham Prize for Fiction
This prize of £1000 which was founded in 1975 is awarded annually to a citizen of the British Commonwealth, Republic of Ireland, South Africa or Pakistan for a first novel or book of short stories written in English and published during the current year. Publishers only may submit books. Entry forms are available from Book Trust, Book House, 45 East Hill, London SW18 2QZ   *tel* 081-870 9055.

William Hill Sports Book of the Year Award
Founded in 1989, this award is given annually in November for a book with a sporting theme (record books and listings excluded). Title must be in the English language, and published for the first time in the UK during the relevant calendar year. Total value of prize is £5000, including £3500 in cash. An award for the best cover design was introduced in 1991; value £500. Details from Graham Sharpe, William Hill Organisation, Greenside House, 50 Station Road, Wood Green, London N22 4TP   *tel* 081-365 7211.

The Calvin and Rose G. Hoffman Memorial Prize for Distinguished Publication on Christopher Marlowe
This annual prize of not less than £7500 is awarded to the best unpublished work that examines the life and works of Christopher Marlowe and the relationship between the works of Marlowe and Shakespeare. The adjudicator is Professor E.A.J. Honigmann, formerly of Newcastle upon Tyne University. The closing date for entries is 1 September, and the competition is open to all. Applications to The Headmaster, The King's School, Canterbury, Kent CT1 2ES   *tel* (0227) 475501   *fax* (0227) 457380.

Winifred Holtby Memorial Prize
Awarded for the best regional novel of the year written in the English language. The writer must be of British or Irish nationality, or a citizen of the Commonwealth. Translations, unless made by the author of the work, are not eligible for consideration. If in any year it is considered that no regional novel is of sufficient merit the prize may be awarded to an author, qualified as aforesaid, of a literary work of non-fiction or poetry, concerning a regional subject. Prize value £800.

Publishers may submit novels published during the current year to The Royal Society of Literature, 1 Hyde Park Gardens, London W2 2LT. Entries must be submitted by 31 October.

The Independent Foreign Fiction Award
Any full-length novel or collection of short stories translated into English from another language, published in the UK in the year preceding the award and must have been published in its original language not more than 15 years preceding entry. Bi-monthly winners shortlisted for annual prize of £10,000. Details from Philippa Baker, *The Independent*, 40 City Road, London EC1Y 2DB/after October 1994: 1 Canada Square, Canary Wharf, London E14 5AP.

Irish Times Literary Prizes
Founded in 1989, these prizes are awarded by the Governors of the Prizes from nominations submitted by literary editors and critics. In 1994, the Irish Literature Prizes were IR£7500 for a non-fiction work (history, biography, autobiography, criticism, politics, sociological interest, travel and current affairs) in English or Irish; IR£7500 for a first book of creative literature (novel, collection of short stories or a volume of poetry) in English or Irish; the International Fiction Prize was IR£10,000 for a work of fiction, in English or Irish, published in Ireland, the UK or the USA.

Jewish Quarterly Literary Prizes
Founded in 1977, prizes are awarded annually for a work of fiction (£4000), non-fiction (£3000) and poetry (£1000) which best stimulate an interest in and awareness of themes of Jewish concern among a wider reading public. Details from The Administrator, Jewish Quarterly, PO Box 1148, London NW5 2AZ *tel* 071-485 4062.

Kent & Sussex Poetry Society Open Poetry Competition
Founded in 1985, this competition is open to all unpublished poems, no longer than 40 lines in length. Prizes: 1st £300, 2nd £100, 3rd £50, 4th five at £20. Closing date: 31 January each year. Entries, an entry fee of £2 per poem, the author's name and address and a list of poems submitted, should be sent to Clive Eastwood, 8 Edward Street, Southborough, Tunbridge Wells, Kent TN4 0HP.

Sir Peter Kent Conservation Book Prize
Established in 1987, the European Year of the Environment, for the best book on an environmental or conservation issue published in the UK in the year ending 31 December. Two awards – £5000 for an adult book and £2000 for a children's book – are sponsored by BP Exploration. Details and entry form from Book Trust, Book House, 45 East Hill, London SW18 2QZ *tel* 081-870 9055.

Kraszna-Krausz Awards
Instituted in 1985, three awards totalling £30,000 are made each year, alternating annually between the best books on a) still photography: art and culture, educational, photographic innovations; and b) moving picture media: culture, business, techniques and technology. The prize in each category will be awarded to the best book published in the preceding two years. Closing date: 30 June each year. 1995 award = a). The Foundation is also open to applications for grants concerned with the literature of photography. Details from W. Gordon Graham, Kraszna-Krausz Foundation, 5 Beechwood Drive, Harleyford Estate, Marlow, Bucks. SL7 2DH *tel* (0628) 477577.

Leek Arts Festival International Poetry Prize
Founded in 1983, annual prizes, total value £2500, are awarded for unpublished poems in English, no longer than 40 lines. Details from the Competition Organiser, LAF International Poetry Competition, 44 Rudyard Road, Biddulph Moor, Stoke-on-Trent, Staffs. ST8 7JN.

The Library Association Reference Awards: The Besterman Medal
The Library Association Besterman Medal is awarded annually for an outstanding bibliography or guide to the literature first published in the UK during the preceding year either in print or in electronic form. Recommendations for the award are invited from members of the Library Association, who are asked to submit a preliminary list of not more than three titles. The following are among the criteria which will be taken into consideration in making the award: (1) the authority of the work and the quality and kind of the articles or entries; (2) the accessibility and arrangement of the information; (3) the scope and

coverage; (4) the quality of the indexing; (5) the adequacy of the references; (6) the up-to-dateness of the information; (7) the physical presentation; (8) the originality of the work; (9) value for money.

The Library Association Carnegie Medal

The Library Association Carnegie Medal is awarded annually for an outstanding book for children written in English and first published in the UK during the preceding year or co-published elsewhere within a three-month time lapse. Recommendations for the award are invited from members of the Library Association, who are asked to submit a preliminary list of not more than three titles, accompanied by a 50-word appraisal justifying the recommendation of each book. The following criteria may act as a general guide: *fiction:* choice to be based upon consideration of: (1) plot; (2) style; (3) characterisation; *information books:* choice to be based upon consideration of: (1) accuracy; (2) method of presentation; (3) style. Format should also be taken into account. The award is sponsored by Peters Library Service and selected by the Youth Libraries Group of the Library Association.

The Library Association Kate Greenaway Medal

The Library Association Kate Greenaway Medal is awarded annually for an outstanding illustrated book for children first published in the UK during the preceding year or co-published elsewhere within a three-month time lapse. Recommendations for the award are invited from members of the Library Association, who are asked to submit a preliminary list of not more than three titles, accompanied by a 50-word appraisal justifying the recommendation of each book. Books intended for older as well as younger children are included, and reproduction will be taken into account. The award is sponsored by Peters Library Service and selected by the Youth Libraries Group of the Library Association.

The Library Association Reference Awards: The McColvin Medal

The Library Association McColvin Medal is awarded annually for an outstanding reference work either in print or in electronic form first published in the UK during the preceding year. The following types of work are eligible for consideration: (1) encyclopedias, general and special; (2) dictionaries, general and special; (3) biographical dictionaries; (4) annuals, yearbooks and directories; (5) handbooks and compendia of data; (6) atlases. Recommendations for the award are invited from members of the Library Association, who are asked to submit a preliminary list of not more than three titles. The following are among criteria which will be taken into consideration in making an award; (1) the authority of the work and the quality and kind of the articles or entries; (2) the accessibility and arrangement of the information; (3) the scope and coverage; (4) the style; (5) the relevance and quality of the illustrations; (6) the quality of the indexing; (7) the adequacy of the bibliographies and references; (8) the up-to-dateness of the information; (9) the physical presentation; (10) the originality of the work; (11) value for money.

The Library Association Reference Awards: The Walford Award

The Library Association Walford Award is awarded annually to an individual who has made a sustained and continued contribution to the science and art of British bibliography over a period of years. The bibliographer's work can encompass effort in the history, classification and description of printed, written, audiovisual and machine readable materials. Recommendations may be made for the work of a living person or persons, or for an organisation. The award can be made to a British bibliographer or to a person or organisation working in the UK.

The Library Association Reference Awards: The Wheatley Medal
The Library Association Wheatley Medal is awarded annually for an outstanding index published during the preceding three years. Printed indexes to any type of publication may be submitted for consideration, providing that the whole work, including the index, or the index alone has originated in the UK. Recommendations for the award are invited from members of the Library Association and the Society of Indexers, publishers and others. The final selection is made by a committee consisting of representatives of the Library Association Cataloguing and Indexing Group and the Society of Indexers, with power to co-opt.

The Lichfield Prize
Lichfield District Council's biennial prize of £5000, instituted in 1988, for the best novel based recognisably on the geographical area of Lichfield District, Staffordshire. Next closing date: 31 May 1995. Details from the Tourist Information Centre, Donegal House, Bore Street, Lichfield, Staffs. WS13 6NE *tel* (0543) 252109.

The London Short Story Competition
Founded in 1992, and open to adults resident in Greater London, this biennial competition awards 15 prizes of £200 each (plus publication in an anthology) for the best short stories about London. Next closing date: end November 1994. Entry form from London Arts Board, Elme House, 133 Long Acre, London WC2E 9AF *tel* 071-240 1313.

LWT Plays on Stage
Founded in 1987, a competition for professional UK drama companies to help three winning companies stage a play of their choice. Prizes: (1st) £18,000, (2nd) £16,000, (3rd) £14,000. The judging panel consists of an actress, an actor, a director, a playwright and a designer. Details available from May to end June. Apply to Michael Hallifax, 3 Dungarvan Avenue, London SW15 5QU *tel* 081-876 4604 *fax* 081-392 9232.

The Sir William Lyons Award
The Lyons Award is to encourage young people in automotive journalism, including broadcasting, and to foster interest in motoring and the motor industry through these media. It is awarded to any person of British nationality resident in the UK under the age of 23 and consists of writing two essays and an interview with the Award Committee. The winner receives a trophy, £1000 and two years' probationary membership of The Guild of Motoring Writers. Further details from the General Secretary, 30 The Cravens, Smallfield, Surrey RH6 9QS *tel* (0342) 843294 *fax* (0342) 844093.

The Macallan/Scotland on Sunday Short Story Competition
Instituted in 1990, this annual prize (£5000; second prize £250; publication in *Scotland on Sunday*) is awarded for the best short story, of less than 3000 words, written by a person born in Scotland, now living in Scotland or by a Scot living abroad. Next closing date: 1 March 1995. Details from The Administrator, The Macallan/Scotland on Sunday Short Story Competition, 20 North Bridge, Edinburgh EH1 1YT.

The McKitterick Prize
This annual award of £5000 was endowed by the late Tom McKitterick for first novels by authors over the age of 40. The closing date for entries is 21 December and the award is open to first published novels and unpublished typescripts. Full details from The Society of Authors, 84 Drayton Gardens, London SW10 9SB.

The Enid McLeod Literary Prize
This annual prize of £200 is given for a full-length work of literature which contributes most to Franco-British understanding. It must be written in English by a citizen of the UK, British Commonwealth, the Republic of Ireland, Pakistan, Bangladesh or South Africa, and first published in the UK. Further details from the Secretary, Franco-British Society, Room 623, Linen Hall, 162-168 Regent Street, London W1R 5TB   *tel* 071-734 0815.

The Macmillan Prize for a Children's Picture Book
Three prizes of £1000 (1st), £500 (2nd) and £250 (3rd) are awarded annually for children's book illustrations by art students in higher education establishments in the UK. Applications to Publicity Manager, Pan Macmillan Children's Books, 18-21 Cavaye Place, London SW10 9PG   *tel* 071-373 6070   *fax* 071-370 0746.

Macmillan Silver Pen Award for Fiction
This award of £500 founded in 1969 and sponsored by Macmillan since 1986 is given annually for an outstanding collection of short stories written in English and published during the previous year by an author of British nationality or an author who has been a long-term resident in the UK. Books are nominated by members of the P.E.N. Executive Committee. Information from P.E.N., 7 Dilke Street, Chelsea, London SW3 4JE   *tel* 071-352 6303   *fax* 071-351 0220.

The McVitie's Prize for Scottish Writer of the Year
Annual prize of £500 to each of five shortlisted writers, and further £9500 to winner. Submissions can include novels, volumes of short stories, poetry, biography, autobiography, journalism, science fiction and children's books as well as theatre, cinema, radio and television scripts. The award is open to writers who were born in Scotland, who have Scottish parents, who have been resident in Scotland or who take Scotland as their inspiration. The closing date is 31 July for work first published, performed, filmed or transmitted during the previous twelve months. Details from The McVitie's Prize, Book Trust Scotland, Scottish Book Centre, 137 Dundee Street, Edinburgh EH11 1BG   *tel* 031-229 3663   *fax* 031-228 4293.

The Mail on Sunday–John Llewellyn Rhys Prize
The prize, worth £5000 to the winner since 1989 when *The Mail on Sunday* became the sponsor, was inaugurated by the late Mrs Rhys in memory of her husband, a writer who was killed in action in 1940. The prize is offered annually to the author of the most promising literary work of any kind published for the first time during the current year. The author must be a citizen of this country or the Commonwealth, and not have passed his or her 35th birthday by the date of the publication of the work submitted. Publishers only may submit books. Entry forms and further information are available from The Mail on Sunday–John Llewellyn Rhys Prize, c/o Book Trust, Book House, 45 East Hill, London SW18 2QZ   *tel* 081-870 9055.

Arthur Markham Memorial Prize
A prize of £350 for a short story, essay, poems, one-act play or first chapter of novel is offered biennially as a memorial to the late Sir Arthur Markham. Candidates must be manual workers in or about a coal mine, or have previously worked as miners. Full details can be obtained from The Academic Registrar's Office, PO Box 594, Firth Court, University of Sheffield, Sheffield S10 2UH.

The Kurt Maschler Award
An annual prize of £1000 was founded in 1982 and is given to a British author/artist or an author/artist who has been resident in Britain for more than ten years. Awarded for a children's book in which text and illustrations are of

excellence and enhance and balance each other. Details from Book Trust, Book House, 45 East Hill, London SW18 2QZ   *tel* 081-870 9055.

The Somerset Maugham Awards
The purpose of these annual awards, totalling about £15,000, is to encourage young writers to travel. Mr Maugham urged that originality and promise should be the touchstones: he did not wish the judges to 'play for safety' in their choice.

A candidate must be a British subject by birth and ordinarily resident in the UK or Northern Ireland. He or she must be under 35 years of age, and must submit a published literary work in the English language, of which he or she is the sole author. Poetry, fiction, non-fiction, belles-lettres or philosophy, but not dramatic works, are eligible.

An information sheet is available from The Society of Authors, 84 Drayton Gardens, London SW10 9SB. Four copies of one published work (which are non-returnable) should be submitted, and must be accompanied by a statement of the author's age, place of birth, and other published works. The closing date is 31 December.

Medical Writing and Illustration Prize
The Medical Writers Group of the Society of Authors is hoping to be able to continue offering prizes for a textbook, an illustrated textbook and an atlas, as in previous years. Please contact the Secretary, MGW, 84 Drayton Gardens, London SW10 9SB.

The Vicky Metcalf Awards for Short-Fiction and a Body of Work
These awards are given annually to Canadian writers to stimulate writing for children: $10,000 for a body of work; $3000 for a short story; $1000 to the responsible editor if published in a Canadian journal or anthology. Details from Canadian Authors Association, 275 Slater Street, Suite 500, Ottawa, Ontario K1P 5H9, Canada   *tel* 613-233-2846   *fax* 613-235-8237.

Meyer-Whitworth Award
Set up to help further the careers of UK contemporary playwrights who are not yet established, this award of £8000 is given annually for an English-language play which shows writing of individual quality and the promise of a developing new talent. Nominated plays must have been produced professionally in the UK for the first time between 1 August and 31 July; next closing date: 3 August 1995. Details from the Theatre Writing Section, Drama Department, Arts Council of England, 14 Great Peter Street, London SW1P 3NQ   *tel* 071-333 0100 ext 431.

MIND Book of the Year–the Allen Lane Award
This £1000 award, inaugurated in memory of Sir Allen Lane in 1981, is given to the author of any book – fiction or non-fiction – published in the current year which outstandingly furthers public understanding of the prevention, causes, treatment or experience of mental health problems. Entries by 31 December. The award is administered by MIND, the National Association for Mental Health. Further details from Caroline Scott, MIND Publications, Granta House, 15-19 Broadway, Stratford, London E15 4BQ   *tel* 081-519 2122   *fax* 081-522 1725.

Montana Book Awards
This annual award, previously known as the Wattie Book Award, has been operating since 1967. Run by the Book Publishers Association of New Zealand, it is given for the best NZ book of the year taking into account writing and illustration, design and production, and impact on the community. Authors must be New Zealanders or resident in New Zealand. It is New Zealand's major literary award: 1st prize $20,000, 2nd $10,000, 3rd $5000. Details from

The Administrator, Montana Book Awards, 133 Mt Eden Road, Mt Eden, Auckland 3, New Zealand   *tel* (09) 630-7699   *fax* (09) 630-3050.

The Mother Goose Award
The award, sponsored by Books for Children, is open to all artists having published a first major book for children during the previous year. Only books first published in Britain will be considered and this includes co-productions where the illustration originated in Britain. The award is presented annually in April and is in the form of a bronze egg together with a cheque for £1000. Recommendations for the award are invited from publishers and should be sent to each panel member. Full details and names and addresses of the panel members from Sally Grindley, Books for Children, Whiteway Court, The Whiteway, Cirencester, Glos. GL7 7BA.

Shiva Naipaul Memorial Prize
This annual prize of £1000 was founded in 1985, and is given to an English language writer of any nationality under the age of 35 for an essay of not more than 4000 words describing a visit to a foreign place or people. Details from *The Spectator*, 56 Doughty Street, London WC1N 2LL.

X.E. Nathan International Poetry Award
Founded in 1993, total prize money of £5000 is awarded annually for any manner of verse, no line restriction. Closing date: 30 November annually. Send poems, plus £2.50 entry fee, to Karen Sanderson, X.E. Nathan International Poetry Award, PO Box 392, Cardiff CF5 6NU.

National Book Awards
Books written by US citizens and published by US publishers are eligible for this annual prize of $10,000 in each of three categories: fiction, non-fiction and poetry. Runners-up in each category will receive $1000. Books are entered by publishers by 15 July each year. Details from the National Book Foundation, Inc., 260 Fifth Avenue, Room 904, New York, NY 10001, USA.

National Book Council Awards for Australian Literature
Angus & Robertson Bookworld Prize
A prize of $10,000 is awarded for an unpublished first novel by an Australian writer; includes publication of winning entry.

Banjo Awards
Named after Australia's best-loved folk poet, A.B. (Banjo) Paterson, these awards are given for books of the highest literary merit and which make an outstanding contribution to Australian literature. There are two equal awards ($20,000) – one for fiction, the other for non-fiction.

Turnbull Fox Phillips Poetry Prize
Founded in 1990, this $7500 prize is given for a published work of poetry by a single author.

Details from The Secretary, National Book Council, Suite 3, 21 Drummond Place, Carlton, Victoria 3053, Australia   *tel* (03) 663 8655   *fax* (03) 663 8658.

National Poetry Competition
Now established as the major annual poetry competition in Britain. Prizes of £3000, £1000, £250, ten of £100. Entry fees of £4 for first poem and £3 each for subsequent entries, length of each poem not to exceed 40 lines. Details and entry forms from The Competition Organiser, The Poetry Society, 22 Betterton Street, London WC2H 9BU.

Natural World Book of the Year Award
This £500 prize is awarded annually to the best book on British wildlife or the countryside by *Natural World*, the national magazine of The Wildlife Trusts.

Submissions must be made by 1 September, and books must have been published between 1 October of the previous year and 30 September of the year of the award. Details from Natural World Book of the Year Award, 20 Upper Ground, London SE1 9PF   *tel* 071-928 2111   *fax* 071-620 1594.

The NCR Book Award for Non Fiction

An annual award founded in 1987 and sponsored by AT&T Global Information Solutions Ltd to stimulate more interest in non-fiction writing and publishing in the UK. The award carries a prize of £25,000, currently the highest award available in the UK. Additionally, £1500 goes to the other three shortlisted authors. Applications welcomed from publishers. Details from The Administrator, NCR Book Award, 206 Marylebone Road, London NW1 6LY   *tel* 071-725 8385   *telex* 263931   *fax* 071-724 6519.

John Newbery Medal

Founded in 1922, this annual prize is given to the author, a citizen or resident of the USA, of the most distinguished contribution to American literature for children published in the US during the preceding year. The judges are 15 members of the Association for Library Service to Children (ALSC), a division of the American Library Association (committee members change annually). Further details from ALSC, The American Library Association, 50 East Huron Street, Chicago, IL 60611, USA   *tel* 312-280-2163   *fax* 312-280-3257.

The Nobel Prize

The Nobel Prize in Literature is one of the awards stipulated in the will of the late Alfred Nobel, the Swedish scientist who invented dynamite. The awarding authority is the Swedish Academy, Box 2118, S-10313 Stockholm, Sweden *tel* (08) 10-65-24   *fax* (08) 24-42-25. No direct application for a prize will, however, be taken into consideration. For authors writing in English it was bestowed upon Rudyard Kipling in 1907, W.B. Yeats in 1923, George Bernard Shaw in 1925, Sinclair Lewis in 1930, John Galsworthy in 1932, Eugene O'Neill in 1936, Pearl Buck in 1938, T.S. Eliot in 1948, William Faulkner in 1949, Bertrand Russell in 1950, Sir Winston Churchill in 1953, Ernest Hemingway in 1954, John Steinbeck in 1962, Samuel Beckett in 1969, Patrick White in 1973, Saul Bellow in 1976, William Golding in 1983, Wole Soyinka in 1986, Joseph Brodsky in 1987, Nadine Gordimer in 1991, Derek Walcott in 1992 and Toni Morrison in 1993. The Nobel Prizes are understood to be worth about £900,000 each. They number five: Physics, Chemistry, Physiology or Medicine, Literature, and Promotion of Peace. (Besides the Nobel Prizes proper, there is the Prize in Economic Sciences in Memory of Alfred Nobel, funded by the Bank of Sweden.)

The Noma Award for Publishing in Africa

Established in 1979, this annual book prize of $5000 is available to African writers and scholars whose work is published in Africa. The principal aim of the Award is to encourage publication of works by African writers and scholars in Africa. The prize is given to the author of an outstanding new book published (during the preceding twelve months) by a publisher domiciled on the African continent or its offshore islands, in any of these three categories: (1) scholarly or academic, (2) books for children, (3) literature and creative writing, including fiction, drama and poetry. Any original work in any of the indigenous or official languages of Africa is eligible for consideration. Full details from The African Book Publishing Record, PO Box 56, Oxford OX1 2SJ   *tel* (0865) 511428   *fax* (0865) 311534/793298.

Northern Arts Writers' Awards

Up to £3000 is available annually to support previously published novelists, short story writers, poets and literary critics living in the Northern Arts region of Cleveland, Cumbria, Co Durham, Tyne & Wear and Northumberland. Details from Lezley Moss, Published & Broadcast Arts Department, Northern Arts, 9-10 Osborne Terrace, Jesmond, Newcastle upon Tyne NE2 1NZ *tel* 091-281 6334.

Northern Short Story Competition
Founded in 1988, this competition (total prize money £500) is open to residents of the area covered by Northern Arts, North West Arts and Yorkshire and Humberside Arts Boards (see page 639). Stories may be on any subject, of no more than 3000 words. Closing date: 30 June each year. Application form from Rosemary Jones, Short Story Competition, Arc Publications, Nanholme Mill, Shaw Wood Road, Todmorden, Lancs. OL14 6DY *tel* (0706) 812338.

Oak Tree Award
Founded in 1989, this is an annual award of £250 to an author/illustrator who has published a book for children aged 8-12 years old, fiction or poetry, in the preceding year. No application necessary; details from Nottinghamshire County Library Service, Glaisdale Parkway, Nottingham NG8 4GP *tel* (0602) 854203 or Dillons The Bookstore, 25 Wheelergate, Nottingham NG1 2NF *tel* (0602) 473531.

Oppenheim–John Downes Memorial Trust
Awards, varying from £50 to £1500 depending on need, from this Trust Fund are given each December (and only then) to deserving artists of any kind including writers, musicians, artists who are unable through poverty to pursue their vocation effectively. Applicants must be over 30 years of age and of British birth. Full details and Application for an Award form from the Trust, c/o 36 Whitefriars Street, London EC4Y 8BH, enclosing sae.

Catherine Pakenham Memorial Award
Young women journalists, or aspiring journalists (over 18 and under 25 years of age), resident in Britain, are eligible for this award which was founded in 1970 in memory of Catherine Pakenham, who died in a car crash while working for the *Telegraph Magazine*. The award of £1000 is given for a non-fiction article between 750 and 2000 words long. Entry forms, after 1 September, from: Jo Henwood, Marketing Dept, The Sunday Telegraph, 1 Canada Square, Canary Wharf, London E14 5DT *tel* 071-538 6966 *fax* 071-513 2511.

Peterloo Poets Open Poetry Competition
Founded in 1986 this annual competition sponsored by Marks & Spencer offers for 1995 a first prize of £2000 and five other prizes totalling £2100. Closing date for entries is 1 March 1995. Full details and rules of entry from Peterloo Poets, 2 Kelly Gardens, Calstock, Cornwall PL18 9SA.

The Portuguese Prize
Founded in 1990, this prize is awarded on an irregular basis for the best translation into English of a work by a Portuguese national. Any genre of book considered. Details from The Society of Authors, 84 Drayton Gardens, London SW10 9SB *tel* 071-373 6642.

Trevor Reese Memorial Prize
This prize of £1000 is awarded biennially for a scholarly work by a single author in the field of Imperial and Commonwealth history. The next award (for a book published in 1993 or 1994) will be given in 1996. Details from The Seminar Secretary, Institute of Commonwealth Studies, 28 Russell Square, London WC1B 5DS.

The Margaret Rhondda Award
This award, first made in July 1968 on the tenth anniversary of Lady Rhondda's

death, and afterwards every three years, is given to a woman writer as a grant-in-aid towards the expenses of a research project in journalism. It is given to women journalists in recognition of the service which they give to the public through journalism. Closing date for next award 31 December 1995. Further details from The Society of Authors, 84 Drayton Gardens, London SW10 9SB.

The Rhône-Poulenc Prizes for Science Books

These prizes, established in 1987 by COPUS and the Science Museum and sponsored by Rhône-Poulenc, are awarded annually to the authors of popular, non-fiction, science and technology books that are judged to contribute most to the public understanding of science. To be eligible books must be written in English and published for the first time in the UK in the year preceding the prize. The Rhône-Poulenc prize (£10,000) is awarded for books with a general readership; the Junior Prize (£10,000), also sponsored by Rhône-Poulenc, is awarded to one or more books written specifically for young people; publishers may enter up to five books for each prize. Entries may cover any aspect of science and technology, including biography and history, but books published as educational textbooks or for professional or specialist audiences are not eligible. The author of a prize-winning book will be ineligible for another Rhône-Poulenc Prize for three years following the Award. Details from COPUS, c/o The Royal Society, 6 Carlton House Terrace, London SW1Y 5AG   *tel* 071-839 5561   *fax* 071-839 2891.

Rhyme International Annual Poetry Competition

The only international competition exclusively devoted to rhymed poetry, it was founded as Rhyme Revival in collaboration with Coventry Chamber of Commerce in 1981. Total annual prizes average around £1000, divided into two classes, 'formal' and 'open'. Entry fee: £2.50 per poem, minimum £5; closing date: 30 September each year. Adjudicated by a different leading poet each year. Full details and entry forms from *Orbis Literary Magazine*, 199 The Long Shoot, Nuneaton, Warks. CV11 6JQ   *tel* (0203) 327440.

Romantic Novelists' Association Award

This annual award for the best romantic novel of the year is open to both members and non-members of the Romantic Novelists' Association, provided they are domiciled in the UK. Novels must be published between the previous 1 December and 30 November of the year of entry. Three copies of the novel are required. Entry forms and details after July from the Award Organiser, Betty O'Rourke, 38 Stanhope Road, Reading RG2 7HN   *tel* (0734) 871154.

The **New Writers' Award** is for writers previously unpublished in the romantic novel field and who are probationary members of the Association. MSS are submitted each September under the New Writers' Scheme. All receive a critique. Any MSS which have passed through the Scheme and which are subsequently accepted for publication become eligible for the Award. Details from New Writers' Scheme Organiser, Hilary Johnson, 5 St Agnes Gate, Wendover, Bucks. HP22 6DP   *tel* (0296) 623260.

The Rooney Prize for Irish Literature

The Rooney Prize was set up in 1976 to encourage young Irish writing talent. The sum of IR£5000 is awarded annually to a different individual, who must be Irish, published in either Irish or English and under 40 years of age. The prize is non-competitive and there is no application procedure or entry form. Information from J.A. Sherwin, Strathin, Templecarrig, Delgany, Co. Wicklow, Republic of Ireland   *tel/fax* (01) 287 4769.

The Royal Bank of Scotland Portico Prize

Founded in 1985, this biennial prize of £2500 (next prize 1995) is awarded for a published work of general interest and literary merit set wholly or mainly in the North-West of England (Lancashire, Manchester, Liverpool, High Peak of Derbyshire, Cheshire and Cumbria). Information from Mrs Jo Francis, Librarian, Portico Library, 57 Mosley Street, Manchester M2 3HY *tel* 061-236 6785.

The Royal Society of Literature Award under the W.H. Heinemann Bequest

The purpose of this foundation is to encourage the production of literary works of real worth. Works in any branch of literature may be submitted by their publishers to the verdict of the Royal Society of Literature which shall be final and without appeal. Prose fiction shall not be excluded from competition, but the Testator's intention is primarily to reward less remunerative classes of literature: poetry, criticism, biography, history, etc. Any work originally written in the English language shall be eligible. Prize value £5000. The recipient of a Prize shall not be eligible again for five years. Entries must be submitted by 31 October to the society at 1 Hyde Park Gardens, London W2 2LT *tel* 071-723 5104.

The RTZ David Watt Memorial Prize

This £5000 prize, introduced in 1988 and organised, funded and administered by The RTZ Corporation, is awarded for outstanding written contributions towards the greater understanding of international and political issues. Those eligible for the prize are writers actively engaged in writing for newspapers and journals in the English language. Entries should comprise a published article in English of not more than 10,000 words. The closing date for entries and nominations is mid-March each year. Full details and entry forms are available from The Administrator, The RTZ David Watt Memorial Prize, The RTZ Corporation plc, 6 St James's Square, London SW1Y 4LD.

Runciman Award

Established in 1985 by the Anglo-Hellenic League for a work – fiction, non-fiction, biography, history or poetry – wholly, or mainly, about Greece or the Hellenic world. The annual £1000 prize is sponsored by the Onassis Foundation. To be eligible a work must be published in its first English edition in the UK. Details from Anglo-Hellenic League, Flat 4, 68 Elm Park Gardens, London SW10 9PB *tel* 071-352 2676 *fax* 071-351 5657.

The Ian St James Awards

These awards, founded in 1989, are made annually. Ten writers of short stories (5000-10,000 words) and six writers (2000-5000 words) will share in over £20,000 prize money and see their stories published by HarperCollins in paperback. The remaining sixty-four shortlisted writers will be published throughout the year in the new fiction magazine, *Acclaim*. To be eligible, writers must be 18 or over and not have had a novel or novella previously published. Entries must be in English but can come from anywhere in the world. Entry forms and further information from: The New Writers' Club, PO Box 101, Tunbridge Wells, Kent TN4 8YD *tel* (0892) 511322.

David St John Thomas Self-Publishing Awards

Established in 1993, these awards are given annually to anyone resident in the UK who has self-published a book during the calendar year preceding the award. The awards are in three categories – novel, non-fiction, poetry – with a prize of £250 in each category. Next closing date: 1 March 1995. Full details and entry form from Self-Publishing Awards, DT Charitable Trust, Writers News Ltd, PO Box 4, Nairn IV12 4HU *tel* (0667) 54441.

The Schlegel-Tieck Prize

This prize was established in 1964 under the auspices of the Society of Authors and its Translators Association to be awarded annually for the best translation published by a British publisher during the previous year. Only translations of

German twentieth-century works of literary merit and general interest will be considered. The work should be entered by the publisher and not the individual translator. Details from the Secretary, The Translators Association, 84 Drayton Gardens, London SW10 9SB.

Scoop of the Year Award

Founded in 1990, and chosen by a panel of senior editors, this annual award of a bronze statuette is given for the reporting scoop of the year, appearing in either a newspaper or electronic media. Details from the Hon. Secretary, London Press Club, 129-130 Strand, London WC2R 1BA *tel* 071-583 7255.

The Scott Moncrieff Prize

This prize was established in 1964 under the auspices of the Society of Authors and its Translators Association to be awarded annually for the best translation published by a British publisher during the previous year. Only translations of French twentieth-century works of literary merit and general interest will be considered. The work should be entered by the publisher and not the individual translator. Details from the Secretary, The Translators Association, 84 Drayton Gardens, London SW10 9SB.

The Scottish Arts Council

Writers Bursaries

A limited number of bursaries – of between £2000 and £6000 each – are offered to enable professional writers to devote more time to writing. Priority is given to writers of fiction and verse, but writers of literary non-fiction are also considered. Application normally open only to writers who have been living and working in Scotland for at least two years.

Applications may be discussed with Walter Cairns, Literature Director, The Scottish Arts Council, 12 Manor Place, Edinburgh EH3 7DD *tel* 031-226 6051.

Book Awards

Six awards of £1000 each are made in both spring and autumn. Preference is given to literary fiction and verse, but literary non-fiction is also considered. Authors should be Scottish or resident in Scotland, but books of Scottish interest by other authors are eligible for consideration.

Publishers should apply for further information to Shonagh Irvine, Literature Officer, The Scottish Arts Council, 12 Manor Place, Edinburgh EH3 7DD *tel* 031-226 6051.

The Scottish Book of the Year and Scottish First Book

Established in 1982 and 1988 respectively, these two annual awards (£5000 and £1500) are open to any author of Scottish descent or living in Scotland, or for a book by anyone which deals with the work or life of a Scot or with a Scottish problem, event or situation. No application necessary. Details from the Convener, The Scottish Book of the Year Award, The Saltire Society, 9 Fountain Close, 22 High Street, Edinburgh EH1 1TF.

Bernard Shaw Translation Prize

Founded in 1990, this triennial prize of £1000 is awarded to the best translation from Swedish to English, of any literary genre, first published in the UK in the three years preceding the closing date. Next closing date: 31 December 1996. Details from The Society of Authors, 84 Drayton Gardens, London SW10 9SB *tel* 071-373 6642.

She Short Story Competition (in conjunction with 'This Morning' programme)

Annual prize of £500, plus publication in *She* magazine, of the best short story of a maximum of 2500 words. Details of application announced in magazine, usually in March issue.

The Signal Poetry for Children Award
A prize of £100 is given annually for an outstanding book of poetry published for children in Britain and the Commonwealth during the previous year, whether single poem or anthology and regardless of country of original publication. Articles about the winning book are published in *Signal* each May. Not open to unpublished work. Further details from The Thimble Press, Lockwood, Station Road, South Woodchester, Stroud, Glos. GL5 5EQ.

The André Simon Memorial Fund Book Awards
Two awards, founded in 1978, are given annually, one each for the best new book on food and on drink (£2000 each), plus one Special Commendation of £1000 in either category. Closing date: 1 October each year. Details from Tessa Hayward, 5 Sion Hill Place, Bath BA1 5SJ *tel* (0225) 336305.

Skoob Books/Index on Censorship International Poetry Competition
Founded in 1988, this biennial competition awards prizes (1st, £1000 Skoob book token; other, books and magazine subscriptions) for poems of any length. All profits go to *Index on Censorship*. Details from Publicity Manager, Skoob Books Ltd, 25 Lowman Road, Holloway, London N7 6DD.

Smarties Book Prize
Established in 1985 to encourage high standards and stimulate interest in books for children of primary school age. Prizes of £2000 are awarded to each of three category winners, with a further £8000 to the overall winner. Eligible books must be published in the 12 months ending 31 October of the year of presentation and be written in English by a citizen of the UK, or an author resident in the UK, and published in the UK. The prize is sponsored by Nestlé Rowntree. Details from Book Trust, Book House, 45 East Hill, London SW18 2QZ *tel* 081-870 9055.

The W.H. Smith Annual Literary Award
A prize of £10,000 is awarded annually to a Commonwealth author (including a citizen of the UK) whose book, written in English and published in the UK, within 12 months ending on 31 December preceding the date of the Award, in the opinion of the judges makes the most outstanding contribution to literature. Submissions are not accepted; the judges make their decision independently. Further details are available from W.H. Smith Group, Strand House, 7 Holbein Place, London SW1W 8NR *tel* 071-824 5458 (direct line).

W.H. Smith Illustration Awards
These annual awards are given to practising book and magazine illustrators, for work first published in Great Britain in the 12 months preceding the judging of the awards. Book covers, illustrations of a purely technical nature and photographs together with works produced as limited editions are excluded. Cover illustrations to magazines are eligible. Enquiries to The National Art Library, Victoria and Albert Museum, South Kensington, London SW7 2RL, or to Lucy Rogers, W.H. Smith Group, Strand House, 7 Holbein Place, London SW1W 8NR *tel* 071-824 5463 (direct line).

South London International Playwriting Festival
Established in 1986, an annual competition for full-length plays which must be previously unperformed. Plays are accepted from all around the world and from both new and established writers. Deadline for entries: 4 July. Finalists are given a professionally directed and acted rehearsed reading in November (many winners have later had a full production). Details and entry form from: Warehouse Theatre, Dingwall Road, Croydon CR0 2NF *tel* 081-681 1257.

Southern Arts Literature Prize
This prize is awarded annually on a rotating basis for a published novel, poetry

collection, or work of literary non-fiction to writers living within the Southern Arts region. Prize: £1000 plus a craft commission to the value of £600. The 1994 award is for poetry. Closing date: end October. Details from The Literature Department, Southern Arts, 13 St Clement Street, Winchester, Hants SO23 9DQ   *tel* (0962) 855099   *fax* (0962) 861186.

Stand Magazine Short Story Competition
Founded in 1980, this biennial short story competition – prizes to the value of £2250 – is open to any writer for an original, untranslated story in English, not longer than 8000 words, not previously published, broadcast or under consideration elsewhere. Entry forms available only on receipt of a UK sae or 2 International Reply Coupons. Further details from Stand Magazine, 179 Wingrove Road, Newcastle upon Tyne NE4 9DA   *tel* 091-273 3280. Closing date 31 March 1995.

Sunday Express Book of the Year Award
A prize of £20,000 is awarded annually to the author of an outstanding, new work of fiction, including short stories, which is first published in English in Britain. No entries are accepted from authors or publishers. Nominations are made by a panel. Details from the *Sunday Express*, 245 Blackfriars Road, London SE1 9UX.

Reginald Taylor and Lord Fletcher Essay Competition
A prize of £300, in memory of E. Reginald Taylor FSA, and of Lord Fletcher FSA, is awarded annually for the best unpublished essay submitted during the year. The essay, not exceeding 7500 words, should show *original research* on a subject of archaeological, art-historical or antiquarian interest within the period from the Roman era to AD 1830. The successful competitor may be invited to read the essay before the Association and the essay may be published in the *Journal* of the Association if approved by the Editorial Committee.

Competitors are advised to notify the Hon. Editor in advance of the intended subject of their work. The next award will be made in May 1996 and the essay should be submitted not later than 31 October 1995 to the Hon. Editor, Dr Martin Henig, British Archaeological Association, Institute of Archaeology, 36 Beaumont Street, Oxford OX1 2PG, enclosing an sae.

Tees Valley Writer National Competition
Founded in 1990, the competition is held each year and prizes awarded for short stories (£250, £150, £100) and poetry (£250, £150, £100), plus a £100 prize for local entrants in each category. Each edition of the *Tees Valley Writer* (2 p.a. – Mar/Sept) contains a free entry voucher for the competition. Details from the Editor, *Tees Valley Writer*, 57 The Avenue, Linthorpe, Middlesbrough, Cleveland TS5 6QU   *tel* (0642) 819102.

Anne Tibble Poetry Competition
This annual prize is awarded for a poem, maximum length 20 lines, to anyone resident in Great Britain. The first prize is for £100; other prizes to a total value of £200. Further details from the Events Team Office, Directorate of Environment Services, Cliftonville House, Bedford Road, Northampton NN4 7NR   *tel* (0604) 233500 ext 4243.

Time-Life Silver Pen Award for Non-Fiction
This award of £1000 founded in 1969 and sponsored by *Time-Life* since 1986 is given annually for an outstanding work of non-fiction written in English and published during the previous year by an author of British nationality or an author who has been a long-term resident in the UK. Books are nominated by members of the P.E.N. Executive Committee. Information from P.E.N., 7 Dilke Street, Chelsea, London SW3 4JE   *tel* 071-352 6303   *fax* 071-351 0220.

The Times Educational Supplement Information Book Awards

There are two annual awards of £500 to the authors of the best information books – one for children up to the age of 10, the other for children aged 11-16. The books must be published in Britain or the Commonwealth. Details from The Times Educational Supplement, Admiral House, 66-68 East Smithfield, London E1 9XY   *tel* 071-782 3000   *fax* 071-782 3200.

The Times Educational Supplement Schoolbook Award

£500 is given for the best school textbook. The age range and subject area vary from year to year, and the books must be published in Britain or the Commonwealth. Details from The Times Educational Supplement, Admiral House, 66-68 East Smithfield, London E1 9XY   *tel* 071-782 3000   *fax* 071-782 3200.

Tir Na N-og Awards

Three annual awards to children's authors and illustrators, founded in 1976. (1) Best Welsh fiction, including short stories and picture books; (2) best Welsh non-fiction book of the year; (3) best English book with an authentic Welsh background. Total value of prize £3000. Details from: Welsh Books Council, Castell Brychan, Aberystwyth, Dyfed SY23 2JB   *tel* (0970) 624151   *fax* (0970) 625385.

The Tom-Gallon Trust

This Trust was founded by the late Miss Nellie Tom-Gallon and is administered by the Society of Authors. An award is made biennially from this Fund to fiction writers of limited means who have had at least one short story accepted for publication. An award of £500 was made in 1993. Authors wishing to enter should send to the Secretary, The Society of Authors, 84 Drayton Gardens, SW10 9SB: (1) a list of their already published fiction, giving the name of the publisher or periodical in each case and the approximate date of publication; (2) one published short story; (3) a brief statement of their financial position; (4) an undertaking that they intend to devote a substantial amount of time to the writing of fiction as soon as they are financially able to do so; (5) an sae for the return of the work submitted. Closing date for next award 20 September 1996.

The Betty Trask Awards

The Betty Trask Awards are for the benefit of young authors under 35 and are given on the strength of a first novel (published or unpublished) of a romantic or traditional, rather than experimental, nature. They stem from a generous bequest by Miss Betty Trask (who died in 1983) and are administered by the Society of Authors. It is expected that prizes totalling at least £25,000 will be presented each year. The winners are required to use the money for a period or periods of foreign travel. Full details of the conditions of entry can be obtained from The Society of Authors, 84 Drayton Gardens, London SW10 9SB. The closing date is 31 January.

The Travelling Scholarships

These are non-competitive awards administered by the Society of Authors. Submissions are not required.

T.E. Utley Memorial Fund Award

Prizes of £2500 and two of £1500 will be awarded annually for an essay on a given subject. Details from Virginia Utley, 44 Leamington Road Villas, London W11 1HT   *tel* 071-792 0409.

'Charles Veillon' European Essay Prize

Launched in 1975, a prize of 20,000 Swiss francs is awarded annually to a European writer or essayist for essays offering a critical look at modern society's way of life and ideology. Details from: The Secretary, Charles Veillon Foundation, CH 1017 Lausanne, Switzerland *tel* (021) 701 41 47.

Edgar Wallace Award
Founded in 1990, and chosen by a panel of senior editors, this annual award of a silver inkstand is given for outstanding writing by a journalist. Details from the Hon. Secretary, London Press Club, 129-130 Strand, London WC2R 1BA *tel* 071-583 7255.

Wandsworth London Writers Competition
The competition is open to writers of 16 years and over who live, work or study in the Greater London Area. Awards are made annually in two classes, Poetry and Short Story, the prizes totalling £850 in each class. Entries must be previously unpublished work. Judging is under the chairmanship of Martyn Goff, Chairman of Book Trust. Further details from Assistant Director of Leisure and Amenity Services (Libraries, Museum and Arts), Wandsworth Town Hall, High Street, London SW18 2PU *tel* 081-871 7037 *fax* 081-871 8349.

Whitbread Literary Awards
Awards to be judged in two stages and offering a total of £30,500 prize money open to five categories: Novel, First Novel, Children's Novel, Biography/ Autobiography, Poetry. The winner in each category will receive a Whitbread Nomination Award of £2000. The five nominations will go forward to be judged for the Whitbread Book of the Year. The overall winner receives £23,000 (£21,000 plus £2000 Nomination Award). Writers must have lived in Great Britain and Ireland for three or more years. Submissions only from publishers. Closing date for entries: 23 July. Further details may be obtained from The Booksellers Association, Minster House, 272 Vauxhall Bridge Road, London SW1V 1BA *tel* 071-834 5477.

The Whitfield Prize
The Whitfield Prize (value £1000) is announced in July each year for the best work on a subject within a field of British history. It must be its author's first solely-written history book, an original and scholarly work of historical research and have been published in the UK in the preceding calendar year. Three non-returnable copies of a book eligible for the competition should be submitted by the author or the publisher before 31 December to the Executive Secretary, Royal Historical Society, University College London, Gower Street, London WC1E 6BT *tel/fax* 071-387 7532.

John Whiting Award
Founded in 1965, this prize of £6000 is given annually. Eligible to apply are any writers who have received during the previous two calendar years an award through the Arts Council new theatre writing schemes, or who have had a premier production by a theatre company in receipt of an annual subsidy. Details from the Drama Director, Arts Council of England, 14 Great Peter Street, London SW1P 3NQ *tel* 071-333 0100.

The Raymond Williams Community Publishing Prizes
Founded in 1990, these annual prizes are awarded to non-profitmaking publishers for work which offers outstanding imaginative and creative qualities and which exemplifies the values of ordinary people and their lives. First prize: £2000 to publisher, £1000 to writer/group, runner-up: £1500 to publisher, £500 to writer/group. The Photography Unit of the Arts Council offers related Raymond Williams Prizes for photographic work in community publishing (details from Hannah Daws, Department of Visual Arts, Arts Council of England). Details of the literary awards from Anne Bendall, Literature

Department, The Arts Council of England, 14 Great Peter Street, London SW1P 3NQ *tel* 071-973 6442.

Write A Story for Children Competition
Founded in 1984, three prizes are awarded annually (1st £1000, 2nd £200, 3rd £100) for a short story for children, maximum 1000 words, by an unpublished writer of children's fiction. Entry form available from The Academy of Children's Writers, PO Box 95, Huntingdon, Cambs. PE17 5RL *tel* (0487) 832752.

Yorkshire Post Literary Awards
A prize of £1200 is awarded for the Book of the Year and a prize of £1000 for the Best First Work each year. Also annual awards of £1000 each are made for works which in the opinion of the Panel of Judges have made the greatest contribution to the understanding and appreciation of Music and Art. Nominations are only accepted from publishers and should arrive (together with one copy of the book) by 15 December in the case of main prizes, by 16 January in the case of the Art and Music Awards. Correspondence to Margaret Brown, Literary Awards Co-ordinator, Yorkshire Post Newspapers Ltd, PO Box 168, Wellington Street, Leeds LS1 1RF *tel* (0532) 432701 ext 1512 *fax* (0532) 443430.

The best reason for writing a historical

There is really only one valid reason for setting a story outside the present day and this is that the situation springs from the period, and could not possibly have happened at any other time. Otherwise you will find yourself with a contemporary story in fancy dress, lacking in depth and not very interesting. You will have wasted all the time you have spent on the research, and might just as well have set it in the present day.

To carry conviction, your characters and the situation in which they find themselves must be of the era in which they live. They must think, act, live and breathe in the way appropriate to their time. This is not to say they will indulge in 'gadzookery', by which I mean language more picturesque than intelligible, but they must not be anachronistic in their outlook or their response to the conflicts and dilemmas of their day. Dramatist John Arden, who wrote *The Roses of Eyam*, a very moving play about the heroism of a tiny village in Derbyshire at the time of the Great Plague of London, says 'A good historical is a scene or a situation from history, focused through individuals.' If we are to succeed, we must never lose sight of this fact.

from *Writing Historical Fiction* by Rhona Martin (A & C Black £8.99)

Index

PHONEDAY

From 1.00 am on Sunday, 16 April 1995:

- When dialling outside a local code area, add the digit **1** after the 0 at the beginning of UK codes. For example, inner London changes from 071 to 0171; Cardiff changes from 0222 to 01222.

- The following cities have an entirely new code and an extra digit in front of the existing local number:

  Bristol   0272 xxxxxx becomes 0117 9xx xxxx
  Leeds   0532 xxxxxx becomes 0113 2xx xxxx
  Leicester   0533 xxxxxx becomes 0116 2xx xxxx
  Nottingham 0602 xxxxxx becomes 0115 9xx xxxx
  Sheffield   0742 xxxxxx becomes 0114 2xx xxxx

- The international access code changes from **010** to **00**.

NOTES

NOTES

NOTES

ORDER FORM
Books for writers

_____	Writing for magazines	**£9.99**
_____	Freelance writing for newspapers	**£9.99**
_____	Writing popular fiction	**£7.99**
_____	Writing for the teenage market	**£8.99**
_____	Writing for children	**£7.99**
_____	Writing for radio	**£6.99**
_____	Writing historical fiction: *new ed Mar'95*	**£8.99**
_____	Writing crime fiction: *new ed Oct'94*	**£7.99**
_____	Writing a thriller	**£9.99**
_____	Writing for television: *new ed Mar'95*	**£9.99**
_____	Writing a play	**£5.95**
_____	Writing about travel	**£5.95**
_____	Research for writers	**£10.99**
_____	Word Power: a guide to creative writing	**£9.99**

All these books can be ordered through your local bookshop or direct from the publisher. Tick the titles you want and fill in the form below.
Prices and availability subject to change without notice

Please return to A&C Black (Publishers) Ltd, Dept YB95, PO Box 19, Huntingdon, Cambs, PE19 3SF   tel (0480) 212666 fax (0480) 405014

Send a cheque or postal order for the value of the book(s), adding (for postage and packing at printed paper rate) 15% UK and Eire; 20% overseas.
Airmail rates available on application.

OR please debit this amount from my Access\Visa Card (delete as appropriate)

Card number ☐☐☐☐☐☐☐☐☐☐☐☐☐☐☐☐☐☐

Amount _____   Expiry date ☐☐ ☐☐ ☐☐

Signed _____

Name (please print) _____

Address _____

_____ Postcode _____